Applied Economics

Twelfth Edition

Edited by Alan Griffiths and Stuart Wall

WITHDRAWN

Visit the *Applied Economics*, Twelfth Edition Companion Website at
www.pearsoned.co.uk/griffithswall to find valuable **student** learning
material including:

- Multiple choice, data response and essay type questions similar to
  the types of questions you may face in an exam
- Links to relevant sites on the web, with comments on their
  usefulness

PEARSON   APPLIED ECONOMICS
TWELFTH EDITION   ALAN GRIFFITHS
                                                   & STUART WALL

HOME   SELECT CHAPTER Welcome   SITE SEARCH   GO   ?

Welcome to the Companion Website for Applied Economics, Twelfth Edition.

Students - select from the links in the drop-down menu above or the resource links below to
access the student study materials.

- Student resources for each chapter, including:
  - Multiple choice, data response and essay type questions similar to the types of
    questions you may face in an exam
  - Links to relevant sites on the web, with comments on their usefulness

Instructors - visit the Instructor Resource Centre to access password-protected resources
accompanying this title.

Copyright © 1995-2011 Pearson Education. All Rights Reserved. Legal and Privacy Notice

APPLIED ECONOMICS

TWELFTH EDITION

EDITED BY

ALAN GRIFFITHS & STUART WALL

Financial Times
Prentice Hall
is an imprint of

PEARSON

Harlow, England • London • New York • Boston • San Francisco • Toronto • Sydney • Singapore • Hong Kong
Tokyo • Seoul • Taipei • New Delhi • Cape Town • Madrid • Mexico City • Amsterdam • Munich • Paris • Milan

Pearson Education Limited
Edinburgh Gate
Harlow
Essex CM20 2JE
England

and Associated Companies throughout the world

Visit us on the World Wide Web at:
www.pearson.com/uk

First published 1984
Second edition 1986
Third edition 1989
Fourth edition 1991
Fifth edition 1993
Sixth edition 1995
Seventh edition 1997
Eighth edition 1999
Ninth edition 2001
Tenth edition 2004
Eleventh edition 2007
Twelfth edition published 2012

© Pearson Education Limited 1984, 2012

ISBN: 978-0-273-73690-5

British Library Cataloguing-in-Publication Data
A catalogue record for this book is available from the British Library

Library of Congress Cataloging-in-Publication Data
Applied economics / Alan Griffiths & Stuart Wall, [editors]. -- 12th ed.
    p. cm.
  ISBN 978-0-273-73690-5 (pbk.)
  1. Economics.   2. Great Britain--Economic conditions--20th century.   I. Griffiths,
Alan, 1944–   II. Wall, Stuart, 1946–
  HB171.5.A65 2012
  330--dc23
                                                                        2011019210

10 9 8 7 6 5 4 3 2 1
15 14 13 12 11

Typeset in 9/11.5pt Sabon by 35
Printed and bound in Great Britain by Ashford Colour Press Ltd, Gosport, Hampshire

BRIEF CONTENTS

CONTENTS

Part III: Macroeconomics

A Companion Website accompanies

APPLIED ECONOMICS, 12/e

Edited by Alan Griffiths and Stuart Wall

Supporting resources
Visit **www.pearsoned.co.uk/griffithswall** to find valuable online resources

Companion Website for students
- Multiple choice, data response and essay type questions similar to the types of questions you may face in an exam
- Links to relevant sites on the web, with comments on their usefulness

For instructors
- Complete, downloadable Instructor's Manual
- PowerPoint slides

Also: The Companion Website provides the following features:

- Search tool to help locate specific items of content
- E-mail results and profile tools to send results of quizzes to instructors
- Online help and support to assist with website usage and troubleshooting

For more information please contact your local Pearson Education sales representative or visit www.pearsoned.co.uk/griffithswall

LIST OF FIGURES

LIST OF TABLES

ACAS	Advisory, Conciliation and Arbitration Service		CEPT	Common External Preference Tariff
AEEU	Amalgamated Engineering and Electrical Union		CET	Common External Tariff
			CFC	chlorofluorocarbons
AEU	Amalgamated Engineering Union		CFI	Court of First Instance
AFTA	ASEAN Free Trade Area		CGT	Capital Gains Tax
AHC	after housing cost		CHD	coronary heart disease
AIM	Alternative Investment Market		COHSE	Confederation of Health Service Employees
ALP	active labour market policy			
AME	Annual Managed Expenditure		COMRSA	Common Market for Eastern and Southern Africa
a.p.c.	average propensity to consume			
APS	Approved Profit Sharing		CPAG	Child Poverty Action Group
ASEAN	Association of South East Asian Nations		CPI	Consumer Price Index
ASHE	Annual Survey of Hours and Earnings		CPIY	CPI excluding indirect taxes
ASI	Adam Smith Institute		CPI–CT	CPI at constant taxation
ASLEF	Associated Society of Locomotive Engineers and Firemen		CSR	corporate social responsibility
			CT	Control Total
ATM	Automatic Telling Machine		CTC	Child Tax Credit
BA	Business Angels		CUFTA	Canadian–US Free Trade Agreement
BALPA	British Airline Pilots Association		DEL	Departmental Expenditure Limit
BBAA	British Business Angels Association		DGFT	Director-General of Fair Trading
BCB	Brazilian Central Bank		DHA	District Health Authority
BMA	British Medical Association		EAGGF	European Agricultural Guarantee and Guidance Fund
CAC	Central Arbitration Committee			
CAP	Common Agricultural Policy		EC	European Community
CAT	Competition Appeal Tribunal		ECB	European Central Bank
CBA	cost–benefit analysis		ECOFIN	European Council of Economic and Financial Ministers
CBI	Confederation of British Industry			
CBR	Central Bank of Russia		ECSC	European Coal and Steel Community
CC	Competition Commission		ECU	European Currency Unit
CCC	Competition and Credit Control		EEA	European Economic Area
CCL	Climate Change Levy		EEC	European Economic Community
CCP	counter cyclical payments		EER	effective exchange rate
CCT	Common Customs Tariff		EES	European Employment Strategy
CDO	Collateralized Debt Obligation		EETPU	Electrical, Electronic, Telecommunications and Plumbing Union
CEFTA	Central European Free Trade Agreement			
CEEP	European Centre of Enterprises with Public Participation			
			EFG	Enterprise Finance Guarantee
CEP	Center for Economic Performance		EFTA	European Free Trade Association
CEPG	Cambridge Economic Policy Group		EGT	endogenous growth theory
			EIB	Enterprise Investment Bank

EIF	European Investment Firm	ISTC	Iron and Steel Trades Confederation
EMCF	European Monetary Co-operation Fund	JSA	Jobseekers Allowance
EMS	European Monetary System	LCH	Life-Cycle Hypothesis
EMU	European Monetary Union	LDC	less developed country
EPS	earnings per share	LFA	Least Favoured Area
ERA	Employee Relations Act	LFS	Labour Force Survey
ERDF	European Regional Development Fund	LIBOR	London Inter-Bank Offer Rate
ERM	Exchange Rate Mechanism	LRAS	long-run aggregate supply
ESCB	European System of Central Banks	LSC	Learning and Skills Council
ESF	European Social Fund	LSE	London Stock Exchange
ETF	European Technology Facility	M&As	Mergers and acquisitions
ETI	Ethical Trading Initiative	MAC	marginal abatement cost
ETS	Emissions Trading Scheme	MAD	Market Abuse Directive
ETUC	European Trade Union Confederation	MBBGs	Major British Banking Groups
EU	European Union	MBO	management by objectives
EWC	European Works Council	MBO	management buyout
FDI	foreign direct investment	MDG	Millennium Development Goal
FFB	Finance for Business	MEC	marginal external cost
FIFG	Financial Instrument for Fisheries Guidance	MEC	marginal efficiency of capital
		MEI	marginal efficiency of investment
FMI	financial Management Initiative	MFA	Multi-Fiber Agreement
FR	financial resources	MFI	Monetary Financial Institutions
FSA	Financial Services Authority	MFN	most-favoured nation
FSB	Federation of Small Businesses	MFV	Managing for Value
FSMA	Financial Services Markets Act	MGQ	maximum Guaranteed Quantity
FTAA	Free Trade Area of the Americas	MID	Modularity in Design
FTC	Federal Trade Commission	MIP	Modularity in Production
GATT	General Agreement on Tariffs and Trade	MIU	Modularity in Use
GBI	Grant for Business Investment	MMC	Monopolies and Mergers Commission
GDP	Gross Domestic Product	MNC	multinational company
GFCF	Gross Fixed Capital Formation	MNE	multinational enterprises
GFE	gross final expenditure	MNPB	marginal net private benefit
GGE	general government expenditure	m.p.c.	marginal propensity to consume
GNI	Gross National Income	MPC	marginal pollution costs
GPFH	General Practitioner Fund Holder	MPC	marginal private cost
GPS	global positioning satellites	MPC	Monetary Policy Committee
GRD	Grant for Research and Development	MSC	marginal social cost
GSP	Growth and Stability Pact	MSF	Manufacturing, Science and Finance Union
HCAI	healthcare associated infections		
HDI	Human Development Index	MTF	multifactor productivity
HICP	Harmonized Index of Consumer Prices	MTFS	medium-term financial strategy
HPM	hedonic price method	MTO	medium term objectives
HRA	Human rights Act	NAFTA	North American Free Trade Area
IATA	International Air Transport Association	NAIRU	non-accelerating inflation rate of unemployment
ICT	Information and Communications Technology		
		NALGO	National and Local Government Officers Association
IDBR	Inter-Departmental Business Register		
IDT	International Development Target	NDYP	New Deal for Young People
ILO	International Labour Office	NEB	National Enterprise Board
IMF	International Monetary Fund	NEDO	National Economic Development Office
IRB	Internal Ratings Based Approach		
IRC	Industrial Reorganization Corporation	NERA	National Economic Research Associates
ISA	Individual Savings Plan		
ISEW	Index of Sustainable Economic Welfare	NGO	non-governmental organization

NHS	National Health Service		SEZ	Special Economic Zone
NICE	National Institute for Health and Clinical Excellence		SFI	Selective Finance for Investment
			SFP	single farm payment
NME	non-market economy		SHA	strategic health authority
NMW	National Minimum Wage		SIV	Structured Investment Vehicle
NPS	non-product specific		SLB	Small Loans for Businesses
NRU	natural rate of unemployment		SME	small/medium-sized enterprise
NUM	National Union of Mineworkers		SOE	State Owned Enterprises
NUPE	National Union of Public Employees		SPPI	Service Producers Providers Index
OFT	Office of Fair Trading		SRAS	short-run aggregate supply
OMO	Open Market Operation		SRI	socially responsible investment
ONS	Office for National Statistics		SS	strong sustainability
OPEC	oil-producing and exporting countries		SSA	Standard Spending Assessment
PCT	primary care trust		SWF	sovereign wealth fund
PDI	power distance		T&G	Transport and General Workers Union
PEP	Personal Equity Plan		TCM	travel cost method
PES	Payments for Ecosystem Services		TEC	Training and Enterprise Council
PES	Public Expenditure Survey		TEEB	The Economics of Ecosystems and Biodiversity
PET	positron emissions tomography			
PFI	private finance initiatives		TESSA	Tax Exempt Special Savings Accounts
PIH	Permanent Income Hypothesis		TEV	total economic value
PIRC	Pension and Research Investment Consultants		TFE	total final expenditure
			TFEU	Treaty on the Functioning of the European Union
PPI	Producer Price Index			
PPP	purchasing power parity		TFP	total factor productivity
PRP	performance-related pay		TI	Transparency International
PS	product specific		TME	Total Managed Expenditure
PSBR	public sector borrowing requirement		TNI	Transnationality Index
PSNCR	Public Sector Net Cash Requirement		TOR	Traditional Own Resources
QE	quantitative easing		TPI	Tax and Price Index
QUALYs	quality adjusted life years		TRIPS	Agreement on Trade Related Aspects of Intellectual Property
RCN	Royal College of Nursing			
RCT	randomized controlled trial		TUC	Trades Union Congress
RDP	Rural Development Policy		TVEI	Technical and Vocational Educational Initiative
RER	real exchange rate			
RHA	Regional Health Authority		UBR	Uniform Business Rate
RMT	Rail and Maritime Transport Union		UKTI	UK Trade and Investment
RNULC	relative normalized unit labour costs		UNCED	UN Conference on Environment and Development
ROA	return on assets			
ROCE	return on capital investment		UNFCCC	UN Framework Convention on Climate Change
RPI	Retail Price Index			
RPIX	RPI minus mortgage interest rates		USM	Unlisted Securities Market
RPIY	RPI minus direct taxes and mortgage interest rates		VFM	Value for Money
			VSTF	Very Short Term Financing
RSA	Revised Standardized Approach		WCED	World Commission on Environment and Development
RTA	regional trading arrangements			
RULC	relative unit labour costs		WFD	Work Force Development
SAL	Structural Adjustment Lending		WFTC	Working Family Tax Credit
SBU	Strategic Business Unit		WS	weak sustainability
SD	sustainable development		WSSD	World Summit on Sustainable Development
SEA	Single European Act			
SEM	small/medium-sized enterprises		WTA	willingness to accept
SEM	Single European Market		WTC	Working Tax Credit
SERPS	State Earnings Related Pension Scheme		WTP	willingness to pay

As any teacher or student of economics well knows, the vitality of the subject depends largely upon a continual synthesis of theory with observation, and observation with theory. Unfortunately this exercise is costly in terms of the time and the effort involved in finding sources, in assembling and interpreting data, and in searching journals and periodicals for informed comment on contemporary events.

Our hope is that this 12th edition of *Applied Economics* will take the reader some distance along this route, by combining information with analysis over 30 separate topic areas. The book also examines in detail the major economic issues arising within each topic area. The focus of *Applied Economics* is increasingly global, with extensive reference made throughout not only to the experiences of the UK, but also to those of other advanced industrialized and emerging economies, helping the reader place any observations on the UK in a broader international context.

Each chapter concentrates on a particular topic area and begins with a synopsis, setting out the issues to be investigated, and ends with a conclusion, reviewing the major findings. The largely self-contained nature of each chapter gives the book a useful degree of flexibility. For instance, chapters can be read selectively, in any order appropriate to the reader's interest or to the stage reached in a programme of study. This may be helpful to the reader as courses rarely follow the same sequence of topics. On the other hand, the topics have been arranged with an element of progression, so that the reader may begin at Chapter 1 and read the following chapters, arranged in four separate 'parts', consecutively. The book then takes the form of a 'course' in applied economics.

Applied Economics is designed for undergraduate and postgraduate students taking degree courses in economics, the social sciences, business studies and management, and for those taking professional and postgraduate courses with an economic content. Much of the content is suitable for those with little or no previous exposure to economics, although the diverse nature of the various topic areas inevitably means some variation in the level of analysis, and indeed in the balance between information and analysis.

We are indebted to many individuals for help during the course of this project, not least the help of so many library staff at Anglia Ruskin University, crucial to our exploring the wide range of journal and on-line sources of data and information captured by this book. We would also like to thank Professor Dr Dieter Lange, Head Central and Eastern Europe, CapGemini and Visiting Professor to Ashcroft International Business School, for much helpful advice on contemporary corporate strategic initiatives incorporated into various chapters. The major debt is, however, clearly owed to those who contributed the various chapters, and this is acknowledged more fully at the end of the book. Finally, for patience and forbearance during many months of absence from normal family activities, our thanks go to Sylvia and Eleanor. Of course any errors and omissions are entirely our responsibility.

We were delighted that the first 11 editions of *Applied Economics* were so well received by teachers and students across a wide range of courses. Our intention is to keep the book at the forefront of economic debate and events. Accordingly, in this twelfth edition we have thoroughly updated all the data and empirical material and added new economic analysis where appropriate. In addition we have incorporated five new chapters, capturing key contemporary areas of debate, namely Chapter 9 'Beyond markets: critical approaches to microeconomics', Chapter 12 'Health economics', Chapter 15 'Corporate social and ethical responsibility', Chapter 28 'The BRIC economies' and Chapter 30 'Managing the global economy: post 'credit crunch'.

You can find a variety of self-check questions on each chapter and further up-to-date information and data on the Companion Website to this book at www.pearsoned.co.uk/griffithswall.

Alan Griffiths, Stuart Wall
Cambridge 2011

M. Al-Kilani

Mahmoud is Principle Lecturer and Programme Leader in the Ashcroft International Business School, Anglia Ruskin University. He is author of a wide range of articles involving corporate social responsibility and issues of executive compensation, dividend signaling and international accounting standards. He is co-authoring (with G. Black) the third edition of *Introduction to Accounting and Finance*, FT/Prentice Hall. Responsible for Chapter 15.

G. H. Black

Geoff is Principal Lecturer in Business Finance, Harper Adams University College. He has held many senior examining posts and has lectured in Cyprus, Hong Kong, Malaysia, India and Singapore. He has written several textbooks, including *Applied Financial Accounting and Reporting*, Oxford University Press, and *Introduction to Accounting and Finance*, FT/Prentice Hall. Responsible for Chapter 2.

G. Burton

Glyn lectures in European Business, Ashcroft International Business School, Anglia Ruskin University, with special reference to macroeconomics and quantitative methods. Author (with G. Carrol and S. Wall) of *Quantitative Methods for Business and Economics*, 2nd edn, FT/Prentice Hall. He has taught economics at various levels and has lectured in Business Schools in France, Finland and the Netherlands. Responsible for Chapters 16, 22 and 23.

A. Dunnett

Andrew lectures, writes and researches at Thames Valley University, West London and was formerly the Head of the Economics Subject group at TVU, having more than three decades of experience in teaching economics and in demonstrating its relevance to real world issues. He is the author of a number of successful texts in economics and business. His interest in Health Economics stems from his involvement in the Richard Wells Research Centre in the Faculty of Health and Human Sciences at TVU where he contributes, as an economist and statistician, to Department of Health funded research into healthcare associated infections (HCAIs). He also delivers the core economics module on the MSc Health and Social Policy at TVU which attracts a wide variety of health service managers and, as a statistician, to more specialist programmes in epidemiology. Responsible for Chapter 12.

E. Fuller

Ted is Head of Business School, Lincoln University and has written and edited numerous publications, books, trainer manuals, expert systems and academic papers. He was formerly Professor and Director of the Centre of Entrepreneurship and Small Business Development at Teesside Business School, University of Teesside. Responsible for Chapter 3.

A. Griffiths

Alan is Reader in Economics, Ashcroft International Business School, Anglia Ruskin University, and previously Tutor in Economics at the University of Wales, Aberystwyth, Fellow of the Japan Foundation, Sophia University, Tokyo, and visiting Professor of Economics at Yokohama National University and Research Officer at the Research Institute for the National Economy, Tokyo. Co-author (with S. Wall) of *Economics for Business and Management*, FT/Prentice Hall, now in its third edition, editor of *European Economy Survey* and *British Economy Survey* and co-author (with S. Wall) of *Intermediate*

Microeconomics: Theory and Applications, Addison Wesley Longman (2nd edn). Responsible for Chapters 1, 5, 7, 14, 19, 30 and Chapters 4, 6, 10, 13, 25, 27 (with S. Wall).

B. Harrison

Barry is Senior Lecturer in Economics, Department of Economics, Nottingham Business School and Faculty Professor, TiasNimbas Business School. He has also held a visiting post at the National Institute for Management of the Economy in Baku, Azerbaijan and has been visiting professor at the European University at St Petersburg, Russia. His research interests currently focus on capital markets in Central and Eastern Europe and his publications have appeared in journals such as *Economics Letters*, *Applied Financial Economics* and *Economic Issues*. Responsible for Chapter 20.

S. Ison

Steve is Professor of Transport Policy, Loughborough University and teaches and researches across a range of transport and environmentally related subjects. He is co-author (with S. Wall) of *Economics*, FT/Prentice Hall, 4th edition, and editor (with T. Rye), of *The Implementation and Effectiveness of Transport Demand Management Measures: An International Perspective*, Ashgate Publishing Ltd, as well as other major texts and monographs. Steve is co-editor of the *Journal of Research in Transportation Business and Management*, associate editor of the *Journal of Transportation Planning and Technology*, and co-series editor of *Transport and Sustainability*. He is a Member of the Editorial Board of the *Journal of Transport Policy*, Member of the Scientific Committee of the World Conference on Transport Research Society and Chair of the World Conference on Transport Research Society Special Interest Group (SIG 10) Urban Transport Policy. Responsible for Chapter 11.

I. Negru

Ioana is Senior Lecturer in Economics in the Ashcroft International Business School, Anglia Ruskin University. She is the author of a wide range of articles and monographs on economic methodology and on the historical and contemporary contribution of various 'schools' of economic thought. Ioana is Associate Editor for the *Journal of Pluralism and Economics Education* and academic referee for a wide range of journals, including the *Cambridge Journal of Economics*, *Journal of Economic Issues*, *Journal of Philosophical Economics*, the *American Journal of Economics and Sociology*, *International Review of Economics Education* and *International Journal of Green Economics*. Responsible for Chapter 9.

G. O'Shea

Greg is Senior Lecturer in International Business and Finance in the Ashcroft International Business School, Anglia Ruskin University. He is a specialist in international business, corporate finance, mergers and acquisitions and business strategy, having worked with various international consultancy groups in the UK, US and Europe and lectured at Aalto University in Helsinki. He has extensive consultancy experience in global strategy and leadership in the US, Japan, Scandinavia, Russia and throughout the rest of Europe. Responsible for Chapter 28.

S. Rubinsohn

Simon is the Chief Economist for the Royal Institution of Chartered Surveyors. In this role, he is responsible for leading the economics and research team at the RICS in providing timely analysis of developments in both the commercial and residential property markets as well as in the construction industry. He is also responsible for delivering the RICS suite of high profile surveys measuring sentiment in different segments of the property market, helping to develop RICS policy positions alongside the External Affairs team and is a regular media commentator. Prior to taking up this position, Simon was Senior Strategist for Barclays Wealth where he played a key role in setting and managing the asset allocation for client portfolios focusing on a broad range of asset classes. Simon initially came into the financial services industry in 1985 when he joined ANZ Merchant Bank as a UK economist. Prior to this, he spent four years lecturing in economics. Responsible for Chapters 17 and 26.

K. Toner

Kieron lectures in Business Economics at the Ashcroft International Business School, Anglia Ruskin University, Cambridge. His teaching and research interests include areas within the field of international economics, particularly global trade issues and exchange rate policy, and also in the area of modern American political economy. He is involved in teaching at undergraduate level, and regularly teaches on business courses in Germany. Responsible (with S. Wall) for Chapter 24.

S. D. Wall

Stuart is Professor of Business and Economics Education, Ashcroft International Business School, Anglia Ruskin University. He has acted as consultant to the OECD Directorate for Science, Technology and Industry, as guest lecturer and examiner at the University of Cambridge and the Science Policy Research Unit, Sussex University and is author of a wide range of reports and articles on business strategy, the environment and the economics of technical change. He has authored and co-authored a wide range of major texts, published in many languages, such as *Economics for Business and Management* (with A. Griffiths) FT/Prentice Hall, now in its third edition, *International Business* (with S. Minocha and B. Rees) FT/Prentice Hall (3rd edn), and of *Intermediate Microeconomics: Theory and Applications* (with A. Griffiths) FT/Prentice Hall (2nd edn) and *Quantitative Methods* (with G. Carrol and G. Burton) FT/Prentice Hall (2nd edn) and *Environmental Issues and Policies* (with Ison, S. and Peake, S.) FT/Prentice Hall. Editor (with G. Black) of *Longman Modular Texts in Business and Economics*. Responsible for Chapters 8, 18 and (with A. Griffiths) for Chapters 4, 6, 10, 13, 25 and 27 and (with K. Toner) for Chapter 24.

R. Webb

Rob is Head of Department for Accounting, Finance and Risk and Director of Postgraduate Programmes at Caledonian Business School, Glasgow Caledonian University. Rob publishes widely in international journals in the areas of financial institution performance and applied economics most recently on the effects of demutualization on large UK bank performance. He is also Senior Advisor to the Risk Panel at the Chartered Institute for Securities and Investment. Responsible for Chapter 21.

C. Zimmermann

Carsten is Assistant Professor of Strategic Management at the University of San Diego, California, USA, lecturing and researching in areas that relate to the role of resources and capabilities in early-stage internationalization and development. His work has appeared in a number of major journals and texts, including *Strategic Reconfigurations*, Cheltenham, Edward Elgar. Carsten has worked many years at the strategic management consultancies A. T. Kearney and Capgemini Consulting, specializing in projects involving revenue growth, strategic sourcing and operational effectiveness in Germany, Hungary, Russia and the United States of America. Carsten is also involved in executive education for various organizations in industries as diverse as telecommunications, automotive supply, media, high technology and energy. Responsible for Chapter 29.

GUIDED TOUR

CHAPTER 1 — Changes in the economic structure

A synopsis at the beginning of each chapter explains what is covered and prepares you for what you will learn

Regular revision of data ensures book is up-to-date

Thorough examination of policy issues in the UK, Europe and the global economy, to help give you an international perspective

Fig. 13.2 Real hourly male earnings by percentile (index: 1966 = 100).
Sources: Various ONS publications and Financial Times (1996).

Explanation of earnings differentials

In seeking to explain the earnings distribution there are two main theoretical approaches, similar to those we considered above for factor shares.

Market theory

The first, the 'market theory', starts from an assumption of equality in net advantages for all jobs, i.e. that money earnings and the money value placed on working conditions are equal for all jobs. It also assumes that labour has a high degree of occupational and geographical mobility, so that if there is any inequality in net advantages, labour will move to the more advantageous jobs until equality is restored. Thus, differences in actual earnings must be caused by compensating differences in other advantages. Job satisfaction is one compensating advantage: enjoyable or safe jobs will be paid less than irksome or risky ones; this may partly explain the relatively high wage of manual workers such as coalface miners and chemical, gas and petroleum plant operators. Still more important are differences in training. Training

Key points at the end of each chapter help reinforce your learning

The website logo directs you to further on-line study material

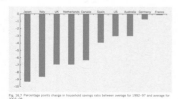

Fig. 16.7 Percentage points change in household savings ratio between average for 1992–97 and average for 2003–08.
Source: ONS Economic Trends (various).

Key points

Now try the self-check questions for this chapter on the Companion Website. You will also find useful links to relevant websites.

References and further reading at the end of each chapter directs you to the most up-to-date and relevant information

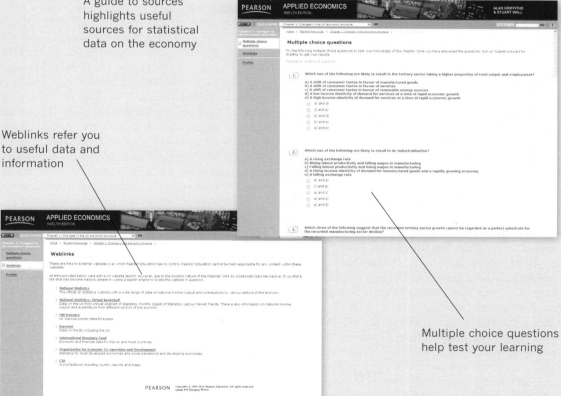

A guide to sources highlights useful sources for statistical data on the economy

Weblinks refer you to useful data and information

Multiple choice questions help test your learning

ACKNOWLEDGEMENTS

We are grateful to the following for permission to reproduce copyright material:

Figures

Figure 1.1 adapted from *Education at a glance 2010: OECD Indicators*, OECD (2010); Figure 2.1 adapted from Tecso plc Annual Report 2010; Figures 2.2, 2.3, 2.5, 2.6 adapted from Tesco plc Annual Report 2010; Figure 2.4 adapted from Tesco plc Annual Report 2006; Figure 4.1 from, and Figure 4.2 adapted from *Global Entrepreneurship Monitor, 2009 Executive Report* (Bosma, N., Levie, J. and Global Entrepreneurship Research Association (GERA) 2010); Figure 5.3 adapted from *Mergers and Acquisitions involving UK Companies*, ONS (2010), Crown Copyright material is reproduced with the permission of the Controller, Office of Public Sector Information (OPSI); Figure 8.2 adapted from *Intermediate Microeconomics*, 1 ed., Financial Times / Prentice Hall (Griffiths, A. and Wall, S. 2000) Fig. 7.8; Figure 8.3 adapted from *Intermediate Microeconomics*, 1 ed., Financial Times / Prentice Hall (Griffiths, A. and Wall, S. 2000) Fig. 7.9; Figure 9.1 from *Intermediate Microeconomics*, 1 ed., Financial Times / Prentice Hall (Griffiths, A. and Wall, S. 2000) Fig. 10.4; Figure 9.2 from *Intermediate Microeconomics*, 1 ed., Financial Times / Prentice Hall (Griffiths, A. and Wall, S. 2000) Fig. 10.5; Figure 9.3 from *Intermediate Microeconomics*, 1 ed., Financial Times / Prentice Hall (Griffiths, A. and Wall, S. 2000); Figure 11.2 adapted from *Transport Statistics Great Britain 2008*, Department of Transport (2009); Figure 12.1 from *Budget 2010: copy of economic and fiscal strategy report and financial statement and budget report – June 2010*, HM Treasury (2010) p. 5; Figure 12.2 adapted from *Public Expenditure Statistical Analysis 2010*, HM Treasury Tables 4.2, 4.3 and 4.4; Figure 12.3 from *Population Estimates*, ONS (2010), Crown Copyright material is reproduced with the permission of the Controller, Office of Public Sector Information (OPSI); Figure 12.4 from *Securing Good Health for the Whole Population: population health trends*, HM Tresury (Wanless, D. 2003) p. 5; Figure 12.5 from *Securing Good Health for the Whole Population: population health trends*, HM Treasury (Wanlass, D. 2003) p. 6; Figures 12.6, 12.7, 12.8 from *OECD Health Data 2009*, OECD (2009); Figure 12.9 from *Securing Good Health for the Whole Population: population health trends*, HM Treasury (2003) p. 9; Figure 12.10 from *Securing Good Health for the Whole Population: population health trends*, HM Treasury (Wanlass, D. 2003) p. 9; Figure 12.11 from http://www.nhs.uk/NHSEngland/thenhs/about/Pages/nhsstructure.aspx, NHS; Figure 14.5 from *Patterns of Low Pay*, ONS (Heasman, D. 2003), Crown Copyright material is reproduced with the permission of the Controller, Office of Public Sector Information (OPSI); Figure 14.6 from *National Minimum Wage: Low Pay Commission Report 2010*, The Stationary Office (2010) Fig. 2.15, Crown Copyright material is reproduced with permission under the terms of the Click-Use License; Figure 15.3 from The link between competitive advantage and corporate social responsibility, *Harvard Business Review*, 84 (12), p. 89 (Porter, M. and Kramer, M. 2006); Figure 15.4 from The link between competitive advantage and corporate social responsibility, *Harvard Business Review*, 84 (12) (Porter, M. and Kramer, M. 2006); Figure 15.6 adapted from *Business Ethics and Values: Individual, Corporate and International Perspectives*, 3 ed., Financial Times / Prentice Hall (Fisher, C. and Lovell, A.); Figure 15.7 from *Business Ethics and Values: Individual, Corporate and International Perspectives*, 3rd, Financial Times / Prentice Hall (Fisher, C. and Lovell, A. 2009) p. 388;

Figure 18.1 after *Public Expenditure Statistical Analysis*, HM Treasury (2010); Figure 19.2 adapted from *The Effects of Taxes and Benefits on Household Income*, ONS (2010), Crown Copyright material is reproduced with the permission of the Controller, Office of Public Sector Information (OPSI); Figure 19.5 adapted from *Tax Database 2009*, OECD (2009); Figure 19.7 from After the minimum wage: social security for working families with children, *Poverty, Journal of the Child Poverty Action Group*, 99 (Child Poverty Action Group 1998); Figure 20.3 from Does electric money mean the death of cash?, *Federal Reserve Bank of Dallas, Southwest Economy*, No. 2, March/April (1997); Figure 20.7 from *Quantitative Easing Explained*, Bank of England (2010); Figure 21.4 adapted from *Monetary and Financial Statistics 2010*, Bank of England (2010); Figure 21.8 from *Bank Management and Financial Services*, McGraw-Hill (Rose, P.S. and Hudgins, S.C. 2010); Figure 25.5 from 'Big Mac' Index, *The Economist*, 16/10/2010; Figure 28.1 adapted from *Cultures and Organisations: Software of the Mind*, McGraw-Hill (Hofstede, G. and Hofstede, G.J. 2005); Figure 29.5 adapted from *World Development Report*, World Bank (2010); Figure 30.4 from *International Business*, 3 ed., Financial Times / Prentice Hall (Wall, S., Minocha, S. and Rees, B. 2009).

Tables
Table 1.4 from *Labour Market Statistics*, ONS (2010), Crown Copyright material is reproduced with the permission of the Controller, Office of Public Sector Information (OPSI); Table 1.8 from *International Comparisons of Productivity*, ONS (2010), Crown Copyright material is reproduced with the permission of the Controller, Office of Public Sector Information (OPSI); Tables 1.9, 1.10 from The productivity gap between Europe and the United States: trends and causes, *Journal of Economic Perspectives*, Vol. 22 (1) (Van Ark, B., O'Mahoney, M. and Timmer, M.P. 2008); Table 1.13 from *Economic Outlook*, No. 87, OECD (2010); Table 4.2 from *Small and Medium Enterprise Statistics for UK and Regions*, Department for Business Innovation and Skills (2010); Table 4.5 from *Annual Small Business Survey 2007/8*, Department for Business, Enterprise and Regulatory Reform (2009); Table 5.1 from *Estimated Costs to Consumers of the Mergers Against Which the CC Took Action Between March 2005 and March 2006*, Competition Commission (Competition Commission 2006); Tables 11.1 and 11.5 from, and Tables 11.2, 11.3, 11.7 and 11.8 adapted from, *Transport Statistics Great Britain 2008*, Department for Transport (2009); Table 11.4 adapted from *Family Spending, a Report on the 2004–05 Expenditure and Food Survey*, ONS (2009), Crown Copyright material is reproduced with the permission of the Controller, Office of Public Sector Information (OPSI); Table 11.6 from Subsidies and the Environment: The State of Knowledge, *OECD: Contract No. RO-97-SC-2035* (Porter, G. 2003); Table 12.1 from NHS Staff 1999–2009 Overview, http://www.ic.nhs.uk/statistics-and-data-collections/workforce/nhs-staff-numbers/nhs-staff-1999--2009-overview, National Health Service; Table 12.2 from *Annual Survey of Hours and Earnings (ASHE)*, ONS (2010), Crown Copyright material is reproduced with the permission of the Controller, Office of Public Sector Information (OPSI); Table 13.2 from *StatExtracts*, OECD (2010) Income distribution – Inequality; Tables 13.4, 13.5 adapted from *Annual Survey of Hours and Earnings 2009*, ONS (2010), Crown Copyright material is reproduced with the permission of the Controller, Office of Public Sector Information (OPSI); Table 13.9 from *Child Wellbeing and Child Poverty: Where the UK Stands in the European Table*, Child Poverty Action Group (CPAG 2009); Table 14.5 adapted from International comparisons of labour disputes in 2006, *Economic and Labour Market Review*, 2 (4), pp. 32–39 (Hale, D. 2008), ONS, Crown Copyright material is reproduced with the permission of the Controller, Office of Public Sector Information (OPSI); Table 17.3 adapted from *Economic Outlook*, December, OECD (2005); Table 19.1 adapted from *Budget Report 2010*, HM Treasury (2010); Table 19.3 adapted from *The Effects of Taxes and Benefits on Household Income 2008/09*, ONS (2010), Crown Copyright material is reproduced with the permission of the Controller, Office of Public Sector Information (OPSI); Table 19.8 adapted from *Tax / Benefit Model Tables (April 2009)*, Department for Work and Pensions (2009); Table 19.9 from *Statistical Bulletin: Low pay estimates 2009*, ONS (2010), Crown Copyright material is reproduced with the permission of the Controller, Office of Public Sector Information (OPSI); Table 19.10 adapted from *Tax / Benefit Model Tables (April 2009)*, Department for Work and Pensions; Table 20.1 adapted from *Financial Statistics*, September, ONS (2010), Crown Copyright material

is reproduced with the permission of the Controller, Office of Public Sector Information (OPSI); Table 20.2 from The formulation of monetary policy at the Bank of Engalnd, *Bank of England Quarterly Bulletin*, Winter, pp. 434–41 (Bean, C. and Jenkinson, N. 2001); Table 21.1 adapted from *Monetary and Financial Statistics 2010*, Bank of England (2010) Tables A5.3 and A5.6; Table 21.4 adapted from *Financial Statistics 2010*, ONS (2010) Tables 5.2C and 5.2D, Crown Copyright material is reproduced with the permission of the Controller, Office of Public Sector Information (OPSI); Table 21.5 from *Monetary and Financial Statistics 2010*, Bank of England (2010); Table 21.6 adapted from *Inland Revenue Statistics 2010*, HMRC (2010) Tables 9.2, 9.3 and 9.4; Table 25.1 adapted from *Statistics Interactive Database: Interest and exchange rates*, Bank of England; Tables 28.2, 28.4, 28.5, 28.6 from *World Development Indicators Database 2010*, World Bank (2010).

Text

Extract on pages 177–8 from The end of rational economics, *Harvard Business Review*, July–August Special Edition (Ariely, D. 2009); Extract on page 435 from *Bank of England Annual Report 2000*, Bank of England (2000) p. 14.

The Financial Times

Figure 2.7 adapted from FTSE actuaries share indices, *Financial Times*, 10/09/2010; Figure 2.8 adapted from FT Share Information Service, *Financial Times*, 10/09/2010; Figure 18.2 from Forecast for spending and revenues % of GDP, *Financial Times*, 21/10/2010 (Wolf, M.); Figure 25.4 from Balance of payments, foreign exchange reserves and currency implications, *Financial Times*, 03/11/2010 (Wolf, M.).

In some instances we have been unable to trace the owners of copyright material, and we would appreciate any information that would enable us to do so.

CHAPTER 1

Changes in the economic structure

In this chapter we review the changing economic structure of nations as they mature, noting in particular the declining significance of industrial output and employment as compared with the service sector. Whilst comparisons are made throughout with international experience, the data in some tables refers to the UK by way of illustration. Alternative explanations of industrial decline are examined, such as economic 'maturity', low-wage competition, the advent of North Sea oil, 'crowding out' by the non-market public sector and low UK productivity *vis-à-vis* its competitors. We consider whether the changes observed in the UK are a cause for concern, or merely a reflection of changes experienced in other advanced industrialized countries.

The popular view of the UK as an industrial economy, a manufacturing nation, is now inaccurate. Over the past 50 years the structure of the economy has been transformed. Manufacturing now contributes only around 12% of total output and employs over 6 million fewer people than in 1964. One of the most prominent of today's industries, North Sea oil and gas, did not even exist 35 years ago, and service activities now dominate the economy in terms of both output and employment. There are even suggestions that the UK is becoming a 'post-industrial' economy, i.e. one in which information-handling activities are predominant. We shall consider the causes and consequences of these changes, and in so doing point out that structural change has implications for other important economic issues.

Structure defined

An economy may be analysed in terms of its component parts, often called 'sectors'. Sectors may be widely drawn to include groups of industries (e.g. the engineering industries) or narrowly drawn to identify parts of industries (e.g. fuel-injection equipment), depending on our purpose. Structural change is often discussed in terms of the even more widely drawn 'primary', 'secondary' and 'tertiary' (service) sectors. It will be useful at the outset to define these, and other conventional sector headings.

1 The *primary sector* – includes activities directly related to natural resources, e.g. farming, mining and oil extraction.

2 The *secondary sector* – covers all the other goods production in the economy, including the processing of materials produced by the primary sector. Manufacturing is the main element in this sector which also includes construction and the public utility industries of gas, water and electricity.

3 The *tertiary sector* – includes all the private sector services, e.g. distribution, insurance, banking and finance, and all the public sector services, such as health and defence.

4 The *goods sector* – the primary and secondary sectors combined.

5 The *production industries* – includes the entire secondary sector except construction, together with the coal and coke industries and the extraction of mineral oil and natural gas. There is an index of industrial production on this basis, and the term 'industry' usually refers to this sector heading.

Structural change means change in the relative size of the sectors, however defined. We may judge size by output (contribution to Gross Domestic Product (GDP)),[1] or by inputs used, either capital or labour. Usually more attention is paid to labour because of the interest in employment and also because it is more easily measured than capital.

Through time we should *expect* the structure of an economy to change. The pattern of demand for a country's products will change with variations in income or taste, affecting in turn both output and employment. If economic growth occurs and real incomes rise, then the demand for goods and services with high and positive income elasticities will tend to increase relative to those with low or even negative income elasticities.[2] For example, between 1983 and 2010, household final consumption expenditure rose by 198% but, while expenditure on recreation and culture rose 412%, expenditure on food and non-alcoholic beverages rose by only 41.6%, and expenditure on alcohol and tobacco actually fell by 4.2%. Such changes have clear implications for the pattern of output and employment.

The pattern of demand is also responsive to changes in the age structure of the population. The UK, like other developed countries, is experiencing important demographic changes which meant that by 2010 there were 0.8 million fewer people in the 16–24-year-old age group than in 1981. So, for example, the 'recreation, entertainment and education' sector may find this a constraint on its growth, unless it can adapt to the changing characteristics of the market. This smaller age cohort of young people will form fewer new households than previous cohorts, so reducing demand for housing, furniture and consumer durables below what it would otherwise have been. In the longer term, a further demographic factor will be the continuing rise in the numbers of people aged over 75, who will place increasingly heavy demands on the medical and care services.

It is not only the demand side which initiates structural change. The reduced supply of young people in the labour market in the early 1990s increased their earnings relative to other workers, which encouraged firms such as supermarkets to recruit older workers. Employers may also respond by substituting capital for labour and so changing employment patterns, or by raising product prices which would reduce the growth of output and in turn influence employment.

Also on the supply side, technical progress makes possible entirely new goods and services, as well as new processes for producing existing goods and services. In Chapter 23 we note that microelectronics not only gives us new products, such as word processors and video games, but also reduces costs of production, whether through the introduction of robotics in manufacturing, or of computerized accounting methods in banking services. Where such 'process innovation' raises total factor productivity, unit costs fall. The supply side is therefore itself initiating new patterns of demand, output and employment, by creating new products or by reducing the prices of existing products and raising quality.

Changes in resource availability may also initiate structural change, as happened so dramatically with oil in 1973 and again in 1979. When the oil-producing and exporting countries (OPEC) restricted world output, oil-based products rose sharply in price, with *direct* consequences for substitutes (e.g. coal and gas) and complements (e.g. cars). In response to higher oil prices, not only did the demand for substitutes rise, and for complements fall, but decisions had also to be taken throughout the economy, by both producers and consumers, to use less energy. As a result there was a decline in output and employment in energy-intensive industries, a prime example being steel.

Oil has had further *indirect* effects on the structure of the UK economy by means of the exchange rate. The development of North Sea oil production enabled the UK to be self-sufficient in oil by 1980, but also bestowed 'petro-currency' status on the pound. This meant that the sterling exchange rate was now responsive to changes in oil prices, which between 1979 and 1983 tended to keep the pound higher than would otherwise have been the case. The result was to make UK exports dearer and imports cheaper in the early 1980s, with adverse consequences for output and employment in sectors facing international competition, both abroad and at home. During 1986 this was partially reversed. The oil price halved and sterling fell 9.2% (on average), providing a stimulus to industrial output during 1987. Although by 1990 the UK was not much more than self-sufficient in oil, the pound still behaved as a petro-currency during the first Gulf war. Following the invasion of Kuwait by Iraq, and the consequent rise in the oil price, the pound appreciated by just over 6% during July and August 1990. The trade surplus in oil peaked at £8.1bn in 1985 and fell to a low of £1.2bn by 1991. Since then it has been rising with the rapid growth in North Sea oil production and reached a peak of £5.7bn in 2002 before becoming negative (−£492m) for the first time in 2005.

International competition is a potent force for change in the economic structure of the UK. Changing consumer tastes, the creation of new products and changing comparative costs result in the redistribution of economic activity around the world. The demise of the UK motorcycle industry in the face of Japanese competition, for example, was the result of UK manufacturers failing to meet consumer demand for lighter, more reliable, motorcycles which Japan could produce more cheaply. As we see in Chapter 26,

for most products the major impact on UK output and employment has come not from Japanese producers, but from those EU countries which, unlike Japan, have unrestricted access to the UK market. Membership of the EU inevitably meant accepting some restructuring of the UK economy, in accordance with European comparative advantages. This is certainly true for industrial production, with the EU a protected free trade area, though less true for agriculture (see Chapter 27).

Decisions on the location of industrial production are increasingly taken by *multinational enterprises*. In the UK motor industry, decisions taken by Ford and General Motors during the 1970s and early 1980s to supply more of the European market from other EU plants contributed to the fall in UK car output from 1.3 million in 1977 to 1.1 million in 1987, despite real consumer spending on cars and vehicles more than doubling in that period. However, by 2010, inward investment by companies such as Nissan, Toyota, Honda, BMW and Peugeot–Citroen had helped avoid further falls in UK output, with the UK now the fourth largest automotive manufacturer in Europe, building over 2 million engines and 1 million cars per year.

Structural change in the UK

Changes in output

Table 1.1 presents index numbers of output at constant factor cost,[3] recording changes in the volume of output for the various sectors. Data for GDP at factor cost are also given so that comparisons can be made between the individual sectors and the economy as a whole.

In the **primary sector**, *agriculture, hunting, forestry and fishing* grew slower than GDP between 1964 and 1979. After 1979 this sector's output was more influenced by the agricultural policy of the European Union than by the UK business cycle. So agricultural output grew strongly through the recession of the early 1980s and, just as perversely, fell during the upswing of 1994 and 1995. Within *mining and quarrying* there are two very contrasting industries: coal, which is the only industry where output has fallen throughout the period, and the oil and gas

Table 1.1 Index numbers of output at constant prices (1990 = 100).

	1964	1969	1973	1979	1981	1990	2009
Primary							
Agriculture, hunting, forestry and fishing	55.0	59.0	69.5	71.3	81.2	100	95.1
Mining and quarrying	187.0	136.1	104.3	109.2	115.7	100	89.4
Coal and nuclear fuel	295.0	213.2	166.1	144.4	143.8	100	19.5
Oil and gas extraction	–	–	–	88.8	99.2	100	120.4
Secondary							
Manufacturing	72.6	85.4	94.6	90.6	77.7	100	94.3
Construction	65.9	74.4	77.4	69.4	60.5	100	104.9
Electricity, gas and water supply	45.3	55.1	69.6	80.4	81.9	100	128.6
Tertiary							
Distribution, hotels and catering, repairs	61.0	65.5	76.0	76.6	69.9	100	150.0
Transport and storage	60.2	66.7	79.3	81.5	77.9	100	152.3
Post and telecommunication	30.6	40.2	50.2	59.7	62.7	100	289.8
Financial, intermediation, real estate, renting and business activities	27.6	34.5	42.3	49.6	54.3	100	187.5
Public administration, national defence and social security	85.1	89.1	98.0	98.0	102.2	100	115.8
Education, health and social work	57.9	67.2	76.5	92.4	94.2	100	146.1
Other services	51.8	54.7	59.0	68.3	70.5	100	156.4
GDP	**58.7**	**66.4**	**74.9**	**80.0**	**76.5**	**100**	**140.6**
Production industries	**62.6**	**73.3**	**81.4**	**87.6**	**78.9**	**100**	**93.8**

Sources: ONS (2010a) *Annual Abstract of Statistics*; ONS (2010e) *United Kingdom National Accounts*, and previous issues.

extraction industry which grew very rapidly in the late 1970s and early 1980s. *Coal* output fell by just over half between 1964 and 1979. High real energy prices after the 1973 and 1979 oil price 'shocks' improved the prospects of the coal industry, but at the same time made feasible the rapid exploitation of high-cost North Sea oil, which was increasingly to act as a substitute for coal. Coal output fell by around 30% between 1979 and 1990 and then by over 90% between 1990 and 2009 as the privatized electricity generating companies made their 'dash for gas'. *Oil and gas extraction* had peaked at an index number of 137 in 1987 before falling to the 100 in 1990 shown in the table (the halving of the oil price in 1986 may have been a factor in this decline). After 1990 the offshore oil and gas extraction industry enjoyed a remarkable revival in which output increased by nearly 76% over the 11 years to 2001 to register an all-time high as new techniques enabled more oil and gas to be profitably produced both from existing fields and also from

new smaller fields which might previously have been uneconomic. However, between 2001 and 2009 output of the sector has fallen to only 20% higher than 1990 as problems with domestic supplies began to emerge.

In the **secondary sector,** 1973 is again a significant date. Output from both manufacturing and construction rose steadily between 1964 and 1973 (at annual rates of 2.9% and 1.8% respectively), but between 1973 and 1979 output from both these subsectors actually fell, and fell still more sharply in the recession between 1979 and 1981. *Manufacturing* output fell by as much as 12.9 points or 14.2% in this recession. The recovery after 1981 took manufacturing output to a new peak by 1990 which was just 5.4 points above the previous peak 17 years earlier in 1973. All of that gain in output was then lost in the recessionary years of 1991, 1992 and 2007. These forces left manufacturing output in 2009 very similar to the level of 1973. Over a period of 36 years this rate of growth represents virtual stagnation.

Output in the *construction* industry follows a similar path to that in manufacturing up to 1981. The industry was then a leading sector in the boom of the eighties, far outstripping manufacturing, with growth of almost 40 points or 66% between 1981 and 1990 (i.e. 5.7% per annum). Output of the industry then fell by 7.7% between 1990 and 2001 before growing strongly between 2001 and 2006, then declining in the recessionary period from 2007 onwards to be only 5% above the 1990 figure in 2009. *Electricity, gas and water supply* shows none of the volatility of construction. The long-run growth of output in this sector tends to keep up with that of GDP and does not always become negative during recessions.

The index of output for the *production industries* (see earlier definition) is presented in the last row of Table 1.1. We see that industrial production grew between 1964 and 1973 by 18.8 points, an annual rate of 2.9%, but then grew more slowly between 1973 and 1979, and fell sharply between 1979 and 1981. This definition includes the contribution of North Sea oil and gas, which helped to compensate for the sharp decline of output in manufacturing since 1973. Exploitation of a non-renewable natural resource is, however, more akin to the consumption of capital than it is to the production of goods and services. The North Sea provided the UK with a once-and-for-all 'windfall' gain in output over other less fortunate countries. To some extent this masked the full extent of the decline in *non-oil industrial output* which fell by 14.6% between 1973 and 1981, resulting in *non-oil GDP* being 2.5% lower in 1981 than in 1973.

After 1981, growth of UK industrial output resumed, led by the recovery of manufacturing output, and averaged 2.9% per year through to 1988. Industrial output in the 1980s was again growing at the rates of the 1960s, and changing oil output did not significantly affect the index. Industrial production then fell back under the impact of recession, falling 4.1 points between 1990 and 1992 before recovering after 1993, though falling again in the first decade of the millennium so that by 2009 the output of the *production industries* was 6.2% below the level recorded at constant factor prices in 1990.

International comparisons highlight the failure of British industry during the 1960s and 1970s. Industrial production in the industrial market economies (OECD) grew at a weighted average of 6.2% per annum between 1960 and 1970, slowing to what

in the UK would still have been regarded as a healthy 2.3% per annum between 1970 and 1983. So British industrial output in the 1960s grew at less than half the average rate of the industrial market economies as a whole, and during the late 1970s contracted as industrial production in these countries continued to grow. However, during the 1980s the growth of UK industry relative to the rest of the OECD clearly improved. The OECD index of industrial production shows growth in the UK of 47% for the period 1981–2005, against an average growth for the whole OECD of 53%. Since 2005 there has been a fall in industrial production of 12.4% in the UK, faster than the fall of 7.4% recorded in the OECD over the period 2005–10. We can conclude that the UK's rate of relative decline as an industrial producer has been greatly reduced since the 1970s but has not yet been halted.

In the **tertiary or service sector**, Table 1.1 shows that output grew in every subsector throughout the whole 1964–79 time period. Even during the recession of 1979–81 output fell in only two of the seven subsectors. The pace-setters have been the communications, financial services and real estate sectors. The thrust of government policy since 1979 under Margaret Thatcher had ensured that public sector services grew more slowly than the rest of the sector. However, since the late 1990s and throughout the first decade of the millennium, public administration along with defence and social security as a group grew relatively rapidly, rising by 15.8% on the 1990 base figure.

The contrast in growth experience between the service sector and the industrial sector has changed the share of total output attributable to each (see Table 1.2). However, even in the service sector, growth of output in the UK at 2.9% per annum between 1964 and 1981 lagged behind the average for the industrial market economies which was 3.9%. Between 1981 and 2009 UK service sector growth was, at 3.1% per annum, a relative improvement as the average for the industrial market economies had fallen to a similar figure. The poor UK industrial performance outlined above may also have contributed to this relatively poor service sector performance, since many services are marketed to industry or to people whose incomes are earned in industry. A growing industrial sector generates an induced demand for the output of the service sector.

The GDP can be obtained by aggregating the various sectors outlined above. It grew from 58.7 in 1964

Table 1.2 Percentage shares of GDP at factor cost.*

	1964	1969	1973	1979	1990	2009
Primary	5.8	4.3	4.2	6.7	3.9	3.7
Agriculture, forestry and fishing	1.9	1.8	2.9	2.2	1.8	0.7
Mining and quarrying including oil and gas extraction	3.9	2.5	1.1	4.5	2.1	2.9
Secondary	40.8	42.0	40.9	36.7	31.5	19.4
Mineral oil processing	0.5	0.5	0.4	0.6	} 22.5	} 11.6
Manufacturing	29.5	30.7	30.0	27.3		
Construction	8.4	8.4	7.3	6.2	6.9	6.2
Electricity, gas and water supply	2.4	2.4	2.8	2.6	2.1	1.6
Tertiary	53.8	53.0	54.9	56.5	64.4	76.8
Distribution, hotels, catering, repairs	14.0	13.3	13.1	12.7	13.5	14.1
Transport and storage	4.4	4.4	4.7	4.8	} 7.6	} 7.0
Post and telecommunication	1.6	1.9	2.3	2.5		
Financial intermediation, real estate, renting and business activities	8.3	8.6	10.7	11.0	} 22.6	} 32.4
Ownership of dwellings	5.4	5.5	5.1	5.8		
Public administration, national defence and social security	7.6	7.0	6.1	6.1	6.3	5.0
Education, health and social work	6.9	7.1	7.7	8.1	8.9	13.1
Other services	5.6	5.2	5.1	5.7	5.5	5.2

Note: Calculated from GDP at factor cost, at current prices and unadjusted for financial services and residual error.
*Totals may not sum to 100 due to rounding.
Source: ONS (2010e) *United Kingdom National Accounts*, and previous issues.

to 80.0 in 1979, i.e. by around 36%. This represents an average annual growth rate of about 2.2% between 1964 and 1979, slowing to 1.1% between 1973 and 1979. The GDP actually declined between 1979 and 1981 by 4.4% whilst the OECD average GDP continued to rise slowly. By international standards the UK growth performance was poor between 1964 and 1981. For instance, the weighted average annual growth rate for industrial market economies, our key trading partners, was 5.1% between 1960 and 1970 and 3.2% between 1970 and 1979. In the eight years following the recession of 1981, UK real GDP grew at an average of 3.3% per annum, well above the UK rates of the 1960s, and above the OECD average of 3.1%. During the 1980s, therefore, the UK's relative economic decline was halted, but even at these higher rates its reversal was likely to be a slow process. Events since 1988 have confirmed this view, with UK real GDP growing at 1.9% per annum between 1988 and 2009 compared to the OECD average of 2.0%.

Changes in shares of output

Table 1.2 uses percentage shares of total output (GDP at factor cost) to show changes in the relative importance of the sectors presented in Table 1.1.

The **primary sector** was in relative decline between 1964 and 1973 because of the contraction of output in coal-mining. From a low point of 4.2% of GDP in 1973, the primary sector sharply increased its share to 6.7% in 1979 and 9.5% in 1984 (not shown), an unusual trend in a developed economy and almost entirely attributable to the growth of North Sea oil and gas production. By 1990 the primary sector's share had slumped to 3.9%. This dramatic change was caused, in part, by the collapse of oil prices during 1986. Since 1990, there has been further decline in agriculture, forestry and fishing but a small improvement in mining and quarrying (including oil), so that the decline in the primary sector share of GDP over the period 1990–2009 was only 0.2%, falling from 3.9% to 3.7%.

The **secondary sector's** share of output fell from a peak of 42.0% in 1969 to only 31.5% in 1990; the recession then further reduced this to 19.4% by 2009. This long-term decline in the secondary sector is inevitable as the share of manufacturing in GDP falls. By 1990 manufacturing produced only 22.5% of UK output, which fell further to 11.6% by 2009.

The **tertiary sector's** share of output has grown throughout the period since 1969, necessarily so as the shares of the primary and secondary sectors have fallen. The financial sector plus real estate, renting and business activities virtually trebled their combined share of output between 1964 and 2009, accounting for nearly a third of total GDP by 2009 – the largest share of UK output in that year.

With the exception of the growth of the North Sea sector, these changes in economic structure have occurred throughout the advanced industrial countries (see Table 1.3). The fall in the share of manufacturing in GDP in the UK is typical of the other industrial market economies, and the growth in the share of the service sector has been similar to the average for such economies. This has led some to interpret the changes in UK economic structure as inevitable, giving more recently industrialized countries a glimpse of the future. However, to be complacent because the *relative* position of the sectors in the UK has changed in line with that in other advanced industrialized countries is to ignore the UK's dramatic and unrivalled fall in the *volume* of non-oil industrial production between 1973 and 1981, outlined above in the section on changes in output. Of especial concern has been the negligible growth rate of manufacturing output in the UK between 1973 and 2009; indeed the volume figure for UK manufacturing in 2009 is very similar to that for 1973 (see Table 1.1 above).

Table 1.3 Industrial market economies, distribution of GDP: percentages.

	1960	1980	1985	2008
Agriculture	6.0	3.1	2.6	1.8
Industry	41.0	36.5	34.2	28.1
(manufacturing)	(30.4)	(24.7)	(23.2)	(17.4)
Services	53.0	60.4	63.2	70.1

Sources: OECD (2002) *OECD in Figures,* and previous issues; OECD (2010c) *OECD Factbook 2010.*

Changes in employment

Employment has obviously been influenced by the changes in output already described. It has also been influenced by changes in technology, which have affected the labour required per unit of output. Table 1.4 gives numbers employed in each sector, together with percentage shares of total employment. The table shows that in the **goods sector** (primary and secondary) there were fewer jobs in 1979 than in 1964, with a still more rapid decline in jobs between 1979 and 2010. In fact, by 2010 total employment in the goods sector as a whole had fallen from over 9.6 million in 1979 to just over 5.4 million in 2010.

In the **primary sector**, employment was reduced by 60% between 1964 and 1990. The contraction in coal output inevitably sent employment in *mining and quarrying* into severe decline. After 1990 this accelerated as the coal industry lost some of its electricity generation market to gas and was itself made ready for privatization. By 2001 coal industry employment stood at only 14,000, having been over 300,000 in the early 1970s. Such was the growth of output per worker in *agriculture, forestry and fishing* that employment was reduced by 2010 to 83% of its 1964 level, despite an increase in output of 73%. The rise of the North Sea sector had directly created only 24,000 jobs in *oil and natural gas* by 1981. Renewed interest in gas helped raise this to 36,000 by 1990 but although output soared after 1990, employment again fell. The outcome was that between 1964 and 2010 the primary sector's share of total employment fell from 5.1% to 1.8%.

In the **secondary sector**, employment fell by 2.07 million between 1964 and 1979, and again by 4.0 million between 1979 and 2010. Manufacturing, as the largest part of this sector, suffered most of these job losses, with manufacturing employment falling by over 6.4 million in the period 1964–2010. The *share* of manufacturing in total employment fell from 38.1% in 1964 to as little as 8.2% in 2010.

As employment fell in the goods sector between 1964 and 1979, employment in the **tertiary sector** expanded by 2,378,000, enabling total employment to be held at around 23 million. This expansion was concentrated in the financial sector, and in various professional and scientific services.

The rough balance between employment losses in the goods sector and gains in the service sector broke down after 1979. Between 1979 and 1981 service

Table 1.4 Employees in employment, UK.

	1964 (000s)	1964 (% of total employment)	1973 (000s)	1973 (% of total employment)	1979 (000s)	1979 (% of total employment)	1981 (000s)	1981 (% of total employment)	1990 (000s)	1990 (% of total employment)	2010 (000s)	2010 (% of total employment)
Agriculture forestry and fishing	540	2.3	432	1.9	368	1.6	363	1.6	314	1.4	450	1.5
Mining and quarrying			336	1.5	304	1.3	285	1.3	126	0.5	62	0.2
Extraction of mineral oil and natural gas			5	–	20	0.1	24	0.1	36	0.2	19	0.1
Total primary	**1,201**	**5.1**	**773**	**3.4**	**692**	**3.0**	**672**	**3.0**	**476**	**2.1**	**531**	**1.8**
Manufacturing	8,909	38.1	7,861	34.7	7,259	31.3	6,221	28.4	4,709	20.5	2,515	8.2
Construction	1,659	7.1	1,320	5.8	1,253	5.4	1,130	5.2	1,143	5.0	2,103	6.8
Other energy and water supply			364	1.6	366	1.6	366	1.7	241	1.1	264	0.8
Total secondary	**10,978**	**46.9**	**9,573**	**42.4**	**8,911**	**38.5**	**7,748**	**35.4**	**6,093**	**26.6**	**4,882**	**15.7**
Distribution, hotels and catering, repairs	1,665	7.1	3,950	17.4	4,252	18.4	4,172	19.1	4,912	21.4	6,558	21.3
Transport			1,062	4.7	1,051	4.5	987	4.5	921	4.0	1,429	4.6
Communication			445	2.0	422	1.8	438	2.0	471	2.0	1,109	3.6
Banking, finance, insurance, business services and leasing	9,513	40.7	1,442	6.4	1,663	7.2	1,738	7.9	3,480	15.2	6,241	20.3
Public administration, defence and social security			1,664	7.3	1,721	7.4	1,623	7.4	1,442	6.3	1,740	5.6
Education and health			2,781	12.3	2,876	12.4	2,908	13.3	5,125	22.4	8,382	27.1
Other services			976	4.3	1,571	6.8	1,600	7.3				
Total tertiary	**11,178**	**47.8**	**12,320**	**54.4**	**13,556**	**58.5**	**13,465**	**61.4**	**16,351**	**71.3**	**25,408**	**82.5**
Total employment	**23,357**		**22,664**		**23,158**		**21,891**		**22,920**		**30,801**	

Sources: ONS (2010c) *Labour Market Statistics*, September; ONS (2006b) *United Kingdom National Accounts*.

Table 1.5 Industrial market economies, distribution of the labour force: percentages.

	1960	1980	2008
Agriculture	17.3	6.5	2.4
Industry	36.7	34.5	23.7
(manufacturing)	(27.2)	(25.0)	(16.9)
Services	46.0	59.0	73.9

Sources: OECD (2010d) *OECD in Figures*, and previous issues; OECD (2010) *Country Surveys* (various).

Table 1.6 Changes in industrial employment (%).

	1964–79	1979–83	1983–2010
UK	−14.8	−18.9	−29.0
Canada	+35.7	−8.7	+12.9
USA	+27.2	−6.4	−18.5
Japan	+28.3	+4.1	−20.0
Austria	−3.2	+8.3	−6.9
Belgium	−18.6	−15.2	−0.4
France	+2.3	−7.4	−22.1
Germany	−10.3	−8.5	+1.7
Italy	+2.2	−3.8	−11.2
Norway	+9.1	−2.7	−6.3
Sweden	−10.9	−7.1	−30.0
Switzerland	−21.1	−3.3	−12.7

Sources: Calculated from data in OECD (2010f) *OECD Statistical Programme of Work Labour Statistics*; OECD (2010e) *Stat. Extracts*; OECD (2005a) *Labour Force Statistics 1984–2004*.

sector employment actually fell slightly. Not until 1984 did the growth of service sector employment again compensate for the loss of goods sector employment. However, over the whole period 1979–2010 service sector employment grew by 11.9 million whilst employment in the goods sector fell by 4.2 million. As a result total employment rose by 7.7 million.

Similar changes in the pattern of employment have, however, taken place throughout the industrial world (see Table 1.5). By comparison with other advanced economies the UK now has relatively small agricultural and industrial sectors, leaving services with a larger than average share of total employment.

Causes of structural change

Stage of maturity

As the world's oldest industrial nation the UK might reasonably lay claim to being its most developed or 'mature' economy. Several variants of the maturity argument provide explanations of industrial decline which appear rather reassuring.

A first variant suggests that the changing pattern of UK employment since 1964 may be seen as analogous to the transfer of workers from agriculture to industry during the nineteenth century, a transfer necessary to create the new industrial workforce. In a similar way, the argument here is that those previously employed in industrial activities were required for the expansion of the service sector in the 1960s and 1970s. However, this line of argument looks rather weak from the mid- to late 1970s onwards,

with rising unemployment surely providing the opportunity for service sector expansion without any marked decline in industrial sector employment.

The hypothesis that economic maturity is always associated with falling industrial employment may be crudely tested by reference to Table 1.6. In the period 1964–79 the experience of the UK, Austria, Belgium, West Germany, Sweden and Switzerland lends support to the hypothesis, whilst the experience of Canada, the USA, France and Norway contradicts it. Italy and Japan also experienced rising industrial employment, but it might be contentious to call these economies 'mature' in this period. Between 1964 and 1979, the evidence does therefore suggest that decline in industrial employment in the UK was not necessarily an inevitable result of economic development. The data between 1979 and 1983 are more difficult to interpret as they cover a period of recession, but only Japan and Austria experienced a rise in industrial employment in these years. However, data for the years 1983–2010 seem to show that most, but not all, countries experienced a fall in industrial employment, Canada and Germany being the exceptions. In the UK the decline in industrial employment accelerated during the early 1990s, resulting in an overall fall of over 29% for the 1983–2010 period as a whole.

A second variant of the 'maturity' argument is that our changing economic structure simply reflects the changing pattern of demand that follows from economic development. It has been argued that consumer demand in a mature economy shifts away from goods and towards services (higher income elasticities) and that this, together with increased government provision of public sector services, adds impetus to the growth of the tertiary sector. This may be a sound explanation for some of the UK's structural change, but not all. The pattern of UK demand simply does not fit such a stylized picture; for instance, UK trade data clearly show UK demand for manufactured imports growing faster than UK manufactured exports. This growth in manufactured imports is hardly consistent with a major switch of UK demand away from industries producing goods.

In a third variant of the 'maturity' argument, Rowthorn and Wells (1987) have pointed out that the demand for manufactured goods is at least as income elastic as the demand for services, when valued at constant prices, that is, in terms of volume. A successful industrial sector would therefore achieve increases in the volume of output at least matching the growth of GDP. Faster growth of productivity in the industrial sector could then cause prices to fall relative to those in the service sector, thereby reducing the industrial sector's *share* of both output at current prices and employment. The 'maturity' argument should, in the view of Rowthorn and Wells, be based on *productivity* changes and not on demand changes. In the case of the UK, the relatively slow growth in the *volume* of industrial output hardly supports this variant of the 'maturity' argument.

A fourth variant of the argument is that the UK has always been a reluctant manufacturing nation, and that we are now specializing in services, a sector in which we enjoy a comparative advantage and a protected domestic market. However, since the mid-1970s, any need to exploit comparative advantages in services could again have been met from unused resources rather than by reducing industrial output and employment.

Low-wage competition

Foreigners, especially from the Third World, make a convenient scapegoat for UK problems and are particularly blamed for providing 'unfair', low-wage competition. Wages in the Third World are extremely low but are often accompanied by low productivity, a lack of key categories of skilled labour, and a shortage of supporting industrial services and infrastructure. The UK is not unique in facing this competition and is itself a low-wage economy by developed country standards. In some sectors (e.g. textiles and cheap electrical goods) Third World competition has been important but, as yet, the scale of Third World involvement in the export of world manufactures is too small (around 18% of OECD-manufactured exports in 2010) to be regarded as a major cause of UK structural change. As we see in Chapters 25–27, the main competition comes from other industrial market economies, not from low-wage developing countries. We should also remember that countries like the previously high growth Asian 'Tiger' economies provide important export markets for manufactured goods, and so have contributed to world economic growth, with the slump in the late 1990s in these economies creating problems for the export sectors of many industrialized economies, such as the UK.

The North Sea

Free-market economists often argue that the contribution of North Sea oil to the UK balance of payments has meant inevitable decline for some sectors of the economy. The mechanism of decline is usually attributed to the exchange rate, with the improvement in the UK visible balance (via removal of the oil deficit) bringing upward pressure on sterling. In terms of the foreign exchange market, higher exports of oil increase the demand for sterling, and lower imports of oil decrease the supply of sterling. The net effect has been a higher sterling exchange rate than would otherwise have been the case, particularly in the late 1970s and early 1980s. The status of sterling as a petro-currency may also attract an increased capital inflow, further raising the demand for sterling, and with it the sterling exchange rate. The higher price of sterling then makes UK exports more expensive abroad, and imports cheaper in the UK. United Kingdom producers of industrial exports, and import substitutes, are the most seriously disadvantaged by a high pound, since the major part of UK trade is in industrial products (around two-thirds of both exports and imports). In this way a higher pound produces a decline in industrial output and employment.

The argument that North Sea oil, through its effect on the exchange rate, inevitably resulted in the decline in UK manufacturing output and employment observed in the late 1970s and early 1980s is rather simplistic. The government could have directed surplus foreign exchange created by oil revenues towards imported capital equipment. This increase in imports of capital equipment would have eased the upward pressure on the pound,[4] whilst providing a basis for increased future competitiveness and economic recovery. Equally, the upward pressure on sterling could have been alleviated by macroeconomic policies aimed at raising aggregate demand, and with it spending on imports, or by lower interest rates aimed at reducing capital inflow.

North Sea oil cannot be wholly to blame for the observed decline in UK industrial output and employment. These structural changes began in the mid-1960s, yet North Sea oil only became a significant factor in the UK balance of payments in 1978. The periods of high exchange rate between 1978 and 1981, whilst certainly contributing to industrial decline, were by no means an inevitable consequence of North Sea oil. Different macroeconomic policies could, as we have seen, have produced a lower exchange rate, as happened after withdrawal from the Exchange Rate Mechanism in September 1992.

'Crowding out'

Bacon and Eltis (1976) argued that the decline of British industry was due to its being displaced ('crowded out') by the growth of the non-market public sector. Some of the (then) public sector, such as steel, is itself industrial and markets its output in the same way as any private sector company. However, some of the public sector, such as health and education, provides services which are not marketed, being free at the point of use. This non-market public sector uses resources and generates income, but does not supply any output to the market. It requires investment goods for input, and consumes goods and services, all of which must be provided by the market sector.

We might usefully illustrate the 'crowding out' argument by first taking a closed economy with no government sector. Here the income generated in the market would equal the value of output. The income-receivers could enjoy all the goods and services they produced. However, they could no longer do so if a non-market (government) sector is now added, since the non-market sector will also require a proportion of the goods and services produced by the market sector. The market sector must therefore forgo some of its claims on its own output. It is one of the functions of taxes to channel resources from the market sector to support non-market (government) activity. The rapid growth of the public sector after 1945, it is argued, led to too rapid an increase in the tax burden (see Chapter 19), which adversely affected investment and attitudes to work, to the detriment of economic growth. Also, in the face of rising tax demands, workers in both market and non-market sectors sought to maintain or improve their real disposable income, thereby creating inflationary pressures.

If the market sector does not accommodate the demands of a growing non-market sector by forgoing claims on its own output, then in an open economy adjustment must be made externally. The higher overall demand *of both sectors combined* can then only be met either by reducing the exports of the market sector, or by increasing imports. A rising non-market public sector in this way contributes to balance of payments problems.

Bacon and Eltis saw the rapid growth of the non-market public sector as the cause of higher taxes, higher interest rates (to finance public spending), low investment, inflationary pressures and balance of payments problems. The growth of the non-market public sector has in these ways allegedly 'crowded out' the market sector, creating an economic environment which has been conducive to UK decline.

These ideas provided intellectual backing to the Conservative Party's approach to public spending and tax policies after 1979. The irony is that attempts to cut public spending and taxation after 1979 simply accelerated industrial decline, eroded the tax base and prevented the desired reduction of the tax burden (see Chapter 19). Bacon and Eltis's ideas provide a coherent theory of industrial decline, helping us to appreciate some of the complex linkages in the process. However, experience since 1979 calls into question their basic propositions. High unemployment during the 1980s made it impossible to argue that industry was denied labour, although it did lack capital investment. It may be that low investment had more to do with low expected returns than with the high interest rates said to be necessary to finance the growth of public expenditure. There are, of course, several other determinants of UK interest rates in addition to public expenditure. The 'crowding out' argument also neglects the importance of public sector services as *inputs* to the private sector. Of the non-marketed services, education is especially important in increasing the skills of the workforce.

Productivity

The total output of any economy is determined partly by the quantity of factor input (labour, capital, etc.), and partly by the use to which factors are put. Different economies may achieve different volumes of total output using similar quantities of factor input, because of variations in productivity. Productivity is the concept relating output to a given input, or inputs.

Productivity is usually expressed in terms of labour as input, i.e. labour productivity, or of capital as input, i.e. capital productivity. However, a productivity measure which relates output to *both* labour and capital inputs is called *total factor productivity* (TFP). We now seek to investigate the UK's productivity performance relative to other countries with the aid of these measures.

The most widely used measure of a country's economic efficiency is *labour productivity* and this is often defined as output (or value added) per person employed. However, since there may be changes in the structure of jobs between full- and part-time or in the length of the working week or number of holidays, then a more useful measure of labour productivity is arguably output (value added) *per person hour*.

A major issue in recent years has been whether the UK has been able to catch up with its major competitors in terms of productivity. Table 1.7 shows the

growth rates of real GDP per hour in four major economies between 1950 and 2009.

The very sound productivity performance of Germany and France in the 1950–73 period reflects their rapid post-war recovery phase. From 1973 to 1995 the growth rates of productivity slowed down in all the countries, but especially in the US, giving the European countries a chance to catch up. However, since 1995 the US figure has accelerated once more while the other countries' productivity rates have continued to fall. The performance of Germany and France has deteriorated, especially after 2003, while that of the UK has kept reasonably stable with an average growth of productivity of 1.8% over the 1995–2009 period. The above figures provide us with *rates of growth* of productivity, but what also matters is not only the rate of growth of productivity but also the *base level* from which that growth takes place. The calculation of these statistics is fraught with problems, such as deciding whether employment refers to persons or jobs and which price deflator to use. With these thoughts in mind we will investigate the most appropriate statistics available for productivity comparisons.

Table 1.8 compares the *absolute* levels of productivity in the UK, France, Germany and the US using index numbers based on UK = 100. It provides statistics for both GDP per hour worked and GDP per worker between 1991 and 2008. From the figures it can be seen that the differential between the UK and these three competitors still remains large in terms of GDP per hour worked. However, whilst the difference between the UK and the other three countries has decreased in terms of both GDP per hour and GDP per worker, the absolute gap still remain relatively

Table 1.7 Growth of real GDP per hour worked (% per year).

	1950–73	1973–95	1995–2009
US	2.37	1.19	2.20
UK	2.66	2.18	1.80
Germany	5.18	2.65	1.30
France	4.89	2.71	1.30

Source: OECD (2010e) *Stat. Extracts, Labour*; Broadberry and O'Mahony (2004).

Table 1.8 International comparisons of productivity: GDP per hour and per worker (UK = 100).

Year	France	Germany	US
1991	133 (127)	133 (117)	134 (138)
1995	124 (118)	129 (114)	124 (132)
2000	119 (111)	112 (104)	119 (129)
2004	110 (104)	96 (106)	116 (126)
2008	116 (109)	117 (108)	122 (133)

Note: Figures for GDP per worker in brackets.
Source: ONS (2010b) *International Comparisons of Productivity*, ICP Data, February.

Table 1.9 Major sectoral contributions to average annual labour productivity: market economies 1995–2004 (% growth rates).

	Market economy (1)	ICT production (2)	Goods production (3)	Market services (4)	Reallocation (5)
Austria	2.2	0.3	1.7	0.3	−0.1
Belgium	1.8	0.3	1.0	0.5	−0.1
Denmark	1.4	0.3	0.8	0.3	0.0
Finland	3.3	1.6	1.3	0.4	0.0
France	2.0	0.5	1.0	0.6	0.0
Germany	1.6	0.5	0.9	0.2	0.0
Italy	0.5	0.3	0.3	−0.1	0.0
Netherlands	2.0	0.4	0.6	1.1	−0.1
Spain	0.2	0.1	0.1	0.1	−0.1
UK	2.7	0.5	0.7	1.6	−0.2
EU	1.5	0.5	0.8	0.5	−0.2
US	3.0	0.9	0.7	1.8	−0.3

Note: (1) = (2) + (3) + (4) + (5), rounded to the nearest whole number.
Source: Van Ark *et al.* (2008).

large in most cases. For example, the UK remains 22% behind productivity in the US in GDP per hour and 33% behind in GDP per worker. For France the UK lags behind by 16% and 9% respectively, but for Germany, whilst the UK has a 17% productivity deficit in terms of GDP per hour, it has only an 8% deficit in terms of GDP per worker.

Table 1.9 provides a *sectoral comparison* of labour productivity growth amongst ten European countries and the US. Three points can be observed from this table.

First, overall labour productivity in the European economies only increased at a rate of 1.5% a year between 1995 and 2004 as compared to 3% a year in the US, and the market services sector of the European economies contributed only 0.5% points to that productivity growth as compared to 1.8% a year in the US. Clearly the difference in labour productivity growth between the EU and US has much to do with the disparity in labour productivity in market services. Second, although labour productivity growth in market services was much greater in the US than in the EU, the contribution of market services to labour productivity varies considerably across the EU countries, being very low in some countries such as Italy and Spain, while much higher in other countries such as the Netherlands and the UK. Third, growth in

labour productivity in goods production seems to be very similar in the US and Europe, with some EU countries such as Austria, Finland and France outperforming the US.

To investigate the productivity issue a little further, it would be helpful to look at productivity in the market services sector in more depth. Table 1.10 shows the contributions which the subsectors of market services have made to the growth of productivity in Europe and the US; 'Distribution services' have clearly made the major contribution followed by 'Finance and business services' and, lastly, 'Personal services'. Within these subsectors, the table identifies the sources of the productivity performance, which include additional labour and capital (factor intensity growth), and the increased efficiency with which these factors are used (multifactor productivity or MFP). Finally, the effect of changes in the distribution of labour input as between industries on productivity growth is identified (labour reallocation).

The gap in productivity between Europe and the US in the 'Distributive' and 'Finance and business' sectors was particularly high in the (later) 1995–2004 period showing the US pulling away in terms of productivity in these subsections from Europe. The better productivity performance in the US seems to be due to multiproductivity rather than factor intensity, i.e.

Table 1.10 Contributions of sectors to average labour productivity growth in market services 1980–2004 (%).

	European Union		United States	
	1980–1995	1995–2004	1980–1995	1995–2004
(1) Market services labour productivity	1.6	0.9	1.5	3.8
(2) Distribution services contribution	1.1	0.6	1.2	2.2
from factor intensity growth	0.5	0.5	0.5	0.6
from multifactor productivity growth	0.6	0.2	0.6	1.0
(3) Finance and business services contribution	0.2	0.1	0.3	1.2
from factor intensity growth	0.5	0.6	0.4	0.8
from multifactor productivity growth	−0.3	−0.5	−0.1	0.4
(4) Personal services contribution	0.0	−0.1	0.0	0.2
from factor intensity growth	0.1	0.1	0.0	0.2
from multifactor productivity growth	−0.2	−0.2	0.0	0.0
(5) Contribution from labour reallocation	0.3	0.2	0.1	0.2

Note: (1) = (2) + (3) + (4) + (5), rounded to the nearest whole number.
Source: As for Table 1.9.

to the efficiency with which factors are used rather than the amount of factors. Reasons for this more rapid growth in US efficiency are numerous but may include the faster rise in information and communications technology in the US, new retail formats, better labour scheduling systems, more effective marketing campaigns, more attractive opening hours, deregulation, and also the higher productivity levels of new firm entrants into the US market.

Manufacturing productivity

The UK's productivity in manufacturing has always been in the forefront of discussion because the sector is so open to global competitive forces. Table 1.11 gives a brief summary of trends in labour productivity for the whole economy and for manufacturing, together with trends in manufacturing output in the UK between 1964 and 2009. We see that output per person employed in manufacturing has risen by 114.2 points on 1964, much more than the 76.9 points recorded for the whole economy. This is certainly supportive of the view that manufacturing is a vital 'engine for growth'. However, we can see that manufacturing *output* increased by only 33.6 points between 1964 and 2005, while manufacturing output actually fell between 2005 and 2009 by 13.7 points as a result of the onset of a cyclical downswing. It is

Table 1.11 United Kingdom productivity and manufacturing output (1990 = 100).

	UK output per person employed		
Year	Whole economy	Manufacturing	Manufacturing output
1964	58.1	45.3	72.6
1969	67.0	53.8	85.4
1973	76.2	63.4	94.6
1979	81.7	65.8	90.6
1990	100.0	100.0	100.0
2005	136.5	153.2	106.2
2009	135.0	159.5	92.5

Source: ONS (2010d) *Monthy Digest of Statistics*, September; ONS (2010c) *Labour Market Statistics*, September ONS (2006a) *Economic Trends*, April, and previous issues.

hardly surprising that we noted significant job losses in the manufacturing industry in Table 1.4 since relatively rapid labour productivity growth and static or falling output are invariably associated with reductions in employment.

Table 1.12 provides more detailed productivity data for manufacturing output between 1980 and 2008 for the UK, US, France and Germany.

Table 1.12 Labour productivity in manufacturing (output per hour), 1980–2008 (2002 = 100).

	US	France	Germany	UK
1980	41.6	42.9	54.6	46.3
1985	50.0	56.0	62.8	59.0
1990	65.9	63.6	69.8	72.8
1995	68.3	75.2	80.6	82.1
2000	89.5	94.0	96.5	93.7
2005	115.1	107.3	107.5	115.5
2008	127.8	115.4	129.2	124.2

Source: US (2010) *International Labor Comparisons*, BLS Supplementary Tables.

Although much discussion of the UK's performance in terms of productivity has centred on the manufacturing sector, it should be noted that this sector is not a cohesive entity; rather it is made up of many subsectors with divergent records over time. A major study of UK manufacturing productivity (Cameron and Proudman 1998) showed that although the overall growth of manufacturing output may have been stagnant, there were significant differences between subsectors of manufacturing. The study investigated output growth and labour productivity in 19 subsectors of manufacturing over the period 1970–92. Their results suggest that there has been an important shift in the contribution of the various subsectors to manufacturing output, with nine sectors experiencing positive rates of output growth (led by computing, pharmaceuticals, aerospace, electronics and precision instruments), whilst the other 10 sectors experienced negative rates of growth of output (led by iron and steel, basic metals, minerals and machinery). Interestingly, the sectors experiencing positive rates of growth of output also tended to be those which experienced higher rates of growth of labour productivity.

Two further conclusions of the study might also be noted. First, the authors investigated whether changes in overall manufacturing productivity were due to the relocation of resources *between* sectors (i.e. from low to high productivity sectors) or due to productivity growth *within* the sectors over time. They concluded that over 90% of the increase in labour productivity was due to *within*-sector productivity growth. This suggests that explanations of changes in productivity should concentrate on factors which affect productivity *within* industries and even plants. Second, the study looked at whether productivities across the various sectors of manufacturing have tended to converge. They concluded that whilst productivity in a number of sectors appeared to settle at levels just below the manufacturing mean, the productivities of a few sectors (such as computing, pharmaceuticals and aerospace) remained consistently above the mean and tended to move further above the mean over time.

Despite these differential performances between sectors within UK manufacturing, the UK falls behind the US, Germany and France in absolute labour productivities in most of the subsectors of manufacturing. For example, a study by O'Mahony and de Boer (2002) points out that in the basic metals sector, the absolute productivity levels in the US, France and Germany in 1999 (UK = 100) were 198, 148 and 166 respectively. For the electrical and electronic equipment sector the figures were 173, 145 and 135 respectively, whilst in textiles, clothing and footwear the absolute productivity figures were 159, 196 and 129 respectively. Such divergent productivity performances between different UK manufacturing sectors, and also between the UK and other countries' manufacturing sectors, raises interesting questions. For example, are these differences due to the nature of technologies used in these sectors, or are they the result of other factors involving capital intensity, labour skills or openness to trade? We will return to some of these questions later in the chapter.

Productivity and capital investment

The contribution of *capital investment* to variations in the rate of output growth between nations has been an important topic of research for many years, the argument being that the greater the investment in plant and equipment, the greater the capacity of the economy to grow (see Chapter 17). Recent research has looked at the role of investment in tangible assets (plant, machinery and equipment) and in human capital (training, etc.) in influencing the growth of nations (Dougherty and Jorgenson 1997). Dougherty and Jorgenson found that for the period 1960–89, the two main factors explaining the recorded differences in levels of output per head between countries were identified as the *level* of capital input and the *quality* of labour input. They concluded that one of the most serious deficiencies in the UK *vis-à-vis* other countries was the low recorded level of capital per head.

The later study by O'Mahony and de Boer (2002) provides further evidence on this issue of capital intensity, i.e. different levels of capital per unit of labour across nations and sectors. It indicated that, as compared to the UK, the capital available per hour worked was 25% higher in the US, 60% higher in France and 32% higher in Germany. The research also looked at three sectors, viz. manufacturing, distributive trades and financial/business services. It concluded that in each sector, the capital per hour worked was, on average across the three countries, some 46% above the UK level in manufacturing, 79% in the distributive trades and 99% in financial/business services.

It has been argued from evidence such as this that the gap between the US and her competitors was partly due to much higher US investment in information and communications technology (ICT). The importance of investment in ICT on productivity growth can be seen in Table 1.9 (p. 13) where it is clear that the growth of ICT production contributed nearly twice as much (0.9%) to overall labour productivity growth in the US as compared to the UK (0.5%) or the EU (0.5%). The need for EU investment in this area is therefore clear.

A relatively low level of capital intensity for the UK is of some concern in the context of studies such as that of Oulton (1997). In a more general survey of growth in 53 countries over the period 1965–90, Oulton found that the most important way of raising growth rates was by increasing the growth rate of capital stock, i.e. raising capital per worker. Of course, the relatively low levels of investment in the UK may be a rational response to low returns, so that whilst low investment may contribute to low productivity, low productivity may in turn discourage investment. For example, Oulton noted that the pre-tax rate of return for investment in UK companies (excluding North Sea oil) averaged only 8.7% per annum between 1988 and 1997, with the private rate of return on human capital around the same figure. Since the cost of capital averaged around 5–7% per annum over the same period, the payoff for investing in either physical or human capital in the UK was hardly attractive!

Finally, one should also not forget that investment in new infrastructure also contributes to productivity growth. For example, increased transport investment can lead to decreasing transport costs, allowing increased specialization and economies of scale (Venables 2007).

Productivity and labour skills

The above account points to the importance of capital intensity in enhancing productivity. Of course the productivity of a nation also depends on the skills of its management and workforce in making the best use of whatever resources are available. Management is responsible for selecting projects, organizing the flow of work and the utilization of resources, so that effective management is a 'necessary' condition for good productivity performance. It is not, however, 'sufficient' since a labour force which possesses inappropriate skills, or which refuses to adapt its work practices and manning levels to new technology, will prevent advances in productivity, whatever the merits of management. A major issue in many industries is workers' lack of flexibility between tasks, resulting in overmanning and also acting as a disincentive to innovation. Lack of flexibility can result from union restrictive practices, but is also caused by badly trained workers and managers who are unable to cope with change. There is evidence of low standards in UK education which mean that many school leavers are ill-equipped for the growing complexity of work.

British industry has periodically placed less emphasis on training than in other countries. Only around 52% of 18-year-olds in the UK were in full-time or part-time education or training in 1999, much less than the 80% figure for Germany, France, the Netherlands and Belgium, suggesting that young people as a group in the UK are among the least educated and trained in Europe. When considering the whole labour force, that is the stock of human capital rather than the flow, the situation is probably even worse. Davies and Caves (1987) had pointed out that British managers were only marginally better qualified than the population at large: for example, very few production managers were graduate engineers. Amongst production workers only a quarter in Britain had completed an apprenticeship compared with about half in Germany. Very few British foremen had formal qualifications for their job, but in Germany foremen were trained as craftsmen and then took the further qualification of *Meister*. In fact only 14% of UK technicians and 3% of UK foremen

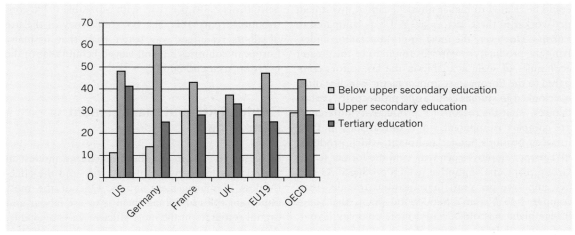

Fig. 1.1 Distribution of highest completed level of education, 2008.
Source: OECD (2010b) *Education at a Glance 2010: OECD Indicators.*

possessed higher intermediate qualifications, compared to 36% of German technicians and 64% of German foremen (Steedman *et al.* 1991).

Figure 1.1 provides some comparative international insight into current labour qualifications showing the distribution of the population aged 25–64 years arranged by their highest level of educational attainment. The UK, together with France, has a relatively high percentage of the population (30%) whose highest level of qualifications attained is below upper secondary education level (i.e. qualification attained before the age of 15/16 years). However, the UK performs relatively well in tertiary education with some 33% of the age group having completed tertiary or higher education as compared to only 25% in Germany and 28% in France. It is at the upper secondary education level that the UK is most disadvantaged, with only 37% of the age group having this level of qualification, yet it is at this level that intermediate technician/craftsmen and other similar skills are located – the skill/educational level at which Germany has excelled. For the UK there is a need to shift the attainment level of a significant proportion of its population from below upper secondary to upper secondary, as is also the case for France and many other European economies. Finally, it should be noted that the US has only 11% of its population in the lowest educational attainment category, with particular strengths in the tertiary or higher education sector where 41% of its population has attained at

least this level of education. The US arguably exhibits the link between educational knowledge, skills and higher productivity!

Of course workforce training is one way in which the UK and other EU countries could help improve their productivity outside the formal education levels noted in Fig. 1.1. Data in 2009 (Department for Business, Enterprise and Regulatory Reform 2009) shows that 67% of UK employers provide some form of training to 63% of the workforce and that 9.8 training days per worker was allocated with a training spend per worker of £1,725. This area of training is essential if the weakness of sub-tertiary education noted above is to be alleviated.

Overall, some progress has been made in narrowing the productivity gaps previously identified for the UK *vis-à-vis* its major competitors. However, the UK is still at a considerable productivity disadvantage in terms of many of its competitors. A similar picture emerges from our review of capital intensity and the quality of the workforce.

Nevertheless it is important to remember that the whole question of productivity differences is much more complex than might at first appear. For example, a NIESR research project investigated the reasons for observed differences in productivity between the US and Europe in two quite different sectors, namely the biscuit sector and the precision industry sector (Mason and Finegold 1997). The survey did find that some of the reasons for the higher US productivity could be related to higher physical capital investment per worker in these sectors in the US as compared to Europe. However, the most important factor underlying the productivity gap was found to be the greater economies of scale available in the US sectors compared to the European sectors, a factor which is often overlooked in studies comparing productivity performances. That the reasons for productivity differences are complex is apparent from comparisons in 1998 between Nissan's Sunderland plant, which produced 98 cars per employee per year, and the former Rover Group plant at Longbridge, which produced 33 cars per employee per year. Investigations revealed that, compared to Nissan's Sunderland plant, the Longbridge plant was older, had a more complex layout, and suffered from a lower demand for its product range, suggesting that simplistic conclusions from productivity comparisons must be treated with some caution. Certainly the existence of relatively inefficient car plants is by no means a British phenomenon. For example, the Renault plant at Sandouville, France, produced only 36 cars per employee per year and the Volkswagen plant at Emden, Germany, produced only 28 cars per employee per year in the late 1990s.

We have now completed our analysis of the relative performance of the UK *vis-à-vis* its main competitors in terms of various factors such as labour and total factor productivities, capital intensity and skill levels. To complete this analysis, it might be useful to summarize the results of research into the main causes of the relative labour productivity differences in the market economies of the US, UK, France and Germany noted earlier in Table 1.8.

Studies such as Broadberry and O'Mahony (2004) have suggested that the gap between the UK and the US in terms of labour productivity was due mainly to the total factor productivity (TFP) element, which reflects the *efficiency* with which the US uses *all* its resources. Subsequent research (see Table 1.9, p. 13) has also emphasized the contribution of TFP (expressed also as multifactor productivity (MFP)) as a key variable influencing the growth of the market economy. Van Ark *et al.* found that the US market economy grew by 3.0% per year between 1995 and 2004, with a significant amount of that growth (i.e. 1.4%) attributable to improvements in MFP. Over the same period Europe's market economy grew by 1.5% per year, but the contribution of MFP was a much lower 0.3%. As far as the UK was concerned, the growth of its market economy over the same period was 2.7% per year, with a sizeable 0.7% contribution from MFP. The UK's efficiency in the use of all its resources was better than that in many European countries but still lagged behind that of the US (van Ark *et al.* 2008).

Productivity and management performance

In recent years there has been increasing interest in the relationship between productivity and the effectiveness of management inputs. One of the most important roles of management is to use labour and capital resources in the most efficient ways available, since poor management can lead to relatively low levels of productivity and therefore of firm competitiveness. In recent years a number of international surveys have provided an interesting indicator of the role of management in the drive towards improved productivity. For example, a survey by Proudfoot Consulting (2002) defined management productivity as the proportion of time spent by management on 'productive' activities which added value to their company. Since management cannot be expected to use 100% of their time 'productively', the consultants defined 85% as the realistic maximum productive use of time which could be expected. The companies studied covered manufacturing, finance and communication sectors and were located in many countries including the US, France, Germany and the UK. The results showed that the US and German management were identified as having used their time the most productively (both achieving 61% use of productive time), followed by France (54%) with the UK the worst performer of the countries in the study (48%). In many of the countries, the reasons for such loss of productive time were arguably managerial in nature, such as 'insufficient planning and control' or 'inadequate management/insufficient supervision'. In the case of the UK, as well as these reasons, 'poor work morale of workforce' and 'inappropriately qualified employees' were also identified. Further studies by Proudfoot Consulting have suggested that the UK has improved its performance since 2002 in terms of using time productively. For example, by 2008, the same research source showed that the UK had improved its performance markedly, using 74% of its time productively as compared to France (61.2%), the US (62.8%) and Germany (39.8%), with the average for the whole study being 65.7%. The critical finding in 2008 was that the quality of UK supervisors was still a major barrier to improved productivity, with 28% of managers citing this reason in the UK, but only 16% in France, and 10% in Germany (Proudfoot Consulting 2008).

A further study which helps clarify the general findings noted above was carried out by the McKinsey Company (2002). The consultancy company interviewed the directors of 100 manufacturing companies in the US, France, Germany and the UK. They defined 'best practice' in areas such as lean manufacturing techniques, organizational performance and management of talent and then gave scores between 0 and 5 according to how close the companies came to the best practice in those three areas. These scores were compared with company financial performance as measured by ROCE (return on capital employed), and also with TFP figures. The results showed that the UK's mean score of 2.9 for the three areas of management was the lowest of the four countries. The study also suggested a positive correlation between these management scores and the financial success (as measured by ROCE) and productivity (as measured by TFP) of these manufacturing companies. Finally, the study pointed clearly to weaknesses in UK management by pointing out that US-owned companies based in the UK are nearly 90% more productive than their UK-owned counterparts.

Interestingly, the problem identified by the McKinsey Company report discussed above continues to be present, as shown in a further survey of 731 medium-sized manufacturing firms across the EU and the US carried out by the Centre for Economic Performance (CEP) and the McKinsey Company (Bloom *et al* 2005). The report showed that better-managed companies had higher rates of growth of sales and higher valuations on the stock market, irrespective of their country of operation.

The 2009 survey also showed that, on average, the performance of managers of UK manufacturing firms warranted an overall management capability score of 3.00 (in relation to a best practice score of 5). This was still behind the US (3.25), Sweden (3.16), Germany (3.15) and Japan (3.15) but just above France (2.98) and Italy (2.98). These conclusions have been given further credence by the International Management Development in its assessment of perceived management quality between 2001 and 2008 (Department for Business, Enterprise and Regulatory

Reform 2009). Data on business executives' perceptions of management quality in different countries, using a scale from 1 to 10, suggest that while the figures for UK were lower than those for the US, France and Germany, it was, nevertheless, the only country to show an increase in perceptions of management quality in 2007 and 2008.

Relative unit labour costs (RULC)

It would still be possible to remain price-competitive with overseas producers even with low labour productivity, if real wages were also low. Labour costs per unit of output (unit labour costs) are determined by the wages of the workers as well as the output per worker. International competitiveness, in terms of unit labour costs, is also influenced by exchange rates. Depreciation of the currency can even compensate for poor productivity and high money wages, though it also has the effect of raising import prices.

Figure 1.2 reveals the sources of the changes in UK cost competitiveness in manufacturing since 1976, relative to its major competitors. The UK's *relative productivity* is shown by Schedule 'C', which indicates the changes in UK manufacturing productivity *relative* to its major competitors since 1976. We see that in 2009 UK manufacturing productivity had risen by around 40% on its 1976 level relative to those competitors. The *relative cost of UK labour* had, however, risen by as much as 110% over this period (Schedule 'B'). The impact of these changes on UK competitiveness was, however, moderated by a slight fall in the *effective exchange rate* to around 94% of its 1976 level (Schedule 'D'). As a result, *relative unit labour costs* (RULC) were around 41% above their 1976 level (Schedule 'A'). Whilst significant, a 41% increase in RULC is certainly much less than the 110% increase in relative labour costs over this period.

The calculation of RULC is as follows:

$$\frac{\text{relative labour costs}}{\text{relative productivity}} \times \frac{\text{sterling effective}}{\text{exchange rate}} = \text{RULC}$$

$$\left(\frac{2.10}{1.40} \times 0.94 = 1.41\right)$$

We should not of course conclude from this that the 1976 position was 'just right'. Nevertheless we have already shown that manufacturing output and

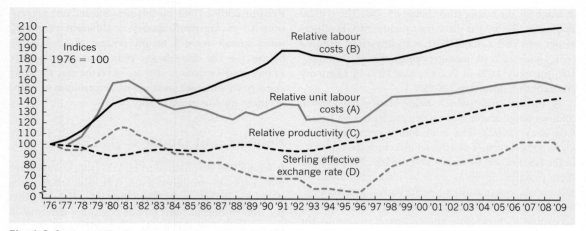

Fig. 1.2 Cost contributions: sources of changes in UK cost competitiveness in manufacturing.
Sources: ONS *Economic Trends* (various); European Commission *European Economy* (various); National Economic Development Office (1987).

employment had fallen dramatically between 1976 and 2009. A restoration of UK competitiveness, even to 1976 levels, would in all probability generate more output and more employment than are currently experienced.

The above formula emphasizes that lower *relative unit labour costs* could be achieved either by reducing relative labour costs, or by raising relative productivity, or by lowering the effective exchange rate, or indeed by a combination of all three. If the *exchange rate alone* were to be used, a *depreciation* of 29% would have been required in 2009 in order to restore RULC in the UK to its 1976 level.

Figure 1.2 draws attention to the fact that the sterling effective exchange rate *appreciated* between 1978 and 1981 (see also Chapter 25). This happened at the very time that relative labour costs were rising rapidly and relative productivity was falling. It is hardly surprising, therefore, that the UK's competitive position deteriorated by about 50% during this period, as indicated by the sharp rise in RULC. This was a major factor in the marked decline in manufacturing output and employment in the UK between 1979 and 1981.

After 1980/81 the competitive position improved (RULC is on a downward trend) as the decline of the sterling effective exchange rate more than compensated for the resumed rise in relative labour costs. Notice that improvements in relative productivity

contributed little to the falling RULC after 1983. By 1990 there was again concern about the competitive position of the UK as the pound rose to around 3.0 Deutsches marks (DM). This concern was reinforced by UK entry into the Exchange Rate Mechanism (ERM) at the (high) central parity of £1 = 2.95 DM in October 1990. However, the enforced withdrawal of the UK from the ERM on 16 September 1992 (see Chapter 27) led to the pound depreciating by more than 14% in the following months. This went some way to meeting the 27% depreciation estimated as being required in 1991 to restore RULC to its 1976 level in Fig. 1.2. This depreciation in sterling certainly brought about a sharp fall in RULC from September 1992 onwards which contributed to the recovery of output and improved the balance of trade. However, a concern in more recent times has been the strong *appreciation* of the sterling effective exchange rate which rose by 28% between 1996 and 2007. This appreciation of sterling has been a powerful factor in raising the RULC over that time period, a trend further reinforced by the tendency for relative labour costs to rise faster than relative productivity in the UK during recent years. However, sterling has depreciated sharply against the US dollar and many other major currencies in the period 2007–10, helping reduce UK RULCs.

An indicator of trends in relative unit labour costs can be seen in Table 1.13 which traces the nominal

Table 1.13 Relative unit labour costs (RULCs) 1995–2009 (2005 = 100).

	US	France	Germany	UK
1995	116.8	112.4	104.5	69.8
1997	114.3	107.1	103.6	83.6
2000	125.5	96.0	100.1	99.3
2005	100.0	100.0	100.0	100.0
2009	92.3	101.2	96.2	86.0

Note: The figures relate unit labour costs relative to 35 industrial countries. OECD (2010a) *Economic Outlook*, No 87 Annex tables.

RULCs in four major economies. From the table we can observe that the UK's relative unit labour costs grew rapidly in the 1990s, before slowing down between 2000 and 2005, and actually falling since 2005. However, the UK's RULCs since 1990 have been lower than in the three competitors shown here, placing the UK at a competitive advantage.

It is important that the productivity gaps already identified be narrowed or removed. It is certainly doubtful as to whether the apparent alternative option of a low-wage, low-productivity industrial economy is viable, given the role of technology. Technical change is frequently embodied in the latest capital equipment, and has the effect of changing not just the volume of output per worker, but also the quality of products. For instance, robot welders and paint-sprayers on car production lines offer a dependable quality which previously more labour-intensive methods did not. If, as a consequence of lower real wages, older and more labour-intensive methods are retained in the face of competition from new technology, markets will often still be lost on the basis of quality, *even if* prices can be held at apparently low levels. In these circumstances, the UK would be producing goods under similar conditions to many newly industrializing Third World countries.

Low productivity, not fully compensated by low wages or by a lower exchange rate, leaves UK companies in a weak market position. They are faced with the choice of raising prices and risking lost orders, or continuing to sell on lower profit margins. Markets differ in their sensitivity to rising prices, but in all markets rising prices tend to reduce sales *volume*, which usually means less employment. Multinational companies located in the UK may, to avoid raising prices, supply an increasing proportion of their market from overseas plants, again reducing UK output and employment (see Chapter 7).

Firms which absorb rising unit costs by taking lower profit margins may be able to maintain their levels of output and employment, at least in the short run. But in the long run profits are vital to industrial investment, both in providing investment finance and in influencing expectations of future rates of return, and hence investment plans. Investment is also required in many industries to raise productivity, and thereby profits, and so we come full circle. Profits depend on productivity, which is affected by investment, which depends on profits! The process is self-reinforcing; low productivity gives low profits, low investment and therefore little productivity improvement. In contrast, once productivity is raised, profits and investment increase, which further raises productivity. This cumulative upward spiral is still further reinforced in that market share and factor incomes rise, so that demand is created for still higher output. New technology is also more easily accepted in situations of rising output, perhaps leading to still higher profits, stimulating further investment, and so driving the process on. The UK's problem is to further improve on its productivity performance, given the substantial gaps which still persist relative to its main competitors across a number of industrial and service sectors.

The consequences of low productivity and poor competitiveness have been felt mainly in the manufacturing sector of the economy, largely because its exposure to international competition is greater than that of the service sector. Structural change, in the form of a *reduced share* of output and employment for the manufacturing sector, is then almost inevitable.

 ## Consequences of structural change

Deindustrialization

There is little agreement as to what 'deindustrialization' actually means. For some time politicians on the left have used the term to mean loss of industrial employment. Others extend the term to include situations of declining industrial output, and still others to include declining *shares* of employment or output.

We have shown that the UK has undergone deindustrialization on each and every one of these criteria. Declining industrial employment is not unusual in other advanced economies (see Table 1.6), and neither is a decline in the industrial sector's share of employment (Table 1.5) or of GDP (Table 1.3). Where the UK is unusual is in the insignificant growth of non-oil industrial production in the 37 years since 1973.

Declining industrial employment need not be a problem; there is every indication that many British people would not freely choose industrial employment. There will, however, be the problem of rising unemployment if declining industrial employment is not compensated by increasing non-industrial employment. Until 1979 this problem did not arise; as we saw in Table 1.4, employment levels were broadly maintained until 1979, but the growth of service sector employment between 1979 and the mid 1990s did *not* compensate for falling industrial employment. The costs of deindustrialization have been particularly felt in those regions where declining industries were concentrated. The Midlands, the North, Yorkshire and Humberside, the North West, Wales and Scotland all experienced a prolonged period with unemployment rates well above 10% during the 1980s and early 1990s, as the industrial base contracted. However, there has been a considerable narrowing of the unemployment differential between regions as the recession of the early 1990s bit deep into the previously expanding service sector activities throughout the UK (see Chapter 23).

Some writers view these changes as part of a move towards a post-industrial society, where the main activities involve the creation and handling of information. However, a decline in the *share* of industrial activity within the economy would be less worrying if *absolute* industrial output had grown since 1973 at the same rate as in other advanced economies.

A decline in manufacturing activity may cause a still more serious employment impact than that given by the official statistics. This is because manufacturing is characterized by many more *backward-linkages* than is the service sector (Greenhalgh 1994). For example, in order to make cars the vehicle manufacturer will buy in some engine components, metal products and textiles from other manufacturers and will also purchase the services of vehicle transporters, accountants, bankers, designers, etc. Manufacturing and services display very different patterns of inter-industry purchases, which can be examined using statistical input–output tables. In particular, the rate of purchase of service output by manufacturing firms is a much larger proportion per unit of gross output than is the purchase of manufactured goods for use as inputs by services. Whereas Greenhalgh found that each £1 spent on manufacturing gross output created £1.61 of employment income in *all* sectors, that same £1 spent on service gross output created only £0.56 of employment income in *all* sectors. Clearly manufacturing sustains a far higher proportion of jobs (*directly and indirectly*) than it might appear to us from data on sectoral shares, such as Table 1.4 above.

Deindustrialization may put not only these backward-linkages at risk but also a variety of *forward-linkages*. The suggestion here is that innovations, whether measured by patents or survey records, are heavily concentrated in the manufacturing sector. Again Greenhalgh (1994) found that 87% of innovations were developed in the manufacturing (and primary) sector, and 80% of all first commercial adoptions of innovations took place in this sector. Deindustrialization clearly puts at risk the 'seed-corn' of domestic technology, which in turn has balance of payments implications (see below) as UK trade becomes progressively geared to high-technology products.

The OECD (2005b) has confirmed this growing interconnectedness between manufacturing and service activities. It suggests that the amount of services embodied in one unit of final output has almost doubled from 8.2% to 15.7% since the early 1970s for the 10 countries included in the survey.

Growth prospects

As we saw in Table 1.11, it is manufacturing which has led the way in productivity growth. Manufacturing lends itself to rapid growth of labour productivity because of the scope for capital investment and technical progress. Growth of manufacturing output, of GDP and of productivity are closely related, and manufacturing has in the past been the engine for growth. As workers found new jobs in manufacturing during the nineteenth century they left agriculture and other relatively low-productivity sectors. Those in the new jobs raised their productivity, and the average productivity of those remaining in agriculture was raised by the removal of marginal workers.

At the same time rising incomes in manufacturing generated new demand for goods and services, the multiplier process encouraging still further growth of output, and with it productivity. Indeed Greenhalgh (1994) points out that in the eight-year period 1985–93, manufacturing contributed about 70% of the average rise in output per worker in the whole economy.

In parts of the service sector there is little scope for improved productivity; even the concept itself is often inappropriate. First, there is often no clear output – how do you measure the output of doctors, or nurses? Second, even where a crude output measure is devised, it often fails to take into account the quality of service – are larger class sizes an increase or a decrease in educational productivity? The national accounts often resort to measuring output by input (e.g. the wages of health workers), so that productivity is by definition equal to 1. There are, however, some services where productivity can be meaningfully measured and in these there is scope for productivity growth, especially where the new information technologies can be applied. But many workers who lose manufacturing jobs move into service sector jobs, where their productivity may be lower, into unemployment or out of the labour market altogether. There is no mechanism for growth in this process, but quite the reverse.

Nevertheless, as the process of deindustrialization progresses, the overall growth of productivity will depend on productivity gains in the service sector. This is in line with the theory of 'asymptotic stagnancy' which indicates that if there are two activities, one of which is 'technologically progressive' whilst the other is 'technologically stagnant', then it can be shown mathematically that in the long run the average rate of growth of an economy will be determined by the sector in which productivity growth is the slowest (Baumol *et al.* 1989). In this context manufacturing can be regarded as the 'technologically progressive' sector with services 'technologically stagnant' in comparison, suggesting that the growth rate of the economy as a whole will depend on the growth of productivity in the service sector. Future developments in information technology will be a key element in further raising productivity in a broad range of service sector activities. The process of deindustrialization is clearly making productivity in the service industry a major determinant of the prospects for future economic growth and increases in welfare

in the UK. In this context, despite the improving comparative performance of the UK, service sector productivity may be seen as of particular concern and a focus for remedial policy action.

Balance of payments

An alternative definition of deindustrialization is offered by Singh, based on the traditional role of manufacturing in UK trade flows. Historically the UK was a net exporter of manufactures, so that surplus foreign exchange was earned which enabled the country to run a deficit on its trade in food and raw materials. Singh (1977) defines an 'efficient' manufacturing sector as one which 'not only satisfies the demands of consumers at home but is also able to sell enough of its products abroad to pay for the nation's import requirements'. Singh also states that this is subject to the restriction that 'an efficient manufacturing sector must be able to achieve these objectives at socially acceptable levels of output, employment and exchange rate'. A country such as the UK would then be 'deindustrialized' if its manufacturing sector did not meet these criteria, leaving an economic structure inappropriate to the needs of the country. It can be argued that this is indeed the position in the UK. The current account can only be kept in balance by surpluses in the oil and service sectors and by earnings from overseas assets. Any reflation of aggregate demand stimulates an even faster growth in imports of manufactured goods which pushes the current account towards deficit. By the end of the 1980s boom the UK again had a worryingly large current account deficit, as indeed it still has in 2010. The decline of UK manufacturing has recreated the balance of payments constraint on macroeconomic policy which many had hoped North Sea oil would remove. This suggests that the UK could be regarded as 'deindustrialized' on Singh's definition.

It might be argued that the service sector can take over the traditional role of manufacturing in the balance of payments accounts. A difficulty here is that unlike manufactures many services cannot, by their nature, be traded internationally (e.g. public sector services), with the result that trade in manufactures is on a vastly bigger scale than trade in services (see Chapter 25). The House of Commons Trade and Industry Committee has pointed out that a 2.5% rise in service exports is required merely to offset a 1%

fall in manufacturing exports. In some services which can be traded, the UK is already highly successful (e.g. financial services), and if even bigger surpluses are to be earned then the UK would have to move towards a monopoly position in those services. In fact, international competition is increasing in traded services and the UK may find it difficult to hold its current share of the market.

Other economists have pointed out that Singh's definition would leave most of the non-oil-producing industrial countries categorized as 'deindustrialized' because, despite growing industrial output, their macroeconomic policies were constrained by their balance of payments positions after the 1973 and 1979 oil price rises. This observation does not invalidate the conclusion that deindustrialization in the UK has had serious balance of payments consequences.

Inflation

If deindustrialization in the UK is so advanced that the economy is not capable of producing goods to match the pattern of market demand, then there may be implications not only for imports but also for prices. Any increase in overall demand will meet a shortage of domestic suppliers in many industrial sectors. This will both encourage import substitution and provide opportunities for domestic suppliers to raise prices. As a result, despite continuing high unemployment, there may be little effective spare capacity in the UK in sectors where deindustrialization has been excessive. Supply-side constraints created by structural change may then have increased the likelihood of the UK experiencing demand-led inflation in the event of a sustained increase in aggregate demand, such as that of the late 1980s. In response to such constraints government policy has moved towards strengthening the supply side, as with the Conservative and new Coalition government's labour market reforms and previous Labour government measures such as the New Deal.

Industrial relations

Deindustrialization is having important implications for the nature of industrial relations. Trade unions originally gained their strength from the industrial sector, in which it was easier to organize and to engage in centralized bargaining because of the broadly similar work undertaken by large groups of workers. Although centralized bargaining has helped to narrow the wage differentials within manufacturing (see Chapter 14), as the UK economy continues to shift towards services this form of bargaining will become more difficult to achieve as the nature of work in the service sector varies considerably across different activities. For example, the levels of skill and security of employment vary significantly between financial services and retailing. The wage differentials will be needed to compensate for these skill differences, and centralized union bargaining designed to narrow wage differentials will clearly be perceived by employers as having adverse effects on the growth of service sector productivity. The roles of trade unions will clearly have to adapt, with the diversity of the service sector making the retention of union membership more difficult and weakening the traditional systems of wage bargaining.

Conclusion

There have been profound structural changes in the UK economy since 1964, resulting in relative stagnation of industrial output and declining industrial employment, and these have transformed the sectoral balance of the economy. The causes of these changes are not agreed. We reviewed various suggestions, such as economic 'maturity', low-wage competition, the advent of North Sea oil, 'crowding out', and low productivity. Our view has been that low productivity, resulting in a substantial loss of competitiveness, has been central to the structural changes observed. Certainly no other major industrial country has experienced the fall in volume of non-oil industrial output recorded in the UK after 1973. The consequences of industrial decline are widespread, contributing to unemployment and balance of payments problems, increasing inflationary pressures and hampering growth. Judged by the growth of output and productivity there has been an improvement in the performance of the UK economy since the 1980s. The UK has reduced the productivity gap with other OECD countries and has increased industrial output at a rate close to the OECD average. Nevertheless, UK manufacturing output in 2009/10 was actually lower in volume terms than it had been in 1973.

Key points

- Whereas the secondary sector contributed some 41% of GDP in 1964, by 2009 this had fallen to 19%.

- Manufacturing (within the secondary sector) saw its share of GDP fall from around 30% in 1964 to 12% by 2009.

- Over 6 million jobs have been lost from the secondary sector since 1964, with 6 million having been lost from manufacturing alone.

- The service (tertiary) sector has provided over 14 million extra jobs since 1964, and has managed to more than match the loss of manufacturing employment.

- Not all advanced industrialized countries have seen a decline in industrial employment.

- Suggested causes of 'deindustrialization' have included maturity of the economy, low-wage competition, North Sea oil, 'crowding out' and low productivity.

- UK productivity *growth rates* in manufacturing and in the whole economy fell behind those of its main competitors during the 1960s and 1970s but kept pace in the 1980s before falling behind again during the 1990–1995 period, but with relative productivity reviving in the UK since then. However, the *absolute levels* of UK productivity and capital intensity remain well below those of its competitors.

- UK productivity per employed worker in manufacturing has grown by some 4.5% per annum since 1979. Unfortunately total UK manufacturing output has grown at a much slower rate, resulting in fewer workers being employed.

- True competitiveness depends not only upon relative productivity but also upon relative labour costs and the sterling effective exchange rate. This is best measured by relative unit labour costs (RULC).

- The UK is still, on average, some 40% less competitive overall (in terms of RULC) in 2009 than it was in 1976.

Now try the self-check questions for this chapter on the Companion Website. You will also find useful links to relevant websites.

Notes

1 The GDP is the total value of output produced by factors of production located in a given country.

2 Income elasticity of demand is given by:

$$\frac{\text{\% change in quantity demanded}}{\text{\% change in income}}$$

3 'Factor cost' means that 'market price' valuations of output have been adjusted to take account of the distortions caused by taxes and subsidies. Taxes raise market prices above the true cost of factor input and so are subtracted. Subsidies reduce market prices below factor cost and so are added. 'Constant factor cost' means that the valuations have been made in the prices of a given base year. This eliminates the effects of inflation, so that the time series shows 'real' output.

4 Buying the foreign currency to pay for the extra imports would increase the supply of sterling on the foreign exchange market, reducing the price of sterling.

References and further reading

Bacon, R. and Eltis, W. (1976) *Britain's Economic Problem – Too Few Producers*, Basingstoke, Macmillan.

Baumol, W. J., Blackman, S. and Wolff, E. N. (1989) *Productivity and American Leadership: The Long View*, Cambridge, MA, MIT Press.

Bloom, N. and Van Reenen, J. (2008) Measuring and explaining management practices across firms and nations, *Quarterly Journal of Economics*, 122(4): 1352–1408.

Bloom, N., Dorgan, S., Dowdy, J., van Reemen, J. and Pippin, T. (2005) *Management Practices Across Firms and Nations*, June, London, Centre for Economic Performance, LSE.

Bosworth, D., Davies, R. and Wilson, R. (2002) Management qualifications and organisational performance: An analysis of the Employers Skill Survey 1999, *Labour Market Trends*, August, 443–4.

Broadberry, S. and O'Mahony, M. (2004) Britain's productivity gap with the United States and Europe: a historical perspective, *National Institute Economic Review*, 189, July, 72–85.

Cameron, G. and Proudman, J. (1998) Growth in UK manufacturing between 1970–92, *Bank of England Quarterly Bulletin*, May, 145–157.

Carr, C. (1992) Productivity and skills in vehicle component manufacturers in Britain, Germany, the USA and Japan, *National Institute Economic Review*, 139(1): 79–87.

Crafts, N. and O'Mahoney, M. (2001) A perspective on UK productivity performance, *Fiscal Studies*, 22(3): 271–306.

Davies, S. and Caves, R. E. (1987) *Britain's Productivity Gap*, Cambridge, Cambridge University Press.

Department for Business, Enterprise and Regulatory Reform (2009) *The 2008 Productivity and Competitiveness Indicators*, London, The Stationery Office.

Dougherty, C. and Jorgenson, D. W. (1997) There is no silver bullet: investment and growth in the G7, *National Institute Economic Review*, 162(1): 57–74.

Eltis, W. and Higham, D. (1995) Closing the UK competitiveness gap, *National Institute Economic Review*, 154(1): 71–84.

Feinstein, C. and Mathews, R. (1990) The growth of output and productivity in the UK, *National Institute Economic Review*, 133(1): 79–90.

Grant, S. (1994) Challenges to UK competitiveness, *British Economy Survey*, Spring.

Greenhalgh, C. (1994) Why manufacturing still matters, *Economic Review*, September, 11–15.

Hadjimatheou, G. and Sarantis, N. (1998) Is UK deindustrialisation inevitable?, in Buxton, T., Chapman, P. and Temple, P. (eds), *Britain's Economic Performance* (2nd edn), London, Routledge, 527–46.

Department of Trade and Industry (1996) *Competitiveness – Forging Ahead*, Cm 2867, London, HMSO.

House of Commons Trade and Industry Committee (1994) *Competitiveness of UK Manufacturing Industry*, Second Report and Vol. II Memoranda of Evidence, April, London, HMSO.

Kaletsky, A. (1998) Where Britain can learn to improve productivity, *Times*, 3 November.

Kitson, W. and Mitchie, J. (1996) Britain's industrial performance since 1960, *Economic Journal*, 106(434): 196–212.

Mason, G. and Finegold, D. (1997) Productivity, machinery and skills in the United States and Western Europe, *National Institute Economic Review*, 162(1): 85–98.

McKinsey Co. (2002) *Reviving UK Manufacturing*, October, New York.

McKinsey Global Institute (1998) *Driving Productivity and Growth in the UK Economy*, New York.

National Economic Development Office (1987) Does manufacturing matter?, *National Institute Economic* Review, 122, 47–58.

O'Mahony, M. (1998) *Britain's Relative Productivity Performance 1950–1996: Estimates by Sector*, September, London, National Institute of Economic and Social Research.

O'Mahony, M. and de Boer, W. (2002) *Britain's Relative Productivity Performance: Updates to 1999. Final Report to DTI/Treasury/ONS*, March, London, National Institute of Economic and Social Research.

O'Mahoney, M. and van Ark, B. (2003) *EU Productivity and Competitiveness: an Industry Perspective*, Brussels, European Commission.

OECD (2002) *OECD in Figures*, Paris, Organisation for Economic Cooperation and Development.

OECD (2005a) *Labour Force Statistics 1984–2004*, Paris, Organisation for Economic Cooperation and Development.

OECD (2005b) *Science, Technology and Industry Scoreboard 2005 – Towards a Knowledge-based Economy*, Paris, Organisation for Economic Cooperation and Development.

OECD (2010a) *Economic Outlook*, No 87, Paris, Organisation for Economic Cooperation and Development.

OECD (2010b) *Education at a Glance 2010: OECD Indicators*, Paris, Organisation for Economic Cooperation and Development.

OECD (2010c) *OECD Factbook 2010*, Paris, Organisation for Economic Cooperation and Development.

OECD (2010d) *OECD in Figures*, Paris, Organisation for Economic Cooperation and Development.

OECD (2010e) *Stat. Extracts*, Paris, Organisation for Economic Cooperation and Development.

OECD (2010f) *OECD Statistical Programme of Work 2010: Labour Statistics*, Paris, Organisation for Economic Cooperation and Development.

ONS (2006a) *Economic Trends*, April, London, Office for National Statistics.

ONS (2006b) *United Kingdom National Accounts*: The Blue Book, London, Office for National Statistics.

ONS (2010a) *Annual Abstract of Statistics*, London, Office for National Statistics.

ONS (2010b) *International Comparisons of Productivity*, ICP Data (February), London, Office for National Statistics.

ONS (2010c) *Labour Market Statistics*, London, Office for National Statistics.

ONS (2010d) *Monthly Digest of Statistics*, London, Office for National Statistics.

ONS (2010e) *United Kingdom National Accounts: The Blue Book*, London, Office for National Statistics.

Oulton, N. (1994) Labour productivity and unit labour costs in manufacturing: the UK and its competitors, *National Institute Economic Review*, 148(1): 49–60.

Oulton, N. (1997) Total factor productivity growth and the role of externalities, *National Institute Economic Review*, 162(1): 99–111.

Proudfoot Consulting (2002) *Untapped Potential: the Barriers to Optimum Corporate Productivity*, October, London.

Proudfoot Consulting (2004) Managing for mediocrity: How six barriers impact productivity globally, *International Labour Productivity Study*, September, London.

Proudfoot Consulting (2005) *2005 Proudfoot Productivity Report*, September, London. Consulting.

Proudfoot Consulting (2008) *Global Productivity Report: A World of Underutilized Opportunities*, London.

Rowthorn, R. E. and Wells, J. R. (1987) *Deindustrialization and Foreign Trade*, Cambridge, Cambridge University Press.

Singh, A. (1977) UK industry and the world economy: a case of deindustrialization? *Cambridge Journal of Economics*, 1(2): 113–16.

Steedman, H., Mason, G. and Wagner, K. (1991) Intermediate skills in the workplace, *National Institute Economic Review*, 136(1): 60–76.

US BLS (2010) *International Labor Comparisons, Supplementary Tables*, BLS Washington DC, US Bureau of Labor Statistics.

Van Ark, B., O'Mahoney, M. and Timmer, M. P. (2008) The productivity gap between Europe and the United States: trends and causes, *Journal of Economic Perspectives*, 22(1): 25–44.

Venables, A. J. (2007) Evaluating urban transport improvements: cost-benefit analysis in the presence of agglomeration and income taxation, *Journal of Transport Economics and Policy*, 41(2): 173–88.

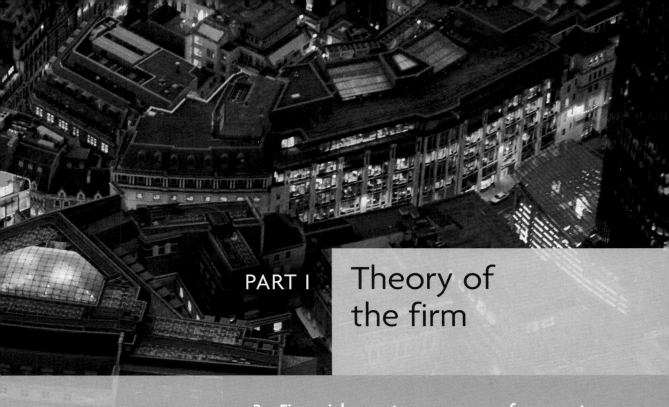

PART I Theory of
the firm

CHAPTER 2

Financial reports as a source of corporate information

Companies in the UK are required to publish information (annually and, for many large companies, biannually) in compliance with statutes and with the rules laid down by various financial regulators. This chapter examines the content and presentation of annual reports, and identifies a range of useful financial measures that can be calculated. The 2010 accounts of Tesco plc have been used for illustration. Tesco is the world's third-largest food retailer, with 4,811 stores in 13 countries. The chapter concludes with a detailed analysis of the Financial Times Share Information Service, and the indices and ratios it contains.

Being familiar with ways of analysing and interpreting published information of the kind in this chapter is important for both internal and external stakeholders of the organization. Changes in the various financial measures can give early warning of the need for policy adjustments and new strategic directions, both to decision-makers within the organization and to those external stakeholders with a financial interest in the future performance of the organisation. Chapters 3 and 15 pay further attention to the ways in which objectives are set and implemented within organizations and to their ethical and social responsibilities, both formal and informal.

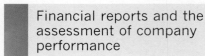

Financial reports and the assessment of company performance

In the past 20 years, companies have been subject to ever more complex regulations that detail the minimum requirements of disclosure in published financial reports. These reports enable various user groups to take informed decisions concerning their financial relationship with the company.

However, the separation of ownership and control in the majority of public companies (plcs)[1] might be thought to encourage management (controllers) to present to shareholders (owners) as favourable a picture as possible of the company's activities. Fear of the effects of competition and of adverse investor reaction might also mean that companies seek to give away as little information as possible – usually by disclosing only the legal minimum of requirements. Even so, most plcs regard the presentation of their published financial reports as a matter of corporate pride, and pay great attention to the quality and relevance of the documents.

An examination of the typical elements that make up a company report reveals a mixture of statutory items (i.e. those required by company law), requirements of the accounting profession, additional Stock Exchange regulations (for 'listed' companies) and voluntary disclosures. Major components of these reports are:

1 Business review
2 Directors' report
3 Balance sheet
4 Income statement
5 Statement of changes in equity
6 Notes to the financial statements (including statement of accounting policies)
7 Cash flow statement
8 Auditors' report.

Each of these is summarized below. Since 2005 there has also been a requirement for companies listed on European Stock Exchanges to implement *International Financial Reporting Standards*, which has resulted in a number of changes in terminology compared with that used in the UK in previous years, including:

- the 'Profit and loss account' is now referred to as the 'Income statement';
- 'Fixed assets' are now referred to as 'Non-current assets';
- 'Stock of unsold goods and materials' is now referred to as 'Inventories';
- 'Debtors' are now referred to as 'Receivables';
- 'Creditors' are now referred to as 'Payables'.

Business review

While there is currently no statutory requirement for a business review, it is regarded as 'best practice' that it be included in the annual reports of large companies. The business review has become an important feature of corporate reporting, providing an opportunity for directors to set out a clear and objective analysis of a company's development, performance, position and prospects. A typical business review includes:

- commentary on the operating results;
- review of the group's financial needs and resources;
- commentary on risks and uncertainties.

For example, Tesco's Business Review in 2010 included the following statement on its business strategy:

> To ensure the Group continues to pursue the right strategy, the Board discusses strategic issues at every Board meeting and dedicates two full days a year to reviewing the Group's strategy. The Executive Committee also discusses strategy on a regular basis. We have structured programmes for engaging with all our stakeholders including customers, employees, investors, suppliers, government, media and non-governmental organisations. We also invest significant resources in ensuring our strategy is communicated well and understood by the parties who are key to delivering it. The business operates a Steering Wheel (a balanced scorecard process whereby we set goals for different areas of the business and assess our overall progress on a quarterly basis) in all countries and significant business units to help manage performance and deliver business strategy. (Tesco 2010)

In addition, there is likely to be a Chairman's report, which is a reflective, personal appraisal of company performance. Tesco's chairman, David Reid, started his 2010 report on the encouraging note:

> I am pleased to report that the Tesco team has once again delivered a good set of results – guided by experienced management who have steered the business through recessions before. As markets around the world are emerging from this recession each part of our business is well positioned to pursue our strategy for growth. (David Reid, Tesco Chairman, 2010)

Directors' report

This includes a statement of the principal activities of the company and of any significant changes that have taken place in the holding of non-current assets (e.g. property sales or the acquisition of subsidiaries). Details of the directors and their shareholdings in the company are also mentioned, as any significant change in their holdings may reflect their view of the company's future prospects.

Balance sheet

Also known as a Statement of Financial Position, this shows the net assets of the company at its financial year-end, often 31 December, but for a retailer like Tesco, the relatively 'quiet' date of the last Saturday in February (27th) was used. It details the assets of the business and balances them against its liabilities; in other words, what the company *owns* (assets) is compared to what it *owes* (liabilities). The excess of assets over liabilities (net assets) equals the total equity invested by the company's ordinary shareholders and the company's reserves (including its profits) built up over time.

Assets are divided between *non-current* and *current*. Non-current assets are those that are expected to be retained by the business and are of significant value, e.g. land, machinery and vehicles. Current assets are those expected to be used in the normal operating cycle, e.g. inventory, trade receivables and bank balances.

Some non-current assets might be *intangible* (i.e. not 'physical'), such as the price paid for the reputation (goodwill) of a business that has been taken over by the reporting company. Most non-current assets

are *depreciated*, which ensures that a reasonable amount is included in the company's total operating expenses to recognize loss in value due to wear and tear, obsolescence, etc.

An increasingly important aspect of a company's balance sheet is the health of its pension scheme. Factors including the volatility of stock markets, low-yielding investments and increased longevity may cause material imbalances between the obligations of a company under the scheme and the underlying assets available to meet those obligations. For Tesco, the non-current liabilities of £15,327m shown on the balance sheet (Fig. 2.1) include a pension deficit of £1,840m, an increase of £346m in the year. However, pension liabilities stretch over a long period, and it is assumed – under an accounting convention known as 'going concern' – that the company will continue for many years and is willing and able to provide the support necessary to meet its pension obligations.

Financial ratios

The construction of several simple ratios from the information contained within the balance sheet can give a clear assessment of the company's performance by making the following comparisons:

- with its *own* performance in previous time periods;
- with that of *other companies* in the same sector;
- with *accepted standards* of performance, i.e. with particular values ('norms') for each ratio.

Figure 2.1 shows the 2010 balance sheet for Tesco plc. Several accounting ratios have been calculated by extracting the 2010 figures from the table and comparing them with the corresponding annual sales revenue (£56,910m for Group sales to outside customers – see the income statement of Fig. 2.2 below). For comparative purposes, the same ratios have been calculated for Kingfisher plc, in a different retailing sector – mainly 'do it yourself' materials and services (B & Q, Screwfix, etc.) – and, by way of contrast, from Alumasc plc, a building materials manufacturer.

Gearing ratio

This reflects the financial risk to which the company is subject, by measuring the capital structure of the company and the degree to which it relies on external borrowings. Gearing (also known as *leverage*) can be calculated in various ways, including:

Group Balance Sheet

27 February 2010

	2010 £m	2009 £m
Non-current assets		
Goodwill and intangible assets	4,177	4,076
Property, plant and equipment	23,203	23,152
Investment property	2,731	1,539
Other investments	4,147	3,318
	34,258	32,085
Current assets		
Inventories	2,729	2,669
Trade and other receivables	1,888	1,820
Loans and Derivative financial instruments	2,642	1,820
Short-term investments and Cash and cash equivalents	2,819	3,509
	11,392	13,081
Other assets held for sale	373	398
	11,765	13,479
Current liabilities[1]		
Trade and other payables	(9,442)	(8,665)
Other current liabilities	(6,573)	(8,930)
	(16,015)	(17,595)
Net current liabilities	(4,250)	(4,116)
Non-current liabilities[2]	(15,327)	(15,063)
Net assets	14,681	12,906
Equity		
Share capital	399	395
Share premium account	4,801	4,638
Other reserves	40	40
Retained earnings	9,356	7,776
	14,596	12,849
Minority interests	85	57
Total equity	14,681	12,906

[1]Includes £575m bank loans and overdraft.
[2]Includes £12,250m loans.

Fig. 2.1 Tesco plc Group Balance Sheet.
Source: Tesco plc *Annual Report 2010* (adapted).

$$\text{gearing ratio} = \frac{\text{external borrowing}}{\text{total capital employed}}$$

$$= \frac{\text{current} + \text{non-current financial liabilities}}{\text{current} + \text{non-current financial liabilities} + \text{total equity}}$$

The total capital employed is made up of external borrowings (debentures,[2] other loans and bank borrowing) and funds generated from shareholders and retained from profits (ordinary shares and reserves). The *cost* of external borrowing is loan interest payments, whilst that for 'internal' funds is the dividend return to shareholders.

The gearing ratio shows the proportion of total capital that is provided externally and gives an indication of the burden of interest payments to which the company is committed irrespective of its profitability. A gearing ratio of up to one-third is usually regarded as acceptable for a company, suggesting that it is not over-reliant on external borrowing. A figure in excess of this indicates a higher-geared company. High gearing ratios are most suitable to those companies with steady and reliable profits, whose earnings are sufficient to cover interest payments and where total dividends are low. However, wide fluctuations in profitability – as in the current recession – would make a highly geared company extremely vulnerable to a downturn in market conditions – profits may be so low that interest payments cannot be covered, leading to financial difficulties. The 2010 accounts of Tesco plc reveal a gearing ratio of 49.16% for Tesco, i.e. $(1,675 + 12,520)/(1,675 + 12,520 + 14,681)$, a value considerably higher than the 28% of Alumasc and Kingfisher's 24%. Tesco had £2,819m investments and cash at bank and in hand at the balance sheet date which, when offset against its financial liabilities, effectively reduces its gearing level to just under 40%.

A drawback of the ratio is that it is concerned only with borrowings on which interest charges are incurred. It ignores completely liabilities that effectively constitute interest-free loans. One such major item is that of 'trade payables' – money that is owed by the company to its suppliers. The ratio tends to understate the dependence of companies on external borrowings, so it is useful to consider *all* liabilities. The numerator would then become 'current and non-current liabilities' and produce a ratio that is a more realistic basis for comparison when linked with 'total equity'. The ratios for the three companies are: Tesco 109%; Alumasc 104%; Kingfisher 75%.

Operating ratios

These can be used to gauge the efficiency with which various aspects of the company's trading are managed.

Inventory turnover ratio

The holding of inventory, in the form of unsold finished and partly finished goods, is an expensive activity for companies due to storage, security and insurance costs, so that considerable attention is paid to the inventory turnover ratio:

$$\text{Inventory turnover ratio} = \frac{\text{average inventory}}{\text{cost of sales}}$$

This ratio reflects the level of inventory used to support sales (see Fig. 2.2 below). We would expect companies to carry the minimum level of inventory

consistent with the efficient running of the business. The figure will vary widely according to the industrial sector involved. Tesco's ratio is only 5.16%, i.e. $((2,669 + 2,729)/2)/52,303$, a figure which reflects the extremely fast throughput of its inventory, on average being sold every 18.9 days (i.e. 5.16% of 365 days). Kingfisher's ratio, reflecting very high-value inventories, was 25% (91 days) whilst Alumasc had a ratio of 17% (63 days).

Trade receivables ratio

This ratio can be used to monitor a company's credit control procedures, by comparing the amount owed to it at the balance sheet date by customers, credit card companies, etc. with its total sales revenue:

$$\text{Trade receivables ratio} = \frac{\text{average trade receivables}}{\text{sales revenue}}$$

Businesses like retail supermarkets are run almost exclusively on a cash-and-carry basis so will have relatively little owed directly by customers. There will, however, be amounts owing by credit card companies at the balance sheet date. For other businesses an average credit period might be six weeks, equivalent to a trade receivables ratio of around 12%. Retailers Tesco and Kingfisher showed figures of 3.3%, i.e. $((1,820 + 1,888)/2)/56,910$ (11.9 days' sales), and 4.8% (17 days' sales) respectively, though Alumasc (with very few 'cash' sales) had a ratio of 23% (82 days' sales).

Trade payables ratio

This ratio indicates the size and period of credit a company receives from its suppliers, by comparing its sales with the total amount the company owes to its trade creditors:

$$\text{Trade payables ratio} = \frac{\text{trade payables}}{\text{cost of sales}}$$

$$= \frac{\text{average amount owed by the group to its suppliers}}{\text{total cost of goods sold in the period}}$$

It is in the company's interests to take full advantage of the credit period offered by its suppliers. Tesco shows a figure of 17.3%, i.e. $((8,665 + 9,442)/2)/52,303$ (63 days), which is a typical credit period. Kingfisher (35% or 129 days) and Alumasc (30% or 109 days) show how the recession has significantly lengthened the time taken for companies to pay their suppliers. Previously, 40–60 days would be considered typical.

Liquidity ratios

These give an indication of the company's short-term financial position, in other words, the availability of cash or marketable assets with which to meet current liabilities.

Current ratio

The current ratio measures the extent to which currently available assets cover current liabilities, i.e. those requiring repayment within one year:

$$\text{Current ratio} = \frac{\text{current assets}}{\text{current liabilities}}$$

Current assets include inventory, trade receivables and cash. Current liabilities include trade payables, taxation and short-term borrowing.

There is no ideal ratio to which every company should aspire, but analysts may become nervous if current liabilities significantly exceed current assets. A strong ratio (e.g. more than 1.5:1) is not necessarily a sign of strength, since it may mean excessive inventories or receivables, or excess cash resources that lie uninvested.

Supermarket chains are unusual in that their rapid turnovers, together with the cash-and-carry nature of their business, will give relatively low inventory and trade receivables figures. For this reason 'current assets' will be relatively small, and so a very low current ratio is to be expected. Tesco's 2010 figure of 0.73 (11,765/16,015) must be viewed in this context. By comparison, Alumasc's 1.9 reflects the high level of inventories which manufacturers carry. Kingfisher's ratio of 0.99 is typical of a predominantly 'non-food' retailer.

Quick assets ratio (acid test)

This ratio provides a better indication of short-term liquidity by ignoring inventory (which could prove hard to sell in a liquidity crisis) and concentrating on those assets which are more easily convertible into cash:

$$\text{quick assets ratio} = \frac{\text{current assets} - \text{inventory}}{\text{current liabilities}}$$

A yardstick of 1.0 is usually sought, indicating that sufficient cash would be available in a crisis to pay off all the company's current liabilities. Alumasc is just above this, with a ratio of 1.16.

Traders with a rapid turnover of cash sales will have a lower level of current assets, and often a very low quick assets ratio. This is the case with Tesco's ratio of only 0.56 ((11,765 – 2,729)/16,015) for 2010. Kingfisher's ratio is only slightly weaker at 0.54.

The current and quick assets ratios are two of the most widely used ratios, as they give a 'snapshot' indication of the day-to-day financial strength of the business.

The calculation of the above six ratios from balance sheet information, i.e. (a) *gearing* ratio, (b) *operating* ratios (inventory turnover, trade receivables ratio, trade payables ratio) and (c) *liquidity* ratios (current ratio, quick assets ratio), permits an assessment of a company's performance with regard to accepted standards across a given sector. This assessment is further improved by considering the information provided by the income statement (see Fig. 2.2).

Income statement

This is a summary of transactions for a stated period, usually a year, and sets revenues against costs in order to show the company's profit or loss (in smaller companies, the income statement is still known as the 'profit and loss account'). The statement discloses summarized figures for the expenses of the business (e.g. the cost of sales), but makes no evaluation of the risks incurred in order to earn the given profit levels. Neither is there any indication of the degree to which the given profit level conforms to the company's objectives. Key information on such aspects can be found in the Business Review section: see p. 32.

Figure 2.2 shows the income statement of Tesco plc for 2010 and indicates the various deductions that take place from sales revenue to derive profit or loss. Part of the profit is distributed to shareholders in the form of dividends (see Fig. 2.4 below), with the balance being retained by the company to boost reserves. Dividends may still be paid to shareholders even when losses have been incurred, if profits were set aside for this purpose in previous years.

The profit figure remains the single most important figure in the company accounts and various profitability measures can be employed to assess relative performance.

Group Income Statement
Year ended 27 February 2010

	2010 £m	2009 £m
Revenue (Sales excluding VAT)	56,910	53,898
Cost of sales	(52,303)	(49,713)
Gross profit	4,607	4,185
Administrative expenses	(1,527)	(1,252)
Profit arising on property-related items	377	236
Operating profit	3,457	3,169
Share of post-tax profits of joint ventures and associates	33	110
Finance income	265	116
Finance costs	(579)	(478)
Profit before tax	3,176	2,917
Taxation	(840)	(779)
Profit for the year	2,336	2,138
Minority interests[1]	(9)	(5)
Profit attributable to owners of the parent[2]	2,327	2,133
Earnings per share from continuing and discontinued operations	Pence	Pence
Basic	29.33	27.14
Diluted	29.19	26.96

[1]Minority interests relate to the proportion of profits attributable to those shares held in one or more of Tesco's subsidiary companies that are not owned by the parent company. For example, Tesco owns only 70% of Tesco's Malaysian subsidiary.
[2]Remaining profit after adjustment for the minority interest (see note 1) is transferred to the equity shareholders of Tesco plc. Tesco has a controlling interest in over twenty subsidiary companies, and is thus referred to as the 'parent' of those companies.

Fig. 2.2 Tesco plc Group Income Statement.
Source: Tesco plc *Annual Report 2010* (adapted).

Profit margins

$$\text{Gross profit margin} = \frac{\text{gross profit}}{\text{sales revenue}}$$

The gross profit margin (also called the 'gross margin') shows the profit earned before administrative and other general overheads are deducted. In highly competitive businesses such as supermarket chains, cost cutting to win sales from rivals results in ultra-slim gross margins – but with turnover measured in £billions, even a fraction of a percentage point up or down can have a dramatic effect on a company's fortunes. Tesco's gross margin in 2010 was a slender 8.10% (4,607/56,910), compared with Alumasc's 33% and Kingfisher's 36%:

$$\text{Operating profit margin} = \frac{\text{operating profit before interest and tax}}{\text{sales revenue}}$$

The operating profit margin is the ratio of profit, after the deduction of trading expenses but before the payment of interest on borrowings (financing charges) and corporation tax, to sales revenue. A figure of 6–8% would be typical for manufacturing industry, but supermarket chains, with high volumes and very competitive prices, might expect a ratio around 4%, which might still yield high absolute levels of operating profit. In fact, Tesco exhibited an encouraging result with a ratio of 6% (3,457/56,910). Kingfisher earned a similar percentage, whilst Alumasc, operating in the struggling housebuilding sector, only recorded 3%.

Return on capital employed (ROCE) and return on assets (ROA)

$$\text{Return on capital employed} = \frac{\text{operating profit before interest and tax}}{\text{total equity and loan capital}}$$

$$\text{Return on assets} = \frac{\text{operating profit before interest and tax}}{\text{total assets}}$$

These two measures, known as ROCE and ROA respectively, are key indicators of company performance as measured by the profitability generated by, firstly, the company's total value invested, whether by shareholders or long-term lenders, and, secondly, the total assets utilized in the period.

Measurement of the return on capital employed is a vital overall benchmark of company performance and is one of Tesco plc's key indicators used internally to gauge progress from one year to the next. On this basis, the Tesco figure is 11.5%, i.e. 3,457/(15,327 + 14,681), whereas Alumasc yields 5.8% and Kingfisher 9.7%.

Measurement of the rate of return on total assets offers a popular alternative assessment of profitability, particularly as it tests whether continual expansion (e.g. in opening new supermarkets in more countries) is a profitable venture. On this basis, the Tesco figure is 7.5%, i.e. 3,457/(34,258 + 11,765), whereas Alumasc yields only 4% and Kingfisher 6%.

Calculations of return on assets will clearly vary, sometimes substantially, with the basis used for measurement of those assets. This is a strong argument for using a standard approach and accountants are expected, under *International Accounting Standard (IAS) 16 Measurement of property, plant & equipment* and other standards, to reassess the value of non-current assets at regular intervals to avoid the use of outdated valuations.

A consideration of these profitability ratios, together with earlier information on gearing, operating and liquidity ratios, can give an overall impression of Tesco's financial position in 2010. The company has maintained a relatively high profit margin and return on capital employed, whilst having a low gearing ratio. Its working capital situation would cause alarm in a different type of business, but the very fast throughput of inventory ensures that the cash flow (see Fig. 2.3) is more than adequate to meet liabilities as they fall due.

Cash flow statement

The usual accounting convention followed when preparing an income statement is that *all* relevant income and expenditure must be included, whether or not it resulted in a cash inflow or outflow in that period. Hence, sales revenue will include sales invoiced but not yet paid for (known as 'receivables') whilst cost of sales and other overheads include goods and services received from suppliers which are owing at the end of the financial year ('payables'). Some expenses, notably *depreciation*, do not result in a cash flow. Also, a company might have major cash flows which are not reflected in the income statement – for example, loans might be issued or repaid in the period, share capital might be issued and non-current assets bought or sold. Profitability alone is not sufficient to ensure the survival of a company – its cash resources must be adequate to ensure that it can meet its liabilities when they fall due and take investment opportunities as they occur. Aggressive companies such as Tesco often show an overall cash flow that is considerably less than their profit (sometimes having an overall net cash *outflow*), as continuing expansion soaks up and possibly exceeds the net cash generated from trading.

Figure 2.3 shows Tesco's cash flow statement for 2010. It shows an overall decrease in cash of £739m. Compare this with the retained profit for the same period of £2,327m as shown in its income statement. Operating activities generated over £4.7bn of cash, but interest payments (£690m), taxation (£512m), payment of dividends (£970m) and, most significantly, the repayment of borrowings (£3,601m) reduced the overall cash flow significantly.

Statement of changes in equity

This gives an overview of the various reasons (including the payment of dividends) for the changes in the 'total equity' as shown in the opening and closing balance sheets, and cuts through much of the fine detail presented elsewhere in the annual report. Equity represents the overall worth of the company as recorded in its accounting records at the balance sheet date, and is used in the ROCE calculation referred to previously.

Figure 2.4 shows Tesco plc's statement, which, for 2010, indicates that the company's total equity

Group Cash Flow Statement
Year ended 27 February 2010

	2010 £m	2009 £m
Cash flows from operating activities	5,947	4,978
Interest paid	(690)	(562)
Corporation tax paid	(512)	(456)
Net cash flow from operating activities	**4,745**	**3,960**
Cash flows from investing activities		
Acquisition of subsidiaries, net of cash acquired	(65)	(1,275)
Proceeds from sale of property, plant and equipment	1,820	994
Purchase of property, plant and equipment and investment properties	(2,855)	(4,487)
Purchase of intangible assets	(159)	(220)
Net increase in loans to joint ventures	(49)	(272)
Investments in short-term and other investments	(1,918)	(1,233)
Proceeds from sale of short-term investments	1,233	360
Dividends received	35	69
Interest received	81	90
Net cash used in investing activities	**(1,877)**	**(5,974)**
Cash flows from financing activities		
Proceeds from issue of ordinary share capital	167	130
Increase in borrowings	862	7,387
Repayments of borrowings	(3,601)	(2,733)
Repayments of obligations under finance leases	(41)	(18)
Dividends paid	(970)	(886)
Own shares purchased	(24)	(265)
Net cash from financing activities	**(3,607)**	**(3,615)**
Net (decrease) increase in cash and cash equivalents	(739)	1,601
Cash and cash equivalents at beginning of year	3,509	1,788
Effect of foreign exchange rate changes	49	120
Cash and cash equivalents at end of year	**2,819**	**3,509**

Fig. 2.3 Group cash flow statement.
Source: Tesco plc *Annual Report 2010* (adapted).

Statement of Changes in Equity

£m	Issued share capital	Share premium	Retained earnings	Other	Total
At 28 February 2009	395	4,638	7,644	229	12,906
Issue of shares	4	163			167
Profit for the year			2,336		2,336
Equity dividends authorised			(970)		(970)
Other adjustments			38	204	242
At 27 February 2010	399	4,801	9,048	433	14,681

Fig. 2.4 Tesco plc Statement of changes in equity.
Source: Tesco plc *Annual Report 2010* (adapted).

increased from £12,906m to £14,681m, mainly as a result of the year's profit of £2,336m, less dividends of £970m.

Notes to the financial statements (including statement of accounting policies)

There is far more information contained in notes to the financial statements than within the balance sheet, income statement and cash flow statement. The notes always commence with a statement of the accounting policies adopted by the company (a short extract is shown in Fig. 2.5), and there then follow many pages of detailed information needed to comply with either relevant accounting standards and/or statutes (45 pages in Tesco's 2010 Report). It is unusual for companies to give more than the minimum requirements (as that might be to a competitor's advantage), but the auditors' report (see Fig. 2.6 below) will confirm whether or not these minimum requirements have been met.

Auditors' report

The auditors are required to report to shareholders ('the members') on whether the group accounts have been properly prepared, in accordance with accounting standards and relevant legislation, and whether they give a true and fair view of the activities of the company. Figure 2.6 shows Tesco plc's report. The auditors may qualify their approval of the accounts if they feel that the records have not been well kept or if all the information they require is not available. Such qualifications usually fall into two categories: (1) those relating to accounting policy, and (2) those relating to unsatisfactory levels of information.

External sources of financial information

Of the various elements in the company accounts, the Business Review is probably the most widely read by non-specialists. None of the other elements, other than the year's profit figure, despite the importance of the information contained, receives more than the passing attention of the average reader. Users of financial information still often prefer to use secondary sources of information, including those provided by the financial press and other external agencies. Two specific features are considered in detail below: the FTSE All-Share Index and data on individual share price movements.

FTSE All-Share Index: sector share movements

The FTSE All-Share Index[3] integrates the movements of some 615 constituent shares, covering 10 sector groups (e.g. Telecommunications) and 39 individual sectors (e.g. Mobile Telecommunications). Figure 2.7 shows a small extract of the information provided. Various other indices and trends are published separately for each sector group, as well as for selected subsectors within those groups. The Index can be found in the 'Companies and Markets' section of the *Financial Times*, as part of that paper's daily Share Service.

A comparison of *sector* index numbers with that for the All-Share Index allows the buoyant and depressed sectors to be quickly and clearly identified. For instance, of the sectors shown in the extract, mining companies have done extremely well (20,930.2) when compared with the depressed media sector, at only 3,955.8.

FT data on individual share movements

The *individual company* Share Information Service – of which Fig. 2.8 is an abstract – can usefully be viewed in conjunction with the All-Share Index. The performance of an individual company can then be assessed in the context of the performance of the industrial sector in which it operates.

Share (equity) price movements are published daily, with shares ordered alphabetically within particular industrial sectors. The price quoted is the middle price, i.e. midway between the buy and sell prices at the close of the market on the previous day. Figure 2.8 shows the specific information provided for Tesco plc in the food and drug retailers sector.

TESCO PLC
Note 1 Accounting Policies

GENERAL INFORMATION

Tesco PLC is a public limited company incorporated and domiciled in the United Kingdom under the Companies Act 2006 (Registration number 445790). The address of the registered office is Tesco House, Delamare Road, Cheshunt, Hertfordshire, EN8 9SL, UK. As described in the report of the Directors, the main activity of the Group is that of retailing, retailing services and financial services.

STATEMENT OF COMPLIANCE

The consolidated financial statements have been prepared in accordance with International Financial Reporting Standards (IFRS) and International Financial Reporting Interpretation Committee (IFRIC) interpretations as endorsed by the European Union, and those parts of the Companies Act applicable to companies reporting under IFRS.

BASIS OF PREPARATION

The financial statements are presented in Pounds Sterling, generally rounded to the nearest million. They are prepared on the historical cost basis except for certain financial instruments, share-based payments, customer loyalty programmes and pensions that have been measured at fair value. The accounting policies set out below have been applied consistently to all periods presented in these consolidated financial statements.

BASIS OF CONSOLIDATION

The Group financial statements consist of the financial statements of the ultimate parent Company (Tesco PLC), all entities controlled by the Company (its subsidiaries) and the Group's share of its interests in joint ventures and associates. Where necessary, adjustments are made to the financial statements of subsidiaries, joint ventures and associates to bring the accounting policies used into line with those of the Group.

USE OF ASSUMPTIONS AND ESTIMATES

The preparation of the consolidated financial statements requires management to make judgements, estimates and assumptions that affect the application of policies and reported amounts of assets and liabilities, income and expenses. The estimates and associated assumptions are based on historical experience and various other factors that are believed to be reasonable under the circumstances, the results of which form the basis of making judgements about carrying values of assets and liabilities that are not readily apparent from other sources. Actual results may differ from these estimates. The estimates and underlying assumptions are reviewed on an ongoing basis. Revisions to accounting estimates are recognised in the period in which the estimate is revised if the revision affects only that period, or in the period of the revision and future periods if the revision affects both current and future periods.

OPERATING PROFIT

Operating profit is stated after profit arising from property related items but before the share of results of joint ventures and associates, finance income and finance costs.

PROPERTY, PLANT AND EQUIPMENT

Property, plant and equipment assets are carried at cost less accumulated depreciation and any recognised impairment in value. Depreciation is provided on a straight-line basis to their residual value over the anticipated useful economic lives. The following depreciation rates are applied for the Group:

- Freehold and leasehold buildings with greater than 40 years unexpired – at 2.5% of cost
- Leasehold properties with less than 40 years unexpired are depreciated by equal annual instalments over the unexpired period of the lease
- Plant, equipment, fixtures and fittings and motor vehicles – at rates varying from 9% to 50%.

Fig. 2.5 Notes to the financial statements: accounting policies.
Source: Tesco plc *Annual Report 2010* (adapted).

Independent auditors' report to the members of Tesco PLC

We have audited the Group financial statements of Tesco PLC for the 52 weeks ended 27 February 2010 which comprise the Group Income Statement, the Group Statement of Comprehensive Income, the Group Balance Sheet, the Group Cash Flow Statement, the Group Statement of Changes in Equity and the related notes. The financial reporting framework that has been applied in their preparation is applicable law and International Financial Reporting Standards (IFRSs) as adopted by the European Union.

RESPECTIVE RESPONSIBILITIES OF DIRECTORS AND AUDITORS

As explained more fully in the Statement of Directors' responsibilities set out on page 68, the Directors are responsible for the preparation of the Group financial statements and for being satisfied that they give a true and fair view. Our responsibility is to audit the Group financial statements in accordance with applicable law and International Standards on Auditing (UK and Ireland). Those standards require us to comply with the Auditing Practices Board's Ethical Standards for Auditors.

This report, including the opinions, has been prepared for and only for the Company's members as a body in accordance with Chapter 3 of Part 16 of the Companies Act 2006 and for no other purpose. We do not, in giving these opinions, accept or assume responsibility for any other purpose or to any other person to whom this report is shown or into whose hands it may come save where expressly agreed by our prior consent in writing.

SCOPE OF THE AUDIT OF THE FINANCIAL STATEMENTS

An audit involves obtaining evidence about the amounts and disclosures in the financial statements sufficient to give reasonable assurance that the financial statements are free from material misstatement, whether caused by fraud or error. This includes an assessment of: whether the accounting policies are appropriate to the Group's circumstances and have been consistently applied and adequately disclosed; the reasonableness of significant accounting estimates made by the Directors; and the overall presentation of the financial statements.

OPINION ON FINANCIAL STATEMENTS

In our opinion the Group financial statements:

■ give a true and fair view of the state of the Group's affairs as at 27 February 2010 and of its profit and cash flows for the 52 weeks then ended;
■ have been properly prepared in accordance with IFRSs as adopted by the European Union; and
■ have been prepared in accordance with the requirements of the Companies Act 2006 and Article 4 of the IAS Regulation.

Richard Winter (Senior Statutory Auditor)
for and on behalf of PricewaterhouseCoopers LLP
Chartered Accountants and Statutory Auditors
London
5 May 2010

Fig. 2.6 Tesco plc Auditors' report.
Source: Tesco plc *Annual Report 2010* (adapted).

The FT of Friday 10 September (see Fig. 2.8) revealed that at the close of the previous day's trading the Tesco share price stood at 417.95p, up 3.2 on that day. We can make a more thorough assessment of Tesco's current position if we examine some of the technical headings of Figs 2.7 and 2.8, in conjunction with Tesco's own annual report.

Price/earnings ratio: Tesco 16.1, sector 15.02, All-Share 14.22

$$\text{P/E ratio} = \frac{\text{share price}}{\text{earnings per share}}$$

where earnings per share is profit after tax divided by the number of ordinary shares in issue. The price/

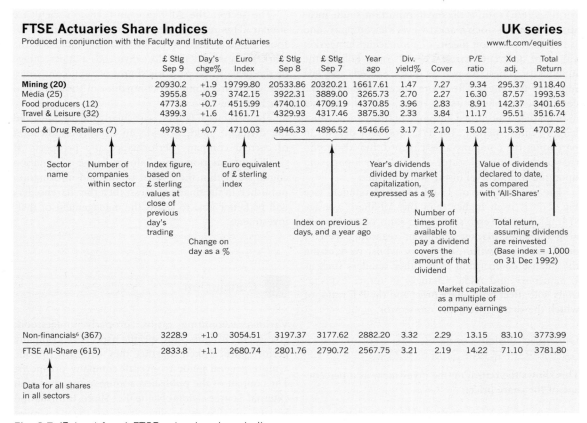

FTSE Actuaries Share Indices
Produced in conjunction with the Faculty and Institute of Actuaries

UK series
www.ft.com/equities

	£ Stlg Sep 9	Day's chge%	Euro Index	£ Stlg Sep 8	£ Stlg Sep 7	Year ago	Div. yield%	Cover	P/E ratio	Xd adj.	Total Return
Mining (20)	20930.2	+1.9	19799.80	20533.86	20320.21	16617.61	1.47	7.27	9.34	295.37	9118.40
Media (25)	3955.8	+0.9	3742.15	3922.31	3889.00	3265.73	2.70	2.27	16.30	87.57	1993.53
Food producers (12)	4773.8	+0.7	4515.99	4740.10	4709.19	4370.85	3.96	2.83	8.91	142.37	3401.65
Travel & Leisure (32)	4399.3	+1.6	4161.71	4329.93	4317.46	3875.30	2.33	3.84	11.17	95.51	3516.74
Food & Drug Retailers (7)	4978.9	+0.7	4710.03	4946.33	4896.52	4546.66	3.17	2.10	15.02	115.35	4707.82
Non-financials[6] (367)	3228.9	+1.0	3054.51	3197.37	3177.62	2882.20	3.32	2.29	13.15	83.10	3773.99
FTSE All-Share (615)	2833.8	+1.1	2680.74	2801.76	2790.72	2567.75	3.21	2.19	14.22	71.10	3781.80

Sector name

Number of companies within sector

Index figure, based on £ sterling values at close of previous day's trading

Change on day as a %

Euro equivalent of £ sterling index

Index on previous 2 days, and a year ago

Year's dividends divided by market capitalization, expressed as a %

Number of times profit available to pay a dividend covers the amount of that dividend

Market capitalization as a multiple of company earnings

Value of dividends declared to date, as compared with 'All-Shares'

Total return, assuming dividends are reinvested (Base index = 1,000 on 31 Dec 1992)

Data for all shares in all sectors

Fig. 2.7 (Extract from) FTSE actuaries share indices.
Source: Adapted from FTSE actuaries share indices, *Financial Times*, 10/09/2010.

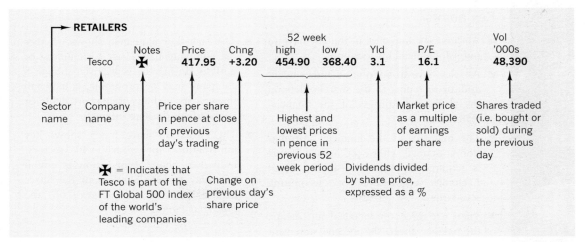

RETAILERS

	Notes	Price	Chng	52 week high	low	Yld	P/E	Vol '000s
Tesco	✠	**417.95**	**+3.20**	**454.90**	**368.40**	**3.1**	**16.1**	**48,390**

Sector name

Company name

Price per share in pence at close of previous day's trading

✠ = Indicates that Tesco is part of the FT Global 500 index of the world's leading companies

Change on previous day's share price

Highest and lowest prices in pence in previous 52 week period

Dividends divided by share price, expressed as a %

Market price as a multiple of earnings per share

Shares traded (i.e. bought or sold) during the previous day

Fig. 2.8 FT Share Information Service.
Source: Adapted from FT Share Information Service, *Financial Times*, 10/09/2010.

earnings (P/E) ratio is the most important single measure of how the stock market views the company, and is the most common means of comparing the market values of different shares. The P/E ratio tells us the number of times the market price exceeds the last reported earnings. The more highly regarded the company, the higher its P/E ratio, with the market anticipating a sustained earnings performance over a lengthy future period. The P/E ratio will depend in part upon the company's past record, but also upon that of the industrial sector of which it is a part, and upon the overall level of the stock market.

The sector figure of 15.02 for food retailers (see Fig. 2.7) is itself higher than the All-Share average (14.22), whilst Tesco's own P/E ratio of 16.1 probably indicates market sentiment regarding Tesco's dominant place within the sector whilst recognizing the intense competition from other retailers such as J. Sainsbury and Asda. Changes in future expectations will affect both share price and the P/E ratio, of which the share price is the numerator.

Dividend yield: Tesco 3.1%, sector 3.17%, All-Share 3.21%

This shows the return on the investment as a percentage of the share price:

$$\text{Gross dividend yield} = \frac{\text{gross dividend per share}}{\text{share price}} \times 100$$

The sector, the All-Share and Tesco's yield are similar. This reflects the fact that the share prices of food retailers have kept broadly in line with the market as a whole. Therefore dividends as a percentage of the price to be paid for shares in such companies (the yield) are similar to companies in the same and other sectors.

These technical figures, particularly the P/E ratio and the dividend yield, provide an excellent indication of current company performance and prospects. If this FT information is used alongside the information contained within the annual report and information published in the financial press, then the shareholders will be better able to assess the management of their investment.

Conclusion

Various accounting ratios, properly understood, give useful insights into specific aspects of company performance. Taken together they can also provide a more general guide to overall company prospects. The content of the published accounts, together with external sources, notably the FT Share Information Service, provide an excellent basis for the assessment of company performance and the evaluation of investments.

Key points

- All limited companies in the UK have to publish financial information.

- All plcs have to appoint an independent auditor to report to the shareholders on the truth and fairness of the financial statements.

- The majority of the financial information contained within the annual report is required by either legislation, Stock Exchange regulations or accounting standards.

- There are three key financial statements: the balance sheet, the income statement and the cash flow statement.

- The cash flow statement shows whether the company had a net cash inflow or outflow during the year. Even though a company may be profitable, it may fail through its inability to pay its debts or repay a loan (or loan interest).

- The FTSE All-Share Index shows key information for nearly 40 sectors. Individual share information is found each day (except Sunday) in the Share Information Service pages of the *Financial Times*.

Now try the self-check questions for this chapter on the Companion Website. You will also find useful links to relevant websites.

Notes

1 Evidence suggests that in the majority of public companies, the controlling management has little or no stake in the ownership of the company. The directors of Tesco plc, for example, had beneficial ownership of only 0.17% of the company's issued equity capital (13.3m shares out of a total issued share capital of over 7.9 billion).

2 Fixed-interest stocks issued by companies, usually redeemable at a set date, and backed by an agreement similar to a mortgage. Also known as 'bonds'.

3 The FTSE All-Share Index is an arithmetic average of price relatives weighted to reflect the market valuation of the shares included. It represents nearly all of the UK stock market value. The index is the aggregation of the FTSE 100, FTSE 250 and FTSE Small Cap Indexes.

References and further reading

Atrill, P. and McLaney, E. (2008) *Accounting and Finance for Non-specialists* (6th edn), Harlow, Financial Times/Prentice Hall.

Black, G. (2009) *Introduction to Accounting and Finance*, Harlow, Financial Times/Prentice Hall.

Financial Times (2010a) FT Share Service, 10 September, London.

Financial Times (2010b) FTSE Actuaries Share Indices, 10 September, London.

Holmes, G., Sugden, A. and Gee, P. *Interpreting Company Reports*, Harlow, Financial Times/Prentice Hall.

International Accounting Standard (2005) *16: Measurement of Property, Plant & Equipment*, London.

McKenzie, W. (2009) *FT Guide to Using and Interpreting Company Accounts*, Harlow, Financial Times/Prentice Hall.

Tesco plc (2010) *Annual Report and Reviews 2010*, Cheshunt.

Watson, D. and Head, A. (2010) *Corporate Finance: Principles and Practice* (5th edn), Harlow, Financial Times/Prentice Hall.

The following websites are relevant to this chapter:

Tesco plc: http://www.tesco.com/corporateinfo
Kingfisher plc: http://www.kingfisher.com
The Alumasc Group plc: http://www.alumasc.co.uk
FTSE: http://www.ftse.com
The International Accounting Standards Board: http://www.iasb.co.uk

CHAPTER 3

Firm objectives and firm behaviour

Economists have put forward various theories as to how firms behave in order to predict their reaction to events. At the heart of such theories is an assumption about firm objectives, the most usual being that the firm seeks to maximize profits. The first part of the chapter examines a number of alternative objectives open to the firm. It begins with those of a maximizing type, namely profit, sales revenue and growth maximization, predicting firm price and output in each case. A number of non-maximizing or behavioural objectives are then considered. The second part of the chapter reviews recent research into actual firm performance, and attempts to establish which objectives are most consistent with how firms actually operate. We see that although profit is important, careful consideration must be given to a number of other objectives if we are accurately to predict firm performance. The need for a perspective broader than profit is reinforced when we consider current management practice in devising the corporate plan.

Chapter 15 (Corporate social and ethical responsibility) also reviews related aspects of firm objectives and firm behaviour.

Firm objectives

The objectives of a firm can be grouped under two main headings: maximizing goals and non-maximizing goals. We shall see that marginal analysis is particularly important for maximizing goals. This is often confusing to the student who, rightly, assumes that few firms can have any detailed knowledge of marginal revenue or marginal cost. However, it should be remembered that marginal analysis does not pretend to describe *how* firms maximize profits or revenue. It simply tells us *what* the output and price must be if they do succeed in maximizing these items, whether by luck or by judgement.

Maximizing goals

Profit maximization

The profit-maximizing assumption is based on two premises: first, that owners are in control of the day-to-day management of the firm; second, that the main

desire of owners is for higher profit. The case for profit maximization as 'self-evident' is, as we shall see, undermined if either of these premises fails to hold.

Profit is maximized where marginal revenue (*MR*) equals marginal cost (*MC*), i.e. where the revenue raised from selling an extra unit is equal to the cost of producing that extra unit. In Fig. 3.1 total profit (*TP*) is a maximum at output Q_p, where the vertical distance between total revenue (*TR*) and total cost (*TC*) is the greatest ($TP = TR - TC$). Had the marginal revenue and marginal cost curves been presented in Fig. 3.1, they would have intersected at output Q_p.

To assume that it is the owners who control the firm neglects the fact that the dominant form of industrial organization is the public limited company (plc), which is usually run by managers rather than by owners. This may lead to conflict between the owners (shareholders) and the managers whenever the managers pursue goals which differ from those of the owners. This conflict is referred to as a type of *principal–agent* problem and emerges when the shareholders (principals) contract a second party, the

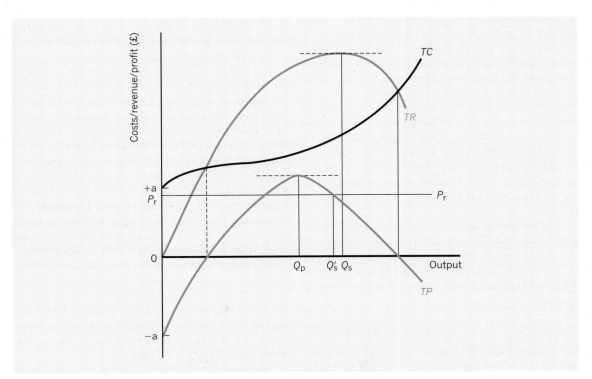

Fig. 3.1 Variation of output with firm objective.

managers (agents), to perform some tasks on their behalf. In return, the principals offer their agents some compensation (wage payments). However, because the principals are divorced from the day-to-day running of the business, the agents may be able to act as they themselves see fit. This independence of action may be due to their superior knowledge of the company as well as their ability to disguise their actions from the principals. Agents, therefore, may not always act in the manner desired by the principals. Indeed, it may be the agents' goals which predominate. This has led to a number of managerial theories of firm behaviour, such as sales revenue maximization and growth maximization.

Sales revenue maximization

Baumol (1959) has suggested that the manager-controlled firm is likely to have sales revenue maximization as its main goal rather than the profit maximization favoured by shareholders. His argument is that the salaries of top managers, and other perks, are more closely correlated with sales revenue than with profits.

Williamson's (1963) managerial theory of the firm is similar to Baumol's in stressing the growth of sales revenue as a major firm objective. However, it is broader based, with the manager seeking to increase satisfaction through the greater expenditure on both staff levels and projects made possible by higher sales revenue. Funds for greater expenditure can come from profits, external finance and *sales revenue*. In Williamson's view, however, increased sales revenue is the easiest means of providing additional funds, since higher profits have in part to be distributed to shareholders, and new finance requires greater accountability. Baumol and Williamson are describing the same phenomenon, though in rather different terms.

If management seeks to maximize sales revenue without any thought to profit at all (pure sales revenue maximization) then this would lead to output Q_s in Fig. 3.1. This last (Q_sth) unit is neither raising nor lowering total revenue, i.e. its marginal revenue is zero.

Constrained sales revenue maximization

Both Baumol and Williamson recognize that some constraint on managers can be exercised by shareholders. Maximum sales revenue is usually considered to occur well above the level of output which generates maximum profits. The shareholders may demand at least a certain level of distributed profit, so that sales revenue can only be maximized subject to this constraint.

The difference a profit constraint makes to firm output is shown in Fig. 3.1. If P_r is the minimum profit required by shareholders, then Q'_s is the output which permits the highest total revenue whilst still meeting the profit constraint. Any output beyond Q'_s up to Q_s would raise total revenue TR – the major objective – but reduce total profit TP below the minimum required (P_r). Therefore Q'_s represents the constrained sales revenue maximizing output.

So far we have assumed that the goals of owners (profits) have been in conflict with the goals of management (sales revenue). Marris (1964), however, believes that owners and managers have a *common* goal, namely maximum growth of the firm.

Growth maximization

Marris (1964) argues that the overriding goal which *both* managers and owners have in common is growth. Managers seek a growth in demand for the firm's products or services, to raise power or status. Owners seek a growth in the capital value of the firm to increase personal wealth.

It is important to note, therefore, that it is through the *growth* of the firm that the goals of both managers and owners can be achieved. Also central to the analysis of Marris is the ratio of retained to distributed profits, i.e. the 'retention ratio'. If managers distribute most of the profits (low retention ratio), shareholders will be content and the share price will be sufficiently high to deter takeover. However, if managers distribute less profit (high retention ratio), then the retained profit can be used for investment, stimulating the growth of the firm. In this case shareholders may be less content, and the share price lower, thereby increasing the risk of a takeover bid.

The major objective of the firm, with which both managers and shareholders are in accord, is then seen by Marris as maximizing the rate of growth of the firm's demand *and* the firm's capital ('balanced growth'), subject to an acceptable retention ratio. Figure 3.2 shows the trade-off between higher balanced growth and the average profit rate.[1]

For 'balanced growth' to increase, more and more investment in capital projects must be undertaken.

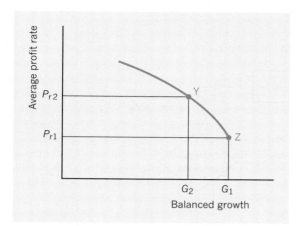

Fig. 3.2 Trade-off between average profit and balanced growth.

Since the most profitable projects are undertaken first, any extra investment must be reducing the average profit rate. Point Z is where the balanced growth rate is at a maximum (G_1), with an implied retention ratio so high that all profitable investment projects have been pursued, giving an average profit rate P_{r1}. Risk avoidance by managers may, however, enforce a lower retention ratio with more profits distributed. Point Y is such a constrained growth-maximizing position (G_2), with a lower retention ratio, lower investment and higher average profit (P_{r2}) than at point Z. How close the firm gets to its major objective, Z, will depend on how constrained management feels by the risk of disgruntled shareholders, or a takeover bid, should the retention ratio be kept at the high rates consistent with points near to Z.

Non-maximizing goals

The traditional (owner control) and managerial (non-owner control) theories of the firm assume that a single goal will be pursued. The firm then attempts to achieve the highest value for that goal, whether profits, sales revenue or growth. The *behaviouralist* viewpoint is rather different, and sees the firm as an organization with various groups, workers, managers, shareholders, customers, etc., each of which has its own goal, or set of goals. The group which achieves prominence at any point of time may be able to guide the firm into promoting its goal set over

time. This dominant group may then be replaced by another giving greater emphasis to a totally different goal set. The traditional and managerial theories which propose the maximization of a single goal are seen by behaviouralists as being remote from the organizational complexity of modern firms.

Satisficing

One of the earliest behavioural theories was that of Simon (1959) who suggested that in practice managers are unable to ascertain when a marginal point has been reached, such as maximum profit with marginal cost equal to marginal revenue. Consequently, managers set themselves *minimum* acceptable levels of achievement. Firms which are satisfied in achieving such limited objectives are said to 'satisfice' rather than 'maximize'. This is not to say that satisficing leads to some long-term performance which is less than would otherwise be achieved. The achievement of objectives has long been recognized as an incentive to improving performance and is the basis of the management technique known as management by objectives (MBO). Figure 3.3 illustrates how the attainment of initially limited objectives might lead to an improved long-term performance.

At the starting point 1, the manager sets the objective and attempts to achieve it. If, after evaluation, it is found that the objective has been achieved, then this will lead to an increase in aspirational level (3B). A new and higher objective (4B) will then emerge. Thus, by setting achievable objectives, what might be an initial minimum target turns out to be a prelude to a series of higher targets, perhaps culminating in the achievement of some maximum target, or objective. If, on the other hand, the initial objective is not achieved, then aspirational levels are lowered (3A) until achievable objectives are set. Simon's theory is one in which no single objective can be presumed to be the inevitable outcome of this organizational process. In fact, the final objective may, as we have seen, be far removed from the initial one.

Coalitions and goal formation

If a firm is 'satisficing', then who is being satisfied – and how? Cyert and March (1963) were rather more specific than Simon in identifying various groups or coalitions within an organization. A *coalition* is any group which, at a given moment, shares a consensus on the goals to be pursued.

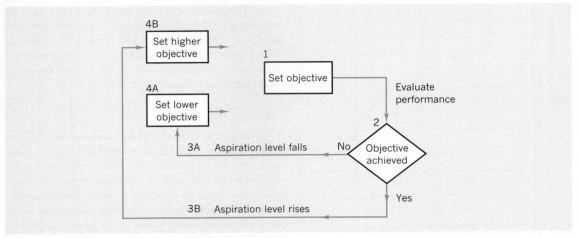

Fig. 3.3 Development of aspiration levels through goal achievement.

Workers may form one coalition wanting good wages and work conditions and some job security; managers want power and prestige as well as high salaries; shareholders want high profits. These differing goals may well result in group conflict, e.g. higher wages for workers may mean lower profits for shareholders. The behavioural theory of Cyert and March, along with Simon, does not then view the firm as having one outstanding objective (e.g. profit maximization), but rather many, often conflicting, objectives.

It is not just internal groups which need to be satisfied. There is an increasing focus by leading organizations on *stakeholders*, i.e. the range of both internal and external groups which relate to that organization. Freeman (1984) defined stakeholders as 'Any group or individual who can affect or is affected by the achievement of the organization's objectives'. Cyert and March suggest that the aim of top management is to set goals which resolve conflict between opposing groups.

Contingency theory

The contingency theory of company behaviour suggests that the optimal solutions to organizational problems are derived from matching the internal structure and processes of the firm with its external environment. However, the external environment is constantly changing as industrial markets become more complex, so that the optimum strategy for a firm will change as the prevailing environmental influences change. The result of this is that firms may not have a single goal such as the maximization of profits or sales, but will have to vary their goals and strategies as the environment changes around them. Contingency theory helps us to understand why firms will not always be able to follow a single optimizing course through time.

To summarize, the various behavioural theories look at the *process* of decision-making. They recognize that the 'organization' is not synonymous with the owner, nor with any other single influence, but rather that the firm has many objectives which relate to the many different groups acting within the organization. These objectives may be in conflict and so management will use a number of techniques in order to reduce that conflict. The behavioural approach has been criticized for its inability to yield precise predictions of firm activity in particular settings. However, where management processes are recognized, such as in strategic planning (see p. 55), then specific short-term predictions can be made.

Does firm objective matter?

The economist is continually seeking to predict the output and price behaviour of the firm. Figure 3.1 indicates that firm *output* does indeed depend upon firm objective, with the profit-maximizing firm having a lower output than the sales-maximizing firm (pure and constrained). If we remember that price is

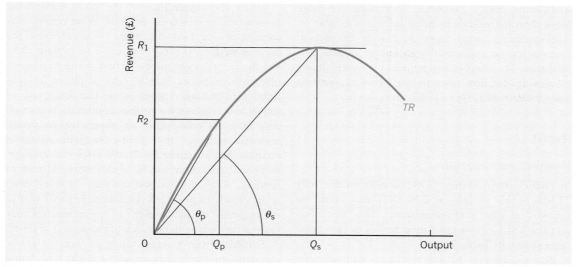

Fig. 3.4 Variation of price with firm objective.

average revenue (i.e. total revenue/total output) we can see from Fig. 3.4 that firm *price* will also vary with firm objective.

Price in the *pure sales-maximizing* firm
$= \tan \theta_s = R_1/Q_s$

Price in the *profit-maximizing* firm
$= \tan \theta_p = R_2/Q_p \qquad \tan \theta_s < \tan \theta_p$

i.e. the price of the pure sales-maximizing firm is below that of the profit-maximizing firm.

It is clear that it really *does* matter what objective we assume for the firm, since both output and price depend on that objective. We turn now to firm performance to assess which of the objectives, if any, can be supported by how firms actually behave.

Firm behaviour

Ownership and control in practice

Profit maximization is usually based on the assumption that firms are owner-controlled, whereas sales and growth maximization usually assume that there is a separation between ownership and control. The acceptance of these alternative theories was helped by early research into the ownership of firms. Studies in

the US by Berle and Means (1934), and by Larner in the 1960s, suggested that a substantial proportion of large firms (44% by Berle and Means and 85% by Larner) were manager-controlled rather than owner-controlled. Later research has, however, challenged the definition of 'owner-control' used in these early studies. Whereas Berle and Means assumed that owner-control is only present with a shareholding of more than 20% in a public limited company, Nyman and Silberston (1978) used a much lower figure of 5% after research had indicated that effective control could be exercised by owners with this level of shareholding. This would suggest that owner-control is far more extensive than previously thought. Leech and Leahy (1991) found that 91% of British public limited companies are owner-controlled using the 5% threshold figure, but only 34% are owner-controlled using a 20% threshold figure. Clearly the degree of ownership control is somewhat subjective, depending crucially on the threshold figure assigned to shareholding by owners in order to exercise effective control.

A further aspect of owner-control involves the role of financial institutions and pension funds. In 2006 they owned 43% of the capital of public companies in the UK (£796 billion of the total value of £1858b). Foreign investors owned a further 41% while individual share ownership has declined from 54% in the mid-1960s to 13% in 2006 (UK Shareholders

Association 2007). Financial institutions are more likely than individuals to bring influence to bear on chief executives, being experienced in the channels of communication and sensitive to indices of firm performance. The effect of this influence is seen by many as moving the firm towards the profit-maximizing (owner-controlled) type of objective.

Profit

Profit maximization

In a major study, Shipley (1981) concluded that only 15.9% of his sample of 728 UK firms could be regarded as 'true' profit-maximizers. This conclusion was reached by cross-tabulating replies to two questions shown in Table 3.1.

Because answers to questionnaires can often be given loosely, Shipley considered as 'true' maximizers only those who claimed both to maximize profit (answered (a) to Question 1) and to regard profit as being of overriding importance (answered (d) to Question 2). Only 15.9% of all the firms replied with both 1(a) and 2(d), and were considered by Shipley as true profit-maximizers.

A similar study by Jobber and Hooley (1987) found that 40% of their sample of nearly 1,800 firms had profit maximization as their prime objective. In a study of 77 Scottish companies by Hornby (1994), 25% responded as 'profit maximizers' to the 'Shipley test'. The percentage of satisficers was very similar in both studies (Shipley 52.3%, Hornby 51.9%).

Given the significance of the profit-maximizing assumption in economic analysis, these results may seem surprising. However, some consideration of the decision-making process may serve to explain these low figures for profit maximization. Firms in practice often rely on preset 'hurdle' rates of return for projects, with managers given some minimum rate of return as a criterion for project appraisal. As a result they may not consciously see themselves as profit-maximizers, since this phrase suggests marginal analysis. Yet in setting the hurdle rates, top management will be keenly aware of the marginal cost of funding, so that this approach may in some cases relate closely to profit maximization. In other words, the response of management to questionnaires may understate the true significance of the pursuit of profit.

Evidence from a recent study of 'not for profit' companies in the healthcare sector in the USA found that 79% of them displayed 'for profit' decisions that maximized the profit function rather than the utility function, i.e. the majority did not spend as much as they could have done to provide a higher level of resident care (Vitaliano 2003).

Profit as part of a 'goal set'

Although few firms appear to set out specifically to maximize profit, profit is still seen (even in response to questionnaires) as an important factor in decision-making. In the Shipley study the firms were asked to list their principal goal in setting price. Target profit was easily the most frequently cited, with 73% of all firms regarding it as their principal goal. Even more

Table 3.1 Sample of 728 firms.

	All respondents (%)
(1) Does your firm try to achieve:	
(a) maximum profits?	47.7
(b) 'satisfactory' profits?	52.3
(2) Compared to your firm's other leading objectives, is the achievement of a target profit . . . regarded as being:	
(a) of little importance?	2.1
(b) fairly important?	12.9
(c) very important?	58.9
(d) of overriding importance?	26.1
Those responding with both 1(a) and 2(d)	15.9

Source: Adapted from Shipley (1981).

firms (88%) included profit as at least part of their 'goal set'.

Profit – long-term versus short-term

Long-term profit may be even more important than short-term profit in firm objectives. Senior managers are well aware that poor profitability in the long term may lead to their dismissal or the takeover of their firm, quite apart from an increased risk of insolvency. Indeed Shipley found that 59.7% of his sample gave priority to long-term profits, compared to only 20.6% giving priority to short-term profits. Shipley found long-term profit to be a significant influence in all sizes of company, though particularly in those of medium/large size. However, as international financial investors dominate the ownership of public companies, who can and do shift their investments to gain short-term profits, the narrative of short-term versus long-term continues to be played out in the financial world. It is not unusual to find the leader of a corporation or the head of a policy institute complaining of the short-term orientation of investors, and the damage that can cause to the sustainability of their organizations (e.g. *Financial Times* 2010).

Studies of the behaviour of firms in technology-based markets have provided further support for the emphasis on longer-term profit perspectives (Arthur 1996). Arthur suggests that when a technology reaches a certain critical mass of usage, then the market is 'locked in' and the only rational choice for new users is then to adopt the established technology. He cites Microsoft Windows as being a typical example of this, with the continued increase in use of Windows providing an example of a market system operating positive feedback. Arthur suggests that average (and marginal) revenues might even rise in technology-based markets as volume exceeds the 'critical mass' for that established technology, rather than decline as in standard theory. This phenomenon has often led to a strategy of giving away products reflecting new technologies at their introduction stage in order to create lock-in. The objective of this strategy for technology-based markets might arguably still be profit maximization, but only in the longer term.

Profit and reward structures

There has been a great deal of concern throughout the 1990s and in the first decade of the millennium that managers in large firms have paid too little regard to the interests of shareholders, especially as regards profit performance of the company. Indeed a number of celebrated cases in the press have focused on the apparent lack of any link between substantial rises in the pay and bonuses of chief executives and any improvements in company performances (see also Chapter 15, p. 314).

The majority of empirical studies have indeed found little relationship between the remuneration of top managers and the profit performance of their companies. In the UK, Storey *et al.* (1995) found no evidence of a link between the pay of top managers and the ratio of average pre-tax profits to total assets, with similar results for studies by Jensen and Murphy (1990) and Barkema and Gomez-Meija (1998) in the US. Table 3.2 confirms this picture, with not one of the 20 firms appearing in the 10 highest sales revenue and 10 highest profit rankings being in the list of the 10 highest paid Chief Executive Officers (CEOs). This apparent lack of a clear relationship between executive pay and company performance became an important issue during 2007–10 as the CEOs of various high-profile financial intermediaries and companies received large pay rises and special cash deals at the same time as company profits and share prices fell. Despite the economic recession, the chief executives of the FT100 companies have also benefited from average increases in the pay element of their remuneration packages by as much as 20%, while average pay settlements across all employees in UK firms only rose by 1.3% (Financial Times 2010).

However, the absence of any proven link between the profitability of a firm and the reward structures it offers to its CEO and other top managers does not necessarily mean that profit-related goals are unimportant. Firms increasingly offer top managers a total remuneration 'package' involving bonus payments and share options as well as salary. In this case higher firm profitability, and therefore dividend earnings per share, may help raise the share price and with it the value of the total remuneration package. Indeed Ezzamel and Watson (1998) have suggested that the total remuneration package offered to CEOs is directly related to the 'going rate' for corporate profitability. It may therefore be that top management have more incentives for seeking profit-related goals than might at first be apparent.

To summarize, therefore, although there may be no open admission to profit maximization, the strong

Table 3.2 The ten highest-ranked US corporations by sales revenue growth, profit growth and CEO remuneration 2010.

Rank	Sales revenue maximizers[1]	Profit maximizers[2]	Highest paid CEOs[3]
1	International Asset Holding	First Solar	Danaher
2	SXC Health Solutions	Sapient	Oracle
3	First Solar	International Asset Holdings	Chesapeake Energy
4	Olin	Fuel Systems Solutions	Occidental Petroleum
5	KapStone Paper and Packaging	Bucyrus International	Yum Brands
6	Sun Power	Sturm Ruger & Co	Gilead sciences
7	Life Partners Holdings	Salesforce.com	Celgene
8	Green Mountain Coffee Roasters	Thoratec	XTO Energy
9	Bucyrus International	Life Partners Holdings	Freeport Copper
10	Ebix	Kapstone Paper and Packaging	Nividia

[1]Revenue growth (latest 3 year annual average growth of revenue).
[2]Profit growth (latest 3 year annual average growth of earnings per share (EPS)).
[3]Remuneration includes salary, bonuses and stocks.
Sources: Adapted from Fortune (2010) *100 Fastest Growing Companies*, 6 September; DeCarlo (2010a) *Special Report: CEO Compensation*, 28 April, Forbes.com; DeCarlo (2010b) *Special Report: Global High Performers*, 21 April, Forbes.com.

influence of owners on managed firms, the use of preset hurdle rates and the presence of profit-related reward structures may in the end lead to an objective, or set of objectives, closely akin to profit maximization.

Sales revenue

Sales revenue maximization

Baumol's suggestion that management-controlled firms will wish to maximize sales revenue was based on the belief that the earnings of executives are more closely related to firm revenue than to firm profit. A number of studies have sought to test this belief. For example, in a study of 177 firms between 1985 and 1990, Conyon and Gregg (1994) found that the pay of top executives in large companies in the UK was most strongly related to *relative sales growth* (i.e. relative to competitors). They also found that it was only weakly related to a long-term performance measure (total shareholder returns) and not at all to current accounting profit. Furthermore, growth in sales resulting from takeovers was more highly rewarded than internal growth, despite the fact that such takeovers produced on average a lower return for shareholders and an increased liquidity risk. These findings

are in line with other UK research (Gregg *et al.* 1993; Conyon and Leech 1994) and with a study of small UK companies by Conyon and Nicolitsas (1998) which also found sales growth to be closely correlated with the pay of top executives.

As well as a linkage between the growth of sales revenue and executive income, there is also general support for the contention that *firm size* is directly related to executive income. Studies by Gregg *et al.* (1993) and Rosen (1990) concur with much earlier studies, such as that of Meeks and Whittington (1975), who found that the larger the asset value of the company, the larger the executive salary.

What does seem clear from these various findings is that top management appears to be able to revise the rules for their own remuneration according to circumstance. Principals (shareholders) would appear to have little effective control over the remuneration of agents (management) in major public corporations where ownership and control are separated. This lack of control has led to a rise in shareholder activism, where investors intervene in the decisions of the Board, either through direct threat of disinvestment, or voting against executive remuneration, forcing or preventing mergers, or imposing corporate responsibility policies at Annual General Meetings or Extraordinary General Meetings.

Sales revenue as part of a 'goal set'

The results of Shipley's analysis tell us little about sales revenue *maximization*. Nevertheless, Shipley found that target sales revenue was the fourth-ranked principal pricing objective, and that nearly half the firms included sales revenue as at least part of their set of objectives. Larger companies cited sales revenue as an objective most frequently; one-seventh of companies with over 3,000 employees gave sales revenue as a principal goal compared to only one-fourteenth of all the firms. Since larger companies have greater separation between ownership and management control, this does lend some support to Baumol's assertion. The importance of sales revenue as part of a set of policy objectives was reinforced by the study of 193 UK industrial distributors by Shipley and Bourdon (1990), which found that 88% of these companies included sales revenue as one of a number of objectives. However, we see below that the nature of planning in large organizations must also be considered and that this may temper our support for sales revenue being itself the major objective, at least in the long term.

Strategic planning and sales revenue

Current thinking on strategic planning would support the idea of short-term sales maximization, but only as a means to other ends (e.g. profitability or growth). Research in the mid-1970s by the US Strategic Planning Institute linked market share – seen here as a proxy for sales revenue – to profitability. These studies found that high market share had a significant and beneficial effect on both return on investment and cashflow, at least in the long term. However, in the short term the high investment and marketing expenditure needed to attain high market share reduces profitability and drains cashflow. Profit has to be sacrificed in the short term if high market share, and hence future high profits, are to be achieved in the long term. A recent meta-study (Armstrong and Green 2007) suggests that a deliberate strategy of buying market share through high advertising and reduced prices (for example) is detrimental to the profits of the business.

Constrained sales revenue maximization

The fact that 88% of all companies in Shipley's original study included profit in their goal set indicates the relevance of the profit constraint to other objectives, including sales revenue. The later study by Shipley and Bourdon (1990) reached a similar conclusion, finding that 93% of the UK industrial distributors surveyed included profit in their goal set.

Growth

There are a number of reasons why firms should wish to grow, although in the 1990s the term 'growth' would appear to apply to asset value and market share rather than workforce. Marris (1964) suggests that managers seek to increase their status by increasing the 'empire' in which they work. Others would argue that although growth is an important company objective it is a means to an end, e.g. higher profit, rather than an end in itself as Marris would suggest.

When we examine the facts, however, there is little to indicate that faster growth really does mean higher profits. An analysis in 2007 of the top 10 highest-growth firms (percentage change in total assets) amongst the leading 100 UK plcs found that, ranked in terms of profitability (percentage profit margin), only Rio Tinto was ranked as *both* fast growing and highly profitable, i.e. being in the top 10 plcs on both measures. Indeed, the other nine high-growth plcs are low in the profitability rankings, with BP third in growth but only 53rd in profitability. This finding is in line with the results of a study by Whittington (1980) who found that profit levels did *not* increase as the firm grew in size. This lends some support to those, like Marris, who see growth as a separate objective to profit.

In fast-moving markets, such as high-technology electronics and pharmaceuticals, companies need flexibility to move rapidly to fill market niches. To achieve this, some firms are moving in quite the opposite direction to growth, i.e. they are 'de-merging'. De-merging occurs when the firm splits into smaller units, each separately quoted on the Stock Exchange. For example, in 2010 Carphone Warehouse de-merged its Talk Talk Telecoms (fixed line and broadband) subsidiary, Fiat de-merged its cars and engines from Iveco Trucks and Fosters de-merged its wine business from its beer business. Such de-merging is a clear sign that professional investors do not merely equate larger size to greater profit.

In a similar vein, Tom Peters, co-author of *In Search of Excellence*, says that 'quality and flexibility will be the hallmarks of the successful economy for the foreseeable future'. This premise leads to a view that size, with its inherent inflexibility and distance from the end-customer, is a *disadvantage*. Indeed, analysis by the Strategic Planning Institute (Buzzel and Gale 1987) shows an *inverse* relationship between market size and the rate of return on investment in the US. In market segments of less than $100m (£61m), the return on investment averaged 27% in their study; however, where firms operated in market segments of over $1bn (£610m), the return averaged only 11%. They found that organizations sought to reduce the disadvantages of size by restructuring, either by de-merging or by the creation of smaller, more dynamic Strategic Business Units (SBUs), which are able to meet the demands of the market more rapidly.

Despite the comments made above, a company which fails to grow over a period of time, even though its profits are relatively healthy, is in danger of becoming an ineffective innovator. Growth is important because it attracts good, young entrepreneurial talent, as dynamic firms such as Nokia, Goldman Sachs and L'Oréal have found. It also helps companies to attract new capital and to be innovative as regards new products and processes. The dynamics of the growth process depend on the interaction between a firm's external environment (industry, markets and customers) and the internal environment of the company (resources and abilities). Table 3.3 shows four corporate growth paths with examples of companies which seem to have taken these paths.

Basically speaking, *corporate renewal* is a determinant of growth when companies use their current resources and abilities to expand their customer base. For example, Swatch succeeded in becoming dynamic once more as a result of greater attention to costs, product design and differentiation. *Innovation* is

an important determinant of growth, as companies like Nokia can attest. The company moved from one which operated across different industries to one which increasingly concentrated on communication systems. It focused more clearly on cellular phones by increasing investment in R&D and increasing its manufacturing capabilities. Some companies grow by *expanding their capabilities* through merger, as was the case with Glaxo and Wellcome. The synergy of two pharmaceutical companies (which had strong R&D capabilities and complementary areas of expertise) meant that the new company, Glaxo Wellcome, could produce an array of new products. Finally, *exploiting external opportunities* involves companies utilizing the benefits of growth in order to exploit external opportunities, such as new markets. For example, in the 1990s, Merck, the giant US pharmaceutical company, acquired Medco, a firm that ran a network of 48,000 pharmacies in the US. Through Medco's direct sales links, Merck was able to control distribution and sell its goods direct to patients.

As we can see from the above examples, growth is still an important strategic variable because it acts as a catalyst to firms that want to become leaders in their respective fields. Firms that stand still often die, so that corporate growth provides the way for firms to ensure their long-term survival.

Non-maximizing behaviour

We have seen that the non-maximizing or behavioural theories concentrate on how firms actually operate within the constraints imposed by organizational structure and firm environment. Recent evidence on management practice broadly supports the behavioural contention, namely that it is unhelpful to seek a single firm objective as a guide to actual firm behaviour. This support, however, comes from a rather different type of analysis, that of portfolio planning.

Work in the US by the Boston Consulting Group on the relationship between market share and industry growth gave rise to an approach to corporate planning known as 'portfolio planning'. Firms, especially the larger ones, can be viewed as having a collection or 'portfolio' of different products at different stages in the product life cycle. If a product is at an early stage in its life cycle, it will require a large investment in marketing and product development in order to achieve future levels of high profitability. At

Table 3.3 Patterns of corporate growth.

Corporate renewal	Innovation	Expanding capabilities	Exploiting external opportunities
Swatch	Nokia	Glaxo	Merck
L'Oréal	Hewlett-Packard	Volkswagen	Bertelsmann
Disney	Canon	BP	Merrill Lynch
Lloyds	Goldman Sachs	Compaq	Wal-Mart

the same time another product may have 'matured' and, already possessing a good share of the market, be providing high profits and substantial cashflow.

The usual strategy in portfolio planning is to attempt to balance the portfolio so that existing profitable products are providing the funds necessary to raise new products to maturity. This approach has become a classic part of strategic decision-making.

If a firm is using the portfolio approach in its planning then it may be impossible to predict the firm's behaviour for individual products or market sections on the basis of a single firm objective. This is because the goals of the firm will change for a given product or market sector *depending on the relative position of that product or market sector within the overall portfolio*. Portfolio planning, along with other behavioural theories, suggests that no single objective is likely to be useful in explaining actual firm behaviour, at least in specific cases.

The non-maximizing behaviour of large companies can be seen clearly in the approach taken by some large companies (Griffiths 2000). For example, between 1997 and 2000 Cadbury Schweppes, the chocolate and confectionery multinational, explained its objectives in terms of 'Managing for Value' (MFV). To meet the MFV criterion the company stressed the importance of:

- increasing earnings per share by at least 10% every year;
- generating £150m of free cashflow every year;
- doubling the value of shareholders' investment in the next four years;
- competing in the world's growth markets by effective internal investment and by value-enhancing acquisitions;
- developing market share by introducing innovations in product development, packaging and routes to market;
- increasing commitment to value creation in managers and employees through incentive schemes and share ownership;
- investing in key areas of air emissions, water, energy and solid waste.

From the above list it is clear that the first three preoccupations are related to the profit objectives while the third and fourth relate to company growth and market share. In addition the final two objectives encompass both human resource and environmental issues.

A multiple and longer-term perspective is also evident in the response of some companies to the 2008–10 recession. For many firms a skilled workforce (talent) is a fundamental resource which is not easy to replace. So when salary costs had to be cut to survive, firms found innovative ways to do this, such as offering pay cuts and sabbaticals, with guaranteed re-employment, rather than making people redundant. Such a move is neither profit maximizing nor growth maximizing in the short term; the motive is survival.

In this context, it can be seen that maximizing a single corporate goal seems unrealistic in the dynamic world of multinationals.

Firm behaviour, firm objective and market structure

Whatever the firm objective, price-setting behaviour will vary with market structure (see also Chapter 6). We initially assume a profit-maximizing objective and note that price-setting behaviour will vary depending on the type of market structure.

Price and market structure

Given a profit-maximizing objective the price charged may still vary depending on the type of market structure within which the firm operates. This is well illustrated by a comparison between the extreme market forms of perfect competition and pure monopoly.

Perfect competition versus pure monopoly

Under perfect competition, price is determined for the industry (and for the firm) by the intersection of demand and supply, at P_C in Fig. 3.5. As the reader familiar with the theory of the firm will know, the supply curve, S, of the perfectly competitive industry is also the marginal cost (MC) curve of the industry. Suppose now that the industry is taken over by a single firm ('pure monopoly'), and that costs are initially unchanged. It follows that the marginal cost curve remains in the same position; also that the demand curve for the perfectly competitive industry becomes the demand (and average revenue (AR)) curve for the monopolist. The marginal revenue (MR)

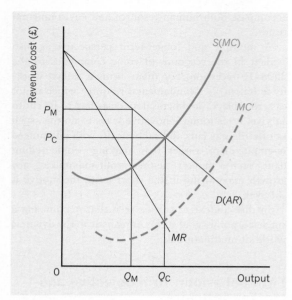

Fig. 3.5 Price under perfect competition and monopoly.

monopoly than under competition. It is in part an empirical question. If economies of scale were sufficient to lower the *MC* curve below *MC'* in Fig. 3.5, then the monopoly price would be below that of perfect competition. Price will, however, except by coincidence, *be different* under these two market forms, as it would under other market forms, such as monopolistic competition or oligopoly.

Price and firm objective

So far we have assumed that the firm with a single objective, i.e. profit maximization, will charge different prices in different types of market structure. If there are *other objectives* then there will tend to be a still wider range of possibilities for price. We saw in Fig. 3.4 (p. 51) that a sales-maximizing objective would usually lead to a lower price than would a profit-maximizing objective. The situation becomes even more complicated when we examine behavioural or non-maximizing objectives, as these yield not a unique price, but a range of price outcomes for any given market structure. Clearly firm price depends also on firm objective.

Price, market structure and firm objective

Price thus depends on both market structure and firm objective. Since there are many possible combinations of these, any given product or service can experience a wide array of possible prices.

From Fig. 3.6 we see that the four market structures can lead to at least four different price outcomes (P_1–P_4) for objective 1. A further four prices (P_5–P_8)

curve must then lie inside the negatively sloped *AR* curve. The profit-maximizing price for the monopolist is P_M, corresponding to output Q_M where *MC* = *MR*. Price is higher under monopoly than under perfect competition (and quantity, Q_M, is lower). This is the so-called 'classical' case against monopoly.

Our intention here is merely to point out that price will tend to *differ* for profit-maximizing firms depending on the type of market within which they operate. In our comparison of extreme market forms, the final outcome for price may or may not be higher under

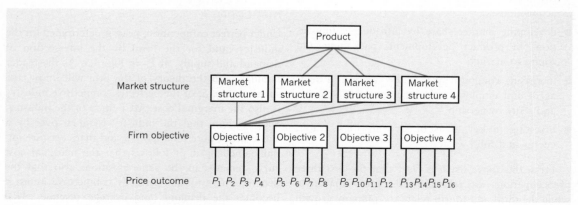

Fig. 3.6 Market structure, firm objective and price.

might result from objective 2, and so on, giving at least 16 prices[2] for the four market structures and the four firm objectives. To derive guidelines for price-setting from theory, which will have general validity, is clearly a daunting if not impossible task.

Conclusion

The traditional theory of the firm assumes that its sole objective is to maximize profit. The managerial theories assume that where ownership and control of the organization are separated, the objective which guides the firm will be that which the management sets. This is usually thought to be maximization of either sales revenue or growth. It is important to know which, if any, of the maximizing objectives are being pursued, since firm output and price will be different for each objective. Behavioural theory tends to oppose the idea of the firm seeking to maximize any objective. For instance, top management may seek to hold the various stakeholder groups in balance by adopting a set of minimum targets. Even where a single group with a clear objective does become dominant within the firm, others with alternative objectives may soon replace it.

In practice, profit maximization *in the long term* still appears to be important. Sales revenue seems quite important as a short-term goal, though even here a profit target may still be part of the goal set. The prominence of the profit target may be an indication that ownership is not as divorced from the control of large firms as may once have been thought. One reason why sales revenue may be pursued in the short term is found in an analysis of current strategic planning techniques, which link short-term sales revenue to long-term profit. Sales revenue may therefore be useful for explaining short-term firm behaviour, but with profit crucial for long-term behaviour. Those who, like Marris, argue that growth is a separate objective from profit find some support in the lack of any clear relationship between growth and profitability. Growth may also be a means of securing greater stability for the firm. It may reduce internal conflict, by being an objective around which both owner–shareholders and managers can agree, and possibly reduces the risk of takeover. Also large firms experience, if not higher profits, then less variable profits (Whittington 1980; Schmalensee 1989). A widely used technique in the management of larger firms, portfolio planning, would seem to support the behaviouralist view, that no single objective will usefully help predict firm behaviour in a given market.

Key points

- Separation between ownership by shareholders (principals) and control by managers (agents) makes profit maximization less likely.

- Maximization of sales revenue or asset growth (as well as profit) must be considered in manager-led firms.

- The objectives pursued by the firm will influence the firm's price and output decisions.

- Different groupings (coalitions) may be dominant within a firm at different points of time. Firm objectives may therefore change as the coalitions in effective control change.

- Organizational structure may result in non-maximizing behaviour; e.g. the presence of diverse stakeholders may induce the firm to set minimum targets for a range of variables as a means of reducing conflict.

- Shipley's seminal work (supported by later studies) found less than 16% of the firms studied to be 'true' profit maximizers.

- However, Shipley found that 88% of firms included profit as part of their 'goal set'.

- Separation between ownership and control receives empirical support, though small 'threshold' levels of shareholdings

- may still secure effective control in modern plcs.
- Profit remains a useful predictor of long-term firm behaviour, though sales revenue may be better in predicting short-term firm behaviour.
- Profit maximization may not be acknowledged as a goal by many firms, yet in setting 'hurdle rates' senior managers may implicitly be following such an objective.
- Profitability and executive pay appear to be largely unrelated, suggesting that other managerial objectives might be

given priority (sales revenue, growth, etc.). However, total remuneration 'packages' for top executives may be linked to profitability, helping to align the interests of managers more closely to the interests of shareholders.
- Portfolio planning points to a variety of ever-changing objectives guiding firm activity rather than any single objective.
- Firm behaviour in specific areas, e.g. price setting, will be influenced by a combination of firm objective and market structure.

Now try the self-check questions for this chapter on the Companion Website. You will also find useful links to relevant websites.

Notes

1 Average profit rate is total profit divided by total capital employed.

2 For instance, it is assumed in Fig. 3.6 that the four firm objectives are of the maximizing type, with only a single price outcome for each objective. Equally, Fig. 3.6 assumes that for

each objective and market structure there is a single price outcome covering both short- and long-run time periods. If either of these assumptions is relaxed, there might be more than 16 different price outcomes from our figure.

References and further reading

Armstrong, J. S. and K. C. Green (2007) Competitor-oriented objectives: the myth of market share, *International Journal of Business*, **12**(1): 117–36.

Arthur, W. B. (1996) Increasing returns and the new world of business, *Harvard Business Review*, **74**(4): 100–9.

Barkema, H. G. and Gomez-Meija, L. R. (1998) Managerial compensation and firm performance, *Academy of Management Journal*, **41**(2): 135–46.

Barreto I. (2010) Dynamic capabilities: a review of past research and an agenda for the future, *Journal of Management*, **36**(1): 256–80.

Bau, F., and Dowling, M. (2007) An empirical study of reward and incentive systems in German enterprenurial firms, *Schmalenbach Business Review*, **59**(April): 160–75.

Baumol, W. J. (1959) *Business Behaviour, Value and Growth*, New York, Macmillan.

Berle, A. A. and Means, G. C. (1934) *The Modern Corporation and Private Property*, New York, Macmillan.

Buzzel, R. and Gale, B. (1987) *The PIMS Principles: Linking Strategy to Performance*, New York, Free Press.

Canals, J. (2001) How to think about corporate growth, *European Management Journal*, **19**(6): 587–98.

Conyon, M. and Gregg, P. (1994) Pay at the top: a study of the sensitivity of top director remuneration to company specific shocks, *National Institute Economic Review*, **149**(1): 83–92.

Conyon, M. and Leech, D. (1994) Executive compensation, corporate performance and ownership structure, *Oxford Bulletin of Economics and Statistics*, **56**: 229–47.

Conyon, M. J. and Nicolitsas, D. (1998) Does the market for top executives work? CEO pay and turnover in small UK companies, *Small Business Economics*, **11**(2): 145–54.

Crossan, K. and Lange, T. (2006) Business as usual? Ambitions of profit maximisation and the theory of the firm, *Journal of Interdisciplinary Economics*, **17**(3): 313–26.

Cyert, R. M. and March, J. G. (1963) *A Behavioural Theory of the Firm*, New York, Prentice Hall.

DeCarlo, S. (2010a) *Special Report: CEO Compensation*, 28 April, New York, Forbes.com.

DeCarlo, S. (2010b) *Special Report: Global High Performers*, 21 April, New York, Forbes.com.

Ezzamel, M. and Watson, R. (1998) Market compensation earnings and the bidding-up of executive cash compensation: evidence from the United Kingdom, *Academy of Management Journal*, **41**(2): 358–96.

Financial Times (1998) Shares in the action, 27 April.

Financial Times (2010) The facts about boardroom pay speak for themselves (letter from Steve Tatton, Editor, IDS Executive Compensation Review), 3 November.

Fisher, C. and Lovell, A. (2009) *Business Ethics and Values: Individual, Corporate and International Perspectives* (3rd edn), Harlow, Financial Times/Prentice Hall.

Fortune (2010) *100 Fastest Growing Companies*, 6 September.

Freeman, R. E. (1984) *Strategic Management: A Stakeholder Approach*, Boston MA, Pitman.

Gregg, P., Machin, S. and Szymanski, S. (1993) The disappearing relationship between directors' pay and corporate performance, *British Journal of Industrial Relations*, **31**: 1–9.

Griffiths, A. (2000) Corporate objectives, risk taking and the market: the case of Cadbury Schweppes, *British Economy Survey*, **29**(2): 45–51.

Henderson, B. (1970) Intuitive strategy, *Perspectives*, **96**, Boston MA, The Boston Consulting Group.

Hornby, W. (1994) *The Theory of the Firm Revisited: a Scottish Perspective*, Aberdeen, Aberdeen Business School.

Jensen, M. C. and Murphy, K. J. (1990) Performance pay and top management incentives, *Journal of Political Economy*, **98** (April): 225–65.

Jobber, D. and Hooley, G. (1987) Pricing behaviour in UK manufacturing and service industries, *Managerial and Decision Economics*, **8**: 167–77.

Leech, D. and Leahy, J. (1991) Ownership structure, control type classifications and the performance of large British companies, *Economic Journal*, **101**(409): 1418–37.

Main, B. G. M. (1991) Top executive pay and performance, *Management and Decision Economics*, **12**: 219–29.

Marris, R. (1964) *The Economic Theory of Managerial Capitalism*, New York, Free Press, Glencoe.

Meeks, G. and Whittington, G. (1975) Directors' pay, growth and profitability, *Journal of Industrial Economics*, **24**(1): 1–14.

Nyman, S. and Silberston, A. (1978) The ownership and control of industry, *Oxford Economic Papers*, **30**(1): 74–101.

Peters, T. and Waterman, R. (1982) *In Search of Excellence*, New York, Harper & Row.

Porter, M. and Kramer, M. (2011) Creating shared value, *Harvard Business Review*, **89**(1): 2–17.

Ramaswamy, V. and Gouillart, F. (2010) Building the co-creative enterprise, *Harvard Business Review*, **88**(10): 100–109.

Rosen, S. (1990) Contracts and the market for executives, *NBER Working Paper* 3542, Cambridge MA, National Bureau of Economic Research.

RSA (1994) *Tomorrow's Company Inquiry*, London, Royal Society for the Encouragement of Arts, Manufacturers and Commerce.

Schmalensee, R. (1989) Intra-industry profitability in the US, *Journal of Industrial Economics*, **36**(4): 212–36.

Shipley, D. and Bourdon, E. (1990) Distributor pricing in very competitive markets, *Industrial Marketing Management*, **19**(3): 215–44.

Shipley, D. D. (1981) Primary objectives in British manufacturing industry, *Journal of Industrial Economics*, **29**(4): 429–43.

Simon, H. A. (1959) Theories of decision making in economics, *American Economic Review*, **69**(3): 253–83.

Stern, S. (2010) Outsider in a hurry to shake up Unilever, *Financial Times*, 4 April.

Storey, D., Watson, R. and Wynarczyk, P. (1995) The remuneration of non-owner managers in UK unquoted and unlisted securities market enterprises, *Small Business Economics*, **7**(1): 1–13.

Vitaliano, D. F. (2003) Do not-for-profit firms maximize profit? *The Quarterly Review of Economics and Finance*, **43**(1): 75–87.

Watson Wyatt Worldwide (2009) *Executive Pay Practices Around the World*. London.

Whittington, G. (1980) The profitability and size of United Kingdom companies, *Journal of Industrial Economics*, **28**(4): 335–52.

Williamson, O. E. (1963) Managerial discretion and business behaviour, *American Economic Review*, **53**(December): 1032–1057.

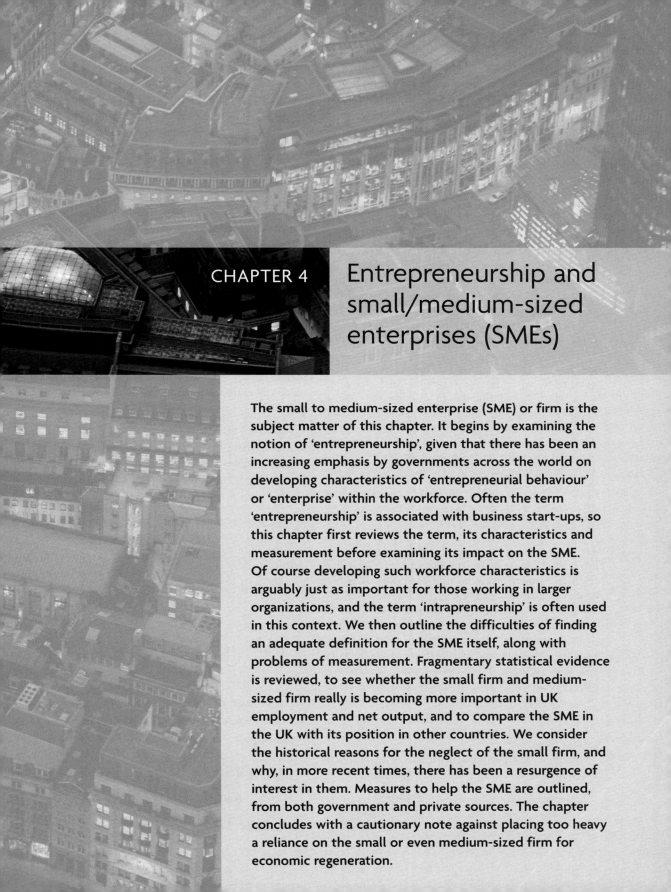

CHAPTER 4

Entrepreneurship and small/medium-sized enterprises (SMEs)

The small to medium-sized enterprise (SME) or firm is the subject matter of this chapter. It begins by examining the notion of 'entrepreneurship', given that there has been an increasing emphasis by governments across the world on developing characteristics of 'entrepreneurial behaviour' or 'enterprise' within the workforce. Often the term 'entrepreneurship' is associated with business start-ups, so this chapter first reviews the term, its characteristics and measurement before examining its impact on the SME. Of course developing such workforce characteristics is arguably just as important for those working in larger organizations, and the term 'intrapreneurship' is often used in this context. We then outline the difficulties of finding an adequate definition for the SME itself, along with problems of measurement. Fragmentary statistical evidence is reviewed, to see whether the small firm and medium-sized firm really is becoming more important in UK employment and net output, and to compare the SME in the UK with its position in other countries. We consider the historical reasons for the neglect of the small firm, and why, in more recent times, there has been a resurgence of interest in them. Measures to help the SME are outlined, from both government and private sources. The chapter concludes with a cautionary note against placing too heavy a reliance on the small or even medium-sized firm for economic regeneration.

Entrepreneurship and business start-ups

Business creation is a key driver of economic prosperity. New businesses contribute to economic growth; social enterprises enrich communities; enterprising employees revitalise organizations, all contributing to the regeneration of communities and creating a significant positive impact on both local and national economies.

As we note in Table 4.2 (p. 68) small firms resulting from new business start-ups are extremely important with around 78% of all UK businesses 'sole traders' with zero to one employees, a further 13% employing between two and four people, and another 5% between five and nine people. In other words, some 96% of all UK businesses employ less than 10 people and account for some 27% of total employment and 20% of turnover. It follows that a key question is what are the entrepreneurial characteristics which help businesses to start-up and, just as important, what are the entrepreneurial characteristics needed to help establish and grow the business? The latter is particularly important given that the UK five-year survival rate for businesses 'born' in 2004 and still active in 2009 was only 46.8% (ONS 2010)!

Role of the entrepreneur

The increased importance of small businesses has given renewed emphasis to the role of the 'entrepreneur', which received little attention in earlier economic analysis. Schumpeter (1934), however, did recognise the importance of the entrepreneur as an innovator, bringing about change through the introduction of new technological processes or products. Knight (1940) saw the entrepreneur as a calculated risk taker, earning profit as a reward for decision making under uncertain conditions which, by definition, cannot be insured against. Shackle (1954) saw the entrepreneur as creative and imaginative, better able than others to recognize opportunities and then exploit them.

Many of these perspectives are usefully captured in the following definition of entrepreneurship:

> Entrepreneurship, rigorously defined, refers to the creation of a new economic entity centred on a novel product or service, at the very least one which differs significantly from products or services offered elsewhere in the market (Curran and Stanworth 1989, p. 12).

A better understanding of the key attributes of entrepreneurs is clearly important as there are numerous studies that point to the lack of effectiveness of government and other interventions in small business support. The Federation of Small Businesses (FSB) in the UK has conducted annual surveys of its members and these have highlighted the apparently very low levels of effectiveness of government funded business support, a view corroborated by a recent report on small firms (Richard 2008).

Entrepreneurial personality

Early work by McClelland (1961) identified the following key characteristics and competencies of successful entrepreneurs:

- *proactive* – demonstrating initiative and assertiveness;
- *achievement oriented* – an ability to identify opportunities and act to exploit them;
- *committed* – to both the achievement of the tasks set and to the people involved.

Linking these personality traits to the views on the role of the entrepreneur mentioned above, we can perhaps add the following to Mclellands' list of personality characteristics:

- *calculated risk taker*;
- *creative*;
- *innovative*.

Meredith (1982) broadly concurs with this set of personality characteristics in the five he identifies as being core traits:

1 *self-confidence*;
2 *risk taking activity*;
3 *flexibility*;
4 *need for achievement*;
5 *strong desire to be independent*.

High self-confidence is a common theme of many analysts seeking to understand the personalities of entrepreneurs since such self-confidence helps sustain a belief in one's own abilities to mobilize resources, motivate others and achieve change, as in new business start-ups! However, Kets de Vries (1977) also emphasizes the non-conformist, even deviant, trait often found in successful entrepreneurs.

Timmons (1994) emphasizes both a high need for achievement and a 'high internal locus of control' as being important to successful entrepreneurs. By 'high internal locus of control', Timmons meant the desire of entrepreneurs to be in charge of their own destiny. Unlike some analysts who believe entrepreneurs are 'born', not 'made', Timmons and others do recognize the role of learning and that entrepreneurs can be taught or at least given structured experiences to help them acquire important characteristics. Timmons certainly believed that many of the entrepreneurial characteristics are closely related to management and leadership skills which can be acquired via appropriate training and exposure. However, he regarded certain attributes as more innate, such as emotional stability, creativity, conceptual thinking and a capacity to inspire.

Early stage entrepreneurs

In recent years there has been an increasing emphasis by governments across the world on developing attributes of 'entrepreneurship' or 'enterprise' within the workforce. A term widely used in discussions of entrepreneurship is 'early stage entrepreneurial activity', which refers to the percentage of the population aged 18–64 years which is involved in starting new businesses at any one time. As we can see from Fig. 4.1, there is a wide variation across countries in this percentage, with such early-stage entrepreneurial activity seeming to be related in interesting ways to the standard of living, measured by Gross Domestic Product (GDP) per capita.

Figure 4.1 demonstrates that entrepreneurship rates are not just a function of differences in economic development (or welfare) but also other factors (as R^2 is only 0.39). Examples of such factors might include population growth, which can stimulate demand and help increase the stock of existing business owner–managers, who serve as role models and who are more likely to start a business than other individuals. Eastern European countries, with falling populations and a low stock of business owner–managers as a

legacy of communism, are clusters below the trend line, while Latin American countries, with healthy population growth rates and a larger stock of business owners, tend to appear above the trend line.

High-expectation entrepreneurs

In more recent times the term 'high-expectation entrepreneurs' has come into use. This is defined by the *Global Entrepreneurship Monitor* as 'All start-ups and newly formed businesses which expect to employ at least 20 employees within five years'. Only around 14% of all start-up attempts are expected to create 20 or more jobs within the first five years, while 44% are expected to create five or more jobs. High-growth entrepreneurs, sometimes termed 'gazelles', are given particular attention by national policy-makers because of the significant (and disproportionate) contribution they make to national new-job creation! Figure 4.2 shows the percentage of the working age population for different countries in such high-growth expectation business start-ups (< 42 months old) over the period 2004–2009. China has over 4% of its adult population engaged in high-growth expectation business start-ups compared to 1.5% in the US, 0.7% in the UK, and less than 0.5% in many EU economies.

▮ Definition of the small firm

There are a number of ways of defining small and medium-sized firms.

Bolton Committee Report of 1971

This had recognised the difficulty of defining the small firm. Rather than depending solely on numbers of employees or other data, it suggested that the emphasis be placed on the characteristics which make the performance of small firms significantly different from those of large firms. Three such characteristics were identified as being of particular importance:

1 having a relatively small share of the market;

2 being managed by owners in a personal way rather than via a formalized management structure;

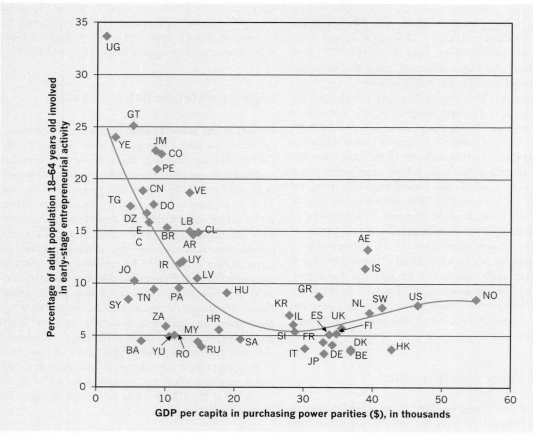

Fig. 4.1 Early-stage entrepreneurial activity rates and per capita GDP, 2009.
Source: Bosma and Levie (2010).

3 being independent of larger enterprises, so that its owner–managers are free from outside control when taking their decisions.

The 1985 Companies Act

This was more specific and defined a company in the UK as small if it satisfied any two of the following criteria:

- turnover of less than £2.8m;
- net assets under £1.4m;
- fewer than 50 employees.

The Department of Business, Innovation and Skills

This defines SMEs in terms of numbers of employees as follows:

- micro firm (0–9 employees);
- small firm (10–49 employees);
- medium-sized firm (50–249 employees);
- large firms (over 250 employees).

European Union (EU)

This definition of an SME involves four criteria, as listed in Table 4.1.

To qualify as an SME, both the employees and independence criteria must be satisfied together with *either* the turnover or the balance sheet criteria. An SME is defined as an 'independent enterprise' when the amount of capital or voting rights in that firm held by one or more non-SME firms does not exceed 25%. The values shown in Table 4.1 for turnover and balance sheet are liable to be changed over time as the

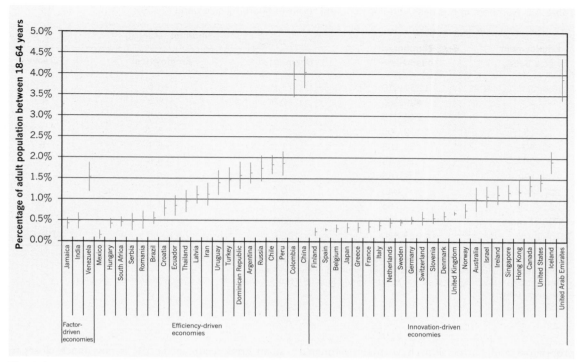

Fig. 4.2 High-growth expectation early-stage entrepreneurship (HEA), 2004/09.
Source: Bosma and Levie (2010).

Table 4.1 EU definitions of micro, small and medium-sized firms.

	Micro firm	Small firm	Medium firm
Turnover (€)	Not exceeding 2 million	Not exceeding 10 million	Not exceeding 50 million
Balance sheet total (€)	Not exceeding 2 million	Not exceeding 10 million	Not exceeding 43 million
Employees	Fewer than 10	Fewer than 50	Fewer than 250
Independence criteria	–	25% or less	25% or less

absolute monetary values require adjustments because of inflation.

 The importance of the small firm

Since 1995, information on the size distribution of all UK firms has been improved with the introduction of the new Inter-Departmental Business Register (IDBR).

This register keeps statistics of all businesses registered for VAT and also those businesses which operate a PAYE scheme. This means that the IDBR includes small businesses below the VAT threshold but with a PAYE system, together with those businesses trading in goods exempt from VAT but operating a PAYE system, e.g. small firms in finance, insurance and education. Of course, the IDBR does not collect information on unregistered businesses, i.e. those which do not register for VAT or operate PAYE systems. Thus, figures for activities such as sole

Table 4.2 Numbers of business, employment and turnover share by size band (2009).

Employment size band	Number of businesses	Share of total (%)		
		Businesses	Employment	Turnover
0 or 1	3,832,670	77.8	14.6	7.9
2–4	629,860	12.8	6.3	6.0
5–9	240,015	4.9	5.5	6.2
10–19	122,600	2.5	5.7	7.3
20–49	59,155	1.2	6.1	6.7
50–99	19,845	0.4	4.6	5.7
100–199	9,165	0.2	4.3	5.4
200–249	1,840	0.0	1.4	2.0
250–499	3,765	0.1	4.3	8.1
500 or more	4,405	0.1	47.3	44.7
Total	4,923,320	100.0	100.0	100.0

Note: 'with no employees' comprises sole proprietorship and partnerships comprising only self-employed owner manager(s) and companies comprising of only one employee director.
Source: Department for Business Innovation and Skills (2010b) *Small and Medium Enterprise Statistics for UK and Regions*, October.

proprietors and partnerships have to be estimated from the Labour Force Survey (LFS) and added to the IDBR figures.

Table 4.2 shows that there were some 4,923,000 businesses in the UK in 2009. The lower employment band category of '0 and 1' includes sole proprietors and partnerships comprising only self-employed owner–manager(s) and companies comprising only one employee–director. This category reflects the growth of self-employment in the UK, but while it accounts for 77.8% of the total number of businesses, it accounts for only some 14.6% of total employment and 7.9% of total turnover. Small businesses with fewer than 50 employees can be seen from the table to account for over 38% of total employment and around 34% of total turnover. If we include SMEs, i.e. businesses employing fewer than 250 employees, then such businesses account for around 48% of employment and 47% of turnover. The total number of businesses in the UK rose from 2.4 million in 1979 to over 4.9 million in 2009 and, since most of the *new* businesses are small, this reflects a significant growth in the small firm sector.

As we see later in the chapter, the 1980s saw a renewed interest in the role of the small firm in the UK, with a variety of policy measures directed towards its support. As a result the relative size of the small firms sector in the UK is now much closer to that in other countries than it was at the beginning of the 1980s. As Table 4.3 indicates, in 2008/09 the small (micro) firm in the UK employing fewer than 10 persons made up 95.5% of all enterprises and provided some 26.4% of all employment and 20.1% of total turnover.

While the figures for the contribution for micro enterprises were similar in the UK and the EU, it is interesting to note that SMEs as a whole tended to contribute less to employment and turnover in the UK than in the EU. The mirror image of this can be seen in the noticeably greater contribution that large firms make to employment and turnover in the UK as compared to the EU.

The neglect of small firms

Early economic theory was broadly favourable to the small firm. The theory of perfect competition had shown that in markets where many small firms produced identical products, the eventual equilibrium would be at the 'technical optimum', i.e. the level of output with lowest average cost. Monopoly, on the

Table 4.3 Shares of enterprises, employment and turnover: UK and EU (2008/9).

	Micro (0–9)	Small (10–49)	Medium (50–249)	Large (250+)
Enterprises				
UK	95.5	3.7	0.6	0.2
EU	91.8	6.9	1.1	0.2
Employment				
UK	26.4	11.8	10.3	51.6
EU	29.7	20.7	17.0	32.6
Turnover				
UK	20.1	14.0	13.1	52.8
EU	18.7	19.2	19.9	42.2

Sources: Adapted from Department for Business Innovation and Skills (2010b) *Small and Medium Enterprise Statistics for the UK and the Regions,* October; EC (2010) *Annual Report on EU Small and Medium Sized Enterprises 2009.*

other hand, was regarded with suspicion, the exploitation of market power giving the opportunity for restricting output and raising prices (see Chapter 6).

The rise of limited liability and the development of the capital market had, by the end of the nineteenth century, made it easier for firms to raise finance for growth. There was also a greater awareness that increased size could secure substantial economies of scale. These developments shifted the focus of attention away from small firms and towards large firms. During the inter-war period, economic theory gave further grounds for viewing large-scale production in a more favourable light. The theory of imperfect competition developed during the 1930s showed that many small firms producing differentiated products could, as with monopoly, produce output below the technical optimum, with prices above the competitive level.

Bannock (1981) argues that after the Second World War attitudes towards large firms became still more positive, with attention being focused on the innovatory role of large firms. Particularly influential was the American economist Schumpeter, who wrote in 1943 that 'the large-scale establishment . . . has come to be the most powerful engine in [economic] progress and in particular of the long-run expansion of total output' (Bannock 1981). Price competition in traditional competitive theory was, to Schumpeter, less important than the 'gales of creative destruction' which replaced old products, processes and organizations with new ones. Technical progress to bring about these innovative changes would, in Schumpeter's

view, require substantial monopoly profits to fund research and development (R & D). The large sums needed to research and develop products in the aerospace, nuclear and computer industries lent weight to this argument. The fact that in the two decades after the Second World War, increasing industrial concentration coincided with the most rapid and sustained period of economic growth in the twentieth century was seen by many as supporting Schumpeter's view.

British government policy reflected this growing preoccupation with larger size as a means of reaping economies of scale and reducing unit costs of production, so that UK products would become more competitive on world markets. For example, in 1966 the government announced the formation of the Industrial Reorganization Corporation (IRC). The White Paper inaugurating the IRC had emphasized the need for increased concentration in British industry, so that firms could benefit from economies of scale in production and increase expenditure on R & D. The IRC was set up to encourage the reorganization of UK industry, which in practice led to it promoting mergers through financial and other assistance. Although the IRC was wound up in 1971, the Industry Acts of 1972 and 1975 continued to offer financial help to industry on a selective basis in order to encourage modernization, efficiency and expansion, in particular through the activities of the National Enterprise Board (NEB). However, emphasis on increasing size as a means of achieving greater efficiency began to wane by the early 1970s, with a reawakening of interest in small firms.

The renewed interest in small firms

Empirical and other evidence began to accumulate in the late 1960s which challenged the views of Schumpeter that large firms must be the engine of economic progress.

First, it began to be felt that large firms might not always be the most innovative. Instead of large firms growing still larger by capturing new markets as a result of product and process innovation, they often grew by taking over existing firms with established products and processes. A study by Hannah and Kay (1977) had shown that virtually all the increase in concentration that occurred in the UK between 1957 and 1973 resulted from mergers between existing companies and not from internal growth.

Second, evidence began to be published which indicated that small firms were themselves beginning to play an important role in innovation. The Bolton Committee had found in its survey of important innovations between 1945 and 1970 that small firms accounted for only some 10% of these innovations, but that this was twice as high as their share of total R & D. It has been argued, therefore, that small firms use skilled manpower and research equipment more efficiently than larger firms. Similarly, in a nation-wide study of 800 firms covering 1,200 innovations, Oakey *et al.* (1980) had found that 23% of these innovations came from single-site independent companies. In the fast-growing instrument engineering and electronic sectors, the small firms' share of innovations was even higher. The fact that small firms had been prominent in the most dynamic, high-technology sectors suggested that they still had an important role to play as innovators. The role of small firms as innovators continued into the 1990s, as illustrated in an important report by the Cambridge University Centre for Business Research which compared the innovative nature of SMEs over the 1990–95 period. The report showed that over 20% of SMEs in their sample produced 'original' product innovation, i.e. innovations which were not only new to the specific firm but also new to the industry in which the firm operated (Cosh and Hughes 1996). A similar conclusion as to the 'efficiency' of both UK and US firms employing between 10 and 99 employees in converting innovation inputs into commercially successful outputs was also reached in recent work by the Cambridge–MIT Institute (Cosh *et al.* 2006).

Third, Prais (1976) produced evidence that the growth in size of firms (business units) was not, in the main, due to the growth in size of plants (production units). According to his calculations, the share of the 100 largest manufacturing plants remained at about 11% between 1930 and 1968, whilst the share of the 100 largest *firms* rose from about 22% to 41% in the same period. Concentration had increased because firms had built or acquired more plants, not because they had built larger ones. Put another way, Prais showed that increasing concentration was not explained by increased technical economies of scale at plant level. The small firm may therefore be able to compete with the large firm even though it produced in relatively small plants.

Fourth, evidence began to accumulate that acquisitions do not always have particularly beneficial effects on financial performance. A number of studies (Singh 1971; Meeks 1977) showed that the profitability of the combined enterprise usually fell after merger. In fact Newbold (1970) found that only 18% of all the mergers investigated could be linked in any way to technical or financial economies of scale. Again, such evidence gave grounds for optimism that the small firm may be at less of a disadvantage in terms of profitability than had earlier been thought.

Fifth, there was evidence that small firms had contributed a major part of the recorded gains in employment whilst larger firms had been shedding labour. Birch (1979), in his study of changes in employment in the USA, concluded that small firms (those with 20 or fewer employees) generated 66% of all new jobs in the US in the period 1969–76. More recent studies have tended to confirm these earlier findings. For example, the European network for research on SMEs found that small and medium-sized companies accounted for no less than 94% of the UK *net* employment growth over the 1987–91 period. Keeble (1997) found that between 1990 and 1995 the number of people employed by small firms in the UK rose by 19%. However, it is also important to note that net employment creation in the UK's SME sector has been mostly generated by new, innovative, technology-based companies (TUC 2000).

Sixth, the role of small firms in foreign trade had been shown to be more significant than had previously been thought. Hannah and Kay (1977) quoted unpublished figures from a survey undertaken in 1973 by the Department of Trade. These showed that firms with a turnover of less than £10m exported 14.5% of turnover, whilst firms with a turnover of over £250m exported only 10%. By the mid-1990s, figures for exports show that the small-firm sector as a whole exported an average of 12% of their turnover, whilst small firms in manufacturing exported as much as 14% of their turnover (Keeble 1997). Such an export performance may also have been under-estimated because small firms also provide 'indirect exports' since they supply intermediate goods for large export firms (EC 2002).

In recent years, SMEs have become more international not only for the traditional reasons of exporting and importing but also to access knowhow and/or technology and/or labour. The Internet and other new facilities for fast and easy communication and collaboration have provided opportunities for more complex international partnerships and alliances for SMEs. As a result many new SMEs in the UK and elsewhere are often 'born global', i.e. orientated towards internationalization from an early stage, with such developments helping small firms play new and dynamic roles in the internationalization process (EC 2003).

For all these reasons there has been a renewed interest in the small firm, which has been reflected in recent government policy.

Measures to help small firms

Small firms: finance and allowances

An array of government financial help has been available for UK SMEs over the last 20 years, many of which have now been superseded. By early 2010 the UK government had introduced *Solutions for Business* which contained a streamlined portfolio of business products available for companies including SMEs. Here we look briefly at some of the more important loans available to such firms under this portfolio and then at other sources of funding, especially that of equity capital and the role of the Alternative Investment Market (AIM). Some points about other allowances and benefits will also be mentioned.

Loan capital
Enterprise Finance Guarantee (EFG)
The Enterprise Finance Guarantee (EFG) helps businesses such as SMEs who would not normally qualify

to get a loan. It helps to overcome financial problems by providing lenders such as banks and other financial institutions with a government guarantee for 75% of the lender's exposure on individual loans. The EFG supports lending to businesses with a turnover of up to £25m and enables bank facilities of between £1,000 and £1m to be available for up to 10 years. The guarantee can be used to support new loans or to refinance existing loans, or it can be used to convert an existing overdraft into a loan to meet working capital requirements. Some £1.3bn is available under this scheme.

Small Loans for Business (SLB)
Small Loans for Business (SLB) provides loans to individuals to support good business ideas that could be difficult to fund through other means. Loans can be used to secure services, purchase equipment and meet a shortfall in funding. It provides small loans of between £3,000 and £50,000 to new and growing businesses, charities and social enterprises. The main criteria is that the business can show that it has tried to obtain funding from traditional sources – bank or Building Society, for example – and been rejected for specified reasons such as a lack of security, poor credit score or insufficient track record. The scheme is funded by the government and private sector partners, and a typical lending rate would be 12.5%.

Finance for Business (FFB)
Finance for Business (FFB) provides flexible finance solutions such as loans and equity finance for businesses with viable business plans that are unable to get support from banks and other investors. It aims to increase start-ups and stimulate business growth through increased access to the right funding at the right time for businesses.

Grant for Business Investment (GBI)
Grant for Business Investment (GBI) replaced the old Selective Finance for Investment (SFI) and provides capital support for businesses wishing to create jobs and to help firms grow, modernise and branch out into new areas, especially in the Assisted Areas of England. The minimum grant is £10,000 and there is no maximum since the final amount will depend on the location and quality of the project. The maximum rate of grant for small companies located in the more deprived or assisted areas of England varies with size. For those companies with less than 50 employees, the

maximum support is 35% of total eligible investment, while for medium-sized firms employing between 50 and 250 employees, the maximum grant is 25%.

European Investment Bank (EIB)

Most of the main UK high street banks have secured finance from the EIB to provide lower-cost funding to SMEs. The funding is in the form of a reduced loan cost or via a cash-back. The scheme is designed for businesses employing 250 employees or less and the loan must be for a minimum of two years and cannot be for short-term working capital needs. The key benefit of the EIB-funded loan is cheaper credit from the participating banks. For example, in 2010 Barclays indicated that cash-back payments of from £150 to £51,000 were available on capital projects ranging from £50,000 to £17m with a maximum cash-back of 2.5% on qualifying businesses.

Grant for Research and Development (GRD)

Grant for Research and Development (GRD) is designed to provide finance to individuals and SMEs to research and develop innovative technology products and processes. There are five different types of projects qualifying for funding – examples of three types will be given here. For example, a grant of up to £20,000 is available for businesses with fewer than ten employees for *micro projects* which involve simple low-cost development lasting no more than 12 months. Another type of grant for *research projects* is available to investigate the technical and commercial feasibility of innovative technology and lasts for 18 months. This grant is for up to £100,000 and is available to businesses with fewer than 50 employees. Finally, an *exceptional development projects* grant is available for those companies who involve themselves in significant technological advance and are strategically important for the industry as whole. For those companies who qualify, the grant is for up to £500,000 and lasts for 36 months.

Equity capital

Business Angels (BA)

These are wealthy individuals who invest in high-growth businesses in return for an equity share, i.e. an ownership share in the company. They generally invest between £10,000 and £750,000 and are not averse to high risk. The benefits of BAs are that the investment decision can be made quickly and they

can bring valuable first-hand experience of working in a small business. However, they do not make investments very regularly and may not be actively looking for an opportunity, so it may be difficult for an SME seeking funding to find them, though this has become easier with the foundation of the British Business Angels Association (BBAA) in 2004. Other venture capital companies (see below) also have links with Business Angels.

Venture capitalists

These companies tend to invest larger sums of money in products or services with a unique selling point or competitive advantage – and therefore with a potential of high returns. They usually look for SMEs with talented management teams and often give active support by providing advice, guidance and opportunities. For example, in 2010 Midven, a venture capital company, was prepared to invest up to £500,000 worth of equity initially and then, depending on the success of that company, to involve itself in a further round of equity investment. The company was happy to consider different types of SME activity, e.g. start-ups, early stage growth and management buy-outs, and was particularly interested in Medical/Biotech, ICT and Software sectors, managing five funds which had invested £360m in more than 100 companies. Venture capital firms vary in size from smaller providers such as Braveheart and the YFM group, to larger entities such as Amadeus Capital Partners and the 3i Group.

Alternative Investment Market (AIM)

The Unlisted Securities Market (USM) was introduced in November 1981 to enable small and medium-sized firms to acquire venture capital on the London Stock Exchange. Its attractiveness declined in the early 1990s partly because the Stock Exchange rules regarding a full listing had been relaxed in response to changes in European Union directives. This meant that the advantages to companies of being on the USM rather than on the Official Stock Exchange List had been eroded. The USM ceased trading in December 1996.

The demand for a replacement market to the USM was evident in the early 1990s with the growth of trading under Rule 4.2 of the London Stock Exchange. This rule permitted member firms to deal in specific securities which were neither listed nor quoted on the USM. It had been formulated to provide an occasional

Table 4.4 Comparison between main stock exchange listing and AIM.

Listing criteria	Main market	AIM
Minimum public float	25% of shares in public hands	No minimum
Trading record	Normally three years trading record required	No trading record requirement
Admission documents	Pre-vetting of admission documents by the Financial Services Authority (FSA)	No pre-vetting of documents made by LSE or FSA unless a public offer of securities is made
Capitalization	Minimum market capitalization of £700,000	No minimum market capitalization
Shareholder approval	Prior shareholder approval needed for substantial acquisitions or disposals	No prior shareholder approval for transactions (unless they are reverse takeovers or 75% disposals)

dealing facility in unquoted companies for members of the Stock Exchange. The main benefit of trading under Rule 4.2 was that trading rules were less stringent than under the full listing or the USM.

In June 1995 the AIM was opened to meet the demand for low-cost and accessible investment funds for small and growing companies who do not need as much capital as large companies. Its trading rules are less demanding than those for a full listing on the London Stock Exchange (LSE). Some of these differences are indicated in Table 4.4.

The above differences between the main market and AIM show how the latter would be more accessible to those companies requiring small amounts of capital and relative flexibility. In 2010 the fee payable by all companies seeking initial admission to AIM varied from £6,085 to £68,750, depending on the market capitalization, while the equivalent on the main market varied from £6,085 to £352,085. The annual fees payable per company on AIM was £4,925 while for the main market the annual fee varied between £4,005 and £39,000 depending on the capitalization of the company.

By September 2010 there were 1,204 companies trading on the AIM with a market value of £65bn. The total money raised between 1995 and 2010 was £69bn and some of the companies listed on the AIM in 2010 included Majestic Wine (drinks), Carluccio's (café/food), Young and Co Brewery (drinks), Straight plc (food waste disposal), Falkland Oil and Gas (gas exploration) and Millwall Holdings (football). Investors in AIM company shares vary from wealthy individuals to institutional investors such as venture

capitalists. For example, in June 2010 Bridges Ventures, a venture capital company, invested £5.5m thus owning 23% of the shares in TEG Group, an AIM listed organic waste specialist. Bridges Ventures itself benefits from lower capital gains and inheritance tax rates on such investments.

The economic impact of the AIM on SMEs and smaller businesses in general was investigated by Grant Thornton, the chartered accountants, in 2010 who concluded that the market had supported some 3,100 companies since its inception. In addition, they concluded that the companies which AIM had helped to grow, having employed over 250,000 employees, contributed £12bn to GDP, and supplied £1.8bn of tax revenues to the Exchequer (Grant Thornton 2010). The ability of AIM to allow smaller companies to raise external funds at different stages of their life-cycle was identified in the report as having helped to create these impacts.

Taxation and allowances

In order to help small firms, some taxation benefits and allowances are also available. For example, in the emergency budget of June 2010 the coalition government promised to bring down taxes on companies, i.e. corporation tax, with the main rate of corporation tax for larger companies whose profits exceed £1.5m due to be reduced from 28% to 24% between 2011 and 2014. In the meantime, the corporation tax rate for small companies whose profits do not exceed £30,000 per year was to fall from 21% to 20% in the year commencing April 2011. Whilst the SME rates of corporation tax are still less than those for large companies, that gap is narrowing. Another example of benefits to SMEs revolves around Research and Development tax credits, with benefits to such companies including a 100% relief for qualifying capital costs in the year of expenditure. Also, under the Enterprise Guarantee Scheme, SMEs can spread their tax payments over longer periods thus giving them more time to pay their tax liabilities. In addition, the 'Annual Investment Allowance' allows companies to write off the costs of their capital assets against tax, which helps to alleviate the burden of investment in expensive plant and equipment. All these and many more such tax reliefs and allowances positively impact on the development of SMEs.

Small firms: other sources of advice and training

Up to April 2010, the Learning and Skills Council was responsible for all post-16 education and training in England other than in the universities. However, in April 2010, the Council was dissolved and two separate organizations were formed.

1 The *Skills Funding Agency*, working under the Department for Business, Innovation and Skills, was set up to fund and regulate adult further education and skills training in England. The agency allocates funding of around £4bn per year to colleges and other skills and training organisations who have discretion over expenditure to meet the needs of local businesses and communities. The agency also houses the National Apprenticeship Service as part of the government's ambition to increase apprenticeships. State aid for training under a Training Aid Exemption clause allows for 45% of the cost of specific training and 80% of general training to be paid for by the state for small companies, while the figures for medium-sized companies are 45% and 70% respectively and for large firms the figures are lower at 25% and 60%.

2 The *Young People's Learning Agency* is the other organization founded in April 2010 whose work includes the following: first, to fund support for some 600,000 young learners through Educational Maintenance Allowances (removed in 2011); second, to provide a stable platform and provide grants for the expansion of the 'academies programme'

which is designed to encourage educational excellence and enhanced training; third, to fund the education and training of 1.4m young people aged 16–19 and up to the age of 25 subject to a learning difficulty assessment. The budget for these programmes for 2010–11 was £5.5bn.

The two agencies described above are not strictly designed to help only SMEs, but the businesses who take advantage of such education and training of student and apprenticeship facilities are mostly companies in that category.

Chambers of Commerce

Local and Regional Chambers of Commerce can provide SMEs with assistance in the areas of customer service, industry participation, employer/employee participation, employment growth and community support. In addition they can provide knowledge and information which can lead to cost savings and market opportunities not usually open to small companies.

Business Links

Businesslink.gov.uk is the official website and was launched in May 2004 and supplies all businesses, but especially SMEs, with information collected from 170 government websites. From April 2007 the service was delivered by Serco on behalf of HM Revenue and Customs but by 2010 the new UK coalition government was reviewing how it is to deliver business support in the future.

Small Business Service and the Enterprise Directorate

The *Small Business Service* began in April 2000 and was designed to act as an effective voice for small firms in government and serve as a centre for bringing knowledge about SMEs together, developing innovative approaches to suit the needs of SMEs. It also partnered other organizations within and outside government to help the small firm sector. In July 2001 the organization was renamed the '*Enterprise Directorate*' and was located in the Department for Business, Innovation and Skills. Its remit has shifted more towards encouraging the growth of existing small businesses and somewhat away from start-up enterprises. The Directorate has a strong research and analytical function while at the same time maintaining international links especially with members in the

Table 4.5 Biggest obstacles to business success, 2006/07 and 2007/08.

Rank	Obstacle	2007/08 %	2006/07 %
1	The economy	16	10
2	Competition in the market	14	15
3	Taxation, VAT, PAYE, National Insurance, business rates	12	12
4	Regulations	12	14
5	Cash flow	9	10
6	Recruiting staff	5	6
7	Shortage of skills generally	4	4
8	Obtaining finance	3	3
9	Availability/cost of suitable premises	3	4
10	Shortage of managerial skills/expertise	1	1
	No obstacles	2	2
	No opinion	2	2

Source: Department for Business, Enterprise and Regulatory Reform (2009) *Annual Small Business Survey 2007/8*.

EU and the US. The continued need for such support was highlighted as early as 2000 in a major study of 1,000 SMEs by the Centre for Business Research of Cambridge University (Cosh and Hughes 2000). They found that less than half the firms investigated had formal structures for their management organization and less than half provided formal training within their companies.

Other useful surveys reflecting the obstacles facing SMEs include the Annual Small Business Surveys published by the government (Department for Business, Enterprise and Regulatory Reform 2009). The 2007/08 survey which interviewed 7,783 SMEs asked companies what they regarded as the greatest obstacles to progress. The results can be seen in Table 4.5 which shows that the greatest concerns were *external* to the firm, such as the condition of the economy, the intensity of competition, taxation, and the regulatory environment, with concern about the economy becoming more prominent in 2007/08 as the UK's financial and economic problems deepened.

Small firms and the banks

Policy-makers have complained for many years that small firms have poor access to external finance due to a market failure in credit markets whereby lenders are imperfectly informed about the characteristics of the borrowers. As a result it is difficult for lenders, such as the banks and other financial institutions, to distinguish borrowers likely to default from those who are able to make repayments. However, since the early 1990s the relationships between borrowers and lenders have improved so that finance is not presently regarded as the main problem by SMEs. Firstly, banks have understood more clearly the nature of SME businesses and are able to assess the risk of borrowers more effectively, with the assessments of businesses relying less on judgements by bank managers and more on the quantitative evaluation of business-owner characteristics and business cash-flows. Secondly, banks have played an important role in helping SMEs to find more appropriate forms of finance, notably through their leasing and invoice discounting subsidiaries. Thirdly, banks have significantly enhanced their range of small business products with the aim of gaining market share. Finally, criticisms of the banks for not making their charges transparent enough for SMEs and thereby inhibiting SMEs from switching their accounts to other banks, have acted as a catalyst for banks to make their charges more transparent.

In addition, over the past decade, SMEs themselves have also 'learned' to access more varied sources of external finance. However, the importance of bank finance to SMEs should not be minimized as different types of finance are required for different purposes at different times. For example, the SME Business Barometer published by the Department for Business, Innovation and Skills noted in February 2010 that the types of finance sought by SMEs in the previous six months were still strongly bank orientated, with 46% seeking bank loans; 33% bank overdrafts; 11% mortgages for property improvement; 10% monies for leasing or hire purchase; 6% loans from family and friends; and 2% each from credit card finance and various grants (Department for Business, Innovation and Skills 2010a).

As a result of the banking crises and recession conditions after 2008, the SME sector has felt the pressure of a tightening in the supply of bank credit. This, together with the deceleration in demand had, by 2010, led SMEs to cut their employment and capital investment spending by more than large companies (Bank of England 2010). The performance of the SMEs sector is therefore very closely connected with the economic and financial conditions of the period in question.

European Union policy for small firms

Within the European Commission, policies relating to small and medium-sized firms are now the responsibility of the Enterprise DG which was created in January 2000 and comprises three previous Directorate-Generals (DGs), namely Industry, SME and Information Society. Help for SMEs in the EU is provided by many agencies and it might be useful here to mention a few initiatives in this area. For example, a framework plan entitled 'The Multinational Programme for Enterprise and Entrepreneurship 2001–06' was designed to enhance European business in general but with special reference to SMEs. The objectives of the framework plan are pursued through a series of activities that fall under three headings. The first is to provide adequate *advice, information and assistance* to SMEs through 259 Euro Info Centres located in most European countries. These centres can also refer SMEs to other specialized networks or organizations when specific assistance is required. The second is to improve the *financial environment* for SMEs with many schemes managed by the European Investment Fund (EIF). For example, Seed Capital Action is designed to stimulate the supply of capital for the creation of innovative new businesses by partially funding the recruitment of more investment managers, whilst the European Technology Facility (ETF) start-up scheme invests in funds which provide risk capital to smaller businesses, and the SME Guarantee Facility, also managed by the EIF, provides guarantees to those financial institutions which lend to qualifying SMEs. Since 2007 the EIF has managed 'Jeremie', an initiative designed to give advice, equity/venture capital and guarantees to SMEs over the period 2007–13. The third objective is to identify *best practice* amongst SMEs by introducing benchmarking activities across the EU. The information gathered from the most efficient SMEs as a result of benchmarking is then disseminated to other SMEs.

Other funds for SMEs are available through the *European Regional Development Fund* (ERDF), which spends 10% of its budget on SMEs. The ERDF will have dedicated €23bn to help small businesses by 2013. The *European Social Fund* (ESF) spends 14% of its funds on promoting a systematic approach to training by SMEs in the poorer regions of the EU. Finally, Enterprise DG has supported the development of European stock markets specifically designed to help SMEs. For example, the Nouveau Marche in Paris and the EASDAQ in Brussels specialize in helping young, relatively small companies gain access to equity funds more easily and cheaply.

Finally, it is also worth mentioning the relevance of the Competitiveness and Innovation Framework (CIP) programme which was adopted in October 2006 and runs from 2007 to 2013. This programme has a budget of over €4bn, of which some €1bn are designated to facilitate access to loans and equity finance for SMEs where market gaps have been identified. It is envisaged that this programme will have helped 400,000 small businesses by 2013.

Conclusion

Renewed interest in small firms derives from changes in economic thought and has been given impetus by the particular policies pursued by the government, partly for ideological reasons, partly as a means of producing new jobs, and partly as a corollary of 'supply side' monetarist policies. However, there is a danger in placing too heavy an emphasis on the role of small firms in rebuilding the UK's industrial base. Figures from the DTI have shown that 45% of VAT registered businesses failed to survive the first three years. Storey (1982) had already shown that most small firms stay static or die. In his study of all the new manufacturing firms started in Cleveland, County Durham, and Tyne and Wear from 1965 to 1978, he found that only 774 survived out of 1,200. Of the survivors, more than half still had fewer than 10 employees in 1982, and nearly three-quarters had fewer than 25. In fact, the probability of a new business employing more than 100 people after a decade was less than 0.75%. For every new job created by a small firm in these three counties over the 13-year period, four jobs were lost from large companies employing over 1,000 persons. Storey *et al.* (1987) found that in their survey of single-plant independent manufacturing companies in northern England, one-third of the new jobs were found in less than 4% of the new starters. Further research (Storey 1994) also showed that it is incorrect to assume that countries which have experienced the most rapid increase in new firm formation (measured in terms of increase in self-employment) are those which have experienced the fastest growth of employment creation. The same survey also pointed out that investment in government training schemes for small-company entrepreneurs at the start-up or at later stages is not necessarily related to the future success of small companies. The evidence shows that success is more closely related to the original educational attainment of the business owner. In other words, it may be more important to improve the level of the UK's general education as a whole, if small firms are to thrive.

For all these reasons, the net advantages of small firms may be less than is commonly supposed. Nevertheless, small firms are able to find market niches, especially where economies of scale are not easily obtained, as in providing specialized items for small markets, and in developing products used as components by large firms. Also the movement towards a higher proportion of employment being in the service sector, where traditionally smaller firms have been dominant, suggests an increasingly important role for smaller firms in the UK economy. For example, a major report has shown that UK-based SMEs performed relatively well over the period 1988–2001 as compared to large companies when measured in terms of growth in real value added, employment and profitability (EC 2002). However, in *absolute* terms there are still major gaps between small and large firms. For example, in the European context, the value added per occupied person in SMEs was still only 83% of the EU average, compared to 128% for large firms (EC 2010).

Key points

- Definitions of the small firm vary within and between countries.

- Across all industrial sectors in the UK, firms with fewer than five employees account for around 91% of the total number of firms. However, such firms account for only around 21% of total employment and 14% of total turnover.

- The small firm is increasingly seen by governments as a focus of new growth and employment opportunities.

- Small-firm support has focused on three main areas: easier access to equity and loan capital, increased tax allowances and grants, and less government interference.

- Banks provide the main source (59%) of external finance for small firms (via over-draft) in the UK, increasingly in the form of medium- to longer-term loans, though high exposure to such overdraft finance remains a problem in the UK.

- Small firms in the UK see interest rate policy, general macroeconomic policy and taxation policy as the governmental policies with most impact on themselves.

- External factors such as the condition of the economy, competition in the market-place, taxation and regulatory control are the dominant obstacles to the business success of SMEs.

- European policy towards SMEs is becoming increasingly influential with large-scale funds available to support a broad range of initiatives.

Now try the self-check questions for this chapter on the Companion Website. You will also find useful links to relevant websites.

References and further reading

Bank of England (2004) *Finance for Small Firms – An Eleventh Report*, April, London.

Bank of England (2010) *Inflation Report*, February, London.

Bannock, G. (1981) *The Economics of Small Firms*, Oxford, Blackwell.

Bannock, G. and Daly, M. (eds) (1994) *Small Business Statistics*, London, Paul Chapman.

Barrett, R., Cowan, E. and Mayson, S. (2010) *International Handbook of Entrepreneurship and HRM*, Cheltenham, Edward Elgar.

Birch, D. L. (1979) *The Job Generation Process*, Boston, MA, MIT Programme on Neighborhood and Regional Change.

Bosma, M. and Levie, J. (2010) *Global Entrepreneurship Monitor 2009 Global Economic Report*, London, Global Entrepreneurship Research Association.

Competition Commission (2002) *The Supply of Banking Services by Clearing Banks to Small and Medium Sized Enterprises*, CM 5319, March, London.

Cosh, A. and Hughes, A. (2000) *British Enterprise in Transition: Growth, Innovation and Public Policy in the Small and Medium Sized Enterprise Sector 1994–99*, Cambridge, ESRC Centre for Business Research, University of Cambridge.

Cosh, A. and Hughes, A. (eds) (1996) *The Changing State of British Enterprise: Growth, Innovation and Competitive Advantage in Small and Medium Sized Firms 1986–95*, Cambridge, ESRC Centre for Business Research, University of Cambridge.

Cosh, A., Hughes, A. and Lester, R. K. (2006) *UK plc: Just how innovative are we? Findings from the Cambridge-MIT Institute International Innovation Benchmarking project*, MIT-

IPC-06-009, Cambridge, Cambridge-MIT Institute.

Curran, J. and Stanworth, J. (1989) Education and training for enterprise: some problems of classification, evaluation, policy and research, *International Small Business Journal*, 7(2): 11–22.

Deakins, D. and Freel, M. (2009) *Entrepreneurship and Small Firms* (5th edn), Maidenhead, McGraw Hill Education.

Department for Business, Enterprise and Regulatory Reform (2009) *Annual Small Business Survey 2007/8*, London, The Stationery Office.

Department for Business, Innovation and Skills (2010a) *Business Barometer*, February, London, The Stationery Office.

Department for Business, Innovation and Skills (2010b) *Small and Medium Enterprise Statistics for UK and Regions*, October, London, The Stationery Office.

Department of Trade and Industry (1999) *Small and Medium-sized Enterprises (SME) Statistics for the United Kingdom 1998*, Small Firms Statistical Unit, July, London, The Stationery Office.

EC (2002) *Observatory of European SMEs 2002/No. 2*, Brussels, European Commission.

EC (2003) *Internationalisation of SMEs, Observatory of European SMEs 2003*, No. 4, Brussels, European Commission.

EC (2010) *Annual Report on EU Small and Medium Sized Enterprises 2009*, Brussels, European Commission.

Gilbert, C. and Eyring, M. (2010) Beating the odds when you launch a new venture, *Harvard Business Review*, 88(5): 92–100.

Grant Thornton (2010) *Economic impact of AIM and the role of fiscal incentives*, September, London.

Hannah, L. and Kay, J. A. (1977) *Concentration in Modern Industry*, Basingstoke, Macmillan.

Keeble, D. (1997) Small firms, innovation and regional development in Britain in the 1990s, *Regional Studies*, 31(3): 281–93.

Kelley, D. J., Bosma, N. and Amoros, J. E. (2011) *Global Entrepreneurship Monitor 2010 Global Report*, London, Global Entrepreneurship Research Association.

Kets de Vries, M. (1977) The entrepreneurial personality: a person at the crossroads, *Journal of Management Studies*, 14(1): 34–57.

Knight, F. (1940) 'What is truth' in economics? On the history and method of economics, *Journal of Political Economy*, 48: 1–32.

Lenihan, H., Andreosso-O'Callaghan, B. and Hart, M. (2010) *SMEs in a Globalised World*, Cheltenham, Edward Elgar.

McClelland, D. C. (1961) *The Achieving Society*, New York, Van Nostrand.

Meeks, G. (1977) *Disappointing Marriage: a study of the gains from merger*, University of Cambridge, Department of Applied Economics, Occasional Paper 51, Cambridge, Cambridge University Press.

Meredith, G. G., Nelson, R. E. and Neck, P. A. (1982) *The Practice of Entrepreneurship*, Geneva, International Labour Organization.

Newbold, A. (1970) *Management and Merger Activity*, Liverpool, Guthstead.

Oakey, R. P., Thwaites, A. T. and Nash, P. A. (1980) The regional distribution of innovative manufacturing establishments in Britain, *Regional Studies*, 14(3): 235–53.

ONS (2010) *Statistical Bulletin: Business Demography 2009 Enterprise Births, Deaths and Survival*, London, Office for National Statistics.

Prais, S. J. (1976) *The Evolution of Giant Firms in Britain*, Cambridge, Cambridge University Press.

Reynolds, P. D., Storey, D. J. and Westhead, P. (2007) Cross-national comparisons of the variation in new firm formation rates, *Regional Studies*, 41(Supplement No.1): S123–36.

Richard, D. (2008) *Small Business & Government: The Richard Report*, Submission to the Shadow Cabinet, London, Conservative Party.

Schumpeter, J. (1934) *The Theory of Economic Development*, Cambridge MA, Harvard University Press.

Shackle, G. (1954) *Uncertainty in Economics and Other Reflections*, Cambridge, Cambridge University Press.

Singh, A. (1971) *Takeovers*, Cambridge, Cambridge University Press.

Small Business Service (2002) *Small and Medium-Sized Enterprises (SME) Statistics for the UK, 2000*, London, The Stationery Office.

Small Business Service (2006) *Annual Survey of Small Businesses: UK 2004/05*, March, London, The Stationery Office.

Storey, D. (1982) *Entrepreneurship and the New Firm*, London, Croom Helm.

Storey, D. (1994) *Understanding the Small Business Sector*, London, Routledge.

Storey, D., Keasey, K., Watson, R. and Wynarczyk, P. (1987) *The Performance of Small Firms*, London, Croom Helm.

Timmons, J. A. (1994) *New Venture Creation: Entrepreneurship for the 21st Century* (4th edn), Chicago IL, Irwin.

TUC (2000) *Small Business – Myths and Reality*, March, London, Trades Union Congress.

Ucbasaran, D., Westhead, P. and Wright, M. (2006) *Habitual Entrepreneurs*, Aldershot, Edward Elgar.

CHAPTER 5 Mergers and acquisitions in the growth of the firm

A well-established maxim suggests that a company must grow if it is to survive. Mergers and acquisitions have become two of the more widely used methods of achieving growth in recent years, accounting for about 50% of the increase in assets and 60% of the increase in industrial concentration. The years 1984–89, 1994–2000 and 2003–07 provided a sustained merger boom, in that the *expenditure* on mergers was extremely high compared to the number of mergers involved. This chapter examines the types of merger activity, such as horizontal, vertical, conglomerate and lateral mergers, and the motives for such activity. These include financial motives which may be related to valuations placed on a firm's assets, the desire to increase 'market power' or to secure economies of scale and managerial motives related more to firm growth than to profitability. Trends in merger activity and legislation affecting merger activity are considered in both the UK and the EU. The UK approach to mergers is then contrasted with that of the US. The chapter concludes with a brief review of recent tendencies to de-merge.

Definitions

One of the most significant changes in the UK's industrial structure during this century has been the growth of the large-scale firm. For example, the share of the 100 largest private enterprises in manufacturing net output has risen from 22% in 1949 to a maximum of 42% in 1975, before falling back to around 34% by 2010. Most of the growth in size was achieved by acquisition or merger rather than by internal growth.

A *merger* takes place with the mutual agreement of the management of both companies, usually through an exchange of shares of the merging firms with shares of the new legal entity. Additional funds are not usually required for the act of merging, and the new venture often reflects the name of both the companies concerned.

A *takeover* (or acquisition) occurs when the management of Firm A makes a direct offer to the shareholders of Firm B and acquires a controlling interest. Usually the price offered to Firm B shareholders is substantially higher than the current share price on the stock market. In other words, a takeover involves a direct transaction between the management of the acquiring firm and the stockholders of the acquired firm. Takeovers usually require additional funds to be raised by the acquiring firm (Firm A) for the acquisition of the other firm (Firm B), and the identity of the acquired company is often subsumed within that of the purchaser.

Sometimes the distinction between merger and takeover is clear, as when an acquired company has put up a fight to prevent acquisition. However, in the majority of cases the distinction between merger and takeover is difficult to make. Occasionally the situation is complicated by the use of the words 'takeover' and 'merger'. For example, in 1989 the press announced that SmithKline Beckman, the US pharmaceutical company, had 'taken over' the UK company Beecham for £4,509m. However, technically speaking it was a 'merger' because a new company SmithKline Beecham was created which acquired the shares of the two constituent companies to form a new entity.

There are two types of 'barriers' which can be employed by companies attempting to deter hostile takeovers:

- *'Poison pill' barrier:* This often involves company rules that allow the shareholders to buy new shares in their company at a large discount, should that company be threatened by a hostile takeover. The now enlarged pool of shareholders makes it more difficult and more expensive for the acquiring firm to complete the takeover. In the US, some 40% of the 5,500 companies tracked by *Institutional Shareholder Service*, a research organization, have been found to employ the 'poison pill'.

- *'Staggered board' barrier:* These involve company rules which allow different groups of directors to be elected in different years. This is likely to deter hostile takeovers since it may be many years before the acquiring company will be able to dominate the existing boardroom of the target company. *Institutional Shareholder Service* estimates that some 60% of US companies have a staggered board. Lucian Bebchuk of Harvard Business School argues that staggered boards cost shareholders around 4–6% of their firm's market value by allowing entrenched managers and directors to resist takeover bids which would be attractive to the majority of shareholders (Bebchuk and Fried 2004).

Types of merger

Four major forms of merger activity can be identified: horizontal integration, vertical integration, the formation of conglomerate mergers, and lateral integration.

Horizontal integration

This occurs when firms combine at the same stage of production, involving similar products or services. During the 1960s over 80% of UK mergers were of the horizontal type, and despite a subsequent fall in this percentage, some 80% of mergers in the late 1990s were still of this type. The merger of Royal Insurance and Sun Alliance to form Royal & Sun Alliance in 1996, Imperial Tobacco's acquisition of the German tobacco firm Reemtsma Cigarettenfabriken in 2002, and the Resolution Life Group's acquisition of the

Britannic Group in 2005 were all examples of horizontal mergers. So too was the merger of Delta Airlines with Northwest Airlines in the US, which was finally consolidated in 2010, resulting in Delta Airlines becoming the world's largest passenger carrier.

Horizontal integration may provide a number of economies at the level of both the plant (productive unit) and the firm (business unit).

Plant economies may follow from the rationalization made possible by horizontal integration. For instance, production may be concentrated at a smaller number of enlarged plants, permitting the familiar technical economies of greater specialization, the dovetailing of separate processes at higher output,[1] and the application of the 'engineers' rule' whereby material costs increase as the square but capacity as the cube. All these lead to a reduction in cost per unit as the size of plant output increases. When Kraft, the US food giant, acquired Cadbury, the UK confectioner, for £11.9bn in 2010, becoming the world's largest confectioner, cost savings of £675m per year were identified from rationalization of production and scale economies. Similarly the huge fabricated chip manufacturing plants ('Fabs') cost over $3bn each, roughly twice as much as previous plants, but are able to produce over three times as many silicon chips per time period, with such 'plant economies' reducing the unit cost per chip by over 40%.

Firm economies result from the growth in size of the whole enterprise, permitting economies via bulk purchase, the spread of similar administrative costs over greater output, and the cheaper cost of finance, etc. The renamed and expanded Air France–KLM airline formed in 2004 estimated cost savings from such 'firm economies' of around £200m over the following five years from economies in functional areas such as sales, distribution, IT and procurement.

Vertical integration

This occurs when the firms combine at different stages of production of a common good or service. Only about 5% of UK mergers are of this type. Firms might benefit by being able to exert closer control over quality and delivery of supplies if the vertical integration is 'backward', i.e. towards the source of supply. Factor inputs might also be cheaper, obtained at cost instead of cost + profit. The takeover of Texas Eastern, an oil exploration company, by Enterprise

Oil in 1989, serves as an example of backward vertical integration. Of course, vertical integration could be 'forward' – towards the retail outlet. This may give the firm merging 'forward' more control of wholesale or retail pricing policy, and more direct customer contact. An example of forward vertical integration towards the market was the acquisition by the UK publishing company Pearson plc of National Computer Systems (NCS) in 2000 for £1.6bn. NCS was a US global information service company providing Internet links and curriculum and assessment testing facilities for schools. The takeover allowed Pearson to design integrated educational programmes for schools by providing students with customized learning and assessment testing facilities. It could also use the NCS network to reach both teachers and parents. In this way, Pearson was able to use its NCS subsidiary to sell its existing publishing products while also developing new on-line materials for the educational marketplace. An example of 'backward' vertical integration can be seen in the case of the US aircraft company Boeing, which bought out its parts suppliers Vought Aircraft in 2009 and Global Aeronautics in 2008, in order to control the supply chain for its 787 Dreamliner plane which had fallen behind in terms of its production schedule.

Vertical integration can often lead to increased control of the market, infringing monopoly legislation. This is undoubtedly one reason why they are so infrequent. Another is the fact that, as Marks and Spencer have shown, it is not necessary to have a controlling interest in suppliers in order to exert effective control over them. Textile suppliers of Marks and Spencer send over 75% of their total output to Marks and Spencer. Marks and Spencer have been able to use this reliance to their own advantage. In return for placing long production runs with these suppliers, Marks and Spencer have been able to restrict supplier profit margins whilst maintaining their viability. Apart from low costs of purchase, Marks and Spencer are also able to insist on frequent batch delivery, cutting stockholding costs to a minimum.

Conglomerate merger

This refers to the adding of different products to each firm's operations. Diversification into products and areas with which the acquiring firm was not previously directly involved accounted for only 13% of all mergers in the UK in the 1960s. However, by the late 1980s the figure had risen to 34%. The major benefit is the spreading of risk for the firms and shareholders involved. Giant conglomerates like Unilever (with interests in food, detergents, toilet preparations, chemicals, paper, plastics, packaging, animal feeds, transport and tropical plantations – in 75 separate countries) are largely cushioned against any damaging movements which are restricted to particular product groups or particular countries. The various *firm economies* outlined above may also result from a conglomerate merger. The ability to buy companies relatively cheaply on the stock exchange, and to sell parts of them off at a profit later, became an important reason for conglomerate mergers in the 1980s. The takeovers by Hanson plc of the Imperial Group, Consolidated Goldfields and the Eastern Group in 1986, 1989 and 1995 respectively provide good examples of the growth of a large conglomerate organization.

The classic example of a conglomerate is the Indian Tata Group which has over 90 operating companies in six business groups, namely communication and information technology, consumer products, engineering, materials, services and chemicals. It owns, for example, Tata Steel, Tata Motors and Tata Chemicals – all major players in international business. With a group revenue of $67.4bn in 2010 with 57% of its companies operating outside India, Tata is a truly global conglomerate.

Another example of conglomerate integration involves Procter & Gamble (P&G), the US multinational, which is the world's largest consumer group conglomerate, owning brands such as Pringles crisps, Pampers nappies and Crest toothpaste. In recent years it has broadened its portfolio of products still further into haircare, acquiring Nioxin, a US scalp care company in 2009, Gillette hair care products in 2005, the German haircare company, Wella, in 2003 and Clairol in 2001. The various 'firm (enterprise) economies' outlined above may also result from a conglomerate merger. P&G expects to save €300m annually from its purchase of Wella by economies from combining back-office activities, media buying, logistics and other purchasing activities.

Lateral integration

This is sometimes given separate treatment, though in practice it is difficult to distinguish from a conglomer-

ate merger. The term 'lateral integration' is often used when the firms which combine are involved in different products, but in products which have *some element of commonality*. This might be in terms of factor input, such as requiring similar labour skills, capital equipment or raw materials; or it might be in terms of product outlet. The Swiss company TetraLaval's offer for the French company Sidel in 2001 (which was finally cleared by the EU competition authorities in 2002) provides an example of the difficulty of distinguishing the concepts of conglomerate and lateral integration. TetraLaval designs, manufactures and sells packaging for liquid food products as well as manufacturing and marketing equipment for milk and farm products. Sidel designs and sells machines used in the manufacture of plastic bottles and packaging. The European Commission regarded the merger as conglomerate in that the companies operated in different sectors of the market and were to be organized, post merger, into three distinct entities within the TetraLaval Group. However, it was still the case that the merger would resemble a case of lateral integration in that the companies had a commonality of experience in the packaging and container sector.

Economic theory and merger activity

A number of theories have been put forward to explain the underlying motives behind merger activity. However, when these various theories are tested empirically the results have often been inconsistent and contradictory. An interesting survey article on merger activity in 1989 noted that as many as *fourteen* separate motives were frequently cited in support of merger activity (Mueller 1989). Despite these obvious complications, it may be useful at this stage to explain some of the main factors which seem to motivate mergers, if only to understand the complexity of the process.

The value discrepancy hypothesis

This theory is based on a belief that two of the most common characteristics of the industrial world are imperfect information and uncertainty. Together, these help explain why different investors have different expectations of the prospects for a given firm.

The value discrepancy hypothesis suggests that one firm will bid for another only if it places a greater value on the firm than that placed on the firm by its current owners. If Firm B is valued at V_A by Firm A and V_B by Firm B then a takeover of Firm B will only take place if $V_A > V_B +$ costs of acquisition. The difference in valuation arises through Firm A's higher expectations of future profitability, often because A takes account of the improved efficiency with which it believes the future operations of B can be run.

It has been argued that it is in periods when technology, market conditions and share prices are changing most rapidly that past information and experience are of least assistance in estimating future earnings. As a result differences in valuation are likely to occur more often, leading to increased merger activity. The value discrepancy hypothesis would therefore predict high merger activity when technological change is most rapid, and when market and share price conditions are most volatile.

Evidence

Gort's (1969) test of the value discrepancy hypothesis in the USA gives some support, finding a statistically significant relationship between merger rate and the parameters noted above. His hypothesis that value discrepancy drives merger activity, especially during periods of rapid shifts in market prices, seems to have some validity. Later researches by Shleifer and Vishny (2003) and Rhodes-Kroopf and Viswanathan (2004) seem to show that relatively different valuations of companies by potential acquirers and bidders often drive merger waves.

Interestingly, recent work on mergers and acquisitions has tended to concentrate on the relationship between industry-level shocks (and associated expectational changes) and merger activity, so reminiscent of the Gort hypothesis. For example, one such study (Andrade *et al.* 2001) indicates that mergers which occurred between the 1970s and the 1990s were often the result of industrial shocks triggered by technological innovations (which can create excess capacity and the need for industry rationalization), supply-side shocks (e.g. oil price changes) or industrial deregulation (greater competition). Similarly, Jovanovich and Rousseau suggest that technological

shocks, to the extent that they do not affect all players in an industry equally, can lead to capital relocation as managers try to restructure industry though mergers and acquisitions (Jovanovich and Rousseau 2004).

Arguably the UK merger booms of the late nineteenth century, the 1920s, the 1960s, the mid-1980s and the 1990s often occurred during periods characterized by industry-level shocks. However, although the industrial shock theory with its effects on expectations does give some indication of the forces at work in merger activity, it does not always give sufficient insight into the particular reasons behind such merger activity.

The valuation ratio

One factor which may affect the likelihood of takeover is the valuation ratio, as defined below:

$$\text{Valuation ratio} = \frac{\text{market value}}{\text{asset value}}$$

$$= \frac{\text{no. of shares} \times \text{share price}}{\text{book value of assets}}$$

If a company is 'undervalued' because its share price is low compared to the value of its assets, then it becomes a prime target for the 'asset stripper'. If a company attempts to grow rapidly it will tend to retain a high proportion of profits for reinvestment, with less profit therefore available for distribution to shareholders. The consequence may be a low share price, reducing the market value of the firm in relation to the book value of its assets, i.e. reducing the valuation ratio. It has been argued that a high valuation ratio will deter takeovers, whilst a low valuation ratio will increase the vulnerability of the firm to takeover. In the early 1980s, for example, the property company British Land purchased Dorothy Perkins, the womenswear chain, because its market value was seen as being low in relation to the value of its assets (prime high street sites). After stripping out all the freehold properties for resale, the remainder of the chain was sold to the Burton Group.

In recent years the asset value of some companies has been seriously underestimated for other reasons. For example, many companies have taken years to build up brand names which are therefore worth a great amount of money; but it is often the case that these are *not* given a money value and are thus not included in the asset value of the company. As a result, if the market value of a company is already low in relation to the book value of its assets, then the acquirer gets a double bonus. One reason why Nestlé was prepared to bid £2.5bn (regarded as a 'high' bid, in relation to its book value) for Rowntree Mackintosh in 1988 was to acquire the 'value' of its consumer brands cheaply, because they were not shown on the balance sheet. Finally, it is interesting to note that when the valuation ratio is low and a company would appear to be a 'bargain', a takeover may originate from *within* the company; in this case it is referred to as a management buyout (MBO).

Evidence

Kuehn (1975), in his study of over 3,500 companies in the UK (88% of companies quoted on the Stock Exchange) between 1957 and 1969, found that those firms which maintained a high valuation ratio were much less susceptible to takeover. Figure 5.1 indicates this inverse relation between valuation ratio and the probability of acquisition. The suggestion is that potential raiders are deterred by the high price to be paid, reflecting a more realistic market valuation of the potential victims' assets. However, the valuation ratio may not be as important as Kuehn's study implies. For example Singh (1971), in a study of take-overs in five UK industries (which included food, drink and electrical engineering industries) between

1955 and 1960, found that a relatively high valuation ratio may not always guarantee protection against takeover. An even stronger conclusion against the valuation ratio hypothesis was drawn by Newbold (1970), when he compared the valuation ratios of 'victim' firms with those of the 'bidding' firms during the merger period of 1967 and 1968. His conclusion was that the valuation ratio of actual 'victim' firms exceeded the average for the industry in 38 cases but was below the average in only 26 cases. In other words, a high valuation ratio did not seem to deter takeover activity. Levine and Aaronovitch (1981) came to a similar conclusion in their study of 109 mergers in manufacturing and services, noting that as many as 14% of the successful 'bidding' firms had a valuation ratio below 1, which one might have expected to result in their becoming 'victim' firms.

Some confirmation of the view that a high valuation ratio may not deter takeover activity has come from a survey of merger activity in the US manufacturing and mining sectors, between 1940 and 1985. This survey related merger activity to a measure called the Tobin *q*. This measure is similar to the valuation ratio explained above, except that the market value of a company is measured against the 'replacement value' of the company's assets. The study found a *positive* relationship between mergers and the Tobin *q*, i.e. a high Tobin *q* or valuation ratio was associated with a high level of merger activity – the reverse of the more usually accepted hypothesis (Golbe and White 1988).

The market power theory

The main motive behind merger activity may often be to increase monopoly control of the environment in which the firm operates. Increased market power may help the firm to withstand adverse economic conditions, and increase long-term profitability.

Three situations are particularly likely to induce merger activity aimed at increasing market power.

1   Where a fall in demand results in excess capacity and the danger of price-cutting competition. In this situation firms may merge in order to secure a better vantage point from which to rationalize the industry.

2   Where international competition threatens increased penetration of the domestic market by foreign

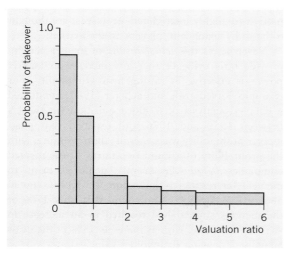

Fig. 5.1 Valuation ratio and probability of takeover.

firms. Mergers in electronics, computers and engineering have in the past produced combines large enough to fight off such foreign competition.

3 Where a tightening of legislation makes many types of linkages between companies illegal. Firms have in the past adopted many practices which involved collusion in order to control markets. Since restrictive practices legislation has made many of these practices illegal between companies, merger, by 'internalizing' the practices, has allowed them to continue.

For these reasons merger activity may take place to increase a firm's market power. However, the very act of merging usually increases company size, both in absolute terms and in relation to other firms. It is clear, therefore, that increased size will be both a by-product of the quest for increased market power, and itself a cause of increased market power.

Evidence

Newbold (1970), in his study of 38 mergers between 1967 and 1968, found that the most frequent reason cited by managers for merger activity was risk reduction (48% of all mergers), as firms sought to control markets along the lines of market power theory. These conclusions were substantiated in a study by Cowling et al. (1980) of nine major UK mergers, which concluded that the mergers did generate elements of market power, often to the detriment of consumers. Further support for this view has come from a study of UK merger trends across 200 industry sectors, ranging from pharmaceuticals to road haulage, which showed that merger activity over the period 1991–95 was closely related to industry concentration. Industries with lower concentration ratios tended to be the industries with the highest rates of merger activity as incumbent firms tried to grow larger in order to increase their market power (Schoenberg and Reeves 1999). Similarly, a global research report covering merger deals involving 107 companies worldwide by the accountancy firm KPMG found that as many as 54% of the executives concerned stated that mergers and acquisitions were aimed at gaining new market share, or protecting existing market share (KPMG 1999).

There is also fragmentary evidence that the termination of restrictive agreements encouraged some firms to combine formally. Elliot and Gribbin (1977) found that the five-firm concentration ratio increased faster in industries in which restrictive practices had been terminated than in those in which no such practices existed.

Empirical work does suggest that an increase in the size of a firm raises its market power. For example, Whittington (1980) found that large firms often experience less variability in their profits than small firms, indicating that large firms may be less susceptible to changing economic circumstances as a result of their greater market power. Studies by Aaronovitch and Sawyer (1975) also show that large firms are less likely to be taken over than small or medium-sized ones, and that a given percentage increase in size for an already large firm reduces the probability of takeover much more than the same percentage increase for a small to medium-size firm. It would appear that size, stability and market power are closely interrelated.

It may also be that profitability and market power are closely related. This would seem to be the implication of the results of a survey into 146 out of the top 500 UK firms. A questionnaire was sent to these companies asking for the responses of their respective Chief Executive Officers to a number of questions relating to merger activity (Ingham et al. 1992). From the responses to questions relating to the motives for mergers, the survey found that the single most important reason for mergers and acquisitions was the expectation of increased profitability. This was closely followed by the second most important reason – the pursuit of market power. It is therefore possible that the desire for market power and the profit motive are highly interrelated, or at least are thought to be so by significant 'players' in the market.

Nevertheless the *actual results* of merger activity provide little evidence that any increase in market power is effective in raising firm profitability. For example, Ravenscraft and Scherer (1987) conducted a detailed analysis of 6,000 acquisitions in the US between 1950 and 1976 and revealed that post-merger profitability was generally disappointing, with the profitability of around two-thirds of the merged companies *below* the average achieved prior to merger. Interestingly, the report by KPMG noted above (KPMG 1999) also found that only 17% of the mergers studied had resulted in an increase in shareholder value, with as many as 53% of the deals actually destroying shareholder value.

Economies of scale

It is often argued that the achievement of lower average costs (and thereby higher profits) through an increase in the scale of operation is the main motive for merger activity. As we noted in the earlier part of this chapter, such economies can be at two levels: first, at the level of the plant, the production unit, including the familiar technical economies of specialization, dovetailing of processes, engineers' rule, etc.; and second, at the level of the firm, the business unit, including research, marketing, administrative, managerial and financial economies. To these plant- and firm-level economies we might add the 'synergy' effect of merger, the so-called '2 + 2 > 4' effect, whereby merger increases the efficiency of the combined firm by more than the sum of its parts. Synergy could result from combining complementary activities as, for example, when one firm has a strong R & D team whilst another firm has more effective production control personnel.

Evidence

Economies of scale seem less important in merger activity than is traditionally supposed. Prais (1976) points out that technical economies, through increased plant size, have played only a small part in the growth of large firms. For instance, the growth of the 100 largest plants (production units) in net output has been much slower than the growth of the 100 largest firms (business units) in net output. Firms seem to grow not so much by expanding plant size to reap technical economies, but by acquiring more plants. Of course, evidence that firms seek to grow as an enterprise or business unit, through adding extra plants, could still be linked to securing 'firm-level' economies of scale.

Newbold (1970), however, found that only 18% of firms surveyed admitted to any motive that could be linked to plant- or firm-level economies of scale. Cowling et al. (1980) concluded in similar vein that the 'efficiency gains' (economies of scale) from mergers were difficult to identify in the firms examined. Finally, Whittington (1980) found profitability to be independent of firm size, and we have already noted that the study by Ravenscraft and Scherer (1987) saw a decline in the profitability of two-thirds of the now larger combined firms in the period following

the mergers. This might also seem to argue against any significant economies of scale, otherwise larger firms, with much lower costs, might be expected to secure higher profits. Similarly, research carried out on the performance of 11 major media companies which had been actively involved in mergers during the period up to 2000 found no significant correlation between firm size (and thus the benefits of economies of scale and scope) and company performance (Peltier 2002).

Although we cannot test the synergy effect directly, there is case evidence that it plays a part in encouraging merger activity. Nevertheless, the hopes of substantial benefits through this effect are not always realized. Unsuccessful attempts at pursuing synergy are widespread, notably by companies who mistakenly believe that they have the management and marketing expertise to turn around loss-making companies into efficient, profitable ventures. Indeed the survey by Ingham et al. (1992), mentioned earlier, placed the 'pursuit of marketing economies of scale' as the third most important reason for mergers. However, this reason was given rather infrequently, i.e. it was ranked well behind 'profitability' and 'market power'. Again, although recent EU annual reports on competition policy seem to indicate that the synergies to be derived from 'combining complementary activities' are an important motive for merger activity, this reason was also ranked well behind 'strengthening of market share' and 'expansion'.

It is, of course, possible that economies of scale as a rationale for mergers might also be linked to the cyclical patterns of demand. For example, it has been shown that the increased benefits of size in industries in which economies of scale matter often drive mergers around cyclical patterns, with firms seeking to grow larger and benefit from economies of scale when they expect demand to be high and rising (Lambrecht 2004).

Managerial theories

In all the theories considered so far, the underlying principle in merger activity is, in one way or another, the pursuit of profit. For example, market power theory suggests that through control of the firm's environment, the prospects of profit, at least in the long run, are improved. Economies of scale theory concentrates on raising profit through the reduction of cost. Managerial theories, on the other hand (see also Chapter 3), lay greater stress on non-profit motives.

With the rise of the public limited company there has been a progressive divorce between ownership by shareholders and control by management. This has given managers greater discretion in control of the company, and therefore in merger policy. The suggestion by Marris, Williamson and others is that a prime objective of managers is growth of the firm, rather than absolute size. In these theories the growth of the firm raises managerial utility by bringing higher salaries, power, status and job security to managers (Marris 1964; Williamson 1967). Managers may therefore be more interested in the rate of growth of the firm than in its profit performance.

Managerial theories would suggest that fast-growing firms, having already adopted a growth-maximization approach, are the ones most likely to be involved in merger activity. These theories would also suggest that fast-growing firms will give higher remuneration to managers, and will raise job security by being less prone to takeover.

Evidence

It does appear that it is the fast-growing firms that are mainly involved in merger activity. For example, Singh (1971, 1975) noted that the acquiring firms had a significantly higher growth rate than the acquired firms, and possessed many of the other attributes of a growth maximizer, such as a higher retention ratio (see Chapter 3), higher gearing and less liquidity (Chapter 2). Similarly, Aaronovitch and Sawyer (1975) reported that in the period before an acquisition, the acquiring firm generally grew much faster than the acquired firm. Ravenscraft and Scherer (1987) in their major study of 6,000 US acquisitions concluded that the pursuit of growth rather than profit was a key factor in explaining merger activity.

As regards higher managerial remuneration through growth, Firth (1980) found a significant increase in the salaries of directors of the acquiring company after merger. The chairman's salary increased by an average of 33% in the two years following merger, compared to only 20% for the control group of companies not engaged in merger activity. More recent research carried out between 1985 and 1990 on a sample of 170 UK firms (Conyon

and Gregg 1994) showed that the remuneration of the top director was closely related to sales growth. The research also showed that company sales growth through acquisition raised the top directors' remuneration significantly above that which could have been achieved by internal or organic growth. The research by Schoenberg and Reeves (1999) into UK merger activity in some 200 industrial sectors, referred to above, also found that the frequency of industry-wide mergers was closely related to the growth of sales revenue. This is in line with the growth and managerial utility motives for mergers suggested by Marris and Williamson, respectively.

Managerial theories place less stress on profit performance, and more on growth of the firm. The fact that, at least in the short run, the profit level often deteriorates for the acquiring firms is taken by some as further evidence in support of the managerial approach. A number of studies have showed that firms involved in mergers tended to have lower profitability levels than non-merging firms; in studies by Meeks (1977), Kumar (1985), Cosh *et al.* (1985) and Ravenscraft and Scherer (1987), mergers were found to have negative effects on profitability.

We have already noted that large firms, whilst not necessarily the most profitable (Meeks and Whittington 1975), were less likely to be taken over than small to medium-sized firms. In fact, any given percentage increase in size was much more significant in reducing the probability of takeover for the large firm than it was for the small to medium-sized firm (Aaronovitch and Sawyer 1975; Singh 1975). The small to medium-sized firm has therefore an incentive to become large, and the large firm still larger, if takeovers are to be resisted. Further evidence in support of the suggestion that small to medium-sized firms are active in acquisitions came from a survey of some 2,000 firms in UK manufacturing industry between 1960 and 1976 (Kumar 1985). The study concluded that there was indeed a tendency for firm growth through acquisitions to be *negatively* related to firm size. Once firms become large they appear to be more 'stable' and less prone to takeover. Such evidence is consistent with managerial theories which stress the importance of growth as a means of enhancing job security for managers. However, it should be noted that the merger boom of the late 1980s showed that even large firms were no longer safe from takeovers; this was in part due to firms now having easier access to the finance required for takeover activity.

The evidence clearly points away from traditional economies of scale, whether at the level of 'plant' or 'firm', as the motive for merger. Survival of the firm, and control of its environment, seems to be at the heart of most merger activity. This often implies the sacrifice of profit, at least in the short run. Such an observation is consistent with market power and managerial theories, both of which concentrate on objectives other than short-run profit (see also Chapter 3).

Mergers and the public interest

Although there is clearly much debate about the motivation behind merger activity, there is a broad consensus that the resulting growth in firm size will have implications for the 'public interest'. Before a more detailed investigation into the legislation and institutions involved in regulating merger activity in the UK, EU and US, it may be helpful to consider the potential impacts of a merger on economic efficiency and economic welfare, which are two key elements in any definition of the 'public interest'.

Economic efficiency

The idea of economic efficiency may usefully be broken down into two separate elements.

1 *Productive efficiency.* This involves using the most efficient combination of resources to produce a *given level* of output. Only when the firm is producing a given level of output with the *least-cost* methods of production available do we regard it as having achieved 'productive efficiency'.

2 *Allocative efficiency.* This is often taken to mean setting a price which corresponds to the marginal cost of production. The idea here is that consumers pay firms exactly what it costs them to produce the last (marginal) unit of output; such a pricing strategy can be shown to be a key condition in achieving a so-called 'Pareto optimum' resource allocation, where it is no longer possible to make someone better off without making someone else worse off. Any deviation of price *away from* marginal cost is then seen as resulting in 'allocative inefficiency'.

What may pose problems for policymakers is that the impacts of proposed mergers may move these two aspects of economic efficiency in *opposite directions*. For example, economies of scale may result from the merger having increased firm size, with a lower cost of producing any given output thereby improving productive efficiency. However, the greater market power associated with increased size may give the enlarged firm new opportunities to raise price above (or still further above) its costs of production, including marginal costs, thereby reducing allocative efficiency.

We may need to balance the gain in productive efficiency against the loss in allocative efficiency to get a better idea of the overall impact of the merger on the 'public interest'.

Economic welfare

Economic welfare is a branch of economics which often involves ideas of consumer surplus and producer surplus.

- *Consumer surplus.* This is the benefit to consumers of being willing to pay *more* for a product than they actually have to pay in terms of the going market price. It is usually measured by the area underneath the demand (willingness to pay) curve and above the ruling market price. So in Fig. 5.2, if the ruling market price is P and quantity sold Q, then area *afd* corresponds to the 'consumer surplus', in the sense that consumers are willing to pay O*afQ* for Q units, but only have to pay O*dfQ* (price × quantity), giving a consumer surplus of *afd*.

- *Producer surplus.* This is the benefit to producers of receiving a price *higher* than the price they actually needed to get them to supply the product. In Fig. 5.2 we shall assume for simplicity that the MC curve is the firm's supply curve (you should know that this actually *is* the case in a perfectly competitive industry!). So in Fig. 5.2, if the ruling market price is P and the quantity sold Q, then area *dfig* corresponds to the 'producer surplus', in the sense that producers are willing to supply Q units at a price of g but actually receive a price of P, giving them a producer surplus of *dg* per unit, and a total producer's surplus of *dfig* on all Q units sold.

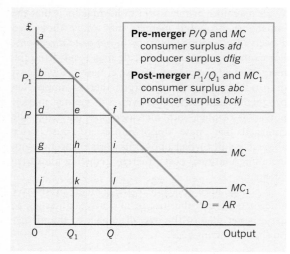

Fig. 5.2 Mergers, economic efficiency and economic welfare. Welfare gain (*ghkj*) and welfare loss (*cflk*) from merger.

Figure 5.2 is useful in illustrating the fact that a proposed merger might move productive and allocative efficiencies in opposite directions. For simplicity we assume the curves displayed to be linear, and the firm to be at an initial price/quantity equilibrium of P/Q with marginal cost MC (for a profit-maximizing firm MR would have intersected MC at point *i*). Now suppose that the merger/takeover results in the (enlarged) firm[2] using its market power to raise price from P to P_1, cutting output from Q to Q_1, *but* that at the same time the newly available scale economies cut costs so that MC shifts downwards to MC_1.

Clearly we have to balance a loss of allocative efficiency against a gain in productive efficiency in order to assess the overall impact on the 'public interest'. To do this we can usefully return to the idea of economic welfare, and the associated consumer and producer surpluses.

If we regard the total welfare resulting from a resource allocation as being the sum of the consumer surplus and the producer surplus, we have:

- pre-merger   *afd + dfig*
- post-merger   *abc + bckj*

In terms of total welfare (consumer surplus + producer surplus) we can note the following impacts of the merger:

- gain of welfare   *ghkj*
- loss of welfare   *cflk*

The 'gain of welfare' (*ghkj*) represents the improvement in productive efficiency from the merger, as the Q_1 units still produced require fewer resources than before, now that the scale economies have reduced costs (shifting MC down to MC_1).

The 'loss of welfare' (*cflk*) represents the deterioration in allocative efficiency from the merger; price has risen (P to P_1) and marginal costs have fallen (MC to MC_1), further increasing the gap between price and marginal cost. As a result of the price rise from P to P_1, output has fallen from Q to Q_1. This loss of output has reduced economic welfare, since society's willingness to pay for these lost $Q - Q_1$ units (the area under the demand curve from $Q - Q_1$, i.e. $cfQQ_1$) exceeds the cost of producing them (the sum of all the marginal costs from $Q - Q_1$, i.e. $klQQ_1$) by *cflk*.

Clearly the overall welfare effect ('public interest') could be positive or negative, depending on whether the welfare gains exceed the welfare losses, or vice versa (in Fig. 5.2 the losses outweigh the gains). No pre-judgement can therefore be made that a merger will, or will not be, in the public interest. As Stewart (1996) notes, everything depends on the extent of any price rise and on the demand and cost curve configurations for any proposed merger. It is in this context that a Competition Commission (CC) investigation and other methods of enquiry into *particular* proposals might be regarded as important in deciding whether any merger should proceed or be abandoned.

In 2006 the CC attempted to place a money value on the potential welfare losses to consumers resulting from mergers. The summary of the commission's findings can be seen in Table 5.1.

The four merger enquiries shown in Table 5.1 were carried out between March 2005 and March 2006. The SDEL/Coors merger involved the equipment used to dispense beer and some other drinks in pubs; the Somerfield/Morrisons deal involved the sale of 115 grocery stores in certain UK locations, raising the problem of local market power; the LSE/Euronext/Deutsche Borse involved two bids for the London Stock Exchange; and Vue/Ster related to the transfer of six cinemas in the UK from Ster to Vue. The figures in the table attempt to assess the likely price rises resulting from the lessening of competition (SLC) and the associated welfare loss of consumer surplus.

Table 5.1 Estimated costs to consumers of the mergers against which the CC took action between March 2005 and March 2006.

Inquiry	Estimated costs to consumers per annum (£)
SDEL/Coors	13.9
Somerfield/Morrisons	5.5
LSE/Euronext/Deutsche Borse	11.8
Vue/Ster	0.3
Total	**31.5**

Source: Competition Commission (2006) July, p. 2.

The combined welfare loss to the consumers of these projected mergers was calculated to be £31.5m per annum. For example, in the SDEL/Coors deal it was calculated that the merger would have increased the price of beer per barrel by £1, amounting to a loss of consumer surplus of £12m per annum in the UK – plus an estimated additional loss of £1.9m due to quality deterioration. None of these four cases was given permission to merge their activities because of the substantial estimated loss of consumer welfare.

Merger booms

The most notable features which have tended to galvanize merger and takeover activity have often included the following.

1 The growth of national and international markets has created circumstances favourable to economies of scale, while at the same time world tariff barriers have been reduced under the guidance of GATT (now the WTO). The result has been fierce competition between nations which has often led to a rationalization of production since larger firms have been seen as having important cost advantages.

2 Improved communication methods, often involving information/telecommunication technologies, have made it easier for large companies to grow, while the adoption by many companies of a multi-divisional structure has encouraged horizontal mergers.

3 There has been a rapid growth in the number and type of financial intermediaries, such as insurance companies and investment trusts. They have begun investing heavily in company equity, thereby providing a ready source of finance for companies who want to issue more shares and then to use the money received to support a takeover bid. At the same time, there has been a dilution of managerial control (see Chapter 3). This 'divorce of ownership from control' has made takeover activity easier because directors now have a less close relationship with the company, and are therefore less committed to its continuing in an unchanged form.

4 Many of the periods of intense merger activity have seen an increase in the 'gearing ratio' of companies, i.e. an increase in the ratio of debt (debenture and bank borrowing) to shares (equity). Loan finance has proven attractive because the interest paid on debentures and loans has been deducted from company profits *before* it is taxed. Therefore companies have had a tax incentive to issue loan stock, the money from which they have then been able to use to mount a takeover bid.

Figure 5.3 shows the trend in UK mergers between 1973 and 2009 in terms of number of acquisitions, their value and also the breakdown according to whether the acquisitions were domestic or cross border.

The motives for such intense takeover activity have been varied. For example, many of the 1985–89 mergers were of the *horizontal* type, suggesting that one important motive for such activity was production economies arising from rationalization. This motive may have been strengthened by the desire to integrate technology and to improve marketing expertise in order to increase market power. There is also some evidence that *target* companies in this period tended to be less dependent on debt finance, which suggests that some acquisitions may have been due to the desire of the *acquirer* to increase cashflow and to reduce its dependency on debt finance. A study of 38 UK takeovers between 1985 and 1987 (Manson *et al.* 1994) seemed to provide some evidence of such motives. These authors found that the takeovers studied did produce operating gains in terms of both cashflow and market values.

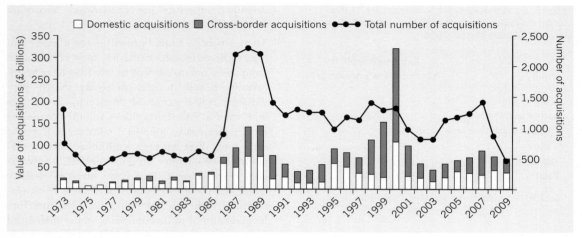

Fig. 5.3 UK mergers 1973–2009.
Source: ONS (2010) *Mergers and Acquisitions involving UK Companies,* September, and previous issues.

During this period, mergers were largely financed by share issues. The value of the more dynamic bidder's share would often tend to be higher than the value of the target company's share, giving the bidder the opportunity to exchange the minimum number of its shares for every one of the target company's. This meant that the takeover deal was relatively 'cheap' for the bidder so that its earnings per share (EPS – total earnings/total number of shares) would not fall too much to worry its existing shareholders and the stock market in general. After the stock market crash in late 1987, however, the decrease in share prices and the rise in interest rates meant that takeovers increasingly involved cash deals rather than share issues.

Merger and acquisition activity during 1992–2009 has been triggered by many factors, including merger opportunities in utilities such as electricity and water, and attempts to secure greater market share in the pharmaceutical, telecommunications and finance industries in order to gain scale economies and provide a base for global expansion. Examples of such mergers in the UK utilities sector include the acquisition of the Lattice Group by the National Grid Group for £5.1bn in 2002 to form National Grid Transco plc, a major supplier of electricity and gas. In the telecommunication industry, the takeover of the German company Mannesmann AG by the UK's Vodafone Air Touch plc in 2000 created Europe's largest telecommunication company and accounted

for much of the high value figure for mergers in that year. In the same year the £120bn merger of UK companies Glaxo Wellcome and SmithKline Beecham to form GlaxoSmithKline resulted in one of the largest pharmaceutical companies in the world. In the insurance industry, the £1.8bn merger of two UK firms, the Britannic Group and Resolution Life Group, in 2005 created a company with combined assets of over £35bn and helped to reflect the increased merger activity after 2003. The number of acquisitions rose until 2007 before decreasing both in number and value as a result of the insecurity of the global financial crisis and the slowdown in the major economies.

Another feature of the merger trends of the last 35 years is the increasing importance of cross-border acquisitions as a proportion of all mergers involving UK firms. The Single Market and the greater integration of the EU, together with the effects of globalization noted previously, have provided a platform for greater involvement by UK firms in international acquisitions, as was seen in Fig. 5.3.

The control of mergers and acquisitions

We have seen that mergers may be a means of extending market power. We now consider how the UK, the

EU and the US have sought to exercise control over merger activity in order to prevent the abuse of such power.

The UK experience

United Kingdom legislation has been tentative in its approach to merger activity, recognizing the desirable qualities of some monopoly situations created through merger; it therefore seeks to examine each case on its individual merits. The first UK legislation, the Monopolies and Restrictive Practices (Inquiry and Control) Act, dates from 1948 and set up the Monopolies Commission. The power of the 1948 Act was extended to mergers by the Monopolies and Mergers Act of 1965 under which the newly established Monopolies and Mergers Commission (MMC) could now report on situations where a merger resulted in a combined market share of 25% or more of a particular good or service, or involved combined assets of over £30m.

The next major Act having implications for merger activity was the Fair Trading Act 1973, under which the Office of Fair Trading (OFT) was formed with a Director-General of Fair Trading (DGFT) as its head. Over the next quarter of a century, the DGFT advised the Secretary of State for Trade and Industry as to which mergers should be referred to the MMC for investigation. However, the Secretary of State could overrule both the DGFT and the MMC if he or she felt that the merger was in the 'public interest', which was nowhere clearly defined. This vague 'public interest' test often led to complaints by business of undue and arbitrary government involvement in the decision-making process as regards permitting or prohibiting merger activity.

Problems with UK merger policy

As already noted, by the 1990s the effectiveness of the MMC and the role of the Secretary of State in merger investigations were increasingly being called into question. For example, the MMC was criticized for lacking both resources and a professional attitude. It had one full-time chairman, three part-time deputy chairmen, 31 part-time commissioners and only 100 full-time staff. Many argued that the MMC was often 'outgunned' by lawyers representing firms under investigation and, with its scarce resources, was unable to properly scrutinize many potentially important merger proposals. For example, between 1950 and 1995 the MMC had investigated only 171 merger cases.

The traditional UK approach to mergers was based on the principle that they can be forbidden by the Secretary of State if they operate against the public interest. The vagueness of the term 'public interest', together with the differing approaches to mergers of individual Secretaries of State, led to what many saw as inconsistent decision-making in merger policy over time. For example, the Labour government had recommended in 1978 that the MMC should recognize the benefits as well as the costs of merger activity in their deliberations. However, the following Conservative government issued guidelines in 1984 suggesting that the MMC should concentrate on 'loss of competition' as the most important aspect when assessing mergers. By 1992, the Conservative government's approach to mergers seems to have shifted ground yet again, with the DTI placing greater emphasis on creating 'national champions' capable of competing in international markets – thereby supporting larger mergers even when some 'loss of competition' was inevitable. Yet by 1996, Ian Laing, the new Conservative Secretary of State for Trade and Industry, announced that 'fostering competition' rather than the creation of national champions should be the guideline for assessing merger policy. This followed the refusal of the minister to allow either National Power's £2.8bn bid for Southern Electric or PowerGen's £1.9bn bid for Midland Electricity to proceed. These ever-shifting approaches to merger activity indicate some degree of strategic confusion in the implementation of merger policy.

In addition to the problems noted above, there were also increasing complications as regards the power of the Secretary of State during merger references. For example, the Secretary of State had the power to overrule recommendations from both the DGFT and the MMC if he or she was so minded. For example, in 1993 the then Secretary of State at the DTI, Michael Heseltine, rejected the recommendation of the DGFT to refer both GEC's acquisition of Philips' infra-red components business and the hostile bid by Airtours for Owners Abroad to the MMC. The Secretary of State argued that the mergers might help rationalize the industry and create strong competitive companies so that, despite the competition-based concerns of the DGFT, he declined to refer these proposed mergers to the MMC for further scrutiny.

Again, in August 1998 Margaret Beckett, the Secretary of State for Trade and Industry, overruled the recommendation of the MMC in the case of First Group, a transport company which had made a £96m acquisition of Glasgow-based SB Holdings. The MMC believed that First Group should be allowed to acquire SB Holdings only if it agreed to sell a division of its Scottish operations to decrease the company's market power. However, the Secretary of State allowed the merger to proceed without any such restriction on the grounds that a rival company, Stagecoach, had entered the Glasgow bus market, thus creating sufficient competitive conditions.

These inconsistencies in merger policy continued even after the replacement of the MMC by the Competition Commission (CC) under the provisions of the 1998 Competition Act. Again there was criticism of inadequate resources in the CC, which had a relatively small staff of 78 persons and a grant income of only £5.9m, the concern being that it might become a 'toothless tiger', used only for appeals against merger decisions rather than itself being a key decision taker. A series of consultation documents were published between 1999 and 2001 culminating in the Enterprise Act of 2002, which received the Royal Assent on November 2002 and was brought into force, in stages, from the spring of 2003 onwards.

Current merger legislation: Enterprise Act 2002

The Enterprise Act 2002 overhauled UK competition law and, amongst other things, restated the UK merger control framework by introducing significant amendments to previous legislation in this area. The main aspects of current merger legislation now include the following.

1 **Relevant merger situation.** Under the Act, a 'relevant merger situation' to which the new procedures potentially apply is one in which *three* criteria are met:

   ■ First, that the two or more enterprises involved in the merger cease to be distinct as a result of the merger.

   ■ Second, that the merger must not have taken place, or have taken place not more than four months before the reference is made to the OFT.

   ■ Third, *either* that the enterprise being taken over has a UK turnover exceeding £70m (the 'turnover test') *or* that the merged enterprises together supply, or acquire, at least 25% of all those particular goods or services supplied in the UK or a substantial part of the UK (the 'share of supply' test). It is implicit in this criterion that at least one enterprise must trade within the UK.

2 **Competition authorities evaluation test.** Under the Act, for a 'relevant merger situation', the test which the OFT will apply when evaluating whether a merger should be referred to the CC is whether the merger or proposed merger has resulted, or may be expected to result, in a substantial 'lessening of competition' within the relevant market or markets in the UK. 'Lessening of competition' would generally mean a situation where product choice would be reduced, prices raised, or product quality or innovation reduced as the result of merger activity. However, the OFT might decide *not* to make a reference to the CC if it believes that customer benefits (e.g. higher choice, lower prices, higher quality or innovation) resulting from the merger outweigh the substantial lessening of competition noted above. Similarly, the CC when considering a merger in more depth will also weigh the 'lessening of competition' effect against the 'public benefits effect' before making its final decision.

3 **Competition authorities.** Under the Act, the OFT was established as an independent statutory body and the post of DGFT was abolished.

   ■ As a result of its new statutory power the OFT can require the provision of information and documents, enter premises under warrant, and seize material. It has explicit duties to keep markets under review and to promote competition. It publishes an annual report on its activities and performance which is laid before Parliament. It also has the functions of advising the Secretary of State on mergers which might fall under the scope of the 'public interest'.

   ■ The CC, which was already an independent statutory body, continues its in-depth investigation of any merger cases referred to it by the OFT or less frequently by the Secretary of State. The CC determines the outcome of such cases and reports its decision to the Secretary of State.

■ The Secretary of State for Business, Innovation and Skills has retained power to make decisions for mergers involving newspaper transfers and in certain public interest cases such as those that deal with national security. Apart from these specified types of merger situations, the main decisions relating to mergers are now dealt with by the OFT and CC without resort to the Secretary of State.

■ There is also a new appeals mechanism giving a right to those parties involved in the merger to apply to the Competition Appeal Tribunal (CAT) for a statutory judicial review of a decision of the OFT, CC or the Secretary of State. There is also a further right of appeal (on a point of law only) to the Court of Appeal.

Putting merger policy into practice

To understand the main procedures for merger investigation, a brief account will be given here of the process. When the OFT is made aware of the 'relevant merger situation', it may choose to undertake a 'first stage' investigation. It might seek to assess the potential effect of the merger on market structure. For example, if it is a horizontal-type merger then market shares, concentration ratios or the Herfindahl–Hirschman Index (see below, p. 100) might be used as initial indicators of potential competition concerns. This market structure assessment could be followed by an examination of whether the entry of new firms into the market is easy or difficult and whether any 'lessening of competition' is likely to occur. The OFT will then make its own decision on the case without reference to the Secretary of State. The OFT will give one of three possible decisions.

1 The merger is given an unconditional clearance.

2 The merger is given a clearance only if the parties agree to modify their uncompetitive behaviour or decrease their market power.

3 The merger may turn out to be serious enough to refer it directly to the CC for a 'second-stage' investigation. At this point the Secretary of State can intervene in the proceedings, but under the new regime this intervention can be done only in *very specific* circumstances involving mergers with media, national security or other narrowly specified implications.

If the OFT refers the merger to the CC, the Commission will consider the evidence of the OFT but will also make its own in-depth report on the merger. After consideration of the evidence and basing its views on both the 'lessening of competition' and 'customer benefits criteria', the CC will recommend that one of three possible actions be taken: (i) an unconditional clearance, or (ii) a clearance subject to conditions proposed by the CC, or (iii) an outright prohibition. If the CC recommends conditional clearance then the companies involved may be asked to divest some of their assets or to ensure in some specified way that competition is maintained (e.g. giving licences to their competitors). Again, the Secretary of State may intervene only in very limited circumstances as in the media, national security or other specified issues (e.g. if one of the parties to the merger is a government contractor). If the decision of the CC is to prohibit the merger, the parties can appeal to the CAT.

In essence, the Enterprise Act has *depersonalized* competition authority by abolishing the post of DGFT. It has also improved the overall *predictability* of the mergers investigation procedure by de-politicizing the process of merger control. It has done this by severely curtailing the involvement of the Secretary of State and by giving expert independent bodies (the OFT and CC) more power. Basically, the OFT and CC have been transformed from essentially advisory bodies to the Secretary of State to independent bodies with their own decision-making powers. The Act has also *clarified* merger control policy by introducing the 'lessening of competition' test in place of the old 'public interest' test and by allowing potential benefits (including public benefits) to be considered. In addition, the Act made the mergers regime more *transparent* by obliging both the OFT and the CC to consult fully with companies involved in mergers and provide the parties involved with their provisional findings. Finally, the new mergers regime seeks to introduce a *fairness* criterion in that companies now have the right of appeal to the CAT.

However, an appeal to the CAT in 2004 created shock waves for the OFT. The OFT had decided *not* to refer to the Competition Commission a merger between two healthcare IT companies, namely iSOFT and Torax, involved in supplying data systems to the NHS. A third company, IBA Health Ltd, appealed to the CAT that the merger was unfair and would lessen competition. The CAT upheld IBA's appeal and asked the OFT to reconsider its decision, arguing that the OFT needed to be satisfied that there had been no *significant* lessening of competition. The OFT then took the case to the Court of Appeal, arguing that the CAT had wrongly interpreted the Enterprise Act 2002. However, in February 2004 the Court of Appeal upheld the CAT's findings so that this judgment may make the OFT more likely to refer future proposed mergers to the Competition Commission, which some see as leading to a less flexible system of merger control.

The City Code on Takeovers and Mergers

The City Code on Takeovers and Mergers ('the Code') was published by the Financial Services Authority (FSA) in April 2001 in order to reinforce London's reputation for clean and fair financial markets and offer better protection to consumers. The Code is 'designed to ensure that shareholders are treated fairly and are not denied an opportunity to decide on the merits of a takeover, and that shareholders of the same class are afforded equivalent treatment by an offeror'. In other words, the Code seeks to outline acceptable standards of commercial behaviour as regards the behaviour of offerors and offerees during takeovers or proposed takeovers.

The Code is administered by the Panel on Take-overs and Mergers ('the Panel') which was established in 1968 and which now carries out certain regulatory functions in relation to the EU Takeover Directive Regulations 2006. Prior to 2006 the Panel did not have statutory powers, although failure to observe the Code's provisions could expose FSA-regulated firms to discipline. The Panel's powers were originally limited to issuing a private reprimand, public censure, or reporting a breach of the Code to the FSA or another body by which the offender is regulated. Since 2006, however, the status of the Panel has been underpinned by legislation in respect of the EU Direc-tive on Takeover Bids noted above. For bids falling within the scope of the EU Directive, the Panel has additional powers to require certain people to produce documents and information, and can apply to a court for enforcement where there is a reasonable likelihood that a person has contravened a Code rule contained within the EU Directive. Although the general aim of the Code continues to be to ensure that takeovers bids are conducted fairly (i.e. with equal treatment for all shareholders), with adequate production of

relevant documentation and no special deals or false markets, the penalties for non-compliance are now much higher after adapting the Code to the EU Directive. For example, it will be a criminal offence if a takeover offer document in a bid falling within the scope of the EU Directive fails to contain all the information required by the relevant rules of the Code.

Insider dealing

On a wider issue, the whole question of 'insider deal-ing' came to the fore during this period. This type of dealing occurs when company shares are bought by those who have special privileged information about the future of the company, e.g. the possibility of an imminent takeover. By buying shares *before* a take-over announcement, for example, they can make huge gains as share prices rise when the excitement of the takeover begins. Basically, the UK has some of the most advanced insider-dealing regulations in the world.

Important UK legislation regulating insider deal-ing came into force in 1994 and extended the scope of the main Companies Securities (Insider Dealing) Act of 1985. Under the 1993 Criminal Justice Act it is a criminal offence for an individual who has inside information to deal in price affected securities (such as shares, debt securities, gilts and derivatives whose price movements could be sensitive to certain infor-mation), or to encourage another person to deal. It is also a criminal offence for such an individual to disclose the information to another person, other than as part of his or her professional work. The deal-ing in question must be either on a regulated market (basically all EU primary and secondary markets) or off-market but involving professional intermediaries who deal in securities.

However, it has proved difficult to prosecute cases under criminal law and so the Financial Services Markets Act 2000 (FSMA) was passed which pro-vided the opportunity to transfer regulatory powers to the FSA and to overhaul the law. The FSA was given power to impose civil sanctions, including fines, on persons engaged in market abuse, which included insider dealing. The FSMA regime was changed again in January 2003 to comply with the EU Market Abuse Directive (MAD) of that year. MAD was finally implemented in the UK in 2005 through the Market Abuse Regulations 2005, appended to the Act of 2000. An insider is now defined as any person who has access to inside information as a result of certain positions held or activities undertaken. The UK maintains the requirement that for an offence to be committed, the inside dealer must 'use' the information when dealing – dealing merely when in possession of inside information is not sufficient to constitute an offence. In February 2006 an FSA committee found that a top manager at the London-based hedge fund GLG Partners LP was guilty of market abuse for selling borrowed Sumitomo Mitsui Financial Group (SMFG) securities after he received confidential information from a salesman at Goldman Sachs Group. The manager and the company were each fined £750,000. In March 2010 a former equities dealer at the stock broker Cazanove was found guilty of insider dealing, having made £103,883 profit from such activity between 2003 and 2004. In this case, criminal proceedings were instigated and the dealer was given a 21 months sentence.

The EU experience

Many European countries have long histories of state intervention in markets so it is hardly surprising that the European Commission accepts the case for intervention by member governments. Apart from agriculture, competition is the only area in which the EU has been able to implement effectively a common policy across member countries. The Commission can intervene to control the behaviour of monopolists and to increase the degree of competition through authority originally derived from the Treaty of Rome. However, the Treaty of Lisbon in 2007 amended the EU's two core treaties, i.e. the Treaty on European Union (Maastricht Treaty) and the Treaty establishing the European Union (Treaty of Rome). The latter was renamed the Treaty on the Functioning of the European Union (TFEU) and contains three main articles which deal with monopoly and competition.

1 Article 101 prohibits agreements between enterprises which result in the restriction of competition (notably relating to price-fixing, market-sharing, production limitations and other restrictive practices). This article refers to any agreement affecting trade between member states and therefore applies to a large number of British industries.
2 Article 102 prohibits a dominant firm, or group of firms, from using their market power to exploit consumers.

3 Article 107 prohibits government subsidies to industries or individual firms which will distort, or threaten to distort, competition.

Mergers and EU industry

There are significant number of mergers which occur in Europe in any given year, most of which are completed without any problems. However, there are some mergers which may cause distortions in competition and are then notified to the Commission for scrutiny. There were 4,274 notifications to the Commission relating to merger activity between 1991 and 2009, of which some 87% have been given unconditional clearance to continue and only 5% were referred onwards for a more in-depth study. Of these, only 20 or 10% were prohibited. Looking at it another way, of the 4,274 early notifications to the Commission only 20 cases were finally prohibited. An in-depth breakdown of the nature of such notifications can be seen in a more limited sample of notifications to the EU Commission between 1990 and 2002 which were deemed by the Commission to exercise 'unacceptable' power within the EU.

The word 'merger' is often used to cover a wider range of different types of concentrative activity. In recent years joint ventures and acquisition of the majority of assets accounted for 86% of notifications of mergers and acquisitions to the EU Commission, while 'agreed bids' accounted for only 6% of total activity. Of course, mergers and acquisitions can take a variety of formal and less formal structures, with 'alliances' sometimes a more accurate term for the emerging relationship. Microsoft and Yahoo entered into an Internet search alliance in 2010, approved by US and EU regulation authorities. Daimler and Renault entered into a cross-shareholding alliance in March 2010 to gain scale economies in small car production, as did Mazda and Toyota in 2010 to share expensive R&D investment costs for hybrid and electric cars.

An interesting strategic view of the merger process has been indicated by surveys of top executives across six of Europe's most actively acquisitive countries (Angwin and Savill 1997). The results showed that the top four reasons for expanding into other countries through acquisitions were, in order:

■ the growing similarity between both national and EU markets;

- the ability to find a good strategic fit;
- establishing a market presence overseas ahead of others; and
- obtaining greater growth potential at a lower cost abroad than at home.

The most appropriate *target company* for acquisition was quoted as being a company which has a good strategic fit with the acquirer, is financially healthy, and has a relatively strong market (or market niche) position. Over the last decade corporate mergers have tended to involve the core activities of the merging companies, resulting in more horizontal-type mergers. For example, the purchase by Volkswagen of Rolls-Royce for £430m in 1998 was aimed at strengthening its core activities, with higher volumes permitting the scale economies which might allow more effective competition in world markets, while at the same time improving the strategic fit, since Volkswagen wanted to compete more actively in the luxury car market in which Rolls-Royce had a greater presence.

A number of advantages were cited by the top executives surveyed for using acquisitions rather than joint ventures or other methods of entry into other EU markets, with an important one being that acquisitions were seen as a faster and less risky method of building up a critical mass in another country.

European competition policy has been criticized for its lack of comprehensiveness, but in December 1989 the Council of Ministers agreed for the first time on specific cross-border merger regulations. The criteria for judging whether a merger should be referred to the European Commission covered three aspects. First, the companies concerned must have a combined world turnover of more than €5bn (though for insurance companies the figure was based on total assets rather than turnover). Second, at least two of the companies concerned in the merger must have a Community-wide turnover of at least €250m each. Third, if both parties to the merger have two-thirds of their business in one and the same member state, the merger was to be subject to national and not Community controls.

The Commission must be notified of merger proposals which meet the criteria noted above within one week of the announcement of the bid and it will vet each proposed merger against a concept of 'a dominant position'. Any creation or strengthening of a dominant position will be seen as incompatible with the aims of the Community if it significantly impedes 'effective competition'. The Commission has one month after notification to decide whether to start proceedings and then four months to make a final decision. If a case is being investigated by the Commission it will not also be investigated by national bodies such as the British Monopolies and Mergers Commission, for example. Member states may prevent a merger which has already been permitted by the Community only if it involves public security or some aspects of the media or if competition in the local markets is threatened.

Review of EU merger regulation

A number of reservations were expressed about the 1990 legislation. First, a main aim of the legislation was to introduce the 'one stop shop' which meant that merging companies would be liable to either European *or* national merger control and not both. However, as can be seen above, there were situations where national merger control could override EU control in certain instances so that there may be a 'two stop shop'! Second, it was not clear how the rules would apply to non-EU companies. For example, it was quite possible that two US or Japanese companies each with the required amount of *sales* in the Community, but with no actual Community *presence*, could merge. While such a case would certainly fall within the EU merger rules, it was not clear how seriously the Commission would pursue its powers in such cases. Third, guidelines were also needed on joint ventures.

In March 1998 a number of amendments were made to the scope of EU cross-border merger regulations, in effect increasing the number of mergers which can be referred to the EU Commission. The threshold (turnover) figures noted earlier had been criticized for being set at too high a level, so that only large mergers could be referred *exclusively* to the Commission, thereby meeting the 'one stop shop' principle. Of course, such an approach suited many individual member countries of the EU which did not want to cede to the Commission their own national authority to investigate mergers. However, by 1996 the EU Commission had suggested a 'middle road' whereby the old higher thresholds could remain but in which other thresholds would be introduced to allow more mergers to be dealt with exclusively by the Commission.

The result of these amendments is that the three original criteria for exclusive reference to the Commission remain, but other criteria have been added to cover some mergers which would not be large enough to qualify under the €5bn and €250m rules described earlier. For example, the Commission can now assume exclusive jurisdiction for any merger if the following three new, and rather complicated, conditions *all* hold true: first, if the combined aggregate worldwide turnover of the undertakings concerned exceeds €2.5bn; *and* second, if in each of at least three Member States, the combined aggregate turnover of the undertakings concerned is more than €100m; *and* third, if in each of the same three Member States, the aggregate turnover of each of at least two of the undertakings concerned exceeds €25m. The Commission believes that the new thresholds may result in more companies having the choice of making only one filing to the Commission instead of multiple national filings (i.e. there will now be more 'one stop shop' opportunities). Of course, the difficulty of calculating more turnover figures than before will add to the complexity of the whole process. To date the Commission has handled around 80 merger cases per year since 1991, and the new legislation will perhaps increase this by another eight mergers per year.

As regards joint ventures, the new regulations make a distinction between 'concentrative' joint ventures and 'cooperative' joint ventures, with the new Commission rules applying to the first type (which was seen to concentrate power) but not to the second (which was merely seen as a method to coordinate competitive behaviour). The second type was to be covered by Articles 81 and 82 (formerly Articles 85 and 86) of the Treaty of Rome, as before.

In 2000, a review of the merger approval system was instigated by the EU. By November 2002 it was announced that a package of reforms would be introduced that would take effect from May 2004. Therefore on 1 May 2004 a new regime for regulating mergers, acquisitions and joint ventures was passed under Regulation 139/2004. The changes consisted of a new substantive test to assess transactions; changes to the rules on jurisdiction which determine when the European Commission rather than the Office of Fair Trading (OFT) will be responsible for a deal; and changes which strengthen the Commission's powers of investigation and enforcement.

Under the old regime, the test for prohibiting a transaction was whether it would 'create or strengthen a dominant position as a result of which effective competition would be significantly impeded in the common market....' Under the new regime, the test is whether a transaction would 'significantly impede effective competition in the common market, in particular as a result of . . . a dominant position.' This change in wording was designed to cover markets in which the enlarged firm, while not dominant, is still likely to result in anti-competitive results. In addition, the wording also reflects the desire of some countries to move towards the UK mergers policy where a 'significant lessening of competition' is an important criterion for assessing mergers.

As far as jurisdiction is concerned, the new regulations leave intact the primary test for determining when a merger notification needs to be made to the European Commission. However, the new regulation grants parties to the merger additional rights, in certain limited circumstances, to request that a deal be subject to a competition authority within the national jurisdiction rather than EU. The idea is to ensure that the best-placed competition authority is the one that examines a proposed deal. Finally, the new regulations slightly extend the time available for the Competition Commission to complete its investigations, and its powers to issue fines have also been strengthened such that fines of up to 1% of aggregate turnover will now be possible.

The US experience

American legislation reflects a much more vigilant attitude towards mergers, dating from the Sherman Anti-Trust Act of 1890. Monopolies were considered illegal from the outset, resulting in a much less flexible approach to the control of monopoly power. Present merger legislation in the US is covered under the Clayton Act (1914), the Celler/Kaufman Act (1950) and the Hart–Scott–Rodino Act (1976), with the laws being enforced by the Federal Department of Justice and the Federal Trade Commission.

Since 1968 US merger guidelines have directed attention to the market power exerted by the four largest companies in any market. The rigidity of using merely the four largest companies (see Fig. 5.4 and the discussion below) for evaluating merger proposals has been extensively criticized, and in June 1982 the US Justice Department issued new proposals. These included establishing a new 'screening' index to alert

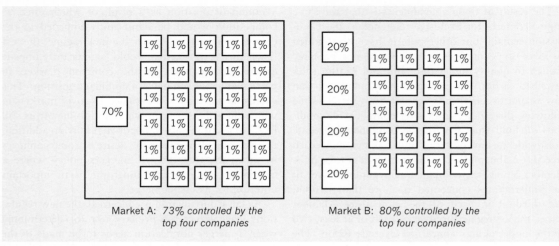

Market A: 73% controlled by the top four companies

Market B: 80% controlled by the top four companies

Fig. 5.4 Hypothetical markets in the construction of market concentration indices.

the Justice Department as to which merger proposals were worthy of closer scrutiny and which should be immediately prohibited or 'nodded through'. That index was to reflect the whole market and not just the four largest firms.

The so-called 'Herfindahl–Hirschman Index' of market concentration was devised for this screening purpose, together with a number of guidelines for policy action. This index is constructed simply as:

$$\sum_{i=1}^{n} (\% \text{ market share})^2$$

for all n companies in the market. Using a squaring procedure places greater emphasis on the large firms in the market. We can illustrate this by first considering an index which adopts an additive procedure. If a simple additive procedure had been used over all n companies:

Market A: Index = 1(70) + 30(1) = 100
Market B: Index = 4(20) + 20(1) = 100

Here the markets would be evaluated as equally competitive, yet a strong case could be made for Market B being the more competitive. Using the Herfindahl–Hirschman Index we have:

Market A: Index = $1(70)^2 + 30(1)^2 = 4,930$
Market B: Index = $4(20)^2 + 20(1)^2 = 1,620$

The lower the index, the more competitive the market, so that Market B is deemed more competitive. The index could, in fact, vary in value from 10,000

(i.e. 100^2) for a pure monopoly, to almost zero for a perfectly competitive industry. For example, an industry consisting of 1,000 companies each with a tiny 0.1% share of the market would produce an index value of only 10 (i.e. $1,000 (0.1)^2$).

Once constructed, the interpretation of the index is still, however, subjective. Figure 5.5 illustrates the range of the index and the three zones of index value identified by the US Justice Department for policy purposes. The chosen dividing lines appear somewhat arbitrary, though it is clear from the guidelines that the two extreme zones are viewed in radically different lights. The central zone (1,000–1,800) represents a policy 'grey' area, requiring more detailed scrutiny of the proposed merger. In practice, mergers in this zone will receive approval only if there is evidence of easy entry into the market, freely available substitutes and no collusive arrangements between existing members. The intention in this central zone is to prevent further acquisitions in the market by a market leader, whilst allowing smaller companies to combine more freely. The 'highly concentrated' zone (>1,800) of the index would, for instance, include any market in which two companies have shares of over 30%, so that their potential for growth of market share by further acquisition is slim – even the addition to one of these firms of a further 2% of acquisition would trigger the 100-point condition. Yet in the same market, two smaller companies with market shares of less than 5% each could combine without infringing anti-trust policies. The purchase of just one of the

Fig. 5.5 The Herfindahl–Hirschman index as an instrument of merger policy.

competing companies in hypothetical Market A of Fig. 5.4 by the dominant firm would increase the index to 5,070 (i.e. $1(71)^2 + 29(1)^2$), triggering the 100-point condition in the process and attracting the attentions of the Justice Department.

To see how such guidelines would operate within the UK context, it might be interesting to take the Monopolies and Mergers Commission report on the UK insulation market, published in May 1991. The merger which was investigated was between Morgan Crucible Plc, an international group based in the UK, and Manville Corporation, a US company. Both companies produced RCF (Refractory Ceramic Fibre) which is used in the steel, petrochemical and aluminium industries as a high temperature heat insulator. The market for RCF in the UK was supplied by the following companies; Carborundum (50%), Morgan Crucible (27%), Kerlane (12%), Manville (9%) and others (2%).

Under the Herfindahl–Hirschman index the industry would already have been regarded as concentrated, with a value of 3,458 (i.e. $1(50)^2 + 1(27)^2 + 1(12)^2 + 1(9)^2 + 1(2)^2$). However, the merger would have increased the market share of the combined group to 36%, so that the index would have risen to 3,944 (i.e. $1(50)^2 + 1(36)^2 + 1(12)^2 + 1(2)^2$). The increase of 486 would have been much higher than the 100-point criterion for attracting the attention of the US Justice Department. Interestingly, this merger was allowed to go ahead in the UK on the basis that Carborundum, the BP-owned company, was continuing to grow, and that the French company, Kerlane, was also increasing its share of the market. In other words, all companies would retain some power in the UK market and competition could still continue. Although US merger policy is not *solely* dictated by the value of the index, the adverse initial movement of the index would certainly have created a context in which subsequent investigation in the US was less likely to decide in favour of the merger than in the UK.

Despite the attractive simplicity of this index, a number of criticisms have been directed towards it. First, the index cannot cope adequately with vertical or conglomerate mergers since they cannot be viewed merely in terms of increasing market concentration. As a result, even with this index, non-horizontal mergers between companies in different industries or market sectors remain an area of uncertainty in terms of Justice Department reaction. Second, there is often no clear way to determine in exactly which market the market share should be measured. For example, in the investigation into the proposed alliance of British Airways and American Airlines in 1998, the carriers themselves asserted that the relevant market was travel between the US and Europe (where their combined market share is modest), while EU officials focused on travel between the US and the UK (where their combined market share is substantial). Third, even where the definition of the market is clear, the relation between changes in the index and changes in market power may be rather obscure. For example, although two firms, Coca-Cola and Pepsi-Cola, control 75% of sales of the US soft drinks industry, such market concentration has in no way diminished the aggressive price competition between these rivals.

Officials have increasingly resorted to a range of indicators in addition to the Herfindahl–Hirschman index in order to evaluate proposed mergers. For example, a key issue may be whether mergers are likely to drive prices higher. In 1997, the proposed merger of Staples and Office Depot, the two superstore office chains, seemed to provide no problem in terms of market concentration as thousands of other US retailers also sell office supplies. However, when the Federal Trade Commission (FTC) used electronic scanners to scrutinize data on sales price and quantities for every item sold, they found a distinctive pattern. Staples' prices were found to be lower in cities where Office Depot had a store compared to cities where Office Depot had none. This was seen by the FTC as evidence that the proposed merger would in all probability allow Staples to raise prices after the merger. The merger was therefore blocked. It is often technological developments, such as the availability of powerful computer resources and electronic retail price scanners in this example, which have permitted such data to be

collected and analysed, providing additional indicators to be used alongside the Herfindahl–Hirschman index as an aid to decision-making.

Corporate restructuring

Two of the most important developments during the 1980s and 1990s were the acceleration in the trend towards corporate restructuring, and the financing of takeovers by 'leveraged debt'.

While larger mergers continued, other forms of restructuring seemed to go against this trend. Restructuring took two directions: the taking apart of diversified conglomerates, and the putting together of focused global companies. There are obvious advantages in creating diversified conglomerates, such as less risk of financial distress and a decreased threat of being taken over. However, in recent years many larger conglomerates have found that they need to concentrate on operating a more limited range of companies or divisions, especially those which can generate cash. For example, Pearson plc, which owns the *Financial Times* and a large number of publishing companies (e.g. Penguin, Pitman, Addison Wesley Longman, Prentice-Hall), sold many of its non-media-related companies during 1997/98, such as those involved with leisure interests (e.g. Madame Tussaud's, Warwick Castle) and financial services, in order to focus on its core, media-related activities. During 2001–02, Kingfisher, the home improvements and electrical/furniture retailer giant, was involved in a large restructuring programme designed to focus on its core activities (B&Q stores) in order to strengthen its market power and financial position in the home improvements sector. For example, in 2001 it de-merged from Woolworth and sold off its Superdrug and Time Retail Finance businesses and went on to acquire the French home improvement company, Castorama, in 2002. Finally, a major phase in Kingfisher's strategy of focusing on the home improvements sector occurred when it de-merged Kesa Electrics (including its Comet stores) in 2003 and bought OBI Asia Holdings, a Chinese DIY company in 2005, in order to enter the Chinese market. For similar reasons, Hays, the large UK conglomerate operating in such diverse areas as personnel, commercial, mail and logistics, announced in early 2003 the decision to break up a £1.5bn empire in order to focus on its personnel/recruitment services division.

The restructuring of companies into a relatively more focused area of operation during the 1980s and 1990s was made more possible by the emergence in the UK and abroad of the 'leveraged buyout'. This means that companies obtain a high percentage of the finance they need in order to take over another company by issuing high interest unsecured bonds (Junk Bonds) or by borrowing through high interest unsecured loans (mezzanine finance). The former was a method favoured in the US while the latter form of borrowing is the favoured UK method. This development has had two important repercussions for corporate strategy. First, it has meant that even managers of very large companies can be subject to a takeover bid from a smaller company which has managed to borrow large amounts of debt finance. Being large *per se* is, therefore, no guarantee of safety from being taken over. Second, it has become easier, through leveraged buyouts, to take over a large diversified conglomerate, to sell off parts of it, and then to refocus the company on its 'core' activity. There has been a tendency in recent years for such 'deconglomeration' to be used in order to increase the cashflow of an acquiring company, thereby helping to service the larger debt created by the takeover, while also increasing the competitiveness of the company in its core activities, to the benefit of shareholders.

The importance of financial and economic reasoning for restructuring through de-merger has continued through time. For example, Cable and Wireless de-merged in 2010 into two new listed companies – Cable and Wireless Worldwide (CWW), providing high-speed voice and data networks for companies internationally, and Cable and Wireless Communications (CWC), running four regional operations in the Caribbean, Panama, Macau and Monaco & Islands. The arguments here were strategic, i.e. the de-merger would create two entities which would be more independent and flexible thus unlocking shareholder value. In a more complex situation, Carphone Warehouse de-merged its two holding companies in 2010 into TalkTalk and New Carphone Warehouse, i.e. into telecoms and retail respectively. In the same year Carphone Warehouse acquired the UK assets of the Italian carrier Tiscali, thus strengthening its telecom business.

However, one should also remember that financial factors alone cannot account for all the restructuring and subsequent merger activity in the UK over the last decade. For example, one of the most powerful forces influencing recent restructuring has been the shift towards privatization and deregulation (see Chapter 8). Schoenberg and Reeves (1999) found that the most important single determinant of merger activity in the UK between 1991 and 1995 was the deregulation of industry. Industrial restructuring (in the form of privatization programmes, Single Market developments, etc.) can clearly play an important role in stimulating merger activity.

Conclusion

Corporate restructuring through mergers and acquisitions became increasingly important in the late 1980s and again in the mid- to late 1990s, as had previously been the case during certain periods of the 1950s and 1970s. The 1980s saw the build-up of conglomerate types of mergers, while the 1990s saw a shift towards mergers between companies within the same sector, as companies moved closer to their 'core' activities. Economic theory and statistical analysis do little to suggest that there are substantial benefits from merger activity, although such activity does appear consistent with managerial motives, such as higher status and remuneration.

UK legislation on mergers and takeovers has required some modification in order to tighten controls on anti-competitive arrangements and to bring UK and EU policy into closer alignment. On a more global scale, the chapter has looked at merger regulation in the US and in the EU.

Key points

- Types of merger activity include horizontal, vertical, conglomerate and lateral.

- Suggested reasons for merger include at least one company believing it can add value beyond the costs of merger (value discrepancy hypothesis), a low valuation of share price relative to assets (valuation ratio) and the desire for greater market power.

- Other reasons include the securing of substantial economies of scale at plant and/or enterprise level. The former would be mainly technical economies by rationalization of production into larger plants.

- There is little evidence to suggest that merger activity increases shareholder value but considerable evidence to suggest that merger activity may diminish profitability and shareholder value.

- Mergers which result in 25% or more of the industry's UK supply being in the hands of the merged enterprise may be referred to the Competition Commission. So too may mergers where an enterprise being taken over has a UK turnover exceeding £70m.

- Few mergers were actually referred to the Competition Commission – only 219 between 1950 and 2000. Less than 3% have been disallowed.

- 'Competition factors' seem to be the most important reason for referral to the OFT, Competition Commission.

- UK regulations of mergers have moved closer to the EU model, with prohibition and legal redress (e.g. fines) more available as remedies to injured parties.

Now try the self-check questions for this chapter on the Companion Website. You will also find useful links to relevant websites.

Notes

1 This refers to the fact that a higher level of output may be required before the separate processes involved in producing the good 'dovetail' so that there is no idle capacity. Suppose two processes are required to produce good X. Process A needs a specialized machine which can produce 20 units per hour and Process B needs a machine able to produce 30 units per hour. Only when output has risen to 60 units per hour will there be no idle capacity. For smaller output than 60 at least one machine cannot be fully used.

2 There is an element of 'contrivance' in this analysis. Strictly speaking, the demand curve for the (now) enlarged firm is likely to be further to the right than $D(= AR)$ in Fig. 5.2. We also assume that the now enlarged firm is seeking a non-profit maximizing solution since, if demand *were* unchanged at $D(= AR)$, the existing MR curve would intersect the new (lower) MC_1 curve to the right of Q, implying a lower price and higher quantity.

References and further reading

Aaronovitch, S. and Sawyer, M. (1975) Mergers, growth and concentration, *Oxford Economic Papers*, **27**(1): 136–55.

Andrade, G., Mitchell, M. and Stafford, E. (2001) New evidence and perspectives on mergers, *Journal of Economic Perspectives*, **15**(2): 103–20.

Angwin, D. and Savill, B. (1997) Strategic perspectives on European cross-border acquisitions: a view from top European executives, *European Management Journal*, **15**(4): 423–35.

Barreto, I. (2010) Dynamic capabilities: a review of past research and an agenda for the future. *Journal of Management*, **36**(1): 256–280.

Bebchuk, L. and Fried, J. (2004) *Pay without Performance: The Unfulfilled Promise of Executive Compensation*, Cambridge MA, Harvard University Press.

Competition Commission (2006) *Estimated Costs to Consumers of the Mergers Against Which the CC Took Action Between March 2005 and March 2006*, July, London.

Conyon, M. J. and Gregg, P. (1994) Pay at the top: a study of the sensitivity of top director remuneration to company specific shocks, *National Institute Economic Review*, **149**(August): 83–92.

Cosh, A. D., Hughes, A. and Singh, M. S. (1980) The causes and effects of takeovers in the UK: an empirical investigation for the late 1940s at the microeconomic level, in Mueller, D. C. (ed.), *The Determinants and Effects of Mergers*, Oelgeschlager, Gunn and Hain.

Cosh, A. D., Hughes, A. and Singh, M. S. (1985) *Institutional Investment, Company Performance and Mergers: Empirical Evidence for the UK*. A report to the Office of Fair Trading, mimeo, Cambridge.

Cowling, K., Cubbin, J. and Hall, S. (1980) *Mergers and Economic Performance*, Cambridge, Cambridge University Press, Ch. 5.

Elliot, D. and Gribbin, J. D. (1977) The abolition of cartels and structural change in the United Kingdom, in Jacquemin, A. P. and de Jong, H.

W. (eds), *Welfare Aspects of Industrial Markets*, The Hague, Leidin Nijhoff, 354–65.

Firth, M. (1979) The profitability of takeovers and mergers, *Economic Journal*, **89**(June): 316–328.

Firth, M. (1980) Takeovers, shareholders' return and the theory of the firm, *Economic Journal*, **82**.

Golbe, D. L. and White, L. (1988) A time-saving analysis of mergers and acquisitions in the US economy, in Auerbach, A. J. (ed.), *Corporate Takeovers: Causes and Consequences*, Chicago IL, University of Chicago Press, 265–310.

Gort, M. (1969) An economic disturbance theory of mergers, *Quarterly Journal of Economics*, **82**(4): 624–42.

Griffiths, A. (1992) Competition policy and EC industry, in Griffiths, A. (ed.), *European Community Survey*, Longman, 103–118.

Ingham, H., Kran, I. and Lovestam, A. (1992) Mergers and profitability, *Journal of Management Studies*, **2**(March): 195–208.

Jovanovich, B. and Rousseau, P. (2004) *Mergers as reallocation*, mimeo, New York University.

Kaplan, R. S., Norton, D. P., Rugelsjoen, B. (2010) Managing alliances with the balanced scorecard, *Harvard Business Review*, **88**(1): 1–9.

KPMG (1999) Unlocking shareholder values: the keys to success, in *Merger and Acquisition: a Global Research Report*, London.

Kuehn, D. A. (1975) *Takeovers and the Theory of the Firm*, Basingstoke, Macmillan.

Kumar, M. S. (1985) Growth, acquisition and firm size: evidence from the United Kingdom, *Journal of Industrial Economics*, **33**(March): 327–38.

Lambrecht, B. M. (2004) The timing and terms of mergers motivated by economies of scale, *Journal of Financial Economics*, **72**(1): 41–62.

Levine, P. and Aaronovitch, S. (1981) The financial characteristics of firms and theories of merger activity, *Journal of Industrial Economics*, **30**: 149–72

Manson, S., Stark, A. and Thomas, H. (1994) *A Cashflow Analysis of the Operational Gains From Takeovers*, Research Report No. 35,

London, The Chartered Association of Certified Accountants.

Marris, R. (1964) *The Economic Theory of 'Managerial' Capitalism*, Basingstoke, Macmillan.

Meeks, G. (1977) *Disappointing Marriage: a Study of the Gains from Merger*, University of Cambridge, Department of Applied Economics, Occasional Paper 51, Cambridge, Cambridge University Press.

Meeks, G. and Whittington, G. (1975) Director's pay, growth and profitability, *Journal of Industrial Economics*, 24(1): 1–14.

Mueller, D. C. (1989) Mergers, *International Journal of Industrial Organization*, 7(1): 1–10.

Newbold, A. (1970) *Management and Merger Activity*, Liverpool, Guthstead.

ONS (2010) *Mergers and Acquisitions Involving UK Companies*, 2nd Quarter, 7 September, London, Office for National Statistics.

Peltier, S. (2002) Mergers and acquisitions in the media industries: a preliminary study of the impact on performance, *12th ACEI Conference*, June 11–14, Rotterdam.

Prais, S. J. (1976) *The Evolution of Giant Firms in Britain*, Cambridge, Cambridge University Press.

Ravenscraft, D. J. and Scherer, F. M. (1987) *Mergers, Sell-offs and Economic Efficiency*, Washington DC, Brookings Institution.

Rhodes-Kroopf, M. and Viswanathan, S. (2004) Market valuation and merger waves, *Journal of Finance*, 59(6): 1685–2718.

Schoenberg, R. and Reeves, R. (1999) What determines acquisition activity within an industry?, *European Management Journal*, 17(1): 93–8.

Shleifer, A. and Vishny, R. (2003) Stock market driven acquisitions, *Journal of Financial Economics*, 70: 295–311.

Singh, A. (1971) *Takeovers*, Cambridge, Cambridge University Press.

Singh, A. (1975) Takeovers, economic natural selection and the theory of the firm: evidence from the post-war United Kingdom experience, *Economic Journal*, 85(September): 497–515.

Stewart, G. (1996) Takeovers, *Economic Review*, 14(1, 2).

Whittington, G. (1980) The profitability and size of UK companies, *Journal of Industrial Economics*, 28(4): 335–42.

Williamson, O. (1967) Hierarchical control and optimum firm size, *The Journal of Political Economy*, 75(2): 123–38.

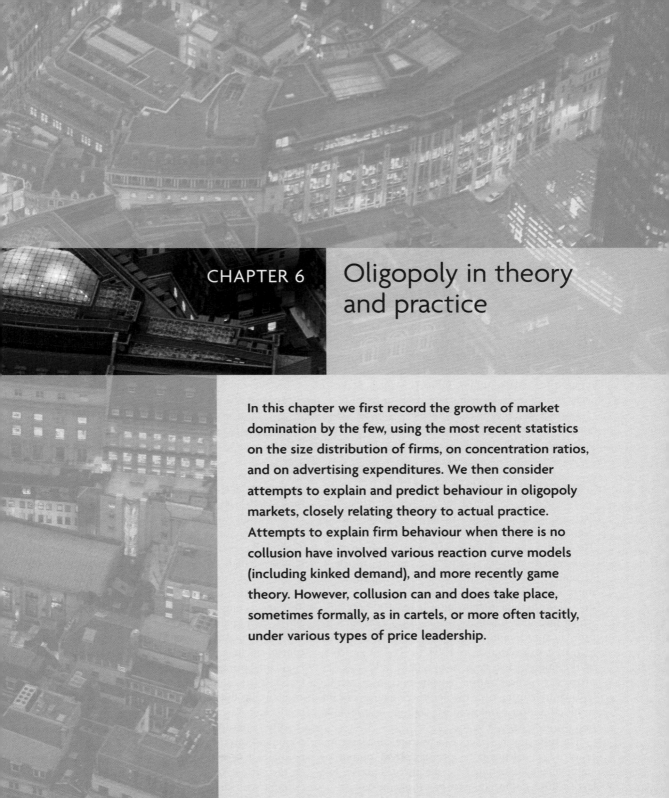

CHAPTER 6

Oligopoly in theory and practice

In this chapter we first record the growth of market domination by the few, using the most recent statistics on the size distribution of firms, on concentration ratios, and on advertising expenditures. We then consider attempts to explain and predict behaviour in oligopoly markets, closely relating theory to actual practice. Attempts to explain firm behaviour when there is no collusion have involved various reaction curve models (including kinked demand), and more recently game theory. However, collusion can and does take place, sometimes formally, as in cartels, or more often tacitly, under various types of price leadership.

The definition and measurement of oligopoly

Oligopoly may be defined as an industry in which there are few firms and many buyers. However, this definition begs two important questions. First, how many is 'few'? Broadly speaking, the number of firms should be sufficiently small for there to be 'conscious interdependence', with each firm aware that its future prospects depend not only on its own policies, but also on those of its rivals. Second, what is an industry? In theory, an industry is defined as a group of firms whose products are close substitutes for one another (i.e. the products have high and positive cross-elasticities of demand).[1] In practice, precise calculations of cross-elasticities of demand are impossible to make, and an industry is defined either by approximate similarity of output (such as the confectionery industry) or by similarity of the major input (such as the rubber industry, which makes a wide variety of goods from shoe soles to tyres).

Bearing in mind these problems of precise definition, the rise of oligopoly can be charted in a variety of ways.

Table 6.1 Company shares of the UK market by sector/product 2009/10.

Sector/ Product group	Percentage share of the UK market	
	Three largest companies	Five largest companies
Tobacco	91	98
Chocolate confectionery	78	87
Electrical retailers	75	82
Tour operators	68	75
Coffee shops	65	74
DIY	57	63
White goods	57	78
Motor Insurance	51	63
Bottled water	48	58
Women's fragrancies	48	71
Vacuum cleaners	45	57
Branded watches	28	38
Footwear retailing	22	26

Source: Mintel International Group Ltd (2010), Mintel Reports (various) and other sources.

Concentration ratios

Perhaps the most usual method of measuring the degree of oligopoly is through concentration ratios. These show the proportion of output or employment in a given industry or product group which is accounted for by the dominant firms operating in those areas. The oldest concentration ratio used in the UK within manufacturing was the 100-firm ratio which measures the share of the 100 largest private firms in total manufacturing net output. This ratio increased from 16.0% in 1909 to 41.7% in 1975, before falling back to 32% by 2010, indicating the progressive concentration of economic power within UK manufacturing over the first three-quarters of the twentieth century, followed by a fall in such domination over the past 35 years.

The more normal way of measuring concentration ratios is to calculate the proportion of output or employment contributed by the three, four or five largest firms in that industry or product group.

Table 6.1 provides details of the three- and five-firm concentration ratios in various sector and product groups. As one would expect, the cigarette sector in 2009/10 is dominated by Imperial Tobacco, Gallaher and Rothmans UK while the chocolate confectionery sector is similarly controlled by Cadbury, Trebor Bassett, Masterfoods (Mars) and Nestlé. However, high concentration ratios are also to be found in DIY retailing, with B&Q and Homebase being the main players in the market, while in motor insurance, companies such as the RBS Group, Aviva and Zurich Financial Services are dominant. Some of the product groups which show less concentrated control include bottled water (Volvic, Evian and Highland Spring) and luxury watches (Rolex, Omega, Gucci, Cartier, etc.). These are markets where there is arguably product space for smaller specialized niche producers.

Often consumers are not aware that a few firms dominate certain markets because each company produces a variety of models or brands that appear on the surface to be unrelated to each other, as for example with Diageo plc which produces brands such as Smirnoff vodka, Bell's whisky and Gordon's gin, and controls 20% of the UK spirit market. It is often useful to examine *product groups* if we wish to see the true extent of market domination by a few firms.

Advertising expenditure

Data on advertising provide a useful, if indirect, method for gauging both the rise of oligopoly markets and the tendency towards product differentiation. Advertising is essentially aimed at binding consumers to particular brands for reasons other than price. Estimates in the US of branded, processed foods put their prices almost 9% higher than 'private label' equivalents – similar products packaged under the retailer's own name – due solely to more extensive media advertising.[2]

One way of understanding the impact of advertising on oligopolistic markets is to study the total advertising expenditure of the top 15 *companies*, as listed in Table 6.2. For example, the two companies (COI is a governmental department) which dominated UK advertising in 2009 were Unilever and Procter & Gamble. The figures shown here include the advertising expenditure of all the major subsidiaries of the two groups operating in a wide range of sectors from food and household goods to health, beauty and cosmetics. The list of top advertisers in Table 6.2 reflects competitive activity in their product/sectors of operation. For example, in the market for concentrated liquids used for clothes washing, Procter & Gamble brought out its Ariel 'Excel Gel' format in late 2008 in order to compete with Unilever's successful launch of Persil 'Small and Mighty' concentrated gel which was launched in 2007. In the stain remover market, Procter & Gamble introduced its new Ariel stain remover in March 2010 to compete with Reckitt Benckiser's dominant 'Vanish' stain remover which controlled 79% of the market. The list of top advertisers is also dominated by four grocery supermarket chains. Here we see that Tesco, Asda, Morrison and Sainsbury's together spent an impressive £324m or about a quarter of the total advertising expenditure of the top 15 companies, as they vied with each other for customers. In contrast, the top four car companies (not shown) only spent £136m on advertising due to the effects of the recession on the marketing budgets of these companies.

The companies noted above all advertise their branded products intensively in order to 'bind' the consumer to the product for reasons other than price.

Table 6.2 Top 15 advertising companies in the UK, 2009.

Rank	Company	Advertising expenditure (£m)
1	COI	207.90
2	Proctor & Gamble	154.98
3	Unilever UK	129.06
4	British Sky Broadcasting	108.85
5	Tesco	104.56
6	Asda Stores	98.66
7	DFS Furniture	93.81
8	Reckitt Benckiser (UK)	84.44
9	Kelloggs Co of GB	80.13
10	L'Oréal Paris	73.54
11	Nestlé	63.53
12	Wm Morrison Supermarkets	61.60
13	Sainsbury's Supermarkets	59.12
14	GlaxoSmithKline	58.43
15	Orange	54.15

Note: COI is advertising by the Central Office of Communication.
Source: Modified from Marketing (2010b) *Top 100 Advertisers*, 24 March.

Where successful, such advertising may help *shift* the demand curve outwards, raising market share, while simultaneously causing the demand curve to pivot and become steeper. Demand then becomes less price elastic, creating new opportunities for raising both price and revenue.

Oligopoly in theory and practice

The central task of market theory is to predict how firms will set prices and output. In perfect competition and pure monopoly we can make definite predictions. In perfect competition it can be shown that in the long run price will be equal to the lowest possible average costs of the firm – what Adam Smith called 'the natural price'. In pure monopoly the firm seeking to maximize profits will restrict output and raise prices until marginal revenue exactly equals marginal cost.

In oligopoly, where there are few firms in the market, and where there is product differentiation, there can be no such precision. Where the number of firms is sufficiently small for each firm to be aware of the pricing policy of its rivals, it will have to try to anticipate its rivals' reactions to its own pricing decision. Further, where products are differentiated, the firm will have to estimate the degree of brand loyalty customers have for its products – the greater that loyalty, the smaller the effect of price changes on consumer demand. This constant need to anticipate the reaction of both rivals and consumers creates a high degree of uncertainty in oligopoly markets.

Despite this uncertainty, the importance of the oligopoly-type of market structure in modern economies has encouraged the quest for theories to explain and predict firm behaviour. Although little progress seems to have been made in devising a general theory of oligopoly behaviour, some progress has been made in understanding the behaviour of *particular* firms in *particular* oligopoly situations. We might usefully review a number of such theories, keeping a close eye on firm practice.

Non-collusive oligopoly

First, we consider situations in which each firm decides upon its strategy without any formal or even tacit collusion between rivals. There are essentially three approaches the firm can adopt to handle interdependence when oligopoly is non-collusive.

1   The firm could assume that whatever it decides to do, its rivals *will not* react, i.e. they will ignore its strategies. This assumption may reasonably be valid for day-to-day, routine decisions, but is hardly realistic for major initiatives. The Cournot duopoly model is, however, of this type. Each firm simply observes what the other does, and then adopts a strategy that maximizes its own profits. It makes no attempt to evaluate potential reactions by the rival firm to its own profit-maximizing strategy.

2   The firm could assume that rivals *will* react to its own strategies, and use past experience to assess the form that reaction might take. This 'learning' process underlies the reaction-curve model of Stackleberg. It also underlies the kinked-demand model (see below), with firms learning that rivals

do not match price increases, but certainly do match any price reductions.

3   Instead of using past experience to assess future reactions by rivals, the firm itself could try to identify the *best possible* move the opposition could make to each of its own strategies. The firm could then plan counter-measures if the rival reacts in this (for the rival) optimal way. As we see below, this is the essence of game theory.

Approaches 2 and 3 might lead us to expect a considerable amount of price movement, as rivals incessantly formulate strategy and counter-strategy. In practice, however, the oligopolistic industries experience *short bursts* of price-changing activity (often linked to price warfare), together with longer periods of relatively stable or rigid prices. We briefly review these two types of situation, noting the relevance of kinked-demand theory to stable prices, and conclude our discussion of non-collusive behaviour with an outline of game theory.

Price warfare

Price-cutting is a well-attested strategy for oligopoly firms, for both raising and defending market share. This can, of course, lead to a competitive downward spiral in firm prices, resembling a 'price war'. Examples of this abound. We will see, in Chapter 9, how price warfare developed amongst petrol retailers. In 1996, for example, stagnant demand for petrol due to increasing taxes, and more fuel-efficient cars coupled with competition from supermarkets, led the UK's largest petrol retailer, Esso, to announce aggressive price cuts to maintain its dominant position. Shell, BP and Conoco (Jet) responded by matching or undercutting Esso's price cuts. The catalyst for the new strategy was that Esso's share of the petrol market had fallen to around 17% as compared to the supermarkets' share of 25%.

In 1996, the cross-channel transport business saw a fierce outbreak of price warfare. Of the 35 million passengers using the cross-channel route, 35% went by Eurotunnel, 32% by P&O European Ferries and 20% by Stena Line. Between 1993 and 1996, peak season cross-channel fares fell by 60% as the ferries tried to resist the challenge of the Channel Tunnel. For example, the standard brochure fares for a crossing in the summer of 1996 involving a car and four passengers were heavily discounted on the shorter Dover/Calais (ferries) and the Folkestone/Calais (Le

Shuttle) routes. Actual ferry prices were cut to around 40% of the standard return price while Le Shuttle prices were cut to 80% of their normal fares. Most of the operators were charging around £100 for a return fare involving a car and four passengers. In order to use its ships to capacity, P&O's policy was to match any rival company's discount. The presence of price warfare is also endemic in the financial sector as illustrated by the price competition between Visa and Europay, the two payments card groupings, over the fees they charge to their member banks in Europe for using their product. After a four-year cost-cutting programme prior to 1998, Europay (which runs the Eurocard debit card scheme and Mastercard) decided to undercut Visa's fees by 20% in early 2000. Visa's response was to announce a programme aimed at undercutting Europay by 25% between 2000 and 2001.

One of the most dynamic areas for oligopolistic price warfare activity in more recent times occurred in the games console market during the period 2001–02 when Sony (Playstation 2), Microsoft (Microsoft XBox) and Nintendo (GameCube) fought for market share. In November 2001 Sony decreased the price of its Playstation 2, a move which led Microsoft to decrease the price of its new Microsoft XBox from £300 to £199 in April 2002. Nintendo followed in May 2002 with a discounted price of £129 for its new GameCube console. By October 2002, the most aggressive aspect of the console price war seemed to be over as the protagonists concentrated on the next generation of consoles due in 2005. The new generation arrived on the scene between 2005 and 2006 when Microsoft's Xbox360, Sony's PS3 and Nintendo's Wii were launched. After an initial period when the companies typically distinguish themselves through product differentiation strategies, they usually resort to price warfare as they compete for increased market share, in this case perhaps up to around 2014 when a further generation of games consoles may emerge. An example of such price warfare happened in August 2009 when Microsoft decreased the price of its Xbox 360 Elite gaming machine from $399 to $299, and the price of its Xbox Pro from $299 to $249. This was in part a reaction to Sony's introduction of the new PlayStation 3 Slim (PS3) gigabyte hard drive at a relatively low price of $299 – a drop of $100 for the PS3 which had found itself trailing behind its competitors, the Xbox 360 and Nintendo's Wii. Similarly in October

2010 Waitrose reduced the price of 1000 own-brand items to counter the discounted price of Tesco own-brand products.

Price decreases are made possible not only by the economies of scale achieved in the production of consoles, but also by companies cross-subsidizing their consoles in order to drive up software sales (e.g. in 2003 Microsoft was known to be losing £60 on each XBox sold).

Clearly in oligopolistic markets, where only a few firms dominate, a price-cutting strategy by one is likely to be followed by others. After short bursts of price warfare, the market may settle down into prolonged periods of price stability, although the fact that firms no longer compete in price may not mean an absence of competition. In periods of price stability, non-price competition often becomes more intense, with advertising, packaging and other promotional activities now used to raise or defend market share. For example, in the food retailing business, advertising is a well-known form of non-price competition. In 2009 Tesco spent £104.6m on advertising, Sainsbury's £59.1m and Asda £98.7m. Coupled with this overall advertising strategy, there have been other efforts at product differentiation, such as the 'green grocer' campaigns to promote environmentally friendly products. Similarly, the loyalty cards introduced by Tesco (Clubcard), and Sainsbury (Reward card) were designed to reinforce brand loyalty and make customers less price sensitive. In economic terms, this was designed to make demand curves less elastic, giving the supermarkets more opportunity to raise prices at a later date if necessary.

Non-price competition may take forms other than advertising and quality considerations. In the mid-1990s when price competition was intense in the travel industry, there were still signs that companies were using other non-price methods to increase market share. For example, Thomson's industrial strategy of *vertical integration* towards the market (owning Lunn Poly and Britannia Airways) was strengthened further in 1994 by its purchase of the Country Holidays Group which gave it a major interest in the UK holiday lettings industry. Vertical integration was also involved in the acquisition by Thomas Cook in 1998 of the US Carlson group (owner of Caledonian Airways and the tour operator 'Inspirations'). Between 2001 and 2002 both Thomson and Thomas Cook experienced further integration when each was taken over by a German-owned leisure group in a period of fierce competition in the European holidays industry. Such takeover strategies are an important 'non-price' method by which firms in oligopolistic industries continue to compete with one another.

In the game console industry, some of the non-price types of competition had already been 'inbuilt' in the original product differentiation between the consoles. Microsoft Xbox had the best on-line service; Playstation had more multimedia capacity and played Blu-ray discs; and the Wii's product range placed paramount importance on the social gamer. By 2010, all three console manufacturers were aiming for both the core gaming audience and the family audience. Hence the emergence of 'warfare', not in terms of prices but in terms of non-price factors, i.e. 'add-ons' such as *Move* for Sony Playstation 3 and *Kinect* for Microsoft's Xbox 360.

Price stability

That price in oligopoly will tend to have periods of stability is, in fact, predicted by economic theory.

Kinked demand

In 1939 Hall and Hitch in the UK and Sweezy in the USA proposed a theory to explain why prices often remain stable in oligopoly markets, even when costs rise. A central feature of that theory was the existence of a kinked-demand curve.

To illustrate this we take an oligopolistic market which sells similar but not identical products, i.e. there is some measure of product differentiation. If one firm raises its price, it will then lose some, though not all, of its custom to rivals. Similarly, if the firm reduces its price it will attract some, though not all, of its rivals' custom. How much custom is lost or gained will depend partly on whether the rivals follow the initial price change.

Extensive interviews with managers of firms in oligopoly markets led Hall and Hitch to conclude that most firms have learned a common lesson from past experience of how rivals react. Namely, that if the firm were to raise its price above the current level (*P* in Fig. 6.1), its rivals *would not* follow, content to let the firm lose sales to them. The firm will then expect its demand curve to be relatively elastic (*dK*) for price rises. However, if the firm were to reduce its

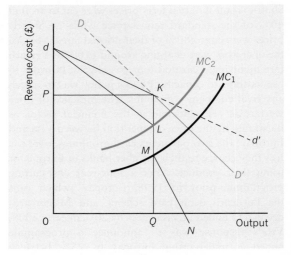

Fig. 6.1 Kinked demand curve and price stability.
Notes: *d–d'* = Demand curve when rivals *do not* follow price changes.
D–D' = Demand curve when rivals *do* follow price changes.
dKD' = Kinked demand curve.
dLMN = Associated marginal revenue curve.

price, rivals *would* follow to protect their market share, so that the firm gains few extra sales. The firm will then expect its demand curve to be relatively inelastic (*KD'*) for price reductions. Overall the firm will believe that its demand curve is kinked at the current price *P*, as in Fig. 6.1.

One can intuitively see why this belief will lead to price stickiness, since the firm will rapidly lose market share if it raises price, and gain little from reducing price. A kinked-demand (average revenue) curve of the form *dKD'* will have a discontinuity (*L–M*) in its associated marginal revenue curve below the kink point *K*.[3] The marginal cost curve could then vary between *MC₁* and *MC₂* without causing the firm to alter its profit-maximizing price *P* (or its output *Q*).

A number of industries have exhibited price stability, despite rising costs. The UK confectionery industry in the 1980s, dominated by Mars, Nestlé Rowntree (which absorbed Rowntree Mackintosh in 1988) and Cadbury Schweppes, was a good example of this tendency. During some periods in the 1980s, price wars were often avoided, though competition between these companies still continued in other forms. For example, in the mid-1980s non-price competition took the form of product weight. In one such period, Mars raised the weight of Mars bars by 10%, Cadbury raised the weight of its Fruit & Nut by 14% and Rowntree Mackintosh raised the weight of Cabana by 15% and increased the chocolate content of KitKat by 5%. In all of these cases the firms accepted rises in their costs, i.e. more ingredients per bar, *without changing price*.

Similarly in the 1990s, competition in the UK snacks market increased as the three major companies, KP Foods, Smiths and Walkers (owned by the US company, PepsiCo) and Golden Wonder (the Dalgety subsidiary), looked for new ways of competing. KP foods introduced its new crisp-like snack called 'Frisp' and spent £4.4m on marketing it in the first three months alone. To prevent being squeezed out by its two big rivals, Golden Wonder planned to launch a few new products in the middle of 1990 and in the meantime increased the packet size of all its crisps and snacks from 28 grams to 30 grams *without raising prices*. In 2010 Mars, the chocolate manufacturer, spent over €10m over five years to produce lower saturated fat versions of its Mars bars, Snickers and Milky Way brands. This cost was absorbed without significant changes to prices as the company tried to remain competitive by developing its health-conscious image.

In terms of our kinked oligopoly model, the companies noted above preferred to accept the higher costs of non-price competition (which can be illustrated by the upward shift in the *MC* curve), rather than engage in price warfare, in order to gain market share. The reason for this is that companies sometimes believe they have a better idea of the costs and benefits involved in *non-price competition* as compared to the unknown risks of getting involved in price competition. When a company becomes involved in price competition, gains and losses are more difficult to assess because they depend on the *reactions* of competitors to the initial company's pricing strategy.

Despite the usefulness of the kinked oligopoly model as a descriptive tool in the understanding of oligopoly behaviour, it still faces a number of problems.

1 The theory does not explain how oligopolists actually *set* an initial price, but merely why a price, once set, might be stable. Kinked demand is *not* a theory of price determination.

2 The observed stickiness of prices may have little to do with the rival-firm reaction patterns of kinked-demand theory. It is, for instance, administratively expensive to change prices too often.

3 The assertion, implicit in kinked-demand theory, that prices are more 'sticky' under oligopoly than under other market forms, has not received strong support from empirical studies (Wagner 1981). For instance, Stigler, in a sample of 100 firms across 21 industries in the USA, had concluded as early as the 1940s that oligopoly prices hardly merited the description 'sticky'. Domberger, in a survey of 21 UK industries, found that the *more* oligopolistic the market, the more variable was price (Domberger 1980).

4 The precise nature of any kink in the demand curve may depend on the economic conditions prevailing at the time. For example, a study of 73 small owner-managed firms in Scotland found that price increases were more likely to be followed during booms, whilst falls were more likely to be followed during times of recession (Bhaskar *et al.* 1991).

Game theory

One of the more recent attempts to assess non-collusive behaviour by oligopolists has involved game theory. The intention is to go beyond the rather general reaction patterns of earlier theory, to more explicit assessments of strategy and counter-strategy. We might usefully illustrate the principles involved by a simple two-firm (duopoly) game, involving market share. By its very nature, a market share game must be 'zero sum', in that any gain by one 'player' must be offset exactly by the loss of the other(s).

Suppose Firm A is considering two possible strategies to raise its market share, a 20% price cut or a 10% increase in advertising expenditure. Whatever initial strategy A adopts, it anticipates that its rival, Firm B, will react by using either a price cut or extra advertising to defend its market share. Firm A now evaluates the market share it can expect for each initial strategy and each possible counter-strategy by B. The outcomes expected by A are summarized in the payoff matrix of Table 6.3.

If A cuts price, and B responds with a price cut, A receives 60% of the market. However, if B responds with extra advertising, A receives 70% of the market.

Table 6.3 Firm A's payoff matrix.

		Firm B's strategies	
		Price cut	Extra advertising
Firm A's	Price cut	60*†	70†
strategies	Extra advertising	50*	55

*'Worst' outcome for A of each A strategy.
†'Worst' outcome for B of each B strategy.

The 'worst' outcome for A (60% of the market) will occur if B responds with a price cut. If A adopts the strategy of extra advertising, then the 'worst' outcome for A (50% of the market) will again occur if B responds with a price cut. If A expects B to play the game astutely, i.e. choose the counter-strategy best for itself (worst for A), then A will choose the price-cut strategy as this gives it 60% of the market rather than 50%. If A plays the game in this way, selecting the best of the 'worst possible' outcomes for each initial strategy, it is said to be adopting a 'maxi–min approach' to the game.

If B adopts the same maxi–min approach as A, *and* has made the same evaluation of outcomes as A, it also will adopt a price-cut strategy. For instance, if B adopts a price-cut strategy, its 'worst' outcome would occur if A responds with a price cut – B then gets 40% of the market (100% minus 60%), rather than 50% if A responds with extra advertising. If B adopts extra advertising, its 'worst' outcome would again occur if A responds with a price cut – B then receives 30%. The best of the 'worst possible' outcomes for B occurs if B adopts a price cut, which gives it 40% of the market rather than 30%.

In this particular game we have a stable equilibrium, without any resort to collusion. Both firms initially cut price, then accept the respective market shares which fulfil their maxi–min targets – 60% to A, 40% to B. There could then follow the price stability which we have seen to be a feature of some oligopoly situations. In some games the optimal strategy for each firm may not even have been an initial price cut, but rather non-price competition (such as advertising). Game theory can predict both price stability and extensive non-price competition.

The problem with game theory is that it can equally predict unstable solutions, with extensive price as well as non-price competition. An unstable solution might follow if each firm, faced with the pay-off matrix of Table 6.3, adopts entirely different strategies. Firm B might not use the maxi–min approach of A, but take more risk.[4] Instead of the price cut it might adopt the 'extra advertising' strategy, hoping to induce an advertising response from Firm A and gain 45% of the market, but risk getting only 30% if A responds with a price cut. Suppose this is what happens. Firm A now receives 70% of the market, but B only receives 30%, which is below its initial expectation of 45%. This may provoke B into alternative strategy formulation, setting off a further chain reaction. The game may then fail to settle down quickly, if at all, to a stable solution, i.e. one in which each firm receives a market share which meets its overall expectation. An unstable solution might also follow if each firm evaluates the payoff matrix differently from the other. Even if they then adopt the same approach to the game, one firm at least will be 'disappointed', possibly provoking action and counteraction.

If we could tell *before the event* which oligopoly situations would be stable, and which unstable, then the many possible outcomes of game theory would be considerably narrowed. At present this is beyond the state of the art. However, game theory has been useful in making more explicit the *interdependence* of oligopoly situations.

Developments in game theory

A number of other ideas are widely presented in game theory approaches:

- *Dominant strategy.* In this approach, the firm seeks to do the best it can (in terms of the objectives set) irrespective of the possible actions/ reactions of any rival(s).

- *Nash equilibrium.* This occurs when each firm is doing the best that it can in terms of its own objective(s), given the strategies chosen by the other firms in the market.

- *Prisoner's dilemma.* This is an outcome where the equilibrium for the game involves both firms doing worse than they would have done had they colluded, and is sometimes called a 'cartel game' because the obvious implication is that the firms would be better off by colluding.

There are different types of game to which these ideas might be applied.

Table 6.4 Payoff matrix (daily profits)

		Firm B	
		Low output	High output
Firm A	Low output	£3,000; £3,000	£2,000; £4,000
	High output	£4,000; £2,000	£1,500; £1,500

One-shot game

The suggestion here is that the decision to be made by each firm is 'once for all'. We can illustrate this type of game using Table 6.4, which is a payoff matrix that expresses the net gains for each of two firms in terms of daily profit, the first value being that for Firm A and the second value that for Firm B. The single policy variable shown here is output level, which can be set high or low, with the payoff dependent on the rival's reaction. Clearly this is a non-zero sum game since the total daily profit for each combination of policies varies rather than remains constant (for example, total profit is £3,000 in the bottom right quadrant but £6,000 elsewhere).

Suppose, initially, that we treat this situation as a one-shot game.

■ 'High output' would be the dominant strategy for each firm, giving both Firm A and Firm B £4,000 in daily profit should the other firm select 'low output'. However, if both firms follow this dominant strategy and select 'high output', they each receive only £1,500 daily profit.

■ If each firm follows a maxi–min decision rule, then Firm A selects 'low output' as the best of the worst possible outcomes (£2,000 > £1,500), as does Firm B (£2,000 > £1,500). The combination (low output, low output) will then be a Nash equilibrium, with each firm satisfied that it is doing the best that it can in terms of its own objective, given the strategy chosen by the other firm (each actually receives £3,000).

■ If each firm follows a mini–max decision rule, you should be able to show that both Firm A and Firm B will still select 'low output' as the worst of the best possible outcomes (£3,000 < £4,000 for each firm). The combination (low output/low output) remains a Nash equilibrium.

Even if one firm follows a maxi–min and the other a mini–max decision rule, the combination (low out-

put/low output) will remain a Nash equilibrium in this particular game. We could reasonably describe this output combination (low/low) as a stable, Nash-type equilibrium.

Repeated game

However, should we view the pay-off matrix in Table 6.4 as part of a repeated game, then the situation so far described might be subject to considerable change. We might expect the respective firms to alter the strategies they pursue and the game to have a different outcome.

Suppose the firms initially establish the low output/low output 'solution' to the game, whether as the result of a 'Nash equilibrium' or by some form of agreement between the firms. Unlike the one-shot game, a firm in a repeated game can modify its strategy from one period to the next, and can also respond to any changes in strategy by the other firm.

■ *Cheating.* If Table 6.4 is now viewed as the payoff matrix for a repeated game, there would seem to be a possible incentive for either firm to depart from its initial 'low output' policy in the next period. Had the initial 'low output' policy been mutually agreed by the two firms in an attempt to avoid the mutually damaging high output/high output combination should each firm have followed its 'dominant strategy', we might regard such a departure as *cheating* on an agreement. By unexpectedly switching to high output, either firm could benefit by raising daily profit (from £3,000 to £4,000), though the loss of profit (from £3,000 to £2,000) by the other firm might provoke an eventual retaliation in some future time period, resulting in the mutually damaging high output/high output combination.

■ *Tit-for-tat strategy.* Whether or not any 'cheating' is likely to benefit a firm will depend on a number of factors, not least the rapidity with which any rival responds to a breach of the agreement: the more rapid the response of the rival, the smaller any net benefits from cheating will be. Suppose, in our example, it takes the other firm five days to respond with higher output: then on each of these days the cheating firm gains a first-mover advantage (see p. 116) of an extra £1,000 in profit from breaching the agreement as compared with upholding the agreement. If the response of the rival were to be more rapid, say, in three days, then only

£3,000 rather than £5,000 benefit would accrue as a first-mover advantage. Of course, once the rival has responded, both firms are damaged in Table 6.4 compared with the pre-cheating situation, losing £1,500 profit per day from the high output/high output combination. This may, of course, induce both firms to restore the initial agreement.

If it becomes known that rivals are likely to respond rapidly to any cheating on agreements (or even departures from Nash-type equilibriums) by adopting *tit-for-tat* strategies, then this may itself deter attempts by either firm to cheat. Provided that each firm believes the rival is sufficiently well informed to be aware of any change in its strategy, it will anticipate a tit-for-tat response that will ensure that any benefits from cheating are of shorter duration. When factored into the decision-making process, the anticipation of a lower profit stream may deter any attempt by either firm to cheat.

Sequential games

In the games considered so far, each firm has been able to make decisions at the same time (i.e. simultaneously). However, in a sequential game the moves and counter-moves take place in a defined order: one firm makes a move and only then does the rival decide how to react to that move. Table 6.5 is a payoff matrix showing net gains as profit per period for each of two firms. The individual payoffs depend on the price (low or high) selected by one firm and the price response of the rival, in this non-zero sum game.

The dominant strategy for both Firm A and Firm B is to set a low price (£3,000 profit), but if they both follow this strategy the outcome is mutually damaging (£1,000 profit each). You should be able to see that a maxi–min decision rule followed by each firm would lead to a low price/low price outcome in which the expectations of each firm are fulfilled given that they have adopted this decision rule.

Table 6.5 Payoff matrix (profit per period)

		Firm B	
		Low price	High price
Firm A	Low price	£1,000; £1,000	£3,000; £2,000
	High price	£2,000; £3,000	£500; £500

First-mover advantages

If decisions can only be taken in sequence, an important issue is whether the firm making the first move can secure any advantage!

■ *Suppose Firm A is in a position to move first.* It can choose 'low price', forcing Firm B to choose between 'low price' (£1,000) and 'high price' (£2,000). Firm A might now anticipate that Firm B will attempt to maximize its own return given the constrained situation (via A's First move) in which B finds itself. In this case Firm B selects 'high price', and Firm A receives £3,000 profit per period. The first move by A has given a net profit advantage to A of £2,000 (£3,000–£1,000) as compared to the previous low price/low price outcome.

■ *Suppose Firm B is in a position to move first.* It can now choose 'low price' in the expectation that Firm A will respond with 'high price' (£2,000 > £1,000) as Firm A now seeks to maximize its own return given the constrained situation (via B's first move) in which it finds itself. In this case, Firm B receives a payoff of £3,000 profit per period and a net profit advantage of £2,000 via the first move.

Clearly this game does contain first-mover advantages, which lie in first anticipating the likely responses of the rival and then channelling those responses in a particular direction as a result of making the first move.

Here we have used game theory in a situation in which the firms did not collude. Game theory can also show (in games which are *not* zero sum) that collusion between firms may sometimes improve the position of all. It is to such collusive behaviour that we now turn.

Collusive oligopoly

When oligopoly is non-collusive, the firm uses guesswork and calculation to handle the uncertainty of its rivals' reactions. Another way of handling that uncertainty in markets which are interdependent is by some form of central co-ordination; in other words, collusion. At least two features of collusive oligopoly are worth emphasizing: first, the objectives that are sought through collusion; and second, the methods that are used to promote collusion – these may be formal, as in a cartel, or informal, via tacit agreement.

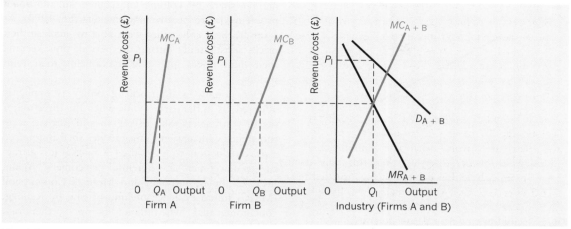

Fig. 6.2 Joint profit maximization in duopoly.

Objectives of collusion

Joint profit maximization

The firms may seek to coordinate their price, output and other policies to achieve maximum profits for the industry as a whole. In the extreme case the firms may act together as a monopoly, aggregating their marginal costs and equating these with marginal revenue for the whole market. If achieved, the result would be to maximize joint profits, with a unique industry price and output (P_1Q_1), as in Fig. 6.2.

A major problem is, of course, how to achieve the close coordination required. We consider this further below, but we might note from Fig. 6.2 that coordination is required both to *establish* the profit-maximizing solution for the industry P_1Q_1, and to *enforce* it once established. For instance, some agreement must be reached on sharing the output Q_1 between the colluding firms. One solution is to equate marginal revenue for whole output with marginal cost in each separate market,[5] with Firm A producing Q_A and Firm B producing Q_B. Whatever the agreement, it must remain in force – since if any firm produces above its quota, this will raise industry output, depress price and move the industry away from the joint profit-maximizing solution.

Deterrence of new entrants – limit-pricing

Firms may seek to coordinate policies, to maximize not so much short-run profit but rather some longer-run notion of profit (see Chapter 3). A major threat

to long-run profit is the potential entrance of new firms into the industry. Economists such as Andrews and Bain have therefore suggested that oligopolistic firms may collude with the objectives of setting price below the level which maximizes joint profits, in order to deter new entrants. The 'limit price' can be defined as the highest price which the established firms believe they can charge without inducing entry. Its precise value will depend upon the nature and extent of the 'barriers to entry' for any particular industry. The greater the barriers to entry, the higher the 'limit price' will be.

Substantial economies of scale are a 'barrier to entry', in that a new firm will usually be smaller than established firms, and will therefore be at a cost disadvantage. Product differentiation itself, reinforced by extensive advertising, is also a barrier – since product loyalty, once captured, is difficult and expensive for new entrants to dislodge. Other barriers might include legally enforced patents to new technologies in the hands of established firms, and even inelastic market demands. This latter is a barrier in that the less elastic the market demand for the product, the greater will be the price fall from any extra supply contributed by new entrants.

The principle of 'limit-pricing' can be illustrated from Fig. 6.3. Let us make the analysis easier by supposing that each established firm has an identical average cost (AC) curve, and sells an identical output, Q_F, at the joint profit-maximizing price P_1 set for the industry. Suppose a new firm, with an identical cost

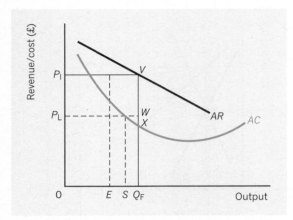

Fig. 6.3 Limit-pricing as a barrier to entry.

profile, is considering entering the industry, and is capable of selling E units in the first instance. Despite the initial cost disadvantage the new firm believes it can survive. One way of preventing the survival of the new firm, perhaps even deterring its entry, would be for the colluding established firms to reduce the industry price to P_L. Although this would reduce their own excess profits in the short run (by VW per unit) the new entrant would make a loss selling E at price P_L, since price would be less than average cost at that output. It would have needed to produce as much as output S *immediately* at the price P_L, even to have just covered its average costs.

The greater the barriers to the entry of new firms, the higher the 'limit price', P_L, can be, i.e. the closer P_L can be to P_I. The most favourable situation for established firms would be if barriers were so great that P_L were at, or above, P_I. In other words, established firms could set the joint profit-maximizing price without inducing entry.

An example of the occurrence of high barriers to entry and relatively high limit prices could be seen in the French market for natural spring water during the early 1990s. In 1992 the French market for such bottled water was dominated by three companies, Nestlé, Perrier and BSN, and the barriers to entry into the industry were high. For example, the transport costs of bringing non-French water to the market were substantial and persuading French retailers to stock new brands was difficult. Advertising costs were also heavy, helping create strong brand loyalties in France for the products of the three companies. Finally, the fact that the companies held 82% of the

market share by volume constituted an additional problem for prospective new entrants (EC 1994). As a result, these companies were able to increase their prices substantially during the period, thus keeping their limit prices high and maximizing their joint profits.

Occasionally a limit-pricing policy is explicitly adopted, as in the early 1960s when the three major petrol wholesalers, Shell/BP, Esso and Regent, were threatened with new entrants. In 1963 Shell announced a price reduction 'to make the UK market less attractive to newcomers and potential newcomers'. Again, in 1973 the Monopolies and Mergers Commission (MMC) found evidence of limit-pricing by Kellogg, concluding that 'when fixing its prices, therefore, Kellogg has as an objective the preservation of its share of the market against potential competitors'.

An obvious constraint to limit-pricing is that prices cannot be set below X in Fig. 6.3, the level at which the established firms begin to make excess profits (normal profit included in average cost), at least not for any length of time. The established firms may therefore resort to non-price competition to reinforce barriers against new entrants. For instance, the petrol companies sought extensive 'solus' agreements, giving discounts to retailers dealing exclusively with them, and sought to buy up retail outlets directly. In the detergent industry, Unilever, by introducing new brands, have increased product differentiation and raised barriers to entry. As much as 58% of their turnover comes from new brands introduced in the past 20 years. Extensive advertising (as shown by Table 6.2) is yet another way of increasing barriers to entry into a market or industry. Advertising can be used to increase brand loyalty, thus making it difficult for new firms with a new product to enter a market. Increased advertising can be used by firms already in the industry not only to keep other firms out, but also to drive out existing firms which have newly entered the industry.

To investigate this latter proposition, a study was undertaken into the behaviour of 42 companies operating in various consumer goods markets, such as electric shavers, deodorants, washing-up liquids and kettles, over the period 1975 to 1981. The study investigated the advertising strategy of companies *already in* these oligopolistic markets after new firms with new products had managed to enter those markets (Cubbin and Domberger 1988). The results of the study showed that increased advertising was used as a weapon in an attempt to drive out new entrants in 38% of markets studied, and that the response of the firms already in the market to the new entrants depended on the *structure of the oligopoly* and the *nature of the market*. For example, in a tightly competitive oligopoly situation, where a dominant firm controlled more than 30% of the market, it was more likely that the new entrant would be exposed to increased advertising competition than in a looser oligopoly where there was no clear dominance by one firm. Similarly, increased advertising competition was more likely to face new entrants in static markets, i.e. those in which demand is not growing. This is partly because growing markets tend to be dominated by new consumers with less attachment to the products of existing firms. Advertising in this situation is therefore a less certain weapon for driving out a new entrant, as compared to a market in which demand is static.

We now turn briefly to the methods which firms have actually used to promote collusion in oligopolistic markets.

Methods of collusion

Formal collusion – cartels

Formal collusion often takes the form of a cartel – in other words, the establishment of some central body with responsibility for setting the industry price and output which most nearly meets some agreed objective. Usually it also has the responsibility for sharing that total output between the members. Cartels are against the law in most countries, including the UK. However, in the UK the Cement Makers' Federation was an exception. Up to 1987 it still held monthly meetings in which deliveries, prices and market shares were discussed. The three main companies sharing the market were Blue Circle (60%), Rio Tinto Zinc (22%) and Rugby Portland (18%), with their common price calculated on a formula which averaged the costs of different producers. The Restrictive Practices Court permitted the cartel to continue on the basis that a common price agreement enables cement capacity to be controlled in an orderly way. Nevertheless, increased concentration of the cement industry in the last few years raised the possibility of intervention by the MMC (now the Competition Commission) and this, together with international competition from cheap European imports (especially from Greece), caused the cartel to be abandoned in

1987. However, cartel-type collusion still persists in the UK cement industry. In 2000, the three largest UK producers of ordinary Portland cement (OPC), i.e. Blue Circle plc, Castle Cement Ltd and the Rugby Group, refused to supply bulk OPC to customers such as ready-mix concrete producers who had intended to resell it in bags to builders' merchants. This was because they themselves sold OPC in bag form to customers. In September 2000 the Office of Fair Trading (OFT) found that such a policy was anti-competitive and told the companies to desist from such supply-fixing cartel behaviour.

An example of a price-fixing cartel operating in the UK was discovered and prohibited by the OFT in 1999. Vitafoam Ltd of Rochdale, Carpenter plc of Glossop, and Recticel Ltd of Alfreton had met to agree on price rises of 8% for foam rubber and 4% for reconstituted foam which they supplied to the upholstery business. Cartel members agreed that the price rises announced by Vitafoam, the market leader, would be matched immediately by similar announcements from Carpenter and Recticel. Another example of a price-fixing cartel operating in the UK was brought to light in April 2005 when 10 roofing contractors in north-east England were found guilty of fixing prices, sharing markets and paying off their potential competitors. The contractors were found to have colluded together and allocated the contract to one of them *before* they tendered their price for the job to customers. For example, in one instance the company Rock Asphalte Limited was found to have been allocated the contract as a result of collusion between the roofing contractors which then 'compensated' others in the group for placing a higher tender price than itself. The money to pay for such 'compensation' came by charging the customer an excessive amount for the work done. In February 2006 the OFT fined the roofing contractors a total of £1.6m for their part in the collusive tendering. Similarly, in 2009 the OFT imposed fines of £39.3m on six recruitment agencies known as the 'Construction Recruitment Forum'. The companies concerned were Warwick Associates, Beresford Blake Thomas, CDI AndersElite, Eden Brown, Fusion People, Hays Specialist Recruitment, Henry Recruitment and Hill McGlynn Associates, all of whom operated in the UK employment recruitment business. The six companies had met between 2004 and 2006 to fix target fee rates which they would charge construction companies for sending them potential recruits. This practice of price-fixing was seen to be restricting or distorting competition and a fine was imposed.

Various cartels operate internationally. The most famous is OPEC, in which many but not all (the UK is not a member) oil-exporting countries meet regularly to agree on prices and set production quotas. Whilst OPEC worked successfully in the mid-1970s in raising oil prices, in the worldwide economic slump of the early 1980s coordination proved increasingly difficult. As demand for oil fell, exporters were faced with the necessity of cutting production quotas to maintain prices; and some, such as Iran and Nigeria with major internal economic problems, were unwilling to do this, preferring to cut prices and seek higher market share. Of course, the Iraqi pressure on OPEC countries to curtail production and raise prices, and the subsequent Kuwait invasion, contributed to higher oil prices in the early 1990s. However, by 1992/93, the continued fall in demand for oil under worldwide recessionary conditions, allied to some additional oil supplies (e.g. from the Gulf States), revived the disagreements between those cartel members in favour of price cuts and those in favour of tighter quotas. In more recent times, OPEC's ability to enforce the cartel led to a cut in the supply of oil available to industrial countries in March 1999. This resulted in a trebling of the price of a barrel of crude oil from $10 to $34 by March 2000.

The International Air Transport Association (IATA) is the cartel of international airlines, and has sought to set prices for each route. During the 1970s it was seriously weakened by price-cutting competition from non-member airlines, such as Laker Airways. It was further weakened by worldwide recession in the late 1980s and early 1990s, with lower incomes causing demand for air travel, with its high-income elasticity, to fall dramatically. To fill seats, the member airlines began to compete amongst themselves in terms of price, often via a complex system of discounts. The experiences of OPEC and IATA suggest that cartels are vulnerable both to price-cutting amongst members when demand for the product declines, and to competition from non-members.

Another example of an international cartel was brought to light by investigations during 1990 into the activity of the International Telegraph and Telephone Consultative Committee (CCITT), a Geneva-based 'club' consisting of the main international telephone companies of the major industrial countries (*Financial Times* 1990). Major international telephone companies such as AT&T (USA), British Telecom (UK), Deutsche Bundespost (Germany), France Télécom (France), Telecom Canada (Canada) and KDD (Japan) belong to the group. The CCITT had a book of 'recommendations' for its member companies which included two important features. First, it suggested a complicated method of sharing the revenues received from international telephone calls. When international phone calls are made from the UK to Japan, for example, BT receives the money for the call but it has to pay KDD in Japan for delivering the call to its final destination in that country. The particular method used to calculate the distribution of the revenue received for the call between the various international telephone companies tended to penalize any company that attempted to cut its telephone prices. This in turn made it difficult for both existing and new companies to decrease prices because their profits would also fall. Second, it suggested that members of the group should not lease too much of their international telephone circuits to other private companies, since this could increase potential competition.

The effect of the first 'rule' was to provide high profit margins for telephone companies because prices were kept artificially high by the peculiar revenue-sharing scheme. Meanwhile, new technological advances had decreased the *real* costs per minute of using a transatlantic cable from $2.53 in 1956 to $0.04 in 1988. While costs had fallen drastically, the price charged for a peak call from the US to the UK and Italy remained at $2 and $4 per minute respectively! As a result, profit margins on international calls (i.e. profits divided by revenue) of some of the top earners were as follows: Japan 75%, Canada 68%, USA 63%, Britain 58%, West Germany 48%, and France 43%. British Telecom earned a profit of between £600m and £800m on its international business during the 1988/89 financial year, depending on the accounting definitions used. The second 'rule' made it difficult for new companies to enter this market because most of the international cables were built by members of the CCITT and new operators had to get permission from these companies in order to lease cable space from them. If they were not allowed more space on international cables, then new companies had to use satellite links which were more expensive and of lower quality than cable links.

Tacit collusion – price leadership

Although cartels are illegal in most countries, various forms of tacit collusion undoubtedly occur. In 1776, Adam Smith wrote in his *Wealth of Nations* that entrepreneurs rarely meet together without conspiring to raise prices at the expense of the consumer. Today the most usual method of tacit collusion is price leadership, where one firm sets a price which the others follow.

1. Dominant-firm leadership. Frequently the price leader is the dominant firm. In the late 1960s Brooke Bond controlled 43% of the market for tea, well ahead of the second largest firm Typhoo with only 18% of the market. Brooke Bond's price rises were soon matched by those of other firms, bringing the industry to the attention of the Prices and Incomes Board in 1970. Sealink, with 34% of the cross-channel ferry market, seems to have been the price leader in ferry travel to the Continent in the 1980s. In the car industry, Ford has frequently acted as the dominant market leader by being first with its price increases. In 1990, companies that bought fleet cars from Ford, Rover, Vauxhall and Peugeot Talbot, accused the big car manufacturers of operating a price cartel led by Ford. By initiating two separate price rises (amounting to a total of 8.5% by the middle of 1990), Ford was seen as the dominant leader of a 'cartel' by the fleet car buyers. We have already noted that Vitafoam acted as a dominant price leader for reconstituted foam in the upholstery business in the UK in 1999. Worries about dominant price leadership in banking also emerged in 2005 when the big four Irish banks, Bank of Ireland, First Trust Bank, National Bank and the Ulster Bank, were accused of tacit collusion. In this case, the other three banks appeared to follow the lead of the National Bank when changing the prices of their products and services (OFT 2005).

2. Barometric-firm leadership. In some cases the price leader is a small firm, recognized by others to have a close knowledge of prevailing market conditions. The firm acts as a 'barometer' to others of changing market conditions, and its prices are closely followed. In the mid-1970s Williams and Glyn's, a relatively small commercial bank, took the lead in reducing bank charges in response to rising interest rates. Maunder also found this sort of price leadership in the glass bottle and sanitary ware markets of

the 1960s and early 1970s (Maunder 1972). Since the mid-1970s there have been signs that the 'minor' petrol wholesalers have had an increasing influence on petrol prices (see Chapter 9). Again the barometric form of price leadership can be seen in the North American newsprint industry where some 30 firms produce most of the newsprint. In a major study, Booth *et al.* (1991) found a tendency for a leader to emerge which then acts as an 'anchor' for the calculations of other firms in the industry and as a 'trigger' for any price adjustment within the group when cost or demand conditions change.

3. Collusive-price leadership. This is a more complicated form of price leadership; essentially it is an informal cartel in which prices change almost simultaneously. The parallel pricing which occurred in the wholesale petrol market (noted in Chapter 9) until the mid-1970s suggested this sort of tacit group collusion. In practice it is often difficult to distinguish collusive-price leadership from types in which firms follow price leaders very quickly. The French market for spring water, referred to earlier in the chapter, is one where both the setting of parallel prices and price leadership were present. Between 1987 and 1992 the prices of bottled water sold by Nestlé, Perrier and BSN rose in almost a simultaneous or parallel way, with Perrier being the price leader. Although the three companies did not have a collusive price arrangement, their behaviour was reminiscent of a close 'tacit' form of oligopolistic interdependence. This type of tacit collusion was also thought to be present in the case of the Irish banks noted previously. For example, it was known that bank prices were not directly cost derived and so the upward movement of prices was not necessarily due to differences in costs. Between 1999 and 2004 there was some evidence that price changes tended to follow, in a parallel fashion, the lead given by the National Bank either in the same quarter or in succeeding quarters (Competition Commission 2007).

Conclusion

That oligopoly has become a progressively more important form of market structure in the UK is clear from the data, particularly from concentration ratios.

Interdependence is a key feature of such markets, which makes the outcome of any strategy by a firm uncertain, depending to a large extent on how the rivals react. Price competition may be a particularly hazardous strategy, perhaps leading to a 'price war'. In any case, to the extent that kinked-demand theory is valid, the profit-maximizing price may not change even for wide variations in cost. For both these reasons there may be extensive periods of price stability. Even so, there may still be close competition between firms for market share, though this will be mainly of the non-price variety – advertising, packaging, new brands, etc. Non-price competition, by increasing product differentiation, real or imagined, may benefit firms not only by raising market share, but by providing greater future control over price – extra brand loyalty making demand curves less price-elastic.

The uncertainty of rival reactions, whether price or non-price, can be mitigated by guesswork, based on past experience (reaction curves), or by trying to evaluate the rivals' optimal counter-strategy (game theory). Collusion between firms may be a still more secure way of reducing uncertainty and avoiding mutual damage. This could be arranged formally, as in cartels, or informally by some form of tacit collusion (information agreements, price leadership, etc.). Although we may be no nearer a general model of oligopoly behaviour, we have made some progress in predicting how firms react under particular circumstances at particular times.

Key points

- Concentration ratios for both product and industry groups have risen over time, implying a more oligopolistic market structure.

- 'Recognized interdependence between the few' is a key feature of oligopoly markets.

- Where firms develop their own strategies independently we speak of 'non-collusive behaviour'.

- Even in this case firms will seek to anticipate how their rivals might react to any strategy they might adopt.

- Past experience might be a guide to rival reactions, as in the 'kinked demand' model. Firms learn that rivals match price cuts but not price rises. The model predicts price stability.

- Even where there is little price competition, there may be extensive non-price competition.

- 'Game' simulations may be used to predict the outcomes of different combinations of action/reaction. Games may or may not have stable equilibria depending on the strategies each firm adopts.

- To avoid uncertainty, collusion may occur, whether formal (cartels) or informal (tacit).

- Informal collusion may include various types of price leadership models as well as agreements of various kinds.

- To be successful firms must abide by the rules of collusive agreements, e.g. producing no more than their allocated quotas.

Now try the self-check questions for this chapter on the Companion Website. You will also find useful links to relevant websites.

Notes

1 Cross-elasticity of demand is defined as the percentage change in the quantity demanded of X, divided by the percentage change in the price of Y. If X and Y are close substitutes, then a small fall in the price of Y will lead to a substantial decrease in demand for X. This gives a high positive value for the quotient.

2 See, for instance, Jump (1982), which suggested that brand loyalty permitted prices to be 9% higher for branded processed foods in the US than for supermarket own-brand equivalents.

3 This is because each demand curve, dd' and DD' respectively, will have its own separate marginal revenue curve, bisecting the horizontal between the vertical axis and the demand curve in question.

4 The maxi–min approach is a rather conservative strategy in that it assumes that the rival reacts to your strategy in the worst possible way for you.

5 A distribution of the joint profit-maximizing output such that aggregate $MR = MC$ in each separate market is often called the 'ideal' distribution. From Fig. 6.2 we can see that there is no other distribution which will raise total profits for the industry. For instance, one extra unit produced by Firm B will add more to cost than is saved by one fewer unit produced by Firm A (i.e. $MC_B > MC_A$). Whether the firms will acquiesce in such a share-out is quite another matter.

References and further reading

Bhaskar, V., Machin, S. and Reid, G. (1991) Testing a model of the kinked demand curve, *Journal of Industrial Economics*, **39**(3): 241–54.

Booth, D. I., Kanetkar, V., Vertinsky, I. and Whistler, D. (1991) An empirical model of capacity expansion and pricing in an oligopoly with barometric price leadership: a case study of the newsprint industry of North America, *Journal of Industrial Economics*, **39**(3): 255–76.

Competition Commission (2007) *Cross-border Personal Banking in Ireland*, 18 May, London.

Competition Commission (2009) *Personal Current Account Banking Services in Northern Ireland; Market Investigation*, 15 May, London.

Coyne, K. and Horn, J. (2009) Predicting your competitor's reaction, *Harvard Business Review*, April, 1–8.

Cubbin, J. and Domberger, S. (1988) Advertising and post-entry oligopoly behaviour, *Journal of Industrial Economics*, **37**(December): 123–40.

Davies, S. and Lyons, D. (1996) *Industrial Organisation in the EU*, Oxford, Clarendon Press.

Dixon, H. (1990) Reconnecting charges with costs, *Financial Times* 3 April.

Domberger, S. (1980) Mergers, market structure and the rate of price adjustment, in Cowling, K. *et al.* (eds), *Mergers and Economic Performance*, Cambridge, Cambridge University Press, Ch. 13.

Economic Trends (2005) *Input–Output: Concentration Ratios for Businesses by Industry in 2003*, **624**(November): 52–62.

EC (1994) *European Economy*, No. 57, Part C, Brussels, European Commission.

Ferreira, N., Kar, J. and Trigeorgis, L. (2009) Option games, *Harvard Business Review*, March, 101–107.

Financial Times (1990) Reconnecting charges with costs, 3 April.

Jump, N. (1982) Corporate strategy in mature markets, *Barclays Bank Review*, **57**(4): 84–9.

Marketing (2010a) *Top 100 Advertisers*, 15 March.

Marketing (2010b) *Top 100 Advertisers*, 24 March.

Maunder, P. (1972) Price leadership: an appraisal of its character in some British industries, *Business Economist*, **4**(Autumn): 132–40

Mintel International Group Ltd (2010), *Mintel Reports* (various).

OFT (2005) *The OFT's Reasons for Making a Reference to the Competition Commission*, May (OFT 787), London, Office of Fair Trading.

Wagner, L. (ed.) (1981) *Readings in Applied Micro-economics* (2nd edn), Oxford, Oxford University Press.

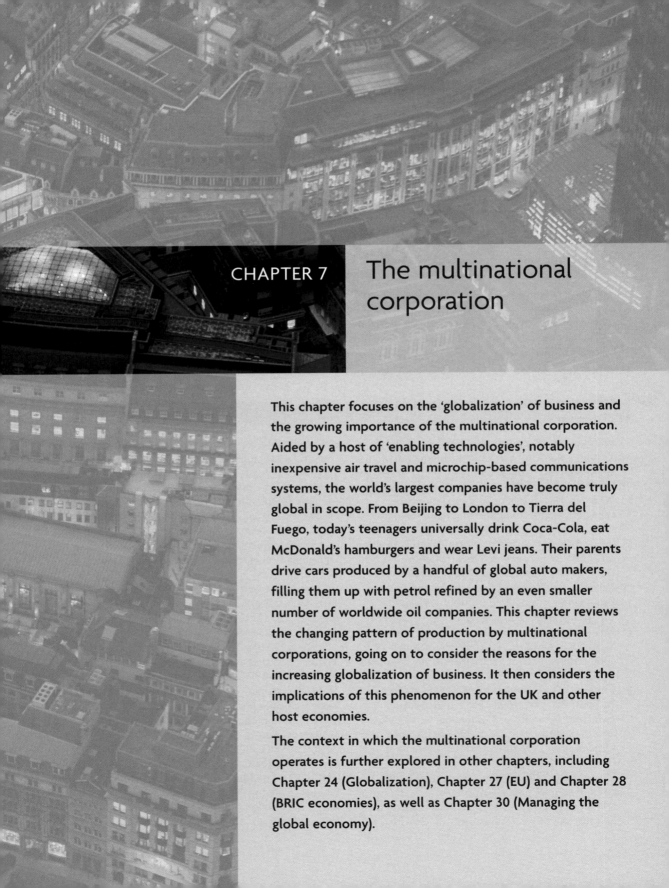

CHAPTER 7

The multinational corporation

This chapter focuses on the 'globalization' of business and the growing importance of the multinational corporation. Aided by a host of 'enabling technologies', notably inexpensive air travel and microchip-based communications systems, the world's largest companies have become truly global in scope. From Beijing to London to Tierra del Fuego, today's teenagers universally drink Coca-Cola, eat McDonald's hamburgers and wear Levi jeans. Their parents drive cars produced by a handful of global auto makers, filling them up with petrol refined by an even smaller number of worldwide oil companies. This chapter reviews the changing pattern of production by multinational corporations, going on to consider the reasons for the increasing globalization of business. It then considers the implications of this phenomenon for the UK and other host economies.

The context in which the multinational corporation operates is further explored in other chapters, including Chapter 24 (Globalization), Chapter 27 (EU) and Chapter 28 (BRIC economies), as well as Chapter 30 (Managing the global economy).

What is a multinational corporation?

The terms 'multinational', 'transnational' and 'international' corporation (or enterprise) are often used interchangeably. A multinational may be defined as a company which owns or controls production or service facilities in more than one country. In other words, a multinational is *not* simply a company which trades internationally by exporting its products (or by licensing overseas producers); it actually *owns* (via a wholly or partly owned subsidiary) or *controls* (via a branch plant, joint venture or minority shareholding) productive facilities in countries outside its home country. Such overseas productive facilities may be acquired by taking over existing locally owned capacity (e.g. Coca-Cola's acquisition of parts of Cadbury Schweppes in the UK) or by investing directly in new (or 'greenfield site') plant and equipment (e.g. Nissan's plant in Washington or Toyota's car factory in Derby).

From a statistical point of view, there are two main methods of ranking the world's top multinationals: first, according to the amount of foreign assets they control, and second, in terms of a 'transnationality index'. Table 7.1 ranks the top 10 multinationals according to the value of foreign assets they control. We can see that two of the top 10 companies are from the US, three from the UK, two from France

and one each from Japan, Germany and Luxembourg. They are primarily based in the telecommunications, petroleum, energy and motor vehicle sectors. However, Table 7.1 also provides each company's transnationality index and its transnationality ranking. The *transnationality index* takes a more comprehensive view of a company's global activity and is calculated as the average of the following ratios: foreign assets/total assets; foreign sales/total sales; and foreign employment/total employment. For example, we can see that the largest multinational company is General Electric in terms of the foreign assets it owns. However, its transnationality index of 52% means that it is ranked only 75th in terms of this criterion. The reason for this is that even though it has large investments overseas in absolute value, in *percentage* terms most of its assets, sales and employment are still located in the US. This is in contrast with Exxon Corporation where over 68% of its overall activity is based abroad.

If we wanted to find the companies which operate mostly outside their home country, then we would have to look at the top 10 multinationals in terms of the *transnationality index*. These are shown in Table 7.2 and here we see the dominance of European Union (EU) companies in sectors such as food/beverages, chemicals, telecommunications and extractive industries. The companies with the highest transnationality index are often from the smaller countries,

Table 7.1 World's top 10 non-financial multinationals ranked by foreign assets, 2008.

Rankings					
Foreign assets	Transnationality index	Company	Country	Industry	Transnationality index (%)
1	75	General Electric	US	Electric/electronics	52
2	32	Royal/Dutch Shell	UK	Petroleum	73
3	6	Vodafone	UK	Telecommunications	89
4	20	British Petroleum	UK	Petroleum	81
5	74	Toyota Motor	Japan	Motor vehicles	53
6	42	ExxonMobil	US	Petroleum	68
7	27	Total SA	France	Petroleum	75
8	67	E.ON AG	Germany	Electricity/gas/water	56
9	90	Electricite De France	France	Electricity/gas/water	42
10	10	ArcelorMittal	Luxembourg	Metals/metal products	87

Source: Modified from UNCTAD (2010) *World Investment Report 2010*, Annex, Table 26.

Table 7.2 World's top 10 non-financial multinationals ranked by transnationality index, 2008.

Rankings					
Transnationality index	Foreign Assets	Company	Country	Industry	Transnationality index (%)
1	37	Xstrata plc	UK	Mining/quarrying	93
2	87	ABB Ltd	Switzerland	Engineering services	90
3	40	Nokia	Finland	Telecommunications	90
4	66	Pernod Ricard SA	France	Food/beverages/tobacco	89
5	67	WPP Group plc	UK	Other business services	89
6	3	Vodafone	UK	Telecommunications	89
7	72	Linde AG	Germany	Chemicals	88
8	13	Anheuser-Busch InBev	Netherlands	Food/beverages/tobacco	88
9	46	Anglo America	UK	Mining and quarrying	88
10	10	ArcelorMittal	Luxembourg	Metals	87

Source: Modified from UNCTAD (2010) *World Investment Report 2010,* Annex, Table 26.

as a more restricted domestic market induces them to operate abroad if they are to maximize their growth in terms of revenue or profits.

Technical definitions of multinationals, however, fail to convey the true scope and diversity of global business, which covers everything from the thousands of medium-sized firms which have overseas operations to the truly gigantic multinationals like IBM, General Motors and Ford. Some multinationals are vertically integrated, with different stages of the same productive process taking place in different countries (e.g. British Petroleum). Others are horizontally integrated, performing the same basic production operations in each of the countries in which they operate (e.g. Marks & Spencer). Many multinationals are household names, marketing global brands (e.g. Rothmans International, IBM, British Airways). Others are holding companies for a portfolio of international companies (e.g. Diageo) or specialize in capital goods that have little name-recognition in the high street (e.g. BTR).

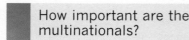

How important are the multinationals?

One way of assessing the importance of multinationals in an economy can be gauged by a survey of

the relevance of US multinationals in their *own* economy. For example, US multinationals in 2010 accounted for 23% of US private sector GDP and 41% of US gains in productivity since 1990. In addition, the higher than normal productivity growth which US multinationals show over other domestic US companies appears to have contributed 75% of US real GDP gains since 2000. Finally, US multinational companies account for nearly half of the nation's exports and a third of the nation's imports (McKinsey Global Institute 2010). Because of these ownership-specific advantages (see p. 137), US companies are able through foreign direct investment (FDI) to transfer their output and productivity benefits to foreign countries such as the UK.

In 2009 the United Nations Division on Transnational Corporations and Investment estimated that there were 82,053 multinationals at that time, collectively controlling a total of 807,363 foreign affiliates. Table 7.3 provides an overview of multinational activity. It shows that in 2009 the sales of multinationals' foreign affiliates exceeded global exports and amounted to over 50% of world Gross Domestic Product (GDP). In terms of importance in research and development (R&D), the aggregate spending of the world's eight largest multinationals on R&D in 2009 was larger than the R&D investments of all individual countries, except for the US and Japan (OECD 2010). Ranked by either turnover or GDP, half of the world's largest economic 'units' are multinationals,

Table 7.3 Multinational activity in a global context.

	2009 ($bn)	Average annual growth rates (%)				
		1991–1995	1996–2000	2001–2005	2008	2009
FDI outflows	1,101	16.8	35.6	9.2	−14.9	−42.9
FDI outward stock	18,982	11.9	18.4	14.6	−16.1	−17.1
Sales of foreign affiliates	29,298	8.8	8.2	18.1	−4.5	−5.7
World GDP at factor cost	55,005	5.9	1.3	10.0	10.3	−9.5
World gross fixed capital formation	12,404	5.4	1.1	11.0	11.5	−10.3
Exports of goods and non-factor services	15,716	7.9	3.7	14.8	15.4	−21.4

Source: Modified from UNCTAD (2010) *World Investment Report 2010*, Table 1.5.

rather than countries. Only 15 nation states have a GDP which exceeds the turnover of Exxon, Toyota or General Motors.

Historically, the bulk of multinational activity was concentrated in the *developed* world. Indeed, as recently as the mid-1980s, half of all multinational production took place in only five countries – the US, Canada, the UK, Germany and the Netherlands. This pattern is now changing rapidly. The rapid industrialization and economic growth in the newly industrializing nations of the world has led to a sharp increase in multinational investment in Asia and (to a lesser extent) Latin America. Some of these countries, notably the 'four tigers' (Taiwan, South Korea, Hong Kong and Singapore), now have per capita GDP levels which exceed those of most European nations and their indigenous companies are now beginning to establish production facilities in the 'old world'. The old bipolar world (dominated by North America and Europe) is now giving way to a tripolar economy, comprising the 'triad' of North America, the EU and East and South-East Asia. These three regions account for approximately 75% of the world's exports and 60% of manufacturing output and the majority of multinational activity, although such activity in the Middle East and Africa is also growing.

It is estimated that in the next 10 years, world GDP will nearly double from its present level of $55,000bn to $90,000bn, with the share of the developing world rising from one-third to one-half over the same period. Table 7.4 shows the changing pattern of FDI by which domestic companies acquire control over productive facilities overseas. After the problems of the early 1990s, inflows of foreign investment rose strongly in the developed countries before experiencing a setback in the early years of the new millennium and again after the financial crisis of 2007/08. The trend in the developing countries was similar but at relatively lower absolute values.

Table 7.4 also reflects the reintegration of the former centrally planned economies of central and eastern Europe into the world economy. Although the total volume of inward foreign investment is still relatively low (central and eastern Europe attracted only 5.7% of total global inflows in the period 2007–09), inflows have increased strongly since the transition process began in 1989. In this region, 60% of the inflows are associated with the privatization of former state-owned enterprises (compared with 8% in the other developing countries). Unsurprisingly, countries that have pushed ahead with market reform, and privatization in particular, have attracted the bulk of the foreign investment, both by creating international confidence in their future economic and political stability and by providing the opportunities for foreign companies to buy local production and distribution facilities. Poland and the Czech Republic, for example, have been highly successful in attracting multinationals such as Ford, Volkswagen and Philip Morris. Countries which have resisted or delayed market reform, notably many of the states of the former Soviet Union, have, in contrast, found foreign companies less willing to risk large-scale inward investment.

Table 7.4 Inflows of foreign direct investment ($bn).

Region	1990–95 (annual average)	1998	2002	2007	2008	2009
Developed countries	145.0	484.2	547.8	1,444.1	1,108.2	565.9
Developing countries	74.3	187.6	155.5	56.9	630.0	478.3
SE Europe and CIS	6.0	22.6	12.8	91.0	122.6	69.9

Note: CIS – Commonwealth of Independent States (formerly Soviet states).
Sources: Modified from UNCTAD (2010) *World Investment Report 2010*, Annex Table 1; UNCTAD (2005) *World Investment Report 2005*, Annex Table B2.

Multinationals and the UK economy

Multinationals play a central role in the UK economy. Table 7.5 gives one indication of their importance. It lists the top 25 UK corporations ranked by revenue, most of them being well-known multinational companies. In the non-financial sector, Royal Dutch/Shell and BP boast production and distribution facilities in over 100 countries and have a transnationality index of 73% and 81%, respectively. Similarly, companies such as Vodafone, the mobile communications giant, GlaxoSmithKline in pharmaceuticals and Tesco, the retailer of food and other products, are major players on the international scene. It should also be remembered that the UK has some large companies in the financial sector, such as the Lloyds banking group and Aviva, the insurance company, both of which are in the top 100 global companies in terms of revenue.

The UK still ranks as a major home to multinationals, reflecting its colonial past and the vast assets it has accumulated. Although Table 7.6 suggests that the *number* of home-based multinationals is smaller than in the other countries represented, the *value* of their contribution to multinational activity is greater, as can be seen in Table 7.7. Outward foreign investment from Britain has remained high ever since the Second World War, with UK home-based multinationals responsible for over 19% of all FDI outflows from the five major economies over the time period in Table 7.7. Moreover, despite the UK's increasingly close economic and political ties with other member states of the EU, the bulk of *outward* foreign direct investment still goes to the US where UK multinationals retain a pre-eminent position in terms of the value of US assets controlled.

As a host country, the UK is also an important destination for *inward* direct investment by foreign multinationals (see Table 7.6). Of the *Financial Times* top 500 companies operating in the UK, 313 are foreign-owned, with Germany (87), France (77), Switzerland (28) and the Netherlands (17) being the most important European nations. Just as UK multinationals dominate FDI in the US, however, so US multinationals account for the lion's share of FDI in the UK; and led by Nissan, Sony, Toyota and Honda, Japanese and Korean multinationals have also increased their stake in the UK economy. By 2010 some 120 major Japanese companies had set up in the UK. Over 30% of all Japanese foreign direct investment in the EU to date has been in the UK.

The UK economy is thus particularly affected by the globalization of business, being simultaneously home of, *and* host to, a large number of multinationals producing a rapidly growing proportion of its output. Multinational companies (both UK companies and foreign companies in the UK) account for an estimated 30% of GDP in the UK and almost half of all manufacturing employment. Most activity is concentrated in capital-intensive, high technology sectors – computers, automobiles, electronics, pharmaceuticals and chemicals. One-third of UK exports and imports by value are estimated to be *intra-firm* (within firm) transactions, as multinationals import and export the intermediate products which tie together production processes which are vertically integrated across national frontiers.

Table 7.5 The UK's top 25 companies by revenue.

UK rank	Company	Sector	Revenues ($m)	Employees	Global rank
1	BP	Oil & Gas	246,138	80,300	4
2	HSBC Holdings	Banking	103,736	309,516	39
3	Lloyds banking Group	Banking	102,967	132,000	42
4	Aviva	Insurance	92,140	46,327	53
5	Royal Bank of Scotland	Banking	91,767	160,000	55
6	Tesco	Retailers	90,234	468,508	58
7	Prudential	Insurance	75,010	27,389	72
8	Vodafone	Mobile Communications	70,899	85,000	80
9	Legal & General	Insurance	68,290	9,324	90
10	Barclays	Banking	66,533	153,800	96
11	GlaxoSmithKline	Pharmaceuticals	44,340	99,913	96
12	Rio Tinto Zinc	Mining	41,825	101,994	173
13	Centrica	Utilities	37,927	34,125	188
14	Scottish and Southern Energy	Utilities	34,357	20,177	215
15	Old Mutual	Insurance	34,072	53,706	220
16	BT Group	Telecommunications	33,860	97,800	222
17	AstraZeneca	Pharmaceuticals	32,804	62,700	226
18	J. Sainsbury	Retailers	31,828	97,300	236
19	BAE Systems	Aerospace/Defence	31,773	98,000	238
20	Standard Life	Insurance	27,803	9,752	288
21	Wolseley	Support Services	24,461	55,132	341
22	William Morrison	Retailers	24,263	94,724	344
23	Imperial Tobacco	Tobacco	22,760	38,381	377
24	National Grid	Utilities	22,331	28,106	384
25	British American Tobacco	Tobacco	22,760	38,381	387

Source: Modified from Fortune (2010) *Global 500*, July.

Table 7.6 Home and host to multinationals.

	Parent corporation in country: home	Foreign affiliates based in country: host
France	1,267	10,713
Germany	6,115	11,750
UK	2,360	13,667
Japan	4,663	4,500
US	2,418	5,664
Total (five countries)	16,823	46,294
Developed countries	58,783	366,881

Source: Modified from UNCTAD (2009) *World Investment Report 2009*, Annex, Table A.1.8.

Interestingly, it is not only the transfer of technology from FDI via multinationals which is important, but also the *use* made of such technological transfer to increase productivity in the UK. For example, US multinationals operating new plants in the UK appear to be more effective in the use of IT than both their domestic UK counterparts and other non-US multinationals operating in the UK. These higher IT productivity benefits also occurred when US multinationals took over UK companies, whereas UK companies taken over by non-US multinationals did not show such benefits. These differences may be due to the ways in which US firms are organized which allow them to use new technologies more efficiently (Bloom *et al.* 2007). Whatever the cause, it can be seen that FDI by foreign multinationals in the form of technological transfer can bring benefits to the UK.

Table 7.7 Outflows from five main home economies for multinationals ($bn).

Location	1990–1995 (annual average)	1998	2002	2007	2008	2009
France	23.7	48.6	50.4	164.3	161.1	147.1
Germany	23.4	88.8	15.2	162.5	134.6	62.7
UK	25.6	122.8	12.3	318.2	161.1	18.5
Japan	25.0	24.2	32.3	73.5	128.0	74.7
US	54.1	131.0	134.9	393.5	330.5	248.1
Total	155.8	223.0	415.4	1,112.0	915.3	551.1
Developed countries	**221.0**	**631.3**	**599.9**	**1,923.9**	**1,572.0**	**820.7**

Sources: Modified from UNCTAD (2010) *World Investment Report*, Annex, Table 1; UNCTAD (2005) *World Investment Report 2005*, Annex, Table B.1.

Why do companies become multinational?

Multinationals are very heterogeneous in nature. Most large companies are multinational, but there are many medium-sized companies which also have overseas operations. This heterogeneity makes it difficult to generalize about the reasons why firms become multinational. Nevertheless, there is broad agreement amongst economists that the primary motivation for multinational activity is to seek higher or more secure profits in the long term – for example, by strengthening the company's market position.

Ultimately, any such consideration of the motives for establishing overseas operations must focus on one or other side of the profit and loss account; that is, becoming multinational is driven either by a desire to cut costs or, alternatively, by the prospect of greater revenues. One way of categorizing these two motives is to distinguish between multinationals which are *cost-oriented* and those which are *market-oriented*.

- *Cost-oriented multinationals* – those which internationalize their operations by *vertical integration*; e.g. integrating backwards in search of cheaper or more secure inputs into the productive process. Oil companies such as Exxon, Shell and BP were early examples of this approach. In order to secure control of strategic raw materials in oil fields around the world, they established overseas extraction operations in the early years of the twentieth

century with the aim of shipping crude oil back to their home markets for refining and sale. More recently, many US and European companies have integrated forwards by establishing assembly facilities in South East Asia, especially China, in order to take account of the relative abundance of cheap, high quality labour (see Table 7.8). Companies such as America's ITT ship semi-manufactured components to the region, where they are assembled by local labour into finished products which are then re-exported back to the home market. Such home countries are sometimes termed 'production platforms', which underscores their role as providers of a low-cost input into a global, vertically integrated production process.

- Market-oriented multinationals – those whose internationalization is motivated by the promise of new markets and greater sales; i.e. the internationalization process takes the form of *horizontal* (rather than vertical) *integration* into new geographic markets, with companies gradually switching from exporting (or licensing) to establishing first a sales outlet and finally full production facilities overseas (see Fig. 7.1).

Figure 7.2 shows the spectacular divergence in economic performance between the world's major economies which is expected over the next 10 years. It shows that in 1992, in terms of market size, the global economy was dominated by rich industrial countries like the US, Japan, Germany, France, Italy and the UK. However, by the year 2020, China will be the world's largest market, with India, Indonesia, South

Table 7.8 Hourly compensation costs in manufacturing 2008 ($ per hour).

Country	Total labour costs ($ per hour)	Total direct pay (% of total)	Other labour costs (e.g. social insurance and labour taxes) % of total
India	0.9	–	–
China	1.4	–	–
Philippines	1.7	91.4	8.6
Mexico	4.0	73.7	26.3
Brazil	8.3	67.9	32.1
Taiwan	8.7	85.3	14.7
Hungary	9.6	73.0	27.0
Argentina	9.9	82.6	17.4
Poland	10.1	84.5	15.5
Czech Republic	12.2	73.4	26.6
Portugal	12.3	79.8	20.2
Korea	16.3	82.3	17.7
Singapore	18.8	86.0	14.0
Greece	19.6	72.4	27.6
Spain	27.7	74.1	25.9
Japan	27.8	82.2	17.8
US	32.3	76.8	23.2
Italy	35.8	69.6	30.4
UK	35.8	79.0	21.0
France	42.9	67.6	32.4
Ireland	44.8	84.7	15.3
Germany	48.2	78.1	21.9
Euro Area	**43.3**	**75.1**	**24.9**
East Asia (excl. Japan)	**13.3**	**84.8**	**15.2**

Source: Modified from US BLS (2010) *International Labor Statistics*.

Korea, Thailand and Taiwan all moving into the 'top 10'. Therefore it is increasingly likely that market-oriented companies will be drawn to these areas.

Extending the product life cycle

A more subtle variation on this theme is that firms may internationalize in order to extend the 'product life cycle' of their products. The underlying thesis is that products have a finite economic life, going through four stages or phases (see Fig. 7.3). In the *introduction phase*, the product is slow to win over consumers, who are unfamiliar with the innovation; many products fail at this stage. But for those which

are successful, sales gradually build up in the following *growth phase*, as the product becomes established. At some point, the product reaches *maturity* – there are few new users to win over and most sales are on a replacement basis; the product becomes standardized and competition becomes cut-throat. Finally, either because a new substitute challenges the product or because consumer tastes simply move on, the product moves into a period of *decline*, with sales steadily falling. The Sony Walkman provides a useful illustration of this cycle. It was first introduced to a sceptical Japanese market, where it was initially derided as a 'portable cassette player with no speakers and no facility to record tapes'. Gradually, it became established, stimulating a raft of 'me-too'

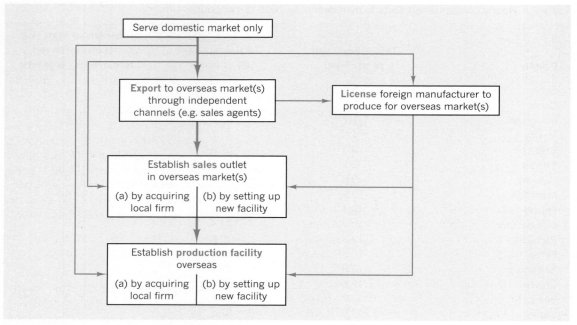

Fig. 7.1 Evolution of a market-oriented multinational.

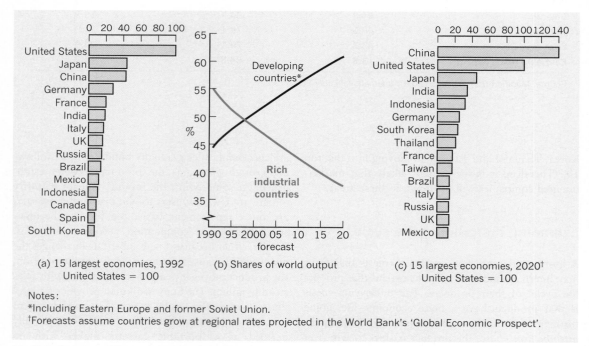

(a) 15 largest economies, 1992
United States = 100

(b) Shares of world output

(c) 15 largest economies, 2020†
United States = 100

Notes:
*Including Eastern Europe and former Soviet Union.
†Forecasts assume countries grow at regional rates projected in the World Bank's 'Global Economic Prospect'.

Fig. 7.2 Growth of the global economy, 1992–2020.
Source: Based on World Bank estimates.

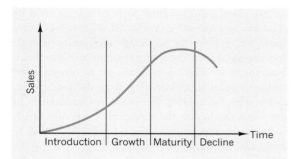

Fig. 7.3 Product life cycle.

copies by other companies until the market became saturated. These products were subsequently superseded by new formats, including portable CD players and minidisc players, which have now given way to the current generation of portable media players.

The link between the product life cycle and internationalization stems from the fact that a product may be at *different stages of its life cycle* in *different geographic markets*, giving rise to changing configurations of supply and demand which variously favour local production, and/or exporting, and/or importing from cheaper overseas suppliers.

Consider Fig. 7.4, which illustrates one possible scenario for a US manufacturer. In *Phase I* (introduction), production is concentrated in the US, with the innovating companies exporting to other countries.

As the US market matures and production techniques become standardized, production starts up in the expanding, lower-cost European market; these new lower-cost producers are able to initially displace imports into Europe from the US (in *Phase II*) and then increasingly challenge US competitors for a share of developing country markets (in *Phase III*) and finally the US market itself (in *Phase IV*). In due course, however, the technology spreads to the developing world, whose producers are gradually able to take on and out-compete the now higher-cost European companies, first in their own markets (*Phase IV*) and ultimately in the US market as well (*Phase V*). In this way, the product life-cycle drives production *out* of the innovating country to lower-cost producers overseas.

Advances in enabling technologies

While cost orientation and market orientation clearly provide important *motives* for investing and producing overseas, the acceleration in the pace of globalization is also intimately tied up with advances in *enabling technologies* which have reduced the costs of doing business across national frontiers. These include:

1 *improved communications*, including cheap air travel, satellite telephone and fax facilities, computers and IT-based communications systems such as the Internet;

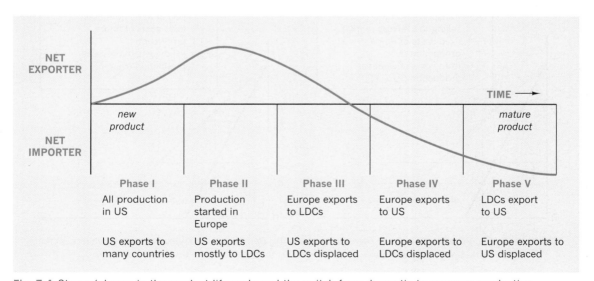

Fig. 7.4 Stages/phases in the product life cycle and the switch from domestic to overseas production.

2 *the globalization of consumer markets*, through television, video and popular music which make it cheaper for established producers to penetrate new markets in developing countries; and

3 *new organizational technologies*, e.g. the rise of the divisional corporate structure based on product or geographic divisions or matrices. This makes managing complex global companies more feasible.

Benefits of producing overseas compared to exporting

One way of exploring the decision by a domestic company to internationalize its production is to consider the advantages of producing at home *vis-à-vis* overseas.

Consider a **market-oriented** company first. By exporting, the company can concentrate production in a single plant at home, reaping the advantages of lower production costs which flow from economies of scale and avoiding the costs of managing an overseas facility. By producing overseas, however,

the company can avoid the costs of transporting its products and incurring tariffs. All other things being equal, the greater the scope for economies of scale and the higher the costs of managing offshore facilities, the more likely a firm will be to forego internationalization in favour of a large domestic plant; conversely, the smaller the scope for economies of scale and the higher the transports costs and tariffs faced when exporting, the greater the incentive to invest directly in overseas capacity.

Figure 7.5(a) illustrates these basic principles graphically. It shows the demand (average revenue) and marginal revenue schedules it faces in its *overseas* market. For simplicity, the *marginal cost of production*, whether at home or abroad, is assumed to be constant at C_1 (with a given fixed cost, this implies that average total costs decline as production increases). The *marginal cost of supplying the overseas market* from a domestic production platform is C_2, where $C_2 - C_1$ is equal to the unit costs of *transport* and *tariffs*. The firm faces *fixed* production costs of F_1 if it produces at home and F_2 if it produces abroad, where F_2 is assumed to be greater than F_1,

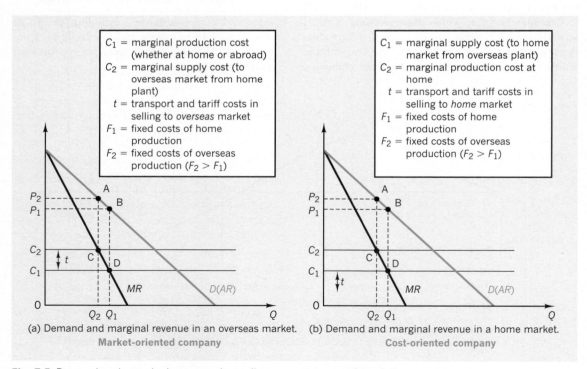

(a) Demand and marginal revenue in an overseas market.
Market-oriented company

(b) Demand and marginal revenue in a home market.
Cost-oriented company

Fig. 7.5 Demand and marginal revenue depending on company and market.

given the higher costs of managing an overseas production facility. Consider the firm's options.

- If the firm *exports to the overseas market*, it will set C_2 equal to marginal revenue, charging a price P_2 and earning profit equal to $P_2ACC_2 - F_1$.
- If the firm *establishes an overseas production facility*, then it will set C_1 equal to marginal revenue, charging a price P_1 and earning profit equal to $P_1BDC_1 - F_2$.

Clearly, the firm's decision rule is:

1 if $P_2ACC_2 - F_1 > P_1BDC_1 - F_2$, then produce at home and export to overseas market;
2 if $P_1BDC_1 - F_2 > P_2ACC_2 - F_1$, then produce overseas.

All other things being equal, the *higher the transport costs and/or tariffs levied on exports* to the overseas market (i.e. C_2 compared to C_1), the greater will be the relative attractiveness of overseas production *vis-à-vis* exporting; similarly, all other things being equal, the *lower the relative fixed costs of producing overseas* (i.e. F_2 compared to F_1), the more attractive will be overseas production. The gap $F_2 - F_1$ will be reduced by advances in enabling technologies which, as we have noted, cut the costs of doing business across national frontiers.

Hence, the decision for a market-oriented firm to locate overseas rather than export hinges critically on the transport and tariff costs of serving overseas markets and the relative fixed costs of production. The greater the former, and the smaller any gap as regards the latter ($F_2 > F_1$), the more favourable the situation is to multinational activity.

The same diagram can also be reinterpreted to illustrate the decision facing a **cost-oriented** multinational. In this case (Fig. 7.5(b)), the demand and marginal revenue schedules are drawn for the *home market*. C_2 is now the company's marginal cost of producing at home for its domestic market, while C_1 represents the marginal cost of supplying the home market from an overseas production platform and shipping back to the home market. Despite the costs of transport and tariffs, it is assumed here that overseas production is subject to lower supply costs, for example because of lower labour costs.

- If the firm *produces at home*, it sets marginal production cost C_2 equal to marginal revenue, charging a price P_2 and earning profit $P_2ACC_2 - F_1$.

- If the firm *produces abroad*, it sets marginal supply cost C_1 equal to marginal revenue, charging a price P_1 and earning profit $P_1BDC_1 - F_2$.

Its decision rules are now:

1 if $P_2ACC_2 - F_1 > P_1BDC_1 - F_2$, then produce at home;
2 if $P_1BDC_1 - F_2 > P_2ACC_2 - F_1$, then produce overseas and export to the home market.

All other things being equal, the *lower the relative marginal costs of supplying from overseas* (i.e. C_1 compared to C_2), the greater will be the relative attractiveness of overseas production *vis-à-vis* domestic production; similarly, all other things being equal, the *lower the relative fixed costs of producing overseas* (i.e. F_2 compared to F_1) the more attractive will be overseas production.

Hence, the decision for a cost-oriented firm to serve its home market from an offshore production facility rather than producing at home hinges on the relative variable costs of overseas production and relative fixed costs. The greater the (variable) cost discrepancy in favour of overseas supply, and the smaller any gap as regards overseas fixed costs compared to domestic fixed costs (i.e. F_2 compared to F_1), the more favourable the situation is to multinational activity.

It should be remembered that labour cost (an important variable cost) can be an important determinant of production location even within major industrialized countries. For example in 2010, the US Department of Labor calculated that the hourly compensation costs of manufacturing workers in the UK were \$35.8 as compared to the US (\$32.3), France (\$42.9), Japan (\$27.8) and Germany (\$48.2). The 1,500 German subsidiaries operating in the UK see the relatively low labour costs in the UK as giving them an attractive production advantage which they can exploit by exporting their UK-produced goods back to Germany and to other European countries.

Location and internalization

The above explanations of internationalization are, however, only partial. They fail to explain why cost-oriented companies do not simply import the inputs they need from independent producers in low-cost countries rather than integrating backwards; similarly,

Table 7.9 Types of international production: some determining factors.

Types of international production	(O) Ownership advantages (the 'why' of MNE activity)	(L) Location advantages (the 'where' of production)	(I) Internalization (the 'how' of involvement)	Strategic goals of MNEs	Illustration of types of activity that favour MNEs
Natural resource seeking	Capital, technology, access to markets; complementary assets; size and negotiating strengths	Possession of natural resources and related transport and communications infrastructure; tax and other incentives	To ensure stability of supplies at right price; control markets	To gain privileged access to resources vis-à-vis competitors	(a) Oil, copper, bauxite, bananas, pineapples, cocoa, hotels (b) Export processing, labour intensive products or processes
Market seeking	Capital, technology, information, management and organizational skills; surplus R&D and other capacity; economies of scale; ability to generate brand loyalty	Material and labour costs; market size and characteristics; government policy (e.g. with respect to regulations and to import controls, investment incentives, etc.)	Wish to reduce transaction or information costs, buyer ignorance, or uncertainty, etc; to protect property rights	To protect existing markets, counteract behaviour of competitors; to preclude rivals or potential rivals from gaining new markets	Computers, pharmaceuticals, motor vehicles, cigarettes, processed foods, airline services
Efficiency seeking (a) of products (b) of processes	As above, but also access to markets; economies of scope, geographical diversification, and international sourcing of inputs	(a) Economies of product specialization and concentration (b) Low labour costs; incentives to local production by host governments	(a) As for second category plus gains from economies of common governance (b) The economies of vertical integration	As part of regional or global product rationalization and/or to gain advantages of process specialization	(a) Motor vehicles, electrical appliances, business services, some R&D (b) Consumer electronics, textiles and clothing, cameras, pharmaceuticals
Strategic asset seeking	Any of first three that offer opportunities for synergy with existing assets	Any of first three that offer technology, markets and other assets in which firm is deficient	Economies of common governance; improved competitive or strategic advantage; to reduce or spread risks	To strengthen global innovatory or production competitiveness; to gain new product lines or markets	Industries that record a high ratio of fixed to overhead costs and which offer substantial economies of scale or synergy
Textile and distribution (import and export)	Market access; products to distribute	Source of inputs and local markets; need to be near customers; after-sales servicing, etc.	Need to protect quality of inputs; need to ensure sales outlets and to avoid under-performance or misrepresentation by foreign agents	Either as entry to new markets or as part of regional or global marketing strategy	A variety of goods, particularly those requiring contact with subcontractors and final consumers
Support services	Experience of clients in home countries	Availability of markets, particularly those of 'lead' clients	Various (see above categories)	As part of regional or global product or geographical diversification	(a) Accounting, advertising, banking, producer goods (b) Where spatial linkages are essential (e.g. airlines and shipping)

Source: Adapted from Dunning (1993).

they do not explain why market-oriented companies should operate their own production facilities in foreign markets rather than licensing local manufacturers to produce their products. A full explanation needs to account for both 'location' (i.e. why a good is produced in *two or more* countries rather than simply one) and 'internalization' (i.e. why production in different locations is done by the *same* firm rather than different firms).

Dunning (1993) attempted to synthesize different theoretical perspectives on multinationals with the evidence provided by case studies. He concluded that companies will only become involved in overseas investment and production when the following conditions are all satisfied:

1 companies possess an 'ownership-specific' advantage over firms in the host country (e.g. assets which are internal to the firm, including organization structure, human capital, financial resources, size and market power);

2 these advantages are best exploited by the firm itself, rather than selling them to foreign firms. In other words, due to market imperfections (e.g. uncertainty), multinationals choose to bypass the market and 'internalize' the use of ownership

specific advantages via vertical and horizontal integration (such internalization reduces transactions costs in the presence of market imperfections); and

3 it must be more profitable for the multinational to exploit its ownership-specific advantages in an overseas market than in its domestic market, i.e. there must additionally exist 'location-specific' factors which favour overseas production (e.g. special economic or political factors, attractive markets in terms of size, growth or structure, low 'psychic' or 'cultural' distance, etc.).

The decisions of multinationals to produce abroad are, therefore, determined by a mixture of motives – ownership-specific, internalization and location-specific factors – as noted above. These are also summarized in a more effective way in Table 7.9.

Honda case study

However, to understand the complexity of motives which underlie multinational activity it may be helpful to consider an actual example, namely Honda Europe. Figure 7.6 shows the Honda motorcycle network in Europe together with its outside supply links. Honda is very much a multinational company with a

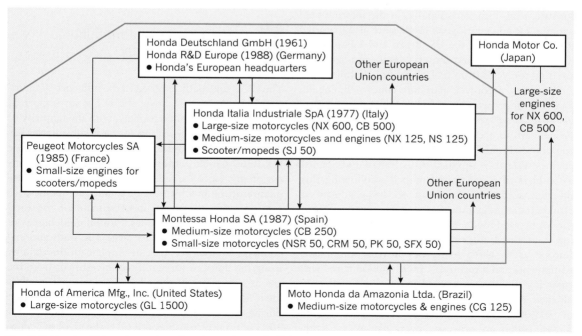

Fig. 7.6 Honda: EU motorcycle networks and supply links.
Source: Various (2010) and UNCTAD (1996), *World Investment Report*, p. 102.

transnationality index of over 50%. It began by exporting motorcycles to Europe, but this was quickly followed by its first European overseas affiliate in 1962. This affiliate, Honda Benelux NV (Belgium), was set up in order to establish strong bonds with European customers as well as to provide a 'learning' opportunity before Honda brought its automobile production to Europe. Figure 7.6 shows that, by the late 1990s, Honda's operations had widened significantly, with its affiliates in Germany acting as its main European regional headquarters. Honda Deutschland GmbH coordinates the production and marketing side, while Honda R & D Europe is engaged in research, engineering and designing for all the affiliates in Europe.

Honda's key *assembly* affiliates are Honda Industriale SpA (Italy) which is wholly owned, and Montessa Honda SA (Spain) which is majority owned (88%). These companies were originally designed to concentrate on the assembly of specific types of motorcycle model appropriate to the different European locations in order to benefit from various economies of scale. At the same time, each assembler exported its own model to the other Honda locations in Europe in order to gain economies in joint production and marketing; in other words any given model is produced in one location, but a full range of models is offered for sale in all locations. Finally, in the international context, Honda's European models are also exported to its subsidiaries in the US, Brazil and Japan, while its European network imports large and medium-sized motorcycles from its US and Brazil affiliates.

As far as motorcycle parts are concerned, engines and key parts were initially supplied from Japan. However, in 1985 Honda acquired a 25% stake in Peugeot Motorcycles SA and began producing small engines in France for scooters and mopeds. These engines were then supplied to its Italian and Spanish assemblers of scooters and mopeds. Following this, medium-sized engines began to be produced in Honda Italia Industriale, both for its own models and for Montessa Honda, while the latter began producing frames and other parts locally. By 2010, Honda Europe as a whole (cars, motorcycles and power equipment) had a turnover of 698 million euros with eight logistic centres located in Europe to integrate all their parts businesses. These centres have a total of 705,000 different parts to manage and some 35,000 orders are processed every day. As far as the motorcycle division (which is shown in Fig. 7.6) is

concerned, Honda Europe delivers 133,100 motorcycles per year with dealers being supplied with the motorcycle they want within 48 hours. The complex linkages outlined in Fig. 7.6 have been shown to be organizationally very successful.

This study of Honda illustrates the complex set of motives underlying multinational activity which were discussed earlier. The traditional technical economies of scale were exploited to reduce average costs as were the more market-based advantages from producing within the EU with its 460 million consumers. In addition, the improved communications within the EU and the rise of more sophisticated corporate structures enabled Honda to integrate operations both horizontally, through affiliate specialization in particular models, and vertically, through specialization of affiliates in the production of parts. Honda was able to capitalize on its well-known ownership-specific advantages of excellent quality engineering and sound business skills, and to combine this with an intelligent strategy for locating production within the largest consumer market in the world. The Honda experience also helps to illustrate the nature of multinational *inter-firm* activity within a sophisticated market dominated by product differentiation.

The impact of multinationals on the UK economy

The UK is unusually exposed to the influence of multinationals. As noted above, the UK is an important *home* country of multinationals, with the majority of its top companies operating overseas subsidiaries. By 2009, official records show that the UK was the home for 2,360 parent corporations which operated internationally. Since the register does not give a complete picture of the involvement of smaller companies, we can take this to be an underestimate of the total number, although it provides a useful guideline as to the number of medium to large UK multinational companies. However, we can supplement this data by using the flows of foreign direct investment from the UK as a measure of the UK's multinational involvement in the world's economy. Here we find that during the 2007–09 period the UK accounted for 19% of total EU outflows of FDI, ahead all EU countries except France.

Table 7.10 The ten largest foreign takeovers of UK companies between 2000 and 2010 (£bn).

Acquired company	Sector	Acquiring company	Sector	Acquirer's nationality	Value (£bn)	Date
O2	Mobile communications	Telefonica	Telecommunications	Spain	18.0	2005
Cadbury	Confectionery	Kraft Foods	Food	US	11.5	2010
Alliance Boots	Pharmacy/Health	KKR	Private Equity	US	11.1	2007
BAA	Airport Management	Ferrovial	Infrastructure Management	Spain	10.0	2006
Powergen	Electrical Generation	E.ON	Electrical Generation	Germany	9.6	2002
ICI	Chemicals	Akzo Nobel NV	Paints/Chemicals	Netherlands	8.0	2008
Thames Water	Water/Sewerage	RWE	Energy	Germany	4.8	2001
Corus	Metals	Tata Steel	Metals	India	4.3	2006
Jaguar/Land Rover	Automobiles	Tata	Conglomerate	India	1.1	2008
Pilkington	Glass	Nippon Sheet Glass	Glass	Japan	1.8	2006

Sources: Various.

The UK is also a major *host* country for foreign multinationals. Table 7.10 gives an indication of this reality by identifying the ten largest foreign takeovers of UK companies between 2000 and 2010.

A snapshot of the involvement of foreign multinational in the UK is evidenced by statistics from the UK Trade and Investment (UKTI) which showed that for the year April 2009 to March 2010 there were some 1,619 projects undertaken in the UK involving foreign multinationals (Department for Business, Innovation and Skills 2010). They created some 53,358 new jobs and safeguarded a further 40,000 jobs, i.e. 93,000 jobs in all. The US continued to be the main source of inward investment into the UK with Japan being the main Asian investor, although India (4th largest investor) and China (6th) were becoming more active investors. In Europe, France with 99 projects and Germany with 90 projects created altogether some 13,000 jobs in the UK during the period shown.

Of all the 1,619 projects initiated in the UK by foreign multinationals between April 2009 and March 2010, some 44% were in the service sector, 17% in R&D, 17% in setting up headquarters in the UK and 15% in manufacturing. These figures show the continued importance for the UK of learning from leading foreign competitors and the increasing importance of the service sector in the globalization process.

What are the implications for the UK economy of such openness to multinationals? Advocates of multi-nationals argue that the economy benefits from their activities, with outward and inward foreign direct investment accelerating industrial restructuring and ensuring the most efficient allocation of resources. On the other hand, critics argue that outward FDI by UK-owned multinationals denies the economy sorely-needed investment and jobs, while the influx of foreign multinationals undermines the nation's economic sovereignty.

An economic cost–benefit appraisal of multinational activity

It is clear that there are strongly contrasting views of multinationals. However, such divergent views are often coloured by implicit assumptions about the nature of the multinationals involved and, as noted in the introduction, international companies are so heterogeneous in their nature that generalizations are both difficult and potentially dangerous. For example, the precise balance of economic costs and benefits that a foreign multinational imposes on the UK economy depends upon:

- how the multinational establishes itself in the UK (e.g. via a greenfield site investment or the takeover of locally owned productive assets, etc.);
- whether funds used for the investment are raised locally or 'imported';

- the function of the multinational (e.g. whether it is cost- or market-oriented); and

- characteristics of host and parent economies (e.g. the extent to which there is 'culture dissonance').

These costs and benefits can be explored in more detail under six main headings. Consider each in turn.

Foreign direct investment (FDI) and economic welfare

Direct investment by a foreign multinational is widely regarded as an unambiguous improvement in economic welfare. Figures 7.7(a) and (b) illustrate the potential economic gains from cross-border investment by multinationals in search of the highest marginal rate of return on capital. These figures show the marginal product of capital in both the home country (MPK_H) and overseas (MPK_F) respectively. Initially, in the absence of multinational activity, capital is relatively less abundant in the home country and with a capital stock, K_1, the marginal product of capital is B. GDP is given by the area under the curve, $0ACK_1$, of which $0BCK_1$ is the reward to capital and BAC is the reward to labour. Similarly, in the overseas sector, the capital stock is K_4, giving rise to a marginal product of capital equal to J and a GDP of $0GLK_4$, of which $0JLK_4$ is the reward to capital and JGL the reward to labour.

Given this disparity between the marginal productivity of capital in different countries, profit-maximizing multinationals will reallocate capital from overseas to the home country, increasing the capital stock from K_1 to K_2, while reducing it overseas from K_4 to K_3. GDP in the home country will rise to $0AFK_2$, an increase of K_1CFK_2. GDP overseas will fall to $0GIK_3$, a reduction of K_3ILK_4. However, remember that a proportion of GDP is a reward to capital and, in the case of multinational investment in the home country, this profit will be repatriated overseas. Hence, for the home country, the net gain from the inward investment is only EFC (the reward to labour), with K_1EFK_2 being repatriated by the foreign multinationals. Conversely, overseas, the loss of GDP (K_3ILK_4) is offset by the repatriated profit K_1EFK_2. Since K_1K_2 (the increase in the capital stock in the home country) is equal to K_3K_4 (the decrease in the capital stock overseas), and D (new marginal product of capital at home) is equal to H (new marginal product of capital overseas), then area K_1EFK_2 must exceed area K_3ILK_4. Thus, the home country benefits as a result of the multinational activity (by the amount of the value-added by its domestic labour force) and overseas producers gain (because the reward from the extra production generated by the use of their capital exceeds its opportunity cost in the overseas market).

This conventional analysis of the impact of multinational investment implicitly assumes, however, that

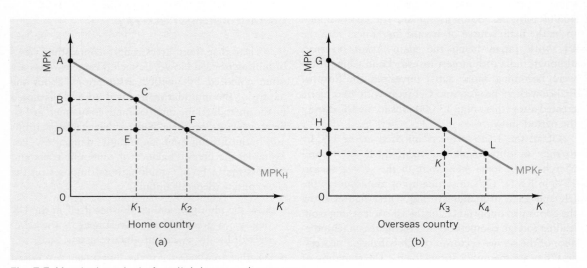

Fig. 7.7 Marginal product of capital, home and overseas.

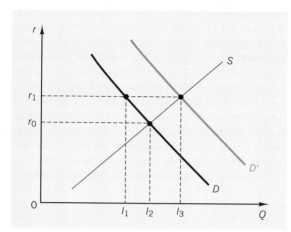

Fig. 7.8 Investment financed from overseas versus investment financed locally.

Technology transfer

It is widely held that multinational activity by more efficient foreign multinationals promotes technology transfer to the benefit of domestic companies. For example, a study of foreign-owned establishments in the UK during the 1990s found that they adopted new technologies earlier than their indigenous UK counterparts (te Velde 2003). Another survey compared the performance of UK-based (non-exporting) companies taken over by UK multinationals, with similar UK companies taken over by foreign multinationals. It seemed that productivity in those UK firms taken over by foreign multinationals was much higher after the takeover than for those firms taken over by UK multinationals. The gap between the productivity performances of the two groups was much greater for high-technology sectors, indicating that foreign multinationals have an even more dominant effect at the high-technology end of production (Girma 2003).

On a practical level, when Nissan established a car plant in north-east England, it demanded much higher standards of UK component suppliers than the incumbent national producers such as Ford and Rover. Nissan's engineers assisted these supplying companies to upgrade their production processes in order to meet their requirements. The result was the creation of a strong positive externality: the international competitiveness of the UK car supply industry was strengthened and, as a direct consequence, the quality of the inputs to domestic auto makers improved.

This so-called 'technology transfer' is clearly maximized by such 'direct linkages' with domestic suppliers, which occurs when incoming multinationals such as Sony, Nissan, Honda and Toyota work closely with domestic suppliers to raise the standard of UK-produced inputs. There are, however, also positive indirect 'demonstration effects' which may promote technology transfer. At its simplest, these relate to attempts by less efficient local producers to imitate the superior processes and organization advantages of the foreign interlopers.

Some attempts have been made to measure the 'spillover' benefits of foreign multinationals on UK industry. For example, one study of UK manufacturing between 1974 and 1995 found that foreign ownership of companies via FDI creates more intra-industry benefits (i.e. positive effect on suppliers, direct linkages, etc.) than inter-industry benefits

the investment constitutes a reallocation of productive capital from overseas to the host country. In practice, this assumption may be violated in two ways.

First, multinationals frequently finance overseas investment either from the retained profits earned by their existing productive or sales operations in the target country or by raising the capital on the local capital market. In both cases, the multinational's investment may simply displace domestic investment that would otherwise have taken place. Figure 7.8 illustrates this dilemma.

An investment financed by a capital inflow from the parent multinational overseas bypasses the domestic market for loanable funds, leaving the balance of domestic savings and investment unchanged at I_2, with rate of interest r_0. However, raising funds locally to finance the investment increases the demand for loanable funds (from D to D'), leading to a rise in interest rates (from r_0 to r_1) and the crowding out of domestic investment (which falls from I_2 to I_1).

Second, multinational investment more frequently involves the takeover of existing assets, rather than greenfield site investment in new plant and equipment. Table 7.10 gives an indication of this reality by identifying the ten largest foreign takeovers of UK companies between 2000 and 2010. In this case, the total capital stock of the host country is unaffected by the FDI, with the ownership of existing assets simply being transferred from local investors to the foreign multinational.

(i.e. demonstration-type or motivational effects on domestic industry) (Harris and Robinson 2004).

There are, however, clear limitations to technology transfer. Most obviously, one of the most powerful drivers for foreign investment is the advantage to a multinational of internalizing an ownership-specific advantage. Such considerations militate against the notion that a foreign multinational will willingly share the technologically based sources of its competitive advantage over local rivals. Moreover, in the case of Japanese multinationals, their historical advantage was built upon close relationships with Japanese suppliers. For example, the big four Japanese motorcycle companies (Honda, Yamaha, Suzuki and Kawasaki) rely heavily on a very limited number of domestic suppliers (e.g. Bridgestone for tyres, Nippon Denso for electronic components, etc.). Early dissatisfaction with UK suppliers with regard to quality and reliability of deliveries has led to a number of these Japanese suppliers following their major customers into the European market, thereby reducing the potential scope for technology transfer via linkages with local suppliers.

A final problem relates to the issue of cultural dissonance. The psychic distance between US and UK companies is relatively small. Both share a broadly common culture, a common language and a reasonably high level of mutual understanding. The success of multinationals from, say, Japan or other parts of East and South-East Asia is built on a very different set of social and cultural values, which are not easily transferable to the UK setting. Companies such as Sony, Nissan and Honda have all reported difficulties in establishing Japanese-style work practices, which many economists regard as an integral part of that country's corporate success. The operation of 'just-in-time' (or 'kanban') production processes and 'quality circles' relies on employee loyalty to his or her company, which in Japan is reinforced by life-time employment and a shared set of values which emphasizes collectivism. Such techniques are much less easily transposed to western cultures with their stress on individualism and self-determination.

Balance of payments

As noted above, the positive balance of payments impact of multinational activity depends, in the first instance at least, on whether the funds are imported (a capital inflow) or raised locally. Even if the capital is imported, however, the ultimate balance of payments

effect may still be negative. At its simplest, multinationals invest in productive facilities overseas because they believe that the net present value of the profits they will be able to repatriate exceeds the capital investment they will make. It follows that, if a multinational invests rationally, the initial capital inflow must be at least matched by the net present value of future outflows on current account (i.e. net payments of interest, profit and dividend abroad). In crude money terms, the total value of the repatriated returns to capital will dwarf the original investment made.

Moreover, the speed with which an initial capital inflow is reversed by outflows on the current account depends critically on the function of the multinational. In the case of a market-oriented company intent on 'jumping tariffs', the multinational may attempt to import part-finished products, using cheap local labour to assemble the final product. Volkswagen was accused of this technique during the 1970s in Brazil, when it established a manufacturing plant in which workers assembled 'complete knock-down kits' into finished cars which were sold, tariff-free, in the Brazilian market. The impact on the current account was strongly negative, with visible imports being inflated by the cost of the kits and invisible imports being increased by the repatriated profits. Most countries (including Brazil) now have extensive 'rules of origin' to prevent such 'screwdriving operations' being used by multinationals as a device for evading tariffs. In Britain's case, however, inward foreign direct investment has historically been generally outweighed by higher outward capital flows.

Employment

Faced with persistently high levels of unemployment in many European countries, it is perhaps understandable that so many states should court foreign multinationals in the belief that their investments will create local employment. Recent investments by major Japanese and US multinationals have, for example, been accompanied by strong competition on the part of national and regional governments in the EU to attract the investment in the hope of generating work. For example, the efforts noted above have been partly responsible for the inflow of Japanese investment into UK industry.

The ultimate employment effect of multinational activity is rather more complex. The net employment effect is a function of three factors:

1 *direct job creation*, which depends on the size of the foreign-owned subsidiary and the labour (or capital) intensity of its production processes;

2 *indirect job creation*, which depends on linkages with local suppliers and the value-added by domestic factors of production; and

3 the 'Trojan horse' effect, namely the displacement of domestic incumbents by the more efficient multinational company, which depends upon the latter's market power.

In practice, it is difficult to gauge the net employment effect of multinational activity in the UK. There is no question that direct job creation has been significant, as witnessed by the eagerness of local authorities in areas of high unemployment to woo potential investors to their region. The UK government estimated that nearly 500,000 jobs were created by overseas businesses in the country between 1979 and 1998. However, indirect job creation (like technology transfer) is clearly limited by the extent to which foreign multinationals rely on imported intermediate products (e.g. inputs shipped from the parent company for local assembly). Under pressure from the EU, Japanese multinationals in the UK, for example, have raised the percentage of 'local' (i.e. EU) content in finished products to 80%. Finally, to the extent that (by definition) foreign multinationals enjoy ownership-specific advantages over domestic rivals, their success is likely to be at the expense of the declining market share enjoyed by the existing incumbents – direct (and indirect) jobs gains may thus be offset by induced job losses in the adversely affected companies. The difficulty of estimating this Trojan horse effect in the UK is that the foreign multinational's output may compete with (and displace) exports from other countries, rather than with domestic production; by the same token, part or all of the multinational's output may be exported (e.g. to other states in the EU). Hence, the UK may enjoy the direct job gains, while the Trojan horse losses (which could well be larger) may fall on third countries, inside or outside the EU. In recent years, certain EU governments, notably France, have expressed precisely this fear, suspecting that the Japanese-led renaissance of the UK's consumer electronics and car industries will be at the expense of French, German and Italian workers.

In the UK, the Trojan horse effect is seen when foreign multinationals, often with UK government subsidies, create employment in the UK but at a high cost per worker and by displacing indigenous companies. For example, it was calculated in the late 1990s that the subsidy given to the Korean Lucky Goldstar (LG) electronics company to locate production in South Wales amounted to £40,000 per job created – while indigenous investment could generate more high quality jobs for a much lower subsidy of between £2,000 and £3,000 per job (*Financial Times* 1998).

Industrial structure

The ownership-specific advantage often enjoyed by foreign multinationals is their market size and power. One consequence of this is, inevitably, the displacement of less efficient domestic producers. Under certain circumstances, it is sometimes argued that foreign direct investment may result in the truncation of the host economy (i.e. the gradual loss of those economic sectors critical to self-sustained growth) and its subsequent dependence on overseas multinationals for continued growth and employment. *In extremis*, it is sometimes claimed that the widespread presence of foreign multinationals may lead to a loss of economic sovereignty on the part of the host country's government. The counter argument is that, at least in the case of the UK, foreign direct investment has positively benefited the UK's economic structure, channelling funds into those sectors (e.g. high technology manufacturing, car production, etc.) in which the economy enjoys a comparative advantage and thereby accelerating economic restructuring. This argument is supported by the work of Girma noted previously (Girma 2003).

Taxation

Multinationals are widely accused by governments of arranging intra-company transactions in order to minimize their tax liabilities, effectively forcing countries to compete to provide the lowest tax regime. Consider a simplified example in which a multinational's production is vertically integrated, with operations in two countries. Basic manufacture takes place in country A and final assembly and sale in country B (see Table 7.11). In country A, the corporate tax rate is 25%, while in country B it is 50%. Suppose the company's costs (inputs, labour, etc.) in country A are $40m and it produces

Table 7.11 Multinational tax avoidance.

$m	Scenario 1		Scenario 2	
	Country A	Country B	Country A	Country B
Costs	40	90	40	100
Sales	50	100	60	100
Profit	10	10	20	0
Tax liability	2.5	5	5	0
Total tax	7.5		5	

intermediate products with a market value of $50m; if it were to sell these intermediate products in the *open market*, it would declare a profit of $10m in country A, incurring a tax liability of $2.5m in that country.

However, suppose the products are actually intended for the parent company's subsidiary in country B. In Scenario 1, the 'transfer price' (i.e. the internal price used by the company to calculate profits in different countries) is set at the market price of $50m in country A for the intermediate products which are now to be 'shipped' to country B for incorporation into the final product. The operation in country B incurs additional costs of $40m, after which the final product is sold in country B for $100m; thus the subsidiary will declare a profit of $10m and incur a tax liability of $5m. The company as a whole will face a total tax liability of $7.5m in countries A and B taken together.

Consider an alternative scenario (Scenario 2), in which the company sets a transfer price *above* the market price for the intermediate products manufactured in the low-tax country, A. With a transfer price of $60m rather than $50m and the same costs of $40m, the subsidiary in country A incurs a higher tax liability (25% of $20m), but this is more than offset by the lower (in fact, zero) tax liability incurred by the subsidiary in country B. Because the latter is now recording its total costs (including the cost of the intermediate products 'bought' from the subsidiary in country A) as being $100m rather than $90m, its profits and tax liability fall to zero. As a result, the total tax liability faced by the company on its international operations is only $5m, rather than $7.5m.

The basic issue is that the multinational has earned a total profit of $20m on its vertically integrated operation, i.e. $100m actual sales revenue in B minus

$80m costs in A + B. However, by setting transfer prices on intra-company sales and purchases of intermediate products appropriately, the company can 'move' this profit to the lowest-tax country, thereby denying the higher tax country (in this case, country B) the tax revenue to which it is entitled. Such transfer pricing can, of course, only succeed when there is no active market for the intermediate products being traded. If the tax authorities in country B can refer to an open market price for the intermediate product, the inflated transfer price being paid can be identified. However, to the extent that many multinationals internalize cross-border operations because they have ownership-specific advantages (e.g. control of a specific raw material or technology), it may be that comparable intermediate products are not available on the open market. For this reason, high-tax countries may find they lose tax revenues to lower-tax centres as business becomes increasingly globalized. This creates, in turn, an incentive for countries to 'compete' for multinational tax revenues by offering low tax rates; the result of such competition is a transfer of income from national governments to the shareholders of multinational companies.

The potential for multinationals to try to avoid tax, as shown in Table 7.11, can be understood by looking at the corporation tax rates across Europe. For example, in 2010, the combined central and local government corporation tax rates varied from 34% in France to 28% in the UK – with rates in the Czech Republic (19%), Poland (19%) and Ireland (12.5%) being significantly lower. Such divergences in tax rates provide ample opportunities for tax avoidance activity.

Conclusion

Multinationals play a more influential role in the UK economy than in any other major, developed country in the world. Most of the household-name companies in Britain – BP, Unilever, Ford, Kellogg, Heinz, Cadbury Schweppes – are multinationals. In the past, companies became multinational to secure resources and markets or to overcome the transport costs associated with exporting. Increasingly, multinationals are becoming genuinely global, performing different stages of an integrated productive process in different countries to exploit natural and government-induced differences in factor costs as we saw in the case of Honda. There is a fierce debate about the benefits and costs of multinational activity for individual economies such as that of the UK. What is clear, however, is that the growth of multinationals will continue into the next century and that an increasing proportion of UK companies will do the majority of their business overseas, while an ever-higher share of UK production will be controlled by foreign companies.

Indeed, it is already becoming increasingly meaningless to think of companies as 'British' or 'foreign'. Is Ford, an 'American' company which designs and builds cars in the UK, 'foreign'? Is Attock Oil, a 'British' oil exploration and production company which operates only in North America and SE Asia, 'British'? As companies become increasingly global in nature, the convention of labelling a company's nationality by reference to the nationality of its controlling shareholders will become redundant. Imagine the Ford Motor Company, owned by Japanese shareholders, run by an American chief executive, producing components across the EU and assembling them in Turkey for sale in Russia. In what sense is such a multinational 'American', 'Japanese' or even 'European'? The multinational of the future is likely to be genuinely 'stateless'. Already the trend towards statelessness is well underway and the implications of this phenomenon are liable to be profound.

Key points

- A 'multinational' is a company which owns or controls production or service facilities in more than one country.

- There are some 82,000 multinational companies, the sales revenue of which amounts to over 50% of world GDP. Only 15 nation states have a GDP greater than the annual turnover of Exxon, Ford or General Motors.

- Multinationals account for around 30% of GDP in the UK and almost half of manufacturing employment.

- Foreign multinationals account for 11% of UK employment and 23% of UK turnover. The US dominates the scene, accounting for 42% of all foreign multinational employment in the UK and 37% of all foreign multinational turnover.

- Successful multinational activity from the home base usually depends on the possession of 'ownership-specific' advantages over firms in the host country, together with 'location-specific' advantages which favour overseas production.

- Cost-oriented multinationals focus mainly on reducing costs of production via overseas production (often via vertical integration); market-oriented multinationals focus mainly on easier sales access to overseas markets via overseas production (often via horizontal integration).

- Being both a 'home' country to (UK) multinationals as well as a 'host' to foreign multinationals results in substantial flows of outward and inward foreign direct investment (FDI).

- The costs and benefits of multinational activity for the UK (or indeed any country) can usefully be assessed under six main headings:

  (i)   FDI and economic welfare

  (ii) technology transfer

  (iii) balance of payments

  (iv) employment

  (v)   industrial structure

  (vi) taxation.

Now try the self-check questions for this chapter on the Companion Website. You will also find useful links to relevant websites.

References and further reading

Bloom, N., Sadun, R. and Van Reenen, J. (2007) *Americans Do I.T. Better: US Multinationals and the Productivity Miracle*, Discussion Paper no 788, London, Centre for Economic Performance, LSE.

Buckley, P. J. (1992) *New Dimensions in International Business*, Cheltenham, Edward Elgar.

Cleeve, E. (1994) Transnational corporations and internationalisation: a critical review, *British Review of Economic Issues*, 16(40).

Crum, R. and Davies, S. (1991) *Multinationals*, Heinemann Educational.

Department for Business, Innovation and Skills (2010) *UK Inward Investment Report 2009/10: UK at the Heart of Global Business*, July, London, The Stationery Office.

Dicken, P. (2011) *Global Shift: Reshaping the Global Economic Map in the 21st Century* (6th edn), London, Sage Publications.

Dunning, J. (1996) Globalisation, foreign direct investment and economic development, *Economics and Business Education*, 4(3): 46–51.

Dunning, J. H. (1993) *Multinational Enterprises and the Global Economy*, Harlow, Addison-Wesley.

Economist (1996) *Economic Indicators*, 27 April.

Financial Times (1998) Regions take an inward look at a growing problem, 21 May.

Fortune (2010) *Global 500*, July.

Girma, S. (2003) The domestic performance of UK multinational firms, *National Institute Economic Review*, 185(July): 78–92.

Greenaway, D. (1993) Trade and foreign direct investment, *European Economy*, 52: 103–28.

Harris, R. and Robinson, C. (2004) Productivity impacts and spillovers from foreign ownership in the United Kingdom, *National Institute Economic Review*, 187(January): 58–75.

Kene, P. B. (1994) *The International Economy*, Cambridge, Cambridge University Press.

Kobrin, S. J. (1991) An empirical analysis of the determinants of global integration, *Strategic Management Journal*, 12(Summer): 17–31.

McKinsey Global Institute (2010) *Growth and Competitiveness in the United States: The Role of its Multinationals*, June, New York.

Meyer, K. (2008) *Multinational Enterprises and Host Economies*, Cheltenham, Edward Elgar.

Norman, G. (1995) Japanese foreign direct investment: the impact on the European Union, in Healey, N. (ed.), *The Economics of the New Europe: from Community to Union*, London, Routledge, 223–38.

OECD (2010) *Economic Globalisation Indicators*, Paris, Organisation for Economic Co-operation and Development.

te Velde, D. W. (2003) Foreign ownership, microelectronic technology and skills: evidence for British establishments, *National Institute Economic Review*, 185(July): 93–106.

Thomsen, S. (1992) Integration through globalisation, *National Westminster Bank Quarterly Review*, August.

UNCTAD (1996) *World Investment Report 1996: Investment, Trade and International Policy Arrangements*, New York and Geneva, United Nations Conference on Trade and Development.

UNCTAD (2005) *World Investment Report 2005: Transnational Corporations and the Internationalization of R&D*, New York and Geneva, United Nations Conference on Trade and Development.

UNCTAD (2009) *World Investment Report 2009: Transnational Corporations, Agricultural Production and Development*, New York and Geneva, United Nations Conference on Trade and Development.

UNCTAD (2010) *World Investment Report 2010: Investing in a Low Carbon Economy*, New York and Geneva, United Nations Conference on Trade and Development.

US BLS (2010) *International Labor Statistics*, Washington DC, US Bureau of Labor Statistics.

Winters, L. (1991) GATT: the Uruguay Round, *Economic Review*, 9(2): 25–7.

Young, S., Hood, N. and Hamill, J. (1988) *Foreign Multinationals and the British Economy*, Croom Helm.

CHAPTER 8

Privatization and deregulation

Public ownership of industries is now in retreat throughout the world as governments privatize. Since the early 1980s the UK has provided a model of privatization which has been influential in policy-making, both in other industrial countries and in developing countries. The collapse of the Soviet Union and the Eastern European Communist regimes has led to privatization programmes which totally dwarf those of the UK. This chapter summarizes the original case for nationalization and considers the arguments for and against privatization. There is also a discussion of the case for regulating the activities of the privatized companies as well as the contrary view in favour of less regulation (i.e. deregulation).

Nature and importance

Public (or state) ownership of industry in the UK has mainly been through *public corporations*, which are trading bodies whose chairpersons and board members are appointed by the Secretary of State concerned. These *nationalized industries*, as they are often called, are quite separate from government itself. They run their businesses without close supervision but within the constraints imposed by government policy. These constraints include limits to the amounts they can borrow and therefore invest and may also include limits to the wages and salaries they can offer. Not all public corporations are, however, nationalized industries. There are some public corporations, such as the BBC, which are not classed as nationalized industries.

Public ownership can also take the form of direct share ownership in private sector companies. So, for example, after the collapse of the DAF motor vehicle group in 1993, the Netherlands government provided 50% of the equity and loan capital for DAF Trucks NV which took over some of the failed group's activities. In a similar way, the UK government held a majority holding in British Petroleum for many years prior to its complete privatization in 1987.

Privatization in the UK has reduced the number of nationalized industries to a mere handful of enterprises accounting for less than 2% of UK GDP, around 3% of investment and under 1.5% of employment. By contrast, in 1979 the then nationalized industries were a very significant part of the economy, producing 9% of GDP, being responsible for 11.5% of investment and employing 7.3% of all UK employees. The scale of the transfer of public sector businesses since 1979 to private ownership is further indicated in Table 8.1 below, which lists the businesses privatized by sector.

Reasons for nationalization

Looking back from the perspective of the new millennium, the reader may well ask why the state ever became so heavily involved in the production of goods and services. Yet between the 1940s and the 1980s this was one of the most contentious issues in British politics, both between the major parties and within the Labour Party. The first post-war Labour government (1945–51) achieved a major programme of nationalization which was opposed by the Conservative Party at the time but broadly left in place by subsequent Conservative governments. The apparent consensus on the scale of the nationalized industries was, however, broken after 1979 as Conservative governments under Mrs Thatcher developed the policy of privatization. We now consider a range of arguments used in favour of nationalization.

Political

The political case for nationalization centred on the suggestion that private ownership of productive assets creates a concentration of power over resources which is intolerable in a democracy. Until 1995 the Labour Party appeared to embrace this idea in Clause 4 of its constitution which promised public ownership of the means of production, distribution and exchange. The founders of the Labour Party saw public ownership as a necessary step towards full-scale socialism and one which would aid economic planning. This developed into a policy of nationalizing the 'commanding heights' of the economy which the 1945 Labour government identified as the transport industries, the power industries and the iron and steel industries; the Post Office had always been state owned and at that time also included telephones. There were always many in the Labour Party who were opposed to a literal interpretation of Clause 4 and saw that there were other means of regulating economic activity besides outright public ownership. By the 1990s, after the collapse of the Eastern European socialist economies, there were few remaining advocates of economic planning and the Labour Party abandoned the old Clause 4 by a large majority at a special conference in 1995.

Post-war reconstruction

After the Second World War some industries, e.g. the railways, were extremely run-down, requiring large-scale investment and repair. For these, the provision of state finance through nationalization seemed a sensible solution. In other industries, e.g. steel, nationalization was a means of achieving reorganization so that economies of scale could be fully exploited. In still other industries, e.g. gas and electricity, reorganization was required to change the industry base from the local to the national.[1] A different government might, of course, have used policy measures other than nationalization, such as grants and tax reliefs, to achieve these objectives.

The public interest

There are many situations where commercial criteria, with their focus on profitability, are at odds with a broader view of the public interest, and in such cases nationalization is one solution. For instance, the Post Office aims to make a profit overall, but in doing so makes losses on rural services which are subsidized by profits made elsewhere – a 'cross-subsidy' from one group of consumers to another. Some object to cross-subsidization, arguing that it interferes with the price mechanism in its role of resource allocation when some consumers pay less than the true cost of the services they buy, whilst others pay more than the true cost. However, in the case of the Post Office cross-subsidization seems reasonable, if only because we may all want to send letters to outlying areas from time to time, and all derive benefit from the existence of a full national postal service. A private sector profit-orientated firm might not be prepared to undertake the loss-making Post Office services.

State ownership may also be a means of promoting the public interest when entire businesses are about to collapse. The state has sometimes intervened to prevent liquidation, as in 1970 when the Conservative government decided to rescue Rolls-Royce rather than see the company liquidated. Prestige, strategic considerations, effects on employment and on the balance of payments all played a part in the argument, as the judgement of the market was rejected in favour of a broader view of the public interest. In the long run, the markets were proved wrong and the decision to intervene commercially correct, as the company is now a world leader in aero-engine technology and has been successfully returned to the private sector.

State monopoly

The 'natural monopoly' argument is often advanced in favour of nationalization of certain industries. Economies of scale in railways, water, electricity and gas industries are perhaps so great that the tendency towards monopoly can be termed 'natural'. Competing provision of these services, with duplication of investment, would clearly be wasteful of resources. The theory of the firm suggests that monopolies may enjoy supernormal profits, charging higher prices and producing lower output than would a competitive industry with the same cost conditions. However, where there are sufficient economies of scale, the monopoly price could be lower and output higher than under competition (see Chapter 9). Monopoly might then be the preferred market form, especially if it can be regulated. Nationalization is one means of achieving such regulation.

Presence of externalities

Externalities occur when economic decisions create costs or benefits for people other than the decision-taker; these are called social costs or social benefits (see Chapter 10, p. 190). For example, a firm producing textiles may emit industrial effluent, polluting nearby rivers and causing loss of amenity. In other words, society is forced to bear part of the cost of private industrial activity. Sometimes those who impose external or social costs in this way can be controlled by legislation (pollution controls, Clean Air Acts), or penalized through taxation. The parties affected might be compensated, using the revenue raised from taxing those firms creating social costs. On the other hand, firms creating external or social benefits may be rewarded by the receipt of subsidies. In other cases, nationalization is a possible solution. If the industry is run in the public interest, it might be expected that full account will be taken of any externalities. For instance, it can be argued that railways reduce road usage, creating social benefits by relieving urban congestion, pollution and traffic accidents. This was one aspect of the case for subsidizing British Rail through the passenger service obligation grant which, in the mid-1990s, amounted to around £1bn. The grant enabled British Rail to continue operating some loss-making services. Nationalization is therefore one means of exercising public control over the use of subsidies when these are thought to be in the public interest.

Improved industrial climate

There was hope after 1945 that the removal of private capital would improve labour relations in the industries concerned, promoting the feeling of co-ownership. The coal industry in particular had a bitter legacy of industrial relations. From nationalization until the strike of 1973, industrial relations in the coal industry, judged by days lost in disputes, seemed to have dramatically improved over pre-war days. Nevertheless, for the nationalized industries as a whole, it is fair to say that the hopes of the 1940s were not fulfilled, perhaps because the form of nationalization adopted in the UK did little to involve workers in the running of their industries. Participation in management, worker directors, genuine consultation and even an adequate flow of information to workers are no more common in the UK public sector than they are in the private sector.

Redistribution of wealth

Nationalization of private sector assets without compensation is a well-tried revolutionary means of changing the distribution of wealth in an inegalitarian society. Nationalization in the UK has not, unlike the Soviet Union in 1917, been used in this way; in the UK there has almost always been 'fair' compensation. Indeed, the compensation paid between 1945 and 1951 was criticized as over-generous, enabling shareholders to get their wealth out of industries which, in the main, had poor prospects (e.g. railways, coal) in order to buy new shareholdings in growth industries (e.g. chemicals, consumer durables). Once 'fair' compensation is accepted in principle in state acquisitions of private capital, then nationalization ceases to be a mechanism for redistribution of wealth.

An alternative to 'fair' compensation is confiscation. However, this would have serious consequences for UK capital markets. Ownership of assets in the UK would, in future, carry the additional risk of total loss by state confiscation, which could influence decisions to invest in new UK-based plant and equipment, and to buy UK shares. The ability of UK companies to invest and to raise finance might therefore be undermined. The transfer of assets might also prove inequitable, since shares are held by pension funds and insurance companies on behalf of millions of small savers who would then be penalized by confiscation.

Privatization

Privatization means the transfer of assets or economic activity from the public sector to the private sector.

As we noted earlier, privatization in the UK has reduced the number of nationalized industries in 2010 to a mere handful of enterprises accounting for less than 2% of UK GDP, around 3% of investment and under 1.5% of employment. Indeed the public ownership of industries is now in retreat throughout the world as governments privatize. However, privatization can often mean much more than denationalization. Sometimes the government has kept a substantial shareholding in privatized public corporations (initially 49.8% in BT), whereas in other cases a public corporation has been sold in its entirety (e.g. National Freight Corporation). Where public sector corporations and companies are not attractive propositions for *complete* privatization, profitable assets have been sold (e.g. Jaguar Cars from the then British Leyland and also British Rail Hotels). Yet again, many public sector activities have been opened up to market forces by inviting tenders, the cleaning of public buildings and local authority refuse collection being examples of former 'in-house' services which are now put out to tender. Private sector finance and operation of facilities and services is also now established in a vast array of public/private finance initiatives (PFI). In other words, the many aspects of privatization also involve aspects of *deregulation*, e.g. in allowing private companies to provide goods and services which could previously only (by law) be provided in the public sector.

Early privatizations, for example BT in 1984, were usually simple transfers of existing businesses to the private sector. Increasingly, privatizations have become much more complex, often being used to restructure industries by breaking up monopolies and establishing market-based relationships between the new companies. For example, the privatization of British Rail involved separating ownership of the track (Railtrack) from the train operating companies and also the train leasing companies. The train operating companies are in this case franchisees who have successfully tendered for contracts to operate trains for a specified period.

Market forces have also been introduced into the unlikely areas of social services, the health services and education – especially higher education. In health and social services this has involved the purchaser/provider model in which, for example, doctors and 'primary care groups' have used their limited budgets to buy hospital services needed by their patients. Funds, and hence the use of resources, are then controlled by *purchasers* rather than by the *providers*.

As a result, these purchasers have an incentive to use hospitals offering, in their judgement, the 'best' service as described by some combination of quality and value for money. (However, as we note in Chapter 13, the Labour government (1997–2010) sought to modify some of these market arrangements.) In higher education, the funding of universities has been closely linked to the numbers of students enrolling. It follows that any failure to enrol students, perhaps through offering unpopular courses, would drive a university into deficit and possible bankruptcy. Resources in this sector were previously allocated by administrators; now a market test is applied.

Table 8.1 shows the extent of privatization in the UK to 2010, in terms of both the number of businesses and their spread across major sectors of the economy. The total value of privatization receipts to the Treasury has been estimated at over £70bn. Clearly the scope for further privatization among the remaining nationalized industries is now limited as there are so few left, but there are many possibilities in the activities currently run by the Civil Service and Local Authorities.

The case for privatization

A commitment to privatize wherever possible became established in the Conservative Party during Mrs Thatcher's first term. By 1982 the late Mr Nicholas Ridley, then Financial Secretary to the Treasury, expressed this commitment as follows:

> It must be right to press ahead with the transfer of ownership from state to private ownership of as many public sector businesses as possible. . . . The introduction of competition must be linked to a transfer of ownership to private citizens and away from the State. Real public ownership – that is ownership by people – must be and is our ultimate goal.

Mr Ridley made a case for privatization which focused on the traditional Conservative antipathy to the state. On this view, the transfer of economic activity from the public to the private sector is, in itself, a desirable objective. By the early 1980s privatization was also supported by adherents of 'supply-side' economics with its emphasis on free markets. Privatization would expose industries to market forces which would benefit consumers by giving them choice,

Table 8.1 Major privatizations: a sectoral breakdown.

Mining, Oil, Agriculture and Forestry
British Coal, British Petroleum, Britoil, Enterprise Oil
Land Settlement, Forestry Commission, Plant Breeding Institute

Electricity, Gas and Water
British Gas
National Power, PowerGen
Nuclear Electric
Northern Ireland Electric, Northern Ireland Generation (4 companies)
Scottish Hydro-Electric, Scottish Power
National Grid
Regional Electricity Distribution (12 companies)
Regional Water Holding Companies (10 companies)

Manufacturing, Science and Engineering
AEA Technology
British Aerospace, Short Bros, Rolls-Royce
British Shipbuilders, Harland and Wolff
British Rail Engineering
British Steel
British Sugar Corporation
Royal Ordnance
Jaguar, Rover Group
Amersham International
British Technology Group Holdings (ICL, Fairey, Ferranti, Inmos)

Distribution, Hotels, Catering
British Rail Hotels

Transport and Communication
British Railways
National Freight, National and Local Bus Companies
Motorway Service Area Leases
Associated British Ports, Trust Ports, Sealink
British Airways, British Airports Authority (and other airports)
British Telecommunications, Cable and Wireless

Banking, Finance, etc.
Girobank

and also lower prices as a result of efficiency gains within the privatized companies.

Supply-side benefits

The breaking of a state monopoly would, in this view, enable consumers to choose whichever company produced the service they preferred. That company would then generate more profit and expand in response to consumer demand, whilst competitive pressure would be put on the company losing business to improve its service or go into liquidation. BT's progressive reductions in telephone charges and Internet access charges in recent years have clearly been at least partly in response to competition. The pressure to meet consumer requirements should also improve internal efficiency (X efficiency) as changes can be justified to workers and managers by the need to respond to the market. The old public corporations had increasingly been seen as producer led, serving the interests of management and workers rather than those of consumers and shareholders (in this case taxpayers). Privatization introduces market pressures which help to stimulate a change of organizational culture.

Trade unions can be expected to discover that previous customs and work practices agreed when in the public sector are now challenged by privatization, as the stance taken by management changes from when the industry was nationalized, and thereby raises corporate efficiency. Similarly, competition in the product market will force moderation in wage demands and increased attention to manning levels, again raising efficiency. Privatization contributes in these various ways to the creation of 'flexibility' in labour markets, higher productivity and reduced unit labour costs.

The stock market provides a further market test for privatized companies. Poor performance in meeting consumer preferences or in utilizing assets should result in a share price which underperforms the rest of the market and undervalues the company's assets, ultimately leaving it vulnerable to takeover by a company able to make better use of the assets. Supporters of privatization place more faith in these market forces than in the monitoring activities of Departments of State and Parliamentary Committees.

Wider share ownership

The Conservative Party in its drive towards privatization also emphasized wider share ownership. By 2010, share ownership in the UK had spread to 22% of the adult population, having been only 7% as recently as 1981. The total number of UK shareholders is about the same as the number of trade unionists. This increase in shareholding is largely due to privatization.

A new group of shareholders has been attracted and become participants in the 'enterprise culture'. Additionally, 90% of the employees in the privatized companies have become shareholders in the companies they work for, at least initially. Worker share ownership is advocated as a means of involving workers more closely with their companies and achieving improved industrial relations. This has been taken further by selling companies to their managers (e.g. Leyland Bus in 1987) or to consortiums of managers and workers (e.g. National Freight in 1982). The latter is regarded as a highly successful example, profits having grown more than tenfold since privatization.

Reductions in PSBR

Privatization has also been seen as a way in which the public sector borrowing requirement (PSBR) (now PSNCR – see Chapter 18, p. 356) can be cut, at a stroke! The finance of external borrowing by the nationalized industries is regarded in accounting terms as being part of public expenditure, which then ceases when these industries become privately owned. Sale of assets or shares also increases government revenue, again reducing the PSBR in the year of the sale. Over the period 1979–2010 the Treasury gained £75bn from asset sales. Privatization made a very significant contribution to the budget surpluses of the late 1980s and to curbing the size of the budget deficits of the 1990s. Privatization proceeds reduced the PSBR as a proportion of GDP by more than 1.5% during the late 1980s, and by a still significant, if smaller, percentage in other years.

Managerial freedom

The activities of state-owned organizations are constrained by their relationship with the government. They lack financial freedom to raise investment capital externally because the government is concerned about restraining the growth of public expenditure (see Chapter 18). Privatization is then seen as increasing the prospects for raising investment capital, thereby increasing efficiency and lowering prices.

A further limitation on nationalized industries is the political near-impossibility of diversification. In many cases, this would be the sensible corporate response to poor market prospects, but it is not an option likely to be open to a nationalized concern. Since privatization, however, companies have been able to freely exploit market opportunities. So, for example, most of the regional electricity companies have become suppliers of gas as well as electricity.

The 'globalization' of economic activity also, in this view, leaves nationalized industries at a distinct disadvantage. For example, no private oil company would have followed the nationalized British Coal in confining its activities to one country where it happened to have reserves. This international perspective is an important reason why the Post Office management saw privatization as 'the only (option) which offers us the freedom to fight off foreign competition'. In the postal services, increased competition has arisen from the Dutch Post Office, which has been privatized, and is expected from further liberalization of other national postal services expected within the European Single Market. The difficulties of an international strategy for nationalized industries are shown by the failure of the attempted Renault–Volvo merger in 1993. The then nationalized status of Renault contributed substantially to Swedish (Volvo) shareholder opposition to the merger.

Privatization, then, is seen by its supporters as a means of greatly improving economic performance.

The case against privatization

Privatization may be opposed for all the reasons that nationalization was originally undertaken (see above). Additionally, both the rationale of the policy and its implementation may be criticized.

Absence of competition

An essential aspect to the case *for* privatization is the creation of competitive market conditions. However, some state-owned industries have always faced stiff competition in their markets (for example, Post Office Parcelforce from DHL), so that privatization of these industries might be considered irrelevant on the basis of this 'competitive market conditions' argument.

The government also faces a dilemma as regards creating competitive market conditions when privatizing public utilities which are monopolies, namely that it has another, and potentially conflicting, objective which is to raise money for the Treasury. Breaking up state monopolies in order to increase competition reduces the market value of the share

offer; monopolies are likely to be worth more as share offers because they reduce uncertainty for investors. Critics would say that the government has allowed the creation of competition to be secondary to creating attractive share issues which sell easily. The result has been the transfer of public utility monopolies intact to the private sector, creating instead private sector monopolies.

Nevertheless, competitive pressures are being applied to some of the previously public utility monopolies in their newly privatized form. For example, at the time of privatization, British Gas appeared to be a classic natural monopoly. Since then consistent pressure from the regulatory authorities has created competitive market conditions in the supply of gas to industry, to such an extent that by 2006 the British Gas share of the industrial market was below 30% and competitive supply had been extended to the domestic market for gas across the whole country. As regards BT, opportunities for new entrants created by rapid technological change have been even more significant in eroding the market dominance of BT. Cable TV companies can now provide highly competitive phone services using their fibre optic cable systems; additionally many large organizations have created their own phone networks and the Internet and digital TV are creating still further opportunities for communication.

The technical and regulatory changes in the telecommunication and gas industries have benefited consumers but should not be confused with the issue of the desirability of privatization. Consumers might well feel that these desirable outcomes could have been achieved under public ownership. If so, critics might then argue that consumers could have experienced still greater benefit from technical innovation because, under privatization, lax regulatory regimes have allowed excessive levels of profit, to the benefit of shareholders and executives rather than consumers.

Presence of externalities

The rationale for privatization is at its weakest when externalities exist. Indeed the former nationalized industries contained many examples of such externalities, which was one of the reasons for their original public ownership. The now privatized rail companies are *not* able to charge road users for any benefits (e.g. less congestion) created by the lower levels of road traffic which rail services create. In the water industry there is a vested interest in encouraging consumption to increase turnover, even if this means the need to build new reservoirs with a consequent loss of land, disruption to everyday life and dramatically changed landscapes. In the case of the electricity industry, the competitive market among the generators has had nearly terminal implications for the coal industry. New contracts for coal supplies to the electricity generating companies have only been secured by British Coal at world prices, well below the prices previously agreed. As employment in mining has plummeted, the cost has been borne by society. Miners' families and local communities have become much poorer, whilst public expenditure on unemployment and social security benefits has risen and tax revenues have been reduced by the rising unemployment. At a time of high unemployment, organizations which lower their *private* costs by making more workers redundant invariably create *social* costs (externalities). There is also the issue of the long-term *strategic* role of the coal industry. The German government has long recognized these wider aspects of industrial policy and has arranged a levy on electricity users to compensate the electricity generators for offering coal prices which are over three times the world price. German electricity prices in the first decade of the millennium were some 30–40% higher than those in the rest of Europe. The UK government has taken a contrary view and decided that the nuclear industry rather than the coal industry should be subsidized. In doing so it has, of course, departed from its free market philosophy and further endangered the coal industry by subsidizing a competitor.

Undervaluation of state assets

The extension of share ownership does not in itself attract much criticism. The issues which have provoked criticism include the pricing and the marketing of the shares. It is argued that valuable national assets have been sold at give-away prices. This criticism is made of both privately negotiated deals and the public share offers. An example of the former is the offer for Austin Rover made by British Aerospace in March 1988 which valued a company which has received a total of £2.9bn of public funds at only £150m and this on condition that the government wrote off £1.1bn of accumulated losses and injected a further

£800m. The deal could be presented as giving away £650m and a company with net assets of more than £1.1bn. The generosity of the government's approach was confirmed when the European Commission ruled that the £800m government injection of capital must be reduced to £572m, in the interests of fair competition in the EU motor market. The Commission also insisted that British Aerospace repay £44.4m which it received from the government as 'sweeteners' during the deal. The government's prime objective was to return Rover to the private sector as quickly as possible in the belief that the benefits would soon outweigh any losses on the deal. There were also the provisos that the company remain under British ownership (see below) and that employment be maintained. These provisos severely restricted the number of potential buyers.

In most cases, public share offers have been heavily over-subscribed and large percentage profits have been made by successful applicants. Rolls-Royce shares, for example, were issued part paid at 85p on 20 May 1987 and moved to 147p by the close of business that day, a profit of 73% before dealing costs. British Telecom shares reached a premium of 86% on the first day. The electricity privatization has, to date, raised some £6.5bn, but the assets involved have a value of £28bn. Hardly surprisingly, the regional electricity company shares had a first-day premium of almost 60%, and those of the electricity generating companies a premium of almost 40%.

Underpriced issues have cost the Treasury substantial revenues and have also conditioned a new class of small shareholders to expect quick, risk-free capital gains. These expectations were encouraged by barrages of skilful advertising. Not surprisingly many of the new shareholders cashed in their windfall gains by selling their shares. As a result share ownership in the new companies quickly became more concentrated. For example, the 1.1 million BA shareholders at the flotation in February 1987 had reduced to 0.4 million by early October. Despite this, there is no doubt that there has been a considerable extension of share ownership, although the majority of shareholders have shares in only one company. In fact 54% of investors hold shares in only one company and only 17% have shares in more than four companies. Parker (1991) concludes that privatization has *widened* share ownership but not *deepened* it. Indeed, the institutional investors raised their proportion of shareholdings during the 1980s at the expense of the private investor, whose proportion of total shareholdings fell from 30% to 20% during this period.

Short-termism

The discipline of the capital markets may prove a very mixed blessing for some of the privatized companies if they become subject to the City's alleged 'short-termism'. The large investment fund managers are often criticized for taking a short-term view of prospects. This would be particularly inappropriate for the public utilities where both the gestation period for investment and the pay-back period tend to be lengthy. The freedom with which ownership of assets changes hands on the stock market is not always in the public interest. The acquisition of B Cal in 1987 by the newly privatized BA, for example, was investigated by the then Monopolies and Mergers Commission (MMC) and approved on condition that BA gave up some of the routes acquired. There was also concern at the 22% holding in BP which the Kuwait Investment Office acquired very cheaply in the aftermath of the 1987 stock market crash. The MMC ruled that the Kuwait holding be reduced to 11%. The limitations of privatization and excessive reliance on the markets was illustrated in 1994 by BMW's takeover of the Rover Group from British Aerospace. The government had originally set a period of five years in which Rover could not be sold to a foreign buyer but, within a few months of the expiry of the limitation, the last British-controlled volume car producer was sold to the German company. Of course it is by no means clear that retaining national control of companies is a desirable objective. The takeover could arguably be welcomed as a benefit of European integration which will strengthen the European car industry. However, if national control *is* desired, as it was when British Aerospace bought Rover, then this is an example of the weakness of privatization as a substitute for industrial policy. The French government's plan to retain a controlling majority interest in Renault after privatization illustrates an alternative approach, although the UK government would tend not to view such a compromise as a 'privatization'.

Opportunity costs

The flow of funds into privatization offers has been diverted from other uses. It is reasonable to suppose that applicants for shares are using their savings rather than reducing their consumption. Large sums of money leave the building societies during privatizations, and other financial institutions are also deprived of funds. This raises the possibility that what is merely a restructuring and change of ownership of state industry may be reducing the availability of funds for other organizations which would use them for real capital investment. The effects of privatization issues on the financial markets are much the same as the effects of government borrowing, raising the same possibilities of 'crowding out'.

The contribution of privatization to reducing the PSBR has been widely criticized as 'selling the family silver'. The sales involve profitable assets and, after privatization, the Exchequer loses the flow of returns from them. Schwartz and Lopes (1993) have pointed out that the sale price of assets should equal the net present value of expected future returns on them. If this were the case, then the 'family silver' argument would lose some of its power and rest on the use to which the proceeds were put – that is consumption or investment. However, most privatization issues in the UK *have* been underpriced in the view of the markets (see above).

Burden on taxpayers

A final criticism of privatization is a moral one, that the public are being sold shares which, as taxpayers, they already collectively own. The purchasers of the shares benefit from the dividends paid by the new profit-seeking enterprises, at the expense of taxpayers as a group. Those taxpayers who do not buy the shares, perhaps because they have no spare cash, are effectively dispossessed.

Regulation of privatized companies

The privatization of public utility companies with 'natural' monopolies creates the possibility that the companies might abuse their monopoly power. In these cases, UK privatizations have offered reassurance to the public in the form of regulatory offices for each privatized utility, for example OFTEL for telecommunications and OFWAT for the water industry. Where privatized companies such as Rover and British Airways are returned to competitive markets, arguably there is no need for specific regulation beyond the normal activities of the Office of Fair Trading (OFT) and the Competition Commission (CC). If a privatized company finds its regulator's stipulations unacceptable, then it may appeal to the Competition Commission.

Objectives of regulators

Regulators have two fundamental objectives. Firstly, they attempt to create the constraints and stimuli which companies would experience in a competitive market environment. For example, companies in competitive markets must bear in mind what their competitors are doing when setting their prices and are under competitive pressure to improve their service to consumers in order to gain market share. Regulation can *simulate* the effects of a competitive market by setting price caps and performance standards. Secondly, regulators have the longer-term objective of encouraging *actual* competition by easing the entry of new producers and by preventing privatized monopoly power maintaining barriers to entry. An ideal is the creation of markets sufficiently competitive to make regulation unnecessary. The market for telecommunication services has moved substantially in this direction, so much so that in July 2006 OFTEL announced that it would no longer apply a price cap for BT-provided services, since the market was now so competitive that such a price cap was unnecessary.

Problems facing regulators

Regulators have an unenviable role as they try to create the constraints and stimuli of a competitive market. Essentially they are arbitrating between the interests of consumers and producers. *Other things being equal*, attempts by regulators to achieve improvements in service levels will cause increases in costs and so lower profits, whilst price caps on services with price-inelastic demand will also reduce profits by *preventing* the regulated industries raising prices and therefore revenue. Lower profits, and the expectation of lower profits, have immediate implications for dividend distributions to shareholders and so for share prices. At this point other things are unlikely to remain equal. The privatized company subject to a price cap may well look for ways of lowering costs to allow profits to be at least maintained, or perhaps raised. In most organizations, there are economies to be gained by reducing staffing levels, and the utility

companies have dramatically reduced their numbers of employees. Investment in new technology may also enable unit costs to be lowered so that profits are greater than they otherwise would have been.

Establishing a price cap

In deciding on a price cap, the regulator has in mind some 'satisfactory' rate of profit on the value of assets employed. A key issue is then the valuation of the assets. If the basis of valuation is *historical*, using the market value at privatization plus an estimate of investment since that date, then the company will face a stricter price cap than if *current* market valuations are used for assets. This is because historical valuations will usually be much smaller than the current valuations and so will justify much smaller total profits and therefore lower prices to achieve that profit.

Price caps are often associated with job losses. In an economy with less than full employment it may then be argued that such cost savings in the privatized companies are only achieved at the expense of extra public expenditure on welfare benefit. However, a counter-argument is that lower public utility prices benefit all consumers, with lower costs of production across the economy stimulating output and creating employment.

It may be over-simplistic to assume that privatized companies will invariably respond to a price cap by cutting costs as much as possible in order to maximize profits over the medium-term period of the price cap. The planning period in public utilities is likely to be much longer than the four or five years of a regulator's price review period. If a company meets its price cap and service requirements by making excessively large efficiency savings so that its profits and share price grow quicker than the average for large companies, then there will be great public pressure on the regulator to be much tougher next time. The goals of regulated companies probably include avoiding the long-term regulatory regime becoming too 'tight'. At the same time, the regulator may depend on the company for a great deal of the information needed for the task of regulation. So there is the possibility of the regulator's independence being compromised, which has been called 'capture' of the regulator. Clearly the relationship between regulator and regulated company is complex, so that simple predictions of action and reaction are difficult to make.

Costs of regulation

Whilst regulation should produce clear benefits for the consumers of each privatized company, there are inevitable costs involved in running regulatory offices and also costs for the regulated company which has to supply information and present its case to the regulator. It is likely that companies will go further than this and try to *anticipate* the regulator's activities, so incurring further costs. It is not at all clear that having separate regulatory offices for each industry is a cost-effective arrangement. Concentration of *all* regulation in one agency might be more efficient and lead to more consistency in the treatment of different industries. It would also enable a consideration of the implications of decisions in one industry on competitive conditions in other industries. OFTEL, for example, has sought to increase competition in the rapidly changing telecommunications market by forcing BT to allow cable TV companies favourable access to its transmission networks. Yet these cable companies themselves have monopoly power in their own markets!

Differences in the regulatory regimes have certainly contributed to the astonishing difference between the weak share performance of the gas and telecommunications industries and the strong share performance of the water and electricity industries which have outperformed the FTSE 100 index by 60% and 101% respectively. High returns in the stock market are usually associated with risk. However, neither the water industry nor electricity can be viewed as risky; indeed, they would normally be seen as unspectacular but steady income generators rather than as growth stocks.

Regulation and deregulation

Regulation

Regulation may be defined as the various *rules* set by governments or their agencies which seek to control the operations of firms. We have already discussed the role of the regulators for the privatized industries who themselves are part of this broad regulatory process.

Regulation is one of the mechanisms available to governments when dealing with the problem of 'market failure'. Of course, market failure can take many forms although, as Stewart (1997) points out, four broad categories can usefully be identified.

1 *Asymmetric information.* Here the providers may have information not available to the purchasers. For example, in recent cases involving the mis-selling of pensions the companies involved were found to have withheld information from purchasers. Stricter regulation of the sector has been the government's response to this situation.

2 *Externalities.* In the case of negative externalities, regulations may be used to bring private costs more closely into line with social costs (as with environmental taxes) or to restrict social costs to a given level (as with environmental standards).

3 *Public goods.* Regulation may be required if such goods are to be provided at all. The idea of a public 'good' (which may, of course, be a service) is that it has the characteristics of being non-excludable and non-exhaustible, at least in the 'pure' case. Non-excludable refers to the difficulty of excluding those who do not wish to pay for the 'good' (e.g. police or defence); non-exhaustible refers to the fact that the marginal cost of providing an extra unit of the 'good' is effectively zero (e.g. an extra person covered by the police or defence forces). The non-excludable condition prevents a private market developing, since it is difficult to make 'free riders' actually pay for the public good. The non-exhaustible condition implies that any price that is charged should, for allocative efficiency (see Chapter 5, p. 89), equal marginal cost and therefore be zero. Private markets guided by the profit motive are hardly in the business of charging zero prices! Both conditions imply that the 'good' is best supplied by the public sector at zero price, using general tax revenue to fund provision (in the 'pure' public good case).

4 *Monopoly.* Regulation may be required to prevent the abuse of monopoly power. In Chapter 5 we considered a variety of regulations implemented by the Office of Fair Trading. Figure 5.2 (p. 90) was used to show that regulations involving the Competition Commission may be used to prevent or modify certain proposed mergers which are arguably against the public interest (e.g. where gains in 'productive efficiency' are more than offset by losses in 'allocative efficiency').

The *forms* of regulation are too innumerable to capture in a few headings. The various rules can involve the application of maximum or minimum prices, the imposition of various types of standards, taxes, quotas, procedures, directives, etc., whether issued by national bodies (e.g. the UK government or its agencies) or international bodies (e.g. the EU Commission, the World Trade Organization, etc.).

Although a strict classification of the numerous types of regulation would seem improbable, McKenzie (1998) makes a useful distinction:

■ regulations aimed at *protecting* the consumer from the consequences of market failure;

■ regulations aimed at *preventing* the market failure from happening in the first place.

In terms of the Financial Sector, the Deposit Guarantee Directive of the EU is of the former type. This *protects* customers of accredited EU banks by restoring at least 90% of any losses up to £12,000 which might result from the failure of a particular bank. In part, this is a response to asymmetric information, since customers do not have the information to evaluate the credit-worthiness of a particular bank, and might not be able to interpret that information even if it were available.

The Capital Adequacy Directive of the EU is of the latter type. This seeks to *prevent* market failure (such as a bank collapse) by directly relating the value of the capital a bank must hold to the riskiness of its business. The idea here is that the greater the value of capital available to a bank, the larger the buffer stock which it can use to absorb any losses. Various elements of the Capital Adequacy Directive force the banks to increase their capital base if the riskiness of

their portfolio (indicated by various statistical measures) is deemed to have increased. In part, this is in response to the potential for negative externalities in this sector. One bank failure can invariably lead to a 'domino effect' and risk system collapse with incalculable consequences for the sector as a whole.

In these ways, the regulatory system for EU financial markets is seeking to provide a framework within which greater competition between banks can occur, while at the same time addressing the fact that greater competition can increase the risks of bank failure. It is seeking both to protect consumers should any mishap occur and at the same time to prevent such a mishap actually occurring.

Overall, we can say that those who support any or all of these forms of regulation, in whatever sector of the economy, usually do so in the belief that they improve the allocation of resources in situations characterized by one or more types of market failure.

Deregulation

Deregulation may be defined as efforts to *remove* the various rules set by governments or their agencies which seek to control the operation of firms.

One of the major arguments in favour of deregulation involves 'public interest theory'. The suggestion here is that regulations should be removed whenever it can be shown that this will remove or reduce the 'deadweight loss' typically shown to result from various types of market interference.

Figure 8.1 can be used to show how a particular market regulation, here a quota scheme, can result in a 'deadweight loss'. In this analysis, *economic welfare* is defined as consumer surplus plus producer surplus.

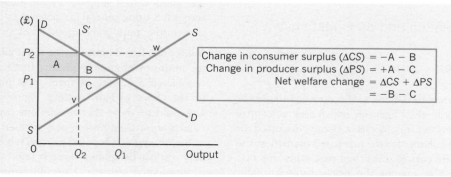

Fig. 8.1 Welfare loss with a quota scheme $0Q_2$ raising price (P_2) above the market clearing level P_1.

The *consumer surplus* is the amount consumers are willing to pay over and above the amount they need to pay; the *producer surplus* is the amount producers receive over and above the amount they need for them to supply the product.

In Fig. 8.1 we start with an initial demand curve DD and supply curve SS giving market equilibrium price P_1 and quantity Q_1. However, the *regulation* here is that should the market price fall below a particular level P_2, then the government is directed to intervene. It is required to use a *quota* arrangement to prevent market price from falling below, P_2; in other words P_2 is a minimum price which is set by regulation at a level which is above the free market price P_1. In terms of Fig. 8.1, if the quota is set at Q_2, then the effective supply curve becomes SvS', since no more than Q_2 can be supplied whatever the price. The result is to raise the 'equilibrium' price to P_2 and reduce the 'equilibrium' quantity to Q_2. However, the quota regulation has resulted in a *loss of economic welfare* equivalent to the area B plus area C. The reduction in output from Q_1 to Q_2 means a loss of area B in consumer surplus and loss of area C in producer surplus. However, the higher price results in a gain of area A in producer surplus which exactly offsets the loss of area A in consumer surplus. This means that the *net* welfare change is negative, i.e. there is a 'deadweight loss' of area B + area C.

'Public interest theory' is therefore suggesting that deregulation should occur whenever the net welfare change of *removing regulations* is deemed to be positive. In terms of Fig. 8.1, it might be argued that removing the regulation whereby the government (or its agent) seeks to keep price artificially high at P_2 will give a *net* welfare change which is positive, namely a net gain of area B + area C. In other words, allowing the free market equilibrium price P_1 and quantity Q_1 to prevail restores the previous deadweight loss via regulation. Put another way, public interest theory is suggesting that deregulation should occur whenever the outcome is a net welfare gain, so that those who gain can, at least potentially, more than compensate those who lose.

Of course, a similar analysis can be carried out in terms of other types of regulation incurring a deadweight loss *vis-à-vis* the free market equilibrium. In Chapter 27 we show how the operation of price support schemes using *central purchasing* arrangements by the Common Agricultural Policy of the EU can incur deadweight loss, when intervention prices are set above the world market price for certain agricultural products.

The empirical difficulties of placing a money value on changes in consumer surplus and producer surplus should not, of course, be underestimated. In terms of Fig. 8.1, it involves accurate estimates of both the demand and supply (or cost) curves facing the firm or industry. Issues of 'weighting' must also be considered, for example whether a £1 gain of producer surplus is the same in welfare terms as a £1 loss of consumer surplus. Certainly, such a 'one for one' weighting was used in Fig. 8.1, with +A gain of producer surplus under the quota regarded as exactly offsetting the −A loss of consumer surplus previously earned under the initial free market situation. Some might argue that a given monetary value to consumers should be given a greater 'weight' in terms of economic welfare than a similar monetary value received by producers!

Whether deregulation will yield a net welfare gain or loss (i.e. be in, or against, the public interest) clearly involves both theoretical and empirical aspects, and may need to be considered on a case-by-case basis. Certainly, deregulation is gathering momentum in the major industrialized economies. For example, it has been estimated that in 1977 some 17% of US GNP was derived from the output of fully regulated industries, whereas that figure has declined to around 5% of GNP in current times. Winston (1993), in a wide-ranging study of the impacts of deregulation across the US industrial and service sectors, found substantial net gains to have resulted from deregulatory activity. For instance, in the US airlines sector he estimated the net benefit of the elimination of all regulations on air fares in 1983 to have been in the range of $4.3bn to $6.5bn over a 10-year period.

Interestingly, empirical estimates of the impact of deregulation have had the greatest difficulty in placing monetary values on predicted or actual changes in the *quality* of goods or services. For example, predictions as to the likely impact of deregulation on the mean and variance of travel times for passengers and freight in the transport sector have been noticeable by their absence from empirical studies or their inaccuracy when compared with eventual outcomes.

Our earlier discussion in Chapter 5 (pp. 89–91) reinforced this point about the difficulty of evaluating the net welfare change from deregulation. It showed how 'public interest theory' may often have to weigh the gains in terms of 'productive efficiency' against

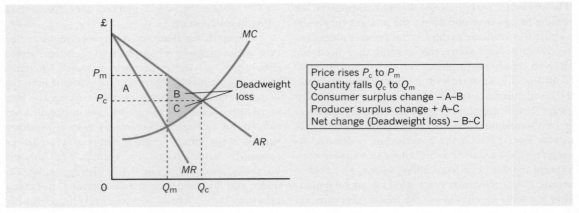

Fig. 8.2 Deadweight loss as a result of monopoly power raising equilibrium price (P_c to P_m) and lowering equilibrium output (Q_c to Q_m).
Source: Griffiths and Wall (2000) *Intermediate Microeconomics*, Financial Times/Prentice Hall.

the losses in terms of 'allocative efficiency' when trying to evaluate whether a regulation (e.g. restricting a proposed merger) is, or is not, operating in the overall public interest.

Regulating a deregulated monopoly

In the real world, the outcomes of deregulation may not be to recapture all the 'deadweight loss' resulting from the previous monopoly situation. This is especially true when a monopoly or oligopoly industry is deregulated, but when a return to a highly competitive industry characterized by numerous small firms is unrealistic! This has, in fact, been the case with most privatizations/deregulations of the previous nationalized industries, with the post-privatization situation often still involving a high degree of market dominance by a relatively small number of large firms.

It is in this type of situation that regulators, using price caps, may be able to release some, if not all, of the 'deadweight loss' previously present when the industry was nationalized or under monopoly control.

Deregulating the monopoly industry: no regulator required

If the classical case against monopoly does hold (Chapter 3, p. 58), namely higher price and lower

output than in the perfectly competitive equilibrium, then Fig. 8.2 can be used to indicate the 'deadweight loss' from removing monopoly power. As compared to the competitive price/output equilibrium (P_c/Q_c), the higher monopoly price (P_m) results in the *loss* of area A and area B (consumer surplus) by discouraging some consumers from purchasing at this higher price. At the same time, the producers who are still able to find a market in which to sell at the higher price gain area A of producers' surplus, but those unable to sell at this price lose area C, giving an overall change of +A − C in terms of producers' surplus.

The net change (deadweight loss) in aggregate consumer and producer surplus of the monopoly situation as compared to the competitive market outcome is therefore:

$$-A - B + A - C = -B - C.$$

Deregulating the monopoly industry: regulator required

In a simple model, removing the monopoly power by privatization/deregulation will then restore the deadweight loss B + C and thereby raise economic welfare. However, in reality the industry may, post-privatization/deregulation, not in fact move in the direction of a competitive industry but retain much of its previous monopoly/oligopoly characteristics, i.e. still be dominated by a few large firms. It is in such a context that using a regulator to oversee the now deregulated industry, and setting a price cap, may help ensure that at least *some* of the deadweight loss from the original monopoly situation is recovered[2].

Suppose a regulator *is* appointed in such a situation and imposes a price ceiling, P_1, for the monopoly in Fig. 8.3. The firm can now charge no more than P_1, so that the effective *average revenue* curve is the horizontal line P_1V up to output Q_1. For output levels up to Q_1 the *marginal revenue* curve will be identical to the average revenue curve (P_1V). Of course, for output levels beyond Q_1 the original average and marginal revenue curves still apply since the firm is permitted to charge *less* than P_1 if it desires to reach those output levels. Effectively the marginal revenue curve is in two segments, P_1V and WZ, with VW a line of discontinuity connecting these two segments.

In Fig. 8.3 the profit maximizing solution ($MC = MR$) will now be output Q_1 at price P_1 for the regulated monopolist. Comparing Fig. 8.3 with Fig. 8.2 it should be readily apparent that the area of deadweight loss under the regulated monopoly is *smaller* than that under the unregulated monopoly.

- Unregulated monopoly: Deadweight loss = 1 + 2 + 3 + 4 + 5.

- Regulated monopoly (P_1 as price ceiling): Deadweight loss = 1 + 2 + 4.

Clearly, a reduction of area 3 + 5 of deadweight loss is achieved by price regulation in this case.

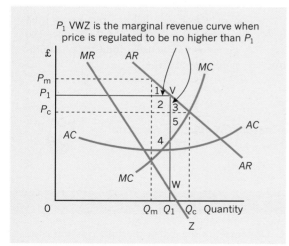

Fig. 8.3 Price regulation of monopoly: P_1 as the price ceiling set by the regulator.
Source: Griffiths and Wall (2000) *Intermediate Microeconomics*, Financial Times/Prentice Hall.

Indeed, if the price ceiling were set still lower, at the competitive price P_c, then the profit-maximizing solution ($MC = MR$) for the regulated monopoly would now be P_c/Q_c with zero deadweight loss.

Without the regulator and the price cap at P_1, there would be the risk that the original privatization/deregulation would have had little or no impact in terms of removing the original deadweight loss, as this is 'recaptured' by the now privatized large company/companies.

Conclusion

Despite the advance of privatization, there remains a strong case for some form of government intervention in selected industries, for example to protect the public interest, prevent abuse of monopoly power and compensate for externalities. It does not, however, follow that nationalization is the best form of government intervention. The extent of privatization since 1979 has radically changed the role of the state in the UK economy and makes it very unlikely that there will ever again be the range of state industries which existed at that date. Indeed, there is now a worldwide shift of policy in favour of privatizing state-owned assets. The performance of both state-owned and privatized industry is difficult to evaluate. It has not been convincingly demonstrated that the form of ownership of an organization is the most important influence on its performance. Of much greater importance would seem to be the degree of competition and the effectiveness of regulatory bodies. Certainly, greater powers are being given to many of the regulators of the previously nationalized industries in an attempt to prevent the abuse of monopoly power by the now privatized utilities. Regulators may impose price caps and use other devices to prevent consumers being 'exploited' in monopoly-type situations. They may also seek to open markets to additional competition by encouraging new entrants. Nevertheless, there is also a counter-movement which seeks to *remove* regulations where these are thought to operate against the public interest. Such attempts at deregulation are widespread, though it should not be forgotten that the reason many regulations exist is to protect consumers from the adverse consequences of various types of 'market failure'.

Key points

- In 1979 the nationalized industries produced some 9% of GDP, 12% of investment and 7% of total employment. However, by 2010 their contribution was much smaller, only around 2% of GDP, 3% of investment and 2% of total employment.

- Privatization is the transfer of assets or economic activity from the public sector to the private sector.

- The term 'privatization' is often used to cover many situations: the outright sale of state-owned assets, part-sale, joint public/private ventures, market testing, contracting out of central/local government services, etc.

- The case *for* privatization includes allegedly greater productive efficiency (lower costs) via the introduction of market pressures. These are seen as creating more flexibility in labour markets, higher productivity and reduced unit labour costs. More widespread share ownership, a lower PSBR (PSNCR), easier access to investment capital, greater scope for diversification and the absence of civil service oversight are often quoted as 'advantages' of privatization.

- The case *against* privatization includes suggestions that state monopolies have often merely been replaced by private monopolies, with little benefit to consumers, especially in the case of the public utilities. The loss of scale economies (e.g. 'natural monopolies'), the inability to deal effectively with externalities, undervaluation of state assets, the subsequent concentration of share ownership and 'short-termism' of the city are often quoted as disadvantages of privatization.

- Regulators have been appointed for a number of public utilities in an attempt to *simulate* the effects of competition (e.g. limits to price increases and to profits), when there is little competition in reality.

- Other regulations are widely used in all economic sectors in order to protect consumers from 'market failure' and to prevent such failures actually occurring.

- There is considerable momentum behind removing regulations (i.e. deregulation) where this can be shown to be in the 'public interest'. However, evaluating the welfare change from deregulation is a complex exercise.

- In some cases, e.g. where deregulation still results in large firms playing a dominant role in the industry, the appointment of a regulator may help to remove at least some of the deadweight loss under the previous nationalized industry or monopoly type situation.

Now try the self-check questions for this chapter on the Companion Website. You will also find useful links to relevant websites.

Notes

1 For example, the transition from private to public ownership meant the takeover of some 550 separate local concerns in the electricity industry and over 1,000 local concerns in the gas industry.

2 Of course, to the extent that the 'classical case' against monopoly of higher price and lower output does *not* hold (see Chapter 3, p. 58) then no such deadweight loss need occur.

References and further reading

Bishop, M., Kay, J. and Mayer, C. (1994) *Privatization and Economic Performance*, Oxford, Oxford University Press.

Crew, M. and Parker, D. (2008) *Developments in the economics of Privatization and Regulation*, Cheltenham, Edward Elgar.

Gerard, R. (2008) *Privatisation: Successes and Failures*, Columbia, University Press Group.

Griffiths, A. and Wall, S. (2000) *Intermediate Microeconomics*, Harlow, Financial Times/ Prentice Hall.

Helm, D. (1994) British utility regulation theory, practice and reform, *Oxford Review of Economic Policy*, 10(3): 17–39.

Humphreys, I. and Francis, G. (2002) Airport privatisation, *British Economy Survey*, Spring, 51–6.

Ingham, A. (2003) Rail privatisation revisited, *Economic Review*, February.

Lipczynski, J., Wilson, J. and Goddard, J. (2009) *Industrial Organisation: Competition, Strategy, Policy* (3rd edn), Harlow, Financial Times/ Prentice Hall.

McKenzie, G. (1998) Financial regulation and the European Union, *Economic Review*, April.

McWilliams, D. and Pragnell, M. (1996) Who will miss the PSBR? *Financial Times*, 30 September.

Ménard, I. and Ghertman, M. (2010) *Regulation, Deregulation, Reregulation Institutional Perspectives*, Cheltenham, Edward Elgar.

Myers, D. (1998) The Private Finance Initiative – a progress report, *Economic Review*, April, 28–31.

Oxford Review of Economic Policy (1997) Competition in regulated industries, 13(1), Spring.

Parker, D. (1991) Privatization ten years on: a critical analysis of its rationale and results, *Economics*, Winter.

Schwartz, G. and Lopes, P. S. (1993) Privatization: expectations, trade-offs and results, *Finance and Development*, June, 14–17.

Sherman, R. (2007) *Market Regulation*, Harlow, Financial Times/Prentice Hall.

Stewart, G. (1997) Why regulate?, *Economic Review*, September.

Wilson, J. (1994) Competitive tendering and UK public services, *Economic Review*, April, 1–5.

Winston, C. (1993) Economic deregulation, *Journal of Economic Literature*, 31(September): 1263–89.

CHAPTER 9

Beyond markets: critical approaches to microeconomics

As we saw in Chapter 3, the widely accepted assumption is that businesses follow maximizing objectives, whether profit, sales revenue or sales revenue, subject to a minimum profit constraint. Although we reviewed a range of non-maximizing or behavioural objectives, we paid little attention to the role of institutions in influencing the context in which both principals and agents (managers) take decisions. This chapter seeks to remedy that deficiency by reviewing the various 'schools' of economic thought and the different perspectives these bring to the role of markets and prices in providing effective 'signals' to both produces and consumers in allocating scarce resources amongst alternative uses.

Defining 'institutions' is by no means as obvious as it might appear! North (1990) defines 'institutions' as including any form of constraints that have been devised by human beings to shape human interactions, whether formal (as in explicit laws and regulations) or informal (as in conventions and codes of behaviour). Such 'institutions' can be created at a single point in time (e.g. US Constitution or UK Magna Carta) or can evolve over time as increasingly accepted norms of behaviour within a particular 'community'. In other words, institutions are 'rules of the game', whether written or unwritten, but are NOT the same as organizations. Organizations are groups of individuals held together by some common purpose, whether in the spheres of economics (trade unions, employer federations, firms, co-operatives), education (schools, universities, training centres), politics (political parties, regulatory agencies, national/regional/local councils) or social endeavours (churches, sports/social clubs).

Institutions and organizations clearly interact, but the emphasis here is on the written and unwritten rules themselves, i.e. the *institutional framework* and its relevance to how markets and indeed economies evolve over time, and to how that framework impacts upon individual consumer and producer behaviour. Of course, this institutional framework plays a key role in determining the types of organizations which evolve and how they operate and develop over time.

Before examining the contribution and relevance of institutional perspectives to actual policy-making, it will help to review the approaches of the various 'schools' of economic thought as to the role of markets and governments in resource allocation. We look closely at the role of markets in neoclassical perspectives before applying some of the more recent institutional perspectives to real world phenomena which neoclassical approaches have found difficult to resolve, such as gift giving and quasi-internal markets.

Classical and neoclassical perspectives on markets

Classical perspectives on the market

For the purposes of creating a benchmark against which the neoclassical and other perspectives on markets can be contrasted, we shall attempt to identify a classical position as to the nature and development of markets by examining the work of key figures within the so-called Classical School. It is widely acknowledged that the 'economic science' emerged as a separate branch of knowledge through the combined efforts of the French Physiocrats, Hume and other Scottish philosophers, and in particular with the publication of Adam Smith's *Wealth of Nations* (1776). The emphasis within classical economic theory was on wealth creation and economic growth, and therefore on the study of the market mechanisms that might bring about these two objectives, seen as vital for the successful functioning of any society. In this context, terms such as laissez-faire, harmony, self-regulating systems, natural order were introduced into the economic, social and political narratives.

One of the purposes of Smith's argument was to study the human propensities that incline mankind to a societal form of existence. Smith's most characteristic ideas concerned the way that man is led by an 'invisible hand' to promote ends which were not part of his original intention, i.e. the 'unintended outcomes' thesis. Whilst recognizing markets as the place where the propensity of human nature to barter or exchange is exerted, for Smith markets were seen in a broader context as a preferable alternative to government regulation in supporting wealth creation and economic growth.

The Wealth of Nations (1776) arguably provided us with the first coherent treatment of the role of markets within an economic system. Although a staunch advocate of the free market, Adam Smith was not a slavish devotee of the unrivalled 'power of the market', and he never suggested that the state can or should be entirely replaced by markets. As Cairncross emphasized: 'The market was allowed more scope and freedom but the state still determined the framework of law and regulation under which private initiative could be exercised to meet market requirements' (Cairncross 1978, p. 113).

Smith's way of describing market forces, the interaction between supply and demand, the formation or adjustment of prices and the sequential 'movement' towards equilibrium has shaped modern thinking on markets. Smith introduced two concepts which can be used to analyse price formation, the *natural price* (i.e. in modern terms the equilibrium price), and the *market price* (i.e. the actual price of a commodity which covers its production cost). Smith contends:

> When the price of any commodity is neither more nor less than what is sufficient to pay the rent of the land, the wages of the labour, and the profits of the stock employed in raising, preparing, and bringing it to the market, according to their natural rates, the commodity is then sold for what may be called its natural price . . . The actual price at which any commodity is commonly sold is called its market price. It may either be above, or below, or exactly the same as its natural price (Smith A. 1776, p. 36).

The market price can be lower, higher or equal to the natural price which is determined by long-run, underlying structural factors. By describing the mechanism of market adjustment, Smith engages his analysis with the process of partial equilibrium; this *comparative statics* method of comparing equilibrium states before and after the adjustments has been used by economists ever since. The argument is extremely simple: if the quantities supplied to the market are smaller than the 'effectual demand' for those commodities, not all individuals can actually buy the desired quantities. Some will be willing to pay a higher price than the natural price; as a consequence, depending on competition, the 'market price' will rise above the 'natural price'. In a similar way, if the quantities supplied to the market are greater than effective demand, the 'market price' will fall. If the demand is equal to supply, the 'market price' will coincide with the 'natural price'.

Smith considers the 'natural price' to be a central price towards 'which the prices of all commodities are continually gravitating' (Smith 1776). Smith has employed the term 'constant tendency' to denote the outcome of economic forces in the economic system. The fluctuations of market prices are governed by wages, profits and rents, and by the stage of development within a society. These influence the circumstances of labour, economic activities, etc., and this position is a more dynamic conception of prices and competition than the one envisaged by neoclassical economics. Smith's concept of 'free competition' amounts to an *absence* of restriction on the market and freedom of entry; similarly, monopoly means *obstacles* to entry, the exertion of power over the consumers through the market being under-stocked, thereby raising 'market prices' above 'natural prices'. In conditions of 'perfect liberty', the sellers have the possibility to adapt their prices and may exit if the 'market price' is below the natural price in the long term.

In other words, Smith acknowledges the existence of monopolies and their tendency to 'keep the market under-stocked'. Ricardo (1817) and Mill (1863), in a similar way, defined monopoly as 'inelastic supply'. With Ricardo, political economy took a major step towards using abstract models, in which the historical, institutional, social or philosophical perspectives were reduced to relatively unimportant issues. The 'comparative statics' approach, which did not go uncriticized, became the dominant methodology. The attractiveness of economics as a science, and the certain guarantee of empirical results similar to those to be found within natural science, undoubtedly had an influence upon Ricardo.

In sum, therefore, the classical conception of markets can be described as constituting a belief in market systems as a mechanism for creating harmonious order in which individual actions motivated by self-interest are co-ordinated by the 'invisible hand' in order to achieve a common good. As the foremost prophet of competition, Smith did not conceive of a perfectly competitive market but advocated a less regulated as opposed to a government-regulated market in order to achieve an efficient allocation of resources.

Classical economists generally had an optimistic attitude towards the market. Of course, a notable exception to this position was Marx, who was sceptical about the merits of co-ordinating economic activities through the market given the nature and inequalities of private property rights. At the same time, and despite their preference towards laissez-faire, the market was certainly not regarded as a 'perfect' entity by classical economists!

Neoclassical perspectives on the market

The origins of neoclassical economics are to be found in the marginalist revolution of the 1870s with its shift in focus for microeconomics towards a concern with differential calculus, mathematical economics and the determination of relative prices. Such an approach flourished with the work of Jevons (1871) and was continued by Walras (1877), Edgeworth (1881) and Pareto, amongst others. On this foundation of mathematical precision, a whole analytical apparatus was developed as regards consumer and choice theory, indifference curves and exchange theory. Indeed, through much of the twentieth century and to the present day, microeconomics has arguably continued to be dominated by marginalism and mathematical formulism.

Neoclassical economics would typically claim that society is populated by individual agents whose behaviour is perfectly predictable and who can be regarded as acting 'rationally' and without reference to any institutional or social context. Only individuals exist and concepts such as *class* or *society* are merely 'intellectual constructions'. The *methodological individualism* underpinning this neoclassical approach implies that change and the outcomes of human actions are best understood through the eyes of individual agents.

Shand (1984) defines such methodological individualism as an approach in which 'all statements about groups are reducible to statements about the behaviour of the individuals composing those groups and their interactions' (p. 4). Boland (2003) offers a similar definition: 'Methodological indi-

vidualism is the view that allows only individuals to be the decision-makers in any explanation of social phenomena' (p. 31).

Methodological individualism therefore presupposes an explanation of institutions as an outcome of individual actions, in line with conventional assumptions. The central debate seems to be between theorists committed to such *methodological individualism* (i.e. the individual actors are the central elements in society and social structure is the result and consequence of the interaction of such individuals) and *methodological holism* (i.e. individual actors are socialized and institutions may be formed which constrain and shape individuals' capacities and dispositions to act).

Some neoclassical economists have sought to allow for various types of market failure and the role of institutions. Williamson (1975), Coase (1937) and others have emphasized the importance of property rights, transaction costs and other institutional characteristics as influencing individual actors, but the neoclassical framework has arguably remained intact.

Whilst market failures of various kinds and institutional contexts are readily admitted by some neoclassical economists as challenging some of the mathematically oriented marginalist precision, advocates of 'methodological individualism' such as North (1990) would respond in the following way:

> Although, I know of very few economists who really believe that the behavioural assumptions of economics accurately reflect human behaviour, they do (mostly) believe that such assumptions are useful for building models of market behaviour in economics and, though less useful, are still the best game in town for studying politics and the other social sciences (North 1990, p. 17).

At this point, it will be useful to illustrate some of the central tenets of the neoclassical approach to markets and the role of price as providing 'signals' to both consumers and producers to bring about stable and 'efficient' resource allocations. Insofar as we can identify a neoclassical approach to institutions, it presumes utility maximization at the level of the individual, stable preferences and the rejection of custom and tradition on the grounds that this might admit ignorance and irrationality. In this context, neoclassical economics is largely unable to deal with issues involving changes in economic and social institutions:

> Neoclassical theory implies that economic behaviour is essentially non-habitual and non-routinised, involving rational calculation and marginal adjustments towards an optimum (Hodgson 1988, p. 130).

Consequently, habits and routines that are the product of unconscious decision-making have no place within the neoclassical schema, despite the obvious existence of such forms of decision-making within the real world.

Markets, prices and economic efficiency

It may be useful at this point to explore the theoretical basis for the belief, particularly amongst neoclassical economists, that markets can coordinate the decisions of innumerable producers and consumers in such a way as to bring about an efficient allocation of resources. The key 'signal' available to markets for influencing producer and consumer decisions is, of course, market price. By way of illustration we shall focus on the role of prices in guiding consumer choices so that total utility (satisfaction) of consumers is maximized, with no single consumer able to add to his/her utility without at the same time some other consumer losing utility. This is the *Pareto optimal* resource allocation, and we return to it in more detail below (p. 170).

For simplicity, we shall begin our analysis by taking a two person and two product model, since by assuming a 2×2 model we can make use of (two-dimensional) graphical analysis. We assume that consumers A and B are active in the market for two products X and Y and that their preferences are expressed by (ordinal) indifference curves which are smooth and convex to the origin. This implies diminishing marginal rates of substitution in consumption between the two products. Consumers are assumed to be independent, in that the consumption pattern of one does not affect the consumption pattern of the other, and to have perfect information as to the prices and qualities of the products traded.

P_X = price of product X;

P_Y = price of product Y

X_A, X_B = quantity of product X purchased by consumers A and B respectively

Y_A, Y_B = quantities of product Y purchased by consumers A and B respectively

Pareto optimal resource allocation between consumers

A Pareto-efficient (Pareto optimal) allocation of resources between consumers is said to occur when it is no longer possible to reallocate product outputs between consumers so as to make one consumer better off without at the same time making the other consumer worse off. We first consider what is involved in a Pareto-efficient distribution of products X and Y between our two consumers A and B using an Edgeworth–Bowley consumption box, then we see how prices can bring about such a resource allocation.

The Edgeworth–Bowley consumption box used in our analysis is shown in Fig. 9.1. The lengths of each side of the consumption box are determined by the amounts of products X and Y ($\bar{X}$, $\bar{Y}$) available for distribution between the two consumers A and B. The more of one product allocated to consumer A, the less is available for consumer B, and vice versa.

The indifference curves of consumer A are plotted with the south-west corner of the box as origin. Each A indifference curve is smooth and convex to this origin, and the furthest indifference curve from the origin (A_5) corresponds to the highest level of utility available to A. In this case, all the output of products X and Y available in the economy is consumed by A (and none by B).

The opposite occurs for consumer B; it is as though we construct the same diagram for B then turn it upside down and superimpose it onto our diagram for A. The origin for B is now the north-east corner of the box. Each B indifference curve is smooth and convex to this origin and the furthest indifference curve from the origin (B_5) corresponds to the highest level of utility available to B. In this case, all the output of products X and Y available in the economy is consumed by B (and none by A).

This time we use the Edgeworth–Bowley consumption box to identify those distributions of resources which are Pareto-efficient. Only certain distributions of the total product ($\bar{X}$, $\bar{Y}$) between

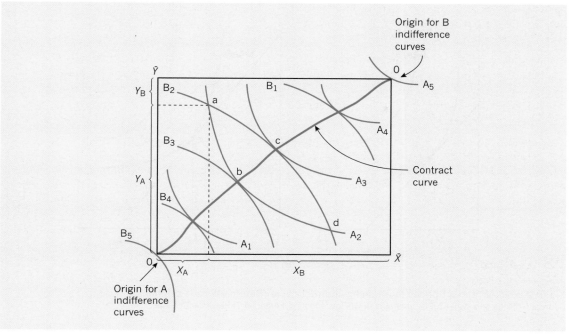

Fig. 9.1 Edgeworth–Bowley consumption box.
Source: Griffiths and Wall (2000) *Intermediate Microeconomics*, Financial Times/Prentice Hall.

consumers A and B are Pareto-efficient. Let us begin by considering the distribution at point 'a' in which X_A, Y_A is the respective consumption of products X and Y by consumer A. Clearly this distribution is non-Pareto-efficient in the sense that we can redistribute output so as to make some better off and none worse off. For example, if we slide down the A_2 indifference curve to point 'b', we distribute less product Y to consumer A but more product X, keeping A's utility constant (at A_2). However, by distributing the residual output to consumer B (now more of product Y and less of product X is available to consumer B than the combination Y_B, X_B at 'a'), we increase B's utility ($B_3 > B_2$) at point 'b'. If consumer B is better off and consumer A is no worse off at 'b' as compared to 'a', then clearly distribution 'a' is non-Pareto-efficient.

Note that B_3 is the highest attainable indifference curve (furthest from the B origin) in the consumption box given that A remains on indifference curve A_2. The distribution at point 'b' is clearly a tangency position between the respective A_2 and B_3 indifference curves and corresponds to a Pareto-efficient distribution of output. Any further redistribution of output

along A_2 in this direction will take us below and to the right of 'b' on A_2 which will mean lower utility for consumer B. For example, at point 'd' we again have A_2, B_2 levels of utility for each consumer, and as we have seen $B_2 < B_3$.

It should be clear that only tangency positions between the respective indifference curves correspond to Pareto-efficient solutions. The line connecting these tangency positions is called the *contract curve*. It is therefore distributions of output along the contract curve which alone are Pareto-efficient in the consumption box. You might usefully consider why a redistribution of resources from 'a' to 'c' would also achieve a Pareto-efficient solution.

Pareto efficiency in consumption implies:

$$\frac{\text{slope of A}}{\text{indifference curve}} = \frac{\text{slope of B}}{\text{indifference curve}}$$

i.e.

$$MRS^A_{XY} = MRS^B_{XY}$$

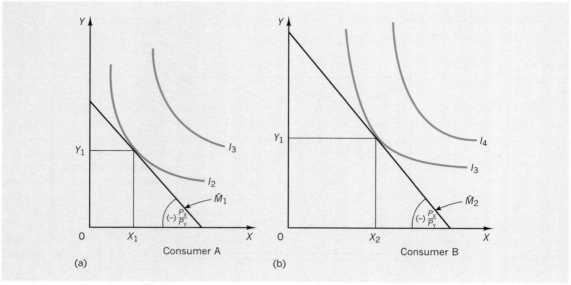

Fig. 9.2 Role of product prices in attaining contract curve (Pareto-efficient solutions).
Source: Griffiths and Wall (2000) *Intermediate Microeconomics,* Financial Times/Prentice Hall.

Prices and Pareto efficiency in consumption

This Pareto efficiency condition in consumption involves the economy attaining an appropriate distribution of output (products X and Y) between consumers (A and B). We now consider how, under our earlier assumptions, *prices* can provide the signals to consumers to bring about contract-curve distributions of output between themselves.

The *slope* of a budget line in Fig. 9.2 is given by the ratio of product prices, P_X/P_y. Provided that consumers face the same price ratios on product markets (e.g. purchase outputs on perfectly competitive product markets) then they will be faced by budget lines of identical slope. To maximize utility consumers must seek the highest attainable indifference curves, given the constraints of income level (*position* of budget line) and product prices (*slope* of budget line). In Fig. 9.2(a), if $\bar{M}_1$ is the income level of consumer A, and P_X/P_y the ratio of product prices, then I_2 is the highest level of utility attainable, where the budget line ($\bar{M}_1$) just touches (is a tangent to) the indifference curve furthest from the origin. This implies consumer A purchasing the combination X_1, Y_1 of the respective products. Similarly in Fig. 9.2(b), if $\bar{M}_2$ is the income

level of consumer B, and P_X/P_y the ratio of product prices, then I_3 is the highest level of utility attainable, where the budget line ($\bar{M}_2$) is a tangent to the indifference curve furthest from the origin. This implies consumer B purchasing the product combination X_2, Y_2.

Without any conscious co-ordination between consumers, but simply by individually seeking their own utility maximizing solutions, the two consumers have achieved a contract-curve distribution of resources (here the allocation of products between consumers). Provided only that they face the same product price ratio (P_X/P_y), they will have equated the slopes of their respective indifference curves; i.e. they will be at a solution such as 'b' or 'c' in earlier Fig. 9.1.

i.e. $MRS_{XY}^A = \dfrac{P_X}{P_Y} = MRS_{XY}^B$

or

slope of A indifference curve

$= \dfrac{P_X}{P_Y} =$ slope of B indifference curve

It is *product prices* which act as the signal to induce consumers to select distributions of products X and Y between themselves (resource allocations) which are Pareto-efficient.

The above analysis has been expressed in terms of product prices and consumers. However, the Edgeworth–Bowley production can be used to show how *factor prices* (wage rate w and interest rate r) can act as signals to profit-maximizing producers to allocate factor input (labour and capital equipment) between the two producers in a Pareto-efficient way.

General equilibrium and 'efficiencies'

Whilst it was readily admitted that the 'invisible hand' in the form of price signals could result in equilibrium outcomes in single markets, there was a problem in extending this equilibrium yielding property of the price mechanism to all markets simultaneously! This became known as the problem of achieving a 'general equilibrium' solution across all product and factor markets simultaneously.

This issue of achieving a general equilibrium through the price mechanisms 'clearing' all markets simultaneously also became linked with the idea of 'efficiency', with the so-called 'Pareto optimal' resource allocation seen as a 'holy grail' in which resources (both products and factors) would be allocated in such a way that it would no longer be possible to redistribute an extra unit of resources to make one consumer or producer 'better off', without at the same time making some other consumer or producer 'worse off'. If you could redistribute resources to make someone better off without making anyone worse off, then clearly you should do so as total 'welfare' would then rise!

The subsequent work of Arrow and Debreu (1954) was seen by many as actually attaining this 'holy grail' by the autonomous actions of individuals guided by self-interest and market signals alone. Arrow and Debreu showed mathematically that if certain competitive conditions were present in markets, then individual agents (consumers and producers) would, without prompting, take self-interested decision in allocating resources such that a Pareto optimal efficiency condition would be inexorably attained. More specifically, Arrow and Debreu showed that, if certain conditions hold, then a set of prices will result across the product and factor markets such

that aggregate supplies will match aggregate demands for every commodity. Nor would any overall 'planner' be needed to achieve this efficient 'general equilibrium'. Self-interested decision-making by the individual 'actors', consumers seeking to maximize utility and producers seeking to maximize profit, will bring about this efficient general equilibrium, provided only that the appropriate market conditions hold! The task of governments then reduces to the minimalist one of ensuring the existence of such conditions – no other co-ordinating effort is required of governments!

However, these necessary conditions are by no means 'trivial'! They required perfect product and factor markets, full and accurate information to all market participants, no externalities in consumption or production, maximizing behaviour by consumers and producers, convexity assumptions ensuring diminishing returns in consumption and production, amongst others. Of all the subsets of opinion within the neoclassical paradigm, the 'Chicago School' has often been identified as holding most closely to the use of unfettered markets in resource allocation.

Chicago School

Based around the University of Chicago, this 'School' is seen by many as the full embodiment of the neoclassical approach, with its resolute application of the assumptions of maximizing behaviour, market equilibria and stable preferences, in a world with few, if any, admitted 'market failures'! Becker (1981) saw no limit to the areas in which 'rational economic decisions' using such microeconomic assumptions, could be usefully applied, as indicated by the following extract from his speech on receiving the Nobel prize for economics.

> In the early stages of my work on crime, I was puzzled by why theft is socially harmful, since it appears merely to redistribute resources, usually from richer to poorer individuals. I resolved the puzzle by pointing out that criminals spend on weapons and on the value of their time in planning and carrying out their crimes and that such spending is socially unproductive (Becker 1981)

The emphasis here is on rational, self-interested calculations being the driving force behind all decision-making, and that ethical values such as 'honesty' will only be a market outcome if it can be shown to yield larger 'payoffs' to the various 'actors' than dishonesty.

Nor does the Chicago School even recognize the existence of 'market failures'! Markets are seen as incapable of failing – and that whilst individuals and businesses may (falsely) perceive such failures – the ultimate outcome can still be modelled using the assumption of 'rational expectations', i.e. where consumers and businesses are assumed to behave 'as if' they had access to all available knowledge and are capable of making precise (marginalist) calculations on that basis!

The fundamental tenet of the Chicago School is that competitive markets have 'efficiency properties' that no other institutional system can possible attain! The Arrow–Debreu work on general equilibrium was seen by Chicago School adherents as the ultimate vindication of this perspective!

 ## Role of the state in neoclassical economics

Whilst the degree to which 'market failure' is accepted as actually occurring varies widely amongst neoclassical economists, most accept that the rigorous conditions advocated for a spontaneous general and competitive equilibrium do not, in reality, exist. In other words we are often, in reality, in a 'second best' world where pragmatic policy-making has a role to play which might differ from the simple presumptions of a 'first best' model in which no market failures occur. Here we provide some insights into the (less extreme) neoclassical perspective that the state's main role is to seek, wherever possible, to correct any market imperfections or failures which might distort the price signals given to consumers and producers and thereby prevent the market from co-ordinating decision-making and increasing economic 'efficiency'!

Imperfect information

We can use our earlier analysis of prices and consumer behaviour to illustrate the typical neoclassical perspective as to the main role of the state being merely to 'correct' any deviation in the set of condi-

tions necessary for general equilibrium. The policy prescription for government intervention in this case is to help restore 'perfect information' to market participants as to the true prices prevailing on product markets. Figure 9.3 shows how *imperfect information* in product markets means that prices would no longer be able to act as appropriate signals for bringing about a contract-curve (Pareto-efficient) solution in terms of the Edgeworth–Bowley consumption box. Remember how we noted (p. 170) that simply by maximizing their own utility subject to the product prices they faced and the incomes they possessed, consumers would equate the slopes of their respective indifference curves and bring about a contract-curve solution. In Fig. 9.3, however, the absence of such perfect information means that consumer A maximizes utility subject to a different set of product prices than those faced by consumer B.

Suppose consumer A is less aware (perhaps via less search activity) of the availability of a cheaper source of product Y than is consumer B, so that consumer A faces a higher price for Y and therefore a lower product price ratio (P_X/P_Y) than does consumer B. This implies a flatter budget line (AM) for consumer A than for B. Clearly from Fig. 9.3 we can see that in maximizing utility by equating their respective

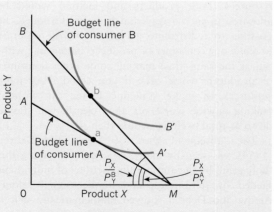

Fig. 9.3 Imperfect information as to prices and market failure.
Source: Griffiths and Wall (2000) *Intermediate Microeconomics*, Financial Times/Prentice Hall.
Note: For diagrammatic simplicity we assume a given *income* for consumers A and B.

budget lines with the highest attainable indifference curves, consumers A and B are in a non-contract-curve situation. In other words, imperfect information as to product prices means that price signals fail to bring about a (first best) Pareto-efficient allocation of resources in product markets as regards consumers (via exchange).

Figure 9.3 is drawn on the assumption that both consumers have identical incomes, but differential access to information as regards the price of Y. This simplifying assumption results in the respective consumer budget lines having the same intercept on the horizontal axis (i.e. M). It also helps to illustrate the welfare loss to the consumer possessing imperfect information. For example, if consumer A were to receive the same product price information as consumer B, then his/her budget line would pivot from AM to BM and he/she would be able to attain a higher indifference curve (such as B').

Institutionalist perspectives on markets

The aim of this section is to assess the contribution of the Institutionalist School to the development of the theory of markets and prices. Here we will focus on the basic contribution of this 'school' to the understanding of markets, and to the process of price formation, reviewing the work of the authors who represent the 'core' of institutional economics such as Veblen (1899), Ayres (1951), Commons (1931) and Mitchell (1927). In addition, we shall also explore later thinkers who have written in this tradition such as Galbraith (1952), Means (1962) and more recently Hodgson (1988).

In order to arrive at an institutionalist conception of markets, it is necessary to examine key themes within institutionalist writing that are pertinent to their views on the nature and operation of markets. It is broadly accepted that the use of the term *institutionalism* as a school of economic thought was first proposed in 1919 by Walter Hamilton in a paper presented at the Thirty-first Annual Meeting of the American Economic Association. Hamilton identified the concern of institutionalism as 'the customs and conventions, or, if you please, the arrangements, which determine the nature of our economic system'. Hamilton went on to argue that economic theory should be based upon an acceptable theory of human behaviour, grounded in a modern theory of psychology.

Although a number of economic and social theorists are identified as having an interest in institutional approaches to economics (e.g. the German Historical School, Marx and Menger), Veblen is widely credited with being the founder of institutional analysis, and he criticized the dominant neoclassical concept of the individual whose preferences are exogenously given and the failure of neoclassical economics to recognize the importance of the role of institutions as embodying tradition, customs and habitual behaviour. According to Veblen (1899, p. 373), 'economics is helplessly behind the times, and unable to handle its subject matter in a way which entitles it to stand as a modern science'. The main reason for this situation lies in a 'faulty conception of human nature', which is static and hedonistic (i.e. seen as passive and inert). Veblen considered that economics should study the processes of human behaviour rather than assuming that pleasure and pain, utility and satisfaction are the 'real drivers' behind human behaviour.

Veblen further suggested that where a habitual way of thinking and acting becomes a persistent element in the culture of a group or society, then it takes on the concrete form of an 'institution', i.e. a settled habit of thought common to all individuals and that this will then influence individual behaviour. Formal and informal 'institutions' and organizations from the past can always be found in the present. Such 'institutions' and organizations are capable of changing but also of enduring through time, a view endorsed by both Veblen and Ayres.

Commons (1931, p. 648) reinforced this emphasis on institutions rather than individuals, seeing an institution as a 'collective action in control, liberation and expansion of individual action'. They determine what an individual can or cannot do; and they can establish *positive* and *negative* freedoms or liberties as regards individual actions. An institution 'indicates what individuals can, must or may do or not do, enforced by collective sanctions' (Commons 1931, p. 649), with the sanctions on individual behaviour resulting from 'disobeying' the accepted norms of behaviour having important economic, ethical and legal implications.

The analysis of markets as particular 'institutions' governed by certain 'working rules' in the form of legal, economical and cultural conventions and norms has been implicitly present in the Institutionalist School. We say implicit because despite extensively discussing the classical and neoclassical conception of exchange, value, market and prices, they have neither provided an alternative systematic approach to market analysis, nor set out the theoretical and methodological consequences of seeing markets as specific historical and cultural institutions. More recently, the analysis of markets as social institutions has been considered by Hodgson:

> We shall here define the market as a set of social institutions in which a large number of commodity exchanges of a specific type regularly take place, and to some extent are facilitated and structured by those institutions. Exchange, as defined above, involves contractual agreement and the exchange of property rights, and the market consists in part of mechanisms to structure, organize, and legitimate these activities. Markets, in short, are organized and institutionalized exchange (Hodgson 1988, p. 174).

Portraying markets as a diverse body of 'institutions' and organizations makes us consider issues such as the values and norms embedded in these institutions and organizations (e.g. in the stock market), or in the associated legal structures (e.g. legal rules which govern contractual interactions). In this institutionalist perspective, market processes evolve and market forces, such as expectations or conventions on prices and legal rules, adapt and change. To many, the fall of the Berlin Wall finally emphasized that markets as institutions have proved to be the most successful form of human organization – a line of argument that falls within the central premise of Francis Fukuyama's *End of History* (1992).

Hodgson (1988) attempts to outline a number of theoretical implications that can be derived from the institutional approach to markets.

■ The institutional view of markets argues against the classical view of markets as being a natural order and an aggregation of subjective preferences in an institutional vacuum; instead, all exchanges take place and interact within an institutional context.

■ The institutional view advocates the endogenous nature of institutions, with institutions playing a central role in economic development and economic analysis, rather than being exogenous to such development and analysis.

■ Markets are a means for transmitting information and knowledge, but they also have a transformational role, shaping individual behaviour, beliefs, preferences or cognitive processes.

■ Markets are specific, cultural institutions, reflecting historical and locational contexts and not a universal and uniform context for human interaction.

These considerations provide a powerful critique of the mainstream neoclassical conception of markets, and arguably constitute an emerging paradigm which differs from the static, non-evolutionary and individualistic character of previous economic doctrines.

Whilst not easily falling within the remit of any single approach, it may be appropriate to reflect on the tenets of the Austrian School under the institutionalist rather than the neoclassical perspective.

Austrian School

The origins of the Austrian approach can be found in the ideas of Menger (1871), although his work also emerged as part of the marginalist movement on which neoclassicism was grounded. Whilst Menger's intention was not to build any particular school of thought, his focus and methodologies clearly exerted considerable influence on the research agenda of those theorists who followed and became known as representatives of the so-called 'Austrian School', including Hayek (1948), von Mises (1949) and Schumpeter (1908, 1991) amongst others. As Boettke and Leeson (2003) state, the contributions initiated by Hayek and von Mises in the 1940s have been slowly transformed into a heterodox, alternative perspective to mainstream economics.

Attempting to identify the essential characteristics of the Austrian School is not an easy task. According to Shand (1984), one of the biggest differences between the Austrian method and the neoclassical one is *subjectivism*, i.e. its emphasis upon individual choices and actions as inherently problematic to predict, and which cannot be presupposed as 'given' and therefore are not capable of being modelled and measured by mathematics or econometrics. Austrian School adherents therefore have 'doubts' about the validity and importance of much empirical work in economics.

Some of the key areas in which the Austrian School adopts a dissenting voice to neoclassical economics involve the principles underlying the treatment of economic behaviour and institutions. As Vaughan (1999) emphasises, 'the key to economic order in Hayek's later writings is found in the role he sees for institutions as repositories of social learning' (Vaughan 1999, p. 130). Institutions are social arrangements that seem to possess a 'wisdom of their own' and, although not designed intentionally, they are the outcome of human action aimed at individual purposes. The most controversial statement came from Hayek in the context of the cultural transmission of rules: a spontaneous system of rules will be more efficient precisely because natural selection determines which rules and institutions are appropriate. Society progresses, in Hayek's view, by continually adapting to the rules emerging in new circumstances. Underlying both Menger's and Hayek's institutional theory seems to be the 'action-information loop', i.e. institutions transmit information and signals to individuals, whose actions both reinforce the goal set of institutions but also have the potential to change that goal set over time. One of the criticisms levelled at Hayek's view of human action and adaptation was called 'the self-referential inconsistency': 'He (Hayek) sees human action as governed by general rules that people have not chosen; they are just adopted. Nowhere in his analysis is there apparently any room for free will; human behaviour is mostly outside human control' (Shand 1984, p. 10).

Gift giving and trust

The institutionalist approach to markets would seem better attuned to explaining increasingly important phenomena in modern societies, including altruism in the form of gift giving and trust, as compared to more market-oriented paradigms. Neoclassical views tend to regard the market as primarily an exchange mechanism, guided by the prices of products or factors of production, by the self-interest of utility-maximizing consumers or profit-seeking producers, and by the initial endowments of income or resources to the respective market participants. Motives such as altruism, which is the basis of gift giving or trust, have proved difficult for the fundamentally exchange-oriented perspective of the market mechanism to explain or predict. However, our institutional perspective has permitted new insights into gift giving and other, non-exchange related actions by market-participants.

Markets have always exhibited a wider economic and social role than that prescribed by the conventional view of markets as simply exchange mechanisms. Economists, anthropologists and historians have been inclined to suggest that the spheres of the market and gift giving are in complete opposition, with many adopting the conventional linear image of historical development in which market relations systematically displace gift relations as economic systems 'mature' (Hicks 1969). The analysis below challenges this conventional view, using giving as an example. 'To give' implies to transfer or to deliver voluntarily to another person something over which you have control or property rights. We define gift as a transfer motivated by altruism. The magic of gift is altered once there is an expectation of returning the gift. Accordingly, a *gift* may be thought of as a transfer, either material or non-material, between individuals, from an individual to a group, from a group to an individual, or from a group to another group. As we can see in modern economics, the role of gift giving is increasingly prominent in the form of the high-profile foundations of Bill Gates, Warren Buffett, Bill Clinton and others, or by the gifts given by millions of private citizens in remitting income back home, or in the gifts given as a response to disaster appeals, or in numerous other ways. Such gift giving is an increasingly important part of economic and social life.

However, within economic theory, there is a long tradition of assuming that human behaviour is inherently selfish. This is manifest in the conventional economists' preoccupation with individual optimizing behaviour. One argument for retaining self-interest as the behavioural baseline in economic analysis derives from Adam Smith's concept of the invisible hand, taken much further by neoclassical economists, resulting in the claim that 'efficient' resource allocation can best be achieved via competitive interactions among self-interested individuals (Collard 1978). Theorems on efficiency attainment via self-interested behaviour in competitive markets yielding a Pareto-optimal general equilibrium tend to be based on denying any role to altruistic goals or preferences. Yet contemporary game theory (see Chapter 6) has shown a wide range of circumstances in which competitive markets do not yield optimal allocations. An efficient market may require cooperative behaviour and trust.

However, not all economists are convinced that economic analysis would be advanced by including gift giving and altruism as part of our understanding of a market-based system. Becker (1981), for instance, has argued that altruism can be present in families or households, but is not a market characteristic. Becker argues that since members of the family maximize the utility of the *oikos* (the household), altruism is nothing but family-oriented self-interest. Even when economists such as Akerlof (1984) apply a model of gift exchange to examine the relationship between workers and firms as part of the process of wage determination in the labour market, his analysis closely resembles a form of reciprocity rather than gift (in the sense used here). In the neoclassical approach espoused by Akerlof (1984), there is no advantage to pay a higher wage than the market-clearing wage. In a gift economy, which functions on norms related to gift, there *is* the perception that benefits may occur by producers paying a higher wage, sellers accepting lower prices or buyers agreeing to pay higher prices in order to maintain a *relationship*.

Recent studies in economics have revisited the self-interest axiom. Studies such as charitable giving and intergenerational transfers (e.g. Andreoni 1989, 1990), voting (e.g. Mueller 1989, 1997), and voluntary tax-paying (Meier 2006) have argued that such actions cannot only be explained by using the selfishness paradigm. Rather the reciprocity model has gained status especially in experimental economics and the theory of games (Kolm 1984, 2000; Fehr and Schmidt 1999; Fehr and Gächter 2000). Meier (2006), who has made some valuable contributions to the theory of pro-social behaviour (i.e. behaviour that systematically deviates from self-interest), has argued that despite previous findings, contributions to public goods are possible without government intervention, and institutions need to be designed to foster and encourage pro-social behaviour. For a pro-social behaviour, the institutional environment in which people decide to contribute time and money to public goods is crucial and can influence intrinsic motivation to behave pro-socially. Meier (2006) concludes:

> The good news is that the prospect of people behaving pro-socially does not look so gloomy as is often predicted by economic theory. People deviate systematically from the self-interest hypothesis by contributing money and time to public goods. The bad news is that they do not

always do so. In certain situations, people are not willing to contribute to a good cause and hence the public good is not provided in a socially optimal amount (Meier 2006, p. 135).

and

> The good news that people behave pro-socially is bad news for orthodox economists, who are reluctant to accept that standard economic theory is limited and sometimes purely wrong in predicting behaviour (Meier 2006, p. 138).

What has been less discussed within the literature is the persistence of earlier non-market forms of transfers and exchanges into modern times. Different forms of exchange such as reciprocity, redistribution and market exchange were certainly present (although in a different guise to those existing within modern society) in pre-modern economies. In modern times, the persistence of some non-market exchanges suggests that the potential co-existence of markets and gift is not simply a historical relic. For example, reciprocity and gift giving have been identified as important components within the workplace (e.g. Akerlof 1984). The current systems of organ and blood donation based upon altruistic acts have supplanted the failed market mechanisms previously put in place to regulate the allocation of these scarce resources (Titmuss 1970: 205). Gift transfers are to be found in many spheres, including organ donations, charity and philanthropic contributions, bequests and so on, with the *voluntary* character of these personal relationships (Godbout 1998) deciding what is left at the level of the individual and what at the level of market and state, with the co-existence of market and gift being seen as a contribution to social order and social harmony. As Elster points out (1989: 287) 'altruism, envy, social norms and self-interest all contribute, in complex, interacting ways to order, stability and cooperation.'

Institutional pluralism or heterodox perspectives

Political economy as constructed by Smith and others perceives selfish behaviour, mediated via the mechanism of the market, as the process by which social harmony emerges within societies. Markets based upon self-interested forms of exchange are then constructed as the central arena within which economic activity emerges and takes place. Meier (2006), however, argues that pro-social behaviour also contributes to social harmony and contends that it is more important to examine the institutional context within which pro-social behaviour emerges and is fostered. If we conceive of markets and gift as being the product of the institutional context from which they spring, then this places 'institutions' such as values and norms as the central feature of economic activity, rather than the market. The economy then becomes a multi-faceted mixture of economic and social institutions for which a pluralistic or heterodox outlook is required, both in terms of recognizing the importance of different institutions and organizations and for coping with the diversity that results.

Economic diversity, or plurality, should be a theme common to any discussions on past and current economic systems. Diversity occurs over time and space and different institutional arrangements create distinct market logics. The institutional settings, the state, the market, and other socio-economic institutions interact with one another to create different national economic processes. The kind of diversity that is relevant here is not reducible to a unique, universal model of development. Take the case of China: it is commonly viewed as an economy and society that is striving towards a system led by the market. Yet China has particular forms of institutionalized behaviour, both formal and informal, such as the network of gifts or *guanxi*. These institutional arrangements are not deviations from a universal market norm, but rather behaviours that deserve to be analysed in their own right. Such elements of diversity have often been viewed by neoclassical economists as *temporary* outcomes of the transition phases from one development stage to another. The strong counter-argument of institutionalists is that diversity should be perceived as a *permanent* attribute of economic and social development over time. Norms, institutions and rules emerge, develop, change and breakdown continuously. Our investigation of economic systems should not be limited to a single market-oriented dimension and the role and place of gift and institutional behaviour in modern economic systems should be acknowledged. This more pluralist or heterodox view of economic development is taken further in Chapter 29.

Irrationality assumptions

Analysts of organizational behaviour are increasingly emphasizing non-rational and behaviourally oriented decision-making, rather than the 'rational economic agents' of the Neoclassical schools:

> We are finally beginning to understand that irrationality is the real invisible hand that drives human decision making. . . . cognition biases often prevent people from making rational decisions, despite their best efforts (Ariely 2009).

The integration of economics with psychological and sociological approaches is resulting in an increasing challenge to the fundamental neoclassical assumption of markets populated by rational economic agents!

The experimental work of Ernst Fehr involving 'the trust game' usefully illustrates the importance of trust and other psychological traits in actual decision-making.

The Trust Game

A group of Swiss researchers led by Ernst Fehr conducted an experiment now known as 'the trust game with revenge' that reveals a lot about the motivation for vengeance. It goes something like this: You and an anonymous partner are each given $10, and you get to make the first move. You must decide whether to send your money over to your partner or keep it for yourself. If you keep it, each of you gets your $10 and the game is over. If you send it, the experimenters quadruple the amount to $40 – so now your partner has $50.

The obvious question is: why would you give away your $10 in the first place? The answer is that you hope you can trust your partner when he makes the next move. He can choose either to keep the $50 – leaving you with nothing – or send $25 back to you, so that you share equally in the spoils.

If your partner is acting rationally and in his own best interest he would never send you the $25. Knowing this, and acting equally rationally, you would

▶

never send him the money to start with. It follows that you will do nothing and go home! The good news is that people are more trusting and reciprocating than standard economic theory would have us believe. In the experiment, many people gave away their $10, and many partners reciprocated by sending $25 back.

But the Swiss game didn't end there. If your partner chose to keep the $50, the experimenter would give you an opportunity in the next phase of the game to use some of your own money to punish him. For every dollar you spend, your greedy partner loses $2. So if you decided to spend $25, your partner would lose all his winnings. You might think that people who had just lost some money would be unwilling to lose even more just to 'get their own back'. Seated comfortably right now, you might not be able to appreciate these feelings, but most of the

people who were given the opportunity exacted severe revenge on their greedy partners.

This finding was not the most interesting part of the study, however. While the participants were making their decisions, their brains were being scanned by positron emissions tomography (PET). The experimenters saw activity in the striatum, the part of the brain associated with experiencing reward. In other words, the decision to punish the greedy partners appeared to be related to a feeling of pleasure. What's more, those who had a high level of striatum activation punished their partners to a greater degree. This suggests that the desire for revenge, even when it costs us something and is fully irrational (you have no idea who this other person is, and you will never meet him again), has biological underpinnings.

Ariely 2009, p. 83

Quasi-markets

The influence of written and unwritten 'rules of the game' (institutions) and of organizations on actual market behaviour are clear when we examine the so-called 'internal' or 'quasi'-markets that have developed in particular economies at particular points in time. In the UK, the 'internal' market and associated 'rules' which have developed within the organization known as the National Health Service (NHS) provides a useful illustration of the institutional, as opposed to the neoclassical approach to markets.

Creating an internal (quasi-)market in the National Health Service (NHS)

The contemporary structure and developments in the health care sector are reviewed in some detail in Chapter 12 and will be seen to embody key elements of the narrative below. The mandate of the NHS is to provide health care services according to need, free at the point of delivery. It was, and continues to be, financed from central government tax revenues via the Consolidated Fund. Some 80% of funding is via these tax revenues with another 14% via a proportion of the National Insurance contributions of employers and employees, with only around 4% of NHS receipts currently funded via charges for prescriptions, dental services, etc. The consequence for resource allocation of providing health care services

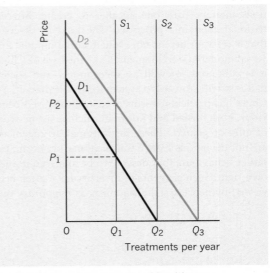

Fig. 9.4 Demand and supply of healthcare.

essentially free at the point of delivery can be discussed using Fig. 9.4.

We assume demand for health care services to be downward sloping with respect to price, i.e. people demand fewer treatments per time period if price rises. If a market were established with demand D_1 and a short-run supply S_1 (here perfectly inelastic supply), then a price P_1 would be established with an equilibrium number of treatments demanded and supplied per year of Q_1. If demand now increases to D_2, then *price adjusts* in the market, rising to P_2 to allocate the unchanged Q_1.

However, the NHS does not operate by price adjustment but by *quantity adjustment* (since service is free at the point of treatment); with the initial demand D_1, at a zero price $0Q_2$ treatments are demanded. This requires the supply curve of treatments to shift rightwards to S_2 if the NHS is to satisfy this demand. If demand now rises to D_2, supply must further increase to S_3, since no price adjustment is permitted, otherwise $Q_3 - Q_2$ patients would be untreated, leading to a rise in waiting lists. It is clear that by relying mainly on quantity adjustment, the NHS must either allocate more resources to health care in the face of increased demand or accept a rise in waiting lists.

In April 1991 the then Conservative government introduced major changes into the UK health care market. The responsibility for *purchasing* health care was to be separated from the responsibility for *providing* it. According to the White Paper preceding the 1991 reforms, the health service reforms were intended to achieve two objectives, namely: to give patients, wherever they live in the UK, better health care and greater choice of the services available; to give greater satisfaction and rewards for those working in the NHS who successfully respond to local needs and preferences.

These objectives were to be accomplished by the implementation of a number of key measures.

1 Increased delegation of responsibilities from central to local levels, for example the delegation of functions from Regions to Districts, and from Districts to individual hospitals.

2 Certain of the larger hospitals were invited to apply to become NHS Hospital Trusts. Trust status would permit the hospital increased freedom of action in terms of local pay settlements, easier access to borrowing, more choice in deciding upon output mix (e.g. types of speciality) and new opportunities to retain profit. There would then be hospitals managed directly by the District Health Authority (DHA) and hospitals with NHS Trust status.

3 All hospitals in the future were to be free to offer their services, at agreed prices, to any DHA in the UK, and to the private sector. Previously hospitals

within a given area normally treated only patients originating from within that area.

4 A facility was to be provided for the larger general practices to hold and operate their own budgets, for the purchase of services directly from hospitals and to cover drug prescribing costs. This meant the creation of a new category of General Practitioner Fund Holders (GPFH). For smaller practices the general practitioners (GPs) could *combine* to form various types of commissioning groups, purchasing on behalf of individual GPs within such groups.

Note that the internal market established in 1991 was *not* a private market in the normal sense. It was not the patients who were to make the purchasing decisions, as they do in the case of US health care, for example; rather it was the DHAs and the GPs who were to have the spending power, allocated to them from the Regional Health Authority (RHA) or, as in the case of the GP Commissioning Groups, allocated to them from the DHA. On the basis of this budget allocation, the purchaser can then effect a health treatment on behalf of the patient in any one of three ways. Treatment may be purchased first, from a (managed) hospital administered by a DHA; second, from a hospital with Trust status; or third, from a private sector hospital, i.e. one totally outside the NHS.

The Conservative government argued in 1991 that the introduction of competition on the supply-side would encourage efficiency. Providers competing for contracts with purchasers would have to be efficient or face a possible loss of business. Purchasers, because they had finite budgets, would have incentives to seek out efficient providers. The government also argued that this system would increase patient choice. Table 9.1 outlines this separation of purchasers and providers, which is also very much a part of health care reforms in 2010 as we note in Chapter 12.

Table 9.1 Purchasers and providers of health care.

Purchasers	Providers
District Health Authority (DHA)	NHS Trust hospitals
GP Fund Holders (GPFH)	District managed hospitals
GP Commissioning Groups	
Private patients	Private hospitals

However, the efficiency benefits claimed for this internal (quasi-)market in health care depend upon the 'signals' or incentives given to both providers and purchasers and the nature of their likely response to such signals. We now consider this in more detail: first, the incentives to purchasers; second, the incentives to providers.

Incentives to purchasers

District Health Authority (DHA)

As purchasers, districts were to be responsible for assessing the health care needs of their populations, prioritizing needs, developing contracting arrangements for the services they wish to purchase, and monitoring provider performance. They received a budget, which was a function of the number and age of the persons for whom they were responsible.

The incentives for increased efficiency facing DHAs were, however, rather limited. There were no direct sanctions for failing to meet the needs of their consumers. Managers were not rewarded on the basis of health care outcomes and so were not directly rewarded for doing what the new system intended them to do. It was relatively costly for districts to gather information about the *outcomes* of care from different providers since they had no direct contact with patients. This high cost of acquiring information meant that at the margin, districts probably under-collected such information.

General Practitioner Fund Holders (GPFH)

Alongside districts, the 1991 reforms gave larger general practices (providers of primary care) the opportunity to become fund holders and to assume a purchasing role. The financing for this role came from top-slicing part of the budget of the DHA in which the fund holding practice was located. Fund holders were free to place contracts with whichever hospitals they wished, and in some cases to substitute their own services for existing ones, e.g. they could now offer minor surgical procedures directly.

GP fund holders had more discretion than non-fund-holding GPs about how and when their patients were treated. They had better access than the DHAs to information about the outcomes of care from different providers, since they saw patients both *before* and *after* treatment. The costs of gathering information were therefore lower and, in this respect, fund

holders were likely to be more efficient than DHAs in acting as consumers' agents.

Competition on the purchasing side between agents rather than individuals may arguably have given purchasers the incentive to be more responsive to patient needs. However, it may also have increased the risk of 'cream skimming'. This is because each purchasing agent – DHA, GPFH or Commissioning Group of smaller GPs – receives a sum of money per person for whom they were responsible, adjusted for age. General Practitioner Fund Holders were, as we have noted, in a good position to identify directly any 'bad risks', i.e. patients who were likely to require recurrent health care. They could then reject these 'bad risks' from their list of patients, thereby reducing costs. In contrast the DHAs had to treat *all* patients, so that the pool of patients available to them may have become over-represented by those deemed 'bad risks' (i.e. adverse selection). Many saw the risks of a two-tier system developing in which healthier patients would receive priority treatment from GP fund holders.

Incentives to providers

The *providers* were to be the NHS managed hospitals, NHS trust hospitals and private hospitals. The difference between the first two, the directly managed hospitals under DHA control and the trust hospitals responsible to the Department of Health, was mainly in terms of the greater contractual freedom of the latter. Trust hospitals could set their own pay scales, and decide themselves on the quantity and mix of factor inputs and types of specialism they offered (output mix).

Neither managed nor trust hospitals could make a profit on their services. Prices had to be based on *average cost*, with no cross-subsidies or price discrimination. However, this average cost pricing policy could itself lead to inefficiencies. In Fig. 9.5 we assume, for simplicity, that two hospitals, A and B, have *identical* average and marginal cost curves. We can see that although each hospital treats a different number of patients, they each have the same average cost in a situation where Q_A treatments take place in hospital A and Q_B treatments take place in hospital B, and therefore both hospitals charge the same price according to the earlier directive on average cost pricing. However, an efficient allocation of resources (patients) would be one which allowed hospital A to charge a *lower price* than B, since scale economies are

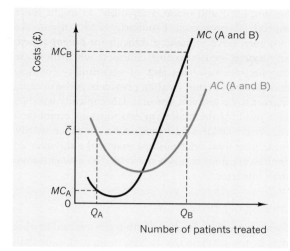

Fig. 9.5 Problems with average cost pricing.

still potentially available to A which would reduce average costs with extra treatments (unlike hospital B where average costs would increase with extra treatments). This lower price would then attract patients to hospital A which can provide treatment at a lower (average) cost than hospital B. Therefore the regulation insisting on average cost pricing did not permit the (quasi-)market for health care to send appropriate signals to patients. Resource allocation would then be inefficient where patients (or their agents) chose the identically priced hospital B rather than A. (Note that a marginal cost pricing principle would be more appropriate here – since MC_A at $Q_A < MC_B$ at Q_B.)

Put another way, the internal market was not structured in such a way as to allow profit signals on particular activities to guide resource allocation. Even if such profit signals had existed, the fact that all three types of provider (including even the private hospitals) may not have followed a clear profit-maximizing objective might have deflected them from reacting 'appropriately' to the profit signals. It is sometimes argued that the publicly owned managed and trust hospitals are dominated by senior managers or medical staff who seek 'breakeven' targets, rather than maximum profits. Such non-profit-maximizing objectives may even extend to private hospitals, some of which have charitable status. It can hardly be surprising if non-profit-maximizing hospitals fail to respond to profit-related signals in ways predicted by economic theory, even when such profit signals *are* transmitted in the market!

Another criticism of the operation of the internal market was that funds did not always follow the patient immediately, the result being that the efficient providers have sometimes been unable to treat more patients even when the demand has been there, since they have run out of funds. As a result, treatments have had to cease in some 'efficient' hospitals once their initial targets have been met.

Characteristics of an internal market and health care provision

It may be that certain aspects of the 1991 reforms establishing an internal market were unlikely to succeed because of *intrinsic characteristics* of the market for health care provision. For example, competition is likely to yield efficiency gains only where excess capacity exists in a market. This is hardly the case in health care provision where almost all indicators point to under-supply (i.e. excess demand). In a case of under-supply in a pure market, *price* will allocate the restricted supply amongst the competing consumers (see Fig. 9.4). In a quasi-market, where regulations of various kinds are imposed which prevent a 'pure' price adjustment, an element of *rationing* may be inevitable. Arguably, it may then be better to use certain 'objective' means of rationing rather than consumer purchasing power or the arbitrary judgements of the service providers.

A number of other problems were seen, by critics, as likely to prevent the internal market from making a significant contribution to the improvement of health care.

Asymmetry of information

When the provider and purchaser were one and the same, as with the DHAs before 1991, the quality of health care provision could be monitored through internal channels. However, they became separated after the creation of the internal market in 1991, the problem then being that while the providers may be aware of any diminution in quality of service, the purchasers may not. This *asymmetry of information* between seller and buyer is a classic instance of 'market failure' which may lead to an inefficient allocation of resources, with purchasers paying more than the competitive price for any given quality of service.

High transaction costs

The main means by which purchasers seek to gain assurances as to the price and quality of provision is by the issuing of contracts, which may of necessity be rather detailed. Drawing up such contracts takes time and money, as does the whole tendering process between rival providers and the eventual requirements for issuing and processing invoices and other documents between contracting parties. These *transaction costs* may absorb some or all of any efficiency gains via the internal market. Before the creation of the internal market some 5% of total health care spending in the UK involved administrative costs; there were fears that the internal market might raise this figure nearer to the 20% of total health care spending involving the various transaction costs commonly experienced in the US.

Non-contestable markets

To avoid excessive transaction costs, there may be the incentive for individual providers and purchasers to develop *long-term relationships* in response to the creation of an internal market. The billing and invoicing system of the respective parties might then be simplified and made compatible, as might other aspects of provision. Familiarity and convenience may then serve to make it difficult for *potential new entrants* to secure existing contracts when these are due for renewal. This lack of opportunity for new entrants may permit existing providers in the internal market to be less efficient than is technically feasible, as a result of the long-term relationships established between providers and purchasers. In other words, these long-term relationships may make the internal health care market less contestable (by new entrants) than hitherto.

Monopoly provision

Some districts and regions within the internal market may be too small, in themselves, to support more than one (or perhaps even one) 'efficient' service provider. This may be the case where significant economies of scale are available in respect of various types of treatment, giving large hospitals a cost advantage. Significant travel costs (transport, time and convenience) may then deter patients (or their agents) from undermining the higher cost provision in these local monopoly cases by seeking treatment in other regions and districts.

Key points

- The role of the market is viewed in different ways by the various 'schools' of economic thought.

- Classical economists tended to emphasise the co-ordinating role of prices in markets, whilst recognizing market imperfections (e.g. monopoly). Such economists saw the market system as also providing a mechanism for channelling self-interest into decisions which are consistent with achieving 'harmonious order' and furthering the common good!

- Neoclassical economists tend to focus on a marginalist approach to decision-making within markets, with differential calculus and other mathematical foundations used to predict resource allocating decisions by rational economic agents.

'Methodological individualism' underpins this approach, with individuals acting rationally seen as the central element in society, and institutional arrangements merely an outcome of these individual actions.

- In the neoclassical perspective, 'prices' convey sufficient information to bring about 'Pareto Optimum' resource allocations. Individual actors need only maximize their own self-interest, subject to the 'signals' they receive from the product and factor markets, and the outcomes will be such that no one can be made better off by further resource reallocation without someone else being made worse off!

- Should 'market failures' occur, these are to be corrected, in the neoclassical view,

by simple 'rules' based on competitive market characteristics, e.g. remove monopolies, improve information, set prices equal to marginal costs of provision, etc.

■ The 'general equilibrium' approach of Arrow–Debreu showed that, subject to competitive market conditions, a market system can itself generate relative prices capable of clearing all markets simultaneously, with no need for any external intervention.

■ Institutional or heterodox economists challenge the neoclassical emphasis on individual actors. They see institutions, especially the written and unwritten rules and norms within various communities and organizations, as playing a key role in resource allocation outcomes. Individual consumer and producer behaviour

is seen, from this perspective, as directly influenced by the institutional context in which the respective actors operate.

■ The institutional or heterodox perspective is seen as better able to deal with issues of gift giving and trust and with other expressions of observed 'selfless' behaviour, seen as non-rational in the neoclassical perspective.

■ Quasi- or internal markets are a further example of institutional contexts playing a key role in actual decision-making. These quasi- or internal markets are often characterized by 'market failure' which are intrinsic to the ways in which they were established, e.g. asymmetry of information via the purchaser/provider structure of health care.

Now try the self-check questions for this chapter on the Companion Website. You will also find useful links to relevant websites.

References and further reading

Akerlof, G. A. (1984) *An Economic Theorists Book of Tales*, Cambridge, Cambridge University Press.

Andreoni, J. (1989) Giving with impure altruism: applications to charity and Ricardian equivalence, *Journal of Political Economy*, 97(6): 1447–58.

Andreoni, J. (1990) Impure altruism and donations to public goods: a theory of warm-glow giving, *Journal of Political Economy*, 97(3): 1147–58.

Ariely, D. (2009) The end of rational economics, *Harvard Business Review*, July–August, Special Edition.

Arrow, K. and Debreu, G. (1954) Existence of an equilibrium for a competitive economy, *Econometrica*, 22(3): 265–90.

Ayres, C. (1951) The co-ordinates of institutionalism, *American Economic Review*, 41(May): 47–55.

Becker, G. (1981) *A Treatise on the Family*, Cambridge MA, Harvard University Press.

Boettke, P. J. and Leeson, P. (2003) The Austrian School of Economics, 1950–2000, in Samuels, W. J., Biddle, J. E. and Davis, J. B. (eds), *A Companion to the History of Economic Thought*, Oxford, Blackwell, 445–53.

Boettke, P. J., Coyne, C. and Leeson, P. (2005) *The Many Faces of the Market*, Working Paper, Fairfax, VA, George Mason University.

Boland, L. A. (2003) *The Foundations of Economic Method: A Popperian Perspective* (2nd edn), London, Routledge.

Cairncross, A. (1978) The market and the state, in T. Wilson and A. Skinner (eds), *The Market and the State: Essays in Honour of Adam Smith*, Oxford, Oxford University Press, 113–34.

Chakravorti, B. (2010) Finding competitive advantage in adversity, *Harvard Business Review*, November, 102–8.

Coase, R. (1937) The nature of the firm, *Economica*, 4(16): 386–405.

Collard, D. (1978) *Altruism and Economy*, Oxford, Martin Robertson.

Commons, J. R. (1931) Institutional economics, *The American Economic Review*, **21**(4): 648–57.

Edgeworth, F. (1881) *Mathematical Physics*, New York, Kegan Paul.

Elster, J. (1989) *The Cement of Society: A Study of Social Order*, Cambridge, Cambridge University Press.

Fehr, E. and Gächter, S. (2000) Fairness and retaliation: the economics of reciprocity, *Journal of Economic Perspectives*, **14**(3): 159–81.

Fehr, E. and Schmidt, K. M. (1999) A theory of fairness, competition and cooperation, *Quarterly Journal of Economics*, **114**, 817–68.

Fukuyama, F. (1992) *The End of History and the Last Man*, New York, The Free Press.

Galbraith, J. (1952) *American Capitalism: the Concept of Countervailing Power*, Boston MA, Houghton Mifflin.

Godbout, J. T. (1998) *The World of the Gift*, Montreal, McGill-Queen's University Press.

Griffiths, A. and Wall, S. (2000) *Intermediate Microeconomics*, Harlow, Financial Times/ Prentice Hall.

Hayek, von F. (1948) Economics and knowledge, in *Individualism and Economic Order*, London, Routledge, 33–56.

Hicks, J. (1969) *A Theory of Economic History*, Oxford, Oxford University Press.

Hodgson, G. M. (1988) *Economics and Institutions: A Manifesto for a Modern Institutional Economics*, Cambridge, Polity Press.

Jevons, W. (1871) *The Theory of Political Economy*, Basingstoke, Macmillan.

Kaletsky, A. (2010) *Capitalism 4.0: The Birth of a New Economy*, London, Bloomsbury.

Kay, J. (2004) *The Truth about Markets*, London, Penguin.

Kolm, S.-C. (1984) *La Bonne Économie. La Réciprocité Générale*, Paris, Presses Universitaires de France.

Kolm, S.-C. (2000) The theory of reciprocity, giving and altruism, in Ythier, J. M., Kolm, S.-C. and Gerard-Varet, S.-A. (eds), *The Economics of Reciprocity, Giving and Altruism*, Basingstoke, Macmillan, 1–44.

Means, G. (1962) *Pricing Power and the Public Interest*, New York, Harper and Brothers.

Meier, S. (2006) *The Economics of Non-Selfish Behavior*, Cheltenham, Edward Elgar.

Menger, C. (1950[1871]) *Principles of Economics*, Glencoe, II, Free Press.

Mill, J. S. (1863) *Utilitarianism*, London, John Murray.

Mises, von L. (1949) *Human Action*, Auburn AL, Ludwig von Mises Institute.

Mitchell, W. (1927) *Business Cycles: The Problem and its Setting*, Cambridge MA, National Bureau of Economic Research.

Mueller, D. C. (1989) *Public Choice*, Cambridge, Cambridge University Press.

Mueller, D. C. (1997) *Perspectives on Public Choice: A Handbook*, Cambridge, Cambridge University Press.

North, D. C. (1990) *Institutions, Institutional Change and Economic Performance*, Cambridge, Cambridge University Press.

Ricardo, D. (1817) *On the Principles of Political Economy and Taxation*, London, John Murray.

Schumpeter, J. (1908) *Das Wesen und Hauptinhalt der Theoretischen Nationalökonomie* (2nd edn), Berlin, Duncker & Humblot.

Schumpeter, J. (1991) The sociology of imperialisms, in Swedberg, R. (ed.), *The Economics and Sociology of Capitalism*, Princeton NJ, Princeton University Press.

Shand, A. (1984) *The Capitalist Alternative: An Introduction to Neo-Austrian Economics*, London, Wheatsheaf.

Smith, A. (1987[1776]) *Wealth of Nations*, Books 1–3, London, Penguin.

Titmuss, R. M. (1970) *The Gift Relationships*, London, George Allen.

Vaughan, K. (1999) Hayek's implicit economics: rules and the problem of order, *The Review of Austrian Economics*, **11**(1–2): 130.

Veblen, T. (1967[1899]) *The Theory of the Leisure Class*, London, Penguin.

Walras, L. (1877, trans. 1954) *Elements of Pure Economics*, Lausanne.

Williamson, O. (1975) *Markets and Hierarchies: Analysis and Antitrust Implications*, New York, The Free Press.

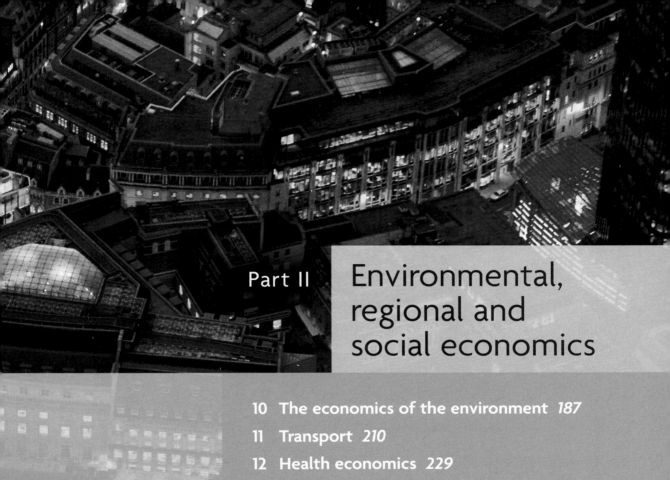

Part II Environmental, regional and social economics

Chapter 10

The economics of the environment

In recent years, there has been considerable interest in
the impact of economic decisions on the environment.
In this chapter we start by reviewing the position
of the environment in models of national income
determination. We then look at a number of important
contemporary issues involving the environment,
such as the debates on sustainable growth and global
environmental change. The application of cost–benefit
principles to environmental issues is also considered,
together with problems of valuation. The use of market-
based incentives in dealing with environmental problems,
such as taxation and tradeable permits, is reviewed, as is
the use of 'command and control' type regulations. We
conclude by examining a number of case studies which
show how environmental considerations can be brought
into practical policy-making, paying particular attention
to global warming and transport-related pollution.

The role of the environment

The familiar circular flow analysis represents the flow of income (and output) between domestic firms and households. Withdrawals (leakages) from the circular flow are identified as savings, imports and taxes, and injections into the circular flow as investment, exports and government expenditure. When withdrawals exactly match injections, then the circular flow is regarded as being in 'equilibrium', with no further tendency to rise or fall in value.

All this should be familiar from any introductory course in macroeconomics. This circular flow analysis is often considered to be 'open' since it incorporates external flows of income (and output) between domestic and overseas residents via exports and imports. However, many economists would still regard this system as 'closed' in one vital respect, namely that it takes no account of the constraints imposed upon the economic system by environmental factors. Such a 'traditional' circular flow model assumes that natural resources are abundant and limitless, and generally ignores any waste disposal implications for the economic system.

Figure 10.1 provides a simplified model in which linkages between the conventional economy (circular flow system) and the environment *are* now introduced. The natural environment is seen as being involved with the economy in at least three specific ways.

1 *Amenity Services* (*A*). The natural environment provides consumer services to domestic households in the form of living and recreational space, natural beauty and so on. We call these 'Amenity Services'.

2 *Natural Resources* (*R*). The natural environment is also the source of various inputs into the production process such as mineral deposits, forests, water resources, animal populations and so on. These natural resources are, in turn, the basis of both the renewable and non-renewable energy supplies used in production.

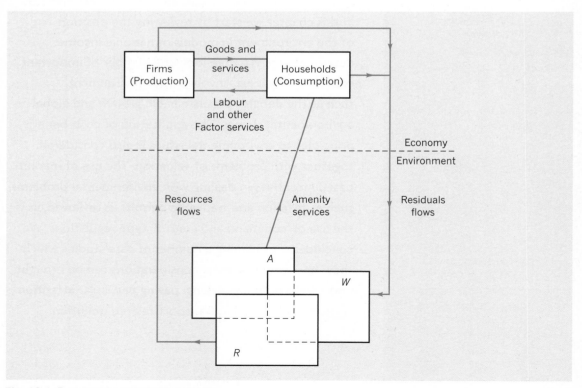

Fig. 10.1 Economy/environment linkages.

3 *Waste Products* (W). Both production and consumption are activities which generate waste products or residuals. For example, many productive activities generate harmful by-products which are discharged into the atmosphere or watercourses. Similarly, sewage, litter and other waste products result from many consumption activities. The key point here is that the natural environment is the ultimate dumping place or 'sink' for all these waste products or residuals.

We have now identified three *economic* functions of the environment: namely, it functions as a direct source of consumer utility (A), as a resource supplier (R) and as a waste receptor and assimilator (W). Moreover, these functions interact with other parts of the economic system and also with each other. This latter point is the reason for showing the three boxes A, R and W as overlapping each other in Fig. 10.1. For example, a waterway may provide amenity services (A) to anglers and sailors, as well as aesthetic beauty to onlookers. At the same time, it may also provide water resources (R) to firms situated alongside which can be used for power, for cleaning, as a coolant or as a direct input into production. Both consumers and producers may then discharge effluent and other waste products (W) into the waterway as a consequence of using this natural resource. All three functions may readily co-exist at certain levels of interaction. However, excessive levels of effluent and waste discharge could over-extend the ability of the waterway to assimilate waste, thereby destroying the amenity and resource functions of the waterway. In other words, the three economic functions of the natural environment constantly interact with each other, as well as with the economic (circular flow) system as a whole. Later in the chapter, we shall look at ways of providing economic incentives or regulations which might bring about *optimum* levels of interaction between each function and within the economic system as a whole.

By bringing the environment into our modelling of the economy, we are essentially challenging the traditional view that the environment and the economy can be treated as separate entities. Everything that happens in the economy has a potential environmental impact. For example, excessive price support for agricultural products under the Common Agricultural Policy (CAP – see Chapter 29) will encourage over-production of agricultural produce. Land which might otherwise be left in its natural state may then be brought into agricultural use, and increased yields may be sought by additional applications of fertilizers and pesticides. Hedgerows may be cut back to provide larger and more economical units of cultivation, and so on. In other words, most types of economic policy intervention will impact upon the environment directly or indirectly. Equally, policies which seek to influence the environment will themselves impact upon the economic system. As we shall see, attempts to reduce CO_2 (carbon dioxide) emissions may influence the relative attractiveness of different types of energy, causing consumers to switch between coal, gas, electricity, nuclear power and other energy forms. There will be direct effects on output, employment and prices in these substitute industries and, via the multiplier, elsewhere in the economy. We must treat the traditional economic system and the environment as being dynamically interrelated.

Sustainable economic welfare

Rather more sophisticated attempts to capture environmental costs within a national accounting framework have been made in recent years. For example, an Index of Sustainable Economic Welfare (ISEW) has been calculated for the US and UK. Essentially, any increase in the GNP figure is *adjusted* to reflect the following impacts which are often associated with rising GNP:

- monies spent correcting environmental damage (i.e. 'defensive' expenditures);
- decline in the stock of natural resources (i.e. environmental depreciation);
- pollution damage (i.e. monetary value of any environmental damage not corrected).

By failing to take these environmental impacts into account, the conventional GNP figure arguably does *not* give an accurate indication of *sustainable economic welfare*, i.e. the flow of goods and services that an economy can generate without reducing its future production capacity. Suppose we consider the expenditure method of calculating GNP. It could be argued that some of the growth in GNP is due to expenditures undertaken to mitigate (offset) the impact of environmental damage. For example, some double-glazing may be undertaken to reduce noise levels from increased traffic flow, and does not therefore reflect an increase in economic wellbeing, merely an attempt to retain the status quo. Such 'defensive expenditures' should be subtracted from the GNP figure (item 1 above). So too should be expenditures associated with a decline in the stock of natural resources. For example, the monetary value of minerals extracted from rock is included in GNP, but nothing is subtracted to reflect the loss of unique mineral deposits. 'Environmental depreciation' of this kind should arguably be subtracted from the conventional GNP figure (item 2 above). Finally, some expenditures are incurred to overcome pollution damage which has not been corrected; e.g. extra cost of bottled water when purchased because tap water is of poor quality. Additional expenditures of this kind should also be subtracted from the GNP figure, as should the monetary valuation of any environmental damage which has *not* been corrected (item 3 above).

We are then left with an *Index of Sustainable Economic Welfare* (ISEW) which subtracts rather more from GNP than the usual depreciation of physical capital.

ISEW = GNP *minus* depreciation of physical capital
              minus defensive expenditures
              minus depreciation of environmental capital
              minus monetary value of residual pollution

The effect of such adjustments is quite startling. The UK GNP per capita (unadjusted) has grown by around 2.0% in real terms as an annual average in the UK since 1950. However, the adjustment outlined above for each year over the period gives an ISEW per head for the UK which corresponds to a mere 0.5% average annual growth in real ISEW over the period. Such 'environmental accounting' is suggesting an entirely different perspective on recorded changes in national economic welfare.

Valuing the environment

A number of approaches may be used in seeking to place a 'value' on environmental changes, whether 'favourable' (benefits) or 'unfavourable' (costs). Some-

times the market mechanism may help in terms of monetary valuations by yielding prices for products derived from environmental assets. However, these market prices may be distorted by various types of 'failure' in the market mechanism (e.g. monopolies or externalities), so that some adjustment may be needed to these prices. For example 'shadow prices' may be used, i.e. market prices which are adjusted in order to reflect the valuation to *society* of a particular activity.

On other occasions there may be no market prices to adjust, in which case we may need to use questionnaires to derive *hypothetical* valuations of 'willingness to pay' for an environmental amenity or 'willingness to accept' compensation for an environmental loss. These 'expressed preference' methods of valuation differ from 'revealed preference' methods which seek to observe how consumers *actually* behave in the marketplace for products which are substitutes or complements to the activities for which no market prices exist.

The issue of *time* is particularly important for monetary valuation of environmental impacts which may take many years to materialize. It is therefore important to pay close attention to the process of calculating the *present value* of a stream of future revenues or costs, using the technique of discounting (see Chapter 17, p. 341).

We return to these valuation techniques below, but first it will be useful to consider why valuing environmental costs and benefits is so important to policy-makers.

Finding the socially optimum output

Figure 10.2 presents a simplified model in which the marginal pollution costs (*MPC*) attributable to production are seen as rising with output beyond a certain output level, Q_A. Up to Q_A the amount of pollution generated within the economy is assumed to be assimilated by the environment with zero pollution costs. In this model we assume that pollution is a 'negative externality', in that firms which pollute are imposing costs on society that are not paid for by those firms.

At the same time the marginal *net* private benefit (*MNPB*) of each unit of output is assumed to decline as the level of economic activity rises. *MNPB* is the addition to private benefit received by firms from

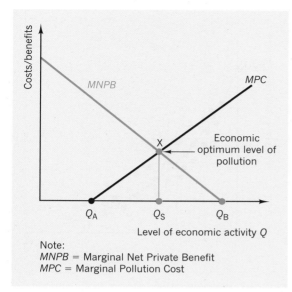

Note:
MNPB = Marginal Net Private Benefit
MPC = Marginal Pollution Cost

Fig. 10.2 Finding an optimum level of pollution.

selling the last unit of output minus the addition to private costs incurred by producing that last unit of output.

If the pollution externality was *not* taken into account, then firms would produce up to output Q_B at which $MNPB = 0$. Only here would total net private benefit (i.e. total profit) be a maximum. However, the *socially optimum* level of output is Q_S, where $MNPB = MPC$. Each unit of output *beyond* Q_S adds more in pollution costs to society than it does to net private benefit, and is therefore socially inefficient to produce. Equally it would be socially inefficient to forsake producing any units *up to* Q_S, since each of these units adds more to net private benefit than to pollution costs for society.

Note that in this analysis the social optimum does *not* imply zero pollution. Rather it suggests that the benefits to society are greatest at output Q_S, with pollution costs being positive at $Q_S X$. We return to this idea of seeking 'acceptable' levels of pollution below.

The valuation issue

A key element in finding any socially efficient solution to the negative environmental effects of increased production clearly involves placing a *monetary value* on the marginal private and social costs (or benefits) of production. In terms of Fig. 10.2 we need some

monetary valuation which will permit us to estimate both the *MNPB* and the *MPC* curves.

Using 'shadow prices'

Where market prices exist, it is at least feasible to obtain monetary valuations of future net revenues from an environmental asset. However, where one or more market failures occur, these prices may be deemed 'inappropriate' and in need of adjustment to reflect more accurately the true benefits and costs to society. Such adjustments give rise to '*shadow prices*', i.e. prices which do not actually exist in the marketplace but which are assumed to exist for purposes of valuation.

Demand curve methods

'Expressed preference' and 'revealed preference' methods are widely used here.

Expressed preference methods

Where no market price exists, individuals are often asked, using surveys or questionnaires, to express how much they would be *willing to pay* for some specified environmental improvement, such as improved water quality or the preservation of a threatened local amenity. In other words, an 'expressed preference' approach is taken to valuation. An example of the use of this approach was used in Ukunda, Kenya, where residents were faced with a choice between three sources of water – door-to-door vendors, kiosks and wells – each requiring residents to pay different costs in money and time. Water from door-to-door vendors cost the most but required the least collection time. A study found that the villagers were willing to pay a substantial share of their incomes – about 8% – in exchange for this greater convenience and for time saved. Such valuations can be helpful in seeking to make the case for extending reliable public water supply even to poorer communities. Questionnaires and surveys of willingness to pay have been widely used in the UK to evaluate the recreational benefits of environmental amenities. They can help capture 'use value' (see p. 193) where market prices are inappropriate or do not even exist, as well as 'option' and 'existence' values.

These 'expressed preference' methods are sometimes referred to as 'contingent valuation' methods, since the user's 'willingness to pay' (WTP) is often sought for different situations 'contingent upon' some improvement in the (environmental) quality of provision. The same approach may involve asking individuals how much they are 'willing to accept' (WTA) to avoid some specific environmental degradation.

Revealed preference methods

This approach seeks to avoid relying on the use of questionnaires or surveys to gain an impression of the *hypothetical* valuations placed by consumers on various environmental costs and benefits. Instead it seeks to use direct observation of the consumers' *actual* responses to various substitute or complementary goods and services to gain an estimate of value in a particular environmental situation. The focus here is on the 'revealed preferences' of the consumers as expressed in the marketplace, even if this expression is indirect in that it involves surrogate goods and services rather than the environmental amenity itself.

1   Travel Cost Method (TCM). Where no price is charged for entry to recreational sites, economists have searched for private market goods or services whose consumption is *complementary* to the consumption of the recreational good in question. One such private complementary good is the travel costs incurred by individuals to gain access to recreational sites. The 'price' paid to visit any site is uniquely determined for each visitor by calculating the travel costs from his or her location of origin. By observing people's willingness to pay for the private complementary good it is then possible to infer a price for the non-price environmental amenity.

   In Fig. 10.3, the demand curve D_{VISITS} shows the overall trend relationship between travel costs and visit rates for all the visitors interviewed. Using this information we can estimate the average visitor's (V_1) total recreational value ($V_1 \times P_1$) for the site. Multiplying this by the total number of visitors per annum allows us to estimate the total annual recreational value of the site.

2   Hedonic Price Method (HPM). A further technique often used in deriving valuations where no prices exist is the so-called 'hedonic price' method. This estimates the extent to which people are, for example, willing to pay a house price premium for the benefit of living within easy access of an environmental amenity. It could equally be used to estimate the house price discount resulting from living within easy access of a source of environmental concern.

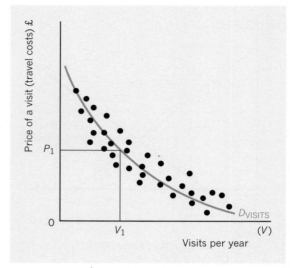

Fig. 10.3 The relationship between the number of visits to a site and the price of the visit.

House and other property prices are clearly determined by a number of independent variables. Some of these will involve variables related to the following.

- *Characteristics of the property*: number of rooms, whether detached, semi-detached or terraced, garage facilities available, etc.

- *Characteristics of the location*: number (and reputation) of schools, availability of shopping and recreational facilities, transport infrastructure, etc.

- *Characteristics of the environment*: proximity to favourable or unfavourable environmental factors.

Statistical techniques (such as multiple regression analysis) can be used to estimate the influence of these possible 'explanatory' (independent) variables on house and property prices. For example, a 'classic' statistical study of the impact of traffic noise in Washington, DC, established an inverse relationship between house prices and the environmental factor 'noise pollution' with each extra decibel of noise found to be statistically correlated with a 0.88% fall in average house prices.

Non-demand curve valuations

Essentially both the expressed preference and revealed preference methods are making use of demand curve analysis in placing monetary values on aspects of environmental quality. However, a number of valuation methods may be used which depart from this approach.

Replacement cost method

The focus here is on the cost of replacing or restoring a damaged asset. This cost estimate is then used as a measure of the 'benefit' from such replacement or restoration. For example, if it costs £1m to restore the façade of buildings damaged by air pollution, then this £1m cost is used as an estimate of the benefit of environmental improvement.

Preventative expenditure method

The focus here is on using the costs incurred in an attempt to prevent some potential environmental damage as a measure of 'benefit'. For example, the expenditure incurred by residents on double-glazing to avoid 'noise pollution' from a new trunk road might be used as a proxy variable of the value placed by residents on noise abatement.

Delphi method

The focus here is on valuations derived from consulting a group of recognized experts. Each member of the group responds independently to questions as to the valuations that might be placed on various (environmental) contingencies in their area of expertise. The initial responses of the group are then summarized in graphical or tabular form, with each member given the opportunity to re-evaluate their individual responses. The idea here is that through successive rounds of re-evaluation, a consensus valuation of the expert group may eventually emerge.

Cost–benefit analysis (CBA)

Under cost–benefit analysis, the techniques already discussed and others are used to assign monetary values to the gains and losses to different individuals and groups, often weighted according to some perception of the contribution of these individuals or groups to social utility (social welfare). It is for this reason that this approach is sometimes referred to as 'social' cost–benefit analysis. Some of the 'market failures' previously identified are taken into account, with some existing market prices adjusted (e.g. via weighting) and values attributed to some situations where no market prices currently exist. If the proposed reallocation of resources via new investment in some (environmental) project is evaluated as creating benefits that are greater, in present value terms, to

those who gain than the costs imposed on those who lose, then the project is potentially viable from society's perspective. In other words, if the net present value to society of a project is positive, then the project is at least worthy of consideration. Whether or not it will be undertaken may depend upon what restrictions, if any, apply to the level of resources (finance) available. If such resources are limited and must be rationed, then of course only those projects with the highest (positive) net present values to society may be selected.

Total economic value

In recent years there has been considerable discussion as to how to find the 'total economic value' (TEV) of an environmental asset. The following identity has been suggested:

$$\text{Total economic value} \equiv \text{use value} + \text{option value} + \text{existence value}$$

The idea here is that 'use value' reflects the practical uses to which an environmental asset is currently being put. For example, the tropical rainforests are used to provide arable land for crop cultivation or to rear cattle in various ranching activities. The forests are also a source of various products, such as timber, rubber, medicines, nuts, etc. In addition, the forests act as the 'lungs' of the world, absorbing stores of carbon dioxide and releasing oxygen, as well as helping to prevent soil erosion and playing an important part in flood control.

There are clear difficulties in placing reliable monetary estimates on all these aspects of the 'use value' of the rainforest. However, it is even more difficult to estimate 'option value', which refers to the value we place on the asset *now* as regards functions which might be exploited some time in the *future*. For example, how much are we willing to pay to preserve the rainforest in case it becomes a still more important source of herbal and other medicines? This is a type of insurance value, seeking to measure the willingness to pay for an environmental asset now, given some probability function of the individual (or group) wishing to use that asset in various ways in the future.

Finally, 'existence value' refers to the value we place on an environmental asset as it is today, independently of any current or future use we might make of that asset. This is an attempt to measure our willingness to pay for an environmental asset simply because we wish it to continue to exist in its present form. Many people subscribe to charities to preserve the rainforests, other natural habitats or wildlife even though they may never themselves see those habitats or species. Existence value may involve inter-generational motives, such as wishing to give one's children or grandchildren the opportunity to observe certain species or ecosystems.

Although much remains to be done in estimating TEV, a number of empirical studies have been undertaken. For instance, the Flood Hazard Research Centre in the UK estimated that in 1987/88 people were willing to pay £14 to £18 per annum in taxes in order that recreational beaches (use value) be protected from erosion (Turner 1991). The researchers also surveyed a sample of people who did *not* use beaches for recreational use. They estimated that these people were willing to pay £21 to £25 per annum in taxes in order to preserve these same beaches (existence value).

Overall, many estimates are finding that the 'option' and 'existence' values of environmental assets often far exceed their 'use' value. For example, existence values for the Grand Canyon were found to outweigh use values by the startling ratio of 60 to 1 (Pearce 1991a). In similar vein, *non-users* of Prince William Sound, Alaska, devastated by the Exxon Valdez oil spill in 1989, placed an extremely high value on its existence value (O'Doherty 1994). The amounts non-users were estimated (via interviews) as willing to pay to *avoid* the damage actually incurred came to $2.8bn, i.e. $31 per US household. This approach, whereby interviewees are asked about the value of a resource 'contingent' on its not being damaged, is often termed 'contingent valuation'.

We now turn to the important policy issue of how we can provide market incentives or regulations which will result in a socially optimum level of environmental damage (output Q_S in Fig. 10.2), rather than the higher levels of environmental damage which would result from an unfettered free market in which externalities were ignored (output Q_B in Fig. 10.2).

Market-based and non-market-based incentives

In free-market or mixed economies the market is often seen as an efficient means of allocating scarce resources. Here we look at ways in which the *market* could be used to provide incentives to either firms or consumers in order to bring about a more socially optimum use of environmental assets.

Market-based incentives

Environmental taxes

An environmental tax is a tax on a product or service which is detrimental to the environment, or a tax on a factor input used to produce that product or service. An environmental tax will increase the *private* costs of producing goods or services which impose negative 'externalities' on society.

In Fig. 10.4 we have a situation similar to that in Fig. 10.3 with Q_S as the socially optimum output. The marginal pollution costs (MPC) curve is more usually referred to as the *marginal external cost* (MEC) curve, as the firm is imposing these pollution costs but not, initially, paying for the damage done. In terms of Fig. 10.4, if a lump-sum tax of t is now imposed on the polluter, it has the effect of shifting the MNPB curve downwards and to the left, thus giving $MNPB - t$. Remember that MNPB is the marginal profit (see p. 190) on each extra unit produced which is now reduced by the tax t levied on each unit. The polluter would now maximize total net private benefits (i.e. total profit) at a level of activity equal to Q_S.

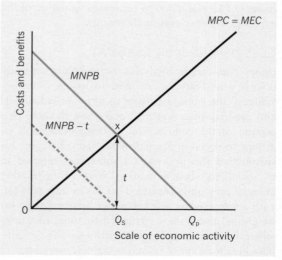

Fig. 10.4 Imposing a lump-sum environmental tax t on output.

If the firm produced an amount greater than Q_S then it would pay more in costs and tax on the extra units sold than it would receive in revenue (profit would fall). If the firm produced an amount less than Q_S then it would pay less in costs and tax on the extra units sold than it would receive in revenue (profit would rise). Only at output Q_S is total net private benefit (total profit) a maximum, i.e. where $MNPB - t = 0$. The tax would be equal to MEC at the optimum level of pollution.

Using environmental taxes in this way is often said to be a policy of 'internalizing' the externality. In other words, the firm itself now has the incentive to take the externality into account in its own decision-making. There are, however, problems with using an environmental tax, not least in determining the tax rate (t) which will make $MNPB - t = 0$.

A move towards environmental taxes is in line with the 'polluter pays' principle adopted by the OECD in 1972. This principle states that 'the polluter should bear the cost of measures to reduce pollution decided upon by public authorities to ensure that the environment is in an "acceptable state"'. The idea behind adopting this principle across member states was to avoid the distortions in comparative advantages and trade flows which could arise if countries tackled environmental problems in widely different ways. Slightly less than 2% of UK total tax revenue is currently yielded by explicitly environmental taxes, although if general taxes on energy are also included in a looser definition of 'environmentally related' taxes, then this figure rises to some 8.5% of UK total tax revenue.

An *environmental subsidy* can be thought of as a *negative* environmental tax. If in Fig. 10.4, the optimum social output was *to the right* of Q_p, then the policy prescription might be a subsidy rather than a tax. A subsidy would shift the $MNPB$ upwards by the amount of the subsidy (v), giving $MNPB + v$, and total net private benefit (profit) would be maximized at an output to the right of Q_p. In an attempt to encourage farmers to reforest agricultural land, China is paying farmers $450 a year per reforested hectare in the area around the Yangzi river, to increase tree planting and help avoid flooding.

Tradeable permits
Another market-based solution to environmental problems could involve tradeable permits, and this is becoming a widely used mechanism by governments,

firms and individuals in attempting to reduce pollution. Here the polluter receives a permit to emit a specified amount of waste, whether carbon dioxide, sulphur dioxide or whatever. The *total* amount of permits issued for any pollutant must, of course, be within currently accepted guidelines of 'safe' levels of emission for that pollutant. Within the overall limit of the permits issued, individual polluters can then buy and sell the permits between each other. The distribution of pollution is then market directed even though the overall total is regulated, the expectation being that those firms which are already able to meet 'clean' standards will benefit by selling permits to those firms which currently find it too difficult or expensive to meet those standards.

Figure 10.5 provides an outline of how the tradeable permits system works. With this policy option the polluter is issued with a number of permits to emit a specified amount of pollution. The total number of permits in existence (Q_S) places a limit on the total amount of emissions allowed. Polluters can buy and sell the permits to each other, at a price agreed between the two polluters. In other words the permits are *transferable*.

The underlying principle of tradeable permits is that those firms which can achieve a lower level of pollution can benefit by selling permits to those firms which at present find it either too difficult or too expensive to meet the standard set. The market for permits can be illustrated by using Fig. 10.5. In order to achieve an optimum level of pollution, the agency

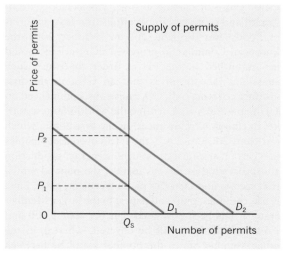

Fig. 10.5 Determining the market price for permits.

responsible for permits may issue Q_S permits. With demand for permits at D_1 the price will be set at P_1. If new polluters enter the market the demand for permits will increase, e.g. to D_2, and the equilibrium permit price will rise to P_2. If, for any reason, the agency wishes to relax the standard set, then more permits will be issued and the supply curve for permits will shift to the right. Alternatively, the standard could be tightened, by the agency purchasing permits on the open market from polluters, which would have the effect of shifting the supply curve to the left.

The EU *Emissions Trading Scheme* uses the idea of tradeable permits in seeking to reduce greenhouse gas emissions.

The EU Emissions Trading Scheme (ETS)

In the EU an Emissions Trading Scheme (ETS) is being seen as a key economic instrument in a move to reduce greenhouse gas emissions. The ETS is intended to help the EU meet its commitments as part of the Kyoto Protocol. The EU took upon itself as part of the Protocol to reduce greenhouse gas emissions by 8% (from 1990 levels) by 2008–12. The idea behind the ETS is to ensure that those companies within certain sectors that are responsible for greenhouse gas emissions keep within specific limits by either reducing their emissions or buying *allowances* from other organizations with lower emissions. The ETS is essentially aimed at placing a cap on *total* greenhouse gas emissions.

The emission of greenhouse gases is seen as a major cause of climate change, which has environmental and economic implications, not least in terms of floods and drought, and in October 2001 the European Commission proposed that an ETS should be established in the EU in order to reduce such emissions. The result is that an ETS, in the first instance covering only CO_2 emissions, commenced on 1 January 2005, representing the world's largest market in emissions allowances. In the first phase, which ran from 2005 to 2007, the ETS covered companies of a certain size in sectors such as energy, production and processing of ferrous metals, the mineral industrial sectors and factories making cement, glass, lime, brick, ceramics, pulp and paper. In the larger Member States it has been estimated that between 1,000 and 2,500 installations will be covered, whereas in the other Member States the number could be between 50 and 400. In terms of the UK, this represents in the region of 1,500 installations, which emit approximately 50% of the economy's CO_2 emissions. The second phase, which is running from 2008–12, includes other sectors such as aviation. In the UK a number of government departments and agencies are responsible for issuing allowances (permits).

With the advent of the ETS an electronic registry system has been developed so that when a change in the ownership of allowances takes place there is a transfer of allowances in terms of the registry system accounts. This registry is similar to a banking clearing system that tracks accounts in terms of the ownership of money. In order to buy and sell the allowances each company involved in the scheme will require an account.

How will the Emissions Trading Scheme work?

This section details a hypothetical situation that will explain how emissions trading operates. In the following analysis we assume there are two companies A and B each emitting 60,000 and 40,000 tonnes of CO_2 per annum respectively. Each company is represented in Fig. 10.6. The marginal abatement cost (*MAC*) curves refer to the extra cost to the firm of *avoiding* (abating) emitting the last unit of pollution. The *MAC* for company A increases more slowly than for company B as emissions are cut back, indicating that the cost of abatement is higher for company B than for company A.

With no controls on the level of emissions, the total level of CO_2 emissions will be 210,000 tonnes (120,000 tonnes from company A and 90,000 from company B). If we now assume that the authorities want to reduce CO_2 emissions by 50% (so that 105 million tonnes is the maximum) then this can be achieved by issuing 105,000 emission allowances each equal to 1 tonne. If they are issued on the basis of previous emission levels ('grandfathering') then company A would receive 60,000 emission allowances (or tradeable permits) and company B 45,000, based on one allowance representing the right to emit one tonne of CO_2. If this were the case then company A would have to reduce its emissions to 60,000 tonnes and company B to 45,000 tonnes. Based on this, company A would have a *MAC* of £1,200 and company B of £3,000. Given this situation, company B would *buy* permits if it could pay less than £3,000 for each, and company A would *sell* them for a price greater than £1,200. Company A would sell them, since the revenue earned from the sale would be

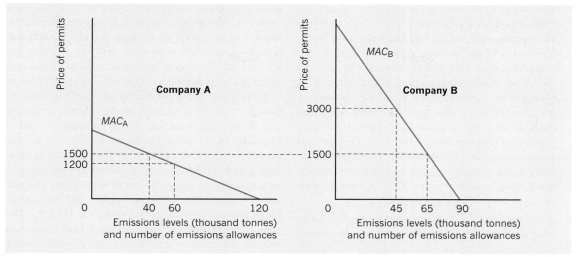

Fig. 10.6 Marginal abatement cost (*MAC*) and the trading in emissions allowances.

greater than the additional abatement cost incurred by reducing emissions. There is thus a basis for trade in emissions allowances and this will continue until the *MAC*s are identical. In Fig. 10.6 this occurs at a price of £1,500 with 40,000 tonnes of CO_2 emitted by company A and 65,000 by company B, with company A selling 20,000 emissions allowances to company B. Overall the price of the allowances will be determined by supply and demand.

Potential advantages of the ETS

A number of potential advantages have been put forward in terms of the use of an ETS when dealing with issues such as the control of emissions affecting climate change, most notably the following.

- Unlike pollution taxes, which begin by making companies pay for something they were once getting for free, emissions allowances begin by creating and distributing a new type of *property right*.
- It is politically easier to get companies to agree on a pollution-control policy that begins by distributing a valuable new property right (permit) than by telling them that they will have to pay a new tax. The reason for this is that the emissions allowance will have a market value as long as the number of allowances created is limited. In other words it is a more acceptable policy instrument for firms directly involved in the ETS.

- Permits are cost-effective since they provide incentives for polluters with low abatement costs to abate (avoid) pollution and sell the permits they no longer require, while providing incentives for polluters with higher abatement costs to purchase these permits rather than abate. In other words a ready-made market exists.
- According to the White Paper on the Future of Air Transport (Department for Transport 2003) one of the advantages of emissions trading is that it guarantees the desired outcome in a way not achieved by alternative market-based and non-market-based instruments, such as the introduction of a charge (environmental tax). Companies have flexibility in that they can achieve their emission reduction levels based on their own strategy, i.e. either by reducing emissions or by purchasing emissions allowances. Either way the desired environmental outcome is achieved, since the cap on overall emissions has been established.

Potential disadvantages of the ETS

The scheme came into force on 1 January 2005; however, a number of potential disadvantages have also been pointed out.

- An appropriate system of initially allocating the emissions allowances is all-important. In terms of the hypothetical situation outlined above, the allowances were allocated on the basis of current emissions, with companies A and B each receiving allowances representing half their emission levels. There are, however, difficulties with this, in that companies may already have successfully reduced their level of emissions and are now penalized for having done so by receiving less of the allowances. An alternative to this *grandfathering* approach could be to allocate allowances equally to those companies that are part of the ETS. This method also has inherent difficulties in that companies may differ in terms of the amount of pollution they currently emit. In terms of the EU ETS, a mechanism closer to the former was adopted.

- In terms of the philosophy underpinning the use of an emissions allowance scheme, it can be argued that it gives the owner of an allowance the right to pollute, in other words a permit to emit pollutants.

- It is possible that a few polluters may purchase all the available permits, making it difficult for new companies to enter a particular sector. In this way allowances could act as a *barrier to entry* and thus be seen as anti-competitive. It has been stated, however, that the idea behind the ETS is to limit emissions and not to limit output. There is, however, a need to be aware of the potential difficulties new entrants to a sector may face.

- Any scheme of this nature will have an administration cost not least in terms of maintaining the electronic registry system. There is also a need to monitor the allowance transactions so that companies are emitting only what they are entitled to. If companies do not surrender allowances necessary to cover their annual emissions then they will be liable to a penalty, which in the first phase of the scheme will be €40 per tonne of CO_2 emitted.

Conclusions

The EU ETS represented a new market-based approach to dealing with the issue of CO_2 emissions and their related impacts on climate change. The scheme was introduced in the EU in January 2005 and is administered by a number of environmental bodies throughout the UK. The scheme has a number of potential advantages, notably the fact that it is establishing a new form of property right, it is more acceptable relative to pollution taxes, it is cost-effective and is flexible. There are, however, potential difficulties, not least in terms of allocating the emis-

sions allowances, the ethical aspect of creating a right to pollute, the possibility of companies cornering the market in emissions allowances and the administrative costs. Overall, time alone will tell whether the ETS will be seen as a successful new market-based solution to the problem of greenhouse gas emissions.

In January 2008, the European Commission proposed a number of changes to the scheme, including centralized allocation (no more national allocation plans) by an EU authority, the auctioning of a greater share (60+ %) of permits rather than allocating them freely, and inclusion of other greenhouse gases, such as nitrous oxide and perfluorocarbons. These changes are to become effective from January 2013 onwards, i.e. in the 3rd Trading Period under the EU ETS. The proposed caps for the 3rd Trading Period foresee an overall reduction of greenhouse gases for the sector of 21% in 2020 compared to 2005 emissions. The EU ETS has recently been extended to the airline industry, but only after 2012.

Bargains

The idea here is that if we assign 'property rights' to the polluters giving them the 'right to pollute', or to the sufferers giving them the 'right not to be polluted', then bargains may be struck whereby pollution is curbed. For instance, if we assign these property rights to the polluters, then those who suffer may find it advantageous to compensate the polluter for agreeing *not* to pollute, the suggestion being that compensation will be offered by the sufferers as long as this is less than the value of the damage which would otherwise be inflicted upon them. Alternatively, if the property rights are assigned to the sufferers, who then have the 'right' not to be polluted, then the polluters may find it advantageous to offer the sufferers sums of money which would allow the polluters to continue polluting, the suggestion being that the polluters will offer compensation to the sufferers as long as this is less than the private benefits obtained by expanding output and thereby increasing pollution. Under either situation, economists such as R. Coase have shown that clearly assigned property rights can lead to 'bargains' which bring about output solutions closer to the social optimum than would otherwise occur.

From Fig. 10.7 we can see that, with no regulation, the polluter will seek to maximize *total* net private benefits (profits) producing at Q_B, whereas Q_S is

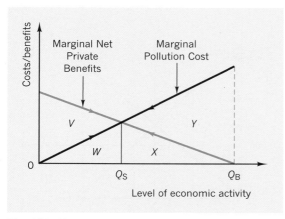

Fig. 10.7 Negotiation under property rights.

			Individual B			
			Negotiate		Free-ride	
Individual A	Negotiate		*80*	80	*20*	90
	Free-ride		*90*	20	*50*	50

Fig. 10.8 Bargaining and game theory.

Bargaining, game theory and the free-rider problem

Chapter 6 (Oligopoly) introduced the idea of game theory, and we now apply this to the bargaining situation. Assume there are two sufferers from the pollution emitted from a factory. The two sufferers, individuals A and B, each have a level of utility equal to 50 utils. Individuals A and B are thinking about involving themselves in negotiation with the factory polluter. In reaching their decision there are *four* scenarios (Fig. 10.8).

1 *Both individuals A and B decide not to negotiate with the polluter.* The outcome is that both continue to suffer and obtain a utility of 50 utils.

2 *Both individuals A and B decide to negotiate with the polluter.* There is a cost in negotiating which is equal to 70 utils each. If they negotiate together, however, they are likely to obtain major concessions, which could be equal to 100 utils for each individual. In this situation both individuals A and B benefit by a further 30 utils, resulting in each having utility of 80 utils.

3 *Individual A decides to negotiate while B free-rides.* In this situation the bargaining strength of the sufferers will be somewhat less and as such the gains from negotiation could be only 40 utils. In this situation the expected utility from negotiation for A would now be 20 utils (the original 50 utils plus the gain of 40 utils minus the cost of 70 utils). For individual B, however, the expected gain is 40 utils with no negotiation costs involved because of free-riding. Thus B's expected utility is 90 utils.

4 *Individual B decides to negotiate while A free-rides.* In this situation A's expected utility is 90 utils and B's 20 utils.

Each individual has one of two options, either to negotiate or to free-ride. The left side of each box (in italics) refers to individual A's outcomes (payoffs)

the social optimum. The introduction of property rights can, however, change this situation. If the *polluter* is given the property rights, then the sufferer will (provided polluter and sufferer have the same information!) find it advantageous to *compensate/bribe* the polluter to cease output at Q_S. For any *extra* output beyond Q_S the losses to the sufferer exceed the benefits to the polluter (e.g. $X + Y > X$ at output Q_B). There is clearly scope for a negotiated solution at output level Q_S.

A similar negotiated outcome can be expected under the Coase theorem if the *sufferer* is given the property rights. This time the polluter will (given symmetry of information) find it advantageous to *choose* the socially optimum output Q_S and offer compensation equivalent to W to sufferers. For any *extra* output beyond Q_S, the gains to the polluter are more than offset by the (actionable) losses to the sufferers (e.g. $X < X + Y$ at output Q_B). There is, again, clearly scope for a negotiated solution at output level Q_S.

The principle of 'sufferer pays' is already in evidence. For example, Sweden assists Poland with reducing acid rain because the acid rain from Poland damages Swedish lakes and forests. Similarly, the Montreal Protocol of 1987 sought to protect the ozone layer by including provisions by which China, India and other developing countries were to be compensated by richer countries for agreeing to limit their use of chlorofluorocarbons (CFCs). On this basis, Brazil has argued that it is up to the developed countries to compensate it for desisting from exploiting its tropical rainforests, given that it is primarily other countries which will suffer if deforestation continues apace.

and the right side to individual B's outcomes (pay-offs). Taking a free-ride might seem an attractive option for each individual, yielding the highest payoff (90) in the belief that the other individual will indeed negotiate. However, if both decide to free-ride this essentially means both decide not to negotiate and the outcome is a less attractive payoff (50). The situation is the same as in the prisoner's dilemma, which is also part of game theory (see Chapter 6).

If each selects the best outcome for itself inde-pendent of the reaction of the other, then each will choose to free-ride, believing it can achieve a payoff of 90 utils. This is the so-called 'dominant strategy' for the game, but in fact the outcome from following this strategy is only 50 utils each. Had each individual sought to negotiate rather than free-ride, then each would have been better off with 80 utils apiece. If sufferers are more likely to attempt to free-ride in this way, then giving them the property rights by making the polluter pay may be the best way of ensuring that the socially optimum bargaining outcome is achieved.

Non-market-based incentives: environmental standards and regulations

Environmental standards

Setting standards is a common option in terms of controlling pollution. For example, minimum stan-dards are set in terms of air and water quality and the polluter is then free to decide how best to meet the standard. A regulator then monitors the situation and action is taken against any polluter who fails to main-tain the standard set.

A standard St_1 could be set as illustrated in Fig. 10.9. This would achieve the optimum scale of economic activity Q_S and the optimum level of pollution. As with an environmental tax, standards require accurate information on MNPB and MEC. For example, the standard could be set at St_2 which would require a scale of economic activity equal to Q_A. This is not an optimum position since the mar-ginal net private benefits derived by the polluter Q_AX are greater than the marginal external costs Q_AY. In other words, the standard is too severe.

In addition, in terms of Fig. 10.9 the penalty Pen_1 imposed on polluters who violate the standard set is not adequate. In fact, the polluter will be tempted to pollute up to Q_B since for each unit up to Q_B the

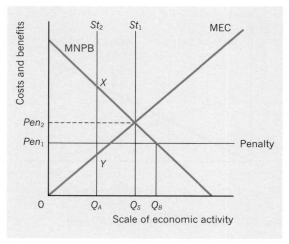

Fig. 10.9 Setting the appropriate standard and imposing the appropriate penalty.

penalty will be less than the profits received by the polluter, as measured by the MNPB curve. The pol-luter will not produce in excess of Q_B since for each unit beyond Q_B the penalty incurred would be greater than the profit obtained from that production. Of course, it is always possible that the pollution will go undetected and therefore no penalty will be imposed. With an optimal standard of St_1 the penalty should be Pen_2 and consistently enforced.

The setting of a standard such as St_1 will achieve the optimum level of economic activity and therefore pollution, provided that the penalty is set at Pen_2 and that this penalty is effectively enforced. Any 'mistakes' in the form of setting an inappropriate standard and/or an inappropriate penalty will lead to a misallocation of resources.

In the EU, a legally binding regulation on maxi-mum emissions of greenhouse gases by new vehicles comes into force in 2015, namely a maximum emis-sion of 130 grammes of CO_2 per kilometre travelled by new cars from that date. In the UK, the Environ-mental Protection Act (1989) laid down minimum environmental standards for emissions from over 3,500 factories involved in chemical processes, waste incineration and oil refining. The factories have to meet these standards for all emissions, whether into air or water or onto land. Factory performance is monitored by a strengthened HM Inspectorate of Pollution, the costs of which are paid for by the factory owners themselves. The Act also provided for public access to information on the pollution created by firms. Regulations were also established on restricting the release of genetically engineered bacteria and viruses and a ban was imposed on most forms of straw and stubble burning from 1992 onwards. Stricter regulations were also imposed on waste disposal operations, with local authorities given a duty to keep public land clean. On-the-spot fines of up to £1,000 were instituted for persons dropping litter.

Regulations have also played an important part in the five 'Environmental Action Programmes' of the EU, which first began in 1973. For example, specific standards have been set for minimum acceptable levels of water quality for drinking and for bathing. As regards the latter, regular monitoring of coastal waters must take place, with as many as 19 separate tests undertaken throughout the tourist season.

Of course regulations may be part of an integrated environmental policy which also involves market-based incentives. A tradeable permits system for sulphur dioxide emissions has been long established in the US and works in tandem with the standards imposed by the US Clean Air Act.

We now review two key environmental issues to examine the relative merits of market-based and non-market-based incentives for dealing with environmental problems, namely global warming and transport-related pollution.

Global warming

This refers to the trapping of heat between the earth's surface and gases in the atmosphere, especially CO_2. Currently some six billion tonnes of CO_2 are released into the atmosphere each year, largely as a result of burning fossil fuels. In fact CO_2 constitutes some 56% of these 'greenhouse gases', with CFCs, used mainly in refrigerators, aerosols and air-conditioning systems, accounting for a further 23% of such gases, the rest being methane (14%) and nitrous oxide (7%). By trapping the sun's heat, these gases are in turn raising global temperature (global warming). On present estimates, temperatures are expected to increase by a further 1 °C in the next two decades, when an increase of merely half a degree in world temperature over the past century is believed to have contributed to a rise of 10 cm in sea levels. Higher sea

levels (resulting from melting ice caps), flooding and various climatic changes causing increased desertification and drought have all been widely linked to global warming.

The whole debate on curbing emissions of CO_2 and other 'greenhouse gases' in an attempt to combat global warming usefully highlights a number of issues:

- a non-zero level of pollution as socially efficient;
- the respective advantages and disadvantages of market-based and non-market-based incentives in achieving socially efficient solutions.

We have already addressed some of the environmental implications of global warming. There are clearly significant social damage costs associated with emissions of CO_2, which rise at an increasing rate with the total level of emissions. This situation is represented by the *Total Damage Costs* curve in Fig. 10.10(a).

However, seeking to reduce CO_2 emissions will also impose costs on society. For instance, we may need to install expensive flue-desulphurization plants in coal-burning power stations, or to use (less efficient) sources of renewable energy (e.g. wind, wave, solar power). These various costs are represented by the *Total Abatement Costs* curve in Fig. 10.10(a). We might expect these Total Abatement Costs to rise at an increasing rate as we progressively *reduce* the level of CO_2 emissions, since the easier and less costly means of cutting back on CO_2 emissions are likely to have been adopted first.

In Fig. 10.10(a), we can see that the consequence of taking *no action* to reduce CO_2 emissions would leave us at Q_p, with zero abatement costs but high total damage costs.

What must be stressed here is the importance of seeking to identify *both* types of cost. On occasions, environmentalists focus exclusively on the damages caused by global warming, whereas producers concern themselves solely with the higher (abatement) costs of adopting less CO_2 intensive methods of production.

The analysis is simplified (Fig. 10.10(b)) by using *marginal* changes in the damage costs or abatement costs related to each extra tonne of CO_2 emitted or abated. The socially optimum level of CO_2 emissions is where marginal damage costs exactly equal marginal abatement costs, i.e. output Q_s in Fig. 10.10(b). To emit more CO_2 than Q_s would imply marginal

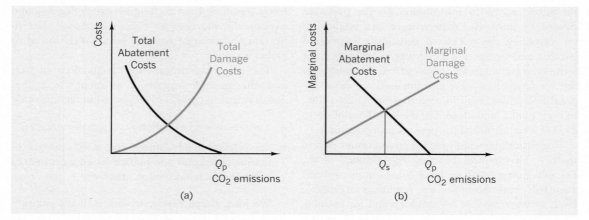

Fig. 10.10 Using abatement and damage cost curves in finding a socially optimum level of pollution.

damage costs to society *greater than* the marginal cost to society of abating that damage. Society is clearly disadvantaged by any emissions in excess of Q_s. Equally, to emit less CO_2 than Q_s would imply marginal damage costs to society *less than* the marginal cost to society of abating that damage. In this case society is disadvantaged by seeking to cut CO_2 emissions below Q_s.

Setting the targets

If we are to apply our analysis in practical ways we must seek to *value* both the marginal damage and the marginal abatement cost curves. Again we are faced with the conceptual problem of placing a valuation on variables to which monetary values are at present only rarely attached, if at all. In addition, in a full cost–benefit analysis we must select a rate of discount (see Chapter 17) to enable a comparison to be made between effects in the distant future and the costs of policies introduced today.

Uncertainty will therefore clearly be involved in any attempt to evaluate the costs and benefits of policy action or inaction. The target for *reducing* CO_2 emissions ($Q_p - Q_s$ in Fig. 10.10(b)) to the socially optimum level will clearly be affected by such uncertainty. Analysts often use 'scenarios' of high, medium and low estimates for marginal damage and marginal abatement cost curves. For instance, Nordhaus (1991) estimated each of these marginal cost curves for both CO_2 emissions and for the broader category of

greenhouse gases, based on US data. His *high* estimate of marginal damage costs was calculated at $66.00 per tonne of CO_2, his *low* estimate at only $1.83 per tonne of CO_2. We can use Fig. 10.10(b), above, to illustrate this analysis. In the high estimate case, the marginal damage cost curve shifts vertically upwards, Q_s falls, and the 'target' reduction in CO_2 emissions (i.e. $Q_s - Q_p$) increases. On this basis, Nordhaus advocates reducing CO_2 emissions by 20%. It is hardly surprising (in view of the valuation discrepancy noted above) that in his low estimate case, the marginal damage cost curve shifts vertically downwards in Fig. 10.10(b), Q_s rises, and the target reduction in CO_2 emissions (i.e. $Q_s - Q_p$) falls. On this basis Nordhaus advocates reducing CO_2 emissions by only about 3%.

The Stern Committee Report in 2006 estimated higher marginal damage costs per tonne of CO_2 than even the high estimate case of Nordhaus. As a consequence, the target CO_2 emission for Stern, with a higher marginal damage cost curve in Fig. 10.10(b), is well below that of Nordhaus (Hof and Van Vuuren 2008). The Stern 'optimum' target turns out to be a peak CO_2 concentration of 540 parts per million, whereas that for Nordhaus is a much higher target of 750 parts per million (World Bank 2010).

Stern Report on climate change

The Stern Report on climate change was published in late 2006, and is widely regarded as the most authoritative of its kind. Its key findings included the following.

- CO_2 in the atmosphere in about 1780, i.e. just before the Industrial Revolution, has been estimated at around 280 ppm (parts per million).
- CO_2 in 2006, however, had risen significantly to 382 ppm.
- Greenhouse gases (CO_2, methane, nitrous oxide etc.) in 2006, were even higher at 430 ppm in CO_2 equivalents.

Two key scenarios were identified in the Stern Report.

Do nothing scenario

- Temperature rise of 2 °C by 2050.
- Temperature rise of 5 °C or more by 2100.

The damage to the global economy of such climate change from the 'do nothing' scenario is an estimated reduction in global GDP per head (i.e. consumption per head) of between 5% and 20% over the next two centuries. This occurs via rising temperatures, droughts, floods, water shortages and extreme weather events.

Intervene scenario

The Stern Report advocates measures to stabilize greenhouse gas emissions at 550 ppm CO_2 equivalents by 2050. This requires global emissions of CO_2 to peak in the next 10–20 years, then fall at a rate of at least 1–3% per year. By 2050 global emissions of CO_2 must be around 25% below current levels. Since global GDP is expected to be around three times as high as today in 2050, the CO_2 emissions *per unit* of global GDP must be less than one-third of today's level (and sufficiently less to give the 25% reduction on today's levels).

The Stern Report estimated the cost of stabilization at 550 ppm CO_2 equivalents to be around 1% of current global GDP (i.e. around £200bn). This expenditure will be required *every year*, rising to £600bn per annum in 2050 if global GDP is three times higher than it is today. Stabilization would limit temperature rises by 2050 to 2 °C, but not prevent them. Otherwise temperature rises well in excess of 2 °C are predicted – possibly as much as 5 °C by 2100. Even limiting temperature rises to 2 °C by 2050 will inflict substantial damages, especially in terms of flooding low-lying countries as the ice caps melt, but also via more extreme weather conditions in various parts of the world.

Co-operative solutions and regulations

The arguments in favour of co-operative solutions to problems such as global warming have led many to support some type of regulatory framework such as that embedded in the Kyoto Protocol (see below). We can review some of these arguments using Fig. 10.11, which represents a situation in which the benefits to a country, A, from pollution reduction accrue only partly to itself, the remaining (and more substantial) beneficiaries from A's pollution reduction being the rest of the region (here the world) of which A is but a part. However, A is faced with having itself to pay the costs of any pollution reduction (abatement) it undertakes.

In Fig. 10.11 A_{MB} and A_{MC} are country A's marginal benefits and marginal costs of pollution reduction (note that the horizontal axis is pollution reduction, so more pollution reduction in Fig. 10.11 – moving left to right – is the same as less pollution emission – moving right to left – in Fig. 10.10(b) above), whilst R_{MB} is the whole region's (rest of the world's) marginal benefit from country A's pollution reduction.

Note that the maximum net benefit for the *whole region* ($MW0$) occurs with pollution reduction by country A of P_R. But the maximum net benefit for *country A* ($LV0$) occurs with pollution reduction by country A of only P_A. To induce A to undertake pollution reduction beyond P_A is in the best interest of

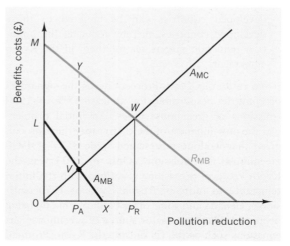

Fig. 10.11 Regional reciprocal pollution and the need for negotiation.

the whole region (world), but any further reduction in pollution by A beyond P_A brings extra benefit to itself only up to X (area VXP_A), and this is insufficient to cover its additional costs. In other words, A will require extensive compensation to induce it to reduce pollution to P_R or at least a regulatory framework in which A can recognize benefits to itself from other countries also acting with a regional or global perspective in mind, rather than merely their own self-interest. It was in an attempt to provide such a global perspective for pollution reduction that the Kyoto Protocol was signed in 1997.

Kyoto Protocol

Provisionally agreed in December 1997 via the UN Framework Convention on Climate Change, the main features of the Kyoto Protocol are as follows.

- Developed countries to collectively reduce 1990 emission levels of six greenhouse gases by 5% by 2012.
- Individual country targets to be set within this average.
- Penalties for non-compliance.
- Emissions trading to be allowed (via permits).
- 'Clean Development Mechanisms' to be applied by which greenhouse gas reductions in developing countries resulting from investments by developed countries can be credited to those developed countries, thereby reducing the pollution reduction targets set for them in the Kyoto agreement.

To ratify the Kyoto Protocol needs the signatures of countries responsible for at least 55% of 1990 emissions of greenhouse gases. An initial problem was the unwillingness of the US to ratify the protocol, given that it alone represented some 35% of 1990 greenhouse gas emissions. Only in 2003 was the Kyoto Protocol provisionally ratified with the initial reluctance to ratify of Russia (18% of 1990 emissions), Canada and some other countries finally being overcome. Having a major source of greenhouse gas emissions such as the US outside the Kyoto Protocol is clearly a weakness for this co-operative approach to tackling global warming.

Copenhagen Accord

The Copenhagen Accord was an outcome of the December 2009 meeting of the UN Framework Convention on Climate change (UNFCCC). It sought to *quantify* responses required if increases in global temperature are to be kept below 2 °C by 2050, i.e. specified actions, targets, verification mechanisms, financing proposals. Nations were to submit these within a tight deadline within two months of the meeting. Many had seen Copenhagen as an opportunity to put a more effective mechanism than Kyoto into the international arena, especially since Kyoto was seen by many to have neglected the developing countries, despite 52% of emissions now coming from the developing countries and 97% of the *growth* in greenhouse gas emissions by 2050 expected to come from these countries.

In the event, while over 102 countries had responded within the time limit, with national plans for targeted actions by 2020, covering over 80% of global emissions, these voluntary and rather 'patchwork' outcomes were seen by many as having failed to provide an effective successor to Kyoto. Nevertheless, seven of the major developing countries (Brazil, China, India, Indonesia, South Korea, Mexico, South Africa) did provide specific emission reduction targets by 2020, despite the Accord not making such quantitative targets a compulsory requirement! China will seek to reduce CO_2 emissions per unit of GDP by 40–45% by 2020 as compared to the 2005 levels.

Achieving the targets

Whatever the targets set for reduced emissions, which policy instruments will be most effective in achieving those targets? The discussion by Ingham and Ulph (1991) is helpful in comparing market and non-market policy instruments. Many different methods are available for bringing about any given total reduction in CO_2 emissions. Users of fossil fuels might be induced to switch towards fuels that emit less CO_2 within a given total energy requirement. For instance oil and gas emit, respectively, about 80% and 60% as much CO_2 per unit of energy as coal. Alternatively, the total amount of energy used might be reduced in an attempt to cut CO_2 emissions.

Another issue is whether we seek to impose our target rate of reduction for CO_2 emissions on *all* sectors of the UK economy. For example, some 40% of CO_2 emissions come from electricity generation, 20% from the industrial sector and around 20% from the transport sector. Should we then ask for a *uniform* reduction of, say, 25% across all sectors? This is unlikely to be appropriate, since *marginal abatement* cost curves are likely to differ across sectors and, indeed, across countries. For instance, it has been estimated that to abate 14% of the air pollution emitted by the textiles sector in the USA will cost $136m per annum. However, to abate 14% of the air pollution emitted by each of the machinery, electrical equipment and fabricated metals sectors will cost $572m, $729m and $896m respectively (World Bank 1992). As well as differing between industrial sectors *within* a country, abatement costs will also differ between countries. For example, it has been estimated that a 10% reduction in CO_2 emissions by 2010 (as compared to 1988 emission levels) will cost €400 per tonne of CO_2 abated in Italy, but only €200 per tonne abated in Denmark, and less than €20 per tonne abated in the UK, France, Germany and Belgium (Commission of the European Communities 1992).

This point can be illustrated by taking just two sectors in the UK – say, electricity generation and transport – and by assuming that they initially emit the same amount of CO_2. Following Ingham and Ulph (1991) suppose that the overall target for reducing CO_2 emissions is the distance O'O in Fig. 10.12.

We must now decide how to allocate this total reduction in emissions between the two sectors. In Fig. 10.12 we measure reductions in CO_2 emissions in electricity generation from left to right, and reductions in CO_2 emissions in transport from right to left. Point A, for example, would divide the total reduction in emissions into OA in electricity generation and O'A in transport. A *marginal abatement cost* (MAC) curve is now calculated for each sector. In Fig. 10.12 we draw the MAC curve for electricity generation as being lower and flatter than that for transport. This reflects the greater fuel-switching possibilities in electricity generation as compared to transport, both within fossil fuels and between fossil and non-fossil (solar, wave, wind) fuels. In other words, any marginal reduction in CO_2 emissions in electricity generation is likely to raise overall costs by *less* in electricity generation than in transport. In transport there are far fewer fuel-substitution possibilities, the major means of curbing CO_2 emissions in transport being improved techniques for energy efficiency or a switch from private to public transport.

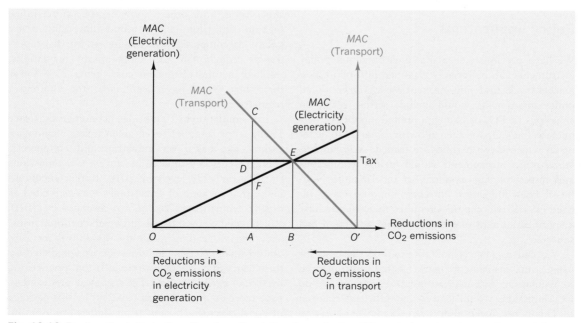

Fig. 10.12 Finding the 'efficient' or 'least-cost' solution for reducing CO_2 emissions in a two-sector model.

Given these *different MAC* curves for each sector in Fig. 10.12, how then should we allocate our reduction between the two sectors? Clearly we should seek a solution by which the given total reduction in emissions is achieved at the least total cost to society: we shall call this the *efficient* or *least-cost* solution. In Fig. 10.12, this will be where marginal abatement costs are the same in both sectors, i.e. at point *B* in the diagram. We can explain this by supposing we were initially *not* at *B*, but at *A* in Fig. 10.12, with equal reductions in the two sectors. At point *A*, marginal abatement costs in transport are *AC* but marginal abatement costs in electricity generation are only *AF*. So by abating CO_2 by *one more* tonne in electricity generation and *one less* tonne in transport, we would have the same total reduction in CO_2 emissions, but would have saved *CF* in costs. By moving from point *A* to the 'efficient' point *B*, we would save the area *CFE* in abatement costs.

It follows, therefore, that for any given target for total reduction in CO_2 emissions, 'efficiency' will occur only if the marginal cost of abatement is the same across all sectors of the economy (and indeed across all methods of abatement). Pollution control policies which seek to treat all sectors equally, even where marginal abatement costs differ widely between sectors, may clearly fail to reach an 'efficient' solution.

Policy implications

We have previously seen that environmental policy instruments can be broadly classified into two types: market-based and non-market-based. *Market-based* policy instruments would include setting a tax on emissions of CO_2 or issuing a limited number of permits to emit CO_2 and then allowing a market to be set up in which those permits are traded. *Non-market-based* policy instruments would include regulations and directives. For example, in the UK, the Non-Fossil Fuel Obligation currently imposed on privatized electricity companies requires them to purchase a specified amount of electricity from non-fossil fuel sources.

We can use Fig. 10.12 to examine the case for using a tax instrument (market-based) as compared to regulation (non-market-based). A tax of *BE* on CO_2 emissions would lead to the 'efficient' solution *B*. This is because polluters have a choice of paying the tax on their emissions of CO_2 or of taking steps to abate their emissions. They will have an incentive to abate as long as the marginal cost of abatement is lower than the tax. So electricity generating companies will have incentives to abate to *OB*, and transport companies to *O'B*, in Fig. 10.12 above. Since every polluter faces the same tax, then they will end up with the same marginal abatement cost. Here 'prices', amended by tax, are conveying signals to producers in a way which helps coordinate their (profit maximizing) decisions in order to bring about an 'efficient' (least cost) solution.

The alternative policy of government regulations and directives (non-market-based instruments) in achieving the 'efficient' solution at *B* in Fig. 10.12 would be much more complicated. The government would have to estimate the *MAC* curve for *each sector*, given that such curves differ between sectors. It would then have to estimate the different percentage reductions required in each sector in order to equalize marginal abatement costs (the 'efficient' solution). It is hardly reasonable to suppose that the government could achieve such fine tuning in order to reach 'efficient' solutions.

The market-based solution of tax has no administrative overhead. Producers are simply assumed to react to the signals of market prices (amended by taxes) in a way which maximizes their own profits. Regulations, on the other hand, imply monitoring, supervision and other 'bureaucratic' procedures. Ingham and Ulph (1991) found that using a tax policy, as compared with seeking an *equal proportionate reduction* in CO_2 emissions by regulations, resulted in total abatement costs being 20% lower than they would have been under the alternative regulatory policy.

In a simulation by Cambridge Econometrics (Cowe 1998), a 'package' of seven green taxes, including a carbon tax based on industrial and commercial energy use, was estimated as cutting CO_2 emissions by 13% on 1990 levels by 2010. Rather encouragingly, this package of green taxes was estimated as raising a further £27bn in tax revenues by 2010, which could be used to cut employers' national insurance by 3%, leading to almost 400,000 extra jobs. Only a small (−0.2%) deterioration was predicted for the balance of payments and for inflation (prices rising by 0.5%) by 2010 and GDP was even predicted to have received a small boost (+0.2%) by this package of green taxes. Such simulation studies are useful in that they 'model' impacts of tax measures throughout the economy, although one must carefully check the assumptions which underlie the equations used in computer models.

The Climate Change Levy

In the 1999 UK Budget, the Chancellor, Gordon Brown, announced that a *Climate Change Levy* (CCL) would be imposed on business use of energy from April 2001. The CCL is a tax applying to fossil fuel used by non-domestic (mainly commercial and industrial) users, applying at different rates to different fossil fuels. The rates are 0.42p per kWh for electricity, 0.15p per kWh for gas and 1.17p per kilogram for coal. Fuel oils are not liable for CCL as they are already liable for separate duty. The CCL is a revenue-neutral tax, meaning that the revenue produced by the tax will be recycled to companies so that for industry as a whole there will be no net increase in taxation. The revenues are recycled through a reduction of 0.3% in employers' national insurance contributions, an increase in tax allowances for certain energy-saving investments by a company, and payments from an energy-efficient fund for small and medium-sized companies. Certain large polluters are able to enter into negotiated voluntary agreement with the government to reduce energy consumption in exchange for a reduction (up to 80%) of CCL. Note that the tax does not apply to domestic energy use, although households will bear some of the burden of this tax in so far as firms pass the tax forward.

Critics have suggested that a carbon tax which was based solely on CO_2 content would be preferable, since the energy content of fuel does not necessarily reflect its carbon content. However, an energy tax is believed to be simpler to administer, being applied at a uniform rate per kilowatt-hour for all 'primary' fuels (coal, gas, oil), rather than a more complex differential rate depending on their carbon content.

Conclusion

The World Bank has concluded that 'regulatory policies, which are used extensively in both industrial and developing countries, are best suited to situations that involve a few public enterprises and non-competitive private firms' (World Bank 1992). It also concludes that economic incentives, such as charges, will often be less costly than regulatory alternatives. For instance, to achieve the *least-cost* or *efficient* solution of point *B* in Fig. 10.12 is estimated as costing some 22 times more in the US if particulate matter is abated by regulations, rather than by using market-based instruments. Similarly, achieving this least-cost solution by regulating sulphur dioxide emissions in the UK is estimated as costing between 1.4 and 2.5 times as much as achieving it by using market-based instruments. Certainly there has been considerable support for using tradeable permits as a key mechanism for tackling the emissions of CO_2 and other greenhouse gases as, for example, with the introduction of an Emissions Trading System by the EU in 2005.

However, regulatory policies are particularly appropriate when it is important not to exceed certain thresholds, e.g. emissions of radioactive and toxic wastes. In these cases, it is clearly of greater concern that substantial environmental damage be avoided than that pollution control be implemented by policies which might prove to be more expensive than expected. However, where the social costs of environmental damage do not increase dramatically if standards are breached by small margins, then it is worth seeking the least-cost policy via market incentives rather than spending excessive amounts on regulation to avoid any breach at all.

With market-based policies, all resource users or polluters face the same price and must respond accordingly. Each *user* decides on the basis of their own utility/profit preferences whether to use fewer environmental resources or to pay extra for using more. On the other hand, with regulations it is the regulators who take such decisions on the behalf of the users, e.g. *all* users might be given the same limited access to a scarce environmental resource. Regulators are, of course, unlikely to be well informed about the relative costs and benefits faced by users or the valuations placed on these by such users.

Market-based policies have another advantage, namely that they price environmental damage in a way which affects all *polluters*, providing uniform 'prices' to which all polluters can respond (see Fig. 10.12), thereby yielding 'efficient' or 'least cost' solutions. By contrast, regulations usually affect only those who fail to comply and who therefore face penalties. Further, regulations which set minimizing standards give polluters no incentives to do better than that minimum.

Our review of environmental concerns and possible remedial policies has, of necessity, been selective. We have considered the competing claims of market- and non-market-based incentives towards achieving socially efficient solutions. Market-based incentives often help avoid the necessity of external bodies seeking to evaluate marginal abatement cost and marginal damage cost curves. This is certainly an advantage in an area where such valuations are notoriously difficult. Nevertheless, there are situations where regulations, or a judicious mix of markets and regulations, may be the most appropriate way forward. In any case, all the interdependences of any proposed solution must be fully taken into account before any final decisions are made. What is beyond dispute is that the environment and the economic system are highly interrelated, and neither can be considered in isolation from the other.

Key points

- The environment interacts with the circular flow, providing amenity services, natural resources and the assimilation of waste products.

- An 'Index of Sustainable Economic Welfare' (ISEW) adjusts the conventional GNP figure for environmental impacts. On this basis, the growth of ISEW per head for the UK in the period 1950–2005 was a mere 0.5% per annum, much less than the growth in real GNP per head of 2.0% per annum over the same period.

- The optimum level of pollution for society is unlikely to be zero. Rather it will occur at the (positive) level at which marginal damage costs exactly equal marginal abatement costs.

- Assessing such an optimum involves finding solutions to problems of *valuation* of environmental impacts, especially where no market prices exist.

- Policy instruments which might be used to achieve a social optimum include both market-based incentives (taxes, tradeable permits and negotiation) and non-market-based incentives (various standards and regulations).

- There is evidence to suggest that in most cases a given objective can be achieved at least cost by a combination of market-based policy instruments.

- Considerable emphasis is now being placed on tradeable permits as a market-based system for tackling greenhouse gas emissions.

- Where the benefits of pollution reduction measures extend beyond the country concerned, there is a case for co-operative and international agreements along the lines of the Kyoto Protocol if socially optimum outcomes are to be achieved.

- The Copenhagen Accord is an attempt to develop specific national action plans to keep global warming within 2 °C of current temperatures by 2050.

Now try the self-check questions for this chapter on the Companion Website. You will also find useful links to relevant websites.

References and further reading

Berck, P. and Helfand, G. (2010) *Economics of the Environment*, Harlow, Pearson Education.

Bergstrom, J., Russell, R. and Randall, A. (2010) *Resource Economics: An Economic Approach to Natural Resource and Environmental Policy* (3rd edn), Cheltenham, Edward Elgar.

Commission of the European Communities (1992) The climate challenge, economic aspects of the Community's strategy for limiting CO_2 emissions, *European Economy*, **51**, May.

Cowe, R. (1998) Green taxes come up against pain barrier, *Guardian*, 2 February.

Department for Transport (2003), *The Future of Air Transport*, Cm 6046, December, London, The Stationery Office.

Hof, A. and Van Vuuren, D. (2008) Analysing the costs and benefits of climate policy: value judgements and scientific uncertainties, *Global Environmental Change*, **18**(3): 412–24.

Ingham, A. and Ulph, A. (1991) Economics of global warming, *Economic Review*, **9**(2): 2–6.

Ison, S., Peake, S. and Wall, S. (2002) *Environmental Issues and Policies*, Harlow, Financial Times/Prentice Hall.

Jackson, T. and Marks, N. (1994) *Measuring Sustainable Economic Welfare – A Pilot Index: 1950–1990*, Stockholm Environment Institute.

Jackson, T., Marks, N., Ralls, J. and Stymne, S. (1997) *Sustainable Economic Welfare in the UK 1950–1996*, London, New Economics Foundation.

Kerry Turner, R., Pearce, D. and Bateman, I. (1994) *Environmental Economics*, Hemel Hempstead, Harvester Wheatsheaf.

Lawrence, P. (2002) Can the World Bank rescue Africa's economies?, *Economic Review*, **19**(4): 20–4.

Lubin, D. and Esty, D. (2010) The sustainability imperative, *Harvard Business Review*, May, 89–99.

Maddison, D., Pearce, D. *et al.* (1996) *Blueprint 5: The True Costs of Road Transport*, London, Earthscan Publications Ltd.

Markandya, A. and Mason, P. (1999) Air pollution and health, *Economic Review*, **17**(2): 2–4.

Newbery, D. M. (1995) Economic effects of (18th Report) recommendations, *Economic Journal*, **105**(September): 1258–72.

Nordhaus, W. (1991) To slow or not to slow: the economics of the greenhouse effect, *Economic Journal*, **101**(407): 920–37

O'Doherty, R. (1994) Pricing environmental disasters, *Economic Review*, **12**(1).

ONS (2003) *UK Environmental Accounts 2003*, London, Office for National Statistics.

Palmer, A. (2001) Organic food, *Economic Review*, **19**(1): 2–5.

Pearce, D. (1991a) Towards the sustainable economy: environment and economics, *Royal Bank of Scotland Review*, **172**(December): 3–15.

Pearce, D. (1991b) Economics and the environment, *Economics, Journal of the Economics Association*, **27**(1): 113.

Pearce, D. (1998) Sustainable development: taking stock for the future, *Economic Review*, **16**(1): 4–7.

Sheppard, P. and Walter, M. (2002) The Dibden Bay project: a matter of choice, *Economic Review*, **19**(4): 25–9.

Stern, N. (2007) *The Economics of Climate Change: The Stern Review*, Cambridge, Cambridge University Press.

Tietenberg, T. and Lewis, L. (2008) *Environmental and Natural Resource Economics* (8th edn), Harlow, Financial Times/Prentice Hall.

Tietenberg, T. and Lewis, L. (2009) *Environmental Economics and Policy* (6th edn), Harlow, Financial Times/Prentice Hall.

Turner, K. (1991) Environmental economics, *Developments in Economics: an Annual Review*, 7.

Unruh, G. and Ettenson, R. (2010a) Growing green, *Harvard Business Review,* June, 94–100.

Unruh, G. and Ettenson, R. (2010b) Winning in the green frenzy, *Harvard Business Review*, November, 110–15.

Willis, K. (1991) The priceless countryside: the recreational benefits of environmental goods, *Royal Bank of Scotland Review*, **172**(December): 34–8.

World Bank (1992) *World Development Report 1992: Development and the Environment*, Washington DC.

World Bank (1994) *World Development Report 1994: Infrastructure for Development*, Washington DC.

World Bank (2010) *World Development Report 2010: Development and Climate Change*, Washington DC.

CHAPTER 11   Transport

Transport is an important sector of any economy and has been the subject of increasing debate in recent years. This chapter will deal with certain aspects of that debate, notably the problems of road transport congestion and the move to a deregulated transport sector. The last 60 years have seen a dramatic change in the patterns of demand for transport. For example, in 1952 only 27% of passenger kilometres travelled were by car, van and taxi, while public transport (both road and rail) accounted for 60%. Today, however, the share has changed, with 84% of passenger kilometres now being by car, van and taxi and with public transport in the form of bus, coach and rail accounting for only 13%. Such a substantial change has significant implications for road congestion and the environment. In this chapter we therefore concentrate mainly on the *road transport sector*, and on the car in particular, although we also include a section which deals with the growth of airline operations, especially the low-cost operators.

One of the important issues involving transport activities is that of externalities, and the divergence between private and social costs and benefits. Such externalities are considered in the context of transport in this chapter and further reviewed in Chapter 8.

The characteristics of transport

First, transport is a service which is seldom demanded for its own sake and can be viewed as a 'derived demand'. In other words, the demand for the private car, public transport and freight haulage is 'derived' from the need to transfer passengers and goods from one destination to another. Each journey undertaken can be seen as 'unique' in terms of both time and space, and cannot therefore be stored or transferred.

Second, the transport sector (both passenger and freight operators) is affected by the peak and off-peak nature of demand. There will be periods of maximum or peak demand, e.g. on a *daily* basis when commuters travel into a major conurbation to work, or on a *seasonal* basis when holidaymakers use road, rail or airline transport during summer periods. Peak periods are present in the transport sector because of the derived nature of demand and because transport is consumed immediately and is therefore non-storable. Spare capacity at one time of the day or season *cannot* be used at another time of the day or season. Also, the indivisibility of supply means that public transport may be running at full capacity into the urban area in the peak period, but operating empty on the return journey. As a result there are often problems of over-supply during off-peak periods.

Third, the transport sector has, over the years, been subject to varying degrees of state intervention. In the 1970s, the transport sector was characterized by public ownership and substantial government intervention, particularly in the provision of public transport. The 1980s and 1990s saw a period of rapid change, with a substantial scaling-down of state intervention in the sector. For example, the *1980 Transport Act* deregulated the long-distance express coach market, allowing increased competition. The National Freight Corporation was privatized in 1982 and subsequent years saw the deregulation of local bus provision as a result of the *1985 Transport Act*. Other transport companies were privatized, such as UK Airports with the 1986 Airports Act, British Airways in 1987 and NBC in 1988. In addition, there was the franchising of rail services from 1995 onwards.

Fourth, 'externality' effects are a characteristic of transport. These include effects such as pollution through emissions from car exhausts, noise from aircraft and motorways, and traffic congestion. At present 37% of carbon monoxide and 30% of nitrogen oxide emissions are associated with road transport in the UK. These impose costs on the community and are generally not taken into account by the transport provider (company or individual) who is usually only concerned with the *private costs* (such as fuel, wear and tear, etc.) of the journey undertaken. Intervention by the state has therefore been required to deal with these external effects, especially where companies or individuals have failed to take full account of the *social* implications of their actions. This has led, for example, to the introduction of emission tests for carbon monoxide as part of the MoT test for cars and light vehicles and an increase in roadside enforcement programmes in order to remove the worst offenders from the road.

Fifth, other characteristics of transport may be gauged from the changing nature of travel over recent years. Table 11.1 gives a summary of passenger travel in Great Britain over the period 1997–2007. It shows that there was an increase in passenger transport by 11.4% over the period, with travel by cars, vans and taxis increasing by 8.3%. *Cars, vans and taxis* dominate passenger transport, accounting for 84% of all passenger kilometres travelled in 2007, with *bus* and *coach* travel accounting for 6% of all passenger kilometres in 2007. Domestic air travel, although it has grown, still accounts for only 1.2% of overall travel.

Table 11.2 compares Great Britain with a number of other countries in terms of passenger kilometres travelled between 1997 and 2007. In all of these countries the major mode of transport is the private road vehicle. In Great Britain some 87% of total passenger travel in 2007 was by cars, compared with 96% in the US for the latest period available. The figure for Japan for passenger travel by cars is much lower (60%), with rail travel being much more significant (33%) than elsewhere.

Finally, another characteristic of transport is the changing nature of the *freight* market. In terms of freight transport, Table 11.3 gives figures in billion tonne kilometres and percentage, by mode, over the period 1998–2008. It shows that there has been a 2% increase in freight transported by road over the period and, as with passenger transport, roads can be seen as the major form of transport, with 674% of the share in the most recent time period.

Table 11.1 Passenger transport by mode, 1997–2007.

	Billion passenger kilometres/percentages														
	Road														
	Buses and coaches		Cars, vans and taxis		Motor cycles		Pedal cycles		All road		Rail		Air		All modes	
		%		%		%		%		%		%		%		%
1997	44	6	632	86	4	1	4	1	684	93	42	6	6.8	0.9	733	100
1998	45	6	635	86	4	1	4	1	688	93	44	6	7.0	1.0	738	100
1999	46	6	641	85	5	1	4	1	696	93	46	6	7.3	1.0	750	100
2000	47	6	639	85	5	1	4	1	695	93	47	6	7.6	1.0	749	100
2001	47	6	654	85	5	1	4	1	710	93	47	6	7.7	1.0	765	100
2002	47	6	678	86	5	1	4	1	734	93	48	6	8.5	1.1	791	100
2003	47	6	677	85	6	1	5	1	735	93	49	6	9.1	1.2	793	100
2004	48	6	679	85	6	1	4	1	736	92	51	6	9.8	1.2	797	100
2005	48	6	674	85	6	1	4	1	733	92	52	7	9.9	1.2	794	100
2006	50	6	682	85	6	1	5	1	746	92	55	7	9.9	1.2	811	100
2007	50	6	685	84	6	1	4	1	749	92	59	7	9.5	1.2	817	100

Source: Department for Transport (2009) *Transport Statistics Great Britain 2008.*

Table 11.2 Passenger transport by national vehicles on national territory, 1997 and 2007.

| | Billion passenger kilometres | | | | | | | |
| | Cars | | Buses and coaches | | Rail excluding metro systems | | Total of these modes | |
	1997	2007	1997	2007	1997	2007	1997	2007
Great Britain	632.0	689.0	45.7	51.5	34.9	50.1	712.6	790.6
Belgium	100.4	112.5	13.1	18.5	7.0	9.9	120.4	140.8
Denmark	50.3	55.3	7.6	7.4	5.2	6.2	63.1	68.9
France	659.5	727.8	42.0	47.1	61.8	80.3	763.2	855.2
Germany	817.1	868.7	68.0	65.4	72.4	79.3	957.5	1013.4
Greece	50.0	95.0	20.7	27.0	1.9	1.9	72.6	118.9
Irish Republic	28.0	42.0	5.5	7.3	1.4	2.0	34.9	51.3
Italy	638.8	720.2	90.0	104.1	46.4	49.6	775.2	873.9
Netherlands	136.5	148.8	12.0	12.3	13.9	16.3	162.4	177.4
Spain	267.6	343.3	44.0	59.2	17.8	21.9	329.4	424.3
Sweden	87.2	99.6	9.8	8.5	7.0	10.3	104.0	118.4
Japan	704.0	724.0	93.0	89.0	395.2	396.0	1,192.2	1,209.0
USA	6085.0	7317.0	233.0	275.0	21.0	23.7	6,339.0	7,615.7

Source: Adapted from Department for Transport (2009) *Transport Statistics Great Britain 2008.*

Table 11.3 Domestic freight transport by mode (in billion tonne kilometres and percentages), 1998–2008.

	1998	2000	2002	2004	2006	2008
All traffic						
Road[1]	160.3	159.3	159.4	162.5	166.7	163.5
Rail	17.3	18.1	18.5	20.3	21.9	20.6
Water[2]	56.9	67.4	67.2	59.4	51.8	49.7
Pipeline	11.7	11.4	10.9	10.7	10.8	10.2
All modes	246.2	256.3	256.0	253.0	251.3	244.0
Percentage of all traffic						
Road[1]	65	62	62	64	66	–67
Rail	7	7	7	8	9	–8
Water[2]	23	26	26	23	22	–20
Pipeline	5	4	4	4	4	–4
All modes	100	100	100	100	100	–100

[1]All goods vehicles, including those under 3.5 tonnes gross vehicle weight.
[2]Figures for water are for UK traffic.
Source: Adapted from Department for Transport (2009) Transport Statistics Great Britain 2008.

The demand for transport

The quantity of a good or service demanded is dependent upon a number of factors, such as its own price, the price of other goods or services (particularly close substitutes and complements), and income. For example, private car ownership is a function not only of the price of motor vehicles, but also of fuel prices, the price of alternative forms of transport, and income levels. Income is an important factor in determining both the demand for transport in general, and the *particular mode* of transport a passenger uses.

Table 11.4 gives figures for motoring expenditure, fares and other travel costs for households with different levels of income in the UK in 2008. As one would expect, it clearly shows that travel expenditure increases with income, with those households in the lowest 10% income group having an average weekly expenditure on *transport* of £12.10 whilst the highest 10% spend £161.10. For *all* households the average is £63.40.

For *rail transport, Family Spending 2008* (ONS 2009) reveals that higher income groups spend more on that mode of travel. As illustrated in Table 11.4, the highest 10% of income earners spent on average

£9.00 per week on rail and tube fares compared to an average for *all households* of £2.40. For bus travel, however, the highest 10% of income earners only spend £1.60 per week on bus and coach fares compared to an average for all households of £1.40, leading one to suggest that bus and coach travel can be viewed in economic terms as an inferior good.

Predicting the demand for transport in the future is a difficult process, since it depends on how the variables affecting demand change over time. For example, forecasts in terms of car ownership predict it to increase by 46% between 1996 and 2031. As Table 11.5 reveals, however, we have not yet reached saturation level in terms of car ownership, for there are still 24% of households who do not own a car.

With regards to forecasting car ownership, the Department of Transport used the *National Road Traffic Forecasts* 1988 to make the following observation:

Many factors are likely to influence the growth of car ownership and use. They include income, the cost of buying and running cars, journey requirements (work and non-work), quality of public transport services and the way people's expectations and preferences about car ownership

Table 11.4 Detailed household expenditure by gross income decile group, 2008

Commodity or service	Lowest 10%	Second decile group	Third decile group	Fourth decile group	Fifth decile group	Sixth decile group	Seventh decile group	Eighth decile group	Ninth decile group	Highest 10%	All house-holds
					Average weekly household expenditure (£)						
Transport	**12.10**	**17.10**	**24.10**	**38.90**	**51.90**	**61.0**	**73.60**	**81.90**	**112.20**	**161.10**	**63.40**
Purchase of vehicles	3.40	4.70	4.90	12.20	16.60	20.10	26.30	24.70	38.0	60.60	21.10
Purchase of new cars and vans	[0.40]	[1.20]	[0.90]	5.30	5.30	7.020	8.80	6.80	8.30	22.50	6.60
Purchase of second-hand cars or vans	2.96	3.50	3.90	6.70	10.80	12.40	16.70	16.80	28.30	34.20	13.60
Purchase of motorcycles and other vehicles	[0.10]	0.10	0.10	0.10	0.40	0.60	0.80	[1.10]	1.50	3.90	0.90
Operation of personal transport	6.00	8.90	14.50	20.00	29.60	32.20	37.10	43.60	55.90	70.00	31.80
Spares and accessories	0.30	[0.20]	1.20	1.50	3.20	1.90	2.10	2.40	5.40	5.40	2.40
Petrol, diesel, other motor oils	4.00	5.70	9.30	14.10	18.68	21.30	25.80	30.10	36.50	44.90	21.00
Repairs and servicing	1.40	2.40	3.10	3.50	5.20	6.80	6.90	8.20	10.30	14.70	6.20
Other motoring costs	0.30	0.60	1.00	0.90	2.50	2.20	2.40	2.90	3.70	5.00	2.10
Transport services	2.70	3.60	4.60	6.80	5.80	8.70	10.20	13.60	18.30	30.50	10.50
Rail and tube fares	0.50	0.70	0.60	0.80	1.00	1.70	2.10	4.10	3.90	9.00	2.40
Bus and coach fares	1.20	0.80	0.80	1.70	1.2	1.80	1.60	1.70	1.30	1.60	1.40
Combined fares	[0.20]	[0.30]	[0.30]	[0.20]	[0.60]	1.20	1.90	1.50	2.30	3.850	1.20
Other travel and transport	0.80	1.90	3.00	4.00	3.00	4.00	4.70	6.30	10.70	16.20	5.40

Source: Adapted from ONS (2009) *Family Spending, a Report on the 2004–05 Expenditure and Food Survey.*

Table 11.5 Households with regular use of cars, 1998–2007.

	Percentage of households			
	No car	One car	Two cars	Three or more cars
1998	28	44	23	5
1999	28	44	22	5
2000	27	45	23	5
2001	26	46	22	5
2002	26	44	24	5
2003	26	44	25	5
2004	25	44	25	5
2005	25	44	25	5
2006	24	44	26	6
2007	24	44	26	6

Source: Department for Transport (2009) *Transport Statistics Great Britain 2008*.

change over time. . . . It seems likely that car ownership will eventually reach a limit – or 'saturation level' – as a larger proportion of the population acquires cars. Since no country appears to have reached this limit yet, the level of saturation must be assumed. For these forecasts, saturation has been assumed to occur when 90% of the driving age group of 17–74-year-olds owns a car (100% car ownership is unlikely because some people will be prevented or deterred by disabilities or other factors). On this basis, saturation would correspond to 650 cars per thousand people. The forecasts of growth in national car ownership are essentially about the rate and path with which the saturation level is approached. (Goodwin, 1990)

Forecasts of future traffic, particularly the private car, are essential for a central government which has to decide on the allocation of funds for future road development. For, as stated by the Department of Transport in 1989:

Traffic forecasts are important in assessing whether the benefits from a road improvement, over its life-time, justify the initial cost and in determining the standard of provision. They enable a balance to be struck between providing extra capacity before it is needed and the cost of

adding to capacity at a later stage. Traffic forecasts also play a part in predicting the environmental impacts of traffic, such as noise and air pollution.

Such forecasts are difficult to determine owing to the high degree of uncertainty about the future and for this reason the basis of the forecasts involves two differing assumptions, namely that of low economic growth and that of high economic growth. The forecasts therefore provide a range of values ('scenarios') to cover the uncertainties involved. It is possible, however, for the outcome to fall outside the forecast range, with the Department of Transport being unable to forecast traffic levels accurately. A good example of this was seen with the M25, for which forecasts were undertaken in the 1970s when oil prices were high and economic growth low. This led the Department of Transport to underestimate the likely demand for transport along the route. For example, between 1982 and 1987 they forecast an increase in road traffic of between 9% and 16%, but the actual increase was 22%. The main reason for this was that the forecast assumed a growth of GDP of between 8% and 15% over the five-year period, but GDP actually grew by 18%. Also the price of fuel was forecast to rise in real terms, whereas it actually fell.

Road transport congestion

Congestion costs arise because the addition of more vehicles onto a road network reduces the speed of other vehicles and so increases the average time it takes to complete any particular journey.

It is possible to gain some understanding of congestion by studying the relationship between speed and flow along a particular route. Figure 11.1 shows a *speed–flow curve* for the movement of vehicles along a particular road. It shows how motorists interact and impose delays and costs on each other. In a free-flow situation (around point A) there is little or no interaction between vehicles, and therefore speeds (subject to the legal speed limit) are relatively high. However, as extra vehicles join the road, average speed is reduced; nevertheless an increased flow will still occur until point B is reached. The flow of vehicles depends upon the number of vehicles joining the road

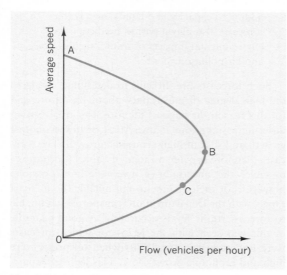

Fig. 11.1 Speed–flow curve.

and the speed of the traffic. For the *individual user*, maximum efficiency is where the speed is at its highest, i.e. point A. In terms of the *system as a whole*, however, the maximum efficiency is at point B, before the speed–flow curve turns back on itself (i.e. where the maximum flow of vehicles is achieved). Once at point B, the road is said to have reached its capacity at the maximum flow level. Motorists may continue to enter the road after B because they may lack perfect information, thus slowing down the whole flow. Point C may therefore be used to represent the speed–flow situation during a peak period. At this point the traffic is in a stop–start situation, perhaps where the traffic flow is subject to a bottleneck. This gives rise to high *external* costs which the motorist is not taking into account. These costs will tend to increase the closer the road is to full capacity.

The costs of congestion

It is clear that a major strategy is needed to tackle the congestion problem, not only in urban areas but also on inter-urban routes. Congestion undermines competitiveness and hinders certain conurbations, particularly London, from attracting people and business. It also imposes a financial cost on the business community in terms of increased commuter times and delays in the delivery of goods.

Although somewhat dated, in 1997 the National Economic Research Associates (NERA) estimated the total cost of road congestion to road users to be £7bn. This was split into the cost to business (£2.5bn) and the cost to private motorists, private van drivers and bus passengers (£4.5bn). A more recent estimate, although a decade old, of congestion costs is even more substantial; for example the RAC (2002) has estimated that congestion costs the motorist around £23bn in time losses alone each year. This is approximately £800 per annum for every motorist in Britain irrespective of the extra fuel and wear and tear costs associated with congestion. Whilst estimates of the cost of congestion have been made, the government has admitted that 'an ideal measure [of congestion] has yet to be identified' (House of Commons Transport Committee 2003).

Figure 11.2 gives some indication of the causes of congestion. There has been a dramatic rise in the number of licensed vehicles over the period 1951–2008, made up almost entirely of private cars.

The theory of urban road transport congestion

An economic model can be used to simplify the various issues involved in transport congestion, as shown in Fig. 11.3. The horizontal axis measures the flow of vehicles per hour along a particular route. The vertical axis measures the cost per trip, including time costs. Two demand curves are shown, both of which have a negative slope because it is assumed that motorists will reduce their driving if the cost of driving increases. The demand curve D_1 refers to the *off-peak* demand for the route. It is the aggregate demand of all motorists who wish to use the route. If the cost per trip is C_0, and demand is D_1, then this will produce a flow of F_0 along the route. When making a journey, a motorist is not likely to take account of the congestion cost of that journey and may in fact consider only his or her own *marginal private cost* (MPC). MPC includes costs such as the price of petrol used and the opportunity cost of the time the motorist spends travelling. There can, however, be costs incurred on *other* road users which the individual motorist will not take into account. These are 'external costs' and include such things as the pollution and noise borne by society as a whole and the congestion borne by other road users. These are shown by the *marginal social cost* (MSC) curve in Fig. 11.3. For

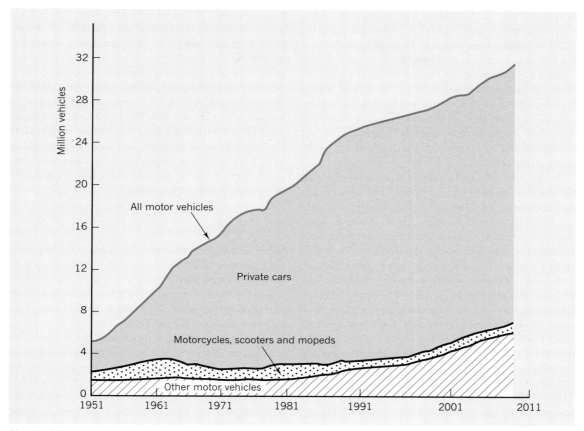

Fig. 11.2 Motor vehicles licensed, 1951–2008.
Source: Adapted from Department for Transport (2009) *Transport Statistics Great Britain 2008*.

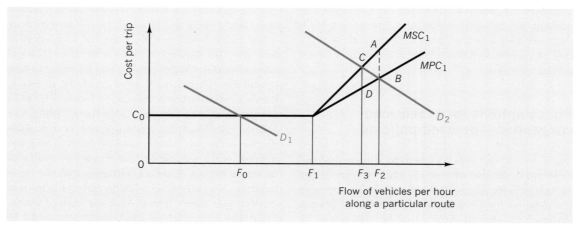

Fig. 11.3 Equilibrium traffic flow.

simplicity, Fig. 11.3 assumes that congestion is the *only* externality; hence MPC is shown as equal to MSC for some range of traffic flow up to F_1 because there is no congestion until that flow is reached. (Of course, if we allowed for the pollution which occurs from exhaust gases at low mileage, then MSC would be above MPC at all levels of traffic flow.) If motorists *did* take into account the social costs of a journey, then they might decide that the journey was not worth making, at least not at that time of day or by that particular route.

In the figure it can be seen that the flow of traffic can increase up to F_1 without congestion, because it is possible for the additional cars to enter the road without slowing down any other driver. It can be seen, therefore, that there is no divergence between marginal private cost and marginal social cost. However, at flows above F_1, congestion is apparent because additional drivers slow down the overall traffic flow and the individual motorist's MPC per trip increases. Each motorist is now beginning to interfere with other road users, affecting their costs but ignoring those costs when deciding whether or not to make a particular trip. As the flow of traffic increases beyond F_1, there is also a *divergence* between the MPC and the MSC, as shown in the figure by lines MPC_1 and MSC_1 (MSC is equal to MPC plus the social cost of congestion). This is brought about mainly through increased travel times, as each additional driver entering the road imposes an extra delay (perhaps only small) on every other driver. If the demand for the route at the peak period is of the normal shape D_2, then the traffic flow will be F_2. Here F_2B will be the (private) cost per trip *to the motorist*, and the external costs which the motorist has *not* taken into account will be equal to AB. At a flow of F_2 there is therefore *allocative inefficiency*, as the 'real' or social cost of congestion has not been accounted for by the private motorist.

Policy options for urban road congestion – demand policies

There are various policies which have been designed to improve the use of existing road capacity. These include policies which can be introduced to influence the *demand* for road space; there are also policies designed to expand road capacity, which can be viewed as *supply-side* policies. These various policies

will be covered in this section. However, at this stage it is also worth mentioning that there is a '*laissez-faire*' approach which is an alternative solution for permitting an equilibrium level of road transport congestion to emerge. For instance, if congestion gets 'too bad' in a particular region, then it may persuade companies and individuals to move to less prosperous regions which do not have the same level of congestion. The problem with this '*laissez-faire*' approach is that the transport network may be operating at, or near, full capacity at certain times, and therefore even small fluctuations in demand can cause long delays and create problems for safety.

Road user charging

When undertaking a journey, each driver is comparing the private benefit of each trip with the private cost of each trip. Drivers will add their vehicles to the flow whenever their marginal private benefit exceeds their marginal private cost. New roads could be built to meet the demand during the peak period, or demand could be restrained, or a mixture of the two policies could be undertaken. In Fig. 11.3 above, the flow of F_3 could be achieved by placing a charge of CD on the road user, so raising marginal private costs from MPC_1 to equal those of MSC_1; this would thereby reduce the traffic flow from F_2 to F_3. This road user charging option would bring about a 'more efficient allocation' of a scarce resource, because the marginal private benefit (as measured by the demand curve) is now equal to the marginal social cost curve. Road user charging is an option which is gaining in popularity. D. Newbery has commented that 'As road space is a valuable and scarce resource, it is natural that economists should argue that it should be rationed by price – road-users should pay the marginal social cost of using the road network if they are to make the right decisions about whether (and by which means) to take a particular journey, and, more generally, to ensure that they make the correct allocative decisions between transport and other activities' (Newbery 1990).

Road user charging was suggested as a possible solution to the urban congestion problem as long ago as 1964, when the Ministry of Transport produced the Smeed Report. Road user charging could be introduced by using meters attached to cars in the form of an electronic numberplate. As a car entered a congested area or stretch of road, the meter would be activated by sensors in the road. A charge would then be registered. As well as dissuading the marginal car user from using the road, it would also provide the authorities with revenue which could be used to construct more roads or to improve the public transport system. The government has recognized this and the Transport Bill (2000) included powers to enable local authorities outside London, if they wanted to, to introduce road user charging and/or a workplace parking levy (see below) as part of their local transport plan. Such powers had already been given to London's mayor and the Boroughs through the Greater London Authority Act 1999.

On 17 February 2003 in London the Mayor, Ken Livingstone, launched the first major congestion charging scheme in Britain, a scheme to charge motorists for the use of the road network within a specified area of Central London between certain times, the aim of the scheme being to reduce congestion. It forms one of only a small number of charging schemes worldwide, the Singapore Electronic Road Pricing scheme being the other main example.

The UK is one of the most congested countries in Europe and London one of the most congested cities. Average vehicle speeds in London have declined over time since 1974, falling from 22 km per hour 30 years ago to as little as 15 km per hour in the central and inner areas of London. This reduction in average speeds has been experienced in both the morning and evening peak periods with, perhaps surprisingly, the daytime off-peak period in Central London being most congested of all (in terms of lowest vehicle speeds). Clearly this is something the London authorities, namely Transport for London, have been keen to address and average speeds have increased by over 2 km per hour following the introduction of congestion charging.

Congestion charging originally covered 21 square kilometres of Central London, although the zone was extended westward in 2007. In October 2010, however, it was announced by the current Mayor that the Western Extension of the Congestion Charging Zone would be removed from January 2011. Motorists entering the zone between the hours of 7.00 am and 6.00 pm, Monday to Friday (excluding public holidays), are charged £8, increased to £10 in January 2011. In the financial year 2005/06 the scheme generated £122m in net revenue. This increased to £148m in the financial year 2009/10 and has been used to invest in improving transport in London.

Enforcement

Enforcement of the scheme is via 700 video cameras, which are able to scan the rear numberplate of the vehicles that enter the zone. Each evening the information obtained is matched against a database of motorists who have paid the charge. Payment can be made by phone, using the Internet, at shops or at petrol stations. If the motorist has failed to pay the charge before midnight, a fine of £120 is imposed. If the offender pays within 14 days, then the fine falls to £60.

Exemptions

A number of exemptions have been built into the scheme.

- Certain listed vehicles receive a 100% discount – this includes all alternative fuel vehicles, namely gas, electric and fuel cell vehicles, which are exempt on environmental grounds. Blue and orange badge holders are also exempt; that is, vehicles driven by disabled people. In addition, certain NHS staff, patients and emergency vehicles (fire engines, police vehicles and ambulances) have been brought within this category. Certain other vehicles are also exempt, such as those with more than nine seats and military vehicles used by the armed forces.

- Residents within the charging zone are eligible for a 90% discount.

- Motorbikes and mopeds, black cabs and London-licensed mini-cabs are also exempt.

According to Transport for London there has been a 6% increase in bus passengers during the charged hours although congestion has risen to the pre-charging levels. It would, however, have been much worse without the charges.

The scheme utilizes a rather simplistic technology, namely cameras on all the roads into the central area. It also incorporates a fixed price of £10, the charge not changing in line with the level of congestion experienced. As we noted in Chapter 10, the 'pure' environmental tax (Pigouvian tax) would equal the marginal external damage and would therefore rise as the marginal external damage increases (e.g. at peak time). The current fixed charge may, however, be changed to a variable charge as the scheme evolves. For example, the scheme might use global positioning satellites (GPS) and cars fitted with satellite receivers in order to allow the charge to vary with distance, time and location.

One of the criticisms levelled at road user charging is its effect on increasing the inflation rate. However, if it succeeds in reducing the total costs of commercial activities, then this is a false worry. Road user charging should not be viewed as a revenue maximizing charge, but as an efficiency maximizing charge. It could then be the key to medium-term relief from congestion and could provide the funds for the long-term upgrading of roads and public transport.

In addition, there are a number of problems to be addressed when considering the implementation of a road user charging policy. First, there need to be accurate estimates of elasticities of demand and of marginal external costs. Second, the issue of equity and the problem of practically implementing the scheme both need to be considered. For example, what charge should be made for congestion and how would it vary depending on the level of traffic and the time of day? Third, road user charging could be seen as an invasion of privacy.

Subsidizing public transport

Another approach designed to shift the demand to the left in Fig. 11.3 is *subsidizing public transport*. This method was used in the 1970s by a number of UK metropolitan councils. For example in Sheffield, bus fares were reduced by 55% in real terms over the period 1975–81. In addition to financial implications, the problem faced by this method is in persuading car users to *transfer* from private to public transport, since they often perceive themselves as being the *victims* of congestion rather than the *cause* of it. To be successful, this policy requires a long-term improvement in public transport and a cross-elasticity of demand between public and private transport substantially greater than zero. An added problem is that increased income levels lead to increased car ownership, thus lowering the demand for public transport, as stated above in the section 'The demand for transport'. The public transport sector therefore becomes more reliant on certain groups of travellers, namely the young, the elderly and those on low incomes.

Parking restrictions

One policy which has been extensively used in urban areas since the 1960s is *parking restraints*. The aim has been, through parking meters and restrictions on on-street parking, to limit the supply of parking spaces, so reducing the demand for urban routes. This policy, too, has limitations in that removing parking facilities from a road essentially increases the size of the road and may therefore encourage extra traffic flows. At the same time, parking restraints encourage illegal parking which may add to congestion. This is one of the main reasons for the introduction of wheel clamps in Central London in 1986 and policies such as the tow-away scheme introduced in Cambridge in 1991, subsequently abandoned in 1996 given its unprofitability.

City Councils have sought to use pricing policies at their car parks to encourage shopping and other short-stay motorists, while at the same time discouraging long-stay commuters. However, the success of this policy has been hindered to some extent by their lack of control over privately operated car parks and by high volumes of through traffic in most congested areas. Parking charges are also unable to discriminate between length of journey or route taken. Pricing policies could be used to encourage motorists to park at peripheral, out of town, car parks that are part of park-and-ride schemes, which are now operating in many British cities.

The lack of control over private parking was addressed by the Transport Bill (2000) which gave local authorities the power not only to introduce road user charging but also to levy a mandatory charge on workplace parking across all or part of their area. The levy would act as a *licence fee* with the owners or occupiers of premises applying to the traffic authority for a licence stating the maximum number of vehicles that would be parked on their premises at any one time. A workplace parking charge per vehicle would then be multiplied by that maximum number. The aim is 'to reduce the amount of free workplace car parking available as a means of reducing car journeys and promoting greater use of alternative modes' (Department of the Environment, Transport and the Regions 1998). It is intended that the levy would act as an incentive for occupiers of property to reduce the total number of parking spaces, restricting the maximum number of vehicles for which a licence is sought. As with road user charging there are a number of issues which need to be addressed. These include the need for *complementary policies* to be adopted, such as the introduction or strengthening of existing on-street parking restrictions and the adjustment of tariffs for both on- and off-street parking

Table 11.6 Cross-elasticity of demand between parking price and purpose of journey using public transport.

Journey purpose	Number of trips	Kilometres
Commuting	+0.02	+0.01
Business	+0.01	+0.00
Education	+0.00	+0.00
Other	+0.04	+0.02
Total	+0.02	+0.01

Source: OECD: Contract No. RO-97-SC-2035.

outside the workplace to levels consistent with those applied to workplace parking. There is also the problem of which premises or vehicles should be exempt, if any, and what the exact parking levy per vehicle should be in order to achieve the desired objective. To date, only Nottingham City Council has seriously considered the introduction of a workplace parking levy as a means of reducing congestion. At the time of writing, Nottingham city council intend to charge for workplace parking from 1st April 2012.

Transport for London (2004) gave cross-elasticity estimates between the price of parking and the demand for public transport for various types of journey. This can be seen in Table 11.6 and reveals close to zero cross-elasticities of demand between the price of parking and all types of journey, whether expressed in terms of number of trips or kilometres travelled.

Limiting car ownership and use

Further ways of influencing the demand for road space include:

- *Limit on car ownership*. This could be achieved by imposing either import restrictions, a registration tax or a system of rationing on cars. As yet, this is not something which has been advocated in the UK, but it does occur in certain parts of the world, not only to deal with traffic congestion but also to save energy. For example, in Singapore a quota system is in operation where vehicle owners tender for a 'certificate of entitlement' without which they cannot own a vehicle. (See www.lta.gov.sg for a more detailed explanation.)
- *System of car sharing*. If successful this would also shift demand to the left in Fig. 11.3.

- *Increase in road fuel duty*. This was introduced by the Chancellor of the Exchequer in the March 1993 budget. The road fuel duty was increased by 10% and it was announced that in future budgets the duty would be increased, in real terms, by at least 3%, though this was subsequently abandoned after the fuel price protests of 2000.

Policy options for urban road congestion – supply policies

As well as demand policies to deal with the urban road congestion problem, *supply-side policies* (such as new road building) can be implemented. An urban road building strategy can be examined by the use of Fig. 11.4.

Increasing the number of lanes, or building new roads, will shift the marginal private cost and marginal social cost curves from MPC_1 and MSC_1 respectively, to MPC_2 and MSC_2. The diagram implies that before the road capacity was expanded, congestion occurred beyond a traffic flow of F_1, but now occurs at a point beyond F_4. The reason for this is that road construction increases road capacity, so that an increased flow is now possible before the costs of congestion appear. If demand is taken to be D_2, then a flow of F_5 will now use the road, and although there will be some congestion (note that MSC_2 is greater than MPC_2 at F_5 by the distance GH) this will be somewhat less than the congestion *before* the new road expansion, which was AB in Fig. 11.4.

There is, however, a limitation with this strategy. If the road network is expanded and improved, then individuals who previously used public transport may now begin to use their own car. New traffic will therefore be *generated*, as those who did not make a particular trip previously are now encouraged to do so, and motorists who travelled via a different route may now be persuaded to use the route(s) in question. Also peak and off-peak travel can, to some extent, be viewed as substitutes, so that off-peak travel may fall. It could therefore be argued that increasing a road's capacity will result in more vehicles using the route, i.e. a case of supply generating its own demand. This means that the level of demand may well be underestimated. In fact, demand could become almost perfectly elastic, as with demand curve D_3 in Fig. 11.4. If this were to be the case, then the flow of traffic along the particular route would be F_6 and not F_5, and the social cost which had not been taken into account

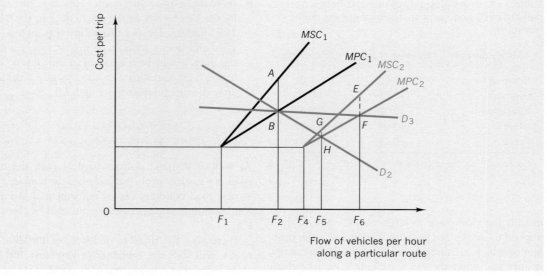

Fig. 11.4 Equilibrium traffic flow: supply-side policies.

would be *EF* and not *GH*. The final situation may not, then, be significantly different from the initial external cost of *AB* in Fig. 11.4. In other words, a similar congestion problem would still persist.

Government transport policy

In July 1998 the government published a White Paper on the Future of Transport entitled 'A New Deal for Transport: Better for Everyone' in which it was recognized that there was a need to improve public transport and reduce car dependency. As such, a commitment was made to create an improved integrated transport system more able to tackle congestion and its associated pollution. The main aim of the White Paper was to 'increase personal choice by improving the alternatives and to secure mobility that is sustainable in the long term'. There was a recognition that road building ('predict and provide') was not the answer to the growth in traffic.

The 2007 White Paper entitled 'Towards a Sustainable Transport System, Supporting Economic Growth in a Low Carbon World' (Department for Transport 2007) continued the theme by stating

that transport has a vital role to play in supporting sustainable economic growth, whilst playing its part in reducing carbon emissions. The White Paper was in essence a response to the Eddington study (2006), which dealt with how to improve transport's contribution to economic growth and productivity, and the Stern Review of the Economics of Climate Change (Stern 2007) which dealt with how transport would play its part in delivering reductions in carbon emissions.

Over the years, the state has attempted to influence transport in a number of ways, concerning quality, quantity, ownership and resource allocation.

Quality

This has been concerned mainly with safety. In 1930 the Road Traffic Act was introduced, which required both bus operators and freight hauliers to license their vehicles with regional Traffic Commissioners. This policy was viewed, essentially, as one of protecting the public interest. This follows from the fact that, for both the road haulier and the bus operator, the capital costs of vehicle purchase are relatively low, so that there is a low barrier to entry into the industry. As a result, profits can be driven down, which in turn could lead to operators trying to reduce their costs, with possibly adverse effects on safety standards. In recent years there have been a number of transport disasters, and this has clearly made the whole area of transport safety a major political issue. An important question is whether increased competition will lead to reduced safety standards!

Quantity

The licensing system has also been used as a form of regulatory control. Successive governments have been of the opinion that quantitative controls on transport were necessary in order to make sure that existing capacity was fully utilized. Such controls have applied to the road haulage and bus industries. One of the implications of licensing has been the cross-subsidization of bus services. Until 1986, the provision of unprofitable services was closely linked to the granting of licences for route monopolies by the traffic commissioners. Although certain services, such as late evenings, weekends and certain rural routes, were unprofitable, they were viewed as being 'socially' worthwhile. The financial losses on such routes were supported from the profits which the operators earned on the more profitable routes, so that cross-subsidization clearly took place. However, cross-subsidization was possible only as long as operators had monopolies; with a deregulated bus sector this was less likely.

Ownership

In the past, railways and parts of the road haulage and bus passenger transport sector have been under public ownership. The main reasons put forward for such ownership include the suggestion that if the subsidization of such services was needed, then it would be easier for the government rather than private companies to control that particular operation. Government control would also allow for improved coordination of services. The government's stance on state ownership has changed, however, in the past 30 years, as with the sale of the National Freight Corporation to its employees in 1982, and of the National Bus Company following the deregulation of the bus industry in 1986 and the franchising of rail services.

Resource allocation

A major area of direct government involvement in the transport sector concerns the large amounts of public expenditure invested in the transport sector.

In the government's Comprehensive Spending Review, October 2010 (see http://www.dft.gov.uk/about/spendingreview) there was a commitment to reducing the deficit while facilitating long-term sustainable growth and addressing carbon emissions. As such, the Spending Review saw the DfT's budget cut by 15% in real terms over the period 2010/11 to 2014/15, with capital funding cut by 11% and the revenue budget cut by 21%. The DfT stated that this would involve the following.

- *Efficiency* – with savings delivered through 'better procurement and management contracts, improved delivery of front line services, savings in rail costs and reduction of lower priority programmes' (Department for Transport 2010).

- *Refocusing lower priority programmes* – which involves making savings through reducing expenditure on lower priority areas, some of which would involve DfT marketing and research activity.

- *Revenue raising* – which involves an increase in the cap on rail fares as well as an increase in the charge to undertake the Dartford crossing. The increase in rail fares is intended to provide investment for important new projects including rolling stock, aimed at reducing overcrowding. The increase in the Dartford crossing charge is aimed at providing funds to assist in an additional crossing.

- *Secure investment in terms of* –
  - £18bn of rail investment;
  - £4bn on Highways Agency projects, capital maintenance and enhancements;
  - £6bn on local transport projects, capital maintenance and enhancements;
  - funding for additional PFI projects; and
  - funding for tube upgrades.

It is intended that both passengers and motorists will benefit from the investment, as will the economy through economic growth.

- *Localism* – in that the government wants to devolve power and greater financial autonomy to local authorities. The idea is that greater local control, participation and accountability is an effective means by which sustainability of local transport systems could 'promote economic growth, minimise the environmental impact of travel, improve public health and address social exclusion' (Department for Transport 2010).

■ *Sustainability* – via priority spending on rail projects which are viewed as sustainable, such as High Speed Rail and Crossrail and ultra low carbon vehicles.

Government intervention in the transport sector, characterized by state monopolies, public ownership and investment based on state priorities, can be contrasted with a '*laissez-faire*' approach. The latter involves leaving the sector to the workings of the free market, with quality, quantity and resource allocation being determined by consumer preferences. In a 'pure' *laissez-faire* situation, transport services are provided by privately owned firms and the finance of those services is based on customer fares. In this free market, there would be no statutory control on entry into the sector and no financial support for those operators facing difficulties. However, the transport sector has not been left to the free market, for many of the reasons mentioned above, although there has been a move in recent years to allow certain parts of the transport sector to operate in a 'freer' market. This has been the case with the private financing and construction of the Channel Tunnel, the deregulation of the bus industry and the private financing of road construction, such as the M6 toll road. There is now a general consensus that road supply cannot realistically be expanded sufficiently to meet demand. The need for demand management policies has therefore become widely accepted, and these will become an increasingly important part of any government's transport policy in the foreseeable future.

Deregulation of the bus industry

Prior to 1930, the local urban and rural bus industry operated in a competitive market structure with no government regulation. There was fierce competition between rival bus companies (using surplus war vehicles) and this period was associated with a high number of accidents, unscheduled and irregular intervention by 'pirate' operators at peak times, and other types of wasteful duplication.

It was for these reasons that, in 1930, the *Road Traffic Act* was introduced, which was to form the basis of bus industry regulation for 50 years. Under the Act, Traffic Commissioners were responsible for the issue of road service licences (a licence being required for each route operated), the quality of vehicles and the level of fares.

The period 1930–80 was therefore a restrictive one for the local bus service industry. A comprehensive public transport network was provided under a protectionist system, with a licence acting as a barrier to entry, since a licence gave the operator a monopoly on a particular route for the duration of the licence. In 1930 the industry was dominated by private bus operators but, as it developed, the state took a progressively larger role, as with the formation in 1968 of the National Bus Company (NBC) and the Scottish Bus Group (SBG). This meant that by 1986 the industry consisted of state-owned operators, the local authority sector and independent companies which mainly operated in the contract hire sector (including school bus provision).

Changes were regarded as necessary by the mid-1980s. There had been a steady decline in patronage, with bus and coach passenger travel falling from 42% of total travel in 1953 to 8% in 1983. The growth in the use of the private car, fare increases in excess of the inflation rate, increased operating costs and the decline in services were seen as the chief reasons for the decline in bus/coach travel.

The 1984 White Paper on Buses stated:

> The total travel market is expanding. New measures are needed urgently to break out of the cycle of rising costs, rising fares, reducing services, so that public transport can win a bigger share of this market. We must get away from the idea that the only future for bus services is to contract painfully at large cost to taxpayers and ratepayers as well as travellers. Competition provides the opportunity for lower fares, new services, more passengers. For these great gains, half measures will not be enough. Within the essential framework of safety regulation and provision for social needs, the obstacles to enterprise, initiative and efficiency must be removed.

The White Paper led to the *1985 Transport Act*, through which (by October 1986) road service licensing requirements were abolished outside London.

Provision was also made in the Act for the privatization of the National Bus Company. The Passenger Transport Executives operating in metropolitan areas were to be converted into independent companies, still owned by the local authorities, but those authorities now had the option to privatize them. Local bus operators had to register their routes and times and to give sufficient notice of withdrawal of services. There was also the introduction of competitive tendering for the unprofitable bus routes.

So the main objective of the 1985 Act was to introduce competition into the bus sector, providing the opportunity for independent bus operators which did not offer licensed services before 1986, now to do so. It was envisaged that there would be a number of benefits from deregulation:

1 increased competition, allowing greater choice for the consumer and providing a service which is more responsive to the preferences of the consumer;

2 a closer relationship between bus operating costs and the fares charged, the reason being the ending of cross-subsidization, whereby certain routes were overcharged in order to subsidize non-profitable routes – this was helped, of course, by the freedom of entry for new operators after 1986, which in principle should compete away any 'monopoly profits' from charging excessive fares on routes, unrelated to costs;

3 providing a greater potential for innovation in bus travel under deregulation, which was less likely in the absence of competition – one such innovation following deregulation has been the introduction of minibus services;

4 a reduction in the subsidies obtained by bus operators to undertake unprofitable services – the revenue support from government had increased from £10m in 1972 to £529m in 1982, and it could be argued that such subsidies created a protective wall behind which bus operators could operate inefficient services.

There were, however, reservations as to the likely success of bus deregulation, most notably the view that it could lead to a wasteful duplication of services on the profitable routes, especially at peak periods, with a resulting increase in the level of congestion in a number of urban areas. Further, it was feared that the intended reduction in the level of subsidy to the bus sector after deregulation might lead to a rise in the level of fares, thereby diminishing bus use.

Bus services since deregulation

In terms of local bus services in England (outside London), there has in fact been an increase in annual bus kilometres travelled. In 1985/86, the year before deregulation, 1,423 million bus kilometres were undertaken, whereas by 2006/07 around 2,190 million bus and coach vehicle kilometres were recorded (Department for Transport 2009).

Although there has been an *increase in bus kilometres travelled* since deregulation, there has also been a *decrease in passenger journeys* in England from 4,808 million in 1985/86 to 4,470 million in 2006/07, a decline of 7%. There is little doubt that deregulation has been a contributing factor to the decline in bus use by passengers in the period following deregulation. One reason, at least immediately after deregulation, is the confusion which passengers experienced due to the changes in service times, routes and operators resulting from deregulation. Higher fares may also have played a part in the reduction in passenger journeys. In Great Britain between 1995 and 2008/07, local bus fares increased by 76.2%, whereas the RPI increased over the same period by only 44.1%.

Airline operations and the growth of low-cost carriers

In recent years there has been a dramatic growth in air travel. This can be seen in Table 11.7 which shows traffic at selected UK airports over the past 10 years. The table reveals a growth at airports such as Luton and East Midlands of 143% and 154% respectively.

Air traffic is forecast to grow rapidly, as illustrated in Table 11.8. Clearly any forecasts have an element of uncertainty; however, even the low forecasts envisage terminal passengers increasing by 60% and 80% for international and domestic passengers respectively between 2010 and 2030.

One of the contributors to air traffic growth in the UK has been the growth in low-cost air travel in terms of passenger numbers, the number of airline operators and the number of airports they operate to and from. There are a number of low-cost operators

Table 11.7 Terminal passenger traffic (arrivals and departures) at selected UK airports, 1994–2008.*

	Millions					
	1998	2000	2002	2004	2006	2008
Gatwick	29.0	31.9	29.5	31.3	34.1	34.2
Heathrow	60.4	64.3	63.0	67.1	67.3	66.9
Luton	4.2	6.1	6.5	7.5	9.4	10.2
Stansted	6.8	11.8	16.0	21.0	23.7	22.3
Birmingham	6.6	7.5	7.9	8.8	9.1	9.6
East Midlands	2.2	2.2	3.2	4.4	4.7	5.6
Manchester	17.2	18.3	18.6	21.0	22.1	21.1

*All traffic: domestic and international.
Source: Adapted from Department for Transport (2009) *Transport Statistics Great Britain 2008*.

Table 11.8 UK forecasts of air traffic demand, terminal passenger traffic 2005–20.

	2010	2020	2030
International			
Low	200	250	320
Mid	210	290	235,360
High	210	300	261,385
Domestic			
Low	50	70	90
Mid	50	70	90
High	50	70	100

Source: Adapted from Department for Transport (2009) *Transport Statistics Great Britain 2008*.

in the UK, most notably Ryanair, easyJet, bmibaby, Thomsonfly and MyTravelLite, and a cursory glance at the website of any low-cost operator indicates the range of origins and destinations served. For example, take the destinations served by two of those low-cost operators from one airport, namely East Midlands, in 2010: Ryanair serves 32 destinations from East Midlands Airport and bmibaby serves 28 destinations.

The growth in low-cost air travel has been remarkable. For example, a news release by Ryanair on November 2010 stated that the number of booked passengers in October 2010 alone was 7 million, up from 6.2 million in October 2009, a 14% increase. In the 12-month period to October 2010, the

total number of booked passengers on Ryanair was 72.5 million.

This growth in low-cost airline operations has been based on employing a number of strategies in order to maintain a tight hold on costs. Such cost-reducing strategies include:

■ operating with only one type of aircraft in order to obtain economies in terms of aircraft maintenance and flexibility in terms of crew utilization;

■ operating a single class with no business or first-class seats, thus allowing more passengers to be carried;

■ selling tickets via the Internet which leads to cost saving as a result of avoiding travel agents' commission;

■ e-ticketing, which dispenses with the need to print airline tickets;

■ utilizing aircraft more efficiently by:

 ■ using less-congested secondary airports, allowing for faster turnaround times;

 ■ not carrying cargo, which takes time to load and unload;

 ■ not providing on-board catering;

 ■ not providing seating allocation.

A key question is whether the growth in low-cost travel can be sustained or whether low-cost operators will need to look for new markets. To some extent this search for new markets is already happening, with operators looking to operate from a wider range of airports to a wider range of destinations.

This growth in air travel has many implications, not least the issues of environmental sustainability and climate change already addressed in Chapter 10.

Conclusion

This chapter has attempted to identify, and analyse, a number of the current issues facing the transport sector, notably road congestion and the role of the state in transport provision. Transport, as a derived demand, is an important sector of the UK economy. In 2008 total household expenditure in the UK was £471.00, of which transport comprised £63.40, the largest category.

The period 1997–2007 saw an 11.4% increase in the demand for passenger transport and this is expected to continue, with the car dominating. Income has been viewed as a major factor in determining that demand and its future growth. Forecasting the future patterns of demand is seen as essential for governments when deciding on the allocation of funds to possible new road or airport developments. The increased reliance on the car has created a major problem of congestion, particularly in urban areas, and in recent years this has become more of a political issue. A number of possible solutions have been examined, originating from both the supply and demand sides. On the supply side, it is clear that it is not possible to provide sufficient road capacity to meet the likely growth in demand. Demand needs therefore to be 'managed', and demand-side policies have been extensively used. Road user charging is viewed by many to be the best method of dealing with the congestion problem, albeit part of a package of measures.

The public sector plays an important role in the transport sector, as regards both its expenditure on such aspects as the national roads system and its ownership of parts of the sector. The last 30 years have, however, seen a move towards a transport sector operating in a 'freer' market. Major parts of the sector have been privatized, the bus industry has been deregulated and there has been increased private-sector involvement in the provision of the transport infrastructure. This chapter has sought to examine the possible reasons for this move towards a free-market sector, together with the likely advantages and disadvantages. It has also made reference to air travel and to the increasingly important low-cost carriers.

Key points

- In the 1950s only 25% of passenger journeys were by car; today the figure has risen to over 80%.

- Transport is a service which is a *derived* demand, with important peak and off-peak characteristics.

- Transport, particularly road transport, is a major source of pollution and of other externalities, e.g. congestion.

- A *speed–flow curve* is a useful means of analysing congestion.

- The RAC estimates that congestion costs the motorist in the UK around £23bn in lost time per annum.

- Policy options to deal with congestion are various. Those involving *demand* include road user charging, subsidies to public transport, parking restrictions and limits to car ownership. Those involving *supply* include more extensive and better integrated transport networks.

- Passenger air traffic has grown dramatically over recent years, especially via the low-cost carriers.

Now try the self-check questions for this chapter on the Companion Website. You will also find useful links to relevant websites.

References and further reading

Button, K. (2010) *Transport Economics* (3rd edn), Cheltenham, Edward Elgar.

Department for Transport (1989) *National Road Traffic Forecasts*, London, HMSO.

Department for Transport (2004) *The Future for Transport: a Network for 2030*, London, The Stationery Office.

Department for Transport (2006) *Transport Statistics Great Britain 2005*, London, The Stationery Office.

Department for Tansport (2007) *Towards a Sustainable Transport System: Supporting Economic Growth in a Low Carbon World*, October, London.

Department for Transport (2009) *Transport Statistics Great Britain 2008*, London, The Stationery Office.

Department for Transport (2010) *Government Comprehensive Spending Review*, available at: http://www.dft.gov.uk/about/spendingreview (accessed February 2011).

Department of the Environment, Transport and the Regions (1998) *A New Deal for Transport: Better for Everyone*, Cm. 3950, London, The Stationery Office.

Department of the Environment, Transport and the Regions (2000) *Transport 2010: The 10 Year Plan*, London, The Stationery Office.

Department of Transport (1984) *Buses*, Cmnd 9300, London, HMSO.

Eddington, R. (2006) *The Eddington Transport Study: The Case for Change*, London, HM Treasury.

Glaister, S. (2009) *Motoring Towards 2050, Roads: A Utility in Need of a Strategy?* London, RAC Foundation, 11 June.

Goodwin, P. B. (1990) Demographic impacts, social consequences, and the transport debate, *Oxford Review of Economic Policy*, 6(2): 76–90.

House of Commons Transport Committee (1993) *Fourth Report, The Government's Proposals for the Deregulation of Buses in London*, London, HMSO.

House of Commons Transport Committee (2003) *First Report of Session 2002–03 Urban Charging Schemes*, HC390-I, London, The Stationery Office.

NERA (1997) *The Costs of Road Congestion in Great Britain*, NERA Briefing Paper, New York, National Economic Research Associates.

Newbery, D. M. (1990) Pricing and congestion: economic principles relevant to pricing roads, *Oxford Review of Economic Policy*, 6(2): 22–38.

ONS (2009) *Family Spending, a Report on the 2004–05 Expenditure and Food Survey*, London, Office for National Statistics.

Page, S. (2009) *Transport and Tourism: Global Perspectives* (3rd edn), Harlow, Financial Times/Prentice Hall.

RAC (2002) *Motoring Towards 2050*, May, London.

Schmidtchen, D., Koboldt, C., Helstroffer, J., Will, B. and Haas, G. (2010) *Transport, Welfare and Externalities*, Cheltenham, Edward Elgar.

Stern, N. (2007) *The Economics of Climate Change: The Stern Review*, Cambridge, Cambridge University Press.

TRACE (1999), *Elasticity Handbook: Elasticities for Prototypical Contexts, Costs of Private Road Travel and Their Effects On Demand, Including Short and Long Term Elasticities*, Report to the European Commission, Directorate-General for Transport, Contract No: RO-97-SC.2035.

Transport for London (TfL) (2004) *The Demand for Public Transport: a Practical Guide*, TRL Report, London.

Transport for London (2006) *Central London Congestion Charging, Impacts Monitoring, Fourth Annual Report*, London.

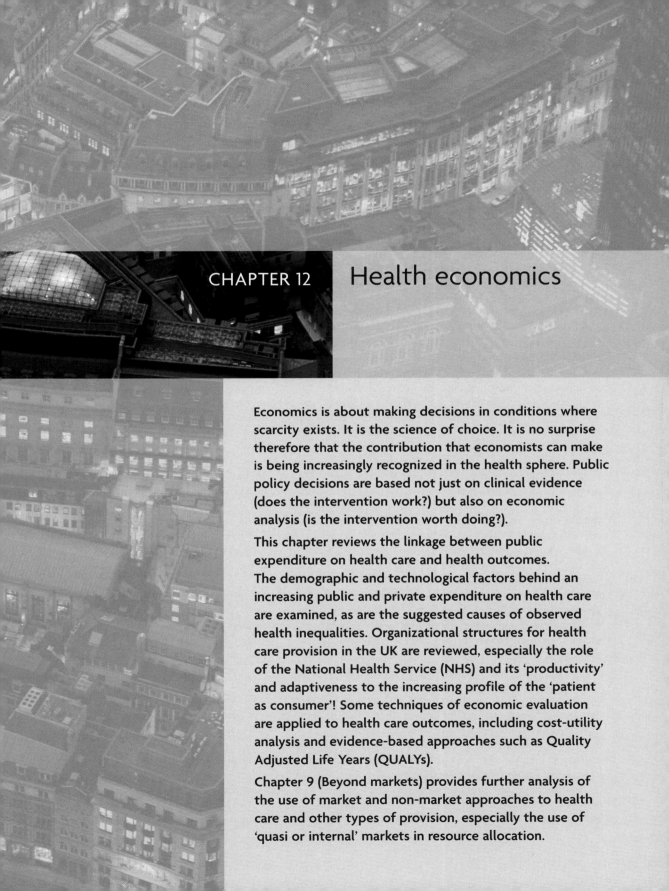

CHAPTER 12   Health economics

Economics is about making decisions in conditions where scarcity exists. It is the science of choice. It is no surprise therefore that the contribution that economists can make is being increasingly recognized in the health sphere. Public policy decisions are based not just on clinical evidence (does the intervention work?) but also on economic analysis (is the intervention worth doing?).

This chapter reviews the linkage between public expenditure on health care and health outcomes. The demographic and technological factors behind an increasing public and private expenditure on health care are examined, as are the suggested causes of observed health inequalities. Organizational structures for health care provision in the UK are reviewed, especially the role of the National Health Service (NHS) and its 'productivity' and adaptiveness to the increasing profile of the 'patient as consumer'! Some techniques of economic evaluation are applied to health care outcomes, including cost-utility analysis and evidence-based approaches such as Quality Adjusted Life Years (QUALYs).

Chapter 9 (Beyond markets) provides further analysis of the use of market and non-market approaches to health care and other types of provision, especially the use of 'quasi or internal' markets in resource allocation.

Health economics, health and health care

The policy-maker's objective is to improve the health of the population – that is, to reduce the incidence of disease and death. Spending on health care is widely regarded as one of the things that promotes this, the assumption being that the more you spend on health care the healthier the population will be, other things being equal. But other things are *not* equal, because the health of the population depends not just on the resources devoted to health care but also on the resources devoted to other areas of public and private spending. Spending on health involves an opportunity cost. The policy-maker (e.g. the Chancellor of the Exchequer) will recognize that the more you spend on health, the less will be available to spend on things such as education, local authority sports facilities, policing and the prison service, all of which will have an impact on the health of the community. Moreover, many economists believe that public spending in total has an opportunity cost – the private spending that it displaces (See also 'Crowding out' theory in Chapter 18, p. 364). If we decide we want to spend more on public services we must recognize that those services have to be paid for by increased taxation and as a result people's private consumption will fall. That private consumption may have included things such as food (buying better quality but more expensive food); heating (which is particularly important for the elderly) or a winter holiday (to provide a spiritual uplift and a physical boost to see the elderly through the often cold winter). All of these are goods and services that the individual *chooses* to consume because they derive satisfaction or wellbeing from them. The consumption of these things makes them feel better. People spend their own money buying things from which they derive utility – that is the economist's definition of a 'rational' economic agent. So if the policy-maker decides (via taxation) to deliberately reduce the capacity of households to purchase goods and services so that the increased tax receipts can be channelled to the provision of additional health care, then the policy-maker has to be certain that the utility so derived is at least as great as that which the individual would have derived from spending his or her own money.

Additionally, we should recognize that people make decisions about their own health – sometimes we call them 'lifestyle choices'. There can be few people who do not recognize, in principle at least, that smoking, excessive alcohol consumption, poor diet and lack of exercise potentially damage their health. Thus in short we need to recognize that the *health of the population* and the provision of *health care* are two quite distinct concepts.

How much do we spend?

In the UK more than 80% of all spending on health care is paid for by the state in the form of the National Health Service (the NHS). Spending on the NHS constitutes the largest single area of spending on goods and services – bigger than spending on education and much bigger than spending on defence. Figure 12.1 shows a breakdown of public spending in the UK in 2010–11, with spending on health (which here means the NHS) the second largest slice of the pie, totalling £122bn. The only slice of the pie that is larger is spending on 'social protection' (£194bn), which is spending on 'welfare' – such as the state retirement pension and incapacity benefit – for which there is no direct output and is therefore regarded as a 'transfer payment' under National Income accounting conventions. In contrast, the NHS *does* produce an output and we call that output 'health care', which is part of the measured output of the economy. At this point, we will assume that the money spent on purchasing health care is equal to the value of the health care produced. We revisit this point later (p. 243).

In recent years, spending on the NHS has increased. However, should we measure this in 'money terms' (£bn) or in 'real terms' (£bn adjusted for inflations)? Using 'real terms' has the advantage of our being better able to compare one year with another, and to more accurately calculate the growth of purchasing capacity over time. But even this is not totally satisfactory. Normally the economy grows year on year (except in a recession such as that in the period 2008–10), and in a growing economy we would expect public spending in total, and in terms of its components, also to grow. Thus it might make more sense to calculate *health spending as a percentage of GDP*, which is normally what we do since both the numerator and the denominator of the expression will be subject to a similar rate of inflation. Even this is a slight simplification, however, because the rate of inflation in the health sector may be higher than the average in the rest of the economy! New technologies

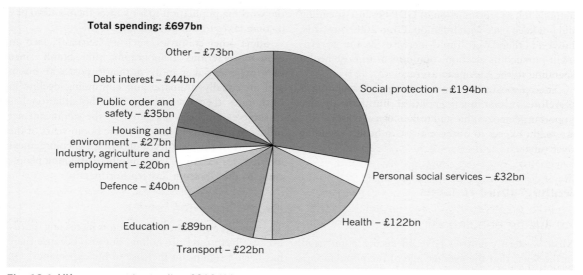

Fig. 12.1 UK government spending 2010/11.
Source: HM Treasury (2010a) *Budget 2010: copy of economic and fiscal strategy report and financial statement and budget report – June 2010*, p. 5. Available at: http://www.hm-treasury.gov.uk/d/junebudget_complete.pdf

are invariably very expensive and health care is highly labour intensive, with labour-saving cost reductions more difficult to achieve in health care than they are, for example, in car manufacture or banking.

One more caveat before we look at the data. We must distinguish between 'spending on health' and 'public spending on health', as the former includes private spending on health care such as paying to go to a private consultant or dentist.

Figure 12.2 shows public spending on health (that is spending on the NHS) as a percentage of GDP. It has risen from about 4.5% of GDP in the late 1980s to about 8.5% of GDP in 2010. In other words, about £1 in every £12 of public spending spent in the economy is spent on the NHS.

As Fig. 12.2 shows, there was only a small rise in the late 1980s and 1990s, and in the early years of the former Labour government (1997–2000) spending

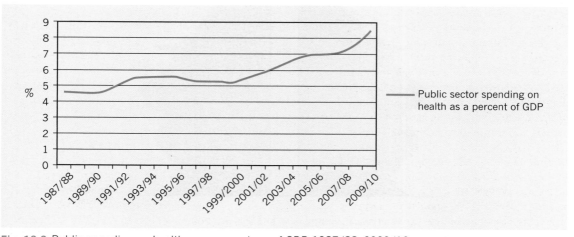

Fig. 12.2 Public spending on health as a percentage of GDP 1987/88–2009/10.
Source: Data from HM Treasury (2010b) *Public Expenditure Statistical Analysis 2010*, Tables 4.2, 4.3 and 4.4. Available at: http//www.hm-treasury.gov.uk/d/pesa_2010_complete.pdf

actually fell as a proportion of GDP because spending did not keep pace with inflation. From 2000 onwards, however, there were rapid increases as the government pursued its election commitment to raise health spending to the European average.

The reason for the increase in health spending is therefore, at least in part, political. But there are also important demographic and technological reasons why we might expect to observe a rise in health spending over time.

Demographic reasons

An ageing population

Most western countries have an ageing population, in the sense that the average age of the population is increasing. Although the post-war baby boom (1946–50) is well known, the biggest bulge in the population in the UK is represented by those who, in 2009, were in their mid-40s, as can be seen from Fig. 12.3.

In 2030 the individuals from that cohort will be in their mid-60s. They will be placing considerable demands on the health and social services sectors as they age, but there will be fewer younger people in the working population to look after them and to pay income taxes to fund their care.

Some other countries, such as Germany, face an even more serious 'demographic time bomb' since they experienced a more dramatic post-war boom and an equally dramatic and continuing decline in birth rates thereafter. In the UK the situation has to some extent been mitigated by the significant net inflow of migrants in the economic boom years of the early part of this century. Following EU enlargement in 2004, for example, large numbers of young people came to the UK from Eastern Europe.

People are living longer

The average age of the population is increasing, partly because birth rates are falling, but also because there has been a significant increase in life expectancy. On average people live to a much greater age than they would have done a century ago. Figure 12.4 shows that in 1900 on average women lived only to the age of 45, yet a woman born a century later in 2001 could expect to live to the age of 80. This increase in average life expectancy is itself also made up of two factors – individuals are living longer certainly, but in addition fewer individuals die young than would have

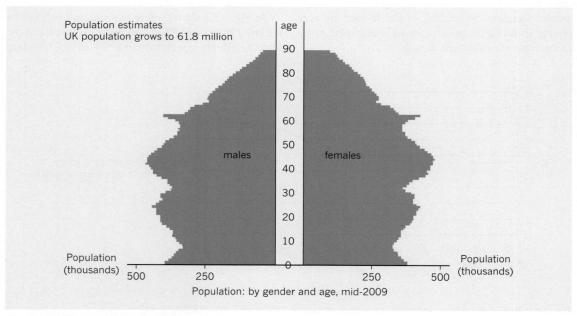

Fig. 12.3 UK population mid-2009.
Source: ONS (2010) *Population Estimates*. Available at: http://www.statistics.gov.uk/CCI/nuqqet.asp?ID=6

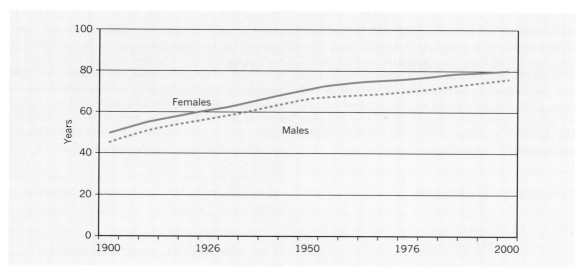

Fig. 12.4 Life expectancy at birth, England, 1900–2001.
Source: Taken from Wanless (2003) *Securing Good Health for the Whole Population: population health trends*, p. 5.

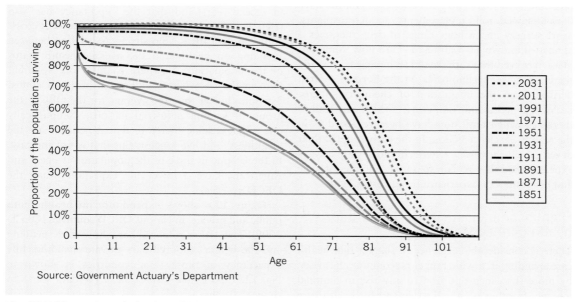

Source: Government Actuary's Department

Fig. 12.5 The rectangularization of life curve, England and Wales, 1851–2031.
Source: Taken from Wanless (2003) *Securing Good Health for the Whole Population: population health trends*, p. 6.

been the case a century ago. This is illustrated by the *rectangularization of life curve* shown in Fig. 12.5. A century ago some people died as infants, some in childhood, some in their twenties, some in their thirties and so on. Now most people in advanced societies live to a 'ripe old age' and then die. This results in the curve shown in Fig. 12.5 becoming increasingly rectangular rather than a smooth downward-sloping curve.

While this longevity is to be celebrated, it nevertheless places greater demands on the health and social services; the very services which, ironically, are partly responsible for this increased longevity! The last year of an individual's life is likely to be the time when he or she places the greatest demands on the health services.

In 2010 some 17% of the UK population is aged over 65 years, compared to only 11% in 1951, and some 4.5% is aged over 80 years, compared to only 1.4% in 1951. As noted above, those over 75 years, together with new born infants, are the main source of increased health care expenditure.

Technological reasons

We can do more – but it's more expensive

The growth of NHS spending is also partly due to technological advance – the increased range and complexity of interventions that are now available. When the NHS was founded in 1948 it promised to provide care for people 'from cradle to grave', yet the technological possibilities available 60 years later could hardly have been imagined. Joint replacements, organ transplants, heart surgery and a huge range of drug therapies – almost unknown 60 years ago – are now commonplace. Yet even these are the old technologies. Already there are newer technologies on the horizon – often derived from the integration of chemistry, microbiology, genetics and computing – which may lead to therapies which until now have been regarded as in the realms of science fiction. In the early stage of their development, however, new technologies are always expensive and they remain so until economies of scale and economies of experience bring costs down.

High income elasticity of demand for health care services

There is considerable evidence to suggest that health care spending in a wide range of economies has risen by more than in proportion to any rise in national income. In other words, the demand for health care services is highly income elastic. This is, of course, partly a reflection of 'higher expectations', such as the greater awareness by patients of new, if expensive, treatments and of patient rights and opportunities (Patients Charter).

Business cycle impacts

With the global recessionary conditions following the collapse of the sub-prime market in 2007/8 (see Chapter 30), the reduction in economic activity has arguably itself resulted in additional health care expenditure. Evidence has begun to accumulate that health care needs are related to aspects of deprivation, such as unemployment, low income, etc. We also note in Chapter 23 that each successive business cycle has tended to exhibit a higher level of unemployment at any given stage than have previous business cycles. Evidence has been collected which indicates that those Regional Health Authorities in the UK with the highest unemployment rates are those which issue the most prescriptions per year, suggesting that rising unemployment is associated with increasing ill health.

If we spent more, would people be healthier?

International comparisons of health spending show that health spending has increased almost everywhere in recent years and that life expectancy has also risen. Paradoxically, however, when we look at cross-sectional data there is no strong association between spending on health and the average health status of the population. Nowhere is this more apparent than in the US where spending on health is almost 2.5 times higher than the average for the OECD (the group of leading industrial nations). Simplistically one might assume therefore that Americans are the 'healthiest' and live longest. But that is not the case. In the US one in three of the population is obese and Americans have a lower life expectancy than the OECD average.

Figure 12.6 shows expenditure on health, both public and private, in various OECD countries (OECD 2009). The darker coloured bars show state spending and the lighter coloured bars private spending. Life expectancy in those same countries is shown in Fig. 12.7 and casual inspection of the data seems to show that there is only a weak relationship between the health expenditure per capita and life expectancy. Thus, for example, Japan spends less on health care per capita than the average for the OECD but has the highest life expectancy of any country, and the US has the highest health care expenditure per capita, being far higher than anywhere else in the world, but has a life expectancy below the OECD average.

Figure 12.8 plots these two indices on the same graph in order to explore the strength of the relationship

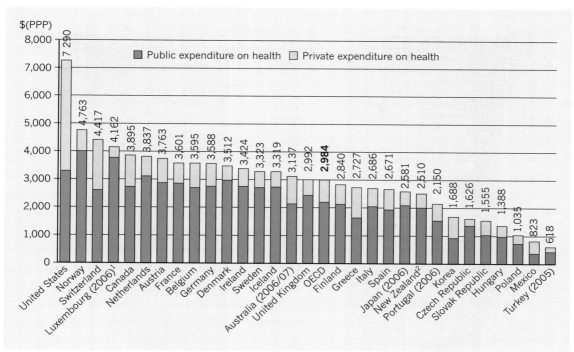

Fig. 12.6 Total health expenditure per capita, public and private 2007.
[1]Health expenditure is for the insured population rather than resident population.
[2]Current health expenditure converted from national currencies to US dollars using purchasing power parities (PPP).
Source: OECD (2009) *OECD Health Data 2009*. Available at: www.oecd.org/health/healthdata

between health spending and life expectancy. If there were a strong relationship between health spending and life expectancy, all the points (all the countries) would lie close to a line[1]. That line would have a positive slope, indicating that the more you spend on health, the healthier the population becomes. The solid line in Fig. 12.8 has a positive slope, but the data points (the countries) do not fit the line very closely. Countries above the line, such as Japan, seem to be healthier than one would predict on the basis of their spending. Countries below the line, such as Hungary, are less healthy than one would predict on the basis of their spending. The US stands out as the country with the highest expenditure, but only average life expectancy. In short, spending on health care is not a very good predictor of life expectancy. The value of the R^2 statistic shows that only about half (55%) of the variation in life expectancy can be explained by variations in health spending per capita[2].

Moreover, the 'line of best fit' (the solid line), though upward-sloping, is not straight. Its slope diminishes, suggesting that for advanced countries further increases in health care spending become less and less effective in producing increases in life expectancy. The more you spend, the less extra benefit you get from it. Spending on health care has *diminishing marginal effectiveness*.

Health inequalities

So why is it that countries that spend more on health do not necessarily have a healthier population? There are a number of possible explanations. One is that there are countervailing lifestyle factors. For example, by international definitions 30% of the American population is obese (20% for the UK). A second is that there are genetic factors involved! There almost certainly are genetic predispositions for most diseases, but given the polyglot nature of the American

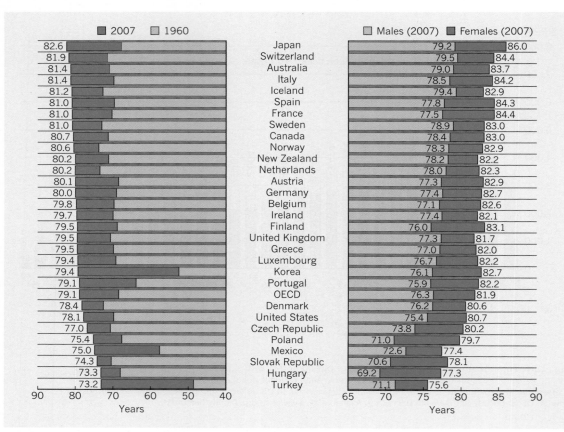

Fig. 12.7 Life expectancy in OECD countries.
Source: OECD (2009) *OECD Health Data 2009*. Available from: www.oecd.org/health/healthdata

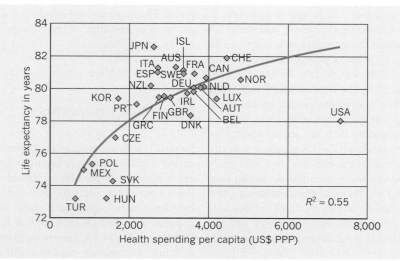

Fig. 12.8 The relationship between spending on health and life expectancy.
Source: OECD (2009) *OECD Health Data 2009*. Available from: www.oecd.org/health/healthdata

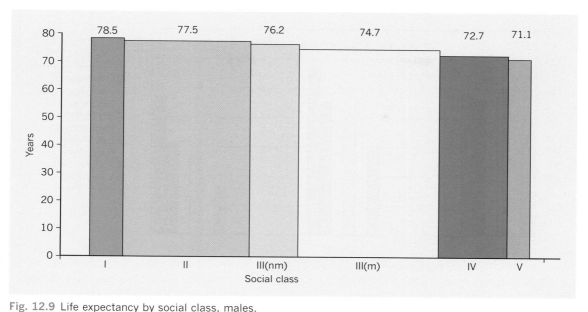

Fig. 12.9 Life expectancy by social class, males.
Note: Width is proportionate to population in each category.
Source: Taken from Wanlass (2003), *Securing Good Health for the Whole Population: Population health trends*, p. 9.

gene pool this explanation seems inadequate. Or perhaps the American health care system is simply inefficient so that resources are squandered? This is clearly one possible explanation, but there is a further possible explanation buried in the aggregate data.

The health status of a population can be summarized by things such as morbidity rates and mortality rates. When we look at these, we are necessarily looking at averages. A *morbidity rate*, for example, is calculated as the number of people with a particular disease per 100,000 population. A *mortality rate* is calculated as the number of people who die (of a particular disease) per 100,000 population. Average life expectancy is based on the age of all the individuals who die in a given year, and if health status is unequally distributed in the population the unhealthy minority will bring down the average life expectancy.

In all countries health status is indeed unequally distributed! The rich are healthier and live longer. The poor are unhealthier and die younger. The London Borough of Kensington and Chelsea has the highest life expectancy (for women) and (not coincidentally) has the highest income. The lowest life expectancy (for men) is in Manchester which also has one of the lowest levels of income per capita. So income is a predictor of health status, but income alone is a rather crude predictor and social scientists

have tended instead to concentrate on *social class*, as defined by occupation.

Figure 12.9 shows life expectancy for males in each of the six social classes. The classifications are the conventional ones adopted by social scientists. Reading from left to right:

I: professional

II: managerial and technical

III(nm): skilled non-manual

III(m):   skilled manual

IV: semi-skilled manual

V: unskilled

It is clear from Fig. 12.9 that life expectancy in the UK depends on occupation. Teachers and lawyers, on average, live to the age of 78.5 years. A refuse collector can expect to live for only 71.1 years. So on average men in social class I live 7.4 years longer than those in social class V. Obviously social class is correlated with income, but social class carries with it the notion of education and social norms. Those higher up the social scale may be more aware of those factors that promote good health – such as diet and exercise – and it may be these things, rather than income itself, that are the main causal factors.

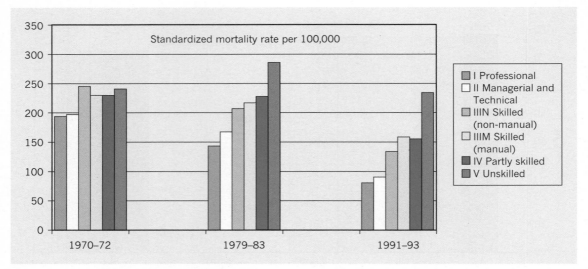

Fig. 12.10 Coronary heart disease mortality in males, England and Wales, by social class over three decades.
Source: Taken from Wanless (2003), *Securing Good Health for the Whole Population: Population health trends*, p. 9.

The fact that health status is related to social class has been known for some time, since at least 1980 and the publication of the Black Report. This same report also suggested that inequalities were increasing over time. The Wanless Report published in 2003 seemed to confirm this. Figure 12.10 is taken from the Wanless Report and shows mortality rates by coronary heart disease (CHD) in men for three periods – the early 1970s, the early 1980s and the early 1990s. The social classes are the same as those in the previous figure. If you imagine for each time period putting a ruler between the middle of the lowest bar and the middle of the highest bar, then the slope of the ruler would be what is known as the *social class gradient*. Figure 12.10 clearly shows that the social class gradient has become steeper – in other words, health inequality has increased. We need to explore the reasons for this in more detail. There seems to have been a significant reduction in CHD in social class I – the incidence of CHD in the 1990s was only about a third of what it was two decades earlier. This may be due to a better knowledge amongst this social group about the dangers and causes of CHD, and to a consequent take-up of anti-hypertensive drugs, and to a reduction in smoking and improved diet. In other words, the message has got through to middle class people. But for people in social class V either the message has not got through or they have chosen to ignore it, because the incidence of CHD is not markedly different to what it was two decades earlier.

What are the implications of this health divide? Firstly, it may partly explain why the health status of the American population is so low, given the amount spent on health care. The distribution of income in the US is very uneven and there is a much bigger gap between the rich and the poor than in European societies. Middle class people in the US may in fact have quite a good health status, but the low health status of the poor will bring down the average.

In a UK context, the implication is probably that the most effective way of raising the overall health status of the population is to target these hard-to-reach groups. By definition, however, they are hard to reach!

 The organization of the NHS in England

The NHS is huge. It employs over a million people and it is often claimed that the only organizations in the world that employ more people are the Indian railways (about 1.6 million) and the People's Liberation Army of China (about 2.25 million active troops). From its inception the NHS was a somewhat monolithic organisation . . .

For the first time, hospitals, doctors, nurses, pharmacists, opticians and dentists are brought together under one umbrella organisation to provide services that are free for all at the point of delivery. (NHS History, 1948) . . . and it continued to operate in this way for the next 40 years. By the early 1990s, however, the rigidities and inefficiencies of state run monopolies were the subject of increasing criticism and a process of structural reform was begun. In 1990 the NHS Community Care Act established health authorities with the responsibility for managing their own budgets. These health authorities became 'purchasers'. Together with GP 'fundholders', they would buy health care from the 'providers' – the hospitals and other health organizations – who in turn also became independent organizations with their own managements (NHS trusts). This was the beginning of the 'purchaser–provider split' (the so-called 'internal market'). Part of the rationale for this was to break up the old NHS monopoly and to introduce market reforms (see also Chapter 9). Competition, it was felt, would act as a spur to efficiency. It may be worth recalling the political climate of the time. Margaret Thatcher had been elected to power in 1979 and the 1980s had seen a wave of privatizations, such as British Telecom and British Gas, that had brought some significant productivity gains.

Moreover, there was a growing feeling in the health service that the hospitals had too much power and influence, perhaps because historically this was where the status of the medical profession was at its highest, particularly amongst consultant surgeons. The reforms would 'challenge the domination of *hospitals* within a health service that was becoming increasingly focused on services *within the community*' (NHS History 1990). Confusingly, both the demanders (purchasers) and suppliers (providers) became known as 'trusts' – Primary Care Trusts (PCTs) would buy services from hospital trusts that were deemed to provide 'secondary care'. To most members of the lay public, this nomenclature is probably confusing, since when most people think of the NHS their immediate mental image is that of a hospital setting. In funding terms, however, only 20% of the NHS budget goes to secondary care. The remaining 80% goes to the primary care sector dominated by the PCTs that currently are responsible for the organization of GP practices, community nurses,

opticians, dentists, pharmacists and so on. The way that the system is supposed to work is illustrated in Fig. 12.11 – an organizational map produced by NHS England.

The organization of the NHS is hugely complex and – in the opinion of some critics – a confusing patchwork of overlapping responsibilities. To the layman, the incomprehensibility of the organizational structure is compounded by the fact that many parts of the structure are referred to by names that give little clue about what they actually do. The name 'trust' is now applied to almost all organizational units that form part of the NHS – the name implying a degree of autonomy for the management of that part of the overall NHS structure. Thus hospitals are called 'acute trusts', except of course for those that are called 'foundation trusts'. In addition, there are 'ambulance trusts', 'mental health trusts' and 'care trusts'. The geographical boundaries of these trusts are not necessarily the same! There is also an additional layer of regional management called the Strategic Health Authorities (SHAs), originally 28 in number but reorganised down to 10 in 2006. Each of the SHAs provides regional management for a geographical area. Don't confuse these SHAs with the other SHAs which are Special Health Authorities. These are national 'arm's length' bodies such as the National Patient Safety Agency, the National Institute for Health and Clinical Excellence, and the NHS Appointments Commission.

The organizational map shown in Fig. 12.11 is sometimes used by PCTs to explain their function to households. Closer inspection, however, shows that Fig. 12.11 is not a good representation of the structure. SHAs (i.e. the regional SHAs) should have an arrow going in to the secondary care sector not into PCTs. And it is not entirely clear what exactly the other arrows are meant to imply!

In 2010 the incoming Coalition government announced plans for (another) fundamental reform of the NHS. The fundamental idea of purchaser and provider would remain, but the role of the PCT in co-ordinating the demands of purchasers would be abolished. Management responsibility for purchasing services would go back to GPs, which is an echo of the pre-existing 'GP fund holding' system that the PCTs replaced. On the supply side, many of the arm's length bodies would be abolished or have their functions subsumed into other parts of the NHS. The regional tier of the NHS would be removed at the same time.

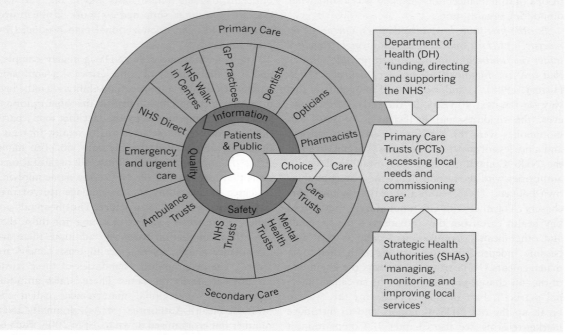

Fig. 12.11 Primary care and secondary care.
Source: NHS (2010b).

In summary, the early reforms of the 1990s were inspired by the desire to reduce the domination of the hospitals in the provision of health care. More recently, however, reforms have emphasised the importance of the patient. It was stated by various official sources that Primary care trusts (PCTs) and ambulance trusts were to be reorganised as part of the government's drive to create a patient-led NHS.

The patient as consumer

The world has changed since the NHS was established in 1948. At that time, people were quite deferential towards authority and the NHS was regarded by many as a paternalistic organization which fostered a culture of dependency. People had limited choice and little say in what happened to them. The NHS would look after you 'from cradle to grave' provided you did what you were told. The ethos has been summed up by the phrase: 'doctor knows best'.

The reforms that were initiated from 1990 onward sought to encourage patients to see themselves as consumers, with the right (and the responsibility) to make informed choices about the services that they consumed. This notion, of course, applies not just to health care but to the education sector and to public services generally. In the health sector it was often accompanied by a change in the words used – patients became 'service users' and sometimes even 'consumers'. In the private healthcare sector the balance of power between buyer and seller in the marketplace has always been more evenly divided. The relationship between patient and physician has always been more equal, as emphasized in this advertising slogan from the private provider, BUPA, which read simply

'The patient will see you now, doctor.'

A senior Department of Health source said: 'Gone will be the paternalistic days of being told by the doctor that you can't have physiotherapy for your back pain, or referral to an orthopaedic consultant. If you have prostate cancer, you will get the information you need to choose whether to go for an operation or opt for a period of watchful waiting. If you need a hysterectomy, you will be told about the benefits and risks of minimally invasive surgery.' (Carvel 2009)

These reforms continue. Passive patients are en-couraged to become active, informed consumers who work with health service specialists to make sensible and informed decisions about the range of inter-ventions available to them. The IT revolution has, of course, been an enabling factor; no matter what you think you may be suffering from, the Internet allows you to research into your condition. The range of information available – often from private providers in the USA – is overwhelming. Information is also available from bodies such as NICE (The National Institute for Health and Clinical Excellence) where members of the lay public can have access to infor-mation which, in former times, would have been restricted to members of the medical and nursing professions. If you really want to choose a hospital on the basis of the rate of HCAI (Healthcare Associated Infections such as MRSA) then that information is also publically available from the web (look under 'h' in the Health Protection Agency website).

The NHS workforce

The NHS is the largest employer in Europe, but exactly how many people work for it? Suppose we restrict our analysis to England (thus excluding Wales, Scotland and Northern Ireland) and to head-counts (multiply the headcount figures by around 0.75 to arrive at full-time equivalents). We would then find that the workforce has increased from about 1.1 million in 1999 to over 1.4 million in 2009. The breakdown is shown in Table 12.1.

One criticism often levelled at the NHS is that there are too many staff employed in administrative positions. Politicians frequently talk about 'cutting bureaucracy' while maintaining 'front line staff'. The figures in the table suggest that roughly half of those employed in the NHS are in non-clinical posts – that is they are not qualified doctors, nurses or technical staff. They are administrative staff working in hospi-tals, GP surgeries or in central services such as IT. Over the last ten years the number of administrative staff has increased less rapidly than the number of clinical staff. What shows up most dramatically from the data, however, is the growth in the numbers of managers and senior manager (shown in the penulti-mate row) which has been two or three times greater than that for other grades of staff. Table 12.1 also shows that doctors account for about 10% of the workforce and that there are about three times as many nursing staff as there are doctors.

One other important feature of the NHS workforce is that doctors are relatively expensive to employ. Medicine has always been one of the highest paid professions but, in recent years, doctors' earnings have increased significantly more than those of other professional workers such as lawyers, accountants and university lecturers. In the UK the *Annual Survey of Hours and Earnings* (ASHE) provides data on the earnings of various occupational groups based on a sample taken from HM Revenue and Customs PAYE records. Table 12.2 shows annual earnings for a selection of occupations, with data on both the median and the mean earnings presented. In general, if the mean is above the median, it is an indication

Table 12.1 NHS workforce (headcounts) in England (thousands).

	1999	2009	% of total in 2009	Average annual % change 1999–2009
Doctors	95	141	10	4
Nurses	330	417	29	2.4
Scientific and technical staff	102	150	10	3.9
Ambulance staff	15	18	1	1.9
Support to clinical staff	297	378	26	2
Other GP practice staff	86	92	6	0.7
NHS infrastructure support	171	236	16	3.3
of which Managers and Senior Managers	*24*	*45*	*3*	*11.9*
TOTAL	1098	1432	100	2.7

Source: NHS (2010a) *NHS Staff 1999–2009 Overview.*

Table 12.2 Annual salary (gross), 2009, all employee jobs (£).

	Median	Mean	20th percentile	80th percentile
All employees	21,320	26,470	11,246	35,733
Medical practitioners	67,179	73,598	33,452	113,341
Solicitors, lawyers, judges	44,698	55,723	27,752	78,847
Corporate managers	37,437	49,527	23,487	61,926
HE teaching professionals	32,461	31,642	19,274	42,004
Nurses	25,700	24,958	16,044	33,163

Source: ONS (2010a) *Annual Survey of Hours and Earnings (ASHE)*.

that the earnings distribution is skewed (has its tail) towards the right – for example, for 'all employees' the fact that the mean exceeds the median suggests that a few individuals receive very large salaries and this pulls the mean upwards in the direction of the skew. Notice that this is also true for doctors and solicitors, but that the reverse is true for nurses and HE teaching professionals – some individuals receive very low incomes and this skew (tail) to the left pulls the average (the mean) down. The table also reports the salary corresponding to the 20th percentile and the 80th percentile points. Thus 20% of all employees earn less than £11,246 per year and 20% of all employees earn more than £35,733.

What is clear is that doctors are relatively well paid. The average salary is about three times that of 'all employees' and they earn more than corporate managers, solicitors and judges. Twenty percent of doctors earn more than £113,341 per annum and doctors earn about three times as much as nurses.

Substituting factors of production

So what might be the implication of these salary levels? In the health care industry various factor *inputs* are used to produce an *output*. The inputs are various types of labour (doctors, nurses, radiographers, dental receptionists), fixed capital (hospital buildings and other equipment such as CAT scanners and ambulances) and consumables (bandages and catheters, etc.). These inputs are combined to produce an output which is health care.

In a competitive industry, if the price of a particular factor input increases (relative to the price of other inputs) the response will normally be to seek ways of using less of the factor that is now more expensive and more of other factors that are now relatively less expensive. This assumes that *factor substitutability* is possible, at least to some extent. The alternative to factors being substitutable would be to assume that factor inputs must always be combined in *fixed proportions* to produce output!

Substitutability will also apply to different types of labour within the labour market. If the price of a particular type of labour goes up, producers will seek ways of using less of the labour that has become relatively more expensive and more of the cheaper substitute. However, the extent to which producers can do so depends on the *elasticity of demand* for the labour in question. In 1890 in *Principles of Economics* Alfred Marshall explained that the demand for labour is a *derived demand*. It is derived from the demand for the final product or service that it helps to create (see also Chapter 14, p. 286).

The extent to which the demand for a particular type of labour will be sensitive to price changes (its elasticity) will depend on three things. Specifically, the demand for a particular type of labour will be *more inelastic*:

- the more inelastic is the demand for the final product;
- the smaller is the *proportion* of total costs accounted for by the labour in question;
- the more *essential* is the labour in producing the final product.

We could argue that in a competitive labour market doctors can command high wages because the demand for their services is not very price sensitive (the demand for their services is inelastic). Analysing this in terms of Marshall's principles the reasons for this are as follows.

1 The demand for the services of health care workers is inelastic because the demand for health care is itself inelastic.

2 There are a relatively small number of doctors in comparison to other health care workers such as nurses (there are three times as many nurses as doctors). Doctors therefore account for only a small proportion of total costs.

3 Doctors (traditionally) have been seen as 'essential' in producing health care, in other words they are difficult to substitute by other factors of production.

Taken together these three characteristics suggest that the demand for doctors' services is inelastic.

This is only part of a complex story, however. In the UK the market for doctors is not 'competitive' (in the sense that economists use that term). It is dominated by the NHS – a monopoly buyer (technically known as a *monopsonist*) that influences the price (the wage level). Usually we would argue that monopsonists drive down the price below the competitive level (see Chapter 14, p. 288). However, many commentators have argued that the 'new GP contract' agreed by the Department of Health in 2004 was over-generous to GPs, paying them extra for things that they would have done anyway as part of their normal profession. There are interesting echoes here not just of the relative affluence of the medical profession but of the way in which it is sometimes viewed by others. Aneurin 'Nye' Bevan was the left-wing Minister of Health in the post-war Attlee government responsible for the establishment of the NHS. In order to persuade the BMA (the British Medical Association representing doctors) it had been necessary to offer concessions. Bevan later gave the famous quote that, in order to broker the deal, he had 'stuffed their mouths with gold'.

NHS productivity

The consideration of factor inputs leads on to the question of *productivity* in the NHS. Although it is often misunderstood, the concept of productivity is straightforward. It is the relationship between inputs and output. Thus, for example, if the quantity of inputs increases by 10% and the quantity of output also increases by 10% then, by definition, productivity has stayed constant. If, however, a 10% increase in inputs results in a rise in output of more than 10%, that outcome can only have been brought about if the transformation process has become more efficient. In other words, productivity must have increased.

Although the concept is straightforward, the measurement of productivity is, in practice, very difficult. If both inputs and output can be measured in physical units, and those units are homogeneous, then the measurement of productivity is straightforward. Thus if output consists of tonnes of coal and the inputs are man-hours we can easily calculate the change in labour productivity in the coal industry. Take as an example the hypothetical data shown in Table 12.3.

In Year 1 productivity is 4 tonnes per man-hour (100,000/25,000) and in year 2 productivity is 5 tonnes per man hour (150,000/30,000). Between Year 1 and Year 2 there has been a 25% increase in productivity.

If, however, different grades of coal are produced – i.e. if output is heterogeneous rather than homogeneous – then we will need a way of adding together the different types of output and the only way of doing this is to use the value (the price) of the coal. Thus:

50 tonnes of type A coal valued at £5 per tonne plus 40 tonnes of type B coal valued at £6 per tonne = £250 + £240 = £490 of coal. Note that we are now measuring output in terms of *values* not volumes.

We could turn this into an index number (=100 in Year 1) and proceed to see how this index changes over time. Thus we have a measure of *changes in output*. If we do the same for inputs (type A labour, type B labour and so on) we can construct an index that measures *changes in inputs* and by comparing the two indices or measures we can see how productivity changes over time.

Table 12.3 Hypothetical inputs and outputs in the coal industry.

	Year 1	Year 2
Coal output (thousands of tonnes)	100	150
Labour input (thousands of man-hours)	25	30

In 2004 the Office for National Statistics (ONS) published an estimate of NHS productivity changes over time. This showed that over the period 1995–2003 NHS output had grown by about 28% whereas NHS inputs had grown by between 32 and 39%. Since inputs had grown faster than output, this of course implies that productivity declined over the period.

This was a cause for concern because in the rest of the economy there has been a tendency for productivity to rise rather than fall. Indeed, it is this rise in the 'efficiency' with which resources are utilized that produces economic growth and improvements in the standard of living. On average the UK economy tends to grow by about 2–2.5% per year and only a small fraction of this can be attributed to increases in factor inputs – an increase in the workforce. The residual therefore must be the result of increases in the efficiency with which those factor inputs are transformed into output – resulting in productivity increases.

The most important factor input is labour, and the term 'productivity' is often taken to refer to labour productivity. Why does labour productivity tend to rise in the economy as a whole? Consider manufacturing. In the UK and throughout the world there has been a huge increase in what economists call *labour-saving technical progress* – basically each worker becomes more productive as a result of having more capital equipment to work with. Thus manufacturing output has increased despite the fact that far fewer people are now engaged in manufacturing. The remaining workers have computer controlled machines to produce the goods. And the same is true, broadly, in the service industries and in retailing. Recently the major supermarkets and stores such as B&Q have introduced self-service checkouts – customers scan their own purchases and pay using automated systems. One member of staff can oversee four or more of these checkouts and there is a consequent increase in labour productivity – an increase in the value of sales per member of staff employed.

These same self-service checkouts may, however, have also led to a change in the *quality* of the shopping experience. There is less personal contact, but there is also less queuing. The frustration of queuing has been replaced by the frustration of being told by a computer that there is an 'unexpected item in bagging area' (when clearly there isn't!). So we cannot really say that the quality of the output has fallen or has increased. It's just different. Statisticians at the ONS have exactly this problem in trying to capture changes in quality and this is particularly difficult when measuring NHS output. When a new service like *NHS Direct* is introduced, enabling patients to phone for advice 24 hours a day, seven days a week, is this better or worse than seeing your GP? The answer is, it is neither better nor worse, it is just different! It doesn't replace going to see your GP, but it is available in the middle of the night and in certain circumstances it may be more appropriate.

Certain sectors of the economy may not have enjoyed the labour-saving technical progress that have characterized most of the manufacturing and service sectors. In hairdressing, for example, there are almost no opportunities for the capital–labour substitution that leads to increases in labour productivity. The number of haircuts per hairdresser has not increased so, in physical terms, output per worker is unchanged. But you pay more for a haircut now than you did 20 years ago so in *value* terms each stylist has become more productive in the sense that the value of what they produce per hour has increased. This illustrates the inherent pitfalls in measuring productivity – it depends on prices as well as physical quantities.

Estimates of output

As we have seen, productivity depends on inputs and on output. In the NHS obtaining an estimate of the volume (the quantity) of output is difficult. How can you add together all the different things that the NHS produces to give a meaningful measure of output? A hip replacement is not the same as treatment for breast cancer. It's like adding together apples and pears. But again *value* may help here, as apples and pears are both fruit! Say apples cost 40p per kilo and pears 30p per kilo. If apple output increases from 10 kilos to 11 kilos and pear output from 10 kilos to 13 kilos, the total output of fruit therefore increases from:

$$(10 \times 40) + (10 \times 30) = 700p$$

to

$$(11 \times 40) + (13 \times 30) = 830p$$

The percentage increase is 830/700 = 18.6% [a *weighted average* of the increase in value of apple production

Table 12.4 The calculation of a volume index

	Unit cost (price) £	Expenditure year 1 £ million	Number of procedures 2000	Number of procedures 2001	Index 2000	Index 2001
Knee replacement	4,785	165.9	34,662	39,902	100	115.1
Varicose vein procedures	835	33.3	39,923	42,150	100	105.6
		199.2	74,585	82,052	100	113.5

Source: Derived from Pritchard (2004).

(10%) and value of pear production (30%)]. We can also express this as an *index number*. The value of output of fruit (apples and pears) increases from 100 in Year 1 to 118.6 in Year 2. And of course if the price of apples (or pears) changes we simply use the *new prices* for the year in question. So in this way we calculate a *volume index*.

Suppose we illustrate this with a further example, this time using realistic healthcare data. In Table 12.4 a knee replacement costs nearly £5,000 and a varicose vein procedure less than £1,000. These costs (prices) are assumed to reflect the *utility value* of each of these procedures – a knee replacement gives about five times as much *extra utility* to the recipient as a varicose vein procedure does. This assumption – that prices reflect how much something is 'worth' to the recipient – comes from the observation that economists make about how people behave when they are spending their own money. If a consumer buys a box of chocolates costing £1, you can infer that he/she derives at least one pound's worth of satisfaction from eating the chocolates. Otherwise he/she would not buy them. And if he/she spends £500 on a flat screen television he/she must get at least £500 worth of utility from so doing. Prices reflect utility.

Between 2000 and 2001 the number of knee replacements increased from 34,662 to 39,902; i.e. an increase of 15.1% (shown in the final column). Varicose vein procedures increased by 5.6%. Taken together the overall volume of output increased by 13.5%. However, this is not a simple average of the increase in the two procedures. It is a *weighted* average of knee replacements and varicose vein procedures, where the weights are equal to the prices. To the non-economist this may seem a bit strange, but we use exactly the same method for calculating

all aggregates – consumer spending, exports, gross national product and so on. These are all weighted averages, where the weights used are the prices paid in the market. We cannot add up physical quantities (tonnes of coal + brown shoes + haircuts) because these things are heterogeneous. So we add up the *value* of coal produced and sold (in money terms), the *value* of shoes and the *value* of haircuts.

So the table calculates what is called a 'volume' index. It is the *quantity* of output, and how that quantity changes over time, but it uses *prices* to weight the heterogeneous outputs so that they can be added up to arrive at an aggregate figure for the change in the amount of output.

Welfare Economics – Pareto

Within the context of the NHS, the word 'rationing' has very negative connotations. So it may be better to use the word 'prioritization' instead, though in practice the effect would be the same. Health service resources are finite and it follows logically that these finite resources should be used in the way that gives the greatest benefit. The implication of this is that some interventions that are technically feasible may yield very little benefit. An *effective* treatment is not necessarily an *efficient* use of society's resources. The resources employed could be transferred to an alternative use and the net benefit to society would be increased.

The framework within which economists analyse resource allocation derives from the work of Vilfredo Pareto and is generally known as Paretian Welfare

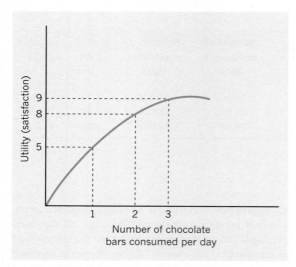

Fig. 12.12 Diminishing marginal utility.

Economics (see also Chapter 9, p. 167). This technical framework is based on a few key axioms. One of these is the notion of *diminishing marginal utility*. Individuals consume goods and services because it gives them utility (or satisfaction) to do so. However if we consider the consumption of chocolate bars as in Fig. 12.12 we note that as we consume additional bars so the satisfaction that we experience increases at a diminishing rate. If we consume one chocolate bar we experience 5 units of satisfaction (call this 5 *utils*). If we consume two bars we experience 8 units of satisfaction (8 utils). So the *extra* satisfaction – the *marginal utility* – is 3 utils. When we consume the third bar, total utility rises from 8 to 9 utils so the marginal utility of the third bar is only 1 util. And in the diagram it looks as though utility peaks at a consumption level of about three and a half bars. Beyond this point marginal utility becomes negative. Chocolate bars have diminishing marginal utility.

Everything that we consume has this fundamental characteristic. The more we have of something the less extra satisfaction we derive from consuming additional units. The rational individual will try to maximize his/her satisfaction (get as much utility as possible). To illustrate the principles involved consider the following example.

A consumer buys only two commodities, apples and bananas, both of which have diminishing marginal utility. At current consumption levels the last

apple eaten yields 10 utils of extra satisfaction ($MU_A = 10$) and the last banana gives 18 utils ($MU_B = 18$). Bananas cost twice as much as apples – say $P_A = 1$ and $P_B = 2$.

We have used symbols such that P_A is the price of apples and MU_A is the marginal utility of apples and so on.

Is the consumer getting as much satisfaction as possible from his/her spending? The answer is 'no'. At the margin each penny spent on apples gives 10 utils of satisfaction but each penny spent on bananas gives only 9 utils of extra satisfaction (18/2). So if some spending was transferred from bananas to apples the increased satisfaction from the extra apple consumption would more than outweigh the loss of satisfaction from the reduction in banana consumption.

In outline:

	Change in utility (approx)
Cut banana consumption by 1	−18
Use resources to increase apple consumption by 2	+20
Net increase in utility	+2

But of course apples possess diminishing marginal utility (as do bananas) so the more apples he eats the less extra satisfaction he gets. He will be maximizing his utility when the ratios of the marginal utilities is equal to the price ratio. That is:

$$\frac{MU_A}{MU_B} = \frac{P_A}{P_B}$$

or equivalently (it's the same equation cross-multiplied)

$$\frac{MU_A}{P_A} = \frac{MU_B}{P_B}$$

The same principles apply within the NHS. If we transferred resources from **Bone marrow transplants** to **Arthritis research** (from service B to service A) it might be possible to achieve a net increase in the wellbeing of the population (its utility). To do so, however, we need to be able to evaluate the utility of the outputs – that is, to put a money value on them. This is where the notion of *economic evaluation* comes in.

Economic evaluation

Strictly speaking, the term *economic evaluation* should be restricted to the set of techniques that involve 'evaluation' – that is putting a money value on something. Often, however, the term is used more broadly to refer to decisions based not just on information about the clinical effectiveness of a medical intervention but its 'cost effectiveness' also. The question being posed is: does the use of such an intervention represent an efficient use of the resources of the NHS and more broadly of society as a whole?

Sometimes the term *economic appraisal* is used instead. The meaning is similar (and both terms are used rather loosely). Economic appraisal should be contrasted with *financial appraisal* and *investment appraisal*, both of which tend to be used in the private sector to refer to techniques that involve the calculation of net present value and internal rate of return to work out whether an investment is worth undertaking (see Chapter 17, p. 341). All three of these appraisal techniques have one thing in common – they recognize that there are alternative uses for the investment funds. They have an opportunity cost. Economic appraisal differs from private sector investment appraisal inasmuch as a broader range of benefits and costs are considered. In financial appraisal the decision is based on the probable effect on the company's costs and revenues. In economic appraisal (in theory at least) a somewhat wider perspective is used.

Cost minimization analysis

If the choice is between two competing procedures where the outcomes of the two procedures are identical, the problem reduces down to that of *cost minimization analysis*. The decision rule is simple: choose the cheapest. Thus, for example, suppose the choice is between in-patient treatment and out-patient treatment (day-surgery) for haemorrhoids. The evidence seems to suggest that the outcomes are not significantly different. The patient is likely to recover just as quickly whether or not he stays in hospital. By choosing day surgery the hospital will avoid paying the 'hotel services' associated with keeping a patient in hospital overnight (probably around £350) and therefore this is the more cost-effective technique. There are other considerations that favour day-surgery – most patients would probably prefer not to stay in hospital and the risk of infection may be less. For other patients there may not be a suitable home environment. Other things being equal, however, the cheaper technique is to be preferred. Consequently, despite the increase in the number of cases treated ('consultant episodes'), the number of beds in NHS hospitals has declined.

Figure 12.13 shows the change in the number of available beds over 20 years. Proportionally, the largest falls have been in learning disability, mental illness and geriatric beds. In all areas, care is increasingly being delivered with shorter stays in hospitals, so the number of beds needed has fallen.

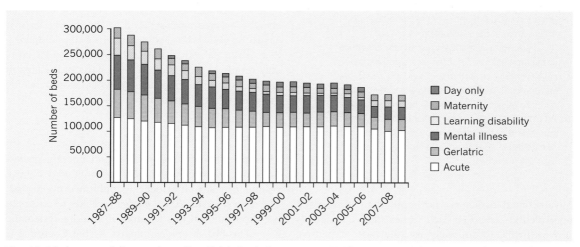

Fig. 12.13 Average daily number of available beds by sector in NHS hospitals, England, 1987/88–2008/09.
Source: The King's Fund (2010).

Cost-utility analysis

This generic term is applied to situations where the choice is between two competing procedures but the outcomes are *not* the same and neither are the costs. Take as an example the case for the routine use of silver coated catheters. A urinary catheter is a narrow tube placed in the body to drain and collect urine from the bladder. They are often used on patients post-operatively or when the patient (who may be unconscious) cannot get out of bed to go to the toilet. In such patients a urinary tract infection (UTI) is not uncommon and these are referred to as CAUTIs (catheter associated urinary tract infections). The manufacturers of catheters have laboratory evidence that a silver alloy coating has antibacterial properties. There is some evidence that they reduce the incidence of CAUTIs in a hospital setting. A summary of one piece of research is shown here:

Silver Alloy Coated Catheters Reduce Catheter-associated Bacteriuria

H. Liedberg and T. Lundberg, *British Journal of Urology*, **65**(4), 379–381, April 1990.

Summary – *The tendency of indwelling catheters to cause urinary tract infection was evaluated in a randomised clinical study of 223 patients. A Foley catheter coated with silver alloy on both inner and outer surfaces was used in 60 patients; 60 others received a Teflonised latex Foley's catheter and the remaining 103 patients were excluded because of antibiotic treatment, diabetes, etc.*

There was a statistically significant difference in the incidence of catheter-associated bacteriuria ($> 10^5$ organisms/ml) in the 2 groups after 6 days' catheterisation: 6 patients with the silver coated catheter developed bacteriuria compared with 22 who had the Teflonised latex catheter. This suggests that the silver impregnated urethral catheters reduce the incidence of catheter-associated urinary tract infection.

Silver coated catheters cost more than non-coated equivalents – say £10 each rather than £5 each. Is it worthwhile to routinely use the more expensive catheter rather than the cheaper alternative?

To answer this question, we should compare the additional cost with the additional benefit – remember that in economics we use marginal analysis to compare marginal costs with marginal benefits. It's easy to work out the additional costs but the calculation of the additional benefits is less straightforward than it may at first appear.

The benefit of the use of the silver coated catheter is the UTIs prevented. On the basis of the evidence quoted in the study above (and estimates from many similar studies), we might conclude that the incidence of UTI falls from 22/60 to 6/60. Thus 16/60 UTIs are prevented. The additional cost to the hospital resulting from these had they not been prevented can be thought of as the cost of keeping these patients in hospital for additional days while the infection is treated and the cost of the drugs required to do so. Such figures will necessarily be based on averages that conceal wide variations in individual cases – in some patients the UTI will be minor and result in only a minor delay in discharge from hospital. Others may, however, already be suffering from multiple morbidities and the UTI will prove fatal.

Notice that an economic evaluation can only be as good as the clinical (statistical) evidence on which it is based. We can think of this as a two-stage process. The first stage is the *clinical evidence* of the improved efficacy of the new technique (such as the silver coated catheter). The second stage is the *evaluation* (placing a money value) of the change in costs and of the change in benefits that result from the adoption of the new technique. At the first stage it has to be clear what the comparator is – what is the new technique being compared against? And at the second stage it has to be clear whose perspective is being adopted – that of the individual hospital, the NHS (since costs may simply be passed on to other parts of the Health Service), or to the wider society, which would include the interests of the patient himself.

Evidence-based medicine

Many members of the medical and nursing professions are involved in clinical research and a huge volume of research evidence is published every year. The term *evidence-based medicine* relates to efforts to use the results of this research in a more systematic way. The British epidemiologist Archie Cochrane is regarded as the originator of the concept. The Cochrane

Collaboration attempts to categorize studies, placing them in a hierarchy according to how valid and reliable they are deemed to be. The work of the Collaboration has led to the randomized controlled trial (RCT) being regarded as the gold standard of research. Ideally the RCT should also be 'blind' – which means that those participating in the research (both researchers and participants) do not know which patients are in the experimental group and which patients are in the control group. Sometimes the results of several studies on a particular topic are grouped together using meta analysis. This adds together the results from similar studies with the measured effects being a weighted average of the results of individual studies. Some statisticians, however, are sceptical of the procedure.

Quality Adjusted Life Years (QALYs)

One particularly controversial application of cost-utility analysis involves an attempt to measure the quality of additional life years gained as a result of the intervention. These are the infamous QALYs. The effect of an intervention (a new clinical procedure, say) is measured not just on one dimension but on two. The first dimension is the additional life years gained. This is multiplied by the second dimension, the quality of life of the patient in those remaining years. This produces a measure of Quality Adjusted Life Years (QALYs).

The two dimensions are illustrated in Fig. 12.14. The vertical axis is the 'quality of life', and the horizontal axis is 'years of life' following the treatment (or no treatment). Without treatment the patient will live for only 12 months with a quality of life rated as 0.5. The treatment being evaluated will extend the patient's life by an additional two years (so they die after three years) and bring about an immediate improvement in the quality of life to 0.9. Thus the benefit of the treatment is the shaded area. This is the *additional quality adjusted life years* gained as a result of the treatment:

$$(3 \times 0.9) - (1 \times 0.5) = 2.2 \text{ QALYs}$$

If the treatment costs, say, £60,000 then the cost per QALY would be £60,000/2.2 = £27,272. This figure can be compared with the cost per QALY associated with other forms of treatment. The NHS may decide not to fund those treatments that appear to offer poor

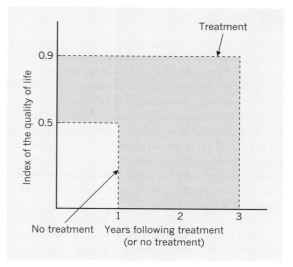

Fig. 12.14 How to calculate a QALY.

value for money. For example, if the cut-off point were £30,000 then this treatment (at only £27,272) would just come within the range of treatments that the NHS is willing to fund.

One measure of quality of life, the EQ-5D, uses the ability of the individual to function in five dimensions – mobility, pain/discomfort, self-care, anxiety/depression, usual activities. Each of the five dimensions has three possible levels – for example for mobility 1 = no problems walking about; 2 = some problems walking about; 3 = confined to bed. A completely healthy and happy individual would rate 11111. At the opposite extreme, 33333 would mean that the patient is confined to bed, is in extreme pain or discomfort, is unable to wash or dress themselves, is extremely anxious or depressed, and is unable to perform usual activities. These are assigned valuations. For example, 12323 (no problems walking, some pain, unable to wash, moderately anxious, unable to perform usual activities) is given a weight of 0.27 – roughly a quarter. So an additional 4 years of life would be worth only about one QALY.

The weights used in the EQ-5D scale were obtained by asking health professionals to 'score' certain health states, but there is a degree of arbitrariness involved and the approach has come under increasing criticism. The National Institute for Health and Clinical Evidence (NICE) has played down their use in recent years.

Conclusion

We can trace the foundation of the NHS back to the Beveridge Report of 1942. The poor could not afford to access the medical treatments that were available at the time and consequently there was a 'pent up demand' for treatment. Access to health care free at the point of delivery would release this pent up demand and there would therefore be a significant increase in the resources required. But – it was argued – once the backlog of sickness had been removed the demand for health care would settle down at a manageable level.

As we now realize, this reasoning is incorrect. It was based on the view that medical technology would remain fixed, whereas we now realize that new treatments – and therefore new demands – are continuously emerging. It may be helpful to distinguish between *need* and *demand*. Suppose a patient is suffering from a disease for which there is no known cure or effective treatment. There is a *need* but not a demand. But if a treatment becomes available then there will be a resulting increase in the *demand* for health service resources. But if that new treatment is very expensive and is not clinically very effective it may not be a rational use of resources to provide it free to those who need it. The NHS may have to prioritize – to ration – its resources.

There is an irony here. When we consider both curative and preventative medicine, ultimately the more successful you are the more it costs you. By preventing disease and curing minor illnesses you increase life expectancy and delay the point at which death occurs. The only certain thing in life is that it ends in death. We may have slightly changed our view about how the NHS should care for people from 'cradle to grave', but the starting point and the end point remain the same. At the beginning, however – and especially at the end – the dignity with which we treat our fellow citizens is the measure of a civilized society.

Key points

- Public spending on health care in the UK (i.e. NHS) has increased from 4.5% of GDP in the late 1980s to around 8.5% of GDP in 2010.

- Demographic factors, such as an ageing population, new medical technologies and a high income-elasticity of demand for health care services, have all contributed to increased expenditure (public and private) on health care services.

- Total spending in the UK on health care services has risen sharply over recent years and is some 10.5% of GDP in 2010, close to the EU average of 10.6% but still well below the US figure of 13.6% of GDP.

- Life expectancy in the global economy depends on many factors other than health expenditure with the coefficient of determination (R^2) being only around 0.55 as between these two variables. Social class is seen to be an important additional factor in the UK.

- The structure of the health service is returning to a purchasers/providers separation, i.e. an internal or quasi-market.

- There is considerable income disparity between doctors and other occupational groups within the health care sector. High remuneration of doctors is derived from an inelastic demand for health care services, doctors accounting for only a small proportion of total costs and being less easily substituted by other factors of production.

- Estimating output and productivity in the health care sector is extremely complex, although volume indices have helped in this respect.

- Economic evaluation of the effectiveness of health care has involved various cost minimization, cost-utility, evidence-based and QALY techniques.

Now try the self-check questions for this chapter on the Companion Website. You will also find useful links to relevant websites.

Notes

1 This is the so-called 'line of best fit' or 'least squares line'. It is that line which minimizes the sum of squared deviations from the line – sometimes called the 'regression' line.

2 R^2 is the so-called co-efficient of determination, given by the following ratio: Explained variation divided by Total variation.

References and further reading

Carvel, J. (2009) NHS constitution ends era of 'doctor knows best', *Guardian*, 21st January.

Department of Health and Social Services (DHSS) (1980) *The Black Report*, London, HMSO.

Folland, S., Goodman, A. and Stano, M. (2009) *Economics of Health and Health Care* (6th edn), Harlow, Financial Times/Prentice Hall.

Gray, A., Clarke, P., Wolstenholme, J. and Wordsworth, S. (2010) *Applied Methods of Cost-effectiveness Analysis in Healthcare*, Oxford, Oxford University Press.

Henderson, J. (2008) *Health Economics and Policy* (4th edn), Maso OH, South Western Educational Publishing.

HM Treasury (2010a) *Budget 2010: copy of economic and fiscal strategy report and financial statement and budget report – June 2010*, London, The Stationery Office.

HM Treasury (2010b) *Public Expenditure Statistical Analysis 2010*, London, The Stationery Office.

ONS (2010) *Population Estimates*, London, Office for National Statistics.

Hollingsworth, B. and Peacock, S. (2008) *Efficiency Measurement in Health and Healthcare* London, Routledge.

Liedberg, H. and Lundeberg, T. (2008) Silver alloy coated catheters reduce catheter-associated bacteriuria, online version of original article in *British Journal of Urology*, 65(4): 379–81, April 1990.

Marmor, T. and Wendt, C. (2011) *Reforming Healthcare Systems*, Cheltenham, Edward Elgar.

Masís, D. P. and Smith, P. C. (2009) *Health Care Systems in Developing and Transition Countries* Cheltenham, Edward Elgar.

McIntosh, E., Clarke, P., Frew, E. and Louviere, J. (2010) *Applied Methods of Cost-Benefit Analysis in Health Care*, Oxford, Oxford University Press.

Mooney, G. (2003) *Economics Medicine and Health Care* (3rd edn), Harlow, Financial Times/Prentice Hall.

Mooney, G. (2010) *Challenging Health Economics*, Oxford, Oxford University Press.

NHS NHS History, 1948, available at: http://www.nhs.uk/NHSEngland/thenhs/nhshistory/Pages/NHShistory1948.aspx (accessed February 2011).

NHS NHS History, 1990, available at: http://www.nhs.uk/NHSEngland/thenhs/nhshistory/Pages/NHShistory1990s.aspx (accessed February 2011).

NHS (2010a) *NHS Staff 1999–2009 Overview*, available at: http://www.ic.nhs.uk/statistics-and-data-collections/workforce/nhs-staff-numbers/nhs-staff-1999-2009-overview (accessed February 2011).

NHS (2010b) *NHS Structure*, available at: http://www.nhs.uk/NHSEngland/thenhs/about/Pages/nhsstructure.aspx (accessed February 2011).

OECD (2009) *OECD Health Data 2009 – Comparing Health Statistics Across OECD*

Countries, Paris, Organisation for Economic Cooperation and Development.

OECD (2010) *OECD Health Data 2010: Statistics and Indicators*, Paris, Organisation for Economic Cooperation and Development.

ONS (2010a) *Annual Survey of Hours and Earnings (ASHE)*, London, Office for National Statistics.

ONS (2010b) *Population Estimates*, London, Office for National Statistics.

Phelps, C. (2009) *Health Economics* (4th edn), Harlow, Financial Times/Prentice Hall.

Pritchard, A. (2004) Measuring government health services output in the national accounts: new methodology and further analysis, *Economic Trends*, **613**.

Smith, P., Mossialos, E., Papanicolas, I. and Leatherman, S. (2010) *Performance Measurement for Health System Improvement: Experiences, Challenges and Prospects*, Cambridge, Cambridge University Press.

The King's Fund (2010) *Frequently Asked Questions*, London.

Wanless, D. (2003) *Securing Good Health for the Whole Population: population health trends*, London, The Stationery Office.

The following websites are relevant to this chapter:

NHS: http://www.nhs.uk/NHSEngland/thenhs/about/Pages/nhsstructure.aspx

The Cochrane Collaboration: http://www.cochrane.org/

NHS Evidence: http://www.evidence.nhs.uk/default.aspx

OECD Health Data: www.oecd.org/health/healthdata.

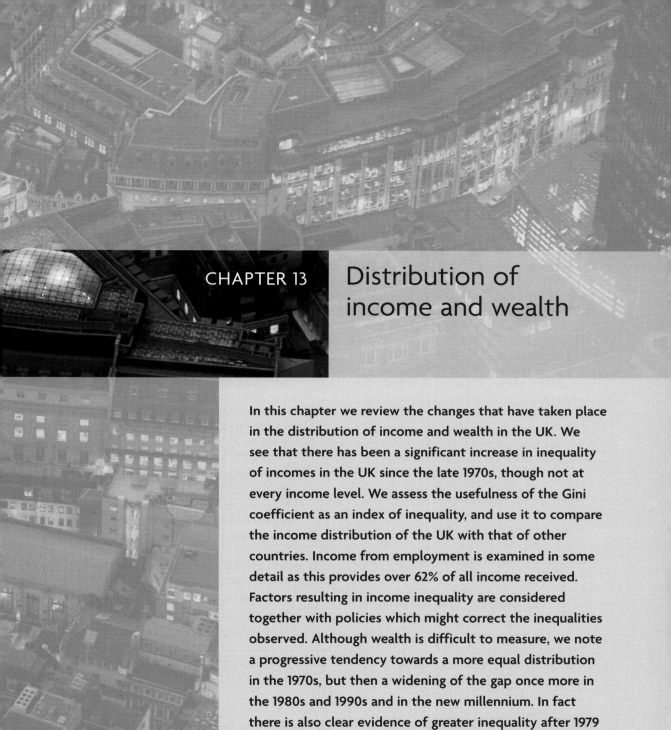

CHAPTER 13

Distribution of income and wealth

In this chapter we review the changes that have taken place in the distribution of income and wealth in the UK. We see that there has been a significant increase in inequality of incomes in the UK since the late 1970s, though not at every income level. We assess the usefulness of the Gini coefficient as an index of inequality, and use it to compare the income distribution of the UK with that of other countries. Income from employment is examined in some detail as this provides over 62% of all income received. Factors resulting in income inequality are considered together with policies which might correct the inequalities observed. Although wealth is difficult to measure, we note a progressive tendency towards a more equal distribution in the 1970s, but then a widening of the gap once more in the 1980s and 1990s and in the new millennium. In fact there is also clear evidence of greater inequality after 1979 at the top and bottom ends of the income distribution. This chapter concludes with a brief review of poverty in the UK.

Distribution and justice

Throughout the history of economics, the distribution of income and wealth has been a major concern. There has been not only a desire to explain the observed pattern of distribution, but also a belief that basic issues of justice and morality were involved. Positive and normative economics are therefore difficult to separate in this area.

Commutative justice

There are two main views of justice in distribution. The first may be called 'commutative justice', where it is held that each person should receive income in proportion to the value of labour and capital they have contributed to the productive process. This view underlies the ideology of the free market economy, with some economists seeking to show that commutative justice will automatically be achieved under free competition, since each factor will receive the value of its marginal product. Disparities in the distribution of income and wealth are then seen as being quite consistent with 'commutative justice'.

Distributive justice

The second view may be called 'distributive justice', where it is believed that people should receive income according to need. Given that people's needs are much the same, 'distributive justice' implies approximate equality in income distribution. This view underlies the ideology of socialism. The socialist sees the free market as a kind of power struggle, through which certain groups are exploited; hence their advocacy of various forms of social control of the economy to achieve 'distributive justice'.

Issues in distribution

In the debate about distribution, there are five specific areas of concern.

1 The distribution of income between persons, irrespective of the source of that income. Included here is income from labour (wages and salaries), and from the ownership of capital (dividend and interest) and land (rent).

2 The distribution of income between factors of production, in particular between labour and capital. Advocates of the free market believe that income accrues to labour and capital according to their relative productivity, whilst critics explain their relative shares as the outcome of a continuous conflict in which capital seeks to exploit labour, and labour to resist.

3 The distribution of earnings between different types of labour. Again, believers in the free market see differences in earnings between occupational groups as being caused by differences in relative productivity. Critics explain such differentials through the relative bargaining power of the labour groups in question.

4 The distribution of wealth. In the nineteenth century virtually all wealth was held by a small elite, who lived off the profits from it, whilst the majority lived by the 'sweat of their brows'. The injustice of this was a major spur to socialism. More recently, defenders of capitalism have argued that wealth has become progressively more evenly distributed, so that the majority benefit from profits – 'We are all capitalists now'!

5 Poverty. Free market ideologists have always acknowledged that a small minority will be unable to compete in the labour market, and will therefore be poor; so from Adam Smith onwards most economists accepted the need for some protection of the poor. Critics, however, have argued that poverty was, and remains, widespread.

In this chapter we shall attempt to assess the facts in each of these five areas of concern, and to look more closely at the conflicting explanations. We shall start by looking at the overall distribution of income between people.

Income distribution between people

The overall picture

The most vivid illustration of income distribution is Pen's 'Parade of Dwarfs' (Pen 1971). In the course of *an hour* the entire population passes by, each person's height in relation to average height signifying their income in relation to average income. In the first minute we see only matchstick people such as women doing casual work. After 10–15 minutes dustmen and ticket collectors pass by, though only three feet high. After 30 minutes, when half the population has passed, skilled manual workers and senior office clerks appear, though these are still well under five feet tall. In fact we only reach the average height 12 minutes before the hour ends, when teachers, executive class civil servants, social workers and sales representatives pass by. After this, height increases rapidly. Six minutes before the end come farmers, headmasters and departmental heads of offices, standing about six feet six inches. Then come the giants: the fairly ordinary lawyer at eight feet tall, the family doctor at 21 feet, the chairman of a typical public company at over 60 feet, and various film stars and tycoons resembling tower blocks.

This illustration demonstrates two little-understood features of personal income distribution. First, the mean or average income is way above median income, the median-income receiver being the person who arrives after 30 minutes, with half the population poorer and half richer. Roughly three-quarters of the population have less than the mean or average income. Put another way, the median income is only about 85% of average income. Broadly speaking, this is because at the top end there are considerable numbers of very rich people who pull the average up. Second, amongst the top quarter of income receivers are people in fairly ordinary professions, such as teachers and sales representatives, who would perhaps be surprised to learn that the great majority of the population were significantly less well off than themselves.

Definition of income

When we come to collect precise data about income we find various problems of definition. Should we deduct taxes and add transfer payments? Should we count capital gains as income? This latter question raises the problem of distinguishing between income which is a flow, and wealth which is a stock. Income is defined in theory as *the amount a person could have spent whilst maintaining the value of his wealth intact*. By this definition capital gains should count as income, but for simplicity of data collection they are

excluded from official tables. A further question is whether an imputed rent should be credited as income to those who own their dwelling. Again, strictly it should, as a dwelling is a potential source of income which could be spent without diminishing wealth, but for simplicity it is usually excluded. Finally, what should count as the income receiver, the individual or the household? In practice we normally use the 'tax unit' – the individual or family which is defined as one unit for tax purposes.

The Lorenz curve and the Gini coefficient

The conventional means of illustrating income distribution is the Lorenz curve, shown in Fig. 13.1. The horizontal axis shows the cumulative percentage of population; the vertical axis the cumulative percentage of total income they receive. The diagonal is the 'line of perfect equality' where, say, 20% of all people receive 20% of all income.

Table 13.1 presents figures for the distribution of income in the UK at selected dates since 1961. The data for 2008/09 are plotted in Fig. 13.1 as a continuous line, and are known as the Lorenz curve. The degree of inequality can be judged by the extent to which the Lorenz curve deviates from the diagonal. For instance, the bottom 20% received only 7.1% of total income in 2008/09, so that the vertical difference

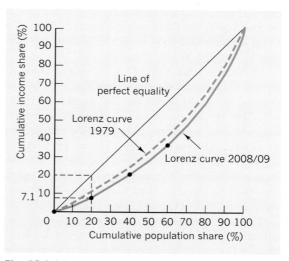

Fig. 13.1 Lorenz curve and Gini coefficient.

Table 13.1 Percentage shares of income after tax in the UK (before housing costs).

Income receivers	1961	1971	1979	1985	1991	2000/01	2008/09
Bottom 10%	3.7	4.0	4.2	4.0	3.0	2.8	2.6
Bottom 20%	9.4	9.5	9.9	9.4	7.4	7.3	7.1
Bottom 30%	16.3	16.1	16.7	15.7	12.9	12.7	12.6
Bottom 40%	24.1	23.2	24.3	22.8	19.5	19.2	19.1
Bottom 50%	32.7	32.2	32.9	30.9	27.2	26.7	26.6
Bottom 60%	42.2	41.7	42.5	40.2	36.2	35.4	35.3
Bottom 70%	52.9	52.3	53.2	50.8	46.6	45.5	45.3
Bottom 80%	64.8	64.2	65.5	63.0	58.9	57.4	57.0
Bottom 90%	78.8	78.3	79.6	77.4	74.0	72.0	73.4
Bottom 100%	100.0	100.0	100.0	100.0	100.0	100.0	100.0
Gini coefficient	0.260	0.262	0.248	0.279	0.337	0.350	0.340

Sources: Department for Work and Pensions (2010) *Households Below Average Income* (HBAI) 1994/5–2008/9; Goodman and Shephard (2002).

between the Lorenz curve and the diagonal represents inequality. To assess inequality over the whole range of the income distribution, the Gini coefficient is calculated. It is the ratio of the area enclosed between the Lorenz curve and the diagonal, to the total area underneath the diagonal. If there was no inequality (i.e. perfect equality), the Lorenz curve would coincide with the diagonal, and the above ratio would be zero. If there was perfect inequality (all the income going to the last person) then the Lorenz curve would coincide with the horizontal axis until that last person, and the above ratio would be 1. The Gini coefficient therefore ranges from zero to 1 with a rise in the Gini coefficient suggesting less equality. The value of the Gini coefficient is, in fact, calculated for each year in Table 13.1.

The figures from Table 13.1, as well as confirming the conclusions we drew from Pen's 'Parade of Dwarfs', show that during the 1960s and early 1970s the Gini coefficient remained relatively constant, suggesting no significant change in the distribution of income. The period from 1971 to 1979 saw a sustained fall in the coefficient, suggesting that the income distribution became progressively more equal. However, the trend has been broken since 1979, with the Gini coefficient rising, i.e. less equality.

The Gini coefficient can, however, only give an overall impression. More detailed inspection shows that the bottom 20% of income receivers were worse off in 2008/09 with only 7.1% of income, compared

to 9.9% in 1979. What has happened is that the relative position of the lower-income groups has worsened, and that of some of the higher-income groups improved. The top 10% received 26.6% of income in 2008/09 but only 20.4% in 1979. When one Lorenz curve lies below another *at every point* we can confidently say that a rise in the Gini coefficient must mean less equality. This appears to be the case for *all* deciles of income in 2008/09 as compared to 1979. If the Lorenz curves intersect we have to balance less equality at one part of the income distribution with greater equality at another part.

If we had compared the 1961 and 1971 Lorenz curves, we would have found just such an intersection. For instance, there was *less equality* for the bottom 50% of income earners in 1971 (32.2% of income) than in 1961 (32.7% of income). However, there was *greater equality* for the bottom 20% of income earners in 1971 (9.5% of income) than in 1961 (9.4% of income). So the rise in the overall Gini coefficient, from 0.260 in 1961 to 0.262 in 1971, must be treated with some care as it does not, in this case, mean less equality throughout the income distribution.

In more recent times the Gini coefficient has continued to rise, despite attempts by successive Labour governments between 1997 and 2010 to reverse this trend through the introduction of new tax and benefit systems designed to be redistributive in nature (i.e. benefit the lower-income groups much more than higher-income groups). In fact the average incomes of the higher-income groups have grown at least as fast as those of the lower-income groups since 1997. We discuss possible reasons behind such an outcome later in the chapter.

International comparisons

International comparisons of income distributions and their associated Gini coefficients have been difficult to undertake because various countries have different definitions of income and different methods of collecting data. However, at this stage it might be useful to compare the Gini coefficient in a sample of countries and also trace the changes over time. In Table 13.2 we find that the UK's Gini coefficient is sixth highest of the sample of 14 countries. In fact, if the whole group of 30 OECD countries had been included, the UK would have come seventh highest in terms of the Gini coefficient, which reinforces the fact that the UK has a relatively high inequality of income *vis-à-vis* some of its competitors. Inequality in the US is also striking, while countries such as Belgium, Denmark and Sweden have low income inequalities by this measure.

Table 13.2 Income distribution: the Gini coefficient (after tax and transfers): mid-1980s to mid-2000s.

	Mid-1980s	Mid-1990s	Mid-2000s
Mexico	0.45	0.52	0.47
Turkey	0.43	0.49	0.43
Portugal	0.35	0.36	0.38
US	0.34	0.36	0.38
Italy	0.31	0.35	0.35
UK	0.33	0.37	0.34
Japan	0.30	0.32	0.32
Spain	0.37	0.34	0.32
Germany	0.26	0.27	0.30
France	0.31	0.28	0.28
Norway	0.32	0.26	0.28
Belgium	0.27	0.29	0.27
Denmark	0.22	0.21	0.23
Sweden	0.20	0.21	0.23

Source: OECD (2010) *StatExtracts*, Income distribution – Inequality.

In terms of *changes* in the income distribution, the Gini coefficient rose in many countries between the mid-1980s and mid-1990s – especially in the UK – but the picture between the mid-1990s and mid-2000s has been more varied across nations, with countries as diverse as the US, Germany and Portugal experiencing an increase in the Gini coefficient while the UK, Mexico, Turkey and Spain showed a fall in the Gini coefficients (less inequality). The OECD report from which these coefficients are derived concludes that the economic growth of recent decades has, overall, tended to benefit the rich more than the poor (OECD 2010).The report also notes that a key driver of income inequality has been the number of low skilled and poorly educated who are out of work and the incidence of people living on their own or in one-parent households.

Income distribution between factors of production

Definition of factors

In analysing the share of income between labour, capital and land there are initial problems of definition. First, under labour do we include workers and managers, thereby combining wages and salaries, since both are paid in return for work? Some argue that salaries for managers include a profit element, since managers exert direct control over capital and they carry entrepreneurial risks. In practice it is impossible to separate any profit element in salaries, and payments to workers and managers are counted together. More difficult is the income of the self-employed, since this undoubtedly includes payment for both labour and capital services; a separate category is, in fact, usually made for the self-employed.

Measurement of factor shares

Table 13.3 shows the income to various factors as a percentage of gross value added at factor cost (national income before adjustment for taxes/subsidies) and provides an insight into the distribution of national income by factor shares. The table is in the new format introduced in 1998 by the government to

Table 13.3 Factor shares as a percentage of gross value added at factor cost.

	1973	1977	1981	1989	2009
Compensation of employees	66.4	66.6	67.9	63.8	62.2
Gross operating surplus	24.5	24.9	23.4	27.1	25.2
Non-financial companies					
Private corporations	17.8	17.5	17.4	23.1	19.0
Public corporations	3.2	3.8	3.7	1.5	0.8
Financial corporations	3.5	3.6	2.3	2.5	5.4
Other income*	9.1	8.5	8.7	9.1	12.6
Total	100.0	100.0	100.0	100.0	100.0

*Includes mixed income and the operating surplus of the non-corporate sector (proxy variable for self-employment income).
Source: ONS (2010b) *United Kingdom Economic Accounts*, Quarter 2, ONS *Economic Trends* (various).

conform to European national income practices. The 'compensation of employees' corresponds to incomes which employees earn from employment, while 'gross operating surplus' covers mainly the profits to various corporate bodies, both private and public. The 'other income' includes what is called 'mixed income' (largely income from unincorporated businesses owned by householders) and the operating surpluses of other unincorporated bodies such as partnerships. Although not precise, the 'other income group' can be thought of as a proxy for 'self-employed income'.

Labour's share of total income has increased from approximately 50% in 1900 to 62.2% in 2009. Table 13.3 shows that over the last 36 years, the percentage shares going to various factors have been relatively steady, although the share of total income going to labour fell and to profits rose significantly between 1981 and 1989 as the relatively slow rise in real wages and the economic recovery helped shift income away from employment and towards corporate profits.

One may question the importance of factor shares in overall income distribution. Whether the changes in factor shares shown in Table 13.3 reflect greater inequality in household incomes depends on how unequally distributed these earnings from different factor sources are across the various income groups. For example, the table suggests that the distribution of factor shares has shifted away from employment and towards self-employment and profits ('gross operating surplus' and 'other income') since 1981. If we knew that income from these two sources is more unevenly distributed across income groups than income from employment, then this shift in factor

shares towards self-employment and profits could result in an increase in the overall inequality of income between different groups of people. Studies have, in fact, shown that income from self-employment and from investments (rent, dividends and interest) are more important sources of income for the lowest and highest income groups than for the middle income groups.

There are two main types of theoretical explanation of factor shares. The first emphasizes the role of market forces and starts with a microeconomic analysis of factor markets. If there is perfect competition in goods and factor markets, each factor will receive precisely its marginal revenue product; in other words, it will receive income in proportion to its productive value. The rising share to the factor labour would be viewed from this standpoint as reward for a greater contribution to production.

An alternative approach has been to explain factor shares in terms of power. Marx saw capitalists as exploiting labour, receiving 'surplus value' from the fact that the efforts of workers yield returns over and above their wages. Marx believed that this exploitation would increase as production became more capital-intensive and labour was displaced, creating a pool of unemployment which would depress wages, and therefore the share of labour in National Income. Eventually, the decline in people's ability to purchase the output of the capitalist factories, combined with the workers' resentment at their poverty, would cause crisis and revolution.

Neither theory is wholly adequate. Assumptions, such as perfect competition in labour markets, required by orthodox theory are clearly unrealistic (see Chapter 14). Similarly, Marx's prediction of a declining wage and factor share for labour has not been fulfilled.

 ## The earnings distribution

Since over 62% of total income accrues to the factor labour (Table 13.3), it follows that differing returns to the various factors (labour, capital or land) are unlikely to be the main explanation of income inequality. Rather, we must turn our attention to variations in income between different groups *within* the factor labour, i.e. the earnings distribution.

Earnings by occupation

Table 13.4 shows the relative median gross earnings for the main occupational groups based on the Annual Survey of Hours and Earnings (ASHE). This survey replaced the previous 'New Earnings Survey' from 2004 onwards and contains comprehensive data on many aspects of earnings. The data in Table 13.4 represent the gross median weekly earnings of certain occupations as a proportion of the gross median weekly earnings of all occupations. From the table it can be seen that managers and senior officials earn

46% above the average for all occupations and enjoy similar earnings to those in professional occupations (e.g. scientists, engineers, teachers, accountants, etc.). Associate professionals and technical occupations (technicians, therapists, prison officers, etc.) earn, on average, 13% above the median earnings for the whole country. It is also true to say that many occupations classed as 'manual' (e.g. process, plant and machine operatives) earn more than 'non-manual' workers, such as those in sales or personal services. Indeed, a more detailed analysis also reveals that certain manual occupations, such as construction operatives, vehicle assemblers, stevedores and heavy goods vehicle drivers, earn the equivalent or more than further education teachers or healthcare managers. Although the picture is complicated, it can be seen that substantial inequality of occupational earnings is clearly present in UK society.

A hidden source of inequality between occupations is the difference in value of fringe benefits and pension entitlement. As early as 1979 the Diamond Commission found that this typically adds 36% to the pre-tax salary of a senior manager, and 18% to that of a foreman, whilst unskilled workers enjoy few or no such benefits.

Earnings by sex

Table 13.5 shows the ratio of female to male gross weekly earnings in 2009. It can be seen that, on

Table 13.4 Relative earnings by occupational groups, 2009.*

Occupational group	Median gross weekly wage (all occupations = 100)
Managers and senior officials	146
Professional occupations	142
Associate professional and technical occupations	113
Administrative and secretarial occupations	76
Skilled trades occupations	93
Personal service occupations	67
Sales and customer service occupations	61
Process, plant and machine operatives	85
Elementary occupations	66
All occupations	**100**

*Full-time employees on adult rates, whose pay for the survey period was unaffected by absence and who have been in the job for at least 12 months.
Source: Adapted from ONS (2010a) *Annual Survey of Hours and Earnings 2009*.

Table 13.5 Relative earnings by sex, 2009.

Occupational group	Median gross weekly wage (female/male ratio)
Managers and senior officials	72 (78)
Professional occupations	83 (89)
Associate professional and technical occupations	80 (89)
Administrative and secretarial occupations	79 (89)
Skilled trades occupations	56 (70)
Personal service occupations	92 (81)
Sales and customer service occupations	68 (92)
Process, plant and machine operatives	67 (71)
Elementary occupations	44 (79)
All occupations	63 (80)

Note: Figures in brackets are for full-time male/female workers.
Source: Adapted from ONS (2010a) *Annual Survey of Hours and Earnings 2009*.

average, women earn only 63% of men's wages in the same occupational groups. Women's wages seem to lag at the upper managerial end of the occupational spectrum and also in the skilled and elementary occupations. Their relative income is higher in the professional and administrative groups, where there appears to have been more equal treatment over time. The position of women improved significantly during the 1970s – a period which saw the introduction of equal pay legislation, as for example between 1970 and 1976 when the ratio of women's average weekly wages to that of men rose from 50% to 61%. Nevertheless, Table 13.5 would suggest that little improvement has taken place in *overall* male/female wage ratios since that period.

However, the comments made above cover *all* male and female workers, both full- and part-time. If we look at the ratios for full-time workers only (in brackets), then the overall ratio of male to female weekly gross wage rises to an average of 80%. This clearly indicates the influence of lower part-time payments made to female labour.

Earnings trends

Figure 13.2 shows that there have been significant changes *over time* in the real earnings gap between high and low wage earners. The figure traces the

growth in real hourly (male) earnings between 1966 and 2009 of people positioned at three different points on the income distribution scale. The 50th percentile line traces the increases in the real hourly earnings of workers receiving the median ('average') wage over the period. Similarly, the 90th percentile represents the growth of real hourly earnings of workers who are 90% of the way up the income distribution, while the 10th percentile shows the growth of real hourly earnings for those whose income is only 10% of the way up the income distribution. Of course the 90th percentile is likely to include some of the people in the 'managers and senior officials' category in Table 13.5, while the 10th percentile will include some of those in the 'elementary occupations' category.

Between 1966 and 1978 the three categories moved roughly in line with each other. However, major differences have emerged since then between those on low and high pay. For example, the real pay for average earners (50th percentile) increased by 46% between 1978 and 2009, whilst the real pay for those near the top of the income scale (90th percentile) increased by as much as 60% over the same time period. On the other hand, those with earnings near the bottom of the income scale (10th percentile) hardly benefited at all over this period. The *relative position* of workers near the bottom of the income scale was in fact the lowest since records began in 1886.

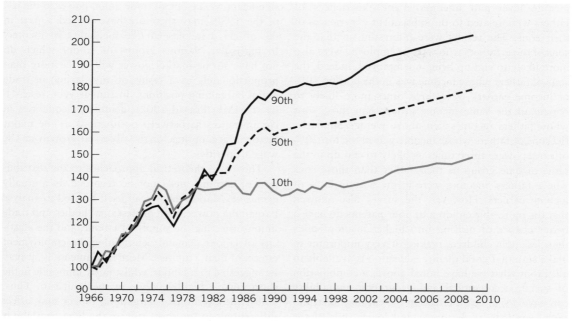

Fig. 13.2 Real hourly male earnings by percentile (Index 1966 = 100).
Sources: Various ONS publications and *Financial Times* (1994).

Explanation of earnings differentials

In seeking to explain the earnings distribution there are two main theoretical approaches, similar to those we considered above for factor shares.

Market theory

The first, the 'market theory', starts from an assumption of equality in *net advantages* for all jobs, i.e. that money earnings *and* the money value placed on working conditions are equal for all jobs. It also assumes that labour has a high degree of occupational and geographical mobility, so that if there is any inequality in net advantages, labour will move to the more advantageous jobs until equality is restored. Thus, differences in *actual* earnings must be caused by compensating differences in other advantages. Job satisfaction is one compensating advantage: enjoyable or safe jobs will be paid less than irksome or risky ones; this may partly explain the relatively high wage of manual workers such as coalface miners and chemical, gas and petroleum plant operators. Still more important are differences in training. Training

and education are regarded as investments in 'human capital', in which the individual forfeits immediate earnings, and bears the cost of training, in the prospect of higher future earnings; this may in part explain the high earnings of professional groups. In fact, one study found that some 30% of the disparities in real hourly male wages shown in Fig. 13.2 could be explained by increases in educational differentials over the period (Gosling *et al.* 2000). Market theory therefore proposes that relative occupational earnings reflect non-monetary advantages between occupations, and the varying length and cost of required training.

Proponents of this theory agree that it is not wholly adequate, and would recognize differences in natural ability as also affecting earnings. However, others, whilst still broadly advocating market theory, have suggested a more fundamental objection, namely that labour is in fact highly immobile. The most recent study of income immobility among the rich and poor found that groups of people at the extreme ends of the income distribution tend to be subject to intergenerational immobility (Johnson and Reed 1996). This research attempted to assess whether the income level and unemployment experiences of fathers were related to the subsequent experiences of their sons. The results were interesting in that the sons of those fathers who were unemployed were also more likely to end up being unemployed. Indeed, the sons of fathers whose income was in the bottom 20% of income earners were three times more likely to remain in the same income group than those sons whose fathers' incomes were above average. Similarly, the sons of fathers whose income was in the top 20% of earners were three times as likely to end up in the same income group as their father than those sons whose fathers' incomes were in the bottom 20% of income earners. However, the survey also showed that the more able children of poor parents do have a better chance of moving into higher income bands than less able children, making it very important to make sure that good quality education is available to all. From what we have noted above, a combination of social, occupational and geographic immobility can have a significant effect on the earnings distribution, especially at the upper and lower ends of the distribution, contrary to the simple predictions of market theory.

Segmented markets

The second theoretical approach places 'immobility' at the very centre of its analysis. This approach sees the labour market as 'segmented', i.e. divided into a series of largely separate (non-competing) occupational groups, with earnings determined by bargaining power *within* each group. Some groups, especially professional bodies, have control over the supply of labour to their occupations, so that they can limit supply and maintain high earnings. Other occupational groups have differing degrees of unionization and industrial power. The relatively high earnings of the relatively small number of printworkers and coalminers in the UK up to the mid-1980s may be explained in part by their history of effective and forceful collective bargaining, whilst the fragmented nature of agricultural and catering work may have contributed to their low pay. In this approach bargaining power is held to outweigh the effects of free market forces. A UK study on the relationship between wage inequality and union density during the 1980s largely substantiated these conclusions (Gosling 1995). It found that wage inequality increased as trade union influence weakened. The

significant weakening of trade union power in the UK in the 1980s may therefore have played a part in the observed increase in the inequality of income. In particular, various groups of labour which do not have strong market power will suffer more than proportionately as a result of any decline in trade union bargaining positions. In similar vein, research by the IMF (Prasad 2002) identified inequalities in circumstances as between occupations as the major factor in accounting for the observed growth in UK wage disparities.

These two theoretical approaches to the distribution of earnings need not be regarded as mutually exclusive. Market theory can itself be used to analyse bargaining power, with professional bodies and trade unions affecting the supply of labour, and the elasticity of labour demand determining the employment effects of their activities. More fundamentally, it may be suggested that labour, whilst fairly immobile in the short run, is highly mobile in the long run. Thus, whilst the exertion of bargaining power may affect differentials in the short run, in the long run labour will move in response to market forces, and thereby erode such differentials.

However, it is obvious from Fig. 13.2 that the wage differential between those on low and those on high wages has *not* been eroded; in fact it actually *widened* between 1978 and 2009. Although the reasons for such a trend are complex, they seem to lie in both inter-industry and intra-industry shifts which have occurred in the UK labour market. For example, the *inter-industry* employment shift from manufacturing to services has tended to increase the number of lower-paid jobs. However, there also seem to have been *intra-industry* employment shifts, namely a shift in demand *within* industries in favour of non-manual, better educated, workers. Even when the proportion of workers with degrees rose from 8% to 11% during the 1980s, their wages continued to rise as demand for such workers rose even faster than their supply. At the other end of the scale, although the percentage of workers with no qualifications fell from 46% to 32%, the unemployment rate among this group actually rose from 6.5% to 16.4% over the 1980s. In other words the demand for such workers fell even faster than the fall in their supply. The drive towards international cost competitiveness and the introduction of new technology have increased the demands for a more skilled and flexible workforce (OECD 1996), leaving workers with low skills, poor family backgrounds and inflexible work attitudes to occupy the low-paid jobs. These trends are also linked to age. For example, young people who are poorly qualified and have low earnings are less likely to experience increasing real earnings with age than are their predecessors (Gosling *et al*. 1994).

Another interesting theory linked to the segmented market hypothesis has been suggested by Daniel Cohen (Cohen 1998). He suggests that there is no longer a single market even for a particular kind of skill or occupation, i.e. there is an *intra-skill* dimension to earnings differentials. For example, top law firms may require secretaries whose pay will reflect their value to the company, while secretaries of similar capabilities working for less profitable law firms will earn considerably less. In other words, an individual's earnings prospects may depend on the nature and profitability of the company which employs them, so that even modest differences in skill may be magnified into significant earnings differentials. In this sense earnings differentials may substantially exceed any skill differentials, even within a given occupation.

The above attempts to explain the presence of wage differentials did not explicitly seek to clarify the reasons for earnings differentials by *sex*, so clearly shown in Table 13.5. Such differentials could be due, for example, to some element of *discrimination* which might exist in the labour market between men and women, even though they were identical workers. For instance, until December 1975, when it was made illegal, collective agreements between employers and employees often included clauses which prescribed that female wage rates should not exceed a certain proportion of the male wage. The examples of wage differentials noted above were made possible because of the preponderance of males in most unions. The state has also been active in allowing this wage differential to exist. For example, up to 1970 when the Equal Pay Act was passed, the police pay structure provided for a differential wage structure for men and women up to the rank of ordinary sergeant, while the pay structure for more senior sergeant ranks included only male rates. Obviously, female policewomen were felt to be able to achieve only the lower grades and even here were not seen as of equal value to males (Tzannatos 1990).

On the other hand, the observed differentials could be regarded as being due to *genuine differences* which exist (or are perceived to exist) between male and female labour. For instance, it is often observed that employers make certain assumptions about the 'average' female worker, i.e. as being one who will not be working for long before leaving to have a child. As a result, employers may be more reluctant to train female workers, who are then placed at a disadvantage as compared to their male counterparts. By acquiring fewer skills, the female worker inevitably receives less pay. Again, female workers are often constrained in competing with male workers by the need to seek employment in the catchment area of their husbands' employment. Such restrictions can again result in a lower wage as compared to that received by the more mobile male counterpart.

Whatever the causes of wage differentials between males and females, there is no doubt that they still exist, even after the initial improvements in the early 1970s following the Equal Pay Act of 1970 and the Sex Discrimination Act of 1975.

The distribution of wealth

Definition of data collection

Wealth is notoriously difficult to define. The most obvious forms of wealth are land, housing, stocks and shares and other financial assets. In addition, many households hold several thousands of pounds-worth of durable goods: cars, carpets and furnishings, electrical goods and so on. All these together are known as 'marketable wealth'. But many ordinary families, whilst owning little land and few shares, may have substantial pension rights. In the case of private schemes these usually derive from contributions into a fund, which in turn is used to buy assets; whilst in the state scheme it derives from contributions which entitle people to future income from government revenues. It is the ownership of marketable wealth plus occupational and state pension rights which is often presented in the data (e.g. Table 13.6).

There are also considerable problems in obtaining information about wealth. Britain has no wealth tax, and so no regular wealth valuations are made. Attempts have been made to do this via sample surveys, but people are often reluctant to reveal their economic circumstances in sufficient detail to draw reliable conclusions. The only time that wealth *is*

Table 13.6 Ownership of marketable wealth.

Percentage of wealth owned by:	1971	1976	1986	2006
Most wealthy 1% of population	31	21	18	21
Most wealthy 5% of population	52	38	36	40
Most wealthy 10% of population	65	50	50	54
Most wealthy 25% of population	87	71	73	77
Most wealthy 50% of population	97	92	90	94

Source: HMRC (2010) *Distribution of Personal Wealth* Inland Revenue Statistics (various).

publicly evaluated is when substantial amounts are transferred from one person to another, usually at death, when wealth is assessed for capital transfer tax. By analysing these figures in terms of age and sex, it is possible to take the dead as a sample of the living, and so estimate the overall wealth distribution. Of course, there is an obvious likelihood of sampling error, especially in estimating the wealth of the young. The procedure also ignores certain bequests, such as those to surviving spouses, which are not liable to tax. Nevertheless, it is the best method available.

Concentration of wealth

Table 13.6 shows the Inland Revenue's estimate of the overall wealth distribution, excluding occupational and state pension rights. As we might expect, wealth is much more unequally distributed than income. For example, the most wealthy 1% of the population own 21% of the wealth, whilst the top 10% own as much as 54% of wealth and the top 50% own 94% of wealth (i.e. the bottom half own only 6% of wealth).

But perhaps more significant than the absolute figures is the astonishingly rapid reduction in inequality, especially in the early 1970s. The wealth of the richest 1% fell in five years from 31 to 21% of the total, whilst for the richest 10% it fell from 65 to 50% (Table 13.6). This reflects the high rate of inflation in those years, which rapidly eroded the value of financial assets, and also the steep decline in the prices of stocks and shares and commercial land. Over a much longer period we observe a steady reduction in wealth inequality. In 1924 the wealthiest 1% owned 60% of *marketable* wealth (i.e. excluding occupational and state pension rights); this had fallen

to 42% in 1951, and is now 21%. A major reason for this has been death duties, and more recently capital transfer tax (inheritance tax). This is a progressive tax, and helps break up the largest wealth holdings as they pass from one generation to another.

Despite the continuing influences of these factors, changes in the distribution of wealth were much more modest in the 1980s and 1990s, as can be observed from Table 13.6. Recently, however, it has been argued that 'new wealth' is being created in the UK as the rapid spread of home ownership and the rise in house prices means that inheriting such properties may allow both middle- and working-class people to benefit in the future. The percentage of UK households owning their own homes rose from 56% in 1980 to 70% in 2009. Although this may improve the wealth situation of many middle- and working-class income earners, it will create even more problems for the children of the 25% or more parents who may never own their own homes. It may also further increase the regional disparity of wealth as a result of regional house price differentials.

Though it is an emotive issue, one may doubt that the wealth distribution is a primary source of income inequality. We have already seen that the main source of income inequality is not between capital and labour, but between different groups of labour.

Poverty

Definition

There has been much debate as to the definition of poverty. Some have tried to define it in *absolute* terms. For example, Rowntree (1901), who made a major study of poverty just over a century ago, concluded that poverty was having insufficient income to obtain the minimum means necessary for survival, namely basic food, housing and clothing. Others have sought to define it in *relative* terms: Townsend (1973), in his survey of poverty, saw it as the inability to participate in the customary activities of society, which then might have included taking an annual holiday away from home, owning a refrigerator, having sole use of an indoor WC, and so on.

In some ways, the grinding poverty experienced in pre-Second World War Britain is no longer present. For example, studies by the Department of Social Security on 'Households below average income' have shown that amongst the poorest 10% of UK income earners, the percentage who have access to some basic consumer benefits were as follows: fridge/fridge freezer (99%), washing machine (88%), central heating (77%), telephone (76%), video (72%) and car or van (53%). Although these figures suffer from measurement problems, the improvement over the last 20 years in these percentages has been significant. However, such data do not always capture the more complicated aspects of poverty and the *relative* positions of different groups in UK society.

On a more practical level the 'official' poverty level (defined as the minimum acceptable income level) used by many researchers in the UK is given by the level of Income Support. On the other hand, the Child Poverty Action Group (CPAG) has defined the 'margins of poverty' as those people whose incomes are below Income Support plus 40%. Income Support is set by governments, and may be affected not only by the needs of the poor, but also by general political policy. It also ignores other aspects of economic deprivation not directly related to money

income, such as inadequate housing, schools, health care and suchlike.

Another important source of statistics on poverty is derived from the *Households Below Average Income* published by the government's Department for Work and Pensions. Using these statistics, the poverty line is most often defined as those households whose income is *either* below 50% of the mean household income *or* below 60% of the median household income. In recent years the government has tended to use the latter definition because it is in line with EU practice, and because it is arguably a better measure for capturing the gap between the standard of living enjoyed by the poorest families and the 'typical' (median) family. Even so, there is sometimes inconsistency, as when using a poverty measure of below 50% (not 60%) of the median household income (as in Table 13.7). The CPAG, on the other hand, continues to use the former definition.

These various measures, together with information on the distribution of income which is supplied by the Institute for Fiscal Studies, provide useful insights into the incidence of low income and poverty. However, they fail to account for other forms of poverty such as those frequently shown in statistics of homelessness or of ill-health.

Incidence of poverty

When we look at some of these suggested measures of poverty we find some disturbing results. Data show that the number of people *receiving* Income Support (including income-based Jobseeker's Allowance) has risen from 3.0 million in 1978 to 5.1 million in 2010. If we add to these figures the people who *depend*

Table 13.7 The growth of poverty (defined as earnings less than 60% of average income), 1979–2009.

	Total population (million)			Child population (million)		
	Total population	Number in poverty	Percentage of population	Child population	Number in poverty	Percentage in poverty
1979	54.0	7.3	13.5	13.8	2.0	14.5
1996/97	55.6	14.0	25.2	12.7	4.3	33.9
2000/01	57.9	13.4	23.1	13.1	4.1	31.3
2008/09	60.3	13.4	22.2	12.8	3.9	30.5

Source: Department for Work and Pensions (2010) *Households Below Average Income 1994/5–2008/9,* and previous issues.

Table 13.8 Child poverty by type of family and income, 1998–2009.

	Percentage of child population[1]		Poverty rate (%)[2]	
	1998/99	2008/09	1998/99	2008/09
Children in lone-parent families				
Full-time	4.0	5.5	16.9	21.0
Part-time	5.0	6.2	44.8	29.0
Workless	13.8	11.7	78.7	75.0
Children in couple families				
Self-employed	11.5	12.5	30.5	30.0
Two full-time earners	11.2	12.5	1.1	3.0
One full-time, one part-time	25.0	22.7	6.7	7.0
One full-time, one not working	18.0	18.8	27.8	29.0
One or two part-time	4.3	5.4	57.4	60.0
Workless	7.2	5.4	82.2	75.0
All children	100.0	100.0	32.5	30.0

[1]Relative to the percentage of all UK children to be found in the groups.
[2]The percentage of children in the various groups where the household earns less than 60% of median income (AHC), i.e. the percentage of children in households classed as being in poverty.
Sources: Department for Work and Pensions (2010) *Households Below Average Income 1994/95–2008/09*; Brewer *et al*. (2006).

upon these benefits, e.g. children, then the total number dependent on these benefits in 2010 was 12.2 million people, or 20% of the total population.

To help clarify the growth of poverty in the UK it may be helpful to study the results of the *Households Below Average Income* report, published in 2010 (Table 13.7). Using the definition of 'poverty' as those households who earn less than 60% of the average income after housing costs, we can see that between 1979 and 2009 the total number of people in poverty has increased from 7.3 million to 13.4 million, suggesting that the percentage of the total population in poverty has nearly doubled over the period. The number of children who live in poverty has increased from 2 million to 3.9 million over the same period, suggesting that the percentage of children in poverty has also doubled between 1979 and 2009. By 2009, therefore, some 22% of the total UK population and 30% of UK children were living in households earning less than half the average income.

Over the past decade the target of reducing child poverty has been a particular policy issue of successive Labour governments and Table 13.8 provides an insight into this issue between 1998 and 2009.

Poverty rates are highest for children in workless families, being 75% in 2008/09 for both lone parents and couples. In addition, families composed of couples with only part-time employment had relatively high child poverty rates of 60% in 2008/09. In contrast, groups such as full-time working lone parents, couples with two full-time earners, and couples with one full-time and one part-time earner, all had below-average child poverty rates. Table 13.8 also shows that there has been general progress in reducing poverty in most groups, with particular success for single parents and couples in workless families.

Although it would seem that governments have succeeded in reducing child poverty, they have not been able to meet their own targets. For example, the government aimed to cut child poverty by 25% between 1989/99 and 2004/05, but the actual fall has been only 17.2%, based on after housing cost (AHC) figures. In actual numbers, this means that the number of children in poverty fell from 4.1 million to 3.4 million, instead of falling further to 3 million between those dates – a shortfall of 0.4 million. Although government policy has undoubtedly made major inroads into alleviating child poverty, the

Table 13.9 The European child wellbeing and poverty index.

Rank	Country	Health	Subjective wellbeing	Children's relationships	Material resources	Behaviour and risk	Education	Housing and environment
1	Netherlands	2	1	1	7	4	4	9
2	Sweden	1	7	3	10	1	9	3
3	Norway	6	8	6	2	2	10	1
4	Iceland	4	9	4	1	3	14	8
5	Finland	12	6	9	4	7	7	4
6	Denmark	3	5	10	9	15	12	5
7	Slovenia	15	16	2	5	13	11	19
8	Germany	17	12	8	12	5	6	16
9	Ireland	14	10	14	20	12	5	2
10	Luxembourg	5	17	19	3	11	16	7
11	Austria	26	2	7	8	19	19	6
12	Cyprus	10	–	–	13	–	–	11
13	Spain	13	4	17	18	6	20	13
14	Belgium	18	13	18	15	21	1	12
15	France	20	14	28	11	10	13	10
16	Czech Rep	9	22	27	6	20	3	22
17	Slovakia	7	11	22	16	23	17	15
18	Estonia	11	20	12	14	25	2	25
19	Italy	19	18	20	17	8	23	20
20	Poland	8	26	16	26	17	8	23
21	Portugal	21	23	13	21	9	25	18
22	Hungary	23	25	11	23	16	15	21
23	Greece	29	3	23	19	22	21	14
24	UK	24	21	15	24	18	22	17
25	Romania	27	19	5	–	24	27	–
26	Bulgaria	25	15	24	–	26	26	–
27	Latvia	16	24	26	22	27	18	26
28	Lithuania	22	27	25	25	28	24	24
29	Malta	28	28	21	–	14	–	–

Source: CPAG (2009).

prospects of it being able to meet its ambitious target were always rather slim. However, its decisions to increase substantially the amount of cash to be transferred to low-income families with children and also its 'welfare to work' policies (see Chapter 19) have meant that more workless parents have found work and hence increased their real incomes (Hills and Stewart 2005).

At this stage it might be useful to investigate the situation regarding child wellbeing and child poverty in European countries. A league table produced by Bradshaw and Richardson (2009) contains 43 separate indicators divided into seven domains as seen in Table 13.9. These domains include health (indicators of infant mortality, etc.); subjective wellbeing (how children feel about their lives, etc.); children's relationships (how children get on in school); material resources (indicators of child poverty); behaviour and risk (indicators of violence); education (indicators of achievement/youth inactivity); and housing and environment (indicators of overcrowding/housing problems). As can be seen, the UK is 24th out of 29 in the overall ranking in this league table, which is well below its economic ranking amongst the same countries in Europe. The UK is not even in the top third of European countries in any of the domains – its 'best' score is 15th for children's relationships! This new assessment of child wellbeing and child poverty signifies a call for more government action in the UK. The Child Poverty Act of 2010 makes meeting the 2020 target of 'eradicating' child poverty legally binding in the UK and provides a huge challenge to future UK governments, especially in a period of economic downturn.

Whatever our definition, there are clearly large numbers of adults and children in 'poverty', suggesting that it is most effectively tackled by a wide range of initiatives over a prolonged period of time. For example, the National Minimum Wage (NMW) introduced in 1998 has, as one of its objectives, the reduction of income inequalities at work (see Chapter 14, page 288). However, in this respect its impacts have been rather modest, perhaps because the NMW has not been uprated in line with average earnings.

Income from employment provides over 62% of all income received, and must be a focus for any attempt to explain the inequality that does exist. Variations in income by occupation, by sex and by skill levels clearly contribute to such inequality. Together with the rise of inequality of income from employment, the growth of self-employment in recent years has also contributed to greater inequality in overall income. Wealth is more unequally distributed than income, and although there has been a progressive tendency towards a more equal distribution since the early 1970s, this process slowed down markedly in the 1980s and actually went into reverse in the 1990s with growing wealth inequality. Poverty is a serious phenomenon in the UK, no matter how we define it. The large numbers and varied characteristics of those in poverty suggest that government policy must be wide-ranging and sustained if poverty levels are to be reduced substantially. In a detailed analysis of income distribution and poverty in the UK, Joyce *et al.* (2010) indicate that the future course of living standards, inequality and poverty will be highly uncertain in the UK. They point out that how the public finances are rebalanced in the near future appears to be the 'single most important determinant of the future path for living standards, poverty and inequality' during the period 2010–15.

Conclusion

After some move towards greater equality of income distribution between 1961 and 1979, the process has been significantly reversed since the end of the 1970s.

Key points

- The Gini coefficient (G) is the ratio of the area between the Lorenz curve and the diagonal to the total area beneath the diagonal.

- Where G = 0, we have perfect equality; where G = 1, we have perfect inequality.

- Where Lorenz curves intersect, we must be particularly careful in using the Gini coefficient.

- Since 1979, the Gini coefficient has tended to rise in the UK.

- Inequality as measured by the Gini coefficient is higher in the UK than for the *average* of EU countries, but is lower than for the US.

- Since employment accounts for around 62% of all factor income, the labour market must be a major source of any income inequalities observed.

- Significant differences in earnings can be observed by type of occupation and by gender, though the latter gap has narrowed in recent years.

- Household characteristics such as age, unemployment, single parenthood, etc., also play a key role in income inequality.

- The distribution of wealth is even more unequal than the distribution of income.

- Poverty can be expressed in both absolute and relative terms. Using a variety of indicators, the incidence of poverty has clearly increased in the UK since 1979, although real progress has been made in combatting poverty in recent times.

Now try the self-check questions for this chapter on the Companion Website. You will also find useful links to relevant websites.

References and further reading

Adam, S. and Brewer, M. (2003) Children, well-being, taxes and benefits, *Economic Review*, 20(3), February; 20(4), April, 27–30.

Atkinson, A. B. (1999) The distribution of income in the UK and OECD countries in the twentieth century, *Oxford Review of Economic Policy*, 15(4): 56–75.

Bradshaw, J. and Richardson, D. (2009) An index of child wellbeing in Europe, *Child Indicators Research*, April, 319–51.

Brewer, M., Goodman, A., Shaw, J. and Sibieta, L. (2006) *Poverty and Inequality in Britain*, London, Institute for Fiscal Studies.

Cohen, D. (1998) *The Wealth of the World and the Poverty of Nations*, Cambridge MA, MIT Press.

CPAG (2009) *Child Wellbeing and Child Poverty: Where the UK Stands in the European Table*, Spring, London, Child Poverty Action Group.

Department for Work and Pensions (2010) *Households Below Average Income (HBAI)*, London, The Stationery Office.

Department of Employment (1999) *New Earnings Survey*, Part D, London, The Stationery Office.

Financial Times (1994) *Economic Viewpoint*, 30th June.

Goodman, A. and Shephard, A. (2002) *Inequality and Living Standards in Great Britain: Some Facts*, Briefing Note no. 19, London, Institute for Fiscal Studies.

Gosling, A. (1995) *Wages and Unions in the British Labour Markets*, Working Paper, University College, London.

Gosling, A., Machin, S. and Meghir, C. (1994) *What has Happened to Wages?*, Commentary No. 43, London, Institute for Fiscal Studies 67(4): 635–66.

Gosling, A., Machin, S. and Meghir, C. (2000) The changing distribution of male wages in the UK, *Review of Economic Studies*, 67.

Gregg, H. and Machin, S. (1994) Is the UK rise in inequality different?, in Barrell, R. (ed.) *The UK Labour Market: Comparative Aspects and Institutional Developments*, Cambridge, Cambridge University Press, 93–125.

Griffiths, A. (2003) Taxes, transfers and the distribution of income: UK experience 1997–2001, *British Economy Survey*, 32(2): 14–18.

Hills, J. and Stewart, K. (2005) *A More Equal Society? New Labour, Poverty, Inequality and Exclusion*, Bristol, Policy Press.

HMRC (2010) *Distribution of Personal Wealth*, London, HM Revenue and Customs.

Jenkins, S. P. (1996) Recent trends in the UK income distribution: What has happened and why?, *Oxford Review of Economic Policy*, 12(1): 29–46.

Johnson P. and Reed, H. (1996) Intergenerational mobility among the rich and poor: results from the National Child Development Survey, *Oxford Review of Economic Policy*, 12(1): 127–8.

Joyce, R, Muriel, A., Phillips, D and Sibieta, L. (2010) *Poverty and Inequality in the UK 2010*, Commentary C116, London, Institute for Fiscal Studies.

Machin, S. (1996) Wage inequality in the UK, *Oxford Review of Economic Policy*, 12(1): 47–64.

OECD (1996) *Technology, Productivity, and Job Creation*, April, Paris, Organisation for Economic Cooperation and Development.

OECD (2008) *Growing Unequal: Income Distribution and Policy*, October, Paris, Organisation for Economic Cooperation and Development.

OECD (2010) *StatExtracts*, Income distribution – Inequality, Paris, Organisation for Economic Cooperation and Development.

ONS (2010a) *Annual Survey of Hours and Earnings 2009*, London, Office for National Statistics.

ONS (2010b) *United Kingdom Economic Accounts*, London, Office for National Statistics.

Pen, J. (1971) *Income Distribution*, London, Pelican.

Prasad, E. S. (2002) Wage inequality in the UK 1975–1999, *IMF Staff Papers*, **49**(3): 339–63.

Rowntree, S. (1901) *Poverty – A Study of Town Life*, London, Macmillan.

Sutherland, H. and Piachaud, D. (2001) Reducing child poverty in Britain: an assessment of government policy 1997–2001, *Economic Journal*, **111**, F85–F101.

Townsend, P. (1973) *The Social Minority*, London, Allen Lane.

Tzannatos, Z. (1990) Sex differences in the labour market, *Economic Review*, May, 31–6.

UNDP (**2010**) *Human Development Report 2010: The Real Wealth of Nations: Pathways to Human Development*, New York, United Nations Development Programme.

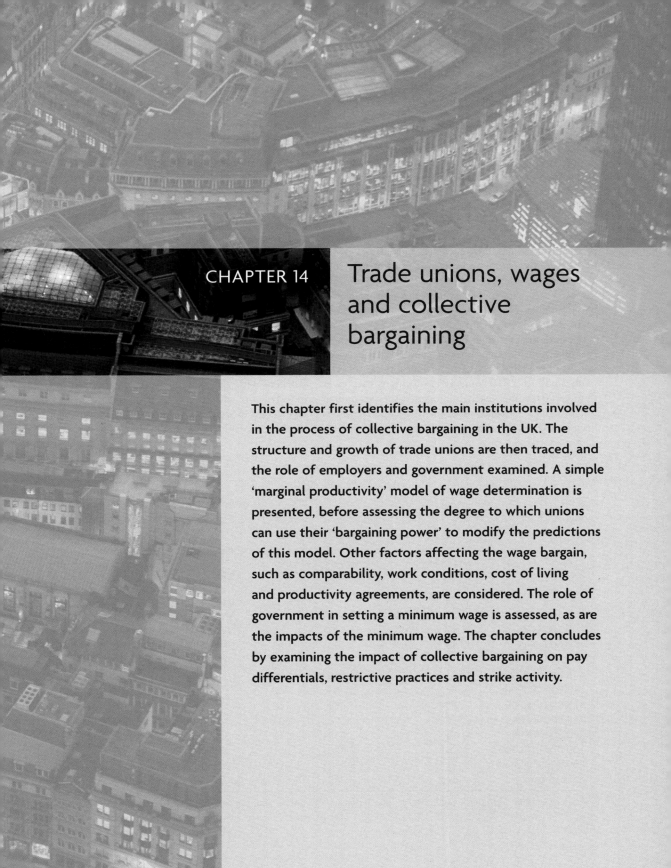

CHAPTER 14

Trade unions, wages and collective bargaining

This chapter first identifies the main institutions involved in the process of collective bargaining in the UK. The structure and growth of trade unions are then traced, and the role of employers and government examined. A simple 'marginal productivity' model of wage determination is presented, before assessing the degree to which unions can use their 'bargaining power' to modify the predictions of this model. Other factors affecting the wage bargain, such as comparability, work conditions, cost of living and productivity agreements, are considered. The role of government in setting a minimum wage is assessed, as are the impacts of the minimum wage. The chapter concludes by examining the impact of collective bargaining on pay differentials, restrictive practices and strike activity.

Types of trade union

A trade union has been described as 'a continuous association of wage-earners for the purpose of maintaining or improving the conditions of their working lives' (Webb and Webb 1896, p. 1). Although useful, this definition does not reflect the whole range of trade union objectives. The Trades Union Congress (TUC) outlines 10 general objectives of unions, with improved wages and terms of employment at the top of the list. Other aims, such as 'full employment', 'industrial democracy' and a 'voice in government', are included, but the emphasis is on the unions' 'capacity to win higher wages through collective bargaining as one of their most effective methods of attracting membership'.[1]

Despite having some objectives in common there is still a considerable amount of diversity between unions in the UK (Table 14.1). Most unions are relatively small. In 2010 some 49% of unions had fewer than 1,000 members each, but together they accounted for only 0.3% of total union membership. There has been a progressive reduction in the number of unions,

from the peak of 1,384 unions in 1920, to 179 in 2010. The reduction has been particularly marked for small unions. The number of unions with fewer than 1,000 members has more than halved since 1979. In 2010 the 10 largest unions (Table 14.2) accounted for 77% of total membership. The trend towards fewer and larger unions, largely as a result of mergers, is well established, but the 179 British unions provide a contrast with the 17 industrial unions in the former West Germany.

Four broad headings have been traditionally used to classify trades unions in the UK, namely craft, general, industrial and 'white-collar' unions.

Craft unions

These were the earliest type of union, and are mainly composed of workers regarded as 'qualified' in a particular craft. Most craft unions now include workers with the same skill across the industry or industries in which they are employed, such as the Associated Society of Locomotive Engineers and Firemen (ASLEF).

Table 14.1 Unions and union membership, 1979 and 2010.

| Members | Number of unions | | All membership (000s) | | Percentage of | | | |
| | | | | | No. of unions | | Membership of all unions | |
	1979	2010	1979	2010	1979	2010	1979	2010
Under 100	73	35	4	1	16.0	19.6	0.0	0.0
100–499	124	30	30	8	27.3	16.8	0.2	0.1
500–999	47	22	33	16	10.4	12.3	0.3	0.2
1,000–2,499	58	17	92	30	12.8	9.5	0.7	0.4
2,500–4,999	43	21	152	74	9.5	16.7	1.1	1.0
5,000–9,999	24	11	155	80	5.3	6.1	1.2	1.1
10,000–14,999	7	4	83	56	1.6	2.2	0.6	0.8
15,000–24,999	19	8	358	160	4.2	4.4	2.7	2.2
25,000–49,999	17	15	623	531	3.7	8.4	4.7	7.2
50,000–99,999	15	2	919	141	3.3	1.1	6.9	1.9
100,000–249,999	16	6	2,350	931	3.5	3.4	17.7	12.6
250,000 and more	11	8	8,490	5,359	2.4	4.5	63.9	72.5
All members	454	179	13,289	7,388	100.0	100.0	100.0	100.0

Source: Adapted from Certification Officer (2010) *Annual Report of the Certification Officer, 2009/10* and previous Issues.

Table 14.2 The top 10 largest TUC unions, 2009/10

Rank	Name	Membership
1	Unite the Union[1]	1,635,483
2	UNISON: The Public Sector Union[2]	1,362,000
3	GMB[3]	601,131
4	Royal College of Nursing of the United Kingdom	400,716
5	Union of Shop Distributive and Allied Workers (USDAW)	370,763
6	National Union of Teachers (NUT)	366,657
7	National Association of Schoolmasters/Union of Women Teachers (NASUWT)	322,142
8	Public and Commercial Services Union (PCS)[4]	300,324
9	Communication Workers Union (CWU)[5]	230,968
10	Association of Teachers and Lecturers (ATL)	206,993

[1]Unite was formed in 2007 as a result of the merger of the Transport and General Worker's Union (T&G) and Amicus (itself a merger of The Amalgamated Engineering and Electrical Union (AEEU), and the Manufacturing, Science and Finance Union (MFS)).
[2]UNISON was formed in 1993 and is composed of three public sector unions, NALGO, NUPE and COHSE.
[3]GMB is the formal designation of the Boilermaker and Allied Trades Union (composed of seven sections which cover both white and blue collar workers).
[4]PCS was formed in 1998 as the merger of the Civil and Public Service Association (CPSA) and the Public Services, Tax and Commerce Union (PTC).
[5]CWU was formed in 1955 as a result of a merger between the National Communications Union and the Union of Communication Workers.
Source: Adapted from Certification Officer (2010) *Annual Report of the Certification Officer 2009–2010*, p. 62.

General unions

These unions originated in the 1880s in the attempt to organize semi-skilled and unskilled workers not covered by the craft unions. General unions do not restrict their membership to workers with specific skills, nor to particular industries or occupations. Examples include Unite the Union with 1,635,483 members and GMB with 601,131 members.

The distinction between craft and general unions is not always clear. Over the last decade or so, this problem has been complicated by the growth of merger activity in the trade union movement. For example, in May 1992 the Amalgamated Engineering Union (AEU) merged with the Electrical, Electronic, Telecommunications and Plumbing Union (EETPU) to form the Amalgamated Engineering and Electrical Union (AEEU). The new union included occupations within the engineering and electrical sectors, which can be classified as 'craft' type occupations, as well as a variety of semi-skilled and unskilled machine operators who could legitimately be placed in the 'general union' category.

Industrial unions

These attempt to place under one union all the workers in an industry, whatever their status of occupation. The National Union of Mineworkers (NUM) comes closest to this in the UK, covering most of the occupations engaged in mining operations, though now very much reduced in size. Other examples of industrial unions include the Iron and Steel Trades Confederation (ISTC) and the Communication Workers Union. Most industrial unions in the UK are 'a matter of degree rather than kind'. In other words, they usually cover a large number of those engaged in the industry, but by no means all.

'White-collar' unions

These restrict their membership to professional, administrative and clerical employees. 'White-collar' unions have expanded faster than any other type of union in the post-war period. Large numbers of professions are now organized as unions, such as the

Royal College of Nursing of the UK (RCN) with 400,716 members and the National Union of Teachers (NUT) with 366,657 members.

As in the case of general and craft trade unions, the distinction between white-collar and manual unions is also becoming clouded by merger. This was exemplified in July 1993 by the formation of UNISON as a result of an amalgamation of the white-collar National and Local Government Officers' Association (NALGO) with the two primarily manual workers' unions, the National Union of Public Employees (NUPE) and the Confederation of Health Service Employees (COHSE). Similarly, in January 2002, the AEEU and the Manufacturing, Science and Finance union (MSF) merged to form Amicus which brought together skilled and semi-skilled workers in the electrical and engineering sectors with supervisory and managerial grades in the manufacturing, science and finance sectors. In fact, the overwhelming majority of unions now have features taken from more than one category of union, suggesting the need for new and alternative classifications. For example, some unions may now be more usefully classified as either 'closed' or 'open'. They may be said to be 'closed', in that they restrict membership to a clearly definable trade or profession such as the British Airline Pilots' Association (BALPA), or to a particular industry as with the NUM. In contrast, 'open' unions seek to recruit a diverse membership, such as the large general unions, thereby making them less susceptible to decline as particular industries ebb and flow.

It is difficult to provide an accurate pattern of trade union membership by *industry*, as over 4 million members belong to unions recruiting over several industries. The fact that the UK does not have just a few industrial unions as in West Germany, or enterprise unions as in Japan, poses problems not only for classification but also for collective bargaining. The 'multi-union' structure of the UK means that many unions are involved in negotiations at both plant and enterprise levels. This can cause problems for both management and unions. Management may experience difficulties in coordinating negotiations with several different unions, often in the same plant. Unions may have to compromise individual aims and policies when part of a 'team' negotiating with employers. Multiunion plants or enterprises may also lead to inter-union rivalry and conflict. For instance, the Rail and Maritime Transport union (RMT) and ASLEF compete for membership among London Underground employees. There is also rivalry among the teaching unions in both schools and university sectors for membership.

The Trades Union Congress

The TUC was founded in 1868 with the aim of improving the economic and social conditions of working people, and of promoting the interests of its affiliated organizations. In 2010 there were 58 affiliated trade unions representing 88% of trade unionists in the UK. The TUC is mainly concerned with general questions which affect trade unions both nationally and internationally, and has participated in discussions relating to the national economy through its membership of the National Economic Development Office (NEDO), although the government's abolition of NEDO in 1992 removed a major residual channel of communication. The General Council of the TUC represents the organization in the period between one annual Congress and another and is responsible for putting Congress decisions into effect. The General Council has no authority to call strikes, or to stop strikes called by its members, but can offer advice on disputes. Under Rule 11 the General Council can intervene in unofficial strikes and make recommendations to the unions and employers concerned.

The TUC has also been successful through its Organising Academy in training union recruiters and improving the professionalism of unions' recruitment strategies. Although the influence of the TUC on the UK government has waned considerably since the 1970s, it has an influence on European legislation as a member of the European Trade Union Confederation (ETUC). The ETUC represents the interests of some 60 million trade unionists in Europe, both within and outside the EU, and is one of the 'social partners' in the EU along with the employers' organizations UNICE and CEEP (see below). The partners have negotiated 'frameworks agreements' that have been adopted as EU Directives and which are binding in UK law. These Directives are considered more fully in the section on the Social Chapter.

 Trade unions and change

Until 1980 the fall in employment, and therefore the number unionized, in the primary and secondary

Table 14.3 Trade union membership and density in the UK, 1979–2010 (000s and %).

Year	Civilian employees in employment	Unemployed	Potential trade union membership	Trade union membership	Density* (%)
1979	23,173	1,295	24,368	13,289	54.5
1981	21,892	2,520	24,412	12,106	49.6
1983	21,067	3,104	24,171	11,236	46.5
1985	21,423	3,271	24,694	10,821	43.8
1987	21,584	2,953	24,537	10,475	42.7
1989	23,661	1,799	25,460	10,238	40.2
1990	22,918	1,665	24,583	9,947	40.5
1992	23,198	2,779	25,977	9,048	34.8
1994	22,937	2,796	25,733	8,278	32.2
1996	23,624	2,388	26,012	7,935	30.5
1998	24,569	1,822	26,397	7,851	29.7
2001	24,161	1,431	25,592	7,779	30.4
2005	24,817	1,425	26,242	7,559	28.8
2010	24,943	2,450	27,393	7,388	27.0

*Union density defined as: $\frac{\text{actual union membership}}{\text{potential union membership}} \times 100$.

Sources: ONS (2010) *Labour Market Statistics*, October; Certification Officer (2010) *Annual Report of the Certification Officer 2009/10*, p. 62.

industries was more than compensated for by the rise in employment, and so the number unionized, in the service industries. Since 1980 this trend has been broken (see Table 14.3) and with it the sustained growth in trade union membership over the post-war period. In fact, membership fell substantially by 44.4% between 1979 and 2010, with union density declining from a peak of 54.5% in 1979 to 27.0% in 2010. A breakdown of membership by sex reveals that of the 7.4 million or so union members in 2010, 50% were women, giving a density of 29.5% compared to a density of 25.2% for men.

Factors affecting union growth and decline

Explanations of the factors which affect union membership (and in particular the decline in the density figure since its peak in 1979) can be grouped under three broad headings.

Labour force composition

This set of explanations highlights the role of changes in the *compositions of the workforce* as a factor

affecting the decline in union density, the argument being that the composition of employment has moved away from the industries, occupations and regions where union density was relatively high, and towards those industries, occupations and regions where union density tends to be relatively low.

For example, union membership differs *by sector*. In the private sector, the average union density is 15.1% whilst in the public sector it rises to an impressive 56.6%. As far as *occupations* are concerned, union density in the category designated 'Professional occupations' (which includes teachers, health workers, business and public service workers and those in science and technology) has an average union density of 47.5% whilst for 'Sales and customer service' occupations (such as those workers in the retail/ wholesale service sectors) union density drops to an average of only 12.3%. In terms of *employment status* (i.e. whether a person is full-time or part-time, self-employed or a trainee), the statistics show that union density is much higher for full-time workers (29.6%) than for part-time workers (21.6%) or for full-time self-employed (10%). It also seems that the *size of workplace* is an important factor. For example, the average union density in workplaces employing 50 or more employees is 37.0%, while that for workplaces employing fewer than 50 employees is only 17.2%. *Gender* is also a factor, with union density higher for females (29.5) than for males (25.2) and increasing with age and length of service for both males and females. Finally, union density varies by country/region, being highest in Northern Ireland (39.9%), followed by Wales (35.4%), Scotland (31.8%) and England (26.1%). However, rates vary in the regions of England, from a high 35.7% in the North East to 21.9% in the South East. Given these figures, it is obvious that the recent changes in the structure of the working population (see Chapter 1, Table 1.4) have had an adverse effect on union density.

The privatization of much of the public sector, the loss of engineering and related jobs via deindustrialization, the sharp increase in the number of self-employed and part-time workers, the growth in the number of small companies, and the growth of female participation in the labour force are just some of the changes which have tended to decrease union density.

Another key factor behind falling trade union membership is the widespread failure of unions to organize workers in businesses that were set up after 1980. The proportion of British establishments which recognize manual and non-manual trade unions for collective bargaining over pay and conditions is 30 percentage points lower in post-1980 establishments than in the rest of the business community (Machin 2000). Although the largest decreases in recognition occurred in private sector manufacturing companies, there were also sharp falls in private sector services companies. Such organizations were often faced with particularly severe competitive conditions during 1980–2000 which tended to restrict their capacity to sustain the potential 'costs' of union recognition (Brown *et al.* 2009). In fact, unions were recognized for collective bargaining in only a fifth of such 'new' enterprises. Another factor relating to the issue of collective bargaining has been the rise of the 'free rider'. Generally speaking, in workplaces where unions have a collective agreement with management on pay and conditions, most of the employees tend to belong to unions. However, over the period 1999–2009, there has been an increasing number of employees in workplaces who *do not* belong to the union and so are seen by many as 'free riding' on the benefits fought for by the unions. This is particularly

so in the private sector where 63% of private sector employees were union members in 1999 but only 57% by 2009. Interestingly, recent research tends to point to the fact that the fall in union density over the last decade is more likely to be due to a waning appetite for unionism among employees in general, rather than any changes in labour force composition indicated above (Bryson and Forth 2010). This suggestion is strengthened by the fact that the percentage of UK employees who have *never* belonged to a trade union rose from an average of 22% in 1985–86 to 51% by 2006–08 (Bryson and Forth 2010).

Macroeconomic factors

Macroeconomic factors such as economic growth and unemployment, as well as movements in prices and wages, also have an effect on union membership and density.

Unemployment has obviously had a significant negative impact on union growth. Historically the major upswings in trade union membership have occurred in periods when unemployment has been relatively low or falling – for instance, 1901–20 and 1934–47. A study by Bain and Elsheikh (1982) found that in 15 of the 19 industries studied during the inter-war and post-war years, slow growth of unionization was correlated with periods of high unemployment, and vice versa. The Bain–Elsheikh model suggests that relatively high unemployment will reduce union bargaining power, and therefore discourage union membership. This conclusion is also supported by a survey which investigated the effects of the 1990–93 recession on TU membership (Geroski *et al.* 1995). That recession was shown to cause a still more rapid decline in trade union membership than might otherwise have been predicted.

However, some have suggested that the *threat* of unemployment may even act as a *stimulus* to union growth. Hawkins (1981) sees this as one factor in raising union density amongst white-collar workers threatened by technological and organizational change during the 1970s. Technology is something of a two-edged sword for unions; on the one hand it may create unemployment, whilst on the other it often confers substantial industrial 'muscle' on the key workers operating the new computer-based systems.

Price and Bain (1976) suggest that the *rate of change of prices* and *the rate of change of wages* may also influence union growth. Rising prices have a 'threat' effect so that workers unionize to defend real wages, particularly in the early years of an inflationary period. Wage rises have a 'credit' effect for unions, in that they are attributed to their bargaining power, and this promotes membership. Bain and Elsheikh (1982) found that the real wage variable, in one form or another, had a significant and positive impact on union growth in 15 of the 19 industries they studied. Also the desire to protect established *pay relativities* may affect union growth. For example, in advanced stages of incomes policies, when pay differentials have been substantially eroded, there is evidence that union membership increases. The suggestion here is that a series of injustices leads workers to seek greater bargaining power by joining unions in the hope of restoring differentials.

The rapid decline of both union membership and density in the 1980s and early 1990s suggests that macroeconomic factors may have a negative influence on union growth. Some of the macroeconomic factors also appear to have different effects on union density than those shown by some of the earlier studies quoted above. For example, Carruth and Disney (1987) tried to capture the effects of the main macroeconomic factors on union density by separating out the changes in union membership into two components: a 'trend' component influenced by changes in total employment, and a 'cycle' component which varies with macroeconomic variables such as wages, prices and unemployment. They note that when unemployment and real wage growth are high relative to the trend, membership growth is depressed. The 'threat' and 'credit effect' noted in earlier studies seem to have become much less effective. Interestingly, a study of the 1988–90 period (Metcalf 1994) noticed that the reverse relationship did not seem to hold; i.e. falling unemployment and slower real wages did not seem to halt the fall in union density. This may suggest that union density may be experiencing a long-term, secular decline rather than being affected only by short-run cyclical changes in macroeconomic variables.

This conclusion is substantiated by more recent research by Blanchflower and Bryson who were unable to establish whether the diminution of union influence was a cyclical phenomenon (Blanchflower and Bryson 2010). This points to a change in union/management attitudes over the last decade which is investigated in the next section.

Industrial relations environment

This set of reasons relates to the influence on union membership and density of such factors as government and employer policies, and the trade unions' own responses to such policies.

Carruth and Disney (1987) found that, in a historical context, *Conservative governments* have tended to exercise a negative impact on membership rates. Freeman and Pelletier (1990) and Minford and Riley (1994) also accord a strong negative impact on membership rates of the post-1979 legislative programme of the UK Conservative governments. Although it is difficult to be precise, there is little doubt that the post-1979 legislative reforms significantly weakened the position of trade unions. To these legislative reforms should be added the effects of government supply-side policies, with their emphasis on privatization and cost savings. For example, the total number of public sector employees decreased from just over 7 million in 1979 to 5 million in 1995 – a fall of 29%. Central government employment fell by 29%, local government employment fell by 9% and employment in the public corporations fell by 21%, over the same period. Given that the density of unionization is higher in the public sector than in the private sector, it is hardly surprising that the Conservative governments' economic policies have been directly associated with a decline in union density. In the 1990s membership may have stabilized temporarily in the first few years of the New Labour government after 1997, but then union density continued to decline as a result of a changing perception of unionism in the community coupled with a 'waning of appetite' for unions amongst employees – a factor returned to below.

Changes in the *attitudes of employers* have also affected union membership over the last 20 years. For example, the incidence of companies refusing to recognize unions has increased. 'De-recognition' refers to the complete withdrawal of a trade union's rights to negotiate pay on behalf of its members, although they may be represented for consultation purposes or during grievance and disciplinary hearings. De-recognition was a feature of several heavily publicized disputes in the 1980s, notably News International's de-recognition of the print unions, P&O's of the seafarers' union and the government's decision that union membership was incompatible with national security at Government Communications

Headquarters (GCHQ). Although these were far from being typical instances, they did serve to indicate a change in management power and the declining attractiveness of union membership in such circumstances.

However, although de-recognition was a factor at work it should be noted that the key determinant was the inability of trade unions to gain recognition for collective bargaining in newly established workplaces, which might be due in part to the attitude of employers (Bryson and Forth 2010). The environment surrounding the workplace appears to have changed in recent years, with empirical evidence seeming to show that unionization has had a negative effect on workplace financial performance in the 1980s. However, any such negative or inverse relationship would appear to have weakened appreciably from 1990 onwards as a result of various factors, including a fall in union wage premium (which decreased labour costs), a decrease in demarcation disputes and other inflexible labour policies, and the emergence of a more positive attitude in the workplace about productivity enhancing practices (Wood and Bryson 2009). A final point to note is that the status of unions in society may have changed. For example, in the mid-1980s some 53% of people felt that unions had 'too much power' while only 10% said they had 'too little power', with 5% of the respondents 'unsure'. By 2007 only some 13% of people felt that unions had 'too much power', with as many as 24% of people saying that unions had 'too little power' and a large 20% saying that they were 'unsure'. This reversal in attitudes and the growth of the 'unsure' category tends to indicate a greater uncertainty about the function of unions in society (Bryson and Forth 2010).

The employers

Employers' associations

Many employers in the UK are members of employers' associations which seek to regulate relations between employers and trade unions. These associations are usually organized on an industry basis rather than a product basis, as with the Engineering Employers' Federation (EEF Ltd) with over 4,000 members in 2010. Their role includes negotiating with unions at industry level, the operation of procedures for the resolution of disputes, and the provision of advice to members on employment law, manpower planning and other personnel matters. In some industries there are local or regional employers' associations, combined into national federations, as with the Building Employers' Confederation. Altogether there are about 126 national employers' associations which negotiate the national collective agreements for their industry with the trade unions concerned, and most of these belong to the Confederation of British Industry (CBI).

Membership of employers' associations has tended to fall over the past 20 years as the trend towards company bargaining has gained ground. Large companies, such as the car manufacturers, BP, ICI and Shell, prefer to bargain on a company basis with unions rather than be part of a multi-employer bargaining team.

The Confederation of British Industry

This is the largest central employers' organization in the UK, representing 80% of the top FTSE 100 companies and 50% of the top FTSE 350 companies. In 2010 the CBI represented 24,000 businesses employing around 33% of the UK private sector workforce across 32 industrial sectors. Policy is determined by a council of 330 members, and there are 230 permanent staff members, including representatives with the EU in Brussels. The CBI seeks to represent the broad interests of businessmen in discussions with the government, with national and international institutions, and with the public at large. It nominates the employers' representatives for such bodies as the Advisory, Conciliation and Arbitration Service (ACAS). Like the TUC, the CBI is affiliated to a Europe-wide representative organization, BUSINESSEUROPE (the Confederation of European Businesses) which represents 40 central industry and employers' federations across 34 countries in Europe. It also works in tandem with the European Centre of Enterprises with Public Participation (CEEP) that represents public sector employers.

Individual employers

Over the last 15 years the influence of management has increased as the pressures of unemployment and international competition shifted power away from unions and towards management. Recent management initiatives to increase employee flexibility, to improve quality, and to introduce more performance-related pay have begun to create a 'cultural change' within individual workplaces. One such change has been the issue of trade union recognition within the company.

The most difficult aspect of collective bargaining in the UK is the fact that workers of a given company often belong to different unions, i.e. multi-union companies. As a result, management often have to negotiate with each union separately. The changing competitive environment mentioned above has caused a shift in the locus of power away from employers' association bargaining with unions and towards individual company bargaining. This shift in power has often resulted in company management attempting to limit bargaining rights to a single trade union within the workplace, i.e. 'single unionism'. The advantage to management of such arrangements is that it simplifies the bargaining process and prevents conflict over demarcations between different skill groups represented by different trade unions within the same enterprise. Although only around 200 firms concluded single-union agreements prior to the advent of statutory recognition (e.g. BICC cables, Ikeda, Hoover and Bosch), the new procedure has substantially increased the number of such arrangements.

Another approach to collective bargaining has been the rise of 'single-table bargaining' which means that, unlike 'single unionism', more than one union is allowed to exist within the company but they have to bargain jointly as a single unit with management rather than separately. These arrangements are supported by the TUC and by individual unions as preferable to single-union deals. Examples are to be found in engineering, the privatized water companies and in car manufacturing, e.g. Rover. Both single-union and single-table bargaining have tended to reflect a shift in power within the workplace, namely towards management and away from unions.

In addition to the issues of union representation, management have been involved in trying to increase employee flexibility by 'multi-skilling', i.e. by widening the skills of each worker (functional flexibility) and by varying the hours worked or employing more part-time or sub-contracted workers rather than full-time workers (numerical flexibility). This trend has threatened union bargaining power, since part-time or sub-contracted workers have a lower union density,

as noted earlier in this chapter. Multi-skilling also tends to restrict the ability of shop stewards to negotiate such subjects as staffing levels, job demarcations and the pace of work. Similarly the growth of performance-related pay (PRP), by linking reward to actual performance, may weaken the trade unions because part or all of the individual's annual pay award is no longer subject to collective bargaining.

Finally, it is worth noting that the growth of quality consciousness in UK industry has enhanced the importance of *teamwork*. The introduction of such devices as quality circles, where groups of around 10 workers meet to discuss their work and suggest improvements, has increased employee involvement in the firm. The large-scale survey of workplace practices by the DTI in 1998 showed that many 'new' management practices had been introduced to create more employee commitment. Such practices included teamwork activity, team briefings and also performance appraisal meetings in which staff were invited to participate in setting targets and goals. The net effect of these increased attempts by management to involve employees has been to circumvent or marginalize unions while retaining union recognition, leaving the future of 'collective' (i.e. union) representation of the workforce rather unclear.

The emergence of 'partnership agreements' between management and trade unions in recent years suggests an attempt to prevent the marginalization of unions noted above. A formal partnership agreement between unions and management usually involves reciprocal agreements whereby employers receive union commitment to flexible work practices whilst union members receive greater work security and greater participation in the affairs of the company. Such partnerships have occurred in a variety of organizations such as Natwest Retail Banking and Tesco.

The government

The government's role in industrial relations is threefold: as an employer, as a legislator and as an economic and social policy-maker.

The government is a major direct *employer of labour*, with central government employing 2.6 million persons, or 4% of the workforce in 2010. It influences not only these pay settlements but also those of the local authorities and the remaining nationalized industries, in total an extra 6.1 million persons. The government can, through its position as a primary source of finance, and by using cash limits (see Chapter 18), affect wage bargaining and employment levels in the local authorities and the nationalized industries.

As a *legislator*, the post-1979 Conservative administration was particularly active, and made extensive use of the law in an effort to reduce what it perceived as excessive union bargaining power, resulting in high UK wage cost and low labour productivity. An examination of the major legal changes introduced since 1979, mainly in the 1980, 1982, 1988, 1989 and 1990 Employment Acts, and in the 1984 Trade Union Act, reveals important changes in the context of collective bargaining. The previous Conservative government consolidated its 'step by step' reforms with the passing of the Trade Union and Labour Relations (Consolidation) Act 1992 (TULR(C)A) as amended by the Trade Union Reform and Employment Rights Act 1993. The former Act was a measure designed to rationalize all previous relevant statutory provisions into a *single act* rather than to change the substance of the law. The latter Act aimed to modify some sections of the 1992 Act by enhancing the rights of individual employees and union members while also imposing certain regulations relating to industrial action. The 1997–2010 Labour government retained most of these legal reforms, and introduced important new statutes (e.g. setting a national minimum wage), as will be discussed later in this chapter.

The closed shop

This is a situation where employees obtain or retain a job only if they become a member of a specified trade union. Its advantages to unions *and* management are discussed below. This practice was progressively weakened by legislation in the 1980s and 1990s making unions liable to legal action from both employees and management if they tried to enforce the closed shop. The relevant legislation which deals with this aspect is contained in Part III of TULR(C)A. A sample study of 529 firms in the mid-1990s found that only 9% of firms still had formal closed-shop arrangements (Geroski *et al.* 1995). However, two important studies (Wright 1996; Addison and Siebert 1998) have shown that while formal union arrangements such as the closed shop may have collapsed among

white-collar workers, manual workers and other groups have still retained informal methods of maintaining a closed shop, as in the case of closed-shop arrangements *agreed* between managers and labour.

Strikes and other industrial action

Since the end of the nineteenth century it has been impossible for a trade union to organize a strike without committing a *tort*, that is the civil wrong of interfering with the contract of employment between employer and employed. The committing of a tort enables the employer to obtain an injunction against, or claim damages from, the union. However, since 1906 Parliament has protected unions from this liability by providing them with immunity from civil action, and a major aim of the post-1979 legislation has been to narrow the scope of this immunity by rendering certain types of dispute 'unlawful'.

Industrial action is unlawful when the union is no longer covered by immunity from civil actions brought by employers or other affected parties in the courts. If successful, the employer will obtain a court injunction prohibiting the dispute, and the union will face fines or the sequestration of its assets for failure to comply. An employer can also subsequently claim damages arising from losses sustained during the action.

An important provision in the 1982 Employment Act restricted 'lawful trade disputes' to those between workers and their own employer, making 'political' strikes and inter-union disputes unlawful (s. 219). Also rendered unlawful by the 1980 Employment Act was secondary action, i.e. action against an employer not party to a dispute (s. 224). Picketing is now almost wholly restricted in law to the union members' 'place of work', often even excluding another plant of the same employer. Restrictions on illegal picketing are effected by making unions liable to pay damages in civil actions brought against them by employers. The 1984 Act also meant loss of legal immunity in certain circumstances. Official industrial action, i.e. that approved by the union leadership, must be sanctioned by a secret ballot of the membership. The ballot must be held no more than four weeks before the event, and a majority of union members must be in favour of the action. If the action takes place without majority consent, then the union loses any legal immunity for organizing industrial action that it may have enjoyed in the past. These provisions were strengthened by the 1988 Employment Act which gave the individual union member the right not to be called out on strike without a properly held secret ballot and, most controversially, in view of the stated opposition of both the CBI and the Chartered Institute of Personnel and Development, the right not to be disciplined by his or her union for refusing to strike or for crossing a picket line. The Act also established a Commissioner for the Rights of Trade Union Members to provide funds and advice to individuals wishing to take legal action to exercise these rights (s. 62). However, this office was abolished by the Employment Act of 1999, which also gave the Certification Officer the power to hear the complaints of trade union members against their unions.

The Employment Act 1999 also strengthened the rights of those employees engaged in 'official' industrial action, i.e. action which has been officially authorized by the unions involved. Previously employees could, in certain circumstances, deem to have been fairly dismissed for such union activity. However under the new Act the dismissal of such employees is deemed automatically unfair for the first eight weeks of the action, a period which may be extended if the employer fails to take 'reasonable steps' to resolve the dispute. Such changes followed the expressed desire of the Labour government to create a workplace environment of greater trust and co-operation.

The 1990 Employment Act took the control of union behaviour even further by requiring that the union leadership must take positive steps to repudiate 'unofficial action', i.e. actions undertaken by union members without union consent (that is of the executive committee or president or general secretary). For instance, the union must do its best to give written notice to all members participating in the action that it does *not* receive the union's support. Failure by the union to take such steps could mean loss of immunity for the union, even though the action is unofficial. In addition, the Act allowed employers to dismiss unofficial strikers selectively at the place of work (e.g. the strike leaders) and deny those dismissed the right to claim unfair dismissal. Any industrial action because of such dismissal would now be deprived of immunity (s. 223).

The Trade Union Reform and Employment Rights Act 1993 passed two main provisions relating to the organization of industrial action. First, ballots held in support of action should be fully postal and subject to independent scrutiny, effectively restricting the initiation of action at 'rank-and-file' level. Second, unions are to be required to give seven days' written notice before industrial action can be taken. This affords a longer waiting period to help settle any dispute. The unions argue, however, that it also gives employers rather longer to prepare for any dispute. The Act also provided government assistance for members of the public to seek damages from trade unions for the effects of unlawful industrial action, but this was abolished by the Employment Relations Act 1999 (ERA). ERA also amended the rules on ballots, enabling employers and trade unions to continue negotiations beyond the four-week deadline for the commencement of industrial action after the date of the ballot. In addition, ERA issued a code of practice on how ballots should be conducted that can be used by courts to determine breaches of the law. It also made it clear that an overtime ban constituted industrial action short of a strike, and not full strike action.

The Employment Relations Act 2004 simplified the law on industrial action ballots and also ballot notices and provided increased protection for employees against dismissal by employers when taking official and lawfully organized industrial action. For example, the Act extended the period in which an employee involved in an official strike could not be dismissed from eight to 12 weeks.

Legal regulation of wages and conditions of work

Many legal regulations which had originally been designed to place a 'floor' on both wages and conditions of work were dismantled after 1979 by successive Conservative governments in order to remove alleged disincentives to employment and to help increase labour flexibility. For example, the abolition of the Wages Councils in 1993 took away minimum-wage guarantees for low-paid workers in the industries for which these Wages Councils existed. In addition, the UK also initially 'opted out' of the 'Agreement on Social Policy' contained in the Social Protocol of the Maastricht Treaty – commonly known as the Social Chapter. This absolved the UK government from the need to implement certain EU Directives regulating employer/employee relations, a policy reversed in 1997 by the incoming Labour government.

Although also committed to workforce flexibility, the Labour government reversed some of this earlier legislation. It established the Low Pay Commission to make recommendations for a *National Minimum Wage* (NMW), which is considered further below (p. 288). It also legislated against the blacklisting of union members and sought to improve the rights of workers on 'zero hours' contracts (i.e. where workers have no guaranteed paid hours). ERA 1999 also gave employees the statutory right to be represented in formal disciplinary and grievance proceedings, which unions have seen as a possible route to recognition and new members as it implies union access to previously non-union workplaces (McKay 2001).

The Employment Act 2002 introduced further individual rights for employees, the most significant of which address certain 'family-friendly' practices to promote 'work/life balance'. From April 2003, maternity leave was increased and working fathers were given the right to two weeks' paternity leave. Employees are also able to request flexible working from their employers, such as job sharing, flexi-time, home-working and part-time work. Employers have the right to refuse such requests, but must explain their reasons for this to the employee in writing. ERA 2004 also changed the operation of some individual employment rights by improving the enforcement regime of the National Minimum Wage, and giving protection against unfair dismissal to employees with less than one year's service who requested flexible working.

Trade union democracy

The Trade Union Act 1984 and Employment Act 1988 embodied a number of provisions for internal union democracy in addition to those pertaining to strike action. Members of the main executive committee of a trade union must have been elected in a secret ballot of the union's members within the previous five years. The Employment Act of 1990 contained the right of members to a postal vote in elections for all members of union governing bodies and for key national leaders. In addition, the 1984 Act required trade unions with political funds to ballot their members at least every 10 years. Only if this is done, and majority assent for the fund achieved, can the union continue to spend money on 'political'

matters, such as a campaign against new legislation or in support of a political party. To date, of all ballots which have been held on this matter, a substantial majority have been in favour of retaining the fund.

The Trade Union Reform and Employment Rights Act 1993 modified some sections of the TULR(C)A by taking the issue of democracy further. First, it strengthened the rights of *individuals* by giving them greater freedom to belong to the union of their choice. For example, an individual could belong to more than one union and unions could not dismiss a member for failing to support a strike. This had obvious implications for relationships between unions and their members. Second, it also gave *trade union members* the right not to have union subscriptions deducted from their pay except with their written consent. The latter 'check off' arrangements were seen as threatening union membership levels and were repealed in 1998 by the Labour government.

Statutory recognition of trade unions

An important legislative change relating to trade union recognition was introduced in June 2000 under Schedule 1 of the Employment Relations Act 1999, which amended the Trades Union and Labour Relations (Consolidation Act) 1992. This schedule covers workers in organizations with at least 21 employees where a trade union has made a request to be recognized as the representative of employees for bargaining purposes. If an employer rejects the request, the union can apply to the Central Arbitration Committee (CAC) which has to decide whether the union has the support of the majority of the workforce that comprises the proposed 'bargaining unit', i.e. the group of employees to be covered by collective bargaining. If 50% or more of the bargaining unit are members of the union applying for recognition, then the CAC may award automatic recognition. If this criterion is not met, then a ballot can be held. In this case recognition will depend on the union receiving a majority of the votes in a ballot *and* at least 40% of the workers entitled to vote having done so. The recognition agreement lasts for three years.

The impact of this legislation on union membership was considered earlier in the chapter, and its use has proved less problematic for trade unions than they envisaged, given the formidable qualifications for recognition that the procedure imposed. From June 2000 to the end of March 2002, 175 applications for recognition were received by the CAC, of which 86 were ultimately withdrawn, 12 were rejected by the CAC, 34 were pending and in 14 cases recognition was decided by the Committee without a ballot. Only 29 cases proceeded to a ballot and 20 of these led to union recognition. The relative success of the unions involved in the procedure reflects their avoidance of making applications where they were not very confident about membership levels and support for recognition in the bargaining unit.

Probably the most difficult part of the recognition procedure is the decision about the appropriateness of the bargaining unit, which must be 'compatible with effective management'. Not only has this been a source of conflict between unions seeking recognition and management, but it can also cause friction between unions competing for membership. For example, the TGWU was recognized by Eurotunnel to represent its train drivers in the teeth of opposition by ASLEF, the train drivers' union (Walsh 2000). Whilst the Labour government extended the rights of employees to collective representation, UK law places more restrictions on industrial action than anywhere else in the EU, and the Labour government remained committed to the outlawing of strikes called in sympathy with other unions, or union actions that can broadly be deemed as political.

In its legislative capacity, therefore, the government can alter the balance of power between employer and employee. However, it is difficult to assess how far any legislation can be effectively used by employers, as this depends upon a complex array of factors, such as management style, the firm's size and position within both product and labour markets, the availability of alternative tactics and the anticipated repercussions of recourse to law on a firm's industrial relations.

ERA 2004 made no substantive changes to the 1992 and 1999 Acts but did give trade unions earlier access to workers and stipulated a duty on parties to refrain from engaging in 'unfair practices', responding to the suggestion that, in the past, employers had engaged in unfair practices by trying to undermine trade union recognition. The Act did not, however, provide for union recognition rights in small firms, i.e. those employing fewer than 21 workers.

The European Union and UK industrial relations

The European Union is discussed more fully in Chapter 27, but the current proposals of the European Commission are of potentially great significance to the UK. The most important measures are contained in the *European Social Charter* and the accompanying 'Action Programme' for its implementation. The Charter contains provisions relating to both the individual and collective rights of workers, but it is important to recognize that it is a statement of *principles* or intent and that by itself it creates no legally enforceable rights. However, the Commission plans to give legal form to the Charter's contents over the next few years, which at present enjoy majority support in the Council of Ministers.

Only a brief outline of the Charter can be given here, but measures pertaining to individual employee rights include greater freedom of movement within the Community, the right to training, protection regarding health and safety and against discrimination, provisions to safeguard the employment conditions of the young, disabled and elderly, and employees at large, and minimum rules on work duration, rest periods and holidays, shift work and systematic overtime. Broadly similar rights are to be extended to part-time, casual and temporary workers. The Charter excludes a commitment to minimum wage legislation. Measures relating to collective labour law are more limited, and the Charter does not propose any legally enforceable right to bargain for trade unions where this is not already part of a member state's law. However, the Charter does include important prospective rights to information and consultation plus the 'participation' of employees before companies make decisions on redundancies and closures.

Implementing the Social Chapter

The Labour government's reversal of the 'opt-out' from the Social Chapter led to the adoption of EU Directives which have had important implications for industrial relations. Under the Social Chapter, the European Commission must consult with the social partners (ETUC, UNICE and CEEP) about the content of its proposals, with much of the ensuing legislation arising out of 'framework agreements' negotiated at European level by the partners. Successful agreements which have been adopted by the Commission include the *Parental Leave Directive* (which gave parents the right to leave work after the birth or adoption of a child), the *Part-time Workers' Directive* (which extended equal rights and pro-rata benefits to part-time staff) and the *Fixed-Term Contracts Directive* (which strengthened the rights of workers under such contracts, as well as discouraging their use). This last Directive is unique in that it is the first to be initiated by UNICE in the employment field (Gennard and Judge 2002). However, the Labour government restricted the impact of the part-time workers' regulations by limiting the scope for comparison between such employees and full-time staff to those working under the same type of contract and at the same location (McKay 2001).

The *Working Time Directive* was implemented in the UK in 1998 and contained provisions for a legal right to four weeks' paid holidays and an upper limit to the working week of 48 hours (averaged over 14 weeks), together with various other entitlements, such as the right to rest periods. The impact so far has been marginal, with the government allowing both individual and collective 'opt-outs' by employees from the legislation. British employee relations have also been affected by the *European Works Council Directive* of 1994 (extended to the UK in 1998). The European Works Council (EWC) is a term used for a pan-European forum of employee representatives set up for the purpose of information and consultation. Multinationals with at least 1,000 employees working in the EU and with at least 150 employees working in two or more of its member states are required to establish an EWC, which consists of managers and elected representatives from the workforce across its European operations. It must meet at least once a year to discuss the progress and prospects of the company, as well as any decisions likely to affect more than one EU member state, e.g. closures or mergers. The EWC Directive was revised by the Council and the European Parliament in May 2009. The changes contained in the new ('Recast') Directive were due to be transposed into national law by June 2011, and have important implications for all companies in terms of the scope of the legislation, both those with an existing European Works Council and those yet to set one up.

A significant new measure that extends the principle of consultation is the *Information and Consultation Directive* (2002), which was opposed by the Labour government. This gives employees in establishments with at least 50 employees rights to information and consultation on the performance of the business and on decisions relevant to employment, including substantial changes to work organization, particularly where jobs are threatened.

As a complement to EU statutes, the *Human Rights Act* 1998 (HRA) came into force in 2000, with important implications for British employee relations. For example, it includes the requirement that internal disciplinary procedures in the public sector organizations must conform to standards of proof and procedures expected of courts and tribunals. The HRA's effects on the private sector are less clear, but employment practices are likely to be subjected to more rigorous examination under the Act which, like the EU Charter, also enshrines a right to freedom of association.

The structure of collective bargaining

Collective bargaining has been defined by Clegg (1978) as referring to 'the whole range of dealings between employers and managers on the one hand, and trade unions, shop stewards and members on the other, over the making, interpretation and administration of employment rules'. These rules are both *substantive*, determining pay, hours, overtime, manning levels, holidays, etc., and *procedural*, governing the way in which substantive issues are settled. One of the most significant changes which has taken place in UK industrial relations over the last 30 years has been the decrease in the percentage of employees covered by collective bargaining agreements. For example, between 1984 and 2009, the percentage of total employees covered by collective bargaining arrangements fell from 71% to 32%. The effects of decreased union density, the legal changes introduced by government, the privatization movement, and the increased power of management all contributed towards this downward trend. Despite this radical change, collective bargaining between unions and employers is still of major importance in most of the UK's key sectors, and occurs at a number of levels.

National or multi-employer bargaining

This level of negotiation predominates in the public sector in which centralized bargaining gives rise to relatively formal, fixed-term and comprehensive agreements, leaving little scope for localized or workplace bargaining. However, there is now a clear trend towards more decentralized bargaining in the public sector. The 'local management of schools' initiative, together with the creation of semi-autonomous NHS Trusts, necessarily imply further moves towards local bargaining. Moreover, both the privatized water companies and electricity generators have withdrawn from industry-level agreements, and decentralization is becoming the norm for the privatized elements of British Rail. Finally, the 'contracting out' to private tender of many services previously supplied by local authorities clearly reduces the coverage of national bargaining in this sector.

In the private sector national bargaining occurs on an industry level, between employers' associations and trade unions, or federations of unions. This was once the main type of collective bargaining, but has declined in importance in many industries so that by the late 1990s it covered only about 15% of employees in the private sector (e.g. electrical contracting). In fact, industry-wide and multi-employer bargaining has already disappeared from a number of sectors, including the clearing banks, the cable industry, provincial newspapers and independent TV companies. Nevertheless, a potentially important development in multi-employer bargaining is the growth of 'coordinated bargaining' across Europe, defined as 'an attempt to achieve the same or related outcomes in separate negotiations' (Sisson and Marginson 2002). At EU-sector level, ETUC and its constituent industry federations, such as the European Metalworkers' Federation, have initiated procedures to combat 'social dumping' by multinational companies (MNCs). In MNCs, many of which operate across Europe, there is pressure from top management to implement 'best practice' policies (such as team-working and annualized hours) across their European subsidiaries as, for example, in the case of General Motors. This type of coordinated bargaining is at an early stage but nevertheless could have an impact on UK industrial relations, although significant decentralization is likely to remain.

Single-employer bargaining

This occurs at two levels: (a) *corporate*, i.e. at the level of the company or whole organization; and (b) *establishment*, i.e. at the level of the workplace, such as the factory, plant or office.

The widespread practice of informal bargaining at workplaces in the 1960s, generally in the manufacturing sector, was criticized by the Donovan Commission in 1968. The Commission recommended that tacit, unwritten deals between local managers and shop stewards should be replaced by written formal agreements of specified duration and on clearly delineated issues. This encouraged the rise of corporate or company-level bargaining and the greater involvement of senior management.

However, this shift to company agreements, largely initiated by US-owned multinationals to exert greater control over collective bargaining, has not been universal. In fact, establishment- or plant-level bargaining remains important in many industries, such as clothing, and the footwear, brick and timber industries. More significantly, recent changes in managerial practice, which have devolved more responsibility to middle management for running individual establishments as separate budget or profit centres, have enhanced formal plant bargaining at the expense of company-wide negotiation. The growth of multi-product or multi-divisional firms such as Unilever, Philips, Coates Viyella and Lucas, for example, is evidence of such trends towards division and establishment level bargaining. However, this development has been accompanied by a decline in the range of substantive issues which many managements are prepared to negotiate with unions. Moreover, and of perhaps greater future importance for workplace bargaining, there has been a marked increase in systems of individual assessment and reward, some linked to the profit performance of the company, which could further undermine collective representation. Studies have shown that 14% of non-managerial employees in the private sector have their pay negotiated at corporate level and 9% at workplace level. This compares with 16% and 35% respectively in the public sector (Cully *et al.* 1999). Bargaining has become more decentralized over time, moving from the multi-employer to the corporate level, and on the other hand from the corporate level to the establishment or plant level. The main reasons cited for the growth of establishment- or plant-level bargaining include better control of profitability levels by taking into consideration local labour market conditions and more ability to reward individual employees according to performance.

Advisory, Conciliation and Arbitration Service (ACAS)

ACAS was established as an independent statutory body on 1 January 1976 and is formally independent of direct ministerial intervention. The agency stemmed from the Department of Employment's Conciliation and Arbitration Service which had often been criticized as not being independent since it was directly under the control of a government minister. Its role is to provide impartial information (advisory) and to help prevent or resolve problems between employers and their workforces (conciliation and arbitration). The service is controlled by a council consisting of 12 members, including an independent chairman and 11 other members with experience of industrial relations (e.g. trade unionists, academics and others), all of whom are appointed by the Secretary of State for Industry. For example, in 2009/10 it completed 849 in-depth advisory meetings, 765 conciliation events and arbitrated or mediated in 44 disputes. *Conciliation* is the process of bringing parties together in a dispute in order to move forward towards a settlement, whilst *arbitration* involves an independent arbitrator or board of arbitrators,[2] who decide on the outcome of a dispute and whose decision may have legal force. Of the 44 arbitration cases dealt with by ACAS in 2009/10, 'dismissal and discipline' accounted for 55% of the cases and 'pay and conditions of employment' for 43% (ACAS 2010).

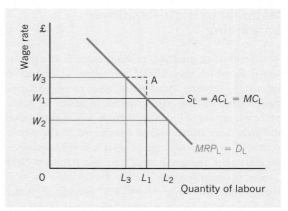

Fig. 14.1 Wage determination in a competitive market.

always be required if the revenue gained from selling the output produced by the last person, the marginal revenue product of labour (MRP_L),[3] is greater than the extra cost of employing that person, the marginal cost of labour (MC_L). In a competitive labour market (see Fig. 14.1), the supply of labour (S_L) to each firm would be perfectly elastic at the going wage rate (W_1), so that the wage rate is itself the marginal cost of labour.[4] The profit-maximizing firm would then hire people until MRP_L equalled MC_L, i.e. L_1 persons in Fig. 14.1. If more than L_1 persons were hired, then the extra revenue from their hire would fail to match the extra cost incurred.

Under these conditions the MRP_L curve becomes the demand curve for labour (D_L), since at any given wage rate the profit-maximizing firm will employ labour until MRP_L equals that wage rate. For example, if the wage rate falls to W_2 in Fig. 14.1, then demand for labour rises to L_2.

Wage determination and collective bargaining

The neo-classical view of wage determination is embodied in 'marginal productivity' theory. With many small buyers of labour (firms) and many small suppliers (i.e. non-unionized individuals), the wage rate would be determined by the intersection of demand and supply curves for labour.

The demand curve for any factor, including labour, is seen as being derived from the demand for the product or service it produces. Additional labour will

Wages and unions

If the labour force is now unionized, then the supply of labour to the firm (or industry) may be regulated. However, even though unions bring an element of monopoly into labour supply, theory suggests that they can influence only price *or* quantity, but not both. For example, in Fig. 14.1 the union may seek wage rate W_3, but must accept in return lower employment at L_3. Alternatively, unions may seek a level of employment L_2, but must then accept a lower wage rate at W_2. Except (see below) where unions are able to force employers off their demand curve for labour (MRP_L), then unions can raise wages only at the 'cost' of reduced employment. However, a *given rise* in wages will reduce employment by less, under the following circumstances.

1 The less elastic is final demand for the product.

2 The less easy it is to substitute other factors for the workers in question.

3 The lower the proportion of labour costs to total costs of production.

All of these circumstances will make the demand curve for labour, MRP_L, less elastic.

Unions and bargaining power

Unions may seek to force the employer off his demand curve for labour so that he makes less than maximum profits. It may then be possible for wages to rise from W_1 to W_3 with no loss of employment, i.e. at point A in Fig. 14.1. How effective unions will be in such strategies will depend upon the extent of their 'bargaining power'.

Chamberlain defines union bargaining power as:

$$\frac{\text{Management costs of disagreeing (to union terms)}}{\text{Management costs of agreeing (to union terms)}}$$

Although this ratio cannot be measured, as it relies on subjective assessments, it is a useful analytical tool. If unions are to exert effective influence on management the ratio must exceed unity. That is to say, it must be more costly for management to disagree (e.g. loss of profits, or market share as a result of strike action) than to agree (e.g. higher labour costs and manning levels). The higher the ratio, the more inclined management may then be to agree to the union's terms.

The level of the wage demand will affect union bargaining power. The more modest the wage claim, the lower the management cost of agreement, and the higher Chamberlain's ratio, i.e. the greater is union bargaining power. This will increase the prospects for securing higher wages with stable employment.

Union density will also affect bargaining power. The greater the proportion of the industry unionized, the less easy it will be to substitute non-union labour. The management costs of disagreeing to union terms will tend to be higher, so that the ratio, i.e. union bargaining power, rises. Equally, the higher is union

density in the industry as a whole, the easier it is for any particular company to pass on higher wage demands as price increases to consumers without losing market share. This is because competing firms in the industry will also be facing similar wage-cost conditions. High union density therefore reduces the management costs of agreeing to union terms, and again raises the ratio, i.e. union bargaining power. High union density will therefore also increase the prospects for securing higher wages with stable employment.

Even macroeconomic factors can be brought into this analysis. The higher the level of real income in the economy, the higher will be demand for 'normal' goods. Management will then be able to pass on cost increases as higher prices with relatively less effect on demand. This will reduce management costs of agreeing to union terms, raise the ratio, and with it union bargaining power.

Another main factor which affects the bargaining power of trade unions is the degree of competition in the *product market*. For example, Gregg and Machin (1991) found that those unionized firms facing increased competition in the market for their product experienced slower wage growth than those unionized firms that did not. In other words, increasing competition in the product market tends to *reduce* the bargaining power of unions to raise wages. This seems to indicate that unions are becoming more aware of the potential 'costs' to them in terms of unemployment if they bargain for higher wages when their firm is experiencing intense competition.

However, one must recognize the existence of many other dimensions to union bargaining power, such as the degree of unanimity or conflict within unions over bargaining goals and methods. Unions will also vary in the militancy of their members and the bargaining abilities of their leaders. All this makes the assessment of bargaining power extremely difficult. It is also important to note that the 'resource' theory of the impact of trade unionism on the firm does not accept that the exercise of this power will necessarily raise production costs. Instead, the theory argues that unions can significantly increase productivity by providing an efficient means for the management and settlement of disputes. Thus, collective bargaining reduces the costs of individual expressions of grievances, which may raise the 'quit' rate of key employees and the incidence of absenteeism or poor-quality work. Further, the 'shock' effect of unions' negotiation of pay rises may force managements to increase efficiency in order to absorb higher costs.

Wages and employers' associations

Wages are determined by a variety of factors, of which union bargaining power is but one, admittedly important, element.

Employers' associations are themselves able to create an element of monopoly on the *demand* side of the labour market (i.e. 'monopsony'). These associations bring together the employers of labour in order to exert greater influence in collective bargaining. Standard theory suggests that monopsony in the labour market will, by itself, reduce both wages and employment in the labour market.

In Fig. 14.2, under competitive labour market conditions the equilibrium would occur where the supply of labour ($S_L = AC_L$) equalled the demand for labour (MRP_L), giving wage W_C and employment L_C. If monopsony occurs, so that employers bid the wage rate up against themselves, then it can be shown that the MC_L curve will lie above the $S_L = AC_L$ curve. For example, if by hiring the fourth worker, the wage ($= AC_L$) of all workers is bid up from £5 to £6, then the AC_L for the fourth worker is £6 *but* the MC_L for the fourth worker is higher at £9 (£24 – £15). The profit-maximizing employer will want to equate the extra revenue contributed by the last worker employed (MRP_L) to the extra cost of employing the last worker (MC_L). In Fig. 14.2 this occurs with L_1 workers

employed. Note, however, that the employer only has to offer a wage of W_1 in order to get L_1 workers to supply themselves to the labour market. The wage W_1 is *below* the competitive wage W_C and the level of employment L_1 is *below* the competitive level of employment L_C. This is the standard case against monopsony in a labour market, namely lower wages and lower employment as compared to a competitive labour market.

When monopoly on the demand side (employers' associations) is combined with monopoly on the supply side (trade unions), the wage and employment outcome becomes indeterminate. This is often called 'bilateral monopoly'.

The existence of employers' associations will clearly affect the strength of union bargaining power. The greater the density of their coverage within an industry, the smaller might be the management costs of disagreement, e.g. in the case of a strike there is less likelihood of other domestic firms capturing their markets. By reducing the numerator of the ratio, union bargaining power is reduced.

Wages and government: the National Minimum Wage

The National Minimum Wage (NMW) covering minimum wages for employees over the age of 18 was introduced in April 1999, and in October 2004 the NMW was extended to cover 16- and 17-year-olds. Table 14.4 shows the increases in the rates of NMW for three categories of workers between April 1999 and October 2011. The NMW has been revised upwards at regular intervals during this period, with the adult rate increasing by 65% between 1999 and 2011, and the Youth Development Rate (18–21 years) increasing by 64% over the same period.

Figure 14.3 illustrates the problem of setting too high a minimum wage. If the NMW is set above the competitive wage (W_C) for any labour market, then there will be an excess supply of labour of $L' - L^*$, with more people supplying themselves to work in this labour market than there are jobs available. In Fig. 14.3 the actual level of employment falls from L_C to L^*.

However, there have been a number of studies suggesting that in the US, a higher minimum wage has actually increased wages *and* employment (Atkinson 1996). But it has been noted that many of

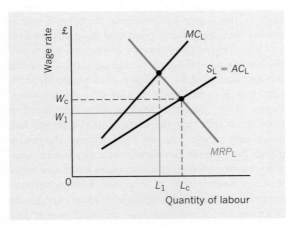

Fig. 14.2 Wage determination with monopsony in the labour market.

Table 14.4 National minimum wage rates per hour, April 1999 to September 2011.

	Aged 16–17	Aged 18–21	Aged 22 and over*
April 1999 to May 2000	–	£3.00	£3.60
June 2000 to September 2000	–	£3.20	£3.60
October 2000 to September 2001	–	£3.20	£3.60
October 2001 to September 2002	–	£3.50	£3.70
October 2002 to September 2003	–	£3.60	£4.10
October 2003 to September 2004	–	£3.80	£4.20
October 2004 to September 2005	£3.00	£4.10	£4.50
October 2005 to September 2006	£3.00	£4.20	£4.85
October 2006 to September 2007	£3.30	£4.45	£5.05
October 2007 to September 2008	£3.40	£4.60	£5.35
October 2008 to September 2009	£3.53	£4.77	£5.52
October 2009 to September 2010	£3.57	£4.83	£5.73
October 2010 to September 2011	£3.64	£4.92	£5.80
			£5.93

Source: Low Pay Commission (2010a) *Historical Rates*.
*From Oct. 2010 this rate is applied to those aged 21+. Also from Oct 2010 an Apprentice Minimum Wage of £2.50 per hour is applied to apprentices under 19 years and those aged 19 and over in the first 12 months of their apprenticeship.

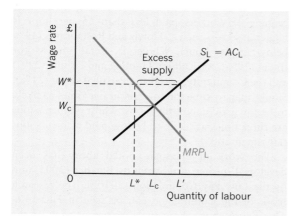

Fig. 14.3 Minimum wage (W^*) set above the competitive market wage (W_c).

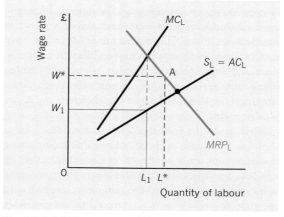

Fig. 14.4 Minimum wage (W^*) raising both wages and employment with monopsony in the labour market.

the US studies have involved labour markets (e.g. fast food) which are dominated by a few large employers of labour, i.e. *monopsonistic* labour markets.

In fact our earlier analysis of monopsony might have led us to expect this. For example, if in Fig. 14.4 the initial monopsony equilibrium was wage W_1 and employment L_1, then setting a minimum wage of W^* would result in a rise in both wages (W_1 to W^*) and employment (L_1 to L^*). Since no labour is supplied

below the minimum wage W^* this is the *effective labour supply curve* at W^* ($W^* = AC_L = MC_L$). The profit-maximizing situation is at point A on the MRP_L curve, where the marginal cost of hiring the last person (MC_L) exactly equals the extra revenue resulting from employing that last person (MRP_L). So imposing a minimum wage on a labour market that is already imperfect (here monopsony) can increase both wages and levels of employment.

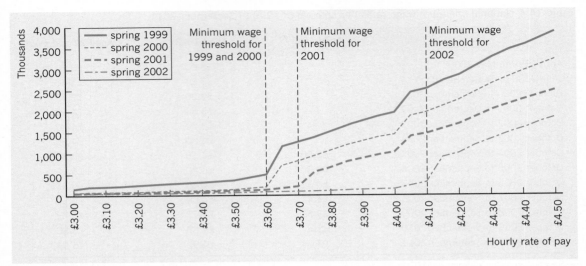

Fig. 14.5 Numbers of jobs paid below different hourly rates of pay for people aged 22 and over, UK, 1999–2002.
Source: Heasman (2003).

The impact of the minimum wage legislation on low pay in the period following its introduction can be seen in Fig. 14.5 which gives the number of people aged 22 and over who were paid *below* a range of hourly wage rates. The figures are given in the form of four lines, each representing a different period in time and indicating the number of people earning below the specified hourly wage rate at the date shown. The NMW levels at the different dates are also provided.

First, it can be seen that there is a tendency for a significant increase in the number earning just above the minimum wage shortly after the introduction of the NMW, suggesting that employers are responsive to raising pay just above the minimum wage around the time the NMW was introduced or subsequently changed. Second, over the period 1999–2002, each successive time line is below the one representing the previous time period, indicating that a change in the NMW threshold has impacts that continue into future time periods, with progressively fewer people paid below that 'new' benchmark as time moves on. Overall it would seem that the numbers of jobs paying wage levels below the NMW threshold appear to be very responsive to the threshold changes but with something of a time lag (Heasman 2003).

Despite the decreases in numbers of workers earning low wage rates (as shown in Fig. 14.5 by the downward shift in the lines over time), there are still a significant number of low-paid workers in some sectors of economic activity. For example, the percentage of workers paid less than £5 per hour is higher in sectors such as Hotels and Restaurants (44% below £5 per hour), Wholesale, Retail and Motor trades (29%), Agriculture, Hunting and Fishing (22%) and the Community, Social and Personal sector (21%). Similarly, part-time jobs are about five times as likely to be low paid as full-time jobs, whilst women's jobs are three times as likely to be low paid as men's jobs (Heasman 2003).

The work of Heasman noted above has been developed further in research by Butcher (2005) and by the Low Pay Commission (2010b). The research work of the Commission can be seen in Fig. 14.6. This figure shows how the earnings at each of the percentiles of the earnings distribution have changed on average each year over four periods: 1992–97 (before the minimum wage was introduced), 1998–2004 (early years of the minimum wage upratings), 2004–08 (more recent periods of uprating) and 2008/09 (the latest figures for the decade).

During the period before the introduction of the minimum wage, i.e. 1992–97, the wages of the lowest paid increased by *less* than those of the median earners (i.e. those at the 50th percentile), while the wages of the top half of the earnings distribution increased by *more* than those of the median earners. However, following the introduction of the minimum wage

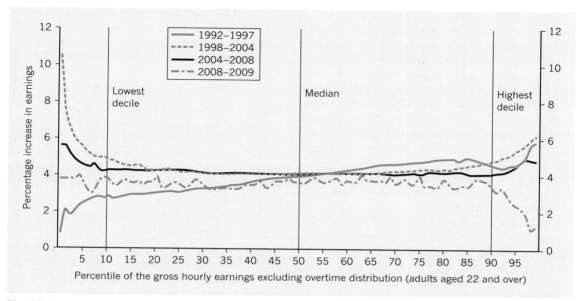

Fig. 14.6 Annual increase in hourly earnings of employees aged 22 and over by percentile, UK, 1992–2009. Source: Low Pay Commission (2010b) Figure 2.15.

between 1998 and 2004, those at the bottom of the earnings distribution received higher pay rises than the median earners. Between 2004 and 2008, the bottom half of the earnings distribution still received pay rises above the median earners, though the differential narrowed. Finally, in 2008–09, the recession appears to have narrowed the differentials for the lower half of the distribution, so that earnings for this group increased at roughly the same rate as the median percentile, while the growth of the highest decile was below that of the median.

Much of the research on the effects of the NMW can be divided into four areas: first, to determine the effect of NMW on the wage growth of low-paid employees; second, to determine the number of workers who have been affected by the NMW: third, to determine the relationship between NMW and employment; and, finally, to clarify the relationship between NMW and the distribution of income.

In relation to the first area, Swaffield (2009) uses a technique which attempts to calculate what the real wage growth of low-paid employees would have been *in the absence* of the NMW or NMW uprating, and then to compare this with the *actual* real wage rate growth. She concluded that low-wage employees had experienced significantly higher pay increases since the introduction of the NMW than previously. She

also found that the wage growth of the lower wage employees followed *trends* in the growth of NMW, i.e. the wage growth of this sector was larger than would have been expected when the NMW was higher than average earnings and smaller when the NMW was lower than average earnings. It appears that employers must have followed the trend of the NMW – being prepared to give higher wages when NMW growth rates were high, and giving lower wage rises when the NMW growth rates were low.

In relation to the second area, figures show that the NMW raised the pay of between 1.2 million and 1.3 million workers by around 15% (Dickens and Manning 2004) with more females being helped by the NMW (8.2% of all female workers) than males (3.2%) (Dickens and Draca 2004). Further, the minimum wage does not seem to have created 'spillover' effects, i.e. the NMW did not create a loss of jobs for other workers earning *more* than the NMW. Interestingly, research shows that firms tend to shift wages up for *all* workers when the NMW increased, so that both groups gained. In other words, firms seem to set their wage depending on the action of their competitors and also on market conditions. They often prefer to absorb the extra labour cost, rather than trying to secure maximum return per worker by squeezing wages (Lam *et al.* 2006).

As far as the relationship between the NMW and employment is concerned, no strong negative or positive effects of the NMW on employment have been found. Studies in this area have tended to compare job losses in the types of jobs or industries most affected by the minimum wage with those least affected by the minimum wage. However, there seems to be some evidence of employers cutting hours of work in response to the minimum wage (Stewart and Swaffield 2004). Other studies have focused on specific parts or sectors of the economy affected by low wages, such as the care homes sector – but even here only minor negative effects on jobs have been found (Arulampalam *et al.* 2004).

Finally, the question is often asked as to whether the minimum wage has reduced labour market inequality. Research in this area appears to show that while the minimum wage has helped those at the lower end of the earnings distribution (Butcher *et al.* 2009), other workers further up the earnings scale have also increased their earnings. It may be that the NMW helped to prevent wage inequality getting more unequal, rather than fundamentally changing the income distribution in favour of lower earners. It is worth remembering that the poorest households are not affected by the NMW, either because they are not in work or because they are pensioners (Machin 2003).

Wages and other factors

Wages can also be influenced by institutional practices which bear little relation to market conditions.

'Spillover' and comparability

The 'spillover' hypothesis argues that wage settlements for one group of workers are transmitted ('spill over') to other groups through the principle of comparability, irrespective of product and labour market conditions. For example, the pay awards achieved by 'wage leaders' often give rise to a sequence of similar settlements in the same 'wage round' for other workers.

Non-pecuniary advantages or disadvantages

Not all jobs have the same conditions of work. Some are hazardous, dirty, boring, require the working of unsocial hours, or receive various perquisites ('perks').

These will inevitably form part of the collective bargain, and ultimately affect the wage outcome. In some circumstances wage demands may be modified as the union places greater emphasis on non-wage factors.

Cost of living

The cost of living is an important factor in determining the wage claim, and has even been a formal part of wage settlements. When inflation is accelerating, unions become still more preoccupied with securing cost-of-living increases. This can trigger a wage–price spiral when unions overestimate future rates of inflation.

Productivity agreements

Part of the wage bargain may include the abandonment of restrictive practices, and the raising of production in return for higher wages. During the 1960s a whole series of formalized productivity agreements were concluded. The first and most celebrated of these was negotiated between Esso and the unions at the oil refinery at Fawley. A whole range of restrictive practices, including demarcation rules, excessive overtime and time-wasting, were 'bought out' by management for higher wages.

 ## The effects of collective bargaining

The process of collective bargaining is vital in deciding both pay and conditions of service for millions of employees in the workplace. In 2009, some 32.5% of all UK employees were covered by such negotiations between employer and employee representatives. Collective bargaining covered only 17.6% of all private sector employees while it covered 67.4% of public sector employees. Although the coverage of collective bargaining is falling, the process itself is still seen by many analysts as having an effect on the UK labour market, despite the fact that the overall coverage is decreasing.

Pay differentials

A number of studies have suggested a significant pay differential between unionized and non-unionized workers. During the 1980s studies by economists such as Nickell and Andrews (1983) and Nickell (1989) placed this differential as high as 20% in favour of unionized workers, though studies in the 1990s by Metcalf (1994) suggested a lower figure of around 10%. Other research of Blanchflower (1996) also suggests a pay differential of around 10% between unionized and non-unionized workers. The evidence also suggests that such differentials have decreased over time and that they depend, in part, on the degree of union density across sectors; the greater the union density, the greater the pay differential (Addison and Siebert 1998).

However, the nature of the pay differential observed between union and non-union labour may be due to more than simply collective bargaining. First, union labour may be of higher quality than non-union labour, with some of the pay differential due to the higher marginal revenue product of union labour. Second, employers may raise the wages of non-union labour in an attempt to forestall unionization, thereby eroding the pay differential. Third, incomes policies imposed by governments may affect the union/non-union pay differential. Flat-rate norms which are often a part of incomes policy will compress the pay differential that union bargaining power might otherwise have secured.

In practice, the particular effect of trade unions on pay is very difficult to disentangle from those of other labour market conditions. It is interesting to note, however, that both union and non-union workers have on average been able to secure very large increases in real wages, even during periods of high unemployment. The latest research has shown that the differential (or premium) between union and non-unionized workers fell from 10% in the mid-1990s to around 8–9% between 1997 and 2002. Since that time, the differential has fallen significantly to 5.9% by 2009 (Bryson and Forth 2010). Interestingly, the wage differential (wage premium) noted previously seems to rise with recession and unemployment as unions may have been more successful than non-union workers in resisting downward pressures on wages during such periods (Bryson and Forth 2010). This may suggest a fall in the price elasticity of demand for labour as the capital/labour ratio has increased, thereby reducing labour costs as a proportion of total costs (see above), and may also indicate a low and negative unemployment elasticity of real wages.[5] In fact, unemployed workers have perhaps ceased to exert a *permanent* influence on wage determination.

Restrictive practices and labour utilization

It has been suggested that the process of collective bargaining reinforces the unions' perception that they have 'property rights'. These rights may include a variety of established practices which have been used to protect jobs or earnings. These practices have important consequences for labour utilization and may form part of the collective bargain. They include the closed shop, minimum staffing levels, demarcation rules, seniority principles, strikes, etc. We briefly review a number of the most important 'restrictive practices'.

The closed shop

Closed shops confer a number of advantages on trade unions. First, they permit monopoly control over labour supply. This increases the union's ability to disrupt production through industrial action, and therefore raises its 'bargaining power'. In terms of Chamberlain's ratio (p. 287), it raises the 'management cost of disagreeing', and therefore union bargaining power. Second, closed shops prevent the 'free rider' problem, whereby non-union labour benefits from union bargaining power. Third, closed shops make it easier to enforce agreements reached between unions and management. Indeed, despite restricting the freedom of employers to choose whom they will employ, the closed shop has the benefit of bringing more order and certainty to industrial relations.

As we have seen, all forms of closed shops in the UK are strictly illegal under section 137(1)(a) of the Trade Union and Labour Relations (Consolidation) Act 1992 (c. 52), reflecting the government's desire to reduce union bargaining power and to protect the right of an individual not to join a trade union. The incidence of closed shops has decreased rapidly since 1979 with contemporary estimates suggesting that only some 9% of firms continue to have some form of closed shop agreement with unions.

Established practices

In industries such as printing, the railways and car production, unions often have, by tradition, some control over staffing levels, job speeds, the introduction of new technologies and demarcation issues, in other words, which type or grade of workers should undertake particular types of work. As a result, management decisions over the allocation of labour within an enterprise are subject to union influence.

The seniority principle

This is the principle whereby union members with the longest service in a firm are the first to be promoted and the last to be made redundant. This principle may conflict with the firm's desire to employ younger, more flexible and cheaper workers. However, companies may sometimes wish to retain senior workers, having already made a substantial investment in them through specific training. One survey using the British Household Panel Survey showed that for male employees, the seniority–earnings profile appeared to be steeper (i.e. more prominent) in the union sector, while occupation-specific expertise had a more significant effect on wages in the non-unionized sector (Zangelidis 2004).

These restrictive practices may enter into the collective bargain. Unions may seek to trade them for higher wages – as in the productivity agreements noted above. Through 'buying out' restrictive practices in this way, management seeks a more efficient utilization of labour, and thereby higher productivity.

The strike weapon

One of the most powerful 'property rights' perceived by the unions is their ability to affect the collective bargain by withdrawing their labour, i.e. going on strike. This is viewed by some as the ultimate form of restrictive practice. The use of the strike weapon by unions in the UK has been the subject of much research and debate.

Table 14.5 demonstrates that compared to its major economic competitors the UK was less strike-prone than the OECD and EU averages over the whole period shown. It is often in the context of strikes that governments and employers see union 'property rights' as detrimental to Britain's economic performance, while the unions themselves perceive the withdrawal of labour as a response to the failure of management. In the UK disputes over pay are the most common cause of working days lost, accounting for 70% of the total in 2005–09, followed by staffing and redundancy issues (19%) and work allocation issues (10%), although attributing strikes to a single cause often masks the existence of other contributory factors. The threat of industrial action by a trade union may alone be sufficient to achieve its aims, but one must

Table 14.5 Strikes: international comparisons 1997–2006 (working days not worked per thousand employees).

Country	1997–2001	2002–2006	1997–2006
Canada	192	180	186
Spain	178	164	170
Denmark	292	38	164
Italy	62	111	88
US	54	15	34
UK	14	28	21
France	20	10	15
Germany	1	6	4
Japan	1	0	1
EU 22	**37**	**41**	**39**
OECD	**43**	**31**	**37**

Source: Modified from *Economic and Labour Market Review*, International comparisons of labour disputes in 2006 (Hale 2008).

be careful not to overestimate its role or that of actual strike incidence in the process of bargaining. The CBI has reported that both are only rarely given as a reason for employers conceding wage increases.

Although the improvement in Britain's strike record is clear and indisputable, there has been a dramatic rise in notified individual grievances. For example, the Advisory, Conciliation and Arbitration Service (ACAS) has reported a substantial rise in cases received for conciliation, i.e. prior to a hearing by an industrial tribunal. Perhaps the lack of actual strike activity may not be a good indicator of the actual stresses and strains experienced within the labour market!

Conclusion

We have seen that the trade unions play an important role in the wage-bargaining process, despite the recent decline in union density. The employers' associations and the government are also important role-players in the process of collective bargaining. In recent years there has been a shift in the private sector from national or industry-wide bargaining to single-employer and, increasingly, establishment bargaining of a largely 'formal' nature. Wage negotiation is, however, a complex procedure, and the outcome depends upon the relative 'bargaining power' of both management and unions. Wages are also affected by a variety of 'non-market' factors, such as comparability, work conditions, cost of living, and the 'trading' of restrictive practices. Government legislation in the form of the National Minimum Wage will also influence the wage outcome. Collective bargaining can have an important effect on pay differentials and may even help enshrine a variety of established (restrictive) practices which have been used to protect jobs or earnings. However, the use of the strike weapon appears to be limited to large plants in specific industrial sectors, though the fact that these are often the basic UK or export-orientated industries may still leave the UK at a disadvantage *vis-à-vis* her international competitors.

Key points

- Most trade unions are relatively small; around 49% have fewer than 1,000 members. However, these unions have only 0.3% of total union membership. In fact, very large unions with over 250,000 members have around 73% of total union membership.

- Trade unions in the UK can be one of four types: craft, general, industrial or white-collar. In Europe most unions are industrial.

- There has been a sharp fall in union membership: in 1979, 54.5% of all employees were unionized, but by 2010 this figure had fallen to only 27.0%.

- Unions can usually secure higher wages only at the 'cost' of less employment unless their bargaining power is strong. If this is the case, they may be able to force employers off their labour demand curves, securing higher wages with no loss of employment.

- Chamberlain defined union 'bargaining power' as the ratio between the management costs of disagreeing and of agreeing to union terms. The larger the ratio, the greater the union bargaining power.

- A *given rise* in wages will usually reduce employment by less: (a) the less elastic the demand for the final product, (b) the less easy it is to substitute labour by other factors of production, (c) the lower the proportion of labour costs in total production costs.

- The government has legislated to reduce union power in various ways, e.g. removing the closed shop, imposing conditions on strikes and other union activities, deregulating the setting of wages and other working conditions, and promoting trade union democracy. It has also legislated to introduce a National Minimum Wage.

- Other factors influencing the wage settlement include spillover and comparability, non-pecuniary advantages/disadvantages, the cost of living and any productivity agreements made between employers and employees.

- Fewer strikes currently occur in the UK than is the average for the advanced industrialized countries; e.g. over the period 1997–2006, only around 21 working days were lost per 1,000 employees in the UK compared to 37 for all advanced industrialized countries.

Now try the self-check questions for this chapter on the Companion Website. You will also find useful links to relevant websites.

Notes

1 Trades Union Congress evidence to the Royal Commission on Trade Unions and Employers' Associations (1968).

2 It may also refer to a Central Arbitration Committee. This is an independent national body which provides boards of arbitration for the settlement of trade disputes.

3 The marginal revenue product of labour (MRP_L) equals the marginal physical product of labour (MPP_L) times the price of output. Because of diminishing returns to labour, the MPP_L curve will eventually begin to slope downwards. This is the part of the curve reflected in Fig. 14.1, since, if MPP_L slopes downwards, so will MRP_L.

4 In Fig. 14.1 we assume the firm to be small, so that changes in its demand for labour are insignificant relative to total demand for that type of labour. As a result it can purchase all the labour it requires at the going wage rate. For this firm, the supply curve of labour can be regarded as perfectly elastic at the market wage rate. Therefore wage rate = average cost of labour = marginal cost of labour.

5 Unemployment elasticity of real wages =

$$\frac{\% \text{ change in real wages}}{\% \text{ change in uneployment}}$$

Oswald estimates a coefficient of about –0.10, i.e. 'we can expect a doubling of unemployment to lower wages by (*ceteris paribus*) a little under 10%.'

References and further reading

ACAS (2010) *Annual Report and Accounts 2009/10*, London, Advisory Conciliation and Arbitration Service.

Addison, J. and Siebert, W. (1998) Union security in Britain, *Journal of Labour Research*, **19**(3): 495–517.

Arulampalam, W., Booth, A. and Bryan, M. (2004) Training and the new minimum wage, *Economic Journal*, **114**, Conference volume.

Atkinson, B. (1996) National minimum wage, *Developments in Economics*, **13**.

Bain, G. S. and Elsheikh, F. (1980) Unionization in Britain: an inter-establishment analysis based on survey data, *British Journal of Industrial Relations*, **18**(2): 137–57.

Bain, G. S. and Elsheikh, F. (1982) Union growth and the business cycle: a disaggregated study, *British Journal of Industrial Relations*, **20**(1): 34–43.

Blanchflower, D. (1996) *The Role and Influence of Trade Unions Within the OECD*, Discussion Paper No. 310, London, Centre for Economic Performance, LSE.

Blanchflower, D. G. and Bryson, A. (2008) *Union Decline in Britain*, IZA Discussion Paper No. 3436, April, Bonn, Institute for the Study of Labor.

Brown, W., Bryson, A., Forth, J. and Whitfield, K. (2009) *The Evolution of the Modern Workplace*, New York, Cambridge University Press.

Bryson, A. and Forth, J. (2010) *Trade Union Membership and Influence 1999–2009*, CEP Discussion Paper No. 1003, September, London, London School of Economics and Political Science.

Butcher, T. (2005) The hourly earnings distribution before and after the National Minimum Wage, *Labour Market Trends*, October, 427–35.

Butcher, T., Dickens, R. and Manning, A. (2009) *The Impact of the National Minimum Wage on the Wage Distribution*, Research Report for the Low Pay Commission, Low Pay Commission; University of Sussex; and London School of Economics.

Carruth, A. A. and Disney, R. (1987) Where have two million trade union members gone?, *Economica*, 55(217): 1–18.

Certification Officer (2010) *Annual Report of the Certification Officer 2009/10*, London.

Chamberlain, N. and Kuhn, J. (1965) *Collective Bargaining* (2nd edn), Maidenhead, McGraw Hill.

Clegg, H. (1978) *The System of Industrial Relations in Great Britain*, Oxford, Blackwell.

Cully, M., Woodland, S., O'Reilly, A. and Dix, G. (1999) *Britain at Work as Depicted by the 1998 Workplace Relations Survey*, London, Routledge.

Daniel, W. W. and Millward, N. (1983) *Workplace Industrial Relations in Britain: The DE/PSI/ESRC Survey*, London: Heinemann Education Books.

Dickens, R. and Draca, M. (2004) *The Employment Effects of the October 2003 Increase in the National Minimum Wage*, November, London, Low Pay Commission.

Dickens, R. and Manning, A. (2004) Has the National Minimum Wage reduced UK wage inequality? *Journal of the Royal Statistical Society*, Series A (Part 4), 613–26.

Disney, R. (1994) The decline of unions in Britain, *Economic Review*, November, 12–15.

Freeman, R. E. and Pelletier, J. (1990) The impact of British union legislation on trade union density, *British Journal of Industrial Relations*, September, 141–64.

Gennard, J. and Judge, G. (2002) *Employee Relations* (3rd edn), London, Chartered Institute of Personnel and Development.

Geroski, P., Gregg, P. and Desjonqueres, T. (1995) Did the retreat of UK trade unionism accelerate during the 1990–93 recession?, *British Journal of Industrial Relations*, **33**(March): 35–54.

Gregg, P. and Machin, S. (1991) Changes in union status, increased competition and wage growth in the 1980s, *British Journal of Industrial Relations*, **29**(4): 603–11.

Hale, D. (2008) International comparisons of labour disputes in 2006, *Economic and Labour Market Review*, **2**(4): 32–39.

Hawkins, K. (1981) *Trade Unions*, London, Hutchinson.

Heasman, D. (2003) Patterns of low pay, *Labour Market Trends*, **111**(4): 171–9.

Lam, K., Ormerod, C., Ritchie, F. and Vaze, P. (2006) Do company wage policies persist in the face of minimum wage? *Labour Market Trends*, March, 69–82.

Low Pay Commission (2010a) *Historical Rates*, London, The Stationery Office.

Low Pay Commission (2010b) *National Minimum Wage: Low Pay Commission Report 2010*, cm.7823, March, London, The Stationery Office.

Machin, S. (2000) Union decline in Britain, *British Journal of Industrial Relations*, **38**(2): 631–45.

Machin, S. (2003) Wage inequality since 1975, in Dickens, R., Gregg, P. and Wadsworth, J. (eds), *The Labour Market under New Labour: The State of Working Britain*, Basingstoke, Palgrave Macmillan, 191–200.

McKay, S. (2001) Between flexibility and regulation: rights, equality and protection at work, *British Journal of Industrial Relations*, **39**(2): 285–303.

Metcalf, D. (1994) Transformation of British industrial relations? Institutions, conduct and outcomes 1980–1990, in Barrell, R. (ed.) *The UK Labour Market*, Cambridge, Cambridge University Press.

Millward, N. and Stevens, M. (1987) *British Workplace Industrial Relations, 1980–1984, The DE/ESRC/PSI/ACAS Survey*, Aldershot, Gower.

Minford, P. and Riley, J. (1994) The UK labour market micro rigidities and macro obstructions, in Barrell, R. (ed.) *The UK Labour Market*, Cambridge, Cambridge University Press.

Nickell, S. and Andrews, M. (1983) Unions, real wages and employment in Britain, 1951–79, *Oxford Economic Papers*, **35**: 183–206.

Nickell, S., Wadhwani, S. and Wall, M. (1989) *Unions and Productivity Growth in Britain, 1974–86*, CLE Discussion Paper No. 353, London, Centre for Labour Economics, LSE.

ONS (2010) *Labour Market Statistics*, October, Office for National Statistics, London.

Price, R. and Bain, G. S. (1976) Union growth revisited, *British Journal of Industrial Relations*, **14**(3): 339–55.

Price, R. and Bain, G. S. (1983) Union growth in Britain: retrospect and prospects, *British Journal of Industrial Relations*, **21**(1): 46–68.

Sisson, K. and Marginson, P. (2002) Co-ordinating bargaining: a process for our times?, *British Journal of Industrial Relations*, 40(2): 197–220.

Smith, P. and Morton, G. (2001) New Labour's reform of Britain's employment law, *British Journal of Industrial Relations*, 39(1): 119–38.

Stewart, M. and Swaffield, J. (2004) *The Other Margin: Do Minimum Wages Cause Working Hours Adjustment for Low-wage Workers?* London, Low Pay Commission.

Swaffield, J. (2009) *Estimating the Impact of the 7th NMW uprating on the Wage Growth of Low Wage Workers in Britain*, Research Report for the Low Pay Commission (University of York).

Walsh, J. (2000) Eurotunnel single union battle provides an early test for CAC, *People Management*, 22 June.

Webb, S. and Webb, B. (1896) *The History of Trade Unionism*, Harlow, Longman.

Wedderburn, L. (1990) *The Social Charter, European Company and Employment Rights*, London, Institute of Employment Rights.

Wood, S. and Bryson, A. (2009) High involvement management, in Brown, W., Bryson, A., Forth, J. and Whitfield, K. (eds), *The Evolution of the Modern Workplace*, Cambridge, Cambridge University Press, 151–75.

Wright, M. (1996) The collapse of compulsory unionism? Collective organization in highly unionized British companies 1979–1991, *British Journal of Industrial Relations*, 34(December): 497–513.

Zangelidis, A. (2004) *Seniority Profiles in Unionised Workplaces: Do Unions Still Have the Edge?* Discussion Paper 2004–9, October, Centre for European Labour Market Research, Aberdeen, University of Aberdeen.

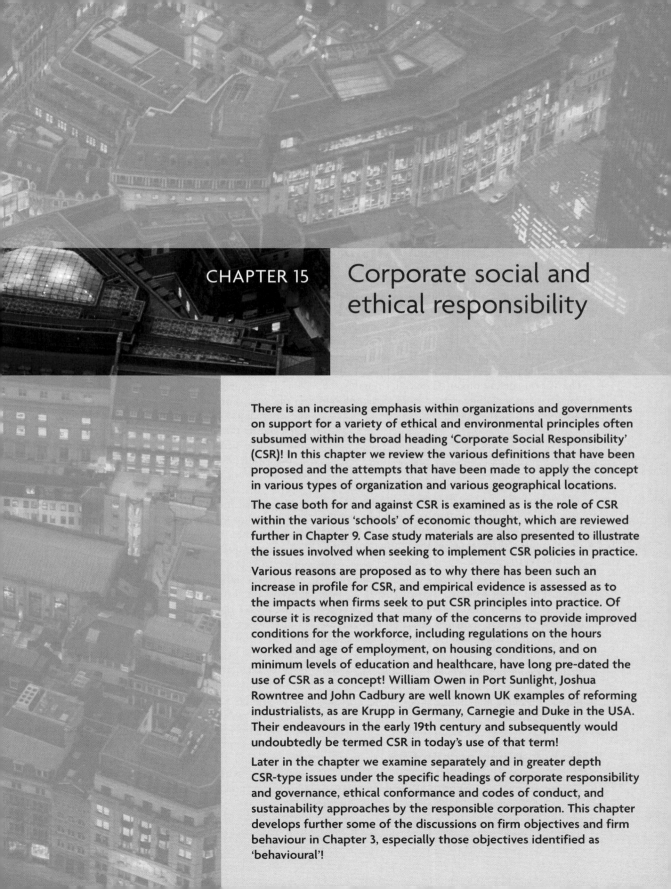

CHAPTER 15 | Corporate social and ethical responsibility

There is an increasing emphasis within organizations and governments on support for a variety of ethical and environmental principles often subsumed within the broad heading 'Corporate Social Responsibility' (CSR)! In this chapter we review the various definitions that have been proposed and the attempts that have been made to apply the concept in various types of organization and various geographical locations.

The case both for and against CSR is examined as is the role of CSR within the various 'schools' of economic thought, which are reviewed further in Chapter 9. Case study materials are also presented to illustrate the issues involved when seeking to implement CSR policies in practice.

Various reasons are proposed as to why there has been such an increase in profile for CSR, and empirical evidence is assessed as to the impacts when firms seek to put CSR principles into practice. Of course it is recognized that many of the concerns to provide improved conditions for the workforce, including regulations on the hours worked and age of employment, on housing conditions, and on minimum levels of education and healthcare, have long pre-dated the use of CSR as a concept! William Owen in Port Sunlight, Joshua Rowntree and John Cadbury are well known UK examples of reforming industrialists, as are Krupp in Germany, Carnegie and Duke in the USA. Their endeavours in the early 19th century and subsequently would undoubtedly be termed CSR in today's use of that term!

Later in the chapter we examine separately and in greater depth CSR-type issues under the specific headings of corporate responsibility and governance, ethical conformance and codes of conduct, and sustainability approaches by the responsible corporation. This chapter develops further some of the discussions on firm objectives and firm behaviour in Chapter 3, especially those objectives identified as 'behavioural'!

Corporate Social Responsibility (CSR): definitions and themes

Some organizations refer explicitly to CSR initiatives; others prefer to use alternative phraseology. Marks & Spencer recently used the phrase 'Plan A' to represent a set of 100 worthy targets to be achieved in the period 2008–13. Publishers have used titles for books, such as 'Corporation Be Good' or the 'A to Z of Corporate Responsibility'. The phrase 'Socially Responsible Investment' (SRI) is also widely used, as are phrases such as 'building a sustainable business' or 'corporate citizenship'.

It will be useful at this point to explore further what exactly is meant by CSR or its many derivatives! Table 15.1 usefully reviews the definitions of CSR adopted by a range of governmental, non-governmental, corporate and social enterprises as a useful starting point.

The various definitions of CSR can, arguably, be characterized as including one or more of the following four core characteristics.

1 *Incorporating voluntary activities* – i.e. those going beyond any legal or regulatory requirement (e.g. (i), (ii) and (vii) in Table 15.1).

2 *Taking externalities into account* – where 'externalities' refers to both the adverse (negative) or beneficial (positive) outcomes of actions by organizations for which they are neither charged (cost) or recompensed (revenue) in the market (e.g. (iii), (vi) and (viii)).

3 *Taking multiple stakeholders into account* – i.e. not just the profit concerns of owners (principals), such as shareholders, but the concerns of employees, customers, suppliers, distributors, and all others with a vested interest in the organisation (e.g. all (i)–(vi) inclusive, and (viii)).

4 *Incorporating organizational value/mission statements* – i.e. not only involving operational or practice-oriented activities, but core belief systems of the organization (e.g. (v), (vi)).

Stakeholder approach to CSR

As we note above, the majority of the definitions in Table 15.1 take 'multiple stakeholders into account'.

It will be useful, therefore, to briefly review the stakeholder approach to CSR. In the view of Milton Friedman (see p. 307), the Nobel prize-winning economist, managers and directors (agents) have the duty and responsibility to always act in the best interests of the owners (principals), namely the shareholders in a public or private limited company. However, stakeholder theory takes a much broader view of the responsibilities of managers and directors. The acknowledged initiator of the stakeholder view, R. E. Freeman, suggested the following definition:

> A stakeholder is any group or individual who can affect, or is affected by, the achievement of a corporation's purpose (Freeman, 1984, p. vi).

Arguably this definition helps more rigorously define the 'S' in 'CSR'! In other words, instead of the vague 'Social' concept, we now focus more pragmatically on the groups or individuals in society who influence the companies' activities or purposes, or who are impacted by those activities or purposes. Figure 15.1 outlines the various groups or individuals who might come within the stakeholder definition of a typical large corporation.

The ethical or moral dimension of stakeholder theory is the implication that if the company itself affects groups or individuals in seeking to achieve its goals, then these groups or individuals have a legitimate interest in the activities of that company. Of course, the *extent* of that interest is somewhat subjective – how do we weight the relative importance of the different stakeholders, whether in terms of the power they should be given to influence corporate policy or the significance we should give to the impacts of corporate policy on their wellbeing? In other words, while 'stakeholder' is arguably a more pragmatic concept than 'social', and an ethical case for the interests of such stakeholders in the activities of the company is more easily made, there is still a subjective issue as regards 'weighting' the importance of the various stakeholders in terms of both their permitted contribution to the decision-making processes and the relative valuation given to their 'well-being' when assessing the expected outcomes of different policy scenarios.

Table 15.1 Organizational definitions of CSR.

	Organization	Type of organization	Definition of CSR	Source
(i)	UK government	Governmental organisation	'The voluntary actions that business can take, over and above compliance with minimum legal requirements, to address both its own competitive interests and the interests of wider society'	www.csr.gov.uk
(ii)	European Commission	Governmental organization	'A concept whereby companies integrate social and environmental concerns in their business operations and in their interaction with their stakeholders on a voluntary basis'	EC Green Paper, 2001, *Promoting a European Framework for Corporate Social Responsibility*
(iii)	Confederation of British Industry	Business association	'The acknowledgement by companies that they should be accountable not only for their financial performance, but for the impact of their activities on society and/or the environment'	www.cbi.org/uk/
(iv)	World Business Council for Sustainable Development	Business association	'The continuing commitment by business to behave ethically and contribute to economic development while improving the quality of life of the workforce and their families as well as of the local community and society at large'	WBBCSD, 1999, 'CSR: Meeting Changing Expectations'
(v)	Gap Inc.	Corporation	'Being socially responsible means striving to incorporate our values and ethics into everything we do – from how we run our business, to how we treat our employees, to how we impact upon the communities where we live and work'	www.gapinc.com
(vi)	HSBC	Corporation	'Means managing our business responsibly and sensitively for long-term success. Our goal is not, and never has been profit at any cost because we know that tomorrow's success depends on the trust we build today'	
(vii)	Christian Aid	Non-governmental organization	'An entirely voluntary, corporate-led initiative to promote self-regulation at either national or international level'	'Behind the Mask: The Real Face of Corporate Social Responsibility', 2004
(viii)	CSR Asia	Social enterprise	'A company's commitment to operating in an economically, socially and environmentally sustainable manner while balancing the interests of diverse stakeholders'	www.csr-asia.com

Source: Adapted from Crane *et al.* (2008), pp. 6–7.

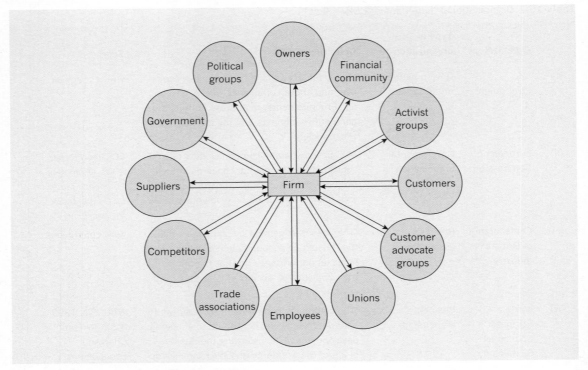

Fig. 15.1 Stakeholders in a large organization.

CSR: a growth phenomenon

Why has CSR in general, and these core characteristics in particular, become so important in the pronouncements and activities of so many organizations and their representatives in recent times? Here we examine some of the key reasons for the increased prominence of CSR, some of the reasons being somewhat 'defensive' in nature, i.e. seeking via CSR to avoid potential damage, but others being more 'positive' and proactive, i.e. seeking via CSR to increase potential benefits to the organization. We shall review both types of motive as we first examine the case for organizations supporting CSR initiatives.

Case for CSR

Here we review some of the arguments widely used to support the resurgence of interest in CSR which many analysts trace back to the 1950s, and to the US in

particular. There are a number of arguments which are advanced under the broad heading of 'enlightened self-interest' for the organizations concerned.

Risk management: avoiding reputational damage

The experience of companies such as Enron, WorldCom, Global Crossing and Parmalat vividly portrays what can happen to companies and share prices when corporate scandals become the focus of 24/7 media coverage. Avoiding reputational damage by putting in place explicit codes of behaviour and reporting regularly on ethical and social activities to shareholders, often in annual 'social responsibility' reports, has become an expectation of the many analysts, credit rating agencies and non-governmental organizations closely scrutinizing multinational corporate behaviour especially! Organisations are increasingly expected to report on their non-financial as well as financial performance, especially given the awareness of shareholders of the impact of corporate disasters such as the explosion at the Bhopal pesticide factory in India, the oil spills of the Exxon Valdez in Alaska and more recently BP in the Gulf of Mexico, the exposure of Nike's and Gap's use of child labour, the resistance of pharmaceutical companies to providing cheaper generic antiretroviral treatments for HIV/AIDS, and so on. In this sense the development of CSR policies becomes an explicit element in 'risk management' used by organizations and their representatives in an effort to *avoid* incidents which might damage their reputation.

Revenue and profit enhancement

Here we review a less defensive and more proactive reason often advanced for the growth of CSR and which can be linked to a number of positive financial associations.

CSR is positively correlated with revenue/profit outcomes

It has often been suggested that firm behaviour which seeks to be more than usually ethical or to give considerable weight to environmental concerns must do so at the expense of profit. However, many firms are now seeing ethical and environmentally responsible behaviour as being in their own self-interest, with demand curves shifting to the right (increasing) the closer the alignment of products with positive social/ethical initiatives. In Fig. 15.2 this is shown as a shift in the demand curve from D to D'. At any given price, consumers will purchase more of the product, raising total revenue at price P in the diagram from $OPVQ$ to OPV_1Q_1. However, there is a further possible revenue-raising strategy that may now be possible! By creating a more positive ethical/environmental association with the product, CSR initiatives may also result in the demand curve pivoting from D' to D'' in Fig. 15.2. The demand curve will now be less price-elastic, giving opportunities for the firm to raise prices and increase revenue, since demand falls by less than in proportion to the price rise.

Firms are increasingly aware of the benefits of aligning themselves with ethical and ecological initiatives. Various 'kitemarks' exist for firms to certify that their product conforms to ethical standards in production, as for example 'Rug-Mark' for carpets and rugs, 'Forest Stewardship Council' mark (to certify wood derived from sustainable forestry extraction

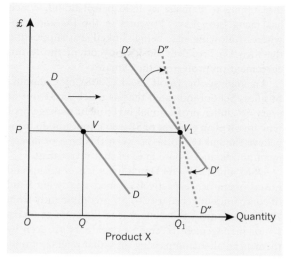

Fig. 15.2 Demand increases and becomes less elastic with successful CSR campaign.

methods) and the 'Fairtrade' mark (guarantees a higher return to developing country producers).

Indeed, it was reported in 2010 that annual sales of *Fairtrade* food and drink in the UK have reached over £500m, having grown at over 40% per year over the past decade. It has expanded from one brand of coffee ten years ago to around 1,000 foodstuffs, including chocolate, fruit, vegetables, juices, snacks, wine, tea, sugar, honey and nuts. A Mori poll in 2010 found that two-thirds of UK consumers claim to be green or ethical and actively look to purchase products with an environmental/ethical association. At the sectoral level, many of the UK's biggest retail names have joined the *Ethical Trading Initiative* (ETI) which brings together companies, trade unions and non-governmental organizations in seeking to ensure that the products sold in their retail outlets have not been produced by 'sweatshop' labour working for next to nothing in hazardous conditions.

At the corporate level, Exxon Mobil seems to be an example of a company that has accepted the linkage between ethical/environmental practices and corporate profits. It announced in late 2003 that it had been holding discreet meetings with environmentalists and human rights groups worldwide in an effort to change its unfavourable image in these respects. The charm offensive has been linked to fears at Exxon's Texas headquarters that a negative public image is threatening to damage its Esso petrol brand, which has faced 'stop Esso' boycotts in the EU and elsewhere following its being linked to supporting the then US President Bush's boycott of the Kyoto agreement on protecting the climate.

An analysis by Geoff Heal (2008) of Columbia Business School indicated that as much as $1 out of every $9 under professional investment management now involves an element of SRI, so important do firms believe the linkage to be between this type of investment and financial outcomes of that investment.

DSM and TNT, the Dutch life sciences group and postal operator, respectively, joined a growing band of companies in February 2010 – predominantly from the Netherlands – that link part of the bonuses which senior management receive to sustainability, seen by them as an all-encompassing term that refers not only to the environment but to issues such as employee satisfaction and safety.

CSR is positively correlated with share price

At a more aggregative level, attempts are now being made to incorporate ethical/environmental considerations into formal stock exchange indices in the UK and other financial markets. A new FTSE 4 Good Index was launched in July 2001, using social and ethical criteria to rank corporate performance. All companies in three sectors were excluded, namely tobacco, weapons and nuclear power (representing 10% of all FTSE companies). Of the remaining companies, three criteria were applied for ranking purposes: environment, human rights and social issues. If a company 'fails' in any one of these criteria, it is again excluded. Of the 757 companies in the FTSE All Share Index, only 288 companies have actually made it into the index. The FTSE itself has produced figures showing that if this new FTSE 4 Good Index had existed over the previous five years, it would actively have outperformed the more conventional stock exchange indices. The same has been found to be true for the Dow Jones Sustainability Group Index in the US. This is a similar ethical index introduced in the US in 1999. When backdated to 1993 it was found to have outperformed the Dow Jones Global Index by 46%.

Providing strategic direction

Porter and Kramer (2006) published a paper on how CSR could, if approached in a strategic way, help enhance an organization's competitive advantage over its rivals. The key element in their analysis is the suggestion that organizations embed CSR in their operational, global supply chain, investor relations and other strategies at every level, so that CSR becomes 'part of the corporate DNA'. CSR then influences all decisions across the organization and gives the organization a competitive edge, thereby adding value.

As Fig. 15.3 illustrates, Porter and Kramer (2006) have identified two types of the CSR–Strategy relationship, i.e. responsive and strategic CSR. *Responsive CSR* is defined as being a reaction to various legal,

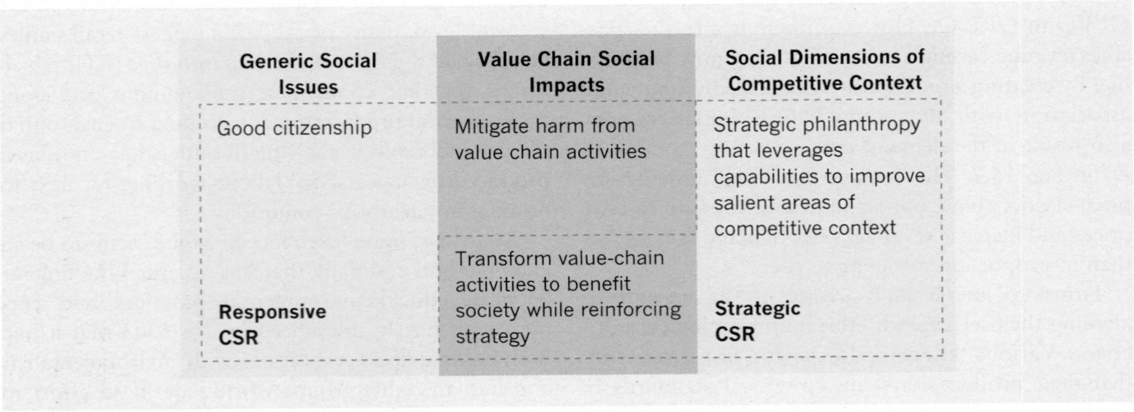

Generic Social Issues	Value Chain Social Impacts	Social Dimensions of Competitive Context
Good citizenship	Mitigate harm from value chain activities	Strategic philanthropy that leverages capabilities to improve salient areas of competitive context
	Transform value-chain activities to benefit society while reinforcing strategy	
Responsive CSR		**Strategic CSR**

Fig. 15.3 Corporate involvement in society: a strategic approach.
Source: Porter and Kramer (2006). The link between competitive advantage and corporate social responsibility, *Harvard Business Review*, **84**(12), p. 89.

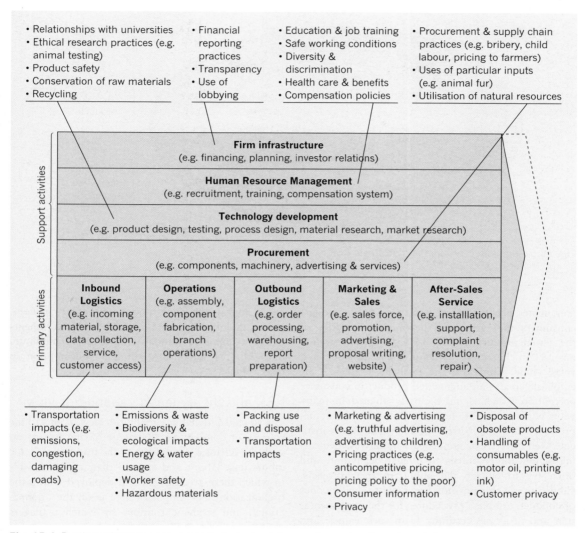

- Relationships with universities
- Ethical research practices (e.g. animal testing)
- Product safety
- Conservation of raw materials
- Recycling

- Financial reporting practices
- Transparency
- Use of lobbying

- Education & job training
- Safe working conditions
- Diversity & discrimination
- Health care & benefits
- Compensation policies

- Procurement & supply chain practices (e.g. bribery, child labour, pricing to farmers)
- Uses of particular inputs (e.g. animal fur)
- Utilisation of natural resources

Support activities

Firm infrastructure
(e.g. financing, planning, investor relations)

Human Resource Management
(e.g. recruitment, training, compensation system)

Technology development
(e.g. product design, testing, process design, material research, market research)

Procurement
(e.g. components, machinery, advertising & services)

Primary activities

| **Inbound Logistics** (e.g. incoming material, storage, data collection, service, customer access) | **Operations** (e.g. assembly, component fabrication, branch operations) | **Outbound Logistics** (e.g. order processing, warehousing, report preparation) | **Marketing & Sales** (e.g. sales force, promotion, advertising, proposal writing, website) | **After-Sales Service** (e.g. installlation, support, complaint resolution, repair) |

- Transportation impacts (e.g. emissions, congestion, damaging roads)

- Emissions & waste
- Biodiversity & ecological impacts
- Energy & water usage
- Worker safety
- Hazardous materials

- Packing use and disposal
- Transportation impacts

- Marketing & advertising (e.g. truthful advertising, advertising to children)
- Pricing practices (e.g. anticompetitive pricing, pricing policy to the poor)
- Consumer information
- Privacy

- Disposal of obsolete products
- Handling of consumables (e.g. motor oil, printing ink)
- Customer privacy

Fig. 15.4 Putting ethical/environmental strategies into practice using the value chain.
Source: Porter and Kramer (2006). The link between competitive advantage and corporate social responsibility, *Harvard Business Review*, **84**(12).

social or intrinsic pressures. The companies which practice responsive CSR 'will gain an edge, but . . . any advantage is likely to be temporary' (Porter and Kramer, 2006). *Strategic CSR*, on the other hand, goes beyond best practices, as 'it is about choosing a unique position . . . arising in the product offering and the value chain.' It provides gains through the synergy of consistently applied CSR and strategy, bringing competitive advantage and, at the same time, generating value for society.

Porter and Kramer identify a range of potential policies associated with aspects of the organization's value chain which might become a focus for policy action when using CSR in a strategic way. As Fig. 15.4 indicates, there are a wide range of CSR-related policy options that organizations might adopt if they are to strategically 'brand' and differentiate themselves in terms of their value chain.

In fact, some organizations may so focus on CSR-related aspects that, in effect, they are developing an

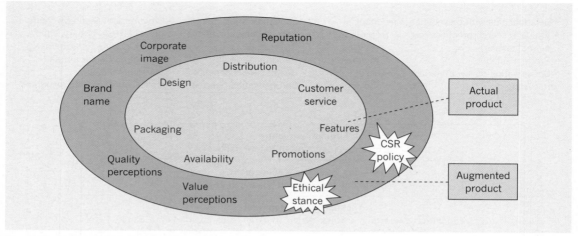

Fig. 15.5 Augmented product and strategic CSR.
Source: McDonald (2007), p. 275.

'augmented product' which has a perception amongst consumers that goes well beyond the realities of the actual product! In Fig. 15.5 the *actual product* has certain characteristics/features and an associated value chain. However, the explicit, strategic CSR emphasis creates an augmented product in consumer perception which is more closely aligned in many ways with those CSR features than with the actual product value chain itself! Such organizations instigate well-advertised, grand-scale initiatives, dedicating significant resources to ethical behaviour, and often try to engage the public in their projects. Companies in this position are likely to devise codes of conduct; establish procedures for the implementation and processes resulting from such values; and publish detailed triple bottom line reports. Also, many of them work closely with non-governmental organizations (NGOs) in a relevant field aiming to achieve a high level of transparency for their operations (e.g. Ecover).

The reality for Porter and Kramer and many other analysts is that CSR and organizational strategy are often only loosely and intermittently connected! In a global study in 2007, McKinsey consultants found a shortfall of over 25% between what respondents believe their organizations *should do* in terms of CSR and what they say their organization *actually does*! At the individual product level Toyota has been criticized for its strategic inconsistency in supporting 'green' sustainable transport with its Prius hybrid model, but at the same time joining other car companies in lobbying the US and other governments to resist imposing standards in terms of minimum miles/km per gallon/litre on fuel consumption in their vehicles.

CSR and the dynamic capabilities view

The so-called 'dynamic capabilities view' points to the sources of competitive advantage having less to do with the intrinsic capabilities of the traditional factor inputs (e.g. labour and capital) than with the ways in which these are engaged and deployed within the organization! The emphasis here is on the organizational and strategic routines by which managers modify, integrate and recombine their factor inputs and resources to generate new value-creating strategies. A number of authors (e.g. Teece *et al.* 1997; Petrick and Quinn 2001) have identified the approaches and policies of the organizations as regards social and ethical issues as sources of competitive advantage, as in the organizational approach to moral decision-making.

Case against CSR

Misuse of scarce resources

The main argument against CSR under this heading is the suggestion that managers do not have the moral right to waste valuable resources on social and related initiatives, as this is detrimental to the efficiency of the business, but should instead seek to use scarce resources to increase the company's (and the owners') profits. This view has been strongly advocated by critics of CSR such as Milton Friedman.

> There is one and only one social responsibility of business – to use its resources and engage in activities designed to increase its profits so long as it stays within the rules of the game, which is to say, engages in open and free competition without deception or fraud (Friedman 1970, p. 126).

Writing some 30 years later Wolf reinforced this view of CSR as essentially misunderstanding the key function of business.

> The role of well run companies is to make profits, not save the planet (Wolf 2000, p. 21).

However, as Fisher and Lovell (2009) point out, Friedman's argument does allow for a form of corporate philanthropy where such activities can be shown to bring higher profitability and returns to owners than any alternative investment opportunities! However, Friedman would argue that such 'calculative' behaviour is nothing more than normal commercial investment appraisal as the motivation behind such calculations is explicitly financial and involves no ethical concern for the beneficiary (-ies) and therefore does not fall into the conventional domain of CSR!

Friedman criticizes the traditional arguments in favour of CSR from at least three perspectives.

1 *Economic.* Friedman argues that companies are responsible for using shareholders' funds in profitable ways and in legally acceptable ways, nothing more! Friedman points out that focusing on charities and schools and engaging in corporate philanthropy distorts allocative efficiency as it 'takes management's eye off the ball', namely securing higher profits for owner-shareholders.

2 *Ethics and political philosophy.* Friedman insists that it is inappropriate for corporations to use shareholders' funds to support good causes since 'any such donations can only come at the expense of lower dividends, higher prices or lower wages (or a combination of all three)'. Friedman asked the rhetorical question 'how can it be ethical that a corporation should act first as unpaid tax collector (i.e. levying a 'tax' on the shareholders/customers and/or employees) and then as unaccountable benefactor?' In the view of Friedman it is the responsibility of publically elected representatives at national or local levels to levy real taxes and in due course be accountable to the electorate, both for the taxes themselves and for the uses to which they are put. In other words, if the tax revenues are used to provide financial support to charities or for other welfare or social services, then in a democratic state the electorate can confirm or withhold its support for such taxes and their uses at the ballot box. Only publically elected representatives of the people or private individuals acting voluntarily have, in Friedman's view, the right to make financial donations of this type.

3 *Philosophical.* In Friedman's view businesses cannot have responsibilities, because they are not real people, they are social constructs dependent on legal definitions and legal protections for their existence. Only individuals can have responsibilities, not corporations.

We now turn our attention to organizational responses to the rather broad CSR definitions and issues already outlined. We first focus on corporate responsibility in the increasingly high profile area of sustainability policies and approaches, then on broader areas of appropriate ethical behaviour, before turning our attention to the internal management and supervision of such policies via the corporate governance framework and various codes of conduct.

Corporate responsibility

The term 'corporate responsibility' is increasingly in use, the omission of 'social' being seen by many as a recognition that the responsibilities of corporations extend over a still broader range of issues, especially those involving environmental and ethical concerns.

Environmental and ecological responsibilities

In today's global economy a number of driving forces are arguably raising environmental concerns to the forefront of *corporate* policy debate, which is the focus of this section – a broader, less corporate review of environmental issues and policies is undertaken in Chapter 10.

- *Environmentally conscious consumers.* Consumer awareness of environmental issues is creating a market for 'green products'. Patagonia, a California-based producer of recreational clothing, has developed a loyal base of high-income customers partly because its brand identity includes a commitment to conservation. 'Every day we take steps to lighten our footprint and do less harm.' A similar successful approach has been used by Timberland ('our love for the outdoors is matched by our passion for confronting global warming') and the Body Shop. Consumers have long claimed to be more virtuous than they are. Retailers called it the '30:3 phenomenon' – 30% of purchasers told pollsters that they thought about workers' rights, animal welfare and the state of the planet when they decided what to buy, but sales figures showed that only 3% of them acted on those thoughts. Now, however, retailers are behaving as if consumers mean it. A Mori poll found that two-thirds of UK consumers claimed to be 'green' or ethical and actively look to purchase products with an environmental/ethical association. We noted earlier that annual sales of Fairtrade food and drink in Britain had reached over £500m in 2010, having grown at over 40% per year over the past decade. In the UK, J. Sainsbury is selling only bananas with the Fairtrade label, which guarantees a decent income to the grower. Marks & Spencer is stocking only Fairtrade coffee and tea and is buying a third of the world's supply of Fairtrade cotton. In the US, Dunkin' Donuts has decided to sell only Fairtrade espresso coffee in its North American and European outlets. Wal-Mart has devoted itself to a range of 'sustainability' projects.

- *Environmentally and credit-risk-conscious producers.* International businesses are increasingly aware that failure to manage environmental risk factors effectively can lead to adverse publicity, lost revenue and profit and perhaps even more seriously a reduction in their official credit rating, making it more difficult and costly (e.g. higher interest rates) to finance future investment plans. BP has found that the Gulf of Mexico oil-spill in

April 2010 cost it $10bn in clean-up operations, $1bn in compensation to those individuals and businesses directly affected, $70bn in market capitalization via a 50% fall in its share price in the following six months. All this does not even include ongoing litigation for breaches in health and safety regulations prior to the explosion and oil spill, and loss of reputation and of 'preferred bidder' status in many ongoing bids for new exploration in the US and elsewhere.

A 2010 Populus poll of energy consumers in the UK found that their choice of energy supplier was significantly influenced by the following factors:

- how hard the supplier is working to use resources effectively and reduce waste;
- level of supplier investment in renewable energy;
- the extent to which the supplier is helping me to become more environmentally efficient;
- how hard the supplier is working to address climate change;
- the supplier's approach to biodiversity.

The above five factors were all in the top seven factors identified by consumers as 'important' when choosing an energy supplier, all scored over 3 on a scale from 0 (completely unimportant) to 5 (very important indeed), and all had increased their scores (by around 10%) since the previous Populus survey in 2008.

- *Environmentally conscious governments.* Businesses have a further reason for considering the environmental impacts of their activities, namely the scrutiny of host governments. Where production of a product causes environmental damage, it is likely that this will result in the imposition of taxes or regulations by government. In the EU, strict new regulations on maximum emissions of greenhouse gases by vehicles are forcing car manufacturers to change engine/chassis designs and sizes to comply with the new regulatory environment. For example, a legally binding EU regulation of a maximum emission of 130 grams of CO_2 per kilometre driven by new cars comes into force in 2015. As we note below, in 2008 the US and EU governments made it a criminal offence to import illegal timber, given environmental concerns involving deforestation.

Environmental sustainability

'Sustainable' and 'sustainability' are now key trigger words in the world of advertising for positive, emotive images associated with words such as 'green', 'wholesome', 'goodness', 'justice', 'environment', amongst others. They are used in a sophisticated manner to sell cars, nappies, holidays and even lifestyles. Sustainability sells – how has this come about and what exactly are we being encouraged to buy?

As long ago as 1987, a United Nations report entitled *Our Common Future* provided the most widely used definition of sustainable development: 'development which meets the needs of the present without compromising the ability of future generations to meet their own needs' (World Commission on Environment and Development, 1987). Of course, there have been many different views as to how this definition should affect individual, corporate and government actions, though one theme that has been constant in most views is that of 'intergenerational equity', i.e. where the development process seeks to minimize any adverse impacts on future generations. These clearly include avoiding adverse environmental impacts such as excessive resource depletion today reducing the stock of resources available for future use, or levels of pollution emission and waste disposal today beyond the ability of the environment to absorb them, thereby imposing long-term damage on future generations.

Forests and deforestation provides a useful case study, illustrating how environmental and ecological dilemmas impact on corporate interests and activities.

Forestry and corporate responsibility

The vital contribution of forests to a sustainable global environment has long been recognized, especially their ability to give out oxygen and absorb and store carbon. Of course, destroying forests for wood, for increased plantation or cattle rearing works in reverse – with around half the dry weight of a tree consisting of stored carbon, much of which is released into the atmosphere when trees are burned or left to rot. In fact, around half the earth's total forest area has been cleared by man-made interventions in the past 10,000 years, and today continued deforestation contributes some 15–17% of the world's annual emissions of carbon dioxide (CO_2). Of course, forest clearance does still more damage than this, with the loss of plant sources of many modern medicines and animal species, as well as threatening the habitats and livelihoods of some 400 million of the world's poorest people, and resulting in increased flooding as bare hillsides fail to absorb rainfall as effectively as in the past.

The increasing emphasis of the media on such environmental issues has, of course, increased pressures on corporations and governments to advance more 'responsible' approaches to forests and their many products and uses. A UN supported organization 'The Economics of Ecosystems and Biodiversity' (TEEB) has estimated that negative externalities from forest loss and degradation cost between \$2trillion and \$4.5trillion each year!

The prominence given to the important role of forests in 'sustainability'-related concerns is providing both positive and negative incentives for corporations to adopt policies consistent with increased environmental responsibility.

- *Positive incentives.* On the positive side, governments and environmental agencies are providing incentives of various kinds to encourage a more responsible corporate attitude towards forestry. For example, agricultural companies and farmers are benefitting from incentives in the form of *Payments for Ecosystem Services* (PES) to reforest agricultural land – in China farmers in the vicinity of the Yangzi River are paid \$450 a year per reforested hectare, in an attempt to lessen flooding damage. Costa Rica offers \$45–163 per reforested hectare

- *Negative incentives.* On the negative side, *failure* to support sustainable forestry can result in serious damage to corporate profitability. Nestlé has been targeted by Greenpeace with negative blogs and adverts exposing links between the production of chocolate for Kit Kat bars and associated deforestation in Indonesia; around half of the forest areas cleared for crops in Indonesia are used for oil palms, mainly for chocolate production. The impact of such negative publicity was deemed so severe by Nestlé that it ceased buying palm oil from its main Indonesian supplier, Sinar Mas, and promised to remove from its supply chain any producer of palm oil linked to deforestation.

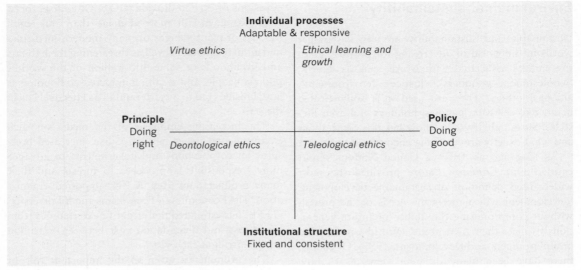

Fig. 15.6 A framework for ethical theories.
Source: Adapted from Fisher and Lovell (2009).

Ethical responsibilities and codes of conduct

Over time a wide range of ethical theories has developed, with individuals and groups supporting or challenging them! Figure 15.6 gives a broad 'map' of the range of ethical theories available and it may be useful at this point to define the terms on the horizontal and vertical axes, before turning briefly to the ethical theories themselves.

Horizontal axis

- *Principles* – standards to be observed, seen as desirable in terms of fairness/justice or some other moral dimension in their own right, irrespective of the outcome of following those principles. This approach is sometimes referred to as a 'duties' view of ethical behaviour – things to be done (or avoided) because they are intrinsically right or wrong.

- *Policies* – approaches that achieve measurable outcomes which are regarded as improvements on the original situations. This approach is sometimes referred to as a 'consequential' view of ethical behaviour – things to be done (or avoided) because

they will have consequences which result in an overall *net* benefit or loss.

Along this horizontal axis, some ethical theories are seen as focusing primarily on the 'rightness' of some action or approach or on the 'outcome' of that action or approach in terms of making a net overall improvement for the individual or group.

Vertical axis

- *Individual processes* – approaches that emphasize the responsibilities of individuals to develop/improve themselves or the group(s) to which they belong.

- *Institutional structure* – approaches that emphasize the importance of establishing institutions and structures that exist and operate independently of the individuals who devise them, but which determine the key principles which underpin ethical considerations.

Of course any such diagram is over simplistic, but it does give us a useful starting point to consider various ethical theories in the context of our previous discussions.

- *Virtue ethics.* This broadly corresponds to theories which emphasize individuals having the responsibility to respond to the question 'What would a virtuous person do in this situation?' Plato is often associated with this approach, identifying the four virtues of wisdom, courage, self-control and justice. His follower, Aristotle, identified key personal qualities associated with achieving these virtues, especially 'justice', namely liberality (especially as regards money), truthfulness, patience, magnanimity. These virtues and personal qualities were seen as desirable ends in their own right, whatever the outcomes of practising them!

- *Deontological ethics.* While the emphasis is still on universal principles to be followed because of their intrinsic 'rightness', irrespective of outcomes, there is a recognition that individuals act within a social and institutional context which gives them a sense of shared identify and commitment to the values of their group. Kantian ethics come under this heading, with actions to be guided by universal principles and deemed morally acceptable only if carried out as a duty, rather than in expectation of any reward or reciprocity. Kant used the term 'categorical imperative' to refer to principles that must be obeyed, with no exceptions.

- *Ethical learning and growth.* Located in the top-right quadrant of Fig. 15.6, the emphasis here is on ethical behaviour being tested by outcomes but ones that are based on individual morality, and cannot be imposed by institutional decree (e.g. codes of conduct). Ethical behaviour can only be encouraged indirectly from this perspective by providing learning experiences from which individuals derive their own ethical codes of behaviour.

- *Teleological ethics.* These are again outcome-oriented ethical theories, but which see institutions as necessary to achieve these desirable ethical outcomes. The term 'teleological' means that the rightness or goodness of an action is not intrinsic to that action, but must be judged on the merits of its outcomes. Utilitarianism is often placed under this heading, with the emphasis here on institutions or organizations seeking to achieve the greatest good of the greatest number: 'The greatest happiness of the greatest number is the foundation of morals and legislation' (Bentham 1843, p. 142). In this sense, utilitarianism is a calculated approach to ethics, with the costs and benefits of institu-

tional actions assumed to be capable of valuation and ranking.

CSR perspectives and ethical frameworks

Perspectives

- *Friedman perspectives.* In terms of our earlier analysis, Friedman's view on businesses (not individuals) having the primary responsibility of achieving profit, and their having no right to engage in distracting philanthropy would locate his perspective in the bottom – left quadrant of Fig. 15.6, i.e. 'Deontological ethics'. His emphasis is on the 'rightness' of a shareholder focus by the business and on the business as an 'institutional' and social construct, dependent on legal definitions and legal protections for its existence (Friedman 1970, p. 126). However, the variant of Friedman's position which emphasizes investigating the profit-related *outcomes* of philanthropy, rather than the *intentions* behind it, would arguably justify placing his approach into the bottom right quadrant, i.e. 'Teleological ethics', with the outcome of philanthropy or gift giving to be judged in terms of outcomes rather than 'rightness'.

- *Stakeholder perspectives.* The broader stakeholder perspective was reviewed earlier (p. 300) and might be more readily located on the right-hand side of Fig. 15.6 with its emphasis on balancing the outcomes of corporate actions amongst the various 'interested parties' within the organization. Of course, it could be located in the top-right quadrant under 'Ethical learning and growth' should the emphasis be on individual behaviour conforming to these stakeholder principles. Here the focus would be on developing an 'atmosphere' conducive to moral behaviour at an individual level within the organization. However, should the emphasis be on institutional behaviour being aligned with a stakeholder approach, as in the case of organizational codes of conduct, then it might more accurately be located in the bottom-right quadrant under 'teleological ethics'.

It is to these 'codes of conduct' that we now turn our attention.

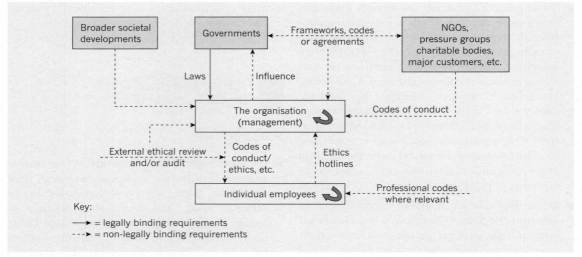

Fig. 15.7 Codes of conduct and ethical frameworks.
Source: Fisher and Lovell (2009), p. 388.

Codes of conduct

As Fig. 15.7 indicates, some of the pressures for organizations to exhibit ethical and socially responsible behaviour stem directly from the explicit legal environment in which the organization operates. The only continuous and unbroken line in Fig. 15.7 indicates the legally binding (mandatory) requirements as regards 'corporate' behaviour imposed on the organization by national and supra-national (e.g. EU) governmental bodies. The broken lines represent the many ethical frameworks and codes of conduct which, while technically voluntary, provide important constraints and contexts for organizational behaviour.

Non-governmental organizations such as Greenpeace, Friends of the Earth, International Baby Food Action Network and other charities and pressure groups will contrast organizational performance against agreed or proposed codes of conduct and ethical frameworks. The codes of conduct the organization itself may impose (usually these are 'top-down' initiatives!) on its own employees and operations will often be an attempt to regularize processes and steer behaviours to align the outcomes of organizational performance more closely with the external pressures and expectations from governments, NGOs and the broader society.

The 'ethics hotlines' in Fig. 15.7 include mechanisms for employees to raise concerns about current behaviours and practices – giving organizations themselves early warning of possible problems as well as providing avenues for expressing concerns which might otherwise result in 'whistleblowing' to a more critical external audience.

Table 15.2 provides a useful summary of some of the advantages and disadvantages of using codes of conduct. Of course, the operation of these codes of conduct can be reviewed annually or periodically by external ethical audits. In addition, a variety of 'informal' mechanism can be used to support such codes in seeking to influence organizational values and behaviour, including reward systems, training, storytelling, recruitment and selection policies and processes, ethics officers, etc.

Codes of conduct versus codes of ethics

Whilst these terms are sometimes used interchangeably, codes of conduct tend to be a more prescriptive set of rules or instructions as regards employee behaviour. They identify specific actions that must be undertaken or avoided! Codes of ethics tend to be more general and to emphasize attitudes and characteristics (honesty, diversity, loyalty, integrity, etc.) to be exhibited, rather than actions to be taken/avoided.

Table 15.2 Codes of conduct: advantages and disadvantages.

Advantages	Disadvantages
Reduces the need for governmental regulation or intervention	Cannot enforce full implementation as voluntary codes
Limits the potential damages awarded when the organization can be seen by the court to have an explicit policy even when not followed by individual employees	Lack rigorous mechanisms to ensure accountability
	Often written as broad philosophical statements therefore hard to measure
Enhances trust, customer loyalty and reputation	Those adopting are often already leaders in CSR issues in those sectors
Creates benchmarks against which the organization's practices can be compared	Often unknown to majority of employees
Creates pressure from internal and external stakeholders to follow through on commitments by formalizing and publishing commitments	Such codes tend to be over-represented in industries and sectors with high visibility and with a focus on brand image or reputation and large environmental or social impacts (often business to customer products)
Creates potential for competitive advantage	Often do not include complaints processes or whistleblower protections
Flexible, can be uniquely adapted to that organization	
Creates order and structure in standards and procedures acceptable to the organization when operating globally	
Allows stakeholders influence in decision-making	
Relatively inexpensive	

Corporate governance

Corporate governance refers to the various arrangements within an organization which provide both authority and accountability in its operations. In other words, it refers to a wide range of formal structures, procedures and regulations governing the means by which decisions are made, communicated and operationalized within an organization. The earlier debate in Chapter 3 on the separation between ownership and control via the rise of public and private limited companies and associated principal–agent issues is certainly relevant here, as is the whole set of formal legal, accounting and other regulations relevant to different categories of company and to the ways in which decisions are made, communicated and enforced (see Chapter 2).

The many corporate scandals over the centuries have tended to result in legislation and regulations seeking to clarify the respective responsibilities of corporations and their shareholders. The 'Bubble Act' of 1719 was an attempt to protect future shareholders

from the distortions and misleading pronouncements of the Board of the South Sea company which had led to financial ruin for so many investors.

Before reviewing some major developments in corporate governance in the UK and US, it may be useful to note that the term can be used in a context much wider than the usual one involving financial and regulatory aspects only. For example, Sir Adrian Cadbury made the following statement in his submission to the World Banks' 1999 Report on Corporate Governance:

> Corporate governance is concerned with holding the balance between economic and social goals and between individual and community goals. . . . The aim is to align as nearly as possible the interests of individuals, corporations and society (Sir Adrian Cadbury, reporting to the King Committee on Corporate Governance 2002, p. 6).

We first check out developments towards such ambitious aims for corporate governance in the high-profile area of executive remuneration.

Corporate governance and executive remuneration

We have already reviewed (Chapter 3, p. 53) executive pay in the context of the principal–agent problem. In Europe 84% of companies place decisions about executive pay in the hands of their compensation, or remuneration, committee, according to a survey *Executive Compensation* by consultants, Hewitt, Bacon and Woodrow (Thomas 2009). So, ultimately it is remuneration committees that are as responsible as anyone when executive pay appears to bear scant relationship to corporate performance. *Pension and Investment Research Consultants* (PIRC), the UK corporate governance watchdog, regularly reports that the pay of executive directors at FTSE 100 companies has spiralled high above inflation.

The rapid rise in executive pay, when the companies themselves have been performing modestly at best, has created widespread criticism from shareholders and others. *Stock options* have been a particular source of criticism – the practice whereby senior executives have been given the 'option' of buying company shares at a heavily discounted price (i.e. lower than the market price) and then selling them at a profit should they succeed in raising the share price above an agreed target. Often, exercising these options has given far more income to executives than their basic salaries.

Table 15.3 provides a useful review of Chief Executive Officer (CEO) remuneration packages around the world (Watson Wyatt Worldwide 2009). In the US some 60% of total CEO compensation is in the form of incentive plans (stock options, etc.), with only 23% of such compensation derived from basic salary and a further 17% from cash bonuses.

Table 15.3 Structure of CEO remuneration packages around the world.

Country	Base salary (%)	Cash bonus (%)	Incentive plan compensation (%)
US	23	17	60
Brazil	27	41	32
Germany	39	47	14
UK	40	38	22
France	44	25	31
Ireland	44	43	13
Hong Kong	51	19	30
Netherlands	51	28	21
Belgium	52	26	22
Italy	52	29	19
Japan	71	12	17

Note: Companies with revenues between $1bn and $3bn.
Source: Watson Wyatt Worldwide (2009) *Executive pay practices around the world.*

The situation is, however, reversed in Japan with 71% of CEO compensation consisting of basic salary, 12% cash bonuses and only 17% via incentive plans. EU countries tend to be somewhere in between these two extremes.

Table 15.4 broadly supports the suggestion that the most important sources of executive remuneration lie outside the base salary. For the five executives with the highest total remuneration package among the FTSE 100 in 2010, it is clear that the base salary is one of the least important sources of executive remuneration. The highest share of the total

Table 15.4 Top five earners in the FTSE 100 2009/10.

Company	Name/role	Base salary	Cash bonus	Benefits and other	Share incentives	Total remuneration
Reckitt Benckiser	Chief executive	£0.99m	£3.52m	£0.083m	£88.00m	£92.59m
Berkeley Group Holdings	Executive director	£0.75m	£0.75m	£0.156m	£34.71m	£36.37m
Xstrata	Chief executive	£1.31m	£1.31m	£0.314m	£22.58m	£25.51m
Icap	Chief executive	£0.36m	£1.50m	£0.669m	£21.80m	£24.33m
BG Group	Chief executive	£1.14m	£1.13m	£0.005m	£20.77m	£23.06m

Source: Various.

Table 15.5 CEO compensation in the FTSE 100.

Year	Average CEO	Average employee earnings (£)	Multiple
1998	1,012,380	21,540	47
1999	1,235,401	20,939	59
2000	1,684,900	24,070	70
2001	1,812,750	24,170	75
2002	2,587,474	24,182	107
2003	2,773,904	24,767	112
2004	3,121,435	25,955	119
2005	3,312,285	27,254	121
2006	3,339,421	30,828	107
2007	3,935,820	25,677	151
2008	3,950,642	30,994	128
2009	3,710,440	32,521	115

remuneration package accounted for by the base salary was 5.1%.

Size of executives' compensation

Of course it is not just variations in the sources of executive remuneration that are often in focus, but also in the *absolute totals* of such compensation.

Totals of executive compensation

Thomas (2009) concluded, having reviewed various global CEO pay surveys, that the US paid by far the largest remuneration packages to executives. Citing work by Towers Perrin, he demonstrates that total CEO pay in Germany is some 51% of that to be expected in comparable companies in the US, with a still lower figure of 44% from Sweden and 21% for China.

Table 15.5 shows the average CEO compensation across the FTSE 100 companies over the period 1998–2009, the average employee earnings across those companies and the multiple between the two. Clearly the general trend has been one whereby the multiple is rising, though with some reduction in the recessionary period 2007–2009. However, the change from a situation whereby the average CEO salary of FTSE 100 companies was 47 times the average employee salary in 1998 but 115 times that salary in 2009.

Arguably, excessive executive pay is even more widespread in the US. For example, the gap between the earnings of ordinary Americans and top executives has grown far wider in the past 25 years. A statistic commonly quoted by the labour group AFL–CIO shows that a chief executive made $42 for every dollar earned by one of his or her blue-collar workers in 1980. Today, chief executives were earning $531 for every dollar taken home by a typical worker.

Executive pay and remuneration committees

So who sits on the remuneration committee which decides the executive remuneration schemes? In the UK the *Combined Code* of corporate governance states that members should be drawn 'exclusively' from non-executives due to the potential for conflicts of interest. By and large, this is so. However, says PIRC, some 14% of FTSE 100 companies continue to include executives on their remuneration committees.

Lessons for corporate governance

Over the past decade or so a number of major 'corporate scandals' have brought issues of corporate governance and accountability to public prominence.

Corporate scandals

Corporate scandals, such as those at Enron, WorldCom and Global Crossing in the US, have become well known in the past few years. However, such problems are by no means confined to the US, as the case of the Italian dairy company, Parmalat, clearly indicates. In little more than a fortnight in December 2003, the Italian dairy conglomerate became engulfed in Europe's biggest financial fraud as some €10–13bn were found to have disappeared from its accounts. Deloitte, Parmalat's chief auditor, did not do its own checks on some big bank accounts at one of the Italian dairy group's subsidiaries that turned out to be fakes. As a result, in December 2003, a major scandal broke after the disclosure that Bonlat, a Parmalat subsidiary in the Cayman Islands, did not have accounts worth almost €4bn (£2.8bn) at Bank of America (B of A). Eventually, this 'lost' money was found to be three times greater. Bonlat's auditor was Grant Thornton and B of A told it in January 2004 that a document purportedly showing accounts with cash and securities worth €3.95bn was fake. Deloitte, one of the big four global accounting firms, allegedly did not make independent checks on the authenticity of Bonlat's supposed accounts with B of A, believing it was entitled to rely on Grant Thornton's work on Bonlat, rather than do its own checks, and such an arrangement was permitted by Italian law and regulators. Even though the division of work between Deloitte, as chief auditor, and Grant Thornton, as auditor to Parmalat's subsidiaries, was allegedly agreed with the company and notified to Consob, Italy's chief financial regulator, the deficiencies in such regulation became only too apparent with the eventual collapse and prosecution of those involved.

These high-profile company collapses, together with shareholder concerns as to the often 'excessive' remuneration packages of company directors in poorly performing companies, have resulted in changes in the rules of corporate governance in recent years. These have involved changes in both internal and external practices, as for example in the companies' dealings with auditors and accountants.

Higgs Committee: UK

In the UK the *Higgs Committee* in 2002 has sought to improve corporate governance in the wake of the bitter experiences for shareholders and investors from the collapse of a number of high-profile companies. The Higgs proposals include the following.

- At least 50% of a company's board should consist of independent non-executive directors.
- Rigorous, formal and transparent procedures should be adopted when recruiting new directors to a board.
- Roles of Chairman and Chief Executive of a company should be separate.
- No individual should be appointed to a second chairmanship of a FTSE 100 company.

Sarbanes–Oxley Act: US

In the US the *Sarbanes–Oxley Act* in 2002 was introduced following major collapses of companies such as Enron, Worldcom and Global Crossing and was also directed at strengthening corporate governance.

- If officers of a company are proved to have intentionally filed false accounts, they can be sent to jail for up to 20 years and fined $5m.
- Executives will have to forfeit bonuses if their accounts have to be restated.

- A ban on company loans to its directors and executives.
- Protection for corporate whistleblowers.
- Audit committees to be made up entirely of independent people.
- Disclosure of all off-balance-sheet transactions.

Other suggestions for improving corporate governance have included the European Commission seeking to ensure that group auditors take responsibility for all aspects of companies' accounts. It is therefore considering requiring each EU member state to set up US-style accounting oversight boards. The OECD has also drafted a revision of its principles on corporate governance, including calls for shareholders to be able to submit questions to auditors, who should be seen as accountable to shareholders and not to management, as seems too often to have been the case. The draft proposals also call on boards to protect whistleblowers.

Conclusion

CSR clearly involves a range of activities and approaches. Whilst CSR definitions vary, at least four characteristics tend to be included: a voluntary element, an inclusion of 'externalities, reference to multiple stakeholders and reference to the organization's core values/mission.

The case for CSR often refers to the organization's need to manage risk and, in particular, to avoid reputational damage. The various stakeholders are all too aware of the adverse impacts of well-publicized environmental or ethical 'lapses' on dividends and the share price, via lost sales and/or paying expensive damages. More positively, such stakeholders are increasingly aware of the benefits from well-publicized proactive CSR initiatives! Being positively associated with ethical or environmental causes is increasingly recognized as important in capturing consumer loyalty, both of existing consumers (making the demand curve less price-elastic) and in attracting new consumers (shifting the demand curve to the right). The former causes the demand curve to pivot and become steeper, increasing options to raise price and revenue given the enhanced commitment of consumers to the organization's product, irrespective of price charged. The latter causes an increase in demand, with more consumers now willing to purchase the product at any given price.

Of course, higher revenue is a key element in securing higher profit (revenue minus cost), giving greater scope for higher dividend payouts to shareholders and higher share price as market sentiment shifts in favour of these shares giving a higher profit. CSR can also be seen as conveying strategic benefits for organizations with 'responsive' and 'strategic' CSR identified by Porter and Kramer, the former being more reactive to events and the latter more proactive in terms of market positioning.

Critics of CSR, such as Friedman, point to the primacy of owner/shareholder interests and profit outcomes as of first importance. For businesses to spend money on CSR initiatives is seen by Freidman as a type of 'tax' on shareholders for activities more properly the domain of elected governments and their representatives. In any case, to Friedman it is inconceivable that a legal entity such as a business should have 'responsibilities', which in his view can only be assigned to individuals.

Environmental, as much as ethical, responsibilities are becoming more prominent in a world where 'sustainability' is a high-profile concept in all walks of life. Ethical theories can be categorized in a framework which is useful in emphasizing whether principle or outcome, individual or institutional responsibilities, are the key characteristics of a particular ethical approach.

The role of codes of conduct within organizations is reviewed, as are a number of legal requirements for corporate governance in various countries. We note that in response to various corporate scandals, a number of 'requirements', both formal and informal, are now expected of organizations as regards the arrangements which provide both authority and accountability. A particular area, executive remuneration, is reviewed in some detail and the absence of effective restraints on CEO and other senior executive remuneration is noted.

Key points

- Corporate Social Responsibility (CSR) has at least four core characteristics: voluntary; recognizes externalities; considers multiple stakeholders; reflects organizational value/mission statements.

- The stakeholder approach helps focus the 'social' in CSR on specific interest groups rather than the vague concept of 'society'.

- CSR has positive linkages with revenue, profit, share price and strategic direction.

- CSR is criticized by some as a misuse of scarce resources resulting in a neglect of the 'rightful' interests of shareholders, namely profit.

- The Friedman approach to CSR can be most readily located in the 'Deontological ethics' category, with an emphasis on 'principles' and institutions whilst the stakeholder perspective fits more clearly in the 'Ethical learning and growth' category, with an emphasis on outcomes (policies) and individuals or groups of individuals.

- Codes of conduct are increasingly used within organizations to secure advantages such as limiting potential legal damages, reducing the need for legal regulations and establishing a positive organizational 'brand' image. Disadvantages include non-compulsion and a tendency to be 'loose' and lacking specificity.

- Corporate governance, i.e. the formal and informal arrangements within an organization giving clarity to authority and accountability, is very much at the forefront of contemporary debate, as governments and organizations seek to avoid recent corporate scandals.

- Executive remuneration remains an area where corporate governance approaches seem unable to curb widely viewed excesses.

- The Higgs Committee recommendations in the UK and Sarbanes Oxley Act in the US are attempts to 'tighten' approaches to corporate governance in the respective countries.

Now try the self-check questions for this chapter on the Companion Website. You will also find useful links to relevant websites.

References and futher reading

Bentham, J. (1994) 'The Commonplace Book' in *The Works of Jeremy Bentham*,Vol. X, ed. Bowring, J., Bristol, Thoemnes Press. Original edition (1843), Edinburgh, Tait.

Berry, L., Mirabito, A. and Baun, W. (2010) What's the hard return on employee wellness programmes? *Harvard Business Review*, December.

Boeger, N., Murray, R. and Villiers, C. (2008) *Perspectives on Corporate Social Responsibility*, Cheltenham, Edward Elgar.

Crane, A., Matten, D. and Spence, L. (2008) *Corporate Social Responsibility: Readings and Cases in a Global Context*, London, Routledge.

Fisher, C. and Lovell, A. (2009) *Business Ethics and Values: Individual, Corporate and International Perspectives* (3rd edn), Harlow, Financial Times/Prentice Hall.

Freeman, E. (1984) *Strategic Management: a Stakeholder Approach*, Harlow, Pitman

Friedman, M. (1970) The social responsibility of business is to increase its profits, *The New York Times Magazine*, 33(September): 122–6.

Heal, G. (2008) *When Principles Pay: Corporate Social Responsibility and the Bottom Line*, New York, Columbia University Press.

Horrigan, B. (2010) *Corporate Social Responsibility in the 21st Century: Debates, Models and Practices Across Government, Law and Business*, Cheltenham, Edward Elgar.

McDonald, M. (2007) *Marketing Plans: How to Prepare Them, How to Use Them* (6th edn), Oxford, Butterworth-Heinemann.

Petrick, J. and Quinn, J. (2001) The challenge of leadership accountability for integrity capacity as a strategic asset, *Journal of Business Ethics*, 34(3–4): 331–43.

Porter, M. and Kramer, M. (2006) The link between competitive advantage and corporate social responsibility, *Harvard Business Review*, 84(12): 78–92.

Porter, M. and Kramer, M. (2011) Creating shared value, *Harvard Business Review*, January–February, 62–77.

Ramaswamy, V. and Gouillart, F. (2010) Building the co-creative enterprise, *Harvard Business Review*, October.

Teece, D., Pisano, G. and Shuen, A. (1997), Dynamic capabilities and strategic management, *Strategic Management Journal*, 18(7): 509–33.

Thomas, R. (2009) *International Executive Pay: Current Practices and Future Trends*, Vanderbilt Law Economic Research Paper No. 08-26, Nashville TN, Vanderbilt University.

Watson Wyatt Worldwide (2009) *Executive pay practices around the world*. London: Watson Wyatt.

World Commission on Environment and Development (WCED) (1987) *Our Common Future*, New York, Oxford University Press.

Wolf, M. (2000) Sleepwalking with the enemy: CSR distorts the market by deflecting business from its primary role of profit generation, *Financial Times*, May 16.

PART III   Macroeconomics

CHAPTER 16

Consumption and saving

Consumption is the most important single element in aggregate demand, accounting for almost half of gross final expenditure (GFE), so that its accurate estimation is essential to the management of the economy. J. M. Keynes related consumption to current disposable income, and for many years this was widely accepted. However, in the 1950s evidence began to appear of a discrepancy between the consumption function estimated from long-run time-series data, and the much flatter consumption function estimated from short-run time-series and cross-section data. The Keynesian consumption function could not resolve this discrepancy, and it was this, together with the need for more accurate forecasts of consumption, that led to the development of the Permanent Income and Life Cycle Hypotheses. In this chapter the Keynesian and alternative theories of consumption are considered in detail, their predictions are compared with actual fact, and their different implications for policy analysis are noted. We also look carefully at the mirror image of consumption, namely the savings ratio.

Consumption

The consumption function – the relationship between consumer expenditure and income – is probably the most widely researched relationship in macroeconomics. The impetus to this research was given by Keynes's initial conceptual breakthrough in *The General Theory of Employment, Interest and Money* (Keynes 1936). In the Keynesian view of the economic system, both output and employment are determined by the level of aggregate demand. Consumer spending is by far the largest element in aggregate demand. Typically it accounts for between half and two-thirds of total final expenditure, so it is essential that the factors influencing consumer spending be identified in order that it may be forecast accurately. This forecast for consumer spending can then be added to forecasts for the other elements of aggregate demand, namely investment, government spending and net exports (exports minus imports), to derive an overall forecast for *total aggregate demand*. Policy-makers can then decide whether this projected level of demand is appropriate for the economy and, if not, what corrective fiscal or monetary action should be taken.

The central position of the consumption function in Keynesian economics has therefore led to many attempts to estimate an equation that would indeed predict consumer expenditure. Unfortunately, most of the early Keynesian types of equation failed to explain some of the more interesting features of aggregate consumer behaviour. Alternative theories were therefore developed in the 1950s and 1960s which, it was claimed, fitted the facts rather better than the simple Keynesian view of consumption.

The development of these new theories, and the relative economic stability of the 1950s and 1960s, led economists to believe (over-optimistically as it turned out) that consumer spending was probably one of the best-understood and best-forecast variables in economics. We see from Table 16.1, however, that there was a sharp fall in the proportion of personal disposable income consumed (the average propensity to consume, a.p.c.) in the early and late 1970s, early 1980s and early 1990s and a sharp rise in the late 1980s, the mid 1990s and recently which were *not* always predicted by the existing equations. These changes in the a.p.c. were reflected in the sharp rise or fall in the savings ratio, and we return to changes in the savings ratio, later in the chapter.

The Keynesian consumption function

In the *General Theory*, Keynes argued that 'The fundamental psychological law . . . is that men are disposed, as a rule and on the average, to increase their consumption as their income increases, but not by as much as the increase in their income' (Keynes 1936, p. 96). From this statement can be derived the Keynesian consumption function[1] which is usually expressed in the following way:

$$C = c_0 + bY$$

where C = consumer expenditure;
  c_0 = a constant;
  b = the marginal propensity to consume (m.p.c.), which is the amount consumed out of the last pound of income received; and
  Y = National Income.

The Keynesian view is that when income rises, consumption rises, but by less than income, which implies that b, the m.p.c., is less than 1. Keynes also argued that 'it is also obvious that a higher absolute level of income will tend, as a rule, to widen the gap between income and consumption' (Keynes 1936, p. 97). This is usually taken to mean that he thought that the proportion of income consumed, C/Y (i.e. a.p.c.), will tend to fall as income increases. In fact, the positive constant c_0 in the above equation ensures that this will happen, since

$$\text{a.p.c.} = \frac{C}{Y} = \frac{c_0}{Y} + b$$

and this will decrease as Y increases if, and only if, c_0 is positive. This also implies, of course, that the a.p.c. is greater than the m.p.c. by an amount c_0/Y.

Drawing the consumption function as a straight line, as in Fig. 16.1, means that we are assuming that the m.p.c., b, is a constant, as it is the slope of the consumption function. The a.p.c. is found, for any level of income, by measuring the slope of the radian from the origin to the appropriate point on the consumption function. For example, if income is Y_1, then consumption would be C_1, and the a.p.c. would be C_1/Y_1, which is the tangent of the angle α. It can be seen that as Y increases, the slope of the radian from the origin to the consumption function falls, which

Table 16.1 UK household income, consumption and savings ratio, 1970–2009 (£m at 2006 prices).

	1 Disposable income	2 Consumption	3* Average propensity to consume (a.p.c.)	4 Change in income	5 Change in consumption	6* Marginal propensity to consume (m.p.c.)	7 Household savings ratio (%)
1970	320,056	297,462	0.93				6.6
1971	323,930	307,172	0.95	3,874	9,710	2.51	5.0
1972	350,987	326,989	0.93	27,057	19,817	0.73	7.3
1973	373,092	344,928	0.92	22,105	17,939	0.81	8.2
1974	369,501	339,885	0.92	−3,591	−5,043	1.40	8.4
1975	372,138	338,945	0.91	2,637	−940	−0.36	9.2
1976	370,056	340,035	0.92	−2,082	1,090	−0.52	8.7
1977	362,096	338,535	0.93	−7,960	−1,500	0.19	7.6
1978	385,500	356,311	0.92	26,404	17,776	0.67	9.4
1979	411,329	372,864	0.91	22,829	16,553	0.73	10.9
1980	418,940	372,589	0.89	7,611	−275	−0.04	12.3
1981	417,974	372,726	0.89	−966	137	−0.14	12.0
1982	418,508	376,298	0.90	534	3,572	6.69	10.8
1983	427,443	392,035	0.92	8,935	15,737	1.76	9.0
1984	443,605	400,798	0.90	16,162	8,763	0.54	10.2
1985	459,081	415,952	0.91	15,476	15,154	0.98	9.7
1986	478,649	443,391	0.93	19,568	27,539	1.41	8.1
1987	486,579	467,794	0.96	7,930	24,303	3.06	5.4
1988	513,846	503,656	0.98	27,267	35,862	1.32	3.9
1989	538,605	521,294	0.97	24,759	17,638	0.71	5.7
1990	563,135	525,408	0.93	24,530	4,114	0.17	8.1
1991	574,060	516,933	0.90	10,925	−8,475	−0.78	10.3
1992	589,636	519,291	0.88	15,576	2,358	0.15	11.7
1993	607,421	532,860	0.88	17,785	13,569	0.63	10.8
1994	615,909	547,735	0.89	8,488	14,875	1.17	9.3
1995	631,068	557,865	0.98	16,059	10,130	0.81	10.3
1996	651,252	589,437	0.89	19,284	22,572	1.78	9.4
1997	678,717	602,610	0.99	27,465	22,173	0.81	9.6
1998	692,847	627,710	0.91	14,130	25,100	1.78	7.4
1999	712,729	661,427	0.93	19,882	33,717	1.70	5.2
2000	742,664	691,461	0.93	29,935	30,034	1.00	4.7
2001	775,651	713,535	0.92	32,987	22,074	0.67	6.0
2002	791,488	739,832	0.93	15,837	26,297	1.66	4.8
2003	815,076	762,772	0.94	23,588	22,940	0.97	5.1
2004	823,672	787,523	0.96	8,596	24,751	2.88	3.7
2005	840,358	805,273	0.96	16,686	17,750	1.06	3.9
2006	853,095	819,610	0.96	12,737	14,337	1.13	3.4
2007	856,644	837,417	0.98	3,549	17,807	5.02	2.6
2008	866,487	842,174	0.97	9,843	4,757	0.48	2.0
2009	882,352	813,167	0.92	15,865	−29,007	−1.83	6.3

*Column 3 = column 2 divided by column 1; column 6 = column 5 divided by column 4.
Source: ONS (various).

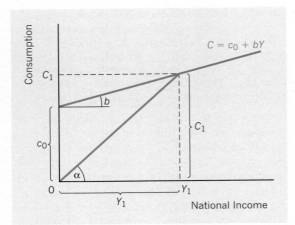

Fig. 16.1 The consumption function.

means that the proportion of income consumed (a.p.c.) falls. Indeed some early Keynesian economists were concerned that private sector investment would not grow as a proportion of income to fill the gap left by a declining average propensity to consume, in which case the economy would be subjected to 'secular stagnation'.

For Keynes, the main influence on consumption in the short run was current disposable income, i.e. income minus direct taxes. When this fluctuated, so would consumption but, because the m.p.c. was less

than 1, consumption would change by an amount less than the change in disposable income. If we look at the actual data for the UK and plot consumption against disposable income, both measured in real terms (using 2006 prices), we can see from Fig. 16.2 that over the period 1970–2009 there appears to be a close positive relationship between consumption and disposable income.[2]

In order to find numerical estimates for c_0 and b for our consumption function, we can fit a regression line, or line of 'best fit',[3] to the data in Table 16.1. Using linear regression we can derive the following equation:

$$C = -19{,}583 + 0.96Y_D$$

where Y_D is real disposable income (£m).

This consumption function (1970–2009) not only appears to fit the data well, as can be seen from Fig. 16.2, but also seems to support the Keynesian view that the m.p.c. is less than 1 (in our case 0.96). Somewhat surprisingly, the equation has a negative intercept of 19,583 (£m), implying that the a.p.c. rises as income rises. However, the intercept term is, statistically, not significantly different from zero and so we cannot be certain that the consumption function fails to go through the origin. If it did, this would mean that the a.p.c. does *not* rise as income rises.

As a first attempt, therefore, the above equation, which explains changes in consumption in terms of

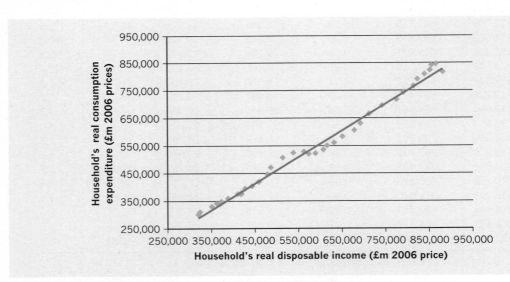

Fig. 16.2 The UK consumption–income relationship, 1970–2009.
Source: Based on Table 16.1.

changes in current disposable income, seems to fit the facts and the Keynesian theory rather well. To take an example from Table 16.1, in 2006 real disposable income was £853,095m; fitting this into our equation gives predicted consumption of £799,388m. Actual consumption was £819,610m, an error of around 2%.

Closer examination of the data, however, indicates that using changes in current disposable income to explain changes in consumption may be less than satisfactory. It may help to look more carefully at the 'errors', i.e. the deviations of the *actual* observations for consumption from the *predicted* values on the regression line. At first sight, these 'errors' in our earlier Fig. 16.2 do not look very large. Nevertheless, policy-makers relying on the simple consumption function equation to forecast any future consumption would, in some years, still make substantial errors. A more striking picture of the errors can be seen in Fig. 16.3. Here the *differences* between actual and forecast consumption, $C = (-19,583 + 0.96Y_D)$, are plotted.

Very large *negative* errors occurred from 1979 to 1982 and during much of the 1990s. In these periods actual consumption was very much *less* than forecast, given the levels of real disposable income. It appears that consumers were acting very cautiously because they were pessimistic about their future incomes. Such uncertainty was caused in part by oil-price shocks and rising unemployment. Similarly, in the early 1990s actual consumption was also lower than forecast by our equation, again in part because of uncertain future incomes as unemployment levels increased, but also because of falling asset prices (houses) and the desire of consumers to pay off accumulated debt. The recent financial crisis in 2007/8, which also threatens jobs and house prices, has again caused a sharp fall in consumption as consumers react to uncertainty by saving and paying off debt.

At the other extreme, large *positive* errors were made in the late 1980s and in the run up to the recent financial crisis in 2008. Here people actually consumed more than would be forecast by our equation, given the levels of real disposable income. This period was one of falling unemployment, inflated house prices and rising incomes, all of which made consumers more optimistic about the future.

It appears from the above that consumers are a good deal more sophisticated than the simple Keynesian consumption function would imply. Consumers take

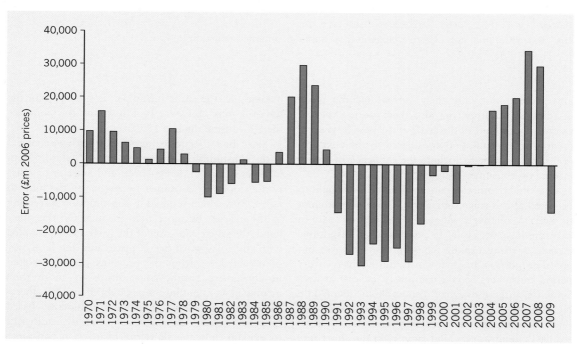

Fig. 16.3 Error analysis of simple consumption function (actual consumption minus forecast consumption).

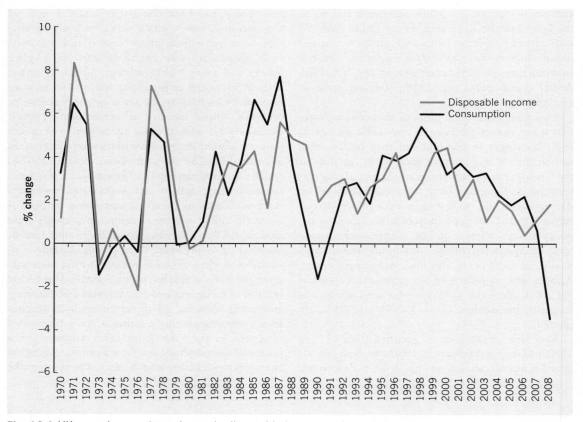

Fig. 16.4 UK annual percentage change in disposable income and consumption.
Source: Based on Table 16.1.

into account not only their *current* income when deciding expenditure, but also their future *expected* income. Indeed one of the goals of the post-Keynesian theories of consumption considered in the next section is to attempt to include the influence of future income on consumer spending.

One other feature of consumer behaviour ought to be noted at this stage. In general, consumers attempt to keep a relatively smooth consumption pattern over the business cycle. In periods when disposable income is rising rapidly, consumption will rise but not in proportion. In other words, during the recovery period consumers behave cautiously, at least at first. Similarly, in periods when disposable income is falling, consumers will on the whole attempt to maintain their consumption as best they can despite their reduced circumstances. Put simply, in the *short run*, consumption usually fluctuates less than disposable

income (i.e. the short-run m.p.c. is smaller than the long-run m.p.c.). Figure 16.4 illustrates this point for the UK, during the late 1970s.

Since the 1970s this pattern appears to have changed with consumption becoming more volatile than income. Financial deregulation and asset price inflation encouraged consumer borrowing in the mid- to late 1980s, which resulted in consumption increasing in those years by more than income. On the other hand, the severe recession of the early 1990s, coupled with the collapse of house prices and the hangover of indebtedness from the previous period, resulted in consumers cutting expenditure by more than income in an attempt to repay debt. It appears, therefore, that a Keynesian consumption function based only on *current disposable income* is insufficient to explain fully the short-run changes in consumer expenditure.

The newer theories of the consumption function differed from that of Keynes in that they were more deeply rooted in the microeconomics of consumer behaviour. Two of the theories, Friedman's Permanent Income Hypothesis (PIH) and Modigliani's Life Cycle Hypothesis (LCH), start from the position that consumers plan their consumption expenditure not on the basis of income received during the current period, but rather on the basis of their long-run, or lifetime, income expectations.

In both these theories, therefore, the link between current consumption and current income is broken. A consumer determines his or her consumption for a given period on the basis of a longer-run view of the resources available, taking into account not just current income but future expected income and any change in the value of their assets. Of course, if consumers cannot borrow on the strength of future income, i.e. if they are liquidity constrained, then they will have to adjust current spending to current income, as in the Keynesian theory.

The Permanent Income Hypothesis (PIH)

In Friedman's PIH an individual's consumption is based on that individual's permanent income (Y_p). Technically Y_p is defined as the return on the present value of an individual's wealth, and hence it is what can be consumed whilst leaving the individual's wealth intact. More generally Y_p could be thought of as some form of long-run average income, or 'normal income', which can be counted on in the future. An individual's actual or measured income (Y) in any time period will be made up of two parts – the 'permanent' part (Y_p), and the 'transitory' part (Y_t). Transitory income might be positive, if the individual is having an unexpectedly good year, or negative, if the individual is having a bad year. It follows that measured income is

$$Y = Y_p + Y_t$$

In the simplest form of the PIH, consumption is a constant proportion of permanent income, i.e.

$$C = kY_p$$

where

$$k = F(i, w, x)$$

The proportion k is determined by factors such as the interest rate (i), the ratio of non-human to human wealth (w), and a catch-all variable (x) which includes age and tastes as a major component. If i rises, then individuals are assumed to feel more secure as to the future returns from their asset holdings, so that k increases. Equally, k will increase if the ratio of non-human to human wealth (w) rises in total wealth holding. This is also thought to increase individual security, since non-human wealth, such as money and shares, is assumed to be more reliable than human wealth, such as expected future labour income.

If the economy grows steadily, with no fluctuations, then Y_p would be approximately equal to Y (measured National Income), and not only would a constant proportion of permanent income be consumed, but also a constant proportion of measured National Income. A study by Simon Kuznets (1946) in the US showed that if *long-run* data were used (10-year averages of consumption and income) then the a.p.c. was roughly constant. Taking 10-year averages effectively eliminates short-run fluctuations in income, and so Kuznets's results are consistent with the constant proportion k in the PIH.

This long-run consumption function derived from time-series data averaged over the business cycle, with its constant a.p.c., seemed, however, at odds with the short-run consumption function derived either from time-series data on an annual basis or from cross-sectional data. The short-run consumption function was flatter than the long-run function (see Fig. 16.5), having therefore a lower m.p.c. and an a.p.c. that was not constant, falling when incomes rose (booms) and rising when incomes fell (slumps). The answer to this puzzle, according to Friedman, is that in booms more people will think that they are doing better than normal than will think they are doing worse than normal. For the economy as a whole, therefore, there will be positive transitory income (Y_t), so that measured National Income (Y) will be above permanent income (Y_p). The unexpectedly high measured income will, however, have little impact on consumer views of their permanent income unless it lasts for several years. Since consumer spending plans are based on permanent income, any boom that is not long-lived

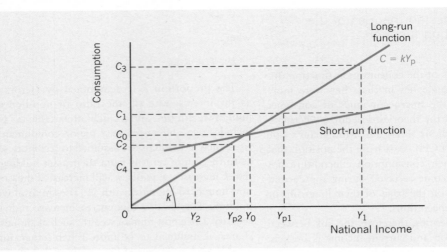

Fig. 16.5 Long- and short-run consumption functions.

will have little effect on consumer spending. The unexpected increases in income are therefore largely saved, with the result that in a boom the average propensity to consume falls. This is seen in Fig. 16.5.

As the economy expands along its long-run trend, consumption should be a fixed proportion, k, of income. In reality, however, the economy fluctuates around this long-run trend. Suppose we start in situation Y_0, with measured and permanent income equal, consumption (kY_0) equal to C_0, and a.p.c. equal to k. The economy then experiences a boom with measured income rising to Y_1. Permanent income will, however, be less affected by the sudden increase in income, and in our figure rises only to Y_{p1}. Consumption, being based on permanent income, now rises to $C_1(kY_{p1})$. Only if measured income remained at Y_1 *for several years* would permanent income be revised upwards to Y_1, and consumption to $C_3(kY_1)$. If this is *not* the case, then the proportion of income consumed will be only C_1/Y_1, i.e. the a.p.c. will have fallen below the initial level k during the boom.

In a slump, income will fall, say from Y_0 to Y_2, and although permanent income may be revised downwards a little to Y_{p2}, it will fall proportionately less than measured income. Consumption will therefore be $C_2(kY_{p2})$, falling much less than if Y_2 had been regarded as permanent (when consumption would fall further to C_4). The a.p.c. will then be C_2/Y_2, which is *above* the initial level k.

It can be seen from this analysis that Friedman is able to explain why the short-run consumption

function is flatter, with a variable a.p.c., whilst the long-run consumption function is steeper, with a constant a.p.c. Booms will, unless long-lived, cause a.p.c. to fall. There will be little upward revision of consumption plans, when higher income is largely regarded as transitory. Slumps will, unless long-lived, in a similar manner cause a.p.c. to rise.

The Life Cycle Hypothesis (LCH)

The LCH, developed by Modigliani and his associates, is similar in many ways to the PIH. Consumption is again seen as being a constant proportion k of Y_p, with the same sort of variables affecting k as in Friedman's theory. Modigliani stresses, however, the age of the consumer, with the consumer trying to even out consumption over a life-time in which income fluctuates widely. In youth and old age, when income is low, consumption is maintained by borrowing or drawing on past savings respectively, so that consumption is a high proportion of income; in middle life, when income is relatively high, a smaller proportion is onsumed, with savings being built up to finance consumption after retirement.

One of the empirical facts that needed to be explained by any theory was why, from *cross-sectional* data, it was seen that low-income groups had a higher a.p.c. than high-income groups. The LCH argued that low-income groups contain a high proportion of very young and very old households, both of which have a high propensity to consume. On the other hand, the high-income groups contain a high proportion of middle-aged households, with a low propensity to consume.

The variations in a.p.c. observed using *time-series* data, when National Income rises or falls, can also be explained by the LCH. Any windfall or transitory income received in a boom is spread over the individual's remaining life-time. For example, an unexpected increase in income of, say, £1,000 for someone with 20 more years to live would mean that they would revise their Y_p upwards by about £50 per annum, so that consumption in the year in which the windfall is received would increase by a relatively small amount (some proportion of £50). The a.p.c. would therefore fall with higher income because consumption (the numerator) will have risen by only a small amount, based on Y_p, but measured income (the denominator) has risen by the full £1,000. An unexpected reduction in income in a recession would likewise be spread over an individual's life-time, with borrowing and/or the running down of past savings leading to only a small cut in that individual's current consumption, thereby causing a.p.c. to rise. The LCH has therefore been able, like the PIH, to reconcile the flatter short-run consumption function with the steeper long-run consumption function (with constant a.p.c.).

Both theories imply that the m.p.c., which is the slope of the consumption function, is lower in the short run than it is in the long run. In the PIH any unexpected increase in income is not consumed, but largely saved, whereas in the LCH it is spread over the consumer's life-time. It follows that the multiplier[4] predicted by these theories will be small in the short run, because m.p.c. is low in the short run. Changes in government spending and taxation aimed at stabilizing the economy will therefore be relatively ineffective, especially if these changes are seen as being only temporary. A by-product of Friedman's work on the consumption function appears, therefore, to be an attack on the effectiveness of Keynesian short-run demand-management policies.

The PIH and LCH appear to have broken the link between current consumption and current disposable income by arguing that consumption depends not only on current disposable income but also on all future disposable income. It could be argued, however, that there are two reasons why the influence of current income may be more important than these

theories imply. First, it is unreasonable to believe that all consumers will be able to borrow and lend in different periods to even out their consumption pattern. An unemployed worker is unlikely to be able to borrow money to maintain his consumption, even though he is convinced he will be able to repay the loan out of future earnings. In this case, once past savings are exhausted, the constraint on consumption will be current disposable income. Second, estimates of future disposable income, on which permanent income is based, are highly uncertain. It is reasonable to expect, therefore, that the consumer uses his or her recent experience, and current income, as an important basis for estimating long-run or permanent income, and hence wealth. For both these reasons, therefore, one could still argue that current disposable income is still a major influence on current consumption, even under the PIH and LCH.

Rational expectations and consumption

The theories of consumption developed by Friedman, Modigliani and others all involve some concept of permanent or (long-term) 'normal' income on which households plan their consumption decisions. In order to arrive at this concept, households need to come to some view of their *expected* future income. The early post-Keynesian theories made convenient, if rather naive, assumptions about this process. Friedman, for example, used *adaptive expectations*, which means that consumers adapt or change their view of their expected income in the light of any 'errors' made in previous time periods. In effect it can then be shown that 'permanent income' (which is supposed to capture future expected income) is simply a weighted average of past incomes.

Despite the empirical convenience of this method of modelling expectations (data on past incomes being readily available), economists have become increasingly dissatisfied with this approach to modelling the formation of expectations. This approach is too mechanistic, is backward looking and, apart from income, ignores all other relevant information that might affect future earnings. As an alternative many economists have adopted the hypothesis of *rational expectations*. Rational expectation theory argues that households form expectations not only on the basis of past experience but also on their predictions about the future. It is assumed that households possess some sort of 'model' of the economy which they then use to process relevant information and derive an expectation of future income. Of course, most households do *not* possess any economic model of the economy. Nevertheless, forecasts from actual models are freely available in the media and households can use these, together with any specific knowledge they might have of their particular industry and region, to make a rational forecast of anticipated future income. Although economists have had problems in applying this concept of rational expectations to empirical work, much of the current theoretical study of consumption is based upon it.

One application of rational expectations to the permanent income model has been developed by Robert Hall. Hall (1978) argued that under certain conditions a household's consumption should follow a '*random walk*'. If households have included all the available and relevant information in their forecast of future income then, assuming consumption smoothing, the only reason for a household to alter its consumption would be an unexpected change in income. Hence the best estimate of next year's consumption (C_{t+1}) will be this year's consumption (C_t), as this reflects all the available information on future incomes. That is to say, $C_{t+1} = C_t + e_{t+1}$ where e_{t+1} is a random amount that results from unexpected shocks. Hall found some evidence to support the view that next year's consumption is closely related to this year's consumption. However, he also found that other variables, including past income, influenced next year's consumption. One reason for this finding is, of course, the linkage between past income and current borrowing potential for householders as a means of financing future consumption.

The substantial variations in the savings ratio over the last economic cycle have, to a large extent, been explained by the impact of monetary policy. Monetary policy, operating through the house price channel, in an environment of financial liberalization, has been held responsible for the boom–bust cycle. Work by Catão and Ramaswamy (1996), however, suggests that although the monetary stance and wealth effects on consumption accounted for over half the contraction in economic activity, the role of 'true' shocks also played a significant role. True shocks are defined as those that cannot easily be explained by obvious economic factors. These could be caused by pessimism about the future or anxiety about the particular course of political or social developments. One policy conclusion that comes from their work is that although monetary policy is influential, it is difficult for monetary policy to fine-tune the economy in the face of expectational shocks.

Windfall gains and consumption

In 1996 consumers received around £3.5bn in special payments, sometimes called windfall gains. In 1997 the figure was around £35bn. These windfall gains were mainly the result of the merger of building societies and their demutualization, which converted building society assets into tradeable shares. There were also windfall gains via enforced (by the regulator) payouts to customers from the regional electricity companies and the sums received from maturing TESSA accounts.

Economic theory tells us that an increase in a consumer's wealth is unlikely to lead to a proportionate increase in consumption, with consumers maximizing utility by spreading the additional consumption over the rest of their life-time. The increase in current consumption is likely, therefore, to be relatively small. The Bank of England Inflation Report in February 1997 adopted this viewpoint, arguing that previous windfall payouts by the Abbey National and TSB had resulted in only modest increases in current consumption. The Bank of England estimated that only around 5–10% of the £35bn of windfall gains expected in 1997 would be spent in the first year (i.e. up to £3.5bn). This view was further supported by a survey carried out by the Harris Research Centre, which found that only 36% of individuals who expected to receive a building society windfall in 1997 intended to spend all or most of it.

Weale and Young (1998) found that the effect of the windfalls on consumption had turned out to be larger than the Bank of England had anticipated a year earlier. It was estimated that consumers' expenditure in 1997 had risen by a further £8bn because of the windfall gains received in that year. One explanation might be that more consumers had suffered from liquidity constraints in 1997 than the Bank of England had anticipated. If an individual is liquidity constrained then arguably they cannot achieve their optimum consumption pattern taking into account expected future income because they cannot, for various reasons, borrow on the strength of that expected future income. Any liquidity-constrained consumer who receives a windfall gain is then likely to spend more of it in the current period than they would have done had no such liquidity constraint been present.

A study by Banerjee and Batini (2003) suggests that about one-seventh of UK consumers consume an amount equal to their current income. This result is obviously at odds with the PIH and the LCH but is consistent with evidence on credit restrictions in the UK. The authors also argue that it ties in with the evidence that consumption in the UK is more responsive to changes in human wealth (labour income) than the PIH would suggest.

The savings ratio

Two motives for saving are usually identified, namely people save for precautionary reasons and for life-cycle reasons. The first motive involves households refraining from consuming all their income to build up a reserve for times when income is unexpectedly low. The second motive involves people needing to build up a reserve of savings during their working life to finance consumption during retirement.

Given these motives for saving there are several economic factors that are likely to influence the savings ratio (see Berry *et al.*, 2009).

Permanent income

As we noticed previously, the permanent income/life cycle theory assumes households base their current consumption on some view of their *permanent income* over their whole life-time and that they would prefer a smooth consumption pattern. The forward-looking consumer will therefore save in periods when income is unexpectedly high (buying financial or housing assets) and will dis-save (selling assets or borrowing) when income is less than that expected in the future. The consumer boom and consequent fall in the savings ratio in the late 1980s and 1990s (see Fig. 16.6) was partly due to positive views about future income prospects (current income below permanent income).

Interest rates

The *real rate of interest* (nominal rate minus the expected inflation rate) is the main determinant of how much extra consumption can be obtained in the future by giving up consumption (saving) today. Higher real interest rates should therefore discourage consumption and borrowing and encourage saving, since still more extra consumption will result in the future by saving today. Higher real interest rates also redistribute income from borrowers to lenders. If lenders have a lower marginal propensity to consume than borrowers, then this will reduce consumption and raise the savings ratio. Expected changes in real interest rates should, by definition, have been taken into account by consumers but *unexpected* increases should raise the savings ratio. The unexpectedly low real interest rates (in some years negative) in the late 1970s and early 1980s are seen by many as having had a downward influence on the savings ratio at that time (see Fig. 16.6). The rise in real rates to its peak in 1990 is seen as having had the opposite effect.

Credit conditions

As argued earlier, some households are likely to be affected by liquidity constraints, i.e. they cannot borrow and spend as much as they would like to, based on their own perception of their future income. Any tightening of credit conditions, either quantitative (volume) or in price, is likely to increase the number of liquidity constrained households, reduce consumption and raise the savings ratio. The tightening of credit conditions and the reluctance of banks to lend whilst they rebuild their balance sheet positions after the recent financial crisis, is likely therefore to raise the savings ratio, as seems to have been the case since 2007 in Fig. 16.6.

Uncertainty

One motive for saving is to construct a buffer to support consumption when income unexpectedly falls. Any increase in economic uncertainty will, therefore, lead to a rise in *precautionary* saving. Any improvements in macroeconomic management which reduce economic fluctuations might then lead to less

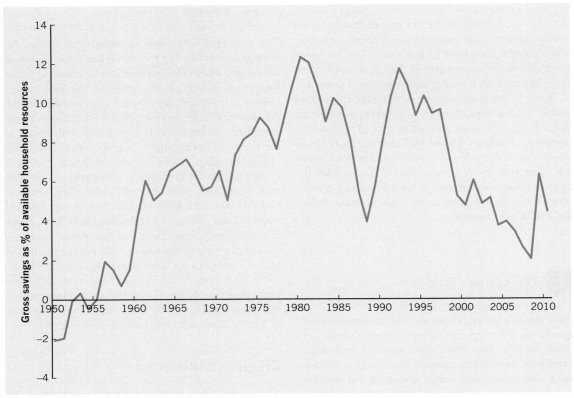

Fig. 16.6 UK households' savings ratio (%).
Source: ONS *Economic Trends* (various).

precautionary saving. The period of improved economic performance from the mid-1990s to 2007 might have helped reduce the savings ratio over that period.

Wealth

Non-human wealth, such as equities, house prices, etc., is part of a household's life-time resources. Any increase in this wealth should therefore increase the amount of consumption out of any given level of income and thereby reduce the savings ratio. Most statistical studies, however, show that the m.p.c. related to changes in wealth is very low, about 0.04–0.06 (although estimates are subject to great uncertainty). The reasons why the low m.p.c. relates to changes in wealth are possibly to do with two main factors. First, the volatility of equity prices means that any increase

in wealth linked to shares and other securities is not seen as permanent. Over half of household financial wealth is tied up in pension funds and life assurance and the effect of rising equity prices on these is not so obvious to consumers. However, house price inflation appears to be different; an increase (bad for people trading up but good for people trading down) seems to provide households with more collateral against which to borrow, and increased borrowing and spending will then lower the saving ratio. Second, because households can release equity from their house, if necessary, when income unexpectedly falls, rising equity prices reduce the need for precautionary savings. The fall in house prices 1990–93 coincided with a large (37%) rise in the savings ratio and may have been one contributory factor, and the same linkage seems to be a possible reason for the rise in the savings ratio post-2007.

Inflation

Inflation erodes the real value of the wealth that households hold; for example, bank and building society deposits, bonds, insurance policies and pension funds are all denominated in nominal terms and are eroded in real terms by inflation. In order to restore the real value of these assets, households have to save more. The savings ratio therefore tends to rise in times of high and unstable inflation, when nominal interest rates do not keep up with the increased inflation rate. Households therefore have to reduce consumption to increase their savings levels, and the savings ratio rises. The high savings ratios of the mid- to late-1970s and 1989–91 were associated with periods of high and unstable inflation.

Demographics

The life cycle theory of consumption suggests that the young on low income will be net borrowers (i.e. consume more than current income), people in their middle years will be net savers (to build up assets for retirement) and older retired people will run down their assets in order to consume. The demographic make-up of the population should therefore affect the overall household savings ratio. The UK post-war baby boom generation is now passing into retirement and this should therefore lower the savings ratio. On the other hand, the increase in life expectancy means a longer retirement period which may force workers in their middle years to save more, thus raising the ratio. These demographic factors only change slowly but do have a significant influence in the long term.

The savings of other sectors

Households are not the only savers in the economy. The *corporate sector* also saves when it retains profits. *Governments* save when they spend less than they receive in taxation, i.e. run a budget surplus. It is therefore the overall level of savings, *national savings*, that should be given close attention.

The theory of 'Ricardian Equivalence' sees private households and government savings as close substitutes for each other. If the government borrows (dissaves) to finance a tax cut, then households might expect higher future taxes and save the current tax cut. The household sector savings ratio therefore rises to compensate for the fall in the government savings ratio. Perversely, the government action which was intended to stimulate spending does no such thing! The theory assumes, of course, that households are forward-looking and are aware of, and concerned about, the implications of the government's current budget surplus (savings) and its likely strategy as regards future tax liabilities! The theory is also undermined if a proportion of households are liquidity constrained, i.e. they are unable to borrow as much as they would wish in order to finance current consumption, based on their expected future earnings. If so, then any unexpected tax windfall will be used to raise consumption to the desired level rather than save the tax windfall.

The decline in the household savings ratio mid-1990s–2008

The UK savings ratio fell from 10.8% in 1993 to a low of 2% in 2008. Several reasons have been put forward for this decline. Benito *et al.* (2007) suggest that the fall in real interest rates during the period could account for about 4% points of the observed drop in the savings ratio. The fall in real interest rates was mainly explained by international factors, specifically the excess savings generated in emerging economies such as China and in the oil exporting countries.

The mid-1990s to the mid-2000s was also a period characterized by steady non-inflationary growth in the UK; the NICE (non-inflationary-continuous-expansion) decade, as Mervyn King, the Governor of the Bank of England, called it. The increased stability of the economy compared to previous decades may have encouraged households to save less for precautionary purposes.

From 2002/03 credit conditions in the UK became easier. The difference between the Bank Rate and mortgage lending rates declined, and the loan-to-income ratio on new mortgage lending rose (from 2.21 for first-time buyers in 1992 to 3.39 in 2007, according to the Council of Mortgage Lenders). Easier and cheaper credit encouraged consumers to bring forward consumption. Rising asset prices, especially house prices, may also have facilitated this process by providing householders with increased collateral against which to borrow. Interestingly,

Berry *et al.* (2009) point out that although most of the benefit of asset price rises has gone to older households, it appears that younger households have reduced their saving most. Either asset prices do not play so much of a role in savings or perhaps there is an expectation of intergenerational transfers so that consumption occurs ahead of inherited income.

Two factors have influenced the savings ratio in the opposite direction. The increased numbers in their middle years over the period should have raised the savings ratio. In addition, companies with a defined benefit pension scheme made increased pension contributions on behalf of their employees, which are treated as household savings by the Office of National Statistics (ONS).

The international perspective

The fall in the household savings ratio over the period from the mid-1990s–2007 has been experienced across many countries (see Fig. 16.7). The influencing factors, namely low real interest rates, rising asset prices and improved economic stability, have been global. The variation in the *magnitude* of the impact, however, suggests that other factors were at play in different countries. For example, the increase in asset prices in the UK and US in the decade to 2007 did not occur in Germany, e.g. German house prices were 12% lower in real terms in 2007 compared to 1997.

The financial crisis and the savings ratio

The severe recession in 2008, the worst since the Second World War, caused house prices to fall, unemployment to rise and credit restrictions to be tightened, together with an increased uncertainty about the future stability of the economy. As we can see in Fig. 16.6, consumption fell and the savings ratio rose to 6.7% in 2009. The increase in the savings ratio and reduction in debt levels of households might be desirable at an individual level, but might make economic recovery more difficult, i.e. the so-called 'paradox of thrift'.

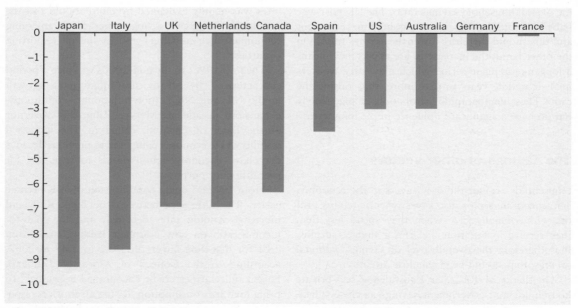

Fig. 16.7 Percentage points change in household savings ratio between average for 1992–97 and average for 2003–08.
Source: ONS *Economic Trends* (various).

Table 16.2 National and sectoral savings and investment.

	Household sector		Company sector		Government sector		Whole economy		Finance from overseas
	Savings	Invest.	Savings	Invest.	Savings	Invest.	Savings	Invest.	
2000	2.9	4.0	9.4	12.3	2.9	1.0	15.3	17.3	2.0
2002	3.8	4.3	10.1	10.1	0.4	1.4	14.5	15.7	1.2
2006	3.8	5.6	11.0	9.9	0.0	2.1	14.8	17.6	2.8
2008	1.3	4.6	15.0	9.8	−1.3	2.2	15.0	16.7	1.6
2010	4.9	3.0	13.4	9.1	−6.6	2.3	11.7	14.5	2.7

Source: *National Institute Economic Review* (2010), July, No. 213, Table A9, p. 165.

National saving

National saving is the sum of saving by the public and private sectors. Table 16.2 illustrates the savings of the various sectors as a percentage of GDP. Overall, if the amount that is invested by a country exceeds the amount that is saved then the excess is represented by the financial account deficit on the balance of payments. In 2008 Britain's national savings rate of 15.8% was lower than that of any other OECD country except Iceland (6.1%), Greece (7.1%), Portugal (10.2%) and the US (12.1%). It may be relevant to ask the question: is Britain's savings rate too low? Britain does not have the same requirement to save as, say, Germany (25.8%) or Italy (18.0%) with their rapidly ageing populations. However, as pointed out in the *National Institute Economic Review*, over the last 20 years the low national savings ratio in the UK has constrained investment and hence wealth formation. Wealth has fallen as a percentage of income and the effects are visible in terms of low levels of public infrastructure and high house prices, both in part the consequence of not generating enough savings to be invested in these forms of capital.

Indeed, a recent study by Weale (2009) calculates the level of savings required by each cohort to fund its consumption without reliance on transfers from other generations, what he calls 'savings adequacy'. Given realistic estimates of real interest rates and economic growth, he concludes that current consumption patterns are unaffordable, both for the current adult population (can 'afford' only 88.8% of

their current consumption) or more importantly for people starting their adult life (can 'afford' 89.3%). Weale sees the only solutions as increasing labour income, either by increased employment rates or longer working lives, or by relying on transfers from younger generation to those not working.

Savings attracted from abroad have helped UK investment to exceed UK savings. However, this implies future payments of net property income abroad, with a negative impact on the UK balance of payments. It follows that the current excess of world savings is not a reason for the UK to avoid facing up to its savings gap!

Conclusion

The importance of having a clear idea of what factors determine consumption cannot be overestimated. Consumption expenditure is the largest element in total expenditure and so any fluctuations in consumption will have important implications for the overall level of demand in the economy. The failure to appreciate the strength of consumer demand in 1987 and 1988 was an important contributory factor to the subsequent deterioration in the inflation and balance of payments position that has posed such problems for the UK economy. Similarly the fall in consumer spending in the recession of the early 1990s was much sharper than in either of the previous two recessions of 1974–77 and 1979–82. Again this change in consumption expenditure was largely unforeseen by forecasters.

Post-Keynesian theories stress that, when deciding on consumption, consumers have a longer-term planning horizon than merely considering current income, the implication of post-Keynesian theories being that consumption is more stable than Keynesians thought. Evidence suggests, however, that in the face of uncertainty and liquidity constraints, current income may still be a key factor influencing consumption.

Changes in savings rates have both a short-run impact on aggregate demand and a long-run impact on future wealth and consumption.

Key points

- In the Keynesian view, current disposable income is the main determinant of consumer spending.

- The suggestion here is that the *average propensity to consume* (a.p.c.) will fall as disposable income increases.

- Further, the *marginal propensity to consume* (m.p.c.) will be less than 1.

- Using a line of 'best fit' to UK data over the period 1970–2009, the consumption function has been estimated as $C = -191{,}583 + 0.96Y_D$, where Y_D is real disposable income (£m).

- This suggests an m.p.c. of 0.96 and a negative intercept term, suggesting a.p.c. will rise, but only slightly, as disposable income increases.

- Evidence began to accumulate that the *short-run* consumption function was flatter than the *long-run* consumption function. In other words, short-run m.p.c. is less than long-run m.p.c.

- Attempts to explain this discrepancy have resulted in independent variables *other than* current disposable income being proposed. The Permanent Income Hypothesis (Friedman) and Life Cycle Income Hypothesis (Modigliani) have been suggested.

- Even models based on past experience and future expectations have been used (rational expectations).

- The policy consequences of errors in forecasting consumption (and therefore savings) are serious: *underestimates* of consumption cause economic policy to be over-expansionary (inflationary); *overestimates* of consumption cause economic policy to be over-cautious (deflationary).

- Savings rates have both short-run and long-run effects on the economy.

Now try the self-check questions for this chapter on the Companion Website. You will also find useful links to relevant websites.

Notes

1 This is a 'generalized' version of the Keynesian consumption function as it uses total income rather than disposable income as the independent variable.

2 However, this is not always the case, as can be seen on the rare occasions when m.p.c. is negative. A negative m.p.c. means that when disposable income falls, consumption actually rises. In 1975, 1976, 1980, 1981, 1991 and 2009, the m.p.c. was indeed negative (Table 16.1).

3 'Best' in the sense that it minimizes the sum of squared deviations from the line.

4 The simple National Income multiplier is defined as 1/1 − m.p.c. for a closed economy with no government sector, and indicates the extent to which National Income changes following a given change in injections or withdrawals. If m.p.c. is low, the multiplier is low.

References and further reading

Banerjee, R. and Batini, N. (2003) *UK consumers' habits*, External MPC Unit Discussion Paper, No. 13, London, Bank of England.

Bénassy-Quéré, A. and Coeuré, B. (2010) *Economic Policy*, Oxford, Oxford University Press.

Benito, A., Waldron, M., Young, G. and Zampolli, F. (2007) The role of household debt and balance sheets in the monetary transmission mechanism, *Bank of England Quarterly Bulletin*, 47(1): 70–8.

Berry, S., Williams, R. and Waldron, M. (2009) Household savings, *Bank of England Quarterly Bulletin*, 49(3).

Catão, L. and Ramaswamy, R. (1996) Recession and recovery in the United Kingdom in the 1990s: identifying the shocks, *National Institute Economic Review*, 157(July): 97–106.

Chrystal, A. K. (1992) The fall and rise of saving, *National Westminster Bank Quarterly Review*, February, 24–40.

Giavazzi, F. and Blanchard, O. (2010) *Macroeconomics: A European Perspective*, Harlow, Financial Times/Prentice Hall.

Goldsmith, E. (2009) *Consumer Economics: Issues and Behaviours* (2nd edn), Oxford, Oxford University Press.

Hall, R. (1978) Stochastic implications of the life cycle permanent income hypothesis, *Journal of Political Economy*, 86(December): 971–87.

Kennally, G. (1985) Committed and discretionary saving of households, *National Institute Economic Review*, 112(May): 35–40.

Keynes, J. M. (1936) *The General Theory of Employment, Interest and Money*, Basingstoke, Macmillan.

Kuznets, S. (1946) *The National Product Since 1869*, Cambridge, MA, The National Bureau of Economic Research.

Leighton Thomas, R. (1984) The consumption function, in D. Demery, *et al.* (eds), *Macroeconomics, Surveys in Economics*, Harlow, Longman.

National Institute Economic Review (2010) 213, July.

OECD (2010) *Economic Outlook*, No. 87, July, Paris, Organisation for Economic Cooperation and Development.

Weale, M. (2009) *Saving and the National Economy*, Discussion Paper 340, September, London, National Institute of Economic and Social Research.

Weale, M. and Young, G. (1998) Debt Management, *National Institute Economic Review*, April.

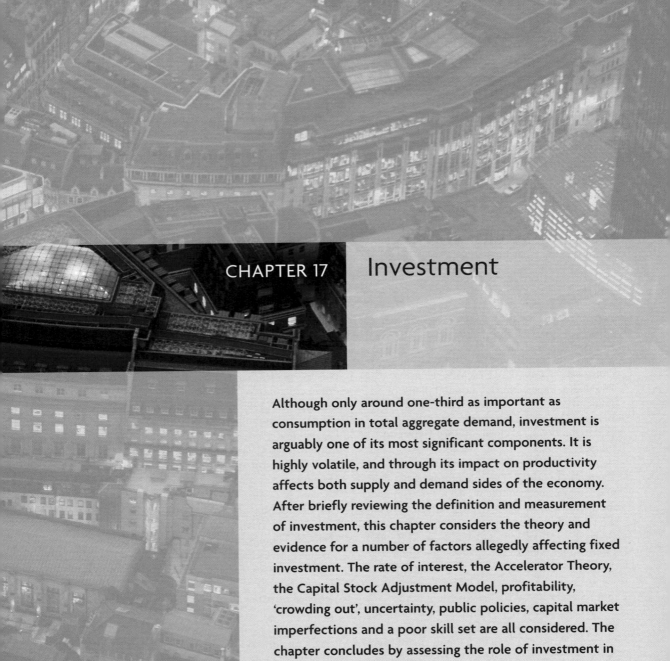

CHAPTER 17   Investment

Although only around one-third as important as
consumption in total aggregate demand, investment is
arguably one of its most significant components. It is
highly volatile, and through its impact on productivity
affects both supply and demand sides of the economy.
After briefly reviewing the definition and measurement
of investment, this chapter considers the theory and
evidence for a number of factors allegedly affecting fixed
investment. The rate of interest, the Accelerator Theory,
the Capital Stock Adjustment Model, profitability,
'crowding out', uncertainty, public policies, capital market
imperfections and a poor skill set are all considered. The
chapter concludes by assessing the role of investment in
economic growth.

The nature of investment

Resources in an economy can be used to produce goods and services for immediate use (consumption), or to add to the stock of fixed capital (investment). This chapter concentrates on the latter.

In one sense, consumption and investment are quite distinct. The act of investment usually involves abstaining from current consumption in order to acquire assets, which raise the productive potential of the economy, and therefore the possibilities for future consumption. Yet in another sense they are similar, both being components of aggregate demand, i.e. types of spending which create income for others in the economic system. We noted in Chapter 16 that consumption was around 48% of gross final expenditure (GFE) in 2009. Although smaller, fixed capital investment was 13% of GFE in 2009.

Stock and flow concepts

The total value of fixed capital at any time is a 'stock' concept. The rate of change of that 'stock' is a 'flow' concept. Investment in the National Accounts is entirely a 'flow' concept, as it is the addition to the stock of fixed capital in any given year. This helps explain why purchases of shares, paintings or antiques, although often termed 'investments' in everyday speech, are not regarded as such in the Accounts. Usually they merely represent a transfer of ownership from one person or institution to another, rather than an addition to the stock of assets. The difference between stock and flow valuations is often substantial.

Gross and net investment

'Gross' investment, though a flow concept, overestimates the change in size of the stock of capital or inventories in the year. In the course of the year some fixed capital will have worn out or become obsolete, and some inventories will have become unusable. A part of 'gross' investment will therefore be needed simply to replace these assets used up in the course of production. If we subtract this 'replacement' investment from 'gross' investment, then we are left with 'net investment'. Net investment is then the estimate of the addition, in any year, to the stock of fixed capital and inventories, having allowed for depreciation of that stock during the year.

Of course, quantifying depreciation presents a number of problems. Estimating the loss in value of a machine in a year is difficult in itself, and may be guided less by the physical state of the asset than by the possibility of tax concessions. Also different accounting conventions will yield different measures of depreciation. For instance, historical cost accounting yields much lower figures for depreciation than does inflation accounting.

The majority of investment expenditure is on fixed capital formation rather than inventories and it is to this that we now turn.

Gross Domestic Fixed Capital Formation (GDFCF)

Gross Domestic Fixed Capital Formation (GDFCF) is defined in the National Accounts as 'expenditure on fixed assets (buildings, plant and machinery, vehicles, etc.), either for replacing or adding to the stock of existing fixed assets'. This apparently clear-cut definition turns out to be rather arbitrary in application. For instance, 'investment' in the National Accounts is restricted to the firm sector. If a household purchases a computer for personal use, it is classified in the National Accounts as 'consumption', yet the same purchase by a firm is classified as 'investment', even though in both cases the capital asset yields a stream of useful services throughout its life. This is because the National Accounts treat the household purchase as self-gratification, but the firm purchase as producing a flow of marketable goods and services.

The arbitrariness of this classification is well illustrated when an individual chooses, for tax purposes, to be regarded as self-employed. The purchase of a car by a teacher for travel to work as an employee is classed as 'consumption' expenditure. Should the teacher change his or her designation to self-employed and engage in privately contracted teaching, then the purchase of that same car could be classed as 'investment' expenditure.

Despite problems of classification, it is important to gauge changes in GDFCF through time, both in total and by sector and type of asset. Table 17.1

Table 17.1 Gross Domestic Fixed Capital Formation (£m) by sector and by type of asset.

		Sector		
	Total	**Business investment**	**General government**	**Other**
1989	130,383	72,025	10,175	48,183
1993	115,311	60,912	14,764	39,635
2002	178,066	111,678	15,740	50,648
2005	195,118	115,116	23,713	56,289
2009	204,270	121,368	37,821	45,081

			Asset		
	Transport & equipment	**Other machinery and equipment**	**Dwellings**	**Other new buildings**	**Intangible fixed assets**
1989	14,828	31,987	40,566	47,080	4,404
1993	11,177	26,000	32,166	49,834	4,442
2002	16,728	56,614	36,800	62,088	5,676
2005	15,031	59,162	42,853	71,516	6,556
2009	12,127	56,411	37,044	80,978	17,710

Sources: ONS (2010) *Monthly Digest of Statistics*, No. 778, October; ONS *Economic Trends* (various).

presents data for selected time periods since 1989 (the peak level of investment in the previous economic cycle). Given the problems we noted in measuring depreciation, the 'gross' concept is perhaps the most useful for purposes of comparison, whether through time or across countries. GDFCF stood at £204bn in 2009 (in real terms), which is around 55% above the level touched at the peak of the cycle in the late 1980s. Following an 11% decline in the recession of the early 1990s, investment spending has continued on an upward path, although slowing somewhat with the onset of recession after 2008.

During the latter part of the 1990s, there was a significant shift in investment spending from the public to the private sector. However, over the past few years this pattern has been reversed, partly as a result of a slowdown in private sector capital expenditure following the boom towards the end of the last decade, but also because of the government's decision to rebuild the infrastructure across much of the public sector. The public sector currently accounts for around 12% of new investment compared with 9% in recent years, but one of the intentions of the 2010 Comprehensive Spending Review is to curb public

expenditure which will inevitably include public sector investment.

One reason why the public sector now contributes relatively little in the way of new investment is the privatization programme which has reduced the number of public corporations. However, it also reflects the desire of the previous government to keep spending under control. Because of difficulties involved in cutting back on current expenditure plans, capital projects have been sacrificed in a bid to fulfil this objective.

Investment by type of asset has changed since 1989. Investment in machinery and equipment has grown most rapidly, increasing by around 84%. It now accounts for around 30% of total GDFCF. There has also been a healthy rise in the level of investment in 'other new buildings' which, in 2009, represented more than one-third of the total. By way of contrast, capital expenditure on transport and dwellings has grown rather more modestly. The level of investment in dwellings has declined in real terms and now accounts for just 18% of GDFCF. Within the housing investment component (dwellings) there has also been a transfer of resources from the public to the private sector. Investment in public sector housing fell from 15% of total dwelling investment in 1989 to less than 9% in 2009.

Factors affecting fixed investment

Investment spending typically has a significant influence on fluctuations in economic activity. Indeed, as a recent Vice-Chairman of the US Federal Reserve, Roger Ferguson, noted, a fall in investment has accounted for the bulk of the drop in GDP in each of the last six American recessions. It is, therefore, clearly important to identify the factors causing such changes in fixed investments.

Gross Domestic Fixed Capital Formation is so heterogeneous that any explanation must address itself to particular components. For instance, investment in dwellings is influenced by population trends, expected life-time income and the availability and cost of mortgage finance, whilst public sector investment is influenced by the priorities of a particular government. Here we focus on the largest component of GDFCF, namely business investment.

The rate of interest

The earliest theories of investment placed considerable emphasis on the importance of the rate of interest, seen here as the compensation required for foregoing current consumption. Fisher used the rate of interest to derive the *present value* (PV) of an expected future stream of income. By calculating the PV of various alternative investment projects they could then be ranked against each other.

This approach was taken a stage further by Keynes who introduced the concept of the marginal efficiency of investment (MEI). The MEI was defined as that rate of discount which would equate the PV of a given stream of future income from a project, with the initial capital outlay (the supply price):

$$S = PV = \frac{R_1}{(1+i)} + \frac{R_2}{(1+i)^2} + \frac{R_3}{(1+i)^3} + \dots + \frac{R_n}{(1+i)^n}$$

where S = the supply price;
     PV = the present value;
       R = the expected yearly return; and
        i = that rate of discount necessary to equate the present value of future income with the initial cost of the project.

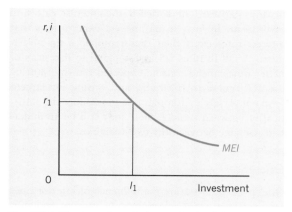

Fig. 17.1 The investment demand schedule.

The curve relating the marginal efficiency of investment (i) to the level of investment in Fig. 17.1 is negatively sloped, for two main reasons. First, the earliest investment projects undertaken are likely to be the most profitable, i.e. offering the highest expected yearly returns (R), and therefore having the highest marginal efficiencies of investment (i). As more projects are initiated, they are likely to be less and less profitable, with lower expected yearly returns, and therefore lower MEIs. Second, a rise in the level of investment undertaken is, at least in the short run, likely to raise the supply price (S), which in turn will reduce the MEI. This could follow if the industries producing capital goods faced capacity constraints in their attempt to raise output in the short run.

The decision on whether to proceed with an investment project will depend on the relationship between the rate of interest (r) and the marginal efficiency of investment (i). If r is less than i, then the annual cost of borrowing funds for an additional project will be less than the expected annual return on the initial capital outlay, so that the project will be profitable to undertake. In Fig. 17.1, with interest rate r_1, it will be profitable to invest in all projects up to I_1, with I_1 itself breaking even. The MEI schedule is therefore the investment demand schedule, telling us the level of investment that will be undertaken at any given rate of interest. Expectations play an important role in this theory of investment. If, as is often the case, expectations are volatile, then the expected yearly returns (R) on any project will change, causing substantial shifts in the MEI schedule. At *any given rate of interest*, investment demand will therefore be changing, which will reduce the closeness of any statistical fit between the interest rate and investment. In fact, it may be via expectations that interest rates exert their major influence on investment. A fall in rates is often a signal to investors of better times ahead, raising expected returns, shifting the *MEI* curve to the right, and raising investment (and conversely). Although this may dilute the statistical fit between *r* and *I*, there may still be an underlying linkage between the two variables.

Evidence

One problem in testing the influence of interest rates on investment is the selection of an appropriate interest rate. The average yield on debentures is a rate frequently used, as this broadly indicates the cost of new borrowing for a company at any point in time.

Historically, most UK studies have failed to show any close connection between interest rates and investment, suggesting that the latter is interest-inelastic. One analysis of the relationship between the real rate of interest and gross fixed investment in plant and machinery in manufacturing was conducted by Turner (1989). He found only a weak correlation between the two variables, as did Whitaker (1998) in his study of investment in the UK in the recovery period 1992–96. However, a study by Osler (1994), covering not only the UK but also Germany, France, Japan and Canada, found that the high level of real interest rates between 1990 and 1993 had substantially depressed private investment and consequently reduced output in the five countries by between $2\frac{1}{2}$ and $4\frac{1}{2}\%$ per year over the period.

Instead of focusing solely on the rate of interest, some research has looked for alternative measures of the cost of capital to firms. Cummins *et al.* (1996), for example, examined the role of the stock market in influencing investment trends. A rise in equity prices tends to make it cheaper to raise capital on the stock market while a fall can make it more expensive. They found that sudden share-price changes had a substantial impact on firms' investment plans in 12 of the 14 OECD countries examined, i.e. a rise in share prices leads to higher investment, and vice versa. A more recent study by Tevlin and Whelan (2000), based on US data, suggested that over the previous decade the cost of capital had become significantly more important in determining the level of investment. They pointed out that much of the recent investment has been in the IT area and suggested that this is far more

sensitive to the cost of capital than is investment in non-computing equipment. The Bank of England, in its model of investment spending, uses a variable described as the 'real cost of capital'. This is weighted to capture the proportion of corporate borrowing that is equity-based and the proportion that is bond-based. The numbers are then combined with equity and bond yields (long-term interest rates) before inflation expectations are deducted. The impact of this variable on business investment is assumed to be relatively modest, with a 1% change in the former shifting the latter by only 0.07% after four quarters and by 0.16% after eight quarters. Put another way, a 10% increase in the real cost of capital (say from 5% to 5.5%) would lower business investment by only 0.7% after one year.

Accelerator Theory and Capital Stock Adjustment Model

The *Accelerator Theory* relates net investment to the rate of change of output. If the capital stock *K* is fully utilized, and the capital/output ratio v is a constant, then net investment (*I*) can be expressed in the following way:

$$K_t = vY_t$$
$$K_t - K_{t-1} = v(Y_t - Y_{t-1})$$
$$I_t = v(Y_t - Y_{t-1})$$
$$I_t = v\Delta Y_t$$

where *Y* is output and *t* and *t* − 1 are time periods.

Net investment in year *t* is then a constant proportion of the change in output during that year. For example, if output rose by £2m for the economy (ΔY_t = £2m), and each extra £1 of output needed an average of £5 of capital equipment to produce it ($v = 5$), then $I_t = 5 \times 2m = £10m$. A number of criticisms have been levelled at the Accelerator Theory. First, the assumption that there is no excess capacity is particularly suspect. If there is spare capacity then a rise in output ΔY_t can be met from the existing capital stock, with no need for new investment. It has been estimated by the CBI that in the period 1979–2002, an average of just over 40% of firms were working at full capacity. Such a large amount of excess capacity must severely impair the effective functioning of the accelerator. Second, the assumption of a constant capital/output ratio, v, is becoming less and less plausible. The advent of new generations of microelectronic technology is progressively reducing capital/output ratios. Third, it is also likely that prior to making an investment the firm would want to be sure that any upsurge in demand and in output is not a temporary phenomenon. *Expectations* of future demand, and therefore future changes in output, will then be important.

A more sophisticated version of this is the *Capital Stock Adjustment Model*. This was developed to overcome some of the problems of the simple Accelerator Theory. It states that investment is positively related to the expected level of output and negatively related to the existing capital stock. Any rise in investment will consequently depend not only on the expected level of output (demand) but also on the current size of the capital stock. Specifically,

$$I_t = bY_{t-1} - cK_{t-1}$$

where
I_t = gross investment in the current year;

b and c = constant coefficients;

Y_{t-1} = last year's level of output;

K_{t-1} = the capital stock at the end of the preceding year.

If it is assumed that the expected volume of output is roughly equal to that experienced in the previous year, Y_{t-1}, then the higher is Y_{t-1} the greater will gross investment tend to be. However, the greater the inherited capital stock, K_{t-1}, the less need there will be for adding to the capital stock, or even replacing worn-out equipment.

Evidence

Even when varying lag structures are introduced into more refined versions of the Accelerator Theory, the evidence in its support is far from convincing. McCormick *et al.* (1983) found that changes in real GDFCF by firms between 1962 and 1980 were not strongly related to the previous year's change in real consumer spending or demand. Kennedy (1997) noted that the Capital Stock Adjustment Principle was useful in explaining manufacturing investment in the UK between 1955 and 1970, though less so since then. Similar support for a modified accelerator theory as a determinant of investment has come from the studies of Catinat *et al.* (1987) and Ford and Poret (1990). A study by Oliner *et al.* (1995) in the US also found this approach helpful in explaining investment, albeit with the inclusion of other variables. However,

Tevlin and Whelan (2000) suggested that the Capital Stock Adjustment Model actually broke down in the 1990s, with the actual level of investment in the US seven percentage points higher in 1997 than could be explained by the model. The Bank of England model, noted earlier, places rather greater emphasis on changes in GDFCF in terms of its near-term influence on investment, suggesting that a 1% rise in demand boosts capital spending by more than 1.28% after four quarters and by 1.68% after two years.

Profitability

There are at least three reasons why changes in profitability might be associated with changes in private sector investment.

1 Higher profits indicate a more favourable return on capital, which may encourage companies to reinvest any surplus rather than devote it to alternative uses.

2 Higher profits may improve business confidence and raise the expected future return on any project. An outward shift of the *MEI* schedule (see Fig. 17.1 above) might then raise investment at any given rate of interest.

3 Higher profits may raise investment by reducing its cost, as funds generated internally are cheaper than those obtained from the capital market, whether equity or debenture.

Evidence

In a major study of investment in the EU over the period 1961–90, the relation between net investment and the rate of profitability per unit of capital stock was found to be highly significant. Indeed variations in profitability were found to account for some three-quarters of the variations in capital stock during this period (COM 1991). In this study the profitability variable was lagged one period in order to take into account the unavoidable delays between changes in profit conditions and the effective realization of resulting investment decisions. More recent work by Carruth *et al.* (2000) and Driver *et al.* (2001) has suggested that investment in the UK is significantly related to corporate profitability.

Given the more open product markets implied by a global economy, it is not only profitability in the *domestic economy* which now influences investment decisions but that in the *global economy*. A recent study has found that an increase in costs in the UK *relative to those in other countries* leads to a more than proportionate reduction in the UK investment, and of course vice versa (Young 1994). In other words, *relative* changes in UK factor prices and tax policies, and thereby in profitability, have a significant effect on UK investment. For example, Young found that a 1% rise in UK *relative factor prices* would lead to a 1.62% decline in UK investment, with an eight-quarter time lag.

Uncertainty

During periods of uncertainty (for example, after a shock rise in oil prices) it has been argued that firms will reduce the value they place on expected future returns on investment projects. In terms of the earlier Fig. 17.1, the *MEI* will shift leftwards and less investment will take place at any given rate of interest. Faced with such uncertainty, therefore, businessmen and women become more inclined to delay any planned capital spending.

Evidence

Until recently, there have been few attempts to model the relationship between investment and uncertainty. There is no general agreement as to how to account for uncertainty as a variable, although the majority of studies have used a variance measure to capture volatility in output, inflation or the exchange rate. Other options include the gold price, equity price volatility and information from the CBI survey. Work by Temple *et al*. (2001) and Bloom *et al*. (2001) amongst others confirms the relevance of uncertainty as an issue impacting upon capital spending decision-making.

Public policies

Public policies may influence investment in the private sector as well as the public sector. For example, changes in the rate of taxation of company profits, or in the capital allowances which can be set against tax, are believed by many to significantly affect levels of investment. The government introduced a tax credit for expenditure on research and development (R&D) in 2002 to stimulate spending in an area seen as being of particular importance.

Evidence

Studies on the impacts of the reform of corporation tax and the phasing out of accelerated depreciation allowances on UK investment were undertaken by Sumner (1988) and Devereux (1989). The results suggested that such policies had relatively little impact on investment demand over the longer term. However, a study by Bond *et al*. (1993) reopened the debate. It suggested that recent corporation tax changes and the loss of capital allowances had created a strong fiscal bias against investment, equivalent to companies facing permanently higher interest rates of 1–2%. This conclusion is not dissimilar to the results produced by Cummins *et al*. (1994). They found that investment behaviour responded in a significant fashion to any changes in the tax regime which affected the cost of capital.

There is much current debate as to whether the pressure on companies to make higher pension contributions to fund shortfalls in defined benefit pension schemes is having an adverse impact on investment. However, Bunn and Trivedi (2005) and Barrel and Riley (2006) argue that pension funds have shifted their portfolios from the now less attractive (lower profits) shares to fixed-interest securities in response to this situation, so that (long-term) interest rates are likely to be lower than would otherwise be the case. Lower interest rates may then encourage companies to borrow more to finance capital spending.

Capital market imperfections

It has been suggested that inefficiencies in the banking system and in the capital markets have prevented industry from obtaining the finance it requires for investment. Amongst the criticisms of UK financial institutions are the allegations that UK banks place too great an emphasis on lending to consumers, whereas overseas banks are primarily concerned with long-term industrial finance. Another criticism is that UK banks tend to concentrate on short-term lending, causing a shortage of long-term funds for investment. A further criticism is that financial institutions, which are major shareholders in many companies, place undue pressure on directors to distribute too high a proportion of total profit as dividend, the consequence then being that little profit is available to be 'ploughed back' as investment.

Evidence

Work carried out by Corbett and Jenkinson (1996) suggests that much of the criticism of the banking sector may be misplaced. Their study, which covers the period 1970–94, suggests that banks provided a roughly similar share of funds for fixed investment in the UK as they did in Germany and the US. On average, bank finance in the UK accounted for 14.6% of investment spending. The corresponding figure for the US is 11.1% and that for Germany 10.8%. The economy where banks *have* played a more significant role is that of Japan. Over the period as a whole, Japanese banks provided 27% of the funds required for Japanese fixed investment.

Even though this research suggests that the UK is not markedly out of line with its main competitors, there remains considerable unease that 'short-termism' by the city discourages investment in another way, by inducing companies to pay too high a dividend in relation to profit. A related criticism is that dividend payments are too inflexible, not varying as profits rise and fall, with the result that funds available for investment are squeezed in times of recession. A Trade and Industry Committee Report (House of Commons 1994) substantiated some of these concerns, showing a rising trend of dividend payments as a percentage of net earnings in UK companies, reaching levels in the UK above most other advanced industrialized countries, with the exception of the US. The Report noted that: 'The Financial Secretary to the Treasury accepts that relatively high dividend pay-out ratios are a weakness in the UK economy' (p. 70). On the subject of corporate distributions, Whitaker (1998) concluded that relatively high dividend payouts during the UK economic recovery of 1992–96 may have diverted funds away from investment in fixed capital. Such concerns have resulted in changes to the tax treatment of dividends, making it relatively more attractive for firms to use profits for investment purposes rather than for dividend payments. Chapter 21 provides further background to this alleged cause of low levels of UK investment.

Skills and the labour market

A paper by the Department of Trade and Industry (2000) has argued that 'deficiencies in management and workforce skills' have contributed to the lack of investment in the UK. A major survey into UK competitiveness by Porter and Ketels (2003) reinforced this view, with American, French and German managers (especially the American managers) able to get more output from an equivalent amount of machinery and labour (i.e. they had demonstrably higher total factor productivities).

Evidence

There is only limited evidence of a relationship between investment and skill shortages. One study in this area was conducted by Nickell and Nicolitsas (2000). As a proxy for skill shortages they used the CBI industrial trends survey which contains a question as to the factors that are limiting output. The result of the study for UK manufacturing found that a 10 percentage point increase in the number of firms reporting skilled labour shortages reduced fixed capital investment by 10% and reduced R & D expenditure by 4%.

The rate of depreciation

Earlier in this chapter (p. 339) we noted that the difference between gross and net investment reflected the rate at which the existing capital stock is depreciated, which helped justify the focus on gross rather than net investment. However, Tevlin and Whelan (2000) concluded that a key reason for the recent pick-up in investment spending had been an increase in the rate at which businesses replace depreciated capital. While econometric models traditionally tend to assume a constant depreciation rate, Tevlin and Whelan argued that a structural shift of capital towards computers over the previous decade justified a faster rate of depreciation.

It is significant that the Office for National Statistics (ONS) in the UK has recently arrived at the same conclusion on the grounds that the lifespan of IT equipment tends to be shorter than for other types of capital. It follows that, although the (gross) investment to GDP ratio has climbed steeply in recent years, the ONS believes that the capital stock to GDP ratio has actually been falling.

The importance of investment

Investment has a dual role to play within any economy. In the short run, investment may be seen mainly as a component of aggregate demand which, if increased, will have the effect of stimulating the economy and, through the multiplier, substantially raising the level of National Income. Fixed investment made up some 13% of total final expenditure in 2009.

In the long run, investment will also affect the supply side of the economy, raising its productive potential and thereby pushing outwards the production frontier. Economic growth is sometimes strictly defined in this way, being that increase in GDP which results from raising productive potential. More usually it is loosely defined as any increase in GDP, even when that is within the existing production frontier.

There have been a number of studies into the importance of investment as a generator of growth, though the results have not been conclusive. For example, in 1961 Kuznets, using time-series data for a number of countries, found little relationship between the *share* of investment in GDP, and the growth in output over time.

Table 17.2 shows both the average annual growth in non-residential investment and in the share of

Table 17.2 Average annual rates of growth of output and the growth and share of investment, 1985–2008.

	GDP growth (%)	Non-residential investment growth (%)	Share of investment in GDP (%)
US	3.0	4.4	18.4
Canada	2.7	4.6	20.3
UK	2.6	4.5	17.5
France	2.2	3.5	19.6
Japan	2.1	2.8	26.7
Germany	2.1	2.8	20.6
Italy	1.7	2.5	20.5

Sources: Adapted from OECD (2010a) *Economic Outlook*, No. 87, Annex tables; OECD (2010b) *Factbook 2010*.

investment in GDP over the period 1985–2008 for the seven major world economies. It suggests that there is some relationship between the growth rate of the economy and the growth rate of investment spending, with the four fastest growing countries experiencing the most rapid increases in *non-residential investment* spending. The US, for example, has enjoyed the most rapid growth in its economy and has also been top of the growth in non-residential investment league, whilst the three major Eurozone countries lag behind on both counts. Interestingly, when the commitment to capital spending is measured from the perspective of the investment share in GDP, the results are much more patchy. The UK spends a relatively low share of total national output on investment but, over the period in question, has achieved a respectable growth performance. By way of contrast, Japan spends a relatively high share of total national output on investment but has generated a disappointing level of growth.

Does the UK suffer from a lack of investment?

Some of the previous discussion suggests that the UK may be suffering from a relatively low level of investment. Certainly Porter and Ketels (Koeva 2003) suggested that one key factor in the observed productivity gap between the UK and its main competitors was under-investment in the UK. Their survey showed that French workers have 60% more capital than in the UK, and those in Germany and the US between 25% and 30% more capital per worker. Recent work at the IMF (Koeva 2003) casts some doubt on this judgement, particularly as it relates to the more productive forms of capital spending. In its analysis the IMF points out that the performance of the UK in *equipment investment* is broadly comparable to that of other OECD countries. The UK does, however, have significantly lower non-residential construction investment which may reflect historical factors or different public policies (since government spending tends to be more important in this area of investment).

Other studies such as that by Bloom *et al.* (2001) remain rather sceptical as to the UK's comparative investment performance. They acknowledge that business investment as a percentage of GDP has risen in the UK since the mid-1990s but contend that it is still not relatively high when compared with the likes

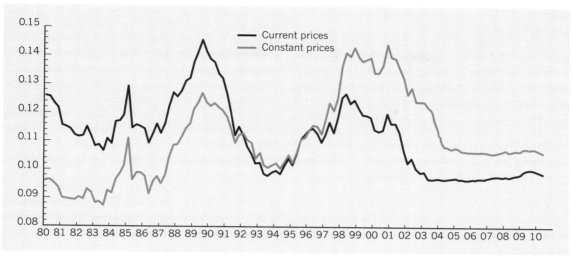

Fig. 17.2 Investment as a share of GDP.
Source: Datastream.

of the US and Germany. One point they make is that the use of 'consistent price investment' data distorts the picture (see Fig. 17.2). The authors of the report argue that over the period in question, the price of capital goods has fallen sharply while the overall price level has risen. In effect, there has been a significant decline in the *real price* of capital goods. Thus Bloom *et al.* point out that 'if firms had indeed bought the same capital goods they bought last year at the higher real prices prevailing last year, they would have had to spend substantially more money'.

Can there be too much investment? While many would answer no, others would disagree, pointing to the example of Japan in the late 1980s when companies spent huge amounts without any regard to the profitability of such decisions. Perhaps inevitably, much of the capital expenditure proved wasteful and hugely damaging initially to corporate finances and ultimately to the financial system as a whole. Although it was only one element of the story, this excessive investment arguably contributed to the decade-long recession that the Japanese economy has only recently begun to emerge from.

Efficiency and investment

The level of investment is not the only factor contributing to growth. A number of economists see investment as a necessary, but by no means *sufficient*,

condition for economic growth. Growth also depends on the efficiency with which any investment is utilized. One method of measuring the efficiency of investment is through the gross incremental capital/output ratio, i.e. the extra capital required to produce an additional unit of output.

Table 17.3 presents incremental capital/output ratios for five major economies. It demonstrates what appears to have been a major weakness of the UK economy in the past, namely that the UK has required *a higher rate of gross investment* to produce a *given increase* in output than have Germany, France, the US or Japan. However, the data suggest a considerable improvement in the efficiency with which investment in the UK has been utilized during the 1990s. Some have suggested that the more flexible labour market in the UK following earlier reforms (see

Table 17.3 Incremental capital/output ratios.

	1970–79	1980–89	1990–2005
France	0.7	1.1	0.8
Germany	0.9	1.5	0.7
Japan	0.8	1.3	0.2
UK	1.6	1.8	0.7
US	1.3	0.9	1.7

Source: Adapted from OECD (2005) *Economic Outlook*, December.

Chapter 14) has allowed capital to be used more productively in recent times.

Table 17.3 suggests that increased capital intensity within the UK has resulted in a *more than proportionate* increase in output during the 1990–2005 period, with only 0.7 units of capital required to yield a one-unit increase in output. It has been pointed out in Chapter 1 that *total* factor productivity must rise in UK plants and enterprises if growth is to be sustained. It follows that increasing the efficiency of labour, and improving the organizational structure of UK firms, may be at least as important in generating economic growth as raising the absolute level of investment.

Studies such as Young (1994) suggest that in a global market with 'footloose' multinationals continually reappraising the location of investment decisions, it is *relative efficiency* which is becoming a crucial factor in investment decisions. Changes in total factor productivity (and thereby costs) in the UK relative to other countries may therefore have an increasingly significant influence on investment decisions in the UK.

Conclusion

Investment occurs in so wide a variety of assets and sectors that it must be disaggregated substantially if any close statistical fit is to be found. However, even when we concentrate on fixed investment in manufacturing, no single theory 'explains' much of the variation in investment. What evidence there is certainly suggests that UK investment is relatively interest-inelastic, reducing the effectiveness of the interest rate as a policy instrument. Nevertheless, insofar as changes in interest rates affect expectations, lower interest rates may still contribute to higher investment.

Although much less important than consumption in aggregate demand, investment has, through the multiplier, a significant effect on National Income, and is the most volatile element in aggregate demand. It also affects the productive potential of an economy. Even though the link between investment and growth is in some ways tenuous, it is interesting that higher growth rates of fixed investment in various countries have been accompanied by stronger growth performances. Some have also suggested that the observed increases in labour productivity suggest that UK investment is now being more efficiently utilized, as reflected by falls in the incremental capital/output ratio for the UK noted in Table 17.3, though clearly there is much scope for further falls in this respect. Increased globalization of production and investment decisions is placing a still greater premium on the UK, matching, and surpassing, the efficiency with which investments are utilized in other countries.

Key points

- Investment is an important element of aggregate demand, contributing around 13% of total final expenditure (TFE).

- Investment also contributes to the 'supply side' of the economy, e.g. directly influencing real output per unit of factor input.

- Investment is a 'flow', as it involves a rate of change.

- Investment is volatile, having a significant impact on changes in National Income (via the multiplier).

- The share of investment undertaken by the public sector has edged up over the past few years to 12%.

- Expectations as to future profitability are a key factor in influencing the level of investment.

- Other relevant factors include the rate of interest, the rate of change of output (accelerator theory), levels and rates of depreciation of capital stock, size of public sector, financial support available, etc.

- In a global economy, changes in UK costs *relative to other countries* have been identified as influencing UK levels of investment.

- As well as the levels of investment, the *efficiency* with which any investment is utilized is also important.

Now try the self-check questions for this chapter on the Companion Website. You will also find useful links to relevant websites.

References and further reading

Ashworth, P., Hubert, F., Pain, N. and Riley, R. (2001) *UK Fixed Capital Formation: Determinants and Constraints*, Report to Department of Trade and Industry and CBI/TUC Working Group on Investment, London, National Institute of Economic and Social Research.

Bank of England (2010) *Inflation Report*, London, Bank of England.

Barrel, R. and Riley, R. (2006) Is UK business investment unusually weak? *National Institute Economic Review*, April, 60–2.

Bénassy-Quéré, A. and Coeuré, B. (2010) *Economic Policy*, Oxford, Oxford University Press.

Bloom, N., Bond, S. and Van Reenen, J. (2001) *The Dynamics of Investment Under Uncertainty*, IFS Working Paper, No. 2001/05, London, Institute for Fiscal Studies.

Bond, S. and Jenkinson, T. (1996) The assessment: investment performance and policy, *Oxford Review of Economic Policy*, 12(2): 1–29.

Bond, S. and Meghir, C. (1994) Financial constraints and company investment, *Fiscal Studies*, 15(2): 1–18.

Bond, S., Denny, K. and Devereux, M. (1993) Capital allowances and the impact of Corporation Tax on investment in the UK, *Fiscal Studies*, 14(2): 1–14.

Bond, S., Elston, J., Mairesse, J. and Mulkay, B. (1997) *Financial Factors and Investment in Belgium, France, Germany and the UK*, NBER Working Paper, No. 5900, Cambridge MA, National Bureau of Economic Research.

Bunn, P. and Trivedi, K. (2005) *Corporate Expenditures and Pension Contributions: Evidence from UK Company Accounts*, Bank of England Working Paper, 276, London, Bank of England.

Carruth, A., Dickerson, A. and Henley, A. (2000) Econometric modelling of UK aggregate investment: the role of profits and uncertainty, *The Manchester School*, 68(3): 276–300.

Catinat, M. *et al.* (1987) The determinants of investment, *European Economy Annual Economic Report*, 31(March): 5–60.

COM (1991) *European Economy, Annual Economic Report 1991–92. The profitability of fixed capital and its relation with investment*, No. 50, December, Brussels, Commission of the European Communities.

Corbett, J. and Jenkinson, T. (1996) *The Financing of Industry: An International Comparison*, mimeo, University of Oxford.

Cummins, J. G., Hassett, K. A. and Hubbard, R. G. (1994) A reconsideration of investment behaviour using tax reforms as natural experiments, *Brookings Papers on Economic Activity*, 2, 1–74.

Cummins, J. G., Hassett, K. A. and Hubbard, R. G. (1996) Tax reforms and investment: A cross-country comparison of investment expenditures, *Journal of Public Economies and Investment*, 62, 237–73.

Department of Trade and Industry (2000) *UK Competitiveness Indicators 1999*, London, The Stationery Office.

Devereux, M. (1989) Tax asymmetries, the cost of capital and investment: some evidence from the United Kingdom panel data, *Economic Journal*, 99, 103–12.

Driver, C., Temple, P. and Urga, G. (2001) *The Profit Orientation of UK Manufacturing Investment: Does π beat Q?*, Working Paper, No. 01/01, Department of Investment, Risk Management and Insurance, London, City University Business School.

Ford, R. and Poret, P. (1990) *Business Investment in the OECD Economies: Recent Performance and Some Implications for Policy*, OECD Working Paper, 88, Paris, Organisation for Economic Cooperation and Development.

Giavazzi, F. and Blanchard, O. (2010) *Macroeconomics: A European Perspective*, Harlow, Financial Times/Prentice Hall.

Gordon, R. J. and Veitch, J. M. (1987) Fixed investment in the American business cycle 1919–1983, in Gordon, R. J. (ed.), *The American Business Cycle: Continuity and Change*, Chicago IL, University of Chicago Press.

House of Commons (1994) Trade and Industry Committee, *Competitiveness of UK Manufacturing Industry*, Second Report, London, HMSO.

Koeva, P. (2003) *UK Investment: Is There a Puzzle?*, IMF Country Report No. 03/47, March.

Kennedy, M. (1997) Economic activity and inflation, in Artis, M. J. (ed.) *The UK Economy* (14th edn), Oxford, Oxford University Press.

McCormick, B. *et al.* (1983) *Introducing Economics*, London, Penguin.

Mullins, M. and Wadhwani, S. B. (1989) The effects of the stock market on investment, *European Economic Review*, 33: 939–56.

Newman, S., Roclert, C. and Schaap, R. (2011) Investing in the post recession world, *Harvard Business Review*, January–February, 150–5.

Nickell, S. and Nicolitsas, D. (2000) Human capital, investment and innovation: what are the connections?, in Barrell, R., Mason, G. and O'Mahoney, M. (eds), *Productivity, Innovation and Economic Performance*, Cambridge, Cambridge University Press.

OECD (2005) *Economic Outlook*, December, Paris, Organisation for Economic Cooperation and Development.

OECD (2010a) *Economic Outlook*, No 87, Annex tables, Paris, Organisation for Economic Cooperation and Development.

OECD (2010b) *OECD Factbook 2010*, Paris, Organisation for Economic Cooperation and Development.

Oliner, S. D., Rudebusch, G. D. and Sichel, D. E. (1995) New and old models of business investment; a comparison of forecasting performance, *Journal of Money, Credit and Banking*, 27(3): 806–26.

ONS (2010) *Monthly Digest of Statistics*, No. 778, London, Office for National Statistics.

Osler, C. L. (1994) High foreign real interest rates and investment in the 1990s, *Federal Reserve Bank of New York Quarterly Review*, Spring 1994, 8–34.

Porter, M. and Ketels, C. (2003) *UK Competitiveness: Moving to the Next Stage*, DTI Economics paper no. 3, London, Department of Trade and Industry/Economic and Social Research Council.

Sumner, M. (1998) Note on improving the effects of effective tax rates on business investment, *Journal of Public Economics*, 35(3): 393–6.

Temple, P., Urga, G. and Driver, C. (2001) The influence of uncertainty on investment in the UK: a macro or micro phenomenon?, *Scottish Journal of Political Economy*, 48(4): 361–82.

Tevlin, S. and Whelan, K. (2000) *Explaining the Investment Boom of the 1990s*, Finance and Economics Discussion Series 2000–11, Washington DC, Federal Reserve Board.

Turner, P. (1989) Investment: theory and evidence, *Economic Review*, 6(3).

Vittas, D. and Brown, R. (1982) *Bank Lending and Industrial Investment*, London, Banking Information Service.

Weale, M. (2006) Commentary: the savings–investment balance. Is there a UK investment shortfall? *National Institute Economic Review*, April, 4–9.

Whitaker, S. (1998) Investment in this recovery: an assessment, *Bank of England Quarterly Bulletin*, February, 38(1): 38–47.

Young, G. (1994) International competitiveness, international taxation and domestic investment, *National Institute Economic Review*, May, 44–8.

CHAPTER 18

Public expenditure

In this chapter we consider the growth of public expenditure and the difficulties surrounding its control. The next chapter will examine the burden of taxation. Given the key policy objectives in the UK of eliminating the budget deficit by 2014/15 and with 70% of the adjustment to take the form of public expenditure restrictions, this chapter and Chapter 19 on taxation assume even greater importance.

Here we look at public expenditure, its form, size and apparently inexorable growth. Problems of definition and calculation are considered, as resolving such ambiguity is extremely important since entire economic and political platforms rest upon the outcome. Attempts to control public expenditure are nothing new; they began early in the nineteenth century, long before Gladstone. Whatever the definition used, successive governments have had difficulty in controlling public expenditure, and the most widely used ratio of public expenditure (Total Managed Expenditure) to GDP has risen from 36.4% in 2000 to 47.2% in 2009/10. The major rise in this ratio has occurred in the period since 2007, with government interventions to offset global recession combining with already planned increases in public expenditure to raise this ratio from 41.1% in 2007/08 to 47.2% in 2009/10. The intention in the Comprehensive Spending Review of October 2010 is to bring this ratio down to 40% by 2015 and to reduce the current public sector net cash requirement (previously PSBR) from 11% to zero.

Trends in UK public spending

Figure 18.1 and Table 18.1 trace the relative importance of public expenditure in the UK economy between 1970 and 2010. Figure 18.1 shows Total Managed Expenditure (TME), previously called general government expenditure (GGE), as a percentage of GDP over an extended period of time in order to understand the changing role of the government in the economy. This ratio rose sharply during the problem periods of the 1970s and 1980s when the UK economy suffered as a result of major oil shocks, but then the ratio fell during the growth years of the mid- to late 1980s and the period 1993–2007. Nor was it only growth in national income which contributed to the reduction in the ratio! The Conservative government was determined that public spending should take a declining share of GDP and announced severe cuts in public expenditure in November 1993, arguing that cuts in expenditure would lower government borrowing which, combined with lower taxation, would increase economic efficiency and improve the 'supply side' of the economy.

When the Labour Party came to power in 1997, the ratio began to rise again for two main reasons: first, the Labour Party's philosophical ideology as regards a more interventionist role for government in the economy; second, there was a backlog of projects which the new government believed needed attention.

Whilst reluctant to change the previous Conservative government's spending projections during its first five years in office (1997–2002), the Labour government undertook a major Comprehensive Spending Review in November 2002 which resulted in sharp increases in public spending over the period 2002/03–2005/06, with the average annual growth of spending over this period to be as follows: Transport (8.4%), Health (7.3%) Education (5.7%) and Housing (3.5%), all well above the projected 2% annual rate of inflation.

However, the ratio of public expenditure (TME) to GDP rose still more rapidly after 2007 as the effects of the credit crunch and the required government intervention to stabilize the economy coincided with additional expenditures planned in the last few years of that government. This rise has now been reversed with the Comprehensive Spending Review of the incoming Coalition government in 2010 projecting a significant reduction in the growth of public spending.

Total Managed Expenditure (TME)

The *Economic and Fiscal Strategy Report* in June 1998 reformed the planning and control regime for public spending.

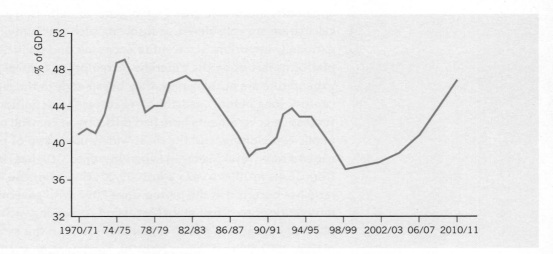

Fig. 18.1 Total Managed Expenditure (TME) as a percentage of GDP since 1970.
Source: Adapted from HM Treasury (2010) *Public Expenditure Statistical Analyses.*

Table 18.1 Historical series of government expenditure (% of GDP).

	Public sector current expenditure	Public sector net capital expenditure	General government expenditure (GGE)	Total Managed Expenditure (TME)
1970–71	32.7	6.2	41.0	42.7
1971–72	33.4	5.3	41.3	42.6
1972–73	33.2	4.9	40.8	41.9
1973–74	35.0	5.2	41.3	44.3
1974–75	38.7	5.6	47.6	48.6
1975–76	39.7	5.6	45.6	49.7
1976–77	39.7	4.4	45.6	48.5
1977–78	38.3	3.0	42.4	45.6
1978–79	38.2	2.5	43.0	45.1
1979–80	38.1	2.3	43.0	44.6
1980–81	40.6	1.9	46.0	47.0
1981–82	42.3	1.0	46.7	47.7
1982–83	42.3	1.6	46.6	48.1
1983–84	42.0	1.8	45.5	47.8
1984–85	42.2	1.6	45.5	47.5
1985–86	40.5	1.2	43.5	45.0
1986–87	39.7	0.7	41.6	43.6
1987–88	38.1	0.6	39.8	41.6
1988–89	35.8	0.3	37.2	38.9
1989–90	35.3	1.2	38.3	39.2
1990–91	35.6	1.3	38.5	39.4
1991–92	38.0	1.8	40.8	41.9
1992–93	39.8	1.8	42.8	43.7
1993–94	39.7	1.4	42.9	43.0
1994–95	39.3	1.4	42.2	42.5
1995–96	38.7	1.4	42.1	41.8
1996–97	37.6	0.7	40.3	39.9
1997–98	36.2	0.6	39.1	38.2
1998–99	35.2	0.7	38.3	37.3
1999–00	34.5	0.6	38.0	36.4
2000–01	35.0	0.5	–	36.8
2001–02	35.5	1.2	–	38.0
2002–03	36.1	1.3	–	38.7
2003–04	36.8	1.3	–	39.4
2004–05	37.6	1.7	–	40.6
2005–06	38.2	1.8	–	41.3
2006–07	37.7	1.9	–	40.9
2007–08	37.8	2.0	–	41.1
2008–09	39.4	3.2	–	43.9
2009–10	41.4	3.8	–	47.2

Source: Adapted from HM Treasury (2010) *Public Expenditure Statistical Analyses*, and previous issues.

- Overall plans were to use a new distinction between current and capital spending.

- Firm three-year plans (*Departmental Expenditure Limits*, DELs) were to provide certainty and flexibility for long-term planning and management.

- Spending outside DELs, which could not reasonably be subjected to firm three-year spending commitments, was to be reviewed annually as part of the Budget process. This *Annual Managed Expenditure* (AME) is also subject to constraints.

- Large public corporations, not dependent on government grants, were to be given more flexibility.

- *Total Managed Expenditure* (TME) was defined as consisting of DEL plus AME and was to be widely used as the overall measure of government expenditure (replacing general government expenditure – GGE).

Making a clear distinction between public sector *current* expenditure and *capital* expenditure is a key element in the government's 'golden rule' (see below). A historical series for these various definitions is shown in Table 18.1.

The debate on the role of public expenditure continues. Nevertheless, the previous Conservative and Labour governments both accepted that, as a cornerstone of the medium-term financial strategy, they should squeeze inflation progressively out of the economy, through a close control of the rate of growth of public expenditure. Continuing fiscal rectitude is seen as important for a government committed to the Maastricht criteria for fiscal convergence (see Chapter 27). These include a 3% target for the overall ratio of public sector borrowing requirement (PSBR) (now public sector net cash requirement) to GDP, and a 60% target for the ratio of public debt to GDP.

Figure 18.2 provides a useful overview of the intentions of the Comprehensive Spending Review of October 2010 in reducing future real levels (at constant 2010/11 prices) of Total Managed Expenditure further below already reduced totals planned by the previous Labour government in its March 2010 budget. The remaining difference between projected TME expenditure and tax revenues (see Chapter 19) will need to be financed by borrowing, but the intention is to all but close the gap between the expenditure and revenue lines by the end of the current Parliament in 2015.

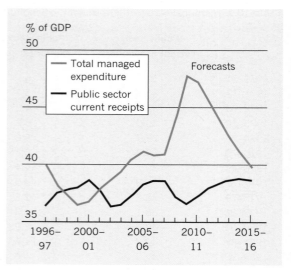

Fig. 18.2 Forecasts for spending and revenues.
Source: Forecast for spending and revences % of GDP, *Financial Times*, 21/10/2010 (Wolf, M.).

Public spending and the National Debt

The National Debt has been reduced sharply by successive governments and at the start of the global recession of 2007/08 had fallen to around 50% of National Income. As can be seen from Fig. 18.3 this is well below the long-run average (1688–2010) of 112% of National Income.

However, the huge sums expended by the government since 2007 in order to rescue fundamentally insolvent financial institutions and purchase large

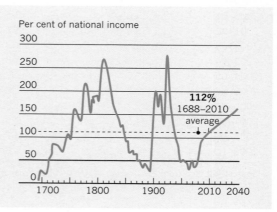

Fig. 18.3 UK public debt since the 17th century.
Sources: IMF data (various); Goodhart (1999).

amounts of securities via quantitative easing (see Chapter 20), have caused a sharp upward revision in the National Debt to around 90% of National Income in 2010, with a projected rise to around 155% of National Income in 2040, were the same expenditure patterns to continue. This projected trajectory for the National Debt is widely considered unsustainable, and it would be 'punished' by the financial markets and credit rating agencies were it to materialize, with long-term interest rates rising well above current levels. Interestingly, in 2010 the budgetary problems of Ireland and its reduced credit rating meant that borrowing for five years or more cost the Irish government an extra 4% more than Germany should it borrow over the same time period.

Public spending by function

Table 18.2 provides data on various aspects of the UK's public sector expenditure by function over the period 1999–2009, with the third column indicating the importance of public spending on each function over the decade to 2009. We can see that Social Protection, Health and Education together comprise a significant 64% of TME. The second column traces the *changes* in public spending on these various functions during the decade as a percentage of GDP. Again, we see the rapid growth in expenditure on Health, Education and Economic Affairs (especially Transport) over the decade.

Fiscal 'rules'

In addition to its commitment to the Maastricht criteria for fiscal convergence, in 1998 the Labour government committed itself to the following two important 'fiscal rules'.

1 The 'golden rule': over the economic cycle the government will only borrow to invest and will not borrow to fund current expenditure.

Table 18.2 Public sector expenditure on services by function, 1999–2009.

Services by function	Expenditure as a % of TME 2009–10	Annual real growth of expenditure (%) 1999–2009
1 **General public services** of which:	8.0	1.3
Public & common services	2.1	3.7
International services	1.2	7.0
Public debt services	4.7	−0.1
2 **Defence**	5.7	2.0
3 **Public order and safety**	5.2	4.9
4 **Economic affairs** of which:	6.8	6.7
enterprise and economic development	1.4	5.9
science and technology	0.5	10.0
employment policies	0.6	−1.6
agri/forestry and fishing	0.9	1.3
transport	3.5	13.2
5 **Environmental protection**	1.7	8.4
6 **Housing and community amenities**	2.3	1.6
7 **Health**	17.9	9.0
8 **Recreation, culture and religion**	7.1	4.2
9 **Education**	13.2	6.5
10 **Social protection**	33.2	4.2

Note: Percentages may not add up to 100 due to rounding.
Source: Modified from HM Treasury (2010) *Public Expenditure Statistical Analyses*, Tables 4.3 & 4.4.

2 The 'public debt rule': the ratio of public debt to National Income will be held over the economic cycle at a 'stable and prudent' level.

In effect, the 'golden rule' was designed to ensure that current expenditure would be covered by current revenue (see Chapter 19) over the economic cycle. Put another way, any PSBR (now public sector net cash requirement) must be used only for investment purposes, with 'investment' defined as in the National Accounts.

The 'public debt rule' was rather less clear in that the phrase 'stable and prudent' was somewhat ambiguous. However, taken together with the 'golden rule' it essentially meant that, as an average over the economic cycle, the ratio of PSBR to National Income could not exceed the ratio of investment to National Income. Given that, historically, government investment has been no more than 2–3% of National Income, then clearly the PSBR as a percentage of National Income must be kept within strict bounds.

These rules were designed to keep government budgets/spending in check as the UK was also committed to the Maastricht criteria for fiscal convergence. These included a 3% target for the overall ratio of the Public Sector Net Cash Requirement (PSNCR) to GDP, and a 60% target for the ratio of public debt to GDP.

To meet the requirements of these fiscal rules, it was essential for the government to introduce systems and procedures to enable it to better manage the planning, monitoring and control of public expenditure.

Planning, monitoring and control

Governments must seek to *plan* levels of public expenditure several years into the future, especially since any rise in public expenditure must be financed either by additional taxation or by increased borrowing. Governments must also develop and apply procedures to *monitor* and *control* public expenditure. All three elements are involved to some extent in the Public Expenditure Survey 'rounds', to which all the spending departments must submit on a regular and ongoing basis.

Public Expenditure Survey (PES)

Planning public expenditure for the next three years begins with the Public Expenditure Survey (PES). As part of this process, the spending departments discuss their spending proposals with the Public Expenditure Division of the Treasury, with all proposals expressed in cash terms. This PES 'round' usually takes place between April and September of each year, with the results of the PES announced at the end of November when the Chancellor presents his Budget statement to Parliament. To avoid any planning 'surprises' the major spending departments, such as the Department of Social Security, actually undergo *two* PES rounds each year, the second lasting from October to April.

Control Total (CT)

We have already noted the importance attached to the 'golden rule', which has resulted in the government paying less attention to monitoring and controlling *cyclical* components of expenditure, such as unemployment benefit and various types of income support. This has led to the government establishing a new Control Total (CT) for public expenditure, which covers around 85% of the value of spending included in TEM. An underlying objective of the CT is to help government focus on those items of expenditure which it can directly control and which are independent of cyclical fluctuations in the economy. As well as excluding unemployment benefit and income support, the CT also excludes central government gross debt interest (since borrowing and interest payments tend to rise during recession and fall during recovery).

Until 1992, the ministers in charge of the spending departments would seek to agree on spending limits for their departments in *bilateral* negotiations with the Chief Secretary to the Treasury. The agreed sums for each department would then be added together and announced in an 'Autumn Statement' on public spending plans.

Since 1993, however, the spending ministers have had to meet face-to-face in Cabinet in October or November to fight for a share of the already established overall value for the CT. Any extra given to one spending department must be funded at the expense of another spending department by reallocating the provisionally agreed CT. Clearly this procedure is intended to restrict the possibility of 'upward drift' in total public spending, which many critics claimed to have been a constant feature of the previous system of simply aggregating the outcomes of bilateral negotiations between spending departments and the Treasury.

Further, since 1993 we have had a unified Budget in March, in which both revenue raising and expenditure plans are discussed together. Prior to 1993, the spending totals were announced in the 'Autumn Statement' and the revenue-raising measures to finance them were announced some six months later in the March Budget. This separation of time between announcing planned expenditure and announcing methods for raising the tax revenue to fund that expenditure was seen as encouraging public expenditure growth, since the public would be less likely to associate any need for higher taxes in the March Budget with announcements of higher public expenditure in the previous autumn. To remedy this, since 1993 we have had a 'unified' Budget, with planned expenditure and planned tax revenue announced together, reinforcing the linkage between the two.

Forecasts

Since the expenditure plans for each department must cover three years, *forecasts* are needed for the future expenditures required to implement the agreed policies over this time period. The expenditure forecasts for each department are based on the work of both *internal* departmental experts (e.g. statisticians and economists) and *external* experts (e.g. members of the independent Government Actuaries Department). Further, the basic assumptions on which these forecasts rest include estimates of future changes in variables such as retail prices, average earnings, unemployment rates, economic growth, etc. To ensure that the various departmental forecasts rest on *common* assumptions, the Treasury provides the spending departments with projections of the data on expected values for all these variables over the next three years.

Agreement by the government on the future spending plans of a department (departmental expenditure limits – DEL) implies agreement on the policy proposals produced by that department over the next three years. Such policy proposals are usually generated by the Policy Group which resides within each department. Members of the Policy Group will seek to reflect the political priorities of both the government and the departmental ministers, as well as taking into account the representation of various pressure groups and any current research findings in the field. These policy proposals, once agreed, are then costed by a specialist group within the department containing statisticians and economists, and these costings will in turn provide the basis for the department expenditure forecasts.

An outline of the various processes involved in a PES has been provided by the Department for Work and Pensions, which is used here to illustrate a system common to most spending departments (Fig. 18.4).

The Department for Work and Pensions is the largest spending department and accounts for around 30% of planned public expenditure. Expenditure on Social Security benefits, such as the Retirement Pension, Housing Benefit and Child Benefit, accounts for 95% of the total Department for Work and Pensions bill. Social Security expenditure is almost entirely demand led, so estimating future expenditure requires projections as to how that demand is likely to change in the future. Factors influencing Social Security expenditure can usefully be grouped into four key headings.

1 *Demographic*. The size and the structure of the population are key variables here, for example an ageing population will reduce spending on Child Benefit, but increase spending on retirement pensions.

2 *Economic*. The projected levels of unemployment, earnings, prices and economic growth will affect the demand for various types of benefit and therefore the amount of benefit paid.

3 *Social*. Changes in family structures, for example the frequency of divorce and of lone parenthood, will affect benefit expenditures.

4 *Policy*. The introduction of new benefits, changes to entitlement, changes to benefit rates, etc. will all affect benefit expenditure.

The government is obliged to report the differences between *forecast* expenditure and *actual out-turn* for any given year; drawing attention to any discrepancies between what was planned to be spent and what was actually spent is seen as helping the process of monitoring and controlling public expenditure.

The planning, monitoring and control of public expenditure can therefore be seen to have undergone considerable change in recent years, with the underlying aim of curbing tendencies towards an upward

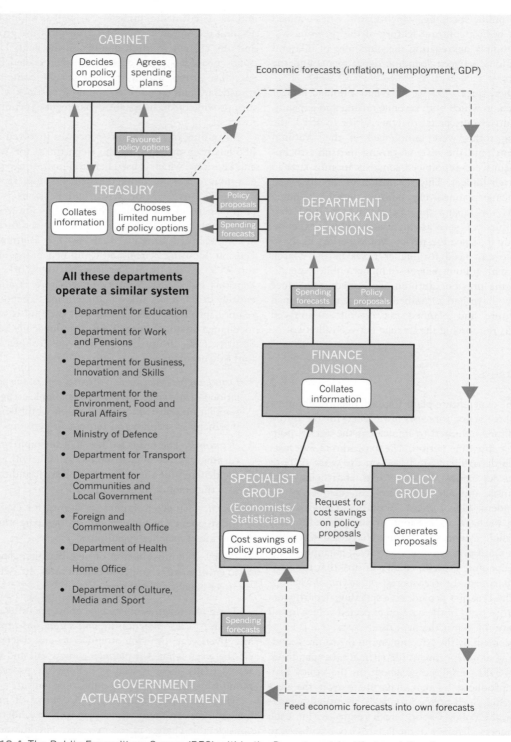

Fig. 18.4 The Public Expenditure Survey (PES) within the Department for Work and Pensions.

drift in spending totals. The procedures involved in the PES, the introduction of a new Control Total, the unified budget, obligations to report any discrepancies between forecast expenditures and actual out-turn are all parts of a more structured and accountable system for public expenditure.

A further element in such a system has been the so-called government drive for greater 'efficiency' in the public sector.

The drive for efficiency

Increasingly strident claims were made throughout the 1980s that, in the absence of competition, public services would always be produced inefficiently. One remedy might clearly be to increase such competition by privatizing the public services (see Chapter 8). Where this 'remedy' was not available then it was argued that efficiency could be improved by making sure that the delivery of public services conformed more closely to the needs of those who used them, rather than to the interests of those who provided them. This view led to a wave of reforms, including the introduction of contracting out and competitive tendering, the creation of Next Step Agencies, and the introduction of Value for Money Audits.

- *Contracting out and competitive tendering*. Putting services previously provided through the public sector out to tender has led to cost savings of varying magnitudes. For example, there have been estimates of savings of 20% in the case of NHS catering and laundry, and savings of 14% in the case of highway services. In a number of other cases savings of 7% have been realized (Griffiths 1998).

- *Next Steps Agencies*. These were introduced within government departments with the intention of improving the management of such departments. The idea here has been to separate the management of policy (the responsibility of central government) from operational management (the responsibility of the Agencies). For example, the Department for Work and Pensions has three main agencies, the Child Support Agency, JobCentre Plus and the Pensions, Disability and Carers Service. Such agencies have often been given the task of meeting a number of key performance indicators or targets, giving a yardstick against which their subsequent performance can be evaluated.

- *Value For Money (VFM) audits*. These are part of the Financial Management Initiative (FMI) aimed at ensuring that public provision of goods and services is economic, efficient and effective. Under the FMI, central government departments have had to demonstrate to the Treasury that they have in place a VFM framework whereby audits are undertaken to check that managers are finding resource savings, while at the same time improving the quality of public services. Again, such procedures have often involved performance indicators.

- *Private Finance Initiative (PFI)*. The intention here has been to identify projects which can attract private sector finance to be used alongside public sector finance. The PFI is a method of providing funds for major capital investments where private companies are contracted to complete and manage the projects. The contracts (e.g. to build hospitals) are typically given to construction firms and the contract often lasts for up to 30 years. The contractors build the public services (hospitals) and they are then leased to the public and the government authority (e.g. Department of Health) who makes an annual payment to the private company. The total value of these forms of public–private partnerships in the UK currently amounted to some £68bn with future spending of £215bn due to be paid over the life of the contracts.

The size of public expenditure

So far we have looked at changing *shares* within total public spending, but has the *absolute* level of public spending grown as fast as critics suggest? Such people usually point to a single statistic for evidence; for instance, that the public sector employs about 25% of the labour force or, as with Milton Friedman, that if public expenditure grows to around 60% of National Income then it will threaten to destroy freedom and democracy. Actually, estimates for the ratio of public spending to National Income vary widely, depending on the definitions used for each item. Figures for 2009/10 put total managed expenditure at around 46% of GDP at market prices (see Table 18.3). If, however, transfer payments are excluded from government expenditure, as they are from the measurement of National Income, then government

Table 18.3 Government spending as a proportion of National Income.

(a) Government spending as a proportion of GNP at factor cost (%)							
1790	1890	1910	1932	1951	1966	1970	1976
12.0	8.0	12.0	29.0	40.2	40.2	42.2	48.7

(b) Government spending as a proportion of GDP at market price (%)								
1978/79	1982/83	1986/87	1990/91	1992/93	1995/96	2000/01	2005/06	2009/10
45.1	48.1	43.6	39.4	43.7	41.8	36.8	41.3	46.2

Note: From 1977 onwards, an approximately 6% upward revision should be made to any government spending/National Income ratio if comparison with pre-1977 figures is to be made.
Sources: HM Treasury (2010) *Public Expenditure Statistical Analyses*; Brown and Jackson (1982).

expenditure falls dramatically to less than 30% of GDP at market prices. What, then, is the truth about the size of public expenditure?

An examination of data from the Office for National Statistics (ONS) suggests that as many as 10 measures could be used for estimating the size of public expenditure. The measure selected will depend on the question at issue. If the intention is to assess the *financial resources* passing through the hands of government, then a ratio involving TME might be appropriate. However, the ONS's definition of National Income in the Blue Book excludes current grants and other transfers. Strictly, therefore, these same items should be excluded from government expenditure. They do not represent additional demand for resources; they are merely transfers of purchasing power from the taxpayer to other sectors of the community. Using this argument, a ratio of TME on goods and services of approximately 30% of National Income would appear to be the most appropriate measure.

No single measure of public expenditure has met with universal agreement, and even when one has been widely used for some time, it can be subject to change for a variety of reasons. In April 1977 the then widely used measure of general government expenditure was redefined to bring the UK into line with OECD accounting methods, and resulted in an apparent overnight reduction of some 6% in measured public expenditure. Again, what was previously tax relief may be reclassified as government expenditure, as with child tax allowances being replaced by Child Benefit in 1977. Public expenditure will also be affected by changes in the degree of 'privatization'

(which is recorded as negative expenditure) or by changes in public sector pricing.

The National Income aggregate used for comparison will also influence our impression of the size of the public sector. Some ratios use domestic product, which measures resources produced *entirely within the domestic circular flow*. If, however, our interest was in the resources produced by UK nationals, *wherever they happen to be located*, then our ratio should use national product. Yet again, both domestic and national products could be valued 'gross' (including depreciation) or 'net' (excluding depreciation); at 'market prices', including the effects of taxes and subsidies, or at 'factor cost', excluding them.

For all these reasons, public spending ratios must be treated with caution when used in policy analysis.

Explanations of the growth in public expenditure

No matter what the definition, statistics show that the government sector of the economy has expanded over the last 150 years (see Fig. 18.5), both in money and real terms, and as a percentage of National Income. In Table 18.3, Brown and Jackson (1982), quoting a variety of sources, showed a dramatically rising trend of government spending as a proportion of GNP at factor cost up to 1976. The trend (using a different statistical series) continued upwards for data after 1976, reaching a peak of 48.1% in 1982/83. Between then and 2000 there has been a sustained fall

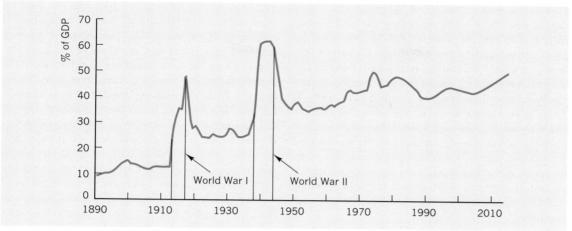

Fig. 18.5 General government expenditure as a percentage of GDP, 1890–2010 (projected).

in government spending as a percentage of National Income, though for a few years during the recession of the early 1990s the percentage had risen before resuming its downward path. Since 2000, and especially since the Comprehensive Spending Review of November 2002, there has been a renewed upward drift in government spending as a percentage of National Income, especially since the onset of the 2007 global recession. However, the 2010 Comprehensive Spending Review has made it clear that the future trend of general government expenditure as a percentage of GDP will be downwards over the coming years.

The explanation of the above trends and the difficulties involved in controlling public expenditure are based on two types of analysis: microeconomic and macroeconomic respectively.

Microeconomic analysis

Explanations based on microeconomic analysis suggest that additional public spending can be seen as the result of governments continually intervening to correct market failure. This would include the provision of 'public goods' such as collective defence, the police and local amenities (Cottrell 2002). An extra unit of such goods can be enjoyed by one person, without anyone else's enjoyment being affected. In other words, the marginal social cost of provision is zero, and it is often argued in welfare economics that the

'efficiency' price should, therefore, be zero. Private markets are unable to cope with providing goods at zero price, so that public provision is the only alternative should this welfare argument be accepted. Microeconomic analysis would also cover extra public spending due to a change in the composition of the 'market', such as an ageing population incurring greater expenditure on health care.

Macroeconomic analysis

There are also explanations of the growth of public spending based on long-run macroeconomic theories and models. The starting point in this field is the work of Wagner (see Bird 1971), who used empirical evidence to support his argument that government expenditure would inevitably increase at a rate faster than the rise in national production. Wagner suggested that 'the pressures of social progress' would create tensions which could only be resolved by increased state activity in law and order, economic and social services, and participation in material production. Using the economists' terms, Wagner was in effect suggesting that public-sector services and products are 'normal', with high income elasticities of demand. Early studies in the UK by Williamson during the 1960s tended to support Wagner, indicating overall income elasticities for public-sector services of 1.7, and for public-sector goods of 1.3, with similar results in other advanced industrialized countries.

Further evidence in favour of Wagner's ideas came during the 1980s when studies by the OECD concluded that the proportion of GNP absorbed by public expenditure between 1954 and the early 1980s on 'merit goods' (education, health and housing) and 'income maintenance' (pensions, sickness, family and unemployment benefits) had doubled from 14% to 28%, as an average across all the advanced industrialized countries, with high income elasticities and low price elasticities playing a major part in this observed growth. Surveys of less developed economies were, however, more confusing, with econometric studies suggesting that little of the growth in public spending could be 'explained' by rising incomes (or low price elasticities).

Peacock and Wiseman's 'displacement theory' (Peacock and Wiseman 1961), covering the period 1890–1953, suggested that public spending was not rising with the smooth, small changes predicted by Wagner, but that it was displaced (permanently) upwards by social upheavals associated, for instance, with depressions or wars leading to demands for new social expenditure (Fig. 18.5 above indicates the displacements of 1914–18 and 1939–45). Displacement theory has, however, been criticized for giving insufficient weight to political influences on the level of public expenditure. A further criticism of 'displacement' theory is the fact that for the UK there is little evidence that ratchet increases in public spending are long lasting. In fact, where the ratio of public expenditure to National Income continued to rise in the 1970s and 1980s, it was more easily explained by downward shifts of trend National Income in recession, with consequent increases in spending on unemployment benefits and social services, rather than through any upward revision of government expenditure plans.

The conclusion that must be drawn from reviewing such work is that there is no definite micro- or macro-explanation of the growth path for public expenditure. It then follows that there is no inevitable 'law' ensuring that public expenditure becomes a progressively rising proportion of National Income. However, in a recessionary period such as that of the early 1990s, increased spending on unemployment and social services may indeed cause a sharp increase in the share of public expenditure in National Income. The same result can be expected from explicit attempts by the UK government to raise the quality of public services and spending per head on those services to levels already reached within the EU economies (Griffiths 2002). Demographic changes may also conspire to raise the share of public expenditure. There has been considerable debate as to the mounting 'burden' on the working population likely to result from the growing number of pensioners in the next few decades. It has been estimated that the UK dependency ratio – the non-working population divided by the working population – will have risen from the current 0.52 to 0.62 by 2030. By 2030, therefore, each worker will be required to contribute 18% more real income to sustain the current level of welfare provision. It is scenarios such as this which have led to renewed scrutiny of the practicability of a welfare state along present lines.

International comparisons

Given that public expenditure has grown over time in the UK, how do we compare with other countries? Conclusions based on OECD surveys indicate that UK public expenditure patterns are similar to those in most other advanced industrialized countries, although inferences drawn from international surveys must be treated with caution. The OECD definitions are frequently different from national ones, public sector boundaries vary between countries, and fluctuating exchange rates compromise any attempt at a standard unit of value.

Table 18.4 indicates that the growing share of UK public expenditure in National Income has been paralleled in other countries. If anything, public expenditure has grown less quickly in the UK, at least up to 2007. For example, in 1964 the UK was joint third highest, with Germany, of the 14 countries shown in Table 18.4, and by 1989 it was only eleventh highest of those same 14 countries. By 2005 it was still in eleventh place until the financial shock of the post 2007/08 period resulted in the UK rising to fifth highest in 2010. Compared to the average performance of Euro area countries, the UK's government outlay as a percentage of GDP has remained below the Euro area average since 1979, only rising above it in 2010 with increased expenditures on stimulating the UK economy.

Table 18.4 Total outlays[1] of government as a percentage of GDP at market prices: some international comparisons.

	1964	1974	1979	1989	1999	2010[2]
Australia	22.1	31.6	31.4	33.1	34.4	34.8
Austria	32.1	41.9	48.9	50.0	53.7	51.9
Belgium	30.3	39.4	49.3	55.7	50.2	54.4
Canada	28.9	36.8	39.0	44.6	42.7	43.2
Denmark	24.8	45.9	53.2	59.4	55.5	60.1
France	34.6	39.3	45.0	49.4	52.6	55.9
Italy	30.1	37.9	45.5	51.5	48.2	51.6
Japan	N/A	24.5	31.6	31.5	38.6	40.8
The Netherlands	33.7	47.9	55.8	55.9	46.0	52.4
Norway	29.9	44.6	50.4	54.6	47.7	45.3
Sweden	31.1	48.1	60.7	59.9	58.6	56.0
UK	32.4	44.9	42.7	41.2	38.8	52.5
USA	27.5	32.2	31.7	36.1	34.2	41.6
Germany	32.4	44.6	47.6	45.5	48.2	47.9
Euro area	32.1	40.7	45.5	47.8	48.2	50.8
Average OECD countries	**29.9**	**36.3**	**41.2**	**41.5**	**39.7**	**44.4**

[1]Total government outlay = final consumption expenditure + interest on national debt + subsidies + social security transfers to households + gross capital formation.
[2]Projected.
Source: Adapted from OECD (2010) *Economic Outlook*, June, and earlier volumes.

Fiscal tightening

The financial crisis of 2007/08 precipitated a sharp recession in the UK economy which resulted in a serious fall in government revenues actually received in 2008/09 and revenues expected in subsequent years. This, combined with rapid increases in government spending to rescue financial institutions, support quantitative easing, provide improved services and pay benefits for higher unemployment, resulted in a rapid increase in the budget deficit, which rose as high as 11% of GDP in 2009/10 (see Fig. 18.2, p. 354). These growing fiscal deficits meant that the UK, as well as other major economies, had to 'repair' their public finances with a combination of expenditure reduction and taxation increases. The UK government has concentrated on the expenditure side of the equation to make these adjustments, with 70% of the projected 'closure' of the budget deficit by 2015 involving planned public expenditure cuts.

To place this 'fiscal tightening' in context it will be useful to provide a background to UK public expenditure issues and the various solutions suggested by both the last Labour government and the Conservative/Liberal coalition government post-2010.

It can be seen (Table 18.5) that the tightening of the finances by both governments was mostly on the public expenditure side with over 70% stemming

Table 18.5 Composition of fiscal tightening to 2014–15: Labour and Coalition government estimates.

	March 2010 Budget (£bn)	June 2010 Budget (£bn)
Tax	21.5	29.8
Spending	−50.9	−82.8
Investment spending	−17.2	−19.3
Current spending	−33.7	−63.5
of which		
Debt interest	−7	−10.0
Benefits	−0.3	−10.7
Public services	−27.0	−42.8
Total fiscal tightening	72.4	112.6

Source: Crawford (2010).

from expenditure cuts and around 30% from tax rises. The Coalition government's plans announced in June 2010 involved a further 'tightening' (cuts in public expenditure/increases in taxation) from £72.4bn to £112.6bn by 2014/15. This was around 56% more than the fiscal tightening envisaged by the Labour government in March 2010. In June 2010 the Chancellor of the Exchequer announced that there would be two basic 'rules' to be followed.

- *Rule 1*: that the forecast time horizon would be 2014/15 and that a fiscal tightening of 5.9% of GDP or £112.6bn would be required over that period.
- *Rule 2*: that debt as a share of GDP should fall by the end of the forecast time horizon. The composition of the 'tightening' was further modified in October 2010 with a shift towards reducing spending on benefits by more than planned and reducing spending on public services by less than planned.

The aim of these policies is to bring the budget back to near balance by 2014/15. Whatever the 'necessity' of cutting public expenditure in the short to medium term in response to the global financial crisis, there is still the question relating to whether it is appropriate to restrict public expenditure *as a general principle*. It is to this question that we now turn.

 Should public expenditure be restricted?

Freedom and choice

Arguments for controlling or reducing the size of public expenditure are wide-ranging but not always convincing.

One argument is that excessive government expenditure adversely affects individual freedom and choice. First, it is feared that it 'spoonfeeds' individuals, taking away the incentive for personal provision, as with private insurance for sickness or old age. Second, it is feared that by impeding the market mechanism it may restrict consumer choice. For instance, the state may provide goods and services that are in little demand, whilst discouraging others (via taxation) that might otherwise have been bought. Third, it has been suggested that government provision may encourage an unhelpful separation between payment and cost in the minds of consumers. With government provision, the good or service may be free or subsidized, so that the amount paid by the consumer will understate the true cost (higher taxes, etc.) of providing him or her with that good or service, thereby encouraging excessive consumption of the item.

Crowding out the private sector

Conservative governments have long believed that (excessive) public expenditure was at the heart of the UK's economic difficulties. They regard the private sector as the source of wealth creation, part of which it saw as being used to subsidize the public sector. Sir Keith Joseph clarified this view during the 1970s by alleging that 'a wealth-creating sector which accounts for one-third of the national product carries on its back a State subsidized sector which accounts for two-thirds. The rider is twice as heavy as the horse.'

Bacon and Eltis (1978) attempted to give substance to this view. They suggested that public expenditure growth had led to a transfer of productive resources from the private sector to a public sector producing largely non-marketed output, and that this had been a major factor in the UK's poor performance in the post-war period. Bacon and Eltis noted that public-sector employment had increased by some 26%, from 5.8 million workers to 7.3 million, between 1960 and 1978, a time when total employment was largely unchanged. They then alleged that the private (marketed) sector was being squeezed by higher taxes to finance this growth in the public sector – the result being deindustrialization, low labour productivity, low economic growth and balance of payments problems (see also Chapter 19). The Bacon/Eltis assumption that the public sector invariably 'crowds out' the private sector has been challenged from various directions. For example, research suggests that although growth in public expenditure and taxes seem to have some negative effects on overall productivity and growth in the short run, their long-run efforts are less predictable (Handler *et al.* 2005). The same research also concluded that government R&D expenditures do *not* crowd out private R&D activities and that additional public expenditure by smaller economies may be growth enhancing.

Control of money

Another argument used by those who favour restricting public expenditure is that it must be cut in order to limit the growth of money supply and to curb inflation. The argument is that a high PSBR – now known as the public sector net cash requirement – following public expenditure growth, must be funded by the issue of Treasury bills and government stocks. Since there are inadequate 'real' savings to be found in the non-bank private sector, these bills and bonds inevitably find their way into the hands of the banks. As we will see in Chapter 20, they may then form the basis for a multiple expansion of bank deposits (money), with perhaps inflationary consequences.

A related argument is that public expenditure must be restricted, to limit not only the supply of money but also its 'price' – the rate of interest. The suggestion here is that to sell the extra bills and bonds to fund a high PSBR, interest rates must rise to attract investors. This then puts pressure on private-sector borrowing, with the rise in interest rates inhibiting private-sector investment and investment-led growth. A major policy aim of the government has, therefore, been to reduce public-sector borrowing. However, a weakness with this argument is that is assumes that the supply of money in an economy is fixed. If the government increases its expenditure but at the same time increases the amount of money in the economy (see quantitative easing, Chapter 20, p. 419), it need not deprive the private sector of finance and interest rates will not be forced upwards.

Incentives to work, save and take risks

There are also worries that increased public spending not only pushes up government borrowing to fund a high PSBR, but also leads to higher taxes, thereby reducing the incentives to work, save and take risks. The evidence linking taxes to incentives is reviewed in Chapter 19. Suffice it to say here that the evidence to support the general proposition that higher taxes undermine the work ethic is largely inconclusive.

Balance of payments stability

A further line of attack has been that the growth of public expenditure may have destabilized the economy.

During the 1970s and early 1980s this view was implied by the Cambridge Economic Policy Group (CEPG), who used an accounting identity (see Chapter 24) to demonstrate that a higher PSBR must lead to a deterioration in the balance of payments. The common sense of their argument is that higher public spending raises interest rates and attracts capital inflows, which in turn raise the demand for sterling and therefore the exchange rate. A higher pound then makes exports dearer and imports cheaper, so that the balance of payments deteriorates.

These various lines of reasoning have been challenged by, amongst others, the New Cambridge School which suggested that the relationships between the public sector and economic management may by no means be so simple. In fact, one adherent of the New Cambridge School, Lord Kaldor, went so far as to say that there was no empirical support for a high PSBR leading either to substantial growth in money supply or to high rates of interest. Similarly, the claim that resources liberated by the public sector would automatically find their way into the private sector was hardly supported by the rising unemployment trend of the early 1980s and early 1990s. Another criticism has pointed to the fact that public expenditure cuts, rather than helping to control unemployment (by cutting inflation in a monetarist model), have either caused or exaggerated current unemployment (see Chapter 23).

Conclusion

The definition of public expenditure is by no means clear-cut and must depend upon the question at issue. Since National Income also has many variants, any public expenditure/National Income ratio must be treated with caution. Whatever the definition chosen, the proportion of government spending in National Income rose steadily throughout the twentieth century. The reduction in the growth of National Income played an important part in raising the ratio in the early 1980s, early 1990s and since 2007, both directly, by restricting the denominator, and indirectly, by causing unplanned increases in expenditure on social security. Whether a growing public sector 'crowds out' or otherwise adversely affects the private sector is a matter of deep controversy. Certainly in comparative terms the UK is by no means exceptional, with the share of UK government spending in National Income well below the average for the EU countries. More 'rigour' has been imposed on procedures to plan, monitor and control public expenditure. This, together with renewed growth in National Income, helped to progressively reduce the ratio of government spending to National Income to around 37% in 2000, though the renewed emphasis on increased government spending since then has seen government spending at around 47% of National Income in 2010.

The move, in late 1992, towards a new 'control total' for public spending made it clear that the gov-ernment would continue to seek a tight fiscal stance, especially on items of expenditure of a non-cyclical nature. The determination of the government to adhere to the Maastricht criteria of a ratio of PSBR to GDP below 3%, and of public debt to GDP below 60%, suggests that public expenditure will remain closely controlled. This view was further strengthened by the announcement of fiscal 'rules' in 1998, especially the 'golden rule' whereby government borrowing would only be undertaken to support public investment and not current consumption. The intention of the Coalition government is to eliminate the budget deficit by 2015, manly by restricting the growth of public expenditure.

Key points

- Although government spending rose in real terms by around 1% per annum between 1990 and 2000, this was less than the growth in real National Income.

- As a result the share of government spending in National Income fell from almost 45% in 1992/93 to around 37% in 2000/01.

- Successive government spending reviews since 2000 have resulted in substantial real-term increases in government spending, which accounted for around 47% of National Income by 2009/10.

- Critics argue that too high a proportion of government spending goes on 'rescue' and 'welfare' and too little on 'renewal'. In this view more of the public purse should be used to support 'investment' type expenditures (on human or physical capital) directed towards raising future National Income.

- Total Managed Expenditure (TME) has now replaced general government expenditure (GGE).

- International comparisons do *not* suggest that UK public expenditure is exceptionally high as a percentage of GDP. In 2010 it was only 5th highest out of 14 countries investigated, and only marginally above the Euro area average.

- Many of the reasons put forward for controlling public expenditure involve the desire to cut the PSBR (now the public sector net cash requirement). The government concern is that too high a PSBR will force higher taxes and interest rates, with adverse effects on incentives and investment in the private sector.

- Part of the 'convergence criteria' within the EU involves keeping the PSBR no higher than 3% of GDP, implying tight control of public expenditure, keeping to this criterion has been difficult since the financial crisis of 2007/08.

- The 'fiscal rules' of the last government have been replaced by the Conservative/Liberal coalition's two broad rules. The intention is to close the budget deficit from the 11% of GDP of 2010 to around zero by 2015.

- The procedures for planning, monitoring and controlling public expenditure have been modified. These include changes to the departmental PES, a new 'Control Total', a unified Budget, relating spending forecasts to out-turns, and various initiatives to increase efficiency in the public sector.

Now try the self-check questions for this chapter on the Companion Website. You will also find useful links to relevant websites.

References and further reading

Bacon, R. and Eltis, W. (1978) *Britain's Economic Problem: too few producers* (2nd edn), Basingstoke, Macmillan.

Beachill, R., Spoor, C. and Wetherly, P. (2002) Keeping the economy healthy, *Economic Review*, 20(2): 2–5.

Bénassy-Quéré, A. and Coeuré, B. (2010) *Economic* Policy, Oxford, Oxford University Press.

Bird, R. M. (1971) Wagner's law of expanding state activity, *Public Finance*, 26(1): 1–26.

Brown, C. V. and Jackson, P. M. (1982) *Public Sector Economics* (2nd edn), London, Martin Robertson.

Cottrell, D. (2002) Public goods: an insoluble economic problem?, *Economic Review*, 20(1), September.

Crawford, R. (2010) 'Where the axe fell', *IFS Spending Review 2010*, Briefing Paper, London, Institute for Fiscal Studies.

Department of Trade and Industry (2006) *The Government's Expenditure Plans 2006–07 to 2007–08*, London, The Stationery Office.

Flemming, J. and Oppenheimer, P. (1996) Are government spending and taxes too high (or too low)?, *National Institute Economic Review*, July, 58–73.

Giavazzi, F. and Blanchard, O. (2010) *Macroeconomics: A European Perspective*, Harlow, Financial Times/Prentice Hall.

Goodhart, C. (1999) Monetary policy and debt management in the UK, in Chrystal, K. Alec (ed.), *Government Debt Structure and Monetary Conditions*. London, Bank of England.

Griffiths, M. A. (1998) Government expenditure and efficiency, *Money Management Review*, 51: 10–13.

Griffiths, A. (2002) The Budget and the Comprehensive Spending Review 2002, *British Economy Survey*, 32(1): 17–21.

Handler, H., Knabe, B., Koebel, M., Schratzenstaller, M. and Wehke, S. (2005) *The Impact of Public Budgets on Overall Productivity*, WIFO Working Paper no. 255, Vienna, Austrian Institute of Economic Research.

HM Treasury (2010) *Public Expenditure Statistical Analyses 2010*, London.

Joseph, K. (1976) *Monetarism is not Enough*, London, Barry Rose.

OECD (2010) *Economic Outlook*, June, Paris, Organisation for Economic Cooperation and Development.

Papava, V. (1993) A new view of the economic ability of the government; egalitarian goods and GNP, *International Journal of Social Economics*, 20(8): 56–62.

Peacock, A. and Wiseman, J. (1961) *The Growth of Public Expenditure in the United Kingdom*, Manchester, UMI.

Rowthorn, R. (1992) Government spending and taxation in the Thatcher era, in Michie, J. (ed), *The Economic Legacy, 1979–1992*, London, Academic Press.

Weir, J. (1998) Government spending: a view from the inside, *Money Management Review*, 51: 5–7.

Wolf, M. (2010) UK public debt since the 17th century, *Financial Times*, 3 November.

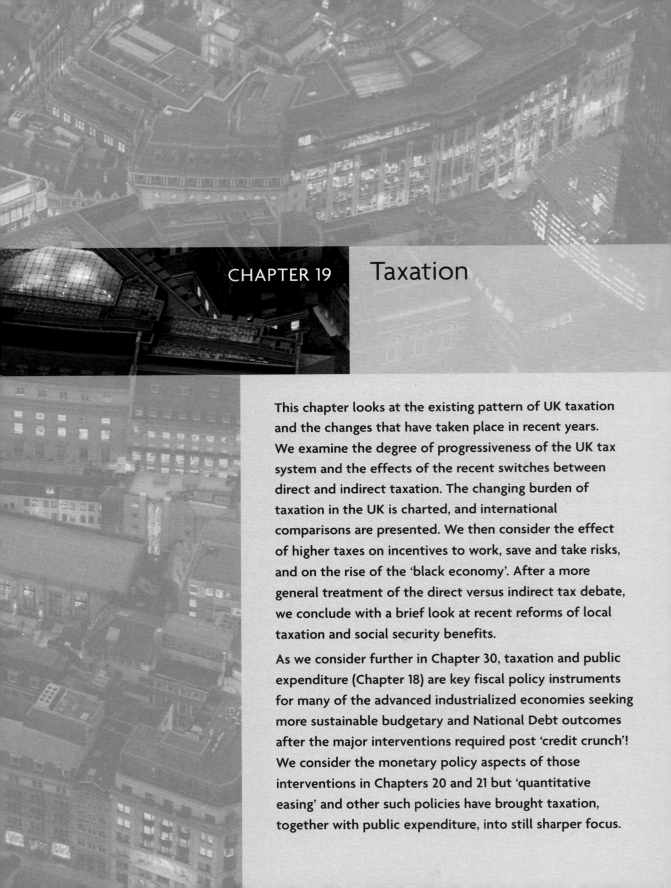

CHAPTER 19   Taxation

This chapter looks at the existing pattern of UK taxation and the changes that have taken place in recent years. We examine the degree of progressiveness of the UK tax system and the effects of the recent switches between direct and indirect taxation. The changing burden of taxation in the UK is charted, and international comparisons are presented. We then consider the effect of higher taxes on incentives to work, save and take risks, and on the rise of the 'black economy'. After a more general treatment of the direct versus indirect tax debate, we conclude with a brief look at recent reforms of local taxation and social security benefits.

As we consider further in Chapter 30, taxation and public expenditure (Chapter 18) are key fiscal policy instruments for many of the advanced industrialized economies seeking more sustainable budgetary and National Debt outcomes after the major interventions required post 'credit crunch'! We consider the monetary policy aspects of those interventions in Chapters 20 and 21 but 'quantitative easing' and other such policies have brought taxation, together with public expenditure, into still sharper focus.

The taxes that are collected: some taxation concepts

Taxes may be classified in a number of different ways:

- the method of collection;
- the tax base;
- the tax rate.

The method of collection

Taxes may be grouped by the administrative arrangement for their collection.

Direct or indirect

Income tax is paid *directly* to the Exchequer by the individual taxpayer (mainly through Pay As You Earn – PAYE), on the full amount of income from employment and investment in the fiscal year. The same is true of corporation tax, paid by firms on company profits. On the other hand, value added tax (VAT), though paid by consumers, reaches the Exchequer indirectly, largely through retailers acting as collecting agencies. Taxes may therefore be classified as either direct or indirect, according to the administrative arrangement for their collection. From Table 19.1 we see that direct taxes – in the form of income tax, capital taxes, corporation tax and petroleum revenue tax – were expected to produce 36.8% (189.4/514.6) of total government receipts in 2009/10. Income tax is by far the most important direct tax, alone contributing almost 27% of government receipts. Strictly speaking we should add the various National Insurance contributions to the total for direct taxation. These are a compulsory levy on employers, employees and the self-employed, expressed as a fixed percentage of total earnings, and paid directly to the Exchequer (shown under the 'Social Security receipts' heading). They total some £95.6bn in 2009/10 and provide around 18.6% of government receipts. They are not, however, included in the Consolidated Fund revenue tables.

Indirect taxes – VAT, a range of excise duties on oil, tobacco, alcohol and motor cars, and import duties – were expected to produce 24.1% of total government receipts in 2009/10. Of these VAT (13.6% of total 'receipts') was the most important.

Table 19.1 How public spending is paid for: income of general government.

	General government receipts (£bn)		
	1998/99	2009/10	2009/10 %
Inland Revenue:			
Income tax	86.4	140.0	
Corporation tax[1]	30.0	35.8	
Petroleum tax	0.5	0.9	
Windfall tax	2.6	0.0	36.8
Capital gains tax	1.8	2.5	
Inheritance tax	1.8	2.4	
Stamp duty	4.6	7.8	
Total Inland Revenue	**127.7**	**189.4**	
Customs & Excise:			
VAT	52.3	70.1	
Fuel duties	21.6	26.2	
Tobacco	8.2	8.8	
Alcohol	5.9	9.0	24.1
Air passenger duty	0.5	1.9	
Insurance premium tax	1.2	2.3	
Others[2]	0.5	5.9	
Total Customs & Excise	**94.0**	**124.2**	
Vehicle excise duties	4.7	5.6	
Oil royalties	0.3	–	
Business rates	15.3	24.3	8.8
Others[3]	8.3	15.7	
Total taxes	**250.3**	**359.2**	69.7
Social security receipts	55.1	95.6	
Council tax	12.1	25.0	
Interest and dividends	4.3	7.7	
Other receipts[3]	14.1	27.1	
Total receipts	**335.9**	**514.6**	**100.0**

Note: Items may not add up to totals because of rounding.
[1]Includes company tax credits.
[2]Includes Landfill Tax and Climate Change Levy, betting and gaming duties and customs duties.
[3]Net of own resource contributions to EU budget, VAT refunds, TV licenses and business rates payments by local authorities.
Source: Modified from HM Treasury (2010) *Budget Report 2010*, June.

Table 19.2 Public sector borrowing requirement, 1996–2010.

	£bn					
	1996/97	1999/2000	2002/03	2004/05	2007/08	2009/10
Public sector current expenditure	299.4	326.6	395.0	455.4	548.0	600.6
Public sector current receipts	288.8	359.3	397.1	451.3	535.6	514.6
Depreciation	12.5	12.6	13.8	15.0	17.8	19.7
Surplus on current budget	**−23.1**	**20.0**	**−11.7**	**−19.0**	**−30.2**	**−105.6**
Net investment	5.3	4.4	12.2	20.7	29.3	49.0
Public sector net borrowing	**28.4**	**−15.7**	**24.0**	**39.7**	**34.6**	**154.7**
(% GDP)	(3.6)	(−1.7)	(2.3)	(3.4)	(2.4)	(11.0)
Financial transactions	−5.7	7.1	−1.5	−1.0	−3.4	−10.7
Net cash requirement	**22.7**	**−8.5**	**22.5**	**38.7**	**31.2**	**144.0**
(% GDP)	(2.9)	(−0.9)	(2.1)	(3.3)	(2.2)	(10.2)

Note: Items may not add up to totals because of rounding.
Sources: Adapted from HM Treasury (2010) *Budget Report 2010*, June; ONS (2010a) *Financial Statistics*, October.

The indirect taxes are collected by Revenue and Customs.

This Consolidated Fund revenue (£359.2bn), together with social security receipts (£95.6bn), business rates (some £24.3bn) and the Council Tax (£25.0bn) plus other miscellaneous receipts, are necessary to pay for the government's expenditure plans outlined in Chapter 18.

Details of the main items of government income and expenditure are shown in Table 19.2. The growing economy of the late 1980s helped contribute to increased tax revenue and the creation of *budget surpluses* from 1987/88 to 1990/91. However, these surpluses shrank rapidly after 1989 as government revenue fell and government expenditure rose in the wake of the most protracted period of recession since the inter-war years. The government's budget situation from the second half of the 1990s can be seen in Table 19.2. This format follows the new European system of accounts and shows the strong growth in public sector current receipts after 1996/97. For example, between 1998/99 and 2000/01 (not shown in Table 19.2) both the *public sector net borrowing* (formerly called the financial deficit) and the *net cash requirement* (formerly the public sector borrowing requirement) were negative, which meant that the government was in the healthy position of being able to repay debt. However, from 2001/02 onwards this trend was reversed as the government's

borrowing increased once more. This reversal was mainly due to a slowdown in the rate of economic growth (slower growth in tax receipts) and the government's increasing commitment to public expenditure on education and health. The significant worsening of the public sector borrowing between 2007 and 2010 was the result of the combined effects of increased expenditure by the then Labour government, the effects of the financial crisis and the slow-down in economic growth.

The tax base

The tax base is essentially the 'object' to which the tax rate is applied. Excluding National Insurance contributions, taxes are usually grouped under three headings as regards tax bases: taxes on income (income, corporation and petroleum revenue taxes); taxes on expenditure (VAT and customs and excise duties); and taxes on capital (capital gains and inheritance tax).

Figure 19.1 shows that for 2009/10, taxes on income were expected to yield 49.2% of the Total Tax Revenue of £359.2bn, taxes on expenditure 36.7% and taxes on capital 1.4%. In addition to these taxes (not in Fig. 19.1) there were compulsory levies in the form of Social Security receipts (National Insurance contributions) from individuals and companies of

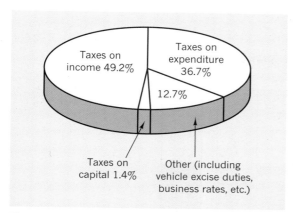

Fig. 19.1 Government revenue in 2009/10 and the tax base (as % of total tax revenue of £359.2bn).

£95.6bn and council tax of £25.0bn, raising the burden further on income.

Classifying taxes in terms of tax base, rather than method of collection, is often of more interest to economists, especially when calculating tax incidence (on whom the tax falls)! However, using the tax base does present problems of definition. For instance, Lord Wrenbury, in a legal judgment in 1925, defined income tax as being that which is 'within the Act, taxable under the Act'. National Insurance contributions, because they are based on calculations by actuaries, are not classified as a tax on income, yet they are levied as a percentage of income. Whatever the tax base, the taxes levied can be one of two types, either specific (lump sum) or *ad valorem*.

Specific and *ad valorem* taxes

A *specific tax* is expressed as an absolute sum of money per unit of the good. Excise duties are often of this kind, being so many pence per packet of cigarettes or per proof of spirit. An *ad valorem* tax is a percentage tax, levied not on volume but on value; e.g. in 2009/10 VAT was 17.5% (now 20%) of sales price, and corporation tax was 28% of assessable profits for larger companies and 21% for smaller companies.

Rate of taxation

Another useful classification is between progressive, proportional and regressive taxes. Tax is imposed as a rate or series of rates; e.g. income tax in 2009/10

was levied at 10% on savings income and a basic rate (20%) and higher rate (40%) on taxable income whilst VAT items that are not exempted are zero-rated or pay 17.5% (now 20%). These tax rates can be regarded as progressive, proportional or regressive, though such terms must be defined strictly as they are often used loosely. For a tax to be regarded as progressive, its rate structure must be such that the tax takes a rising proportion of total income as income increases; a proportional tax takes a constant proportion, whilst a regressive tax takes a declining proportion.

The pattern of UK taxation

A broadly proportional tax system

Since a progressive tax means that the rich pay more, not only in an *absolute* sense, but *as a proportion of their total income*, we need to know more than that the *marginal* rate of tax rises with income.[1] If, for instance, tax allowances and exemptions are more easily acquired by higher-income groups (as with mortgage repayments, etc.) then, despite a rising marginal rate, the individual may pay a smaller proportion of a higher total income in tax. In fact, it is the *average* rate[2] that is the best guide to whether the tax or tax system is, or is not, progressive. If the average rate is rising with income, then the tax *is* taking a higher proportion of higher incomes, i.e. the tax *is* progressive.

As we know from any game, say cricket, only when an individual scores more on his last (marginal) innings than his average for all previous innings, will his overall average actually rise. In the same way, only when the *marginal rate of tax is higher than the average rate*, will the average rate rise as income rises, and the tax be progressive. If the marginal and average rates are equal, then the average rate will be unchanged as income rises, so that the tax is proportional. If the marginal rate is below the average rate, then the average rate falls as income rises, and the tax is regressive.

Figure 19.2 shows that, for the UK, direct taxes (the unshaded area in each bar) are progressive, taking a larger proportion of the total (gross) income of richer households. Indirect taxes are in contrast regressive, taking a declining proportion of such income. Overall, taking *both* direct and indirect taxes

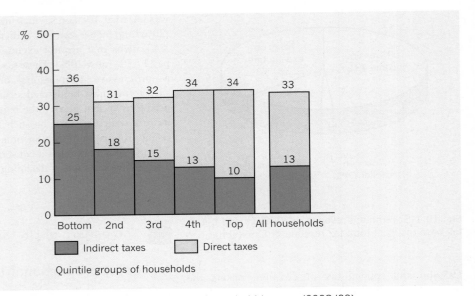

Fig. 19.2 Direct and indirect taxes as a percentage of gross household income (2008/09).
Source: Adapted from ONS (2010c), *The Effects of Taxes and Benefits on Household Income, 2008/09*, June.

Table 19.3 The regressiveness of indirect taxes (2008/09).

Quintile groups of households	Indirect taxes as percentage of *disposable* income per household		
	VAT	Other indirect taxes	Total indirect taxes
Bottom fifth	10.7	17.9	28.6
Next fifth	8.3	12.6	20.9
Middle fifth	7.2	10.4	17.6
Next fifth	7.1	9.5	16.6
Top fifth	5.5	6.6	12.1

Source: Adapted from ONS (2010c) *The Effects of Taxes and Benefits on Household Income, 2008/09*, June.

together, the UK tax system is broadly proportional to income.

Although indirect taxes as a whole are regressive, there is some variation between different types of indirect tax. As we observe from Table 19.3, VAT is a more mildly regressive tax, whereas other indirect taxes are strongly regressive.

A shift towards indirect taxation

We have seen that indirect taxes are more regressive than direct taxes. Here we chart the substantial

changes that took place in the direct/indirect tax ratio.

As Fig. 19.3 indicates, throughout the 1950s and 1960s taxes on income (direct) and expenditure (indirect) maintained a steady relationship, with taxes on income yielding around 10% more revenue. During the early and mid-1970s, however, the balance changed in favour of direct taxes on income as revenue providers for central government, due in part to inflation raising money incomes (and therefore direct tax receipts) and in part to fiscal drag. Fiscal drag is the extra tax yield which results from the fact that changes in both tax allowances and tax bands may

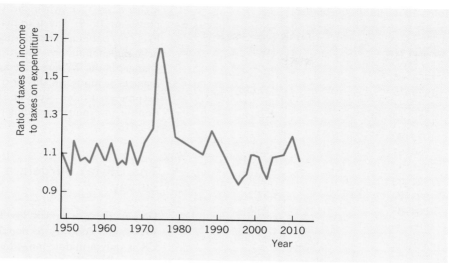

Fig. 19.3 The ratio of central government taxes on income to taxes on expenditure, 1949–2010.
Source: HM Treasury (2010) *Budget Report 2010*, and previous issues.

not occur until *after* inflation has had its impact on money incomes. By 1975 direct taxes on income had peaked, providing some 60% more revenue than taxes on expenditure. The ratio fell substantially after that, and by 1986 direct taxes provided only some 10% more revenue than taxes on expenditure. After 1986 the ratio began to edge upwards again as incomes increased, with growing prosperity in the economy raising the yield from direct taxes. However, in 1988/89 the Chancellor once more reversed the trend by permitting a substantial over-indexation of tax allowances. This, together with the increase in VAT rates to 17.5% in the 1991 Budget, has caused the ratio to continue its downward path before settling to a ratio closer to its 1950–70 trend. Indeed, actual and projected increases in indirect tax (e.g. VAT rose to 20% in January 2011) are likely to further reduce this ratio.

Income taxes are more 'visible' to individuals than expenditure taxes, which to some extent are hidden in product prices. This may well have contributed to the *feeling* that the UK was overtaxed, despite the fact that this is contradicted by the evidence (see Table 19.5 below). It may be helpful to look further into the factors helping to establish the pattern shown in Fig. 19.3.

With the slowing down of inflation in the mid- to late 1970s, the ratio of direct to indirect taxes in total revenue began to fall. The new Conservative government in 1979 then made a deliberate switch away from direct income taxation towards indirect taxation, cutting the standard rate of income tax from 33% to 30%, and raising VAT from 8% to 15%. We might have expected this switch to reinforce the downward trend in the ratio of direct to indirect tax receipts. In fact, higher inflation in the early years of that government prevented the ratio falling. Since the early 1980s, the receipts from direct taxes on income have fluctuated around an average figure some 10% above those from indirect taxes on expenditure; we have returned to the broad pattern of the 1950s and 1960s. The restored importance of indirect taxes, whatever its source, must, in the context of our earlier analysis, have made the UK tax system less progressive than it would otherwise have been.

A rise in the UK tax burden

We have seen that the *structure* of UK taxation has changed in recent years. What about the *level* of taxation? The ratio of total tax take to National Income is a frequently used measure of tax 'burden'. We can see from Table 19.4 that between 1964 and 1970 the total receipts from all taxes (including National Insurance) rose sharply as a proportion of

Table 19.4 The UK tax burden.

Fiscal year	Tax as a percentage of GDP*
1964–65	30.00
1969–70	37.50
1973–74	31.9
1978–79	33.1
1979–80	33.5
1980–81	35.5
1981–82	38.0
1982–83	38.2
1983–84	37.7
1984–85	38.2
1985–86	37.4
1986–87	37.0
1987–88	36.8
1988–89	36.1
1989–90	35.4
1990–91	34.9
1991–92	33.8
1992–93	32.7
1993–94	31.8
1994–95	33.0
1995–96	33.6
1996–97	34.0
1997–98	35.1
1998–99	35.5
1999–2000	35.5
2000–01	36.3
2001–02	35.8
2002–03	34.3
2003–04	34.3
2004–05	35.2
2005–06	35.9
2006–07	36.1
2007–08	36.4
2008–09	35.4

*Net taxes and National Insurance contributions as a percentage of money GDP.
Sources: Adapted from HM Treasury 2010, *Budget Report 2010*; Office for Budget Responsibility (2010) *Pre-budget Forecast*, June.

GDP. Between 1970 and 1974 the tax ratio fell from 37.5% to 31.9% before rising to a peak in 1984/85. There was then a drift downwards in the figures until 1993/94 with substantial income tax reductions. However, the tax burden of 35.4% in 2009 was at a higher level than when the Conservatives came to power in 1979. The fear that the tax burden was likely to continue to rise during the first decade of the new millennium has led to proposals for radical changes in the Welfare State to curb growing government expenditure in this area. These concerns have become even more acute in 2011 with sharp reductions in government spending planned over the period to 2015.

The UK tax burden: a comparative survey

Despite the rise in UK tax burden since the mid-1990s, and contrary to popular public opinion, the UK is only a middle-ranked country in terms of tax burden. From Table 19.5 we see that in 1981 the UK was the eighth-ranked country out of 20 in terms of tax burden, below the Scandinavian countries and close to Germany. OECD data in 2008 gave the UK a lower ranking of eleventh. Despite the high level of tax revenue as a proportion of GDP over this 20-year period, the UK tax burden in 2008 continued to lie well below that in the Scandinavian countries, where between 42% and 48% of GDP was taken in tax and social security contributions in that year, and was very similar to other major competitors such as Germany.

Tax burden and economic growth

It can be concluded from the evidence of Table 19.5 that there is little relationship between low tax burdens and faster economic growth. Belgium, with the third-highest tax burden in 2008, had an annual average growth rate of 2.5% in the period 1981–2008, close to the OECD average of 2.6% per annum, and was also ranked as high as ninth in terms of growth rate. On the other hand, Switzerland, with one of the lowest tax burdens, had only the sixteenth-fastest growth rate of 1.6% in that period, well below the OECD average.

Tax schedules and tax rates

We should, however, bear one or two cautionary points in mind before lapsing into complacency! A study by Messere *et al.* (1982) suggests that published *tax schedules* are a greater disincentive to effort than the 'effective tax rates' (i.e. the tax actually paid after

Table 19.5 Comparative tax burdens and economic growth.

Tax* as a percentage of GNP	1981		2008		GDP growth (yearly average) 1981–2008	
	Percentage	Rank	Percentage	Rank	Percentage	Rank
Australia	33.5	14	30.8	15	3.5	3
Austria	49.6	4	42.9	5	2.4	10
Belgium	49.6	4	44.3	3	2.5	=9
Canada	40.0	12	32.2	13	2.7	7
Denmark	55.6	3	48.3	1	1.9	14
Finland	39.6	13	42.8	6	2.5	=9
France	47.6	7	43.1	4	2.1	=13
Germany	42.3	9	36.4	10	2.1	=13
Greece	31.6	16	31.3	14	2.5	=9
Ireland	41.6	10	28.3	17=	5.6	1
Italy	33.4	15	43.2	3	1.7	15
Japan	28.3	19	28.3	17=	2.2	12
Luxembourg	40.0	11	38.3	8	5.2	2
Netherlands	49.4	6	37.5	9	2.6	=8
Norway	48.7	2	42.1	7	2.8	6
Spain	27.2	20	33.0	12	3.2	4
Sweden	56.9	1	47.1	2	2.3	11
Switzerland	30.8	18	29.4	16	1.6	16
United Kingdom	42.4	8	35.7	11	2.6	=8
United States	31.1	17	26.9	18	3.1	5

*Including social security contributions.
Sources: OECD (2010c) *Taxation: Key Tables for OECD*, April and previous issues; OECD (2010a) *Economic Outlook*, No. 87, Annex, Table 1.

all personal and other allowances have been calculated). The argument here is that it is tax schedules as shown in Table 19.6, widely publicized in newspapers and annual tax returns, which form the basis for the ordinary citizen's notion of tax burden.

In analysing tax schedules, the Messere study found that a higher proportion of taxpayers (over 95%) paid the basic rate in the UK than elsewhere, and that both the initial and top rates of tax on earned income were higher in the UK than elsewhere. Nevertheless, the taxpayer on average income in the UK paid a marginal rate no higher than in other OECD countries. Since 1987/88 the Conservative, Labour and (since 2010), Coalition governments have simplified the tax structure and reduced tax rates (as shown in Table 19.6 and Fig. 19.4) in order to try to encourage incentives. By the late 1990s, and as was

Table 19.6 UK income tax schedules, 1987/88 and 2010/11.

Rate of tax (%)	1987/88 Taxable income (£)	2010/11 Taxable income (£)
20	–	0–37,400
27	0–17,900	–
40	17,901–20,400	Over 37,400
45	20,401–25,400	–
50	25,401–33,300	Over 150,000
55	33,301–41,200	–
60	Over 41,200	–

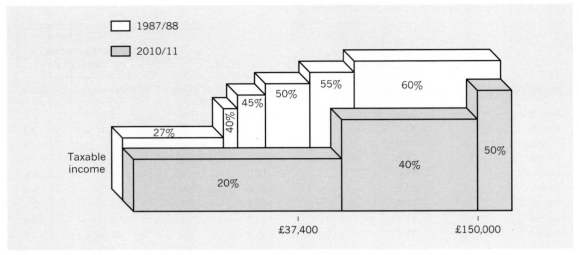

Fig. 19.4 Comparison of income tax between 1987/88 and 2010/11.

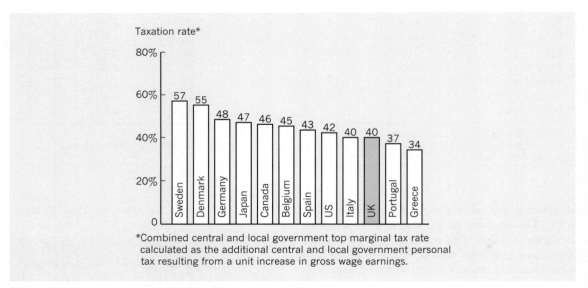

*Combined central and local government top marginal tax rate calculated as the additional central and local government personal tax resulting from a unit increase in gross wage earnings.

Fig. 19.5 Top marginal rates of personal income tax, 2009.
Source: Adapted from OECD (2010b) *Tax Database 2009*.

still the case in 2009, the Treasury could safely claim that the UK's top marginal rate of income tax at 40% was below that of its major competitors, as can be seen from Fig. 19.5. However, in April 2010 a new marginal rate of tax of 50% was introduced for those earning over £150,000 of taxable income, so that the UK is now less attractive than previously for high earners.

A further reason for taxpayers believing that the burden of taxation is higher than it actually is may arise from a failure to understand the method of collection of income tax. Income tax is *not* collected on the total amount of income. Each individual is granted allowances or exemptions that reduce the total amount of income liable to tax. In 2010/11 each single person under 65 was, for example, given an allowance of £6,475. These allowances, plus a few others, are deducted from the total income to produce the *taxable income*. Tax rates of 20%, 40% (on taxable incomes over £37,400) and 50% (on taxable incomes over £150,000) are then applied to this *taxable income*. Thus the average burden of taxation for the average taxpayer is considerably below the main 20% and 40% seen in the tax schedules.

Overall there appears little evidence that the UK has an excessive burden of tax in comparison to other countries. Although the proportion of GNP taken in tax has tended to rise in the UK since the early 1970s, the UK is, in comparative terms, a lower-ranked country in terms of tax-take, with tax (including Council Tax) amounting to 35.4% of GDP in 2009/10. However, particular groups of UK taxpayers at the lowest and highest taxable income scales did suffer unusually high marginal rates during the 1970s and 1980s. This, together with the growing 'visibility' of the income tax and social security payments system in the UK, may have created the impression of a comparatively high tax burden, but this impression was, in fact, misleading for the *average* taxpayer and arguably even for the *top* taxpayer (Fig. 19.5). The post-1988/89 reduction in tax rates and simplifications of the system have helped to improve the tax burden on low-income earners, and have reduced the overall burden of the tax system over the last 25 years as seen in Table 19.4.

Does the level of taxation matter?

Clarke suggested in 1945, with the support of Keynes, that when taxation of all kinds was more than 25% of National Income, damaging pressures would follow. In fact, most industrial countries passed this figure over 30 years ago, with tax ratios of over 40% for some countries in the 1970s, yet they experienced low inflation and rapid growth of real incomes. However, perceptions of the benign nature of taxation have begun to change in more recent years, reverting back to those of Clarke and Keynes. Two of the major criticisms of a high tax burden relate to its (alleged) erosion of economic incentives and its encouragement of tax avoidance and evasion. We now consider these criticisms.

Impact of taxes on incentives to work, save and take risks

As the reader familiar with indifference curve analysis will know, a higher tax on income will have two effects, which pull in opposite directions. First, there is an 'income effect', with real income reduced via higher taxes, which means less consumption of all items, including leisure, i.e. more work is performed. Second, there is a 'substitution effect', with leisure now cheaper via higher taxes, since less real income is now sacrificed for each unit of leisure consumed. The substitution effect leads to cheaper leisure being substituted for work, i.e. less work. On grounds of theory alone we cannot tell which effect will be the stronger, i.e. whether higher taxes on income will raise or lower the time devoted to work rather than leisure (where, of course, the worker has some choice).

The only general conclusions that can be drawn from indifference analysis are the following.

1 Progressive taxes have higher substitution effects, and are therefore likely to cause a greater increase in leisure consumption (i.e. less work) than if the same sum of money were raised via a proportional tax.

2 Taxes on savings create a strong disincentive to future savings via their double-taxation effect. Since saving takes place out of real disposable (net) income, to tax the returns on savings is to impose a further tax on net income.

3 Taxes on investment may discourage high-risk projects. Investment projects involve combinations of risk and yield, those with more risk usually providing more yield. If yields on investment income are more heavily taxed, then this may discourage high-risk investments, such as North Sea oil-prospecting, and encourage low-risk investments (including cash-holding).

Theory can take us little further than this general analysis. Beyond it we must look at actual behaviour to assess the impact of higher taxes on incentives. Empirical studies have taken three forms: (a) controlled experiments, usually observing how selected persons respond to higher benefits (negative taxes); (b) questionnaires based on random samples, and (c) econometric studies using data on how people have responded in the past to tax changes.

Studies up to 1970

Brown and Dawson (1969) conducted an exhaustive review of tax studies in the UK and USA from 1947 to 1968. They concluded that higher taxation had a disincentive effect on work (income < substitution effect) for between 5% and 15% of the population. These were mainly people who had the greatest freedom to vary their hours of employment – those without families, the middle-aged, the wealthy, and rural workers. In contrast, higher taxation had an incentive effect on work (income > substitution effect) for a rather smaller percentage of the population, who were characteristically part of large families, young, less well-off, urban dwellers. From a national viewpoint the small *net* disincentive effect on the population of higher taxes was regarded by Brown and Dawson as of little significance; over 70% appeared neutral (income = substitution effect) in their work response to higher taxes.

As regards the UK, two of the most important studies reviewed by Brown and Dawson were those based on questionnaires by Break (1957) and Fields and Stanbury (1971). In 1956, Break found a small *net* disincentive effect, with an extra 3% of the population claiming higher taxes to be a disincentive to further work than claimed it to be an incentive. In 1968 Fields and Stanbury updated Break's UK study and found the *net* disincentive effect to have grown to 8% of the population. In both studies the *net* disincentive effect was greater for higher-income groups, as one might expect with these paying higher marginal taxes (stronger substitution effects). This small growth in overall *net* disincentive effect between 1956 and 1968, and its being more pronounced at higher-income levels, was really all the empirical support there was in the UK for those suggesting that higher taxes discouraged work effort.

Studies after 1970

Controlled experiments and questionnaire results after 1970 gave no clearer a picture than those before 1970. If anything, they again pointed to a slight disincentive of higher taxes. For instance, Brown and Levin found that an increase in marginal tax rates for 2,000 Scottish workers in 1974 reduced hours worked, at least for higher-income groups. Fiegehen and Reddaway conducted a study on incentives amongst senior managers at board level in 94 companies in 1978, just before the large tax cuts introduced by the (then) newly

elected Conservative government a year or so later. Similarly to Break and Fields and Stanbury (see above), they showed that 12% of managers reported an incentive effect of high taxation on hours of work, while an equal percentage reported a disincentive effect. The most common response from 41% was 'no reply or don't know'. Fiegehen and Reddaway concluded: 'it is clear that, in total, any disincentive effects that operated on senior managers had a minimal impact on the activities of British industry'. Such studies were hardly a basis for advocating that tax *cuts* would lead to an upsurge in work effort! An important study by the Institute of Fiscal Studies (Dilnot and Kell 1988) tried to assess the effects of the 1979/80 reduction in the top rate of UK income tax from 83% to 60% on tax receipts. The argument used to support these top-rate tax cuts was that the lower income tax rates should provide extra incentives to work harder and thus boost tax revenue. The study found that the subsequent increase in tax revenue during the period to 1985/86 could be explained mostly by factors such as employment growth, growth of earnings and growth of self-employment rather than by any 'incentive' effects. Dilnot and Kell felt that any 'incentive' effect which may have been present could only account, at most, for £1.2bn or 3% of the total increase in tax revenues over the period studied.

Flemming and Oppenheimer (1996) also found little evidence to support the suggestion that reduced marginal tax rates at the upper end would unleash entrepreneurial talent and labour effort. They argued that if skilled or energetic workers supplied more effort (i.e. labour input/hours worked) as higher marginal tax rate fell, then one might expect that the *relative price* of their time/effort, i.e. wage per hour, would fall *vis-à-vis* other lower-skilled groups via an increase in relative supply resulting in a decrease in relative price (i.e. wage per hour). However, as noted in Chapter 14, pre-tax hourly earnings between different skill and occupational levels have widened considerably over the last 20 years, indicating that the higher-income earners have *increased* their relative wages. This rather suggests that the higher-income, higher-skilled segment of the workforce may not have increased the number of hours worked, i.e. the supply of effort, but may merely have benefited from *demand* changes which have moved in their favour, as discussed in Chapter 14. Interestingly, the disincentive to work resulting from high real marginal rates of tax is arguably more of a problem for those

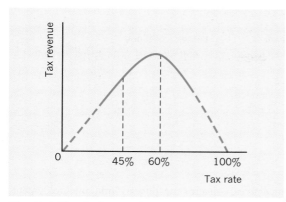

Fig. 19.6 The 'Laffer' curve.

on below-average incomes, as the discussion of the poverty 'trap' indicates below.

The Laffer curve

Professor Laffer derived a relationship between tax revenue and tax rates of the form shown in Fig. 19.6. The curve was the result of econometric techniques, through which a 'least squares line'[3] was fitted to past US observations of tax revenue and tax rate. The dotted line indicates the extension of the fitted relationship (continuous line), as there will tend to be zero tax revenue at both 0% and 100% tax rates. Tax revenue = tax rate × output (income), so that a 0% tax rate yields zero tax revenue, whatever the level of output. A 100% tax rate is assumed to discourage all output, except that for subsistence, again yielding zero tax revenue. Tax revenue must reach a maximum at some intermediate tax rate between these extremes.

The London Business School has estimated a Laffer curve for the UK using past data. Tax revenue was found to reach a peak at around a 60% 'composite tax rate', i.e. one which includes both direct and indirect taxes, as well as various social security payments, all expressed as a percentage of GDP. If the tax rate rises above 60% then the disincentive effect on output is so strong (i.e. output falls so much) that tax revenue (tax rate × output) actually falls, despite the higher tax rate. The Laffer curve in fact begins to flatten out at around a 45% composite tax rate. In other words, as tax rate rises above 45%, the disincentive effect on output is strong enough to mean that little extra tax revenue results. Econometric studies of this type have given support to those in favour of limiting overall rates of tax. It is interesting to note

that shortly after this study, the top rate of tax on earned income in the UK was indeed reduced from 83% to 60%.[4]

The reduction in the top income tax rate to 40% in 1988/89 was inspired by the Laffer curve and supply-side economics. The Chancellor of the Exchequer believed that the tax cuts would increase revenue. He based his tax cuts on American research by Lindsey that concluded that reductions in the top tax rates to the American government in 1981/82 were costless as the top 170,000 taxpayers ended up paying $26.6bn under new legislation instead of $26bn under the old. Lindsey argued that the tax cuts not only created incentives but also increased the *cost of tax avoidance*.

This research has been criticized partly because it is American evidence and partly because the American rates were slashed by 23% over three years, with the top personal rate being reduced from 70% to 50% whilst the UK moved from 60% to 40% in just one year. Finally, Lindsey and other tax experts have consistently argued that as tax rates are cut, economic efficiency is raised by reducing tax breaks and shelters at the same time. However, fresh evidence on the impact of cuts in high rates of British taxation has been provided by Minford and Ashton (see Brown 1988). The latter study concluded that the cut in the higher British tax rates to 40% would increase hours worked by 8%.

In summary, those who advocate 'supply-side economics', with tax reduction a key instrument for improving economic incentives, leading to an upsurge of productive activity, receive limited support from empirical studies. Only a small net disincentive effect has been found from studies using questionnaires, such as those by Break and by Fields and Stanbury. This conclusion was reinforced by the later study of Dilnot and Kell. On the other hand, the Laffer curve constructed for the UK by the London Business School, and work by Minford in the UK and Lindsey in the US, do indicate that *reductions* in the composite rate of tax below 60% and down as far as around 45%, have strong incentive effects on output – the converse of *rises* in tax rate between 45% and 60% having strong disincentive effects. However, we noted in Table 19.4 that the UK composite tax rate is currently less than 40%, and reductions below this level receive little support from econometric studies.

Nevertheless 'supply-side economics' has re-emerged in the taxation debate in recent times with the idea of a 'flat tax'.

Table 19.7 Impacts of various 'flat tax' options.

Average tax rate on taxpayers' total income	Flat tax rate on taxed income	Allowances and deductions	Losers – millions (net number)	Tax revenue lost
18	23	Unchanged	27	Nil
15	20	Personal allowances raised by £2,500	8	£10bn
13	18	Unchanged	None	£20bn

The idea of a single, low income tax rate to be paid by all, i.e. a 'flat tax', has been much discussed in recent times. For example, the Adam Smith Institute (ASI) has proposed a 'flat tax rate' of 22% with a personal allowance of £15,000 (over twice as high as the current allowance). The cost of setting such a high level of personal allowances – to lift the poorest out of tax – would be £63bn, but the ASI believed this could be recouped in three years as lower taxes create incentives for us all to work harder and to stop avoiding tax. The suggestion of supporters of the flat tax is that the British tax system has become so complex that few can understand it, unintended disincentives to work frequently occur, and failure to follow simpler, lower tax regimes in the rest of the world is undermining UK international competitiveness.

However, critics of the 'flat tax' approach point out that it is a myth that the poor will benefit from lower tax rates. For example, Brian Reading, of Lombard Street Research, noted that 50% of the total income tax revenue is actually paid by the top 10% of income earners, so that 10% (3 million people) would gain the most and the other 90% (27 million people) would lose the most from a move to a 'flat tax' regime which collected the same amount of income tax revenue as is currently collected *and* kept the same personal allowances. This would require a flat tax rate of 23% and would potentially result in 24 million losers 'net'.

Table 19.7 provides some useful data in this respect. The average tax rate is currently 18%, but the flat tax rate would have to be set higher than this because of personal allowances which remove taxes from initial slices of income.

Poverty and unemployment traps

One area where the facts do strongly suggest that the current level and type of taxation may have eroded incentives, concerns the 'poverty' and 'unemployment' traps. The families in these traps are enmeshed in a web of overlapping tax schedules and benefit thresholds, developed and administered by two separate departments (Department for Work and Pensions and the Treasury) with differing objectives in mind.

The 'poverty trap' describes a situation where a person on low income may gain very little, or even lose, from an increase in gross earnings. This is because as *gross* earnings rise, the amount of benefits paid out decreases while income tax deductions increase. In extreme circumstances, *net* income may actually fall when a person's gross earnings rise, i.e. an implicit marginal tax rate (or marginal net income deduction rate) of over 100%. After 1988, the government tried to resolve the gross disincentive effects of such high rates of deduction by relating benefits to net income after tax. However, the problems of the poverty trap dilemma still occur, if not to the same extent as before.

Table 19.8 shows the net income situation of a married man with two children in April 2009 when his gross income rises from £150 to £300 per week. We can see that net income rises little over this range. For example, an increase in income from £150 to £200, i.e. £50 per week, gives only an extra £2.25 in income after deductions, i.e. £47.75 is lost. This results in an implicit marginal tax rate (or marginal deduction rate) of about 95% (47.75/50). In 1992, using a similar family situation and gross income change, the rate was as high as 124%. The improvements in the family credit arrangements since 1992 have eased such extreme situations but the rates are still high and often provide little encouragement for those in the area of the poverty trap to work harder.

A high implicit marginal tax rate (marginal deduction rate) can therefore act as a major disincentive to low income earners. This point is further exemplified

Table 19.8 The poverty trap: married couple with two children under 11.[1]

	April 2009			
	(£ pw)	(£ pw)	(£ pw)	(£ pw)
Gross earnings[2]	150	200	250	300
Plus Child benefit	33.20	33.20	33.20	33.20
Child tax credit	96.32	96.32	96.32	96.32
Working tax credit	61.48	41.98	22.48	2.98
Housing benefit	20.78	11.03	1.28	–
Council tax benefit	12.16	9.16	6.16	3.16
Less				
Income tax	5.10	15.10	25.10	35.10
National insurance	4.40	9.90	15.40	20.90
Net income	**364.44**	**366.69**	**368.94**	**379.66**

[1]For a married man with two children under 11 with weekly Local Authority rent of £69.00 and Council tax of £27.00.
[2]30 hours per week at the minimum wage (April 2009) was £171.9.
Source: Adapted from Department for Work and Pensions (2009) *Tax/Benefit Model Tables (April 2009)*.

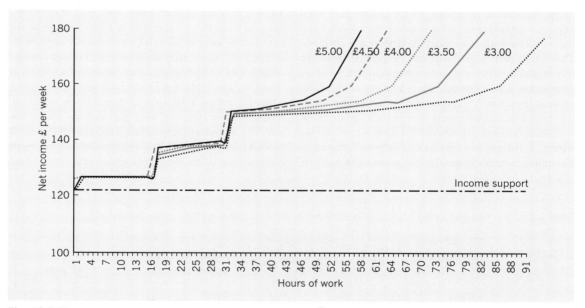

Fig. 19.7 Hours, wages and net family income: couple (one earner) with two children aged 4 and 6.
Source: *Child Poverty Action Group* (1998), Fig. 1.

by Fig. 19.7 which simulates the net income of a family with two young children and only one income earner, under different income circumstances just prior to the introduction of the Minimum Wage in 1999 (Child Poventy Action Group 1998).

The vertical axis presents *net* pay after all benefits (here income support) and tax payments have been taken into consideration. The horizontal axis presents the hours worked per week. The income support level for such a family under the Jobseekers' Allowance would be around £125 per week and would correspond to the income that the family would receive if the only wage earner in the family was unemployed. The two other lines in Fig. 19.7 denote the change in net income which the family would receive if the person *was* in employment. The net income lines are plotted for wages of between £3.00 and £5.00 per hour and, as one would expect, net income tends to rise in line with increases in the number of hours worked. Notice, however, that when the wage per hour is only £3.00, net income barely rises between 10 and 20 hours' work per week, and for more than 30 hours' work per week. For example, if the worker increases the number of hours worked from 30 to 80 hours a week, the net pay rises by only about 3p for every pound earned. In fact the 'plateaux' broadly represent the impact of the poverty trap. If wages increase to £5.00 per hour then there is much less evidence of any such plateaux. This analysis would seem to suggest that the reason for the existence of a poverty plateau is a combination of the complexity of the benefit/tax structure (which creates very high implicit marginal tax rates at lower income levels), and the very low wages per hour paid to many workers. The extent of this problem can be gauged from the fact that there were still some 1.8 million UK workers earning less than £3.40 per hour and some 3.75 million earning less than £3.50 per hour prior to the introduction of the £3.60 hourly minimum wage in 1999.

The continued problems of a low wage and its effects on the poverty trap can be seen in Table 19.9. The table presents figures for the number of workers in jobs paying less than the minimum wages for different age groups between 2004 and 2009. The estimates indicate that a total of 242,000 people were in jobs paying less than the minimum wage in 2009, comprising 0.9% of the workforce. In absolute terms, most of the people earning such low wages were over 22 years of age, but in percentage terms, it was the young people aged between 16 and 21 who had the highest figure. Although the low pay situation has improved since the late 1990s, it has been difficult to make major inroads into this intractable low pay/poverty trap problem.

As we have noted, the 'poverty trap' relates to people who are *in work* but find little incentive to improve their situation by extra work effort. On the other hand, some workers never even enter the labour market because of another problem, often called the 'unemployment trap'.

The 'unemployment trap' occurs when people find that their income when employed is no better than if they were unemployed. Taking figures for April 2009, Table 19.10 shows that when the gross wage of the married man in our example is £200 per week, the net income after various allowances and deductions is £366.69. If he was unemployed, his net income would be £334.95, i.e. the *replacement rate* is 91.34%. The replacement rate measures the proportion of a person's net income that will be 'replaced' by the benefit system if that person loses his or her job. The introduction of family credit in 1988 helped to decrease the number of people with replacement rates of over 100%. The replacement rate for a person

Table 19.9 Number and percentage of jobs paid below the national minimum wage in the UK.

	Jobs held by people aged 16–17		Jobs held by people aged 18–21		Jobs held by people aged 22+		All jobs	
	000s	(%)	000s	(%)	000s	(%)	000s	(%)
April 2004	–	(0.0)	44	(2.3)	233	(1.0)	276	(1.1)
April 2005	20	(4.0)	55	(3.0)	233	(1.0)	308	(1.2)
April 2006	14	(3.8)	44	(2.3)	238	(1.0)	296	(1.2)
April 2007	16	(4.0)	49	(2.6)	231	(1.0)	296	(1.1)
April 2008	16	(3.9)	46	(2.5)	212	(0.9)	274	(1.0)
April 2009	14	(4.1)	44	(2.6)	184	(0.8)	242	(0.9)

Source: ONS (2010b) *Statistical Bulletin: Low Pay Estimates 2009*.

Table 19.10 The unemployment trap: unemployed married couple with two children under 11.*

In work	£ pw	Out of work	£ pw
Gross earnings	200	Jobseekers' allowance	100.95
Child benefit	33.20	Child benefit	33.20
Child tax credit	96.32	Child tax credit	96.32
Working tax credit	41.98	Housing benefit	69.00
Housing benefit	11.03	Council tax benefit	27.00
Council tax benefit	9.16	Meals and welfare	8.48
Less			
Income tax	15.10		
National insurance	9.90		
Net income	366.69	Net income	334.95
Replacement ratio	$\frac{334.95}{366.69} = 91.34$		

*For a married man with two children under 11 with weekly Local Authority rent of £69.00 and Council tax of £27.00. Unemployed married couple with one earner previously working more than 30 hours a week.
Source: Adapted from Department for Work and Pensions (2009) *Tax/Benefit Model Tables* (April 2009).

in the same situation as our present example in 1992 was 104%, representing a marginal improvement. However, the fact that the income of a person when out of work is still around 91% of his income when in work provides little incentive to work.

From these examples, we can see that both poverty and unemployment traps provide a disincentive to work because people caught in these problematic situations find it difficult, if not impossible, to improve their position through their own efforts.

Impact of taxes on avoidance and evasion

Tax avoidance is legal; tax evasion is illegal, involving concealment in one form or another, and therefore fraud.

The black economy

The Inland Revenue has estimated that tax evasion was equal to between 6% and 8% of GDP in the UK – often called the 'black economy'. However, other estimates have suggested that the black economy may even be as high as 10–12% of GDP (Lyssiotou *et al.* 2004). A National Audit Office report in 2008 calculated that there were approximately 2 million people

involved in the black economy and that it had increased by 13% in real terms between 2003/04 and 2006/07. The value of the 'black or hidden economy' was calculated in 2006/07 as £145m which is equal to the GDP of Portugal, or as much as the UK Treasury earned from income tax in 2009/10 (see Table 19.1). One way in which the black economy can be estimated is through the difference between National Income when measured by the income method and when measured by the expenditure method. Apart from errors and omissions, these are defined in the National Accounts in such a way that they come to the same value. If, however, people receive income and do not declare it in tax returns, it will not appear on the income side, though expenditure will increase as the unrecorded income is spent on goods and services. In recent years the 'income' valuation – based on tax returns – has fallen short of the 'expenditure' valuation by progressively larger amounts.

Direct versus indirect taxes

In Fig. 19.3 above we observed a switch from direct to indirect taxation since the late 1970s. We noted that this switch entailed a move towards a more regressive system of taxation, i.e. one which takes a *smaller proportion* of higher incomes. This must follow since we move away from direct taxes which we saw to be progressive, towards indirect taxes, which at best are proportional (VAT), and more usually are regressive (the Community Charge – now the Council Tax, Uniform Business Rate, excise duties, import duties, etc.). It might be useful to consider in *more general terms* the advantages and disadvantages of direct and indirect systems of taxation. For convenience we shall compare the systems under four main headings, with indirect taxes considered first in each case.

Macroeconomic management

Indirect taxes can be varied more quickly and easily, taking more immediate effect, than can direct taxes. Since the Finance Act of 1961, the Chancellor of the Exchequer has had the power (via 'the regulator') to vary the rates of indirect taxation at any time between Budgets. Excise and import duties can be varied by up to 10%, and VAT by up to 25% (i.e. between 13.13% and 21.87% for a 17.5% rate of VAT). In contrast, direct taxes can be changed only at Budget time. In the case of income tax, any change involves time-consuming revisions to PAYE codings. For these reasons, indirect taxes are usually regarded as a more flexible instrument of macroeconomic policy.

Economic incentives

We have already seen how, in both theory and practice, direct taxes on income affect incentives to work. We found that neither in theory nor in practice need the *net* effect be one of disincentive. Nevertheless, it is often argued that if the *same sum* were derived from indirect taxation, then any net disincentive effect that did occur would be that much smaller. In particular, it is often said that indirect taxes are less visible (than direct), being to some extent hidden in the quoted price of the good. However, others suggest that consumers are well aware of the impact of indirect taxes on the price level. Let us look in more detail at the direct versus indirect argument, first in relation to incentives to work and second in relation to incentives to save and take risks.

Work effort

In terms of effects on the supply of work effort, a case against the current system of direct taxes and in favour of a switch towards indirect taxes might be made in the *specific* cases of poverty and unemployment traps. However, no *general* case can be made for such a switch. In fact, both income and substitution effects of a rise in indirect taxes are in the same direction as those for a rise in direct taxes. By raising the prices of goods, higher indirect taxes also reduce real income, and at the same time reduce the cost of leisure in terms of goods forgone. In other words, the income and substitution effects we considered above apply to higher indirect taxes as well as to higher direct taxes. Whether the *magnitude* of the income and substitution effects will be the same for indirect as for direct taxes is quite another matter. It will partly depend upon which items are taxed. If indirect taxes are levied on goods with highly inelastic demand curves, then the indirect taxes will be largely passed on to consumers as higher prices. Both income and substitution effects will then be substantial in magnitude. Of course the converse also applies – if the indirect taxes are levied on goods with elastic demand curves, both income and substitution effects will be small. We can make no general claim for 'superiority' of either type of tax with regard to work incentives.

Saving and risk-taking

With regard to incentives for saving, indirect taxes have the advantage of avoiding the 'double-taxation effect' imposed by direct income taxes. Saving takes place out of net income, i.e. income that has already been taxed. To tax the return on savings, via a tax on investment income (e.g. dividends), is to impose a type of double taxation on that income, an obvious disincentive to saving. This is, however, a weak argument in support of indirect taxes as it is quite possible to devise a system of direct taxation that avoids double taxation.

The argument that indirect taxes are to be preferred because they avoid the discrimination against risky investments of a direct tax system can also be rebutted. Risky investments do usually have higher yields, and do therefore pay more direct tax than less risky investments. However, such discrimination could be reduced, perhaps by raising the value of allowances (e.g. on exploration costs, etc.) that can be set against tax.

In terms of incentives, then, there is no general case to be made for or against one or other type of tax system. If we are to be more specific, we must compare one particular type of indirect tax system with one particular type of direct tax system.

Economic welfare

It is sometimes argued that indirect taxes are, in welfare terms, preferable to direct taxes, as they leave the taxpayer free to make a choice. The individual can, for instance, avoid the tax by choosing not to consume the taxed commodity. Although this 'voluntary' aspect of indirect taxes may apply to a particular individual and a particular tax, it cannot apply to all individuals and all taxes. In other words, indirect taxes cannot be 'voluntary' for the community as a whole. If a chancellor is to raise a given sum through a system of indirect taxes, individual choices not to consume taxed items must, if widespread, be countered either by raising rates of tax or by extending the range of goods and services taxed.

Another argument used to support indirect taxes on welfare grounds is that they can be used to combat 'externalities'. In Chapter 10 we noted that an externality occurs where private and social costs diverge. Where private costs of production are below social costs, an indirect tax could be imposed, or increased, so that price is raised to reflect the true social costs of production. Taxes on alcohol and tobacco could be justified on these grounds. By discriminating between different goods and services, indirect taxes can help reallocate resources in a way that raises economic welfare for society as a whole.

On the other hand, indirect taxes have also been criticized on welfare grounds for being regressive, the element of indirect tax embodied in commodity prices taking a higher proportion of the income from lower-paid groups. Nor is it easy to correct for this. It would be impossible administratively to place a higher tax on a given item for those with higher incomes, although one could impose indirect taxes mainly on the goods and services consumed by higher-income groups, and perhaps at higher rates.

In terms of economic welfare, as in terms of economic incentives, the picture is again unclear. A case can be made with some conviction both for and against each type of tax.

Administrative costs

Indirect taxes are often easy and cheap to administer. They are paid by manufacturers and traders, which are obviously fewer in number than the total of individuals paying income tax. This makes indirect taxes, such as excise and import duties, much cheaper to collect than direct taxes, though the difference is less marked for VAT, which requires the authorities to deal with a large number of mainly small traders.

Even if indirect taxes do impose smaller administrative costs than direct taxes for a given revenue yield, not too much should be made of this. It is, for instance, always possible to reform the system of PAYE and reduce administrative costs. The Inland Revenue is, in fact, considering a change from PAYE to an American system of income tax, with the obligation on taxpayers themselves to estimate and forward tax, subject to random checks. Also, the computerization of Inland Revenue operations may, in the long run, significantly reduce the administrative costs associated with the collection of direct taxes.

In summary, there is no clear case for one type of tax system compared to another. The macroeconomic management and administrative cost grounds may appear to favour indirect taxes, though the comparison is only with the *current* system of direct taxation. That system can, of course, be changed to accommodate criticisms along these lines. On perhaps the more important grounds of economic incentives and economic welfare the case is very mixed, with arguments for and against each type of tax finely balanced. To be more specific we must compare the particular and detailed systems proposed for each type of tax.

Tax and social security reform

The subject of tax reform is a topic in its own right and can only be touched upon here. Tax reform had been low on the political agenda before 1965, with the basic structure of taxes remaining unchanged for decades. Since then there have been more new taxes introduced than in any other equivalent peacetime period. Changes have included the introduction and repeal of selective employment tax; VAT replacing purchase tax; corporation tax replacing profits tax; the amalgamation of surtax and income tax; new taxes such as gambling and betting duties, and capital gains tax; and the replacement of estate duty first by capital transfer tax and subsequently by an inheritance tax.

Local taxation

In the late 1980s the Conservative government increased the pace of its tax reform. It introduced the Community Charge in England and Wales during 1990 (in Scotland during 1989), together with the Uniform Business Rate (UBR) in the same year. The unpopularity of the Community Charge or 'poll tax' led to its replacement in April 1993 by the Council Tax.

The 'rates' system

The Community Charge was introduced to replace what was seen as the 'unfairness' of the old local authority rates system. The rates were a property tax, paid by tenants and owner occupiers. The total amount paid per household in tax was based on two figures: first, on the 'rateable value' of the property, which was a value based on an assessment of what the property could earn if it were let out on the open market; and second, on a 'poundage' expressed as 'so many pence in the pound'. This was calculated by the local authority in accordance with the revenue it needed to raise to pay for local services. For example, if the local authority valued a house at £30,000 and the local poundage was 2p in the pound, then the total rates for that house would be £30,000 × 0.02 or £600 per year. There were persistent complaints that the rates system was complicated and inequitable, for instance because it was difficult to properly assess the rentable value of any property. It was also based on the household unit, irrespective of how many people were actually living in the household. Also the rates had a regressive effect on some members of the public, e.g. on elderly people who sometimes occupied large, highly rated properties but who could no longer afford to pay the rates demanded since their incomes were insufficient. Finally, the total rates collected by this method were often inadequate to meet the increasing cost of local government spending on education, etc. As a result, this system was abolished for domestic premises and replaced by the Community Charge in 1990. For business premises the rating principle was retained in a modified form known as the Uniform Business Rate (UBR).

Hypothecation

A recent approach favoured by many as a means of raising the tax take whilst retaining public support, involves the idea of *hypothecation*. This is the allocation of current or additional taxes to *specific* spending outcomes. An example is the suggestion in the 1992 election manifesto by the Liberal Democrats that an extra 1% should be added to the basic rate of income tax and the entire extra revenue raised be used for education spending.

The Uniform Business Rate (UBR)

The UBR payable on any commercial property is based on two factors – the rateable value of that property, and a UBR 'multiplier'. The rateable value represents the annual rental value of the property on the open market and is fixed by an independent valuation officer, with rateable values reviewed periodically throughout the UK. To determine the actual amount of UBR to be paid per year, the rateable value is then multiplied by a rating 'multiplier' or poundage. The Standard UBR multiplier in England for 2009/10 was 48.5p in the pound.

One of the inevitable problems with this new tax was that business properties in the more dynamic or prosperous areas would find their valuations rising overnight to a much higher level than before, while other businesses in less prosperous areas would experience a fall in their valuations. The UBR also represented a change in that the 'poundage rate' under this scheme was now set by central government and not by the local authority. Although the local authorities actually collect the UBR, the receipts are paid into a central fund outside local authority control. The fund is then redistributed to local authorities at a fixed rate per adult, with extra finance made available to those local authorities with special problems. This is clearly a further curbing of local authority financial control.

The Community Charge

Unlike the UBR, the *Community Charge* sought to depart from the old rating system method of calculating local taxes. The Community Charge was to be based not on the household, but on the individual. In other words, the Community Charge (or poll tax) was a personal tax assessed on each adult and expressed in the form of a lump-sum payment per year.

The Community Charge was unpopular because it meant an increase in tax for many families, especially those with a number of adults living in one household. It was also accused of being a regressive tax, in that the fixed charge per head tended to affect low income earners more than high income earners despite the existence of rebates for poor families. Also, the cost of administering the tax was high, at some 4% of its yield, whereas other taxes cost less than half that amount to collect. Many of these costs were associated with the need to register individuals and with the problems of chasing non-payers. The tax also created tensions between central government and some local authorities who felt that their 'needs' were greater than was implied by their Standard Spending Assessment (see below). As a result, some local authorities (often in hard-pressed urban areas) put an extra levy on their Community Charge. This increase in the Community Charge in major urban areas resulted in a general dissatisfaction with this form of local taxation. The intense unpopularity of the Community Charge led to its replacement by the Council Tax on 1 April 1993.

Council Tax

The *Council Tax* is a hybrid tax, which is both part property or household tax and part personal tax. The Council Tax is based on the capital value of each property, on the assumption that it contains two-adult members. If the property contains only one adult, then he or she will pay only 75% of the bill of a two-adult household. No additional tax is paid on a property where more than two adults reside. Also, personal discounts are given to certain classes of adults, e.g. those on very low incomes, handicapped people, those in full-time education, and so on. It has been calculated that about 25% of all households are entitled to some form of Council Tax rebate.

Properties are valued on a sample basis (e.g. one house may be taken as typical of that street or area) and assigned to specific property bands, as shown in Table 19.11. The average national property value is calculated and assigned to the appropriate band, i.e. band D in this case. From this base, the tax bills for properties in both higher and lower bands are calculated. For example, the average property value in England in 2009/10 was deemed to be £80,000, i.e. it is located in band D – between £68,000 and £88,000 (column one). This means that this band ranges from between 85% and 110% of the average property value (second column). Therefore the tax paid by property owners in band D is regarded as the 'average', i.e. 100 (third column). Properties which are valued at under £40,000 will pay 67% of the average bill, those valued at between £88,000 and £120,000 will pay 122% of the average bill, and so on.

The central government calculates a Standard Spending Assessment (SSA) for each authority based

Table 19.11 Council Tax: bands and property values, 2009/10 (England).

Band	Property value (£)	Property value (% of national average)	Council tax (% of average property)	Average bill* (£)
A	Under 40,000	up to 50	67	934
B	40,001–52,000	50–65	78	1,090
C	52,001–68,000	65–85	89	1,245
D	68,001–88,000	85–110	100	1,401
E	88,001–120,000	110–150	122	1,712
F	120,001–160,000	150–200	144	2,023
G	160,001–320,000	200–400	167	2,335
H	Over 320,000	400–500	200	2,802

*For a property in SE England (2 or more adults).

Source: Adapted from *Guide to 2009/10 Council Tax and Business Rate* (2010).

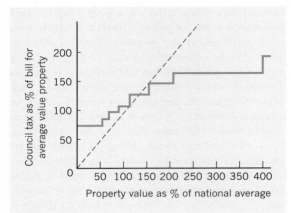

Fig. 19.8 Council Tax: property values and tax in each band.
Source: Adapted from *Guide to 2009/10 Council Tax and Business Rate* (2010) www.communities.gov.uk/documents.

on its estimate of the amount of money the authority needs to provide a 'standard' level of service given the demographic and other characteristics of the local area. The government grant to each local authority is then equal to its SSA *minus* an estimate of how much the authority can raise from other sources, e.g. Community Charge and the UBR. If all authorities kept to their SSA, then the actual average household bill would be shown in column four of Table 19.11.

There are some points worth noting about this scheme. First, the Council Tax, as in the case of rates, is a regressive tax in that occupiers of properties of below-average value pay proportionately more in tax, while occupiers of properties of above-average value pay proportionately less in tax. This can be seen from Fig. 19.8, in that the Council Tax line is flatter than the dotted 45% line, which would represent a proportionate tax. However, it may be said to be fairer than the Community Charge in that the tax does, at least, rise with the value of the house and it is reasonable to assume that those living in more expensive houses have higher incomes than those living in less expensive dwellings. Second, the administration of the scheme will be much easier because, unlike the Community Charge, collection is based on the household and not on the individual. Third, as with the Community Charge, the central government will still estimate the amount each local authority 'needs' to spend, i.e. the SSA. If a local council exceeds this amount, then the local Council Tax will be increased

by a factor *greater than* the excess spending (i.e. the high-spending councils are penalized).

It has been calculated that some 37% of families were better off, and 37% worse off, as a result of the change from Community Charge to the Council Tax.

Tax, social welfare policies and work incentives

In addition to the significant changes which have taken place in local taxation, there have also been attempts by government to modify the tax structure in order to make it more equitable, while at the same time encouraging savings and increasing the base of UK share ownership. For example, the Approved Profit Sharing scheme (APS), the SAYE scheme and the Discretionary Share Option Scheme all provide tax incentives for employees to buy shares in their companies. Also the Personal Equity Plans (PEPs) introduced initially in 1986 encouraged small savers to invest in UK companies through unit and investment trusts. By making the income and capital gains from investing in such trusts free of tax, up to a maximum amount of £6,000 a year, it was hoped that savings would be encouraged, thereby helping to channel investment into UK industry. In April 1999, these were replaced by Individual Savings Accounts (ISAs). For example, during the 2009/10 tax year, savers can invest up to £10,200 tax free in an ISA with the advantage that they can have instant access to the tax-free saving. ISAs have also been sold by a wider range of providers, e.g. by post offices and supermarkets, as well as by the financial institutions. It is difficult to measure the success of such share and savings schemes in stimulating UK industry, since any increase in share ownership by employees will not necessarily improve company performance *per se*.

On the personal taxation front, 1990 saw the introduction of a greater measure of equity, in that independent taxation for married couples was introduced. This gave married women independent status as taxpayers, i.e. they could control their own tax affairs. Since 1805 husbands had been legally responsible for the married couple's tax affairs and any married couple's allowance had been received by the husband. In the budget of 1992 it was announced that from 1993/94 onwards any extra married allowance can be claimed in its entirety by *either* husband or wife, or it can be shared equally between them, thus making the tax system fairer to married women. In 1999, the married couple's allowance was abolished, leaving a working husband and wife each receiving the single person's allowance.

As far as the social security system was concerned, the government introduced important measures in 1988 to modify the whole system. These covered unemployment benefits, pensions, income support, housing benefits, a family credit system and the social funds. The State Earnings Related Pensions Scheme (SERPS), which provided a pension based on National Insurance contributions, was cut back. Designated occupational pension schemes could now 'contract out' of SERPS. This meant that state pensions would be reduced, but the private scheme must then guarantee to at least make up the difference. Contracted-out workers pay a rate of National Insurance contribution reduced by 2%, as do their employers. At the same time the old supplementary benefit and heating allowances were abolished and a new system of income support was introduced.

The incoming Labour government of 1997 built on these reforms in order to tackle both the poverty and unemployment traps discussed earlier. A Jobseeker's Allowance (JSA) had already been introduced in 1996 to encourage more active job search during the first months of unemployment. Under the JSA the unemployed person and the Employment Service Adviser must draw up an agreement specifying what is expected of the unemployed person if they are to continue receiving the allowance. In April 1998 the government's 'New Deal' or 'Welfare to Work' initiative took such measures further by offering wage subsidies to employers to take on the unemployed and by offering new training and education opportunities.

From April 2001 the New Deal programme was extended to cover many groups, including young people aged 18–24 years, adults over 25 years old, lone parents, the disabled, the over 50s and musicians. The greatest emphasis was on the first group, i.e. the New Deal for Young People (NDYP) to improve job search and interview skills through consultation sessions and training by approved organizations. If the person still failed to obtain work, then four options were available – they could opt for a subsidised job placement and a training allowance while being paid a wage by the employer; for full-time education for up to 12 months; for work in the voluntary sector; or for work with the Environmental

Task Force. Participation in one of the four options was mandatory in order to receive benefits and a refusal to participate led to the benefit being stopped.

From October 2009 a Flexible New Deal was introduced, which was designed to upgrade the New Deal and place greater emphasis on a stronger framework of rights and responsibilities, with more attention being placed on providing jobs that offer opportunities for progression. The Flexible New Deal is delivered for Jobcentre Plus by organizations called 'Providers' who help the unemployed to find work. The package includes the provision of work experience for four weeks to improve the chances of finding a permanent job. Over the period 1999–2009, it has been estimated that the New Deal structure has helped 1.8 million people into jobs and placed an extra 300,000 lone parents into work. Research by the Institute for Fiscal Studies found that NDYP increased the probability of finding a job by 20% while work by the National Institute of Economic and Social Research (NIESR) found that NDYP benefited the economy by £500m per year (Department for Work and Pensions 2008).

Perhaps the biggest change in the 'welfare to work' system has been the introduction of tax credits as a means of alleviating poverty and improving incentives to work. Under this system, help is given to the needy through the tax system rather than as a 'handout' from the benefit agencies. The Working Family Tax Credit (WFTC) system operated from 1999 to 2003 but was replaced by the Child Tax Credit (CTC) and the Working Tax Credit (WTC) in April 2003. The Child Tax Credit is paid directly by the Inland Revenue to the main carer in the family, whilst the Working Tax Credit is paid through the wage packet to working people (those with or without children).

In 2009/10, there were many types of benefits available on the WTC scheme, depending on people's particular situations. For example, a working couple with one child could claim the basic element of £1,890 per year plus up to 80% of the costs of childcare up to a maximum limit of £175 per week. The family's income in the previous tax year is then compared with the threshold figure of £6,420. If that income is *below* that threshold, then the full WTC is given, but if the income is *above* the threshold, then the maximum WTC is reduced by 39p for every £1 of excess income.

The CTC is paid to families with children regardless of whether the parents work. Families with incomes up to £13,910 would qualify for £545 per year in the form of a 'family element' of the credit, plus a 'child element' of £2,300 for each child. Families earning between £16,190 and £50,000 receive only the family element of the credit and this element is also gradually taken away for incomes above £50,000 until it becomes zero at £58,000.

Finally, the benefit system in the UK provides Child Benefit (CB) to all children under 16 years old and also to those under 20 years old who are in full-time education. In 2010 the benefits were £20.30 per week to the oldest child and £13.40 per week for other children.

By guaranteeing minimum incomes and adjusting take-home pay through tax credits, the new system attempts to overcome the poverty and unemployment traps illustrated in Tables 19.8 and 19.10. The new system was designed to be more generous whilst at the same time providing an incentive to work by decreasing the implicit tax rates (marginal deduction rates) discussed previously. The main problem with these various types of benefits is the 'take-up rate'. However, figures released in 2010 showed more impressive results than for previous benefit systems in that some 81% of eligible families claimed CTC. For WTC, the take-up rate was much less, showing only a 57% take-up rate. The hope is that the WTC and CTC will, over time, build on the old WFTC which had already begun to increase incentives to work for certain groups, i.e. unemployed households and single-parent families (Blundell 2000). A recent assessment of the effects of the old WFTC shows that it also had strong employment effects on married mothers in *poor households* in that the childcare component of the WFTC made it more likely for mothers to remain in the workforce and/or stimulated such mothers to enter the labour market (Francesconi *et al.* 2009). A study carried out by the Institute for Fiscal Policy in 2001 attempted to analyse the potential effect of the new credits (WTC and CTC) and noted that the poorest 30% of families would probably gain an average of 2.7% in income as a result of the new changes. However, the report also indicated that the work incentive effect of the new credit system may not be very significant, because for people without children, entering work *already* increases income significantly above the welfare benefit level. In part this is because benefits currently available when such

people are unemployed are relatively low (Clark and Myck 2001). This relatively weak relationship between the new CTC/WTC and incentives to work was substantiated by research undertaken over the period 2002–05 for the Joseph Rowntree Foundation. The study found that WTC made no difference to the number of hours that women in families worked and that the employment rates of lone parents or mothers in couple families were in fact lower for those receiving CTC (Chzhen and Middleton 2007). The overall incentive effects of such benefits on employment is therefore uncertain and seems to affect various groups of relatively poor people in different ways.

Conclusion

The UK tax system is broadly proportional. Direct taxes are, as a group, *progressive* in the UK, taking a larger proportion of the income of richer households. Indirect taxes are, as a group, *regressive*, though this is not the case for all indirect taxes. VAT is broadly proportional with the exception of the top fifth of income earners. The movement towards indirect taxation has therefore made the UK tax system less progressive than it would otherwise have been. The overall tax burden measured as a *percentage of GDP* has fluctuated since the late 1960s and rose during the 1990s to levels experienced in the early 1980s. However, the UK is not overtaxed compared to other countries. Neither does higher tax necessarily mean lower economic growth. Certainly the empirical case for higher taxes being a disincentive to effort and output is rather flimsy, whether from questionnaire or econometric study. There can be no general presumption in favour of either indirect or direct taxation, when we assess each system in terms of macro-management, economic incentives, economic welfare and administrative costs. The dilemma of how to construct an equitable and efficient form of local taxation remains, while the complicated relationships between tax changes and social security benefits still create difficulties for those families caught in the poverty or unemployment 'traps'. Various 'welfare to work' reforms are aiming to provide greater opportunities and incentives to those seeking employment.

Key points

- Taxes on *income* account for around 50% of all tax receipts, with taxes on *expenditure* around 37%.

- UK *direct* taxes are progressive while *indirect* taxes are regressive. Overall, the UK has a broadly proportional tax system.

- The UK tax burden as a percentage of GDP has averaged over 35% of GDP over the past decade.

- The UK is a middle-ranked country in terms of tax revenue as a percentage of GDP, i.e. in terms of 'tax burden'.

- There is no clear relationship between high income tax rates and disincentives to work. Detailed surveys show only a potentially small disincentive effect.

- A current topic of debate is the so-called 'flat tax', with a single tax rate levied on all earned income.

- The 'poverty trap' has improved since 1992 with implicit marginal tax rates for some households falling from 124% in 1992 to around 95% by 2009. Low hourly wages tend to worsen the poverty trap situation, though the minimum wage may help in this respect.

- The 'unemployment trap' has eased slightly, with replacement rates for an unemployed married couple with two children falling from 104% in 1992 to 91% by 2009.

- Labour market reforms, such as the Working Tax Credit (WTC) and the Child Tax Credit (CTC), and other 'Welfare to Work' initiatives have gone some way in helping relieve the unemployment and poverty 'traps'.

Now try the self-check questions for this chapter on the Companion Website. You will also find useful links to relevant websites.

Notes

1 As it does in the UK, e.g. 20% on the first £37,400 of taxable income, 40% on taxable income up to £150,000 and 50% on higher income.

2 The average rate is total tax paid, divided by total income.

3 That is, that line which minimizes the sum of squared deviations from the line.

4 Note, however, that the Laffer curve strictly refers only to *overall* tax level, and not to that for any particular tax.

References and further reading

Alm, J. (2011) *The Economics of Taxation*, Cheltenham, Edward Elgar.

Bénassy-Quéré, A. and Coeuré, B. (2010) *Economic Policy*, Oxford, Oxford University Press.

Blundell, R. (2000) Work incentives and 'in work' benefit reforms: a review, *Oxford Review of Economic Policy*, 16(1): 27–44.

Break, G. (1957) The effects of taxation on incentives, *British Tax Review*, June, 101–13.

Brown, C. (1988) Will the 1988 income tax cuts either increase work incentives or raise more revenue?, *Fiscal Studies*, **9**(4): 93–107.

Brown, C. V. and Dawson, D. A. (1969) *Personal Taxation, Incentives and Tax Reforms*, Political and Economic Planning (PEP) Broadsheet 506, London, HMSO.

Child Poverty Action Group (1998) After the minimum wage: social security for working families with children, *Poverty, Journal of the Child Poverty Action Group*, **99**, Spring.

Chzhen, Y. and Middleton, S. (2007) *The Impact of Tax Credits on Mothers' Employment*, October, York, Joseph Rowntree Foundation.

Clark, T. and Myck, M. (2001) *Credit Where it's Due? An Assessment of the New Tax Credits*, Commentary No. 86, London, Institute for Fiscal Studies.

Crawford, M. and Dawson, D. (1982) Are rates the right tax for local government?, *Lloyds Bank Review*, **145**(July): 15–35.

CSO (1995) Taxes and Social Security contributions: an international comparison 1981–1993, *Economic Trends*, **505**, November.

Department for Work and Pensions (2008) *Transforming Britain's Labour Market: Ten Years of the New Deal*, January, London, The Stationery Office.

Department for Work and Pensions (2009) *Tax/Benefit Model Tables (April 2009)*, London, The Stationery Office.

Dilnot, A. W. and Kell, M. (1988) Top-rate tax cuts and incentives: some empirical evidence, *Fiscal Studies*, **9**(4): 70–92.

Fields, D. and Stanbury, W. (1971) Income taxes and incentives to work: some additional empirical evidence, *The American Economic Review*, **61**: 3, Part 1 (June), 435–43.

Flemming, J. and Oppenheimer, P. (1996) Are Government spending and taxes too high? *National Institute Economic Review*, **157**(July): 58–73.

Francesconi, M., Rainer, H. and van der Klaauw, W. (2009) The effects of in-work benefit reform in Britain on couples: theory and evidence, *Economic Journal*, February, 66–100.

Giavazzi, F. and Blanchard, O. (2010) *Macroeconomics: A European Perspective*, Harlow, Financial Times/Prentice Hall.

HM Treasury (2010) *Budget Report 2010*, June, London.

House of Commons (1990) *Low Income Statistics*, Social Services Committee, Fourth Report, London.

Kay, J. and King, M. (1990) *The British Tax System*, Oxford, Oxford University Press.

Lyssiotou, P., Pashardes, P. and Stengos, T. (2004) Estimates of the black economy based on consumer demand approaches, *Economic Journal*, July, 622–40.

Messere, K., Owen, J. and Teir, G. (1982) Tax trends and impact of taxes on different income groups, *The OECD Observer*, 25 January.

OECD (2000) *OECD in Figures*, Paris, Organisation for Economic Cooperation and Development.

OECD (2010a) *Economic Outlook*, No. 87, Annex tables, Paris, Organisation for Economic Cooperation and Development.

OECD (2010b) *Tax Database 2009*, Paris, Organisation for Economic Cooperation and Development.

OECD (2010c) *Taxation: Key Tables for OECD*, April, Paris, Organisation for Economic Cooperation and Development.

Office for Budget Responsibility (2010) *Pre-budget Forecast*, June, London.

ONS (2010a) *Financial Statistics*, October, London, Office for National Statistics.

ONS (2010b) *Statistical Bulletin: Low Pay Estimates 2009*, London, Office for National Statistics.

ONS (2010c) *The Effects of Taxes and Benefits on Household Income, 2008/09*, London, Office for National Statistics.

Reading, B. (2005) *Lombard Street Research*, London.

Smith, D. (1996) Moonlighters cheat taxman out of £85bn, *Sunday Times*, 31 March.

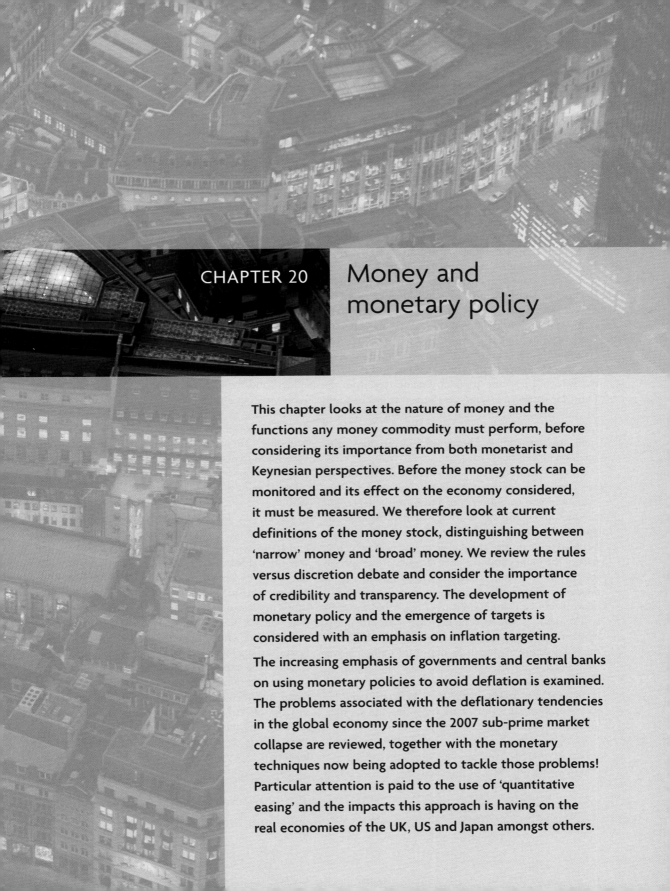

CHAPTER 20

Money and monetary policy

This chapter looks at the nature of money and the functions any money commodity must perform, before considering its importance from both monetarist and Keynesian perspectives. Before the money stock can be monitored and its effect on the economy considered, it must be measured. We therefore look at current definitions of the money stock, distinguishing between 'narrow' money and 'broad' money. We review the rules versus discretion debate and consider the importance of credibility and transparency. The development of monetary policy and the emergence of targets is considered with an emphasis on inflation targeting.

The increasing emphasis of governments and central banks on using monetary policies to avoid deflation is examined. The problems associated with the deflationary tendencies in the global economy since the 2007 sub-prime market collapse are reviewed, together with the monetary techniques now being adopted to tackle those problems! Particular attention is paid to the use of 'quantitative easing' and the impacts this approach is having on the real economies of the UK, US and Japan amongst others.

The nature of money

We are all familiar with money. We use it almost every day of our lives, we recognize it when we see it, and most of us are all too aware that we don't have enough of it! Despite this, the effect of changes in the money supply on macroeconomic variables such as the rate of inflation, the rate of unemployment and the level of output are matters of deep controversy. One reason for this is that there is no completely watertight physical or legal definition of money. Instead, economists adopt a behavioural approach to the definition of money. This approach highlights the confidence element of money and emphasizes the importance of its *acceptability*. At the most basic level, money can be thought of as anything generally acceptable to others as a means of payment. History is littered with examples of commodities that have functioned as money at different times and in different places. The word 'pecuniary' is derived from the Latin for cattle and 'salary' is derived from the Latin for salt, indicating that both these commodities have functioned as money in the past. Other commodities such as stones, shells, beads and metals have also functioned as money.

In the UK, notes, coins, cheques and credit cards are used as means of payment to promote the exchange of goods and services and to settle debts, but cheques and credit cards are not strictly regarded as part of the money supply. Rather it is the underlying *bank deposit* of the cheque or credit card which is part of the money supply. Since cheques are simply an instruction to a bank to transfer ownership of a bank deposit, a cheque drawn against a non-existent bank deposit will be dishonoured by a bank and the debt will remain, as will also be the case if an attempt is made to settle a transaction by using an invalid credit card. Therefore a general definition of money in the UK today is notes, coins and bank and building society deposits.

In practice, for any asset to be considered as money it must perform certain functions and we turn now to a brief discussion of these.

Functions of money

Unit of account

One of the most important functions of money is to serve as a numeraire, or unit of account. Distance is measured in metres, weight in kilograms and so on. In the same way, when we measure the relative value in exchange of a house, a car or a haircut, our measuring rod is money. Money is therefore a common denominator against which value in exchange can be expressed. We then know that a litre of petrol is less valuable than a litre of whisky because we are able to express relative values in money terms. In the UK the basic unit of account is the pound sterling and all values in the UK are expressed in pounds sterling or fractions of a pound sterling.

The existence of a unit of account facilitates rational decision-taking by consumers and producers. To understand the importance of this, consider a *barter economy*, i.e. an economy in which there is no unit of account. As an initial simplification, assume that only *four* consumer goods are offered for sale in this economy. To make decisions about how much of each good to acquire, consumers would need to consider the value of each good in relation to the value of all other goods. Figure 20.1(a) shows that consumers would need to express the value of good A in terms of goods B, C and D. Similarly, the value of good B would need to be expressed in terms of goods A, C and D, and so on. Without money, each good or service offered for sale would require an exchange value (or ratio) expressed in terms of *each* of the other goods and services offered for sale; *six* exchange ratios in all would be required. Figure 20.1(b) shows that when a unit of account does exist, the number of exchange ratios is reduced (here to only three) because the value of each good can be expressed in terms of the money commodity.

This is important because the number of exchange ratios increases rapidly as the number of goods and services offered for sale increases. In fact, we can calculate the number of exchange ratios that would exist in a *barter economy* if we substitute into the formula:

$$R_b = \tfrac{1}{2}N(N-1)$$

where R_b = the number of exchange ratios in a barter
            economy;

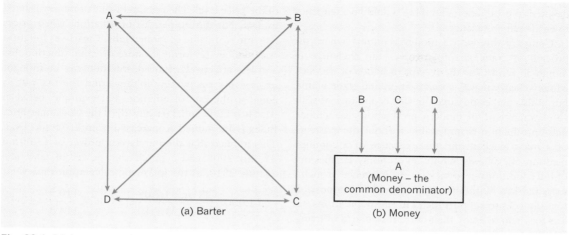

Fig. 20.1 (a) In a non-money economy producing four goods, six exchange ratios are required. (b) In a money economy producing four goods where one of the goods is money, only three exchange ratios are required.

N = the number of goods and services traded in the barter economy.

For example, in an economy where 1,000 goods and services are traded (quite a modest number compared with the number of goods and services actually traded in a modern economy such as the UK), the number of exchange ratios that would exist is 499,500! Imagine trying to make rational decisions about what and how much to produce when it is first necessary to compare such a large number of exchange ratios.

Contrast this situation with the number of exchange ratios that exist in a *money economy* and you immediately see one of the main advantages of money. In this case the number of exchange ratios is simply:

$$R_m = N - 1$$

where R_m = the number of exchange ratios in a money economy;
N = the number of goods and services traded in the money economy.

Again, if 1,000 goods and services are traded, the number of exchange ratios is now only 999 for the money economy. Since each of these exchange ratios is expressed in the *same unit of account*, comparisons between relative goods and services as regards exchange value is very easy, taking the form of relative prices in a money economy. The fact that it is easy to compare relative prices makes it possible for consumers and producers to estimate the *opportunity*

cost of any production or consumption decision. Economic theory tells us that in these circumstances resources are likely to be allocated much more efficiently than would otherwise be the case.

Medium of exchange

In this sense, money is an interface between buyers and sellers which enables them to trade without the existence of a 'double coincidence of wants'. With a barter system those who trade must seek out others who have what they require and in turn require what they have. In functioning as a medium of exchange, money greatly improves the efficiency of the economic system and vastly increases the scope for specialization, thereby allowing firms to achieve economies of scale. So important is the role of money in the process of exchange that it would be impossible for all but the most primitive societies to function in the absence of money.

The restrictions on specialization and exchange that would characterize a barter economy are easy to illustrate. Consider a producer of wheat who requires cloth. First the wheat producer must find someone who requires wheat and who is simultaneously able to offer cloth in exchange. Having established such a double coincidence of wants, it is then necessary to agree a mutually acceptable rate of exchange for wheat in terms of cloth. In such cases, the time and effort devoted to exchange might well exceed that devoted to production and there would be a tendency towards self-sufficiency.

Compare this with a money economy where the process of trade simply involves the exchange of money in return for the receipt of goods or services. Money clearly makes specialization and trade viable, but it also makes possible the vast economies of scale so characteristic of modern production. Remember, mass production is impossible without the existence of a mass market, and the existence of a common medium of exchange within an economy satisfies one of the conditions necessary for the existence of such a mass market. Without money it would be impossible for countries to support their current populations, far less for them to enjoy their current standard of living.

Store of value

The store of value function of money is closely bound up with its medium of exchange function. As a store of value, money permits a time-lag to exist between the sale of one thing and the purchase of something else. When goods and services are sold they are purchased with money which is then held by the sellers of goods and services until they themselves make purchases. In this sense, money is an *asset* used for storing the value of sales until this value is required to make purchases. Most people receive payment for their labour at discrete intervals, usually a week or month, which do not coincide with the continuous flow of expenditures made over the same period. Money is therefore a convenient form in which to store purchasing power.

Money is not unique as a store of value and there are many forms in which wealth can be held, ranging from financial assets such as government bonds, to physical assets such as antiques. As a means of storing wealth these assets have advantages over money. For example, holders of government bonds receive interest income while holders of antiques usually experience a capital gain. Money, on the other hand, has the advantage of being immediately acceptable in exchange for goods and services. Economists use the term *liquidity* to describe assets which can easily and inexpensively be converted into money. Money is therefore the most liquid of all assets.

The liquidity which money possesses gives it a 'convenience value' over other assets, but whether it is an effective store of value depends on the behaviour of the price level. The nominal value of money is fixed by law, but during periods of inflation, when prices rise, the real value of money falls. Clearly as inflation rises, money performs its store of value function less and less effectively. Indeed, inflation can be thought of as a tax on money holdings and the tax rate is equal to the rate of inflation. For example, between 31st July 2009 and 31st July 2010 the Consumer Price Index (CPI) in the UK increased from 110.9 to 114.3. This implied that the purchasing power of £1.00 on 31 July 2009 had a purchasing power of £0.97 on 31 July 2010, as the following calculation shows.

$$£1.00 \times \frac{\text{CPI on } 31.7.09}{\text{CPI on } 31.7.10} = £1.00 \times \frac{110.9}{114.3} = £0.97$$

Between 31 July 2009 and 31 July 2010, the real value of money had fallen by 3%.

The store of value function of money and the medium of exchange function are closely bound together. In periods of hyperinflation, money ceases to function both as an effective store of value and as an effective medium of exchange. Indeed, those hyperinflations that have been documented are characterized by economic agents spending money balances as quickly as possible before they become worthless. A classic example of this occurred during the French Revolution of 1789 when assignants, the paper currency of the time, were issued in such quantity that their value declined so quickly that the peasants used them for the most ignominious purpose to which paper can ever be put. The German experience with hyperinflation in the inter-war period provides another classic example of money becoming ineffective as both a store of value and a medium of exchange. In extreme cases such as this, the value of money falls so quickly that it becomes increasingly difficult to make production and investment decisions. The result is that economic activity declines and economic agents resort to barter and exchange goods and services directly. The growth of the 'barter economy' during the hyperinflation in Zimbabwe in recent years is a case in point.

A standard for deferred payments

Economists sometimes identify a fourth function of money: that it provides a standard for deferred payments. In this sense, money provides a means of agreeing payments to be made at some future date, at the time when contracts are signed. Arguably, this is simply a particular aspect of its unit of account function.

Near money

Commodities which fulfil only some of the functions of money cannot be classed as money. Credit cards and luncheon vouchers, for instance, can sometimes be used as a medium of exchange for transactions, but they are not money because they cannot always be used and neither do they fulfil the other functions of money. Paper assets such as government securities serve as a store of value, but they cannot be used as a medium of exchange. However, liquid assets, i.e. those which can easily be converted into money without loss of value, form a potential addition to the money stock, and are often referred to as 'near money'. Assets normally classed as 'liquid' include time deposits, treasury and commercial bills, and certificates of deposit (Fig. 20.2). Other assets become more liquid the nearer they are to their maturity date. Many of the assets shown in Fig. 20.2 are considered in more detail later in this chapter and in Chapter 21.

Electronic money

The creation and use of electronic money, though still in its infancy, is likely to increase rapidly over the next few years. The possible implications of this are profound and far-reaching. So what is electronic money? Electronic money is a payment instrument whereby monetary value is stored electronically on some device in the possession of the customer. The

European Central Bank defines electronic money as 'an electronic store of monetary value on a technical device that may be widely used for making payments to undertakings other than the issuer without necessarily involving bank accounts in the transaction, but acting as a prepaid bearer instrument'.

The most obvious device for storing money is a computer chip embedded in a *smart card* and, for purposes of simplicity, our discussion here is restricted to this. The amount stored on the chip is increased or decreased every time it is used in some financial transaction or whenever funds are loaded onto, or unloaded from, the card. In this way, electronic money stored on a card can be thought of as being similar to cash stored in a wallet. The amount of money in the wallet goes up or down according to whether purchases or sales take place and additional balances can be loaded into the wallet or unloaded from it. This is entirely different from a credit card which simply gives its owner an immediate overdraft. E-money more closely resembles cash than credit card transactions, and Fig. 20.3 shows the clearing and settlement of cash and E-money.

E-money is convenient and settlement is almost immediate. It is possible for E-money users to transfer balances onto their stored value cards from home and terminals that accept E-money transfer funds stored on a chip, into a bank account in settlement of transactions, almost invariably without delay. Another advantage of E-money is that it eliminates the necessity of carrying coins, which most people find inconvenient since they inevitably pile up in pockets and purses! The problems with E-money include consumer resistance because of loss of anonymity when making transactions and consumer concerns over security and the possibility of counterfeiting. These

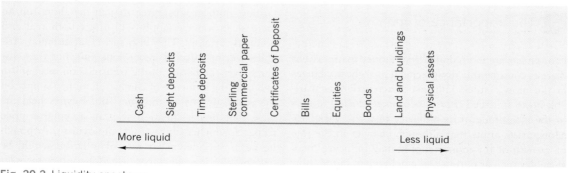

Fig. 20.2 Liquidity spectrum.

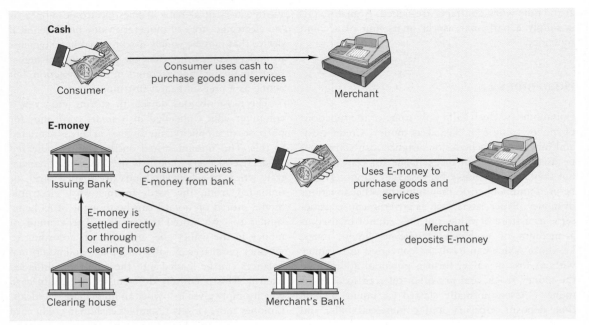

Fig. 20.3 Clearing and settlement of cash and E-money.
Source: Rossell (1997), p. 6.

problems are technical and can probably be overcome relatively easily. For example, some institutions provide anonymity by offering E-money which, once it has been downloaded onto the card and balances are transferred from the individual's to the institution's account, cannot be 'matched' to the account from which it originated. Security and counterfeiting risks can probably be minimized by the development of sophisticated encryption techniques. When these are available and the public has trust in them, the use of E-money is likely to rise substantially.

The importance of money

Economists are in no doubt that 'money matters', but there is considerable disagreement as to how changes in the money stock influence macroeconomic variables (the so-called *transmission mechanism*) and as to the magnitude of its influence on these variables. Monetarists argue that although changes in the rate or growth of the money supply may influence 'real' variables such as output and employment in the short run, in the long run they affect only nominal (or

money) variables such as the rate of inflation, the rate of interest and the rate of exchange. The neoclassical view is an extension of monetarist thinking and agrees that changes in the rate of growth of the money supply affect only nominal variables, but contends that this is the case in both the long run and the short run. Keynesians, on the other hand, argue that as well as affecting nominal variables, changes in the rate of growth of the money supply also affect real variables such as the level of output and employment in both the short run and the long run.

It is natural that we should focus on the differences between Keynesians and monetarists, but it would be a mistake to think that there are no similarities! Both groups agree that in the short run an increase in money supply will affect both real and nominal variables. They also agree that nominal variables will be affected in the long run, but they disagree over the nature of the transmission mechanism and over the influence of changes in money supply on the real economy in the long run. Keynes held the view that higher inflation was an acceptable price to pay for higher output and employment. Although he never specified what rate of inflation would be 'acceptable', it is likely that he had in mind some relatively low rate such as the 2% per annum currently targeted by the Bank of England. Monetarists, on the other hand, argue that any changes in output and employment that occur as a result of higher money growth will be only transitory, i.e. in the long-run real variables will revert back to their equilibrium rates and higher money supply will affect only nominal variables.

The quantity theory of money

The relationship between money on the one hand and nominal income (final output × the average price of that output) on the other is formally recognized in the *equation of exchange*. The income version of this states that:

$$M \times V_Y = P \times Y$$

In other words, over any given time period, the amount of money in circulation (M) times the income velocity of circulation (V_Y) (i.e. the average number of times the money supply is spent on final output) must be identical to the average price of final output (P) times the volume of final output produced (Y).

Note that the income velocity of circulation (V_Y) is a measure of the speed at which money is spent on final output and is determined by several factors. One important factor is the frequency with which payments are made. For example, if wages are paid monthly and all other things are equal, money balances will, on average, be higher than if wages are paid weekly. This implies a lower income velocity of circulation.

There is nothing controversial in the equation of exchange. It is simply an identity and must be true by definition. It simply tells us that the value of spending on final output in one period (MV_Y) equals the value of output purchased in the same period (PY). However, if we assume that V_Y and Y are constant, then we have a relationship between M and P.

The *quantity theory of money* specifies the nature of this relationship and states that the relationship is *causal* from money to prices. In other words, an increase in the money supply will cause an increase in the average price level. Furthermore, causation is one way, that is, the average price level cannot change unless there has been a prior change in the money supply. We shall see below that this strict interpretation of the *quantity theory of money* remains controversial.

The monetarist view of money

The quantity theory of money is the basis of all monetarist thinking. In short, monetarism is a set of beliefs about the ways in which changes in *money growth* (the rate of growth of the money supply) affect other macroeconomic variables. Monetarists argue that, in the *short run*, the effect of changes in money growth is ambiguous, affecting both real variables (output, employment, real wages, etc.) and nominal variables (the rate of inflation, the rate of interest, the rate of exchange, etc.), though in imprecise and largely unpredictable ways. However, in the *long run* the effect of changes in money growth is unambiguous, affecting only nominal variables. It is for this reason that monetarists focus on long-run relationships.

Monetarist beliefs are based on empirical relationships which they claim show a highly significant correlation between money growth and nominal national income. However, since they believe that real national income (output) is not affected by changes in money growth in the long run, the implication is that increased money growth leads to higher nominal income through inflation. In other words, increases in money growth lead, in the long run, to an increase in the rate of inflation.

The demand for money

All monetarists accept the quantity theory of money, but the emergence of monetarism as an economic doctrine focuses on the *demand for money*. Monetarists argue that the demand for money is determined by the same general factors which influence the demand for other goods and services and focus particularly on the *level of income*, the *price level* and the *expected rate of inflation*. It is claimed that the relationship between these variables and the demand for money is stable over time. This is an extremely important claim because such stability could not exist unless the velocity of circulation was also constant. In other words, if it can be shown that the demand for money is stable, then the income velocity of circulation (V_Y) is also stable.[1]

For simplicity, the monetarist view implies that the demand for money is a stable function of nominal national income. The reasoning underlying this view is that in the long run the *actual* rate of inflation and the *expected* rate of inflation coincide. The main determinants of changes in the demand for money are

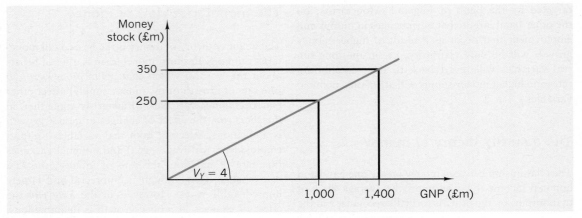

Fig. 20.4 When velocity of circulation is constant, a change in the money supply leads to a proportional change in nominal GDP.

therefore changes in the actual rate of inflation, that is, the rate of change of the price level, and changes in real income, that is, changes in nominal GNP divided by the price level. Monetarists therefore argue that when there is increased money growth, this will lead to changes in nominal GNP which will restore equilibrium between the demand for money and the supply of money.

To understand this more fully, the equation of exchange ($MV_Y = PY$) can be written in the form $M = kPY$ where $k = 1/V_Y$. In equilibrium, the demand for money equals the supply of money and so we can write:

$$M_s = M_d = kPY$$

Note that k is the proportion of nominal income (PY) that the population demand as money. Beginning with equilibrium between demand for money and supply of money, if the supply of money increases there will be disequilibrium between demand for money and supply of money. How is equilibrium restored? If, as the monetarists assume, V_Y is constant, then k must also be constant and equilibrium can only be restored by a rise in nominal income (PY). If V_Y is not stable, then k will not be stable. In this case, equilibrium following an increase in the money supply might be partially or totally restored by a change in the proportion of national income held as money. In other words, equilibrium is restored by a change in the demand for money that is not proportionately related to a change in nominal income.

Figure 20.4 is used as a basis for explanation. If the demand for money is constant at 25% of GNP, that is $k = \frac{1}{4}$, and the initial level of GNP is £1,000m then, assuming that demand for money and supply of money are in equilibrium, the quantity of money supplied and demanded is £250m. If the money supply now increases, nominal GNP will increase and, since k is assumed to be constant, demand for money will also increase. For example, if the money supply increases by £100m, equilibrium will be restored when demand for money increases by £100m and, with k constant at $\frac{1}{4}$, this implies that GNP increases to £1,400m.

The transmission mechanism

An important question to answer is *why* nominal GNP increases following an increase in money growth. In fact, the route by which the effect of a change in the money supply is transmitted to the economy is referred to as the *transmission mechanism*. The monetarists argue that an increase in the money supply will leave people holding excess money balances at the existing level of GNP. Consequently, spending on a whole range of goods and services will increase as economic agents (individuals and organizations) divest themselves of unwanted holdings of money. (This contrasts with liquidity preference theory which implies that it will be spent on *securities* – see the following section.) As aggregated demand increases, output and prices will rise until people are persuaded to hold an amount of money equivalent to the increased money supply in order to finance the increased value of their transactions. In other words, nominal GNP goes on rising until the increase in the supply of money is matched by an increase in the *transactions demand for money*, so that supply an demand for money are brought back into equilibrium.

However, this simple approach is ambiguous because an increase in nominal GNP can consist entirely of an increase in real income with prices unchanged, or entirely of an increase in prices with real income unchanged, or some combination of both. The monetarists claim that in the *short run*, the increase in nominal GNP will consist of an increase in both real income (output) and prices. However, in the *long run* they argue that there is an equilibrium 'natural rate of output' which is determined by institutional factors such as the capital stock, mobility of labour, the rate of social security payments, whether a minimum wage exists and so on (see Chapter 23). Such factors are not influenced by changes in money growth. Whilst it is possible that changes in money growth will bring about changes in real income in the short run, such changes will be only transitory since in the long run real income will return to the level that would have existed before the increase in money growth. Hence, an increase in money growth above the rate of growth of real income will, in the long run, simply lead to higher prices.

Short-run and long-run adjustment to a monetary shock

But why should output increase in the short run following an increase in money growth, and return to the 'natural rate' in the long run? In fact, an increase in money growth encourages increased spending as economic agents attempt to divest themselves of excess money balances at the existing price level. The inevitable consequence is rising prices. This implies a fall in real wages and an increase in the real profits of firms, providing the incentive to increase production. However, over time, rising prices are followed by rising nominal wages. The mechanism is now reversed. When the real wage is restored, real profits revert to their original level and the incentive to increase production (higher real profits) disappears. As a consequence, firms cut back on production and output reverts to the 'natural rate'. In terms of the quantity theory, the implication is that both velocity

and output are constant in the long run and that an increase in money growth merely causes an increase in prices.

Criticisms of the quantity theory

It is important to note that monetarism changes the relationship between M and P (given V_Y and Y) from that of an identity to that of a causal relationship. Although monetarism provides a theoretical rationale for doing this, a number of criticisms can be made of the view that a change in M will automatically lead, in the long run, to a proportionate change in P.

The first and perhaps most damaging criticism relates to assumptions about the behaviour of the velocity of circulation. The velocity has always fluctuated in the short run, sometimes in response to sudden changes in money growth. In the longer run, however, monetarists argue that velocity is relatively stable. Indeed Fig. 20.5 provides rather ambiguous evidence as to the stability of the velocity of the broad money aggregate M4 (see p. 406 below) and more serious statistical analysis is necessary to test for stability. Such testing is beyond the scope of this chapter, but it is fraught with difficulty as the following section explains.

Figure 20.5 does not provide conclusive evidence so that the debate about whether the velocity of circulation (V_Y) can be regarded as stable in the long run is far from over. In fact, there is widespread agreement that velocity is unstable in the short run, though economists cannot agree about its behaviour in the long run. A considerable amount of research has been undertaken to test the stability of the demand for money function (remember, if demand for money is stable, velocity is stable), with mixed results. One reason for this is that there is no accepted definition of what constitutes the short run. Indeed, many economists who accept the predictions of the quantity theory allege that the length of the short run is variable and subject to unspecified changes in duration. This, of course, makes empirical testing of the quantity theory extremely difficult. It is therefore very difficult to identify the short-run influences on the demand for money and to assess their effects. There are also problems with the way in which the money supply is measured and hence with the way in which velocity is calculated.[2] In this respect, some economists have argued that no simple monetary aggregate sum measure of money such as M4 is a particularly

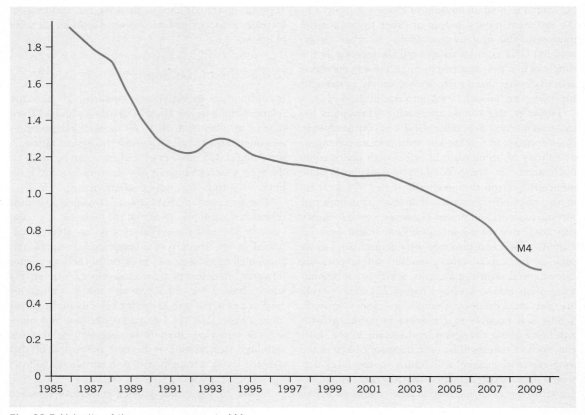

Fig. 20.5 Velocity of the money aggregate M4.
Source: ONS *Financial Statistics* (various).

useful measure of money and that the *Divisia* (see p. 406) is superior.

A further problem with the monetarist explanation of the effects of changes in *M* concerns the assumptions made about *goods market* behaviour. Monetarists assume that goods prices are demand determined rather than cost determined, and change as asset holdings, particularly money balances, change. Monetarists dismiss the possibility that goods prices are determined by costs. Their reasoning is simple. If money growth rises, then aggregate demand will rise. Since no business sells its products at a constant rate over time, businesses must hold stocks to meet changes in demand. A *general* rise in aggregate demand is not initially distinguishable from any other increase in demand, so the rise in aggregate demand will be met out of stocks and there will be no change in prices. However, if the higher level of demand

persists, businesses will increase their purchases from suppliers to restore their stocks. The firms which supply the wholesalers and retailers will therefore experience higher than normal rates of sales and their stocks will be depleted more rapidly than expected. Suppliers of products will therefore increase production in order to restore their stocks to the desired level.

This process filters down the networks of markets until it reaches the markets for raw materials and labour (the primary inputs used to produce products). In the raw materials markets, the amount available is likely to be insufficient to meet the increased amount demanded at the old price, especially so when the increase in aggregate demand implies that all manufacturers want additional raw materials. The price of raw materials (and labour) will therefore be bid up until the market 'clears'. Because the higher price of raw materials (and labour) increases costs of production, manufacturers will charge wholesalers higher prices, citing increased raw material costs as the reason. Wholesalers will in turn charge retailers higher prices because of the higher prices they are compelled to pay. Retailers will then charge their customers higher prices and can, in truth, blame this on the higher costs they have incurred to supply customers with the product! However, rising costs are not the cause of the higher prices. The underlying cause is rising demand caused by increased money growth.

The Keynesian view of money

The perspective of Keynesian economics is essentially short run. Keynesians believe that changes in the money stock affect 'real' variables such as output and employment rather than money variables such as prices. Keynes envisaged economic agents (organizations and individuals) as holding money for *speculative motives* as well as for *transactions purposes*, and switching between financial assets (bonds) and holdings of money in response to expected changes in the price of financial assets. Economic agents would switch money holdings into bonds when they considered the price of bonds so low that they were more likely to rise in the future than to fall further. Now since bonds have a fixed coupon, i.e. they pay the same amount of money annually, a change in bond prices also implies an *opposite* change in the rate of interest.[3] A *fall* in bond prices therefore implies a rise in the rate of interest, raising demand and vice versa.

In the Keynesian model, an increase in money growth creates an imbalance between supply and demand for money which encourages economic agents to purchase bonds. In other words, an increase in money growth does not lead to a change in expenditures on goods and services and so has no immediate effect on the price of final output. Instead, the price of bonds is driven upwards and interest rates fall, encouraging an increase in investment (see Chapter 17) and therefore in output, employment and incomes as the multiplier effect works through the economy. These changes in turn lead to an increase in the value of transactions and a consequent increase in the transactions demand for money to hold. The fall in interest rates also leads to a rise in the speculative demand for money to hold. These changes continue until there is an equilibrium between the supply of and demand for money.

An important issue is why the increase in money growth does not lead to an increase in prices in the Keynesian model. The answer is that, in the Keynesian view of the economy, different variables adjust at different rates. Market quantities, such as output or the number of jobs, adjust much more quickly than market prices. Prices may indeed rise as a result of an expansion in aggregate demand, but they will rise slowly, because it will take time for manufacturers to feel the effects of overall expansion on costs of production. Price rises will only accelerate when the economy nears full employment. The market is therefore in a permanent 'disequilibrium' state, because prices do not adjust fast enough to equate demand and supply.

Differences between monetarist and Keynesian views

The differences between the two positions can be summarized as follows. Monetarists believe that in the long run money growth affects only nominal variables. Real variables are not affected by money growth in the long run and instead are determined by such factors as labour mobility, the existence of minimum wages, technological progress and so on. Velocity of circulation exhibits long-run stability so that the demand for money varies proportionately with nominal income. Since real output is uninfluenced by changes in money growth in the long run, equilibrium between demand for money and supply of money following an increase in money growth is restored by an increase in prices.

In the Keynesian model, changes in money growth affect both nominal variables *and* real variables. However, a given increase in money growth has different effects because the velocity of circulation is unstable. In the Keynesian model an increase in money growth leads to a reduction in the velocity of circulation as more money is absorbed into idle balances and so is willingly held. This implies that part of any increase in money growth is willingly held at the existing price level.[4] This somewhat dissipates the effect of any increase in money growth. However, when there are unemployed resources in the economy, increased money growth will usually be associated with an increase in output and a fall in unemployment. This Keynesian implication that output is demand determined and that unemployment is due to insufficient aggregate demand is emphatically rejected by monetarist economists!

The debate between monetarists and Keynesians is not just about the role of money and the implications of this for monetary policy. It is also about ideology. Monetarists believe that the economy is inherently stable and tends towards a long-run equilibrium level of output. Because of this, they argue that resources are most efficiently allocated through the market and that government intervention destabilizes the economy and leads to a misallocation of resources by moving the economy away from its long-run equilibrium rate. They argue in favour of a 'monetary rule' whereby the money supply grows at a predetermined rate so that (by implication) markets have information about the expected long-run rate of inflation. The Keynesian view is exactly the opposite. They view the economy as inherently unstable and argue in favour of government intervention to stabilize the economy. They reject any kind of 'monetary rule' since this would restrict the scope for intervention and reduce the ability of government to respond to adverse shocks.

Debate between monetarists and Keynesians was fuelled in the 1970s and 1980s by the relatively high rates of inflation experienced then. More recently, inflation targeting has provided the framework for successfully controlling inflation so that, although the debate between monetarists and Keynesians has not yet been resolved, it is certainly less important than it once was. Although economists still disagree on whether money growth is the only cause of inflation, they all agree that inflation must be financed by money growth. In other words, money growth, at the very least, plays a permissive role in the inflationary process (see also Chapter 22). It is to the measurement and control of the money stock that we now turn.

Issues in counting the money stock

Economists, governments and central bankers are interested in counting the money stock, not least because this is important if we are to test the propositions of monetary theory. Earlier, we discussed the quantity theory of money in some detail, but how would we be able to test this theory without a clearly defined measure of the money supply? Another reason why we are interested in counting the money stock is that we wish to control its behaviour so as to achieve macroeconomic objectives, in particular controlling the rate of inflation. Without a measure of the money stock this would be impossible.

Narrow and broad money

Estimates of the money stock have been published in the UK since 1966, but there is no single measure of money that fully encapsulates monetary conditions. Indeed, defining money as a set of aggregates that collectively and individually perform the functions of money is very difficult and in the 1980s there were as many as 23 different definitions of money in 24 OECD countries! The problem centres on notions of liquidity, and economists (and policy-makers) sometimes find it convenient to distinguish between narrow measures of money and broad measures of money. *Narrow* measures of money include the more liquid assets such as sight (current account) deposits with financial intermediaries (banks) and are therefore concerned with the medium of exchange function of money, whereas *broad* measures of money also include a variety of less liquid assets and therefore also focus on the store of value function.

Narrow measures of money were once thought to be considerably more important than they now are, and several governments, including the UK government in the early 1970s, monitored and attempted to control a narrowly defined measure of money. However, broad money is now considered to be of considerably more importance than narrow money and currently the Bank of England only publishes data on notes and coin in circulation rather than a more comprehensive definition of narrow money. The basic problem with measures of narrow money is that, by omitting less liquid assets such as time deposits that can reasonably easily and quickly be transformed into the means of payment, they fail to perform any reliable function as a leading indicator of subsequent changes in other monetary variables, with the result that changes in narrow money growth give no reliable information about future developments in important variables, such as the expected rate of inflation.

Therefore, although the Bank of England does publish monthly data on notes and coin in circulation outside the Bank of England, the figures have no strategic purpose and are not in any way significant for the formation or conduct of policy. This is hardly surprising since no-one would seriously argue that any of the widely used narrow measure of money provides a comprehensive definition of money. For example, sight deposits at banks and building societies perform the medium of exchange function of money and would certainly be included in many narrow definitions of money. However, time deposits which primarily perform the store of value function can, after the required notice of withdrawal has elapsed, be converted into assets which also perform the medium of exchange function of money. The problem, therefore, is not simply to distinguish between assets which function as money and assets which do not, but rather to identify that group of assets which provides a reliable and stable link between money supply growth and prices.

This is no easy task, and measures of the money stock have changed frequently since they were first introduced. This is only in part because of changing asset behaviour by the public; it is also because of changes resulting from financial deregulation and innovation. The public holds deposits with the banking sector not only for *transactions* purposes, but also as an *asset* on which they receive interest. Anything which changes the asset behaviour of the public, i.e. the volume of bank deposits held by the public, will be reflected in changes in the different money aggregates. This would weaken the link between money growth and prices. However, changes in the asset behaviour of the public are not the major problem with arriving at a workable definition of money. A far more serious problem stems from financial innovation and deregulation which have been a feature of the financial sector since the late 1990s. These changes have radically altered the range and nature of those assets which perform the functions of money and this in turn has changed the relationship between measures of the money stock and nominal national income.

Major changes in the banking sector began in the 1980s. For example, the Big Bang of 1986 removed the distinction between retail banks and wholesale banks, while the Building Societies Act of 1986 allowed building societies to offer transactions services (cheque books, cash cards and credit cards) and loans for purposes other than house purchase. This considerably blurred the distinction between banks and building societies and therefore rendered existing measures of the money supply, which excluded build-

ing society deposits, less reliable. In other words, measures of money supply growth failed to accurately predict changes in the rate of inflation, not necessarily because the demand for money was unstable, but possibly because existing measures of money no longer adequately measured the money stock. The increasing availability of new assets will mean that the actual money stock will continue to change in ways not accurately captured by existing measures for the foreseeable future.

In counting the money stock at least three elements are relevant: deposits, liabilities and currencies.

Which deposits should be included?

Some measures of money include only sight deposits (chequing accounts where cash is available on demand) whereas others also include time deposits (requiring notice of withdrawal). In narrow measures of money we are particularly interested in counting transactions balances and therefore the question arises as to whether we should count only retail deposits up to a certain limit; if so, why should wholesale deposits up to the same limit be excluded? (See Chapter 21 where we note that *retail deposits* are usually defined as individual deposits of £50,000 or less, and *wholesale deposits* as individual deposits in excess of £50,000.) There is a further problem about the ownership of deposits. In the UK only private-sector deposits are counted as part of the money stock. Public-sector deposits are therefore excluded, as are deposits of overseas residents. The same is not true in all countries.

Which liabilities should be included?

Traditionally only bank deposits have been counted as part of the money stock but, as the nature of the financial sector has changed, building society deposits are now included in some measures of the money stock. This simply reflects the fact that these institutions now provide banking services similar to those of the clearing banks. Some idea of the importance of this is illustrated by events in July 1989 when the Abbey National Building Society changed its status from a mutual society to that of a bank. To have included its very large deposits in measures of the money stock which did not already include building society deposits would have involved large breaks in the statistical series of those measures. Instead, it was decided to discontinue publication of certain money aggregates and to introduce a new money aggregate (M4).

Which currencies should be included?

No money aggregate currently measured in the UK includes foreign currency deposits. However, these have been included in earlier measures of money and a dilemma certainly exists for the authorities. Capital controls have now largely been abandoned and the Single Market certainly allows the free flow of funds within the EU. Most foreign currencies can readily be converted into other currencies; euros in particular can easily be converted into sterling and are even accepted at the tills by some UK retailers. Foreign currency deposits might well, therefore, become an even more significant component of the money supply in the future than they have been in the past. A strong case could therefore be made for their inclusion in a broad measure of the money stock.

Measures of money

Currently the Bank of England only publishes data on broad measures of money and, for most purposes, the most important monetary aggregate published in the UK is M4. This is a *broad* measure of money first introduced in 1987, and now upgraded to the status of the sole broad measure of money in the UK. M4 consists of:

- notes and coin held by the M4 private sector (i.e. the private sector other than Monetary Financial Institutions (MFIs) such as the Bank of England and other banks and building societies); plus

- all M4 private-sector retail and wholesale sterling deposits at MFIs in the UK (including certificates of deposit and other paper issued by MFIs of not more than five years' original maturity).

This money aggregate was introduced in 1987 because of the evolving role of the building societies which ceased to offer loans solely as mortgage finance for the purchase of property. Indeed, building societies began to compete aggressively with banks as providers of loans for purchases other than property. The nature of the medium of exchange function of various financial intermediaries therefore evolved and, to accommodate this, it became necessary to widen the definition of money to include deposits

Table 20.1 Components of M4 (£m) as at August 2010.

M4 private sector holdings of	
Notes and coin	51,315
Retail bank deposits	1,158,451
Wholesale deposits (banks + building societies) (inc CD's)	984,344
Total	**2,205,377**

Source: Adapted from ONS (2010) *Financial Statistics*, September.

with building societies. Table 20.1 shows the total amounts outstanding for the different components of M4 as at August 2010.

The Divisia Index

M4 items are simply summed to give a measure of the money supply. Each item in the aggregate has a weight of unity and so all assets are weighted equally. This approach takes no account of the 'moneyness' of the different assets. Thus notes and coin in circulation are treated in exactly the same way as interest-bearing time deposits and any substitution of one for the other has no effect on the measured magnitude of M4. However, notes and coin function as a 'pure' medium of exchange and are non-interest bearing, unlike interest-bearing deposits which function primarily as a store of value. The latter earn an explicit rate of return and, at different times, *switching* between assets is apparent. The implicit assumption of simple sum measures of the money supply, namely that all components are perfect substitutes, is therefore erroneous.

A different approach is to weight the different assets in the money stock according to their role in *transactions*, i.e. according to the extent to which they function as a medium of exchange. This is the reasoning behind the Divisia Index which is claimed to be more closely related to total expenditure in the economy than conventional money aggregates. There are, of course, problems as to which variables to include in such a Divisia Index and the weight to be accorded to each variable. In practice, the basic approach has been to weight each component according to the *difference* between its interest yield and the yield on a safe benchmark asset. In a Divisia Index, notes and coin therefore have a weight of 1, while high-interest-bearing savings accounts have a weight closer to zero, because the interest paid on them approaches the benchmark market rate and switching into and out of such accounts makes them less useful as a measure of the medium of exchange function.

The money supply process

The creation of deposits

The existence of a legal definition of money enables us to focus on an important question: how is money created? The answer is not self-evident. Notes and coin are, of course, issued through the Bank of England and the Royal Mint, but they are not released without limit. If they were they would quickly lose value and would become unacceptable as a medium of exchange. However, before we focus on the importance of changes in base money (which includes notes and coin) in the money supply process, let us look at the creation of bank deposits. Even a cursory glance at the data for M4 in Table 20.1 shows that bank deposits are a significant component of broad money aggregates such as M4.

In any discussion of the creation of bank deposits, it is customary to begin by recognizing that not all of the funds deposited with a bank will be withdrawn at any one time. Indeed, under normal circumstances inflows and outflows of funds will be such that on any one day banks will require only a fraction of the total funds deposited with them to meet withdrawals by customers. This implies that the remainder can be lent to borrowers. But this is not the end of the story because funds lent by one bank will flow back into the banking system; again, a fraction will be retained and the remainder will be available for lending to other borrowers. This process is known as the money supply multiplier.

The money supply multiplier

Models of the money supply multiplier link the money supply to the monetary base in a relationship of the following form:

$$M = mB$$

where M = the money supply;
m = the money supply multiplier;
B = the monetary base.

In models such as this, m tells us how many times the money supply will rise following an increase in the monetary base. But what determines the value of m? In fact, there are two factors: the decisions of depositors about their holdings of currency and deposits, and the level of reserves the banks hold to meet customer demands for currency. For simplicity, let us assume that c is the desired ratio of currency (C) to total deposits (D) and that r is the desired ratio of reserves (R) to total deposits (D). Thus we have:

$$c = \frac{C}{D} \text{ and } r = \frac{R}{D}$$

Since $B = C + R$ and $M = C + D$, it follows that:

$$\frac{M}{B} = \frac{C + D}{C + R}$$

which, after dividing the right-hand side by D, can be written as:

$$\frac{M}{B} = \frac{\frac{C}{D} + 1}{\frac{C}{D} + \frac{R}{D}}$$

Replacing C/D with c and R/D with r we have:

$$\frac{M}{B} = \frac{c + 1}{c + r}$$

Since $m = M/B$ we can say that the money supply multiplier is determined by the public's desired ratio of cash to total deposits (c) and the bank's desired ratio of reserves to total deposits (r).

Whether the money supply multiplier is an adequate explanation of the money supply process depends partly on the stability of the ratios c and r. For the UK, the evidence suggests that c, the ratio of the public's demand for cash to deposits, can be unstable and unpredictable. Of course, there are bound to be seasonal variations and it might be expected that over the Christmas period and during the summer months when more holidays are taken, the c ratio will rise because of an increase in the public's demand for cash. However, empirical studies of the c ratio have concluded that the instability it exhibits arises for many reasons and changes do not always coincide with predictable changes in the seasons. One reason why the c ratio might be unstable is that changes in the rate of interest change the opportunity cost of holding cash. This is especially important because of the emergence of interest-bearing current account deposits. Whatever the reasons, for the UK it has been estimated that the c ratio varies between 0.16 and 0.21.

The empirical evidence on the stability of the r ratio is not so conclusive and some studies suggest that r is unstable while others suggest that it is relatively stable. Again, in the short run at least, changes in the rate of interest are likely to cause changes in the r ratio. For example, when interest rates are rising, banks have an incentive to reduce their holdings of reserves.

Certainly the general view for the UK is that the money supply multiplier is unstable, at least in the short run.

The rules versus discretion debate

The rules versus discretion debate is one of the most enduring issues in monetary policy. It focuses on whether monetary policy should be conducted according to established rules, known in advance to all, or at the discretion of policy-makers. In the early years of the debate, it was argued that the case for discretion in policy rested on the view that wages and prices adjust slowly in response to shocks such as a sharp increase in the price of oil. The slow adjustment of the economy results in lost output and unemployed resources. An activist policy allows freedom to vary policy in order to speed up adjustment and move the economy towards full employment or away from inflation. The counter-argument was that discretion succeeded only in raising the long-run rate of inflation and that a policy rule, such as a constant rate of growth for the money supply, facilitated a more effective adjustment and promoted a more stable economy.

The debate has now moved on and it is accepted that if economic outcomes (such as the rate of inflation) depend on expectations about future policies, then credible pre-commitment to a rule can have favourable effects on the economic outcomes that discretionary policies cannot have. In other words, a credible rule can influence expectations and in so doing can deliver more favourable outcomes than are possible when the authorities initiate discretionary changes in policy.

To understand how this can happen, imagine if the authorities announce a target for inflation for the 12-month period ahead which is below the existing rate of inflation. If the pre-commitment to deliver a lower rate of inflation is credible, that is, if it is widely believed that the authorities will adjust policy so as to deliver the target, this will influence wage and price setting to take account of the lower expected rate of inflation. As pressure on prices and wages falls, the authorities have an incentive to renege on their commitment to a lower rate of inflation, since an expansionary policy in these circumstances will boost output with little immediate impact on inflation. Economists refer to policy announcements that are subject to change as the *time inconsistency* problem.

The existence of time inconsistency raises a dilemma for the authorities. If their policy announcements are not deemed to be credible, they will have no effect on expectations and it will therefore be more difficult to deliver the target outcome without reducing output and increasing unemployment. Any policy that is not time consistent will therefore be unable to deliver favourable policy outcomes, that is, low inflation at a low cost in terms of output and unemployment. However, if the authorities pre-commit to a credible policy, favourable outcomes follow naturally because of the effect the pre-commitment has on inflation expectations. In other words, announcing a rule and sticking to it delivers favourable outcomes that cannot be achieved when the authorities exercise discretion.

This conclusion is now widely accepted, but several questions immediately present themselves: what should be the ultimate goal of policy, what variable should the authorities target to achieve their goal and how can they enhance the credibility of pre-commitments to the target? The first of these questions is easily answered. For most central banks, the overriding priority is to maintain low and stable inflation. It is well known that inflation imposes costs on the economy in terms of resource misallocation and so on, but it is also a widely held view that an environment of low and stable inflation is more likely to encourage investment and growth. The problem for central banks is therefore how best to achieve the aim, and this involves an analysis of the issues raised in the remaining two questions. We consider each in turn.

Monetary policy targets

Monetary targeting

One of the earliest proposals for a rule, particularly associated with Milton Friedman, was to establish a *monetary rule*. Such a rule involves setting a target rate of growth for the money supply. Monetary targeting can be analysed within the quantity theory framework. For example, if over some given period, V_Y is expected to fall by 1%, the target rate of inflation is 2% and Y is expected to grow by $2\frac{1}{2}$%, the quantity theory predicts that the inflation target will be achieved if the money growth target is fixed (and achieved) at roughly $5\frac{1}{2}$%.

In fact, it is no longer thought that inflation can be controlled directly by setting target rates of growth for the money supply. This does not necessarily imply that the quantity theory of money does not predict a causal link from money to prices. The predictions of the quantity theory are much more reliable in the *long run*, but over the *medium term* the relationship between money and prices is less precise. Because of this, as the following discussion shows, there are severe problems with monetary targeting and with interpreting the components of the quantity theory of money.

Problems with monetary targeting

Our simple example above assumes that variables in the quantity theory equation can be accurately measured. In reality the growth of output depends on the availability of factors of production and their productivity. These are very difficult to measure and forecast, especially if an economy is undergoing structural change. In the UK in the 1980s and 1990s, structural changes occurred because of privatization and deregulation, trade union reform and so on. In the early years of the new millennium other structural changes are taking place, such as the rising number of school-leavers entering further and higher education rather than the labour market.

It is also unclear which definition of money most accurately captures the causal link from money to prices. Narrow definitions of money are more easily controlled, but they omit some liabilities of the banking system that have an important bearing on inflation. Divisia attempts to weight the various components of any definition of money according to their impact on prices. However, identifying appropriate weights has proved problematical and there is no agreement that Divisia offers any advantages over more conventional measures of money.

Deregulation and development of the financial sector have also caused problems in predicting velocity of circulation. Financial deregulation usually results in a permanent reduction in velocity of circulation of broad money. To the extent that this happens, an increase in broad money growth might not imply an increase in the future rate of inflation. If there are frequent and unexpected changes in velocity, pursuing an inflexible money growth target can cause short-run swings in interest rates and real output as demand for money changes but supply of money does not respond.

Another problem with monetary targeting is that even if velocity is stable in the long run, short-run changes in velocity will cause unanticipated changes in interest rates. A change in velocity implies a change in demand for money and, with supply changing according to some fixed rule, interest rates will adjust in order to maintain equilibrium between demand for money and supply of money. Such unanticipated changes in interest rates will adversely affect investment and might have other adverse consequences on the economy through their effect on the exchange rate.

Exchange rate targeting

An exchange rate target simply involves fixing the external value of one currency against another, low-inflation, currency. Over time this will result in the prices of tradeable goods and domestic inflation converging towards foreign levels. Maintaining the fixed exchange rate implies that domestic monetary policy must follow the monetary policy of the anchor currency, otherwise there will be pressure on the exchange rate.

A major advantage of exchange rate targeting over monetary targeting is that unanticipated changes in money demand have no effect on domestic interest rates because they will be matched by an equivalent and offsetting change in money supply through capital flows. Exchange rate targets are also transparent and easy for the general public to understand. To the extent that exchange rate targets are credible, they therefore provide information on which expectations can be based. The major problem with exchange rate targets is that they leave the authorities powerless to deal with adverse shocks to the economy, such as a deterioration in the terms of trade or a loss of export markets. Unless wages and prices are flexible, an adverse shock must be borne by the domestic economy and will result in declining output and rising unemployment. This will continue until the economy slows up sufficiently and wages and prices fall far enough to restore competitiveness.

Inflation rate targeting

When the authorities target the rate of inflation, the simplest case is when monetary policy is adjusted whenever the forecast rate of inflation rises above the announced target range. If inflation is above the target range, monetary policy is tightened and vice versa. However, central banks that target the rate of inflation have generally adopted a broader approach and, as well as monitoring forecast changes in the rate of inflation, also look at other factors: the overall state of the economy, rates of wage change and so on.

This is a much more flexible approach than a rigid monetary rule. It gives the central bank scope to respond to unanticipated shocks or cyclical changes in the economy which might require an easing or tightening of monetary policy to avoid some adverse effect on the economy. For example, if there is a downturn in economic activity which might develop into a recession, the central bank can cut interest rates to reduce the possibility of this eventuality. In adopting an inflation target which is to be interpreted flexibly, the central bank has some freedom to manoeuvre and is able to respond flexibly to changing circumstances without compromising its inflation target.

To see the advantage of this, consider the effect of a demand-side shock and a supply-side shock. When the economy is subject to a demand-side shock, output and inflation rise and fall together. For example, if there is a sharp fall in the demand for exports, inflation and output fall. In such cases, the optimal response of the central bank is clear and monetary policy should be loosened. Supply-side shocks, on the other hand, move the economy in opposite directions. For example, a sharp rise in the price of oil would push up input prices and would inject an inflationary impetus into the economy. Simultaneously the higher price of oil causes a reduction in aggregate demand and a consequent fall in output and employment. In this case, the bank has to decide on the optimal response. Either it can bring inflation down rapidly by a sharp tightening of monetary policy so that the burden of adjustment falls entirely on output, or it can tighten monetary policy less severely so that the burden of adjustment is shared between prices and output. By changing the policy time horizon, the time by which inflation should be back within the target range, the central bank spreads the output consequences of reducing inflation over a longer time period, thereby reducing the impact on employment, rather than compressing it into a shorter time horizon. Figures 20.6(a) and (b) illustrate the point.

In Figs 20.6(a) and (b), AD and AS are the original aggregate demand and aggregate supply curves. The price level is initially P and output is Y. In Fig. 20.6(a), an unanticipated fall in aggregate demand shifts the aggregate demand to AD_1. As a result prices fall to P_1 and output falls to Y_1. In this case, the appropriate response of the authorities is to loosen monetary policy and so move aggregate demand back towards its original position. In Fig. 20.6(b), there is an unanticipated adverse supply shock which reduces aggregate supply to AS_1. In this case the bank has a range of policy responses depending on its priorities. It can tighten monetary policy severely enough so that aggregate demand and, through this, output fall far enough to preserve price stability (Y_2). Alternatively, it can loosen monetary policy far enough so that output is unchanged but prices are given a further upward twist (P_2). Between these two extremes there exist an infinite number of policy choices which result in the burden of adjustment being shared between output and prices. The distribution of the burden depends on the preferences of the central bank.

Central bank credibility

Central bank credibility refers to the degree of confidence the public has in the central bank's

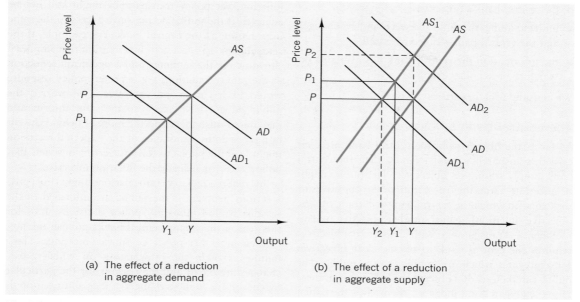

Fig. 20.6 The effects of reductions in aggregate demand and supply.

determination and ability to meet its announced targets. In reality, establishing credibility can sometimes be difficult because, as we have argued above, there are incentives for policy-makers to default on commitments that are widely believed. So how can credibility be improved and maintained?

In establishing and maintaining credibility, the overriding priority is that the authorities must be able to persuade the public that there is no inconsistency between their policy objectives. If policy objectives are inconsistent, any attempt to establish credibility will fail. Most central banks currently emphasize their commitment to price stability as their primary aim and promulgate the view that other aims, such as high and stable levels of employment, will be pursued only to the extent that they do not jeopardize price stability.

There would not seem to be any inconsistency in these objectives, but credibility will be more easily established and maintained in a stable economic environment in which the target rate of inflation is consistently delivered. If there is an economic downturn that monetary policy is unable to correct, it is possible that as unemployment rises the public might form the view that the government will reconsider its policy stance. To the extent that this creates the expectation of a higher rate of inflation, central bank

credibility will be compromised. The old adage that 'nothing succeeds like success' is also true of central bank credibility. When the economy is performing well and the central bank is delivering its targets, credibility will be easier to establish than when the economy is not performing well.

As noted above, there are lags before changes in monetary policy take effect. In the meantime, inflation might be subject to change because of unforeseen events that make control in the short term difficult. Yet the central bank will be judged by outcomes, and where these differ from the central bank's announced targets, its credibility might be damaged. The central bank can minimize the damage by ensuring that the public is fully informed of events and why the measures it has taken are consistent with the announced policy objective.

Transparency in monetary policy

Central bank credibility is far easier to establish when policy is *transparent*. With respect to monetary policy, transparency is important whenever there is incomplete or imperfect information. Information might be incomplete or imperfect with respect to:

- the central bank's objectives;
- understanding the links between policy changes and the central bank's objectives; and/or
- the information the central bank has available on which to base policy changes.

We consider each in turn.

The central bank's objectives

As far as the objectives of the central bank are concerned, transparency involves more than the central bank simply stating its objectives. The public might be uncertain about the true nature of the objectives or the extent to which the central bank will trade off one objective (inflation) against another objective (unemployment). Transparency with respect to objectives requires the central bank to pursue clear objectives for aggregates which are familiar to the public. The public can then readily observe the behaviour of these target aggregates and judge for themselves the extent of transparency. Transparency is most likely to be achieved when the objectives of the central bank are either enshrined in its constitution or imposed on it by government. Currently many central banks pursue an inflation target (see p. 410). In some cases, such as the European Central Bank (ECB), the target value for inflation is set out in their constitution. In other cases, such as the Bank of England, the target rate of inflation is set by government.

The role of policy changes

Even if the central bank's objectives are clearly understood, transparency is not guaranteed, since the public might not understand the operation of the techniques used to achieve the target. For example, if the main policy instrument is interest rates, how big a change in interest rates is required each time the projected value of inflation deviates by $x\%$ from its target rate? Little can be said about this, since the relationship is imperfectly understood even by economists! What we can say is that transparency will be easier to achieve if interest rates move predictably in response to projected deviations in the rate of inflation from target.

The importance of information

The public might understand the central bank's objectives and the expected behaviour of interest rates in response to projected values for the rate of inflation, yet policy transparency might still not be achieved if the public do not have access to the same information as the central bank. For example, if the central bank has access to information that implies a slowdown in the economy and a significant reduction in the rate of inflation, the expected policy response would be a cut in interest rates. However, if the public do not have access to the same information they might misunderstand the motives behind the cut in interest rates. Ignorance of the expected recession might lead the public to form the erroneous view that policy was jeopardizing the inflation objective.

In reality, lack of information might not pose a serious problem if the public are informed of the reasons behind monetary policy decisions. It is for this reason that many central banks publish minutes of their monetary policy committee meetings. These minutes explain the information on which policy changes are based and the reasons for the particular extent of the policy change. Other information is often also made available to the public, such as the Inflation Report published by the Bank of England which details the bank's forecast of inflation for the period ahead.

Techniques of monetary policy

Over the years, a variety of techniques have been used to implement monetary policy. However, we can group the techniques of monetary policy into two broad approaches: those which impose direct controls on the banking sector and market-based instruments which focus on interest rates. Both have been used by the Bank of England (as well as other central banks) to implement monetary policy.

Direct controls

Direct controls focus on the growth of bank deposits and often involve legal measures specifying that financial institutions are required to hold part of their assets in a defined form such as cash or other liquid assets, usually referred to as *reserve assets*. The central bank can then seek to control the growth of bank deposits by limiting the availability of reserve assets. There are two main ways in which this can be done.

1 *Special deposits.* One technique used in the past was to impose *special deposits* on the banking sector. These deposits were 'frozen' at the central bank and the banking sector had no access to them (although they continued to earn interest at the treasury bill rate) until they were released by the central bank. A call for special deposits implied a reduction in the banks' operational deposits at the central bank and this again put pressure on the banking sector to reduce its lending. This technique was abandoned in 1971.

2 *Credit ceilings.* The central bank has also used credit ceilings, known as *supplementary special deposits*, to limit the growth of bank lending. These were imposed on the banking sector when their liabilities (bank deposits) rose above a specified level. In such cases, banks were required to make *non-interest bearing deposits* with the central bank in proportion to the growth of their liabilities. This technique was abandoned in 1980.

The principal advantage of direct controls is that they provide the central bank with a way of controlling the quantity or maximum price of credit. This might be particularly useful in a temporary crisis. They might also provide the only practicable way to implement monetary policy when financial markets are undeveloped. However, there are severe problems associated with these direct techniques of monetary control. Probably the major disadvantage is that they tend to be ineffective because they encourage *disintermediation*, that is, the diversion of business away from the regulated sector to unregulated sectors of the economy. This must be inefficient because if the unregulated sector was operating efficiently, it would already be providing a greater proportion of the business provided by the regulated sector! When direct controls are in place, savers and borrowers search for ways of circumventing the regulations. One obvious route through which regulations at home can be bypassed is by transferring business abroad. Regulations are also inefficient because they tend to stifle competition between banks and limit the benefits to borrowers and depositors.

Indirect controls

Indirect controls exert their influence through channels that leave the financial institutions free of direct controls (other than those necessary for prudential control of the banking system). Reserve asset ratios were abolished in 1981 and in more recent years the Bank of England has exercised control by measures which focus on the availability of *base money* (notes and coin held by the banking sector plus reserve balances at the Bank of England). Again these might take a variety of forms.

- *Reserve requirements.* Reserve requirements impose restrictions on the form in which banks must hold their assets. They usually involve a requirement that total assets can be no greater than the maximum value of some defined group of assets (reserve assets). For example, if reserve assets are defined as the monetary base, then total assets can be no greater than some multiple of the monetary base.

- *Funding.* During the 1980s, the Bank of England exerted its influence on the banking sector by *funding* the national debt. This technique involved the Bank in issuing fewer short-term securities and more long-term securities. Because treasury bills constituted part of the liquid assets ratio but long-term securities did not, the aim was to leave the banks short of liquid assets and compel them to cut their lending.

- *Interest rates.* The Bank of England has considerable influence over short-term rates of interest because of the role it performs in the domestic money markets. As banker to the government and to the banks, it is able to forecast fairly accurately the daily flows of funds between the government's account and the accounts of the banks. When more money flows from the banks' accounts to the government's account the market will be short of funds; when funds flow in the opposite direction, the market will have a surplus of funds. The Bank of England operates on a daily basis to smooth these flows of funds but tends to conduct its open-market operations (see p. 444) in such a way as to leave the market short of funds. It then relieves this shortage by lending to the different institutions at a *repo* rate (official rate) of its own choosing. For example, if the Bank of England *sells* gilts (government bonds) in the open market there will be a transfer of deposits from the banks' operational balances at the Bank of England into the government's own account as cheques authorizing payment are cleared. As operational balances fall, banks are forced to borrow from the Bank of England.

Rather than dealing with every individual bank, the Bank of England uses the discount houses as an intermediary. The discount houses have borrowing facilities at the Bank of England and, when the market is short of funds, the discount houses are 'forced into the Bank'. The Bank of England provides them with cash either by re-discounting bills held by the discount houses or by lending direct. When the Bank changes the rate implied in the price at which it re-discounts bills or the repo rate at which it lends, all institutions quickly follow the Bank's lead and adjust their own rates of interest.

Central banks in developed economies rely almost entirely on indirect controls. Such controls are effective because they are non-selective and affect all institutions across the entire spectrum. For example, when the Bank raises its minimum lending rate (discount rate) this will affect all institutions indiscriminately and will result in interest rates rising throughout the economy. Indirect controls therefore avoid these problems associated with direct controls but are not as flexible as they might seem. Interest rates can be changed quickly, but the Bank of England estimates that it can take up to two years for a change in interest rates to exert its full impact on inflation.

UK monetary policy since the 1950s

Monetary control in the 1950s and 1960s

In the 1950s and 1960s the Keynesian view of money was the consensus view. There was a widespread belief that money growth exerted its influence on the economy through changes in the rate of interest which stimulated changes in the rate of investment. However, monetary policy was viewed as having a weak effect, since the available empirical evidence strongly suggested that investment was interest-inelastic. The prevailing view was that investment by firms in fixed assets and stocks, if it was influenced at all by monetary factors, was influenced more by the *availability of credit* rather than by its *nominal cost*.

Consequently monetary policy consisted primarily of ceilings on lending, although open-market operations and special deposits were also used during this period.

Competition and Credit Control (CCC), 1971

In 1971 the focus of monetary policy switched decisively. Interest rates were, ostensibly at least, to be market determined rather than imposed by the authorities. Furthermore, regulations were introduced compelling banks to observe a minimum 12.5% *reserve assets ratio* between eligible reserve assets and eligible liabilities. The former were defined as private-sector non-bank deposits and building society deposits. The latter included balances at the Bank of England, money at call and short notice with the discount houses, British government and Northern Ireland treasury bills, local authority bills and commercial bills eligible for rediscount at the Bank.

Whenever eligible reserve assets fell below the 12.5% minimum level, it followed that banks would be compelled to reduce their lending. Whenever it wanted to tighten monetary policy, the Bank of England could always engineer such an event, for example by calling for special deposits. In reality, although rates of interest were supposed to be market determined, the Bank of England frequently intervened to leave the banks short of funds, leaving it free to adjust interest rates.

Competition and Credit Control was in place for less than a decade. It failed to provide an effective framework for monetary policy for a variety of reasons. For example, it was unclear whether interest rates were market determined or whether the authorities were setting interest rates. (We have already argued that there are clear benefits arising from transparency.) Probably of more significance is that the regulations applied only to defined institutions and there was an explosion of growth in the unregulated sector. Rising inflation in the 1970s also caused problems because it led to rising public-sector borrowing and, rather than disrupt long-term interest rates through funding, the government borrowed short-term thus ensuring an adequate supply of liquidity to the banking sector. Despite these problems, it was the abolition of exchange controls in 1979 that finally brought the framework to an end.

Capital flows between countries increased (see Chapter 26) to the extent that effective monetary control became impossible, since residents were enabled to open overseas bank accounts and to borrow abroad for current spending in the UK.

The medium-term financial strategy (MTFS), 1980

In March 1980 the government unveiled its new approach to monetary control, the *medium-term financial strategy* (MTFS). The MTFS was designed to provide a framework of control within which money growth could be targeted over a four-year period. The emphasis of control shifted in two ways:

1 from a short-term to a medium-term perspective; and

2 from controlling the availability of reserve assets to controlling the growth of bank assets, the so-called 'counterparts' to the money stock.

The rationale for shifting to a medium-term perspective is an admission that it is impossible to exercise control over money growth over a short time horizon. The rationale for controlling the counterparts to the money stock reflects the fact that, apart from the narrowest measures of money, definitions of the money stock focus on bank deposits. There is a famous banking maxim that 'every loan creates a deposit' because every loan granted by a bank is redeposited within the banking sector after being spent by the borrower. Controlling the counterparts of the money stock was therefore seen as a way of controlling money growth. In the UK, the authorities attempted to control growth of the (now defunct) broad measure of money known as sterling M3 (£M3). The MTFS set declining target rates of growth for £M3 annually so that as one year in the four-year cycle passed, another year began.

Bank deposits consist of lending to the *government*, the *private sector* and the *overseas sector*. The sum of lending to each of these forms the counterparts to the money stock, and the MTFS included specific measures to control each of these individually.

■ Government expenditure was to be progressively reduced to rein back the PSBR (now PSNCR). This was made easier because the proceeds from privatization were treated not, as might be expected, as

a means of financing the PSBR, but as a means of reducing it!

■ Debt sales to the non-bank private sector were encouraged by adjusting interest rates to the level required to persuade the non-bank private sector to take up offers of treasury bills.

■ Exchange rate policy was to be used to influence the external and foreign currency counterparts of the money stock.

Additional measures, designed to improve the effectiveness of monetary control by addressing some of the problems associated with Competition and Credit Control, were introduced in August 1981. Thenceforth banking regulations applied to all monetary institutions within the monetary sector. This is to avoid the emergence of disintermediation. The reserve assets ratio was abolished and a minimum figure (now abolished) was established for operational deposits.

The MTFS proved no more effective as a framework for monetary policy than did Competition and Credit Control. Monetary growth frequently exceeded the target growth rate and, in an attempt to improve control, target rates of growth for the then monetary base (M0) were introduced in 1984. By 1987 targets for £M3 were abandoned, although the Bank of England continues to 'monitor' changes in M0. There are many reasons why it proved difficult to restrain £M3 within its target range. One reason is that private-sector borrowing proved less sensitive to rising interest rates than anticipated. However, the main reason is that deregulation of the financial sector and product innovation distorted the money aggregates to the extent that they became unreliable as indicators of money growth.

Exchange rate and inflation rate targeting

As confidence in the efficacy of targeting money growth waned, the authorities turned to the exchange rate as an anchor for monetary policy. In the late 1980s sterling shadowed the Deutsche mark (DM) before the official announcement in October 1990 that sterling was to join the ERM at a rate of £1 = DM2.95. It soon became clear that at this exchange rate sterling was hopelessly overvalued on the foreign exchanges, and in September 1992, with the UK deep in recession and interest rates at 15% to preserve the exchange rate, the Chancellor of the Exchequer bowed to the inevitable and withdrew sterling from the ERM. The following day interest rates were reduced to 10% and, free of exchange rate constraints, the focus of policy changed.

In October 1992, the Chancellor announced that monetary policy would henceforth target the rate of inflation. The first steps towards increasing transparency and credibility quickly followed when, later the same month, the Chancellor announced that the Governor of the Bank of England would produce a regular report on progress towards the inflation target. The *Inflation Report* is compiled by the Bank in the belief that it will be more credible than if it is produced by the government. In 1994, transparency was further increased when it was announced that minutes of meetings between the Chancellor and the Governor of the Bank of England to review the performance of monetary policy would be published. The Inflation Report and the Minutes of the Monetary Policy Committee (MPC) meetings (see below) remain an important mechanism through which the Bank communicates its views and actions to the general public.

The inflation target was initially set in the range 1–4% per annum, but in 1997 a point target of 2.5% for RPIX inflation was introduced. This was subsequently revised on 10 December 2003 to a point target of 2% for CPI inflation, and the target rate of inflation for the UK remains at this level. In principle, inflation targets are easy to understand: the central bank simply adjusts policy (usually its discount rate – i.e. the minimum lending rate in the UK) whenever forecast inflation rises above or falls below the target rate. In practice, all central banks face constraints on their ability to take action whenever forecast inflation deviates from the target. For example, in September 2010, inflation in the UK on the CPI measure (the government's target measure) was 3.1%, yet on 7 October the Bank of England announced that it was leaving the minimum lending rate unchanged at 0.5%, where it has been since March 2009. The problem is the depressed and fragile nature of the UK economy which some analysts predict is on the verge of a second recession. An increase in interest rates would further depress aggregate demand and increase the likelihood of another recession or, even worse, it might send the economy into a deflationary spiral.

The main advantage of an inflation target over, say, a monetary rule where the money supply grows by a fixed amount, is that it gives the Bank flexibility to respond to adverse shocks, whether these are anticipated or unanticipated. An *anticipated shock* of a sufficient magnitude would simply trigger a counterfactual change in interest rates before the shock materialized, whereas an *unanticipated shock* of a sufficient magnitude would trigger a counterfactual change in monetary policy at the first opportunity. With respect to the Bank of England, this would be at the next meeting of the MPC.

Operational independence of the Bank of England

In furtherance of the aim of achieving credibility, on 6 May 1997, the Bank of England was given operational responsibility for setting short-term interest rates to achieve the inflation target, initially retained by the Labour government at 2.5% but revised downwards in 2003 to 20%. However, the incoming Chancellor, Gordon Brown, made it clear that the government would retain a national interest in controlling inflation. This is effectively an escape clause allowing it to overrule the Bank's interest rates decisions in pursuit of the inflation target when it deems such action necessary. Neither the Labour government nor the post-2010 Coalition government has specified any formal process for implementing the escape clause, nor defined a set of conditions under which the Bank would be overruled. Nevertheless, the point target now has a one percentage point threshold either side and if inflation breaches this, the MPC (which decides on interest rate changes, see below) is required to publish an open letter outlining the reasons for the deviation and to explain the policy changes to be adopted so as to bring inflation back to target.

The MPC, with a membership of nine and a quorum of six, meets monthly at the Bank of England to decide on the timing and extent of any change in the rate of interest for the month ahead. The broad aim is to keep the growth of demand in line with supply-side capacity as reflected by consistently low inflation. Subject to the primacy of hitting the inflation target, the MPC is required to support the government's economic policy, including its objectives for growth and employment. Monetary policy is therefore loosened or tightened in order to moderate the fluctuations that occur over the business cycle. It is anticipated that the target rate of inflation is consistent with delivering steadier growth, higher levels of employment and rising living standards into the medium and longer term.

The making of monetary policy in the UK

The making of monetary policy in the UK follows a clearly defined monthly cycle. Decisions are taken by a simple majority vote. The timetable for a typical monthly round of the MPC is set out in Table 20.2.

Recent developments in UK monetary policy

UK monetary policy in recent years has focused on tackling deflation, especially by injecting more money into the economy via quantitative easing and keeping interest rates at extremely low levels.

Deflation

The primary economic aim of the Bank of England is to maintain a low and stable rate of inflation with a target rate of 2%. Since the 1980s, relatively high inflation has been more of a problem for the UK than relatively low inflation, but in more recent years in the UK, as well as Europe and the US, the prospect of deflation has caused concern. Deflation differs from disinflation which simply means a fall in the rate of inflation. Deflation actually implies falling prices and has potentially serious consequences for the economy. It is to counter the prospect of deflation that the Bank of England (and the Federal Reserve in the US) has introduced its quantitative easing programme. Before we discuss the nature of quantitative easing, we briefly consider the causes and consequences of deflation.

Sources of deflation

Economists generally agree that in the long run inflation and deflation are monetary phenomena. In this sense, deflation is caused by a reduction in aggregate demand that is so severe that traders are obliged to persistently reduce prices to help retain sales volume. Some economists have argued that the expenditure

Table 20.2 Typical monthly round of the MPC.

Briefing	
Throughout the month	Circulation of briefing material and analysis of data releases and market developments by staff
Friday before policy meeting	Half-day pre-MPC meeting
Monday/Tuesday	Staff undertake follow-up work requested by the Committee
Policy meeting	
Wednesday	Policy meeting commences early afternoon. Committee identifies the key issues and debates their implications for inflation prospects
Thursday	Policy meeting concludes. Committee members provide their assessment of the appropriate policy stance and vote on the level of interest rates. Policy announcement at noon. Decision implemented immediately in a round of open-market operations at 12.15
Minutes	
Week following policy meeting	Draft of the Minutes circulated and comments from Committee Members incorporated
Monday (second week after policy meeting)	Committee meets and signs off the Minutes
Wednesday (two weeks after policy meeting)	Publication of the Minutes at 09.30

Source: Bean and Jenkinson (2001).

cuts announced by the new Coalition government in October 2010 are so severe that they might trigger deflation (see Chapter 18). Of course, other mechanisms might trigger deflation; even a positive supply shock to labour productivity can put downward pressure on prices, as nominal wage rates adjust only slowly upwards to unexpected increases in output, so that as output per hour rises faster than hourly wage rates, unit labour costs decline and in competitive markets prices fall. If the productivity shock is widespread, its effect might be to drive the price level downwards. Falling prices in some sectors might also impact on other sectors as lower inflation induces lower wage rises, which in turn generate lower inflation, and so on until the price level begins to fall.

Problems with deflation

Problems with deflation include the following.

■ *Misallocation of resources.* Governments and policy-makers worry about deflation for the same reasons they worry about inflation. Like inflation, deflation impairs the ability of the price mechanism to allocate resources efficiently since it blurs the distinction between absolute and relative price changes. When demand for a product changes, prices rise or fall and this leads to changes in output to accommodate the change in demand. However, the price mechanism can only discharge its role efficiently if suppliers are able to distinguish between a change in the price of a *single product* and a change in the average price of *all products* (the price level). This is not as easy as it seems because, during periods of inflation or deflation, not all prices change by the same amount, at the same time or even in the same direction! During inflation some prices actually fall, and during deflation some prices actually rise. It is the *general* price level that changes. When producers fail to distinguish between a change in the price of a single product and a change in the average price of all products they misread the information contained in price signals and adjust output in ways which are often contrary to changes in demand. The result is then a misallocation of resources in the economy which results in the over-production of some goods and the under-production of others in relation to the optimum level of output.

■ *Postponement of spending decisions.* Other problems with deflation result from it creating incentives to save and to postpone spending, because prices will be lower and purchasing power greater in the future. Deflation can be extremely damaging when people postpone spending in the anticipation of cheaper future prices, as this depresses current spending and, as stocks accumulate and profits fall, firms cut back on production and on employment and cut prices. The longer consumers postpone their spending, the longer and more pronounced the deflation will be.

■ *Borrowers lose out.* Deflation also worsens repayment burdens for borrowers because debts remain fixed in nominal terms (for each £100 borrowed, £100 must be repaid), but wages and prices fall during deflation. This not only causes hardship for individual households, but also causes problems for firms who will cut back on borrowing and investment as debt repayment burdens increase. There is also likely to be a greater number of defaults on loans and the banking sector is therefore likely to restrict lending, making recovery from deflation still more difficult. This has certainly been a factor in the ongoing problems faced by the Japanese economy.

■ *'Zero bound' and policy-making problems.* For policy-makers, a major problem associated with deflation is that posed by the so-called 'zero bound'. A major determinant of nominal interest rates is *expected inflation*, and since prices fall during deflation, nominal interest rates also tend to fall. However, once the nominal interest rate is at zero, no further downward adjustment in the rate can occur, since lenders will not accept a negative nominal interest rate when it is possible instead to hold cash. At this point, the nominal interest rate is said to have hit the 'zero bound'. This poses a major problem because when the nominal interest rate has been reduced to zero (as in the US), the *real* interest rate paid by borrowers equals the expected rate of deflation. For example, if deflation is at an annual rate of 2%, then someone who borrows for a year at a nominal interest rate of zero actually faces a 2% real cost of funds, as the loan must be repaid in pounds sterling whose purchasing power is 2% greater than that of the pounds borrowed originally. In a period of sufficiently severe deflation, the real cost of borrowing becomes prohibitive. Capital investment, purchases of new homes and other types of spending decline accordingly, accelerating still further the economic downturn.

The zero bound also places severe limitations on the conduct of monetary policy. Under normal conditions, the Bank of England (and most other central banks) will implement policy by setting a target for a short-term interest rate and enforcing that target by buying and selling securities in open capital markets (open market operations). When the short-term interest rate hits zero, the central bank can no longer ease policy by lowering its usual interest-rate target. The central bank's inability to use its traditional methods for conducting monetary policy at the very least complicates the policy-making process and introduces uncertainty as to the size and timing of the economy's response to policy actions. One thing we have learned about monetary policy in recent decades is that it operates more efficiently when it is predictable!

In the UK, interest rates have been close to the zero bound since March 2009, but with output growing only slowly (0.8% in the third quarter of 2010) and unemployment forecast to rise sharply, the Bank's options to stimulate the economy are limited. For this reason, the bank has implemented *quantitative easing* which simply means that it injects more money into the economy with the aim of stimulating demand. This implies that the Bank at least partly believes that the velocity of circulation will not decrease so as to fully offset the stimulus that increased money supply growth will bring. The extra money supply is created by the bank buying assets, primarily gilts.

Quantitative easing

Quantitative easing (QE) refers to the process through which the central bank injects more money into the economy (see Fig. 20.7). It does this through asset purchases, primarily gilts, in the open market. As purchases of assets increase, the amount of cash and liquidity in the economic system increases, stimulating spending and creating a 'wealth effect', as the extra demand for assets raises their price and asset-holders will experience a rise in wealth, whether they choose to sell their assets or retain them! Higher wealth might encourage additional spending and, to the extent that this does happen, it will reinforce the effects of QE. Higher asset prices also mean lower

yields, with the new lower effective interest rates making it cheaper to borrow to finance spending. As banks receive cash from selling their assets to the central bank, their operational deposits with the Bank of England rise and they can use these to stimulate further lending to their customers via the money supply multiplier (p. 407).

However, it is possible that the financial crisis will have left banks nervous and reluctant to increase their lending. It is for this reason that the Bank of England is particularly targeting the wider economy and purchasing mainly in private-sector asset markets, in other words purchasing private-sector assets, mainly from non-bank asset-holders. By reassuring the markets of its willingness to buy debt, the Bank's intention is to encourage lending, since its actions guarantee a ready market for assets if financial intermediaries, firms or individuals experience a tightening of their liquidity situations. A further result of QE is that as asset prices rise, interest rates, which move inversely with asset prices, will fall and the effect will be to encourage borrowers and stimulate spending. Figure 20.7 shows how QE works.

By early 2011 the QE programme has resulted in asset purchases by the Bank of £200bn and there is evidence that M4 has slowly started to rise. However, it remains to be seen whether this rise will be sustained and what the impact on the real economy will be. In Japan, where QE has been tried for over a decade now, the effect on the real economy has been limited – but so too has been the scale of the QE programme which was comparatively small in Japan compared to that undertaken by the Bank of England, and by the US Federal Reserve which introduced a one trillion dollar programme in March 2009.

One interesting point to note with respect to QE is that although it does not imply a return to monetarist thinking, it does imply a belief in the impact of money supply growth on aggregate spending. If increased money supply growth was *not* expected to generate an increase in aggregate demand, there would be no point in implementing the QE programme in the first place! While the strictest interpretation of monetarism, with its adherence to a stable velocity of circulation at its core, has not been resurrected by the QE programme, it remains clear that the Bank does *not* believe that a change in money supply growth will be matched by an equal and offsetting reduction in the velocity of circulation.

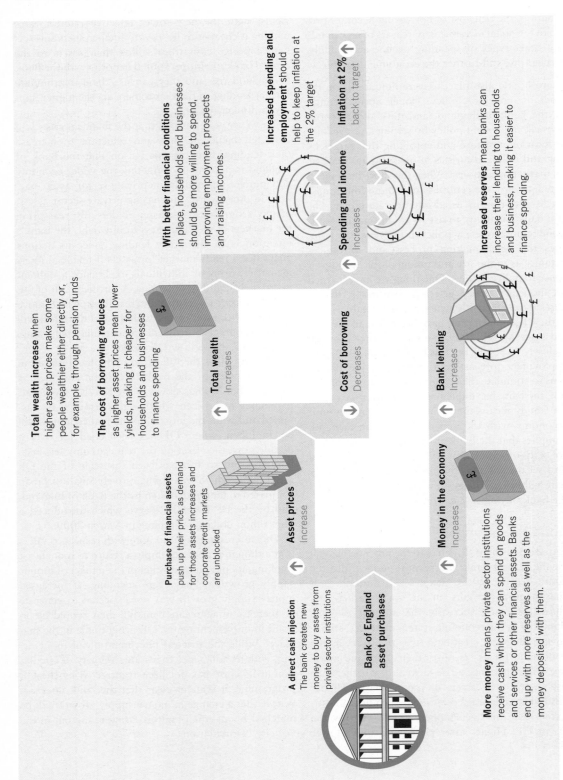

Fig. 20.7 Quantitative easing.
Source: Bank of England (2010).

Conclusion

A number of conclusions might be drawn from the UK experience of money growth and monetary control since the 1980s.

1 Financial innovation and deregulation make it impossible to define a set of assets which alone function as money. This is the major reason the broad money aggregates have been subjected to continuous redefinition.

2 Controversy remains about how useful the definitions of money are. In the UK, one measure of narrow money (M0) and one measure of broad money (M4) are monitored. However, different measures of money are published in different countries and the accepted view is that when interpreting monetary conditions, definitions of money do not always include all of the relevant variables. There is also a view that weighted measures of the money stock (Divisia) might be more useful than 'simple sum' measures.

3 Doubt remains as to whether the direction of causation is from money to prices or from prices to money. However, growing evidence does support the view that the velocity of circulation of money follows a relatively stable trend, though there are short-run fluctuations about this trend.

4 Controlling a particular money aggregate is difficult because of financial innovation, deregulation and disintermediation. Monetary control is especially difficult because of disintermediation (see also Chapter 21).

5 The focus of monetary policy has switched from controlling intermediate variables such as the money stock or the exchange rate which were formally thought to be linked to the rate of inflation, to direct targeting of the rate of inflation.

6 Monetary policy actions focus on changes in the rate of interest which affect all institutions simultaneously and equally.

7 The adoption of quantitative easing (QE) policies is a recognition by governments and central banks of the continued effectiveness of money supply policies on the real economy, especially when interest rates are often close to zero.

Key points

- Money functions as a unit of account, a medium of exchange and a store of value.
- Money avoids the inefficiency of a barter system, permitting greater specialization and associated scale economies.
- For most purposes, M4 is the most important official definition of money and is a broad measure of the money stock.
- Deposits at financial institutions are the most important component of broad money.
- Definitions of money are constantly evolving because of financial deregulation and innovation.
- Monetary policy is most effective when it is both credible and transparent.
- Since 1992, the Bank of England has adopted an inflation target as the nominal anchor for monetary policy.
- The Bank of England was granted operational independence on 6 May 1997.
- There has been an increasing policy concern with avoiding deflation via monetary policy since the onset of the global recession of late 2007.
- Governments and central banks are increasingly turning to 'quantitative easing' as a technique to stimulate their economies, especially when interest rate policies are restricted by 'zero bound' issues.

Now try the self-check questions for this chapter on the Companion Website. You will also find useful links to relevant websites.

Notes

1 It is important to understand that in arguing that velocity is stable, the monetarists are not arguing that it is constant. Instead they have always claimed that velocity changes only slowly over time and in a predictable way. In this sense it can be regarded as stable from one time period to the next. We shall see later that this has important implications for policy purposes.

2 The quantity theory states that $MV_Y = PY$. If we multiply the average price of final output by the volume of final output we obtain GNP. The quantity theory can therefore be written as $MV_Y = \text{GNP}$ and hence $V_Y = \text{GNP}/M$. The problem is which measure of money do we use? If an inappropriate aggregate for M is substituted, the value obtained for V_Y will be inaccurate. Economists cannot agree on an appropriate definition of money and this has caused problems with attempts to test the stability of V_Y.

3 For example, a *consol* (an irredeemable bond) issued at 3% with a par value of £1m pays its owner £30,000 per annum. If the current market price of the consol is less than par, for example £0.9m, then the market rate of interest is 0.03/0.9 = 3.33%. Hence there is an *inverse relationship* between bond prices and the rate of interest.

4 It is sometimes argued that in the extreme a *liquidity trap* exists so that any change in the money supply leaves interest rates unchanged. Since the Keynesian transmission mechanism is through changes in interest rates, in this extreme situation an increase in money growth has no effect on the price level (P) or real output (Y). The increase in money growth has therefore been completely absorbed into idle balances, i.e. its effects have been offset by a reduction in the velocity of circulation. In other words, the increase in money supply is matched by an increase in the demand for money.

References and further reading

Bank of England (2010) *Quantitative Easing Explained*, pamphlet, London.

Bank of England Inflation Reports (various) Supplements to *Bank of England Quarterly Bulletins*.

Bean, C. (2002) *The MPC and the UK economy: should we fear the D words?* Speech delivered to the Emmanuel Society, London, 25 November 2002, *Bank of England Quarterly Bulletin*, Winter, 475–85.

Bean, C. (2009) *Quantitative Easing: An Interim Report*, speech given to the London Society of Chartered Accountants, London, 13 October 2009.

Bean, C. and Jenkinson, N. (2001) The formulation of monetary policy at the Bank of England, *Bank of England Quarterly Bulletin*, Winter, 434–41.

Bénassy-Quéré, A. and Coeuré, B. (2010) *Economic Policy*, Oxford, Oxford University Press.

Benati, L. (2005) Long-run evidence on money growth and inflation, *Bank of England Quarterly Bulletin*, Autumn, 48–80.

Chote, R. (1997) Treading the line between credibility and humility, *Financial Times*, 13 June.

Dungey M., Fry, R., Gonzales-Hermosillo, B. and Martin, V. (2011) *Transmission of Financial Crises and Contagion*, Oxford, Oxford University Press.

European Central Bank (2000) Issues arising from the emergence of electronic money, *Monthly Bulletin*, November, 48–80.

Giavazzi, F. and Blanchard, O. (2010) *Macroeconomics: A European Perspective*, Harlow, Financial Times/Prentice Hall.

Gnos, C. (2009) *Monetary Policy and Financial Stability*, Cheltenham, Edward Elgar.

Janssen, N. (2005) Publication of narrow money data: the implications of money market reform, *Bank of England Quarterly Bulletin*, 45(3): 367–72.

King, M. (2002) The inflation target ten years on, lecture delivered at the London School of Economics, 19 November 2002, *Bank of England Quarterly Bulletin*, 42(4): 465–74.

Krugman, P. and Obstfeld, M. (2010), *International Economics: Theory and Policy*, Harlow, Financial Times/Prentice Hall.

Lynch, R. (2010) £200m quantitative easing 'slowly taking effect', *Independent*, 4 January.

Mercia, P. and Papadia, F. (2011) *Implementing Monetary Policy in the Euro Area*, Oxford, Oxford University Press.

ONS (2010) *Financial Statistics*, September, London, Office for National Statistics.

Pool, W. (1999) Monetary policy rules, *Federal Reserve Bank of St Louis, Economic Review*, March, 3–12.

Rossell, M. (1997) Does electronic money mean the death of cash? *Federal Reserve Bank of Dallas, Southwest Economy*, No. 2, March/April, 5–8.

Sands, C. (2007) The Afghan village that uses opium as its currency, *Independent*, 4 May.

Schreft, S. L. (2002) Clicking with dollars: how consumers can pay for purchases from e-tailers, *Federal Reserve Bank of Kansas Economic Review*, first quarter, 37–64.

CHAPTER 21

Financial institutions and markets

All modern, developed economies have a sophisticated financial system which incorporates both the financial institutions and financial markets. These institutions and markets exist to mediate between those who wish to save or lend and those who wish to borrow or invest. Mediation is necessary because lenders and borrowers have different needs in terms of maturity, liquidity and yield.

Lenders can be expected to prefer to lend for a short term before the loan matures, to get their money back quickly if their own need for liquidity changes, and to receive high returns on their loans. Borrowers can be expected to prefer to borrow over the long term and to offer low returns, though sharing the same desire for liquidity.

The whole process of matching the needs of lenders and borrowers is known as 'financial intermediation' and the institutions which play a part in this process are known as 'financial intermediaries'. Financial markets also play a key role in this system by allowing borrowers to issue IOUs such as bills or bonds which are acceptable to lenders and which can be traded on the secondary markets (i.e. markets dealing in securities which already exist).

The whole financial system is continually undergoing rapid development and since the 1990s financial markets have become ever more complex, offering new types of financial instruments which reduced transactions costs and were more flexible and better targeted. At the same time, the traditional roles of the financial institutions have become increasingly blurred and, as their operations evolved, they were laying the foundations for the largest financial crisis to hit the UK financial system (see also Chapter 20 and Chapter 30).

The role of the financial system

The basic rationale of a financial system is to bring together those who have accumulated an excess of money and who wish to save with those who have a requirement to borrow in order to finance investment. This process arguably helps to better utilize society's scarce resources, increase productive efficiency and ultimately raise the standard of living. Santomero and Babbel (2001) have usefully summarized this role of the financial system:

> Without a developed financial system, institutions, firms, and households would be forced to operate as self-contained economies. As a result, they could not save without deploying their resources somewhere, and they could not invest without saving from their own current output. A financial system allows trade between

individuals to accomplish both these ends. It allows savers to defer consumption and obtain a return for waiting. Likewise, it permits investors to deploy resources in excess of those that they have available from their own wealth in order to gain the productivity that such investment yields. The economy also gains from the financial system, as both households and firms advance the economy, total output, and economic growth.

Figure 21.1 provides an overview of the structure of the financial system in the UK. Essentially there are three kinds of operator in the UK financial system.

1 *Lenders and borrowers*, including persons, companies and government. Lenders are also referred to as savers, depositors or ultimate lenders and borrowers as investors or ultimate borrowers.

2 *Financial intermediaries*, consisting of financial institutions which act as intermediaries between

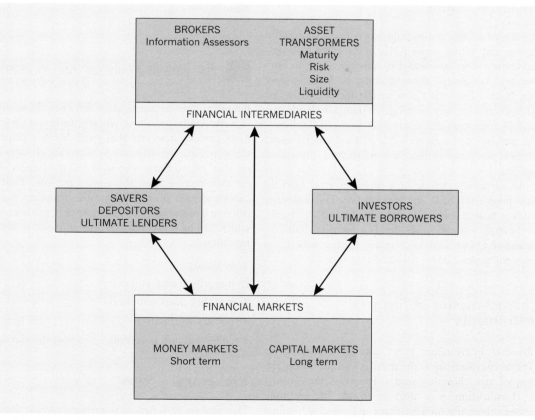

Fig. 21.1 The financial system.

lenders and borrowers. Financial intermediaries take one of two general forms: brokers (bringing together lenders and borrowers by evaluating market information) and asset transformers (transforming the financial assets of lenders by varying the maturity, risk, size and liquidity of the liabilities of borrowers).

3 *Financial markets*, where money is lent and borrowed through the sale and purchase of financial instruments. They play an essential role in reducing the cost of placing, pricing and trading such instruments. In the UK, the financial markets can be defined as short-term money markets and long-term capital markets.

The chapter will now consider in more detail the working of the financial system in the UK, beginning with the various financial instruments that are traded.

Financial claims

Operators within a financial system are essentially buying and selling paper IOUs in the form of financial claims. They are issued by those wishing to borrow and bought by those wishing to lend; lenders then hold a financial claim on the future income of the issuing company or person. Financial claims can be split into financial assets and financial liabilities. The purchaser of a claim holds it as a financial asset, whereas the issuer of the claim holds it as a financial liability.

An obvious example of a financial asset held by most people is a bank deposit account. The depositor holds a financial claim on the bank; and the bank, the borrower of the funds, holds a financial liability. Financial claims can take many forms, which are given the generic name financial instruments.

Characteristics of financial instruments

Financial instruments are classified according to various characteristics, the most important being the level of risk, liquidity and maturity. Other means of classification may also be used, for example between those instruments that can be traded by third parties (e.g. Treasury bills) and those that cannot

(bank deposits), or between those issued with a fixed or variable rate of interest.

Every financial instrument also provides the purchaser with a return or yield. The yield on any financial instrument is related to its characteristics and in general will be lower if the instrument is liquid, has a short time to maturity and has a lower level of risk. Thus, yields are usually higher for long-term investments because lenders require to be compensated for giving up their money for long periods of time and because the risk of default increases with time.

If financial instruments were perfect substitutes for one another, the yields on each would be identical. Any higher yield on one type of instrument would cause lenders to adjust their portfolios in favour of that instrument. The higher demand would then raise the market price of the instrument and thereby reduce the yield. Any variation in yields therefore represents a lack of perfect substitutability between different financial instruments. The various types of financial instruments traded in the UK are discussed in more detail when reviewing the functions of financial markets.

The role of financial intermediaries

Financial intermediaries come between these wishing to save (lend) and those wishing to invest (borrow). They provide a service that yields them a profit, via the *difference* which exists between the (lower) interest they pay to those who lend and the (higher) interest they receive from those who borrow. That they can earn such profits reflects the fact that they are offering a useful service to both lenders and borrowers, which can be disaggregated into at least five separate functions:

1 brokerage
2 maturity transformation
3 liquidity transformation
4 risk transformation
5 collection and parcelling – size transformation.

Brokerage

The brokerage function is rather different from the other four, which might all be regarded as including elements of 'asset transformation'. A broker is an intermediary who brings together lenders and borrowers who have complementary needs and does this by assessing and evaluating information. The *lender* may have neither the time nor the ability to undertake costly search activities in order to assess whether a potential borrower is trustworthy, is likely to use the funds for a project that is credible and profitable, and is able to pay the promised interest on the due date. By depositing funds with a financial intermediary the household avoids such information gathering, monitoring and evaluation costs, which are now undertaken by the specialized financial intermediary. The *borrower* needs to know that a promised loan will be received at the time and under the conditions specified in any agreement.

By bringing lenders and borrowers together in these ways, the various information and transactions costs are reduced, so that this brokerage function can command a 'fee'. The size of that fee will, of course, be greater the more difficult and expensive it is for the financial intermediary to develop procedures for evaluating and monitoring borrowers in order to minimize 'default risks'.

The next four functions involve elements of *asset transformation*, in which the liabilities (deposits) are transformed by the financial intermediaries into various types of asset with differing characteristics in terms of maturity, liquidity and risk.

Maturity transformation

Here the financial intermediaries bridge the gap between the desire of lenders to be able to get their money back quickly if needed, and the desire of borrowers to borrow for a long period. In fulfilling this function, the financial intermediaries hold liabilities (e.g. deposits) that have a shorter term to maturity than their assets (e.g. loans), i.e. they borrow short and lend long. For example, a building society will typically hold around 70% of its liabilities in the form of deposits repayable 'on demand', i.e. which can be withdrawn at any time without penalty. In contrast, around 75% of its assets are repayable only after five years or more.

Financial intermediaries are able to perform this maturity transformation function in part because of the 'law of large numbers', which implies that while some depositors will be withdrawing funds others will be making new deposits. This means that, overall, withdrawals minus new deposits are likely to be small in relation to the value of total deposits (liabilities). As a result the 'funding risk', namely that depositors might wish to withdraw more funds than the banks have available in liquid form, is greatly reduced. This enables the financial intermediaries to hold a sizeable proportion of less liquid assets (e.g. long-term loans) in their portfolio.

Liquidity transformation

Related to the ability to transform maturity, banks also undertake liquidity transformation. Liquidity is the ability of a debt holder, e.g. the deposit holder in a bank, to redeem their deposit quickly and without cost in the event that they desire or need cash. Banks issue claims in the form of deposits which do not require their holders to give the bank any notice or pay any penalties for premature withdrawal. In contrast banks hold assets that are largely illiquid and costly to convert back into cash. This ability to hold liabilities that are liquid but assets that are illiquid is a key feature of banks and is known as *liquidity transformation*. Banks can achieve this for much the same reasons as for maturity transformation – as the number of customers that a bank can attract increases, the ability to measure the amount of daily liquidity required for the bank becomes more predictable, such that a bank will be able to calculate, with some certainty, the value of cash that will be needed on any one day and hold enough cash reserves to meet this demand. The rest of their assets can then be held in more illiquid, higher yielding assets. Once again this can be related to the law of large numbers outlined above.

Risk transformation

This involves the financial intermediaries in shifting the burden of risk from the lender to themselves. Their ability to do so depends largely on *economies of scale* in risk management. The large amounts of deposits (liabilities) the financial intermediaries collect allow them to diversify their assets across a wide variety of types and sectors. 'Pooling' risk and reward in this way means that no individual is exposed to a situation in which the default of one or more borrowers is likely to have a significant effect.

Collection and parcelling

Financial intermediaries also transform the nature of their assets through the *collection* of a large number of small amounts of funds from depositors and their *parcelling* into larger amounts required by borrowers. Often the financial intermediaries have relied on obtaining many small deposits from conveniently located branches of their operations. This process is known as 'size intermediation' and benefits borrowers because they obtain one large loan from one source, thus reducing transaction costs. Of course this loan is an asset to the financial intermediary and a liability to the borrower.

The common characteristics of all financial intermediaries are therefore as follows. First, they take money from those who seek to save, whether it be in exchange for a deposit account bearing interest or in exchange for a paper financial claim. Second, they lend the money provided by those savers to borrowers, who may issue a paper asset in return. Third, in exchange for such lending they acquire a portfolio of paper assets (claims on borrowers) which will pay an income to the intermediary, and which it may 'manage' by buying and selling the assets on financial markets in order to yield further profits for itself.

UK financial intermediaries

The UK financial system incorporates different types of financial intermediary, offering lenders and borrowers a variety of instruments which have different maturities, liquidities and risk profiles. A popular method of classification is to distinguish between the bank and non-bank financial intermediaries.

- *Bank sector.* All the UK financial institutions that have been issued with a *banking licence*, including the high street commercial banks, the corporate wholesale banks and the foreign banks, all of which are regarded as being part of the bank sector. Currently there are 346 authorized banking institutions operating in the UK, a fall of over 200 from the 1990 figure of 548.
- *Non-bank sector.* The other financial intermediaries, including the building societies, insurance

companies, pension funds, unit trust and investment trust companies, are classified as part of the non-bank sector. A further disaggregation of the non-bank sector brings together those institutions which are *deposit-taking institutions*, such as the building societies, and those which are *investing institutions*, namely all the non-bank sector except the building societies.

However, even this simple classification of bank and non-bank sector is becoming more difficult to sustain with the growth of competition since the 1990s between these sectors (*inter-sector competition*) and between the institutions within these sectors (*intra-sector competition*), so that the distinction between banking and non-banking institutions has become increasingly blurred. Nevertheless, it may be helpful to consider the UK financial intermediaries under the following three headings: banking financial intermediaries, non-bank financial intermediaries and the Bank of England.

The UK banking financial intermediaries

The UK bank sector includes a range of financial intermediaries.

The retail banks

These include banks which either participate in the UK clearing system or have extensive branch networks. The retail banks are sometimes known as the MBBGs (Major British Banking Groups) which includes all the UK's large retail banks. Listing these banks was once relatively simple, but a spate of mergers and acquisitions has meant changes in ownership. This has been further complicated by the 2007/08 global banking crisis which has led to further rationalization in the UK banking sector. As a result, the largest retail banking groups operating in the UK are Barclays plc; Lloyds Banking Group (which now includes Lloyds TSB and Halifax Bank of Scotland (HBOS)); Hong Kong and Shanghai Banking Corporation (HSBC) plc; The Royal Bank of Scotland (RBS) plc; the troubled mortgage bank, Northern Rock; and Santander UK which is based in Spain but now owns Abbey National, Alliance and Leicester and Bradford & Bingley's savings business. Further complications have also resulted from the UK government having to step in to re-capitalize RBS, LloydsTSB and HBOS (who merged) and Northern Rock (see p. 455).

Traditionally, retail banks, through their extensive branch networks, have historically been primarily engaged in gathering deposits and creating loans, usually at high margins given that they could obtain deposits at low interest rates and could offer loans to individuals and firms at high interest rates. Activities in this sector were highly regulated until the early 1970s and were often described as being 'supply led', since most arrangements appeared to be in the interests of the providers rather than the customers.

Today, the retail banking market is increasingly competitive and banks are more responsive to the needs of their customers. The retail banks offer a wide array of services to personal customers, including savings accounts, unsecured and secured loans, mortgages, overdrafts, automated cash machines, home banking, foreign currency transactions and general financial advice. They also offer a range of services to corporate customers, including leasing and hire purchase, export and import facilities, payroll services and international financial transfers.

Total assets in the banking sector have increased substantially during the past 10 years, from around £3,145bn in 2000 to over £7,600bn by the end of 2009, despite the problems caused by the financial crisis; however, this figure is boosted by the trend of mutually owned building societies converting to banks (see below).

The wholesale banks

These include around 500 banks which typically engage only in large-scale lending and borrowing transactions, namely transactions in excess of £50,000. The wholesale banks include the following:

- *merchant banks*, of which there are about 40 including the Accepting Houses;
- *other British banks*, a general category covering banks with UK majority ownership;
- *overseas banks*, which include American banks, Japanese banks and a variety of other overseas banks and consortium banks.

The wholesale banks actually include a large number of small providers. This, together with the fact that the majority of transactions are completed with knowledgeable corporate clients, usually results in margins being low. Nevertheless, individual transactions are 'wholesale', that is of a high value (greater than £50,000 but, more typically, in excess of £1m) so that sizeable absolute levels of profit can still be made. Wholesale banking takes place mainly in foreign currencies, which reflects the substantial presence of Japanese and American banks in this sector. Recent figures show that London remains the most popular financial centre with 249 foreign banks located there during 2009. However, the sector also includes the British merchant banks, whose major business includes the acceptance of bills, underwriting, consultancy, fund management and trading in the financial markets.

Historically, retail banks could be distinguished from wholesale banks by the nature of their business, in that they dealt in a high volume of small deposits, operated an extensive branch network, were actively involved in the cheque clearing system and relied heavily on the personal sector for their deposits (liabilities). However, these distinctions are becoming increasingly blurred due to the participation of all banks and other financial intermediaries in wholesale banking and to the growth of the inter-bank market.

Much of this convergence between the retail and wholesale banking sectors has been due to retail banks entering the wholesale arena, largely because of diminishing margins in the retail sector. We consider the response of the retail banks to a variety of challenges later in this chapter (p. 451). Wholesale banking, however, has remained relatively unchanged in that the vast majority of transactions remain with the corporate sector and are undertaken in foreign currencies.

UK non-bank financial intermediaries

The institutions in this sector fulfil a number of specialist functions, such as providing mortgage finance, insurance and pension cover. They typically specialize in matching the needs of borrowers for long-term finance with the needs of lenders for paper assets denominated in small units which are readily saleable. The UK non-bank financial intermediaries include the building societies, insurance companies, pension funds, unit trusts and investment trusts.

The building societies

These are mutually owned financial institutions which have traditionally offered loans in the form of mortgages to facilitate house purchase. Mutuality means that they are owned by their 'members', namely those who have purchased shares in the form of deposits, and those who have borrowed from them. Until the early 1980s, building societies were the only institutions offering mortgages, and competition was restricted by various agreements and regulations between the various building societies.

Competition in this sector has, however, intensified since the early 1980s when deregulation of the retail banking sector allowed banks to offer mortgage finance and thereby to threaten the position of the building societies. This led to demands for deregulation to be extended to the building society sector in order to allow the building societies to respond by competing with banks in financial and other markets, where previously they had been restricted. The Building Societies Act of 1986, the subsequent Orders in Council of 1988 and the Building Societies Act 1997 have permitted building societies to offer a whole range of new banking, investment and property-related housing services, in addition to their traditional savings and home loan business.

The Building Societies Act 1997 relaxed restrictions on *unsecured lending* and permitted building societies, subject to their own prudential controls, to lend out 25% of their assets on an unsecured basis. In addition, it allowed societies to have greater access to the wholesale money markets, permitting up to 50% of their funds (liabilities) to be in the form of borrowings on these markets. This meant that societies need not rely as heavily on costly retail deposits from savers to finance their lending, allowing them to compete more aggressively with the banking sector. In fact, by the end of 2007 total wholesale liabilities in the building society sector were over £66 billion.

However, the 1997 Act, while granting societies more freedom, also ensured that the building societies' main function and basic purpose of attracting savings and making loans for house purchase remained. To this end, societies still have to raise at least 50% of their funds from individual investors (usually in the form of issuing a retail deposit) and remain restricted to having 75% of their commercial assets in the form of loans secured by a mortgage on housing.

The evidence indicates that building societies have remained true to their basic principles and remain predominantly mortgage finance providers. Table 21.1 shows that the building society sector provided over five times more mortgage lending by value in 2009 than consumer credit lending. However, the table shows that the building societies are seeing their share of the gross consumer credit market dwindle after an initial rise. The level in 2009 is only 1.9% of the total lending of consumer credit, reflecting both the effect of the financial crisis and the extent of demutualization. Rather more significantly, the share of the building societies in gross mortgage lending has declined substantially over the period to just under 13% of the market, whereas banks now dominate over 80% of the market. This reflects the trend in demutualization.

This trend is also reflected in Table 21.2 which shows that building societies are also losing their share of UK private-sector deposits. In 1985, some 45.1% of UK private-sector deposits were held in building society accounts and 49.5% in UK banks. However, by 2009 the building societies' share had dropped to 12.1%, whilst the share of the banks had risen to over 80%. In fact such a trend had been long established; for example, the building societies witnessed a fall in their share of UK private sector deposits of over 32% between 1985 and 2000. Table 21.3 outlines the conversion of building societies into banks and their consequent changes in ownership.

Demutualization

As we have already noted, the building societies have been losing market share to the banks in the deposit, consumer credit and mortgage markets. Indeed, in 1997 the banking sector for the first time had a greater share of gross mortgage lending than the building societies, a trend which is set to continue. However, this comparison is not entirely fair, as it does not represent a like-for-like comparison over time. In fact, a major reason for these losses of market share involve the demutualization and conversion of the larger building societies into banks, which means that their business is now counted as part of the banking sector. Table 21.3 shows those building societies which have converted into banks, the date of conversion, the total assets and the market capitalization involved. A number of reasons have been suggested for this trend towards demutualization.

■ Banks are in a better position than building societies to compete in financial services and mortgage markets because they can issue shares. This will provide the funding to permit faster growth and enable speedier diversification into new areas.

Table 21.1 Bank and building society shares of gross lending for mortgages and consumer credit, 2001–2009 (£m).

	2001	2002	2003	2004	2005	2006	2007	2008	2009
Gross mortgage lending									
Building Societies	26,086	34,862	46,347	46,563	43,505	52,391	51,847	37,760	18,531
% of total	16.4	15.9	16.7	16	15.1	15.2	14.3	14.7	12.9
Banks	119,031	161,852	194,853	201,866	201,765	234,592	246,925	193,982	118,533
% of total	74.6	73.6	70.3	69.6	70	67.9	68	75.7	82.5
Other	14,356	23,107	35,937	41,488	42,630	58,630	63,851	24,343	6,585
% of total	9	10.5	13	14.4	14.9	16.9	17.7	9.6	4.6
Total	159,473	219,821	277,137	289,917	287,900	345,613	362,623	256,085	143,649
Gross lending of consumer credit									
Building Societies	3,219	3,703	4,909	6,213	7,963	9,218	9,820	3,383	3,302
% of total	1.8	1.9	2.4	2.8	3.6	4.4	4.8	1.8	1.9
Banks	142,223	158,605	168,659	176,882	173,038	162,342	157,466	152,595	133,816
% of total	80.2	80.8	81.4	80.2	79.3	78.1	77.1	79.5	78.6
Other	31,792	33,868	33,513	37,491	37,222	36,433	36,993	35,973	33,165
% of total	18	17.3	16.2	17	17.1	17.5	18.1	18.7	19.5
Total	177,234	196,176	207,081	220,586	218,223	207,993	204,279	191,951	170,283

Source: Adapted from Bank of England (2010) *Monetary and Financial Statistics 2010*, Tables A5.3 and A5.6.

Table 21.2 UK private sector deposits with banks and building societies, 1985–2009 (£bn).

	1985	1995	2000	2005	2006	2007	2008	2009
Total UK Banks								
UK private sector deposits	114.9	412.6	696.7	1,047.50	1,193.50	1,333.50	1,522.90	1,675.00
% of total	49.5	60.6	79.8	79.9	80.7	80.8	80.4	83.0
Building Societies								
UK private sector deposits	104.8	211.3	112.9	189.8	206.9	231.6	275.6	244.3
% of total	45.1	31.0	12.9	14.5	14.0	14.0	14.5	12.1
Other								
UK private sector deposits	12.5	56.9	63.2	72.9	79.2	84.7	95.9	99.3
% of total	5.4	8.4	7.2	5.6	5.4	5.1	5.1	4.9
Total	232.20	680.80	872.80	1,310.20	1,479.60	1,649.80	1,894.40	2,018.60

Source: Adapted from British Bankers Association (2010) *27th Annual Abstract of Banking Statistics*, Volume 23, Table 4.03.

Table 21.3 Building society conversions, total assets and market capitalization.

Building society	Date of conversion	Total assets (£bn)*
Abbey (acquired by Santander UK)	July 1989	285
Cheltenham & Gloucester (merged into Lloyds Banking Group)	August 1995	1,027
National & Provincial (merged into Abbey – now Santander UK)	August 1996	285
Alliance & Leicester (acquired by Santander UK)	April 1997	285
Halifax (merged into Bank of Scotland to form HBOS – HBOS merged into Lloyds Banking Group)	June 1997	1,027
Bristol & West (merged into Bank of Ireland)	July 1997	n/a
Woolwich (acquired by Barclays August 2000)	July 1997	1,379
Northern Rock (UK government supported)	October 1997	87
Birmingham Midshires (merged into Halifax – Halifax merged into Bank of Scotland – HBOS merged into Lloyds Banking Group)	January 1999	1,027
Bradford & Bingley (a portion merged into Santander UK)	December 2000	285

*Total assets 2009 of the parent bank.
Sources: Building Society Association (2010a) *BSA Annual Report*, and earlier; Building Society Association (2010b) *BSA Yearbook 2009/2010*, and earlier.

■ Building societies which convert to banks cannot be taken over for five years, giving them time to establish themselves and compete with the larger banks.

■ Building societies which convert can now compete under the same regulatory environment as banks, which means that they no longer have restrictions on access to the wholesale markets. This provides them with improved access to corporate clients and to cheaper funding, allowing them to compete more aggressively in the consumer credit market.

■ Diversification into new and risky areas of business should, it is argued, be undertaken by using newly issued capital raised by newly constituted institutions rather than by using historical capital derived from relatively safe savings and mortgage business.

Such arguments were present in the conversion documents of both the Alliance & Leicester Building Society and the Halifax Building Society. The Alliance & Leicester document (1996) stated that the society intends to expand its commercial lending activities, extend its use of wholesale money markets, and increase its provision of 'personal financial services, such as unsecured lending, telephone banking, life assurance and unit trust products'. This will allow it to reduce its 'dependency on the mature residential mortgage market . . . and to build new sources of revenue from cross-selling'.

Expansion and consolidation was also a central theme in the Halifax Building Society's transfer documentation (1996). Their strategy statement read:

> Halifax plc are seeking significant earnings growth in the areas of long term savings and protection products and personal lines insurance . . . Halifax must continue to focus on its key competitive advantages of providing innovative and competitive products together with a high level of customer service.

Those who doubt the benefits of conversion have, however, expressed their concern. First, the costs of paying large dividends to shareholders will increase the interest rate to borrowers and decrease the rate for deposit holders (lenders). Second, capital markets have a tendency to be short term in their evaluation of strategy and performance, which may hinder long-term growth. Third, there is little evidence that banks are more accountable to their owners than are building societies. Fourth, takeover threats by other banks may still exist. At least one building society waived its right not to be taken over after conversion and in any case the protection from takeover for five years is removed if another building society initiates the takeover, as when Birmingham Midshires was acquired by the Halifax in 1999. Fifth, there are increased costs resulting from conversion, including the cost of compliance with a new regulatory code and the cost of retraining staff.

However, the comparison of building societies with banks and the debate as to the respective advantages and disadvantages of conversion have arguably become redundant issues, having been overtaken by events. Those building societies that wish to remain specialist mortgage providers are likely to stay in the building societies sector and, by remaining as mutual institutions, may acquire a competitive edge in offering mortgages at lower interest rates. Much of the rationalization of this sector may already have occurred, there having been 481 building societies in 1970 but only 63 by the end of 2005. However, it is worth noting that these societies continue to manage over £270bn worth of assets.

On the other hand, most former building societies that have wished to expand their range of products and services, having found regulations in the sector somewhat restrictive, have already chosen to convert. Of the top 10 building societies in December 1996, only three exist today, namely Nationwide, Britannia and Yorkshire.

Insurance companies and pension funds

About half of all personal savings are channelled into these institutions via regular and single-premium life assurance and pension payments. These savings from the personal sector are used to acquire a portfolio of assets. The institutions then manage these assets with the objective that they yield a sufficient return to pay the eventual insurance and pension claims as well as providing a working rate of return for the financial institutions themselves. The insurance companies and pension funds are major investors in the financial markets and exert considerable influence in these markets. They hold large amounts of long-term debt and help absorb ('make markets in') large volumes and values of new issues of various equities, bills and bonds.

Although these insurance companies and pension funds compete strongly against each other in the personal savings market, their portfolio choices differ because the structures of their liabilities differ. For example, the life assurance companies hold a larger proportion of assets as fixed-interest securities, because many of their liabilities are expressed in nominal terms (e.g. money value of payments in the future on policies is known). Pension funds, however, hold a larger proportion of assets in the form of equities, which historically have yielded higher real rates of return, because many of their liabilities are expressed in real terms (e.g. pensions paid in the future are often index linked). However, both these institutions are affected by the volatility of financial markets, both domestic and worldwide. For example, at the beginning of 2000 they held quoted UK company shares to the value of £743bn, which made up 45% of their total financial assets of £1,657bn. As the UK share market dropped, the value of their investments in UK company shares halved and by the end of 2002 it was worth only £388bn. As a result, total financial assets held by insurance companies and pension funds also fell to 1998 levels of around £1,250bn. The financial crisis has meant that the value of these holdings had dropped to £353bn by 2009. Importantly, such volatility can affect both premiums and payouts in the sector.

Unit and investment trusts

Both unit and investment trusts offer lenders a chance to buy into a diversified portfolio of assets and thereby reduce risk while at the same time receiving attractive returns. These institutions can achieve this by pooling the funds received from a large number of small investors and then implementing various portfolio management techniques not available to such small investors.

There are over 1,400 *unit trusts*, provided by individual companies, banks and insurance companies. A lender looking to buy into a unit trust purchases the number of units they can afford at the current value and then pays a further 5% of the purchase price for the management of the fund. The price of each unit is given by the net value of the trust's assets divided by the number of units outstanding. The size of the unit trust fund varies with the amount of units currently in issue, which allows the fund to expand and contract depending on demand, thus unit trusts are termed 'open ended'.

There are over 300 *investment trusts* and they undertake a similar role, allowing individuals to benefit from a pooled investment fund. However, investment trusts are plcs and raise funds for investment by issuing equity and debt and by using retained profits. Unlike unit trusts they can also borrow money. If individuals or firms are to buy into an investment trust, they must purchase their shares, which are limited in supply, thus investment trusts are termed 'closed ended'.

Table 21.4 shows total investments by both unit and investment trusts. Two factors are worth noting. First, unit trusts hold over ten times the value of assets held by the investment trusts. Second, both institutions invest heavily in foreign company shares, with unit trusts investing around 37% and investment trusts about 49% in this type of investment.

An important issue is the extent to which insurance, pension fund, investment and unit trust companies are involved in *equity finance*. These institutions are responsible for holding around 50% of UK equity, which means that share prices will be significantly affected by the portfolio preferences of these institutions. That preference will be influenced by overall

Table 21.4 Total investments of investment and unit trusts, 2008 (market value, £m).

	Unit trusts holdings	Investment trusts holdings
Investment:		
British Government Securities	33,469	628
UK listed company securities	190,985	14,204
Overseas company securities	144,108	19,008
Other	19,637	5,239
Total	388,199	39,079

Source: Adapted from ONS (2010) *Financial Statistics 2010*, Tables 5.2C and 5.2D.

'environmental' factors, such as the inflation rate, the exchange rate and the state of business expectations, as well as by the particular needs of the institutions themselves. A concern is that such institutions may tend to be affected in the same way by the same set of factors, so that share prices may be more volatile than would otherwise be the case. This could have significant repercussions on the individual companies concerned because share prices may then fluctuate in ways which do *not* reflect their true valuation in terms of yield. It follows from this that the ability of companies to raise funds on the Stock Exchange may be affected by the activities of these institutions, and possibly in ways unconnected to their underlying profit potential.

The Bank of England

The Bank of England is at the head of the UK financial system, is owned by the government (having been nationalized in 1946), and has a monopoly on the note issue in England and Wales. As the central bank of the UK, the Bank is committed to maintaining a stable and efficient monetary and financial framework. In pursuing its goal, it has three core purposes (Bank of England 2000, p. 14).

1 *Maintaining the integrity and value of the currency.* Above all, this involves maintaining price stability (as defined by the inflation target set by the government) as a precondition for achieving the wider economic goals of sustainable growth and high employment. The Bank pursues this core purpose through its decisions on interest rates taken at the monthly meetings of the MPC, by participating in international discussions to promote the health of the world economy, by implementing monetary policy through its market operations and its dealings with the financial system, and by maintaining confidence in the note issue.

2 *Maintaining the stability of the financial system, both domestic and international.* The Bank seeks to achieve this through monitoring developments in the financial system both at home and abroad, including links between the individual institutions and the various financial markets; through analysing the health of the domestic and international economy; through close co-operation with the financial supervisors, both domestically and internationally; and through developing a sound financial infrastructure including efficient payment and settlement arrangements. In exceptional circumstances (in consultation with the Financial Services Authority and HM Treasury as appropriate) the Bank may also provide, or assist in arranging, last-resort financial support where this is needed to avoid systemic damage.

3 *Seeking to ensure the effectiveness of the UK's financial services.* The Bank wants a financial system that offers opportunities for firms of all sizes to have access to capital on terms that give adequate protection to investors, and which enhances the international competitive position of the City of London and other UK financial centres. It aims to achieve these goals through its expertise in the marketplace, by acting as a catalyst to collective action where market forces alone are deficient, by supporting the development of a financial infrastructure that furthers these goals, by advising government, and by encouraging British interest through its contacts with financial authorities overseas.

In order for it to achieve its core purposes, the Bank is split into three main divisions, each of which has its own responsibilities to the UK financial system. These are the *Monetary Analysis and Statistics* division, the *Financial Market Operations* division and the *Financial Stability* division.

Monetary Analysis and Statistics division

This division is responsible for providing the Bank with economic analysis that helps the MPC (see p. 437) formulate its monetary policy to aid economic growth and control inflation. Within this division, economists at the Bank conduct research and analyse developments in international and UK economies and publish reports which are then made publicly available. These include the *Bank of England Quarterly Bulletin*, the *Inflation Report* and the monthly *Monetary and Financial Statistics*.

Financial Market Operations division

This division has three main areas of responsibility.

1 *Operations in the financial markets.* It is responsible for planning and conducting the Bank's operations in the core financial markets, especially the sterling wholesale money markets, where it aims to establish short-term interest rates at the level required by government in order to meet its monetary policy objectives (see p. 436). This division also manages the UK's foreign exchange and gold reserves and contributes market analysis to aid the MPC and the Financial Stability Committee in their operations.

2 *Banking and market services.* It undertakes the traditional role of providing banking services to the government, banks and other central banks and managing the note issue. In addition, the division also plays an important role in providing (and monitoring) a safe and efficient payment and settlement system for the UK financial markets and the wider economy.

3 *Risk analysis and monitoring.* It is responsible for analysing any risks that may arise from the Bank's operations in the financial markets and for assessing the effects that these may have on the Bank and the UK economy.

Financial Stability division

The Bank of England no longer has any supervisory or regulatory powers over the UK financial system, so the Financial Stability division undertakes to *maintain the stability* of the financial system as a whole. Its main areas of responsibility are domestic finance, financial intermediaries, international finance, financial market infrastructure and regulatory policy. This division works closely with the Financial Stability Committee which is chaired by the Governor of the Bank of England. In general, the work of the division covers the functioning of the international financial system as well as that of the UK. To this end, it carries out research into developments in the structure of financial markets and institutions and makes proposals for changes to increase safety and effectiveness. The division is also responsible for publishing the *Financial Stability Review*.

In operational day-to-day terms the Bank of England has an important influence on three major markets: the sterling money market, the foreign exchange market and the gilt-edged market.

1 *The Bank is a major player in the sterling money market* (see p. 440), buying and selling Treasury bills on a daily basis. The object is twofold. First, the Bank buys or sells bills in order to ease cash shortages or to withdraw cash surpluses, which arise as a result of daily transactions between the government and the public. Such transactions by the Bank affect commercial bank clearing balances, alter the liquidity of these banks and hence their willingness to lend. Second, the 'Financial Market Operations' division of the Bank trades in bills with the government's interest rate policy specifically in mind. The buying and selling of bills by the Bank affects yields and therefore influences interest rates throughout the market (see p. 443). The Bank, in its daily dealings, attempts to reconcile these two separate objectives.

2 *The Bank has a major role in the foreign exchange market* as it is responsible for carrying out government policy with regard to the exchange rate. A strong pound has been seen by successive governments as essential if inflation is to be kept low. The combination in recent years of a floating pound and a weak balance of payments on current account has made it necessary to attract short-term funds on capital account by maintaining high interest rates. The Bank also uses the Exchange Equalization Account to intervene in the foreign exchange market by buying up surplus sterling should it need to support the external value of the pound.

3 *The Bank is also influential in the gilt-edged market* as it administers the issue of new bonds when the government wishes to borrow money. Various methods are used, depending on market circumstances. The 'tap' method is where bonds (gilts) are issued gradually in order not to flood the market and depress the price; the 'tender' method is where institutions are invited to tender for a given issue; and the 'auction' method is where bonds are sold to the highest bidders among the 20 or so gilt-edged market makers (GEMMAs). The Bank also manages the redemption of existing bonds in such a way as to smooth the demands on the government's financial resources. For instance, it buys up bonds which are nearing their redemption date, so as not to have to make large repayments over a short period of time.

The Bank faces a continual problem in that its actions in each of these markets have repercussions for the functioning of the other markets. For instance, intervention to purchase sterling in the foreign exchange market in order to support the sterling exchange rate is often ineffective because of the size of speculative outflows of short-term capital from the sterling money and gilt-edged markets. As a result, interest rates may need to be raised in order to deter these short-term capital outflows. This often proves difficult, however, because of the way in which daily transactions between the government and the public affect the balances of the clearing banks with the Bank of England. For example, if the banks are short of liquidity the Bank of England may be purchasing bills on the Open Market in order to help replenish their cash balances. However, purchasing existing bills by the Bank of England will raise their market price and lower their yield, i.e. lower interest rates. This may then conflict with the need to keep interest rates high to prevent short-term capital outflows from depressing the sterling exchange rate.

Bank of England and the economy

The three main purposes of the Bank of England were defined in May 1997, when the then Chancellor of the Exchequer, Gordon Brown, proposed a number of institutional and operational changes to the Bank of England. First, it was given operational independence in setting interest rates which would now be the responsibility of a newly created Monetary Policy Committee (MPC) working within the Bank. Second, the regulation of the banking sector was taken away from the Bank and given to a newly established 'super' regulator called the Financial Services Authority (FSA). Third, although the government retained responsibility for determining the exchange rate regime, the Bank could now intervene at its discretion in support of the objectives of the MPC. Fourth, the management of the national debt was transferred from the Bank to the Treasury. These changes were set out in The Bank of England Act which came into force on 1 June 1998. The most important of these changes involved the creation of the MPC and the FSA.

The Monetary Policy Committee (MPC)

The Bank of England Act established that the responsibility for monetary policy and therefore for setting short-term interest rates was to reside with the MPC, a committee within the Bank of England. The MPC would be free from government intervention in all but extreme economic circumstances. The aim of short-term interest rate setting would be to restrict the growth of inflation to within a target range set by the government and announced in the annual Budget Statement. The target had been set at 2.5% for annual retail price inflation, excluding mortgage interest payments (RPIX), but was subsequently revised in 2003 to a point target of 2% for CPI inflation. Significantly, if inflation is more than 1% either side of this figure then the MPC is required to write an open letter of explanation to the Chancellor.

The MPC consists of the Governor of the Bank, two Deputy Governors, two members appointed by the Bank in consultation with the Chancellor, and four 'experts' appointed by the Chancellor. The MPC meets monthly, publishes its decisions within days of concluding any meeting and publishes minutes of the meeting within six weeks.

There has been much discussion as to the merits of these changes. In essence, they are an attempt by the Chancellor of the Exchequer to take the 'politics' out of setting interest rate policy. Hall (1997) makes the following points:

> As a device for enhancing the credibility of monetary policy the current regime, if allowed to work with optimal efficiency, is vastly superior to its predecessors, which had confirmed the

worst fears of outside observers by allowing the Chancellor to attempt to extract the maximum political advantage from the interest rate setting process . . . Moreover, if one believes in a high and positive correlation between the degree of independence enjoyed by a Central Bank and that country's success in fighting inflation, then the recent changes can only but serve to reinforce one's optimism about the UK's future inflation prospects.

It has been argued that as a result of such independence, the financial markets will gain additional confidence in the UK's ability to control future inflation. Some have pointed to the fact that long-term interest rates for UK government borrowing have reached a 30-year low since the Bank's independence was announced, as evidence of such confidence. Nevertheless, concerns over the new policy include fears that the Bank may set interest rates which are higher than necessary to control inflation, thereby stifling investment and raising the sterling exchange rate to levels which damage trading sectors of the economy, such as manufacturing. Others have argued that the MPC should have been given a target for economic growth as well as a target for inflation, to prevent an over-emphasis on deflationary policies.

The Financial Services Authority (FSA)

Overall, supervision of any banking system is essential to protect the interests of depositors, and although there was some degree of depositor protection in the 1960s it was not until the secondary banking crisis of the 1970s that formal supervisory structures were developed and embodied in the Banking Acts of 1979 and 1987.

Traditionally, the Board of Banking Supervision within the Bank concerned itself with three issues.

1 *Capital adequacy.* To what extent do banks have sufficient reserves of capital to cover the possibility of default by borrowers? This issue has become particularly important in recent years as the volume of Third World debt has grown to unmanageable proportions. The 1989 Solvency Ratio Directive established an EU-wide rule that a bank's capital reserves must be at least 8% of its risk-adjusted assets and off-balance-sheet transactions. Off-balance-sheet transactions include such things as an advance commitment to lend (rather than an

actual loan) which may or may not ultimately lead to a future balance sheet entry.

2 *Liquidity*. There is currently no formal requirement as to adequate liquidity holdings by banks. However, the Bank of England required all banks under the Banking Act of 1987 to keep a ratio of 'primary liquid assets' to some definition of deposit liabilities. Such ratios may differ as between different types of banks, and deposits will be ranked according to their maturity. The shorter is the maturity structure of deposits, the higher will be the ratio of liquid assets required.

3 *Foreign currency exposure*. This issue relates particularly to banks which take deposits and lend in different currencies. Supervisors are concerned that banks should balance their assets and liabilities in each currency in such a way that their 'exposure' (to risk of loss on the foreign exchange market) should not exceed 10% of their capital base.

However, in May 1997 the Chancellor also reformed the regulatory structure of the financial system. As already noted, regulation and supervision of the *banking sector* was traditionally the responsibility of the Bank of England. In contrast, the regulation and supervision of the *non-bank sector* has historically been the responsibility of numerous different bodies, such as the Building Societies Commission and the Securities and Investment Board which itself headed three other self-regulating bodies. The Chancellor of the Exchequer highlighted problems with the then regulatory structure in a statement on 20 May 1997:

> It has long been apparent that the regulatory structure introduced by the Financial Services Act 1986 is not delivering the standard of supervision and investor protection that the industry and the public have a right to expect. The current two tier system splits responsibilities . . . This division is inefficient, confusing for investors and lacks accountability and a clear allocation of responsibilities. It is clear that the distinctions between different types of financial institutions – banks, securities firms and insurance companies – are becoming increasingly blurred . . . [therefore] there is a strong case in principle for bringing the

regulation of banking, securities and insurance together under one roof.

The Bank of England Act of 1998 transferred the regulatory functions of the Bank to a new regulatory authority called the Financial Services Authority (FSA), which was now to be responsible for regulating all financial institutions, whether bank or non-bank. The Bank of England retains responsibility for monitoring the financial system, with the government establishing a structure whereby the Treasury, the Bank of England and the FSA work together to achieve stability. In a Memorandum of Understanding published in October 1997 the Chancellor set out the various roles of the Treasury, the Bank and the FSA, making it clear that these organizations should exchange information and consult regularly. A standing committee was established to provide the means for the three bodies to discuss any foreseeable problems.

The new regulatory structure was completed by the establishment of a new Financial Stability Committee whose functions were to oversee the stability of the system and detect any risk of system-wide failure. This Committee had the responsibility of liaising with the Standing Committee created by the Memorandum of Understanding. Figure 21.2 provides an overview of the new regulatory structure.

UK financial markets

The financial markets within the UK perform a variety of functions which make them attractive to both lenders and borrowers. Such functions include providing a place to trade financial instruments and a system by which to 'price' such instruments. The major UK financial markets are located in London, one of the three dominant financial centres together with New York and Tokyo. One reason for London's dominant position is the large number of overseas banks transacting in foreign currencies on the financial markets.

As with the financial intermediaries, there are a number of ways in which the financial markets might be classified. One of the most common is to separate the UK financial markets into the sterling wholesale money markets and capital markets.

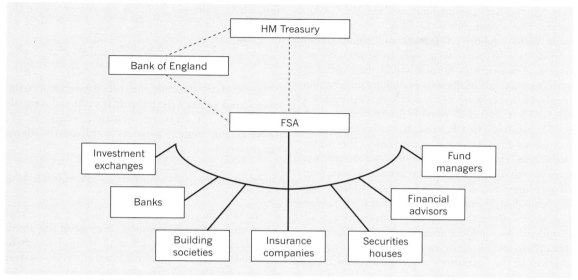

Fig. 21.2 The regulatory structure in the UK.

The sterling wholesale money markets

Transactions undertaken in the UK 'money market' involve the borrowing and lending of short-term wholesale funds by financial institutions. 'Short-term' means for periods varying from one day to one year, and 'wholesale funds' means amounts in excess of £50,000. Money market activity in London has developed rapidly over the last 35 years, partly due to the growth of the financial sector in general, but also because of the increasing demand for sophisticated financial services by clients both in the UK and abroad.

In the UK, the money markets have been traditionally split into the *primary markets*, which issue new financial instruments, and the *secondary* (or *parallel*) *markets*, which deal in previously issued financial instruments or securities (financial instruments which can be traded by third parties are known as *securities*). This distinction is no longer relevant today and it is best to think of the wholesale money market as one market issuing and trading short-term financial instruments. There are various money markets operating in the UK but it is useful to begin with the discount market.

The discount market

The discount market has always played an important role within the UK financial system. In this market, short-term (commonly 91 days) financial instruments known as 'bills' are bought and sold 'at a discount' to their redemption value on maturity (i.e. bought and sold at a price *below* their maturity value). The discount market has no physical location and only bills of the highest quality are traded. This is ensured by bills being accepted and underwritten (guaranteed) by creditable banking institutions (counterparties), with the Bank of England dealing only with 'eligible' bills that have been accepted by these registered counterparties.

During the nineteenth century, the major function of the discount market was the discounting of commercial bills of exchange which financed the increasing volume of international trade. In general, the functions of the discount market today are to allow commercial banks to adjust their cash positions, to provide short-term finance to the government and corporate sector, and to underwrite and 'make-a-market' in the weekly trade of government Treasury bills.

Traditionally, the main players in the discount market were the discount houses that bought and sold discounted bills, thereby acting as a buffer between the Bank of England and the UK banking sector. This meant that if the banking sector needed more cash (liquidity), the Bank of England would provide this by purchasing bills from the discount houses. The discount houses would then make the cash from the sale of the bills available to the banking sector. However, over the past few years the Bank of England has started to provide direct support to the banking sector. The UK banks have also made growing use of the inter-bank market and other money markets to adjust their liquidity, which has somewhat nullified the role of the discount houses. Today, many of the former discount houses have merged with larger financial institutions, so that the Bank of England now deals only with registered counterparties, which include banks, building societies and securities firms. The Discount House Association, which was the overseer of the operations of the (now defunct) eight discount houses, has been replaced by the Finance House and Leasing Association.

The main functions of the counterparties are to:

- underwrite the weekly tender issue of Treasury bills by bidding competitively for those bills not sold;
- provide short-term finance for companies by discounting bills; and
- maintain a secondary market in certificates of deposit (CDs) and other short-term financial instruments.

The characteristics of bills

Bills are short-term financial instruments that are generally issued by large corporations (known as commercial bills) or by the Bank of England on behalf of the government (known as Treasury bills or Tbills) and traded on the discount market. The original purchaser (the lender) buys the bill at *below* its face or redemption value, i.e. at a discount, and earns a return by holding it until maturity. Alternatively, the original purchaser can sell the bill in the discount market before the bill matures. For example, the government might make an issue of £100,000, 91-day bills, at a discount of £2,000. This would mean that the purchaser would pay £98,000 for the bills and on maturity, in 91 days, would receive £100,000 back from the government. For the purchaser of the bill, it is important that they are aware of the annual percentage 'yield' or 'return' on the bill so that they can compare it with other financial instruments. The

annualized 'discount yield' is calculated using the formula:

$$\text{Discount yield} = \left(\frac{discount}{redemption\ value}\right) \times \left(\frac{365}{n}\right) \times 100$$

In the above example the discount is £2,000, the redemption value of the bill is £100,000 and n equals the number of days to maturity, which is 91. Therefore the annual 'discount yield' on the above bill is given by

$$\text{Discount yield} = \left(\frac{2,000}{100,000}\right) \times \left(\frac{365}{91}\right) \times 100 = 8.02\%$$

The discount yield, however, is not the actual return that the investor enjoys, because in the above formula the redemption value of the bill has been used and not the *purchase price* of the bill. To convert the discount yield into the rate of interest enjoyed by the purchaser of the bill and one that is comparable with other financial instruments, it is necessary to change the denominator in the formula, thus:

$$\text{Interest rate} = \left(\frac{2,000}{98,000}\right) \times \left(\frac{365}{91}\right) \times 100 = 8.19\%$$

which is slightly higher than the discount yield.

Bills have a number of additional features.

- They are issued in denominations of no less than £5,000 (but more typically £250,000).
- They are *highly liquid* and *low-risk securities*. They gain their *liquidity* from being short-term and from being actively traded on the discount market. They are *low-risk* instruments because either they are issued by governments or, in the case of commercial bills, they have been underwritten by creditable banks – giving them eligible bill status, meaning that they are eligible for discount at the Bank of England.
- They are *fixed income securities* because the purchaser of the security knows the amount they will receive from the bill at the time of purchase. However, their price fluctuates in line with any change in market or current interest rates.

The sterling inter-bank market

This market is now the largest and the most significant of the money markets. The inter-bank market allows financial institutions to borrow and lend wholesale funds amongst themselves (dealing through money brokers) for periods ranging from overnight to five years. By using such borrowings, banks have been able to make (profitable) lending decisions which are to some extent independent of the amount of personal deposits that they have been able to attract, because they could now obtain any extra funding they might acquire on the inter-bank market. The amounts involved are large, starting from £500,000, but £10–12m is not untypical. Banks today borrow to finance lending, to balance out fluctuations in their books, and to speculate on future movements in interest rates. The London Inter-Bank Offer Rate (LIBOR) therefore represents the marginal or opportunity cost of funds to the banks and is the major influence on banks' base rates. The average size of the market in 2009 was over £237bn.

The sterling certificate of deposit market

Certificates of deposit (CDs) are paper assets issued by banks, building societies and finance houses to depositors who are willing to leave their money on deposit for a specified period of time. They are issued for periods ranging from three months to five years, but tend to be shorter rather than longer term and are issued at a rate of interest which can either be fixed or floating. Unlike Tbills and commercial bills, CDs are issued 'at par' (that is, its issue, nominal or face value) and the interest is added on to the face value at maturity, when the deposit is repaid. So, for example, the future (or *redemption*) value of a 91-day £100,000 CD that pays 5% interest can be found by the formula:

$$\text{Redemption value} = 100,000 \times \left[1 + \left(0.05 \times \frac{91}{365} \right) \right]$$

$$= £101,246.58$$

The purchaser of the CD can sell it on the market at any time if they have a requirement for liquidity. This enables banks to lend for longer time periods because they can be certain of having access to liquidity. In addition, CDs are attractive to portfolio holders because the yield is competitive. By 2009, UK banks held £132bn in CDs and other short-term paper liabilities on their balance sheet.

The sterling commercial paper market

Since May 1986, companies have been permitted to issue short-term (7–364 days) unsecured promissory notes, which can then be traded at a discount. This provides a way of raising cheap short-term funds for businesses that require finance for general business purposes. The 1989 Budget extended the right to issue this form of sterling commercial paper to governments, overseas companies and certain overseas authorities, as well as to banks, building societies and insurance companies.

Large companies, or companies with high credit ratings, can borrow funds at more competitive rates than they can obtain from the banks. The creation and growth of this market has led to *disintermediation*, whereby companies circumvent the various financial institutions and deal directly with the wholesale markets themselves. This could be a concern for banks in that they may be left with borrowers who are of 'lower quality' and therefore riskier should a larger proportion of the 'higher quality' companies deal directly with the wholesale markets.

Euromarkets

Eurocurrency is currency held on deposit with a bank outside the country from which that currency originates. For example, loans made in dollars by banks in the UK are known as eurodollar loans. The eurocurrency market is a wholesale market and has its origins in the growing holdings of US dollars outside the US in the 1960s. Since that time, eurocurrency markets have grown rapidly to include dealing in all the major currencies, and have become particularly important when oil price rises create huge world surpluses and deficits, resulting in large shifts in demand for and supply of the major world currencies.

The major participants are banks, who use the euromarkets for a variety of reasons: for short-term inter-bank lending and borrowing, to match the currency composition of assets and liabilities and for global liquidity transformation between branches. However, the market is also extensively used by companies, and by governmental and international organizations. Lending which is longer-term is usually done on a variable-rate basis, where the interest is calculated periodically in line with changing market rates.

There are two important factors which make eurocurrency business attractive. The first is that the market is unregulated, so that banks which are subject to reserve requirements or interest rate restrictions in the home country, for instance, can do business more freely abroad. The other factor is that the margin between lending and borrowing rates is narrower on this market than on the home market, primarily because banks can operate at lower cost when all business is wholesale and when they are not subject to reserve requirements.

UK capital markets

In contrast to the short-term transactions undertaken in the UK wholesale money markets, the capital market provides an arena in which private and public sector companies can trade medium- and long-term financial claims. These financial claims can be either equity shares, interest-bearing debt instruments (bonds) or a mixture of the two types of instrument.

Purchasers of *equity* have bought themselves a legal share in the ownership of the company, giving them the right to contribute in the determination of broad company strategy as well as a claim on the profits of the company. Purchasers of *debt*, in the form of *bonds*, in contrast, have purchased a long-term financial instrument which provides them with a flow of cash interest payments at specific times in the future. The purchasers of debt are classed as creditors or lenders and do not have ownership rights on the company.

The characteristics of equities

Equities (or shares) are non-redeemable financial instruments issued by companies. Any profits that are paid to shareholders are done so in the form of a *dividend*, which is usually paid annually. Shareholders usually have voting rights in the election of directors and have a claim on any income left over if the company is liquidated. However, the major advantage of holding this kind of instrument lies in the possibility of capital appreciation if strong profit growth is anticipated some time in the future. In the case of *preference shares* the company pays a fixed annual sum to the shareholder and there is also the possibility of capital appreciation when the share is sold. *Ordinary shareholders* bear the largest risks since if the company goes out of business, the 'preferred' shareholders have first claim to a share of the money raised by selling assets (although only after the Inland Revenue, Customs and Excise and secured

bank borrowers are paid). However, in good times, the ordinary shareholder will earn the greatest returns as dividend payments may be much greater than the fixed return received by the preference shareholders. As always in the financial markets, those who bear most risk have higher potential for returns.

The characteristics of bonds

Bonds are interest-bearing financial instruments issued by central and local governments, companies, banks and other financial institutions. The issuer of the bond (the borrower) undertakes to redeem the bond at 'par value' (£100) on a certain date and to pay the bondholder an annual fixed sum (the coupon rate) in interest each year. They are usually issued to mature in between five and 25 years' time with the year of maturity included in the bond's title, though some government bonds are undated and will never be redeemed. Bonds are also classified by their *residual maturity*, meaning the amount of time left until the bill will be redeemed by the issuer. Bonds with up to five years until maturity are known as 'shorts', those with between five and 15 years to maturity 'mediums', with those with over 15 years to run being known as 'longs'.

Bonds may be bought either as a new issue or second-hand on the secondary markets. The lender buying from the *secondary market* may have bought the bond at a price *below* par value and this makes the annual fixed interest payment more attractive, taking into account this lower price. For example, if 5% government bonds (gilts) of par value £100 are bought on the secondary market at £50, the buyer receives £5 a year from the government (that is, 5% of £100). However, the actual yield for the lender in this case is 10% (£5 from £50). In addition, the lender will gain a further £50 if they hold the bond until it matures when the government will redeem it for £100. Bonds normally bear a *fixed rate of interest* and this means that there will usually be an *inverse* relationship between the market price of an existing bond and movements in current interest rates. Therefore, in the above example, a *doubling* of the current interest rate from 10% to 20% would mean that the Treasury bond would *halve* in value (ignoring any later capital gain on maturity) to £25 because £5 return on £25 corresponds to an annual yield of 20% (£5/£25 × 100 = 20%). This would certainly be the market price for an existing Treasury bond with no future redemption date (known as consols) and therefore no future capital gain. If the price of such bonds did *not* fall by £25 when interest rates doubled, then investors would simply move their funds to financial instruments with similar characteristics where they could earn a return of 20%. Higher interest rates therefore reduce the market price of existing bonds and lower interest rates increase the market price or value of existing bonds.

UK capital markets can be split into primary and secondary markets.

- *Primary capital markets*. New issues of debt and equity are originally placed on the primary capital market and then traded in the secondary market which includes the London Stock Exchange (LSE). The majority of primary markets are 'over-the-counter' markets which are a type of market with no location, reporting system or centralized market. In these markets information is dispersed using burgeoning computer networks.

- *Secondary capital markets*. These are organized markets that enable the equity and debt of issuing companies to be traded. The ability to trade debt on a secondary market is an important part of any capital market, because it allows holders of long-term financial debt to liquidate their holding for cash at any time, for a known return. This means that new issues are more likely to be purchased. Also the holders of marketable financial claims can more readily maximize their utility by rearranging their consumption and risk profiles over time.

At the heart of the capital market in the UK is the LSE. The LSE has a physical location where equity and debt instruments can be traded. However, the amount of business transacted on the floor of the LSE is minimal, with the majority of business taking place outside the physical location of the exchange using telephones and new technology. The market can be split into two: the *Main Market*, which is the largest and is where the majority of equity and debt prices are quoted; and *the Alternative Investment Market* (AIM) which opened in July 1995 to allow smaller companies access to the secondary market (see Chapter 4).

A major factor concerning capital markets today is the growing competition between financial centres, especially those within Europe. Traditionally, London has been the busiest European capital market: for example, the amount of international banking business undertaken from London at the beginning of the 1990s was three times that of the next busiest European country. Reasons advanced for this dominance have included London's geographical position between New York and Tokyo, the large amount of foreign banks operating in London, the availability of trained staff, and London's convenience in reaching the rest of Europe.

However, with the evolution of the Single Market, the increasing globalization of businesses and the advancement of technology, the competition from other financial centres has become intense. This has meant that European companies requiring long-term finance are increasingly looking throughout the European financial centres and not just at London.

The Bank of England and the sterling wholesale money markets

Having introduced both the Bank of England and the sterling wholesale money markets, it will be useful to consider the operations of the Bank of England in the money markets and the ways in which it seeks to influence the short-term interest rate.

We have already noted that setting interest rates is now the concern of the MPC which operates within the Bank of England. The aim of the Bank's operations on the money markets is to *guide* short-term interest rates to the level set by the MPC. The Bank does this by providing liquidity or cash to the banking system at the interest rate set by the MPC and by buying government securities at prices consistent with the interest rate set by the MPC. This exerts pressure on the short-term money market rate of interest to move to the 'official' rate set by the MPC.

To be able to do this, the Bank of England manages its accounts in ways which will ensure that the banking system as a whole is short of liquidity. The Bank of England can 'tighten' bank liquidity in the following ways.

- *Through taxation*. When people pay their taxes they do so from their bank accounts; the flow of these payments to the Bank of England (on behalf of the government) drains the banking sector of liquidity.

■ *Through government borrowing.* Selling government securities (e.g. Treasury bills) to individuals or institutions who pay for them from their bank accounts.

■ *Through buying short-term claims on banks.* Such 'claims' are via the Bank of England lending to the banks for short periods. A number of these claims mature throughout the day and must be redeemed by the banks, draining them of liquidity.

■ *Through regulations.* For example, regulations which require the clearing banks to maintain positive end-of-day balances with the Bank of England.

The Bank of England is aware that banks will always look to the money markets in general, and the Bank of England in particular, should they need to restore their liquidity. At this point the Bank will offer such liquidity at a 'price', namely one which will reinforce the interest rate level set by the MPC.

The Bank of England can, for example, raise short-term interest rates by first starving the banking sector of liquidity and then offering to restore that liquidity at its official rate of interest. This intervention often comes in the form of Open Market Operations (OMOs) on the money market. Figure 21.3 provides a simplified overview of such OMOs. Where the

Bank of England wants to *raise* interest rates it *sells* securities, and vice versa.

The Bank of England conducts its OMOs by buying and selling high-quality government securities such as Treasury bills and eligible bank bills, government foreign currency debt and gilt repos. By far the most significant of these securities are the gilt repos.

The gilt repo market

In March 1997, the Bank introduced reforms to its daily operations in the money markets. The aims of these reforms were threefold: first, to increase the efficiency of liquidity provision in the banking sector; second, to increase competition by raising the number of eligible institutions with which the Bank would trade (these institutions are known as 'counterparties' and now include banks, building societies and securities houses); and third, to introduce the gilt repo into its OMOs, thereby providing the Bank with an additional instrument with which to influence short-term interest rates.

A *repo* is a transaction in which one party sells a financial asset to another party and agrees to repurchase an equivalent value of financial assets at some time in the future. The gilt repo market was introduced in January 1996 and quickly became a major tool with which the Bank of England could provide refinancing to the banking sector. Within three months of its introduction, over 50% of refinancing by the Bank was provided by the gilt repo and almost 50% of OMOs by the Bank were undertaken using the gilt repo. Figure 21.4 indicates that the value of gilt repos outstanding at banks and other financial institutions had expanded to an average of over £319bn during 2009.

In addition, the gilt repo market has made a considerable impact on the sterling money markets. As Table 21.5 shows, the gilt repo market has now outgrown the CD market.

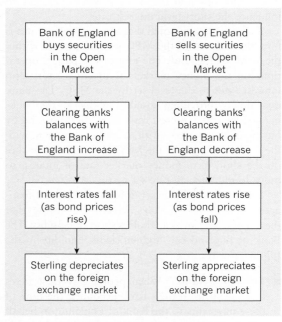

Fig. 21.3 Open Market Operations of the Bank of England.

The changing UK banking market

Prior to the largest banking crisis in UK history, the UK financial system was already undergoing a phase of major structural change. This had been brought

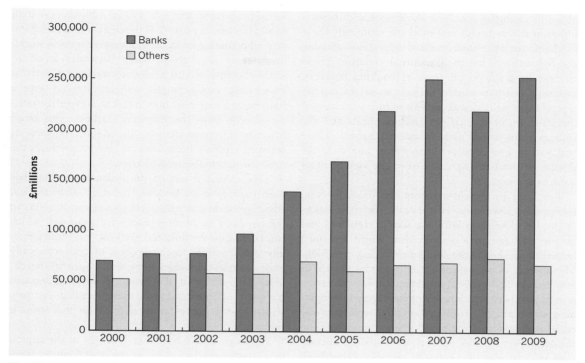

Fig. 21.4 Average gilt repos outstanding at banks and other institutions, 2000–09.
Source: Adapted from Bank of England (2010) *Monetary and Financial Statistics*, Table D3.1.

Table 21.5 Average yearly size of the UK sterling money markets, 2000–09 (£bn).

	Commercial paper	Treasury bills	CDs	Inter-bank	Gilt repo's
2000	16	3	132	159	120
2001	20	4	138	178	132
2002	26	14	138	219	134
2003	35	18	140	263	153
2004	N/A*	19	138	298	208
2005	N/A*	20	142	383	229
2006	N/A*	19	149	519	286
2007	N/A*	16	157	492	319
2008	N/A*	26	162	203	293
2009	N/A*	49	132	237	319

*Issues of commercial paper are not available from September 2004.
Source: Bank of England (2010).

about by changing economic conditions and increasing pressures in traditional markets; ultimately these led banks to alter their internal operations and lay the foundations for their eventual collapse. These change impacted on all areas of banking business, including customer profile, delivery strategies and the type of business undertaken. This in turn has changed the structure of the various balance sheets and the sources from which their income is derived. These will now be looked at pre-crisis before analysing the genesis of the banking crisis from the viewpoint of bank operations.

Response to pressures within the retail banking sector was rather slow. Historically, the retail banks in the UK developed within a stable, regulated and largely uncompetitive environment, which remained largely untouched in the decades preceding the 1970s. The absence of competition meant that by the 1970s retail banks had evolved into monoliths, with extensive branch networks employing managers who operated within a highly regulated market, typified by the cartel arrangements for fixing interest rates between the large retail banks. In such a regulated, uncompetitive environment it is hardly surprising that bank managers have been characterized as adopting conservative, risk-averse strategies towards lending decisions. However, the progressive build-up of competitive pressures on retail banks since the Competition and Credit Control Act of 1971 has brought about an entirely different landscape for the retail banks.

Some of the challenges facing major UK banks include:

- increase in suppliers;
- growing consumerism;
- the use of technology; and
- implementing the Basel Accords.

Increase in suppliers

The increase in suppliers of services that were traditionally the preserve of the retail banks has come from three main sources: the financial markets, non-bank financial intermediaries and non-financial companies.

The financial markets

Traditionally, the retail banks have liaised between lenders and borrowers, using their deposits to benefit the economy by providing a variety of financial instruments with less risk and at a lower cost than would have been possible if the market had to rely on direct borrowing or lending. However, new financial instruments (e.g. repos) have been developed to enable borrowers and lenders to transact directly at lower cost. For example, companies faced with a funding gap may now find that it is cheaper to transact directly with the financial markets. This trend towards *disintermediation*, i.e. direct transactions between ultimate borrowers and lenders, reduces the need for financial intermediaries.

This increased use of the financial markets has been fuelled by the growing trend of *securitization*. Although technically the term securitization refers to the bundling up of mortgages into 'securities' which can be sold on the financial markets, it is more generally used to refer to the process of converting any existing (non-tradeable) loan into a *security* (tradeable). The seller of the asset (security) guarantees payment of interest in the new bundled security, which now becomes more liquid than the assets it replaces.

Although banks have lost business to the capital markets, securitization has enabled all financial institutions, including banks, to develop and market paper claims against what were previously non-marketable financial assets such as long-term loans, thereby reducing the risks and cost of holding them. Banks have also benefited by acting as advisor and broker to those companies wishing to finance future projects by issuing securities directly onto the markets.

Non-bank financial intermediaries

These financial intermediaries include the building societies, insurance companies and unit and investment trust companies. They have utilized changes in market regulations and technology to offer new, cheaper and more flexible products and services to lenders. In many cases these institutions are not exposed to the high operating costs of the banking sector. For example, the Halifax reported a cost/income ratio of 42.3% in 1996, covering its last year of trading as a mutual building society, whereas retail banks such as Lloyds and NatWest reported cost/income ratios of 57% and 68% respectively in the same year.

Non-financial companies

The threat of competition from non-financial companies to the retail banks has become real as the costs of entry into the banking sector have fallen. General retailers, such as Marks & Spencer, and super-markets, such as Sainsbury's, Tesco, Asda, Safeway and Morrisons, all now offer many financial services, and even car manufacturers such as Vauxhall are developing their own financial products. These retailers can benefit from cheaper entry costs to many banking activities, due partly to advances in technology and also to their ability to utilize their extensive branch networks.

The term 'asymmetric competition' might be used to describe the competition pressures on the retail banking sector from these non-bank financial intermediaries and non-financial companies (Llewellyn 1997). It is asymmetric because changes in technology and regulation have made it easier for non-financial firms to diversify into banking business than for banks to diversify into non-financial business. This is mainly because of branding in that a strong reputation in general retailing gives a non-financial institution the possibility of using that reputation to sell financial products. However, the reverse is far less true, in that a bank with a strong reputation will find this of little help should it seek to diversify into general retailing. Further, whereas general retailers can put aside a small area within their current buildings to sell financial products, banks do not possess the spatial resources to sell tangible retail goods such as clothes, motor cars, etc. Generally speaking, these non-financial companies have entered the financial services sector for three main reasons: first, they have an established distribution network to provide such financial services; second, they have a strong brand image, especially as regards reputation; and third, in many cases (e.g. supermarkets) they can exploit information that they have gained from loyalty card and related schemes.

These new suppliers are clearly increasing the competitive pressures on the retail banking sector while at the same time restricting the ability of the banks themselves to diversify into new market segments. Further, the non-financial companies especially have the ability to cross-subsidize their financial services from other profitable activities and thereby out-compete the retail bank financial services.

Growing consumerism

At the same time, there has been an increase in the awareness, expectations and demands of customers for newer, better and more targeted financial services.

One possible reason for this growing 'consumerism' might include an increase in the number and quality of information flows available to consumers, especially due to the growth in the Internet. Additionally, this provides, amongst other things, easier access to brokerage and other financial advice. Demographic changes might also have played a part; for example, an ageing population has increased its demand for savings and pension-related financial products, especially in the context of a more restricted Welfare State in the future, including even less generous provision for the state pension. A longer life expectancy and reduced job security might be other important factors in this increased desire for newer, better and more targeted financial services.

Table 21.6 shows the rapid growth in demand for savings products such as PEPs, TESSAs and ISAs. *PEPs* are Personal Equity Plans, introduced in 1987 to encourage savings by being exempt from income tax on any dividends or interest received. PEPs can involve investments in a variety of market-based financial instruments, such as UK and European company shares and corporate bonds. The growth in PEPs has been extremely rapid, growing by more than £76bn between 1991 and 2001, with the value of PEPs in the UK being worth over £67bn by 2008. PEPs were closed to new subscriptions in April 1999. *TESSAs* are Tax Exempt Special Savings Accounts and are also exempt from income tax on savings up to £9,000 over five years. TESSAs grew to a value of over £30bn before the introduction of ISAs. *ISAs* are individual savings accounts and were introduced as a replacement for PEPs. Once again, they are tax free. Figures show the value of ISAs held in the UK to be over £45bn.

These identified trends suggest a shift in the balance of power from the *suppliers* to the *consumers* of financial services, and this shift is likely to continue as consumers demand more flexible, competitive and convenient financial products.

Technology

New technologies have tended to replace labour-intensive and costly processes with more capital-intensive and efficient processes. This is especially so as regards methods of storing and analysing information and assessing risk, thereby substantially increasing the volume of financial transactions that can be processed and reducing the cost per unit transaction.

Table 21.6 The demand for TESSAs[1], PEPs[2] and ISAs in the UK, 1991–2010 (£m).

Year	PEPs	TESSAs	ISAs
1991	4,520	7,326	–
1992	6,970	13,031	–
1993	11,890	18,455	–
1994	20,090	23,712	–
1995	23,800	28,047	–
1996	34,120	25,981	–
1997	49,530	27,257	–
1998	77,850	29,737	–
1999	91,920	30,040	–
2000	94,000	28,325	28,431
2001	81,120	13,284	29,778
2002	74,800	7,811	28,549
2003	57,380	3,689	27,962
2004	66,880	n/a	27,668
2005	72,620	n/a	28,237
2006	79,540	n/a	31,105
2007	79,250	n/a	33,041
2008	67,670	n/a	35,701
2009	n/a	n/a	40,094
2010	n/a	n/a	45,052

[1]Tax exempt special savings accounts (TESSAs) could be opened between 1 January 1991 and 5 April 1999.
[2]Personal equity plans (PEPs) commenced on 1 January 1987 but were closed to new subscriptions from 6 April 1999.
Source: HMRC (2010) *Inland Revenue Statistics 2010*, Tables 9.2, 9.3 and 9.4.

A simple illustration of the impact of new technology can be found in the growth of automated clearing. Although only introduced in 1985, by 1988 it had exceeded the annual value of the more costly paper-based clearing mechanism, and is now more than 10 times larger than paper-based alternatives, with an annual value of around £30,000bn.

A significant impact of the new technologies, especially the Internet, has also been to reduce the costs of entry into the banking sector, thereby increasing competition. For example, new competitors no longer need an extensively staffed branch network, given the availability of telephone and Internet banking systems, which permit competitors to reach consumers in their homes.

Given the nature of banking products and services and the requirement to reduce costs in an increasingly competitive environment, developing the Internet as a way of delivering service has been a major challenge to large UK banks. Today, all major banks have well-established Internet sites that offer a whole host of products and services. In addition, banks have created Internet-only subsidiaries which they market independently, examples being Cahoot, Intelligent Finance and Smile, which belong to Abbey, HBOS and Co-op respectively. Griffiths (2009) for Key Note recently found that on-line banking has become the most popular service for those who manage some of their finances on-line, with 91% of those using the Internet to manage their finances using on-line banking. Correspondingly, there has been a substantial rise in the number of bank accounts that have Internet access; for example, in 2000 there were approximately 6.5 million bank accounts that had Internet access, but by 2005 this had risen to over 24 million, and is expected to rise to nearer 30 million by the end of 2010. This rise could obviously not occur unless general Internet access had grown substantially in the past few years. This is corroborated by recent figures published by *National Statistics* which reported that in February 2006, some 63% (29 million) of adults in the UK had accessed the Internet.

A number of reasons have been suggested as to why the rise in Internet banking has been, and will continue to be, so rapid. These include:

- the extremely low marginal cost of transactions;
- no requirement for a branch network;
- easy access to service and product information, which lowers search costs; customers can access information on all financial service providers quickly and cheaply and so price variation will fall, reducing margins in the sector;
- low costs of entry onto the Internet, further eroding margins;
- the consumer pays to connect to the service.

The increasing use of technology will therefore affect traditional banking business by increasing supplier access to customer information, reducing the costs of supplying various financial services and lowering entry barriers. Such impacts are forcing retail banks to reduce their cost structures in order to compete more effectively and maintain their profitability.

The Basel Accords

Another major development affecting the operations of the banking industry during the past two decades has been the international implementation of the various Basel Accord so. Basel I was a non-binding agreement developed by the Basel Committee on Banking Supervision due to concerns regarding the capital levels of internationally active banks, as it was believed that inadequately capitalized banks could lead to an erosion of confidence in the international banking system, affecting not only the sector but the global economy. The first Basel Accord was developed during the mid- to late 1980s and endorsed by the central banks from 12 leading nations during July 1988. However, it was not until the mid-1990s that the Accord had been fully implemented. Basel II has been under development since 1998 and was implemented during the mid-2000s, although, due to the global financial crisis, Basel III has now been developed.

Basel I

The first Accord had three main purposes: first, to raise capital ratios for banks across the globe to a minimum level; second, to strengthen the soundness and stability of the international banking system; and third, to reduce differences in regulatory treatment of banks in different countries. Overall, it can be argued that Basel I has led to increases in capital ratios and the strengthening of the international banking system, as well as enhancing competition.

Basel I's main innovation was to get banks to distinguish between different credit risks for the assets which they were holding on their balance sheet (credit risk being the risk that, after making a lending/investment decision, the bank will not get its money back). This was achieved by allocating risk weights to different types of lending/investment decisions. In addition, banks also had to identify the credit risk inherent in 'off-the-balance-sheet' instruments. Banks complying with the Accord agreed to categorize their capital between 'core' capital (known as tier I capital), consisting of equity, and any retained earnings and supplementary capital (known as tier II capital), consisting of a bank's loan loss reserves, convertible and subordinated debt instruments and any revaluation reserves from equity and buildings. The Accord then introduced a minimum ratio of capital to risk-adjusted assets of 8%, with tier I capital to risk-adjusted assets being at least half, or 4%, such that:

$$\frac{\text{total capital (tier I and tier II)}}{\text{risk adjusted assets}} \geq 8\%$$

and

$$\frac{\text{core capital (tier I)}}{\text{risk adjusted assets}} \geq 4\%$$

In other words, during times when banks were already facing a number of challenges they now had to consider increasing the level of capital, with the inevitable effect of reducing resources to invest in profitable opportunities. If new capital was not forthcoming, banks had to forego riskier projects or even sell off some assets in order to comply with the Basel Accord. Either way, banks had to modify the credit risk associated with their asset portfolio and, on occasion, reallocate assets to less risky categories.

Basel II

By the mid-1990s it became clear that Basel I was becoming outdated as the environment in which banks operated became increasingly sophisticated. Consequently, the Basel Committee on Banking Supervision developed a replacement, known as Basel II, which was implemented in 2006/07 after much consultation with the international banking community. Basel II places even greater pressure on banks to rethink their operations and put in place procedures to manage their portfolio of risk. In the UK, the major banks have been preparing for some time, which has had major strategic and cost implications.

The new Basel Accord, formally launched in June 1999 with a consultative document published in 2003 and agreement finally being reached in 2004, has undergone an extensive review and consultation period. It is built around three pillars.

■ *Pillar I* provides banks with a framework for the calculation of *minimum regulatory capital requirements* associated with the banks' risk exposure. Minimum capital requirements will have to cover not only credit and market risk but, for the first time, operational risk. Banks are then given a number of approaches which they can take in order to calculate their capital requirement. For *credit risk*, banks can take either the Revised Standardized Approach (RSA) or the Internal

Ratings Based Approach (IRB); in each case, the minimum capital requirement remains the same at 8% to risk-weighted (adjusted) assets. The essential difference is that under the RSA the new risk weight categories are based on recognized external credit rating agencies, whereas the IRB approach allows banks to use more sophisticated techniques based upon their own internal estimates from models to assess their regulatory capital requirement – under strict methodological and disclosure requirements. The approaches available for *market risk* remain essentially unchanged from Basel I, while for *operational risk* banks can again choose from three different approaches for calculating the separate capital requirement for operational risk: the Basic Indicator Approach, the Standardized Approach and the Advanced Measurement Approach. The first two of these approaches base requirements on the risk-weighted three-year average of gross income, with the Basic Indicator Approach using a single risk weight whereas the Standardized Approach divides income across a number of business lines, each with its individual weight. The third approach, like that for credit risk, allows banks to utilize internal models.

- *Pillar II* is based around a process of *supervisory review*, aimed at ensuring that banks have adequate capital and reliable and appropriate systems in place to measure, manage and monitor risk levels. It is the responsibility of the bank to develop and review levels of capital and set appropriate targets under which the authorities will evaluate the bank's assessment and intervene if necessary. The Accord also allows supervisors to strengthen risk management procedures, apply internal limits, strengthen the level of provisions and improve internal controls. It also allows for an assessment of compliance with the more advanced approaches outlined in Pillar I.

- *Pillar III* concerns *market discipline* and is a check on the minimum capital requirements outlined in Pillar I and the supervisory review outlined in Pillar II. It is designed to increase market discipline by introducing a set of disclosure requirements that will allow comparison of risk exposure, risk assessment processes and capital adequacy across institutions. This will allow market participants to make more informed judgements of banks.

The implementation of Basel II obviously came at a cost to the major UK banks which developed a strategic response to the Accord, put in place structures to deal with compliance and develop new risk-management systems. In the UK, it was generally thought that it is likely that there would be some reduction in the regulatory capital requirement, but that this may be further affected by Pillar II where additional requirements may be necessary – this did not, however, emerge. The overall cost of compliance with such new and complex regulations was high, and this increased barriers to entry into the UK banking market for smaller institutions. For example, in 2004 *The Economist* suggested a figure of 0.05% of total assets, and PricewaterhouseCoopers (PWC) believe that between €20–30bn would be spent by European banks between 2002 and the end of 2006 on compliance. Of major significance is that Basel II failed to stop the 2007 banking crisis, although some argue that it may have helped slow the crisis and stopped it becoming even worse. In any event, the recent crisis has led to a rethink by global bankers and regulators and Basel II will be replaced by Basel III.

Basel III

The oversight body of the Basel Committee announced on 12 September 2010 that it has endorsed the capital and liquidity reform package originally proposed in December 2009 and amended in July 2010, known as 'Basel III'. The Basel III package was proposed to remedy alleged deficiencies in the Basel II accounts during the 2007/10 financial crisis. It was agreed that there would be:

- an unweighted leverage ratio;

- two new capital buffers – a conservation buffer and a countercyclical buffer;

- new and substantial capital charges for non-cleared derivative and other financial market transactions; and

- significant revisions to the rules on the types of instrument that count as bank capital.

Banks had argued that imposing excessively high capital ratios could lead to a double-dip recession; regulators countered that without robust ratios, a new crisis could result. The committee has decided to increase the capital requirements substantially, although, in recognition of the fragile state of the economic recovery, the package of reforms will not take full effect until 2018.

New capital ratios

- *Total Tier 1.* The total Tier 1 requirement increases from 4% to 6% under Basel III.

- *Total capital.* The total minimum capital requirement remains at 8%, subject to a new capital buffer. However, 6% of capital must be Tier 1, which means that Tier 2 (which will no longer be divided into upper and lower tiers) can account for no more than 2% of capital. Tier 3, which is used solely for market risk purposes, will be removed completely.

New capital buffers

- *Capital conservation buffer.* All banks will be required to hold sufficient capital to meet the minimum capital ratios, as well as having a 'capital conservation buffer' above the minimum 8% total capital. This buffer is set at 2.5% and must consist solely of common equity, after deductions. In effect, common equity capital (common shares plus retained income) must be equal to 7% of risk-weighted assets, other than in times of stress, when the buffer can be drawn down. This buffer is to ensure that banks maintain capital levels during recessions and have less discretion to run down their capital buffers through dividend payments.

- *Countercyclical buffer.* This involves up to 2.5% of capital being held in the form of common equity or other fully loss-absorbing capital. This buffer will apply only when a national regulator considers that there is excessive credit growth in the national economy, and will be introduced as an extension of the 'capital conservation buffer'.

Responses of UK retail banks

Retail banks in the UK (and Europe) have made serious attempts to reduce their cost/income ratios in response to these various market pressures. The focus has been both to reduce cost and to increase income (revenue) in order to reduce this ratio.

Retail banks have reduced fixed and variable costs by reducing the number of branches and staff. There was a substantial fall in the number of staff employed by the 'big four' retail banks from around 280,000 in

1989 to around 196,000 in 2001, though numbers have risen since then to over 265,000 this is mainly due to the changing structure of the sector (see Fig. 21.5(b)). Although the number of branches has declined, there has been a sustained increase in the number of automatic telling machines (ATMs) from around 2,000 in 1979 to around 21,855 in 2009 (Fig. 21.5(a)).

The cost/income ratio is a measure of operating expenses as a proportion of gross income. The cost/income ratio fell significantly during the second half of the 1990s. At that time, many believed that the ratio would need to be reduced even further if retail banks were to become competitive; a target of around 50% was widely accepted, given that other credit institutions such as building societies had cost/income ratios around 45%. Pre-crisis, the 2007 ratio had witnessed a steadily declining trend and had fallen back to the mid-50s from over 60% in 2004 and 2005. However, the spike in 2008 to over 100% reflects the effects of losses due to the crisis.

Diversification and consolidation

Although banks have reduced the number of branches and, from time-to-time, their staffing levels, the policy has met with resistance on both political and economic (customer) fronts. An alternative approach which seeks to tackle both sides of the cost/income ratio has involved the retail banks following a strategy of *diversification* which has ultimately created 'universal financial supermarkets'. This diversification into new markets has helped the *cost* side of the ratio by spreading costs over a wider product range. Further, it allows banks to utilize their extensive asset base (that is, branch network and staff expertise) in new areas using the same, or reduced, inputs. In addition, they can tap into their solid high street reputation and their access to customer financial data to help cross-sell products. Diversification into universal provision has therefore developed in the belief that banks can exploit scale economies and reputation advantages to generate a joint demand for their new and wider range of products. There are therefore many advantages to undertaking a diversification strategy in banking, including making more efficient use of a bank's branch network, the skills set of its staff, and its marketing and distribution strategy which

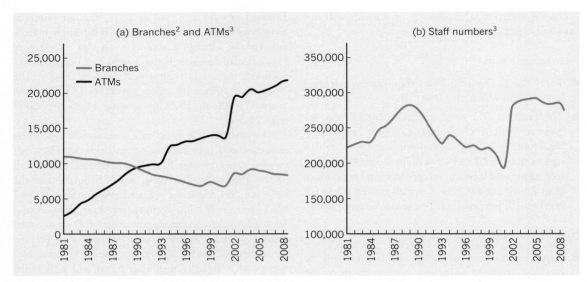

Fig. 21.5 (a) Number of branches and ATMS and (b) staff at the 'big four/five' retail banks[1] between 1981 and 2009.
[1]1981–2002 figures are for the 'big four' UK retail banks: Barclays, NatWest (now part of Royal Bank of Scotland (RBS branch level excluded for reasons of comparison)), HSBC (formerly Midland Bank in the UK) and Lloyds TSB (formerly Lloyds Bank). 2002–09 figures are for the pre-2007 big five: Barclays, RBS, HSBC, HBOS and Lloyds TSB (remembering that HBOS is now part of Lloyds).
[2]Figures prior to 1999 cover Lloyds Bank only.
[3]Figures prior to 1994 cover Lloyds Bank only.
Source: Adapted from British Bankers' Association (2010) *Annual Abstract of Banking Statistics*, Volumes 12, 23 and 27, Tables 5.01, 5.02 and 5.03.

can be utilized to entice customers into purchasing an array of financial products and services. Banks have also diversified as a reaction to customer demand as both retail and corporate customers have become increasingly sophisticated and banks must adapt to retain their custom. A diversified bank will have greater scope to identify specific advantages that are brought about by the unique nature of its products, with these unique features allowing banks to benefit from 'tie-in' and 'batch' selling. This is due to certain products being complementary to each other, generating tie-in sales which allow a person or company to obtain products which will solve all their financial demands.

UK retail banks now offer a much broader array of products and services and receive income from sources other than interest payments, such as from foreign exchange and equity dealings and derivative-based income. This decline in importance of interest as a source of income is shown in Fig. 21.7. Whereas non-interest income was only around 25% of all income in 1980, by 2004 non-interest income pro-

vided the larger source of banks' total income, and this remained the case during 2005, 2006 and 2007. However, again the impact of the crisis had significant impact on this source of bank income and the figure shows that in 2008 interest income is higher than non-income income. This is reversed in 2009 as banks begin to slowly get back on their feet.

Given that banks have decided upon a strategy of diversification, they must decide how they will become established in the new area of provision. Obviously, they can achieve this by growing internally; however, one of the quickest ways to gain market entry is by merger and acquisition.

Mergers and acquisitions in the UK banking sector

Mergers and acquisitions (M&As) have been increasingly utilized in the UK banking industry over the past 15 years as they can be a speedy way for banks to diversify their product range by purchasing a market leader in the chosen area. However, they have

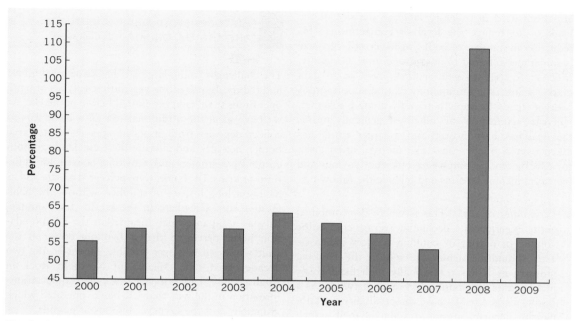

Fig. 21.6 Cost/income ratios for UK MBBGs[1], 2000–09 (cost/income measured by operating expenses as a proportion of gross income).
[1]Major British Banking Groups, which consists of all the main retail banks in the UK.
Source: Adapted from British Bankers' Association (2010) *Annual Abstract of Banking Statistics*, Volume 27, Table 3.07.

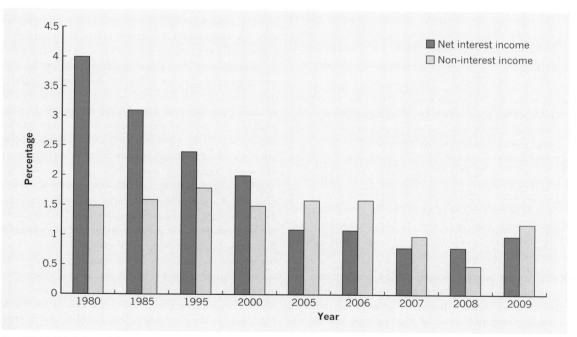

Fig. 21.7 Net interest income and non-interest income as a proportion of average balance sheet total for UK MBBGs[1], 1980–2009.
[1]Major British Banking Groups, which consists of all the main retail banks in the UK.
Source: Adapted from British Bankers' Association (2010) *Annual Abstract of Banking Statistics*, Volume 27, Table 3.07.

also been used in order to increase the size of the bank or to reduce the level of competition. This reduction in number of banks to fewer of larger size is sometimes referred to as *consolidation*. Generally, M&As are used to gain market entry or to gain market share. The terminology can be important, as 'merger' tends to imply a friendly coming together, whereas 'acquisition' or 'takeover' generally means the deal has been hostile and a larger entity has taken over a smaller one. The motives often given for M&As tend to emphasize efficiency savings and increased income streams and include the following:

- *Economies of scale.* This is where the combined entity experiences a decline in average cost as the volume of output of banking services increases. This should be achievable within the banking industry as it has traditionally high fixed costs, including its distribution or branch network. As a result, merged banks have the possibility of rationalizing departments and/or reducing their branch network while increasing income streams.

- *Economies of scope.* Such economies occur when, as a result of jointly providing products and services, the average cost of the new combined mix of services declines. Economies of scope can be either internal, where joint production creates cost savings, or external, where banks can benefit from joint consumption and the previously mentioned 'tie-in' and 'batch' selling.

- *Eliminating redundant capacity.* This is where banks eliminate waste by merging, allowing the streamlining of production, a reduction in costs and an increase in overall efficiency.

- *Improving managerial efficiency.* Linked to the above, a merger allows the removal of inefficient managers and the chance to replace them or to combine their roles. In addition, the newly merged bank may also have the chance to rewrite contracts which focus more clearly on incentives to perform.

- *Increasing market power.* M&A activity can be stimulated by the belief that the larger merged entity will benefit from an increase in market power, mainly because it may remove one of the main competitors. In addition, due to the importance of the banking sector to an economy, a large bank will have increased political power and could use this to its advantage.

An overview of bank operations and the UK banking collapse

The challenges to the large UK banks detailed above had the result of creating very different types of bank operations than had ever existed before in the UK. As we have seen, the traditional role of a bank was to collect deposits from its customers using its large branch network and allocate these efficiently to both corporate customers and individual households in the form of loans. UK banks were perceived as safe and as having a long history of stability, without the bank failures seen elsewhere in the world (for example, Russia or Japan) which meant that the UK population never perceived that a banking crisis on the scale witnessed was ever possible. However, the two decades up to the collapse of Northern Rock in August 2007 had witnessed a rather quiet transformation in the way that UK banks operated which ultimately cost the taxpayer billions of pounds.

The evolution of bank operations can be traced back to the rise in competition in the UK banking market and the banks' response. As the environment changed, banks reacted by diversifying and merging (or acquiring) other banks, which took them into new areas of operation. What was not widely understood was that their internal operations had changed significantly over the period, relying less on interest income from traditional operations (taking in deposits, allocating loans) and more on fee income from smoothing transactions in the financial markets. This can easily be seen by looking at Fig. 21.7 – the proportion of profits from interest income had fallen dramatically and by 2006, the year before the crisis began, non-interest income was significantly larger as a proportion of average assets.

The change in internal bank operations was possible due to the evolution of the financial markets. These markets had become much easier for both corporate customers and individuals to access – meaning that they were choosing markets over banks. This became known as financial disintermediation, or the circumvention of banks, and it threatened to severely impact on bank profitability. As a result, the banks reacted by utilizing the financial markets as shown in Fig. 21.1 via the line connecting the banks to the financial markets. This trend was made much easier due to large UK banks acquiring investment banks in the 1980s and early 1990s. Investment banks are banks that engage with financial markets on a daily basis –

underwriting new issues, buying and selling in secondary markets and, importantly, trading securities on their clients' and their own behalf. Investment banks had become dominant players in the burgeoning securitization market – a market that banks had started to increasingly utilize after the turn of the millennium.

By the end of the 1990s, UK banks had long realized that the old model of banking was becoming less profitable and would need to be replaced by managing their assets and liabilities more dynamically. Essentially this meant that instead of waiting for deposits to flow into the bank (by servicing a large and expensive branch network) they could access the money markets, which were highly liquid due to the vast inflows of foreign currencies – especially the US dollar. In practice, banks could issue debt instruments into the money market, boost their liabilities and use this cash to invest in profitable opportunities in the markets. Evidence of this trend can be seen in Table 21.5 by the massive growth in the inter-bank market between 2000 and 2006 from an average size of £159bn per year to £519bn! This fitted neatly into their strategy of reducing costs by shutting branches (see Fig. 21.5) which were no longer as important in raising cash from deposit holders. On the asset side they also had a historic problem – loans were unmarketable and lay dormant on their balance sheet exposing banks to credit risk and forcing them to cover this risk by holding the appropriate level of capital (see Basel II), thereby reducing opportunities to generate profits.

The development of securitization further added to the change in bank operations – they could manage their cash position by bundling up loans and selling them to the market. This meant that banks became increasingly exposed to the markets on both sides of their balance sheet – the liability side and the asset side. Securitization allowed banks to bundle up their loans into separate tranches, each with an individual risk profile (and expected return), and sell them onto

the market – thus increasing liquidity, reducing risk and freeing up capital. A bank could now bundle together, say, £500m of mortgage loans, and sell them onto the market. In practical terms, this meant that they received £500m (less costs) into their cash reserves and sold the rights to the principal amount of the loan and the future stream of interest. Importantly, they had also sold on the credit risk of the loans – the risk that the loanee would not pay back their loan. The banks were then free to use the £500m as they wished with many UK banks then making more loans that would again be securitized! Figure 21.8 outlines the basics of the process.

This process had changed bank operations into their becoming originators and distributors – originating loans and then distributing them to the financial markets. However, banks were now extremely exposed to the vagaries of the financial (money) markets and in August 2007, as the sub-prime crisis hit the US, Northern Rock became the first victim of the 'originate to distribute' model. Llewellyn (2008) notes:

> For three days in August 2007, the UK experienced its first bank-run since Overend and Gurney in 1866. Around £3 billion of deposits were withdrawn (around 11 per cent of the bank's total retail deposits) from a medium-sized bank – Northern Rock (NR). The unedifying spectacle of widely-publicised long queues outside the bank's branches testified to the bank's serious problems. The NR crisis was the first time the Bank of England had operated its new money market regime in conditions of acute stress in financial markets, and it was the first time it had acted as a lender-of-last-resort for many years.

In the preceding years, Northern Rock had become heavily exposed to the 'originate and distribute' model and had used it well for many years – gaining a reputation for strong and efficient performance. For

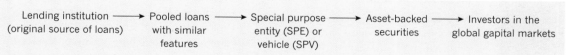

Sequence of events in the securitization process – an example: The home buyer receives a mortgage loan. This loan and similar loans are then pooled together and removed from the lender's balance sheet. The pool of loans is placed in a special-purpose entity (corporation or trust). The pooled loans become collateral for issuing asset-backed securities. These securities are sold to capital-market investors around the world who are attracted by their superior liquidity and credit rating. Investors receive loan interest and principal payments through servicing firms that collect loan payments.

Fig. 21.8 The securitization process.
Source: Rose and Hudgins (2010).

example, they were operating only 56 branches in 2007 compared to Barclays operating 1,733 and had generated profits of £626.7 m in 2006. But this had come at the cost of being highly exposed to the UK money markets and to the US sub-prime markets. The latter had led to US banks collapsing as the US financial markets lost confidence in securitization (finding it difficult to assess value and risk in these markets meaning that liquidity dried up). Uncertainty in the US spiralled and cash and liquidity in its billions were no longer available to be shipped over to the UK money markets. The Northern Rock bank could no longer fund its operations as they could no longer get money from the money markets either by selling debt instruments or by selling mortgage-backed securities – in fact, the inter-bank market contracted considerably from a high of £519bn in 2006 to £203bn in 2008, which signalled a rethink of the originate and distribute model (see Table 21.5). Northern Rock had no choice but to go to the Bank of England as Lender of Last Resort. This quickly escalated into the largest banking crisis the UK banking sector had witnessed as the sector ran out of liquidity and banks could no longer fund their operations. In this situation banks must turn to their capital reserves, but these eroded alarmingly quickly and threatened the existence of all the major UK banks. This resulted in the Bank of England having to step in during 2007 and 2008 to re-capitalize the banks – pouring over £40 billion of capital into the UK banking sector and forcing banks to merge in order to increase stability. This has resulted in Santander acquiring many UK household names and HBOS being acquired by Lloyds TSB.

Conclusion

The 2007 and 2008 crisis has left a myriad of issues to be considered and which have yet to be resolved, including: who was regulating the banks? Why had they been allowed to expose themselves to the financial markets on such a scale? Were banks holding appropriate levels of capital? Who was calculating individual bank risk and how was this linked to systemic risk? Were the risk models utilized appropriate and were they understood? Should banks return to their traditional operations?

These and many more questions are yet to be fully answered, but the authorities have reacted by changing commercial bank liquidity requirements, increasing the Tier 1 capital requirement to 7%, and utilizing the Treasury bill market once again to influence market liquidity (this has seen a rise in activity from £16bn in 2006 to £49bn in 2009). In addition, there is a new Basel III which has been written in light of what the authorities have learnt from the crisis. Concurrently, the banks have reacted by increasing capital reserves; for example Barclays reported a capital ratio of 16.6% in 2009, compared to 11.5% in 2004. Banks are also now holding much more of their assets as cash; for example, the Major British Banking Groups (MBBGs) held £112.8bn of cash on their balance sheet by the end of 2009, compared to only £10.2bn in 2005. In the UK the Independent Banking Commission has been tasked with investigating the crisis and recommending regulatory reform. Its findings are due by September 2011.

Key points

- Financial institutions exist to match the needs of borrowers and lenders, i.e. to *mediate* between them.

- Mediation may be necessary because borrowers and lenders have different requirements in terms of maturity, liquidity and yield.

- There are three main types of 'operator' in the UK financial system: lenders and borrowers, financial intermediaries and the various financial markets in which transactions take place.

- Financial intermediaries can take one of two main forms: brokerage intermediaries and asset-transforming intermediaries. *Brokerage intermediaries* assess information on lenders and borrowers but do not purchase or hold financial assets. *Asset-transforming intermediaries* acquire liabilities and transform them into assets with different characteristics in terms of maturity, liquidity and yield.

- UK financial intermediaries can also be categorized as *bank financial intermediaries*,

which include the retail and wholesale banks, and *non-bank financial intermediaries*, which include building societies, pension funds, investment and unit trusts.

■ Financial intermediation is becoming increasingly competitive and diversified. Not only are existing 'players' widening the range of activities in which they are involved but entirely new 'players' are entering the markets (e.g. supermarkets and banking services).

■ The Bank of England has been granted independence in the setting of short-term interest rates and this is overseen by the Monetary Policy Committee (MPC) which is a committee within the Bank. The Bank manipulates short-term interest rates via open market operations in the

money markets using predominantly gilt repos.

■ Financial institutions are regulated by the Financial Services Authority (FSA). However, financial stability is maintained via frequent discussions between the FSA, the Bank of England and the Treasury department.

■ Financial markets can be split into two main markets: the money markets, which mainly deal in short-term financial assets, and the capital markets, which mainly deal in long-term financial claims.

■ UK banks have undergone considerable change since the 1990s and the change in both external strategies and internal operations – especially their reliance on the financial money markets – contributed to the recent financial crisis.

Now try the self-check questions for this chapter on the Companion Website. You will also find useful links to relevant websites.

References and further reading

Bank of England (1997) The Bank of England's operations in the sterling money markets, *Bank of England Quarterly Bulletin*, May (2), 204–207.

Bank of England (2000) *Bank of England Annual Report 2000*, London.

Bank of England (2010) *Monetary and Financial Statistics 2010*, London.

Bénassy-Quéré, A. and Coeuré, B. (2010) *Economic Policy*, Oxford, Oxford University Press.

British Bankers' Association (1998) *15th Annual Abstract of Banking Statistics*, London.

British Bankers' Association (2010) *27th Annual Abstract of Banking Statistics*, London.

Building Society Association (2010a) *BSA Yearbook 2009/2010*, London.

Building Society Association (2010b) *BSA Annual Report*, London.

Casu, B., Girardone, C. and Molyneux, P. (2011) *Introduction to Banking*, Harlow, Financial Times/Prentice Hall.

Criado, S. and van Rixtel, A. (2008) *Structured Finance and the Financial Turmoil of 2001–2008: An Introductory Overview*, Documentos Ocasionales No. 0808, Madrid, Banco de Espana.

Dungey, M., Fry, R., Gonzales-Hermosillo, B. and Martin, V. (2011) *Transmission of Financial Crises and Contagion*, Oxford, Oxford University Press.

European Commission (1997) *Credit Institutions and Banking*, Vol. 3, Subseries II, Impact on

Services, The Single Market Review, London, Kogan Page/Earthscan.

FSA (2009) *The Turner Review: A Regulatory Response to the Global Banking Crisis*, London, Financial Services Authority.

Giavazzi, F. and Blanchard, O. (2010) *Macroeconomics: A European Perspective*, Harlow, Financial Times/Prentice Hall.

Gnos, C. (2009) *Monetary Policy and Financial Stability*, Cheltenham, Edward Elgar.

Greenbaum, S. I. and Thakor, A. V. (2007) *Contemporary Financial Intermediation*, Orlando FL, Dryden Press.

Griffiths, J. (ed.) (2009) *Financial Services Organisations on the Internet*, Key Note Market Assessment, July, Richmond upon Thames, Keynote.

Hall, M. J. B. (1997) *All Change at the Bank*, Banking Centre Research Paper No. 11–97, Loughborough, Loughborough University.

Heffernan, S. (2005) *Modern Banking*, Chichester, Wiley.

HMRC (2010) *Inland Revenue Statistics 2010*, Inland Revenue Analytical Services Division, London.

HM Treasury (2003) *The New Capital Adequacy Directive, CAD 3: The transposition of the new Basel Accord into EU legislation*, Consultation Document, December, London.

Howells, P. and Bain, K. (2007) *Financial Markets and Institutions*, Harlow, Financial Times/Prentice Hall.

IFSL (2010) *Banking*, City Business Series, February, London, International Financial Services.

Llewellyn, D. (1997) *Trends in the British Financial System: the Context for Building Societies*, London, Building Societies Association for Building Societies Trust.

Llewellyn, D. (2008) The Northern Rock crisis: a multi-dimensional problem waiting to happen, *Journal of Financial Regulation and Compliance*, 16(1): 35–58.

ONS (2010) *Financial Statistics*, London, Office for National Statistics.

Pilbeam, K. (2010) *Finance and Financial Markets*, Basingstoke, Palgrave Macmillan.

Rodgers, P. (1997) Changes at the Bank of England, *Bank of England Quarterly Bulletin*, 37(3): 241–7.

Rodgers, P. (1998) The Bank of England Act, *Bank of England Quarterly Bulletin*, 38(2): 93–9.

Rose, P. S. and Hudgins, S. C. (2010) *Bank Management and Financial Services*, Maidenhead, McGraw-Hill.

Santomero, A. M. and Babbel, D. F. (2001) *Financial Markets, Instruments, and Institutions* (2nd edn), Chicago IL, Irwin.

Stiglitz, J. (2010) *Freefall: Free Markets and the Sinking of the Global Economy*, London, Penguin.

Webb, R. (2003) Levels of relative efficiency in large UK banks: a DEA window analysis, *International Journal of the Economics of Business*, 10(3): 305–22.

The following websites are relevant to this chapter:

Bank for International Settlements: www.bis.org
Bank of England: www.bankofengland.co.uk
British Bankers' Association: www.bba.org.uk
Building Societies' Association: www.bas.org.uk
Chartered Institute of Bankers: www.cib.org.uk
European Central Bank: www.ecb.int
Financial Times: www.ft.com
International Financial Services London: www.ifsl.org.uk
London Stock Exchange: www.londonstockexchange.com

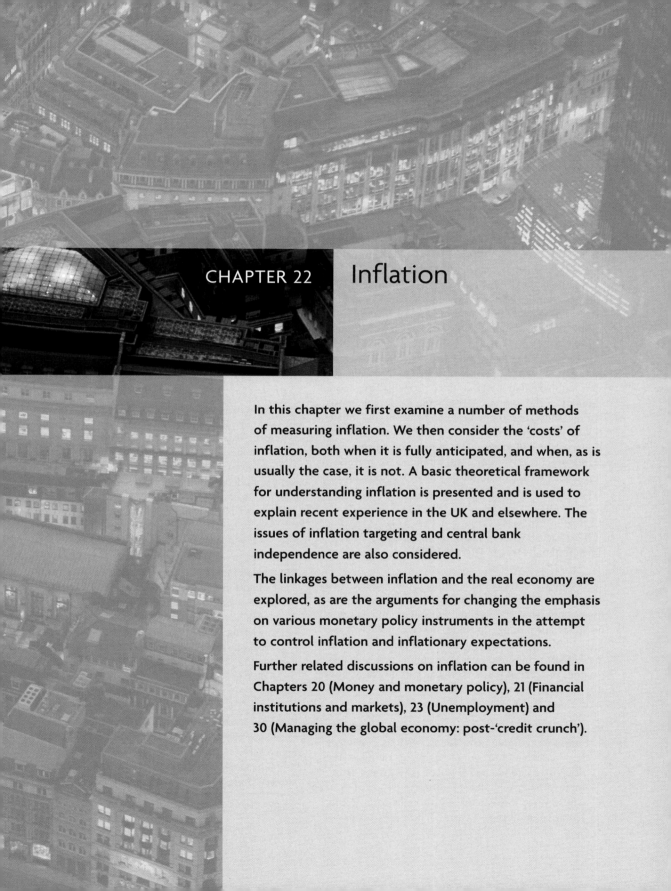

CHAPTER 22   Inflation

In this chapter we first examine a number of methods
of measuring inflation. We then consider the 'costs' of
inflation, both when it is fully anticipated, and when, as is
usually the case, it is not. A basic theoretical framework
for understanding inflation is presented and is used to
explain recent experience in the UK and elsewhere. The
issues of inflation targeting and central bank
independence are also considered.

The linkages between inflation and the real economy are
explored, as are the arguments for changing the emphasis
on various monetary policy instruments in the attempt
to control inflation and inflationary expectations.

Further related discussions on inflation can be found in
Chapters 20 (Money and monetary policy), 21 (Financial
institutions and markets), 23 (Unemployment) and
30 (Managing the global economy: post-'credit crunch').

The definition and measurement of inflation

Inflation is a persistent tendency for the general level of prices to rise. In effect the rate of inflation measures the change in the purchasing power of money, i.e. how much more money you would need to have this year when faced with this year's prices to be as well off as you were last year when faced with last year's prices.

The UK has two main measures of inflation, the Consumer Price Index (CPI) and the Retail Price Index (RPI). The CPI is used as inflation target by the UK government, and the Monetary Policy Committee (MPC) of the Bank of England is given this inflation target and tasked with achieving it when it sets interest rates each month. The calculation of the CPI is based on EU definitions and so is useful for making international comparisons of inflation. The RPI was first published in 1947 and is probably the more familiar of the two measures, being used as the basis for tax allowances, state benefits, pensions and index-linked gilts. However, from April 2011 the CPI has replaced the RPI as the price index used when calculating benefits, tax credits and public sector pensions, although the RPI will still be used to update index-linked gilts.

The Consumer Price Index (CPI) and the Retail Price Index (RPI)

The simplest way to think about a price index is to imagine a huge 'basket' of goods and services that represents what the average consumer purchases; it includes such things as food, foreign holidays, car fuel, clothing, housing and so on. The *content* of the basket stays the same each year, but as prices change so does the *cost* of the basket. The CPI measures how the average price of this representative basket changes over time.

■ *CPI.* The CPI is calculated using around 700 separate and representative items, as it is obviously impracticable and unnecessary to monitor the price of all goods and services. The group 'fruit', for example, includes 15 different types of fruit whose price movements are thought to be representative of all types of fruit. These 15 fruit prices

are then combined together to obtain the *overall* movement in the price of the group, 'fruit'. The coverage of items in the CPI is broadly similar to that of the RPI except in its treatment of housing costs. The CPI does *not* include council tax, mortgage interest payments, house depreciation, buildings insurance and one or two other housing costs. On the other hand, the CPI does include charges for financial services, which the RPI does not.

Households also spend differing amounts on the various goods in their 'basket'. A 10% rise in the price of gas, for example, would have more impact than a 10% rise in the price of fruit. The items in the index are therefore given differing weights to reflect their relative importance in consumer expenditure, as Table 22.1 indicates. The CPI weights are based on expenditure within the UK by all private households, foreign visitors to the UK and residents in institutions such as nursing homes, hospitals and university halls of residence.

■ *RPI.* In contrast, the expenditure underlying the RPI is more limited, excluding the top 4% of households by income and excluding pensioner household where at least three-quarters of income is from state benefits. The expenditure of these groups is thought not to be typical of other households and so is excluded from the RPI. To keep the RPI index

Table 22.1 CPI divisions and weights, 2000 and 2010.

	2000	2010
CPI (overall index)	1000	1000
Food and non-alcoholic beverages	121	108
Alcoholic beverages and tobacco	57	40
Clothing and footwear	70	56
Housing, water, electricity, gas and other fuels	118	129
Furniture, household equipment and maintenance	78	64
Health	14	22
Transport	161	164
Communications	25	25
Recreation and culture	149	150
Education	13	19
Restaurants and hotels	137	126
Miscellaneous goods and services	57	97

Source: ONS (various).

up to date, the weights are changed each year in line with changes in expenditure and new items are included and old ones dropped. In 2010 for example, in came Blu-ray disc players, garlic bread, liquid soap and household services maintenance policies but out went pitta bread, fizzy canned drinks, bars of soap and gas call-out charges.

Calculating CPI and RPI indices

In order to construct the indices, prices are collected around the middle of each month. Price collectors record about 110,000 prices for 560 items in a variety of shops of all sizes in around 150 locations throughout the UK. The collectors go to the same shops each month to compare like with like. For reasons of efficiency, some prices are collected centrally; examples being newspapers, water supply, rail tickets and the prices from some larger retailers that have national pricing policies.

Once prices have been collected an index is calculated. Changes in the prices of individual goods and services are measured by relating them to the prices in the previous January, and these *price relatives* are weighted by the current year's weights to form the overall index based on January of that year. The final stage is to then chain link[1] the index so that comparisons can be made with previous years and specifically with the base year (2005 = 100 for the CPI and Jan 1987 = 100 for the RPI). Chain linking also allows comparisons to be made which are free of the distortion that a change in the shopping 'basket' would otherwise introduce.

The CPI index for September 2010 stood at 114.9 which means that average prices have risen by about 15% since 2005. As the index is an average it conceals the fact that some prices have increased more rapidly (gas 78%, electricity 55%, postal services 50% and education 57%) while other prices have increased less rapidly or even fallen (audio visual equipment by over 40%). In September 2009 the CPI stood at 111.5 so the percentage change on a year earlier (the *annual* inflation rate) is calculated as:

$$[(114.9 - 111.5)/111.5] \times 100\% = 3.1\% \text{ (rounded)}$$

In comparison, the RPI index for September 2010 and September 2009 stood at 225.3 and 215.3 respectively, giving an annual rate of inflation as measured by the all items RPI of 4.6%:

$$[(225.3 - 215.3)/215.3] \times 100\% = 4.6\% \text{ (rounded)}$$

Inflation as measured by the RPI and RPIX is shown in Fig. 22.1.

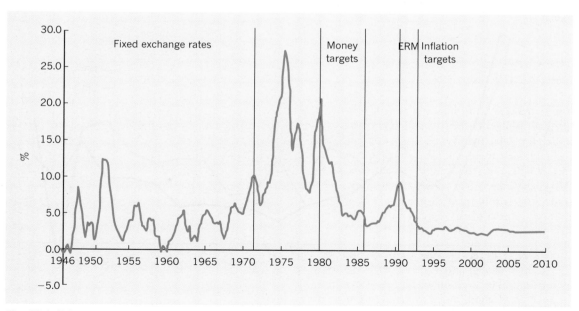

Fig. 22.1 Inflation is measured as the annual increase in the retail price index from 1946 to 1974, and in the retail price index excluding mortgage interest payments since 1974.
Source: ONS *Economic Trends* (various).

Comparing CPI and RPI indices

Although the CPI and RPI use roughly the same set of prices to construct each index, the results usually differ. The reasons for this difference are that they differ in coverage; the CPI covers a broader population base than the RPI; they differ in item coverage (specifically the CPI does *not* cover some housing costs); they have differing construction methodologies to combine prices into an overall index (the CPI uses a geometric mean, whereas the RPI uses an arithmetic mean). The difference between the two (CPI − RPI) was −1.5% points in September 2010, with some −0.73 of the difference being explained by housing components excluded from the CPI, some −0.9 by the different construction methodologies, some +0.13 by the differences in the item coverage and some −0.06 by other differences including weights.

As can be seen from Fig. 22.2 the percentage increase in inflation given by the RPI has usually been higher than that given by the CPI. Changing from the RPI to the CPI as the basis for upgrading benefits and public sector pensions is therefore controversial. Since 1990, £1,000 updated each year by the April RPI index would have amounted to £1,876 whereas £1,000 updated by the CPI would have amounted to only £1,615.

Other measures of inflation

No single inflation measure can meet all user needs. The Office for National Statistics (ONS) publishes several indices designed for specific purposes, some of which are explained below.

■ *CPIY (Consumer Price Index excluding indirect taxes).* CPIY is designed to measure 'underlying' price movements, but excluding those changes that are due to indirect tax changes such as VAT, and the duty on tobacco, alcohol and petrol. In the year to September 2010 the CPIY rose by 1.5%.

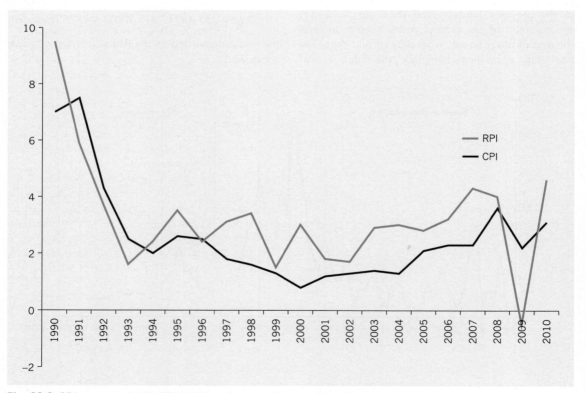

Fig. 22.2 CPI compared with RPI (all items) – annual percentage change.
Source: ONS (various).

- *CPI–CT (Consumer Price Index at constant taxation).* CPI–CT is an index where tax rates are kept constant at the rates that prevail in the base year. Comparing the CPI–CT to the CPI gives an indication of the impact of tax changes on the CPI. In the year to September 2010 the CPI–CT rose by 1.4%.

- *RPIX (Retail Price Index minus mortgage interest rates).* RPIX was used to define the government inflation target prior to switching to the CPI in 2003. It is an attempt to get a picture of underlying inflationary pressure at a time when policy-makers might be using higher interest to subdue inflation. In the year to September 2010 RPIX rose by 4.6%.

- *RPIY (Retail Price Index minus direct taxes and mortgage interest rates).* RPIY is an attempt to gauge core inflation excluding government initiated change in direct taxes and mortgage interest rates. In the year to September 2010 RPIY rose by 3.4%.

- *Tax and Price Index (TPI).* TPI is a measure of how the average person's gross income needs to change in order to buy a given basket of goods, allowing for income tax and national insurance changes. When these taxes rise, the TPI will rise faster than the RPI. It is useful to compare TPI with average earnings to indicate changes in the real purchasing power of gross earnings.

- *Pensioner indices.* These are constructed to reflect the different purchasing pattern of pensioners. The single pensioner household index rose by 3.9% in the year 2009–2010.

- *Producer Price Index (PPI).* PPI is a measure of the changes in price of goods bought and sold by UK manufacturers.

- *Services Products Providers Index (SPPI).* SPPI is a measure of price changes in services provided by UK businesses to other UK businesses, and is thought to give some early indications of inflationary pressures.

European comparisons of inflation: the HICP

The *Harmonized Index of Consumer Prices* (HICP) is calculated in each EU country for purposes of comparison (it is the equivalent of the CPI in the UK). The European Central Bank aims to keep EU inflation below 2% as measured by the HICP though several EU countries have inflation rates well above this figure, including the UK (Table 22.2).

 ## Low inflation as a policy objective

Much of the recent debate on inflation centres around how best to defeat it. Less is heard, at least in public debate, about the actual economic costs of inflation. It is important to identify these costs and to try and quantify them, so that they can then be compared with the costs of the policies aimed at reducing inflation. These latter costs are usually seen in terms of higher unemployment if restrictive monetary and fiscal policies are used to control inflation, or a misallocation of resources if prices and incomes policies are used. Traditionally the costs of inflation were seen in terms of its adverse effect on income distribution, as rising prices are particularly severe on those with fixed incomes, such as pensioners. However, Milton Friedman, in his Nobel lecture, shifted the focus of attention towards the adverse effects of inflation on output and employment.

In assessing the costs of inflation it is usual to distinguish two cases: that of perfectly anticipated inflation, where the rate of inflation is expected and has been taken into account in economic transactions, and that of imperfectly anticipated, or unexpected, inflation. We will consider perfectly anticipated inflation first, as it provides a useful benchmark against

Table 22.2 HICP: EU comparisons of inflation (year to August 2010).

EU 27	UK	France	Germany	Greece	Italy	Portugal	Spain
2.0%	3.1%	1.6%	1.0%	5.6%	1.8%	2.0%	1.8%

Source: ONS (2010) *Consumer Price Indices Technical Manual.*

which to assess the more usual case of imperfectly anticipated inflation.

Perfectly anticipated inflation

Suppose we initially have an economy in which inflation is proceeding at a steady and perfectly foreseen rate, and in which all possible adjustments for the existence of inflation have been made. In this economy all contracts, interest rates and the tax system would take the correctly foreseen rate of inflation into account. The exchange rate would also adjust to prevent inflation having any adverse effect on the balance of payments.

'Shoe-leather' costs

In such an economy the main cost of inflation would arise from the fact that interest is not normally paid on currency in circulation. The opportunity cost to the individual of holding currency would then be the interest the individual could have earned on other assets, such as deposits at the bank. Higher anticipated inflation will tend to raise interest rates and therefore the opportunity cost of holding currency, with the rational response to this being for the individual to economize on currency holdings by making more frequent trips to the bank. The costs of these extra trips to the bank are often called the 'shoe-leather' costs of inflation. Although these costs are small for low rates of inflation, they have been estimated as rising to about 0.3% of GDP for perfectly anticipated inflation rates rising to around 10% per annum.

'Menu' costs

A second cost, when inflation is fully anticipated, is that of having to change prices frequently. This is sometimes called the 'menu' cost of inflation. Presumably the more rapid the inflation, the more frequently things like price tags, cash tills, vending machines and price lists have to be changed, and this takes time, effort and money.

A study (Bakhshi *et al.* 1997) has attempted to estimate the benefits and costs of reducing perfectly anticipated inflation in the UK by 2% (which, given the current inflation target in the UK, would amount to achieving price stability). The annual welfare benefits of such a reduction in inflation were estimated at around 0.21% of GDP. Of course, the welfare

benefits of lower inflation must be set against the lost output associated with the necessary deflation. Based on estimates of the UK 'sacrifice ratio' (the cost of cumulative lost output required for each percentage point reduction in inflation), Bakhshi *et al.* calculated the annual welfare loss of such a reduction in inflation to be around 0.18% of GDP. In other words, based on his estimates, there would be a net welfare gain of 0.03% of GDP per annum as a result of policies which reduce perfectly anticipated inflation in the UK by 2%.

Further costs arise from inflation when it is either not foreseen correctly, or not adjusted to fully. It is to these additional costs from imperfectly anticipated inflation that we now turn.

Imperfectly anticipated inflation

Redistribution effects

Unanticipated inflation leads to a redistribution of income and wealth. Debtors will gain at the expense of creditors if contracts do not take inflation fully into account and those on fixed incomes will suffer. In general there is likely to be a transfer from the private to the public sector. For example, inflation causes fiscal drag, taking individuals into higher tax brackets, thereby raising tax revenue for the public sector. Inflation also reduces the real value of the national debt, with government securities maturing at specified future dates for sums that are fixed in *money* terms, so that inflation reduces the real cost to the government of redeeming them. Inflation can, in effect, be regarded as an implicit tax on the holding of cash.

Costs of decision-taking

Uncertainty about future price levels is likely to lead to a misallocation of resources. For example, such uncertainty may discourage long-term contracts. This in turn is likely to inhibit investment which by its very nature tends to be long term. Savers and lenders may react to the uncertainty about future price levels by demanding a premium to cover the perceived extra risk. This premium will push up real interest rates and again discourage investment. Capital will also be misallocated if savers and investors form different expectations of inflation and hence different views as to expected real interest rates. There is evidence to suggest that the rate of inflation and the level of uncertainty are positively correlated (see Briault 1995).

Inflation and relative price movements

In market economies, changes in relative prices act as signals which serve to guide the allocation of resources. It is argued that economic agents find it difficult to discern *relative* price movements from *general* price level movements in times of inflation, especially when the rate of inflation is uncertain. In this case incorrect decisions will be made and resources will be misallocated.

The effects of inflation on economic growth

The previous analysis suggests that inflation (and especially uncertainty surrounding the future inflation rate) will lead to a misallocation of resources and a lower rate of economic growth. Testing this hypothesis empirically is extremely complex.

One approach is to use *time-series* data for single countries. Grimes (1991) found a significant *negative* relationship for 13 countries, which implied that a sustained increase in inflation from 0% to 9% would lead to a full percentage point reduction in annual growth rates. Others have found weaker but still negative relationships. The problem with simple regression equations used in such analyses is that it is difficult to get unbiased results. Difficulties arise in interpreting the overall negative relationship between inflation and growth. For example, in most countries, at least in the short run, inflation and economic growth are likely to be positively related, as in periods of boom. It might also be the case that the negative relationship might just be picking up the effects of policy measures; for example, a period of high inflation might precipitate a deflationary policy response which would slow the growth rate. The interested reader should consult Briault (1995) for further discussion of these issues.

An alternative approach is to use *cross-country* data. One example of this is the work done by Robert Barro (1995). He looked at data for 100 countries from 1960 to 1990. His regression results indicated that an increase in average inflation of 10% points per year reduces the growth or real per capita GDP by 0.2–0.3% points per year, and lowers the ratio of investment to GDP by 0.4–0.6% points. Although

these effects may not appear particularly large, a reduction in growth rate of the above order of magnitude (brought about by a 10% rise in the average inflation rate) would mean that after 30 years real GDP would be 4–7% lower than otherwise. This would represent an estimated £30–50bn shortfall in GDP at current UK values of output.

Another study by Sarel (1996) suggested that the effect of inflation on growth is non-linear. He found a *structural break* in the relationship at an inflation rate of around 8%, with inflation below 8% per annum having no significant negative effects on growth, but inflation above 8% per annum having significant negative effects on growth, the suggestion here being that policy-makers should always keep inflation below the level (8%) consistent with this structural break.

A more recent study by Gillman and Harris (2010) of transition economies finds that inflation has a significant and negative effect on economic growth but that this effect decreases as the inflation rate rises. They conclude that monetary policy, via its effect on inflation, can therefore influence economic growth and suggest that the adoption of the low inflation Eurozone monetary policy or a monetary policy which sets a low target for inflation will be beneficial for these transition economies.

Economic theory and inflation

The causes of inflation can be illustrated using the standard aggregate supply/demand framework found in most economic texts, such as Lipsey and Chrystal (1995) and Parkin *et al.* (2003). Figure 22.3 illustrates this framework. The first point to make is that the distinction between the short-run and long-run aggregate supply curves is important.

The upward sloping *short-run aggregate supply* (SRAS) curve assumes that some input prices, particularly money wages, remain relatively fixed as the price level changes. It then follows that an increase in the price level, whilst input prices remain relatively fixed, increases the profitability of production and induces firms to expand output and employ more labour. An increase in the general price level will therefore lead, in the short run, to some increase in real GDP.

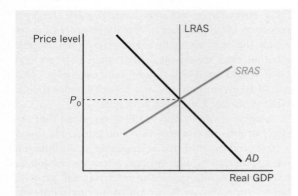

Fig. 22.3 Aggregate demand and supply.

There are two explanations as to why wages may remain constant even though prices have changed. First, many employees are hired under fixed-wage contracts. Once these contracts are agreed it is the firm that determines (within reason) the number of labour hours actually worked. If prices rise, the negotiated real wage will fall and firms will want to hire more labour time. Second, workers may not immediately be aware of price level changes, i.e. they may suffer from 'money illusion'. If workers' expectations lag behind actual price level changes, then workers will not be aware that their real wages have changed and will not adjust their wage demands appropriately. Both these reasons imply that as the price level rises, real wages will fall and the employment of extra labour hours will become more attractive to employers.

The long run is defined as the period in which all input prices (e.g. money wages) are fully responsive to changes in the price level. Workers in the long run can gather full information on price level changes and can renegotiate wage contracts in line with higher or lower prices. It follows that in the long run, a change in the price level is likely to be associated with an equal increase in money wages, leaving the real wage unchanged and by implication leaving employment and output unchanged. The *long-run aggregate supply* (LRAS) curve is independent of the price level; in other words, it is vertical.

Because, in the long run, all wages and prices can be renegotiated in line with supply and demand, the labour market will be in equilibrium (the real wage equating labour demand and supply) at the full employment level, with unemployment at the natural rate (see Chapter 23). The level of output associated

with this level of employment is variously called the *full employment* level of output or the *natural* level of output. This level of output is obviously not constant but is determined by supply-side factors, such as the labour force, the capital stock and the state of technology. Through time this full employment or natural level of output can be expected to increase as the economy grows, i.e. the vertical LRAS curve can be expected to shift to the right.

Demand-pull inflation

One-off demand inflation

Consider the case of a one-off increase in aggregate demand. The source of the increase could be an increase in the money stock, an increase in the budget deficit, or any autonomous change in consumption, investment or net exports. Whatever the cause, the aggregate demand curve AD_0 in Fig. 22.4 shifts to the right to AD_1 along the short-run aggregate supply curve $SRAS_0$. Excess demand now exists at the old price level P_0 and this pushes prices up to P_1. Such higher prices, with money wages lagging behind, increase the profitability of firms who then increase output beyond the full employment level Q_0, so that unemployment falls below the natural rate. However, the new short-run equilibrium (B) with the output Q_1 is not sustainable; labour is relatively scarce and workers will negotiate money wage increases to compensate for the increase in prices. The short-run aggregate supply curve now shifts up and to the left

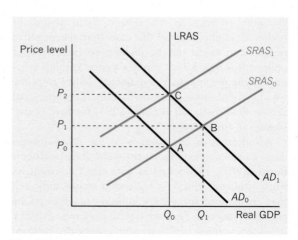

Fig. 22.4 A one-off increase in demand.

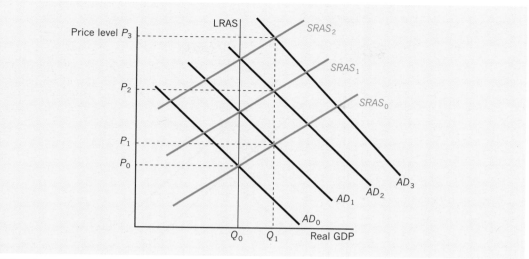

Fig. 22.5 Continuous demand inflation.

(i.e. from $SRAS_0$ to $SRAS_1$) in response to the increased costs of production, returning the economy to a new long-run equilibrium (C).

The economy experiences a period of 'stagflation' as output falls back to its *natural* level Q_0 and the price level continues to rise to P_2. The rise in price from P_1 to P_2 causing output to fall is usually explained in terms of rising prices reducing the real money supply, which in turn causes interest rates to rise and therefore interest-sensitive elements within aggregate demand to fall. Note that the inflation stops when the price level reaches P_2. A one-off increase in aggregate demand will not therefore generate a lasting inflation.

Continuous demand inflation

Inflation proper, by which we mean a *sustained* upward movement in the price level, can occur only if the growth in aggregate demand is maintained. In this case output does *not* fall back to its natural rate but remains above it. It seems unlikely that autonomous shifts in private aggregate demand will be repeated period after period, which leaves either fiscal or monetary policy as the most likely cause of persistent demand inflation. However, expansionary fiscal policy, if funded by borrowing, is likely to lead to higher interest rates and therefore to the crowding-out of private spendings. This leaves monetary expansion as the most likely factor in turning a one-off inflation into a sustained inflation. The initial inflationary

impulse could come from any demand-side factor, but an increase in the money supply is still necessary to prevent the price increases from reducing the real money supply, pushing up interest rates and eventually stopping the inflationary process. Figure 22.5 illustrates this case. As long as the money supply is allowed to expand in line with increasing prices, the aggregate demand curve continues to shift upward and the economy is kept above its natural level of output Q_0. The cost of this money supply strategy, however, is continuing inflation, with the price level rising in each time period.

Cost-push inflation and supply shocks

Cost-push or supply-side inflation results from an increase in costs of production which firms pass on in the form of higher prices. The source of the cost increases could be a rise in imported raw material costs, such as the two oil price shocks of 1973–75 and 1979–80. Alternatively, trade unions may use their market power to push wages up irrespective of the pressure of demand in the labour market. In both these cases one group, OPEC or unions, is using market power to try and secure a larger share of output; firms, in response, attempt to protect their profits by increasing prices. Figure 22.6 shows cost-push/supply-side inflation.

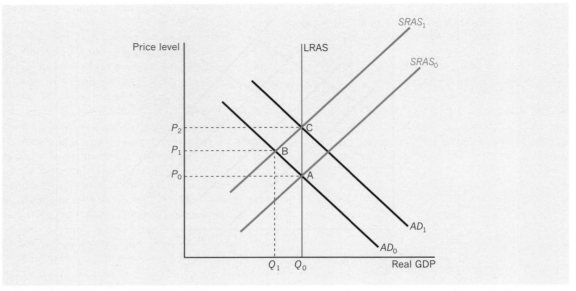

Fig. 22.6 Cost-push/supply-side inflation.

Suppose the economy is initially in equilibrium (A) with output at the full employment or natural rate Q_0 and the price level at P_0 with zero inflation. An increase in oil prices then shifts $SRAS_0$, the short-run aggregate supply curve, to $SRAS_1$. The economy now faces a period of stagflation with falling output, increased unemployment and rising prices. The period of stagflation ends when the new short-run equilibrium B is reached. If aggregate demand remains unchanged at AD_0 then the excess supply in both goods and labour markets will eventually put downward pressure on costs and wages, causing the SRAS curve to return to its original position. This period of deflation returns the economy to its full employment equilibrium (A). However, this process is likely to be slow and painful, requiring a major adjustment in relative prices and a fall in real wages.

Expansionary monetary policy which shifts the aggregate demand curve to AD_1 would speed up the process of returning the economy to full employment, but at the cost of additional inflation (Q_0/P_2 at point C). Indeed if the government got the timing and strength of the demand expansion just right, the economy could move from one long-run equilibrium to another, with very little loss of output. It is highly unlikely, however, that the government has the appropriate information and macroeconomic tools

to stabilize output precisely at the full employment level Q_0.

Continued cost-push inflation is unlikely, unless accompanied by accommodating monetary policy. Union pressure for wage increases would be undermined by falling output and increased unemployment, and even oil producers would eventually find that the reduced activity of non-oil-producers would restrict their market power. Monetary accommodation would, however, alter the story and might lead to repeated supply shocks and continuing inflation. Unions, thwarted in their attempt to seek real wage increases because of the higher prices associated with the monetary expansion and without the deterrent of unemployment, might ask for wage increases in the next round, causing the SRAS curve to shift to the left a second time. The choices for the government are, as before, either to allow unemployment to increase or to accommodate the new price increases by increasing the money supply and stimulating demand. The latter path could then lead to a continuous wage–price spiral.

There is no consensus as to the advisability of monetary accommodation of a supply-side shock. The policy decision depends to some extent on judging the relative costs to the state of extra unemployment against those of extra inflation. The danger with accommodation is that once inflationary expectations become entrenched in the wage–price setting process, they might be eliminated only after a prolonged period of unemployment (see the section on the Phillips curve below).

In conclusion, the theoretical analysis of inflation indicates that the government can always stop inflation, whether the cause is demand or supply-side factors. All the government has to do is to halt the growth of the money supply. The bad news, however, is that the cost of halting inflation is likely to entail a reduction in output and a rise in unemployment.

The relationship between inflation and unemployment (the Phillips curve)

Very few articles in economics have generated as much subsequent interest as A. W. Phillips' study of UK wage inflation and unemployment over the period 1861–1957. In the article (Phillips 1958) he appeared to find a stable and inverse relationship between unemployment and inflation (strictly, changes in wage rates). If unemployment was low, inflation would be high, and vice versa. The so-called Phillips curve suggested that with unemployment of around 5.5% there would be zero *wage inflation* and that with unemployment of around 2.5% the wage inflation generated would be covered by productivity growth, resulting in zero *price inflation*. This is depicted in Fig. 22.7. The relationship seemed to hold good over a long period of time and subsequent

research found that it held good for many economies, and not just that of the UK.

The inverse relationship between inflation and unemployment was explained in terms of unemployment being an *indirect* measure of the level of excess demand in the economy. When unemployment is high and demand is low, the excess supply of labour holds wages and prices down; however, when unemployment is low and demand is high, the excess demand for labour will push wages and prices up more quickly. The Phillips curve appeared to offer the policy-maker a menu of choices from which could be chosen the preferred combination of unemployment and inflation, whilst at the same time highlighting the trade-off between the two policy objectives. If the economy was, say, at point A and the government wished to reduce unemployment by expanding aggregate demand, then it could do so but only at the cost of higher inflation, as at point B. Using the previous AD/AS framework, the expansionary fiscal or monetary policy would cause the AD curve to shift to the right, so that it now intersected further along the SRAS curve, thereby causing the price level to rise. The rise in prices will then push real wages down (because of either fixed contracts or workers' expectations lagging behind actual price increases), resulting in firms taking on more workers, unemployment falling and output rising. It is clear that some economists and policy-makers thought that point B could be maintained indefinitely if desired, but as we have seen and will confirm later, the existence of any such long-run trade-off (whereby a constant though

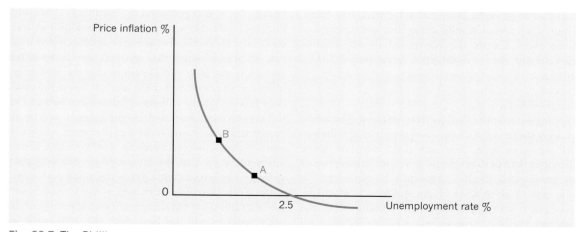

Fig. 22.7 The Phillips curve.

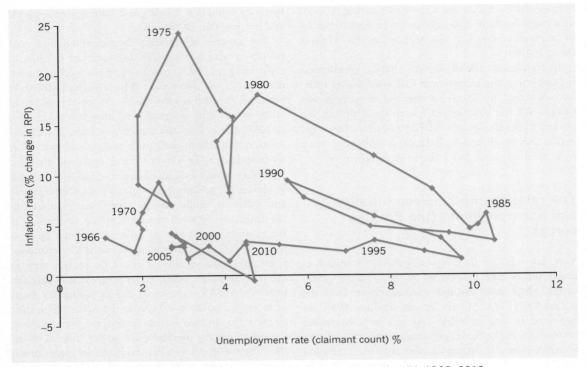

Fig. 22.8 The relationship between unemployment and inflation rates in the UK, 1966–2010.
Source: ONS (various).

higher rate of inflation can be achieved for a given fall in unemployment) is highly questionable.

Breakdown of the Phillips curve

Evidence of the breakdown of the Phillips curve came very soon after the 'discovery' of this relationship that had supposedly been stable for over 100 years. Figure 22.8 plots UK inflation against unemployment since 1966. Clearly the downward sloping Phillips curve is not always in evidence in the period 1966–2010.

Supply-side factors

One reason why the Phillips relationship might not be entirely stable is the existence of supply-side inflation. As we have seen, raw material prices or wage increases may push costs and prices up irrespective of the pressure of demand, at least in the short term. In this case, a given level of unemployment would be associated with higher levels of inflation than the original Phillips curve would predict. The two oil price shocks of 1973–75 and 1979–80 resulted in periods of increased inflation that were not associated with falling unemployment, as the demand-side theory would have led us to predict.

Time-period factors

A more fundamental reason for the breakdown of the Phillips curve was proposed by Friedman (1968) and Phelps (1967). The new version of the Phillips curve makes the distinction between the short run and long run. It also assumes that markets are competitive enough in the long run to ensure that the real wage will be at the market clearing level. If this is the case, then labour supply will equal labour demand at the full employment level and unemployment will be at its natural rate. Note, however, that even when the market clears, not all workers who consider themselves to be part of the labour force will be either willing or able to accept a job at the going real wage. Some workers will be searching around for a better job offer (these are the *frictionally unemployed*), while other workers will not have the right skills or be in the right place (these are the *structurally unemployed*).

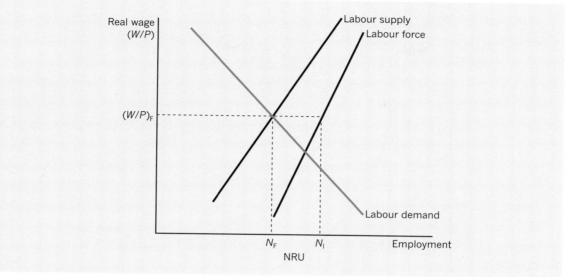

Fig. 22.9 The labour market.

The two groups together make up the *natural rate of unemployment* (NRU).

Figure 22.9 shows the market clearing or full employment real wage $(W/P)_F$ and the associated full employment level of employment (N_F); the NRU is $N_1 - N_F$, the difference between the amount of labour demanded and the labour force.

Expectational factors

The final strand of the revised Phillips curve is to emphasize the role of *expectations* in the inflationary process. Friedman pointed out that what workers and firms are interested in is the *real* wages, not the *money* wage. Wage bargaining takes place in money terms but when considering a money wage offer the expected inflation rate will be taken into account. The implication is that for any given level of unemployment (labour market tightness) there will be any number of possible money wage claims (for a given target real wage), depending on the expected level of inflation. As these money wage deals are passed on in price increases, it means that a given level of unemployment can be associated with any level of inflation which in turn means the existence of not just one Phillips curve but a whole family of Phillips curves, one for each expected inflation rate.

In Friedman's view, once expectations are taken into account the unemployment/inflation trade-off is only a short-term possibility. Assume that the economy is currently at the natural rate of unemployment U_n and that zero inflation has been experienced for some time and hence is expected to continue (point A in Fig. 22.10). The government attempts to increase output beyond the natural (full employment) rate by increasing the money supply. Aggregate demand shifts to the right and prices are forced up (as in Fig. 22.4 earlier). The increase in prices reduces real wages and so makes it profitable for firms to employ more labour. But why should previously unemployed labour take jobs they had previously rejected? As workers were expecting zero inflation, any money wage increase resulting from increased demand for labour will be interpreted as a *real* wage increase. As long as the money wage increase is less than the price increase, firms will be happy to employ the extra workers who have been 'fooled' into believing they have secured higher real wages by unexpectedly high inflation. Unemployment falls below the natural rate U_n to U_b, and inflation increases to b as the economy moves along the short-run Phillips curve (Ph_0) to B. (Note: this is equivalent to a movement up and to the right along the short-run aggregate supply curve in Fig. 22.4 earlier.)

If the inflation rate was to stay at b, workers would, sooner or later, adjust their inflationary expectations accordingly. Workers will then take the new and higher expected rate of inflation into account in their

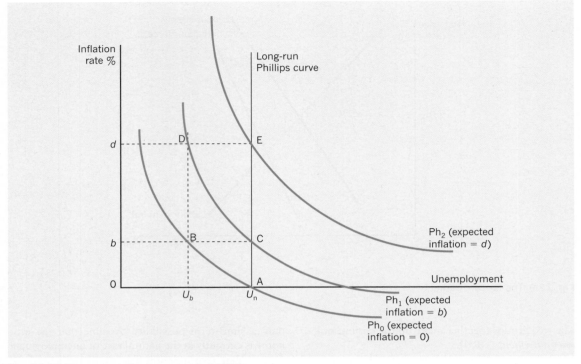

Fig. 22.10 The expectations-augmented Phillips curve.

wage bargains. This is equivalent to the short-run aggregate supply curve shifting up and to the left, and the Phillips curve shifting up and to the right (Ph_1). The economy will now be at C, with unemployment and output falling back to their natural rates and with actual and expected inflation equal to b. In other words, C is a long-run equilibrium possibility, with an inflation rate constant at b.

Suppose, however, that the government wishes to return unemployment to U_b. It must then increase the growth of the money supply more rapidly, so that actual inflation again exceeds expected inflation. If the government does do this the economy will move along the new short-run Phillips curve to point D. As before, this short-run equilibrium cannot be maintained because expectations will again catch up with actual inflation, and the economy will then move to E as the short-run Phillips curve again shifts upwards (Ph_2). At E the economy is once more in long-run equilibrium, with expected and actual inflation equal and the inflation rate constant at d.

Several interesting conclusions can be drawn from this modern view of the Phillips curve.

- There is a short-run trade-off between unemployment and inflation but no long-run one.

- Any rate of inflation is consistent with long-run equilibrium; all that is required is that *expected* inflation should equal *actual* inflation.

- Attempts to push unemployment below the natural rate will result in increasing inflation. In fact the natural rate of unemployment is sometimes known as the non-accelerating inflation rate of unemployment (NAIRU).

- Once inflationary expectations have become embedded in the system, a period of unemployment above the natural rate is required in order to lower the inflation rate. A movement down a given short-run Phillips curve to a level of unemployment above the natural rate will result in actual inflation being below expected inflation, leading to a downward revision of expectations, and hence falling inflation.

- The natural rate of unemployment (and the NAIRU) are not constant over time. See Chapter 23 for a discussion of this issue.

UK inflationary experience: 1970–92

During the 1970s and early 1980s the UK experienced its highest periods of inflation in recent history. Inflation peaked in 1975, reaching nearly 27% (% change over the 12 months to August); then after falling back it peaked again in the year to June 1982, reaching 21.9%. Another period of inflation occurred in the year to September 1990 when inflation reached 10.9%.

The first of these three periods to 1975 was preceded by very buoyant aggregate demand, stimulated by money supply growth (as a result of relaxation of the rules on bank lending), an expansionary budget and a booming world economy. All these led to the AD curve shifting to the right beyond the full employment level of output and increasing inflation. This period of rapid demand-led growth can be seen in Fig. 22.11. Our analysis tells us that even without

the adverse supply shock given by oil and other commodity prices in 1973, prices would have been given a further boost (and output would fall) as *expectations* of inflation were revised upwards in response to wage increases shifting the short-run AS curve up and to the left. The adverse supply shocks from oil and commodity price rises merely accelerated this process towards rising prices and falling output (note the fall in real GDP between 1973 and 1975 in Fig. 22.11).

The second inflationary episode occurred in the late 1970s and early 1980s. Again this period was marked by adverse supply shocks, including a doubling of oil prices, a near-doubling of VAT in 1979 (Q3) and an increase in wage costs, the last being the result of a catching-up process after a period of wage controls during 1974–79. The tightening of monetary and fiscal policy in late 1979 led to a further period of 'stagflation' in the following years (again note the fall in real GDP between 1979 and 1981 in Fig. 22.11).

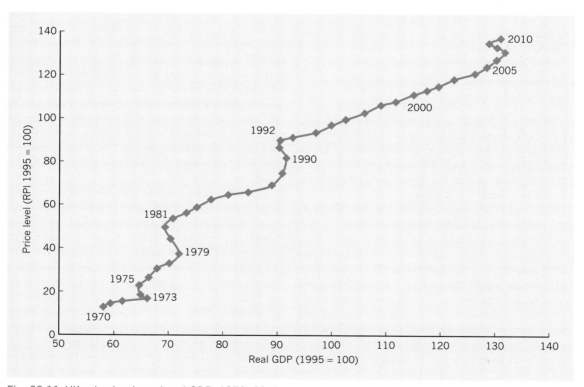

Fig. 22.11 UK price levels and real GDP, 1970–2010.
Source: ONS and author's calculations.

It has been argued (Nelson and Nikolov 2002) that the reason why inflation was so troublesome in the late 1960s and the 1970s was partly due to policy-makers *underestimating* the degree of excess demand in the economy and partly due to the neglect of monetary policy. Underestimating the rate of productivity slowdown in the 1970s meant policy-makers *overestimated full employment output* and hence *underestimated the level of demand pressure* (as measured by the output gap) in the economy. This was especially important over the 1972–74 period.

The reasons given for the neglect of monetary policy (meaning appropriate changes in interest rates) included:

■ the view held by some that inflation was caused by factors other than excess demand;

■ a feeling that incomes policy could be used as an alternative to demand management as a method of restraining inflation;

■ an assumption that cost-push inflation could continue indefinitely even in the absence of monetary accommodation (a view emanating from the Radcliffe Report of 1959 that argued that the velocity of circulation of money would adjust to offset any monetary policy); and

■ a scepticism about the impact of interest rates on aggregated demand.

Nelson and Nikolov conclude that if appropriate interest rate changes had been made and if the output gap had not been mismeasured, then the 9.3% points actual increase in average inflation from 1970 Q1 to 1979 Q1 compared to the 1960s could have been reduced by around 7.2% points.

The third inflationary episode was, like the first, associated with excess demand in the economy. Financial liberalization, a relaxation of monetary policy, rising house and other asset prices, growing consumer confidence, tax-cutting budgets in 1987 and 1988 and buoyant world demand all conspired to push aggregate demand beyond the full employment level. GDP was estimated to be over 4% above its full employment potential in both 1988 and 1989. Action to curtail inflation was taken in late 1988 when interest rates were increased by around 4% points to 12.8%. Further rate increases followed in 1989, but too little and too late to stop inflation rising to over 10% by the autumn of 1990.

Inflation targets and central bank independence 1992–

Since the early 1990s some 26 countries (including the UK, New Zealand, Canada, Australia and Brazil) have adopted explicit inflation targets. While the US has no explicit inflation target, the Federal Reserve Bank often indicates that it would prefer core inflation to be around 2%, similar to the inflation target in the Eurozone, with the European Central Bank aiming for inflation of below but close to 2%. Instead of using *intermediate policy targets*, such as the money supply or the exchange rate to achieve inflation stability, the emphasis has moved towards the use of explicit inflation targets. In the UK the initial inflation target set in 1992, by the then government, was 2.5% as measured by the RPIX; this was later replaced by the current target of 2% as measured by the CPI. A further significant change occurred in 1997 when the government delegated the power to decide interest rates to the nine member MPC of the Bank of England (see Chapter 20). The MPC is charged with setting short-term interest rates in order to meet the government's inflation target in the medium term. Put simply, if the MPC forecasts that the CPI is going to be above 2% in approximately two years' time (given the time lags before interest rates have their maximum impact), it might seek to raise interest rates now to bring future inflation back into line. The inflation target is a symmetrical one, in that inflation below 2% is regarded as being just as undesirable as inflation above 2%, so that interest rates will be lowered if an inflation rate below target is forecast.

The UK framework has been intended to remove politics from interest rate decision-making, as these decisions are taken by the independent MPC and should give monetary policy more credibility and help keep inflationary expectations around the official target. Credibility is also enhanced by increased transparency and accountability. The publication of the *Quarterly Inflation Report* and the *Minutes of the monthly MPC meetings* improves transparency and the requirement for the Governor of the Bank of England to write a letter of explanation if *actual* inflation rate deviates by more than 1% from the target (in either direction) helps ensure accountability. The first such letter had to be written in April 2007 after the March inflation rate had risen to

Table 22.3 UK inflation dynamics, 1950–2007.

Period	Mean	Standard deviation	Persistence*
Jan 1950–April 1997	6.1	5.1	0.7
May 1997–March 2007	1.5	0.5	0.5

*Persistence is the correlation co-efficient between inflation in December of the year in question and inflation the previous December.
Source: King (2007).

3.1%. In August 2010 the Governor again explained in a written letter that the inflation rate of 3.1% for the year to July 2010 was due to the VAT increase in January, to past increases in the oil price and to the continued impact of Sterling depreciation since 2007 on import prices. However, given that the impact of these should diminish by the time of the next 12-month comparison and given that there is considerable spare capacity in both product and labour markets, the then Governor felt able to forecast that, although inflation would be above target until the end of 2011, it would fall back to the target level after that and so no change needs to be made to the current interest rate.

The current Governor of the Bank of England, Mervyn King, reviewed the effectiveness of the UK inflation framework in 2002 and 2007. He found that inflation in the UK since the mid-1990s had been lower than for a generation; less variable and less persistent (see Table 22.3). He also pointed out that the lower and more stable inflation rate was not at the expense of a restricted demand and lower economic growth. The average growth rate of the UK economy (1997–2007) at 2.8% per annum was above the post-war average and better than that in any G7 country apart from Canada, as compared with the period 1950–1996 when the UK had the lowest recorded G7 growth rate.

A key question is whether the change in the monetary policy framework has been the cause of low inflation and stability in the real economy, or whether the causation runs from a more stable world environment (at least up to 2007) resulting in lower inflation! King (2007) argues that the better outcomes for inflation and economic stability are *not* simply the result of luck but that the crucial achievement of the new monetary policy framework has been to anchor inflationary expectations at a low level, with

the result that monetary policy is not adding to the volatility of the economy as it sometimes did in previous decades.

 Conclusion

It is generally agreed that the high and volatile UK inflation experience of the 1970s and 1980s did substantial harm to the UK economy. In the medium term, inflation is determined by the balance between aggregate expenditure and supply-side capacity. The new inflation framework has been relatively successful in controlling expenditure and hence in keeping inflation in check. Low and stable inflation (however defined) may be insufficient on its own to guarantee continued macroeconomic stability, but it is likely to remain as a central objective of monetary policy in the medium- and long-run time periods. Short-run variations of actual inflation from target inflation are inevitable, being caused by unpredictable factors such as sudden VAT increases, oil price increases and currency depreciations. These factors are not easily influenced by interest rates and their impacts on inflation should be largely ignored as long as the medium-term forecast for inflation is that it will return to its target level.

In the light of the recent financial crisis, however, adjustments to the current inflation framework have been considered. Nevertheless, there is widespread agreement at present that the alternatives undermine either the simplicity or the credibility of the current inflation framework that are so important in anchoring inflationary expectations with the current inflation framework still the best available.

Key points

- The RPI measures movement in the prices of a 'basket' of goods and services bought by a representative UK household.

- Items with higher income elasticities of demand (e.g. housing, leisure services, catering) are being given increasing weights in the calculation of the RPI.

- The RPI is linked back to January 1987 = 100 as base. With an RPI of 225.3 in September 2010, this indicates that average retail prices have risen by 125.3% since January 1987.

- RPIX is RPI *excluding* mortgage interest payments.

- RPIY is RPI *excluding* mortgage interest payments and indirect taxes.

- The CPI replaced the RPIX as the UK inflation target in 2003.

- The modern view of the Phillips curve is that there is a short-run trade-off between unemployment and inflation, but no long-run trade-off.

- Attempts to push unemployment below the *natural rate* will result in increasing inflation.

- This natural rate of unemployment is sometimes known as the non-accelerating inflation rate of unemployment (NAIRU).

- The government sets the inflation target and the Monetary Policy Committee (MPC) changes interest rates in trying to meet that target.

- There is evidence that setting an inflation target may itself help to reduce inflation without inhibiting growth.

Now try the self-check questions for this chapter on the Companion Website. You will also find useful links to relevant websites.

Note

1   Using chain indexing – the index for, say, May 2007 with base year 2005 is given by:

Index May, 2007 | 2005 = Index Dec 2006 | 2005 × Index Jan 2007 | Dec 2006 × Index May, 2007 | Jan 2007

References and further reading

Bakhshi, H., Haldane, A. and Hatch, N. (1997) Some costs and benefits of price stability in the UK, *Bank of England Quarterly Bulletin*, 37(3): 274–84.

Barro, R. (1995) Inflation and economic growth, *Bank of England Quarterly Bulletin*, 35(2): 166–76.

Bean, C., Paustian, M., Penalver, A. and Taylor, T. (2010) Monetary policy after the fall, *Federal Reserve Bank of Kansas City Conference*, Jackson Hole, WY, 26–28 August.

Bénassy-Quéré, A. and Coeuré, B. (2010) *Economic Policy*, Oxford, Oxford University Press.

Briault, C. (1995) The costs of inflation, *Bank of England Quarterly Bulletin*, 35(1): 33–5.

Cobham, D. (2010) *Twenty Years of Inflation Targeting Lessons Learned and Future Prospects*, Cambridge, Cambridge University Press.

Dungey M., Fry, R., Gonzales-Hermosillo, B. and Martin, V. (2011) *Transmission of Financial Crises and Contagion*, Oxford, Oxford University Press.

Friedman, M. (1968) The role of monetary policy, *American Economic Review*, 58(March): 1–17.

Friedman, M. (1977) Inflation and unemployment, *Journal of Political Economy*, 85(3): 451–72.

Giavazzi, F. and Blanchard, O. (2010) *Macroeconomics: A European Perspective*, Harlow, Financial Times/Prentice Hall.

Gillman, M. and Harris, M. (2010) The effect of inflation on growth. Evidence from a panel of transition countries, *Economics of Transition*, 18 (4): 678–714.

Gnos, C. (2009) *Monetary Policy and Financial Stability*, Cheltenham, Edward Elgar.

Grimes, A. (1991) The effects of inflation on growth: some international evidence, *Weltwirtschaftliches Archive*, 127: 631–44.

IMF (2006) How has globalization affected inflation? *World Economic Outlook*, April, Washington DC, International Monetary Fund.

King, M. (2002) The inflation target ten years on, lecture delivered at the London School of Economics, 19 November 2002, *Bank of England Quarterly Bulletin*, 42 (4), Winter.

King, M. (2007) *The MPC Ten Years On*, lecture delivered to the Society of Business Economists, London, 2 May.

Lipsey, R. and Chrystal, K. (1995) *Positive Economics*, Oxford, Oxford University Press.

Nelson, E. and Nikolov, K. (2002) *Monetary Policy and Stagflation in the UK*, Working Paper No. 155, May, London, Bank of England.

Nickell, S. (2006) *Monetary Policy, Demand and Inflation*, speech given to Bank of England South East and East Anglia Agency, 31 January 2006.

ONS (2010) *Consumer Price Indices Technical Manual*, London, Office for National Statistics.

Parkin, M., Powell, M. and Matthews, K. (2003) *Economics*, London, Addison Wesley Longman.

Phelps, E. S. (1967) Phillips curves, expectations of inflation and optimal unemployment over time, *Economica*, 34(August): 254–81.

Phillips, A. W. (1958) The relation between unemployment and the rate of change of money wage rates in the United Kingdom, *Economica*, 25(November): 283–99.

Radcliffe Committee (1959) *Report on the Working of the Monetary System*, CMND. 827, London, HMSO.

Sarel, M. (1996) Nonlinear effects of inflation on economic growth, *IMF Staff Papers*, 43(1): 199–215.

Soteri, S. and Westaway, P. (1993) Explaining price inflation in the UK: 1971–92, *National Institute Economic Review*, 144(May): 85–94.

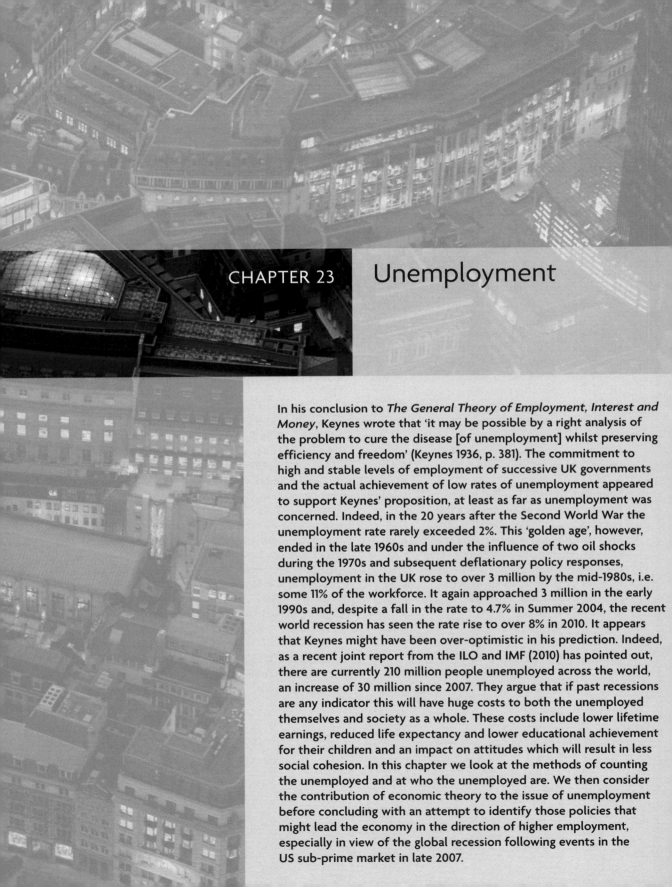

CHAPTER 23

Unemployment

In his conclusion to *The General Theory of Employment, Interest and Money*, Keynes wrote that 'it may be possible by a right analysis of the problem to cure the disease [of unemployment] whilst preserving efficiency and freedom' (Keynes 1936, p. 381). The commitment to high and stable levels of employment of successive UK governments and the actual achievement of low rates of unemployment appeared to support Keynes' proposition, at least as far as unemployment was concerned. Indeed, in the 20 years after the Second World War the unemployment rate rarely exceeded 2%. This 'golden age', however, ended in the late 1960s and under the influence of two oil shocks during the 1970s and subsequent deflationary policy responses, unemployment in the UK rose to over 3 million by the mid-1980s, i.e. some 11% of the workforce. It again approached 3 million in the early 1990s and, despite a fall in the rate to 4.7% in Summer 2004, the recent world recession has seen the rate rise to over 8% in 2010. It appears that Keynes might have been over-optimistic in his prediction. Indeed, as a recent joint report from the ILO and IMF (2010) has pointed out, there are currently 210 million people unemployed across the world, an increase of 30 million since 2007. They argue that if past recessions are any indicator this will have huge costs to both the unemployed themselves and society as a whole. These costs include lower lifetime earnings, reduced life expectancy and lower educational achievement for their children and an impact on attitudes which will result in less social cohesion. In this chapter we look at the methods of counting the unemployed and at who the unemployed are. We then consider the contribution of economic theory to the issue of unemployment before concluding with an attempt to identify those policies that might lead the economy in the direction of higher employment, especially in view of the global recession following events in the US sub-prime market in late 2007.

Unemployment in the UK

It could be argued that the adoption, after the Second World War, of Keynesian demand-management policies secured nearly two decades of historically low unemployment (see Fig. 23.1). In recent years, however, although government commitment to full employment (first stated in the 1944 White Paper on employment policy) has never been revoked, we no longer appear to have the tools with which to do the job. The traditional reliance on macroeconomic policies as a means of reducing unemployment has largely been replaced by a greater emphasis on microeconomic supply-side measures that take into account the changing nature of the labour market, society and the global economy. Labour market reforms of this type during the 1980s and 1990s and measures such as the 'New Deal' of the 1997–2010 Labour government have, however, resulted in a UK unemployment rate that compares favourably with our EU partners. Nevertheless, the UK unemployment rate is still four times as high as it was in the 1950s and 1960s and there is an uneasy feeling that this period of very low unemployment may prove to have been the exception rather than the rule!

Before attempting to assess the causes of high unemployment, and to consider what, if anything, can be done, it is important to examine the unemployment statistics themselves to see what light they shed on the issue.

How unemployment is measured

Since January 2003 the UK government's only official and internationally comparable measure of unemployment has been provided by the *Labour Force Survey* (LFS). The LFS uses the internationally agreed definition of unemployment recommended by the International Labour Office (ILO). Unemployed people are 'those without a job who have actively sought work in the last four weeks and are available to start work within the next two weeks, or those who are out of work, but who have found a job but are waiting to start in the next two weeks'.

The LFS samples around 61,000 households in any three-month period and interviews are taken from approximately 120,000 people aged 16 and over. The LFS enables the publication of results for the latest available three months every month. Results for individual months are not published, however, as they are not thought to be statistically robust. Everyone surveyed is classified as either *economically active* (in employment or ILO unemployed) or *economically*

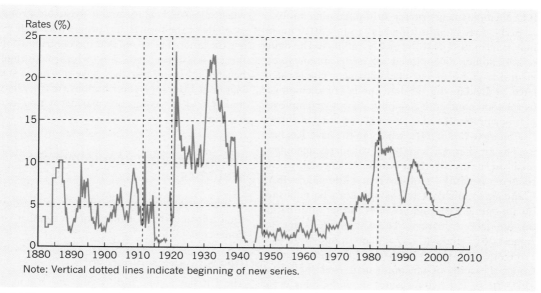

Fig. 23.1 UK unemployment rate, 1881–2010 (excluding school-leavers).
Sources: ONS *Labour Market Trends* (various); London and Cambridge Economic Service (various).

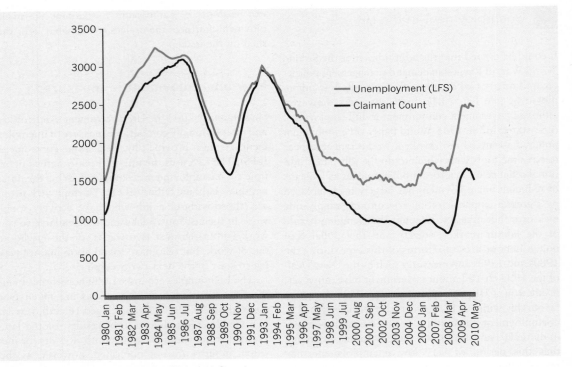

Fig. 23.2 Unemployment and the Claimant Count.
Source: ONS (various).

inactive (either wanting a job but not meeting the ILO unemployment criteria, or not wanting a job).

In the three months from May to July 2010 unemployment in the UK stood at 2.47 million. The figure of 2.47 million unemployed represents an *unemployment rate* of 7.8%. The unemployment rate is calculated by dividing the absolute number of unemployed by the total number of economically active (employed plus unemployed) and expressing this as a percentage.

Claimant Count data, which, in the past, has been used as an alternative measure, calculates unemployment in terms of those claiming unemployment-related benefits (Jobseeker's Allowance–JSA). Claimant Count data will continue to be published on a monthly basis and provides further information on the labour market. The Claimant Count for August 2010 stood at 1.47 million, a rate of 4.5%.

Figure 23.2 shows both the LFS and Claimant Count measures of unemployment over the period 1980–2010. The two measures show the same broad trend, rising and falling together over the economic cycle. The LFS unemployment figure is usually higher because people who are unemployed are not necessar-

ily eligible for JSA, or may choose not to claim even when eligible. The 16- and 17-year-old group is an example of the former and people over state pension age the latter. The group that has contributed most to the gap is women aged 25–49 who are not eligible for benefit, either because they have not made sufficient National Insurance contributions, or they have too high a level of savings or a partner whose income is too high.

Disaggregating unemployment statistics

Further insight can be gained by breaking down the total unemployment figures into a number of components as follows.

Regional unemployment

The UK has a long history of some regions having a higher than average level of unemployment. Traditionally the explanation of such variations was in terms of the depressed regions being over reliant on declining industries (coal, textiles, shipbuilding) together with limited labour mobility. In 1971, for example, Northern Ireland had an unemployment rate that was double the UK average, whilst in Scotland the rate was 70% above the UK average. In comparison, the South East had an unemployment rate of half the UK average. Declining UK unemployment over the period 1994–2006 saw some narrowing of the regional disparities, although apart from London and the South East the private sector had struggled to create jobs and in the North and the Midlands, the public sector had been the main source of new employment.

The recession since 2007 has reopened the problems for certain regions and cities. At the regional level, Yorkshire and Humberside and the North East have the highest rates of unemployment (9.1% compared to the UK average rate of 7.8% in 2010). However, the regional figures hide considerable differences. Cities in and around the larger industrial conurbations have experienced the largest increases in percentage unemployment, with the continued decline in manufacturing raising percentage unemployment most in cities. The current public sector spending cuts mean that cities with higher percentages of public sector employment will be extremely vulnerable to increased unemployment. Cities with large numbers of people with low skill levels – such as Dudley and Sandwell (12%), Dover (7.4%), Ebbw Vale (12.2%) and Abergavenny – have also experienced higher percentage unemployment. Cities with highly skilled populations and few people with low skill levels, such as Cambridge (2.1%), have fared lot better.

Unemployment and inactivity by gender

Male unemployment rates have always been higher than female rates. The overall UK unemployment rate for the three months to July 2010 was 7.8%, with male unemployment for the same period being 8.5% compared to female unemployment of 7.0%. Additionally, a striking feature has been the rise in male *inactivity rates* (neither employed nor counted as unemployed) and the fall in female inactivity rates. In June 1976 the female inactivity rate (16–59) was 41.2% and the male inactivity rate (16–64) was 6.4%. By June 2010 the female rate had fallen to 29.3%, but the male rate had risen to 17.0%. This increase in female participation in the labour market arises mainly from married women whose partners are typically working, which more than compensates

the fact that the participation rate of single women with children has fallen. The rise in male inactivity rates has mainly involved married men whose partners do not work (or have never worked) and single men. Nickell (2003) finds that the rise in prime-age male inactivity rates is largely accounted for by low-skilled workers claiming incapacity benefit. The weakness of the labour market for unskilled workers plus the relative ease in acquiring incapacity benefit could explain part of this rise in inactivity rates. Recent government measures targeting such males have had limited success. In June 2010 there were over 1.1 million males giving long-term sickness as the reason for inactivity.

As a result of these changes, there has been a growing polarization between work-rich households where both partners work, and work-poor households where no one works. Nickell couples this trend together with growing UK wage dispersion (falling relative wages of unskilled workers) to explain increased poverty in the UK (see Chapter 14 for more details).

Age-related unemployment

The average OECD youth unemployment rate (15–24 years) is about three times that of the adult unemployment rate. The current global recession has worsened this relative position with the youth rate rising by 6% since 2008, reaching 19% in 2010. The UK figure of 19% in 2010 was high, but less than in some countries such as France (21.4%), Italy (28.9%), Sweden (29.7%) and Spain (41.1%). One notable exception was Germany where an effective apprenticeship scheme and agreements on short-term working had kept the youth unemployment rate at 9%. Evidence suggests that a long period out of work for young workers has a significantly negative impact on their future labour market performance. Table 23.1 indicates that the unemployment rate tends to decline with age; for example only 6.3% of those aged 25–49 years were unemployed in 2010 compared to 32.3% of those aged 16–17 years.

However, those older workers who *do* become unemployed are particularly prone to long spells of unemployment. The long-term unemployed (a year or more) are disproportionately older, disproportionately male and disproportionately low skilled. Such *long-term unemployment* destroys skills and motivation and is often used by employers as an unfavourable filtering device, leading to the stark statistic that

Table 23.1 UK unemployment rates (%) by age, May–July 2010.

	16–17	18–24	25–49	50 and over	16–59/64
All persons	32.3	17.4	6.3	4.6	8.0
Men	35.8	19.0	6.7	5.7	8.7
Women	28.9	15.5	5.9	3.2	7.1

Source: ONS (various).

Table 23.2 Percentage of UK unemployed who have been out of work for over a year, May–July 2010.

	16–17	18–24	25–49	50 and over	16–59/64
All persons	11.0	26.3	36.0	42.9	33.2
Men	12.1	32.5	42.2	44.3	37.6
Women	N/a	17.6	27.8	39.9	24.4

Source: ONS (various).

those workers who are still unemployed after two years stand only a 50% chance of leaving unemployment for a job within the following year. Table 23.2 indicates that 42.9% of the unemployed aged 50 and over had been unemployed for a year or more, compared to only 26.3% of the unemployed aged 18–24 years. The government's strategy towards both youth and long-term unemployment in the UK is discussed later in the chapter.

It is worth noting that the fall in the proportion of youths in the labour force over the last 20 years (a result of the low birth rate in the 1970s) may have contributed as much as 0.55 percentage points of the 5.65 percentage points fall in the UK unemployment rate between 1984 and 1998. It was thought unlikely, however, that shifts in the age composition of the labour force would have much effect on the unemployment rate over the first 10 years of the new millennium (Barwell 2000).

Qualifications and unemployment

The demand for low-skilled and poorly educated workers has been declining throughout the OECD since the early 1980s, whereas the demand for skilled workers has outstripped the supply. The overall result is that the employment prospects and wages of poorly educated and unskilled workers have deteriorated relative to those for better educated and skilled workers. Almost 90% of those with a degree or

equivalent as their highest qualification were in employment, which compares with only 48% of people with no qualifications. People with higher qualifications are less likely to be unemployed or economically inactive. Similarly the wage gap between men aged 25–49 years with no qualifications and those with a university degree was 61% in 1979, but this gap had increased to 90% in 2010.

Ethnic unemployment

As we can see from Fig. 23.3, there are large differences in unemployment rates by ethnicity, in this case for the age range 16–24 years. In Quarter 3 of 2009 unemployment rates had increased for all ethnic groups, including 'white' over the previous 18 months, but still more so for some of the ethnic groups shown in the figure.

Disadvantaged groups

As we have seen, different groups within the population have different employment opportunities. The UK government has highlighted six disadvantaged groups with the aim of reducing the gap between the employment rates of these groups and those of the population as a whole. The six groups are: disabled people; lone parents; ethnic minorities; people aged 50 and over; the lowest qualified; and people living in the most deprived local authority areas. Some 60% of

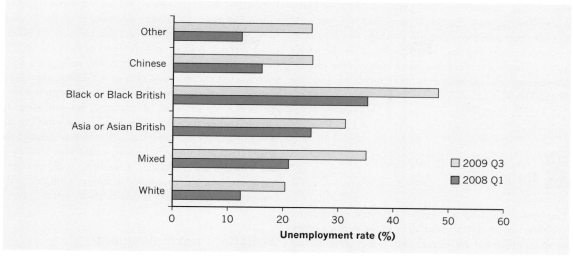

Fig. 23.3 Unemployment rates for 16–24 years of age by ethnicity.
Source: ONS (various).

the population below pensionable age population belongs to one of these disadvantaged groups. A recent study (Barrett 2010) found that only 12% of people possessing none of these characteristics were economically inactive compared to 18% being economically inactive for those possessing two of these characteristics and 77% for those possessing five or six characteristics. The study showed that targeted measures in recent years had narrowed the unemployment gap between nearly all the disadvantaged groups and the population as a whole, the exception being workers with no or low qualifications. Lone parents saw the biggest narrowing of the gap and

indeed were the only group to have seen an increase in their employment rate in the recent recession.

International comparisons

Unemployment rates in most countries have fallen since the mid-1980s, although not back to the low levels experienced in the 1960s. However, some countries have been less successful in reducing unemployment than others. As can be seen from Table 23.3,

Table 23.3 Comparative unemployment rates (%) (standardized).

	1965–72	1973–79	1980–87	1988–92	1993–02	2008	2010[2]
France	2.3	4.3	8.9	9.3	10.7	7.4	10.0
Germany[1]	0.8	2.9	6.1	5.5	8.5	7.5	6.9
Italy	4.2	4.5	6.7	9.1	10.7	6.7	8.4
Japan	1.3	1.8	2.5	2.2	3.9	4.0	5.2
Netherlands	1.7	4.7	10.0	6.1	4.6	3.9	4.4
Spain	2.7	4.9	17.6	17.4	18.4	11.3	20.3
Sweden	1.6	1.6	2.3	2.7	7.8	6.2	8.5
UK	3.1	4.8	10.5	8.2	7.0	6.2	7.8
US	4.3	6.4	7.6	6.1	5.2	5.8	9.6

[1]West Germany up to 1992; the whole of Germany from 1993.
[2]July.
Sources: Adapted from *OECD Economic Outlook* (various); *Eurostat*.

the big four countries in the eurozone, namely Germany, France, Italy and Spain, have had little success in reducing unemployment rates, whilst the Japanese unemployment rate has risen steadily since the early 1990s. The recent recession saw a steep rise in unemployment in all countries except for Germany and the Netherlands.

 ## Unemployment and economic theory

The traditional way of analysing the unemployment problem has been to try and identify the various types of unemployment by cause, this being seen as the first step towards formulating appropriate policy. Economists often distinguish between frictional, structural, classical and demand-deficiency (Keynesian) unemployment. Some would argue that a further type of unemployment should be distinguished, namely technological unemployment. We now consider each 'type' in more detail.

Frictional unemployment

Frictional unemployment results from the time it takes workers to move between jobs. It is a consequence of short-run changes in the labour market that constantly occur in a dynamic economy. Workers who leave their jobs to search for better ones require time because of the imperfections in the labour market. For example, workers are never fully aware of all the possible jobs, wages and other elements in the remuneration package, so that the first job a worker is offered is unlikely to be the one for which he or she is best suited. It is rational, therefore, for workers to spend time familiarizing themselves with the job market even though there will be costs involved in this search, namely lost earnings, postage, telephone calls, internet searches etc. These 'search' costs can, however, be seen from the workers' point of view as an investment, the gain being higher future income. In principle, the economy should also gain from this search behaviour, through higher productivity as workers find jobs that are more appropriate to their skills.

Any measures that reduce the search time will reduce the amount of frictional unemployment.

Improving the transmission of job information, permitting workers to acquire knowledge of the labour market more quickly, is one such measure. A more controversial issue is how the level of unemployment benefit affects search time. It could be argued that by reducing the workers' cost of searching, increased unemployment benefit will lead to more search activity and a higher level of frictional unemployment. On the other hand, a reduction in unemployment benefit, though perhaps leading (via less search) to lower frictional unemployment, could also lead to a less efficient allocation of resources, with workers having to take the first job that comes along regardless of how appropriate it was to their skills.

Structural unemployment

Structural unemployment arises from longer-term changes in the structure of the economy, resulting in changes in the demand for, and supply of, labour in specific industries, regions and occupations. It could be caused by changes in the comparative cost position of an industry or a region, by technological progress or by changes in the pattern of final demand. Examples of structural unemployment are not difficult to find for the UK economy and might include shipbuilding, textile, steel and motor-vehicle workers, i.e. workers in manufacturing industries where the UK has largely lost its comparative advantage over other countries (e.g. newly industrialized countries). On the other hand, the emerging unemployment in the printing industry and in clerical occupations has more to do with technological progress, which enables information to be processed, stored and retrieved more quickly, so that fewer people are required per unit of output (see below). Yet again, structural unemployment may be due to a shift in demand away from an established product, as with the decline of the coal industry following the move to gas-fired power stations.

The structurally unemployed are therefore people who are available for work, but whose skills and locations do not match those of unfilled vacancies. Structural unemployment is likely to reach high levels if the rate of decline for a country's traditional products is rapid and if the labour market adjusts slowly to such changes. Indeed, adjustments are likely to be slow since they are costly to make. From the workers' point of view it may require retraining in new skills and relocation, whilst from the firms' point of view it often means abandoning their familiar products and processes and investing in new and often untried ones. This process of adjustment is, of course, easier the more buoyant the economy.

At a broader level, one of the most important issues facing developed countries is whether they will be able to generate enough output to finance the necessary increase in service occupations required to absorb those released by the manufacturing sector. Whilst manufacturing accounted for 30.1% of employment in the EU in 1970, it accounted for only around 22% in 2006, and most forecasts see this structural trend continuing (see Chapter 1). In the UK employment in manufacturing fell from 24.7% of the workforce in 1978 to 8.2% in 2010. The way in which the developed world manages this structural transition over the medium term will be one of the key determinants of future levels of employment.

Technological unemployment

New technologies have substantially raised output per unit of *labour input* (labour productivity) and per unit of *factor input*, both labour and capital (total factor productivity). There has been much concern that the impact of these productivity gains has been to reduce jobs, i.e. to create technological unemployment. We now consider the principles which will in fact determine whether or not jobs will be lost (or gained) as a result of technological change.

Higher output per unit of factor input reduces costs of production, provided only that wage rates and other factor price increases do not absorb the whole of the productivity gain. Computer-controlled machine tools are a case in point. Data from Renault show that the use of DNC machine tools resulted in machining costs one-third less than those of general-purpose machine tools at the same level of output. Lower costs will cause the profit-maximizing firm to lower price and raise output under most market forms, as in Fig. 23.4. A downward shift of the average cost curve, via the new technologies, lowers the marginal cost curve from MC_1 to MC_2. The profit-maximizing price/output combination ($MC = MR$) now changes from P_1/Q_1 to P_2/Q_2. Price has fallen, output has risen.

The dual effect on employment of higher output per unit of labour (and capital) input can usefully be illustrated from Fig. 23.4. The curve $Q = F(N)$ is the familiar production function of economic theory, showing how output (Q) varies with labour input (N), with capital and other factors assumed constant. On the one hand, the higher labour productivity from technical change shifts the production function outwards to the dashed line $Q' = F(N)$. The original output Q_1 can now be produced with less labour, i.e. with only N_2 labour input instead of N_1 as previously. On the other hand, the cost and price reduction has so raised demand that more output is required. We now move along the new production function Q' until we reach Q_2 output, which requires N_3 labour input. In our example, the reduction in labour required per unit output has been more than compensated for by the expansion of output, via lower price. Employment has, in fact, risen from N_1 to N_3.

This analysis highlights a number of points on which the final employment outcome for a firm adopting the new techniques will depend.

1 The relationship between new technology and labour productivity, i.e. the extent to which the production function Q shifts outwards.

2 The relationship between labour productivity and cost, i.e. the extent to which the marginal cost curve shifts downwards.

3 The relationship between cost and price, i.e. the extent to which cost reductions are passed on to consumers as lower prices.

4 The relationship between lower price and higher demand, i.e. the price elasticity of the demand curve.

Suppose, for instance, that the new process *halved* labour input per unit output. If this increase in labour productivity (1 above) reduces cost (2 above) and price (3 above), and output *doubled* (4 above), then the same total labour input would be required. If output more than doubled, then more labour would be employed. The magnitude of the four relationships above will determine whether the firm offers the same, more or less employment after technical change in the production process.

Although a more detailed treatment must be sought elsewhere, there is in fact a fifth relationship crucial to the final employment outcome, namely, the extent to which any higher total factor productivity arising from a technological innovation can be separately attributed to capital or to labour. An innovation is said to be capital saving when the marginal product of capital rises relative to that of labour, and

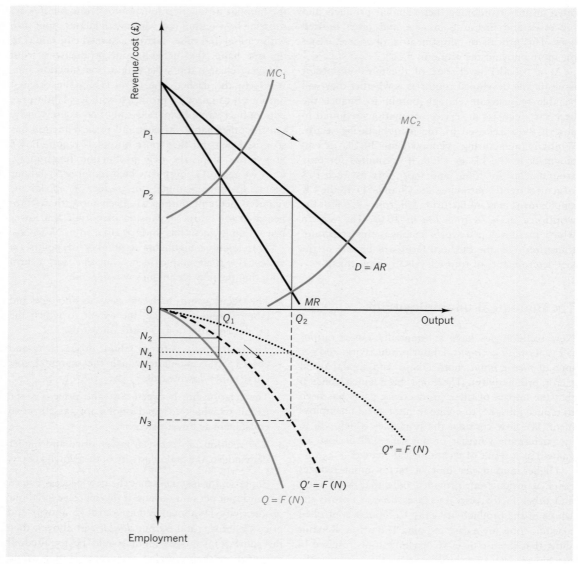

Fig. 23.4 Technical change and the level of employment.

labour saving when the converse applies. This whole issue is surrounded by problems of concept and measurement. We can, however, use Fig. 23.4 to present the outline of the argument.

Suppose we take the dashed line $Q' = F(N)$ to represent a situation in which the new technology is capital saving (with only a small rise in labour productivity), so that the new and higher output Q_2 requires considerable extra labour to produce it

(N_3 employment). If, on the other hand, the new technology were labour saving (with a substantial rise in labour productivity), then the new dotted line $Q'' = F(N)$ in Fig. 23.4 would be more appropriate. Output Q_2 would now only require employment N_4. The prospects for higher employment would therefore appear more favourable when innovations are capital saving, raising the marginal product of capital relative to that of labour.

Broadly speaking, the scenario most favourable to employment would be where a small increase in (labour) productivity significantly reduces both cost and price, leading to a substantial rise in demand.

Classical unemployment

Unemployment may be associated, in the classical view, with real wages that are 'too high'. In this case, trade unions have used their power to force the *real wage* above the market clearing level or have prevented it from falling to the market clearing level after a change in the supply or demand conditions. A government minimum wage above the equilibrium wage could also generate such classical unemployment. In the 1970s there was a revival in this line of thought. The monetarist and new classical economists argued that whilst, for the most part, the economy would be at 'full employment', there might be times when firms and workers would *overestimate* the rate of inflation. If firms pay money wage increases based on such false price expectations, this will lead to (temporarily) higher real wages and reduced employment. Figure 23.5 illustrates classical unemployment using the familiar labour market diagram.

The *labour demand* curve has a negative slope to reflect the usual assumption that the demand for

labour rises as the real wage falls. The *labour force* curve has a positive slope to reflect increased labour force participation as real wages rise. The *labour supply* curve represents those willing and able to take jobs at a given real wage. The market clearing real wage is $(W/P)_F$, giving employment equal to the full employment level N_F and unemployment equal to $N_1 - N_F$. This equilibrium level of unemployment is considered to be entirely *voluntary*. However, if the real wage $(W/P)_2$ is above the market clearing level $(W/P)_F$ for whatever reason, then employment falls to N_2 and unemployment increases to $N_3 - N_2$ of which the portion $N_3 - N_4$ could be regarded as 'voluntary'. In the classical view the remaining 'involuntary' unemployment $N_4 - N_2$ could not persist for long. The unemployed would exert downward pressure on money wages, and the real wage would fall back to the market clearing level.

Demand-deficient unemployment

Keynes criticized the view that unemployment is caused by too high real wages. He considered that the cause of mass unemployment in the 1930s was not to be found in the market for labour, but was rather a result of too little demand in the *market for goods*. This lack of overall demand together with an assumed downward stickiness in wages and prices leaves the economy trapped for long periods with high levels of unemployment. The downward stickiness in wages (and therefore prices) thwarts the operation of the real balance effect, whereby lower prices raise *real incomes* and thereby increase consumer spending.[1] Since no automatic tendency exists to return the economy to full employment by generating sufficient aggregate demand in the goods market, Keynesians would advocate some form of expansionary government demand-management policy. Demand-deficient (Keynesian) unemployment is illustrated in Fig. 23.6.

Aggregate demand (AD) determines the level of output Y_2 (assume Y_F is full employment output – i.e. only 'voluntary' unemployment). Given this level of output and the production function in the economy, firms will need to employ only N_2 workers to meet the demand for their product. The *effective demand* for labour is traced out by the points a-b-N_2. Note that the real wage could be anywhere between $(W/P)_2$ and $(W/P)_3$. A cut in real wages would not restore employment to its full employment level (N_F) if

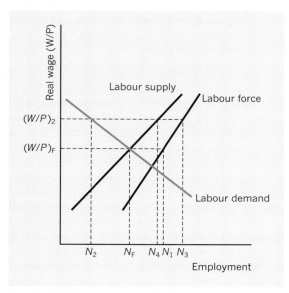

Fig. 23.5 'Voluntary' or equilibrium unemployment and the real wage.

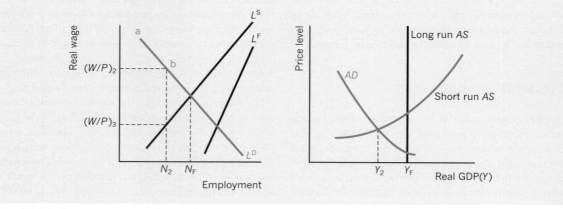

Fig. 23.6 Demand-deficient unemployment.

aggregate demand for output remains unchanged at a level consistent with output Y_2.

A framework for thinking about unemployment

One useful way of thinking about unemployment, which is especially helpful from a policy perspective, is to distinguish between 'cyclical unemployment' which results from a deficiency of aggregate demand (e.g. during the downswing of the business cycle) and 'sustainable unemployment'. *Sustainable unemployment* is the level below which tightness in the labour market will lead to an increasing rate of wage and price inflation. The sustainable level of unemployment is variously referred to as the 'natural rate of unemployment' (NRU), the 'non-accelerating inflation rate of unemployment' (NAIRU) or, as in OECD publications, the 'structural' rate of unemployment.

At any moment in time therefore:

$$\frac{\text{Actual}}{\text{unemployment}} = \frac{\text{Sustainable}}{\text{unemployment}} + \frac{\text{Cyclical}}{\text{unemployment}}$$

Figure 23.7 illustrates these two components for several OECD (advanced industrialized) countries in 2010. In 2006, prior to the recent recession, some countries (Ireland, the UK, Italy, Spain) had unemployment rates below the structural (sustainable) rate. The implication is that demand was too high and that future inflation was a danger. As Fig. 23.7 shows, the recession has had the effect of pushing unemployment above the structural level in all the countries in our sample, apart from Germany. The argument would now be that demand needs to increase to encourage firms to hire the unemployed workers. The key issue is whether this extra demand should come from public sector expenditure or whether the private sector is capable or indeed willing to provide it.

The natural rate of unemployment (NRU) and the NAIRU

Given the central role of these concepts in discussions of unemployment, it might be useful to consider the NRU and NAIRU in rather more detail.

Natural rate of unemployment (NRU)

The NRU was introduced into economics by Milton Friedman (Friedman 1968). It can be thought of as being derived from a competitive labour market with flexible real wages, with the *natural rate* of unemployment being determined by the equilibrium of labour supply and demand. The usual labour market diagram of Fig. 23.8 can be used to illustrate this. Here labour demand, L^D, reflects the marginal revenue product of workers, i.e. the extra revenue contributed by employing the last worker. This is downward sloping in line with the assumption of a diminishing marginal physical product for workers (see Chapter 14). Labour supply, L^S, represents all those workers willing and able (i.e. they have the right skills and are in the right location) to accept jobs at a given real wage. The labour force, L^F, shows the total number

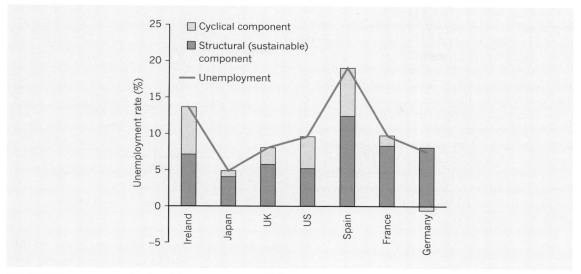

Fig. 23.7 Unemployment rate, structural (sustainable) and cyclical components, 2010.
Source: OECD (various).

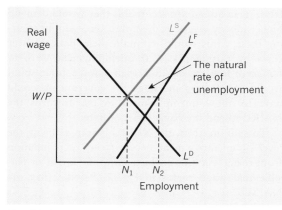

Fig. 23.8 Finding the natural rate of unemployment (NRU).

of workers who consider themselves to be members of the labour force at any given real wage; of course not all of these are willing or able to accept job offers, perhaps because they are still searching for a better offer or because they have not yet acquired the appropriate skills or are not in an appropriate location. Note the convergence of L^S and L^F as the real wage rises. This reflects the reduction in the 'replacement ratio' (i.e. ratio of benefits when out of work to earnings when in work) when real wages rise, given the current level of unemployment benefits. Such a reduc-

tion in the 'replacement ratio' could be expected to result in a higher proportion of the labour force being willing and able to accept jobs as the real wage rate rises (see Chapter 14).

At the equilibrium real wage (W/P) in Fig. 23.8, N_1 workers are willing and able to accept job offers whereas N_2 workers consider themselves to be members of the labour force. That part of the labour force unwilling or unable to accept job offers at the equilibrium real wage ($N_2 - N_1$) is defined as being the natural rate of unemployment (NRU). In terms of our earlier classification of the unemployed, the NRU can be regarded as including both the frictionally and structurally unemployed.

It can be seen that anything that *reduces the labour supply* (the numbers willing and able to accept a job at a given real wage) will, other things being equal, cause the NRU to increase. Possible factors might include an *increase in the level or availability of unemployment benefits*, thereby encouraging unemployed members of the labour force to engage in more prolonged search activity. An *increase in trade union power* might also reduce the numbers willing and able to accept a job at a given real wage, especially if the trade union is able to restrict the effective labour supply as part of a strategy for raising wages. A reduced labour supply might also result from *increased technological change* or increased *global competition*, both of which change the nature of the labour market skills required for employment. *Higher taxes on earned income* are also likely to reduce the labour supply at any given real wage.

Similarly anything that *reduces the labour demand* will, other things being equal, cause the NRU to increase. A fall in the marginal revenue product of labour, via a fall in marginal physical productivity or in the product price, might be expected to reduce labour demand. Many economists believe that the two sharp oil price increases in the 1970s had this effect, with the resulting fall in aggregate demand causing firms to cut back on capital spending, reducing the overall capital stock and hence the marginal physical productivity of labour.

Non-accelerating inflation rate of unemployment (NAIRU)

Unlike the NRU which assumes a competitive labour market, the NAIRU is usually developed from a model that recognizes imperfect competition in the labour market (Layard 1986). The 'sustainable' level of unemployment (i.e. the level consistent with the inflation rate being unchanged) is seen here as being the result of a bargaining equilibrium between firms and workers rather than a market clearing outcome. The two sides of the labour market are seen as engaged in a constant struggle over the available real output per head. If the claims of the two sides are inconsistent, in that they add up to more than the real output per head available, then each side will try to safeguard its own claim by using its market power. Workers will claim higher money wages and firms will raise their product prices. The result of such a power struggle will then be rising inflation.

Figure 23.9 illustrates the determination of the NAIRU. At any particular moment there is a limit to the real wage the economy can provide, given labour productivity and the mark-up that firms typically apply to costs. This limit is the *feasible real wage* (W/P)*. At the same time, the *target real wage* reflects the aspirations of workers. It seems likely that this target will be influenced by the level of demand in the economy, as reflected by the unemployment rate. When demand is high and unemployment is low, workers will feel more able to negotiate wage increases than when demand is low and unemployment high. There will be some level of unemployment where workers' aspirations are *equal* to the real wage

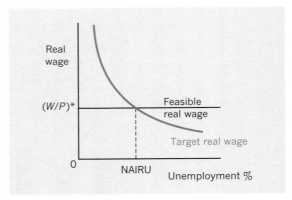

Fig. 23.9 The determination of the NAIRU.

that firms are willing to offer; this is the NAIRU. In other words, NAIRU is determined by the intersection of the target and feasible real wage curves in Fig. 23.9. If unemployment were pushed *below* the NAIRU by government expansionary policy, then workers would seek a real wage above the feasible level; in an attempt to secure this they would demand higher money wages. If they were successful in securing these, firms would maintain their mark-up over costs by raising their prices. If unemployment were to *remain* below the NAIRU, then a wage–price spiral would ensue. At some stage the government would have to allow unemployment to rise towards the NAIRU to end the rising inflation rate.

To sum up, then, the NAIRU is seen as being the level of unemployment necessary to keep inflation from rising. Anything which *shifts* the target or feasible real wage curves in Fig. 23.9 will affect the NAIRU.

Any factor that enables or encourages workers to *increase the target real wage* for a given level of unemployment will clearly increase the NAIRU, shifting the target real wage curve upwards and to the right. Such factors might include any or all of the following:

■ an increase in benefits and their duration;

■ an increase in trade union power or greater employment protection (both reducing the fear of unemployment);

■ increased structural unemployment (the unemployed now compete less effectively with the employed because they have the wrong skills or are in the wrong place);

- an increase in the long-term unemployed as a proportion of total unemployment (the long-term unemployed compete less effectively with the employed for jobs);

- an increase in taxes on earnings which reduces the post-tax real wage and leads workers to seek a higher pre-tax real wage.

Similarly any factor that *reduces the feasible real wage* will increase the NAIRU. Such factors might include any or all of the following:

- reduced labour productivity;

- unfavourable movements in the Terms of Trade (i.e. a fall in the ratio of export to import prices), reducing the share of output going to domestic employees and raising that going to foreign employees;

- higher dividends reducing the share of output going to employees and raising that going to shareholders;

- more 'leapfrogging' by which one group of workers use a pay increase by others to justify their own higher pay demands.

The idea that the best policy-makers can do in the short run is to keep demand at a level such that unemployment is at or near the NAIRU, whilst in the long run reforming labour market incentives and institutions to lower the NAIRU, has dominated economic policy making for the last 30 years. However, this strategy is, of course, not without its critics, not least because of considerable variability in the estimates of the NAIRU that have been made for the UK over various time periods, indicated in Table 23.4. Galbraith (1997) argued that it was time to abandon the NAIRU on theoretical grounds and also because attempts to keep its level down had become a 'professional embarrassment'. In addition, policy-makers, arguably too much concerned with inflation, had run

the economy with too low a level of demand and too high a level of unemployment, causing the NAIRU to increase (see p. 492 on Hysteresis). Storm and Naastepad (2009) similarly argue that adherence to the NAIRU as a guide to policy in France, Germany and Italy (as compared to US policy) has led to between 900,000 and 2.4 million extra European workers being (unnecessarily) unemployed. They argue that more expansionary policies, aimed at full employment, and higher labour productivity growth policies followed by the Nordic countries have provided better outcomes compared to a rigid following the NAIRU framework.

Unemployment in the OECD

Two important puzzles face applied economists when considering data on unemployment in the advanced industrialized countries of the OECD. One puzzle involves explaining why unemployment has been much higher in almost all OECD countries during the 1980s and 1990s than it had been in the decades following the Second World War. The second puzzle involves explaining why such large variations have been recorded in unemployment rates between the OECD countries.

A study of cross-country differences in unemployment rates (Nickell 1998) attempted to assess the impact on unemployment of a variety of factors. For example, Nickell estimated that a 10% increase in the 'replacement ratio' and a one-year increase in the duration of entitlement to unemployment benefits would result in a 25% increase in unemployment, while a 10% increase in trade union density would result in a 60% increase in unemployment. On the other hand, a 5% reduction in the overall tax rate

Table 23.4 Estimates of the UK NAIRU.

Time period	1966–73	1974–80	1981–87	1989–90	1996–99	2002	2007
NAIRU range	1.6–5.6%	4.5–7.3%	5.2–9.9%	3.5–8.1%	6% approx.	5.25% approx.	5.3%

Sources: OECD Economics Department Working Papers 649 (Gianella *et al.* 2008); *Bank of England Quarterly Bulletin* (1993), Vol. 33, No. 2; Bank of England (1998) *Inflation Report*, August; HM Treasury (2002b) *Trend Growth; Recent Developments and Prospects*, April.

would reduce unemployment by 15% and a 2% cut in the real interest rate (a substantial cut) would reduce unemployment by around 10%. He found that policies involving an increase in labour market 'rigidity' (such as improved labour standards and greater employment protection) had little impact on overall unemployment. Nickell argued that such variables, despite problems of definition and measurement across countries, do shed some light on why unemployment varies a great deal between countries. For example, Spain, with its high replacement ratios, long benefit duration, rather high tax rates on earnings and relatively 'rigid' labour market, suffers from high unemployment, as might be expected from Nickell's analysis, whereas the US, with its relatively low replacement ratios, short benefit duration, low tax rates on earnings, flexible labour market and low union coverage, has relatively low unemployment.

Nickell goes on to argue that although his variables usefully explain cross-country comparisons, they are less useful in explaining the time-series pattern of OECD unemployment (see also Bean 1994). For example, when comparing the higher unemployment of the 1990s with the much lower unemployment of the 1960s, Nickell was surprised to find that today's replacement ratios are no more generous, trade union militancy no worse, real interest rates not much higher, and labour markets not much more rigid than all of these factors had been in the 1960s and yet unemployment is so much higher.

Concentrating on the UK alone, rather than on cross-country comparisons, Nickell (1998) estimated that the fourfold rise in the numbers unemployed since the 1960s could comfortably be explained by a model including the replacement ratio, the Terms of Trade, skills mismatch, union pressure, industrial turbulence, the tax 'wedge' and the real interest rate. The variables making the most important (percentage) contributions in explaining the overall rise in unemployment have been skills mismatch 14%, union pressure 19% and tax 'wedge' 23%, but the real interest rate *only* 3.5%.

A rather different view was offered by Phelps and Zoega (1998) who suggested that two global forces, namely sharp rises in oil prices in the 1970s and in real world interest rates in the 1980s and early 1990s, have been the major factors responsible for the observed increases in worldwide unemployment since the 1960s.

Higher oil prices reduce labour productivity by reducing the proportion of the existing capital stock which can be regarded as 'economically efficient'; for example, oil-intensive capital equipment becomes effectively redundant. As well as diminishing the 'economically efficient' capital stock, and with it labour productivity, higher oil prices are seen by Phelps and Zoega as contributing to higher unemployment by diminishing net exports (exports minus imports) for many OECD countries. The non-oil exporting OECD countries have been particularly hard-hit by ever increasing import bills for oil and 'oil-based' products.

The Phelps and Zoega model sees hiring rates for workers as heavily dependent on both net productivity and the real interest rate. As well as the slowdown in productivity growth experienced in most countries following oil-price shocks, the steep rises in global real interest rates also experienced at such times further reduce the hiring rate for labour, resulting in substantial increases in levels of unemployment. Higher real interest rates particularly discourage the hiring of workers who require a substantial investment in human capital, such as the large numbers of higher skilled and well-educated workers required by many high-technology, 'information age' industries.

Unemployment persistence and hysteresis

In the mid-1980s oil prices fell, trade union power diminished compared to the 1970s, the replacement ratio fell, and yet unemployment kept on rising, at least in Europe. One explanation might be that demand-deficient unemployment had risen because governments were trying to control inflation by running the economy with unemployment *above* the NAIRU. However, inflation did not fall in the mid-1980s, leading some economists to the view that a period of high unemployment resulting from contractionary demand management might lead to the NAIRU itself increasing. The idea that there might be a mechanism whereby a rise in unemployment increases the equilibrium (or natural) rate of unemployment is known as *hysteresis*. There are several possible mechanisms to explain hysteresis in European unemployment.

One explanation of hysteresis involves the *insider–outsider hypothesis* (Blanchard and Summers 1986; Lindbeck and Snower 1988). *Insiders* are the unionized employed who pay little attention to the interests of the unemployed *outsiders*. For a variety of reasons (such as turnover costs, firm-specific human capital and the possibility of refusing to co-operate with newly hired outsiders), insiders do not fear that they will be replaced by outsiders. Of course in practice, if the demand for labour falls, then some insiders may lose their jobs and become outsiders. Once labour demand recovers, however, the smaller pool of insiders who remain will exploit their relative scarcity by negotiating higher wages for themselves rather than accepting wage moderation and allowing the employment of more outsiders. The economy therefore settles at a higher-wage, lower-employment equilibrium.

A second explanation of hysteresis concentrates on the role of the *long-term unemployed*; in other words this approach concentrates on the role of the *outsiders* rather than on the wage-determining role of the insiders. The long-term unemployed are seen as effectively having withdrawn from the labour force (they search less effectively, they lose their skills and employers see them as a bad risk). The result is that they do not exert much downward pressure on wage setting, so that a higher level of unemployment is required to exert the same control on inflation when the long-term unemployed increase as a proportion of the total unemployed. Empirical evidence certainly suggests that when European unemployment persists the effect is to increase the proportion of the long-term unemployed in total unemployment, so that the equilibrium (or natural) rate of unemployment rises.

A third explanation of hysteresis involves the effect of recessions on the *capital stock*. As aggregate demand falls, firms go out of business and investment plans are shelved, reducing the capital-to-labour ratio and therefore the marginal productivity of labour (shifting the labour demand curve to the left). From the point of view of the NAIRU model there has been a reduction in the 'feasible real wage'. Whichever way we look at it, the equilibrium (or natural) rate of unemployment rises.

A fourth explanation of hysteresis involves the suggestion that a more highly regulated labour market discourages recruitment, and may lead to higher equilibrium unemployment after a downturn in demand (see Bean 1994).

What can be done to reduce unemployment?

In 1994, at a time of high and persistent unemployment, the OECD published its *Jobs Study* (OECD 1994). This study, together with the OECD's *Jobs Strategy* (1998), made more than 60 policy recommendations and provided a blueprint aimed at creating jobs and reducing unemployment, whilst at the same time maintaining social cohesion. As Coats (2006) points out in *Who's Afraid of Labour Market Flexibility?*, the strategy was a mixture of Keynesian demand management (deficit spending in recessions and fiscal consolidation in booms), growth theory (with its emphasis on entrepreneurship, research and development) and labour market flexibility (with its emphasis on job skills). The key recommendations were as follows.

- Set macroeconomic policy to encourage non-inflationary growth.
- Enhance the creation and diffusion of technology.
- Increase working time flexibility.
- Encourage entrepreneurship and eliminate restrictions on the creation and expansion of enterprises.
- Make wage and labour costs flexible and responsive to local conditions and skill levels, particularly for young workers.
- Reform employment security provisions that inhibit recruitment.
- Strengthen the emphasis on 'active' labour market policies.
- Improve the education and skills of the labour force.
- Reform 'unemployment and related' benefits and the tax system to improve the functioning of the job market, whilst not jeopardizing society's equity goals.
- Enhance product market competition to reduce monopolistic tendencies and weaken insider–outsider mechanisms, thereby leading to a more dynamic economy.

In June 2006 a revised study was published (OECD 2006) reviewing the progress that had been made in improving the labour markets since 1994. Its conclusions were that some progress has been made in most but not all countries. At the same time the challenges and dangers have become broader and include a more rapid pace of technological advance, globalization with the associated increase in competition from the extra labour force in China and India, and the demographic problem of an ageing workforce in many countries.

Over the 12 years the OECD noted that the trend rise in unemployment had been reversed or at least stabilized. In some countries, notably Finland, Spain and Ireland, there had been substantial reductions (9.3, 11.2 and 10.0 percentage points respectively between 1994 and 2006). Other countries that adopted many, if not all, of the *Job Strategy* recommendations had also done well. The UK, for example, reduced unemployment over the same period by 4.1 percentage points. However, it was also the case that other countries that had adopted the Nordic 'flexicurity' approach such as Denmark with its easy hire-and-fire but strong support for the unemployed (who receive 65% of work income compared with only 18% in the UK), Austria and the Netherlands, all of which had similar approaches, had also done relatively well. Other countries that the OECD regarded as not having reformed their labour markets sufficiently, such as Germany, France and Italy, had done less well despite strong global growth over that period.

Active labour market policies

The last decade has seen an emphasis on 'activating' the unemployed and other benefit recipients. The various OECD countries have differed in their specific implementation of this strategy, but most have used a 'carrot and stick approach'. High-quality employment services and strong job search incentives have been reinforced by the threat of benefit reduction or removal. The OECD argued that if properly designed, such 'active labour market policies' (ALPs) have led to improved labour market outcomes. The UK has gone further down the road of these ALPs than have most other OECD countries. The last Labour government set up the various New Deal programmes and later the 'Pathways to Work' programme for people with disabilities in an attempt to increase the employment of the various groups. The introduction of the minimum wage and reforms of tax and benefits were also policies directed towards increasing the incentives to move into work (see Chapter 19). At the same time, it has also been argued that UK benefit recipients face some of the toughest hurdles in order to receive or continue receiving benefits (Daguerre and Etherington, 2009). It is difficult to assess the effectiveness of these programmes, but Daguerre and Etherington argue that there have been mixed results and that it is important to tailor ALPs to the most needy and to ensure early and high quality interventions and individualised assistance as it is clear that 'one size' does not fit all.

The great recession

The 'great recession' can be dated from late 2007 for the US and early 2008 for many other countries and regions, including the UK and Europe. The ILO has estimated that this recession has resulted in an extra 34 million unemployed people worldwide, with unemployment in the OECD countries reaching a post-war high of 8.7% in March 2010. Particularly badly affected have been young workers, with youth unemployment in the OECD rising by 7%, nearly four times the rate for other employees.

It is interesting to note that not all countries have had the same experience; in fact, the disparity of experience seems to have been greater than in previous recessions! As Fig. 23.10 shows, the US and Spain have shed the largest numbers of workers relative to the fall in GDP, the suggestion being that workers in the US have a fairly low level of job protection and so are more easily released. Spain suffered job losses partly as a result of the collapse of the labour-intensive housing market bubble (Ireland also), but also because a large proportion of its workers, especially the young, immigrants and the unskilled, are on short-term (temporary) contracts with very little job protection. Stronger employment protection measures, in the view of many analysts, maintained employment in Germany and France, as did short-term and more flexible working arrangements (e.g. a reduction in weekly hours worked) in Germany, some other European countries and Japan, which helped dampen the effects of the recession on unemployment. Labour hoarding of this type is, however, not without its

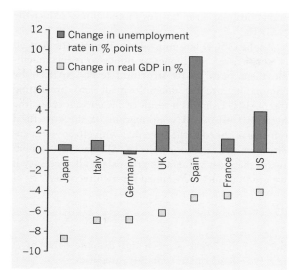

Fig. 23.10 Change in unemployment and GDP from peak to trough: selected OECD countries.
Source: OECD *Economic Outlook* (various).

tion, and subsequently prices fell more rapidly than money wages, with output prices changing on average each four months whereas wages only changed on average annually! As a result, real wages rose, forcing firms to reduce employment. The current recession was, however, preceded by low and stable inflation so there was less need for downward price adjustments and hence real wages may have risen less rapidly than before, putting less pressure on firms to cut employment.

A second explanation might be found in structural changes in the labour market which have meant that firms are more willing, at least in the short term, to accept lower productivity and workers are more willing to accept lower real wages. Increased hiring and firing cost are seen as a reason for such responses by employers and weaker unionization. Lower unionization since the 1990s (see Chapter 14) may explain some of the differences from the earlier recessions, although most of the decline in unionization occurred before the current recession.

Other factors which might explain these differences between respective recessions might include more pessimistic expectations of employees, leading to increased concerns about future jobs and hence greater wage moderation. Labour supply also impacts on wages, and the labour force participation rate seems to have held up better than in previous recessions. Older workers may be more concerned about future pensions, given the financial crisis and the removal of many final salary pensions, and households in general may be more concerned about future incomes, leading both groups to work longer, whether in years before retirement or before withdrawing from the labour force, respectively. The 25% reduction in the effective sterling exchange rate between mid-2007 and early 2009 might also have had an influence in the UK; the higher import prices helping UK-based firms to compete against more expensive imports, which may have helped reduce the need for cost savings via cutting jobs. Lower sterling export prices may also have reduced the need for UK-based exporters to reduce employment.

Overall, the unusual behaviour of the UK labour market in the recent recession is likely to be partly due to an increased flexibility in real wages relative to employment and partly due to other factors such as the supply of labour and the exchange rate depreciation.

costs, as it results in lower labour productivity and may lead to the danger of a jobless recovery. The OECD (2010) has estimated, for example, that output in Japan could rise by as much as 7% during the recovery without firms needing to hire any new workers, if hours per worker and productivity levels return to the pre-crisis level. Keeping workers engaged in the labour market nevertheless has many overall benefits and lowers the danger of hysteresis (see p. 492).

In the UK, GDP fell by 8% in the two years to Q1 2010, a much larger fall than in the previous two recessions at the start of the 1980s and 1990s. Employment, however, has fallen by much less than in those recessions, i.e. by 1.9% as against the 2.4% in the 1980s recession and the 3.4% in the 1990s recession. A further difference is also worth noting, namely that real wages per hour rose less rapidly in the current recession as compared to the previous recessions, putting less pressure on firms to shed labour. Hours worked per worker fell as in previous recessions but by a similar amount.

Faccini and Hackworth (2010) have examined the reasons that have helped dampen the fall in employment. First, they conclude that some of the explanation can be found in the changes in the economy which have occurred since the 1990s. The 1990s recession was preceded by rapid price and wage infla-

Conclusion

Unemployment is determined by the level of demand in the economy. If demand is too low, then unemployment will be above the equilibrium rate (structural rate or NAIRU); if demand is too high, then unemployment will be below the NAIRU and, in the absence of other offsetting factors, the inflation rate will begin to rise. The implication for policy is that demand management should aim to keep unemployment as close to the NAIRU as possible, whilst labour and goods market initiatives should aim to reduce the NAIRU.

As the OECD has pointed out, the immediate need is to use fiscal and monetary policy to reduce unemployment back to its structural level (NAIRU) by eliminating cyclical unemployment and preventing the NAIRU rising as a result of the current crisis (the hysteresis effect). A continuation of the structural reforms outlined earlier together with effective expenditure on active labour policies (ALP) and an emphasis on the most vulnerable groups are all necessary if we are to ensure a sustained job-rich recovery.

Key points

- Successive 'unemployment cycles' (peak to peak) have tended to result in higher unemployment rates.

- The ILO (survey) method of measuring the unemployed differs from the claimant (administrative record) method used in the UK.

- Unemployment in the UK can be *disaggregated* into regional, occupational, gender, age, ethnically-based and qualification-related unemployment.

- The major *types* of unemployment include frictional (temporary), structural (changing patterns of demand), technological (changing technology), classical ('excessive' real wages) and demand-deficient (inadequate demand) categories.

- The *natural rate of unemployment* (NRU) is the voluntary unemployment (labour force – labour supply) existing at the real wage level which 'clears' the markets.

- The *non-accelerating inflation rate of unemployment* (NAIRU) is that level of unemployment which equates the *feasible* real wage with the *target* real wage. It is the unemployment rate at which inflation is constant.

- Progress has been made in reducing the UK NAIRU since the 1980s.

- Combinations of policies are required to combat unemployment.

Now try the self-check questions for this chapter on the Companion Website. You will also find useful links to relevant websites.

Note

1 The downward stickiness in wages (wage rigidity) and therefore prices also thwarts the interest rate and foreign trade effects which might stimulate recovery. In the 'interest rate effect', lower prices mean an increase in *real money supply*, lowering the 'price' of money (interest rates) and thereby raising the investment component of aggregate demand. In the 'foreign trade effect', lower prices mean more competitive exports and more competitive (home-produced) substitutes for imports, a rise in exports and a fall in imports again stimulating (net) aggregate demand.

References and further reading

Bank of England (1998) *Inflation Report*, August, London.

Bank of England Quarterly Bulletin (1993) Volume 33, no. 2.

Barrett, R. (2010) Disadvantaged groups in the labour market, *Economic and Labour Market Review*, 4 (6): 18–24.

Barro, R. J. (1998) *Macroeconomics*, Cambridge MA, MIT Press.

Barwell, R. (2000) Age structure and the UK unemployment rate, *Bank of England Quarterly Bulletin*, 40(3), August.

Bean, C. (1994) European unemployment: a survey, *Journal of Economic Literature*, 32, June.

Begg, D., Fischer, S. and Dornbusch, R. (1994) *Economics*, London, McGraw-Hill.

Bénassy-Quéré, A. and Coeuré, B. (2010) *Economic* Policy, Oxford, Oxford University Press.

Berthoud, R. (2003) *Multiple Disadvantage in Employment: A Quantitative Analysis*, Institute for Social and Economic Research, Colchester, University of Essex.

Blanchard, D. and Summers, L. (1986) Hysteresis and the European unemployment problem, *NBER Macroeconomic Annual*, Cambridge, MA, National Bureau of Economic Research.

Clark, A. and Layard, R. (1989) *UK Unemployment*, Oxford, Heinemann Educational.

Coats, D. (2006) *Who's Afraid of Labour Market Flexibility?* London, The Work Foundation.

Daguerre, A. and Etherington, D. (2009) *Active Labour Market Polices in International Context: What Works Best? Lessons for the UK*, Department for Works and Pension, Working Paper 59, London, The Stationery Office.

Dawson, G. (1992) *Inflation and Unemployment: Causes, Consequences and Cures*, Cheltenham, Edward Elgar.

Faccini, R. and Hackworth, C. (2010) Changes in output, employment and wages during recessions in the UK, *Bank of England Quarterly Bulletin*, first quarter.

Fothergill, S. and Gudgin, G. (1982) *Unequal Growth: Urban and Regional Change in the UK*, London, Heinemann.

Friedman, M. (1968) The role of monetary policy, *American Economic Review*, 58, March.

Galbraith, J. (1997) Time to ditch the NAIRU, *Journal of Economic Perspectives*, 11(1), Winter.

Gianella, C., Koske, I., Rusticelli, E. and Chatal, O. (2008) *What Drives the NAIRU? Evidence From a Panel of OECD Countries*, OECD Economics Department Working Papers 649, Paris, Organisation for Economic Cooperation and Development.

Giavazzi, F. and Blanchard, O. (2010) *Macroeconomics: A European Perspective*, Harlow, Financial Times/Prentice Hall.

HM Treasury (1998) *Stability and Investment for the Long Term: Economic and Fiscal Strategy Report*, London.

HM Treasury (2002a) *UK Employment Action Plan*, London.

HM Treasury (2002b) *Trend Growth: Recent Developments and Prospects*, London.

ILO–IMF (2010), *The Challenges of Growth, Employment and Social Cohesion*, discussion paper, Joint ILO–IMF conference in cooperation with the office of the Prime Minister of Norway, Oslo, September 13.

IPPR (2010) *Youth Unemployment and the Recession*, Press Release, 20 January, London, Institute for Public Policy Research.

Keynes, J. M. (1936) *The General Theory of Employment, Interest and Money*, Basingstoke, Macmillan.

Mishel, L. (2006) *CEO Pay-to-Minimum Wage Ratio Soars*, Economic Snapshot, June 26, Washington DC, Economic Policy Institute.

Layard, R. (1986) *How to Beat Unemployment*, Oxford, Oxford University Press.

Layard, R., Nickell, S. and Jackman, R. (1994) *The Unemployment Crisis*, Oxford, Oxford University Press.

Lee, N. (2010) *No City Left Behind? The Geography of the Recovery*, London, The Work Foundation.

Lindbeck, A. and Snower, D. (1988) *The Insider–Outsider Theory of Employment and Unemployment*, Cambridge MA, MIT Press.

Nickell, S. (1998) Unemployment: questions and some answers, *Economic Journal*, 108(48), May.

Nickell, S. (2003) *Poverty and Worthlessness in Britain*, speech given at Royal Economic Society Conference at Warwick, 8 April.

OECD (1994) *Jobs Study: Facts, Analysis and Strategies*, Paris, Organisation for Economic Cooperation and Development.

OECD (1998) *Jobs Strategy: Progress Report*, OECD Working Paper No. 196, Paris, Organisation for Economic Cooperation and Development.

OECD (2006) *OECD Employment Outlook, Boosting Jobs and Income*, Paris, Organisation for Economic Cooperation and Development.

OECD (2010) Return to work after the Crisis, *Economic Outlook*, No. 87, May, 251–92.

ONS (2000) *Labour Market Trends*, July, London, Office for National Statistics.

Phelps, E. and Zoega, G. (1998) Natural rate theory and OECD unemployment, *Economic Journal*, 108(48), May.

Rowthorn, R. (1995) Capital formation and unemployment, *Oxford Review of Economic Policy*, 11(1), Spring.

Storm, S. and Naastepad, C. (2009) The costs of NAIRU variation, *Challenge*, 52(5), September–October.

PART IV International economics

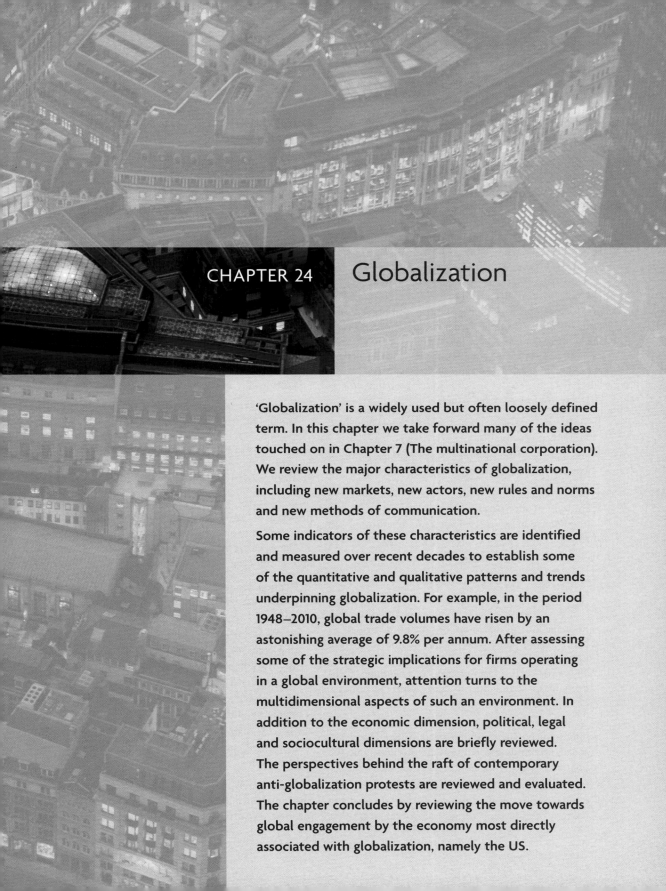

CHAPTER 24   Globalization

'Globalization' is a widely used but often loosely defined term. In this chapter we take forward many of the ideas touched on in Chapter 7 (The multinational corporation). We review the major characteristics of globalization, including new markets, new actors, new rules and norms and new methods of communication.

Some indicators of these characteristics are identified and measured over recent decades to establish some of the quantitative and qualitative patterns and trends underpinning globalization. For example, in the period 1948–2010, global trade volumes have risen by an astonishing average of 9.8% per annum. After assessing some of the strategic implications for firms operating in a global environment, attention turns to the multidimensional aspects of such an environment. In addition to the economic dimension, political, legal and sociocultural dimensions are briefly reviewed. The perspectives behind the raft of contemporary anti-globalization protests are reviewed and evaluated. The chapter concludes by reviewing the move towards global engagement by the economy most directly associated with globalization, namely the US.

Characteristics of 'globalization'

It is widely accepted that the world has become increasingly interconnected in recent decades as the result of economic, technological, political, socio-logical and cultural forces. To take but one example, Carlos Ghosn, the Renault–Nissan CEO, announced in April 2010 an alliance with Daimler, the German automaker, combining car technology and manufac-turing capability on a global scale. The Boeing 787 Dreamliner has wings built in Japan, fuselage in Italy and the US, landing gear in France.

However, there is considerable debate as to whether such events merely reflect the continuation of a long-established internationalization process or a deep-seated shift in the structure and operations of the world economy. 'Globalization' is a much used but often loosely defined term, which many believe should be restricted to situations characterized by this latter perspective. Glyn (2004) sees globalization as characterized by two key trends:

1 shifts within countries towards market-driven systems of production;
2 the increasing international economic integration of countries through trade, investment and migration.

As we can see below, there are a wide range of definitions of globalization, but certainly increasing 'interconnectedness' is a theme running through all of them!

Definitions of globalization

- '. . . the process of transformation of local phe-nomena into global ones. It can be described as a process by which the people of the world are unified into a single society and function together. This process is a combination of economic, tech-nological, sociocultural and political forces' (Croucher 2003, p. 10)
- '. . . a widening, deepening and speeding up of interconnectedness in all aspects of contemporary social life from the cultural to the criminal, the financial to the spiritual' (Held *et al.* 1999, p. 2)
- '. . . increasing global interconnectedness, so that events in one part of the world are affected by, have to take account of, and also influence, other

parts of the world. It also refers to an increasing sense of a single global whole (Tiplady 2003, p. 2)
- '. . . the worldwide movement towards economic, financial, trade and communications integration. Globalisation implies opening out beyond local and nationalistic perspectives to a broader outlook of an interconnected and inter-dependent world with the free transfer of capital, goods and services across national frontiers' (*Business Dictionary*)
- '. . . refers to the shift toward a more integrated and interdependent world economy . . . [through] the merging of historically distinct and separate national markets into one huge global market place' (Hill 2005, p. 6)
- '. . . process by which the whole world becomes a single market. This means that goods and services, capital and labour are traded on a worldwide basis, and information and the results of research flow readily between countries (Black 2002)
- '. . . reflects a business orientation based on the belief that the world is becoming more homo-genous and that distinctions between national markets are not only fading but, for some prod-ucts, will eventually disappear' (Czinkota *et al.* 1999, p. 454)

Of course, globalization is by no means the preserve of economists alone. Indeed, it has been approached from the perspective of at least four academic disciplines, within each of which it tends to take on different characteristics.

1 *Economists* focus on the growth of international trade and the increase in international capital flows.
2 *Political scientists* view globalization as a process that leads to the undermining of the nation state and the emergence of new forms of governance.
3 *Sociologists* view globalization in terms of the rise of a global culture and the domination of the media by global companies.
4 *International relations experts* tend to focus on the emergence of global conflicts and global institutions.

Some argue that globalization is a long-standing phenomenon and not really anything new, pointing out that world trade and investment as a proportion of world GDP is little different today from what it was a century ago and that international borders were as open at that time as they are today with proportionately just as many people migrating abroad. Indeed Adam Smith as long ago as 1787 defined the businessmen of his time as 'men without a country'.

However, those who believe that globalization really is a new phenomenon tend to agree that at least three key elements are commonly involved.

1 *Shrinking space.* The lives of all individuals are increasingly interconnected by events worldwide. This is not only a matter of fact but one which people increasingly perceive to be the case, recognizing that their jobs, income levels, health and living environment depend on factors outside national and local boundaries.

2 *Shrinking time.* With the rapid developments in communication and information technologies, events occurring in one place have almost instantaneous (real-time) impacts worldwide. A fall in share prices in Wall Street can have almost immediate consequences for share prices in London, Frankfurt or Tokyo.

3 *Disappearing borders.* The nation state and its associated borders seem increasingly irrelevant as 'barriers' to international events and influences. Decisions taken by regional trading blocs (e.g. EU, NAFTA) and supra-national bodies (e.g. IMF, World Trade Organization) increasingly override national policy-making in economic and business affairs as well as in other areas such as law enforcement and human rights.

It may be useful at this point to consider some of the conceptual issues as regards 'globalization' a little further using a broadly *economic* perspective.

■ *Shallow versus deep integration.* 'Shallow integration' is often used to describe an increasing volume of trade in goods and services between largely independent firms which conduct the main part of their activities within single national economies. A stereotypical version of 'shallow integration' would be the growth in international trade involving firms exchanging materials and foodstuffs with other firms mainly engaged in the manufacture and finishing of products in single national economies. 'Deep integration' is more commonly associated with the rise of the multinational enterprise and the associated *fragmentation* of production

processes and their *geographical relocation* on a global scale which pays scant regard to national boundaries. The term is also used to reflect the development of communication networks, financial transactions and logistical arrangements on a global scale. In other words, 'deep integration' views the linkages between national economies as being progressively influenced by the cross-border value-adding activities of multinational enterprises over a broad range of goods and services.

■ *Internationalization versus globalization processes.* Whilst the growing *quantitative* importance of multinational enterprises in global trade patterns (see Chapter 7) points inexorably towards 'deep integration', a key question is whether their involvement has also led to a *qualitative* change in the relationship between nation states and firms. Whereas the term 'internationalization' might be applied to the many processes resulting in more geographically extensive patterns of economic activity, 'globalization' should arguably be applied only to processes whereby geographically dispersed activities become more *functionally integrated* than hitherto. For example, a 'qualitative' change might be said to occur where the co-ordination and regulation functions involving the production chain become progressively 'internal' to the multinational enterprise rather than an 'external' issue whose resolution requires engagement between the multinational enterprise and national or international regulatory bodies. In such a case, there has arguably been a 'qualitative' change in the relationship between nation states and the firm.

Table 24.1 attempts to capture some of the characteristics which currently underpin the use of the term 'globalization' as being something different from what has gone before. Some would argue that the 'globalization tendencies' outlined in Table 24.1 can be at work without this resulting in the end-state of a new geo-economy in which 'market forces are rampant and uncontrollable, and the nation state merely passive and supine' (Dicken 2011, p. 5). Certainly the focus in this chapter will be on examining the impacts of these 'globalization tendencies' in today's world economy rather than on a semantic debate as to whether a deep-seated shift, involving qualitative change, has or has not occurred in the structure and operations of the world economy.

Table 24.1 Characteristics of globalization.

New markets
- Growing global markets in services – banking, insurance, transport.
- New financial markets – deregulated, globally linked, working around the clock, with action at a distance in real time, with new instruments such as derivatives.
- Deregulation of antitrust laws and growth of mergers and acquisitions.
- Global consumer markets with global brands.

New actors
- Multinational corporations integrating their production and marketing, dominating world production.
- The World Trade Organization – the first multilateral organization with authority to force national governments to comply with trade rules.
- A growing international network of Non-Governmental Organizations (NGOs).
- Regional blocs proliferating and gaining importance – European Union, Association of South-East Asian Nations, Mercosur, North American Free Trade Association, Southern African Development Community, among many others.
- More policy coordination groups – G7, G8, OECD, IMF, World Bank.

New rules and norms
- Market economic policies spreading around the world, with greater privatization and liberalization than in earlier decades.
- Widespread adoption of democracy as the choice of political regime.
- Human rights conventions and instruments building up in both coverage and number of signatories – and growing awareness among people around the world.
- Consensus goals and action agenda for development.
- Conventions and agreements on the global environment – biodiversity, ozone layer, disposal of hazardous wastes, desertification, climate change.
- Multilateral agreements in trade, taking on such new agendas as environmental and social conditions.
- New multilateral agreements – for services, intellectual property, communications – more binding on national governments than any previous agreements.
- The (proposed) Multilateral Agreement on Investment.

New (faster and cheaper) methods of communication
- Internet and electronic communications linking many people simultaneously.
- Cellular phones.
- Fax machines.
- Faster and cheaper transport by air, rail, sea and road.
- Computer-aided design and manufacture.

Source: Adapted from UNCTAD (1999) *World Investment Report 1999*.

Indicators of globalization

Bearing in mind the characteristics of globalization already outlined in Table 24.1, here we review some selected quantitative indicators relevant to the debate.

New markets

Table 24.2 would certainly seem to confirm the growth of new markets within a more liberalized and deregulated global environment. We have already seen the relevance of foreign direct investment (FDI) to cross-border mergers and acquisitions by multinational

Table 24.2 Increasing liberalization of markets on a global scale.

	National regulatory changes in FDI regimes		
	Number of regulatory changes	Number more favourable to FDI	Number less favourable to FDI
1991	82	80	2
1993	103	100	3
1995	107	102	5
1997	158	144	14
1999	146	138	8
2001	206	194	12
2005	214	201	13
2009	102	71	31

Source: Adapted from UNCTAD (2010b and various) *World Investment Report.*

Table 24.3 Transnationality Index for the world's largest 100 MNEs in their home economies, 1990 and 2008.

	Average TNI (%)		Number of MNEs	
Economy	1990	2008	1990	2008
European Union	**56.7**	**67.6**	**48**	**58**
France	50.9	66.6	14	15
Germany	44.4	56.9	9	13
UK	68.5	75.5	12	15
US	**38.5**	**58.1**	**28**	**18**
Japan	**35.5**	**50.0**	**12**	**9**
All economies	**51.1**	**63.4**	**100**	**100**

Source: Adapted from UNCTAD (2010b and various) *World Investment Report.*

enterprises (MNEs) (Chapter 7). Table 24.2 uses data from the United Nations Conference on Trade and Development (UNCTAD 2010) to indicate the progressive increase in regulatory changes affecting FDI by national governments, the overwhelming majority of which have been 'more favourable' to FDI flows. Nevertheless, the latest data for 2009 show a sharp rise in the number of regulatory changes which have been 'less favourable' to FDI flows, with some 30% of all such changes in this category as compared to only around 6% as recently as 2005.

New actors

The rapid growth of MNEs themselves has already been documented in Chapter 7, as for example with employment in the overseas affiliates of MNEs rising from less than 18 million in 1982 to around 64 million in 2009. Table 24.3 throws further light on the increasing globalization of productive activity by showing the progressive growth in the Transnationality Index (TNI) for the world's largest 100 MNEs in their home economies between 1990 and 2008. The TNI has been defined (see p. 125) as the average of the following three ratios: foreign assets/total assets; foreign sales/total sales; and foreign employment/total employment. A rise in the TNI suggests still more international involvement of the top 100 MNEs

outside their home country, which is certainly a pattern strongly supported by the data in Table 24.3.

The EU is home to 58% of the world's largest MNEs, and we can see from Table 24.3 that the average TNI for the EU has risen from 56.7% to 67.6% over the 1990–2008 period alone. A rapid growth in the TNI is also indicated for MNEs with the US and Japan as their 'home' bases. For 'all economies' the greater internationalization of production is indicated by the rise in TNI from 51.1% to 63.4% during 1990–2008. Closer scrutiny of these data reveals that the driving forces behind these observed increases in TNI have been the growth in the foreign sales/total sales and the foreign employment/total employment ratios that contribute to the TNI. The data in Table 24.3 also indicate a greater number of the world's largest 100 MNEs originating from *outside* the countries shown, only 12 in 1990 but 15 in 2008. East and South East Asia especially are home to a growing number of large MNEs with extensive international subsidiaries.

New actors within a globalized economy are also expected to include growing numbers of multilateral organizations (e.g. the World Trade Organization – WTO), non-governmental organizations (NGOs) and policy co-ordination groups (e.g. G8/G7). These will be in greater demand in an attempt to bring some kind of order to a progressively less nationally supervised and more deregulated world trading regime. In addition, the growth of regional trading blocs is often predicted as a collective response to the progressive loss of economic power of individual nation states. Chapter 26 provides ample evidence of the growing presence of these new actors within the global economy.

New rules and norms

Not only are new international institutions and trading blocs characteristic of a more globalized economy in which nation states have progressively less influence, but so too are the 'rules and norms' by which they seek to operate. Market-oriented policies, democratic political frameworks, consensus goals involving social and environmental responsibility, and growing multilateral applications of agreed rules were all identified as characteristics of globalization in Table 24.1 above. Again, Chapter 26 provides considerable empirical evidence of movements in this direction. Here we note the importance of good governance and transparency, an absence of corruption and appropriate property rights to the establishment of a sustainable globalized economic environment.

The World Bank's *World Development Report* (World Bank 2001, 2005, 2010) has pointed out that good governance – including independent agencies, mechanisms for citizens to monitor public behaviour and rules that constrain corruption – is a key ingredient for growth and prosperity. In an early study Barro (1991) had found a positive correlation between economic growth and measures of political stability for 98 countries surveyed between 1960 and 1985. More recent empirical research points in a similar direction, for example confirming that FDI inflows are inversely related to measures of corruption, as with Lipsey (1999) observing a strong negative correlation between corruption and the locational choice of US subsidiaries across Asian countries. Similarly Claugue *et al.* (1999) and Zak (2001) found that productivity and economic growth will improve when governments impartially protect and define property rights.

Underpinning these findings is the perception by firms that a non-transparent business environment increases the prevalence of information asymmetries, raises the cost of securing additional information, increases transaction costs (e.g. risk premiums) and creates an uncertain business environment which deters trade and investment. For example, Wallsten

(2001) found a strong inverse relationship between investment intentions and the threat of asset expropriation, as well as a propensity for firms to charge higher prices to help pay back their initial capital outlays more rapidly when they felt less secure about the intentions of host governments, the higher prices often inhibiting the penetration and growth phase of product life cycles.

New methods of communication

Management specialist Stephen Kobrin (1994) describes globalization as driven not by foreign trade and investment but by information flows. It is this latter perspective which sees globalization as a process inextricably linked with the creation, distribution and use of knowledge and information, which is the focus here. Many contributors to the globalization debate regard the technological convergence of information, computer and telecommunications technologies in the late twentieth century as having acted as a key catalyst in the rapid growth of these information-based activities, seen here as the hallmark of the globalized economy (Held *et al.* 1999).

International communications have grown dramatically, as evidenced by indicators such as the 4.22 billion mobile phone subscribers globally in 2010, a 95% rise on 2005. Nearly a quarter of the world's population – i.e. over 1.6 billion people – have Internet access. In this period 2000–09, the number of Internet users rose by 1,400% in China, 1,520% in India, 1,225% in Turkey, and even more rapidly elsewhere (e.g. 10,600% in Vietnam over the same period). Facebook more than doubled its subscribers from 140 million to over 300 million in 2009/10 (Laudicina 2010). Contemporary discourse often seeks to express globalization in terms of the exponential growth in the creation, processing and dissemination of knowledge and information. For example, an 'index of globalization' recently compiled jointly by the Carnegie Foundation and ATKearney (a global consultant) gives considerable weight to the proportion of national populations online as well as to the number of Internet hosts and secure servers per capita. These indicators of access to information technology and associated information flows are seen here as proxy variables for 'global openness', to be used in association with the more conventional indicators of investment, capital flows, foreign income as a proportion of national income, and convergence between domestic and international prices, when compiling the overall globalization index. Singapore has regularly been recorded as the 'most globalized' country, helped by the fact that its outgoing telephone and Internet traffic per head per year has been some four times as much as in the US.

We now look in rather more detail at a sophisticated index widely used in ranking countries in terms of globalization characteristics.

KOF Index of Globalization

The KOF (Swiss Federal Institute of Technology) Index of Globalization was first introduced in 2002 and has been regularly updated since then. It incorporates three key dimensions in determining a country's overall 'score':

1 *economic globalization*, characterized as long-distance flows of goods, capital and services as well as information and perceptions that accompany market exchanges;

2 *political globalization*, characterized by a diffusion of government policies; and

3 *social globalization*, expressed as the spread of ideas, information, images and people.

In the 2010 KOF Index (see Table 24.4) each variable used for 'scoring' these dimensions is transformed to an index on a scale of 1–100, where 100 is the maximum value any country achieved for that variable over the period 1970–2007, and 1 is the minimum value[1].

The variables used in calculating the globalization 'score' for each dimension/component include the following:

■ *Economic globalization*: *trade variable* (sum of exports and imports); *FDI variable* (sum of inflows and outflows in a given year plus FDI stock value); *portfolio variable* (sum of a country's stock of assets and liabilities).

■ *Social globalization*: *personal contacts variable* (international telecom traffic in minutes per person; international volumes of letters sent or received per person; incoming and outgoing tourism value per person; stock of foreign people in country); *information flows variable* (number of Internet users per 100 people; % of households

with TV, international newspapers traded as % of GDP); *cultural proximity variable* (traded value exports and imports of books and related as % of GDP); number of global MNEs located in country – e.g. McDonalds/IKEA.

■ *Political globalization: embassies and high commission variable* (number in country); *international organizations variable* (number in country); UN peace missions (number in which involved); UN treaties (number signed).

Belgium is ranked 1st in terms of this index, although its ranking was only 6th on economic globalization, 4th on social globalization and 3rd on political globalization. While Singapore was ranked 1st for economic globalization, it was ranked 21st in social globalization and 77th in political globalization.

Whatever the merits or demerits of these types of indices, they certainly recognize the multidimensional characteristics of globalization, with particular emphasis on 'interconnectedness' in an international context, which underpins the metrics developed around each of the variables outlined above.

Globalization and corporate strategy

It may be useful to assess the impacts of the characteristics of globalization outlined in Table 24.1 on the strategic direction of firms, where 'strategy' is defined as the guiding rules or principles which influence the direction and scope of the organization's activities over the long term. Of course, various chapters have touched on aspects of firm objectives and behaviour (Chapter 3), cross-border mergers and alliances (Chapter 5), multinational involvement (Chapter 7) and corporate social responsibility (Chapter 15). However, here we concentrate more explicitly on devising corporate strategy within a business environment exhibiting still more rapid growth in the various quantitative indicators of globalization outlined above.

Prahalad (2000) paints a vivid picture of a 'discontinuous competitive landscape' as characterizing much of the 1990s and early years of the millennium. Industries are no longer the stable entities they once were.

Table 24.4 2010 KOF Index of Globalization: top 20 overall, and by each dimension.

	Country	Globalization index	Country	Economic globalization	Country	Social globalization	Country	Political globalization
1	Belgium	92.95	Singapore	97.48	Switzerland	94.94	France	98.44
2	Austria	92.51	Ireland	93.93	Austria	92.77	Italy	98.17
3	Netherlands	91.90	Luxembourg	93.57	Canada	90.73	Belgium	98.14
4	Switzerland	90.55	Netherlands	92.40	Belgium	90.61	Austria	96.85
5	Sweden	89.75	Malta	92.26	Netherlands	88.99	Sweden	96.27
6	Denmark	89.68	Belgium	91.94	Denmark	88.01	Spain	96.14
7	Canada	88.24	Estonia	91.66	United Kingdom	87.05	Netherlands	95.77
8	Portugal	87.54	Hungary	90.45	Germany	85.97	Switzerland	95.00
9	Finland	87.31	Sweden	89.42	Sweden	85.95	Poland	94.63
10	Hungary	87.00	Austria	89.33	France	85.84	Canada	94.40
11	Ireland	86.92	Bahrain	89.32	Portugal	85.95	Portugal	94.36
12	Czech Republic	86.87	Denmark	88.58	Norway	85.30	Germany	94.21
13	France	86.18	Czech Republic	88.43	Finland	84.89	Denmark	93.96
14	Luxembourg	85.84	Cyprus	87.77	Slovak Republic	83.90	United States	93.85
15	Spain	85.71	Finland	87.33	Czech Republic	83.54	Egypt, Arab Rep.	93.39
16	Slovak Republic	85.07	Slovak Republic	87.25	Australia	82.96	Argentina	93.38
17	Singapore	84.58	Chile	87.14	Spain	82.52	Greece	93.11
18	Germany	84.16	Israel	85.15	Luxembourg	81.60	Turkey	93.11
19	Australia	83.82	Portugal	85.03	Hungary	80.79	Brazil	92.95
20	Norway	83.53	Bulgaria	84.10	Liechtenstein	80.11	India	92.69

Source: KOF (2010).

- Rapid technology changes and the convergence of technologies (e.g. computer and telecommunications) are constantly redefining industrial 'boundaries' so that the 'old' industrial structures become barely recognizable.

- Privatization and deregulation have become global trends within industrial and service sectors (e.g. telecommunications, power, water, health care, financial services) and even within nations themselves (e.g. Transition Economies, China).

- Internet-related technologies are beginning to have major impacts on business-to-business and business-to-customer relationships.

- Pressure groups based around environmental and ecological sensitivities are progressively well organized and influential.

- New forms of institutional arrangements and liaisons are exerting greater influences on organizational structures than hitherto (e.g. strategic alliances, franchising).

In a progressively less stable environment dominated by such discontinuities, there will arguably be a shift in perspective away from the previous strategic focus of Porter and his contemporaries, in which companies are seen as seeking to identify and exploit *competitive advantages* within stable industrial structures. The more conventional strategic models focused on securing competitive advantages by better utilizing one or more of the following five factors:

1 *architecture* (a more effective set of contractual relationships with suppliers and customers);

2 *incumbency advantages* (reputation, branding, scale economies, etc.);

3 *access to strategic assets* (raw materials, wavebands, scarce labour inputs, etc.);

4 *innovation* (product or process, protected by patents, licences, etc.);

5 *operational efficiencies* (quality circles, just-in-time techniques, re-engineering, etc.).

However, the discontinuities outlined previously have changed the setting in which much of the strategic discussion must now take place. Prahalad (2000) goes on to suggest four key 'transformations' which must now be registered.

1 *Recognizing changes in strategic space.* Deregulation and privatization of previously government-

controlled industries, access to new market opportunities in large developing countries (e.g. China, India, Brazil) and in the transitional economies of Central and Eastern Europe, together with the rapidly changing technological environment, are creating entirely new strategic opportunities. Take the case of the large energy utilities. They must now decide on the extent of integration (power generation, power transmission within industrial and/or consumer sectors), the geographical reach of their operations (domestic/overseas), the extent of diversification (other types of energy, non-energy fields), and so on. PowerGen in the UK is a good example of a traditional utility with its historical base in electricity generation which, in a decade or so, has transformed itself into a global provider of electricity services (generation and transmission), water and other infrastructure services. Clearly the strategic 'space' available to companies is ever expanding, creating entirely new possibilities in the modern global economy.

2 *Recognizing globalization impacts.* As we discuss in more detail below, globalization of business activity is itself opening up new strategic opportunities and threats. Arguably the distinction between local and global business will itself become increasingly irrelevant. The local businesses must devise their own strategic response to the impact of globalized players. Nirula, the Indian fast food chain, raising standards of hygiene and restaurant ambience in response to competition from McDonald's, is one type of local response, and McDonald's providing more lamb and vegetarian produce in its Indian stores is another. Mass customization and quick response strategies require global businesses to be increasingly responsive to local consumers. Additionally, globalization opens up new strategic initiatives in terms of geographical locations, modes of transnational collaboration, financial accountability and logistical provision. In 2010, Boeing has a supply chain of some 6,500 different suppliers located in over 100 countries.

3 *Recognizing the importance of timely responses.* Even annual planning cycles are arguably becoming progressively obsolete as the speed of corporate response becomes a still more critical success factor, both to seize opportunities and to repel threats.

4 *Recognizing the enhanced importance of innovation.* Although innovation has long been recognized

as a critical success factor, its role is still further enhanced in an environment dominated by the 'discontinuities' mentioned. Successful companies must still innovate in terms of new products and processes, but now such innovation must also be directed towards providing the company with faster and more reliable information on customers as part of mass customization, quick response and personalized product business philosophies.

These factors are arguably changing the context for business strategy from positioning the company within a clear-cut industrial structure to stretching and shaping that structure by its own strategic initiatives. It may no longer be sensible or efficient to devise strategic blueprints over a protracted planning time-frame and then seek to apply the blueprints mechanically, given that events and circumstances are changing so rapidly. The *direction* of broad strategic thrust can be determined as a route map, but tactical and operational adjustments must be continually appraised and modified along the way.

Nor can the traditional strategy hierarchies continue unchallenged – i.e. top management creating strategy and middle management implementing it. Those who are closest to the product and market are becoming increasingly important as well-informed sources for identifying opportunities to exploit or threats to repel. Arguably the roles of middle and lower management in the strategic process are being considerably enhanced by the 'discontinuities' mentioned. Top managers are finding themselves progressively removed from competitive reality in an era of discontinuous change. Their role is rather to set a broad course, to ensure that effective and responsive middle and lower management are in place to exercise delegated strategic responsibilities, and to provide an appropriate infrastructure for strategic delivery. For example, a key role of top managers in various media-related activities may have been to secure access to an appropriate broadband wavelength by successfully competing in the UK or German auctions. Such access is likely to be a prerequisite for competitive involvement in a whole raft of Internet-related products for home and business consumption via mobile telephony. Figure 24.1 provides a useful summary of the traditional and emerging views of international business strategy.

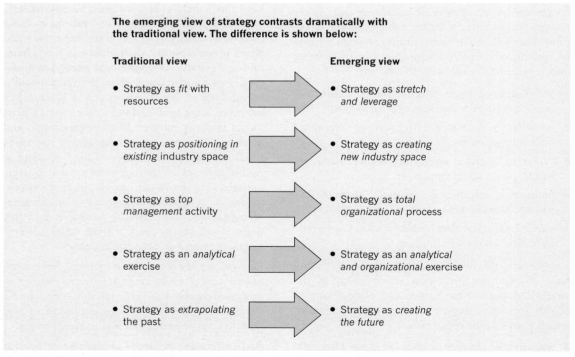

The emerging view of strategy contrasts dramatically with the traditional view. The difference is shown below:

Traditional view	Emerging view
• Strategy as *fit* with resources	• Strategy as *stretch and leverage*
• Strategy as *positioning in existing* industry space	• Strategy as *creating new industry space*
• Strategy as *top management* activity	• Strategy as *total organizational* process
• Strategy as an *analytical* exercise	• Strategy as an *analytical and organizational* exercise
• Strategy as *extrapolating* the past	• Strategy as *creating the future*

Fig. 24.1 New strategic directions in a global economy.

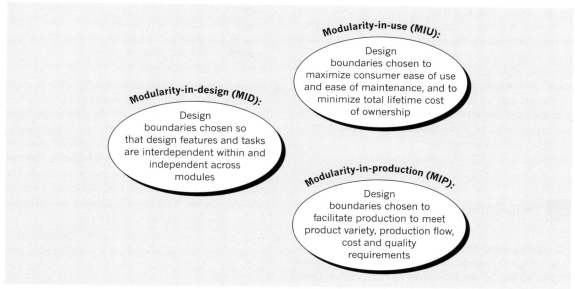

Fig. 24.2 Modular strategies.

Modular strategies

Globalization has been a driving force for *modular strategies*, since these can help companies engage in large worldwide investments without a huge increase in fixed costs and with fewer of the problems typically associated with managing complex global operations. Modular strategies can embrace production, design and/or use (see Fig. 24.2).

- *Modularity in Production (MIP).* This provided the initial impetus to adopt modules in the car industry. Here production activities are broken down into a number of large but separate elements that can be carried out independently, with the finished vehicle then being assembled from these large sub-assemblies. Such modular production systems can help reduce the fixed capital overhead required for production, especially where selected modules are *outsourced*. Specialization of labour and management on smaller, independent modules can also result in productivity gains and lower variable costs.
- *Modularity in Design (MID).* There may be more problems in establishing modularity in the design process. This will be particularly true where the finished product embodies systems as well as

sub-assembly components. For example, a finished vehicle offers climate control and vehicle safety 'systems' which, to be provided effectively, require design input into a whole range of sub-assembly module operations. Modularity in design may therefore require that boundaries be carefully drawn so as to capture as many interdependencies as possible within the modular groupings.

- *Modularity in Use (MIU).* This was the main reason for the introduction of modularity in the computer industry. It became increasingly obvious that consumers required computer-related products that were both compatible and upgradeable. Much effort was therefore expended in standardizing interfaces between different elements of the product architecture to give these desired user attributes. The then leader, IBM, found that the electromechanical system could be disaggregated without adversely affecting performance.

Of course, creating a modular product in any or all of these ways may have organizational consequences, not all of which may be foreseen. A national or international infrastructure exists which supports new firm start-ups – e.g. access to venture capital, skilled labour, etc. Further, for example, a module product architecture may result in *modular business organization.* This has certainly been the case in the computer industry. It can also stimulate certain types of organizational practice, such as outsourcing, and shift power relationships between companies. For example, IBM's decision to outsource the development and production of its operating system to Microsoft and of its chip to Intel was an important factor in shifting power away from the overall product architecture to these designers and producers of modular systems elements.

Dimensions of globalization

Of course, we should admit that a one-dimensional view of globalization, which thinks purely in terms of the economic impacts of market forces, is likely to result in only a partial picture at best. To quote Giddens (1990):

> Globalisation is a complex process which is not necessarily teleological in character – that is to say, it is not necessarily an inexorable historical process with an end in sight. Rather, it is characterised by a set of mutually opposing tendencies.

McGrew (1992) has tried to identify a number of these opposing tendencies.

- *Universalization versus particularization.* While globalization may tend to make many aspects of

modern social life universal (e.g. assembly line production, fast food restaurants, consumer fashions) it can also help to point out the differences between what happens in particular places and what happens elsewhere.

- *Homogenization versus differentiation.* While globalization may result in an essential homogeneity ('sameness') in product, process and institutions (e.g. city life, organizational offices and bureaucracies), it may also mean that the general must be assimilated within the local. For example, human rights are interpreted in different ways across the globe, the practice of specific religions such as Christianity or Buddhism may take on different forms in different places, and so on.

- *Integration versus fragmentation.* Globalization creates new forms of global, regional and transnational communities which unite (integrate) people across territorial boundaries (e.g. the multinational enterprises, international trade unions, etc.). However, it also has the potential to divide and fragment communities (e.g. labour becoming divided along sectoral, local, national and ethnic lines).

Morrison (2002) usefully reviews these multidimensional perspectives of globalization, in particular pointing to two widely held but contrasting schools of thought (Table 24.5).

- *Hyperglobalists* envisage the global economy as being inhabited by powerless nation states at the mercy of 'footloose' multinational enterprises

Table 24.5 Globalization: two schools of thought.

	Hyperglobalists	Transformationalists
What's new	A global age	Historically unprecedented levels of global interconnectedness
Dominant features	Global capitalism; global governance; global civil society	'Thick' (intensive and extensive) globalization
Power of national governments	Declining or eroding	Reconstituted, restructured
Conceptualization of globalization	As a reordering of the framework of human action	As a reordering of interregional relations and action at a distance
Historical trajectory	Global civilization	Indeterminate; global integration and fragmentation

Source: Morrison (2002), adapted from Held *et al.* (1999).

bestowing jobs and wealth creation opportunities on favoured national clients. National cultural differences are largely seen by these progressively powerful multinationals as merely variations in consumer preferences to be reflected in their international marketing mix.

■ *Transformationalists* recognize that globalization is a powerful force impacting on economic, social and political environments, but take a much less prescriptive stance as to what the outcomes of those impacts might be. Predictions as to any end-state of a globalized economy can only be tentative and premature. Globalization involves a complex set of intermittent, uneven processes with unpredictable outcomes rather than a linear progression to a predictable end-state. It is this more pragmatic transformationalist approach which is reflected in the rest of the chapter.

Globalization and the political environment

At the heart of governance is the notion of 'sovereignty', which implies the power to rule without constraint and which, for the last three centuries, has been associated with the nation state. We live in a world which is organized as a patchwork of nation states within which different peoples live, with their own systems of government exerting authority over the affairs within their territory. Of course, groupings within those territories may arise from time to time, which seek a measure of independence from the central authorities, sometimes claiming nation statehood themselves. Many would also argue that the idea of the nation state has itself been challenged by the growth of globalization. Before turning to this issue, it may be useful to highlight two opposing and arguably contradictory tendencies in globalization.

1 *Centralization versus decentralization.* Some aspects of globalization tend to concentrate power, knowledge, information, wealth and decision-making. Many believe this to be the case with the rise of the MNE, the growth of regional trading blocs (e.g. EU), the development of world regulatory bodies such as the WTO, etc. However, such centralizing tendencies may conflict with powerful decentralizing tendencies as nations, communities and individuals attempt to take greater control over the

forces which influence their lives (e.g. the growth of social movements centred on the global environment, peace and gender issues, etc.).

2 *Juxtaposition versus syncretization.* In the globalization process, time and space become compressed, so that different civilizations, ways of life and social practices become juxtaposed (placed side by side). This can create 'shared' cultural and social spaces characterized by an evolving mixture of ideas, knowledge and institutions. Unfortunately this can also stimulate the opposite tendencies, such as a heightened awareness of challenges to the established norms of previously dominant groups, which can result in determined attempts to avoid integration and instead combine against a 'common opponent' (syncretization).

Whilst there may be many theories as to the causes of globalization, most writers would agree that globalization is a discontinuous historical process. Its dynamic proceeds in fits and starts and its effects are experienced differentially across the globe. Some regions are more deeply affected by globalization than others. Even within nation states, some communities (e.g. financial) may experience the effects of globalization more sharply than others (e.g. urban office workers). Many have argued that globalization is tending to reinforce inequalities of power both within and across nation states, resulting in global hierarchies of privilege and control for some but economic and social exclusion for others.

Globalization and the nation state

It has been argued that one of the major effects of globalization is to threaten the notion of the territorial nation state, in at least four key respects: its competence, its form, its autonomy and, ultimately, its authority and legitimacy. In a global economic system, productive capital, finance and products flow across national boundaries in ever-increasing volumes and values, yet the nation state seems increasingly irrelevant as a 'barrier' to international events and influences. Governments often appear powerless to prevent stock market crashes or recessions in one part of the world having adverse effects on domestic output, employment, interest rates and so on. Attempts to lessen these adverse effects seem, to many citizens, increasingly to reside in supranational bodies such as the IMF, World Bank, EU, etc. This inability of nation states to meet the demands of their citizens without international co-operation is seen by many as evidence of the declining *competence* of states, arguably leading to a 'widening and weakening' of the individual nation state.

In such a situation, the *form* and *autonomy* of the nation state are also subtly altered. The increased emphasis on international co-operation has brought with it an enormous increase in the number and influence of intergovernmental and NGOs to such an extent that many writers now argue that national and international policy formulation have become inseparable. For example, whereas in 1909 only 176 international NGOs could be identified, by 2010 this number exceeded 30,000 and was still growing! The formerly monolithic national state, with its own independent and broadly coherent policy, is now conceived by many to be a fragmented coalition of bureaucratic agencies each pursuing its own agenda with minimal central direction or control. State autonomy is thereby threatened in economic, financial and ecological areas.

However, as we saw earlier, globalization consists of a series of conflicting tendencies. Whilst there is some evidence that the relevance of the nation state is declining, other writers claim the alternative view. Some argue that the state retains its positive role in the world through its monopoly of military power which, though rarely used, offers its citizens relative security in a highly dangerous world. Further, it provides a focus for personal and communal identity, and finally, in pursuing national interest through co-operation and collaboration, nation states actually empower themselves. The suggestion here is that international co-operation (as opposed to unilateral action) allows states simultaneously to pursue their national interests and at the same time, by collective action, to achieve still more effective control over their national destiny. For example, the international control of exchange rates (e.g. the EU single currency) is seen by some as enhancing state *autonomy* rather than diminishing it, since the collective action implicit in a common currency affords more economic security and benefits for nationals than unilateral action.

Globalization is therefore redefining our understanding of the nation state by introducing a much more complex architecture of political power in which authority is seen as being pluralistic rather than residing solely in the nation state.

Globalization and knowledge-based economies

Most commentators agree that developments in the information and communications technologies (ICT) have played a key role in the dramatic surge in information flows associated with the globalized economies of the latter part of the twentieth century. Some have even spoken of a new economic paradigm (e.g. 'new economy') resulting in a long-term upward shift in the productivity of both labour and capital, leading to enhanced prospects of higher long-term and non-inflationary growth. Convergence of ICT technologies and the enhanced use of the Internet and websites are often linked, in this perspective, to a new Kondratief 'long wave' cycle of the type associated with the earlier technological breakthroughs in steam power, railroads and electricity.

Recent major reports have identified a number of important impacts of the expanded Internet and website usage within the global economy and associated increases in information-related activities on contemporary labour markets. A number are briefly reviewed below.

- A positive net impact on total levels of employment, with the employment-creating potential of ICT outweighing the risk of job losses. Evidence suggests that countries experiencing the greatest growth in 'total factor productivity' over the past decade have been those where ICT have been most widely adopted. These are also the countries in which employment has grown most rapidly.

- A change in the patterns of employment as ICT developments increase the demand for highly skilled workers who can push forward the technological frontier and make the new technology accessible to the rest of the workforce. Less skilled, repetitive occupations in both manufacturing and service sectors (e.g. offices) tend to be replaced by ICT, with fewer, more highly skilled workers remaining.

- A greater geographical dispersion of employment as work becomes progressively less dependent on specific locational factors (e.g. growth in work from home).

- A shift in employment towards smaller, less established firms and new entrants via 'leapfrogging', which in this context refers to the opportunities inherent in the new ICT technologies for small/

medium-sized enterprises (SMEs) and new entrants to bypass earlier investments by rivals in the time or cost of developments.

■ A more highly skilled and better-educated workforce within economies which now depend less on physical inputs than on knowledge.

■ A shift in the focus of education and training to foster generic skills, with individuals no longer seen as passive recipients of facts but as active, lifelong learners. The ability at all levels of expertise to learn new approaches and transform existing knowledge into new knowledge becomes still more important in work environments that rely increasingly on rapid innovation and the interpersonal exchange and creation of knowledge.

However, some have cast doubt on the growth of knowledge-based societies as indicative of globalization. For example, it has been suggested that 'globalization' is merely a contemporary catchphrase for what in reality has been a long-established process in the growth of knowledge and information. Adams, an American historian, claimed as early as 1918 to have observed an exponential growth in various aspects of knowledge, subsequently formulated as 'Adams' Law of Acceleration of Progress' (see Rescher 1978). Similarly Rider (1977), investigating the stock of books of American universities over the period 1831–1938, found the stock to have doubled every 22 years, whilst the stock of the pure research universities had doubled every 16 years, resulting in growth rates of 3.2% and 4.4% per annum respectively. Price (1977), using similar indicators, estimated the growth rate of the stock of knowledge to be 6.5% per annum. Later writers (Machlup 1962; Bell 1973; Gershuny 1978) have identified these patterns and trends as being part of an inexorable process towards 'maturity' as developed economies pass through industrial and service-sector stages and towards 'post-industrial' societies. The acquisition and codification of theoretical knowledge, giving rise to a host of information-related activities, is seen as a key characteristic of such post-industrial societies.

Globalization and terrorism/criminality

The global growth of foreign direct investment and the increasingly 'footloose' activities of MNEs have already been documented as widely used indicators of globalization. Many commentators have also drawn attention to parallels between the rapid growth in formal, legal cross-border relationships and the rapid growth in a wide range of illegal cross-border relationships including, at one extreme, activities more commonly associated with terrorism. Some of the characteristics of globalization previously reviewed in Table 24.1 are seen as conducive to such growth, especially the weakening of power and control by nation states and the proliferation of new, less detectable methods of communication. Whilst a proper investigation of so complex an issue is beyond the scope of this chapter, we can perhaps draw attention to some of the economic impacts associated with global terrorism and criminality within more globalized economies.

September 11th 2001 (9/11)

This is perhaps the single event most closely associated with global terrorism. It may therefore be instructive to consider some of the short-term and long-term economic impacts of that event. Kaletsky (2002) identified what is arguably the major cost of 9/11 to the world economy over the two years following the attack on the World Trade Center, namely the difference between *projected and actual* growth of global GDP over that period. Whilst other external events may also have contributed to the cumulative discrepancy (projected – actual) of $740bn (£476bn) estimated as the resulting shortfall in global GDP over the two-year period following 9/11, there is little doubt that the greatest single influence has been 9/11 itself.

Of course, many other more *direct* short-term costs of 9/11 can be identified. In New York alone some $95bn in costs have been estimated as directly attributable to 9/11 and some $36bn in costs to an assortment of insurance companies involved with individuals and companies affected by 9/11.

Nevertheless, it is the adverse impacts of global terrorism on future growth prospects that are likely to impose the greater short- and longer-run costs on the world economy.

Globalization and disease control

We noted earlier that increased international travel and communication featured in the 'globalization characteristics' outlined in Table 24.1. Parallel with the growth of such travel is an increasing exposure to communicable diseases.

SARS: a case study of globalized disease

In 2003 the SARS (Severe Acute Respiratory Syndrome) outbreak provided a useful illustration of this point, with the World Health Organization believing it to be the first health episode of the twenty-first century with epidemic potential, with the ease of global travel acknowledged as playing a key role in its dissemination. Stephen Roach, chief economist of Morgan Stanley, argued that SARS would cut growth in Asia, excluding Japan, from 5% to 4.5% in 2003. Hu Angang, of Tsinghua University in Beijing, believes that without SARS, China could have achieved 9–10% growth in 2003, but estimated SARS to have reduced growth by at least 1% on those projections to 8–9%. The World Bank was also pessimistic, cutting 0.5% off its pre-SARS estimate for Chinese growth in 2003.

We cannot, of course, hope to capture more than a flavour of the multidimensional and broad-based influence of globalization in a single chapter. What we can do is note that the economic, sociocultural and political impacts are significant and ongoing.

Anti-globalization movements

In recent years the meetings of various international finance, trade, political and economic forums which were once routine, have become the focus of unprecedented protest and widespread media coverage. Since the Seattle meeting in November 1999, a wave of other protests has crashed around the world, including Bolivia, Ecuador, Washington, Paris, Prague, Nice, Quebec, Gothenburg and Genoa.

Seattle represented a turning point in what some now describe as the 'anti-globalization movement'. Although one account of events in Seattle maintained that people both outside and inside were confused about what they wanted, it captured the attention of the world's media and brought the issues surrounding globalization onto screens and into people's homes. International economic and political meetings now invariably focus on the major themes of trade, debt relief and globalization. Although hard to understand, this new 'movement' is now given much attention in the media.

Is the anti-capitalist movement merely the focus of today's privileged, excluded or bored OECD youth – an anarchist travelling circus? Such explanations are too simplistic. The coalitions of stakeholders taking to the streets appear to be unlikely alliances of disparate groups transcending age and economic and social classifications, including trade unionists, representatives of NGOs, shareholder activists and students. Although the movement certainly contains anti-globalization and anti-capitalist elements, it appears to be united over the central issue of political, economic and social exclusion. All these groups have experienced the transfer of power from government to big corporations, the acceleration of inequalities within and between countries as a result of current economic policies and political ideologies, and the sense that society is itself being shaped and defined by big corporations. In rising up and dissenting against a sense of dispossession, the anti-globalization movement is in effect creating a society for those who feel excluded.

Globalization – North and South

North and *South* are terms often used to refer to the advanced industrialized and the developing economies respectively and their perspectives on globalization often differ markedly. Some Northern perspectives see globalization as liberalization, creating a climate of trust and enhancing wealth creation, whereas Southern perspectives often emphasize marginalization, exploitation, divisiveness and the exercise of power, viewing neo-liberal economic policies as destructive of livelihoods, communities, cultures and natural resources.

Many supporters of globalization are aware of its shortcomings and unintended side-effects and argue that the challenge is finding rules and institutions to preserve the advantages of globalization whilst taking account of these problems, hence the search for 'globalization with a human face', which can embrace concerns for ethics, equity, inclusion, human security, sustainability and development.

Sustainable development, open economies and trade

A key issue is whether globalization helps contribute to raising global standards of living, enhancing human and social capital in both North and South and therefore contributing to sustainable development, or whether its impacts are quite the opposite. This debate has largely crystallized around perspectives as to the role and impacts of international institutions such as the World Trade Organization, World Bank, IMF and so on. The anti-capitalist protestors regard these roles as inimical to sustainable development. But is this really so? We now address this key issue in rather more depth, with the particular emphasis on whether an 'open' world trading regime supports or hinders sustainable development.

Trade liberalization and the World Trade Organization (WTO)

The WTO is a powerful institution of international global governance whose rules and procedures are having a profound impact on global economic, social and political development (see Chapter 26). Agreeing trade rules that work for the benefit of the many and not the few is about reaching agreement on the ultimate purposes and goals of trade liberalization itself.

Trade liberalization has certainly met many of its own objectives, with various trade rounds having resulted in a tenfold reduction in border tariffs on industrial products from 50% in 1947 to around 5% in 2010. However, many believe that it is the multinational corporations and the North in general that have benefited most from these trade freedoms. Nevertheless some, even from the South, argue that the WTO is needed to protect developing countries and that it is a broadly successful institution of global governance to be reformed and improved, but not abandoned. Others stress that the WTO goes much too far, pointing out that it forces domestic laws to conform to trade law; in over 90% of the WTO cases between 1995 and 2010, national government regulation has been struck down. In essence, some see the WTO as a mechanism for putting trade rules above every other kind of law, in the interests of its most powerful members. For example, Southern governments argue that the focus tends to be on Southern rather than Northern non-compliance!

Whilst any country has a chance of winning a case at the WTO, not all can impose effective sanctions. For example, a small developing country can win a WTO ruling but, even with WTO permission, would hardly benefit from imposing retaliatory sanctions on a large, advanced industrialized country. In contrast, developing countries fear the impact of trade sanctions imposed by the more powerful WTO members who have won a WTO ruling against them.

The influence of multinational companies on devising the current trade rules at the WTO arouses strong emotions. Many would like to see an end to a system in which trade rules are set after discussions between government trade representatives and the government relations representatives of multinational companies. Trade rules are widely held to have been set to the advantage of the business community, restricting the capacities of national governments to make their own trade-related decisions. Such cross-border and internally invasive intervention has been an important source of public disenchantment with the WTO and similar bodies.

The anti-capitalist protests have significantly changed the dynamic of the trade negotiations. The conventional wisdom that 'trade is good for the poor, it makes people richer – and hence improves the environment' is now being openly challenged. Whilst more trade may very well benefit higher-income groups in many countries, in some cases it would seem to have had negative effects on low-income groups in both developed and developing countries. However, many believe that the reform, not the abandonment, of institutions such as the WTO may be in the ultimate interests of the world's poor, in other words the essential maintenance of an 'open' world trading system with institutional support to prevent its worst excesses. Chapter 30 reviews in rather more detail the linkages between trade openness, economic growth and development.

We conclude with a brief review of the one nation which, more than any other, is perceived as the driving force behind, and major beneficiary of, globalization, namely the US.

The US and globalization

Although the US is less dependent in trade terms on the global economy than many believe, its influence is felt everywhere. The US has a population of 287,400,000, which is smaller than the EU's single market, but it has a huge land area (9,158,960 square kilometres) which is very resource rich with plentiful supplies of water, timber, coal, iron ore, oil, gas, copper, bauxite, lead, silver, zinc, mercury and phosphates, amongst others. Given the abundance of these resources, the US was for many years self-sufficient with little need to import. However, a recurring problem has been the country's relatively low population density so that, despite its huge potential in natural resources, it has had a scarce labour supply which has made full exploitation of those resources rather difficult. For much of the nineteenth century and even in the early twentieth century, the US was largely disengaged from the global marketplace in terms of imports and exports. Even in the 1960s, imports and exports *combined* amounted to barely 10% of GDP. Nowadays things have changed. Today the US exports around 13% of its GDP, with almost 30% of all the wealth generated (more than $2 trillion) coming from trade.

Figure 24.3 usefully indicates the dominance of the US, via its currency, in global economic affairs. Although the US only accounts for some 24% of world GDP in 2010, US dollars are used in around 84% of all foreign exchange transactions, comprise some 62% of global reserves, and are the currency in which 60% of global bank deposits, 50% of global bank loans and 44% of debt securities transactions are denominated.

The increased role of the US in the globalization process essentially has two strands which, while interconnected, remain distinct. The first of these strands relates to a number of happy accidents that drew a reluctant US into increased involvement in international affairs which, combined with pragmatic domestic policies, allowed it to benefit fully from that involvement. The second of these strands involves the notion of the dynamism of American culture and the endurance of the 'American dream' which in turn have given rise to the perception of US dominance in the global economy.

US international engagement

During the nineteenth century, and particularly after the American Civil War (1861–65), the American economy grew rapidly, spurred on by the advent of the railways which made development of the western territories more viable. Even more striking, however, was the growth of US economic influence abroad. From the 1870s onward, US farmers in the midwest exported grain and meat, as improved transport links and refrigeration lowered transport costs. The US began to eclipse the major European countries as a manufacturing nation, and as a producer of raw materials such as coal, iron and steel. By 1914 the US was producing nearly five times as much steel as the UK and more than twice as much as the German Empire.

With a smaller population in a pre-consumer society, the US was able to almost completely isolate itself from the rest of the world, and thanks to a highly protectionist trade policy, its imports were minimal. However, vast amounts of European, and especially

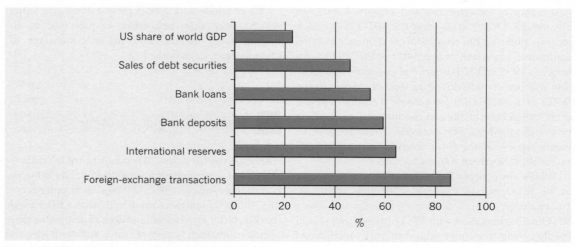

Fig. 24.3 US dollar's share of world total, %, in 2010.
Sources: Various.

British, portfolio investment had flooded into the US to finance economic development in the late nineteenth and early twentieth centuries. By the end of the First World War, with Europe an economic wreck, the allies had borrowed such large sums from US bankers that Wall Street had become the world's financial centre, and the US had become the world's largest international creditor. Under the presidency of Woodrow Wilson (1913–21) the US took its first tentative steps towards freer international trade, but such steps were not long lasting or indeed very forthright.

The 1920s saw unprecedented growth in the American economy as the consumer age really began. Fostered by the loose regulation and pro-business framework of the classical *laissez-faire* economic policies of the government, and largely free from foreign competition due to its extensive tariff barriers, American business grew rapidly. As the population expanded so did the markets available for these firms, and developments in technology allowed for vastly increased output at lower costs.

The Second World War served as a kick-start for the US to engage with the global economy, and is one of the happy accidents mentioned earlier. More activist government policies brought about by the war effort helped to start a number of virtuous circles whose effects lasted many decades. For example, the strong American presence in the world aircraft industry today came about because of the increased demand for aircraft that arose from the needs of the US military during the Second World War. Having thus acquired a dominant position in the aircraft industry during the war, the US now had a large pool of workers and engineers with the skills required, and was thereby well positioned to maintain its competitive advantage. Even though the initial war trigger is long gone, the dominant position of the US aircraft industry endures. To varying degrees, the same can be said about other industries, ranging from space technology, through defence, and on to consumer goods. In summary, by the end of the Second World War, the US was in an excellent position to head into the post-war period. Its industrial base was large and diverse, its technology was superior, and a number of virtuous circles had developed.

US cultural dominance

The move into the global arena was aided by the widespread perception in the 1950s and 1960s that American culture was dynamic and worthy of emulation. The fact that the US was an English-speaking country, and English is the language of international business and commerce, also helped smooth such cultural transmission. In a time of rising prosperity and optimism about the future, the American dream seemed available to all. The growth of American firms in the consumer goods and leisure industries coincided with an increased demand for these outputs within the more affluent societies. American culture began to permeate Western Europe, driving demand further, and thus ensuring business for American firms, whether located in Europe or supplied from the US.

In the post-war period, the US became a champion of free trade, reversing the policy plank that had been present since the early days of the union. It was a founder member of the General Agreement on Tariffs and Trade (GATT) in 1947 which sought to break down barriers to trade, especially trade in manufactures. Having developed strong and competitive industries in the US, being home to major financial centres in New York and Chicago, and finding itself drawn more into the global arena than previously, the aim was to increase its access to foreign markets. As the domestic economy developed and became ever more consumer orientated, the US found itself constrained in exploiting its resources fully due to insufficient labour supply. Paradoxically for a country that, in theory, did not need to trade internationally, the ever-increasing demand from rising prosperity at home forced the US to import, and the hungry ambitions of American business sought new markets outside the US.

Modern American trade policy, particularly in the post-cold war period, has focused on locking the US into each significant region of economic development. Under Presidents George H. W. Bush (1989–93), Bill Clinton (1993–2001), George W. Bush (2001–09), and arguably under the early years of the Obama administration, the US primarily favoured a regional and bilateral thrust to trade policy, although remaining a member of the WTO. American involvement in the APEC agreement (1993), the creation of the North American Free Trade Agreement (NAFTA) (1994), the signing of the Transatlantic Pact between the US and the EU (1995), and the current development of the Free Trade Area of the Americas (FTAA) have all cemented the American position in the global economy. However, they mark a subtle change in what had occurred previously. The new regionalist approach to trade policy exchanges access to the

American market for reciprocal access to foreign markets. It uses the power of the US, and the allure of its domestic economy, to force open foreign markets that otherwise may have remained closed. It also ensures that very little now goes on in the global economy without US involvement.

In the realm of international financial markets, American practices are now more widespread than in previous generations. As American financial service providers have traditionally been better financed than their British counterparts, with a work ethic less genteel and less based on historical precedents, it was much easier for them to attract the best staff and be more competitive in the European financial markets. In the 1980s, when American financial service providers arrived to do business in the City of London, they found that the London markets functioned like a gentlemen's club, with short working weeks, long lunches and a sense of tradition. The faster-paced 'greed is good' ethic of the American markets swept away much of the old city practices very rapidly, as the traditional British financial markets found that their quaint ideals, smaller capital base and respect for tradition were no match for the flash young traders from the US who worked through lunch breaks and often on into the evening in search of the lucrative bonuses. Nowadays American financial service providers are everywhere, and the culture they brought with them has displaced much indigenous financial culture.

Globalization has resulted in challenges for the US too. In spite of the advantages it possesses, whether by virtue of natural resources, language, culture, government policy or serendipity, the move into the global market has not been without problems. Perhaps the most obvious problem has involved the trade deficits that opened up quite rapidly between 1981 and 1984. Although the US had run deficits before, the deficits of the 1980s appeared year-on-year, and were much larger than any previously experienced. In part, the trade deficits were the result of the budget deficits resulting from Ronald Reagan's tax-cutting agenda. National savings fell, and capital had to be imported to finance domestic American investment. The American position as the world's largest international creditor disappeared; indeed, the US became the world's largest net debtor. During the 1980s, the American trade deficit was financed by the sale of American assets, including shares, bonds, real estate and eventually entire companies. There are those in the US who saw this financing of the deficit as giving away the foundations of the American economy to foreigners and resulting in a loss of American economic sovereignty. The major budget and trade deficits of George W. Bush had reawakened such concerns, which continue under the current Obama administration.

Many in the US, on both sides of the political divide, question the benefits from being involved in globalization. Some argue, for example, that the freer world trade arising from GATT/WTO and the patchwork of bilateral and regional deals negotiated by the US has left the American worker dangerously exposed to lower wage competition from the economies of Latin America and the Asia Pacific rim. As the MNEs source labour and raw materials from whichever locations are cheapest, they now produce much of their output from outside the US but can then sell within the American market without paying high import tariffs. They no longer employ as many American workers, or invest as much in the US. This argument, known as the 'pauper labour argument', implies that American workers will lose out in terms of employment, pay and working conditions from the inexorable process of globalized world production.

There is also concern that in an era of global markets, where production occurs in many locations which are likely to be different from those in which the goods are sold, firms that began life as 'American' now see themselves in a different light, namely as global companies rather than national ones. It used to be said that what was good for General Motors was good for America, but if ideas such as the pauper labour argument are valid, then this is less likely to be the case now.

Again some argue that, given the size and wealth of the American market, the US should once again be protectionist, as foreign firms would be willing to pay more in the form of tariffs for access to its huge, high-income market. They also suggest that since much of global trade is *intra-industry trade*, with parts made in a number of countries for assembly in the US, such tariffs would make it less cost-efficient for firms to source their components outside the US, thereby encouraging productive capacity to return to America.

We might conclude that for the reluctant globalists of the US, globalization has been remarkably successful. However, disadvantages have also been recognized, as with successive Presidents attempting to equip the American workforce to take full advantage of the opportunities resulting from intensified global competition. Their attempts to overhaul health care, education and job training, and bring about an improvement in skills, were aimed at raising American productivity and lowering business costs. In practice, American success in promoting free trade has arguably intensified the pressure on lower-skilled Americans, whilst offering them little defence from an ever intensifying global competition in the future.

Conclusion

Globalization is more widely viewed as a process rather than an end-state, in terms of our earlier framework, conforming more closely to the perspective of 'transformationalists' rather than 'hyperglobalists'. That said, it is characterized by major changes occurring in at least four broad areas, namely new markets, new actors, new rules and norms, and new methods of communications. Quantitative and qualitative changes in these areas are arguably having major impacts in shaping corporate strategies and influencing the lives of employees and individuals worldwide. Nor can we confine these impacts to the economic sphere alone, important though that undoubtedly is. The greater difficulties faced by nation states in combating global forces extend to the security and health-related domains, as much as the economic. At the macro level, policy responses have often involved a resort to more multilateral institutions and arrangements, including regional trading blocs, in an attempt to employ more effective collective influence where national influence is perceived to be lessening. At the micro level, the wide range of firm strategies (e.g. Porter's Five Forces) thought appropriate when industry structures were stable and predictable, at both national and institutional levels, are now being challenged and reshaped in the 'discontinuous competitive landscape' more typical of a globalized business environment.

Of course the debate as to the costs and benefits of globalization, however defined, continues apace. Supporters of the development of advanced business capitalism since the early nineteenth century point to the remarkable growth in living standards achieved. For example, in the eight centuries from 1000 to 1820 per capita incomes in Western Europe rose by 0.15% per year on average, but by 1.5% per year on average since then – 10 times as fast. On the other hand, anti-globalization protesters point to the gross inequalities between rich and poor, such inequalities buttressed by the prevailing rules and norms governing the actions of an institutional superstructure (IMF, World Bank, G7/G8, WTO, etc.) which is allegedly biased against the disadvantaged.

Key points

- Shrinking space, shrinking time and disappearing borders are widely accepted features of globalization, however defined.

- 'Hyperglobalists' and others see globalization as an end-state characterized by global governance, global capitalism (dominated by multinational enterprises) and rapidly eroding nation states.

- 'Transformationalists' and others see globalization as consisting of a complex set of intermittent, uneven processes linked to rapidly increasing levels of global interconnectedness. Whilst no single end-state is predictable, corporate, national and individual destinies will be reshaped by these globalization processes.

- These globalization processes are leading to new markets, new actors, new rules and norms, and new methods of communication.

- In a progressively less stable environment, there will arguably be a shift away from the previous strategic focus of Porter and his contemporaries in which companies seek to identify and exploit competitive advantages within stable industrial structures.

- In the new, globalized landscape the strategic focus shifts to the stretching and shaping of industrial structures by the MNEs themselves, using their own strategic initiatives.

- Globalization is redefining our understanding of the nation state by introducing a much more complex architecture of political power in which authority is seen as being pluralistic (e.g. intergovernmental and non-governmental organizations) rather than residing solely in the nation state.

- The growth of knowledge-based economies dominated by the creation, processing and dissemination of information is seen by some as synonymous with globalization.

- Globalization is a multidimensional process, reshaping the context of security, health control and other governmental policies just as much as their economic policies.

- The US, whilst seen as the major driver of, and beneficiary from, globalization, has in many respects been a reluctant participant in that process.

Now try the self-check questions for this chapter on the Companion Website. You will also find useful links to relevant websites.

Note

1 The weights for calculating the sub-indices are determined using principal components analysis for the entire sample of countries and years.

References and further reading

Barro, R. (1991) Economic growth in a cross-section of countries, *Quarterly Journal of Economics*, **106**(20): 407–43.

Bell, D. (1973) *The Coming of Post-Industrial Society*, New York, Basic Books.

Bénassy-Quéré, A. and Coeuré, B. (2010) *Economic Policy*, Oxford, Oxford University Press.

Black, J. (2002) *A Dictionary of Economics*, Oxford, Oxford University Press.

Booth, P. and Wellings, R. (2009) *Globalization and Free Trade*, Cheltenham, Edward Elgar.

Buchanan, P. (1998) *The Great Betrayal: How American Sovereignty and Social Justice Are Being Sacrificed to the Gods of the Global Economy*, New York, Little, Brown.

Claugue, C., Keefer, P., Knack, S. and Olson, M. (1999) Contract-intensive money: contract enforcement, property rights and economic performances, *Journal of Economic Growth*, 4, 185–211.

Croucher, S. (2003) *Globalization and Belonging: the Politics of Identity in a Changing World*, New York, Rowman & Littlefield.

Czinkota, M., Johansson, J. and Ronkainen, I. (1994) *International Marketing*, New York, McGraw-Hill.

Dicken, P. (2011) *Global Shift: Reshaping the Global Economic Map in the 21st Century* (6th edn), London, Sage Publications.

Duignan, P. and Gann, L. H. (1994) *The USA and the New Europe 1945–1993*, Cambridge MA, Blackwell.

Dunning, J. and Lundan, S. (2008) *Multinational Enterprises and the Global Economy* (2nd edn), Cheltenham, Edward Elgar.

French, M. (1997) *US Economic History since 1945*, Manchester, Manchester University Press.

Gershuny, J. (1978) *After Industrial Society? The Emerging Self-service Economy*, Leiden, Brill Academic Publishers.

Giavazzi, F. and Blanchard, O. (2010) *Macroeconomics: A European Perspective*, Harlow, Financial Times/Prentice Hall.

Giddens, A. (1990) *The Consequences of Modernity*, Cambridge, Polity Press.

Glyn, A. (2004) The assessment: how far has globalization gone? *Oxford Review of Economic Policy*, 20(1): 1–4.

Held, D., McGrew, A., Goldblatt, D. and Perraton, J. (1999) *Global Transformations: Politics, Economics and Culture*, Cambridge, Polity Press.

Hill, C. (2005) *International Business: Competing in the Global Marketplace* (5th edn), Maidenhead, McGrawHill/Irwin.

ILO (2001) *World Employment Report 2001: Life at Work in the Information Economy*, Geneva, International Labour Office.

IMF (2001) *World Employment Report 2001: The Information Technology Revolution*, October, Washington DC, International Monetary Fund.

Kaletsky, A. (2002) If leaders persist with failed economic policy they will be doing Bin Laden's work for him, *The Times*, 10 September.

Kobrin, S. J. (1994) Is there a relationship between a geocentric mind-set and multinational strategy? *Journal of International Business Studies*, 3, 493–511.

KOF (2010) *KOF Index of Globalisation*, Zurich, Swiss Federal Institute of Technology.

Krugman, P. (1994) *Peddling Prosperity: Economic Sense and Nonsense in the Age of Dminished Expectations*, New York, Norton.

Krugman, P. (1998) *The Age of Diminished Expectations*, Cambridge MA, MIT Press.

Krugman, P. and Obstfeld, M. (2010) *International Economics: Theory and Policy*, Harlow, Financial Times/Prentice Hall.

Laudicina, P. (2010) Globalisation enters a new era: what course will it take? *Corporate Finance Review*, March/April, 5–12.

Lipsey, R. E. (1999) *The Location and Characteristics of US Affiliates in Asia*, NBER Working Paper 6876, Cambridge MA, National Bureau of Economic Research.

Machlup, F. (1962) *The Production and Distribution of Knowledge in the United States*, Princeton NJ, Princeton University Press.

McGrew, A. (1992) A global society, in Hall, S., Held, D. and McGrew, A. (eds), *Modernity and its Futures*, Milton Keynes, Open University Press, 62–102.

Mohan, R. (2009) *Monetary Policy in a Globalised Economy*, Oxford, Oxford University Press.

Morrison, J. (2002) *The International Business Environment: Diversity and the Global Economy*, New York, Palgrave Macmillan.

Prahalad, C. K. (2000) *Mastering Strategy*, London, Financial Times/Prentice Hall.

Price, D. de Solla (1977) *Science Since Babylon*, New Haven CT, Yale University Press.

Rescher, D. (1978) *Scientific Progress. A Philosophical Essay on the Economics of Research in Natural Science*, Oxford, Blackwell.

Rider, M. (1977) Growth of knowledge, in de Solla Price, D. (ed.), *Science Since Babylon*, New Haven CT, Yale University Press.

Spulber, N. (1995) *The American Economy: The Struggle for Supremacy in the 21st Century*, Cambridge, Cambridge University Press.

Tiplady, R. (2003) *One World or Many? The Impact of Globalisation on Mission*, New York, Authentic.

UNCTAD (1999) *World Investment Report 1999: Foreign Direct Investment and the Challenge of Development*, New York and Geneva, United Nations Conference on Trade and Development.

UNCTAD (2005) *World Investment Report 2005: Transnational Corporations and the Internationalization of R&D*, New York and Geneva, United Nations Conference on Trade and Development.

UNCTAD (2010a) *Trade and Development Report 2010: Employment, Globalization and*

Development, New York and Geneva, United Nations Conference on Trade and Development.

UNCTAD (2010b and various) *World Investment Reports*, New York and Geneva, United Nations Conference on Trade and Development.

UNDP (2010) *Human Development Report 2010 The Real Wealth of Nations: Pathways to Human Development*, New York, United Nations Development Programme.

Wallsten, S. (2001) *Ringing in the 20th Century*, World Bank Research Working Paper No. 2690, Washington DC, World Bank.

World Bank (1997) *Trade Development and Poverty Reduction*, www.worldbank.org/devcom (accessed February 2011).

World Bank (2001) *World Development Report (WDR) 2000/2001: Attacking Poverty*, Washington DC.

World Bank (2003) *Global Economic Prospects*, Washington DC.

World Bank (2004) *World Development Indicators*, Washington, DC.

World Bank (2005) *World Development Report 2005: A Better Investment Climate for Everyone*, Washington DC.

World Bank (2010) *World Development Report 2010: Development and Climate Change*, Washington DC.

World Bank (2010 and various) *World Development Reports*, Washington DC.

Zak, P. (2001) Institutions, property rights and growth, *Gruter Institute Working Papers*, **2**(1): Article 2.

Zamagni, S. and Zamagni, V. (2010) *Cooperative Enterprise: Facing the Challenge of Globalization*, Cheltenham, Edward Elgar.

CHAPTER 25

Exchange rates and trade performance

The manipulation of exchange rates in attempting to create national competitive advantages is an issue at the forefront of contemporary policy debate. The causes and consequences of exchange rate and currency conflicts are reviewed in some detail.

The exchange rate is the price of one currency in terms of another. For example, the exchange rate for sterling is conventionally defined as the number of units of another currency, such as the dollar, that it takes to purchase one pound sterling on the foreign exchange market. In the market, however, it is usually quoted as the number of units of the domestic currency that it takes to purchase one unit of foreign currency. In general terms the exchange rate is perhaps the most important 'price' in any economic system. It influences the price of a nation's exports and hence their sales, thereby determining output and jobs in the export industries. It affects the extent to which imports can compete with home-produced products, and thereby affects the viability of domestic companies. Because the price of imports enters into the various price indices, any variation in the exchange rate will also have an effect on the official rate of inflation. This chapter will consider these various issues and especially the impacts of exchange rates on trade performance.

The chapter concludes by reviewing the operation, over time, of various exchange rate regimes, such as the gold standard, the 'adjustable-peg' exchange rate system and freely floating exchange rates.

The foreign exchange market

The foreign exchange market is the money market on which international currencies are traded. It has no physical existence: it consists of traders, such as the dealing rooms of major banks, who are in continual communication with one another on a worldwide basis. Currencies are bought and sold on behalf of clients, who may be companies, private individuals or banks themselves. A distinction is made between the 'spot' rate for a currency, and the forward rate. The spot rate is the domestic currency price of a unit of foreign exchange when the transaction is to be completed within three days. The forward rate is the price of that unit when delivery is to take place at some future date – usually 30, 60 or 90 days hence. Both spot and forward rates are determined in today's market; the relationship between today's spot and today's forward rate will be determined largely by how the market *expects* the spot rate to move in the near future. The more efficient the market is at anticipating future spot rates, the closer will today's forward rate be to the future spot rate.

The spot market is used by those who wish to acquire foreign exchange straightaway. Forward markets are used by three groups of people.

1 Those who wish to cover themselves (*hedge*) against the risk of exchange rate variation. For instance, suppose an importer orders goods to be paid for in three months' time in dollars. All his calculations will be upset if the price of dollars rises between now and payment date. He can cover himself by buying dollars today for delivery in three months' time; he thus locks himself into a rate which reduces the risk element in his transaction.

2 *Arbitrageurs* who attempt to make a profit on the difference between interest rates in one country and another, and who buy or sell currency forward to ensure that the profit which they hope to make by moving their capital is not negated by adverse exchange rate movements.

3 Straightforward *speculators* who use the forward markets to buy or sell in anticipation of exchange rate changes. For instance, if I think that today's forward rates do not adequately reflect the probability of the dollar increasing in value, I will buy dollars forward, hoping to sell them at a profit when they are delivered to me at some future date.

London is the world's largest centre for foreign exchange trading, with an average daily turnover of over US $1,100bn. The market is growing all the time; indeed, the average daily turnover in 2010 was more than treble the value recorded in 1993. Some 66% of transactions are 'spot' on any one day, 24% are forward for periods not exceeding one month, and 10% are forward for longer than one month. Increasingly, however, more sophisticated types of transactions are being done. For instance, there is a growth in the following types of transactions:

■ foreign currency options, which give the right (but do not impose an obligation) to buy or sell currencies at some future date and price;

■ foreign currency futures, which are standardized contracts to buy or sell on agreed terms on specific future dates; and

■ foreign currency swaps – spot purchases against outright forward currency sales.

Foreign exchange market business in London is done in an increasingly wide variety of currencies: for example, £/$ business now accounts for only 12% of activity. However, trading transactions which do not involve the US dollar are becoming increasingly frequent.

Supply and demand for a currency

Prices of currencies are determined, as on any other market, by supply of and demand for the various currencies. Businessmen wishing to import goods will sell sterling in order to buy currency with which to pay the supplier in another country. Tourists coming to the UK will sell their own currency in order to buy sterling. Other types of transactions, too, will have exchange rate repercussions. For instance, if a German company wishes to buy a factory in the UK it will need to convert euros into sterling, as will foreign banks who wish to make sterling deposits in London, or residents abroad who wish to buy UK government bonds.

Another way of saying this is that in any given period of time the factors which determine the demand and supply for foreign exchange are those which are represented in the balance of payments account. The demand for foreign exchange arises as a result of imports of goods and services, outflows of UK capital in the form of overseas investment (short and long term), and financial transactions by banks on behalf of their clients. The supply of foreign exchange comes as a result of the export of goods and services, inflows of foreign capital and bank transactions.

It is clear from the balance of payments accounts that companies and individuals are not the only clients of foreign exchange market dealers. The Bank of England also buys and sells foreign currency, using the official reserves in the Exchange Equalization Account. In order to reflect on why this might be the case, we have to remember that governments have an interest in the level of the exchange rate, and that they may on occasion wish to intervene in the workings of the foreign exchange market to affect the value of sterling. Indeed, it was estimated that on the day sterling was forced to withdraw from the Exchange Rate Mechanism (ERM) (16 September 1992), the Bank of England spent an estimated £7bn, roughly a third of its foreign exchange reserves, in buying sterling. In particular it bought sterling with Deutsche marks (DM) in an unsuccessful attempt to preserve the sterling exchange rate within its permitted ERM band.

Historically, the policy stance on this has varied. As we note later in the chapter, it was only after the Second World War that foreign exchange markets began to function freely on a worldwide basis. Governments then had the option of allowing exchange rates to be market-determined, i.e. to 'float', or to establish some kind of fixed exchange rate system. The decision was taken at Bretton Woods in 1945 to adopt a fixed exchange rate regime; governments thus committed themselves to continual intervention in the market in order to offset imbalances in the demand and supply for their currencies. The Bretton Woods agreement collapsed in 1972, since when currencies have been allowed to float. However, the European Exchange Rate Mechanism was established in 1979 to restrict the range within which member currencies could float against each other (see Chapter 27), with the ERM eventually leading to the establishment of the euro as the single currency. For a variety of reasons, governments continue to 'manage' the floating exchange rate system by intervening in the foreign exchange market. In the UK the Bank of England deals in this market in order to smooth out short-term fluctuations in the value of sterling as well as to influence the exchange rate as part of its overall economic strategy. However, intervention in the market alone is insufficient to affect the sterling exchange rate, simply because the size of speculative trading on the world's foreign exchange markets dwarfs the size of any one country's official reserves. Governments must therefore attempt to increase the demand for their currencies by, for instance, attracting flows of short- or longer-term investment from abroad by means of high interest rates.

We have argued that in everyday terms currency prices are determined by demand and supply on the foreign exchange markets. We must now examine in more detail the forces determining any given exchange rate in the short and long term. As we shall see, all the various theoretical explanations focus on the importance of one or other of the variables contained within the balance of payments accounts. The theories vary only in the time perspective considered. The function of theory is to explain and predict; we shall consider later to what extent recent experience in the UK validates the different theoretical arguments.

Exchange rate definitions

Before we do this, however, we must consider what we mean by 'the exchange rate'. In a foreign exchange market where exchange rates are allowed to 'float', every currency has a price against every other currency. In order to allow for measurability, economists use three separate concepts.

1 *The nominal rate of exchange.* This is the rate of exchange for any one currency as quoted against any other currency. The nominal exchange rate is therefore a bilateral (two-country) exchange rate.

2 *The effective exchange rate* (EER). This is a measure which takes into account the fact that sterling varies differently against each of the other currencies. It is calculated as a weighted average of the individual or bilateral rates, and is expressed as an index number relative to the base year. The weights are chosen to reflect the importance of other currencies in manufacturing trade with the UK. The EER is therefore a *multilateral* (many-country) exchange rate.

3 *The real exchange rate* (RER). This concept is designed to measure the rate at which home goods exchange for goods from other countries, rather than the rate at which the currencies themselves

are traded. It is thus essentially a measure of competitiveness. When we consider *multilateral* UK trade, it is defined as:

$$RER = EER \times P(UK)/P(F)$$

In other words, the real exchange rate is equal to the effective exchange rate multiplied by the price ratio of home, $P(UK)$, to foreign, $P(F)$, goods. If UK prices rise, the real exchange rate will rise unless the effective exchange rate falls. We consider below the question of how one might measure this definition empirically.

Nominal exchange rate

Table 25.1 outlines the *nominal rate of exchange* for sterling against a variety of other currencies (columns 1 to 5) and the overall *effective exchange rate* (EER) against a 'basket' of other currencies (column 6). Of course, from 1 January 1999 onwards the French franc, German mark and Italian lira were replaced by the euro.

We can see from Table 25.1 that the pound sterling varied in both directions in terms of its *nominal exchange rate* against the US dollar over the period 1997–2007, but rose overall with £1 worth $1.64 in 1997 but $2.00 in 2007. However, since 2007 the pound sterling has fallen sharply against the US dollar. The nominal exchange rate for the pound sterling against the euro has fallen consistently over the period 1999–2010, with a particularly sharp fall since 2007. A sharp fall in the nominal exchange rate for the pound sterling against the Japanese yen can also be observed in the period since 2007.

Impacts of a change in the nominal exchange rate
A fall in these nominal exchange rates for sterling since 2007 in particular is helping to make UK exports to these countries cheaper (in the foreign currency) and imports dearer (in sterling). For example, in 2007 an American resident would have had to give up $2.00 for each pound, whereas by 2010 he or she would have needed to give up only $1.51 for each pound. British goods and services would therefore

Table 25.1 Sterling exchange rates, 1997–2010.

Year	US dollar	French franc	Japanese yen	German mark	Sterling effective exchange rate (2005 = 100)	Euro	Consumer prices 1990 = 100	
							UK	US
1997	1.64	9.56	198.12	2.84	96.37	–	124.9	122.9
1998	1.66	9.77	216.75	2.91	100.00	–	129.1	124.4
1999	1.62	9.97	183.94	2.97	99.37	1.52	131.2	127.6
2000	1.52	10.77	163.27	3.21	101.15	1.64	133.1	131.1
2001	1.44	10.55	174.84	3.15	99.49	1.61	136.0	134.2
2002	1.50	–	187.87	–	100.56	1.59	139.0	137.3
2003	1.64	–	189.32	–	96.88	1.45	141.2	138.5
2004	1.83	–	198.10	–	101.60	1.47	144.6	140.2
2005	1.82	–	200.16	–	100.43	1.46	147.8	142.6
2006	1.84	–	214.33	–	101.22	1.47	152.4	145.3
2007	2.00	–	235.71	–	103.59	1.46	155.8	149.2
2008	1.85	–	192.36	–	90.78	1.26	158.9	155.5
2009	1.57	–	146.47	–	80.13	1.12	161.4	153.2
2010*	1.51	–	136.62	–	77.21	1.11	166.2	155.6

*End of first quarter.
Note: Figures have been rounded to 2 decimal places. The annual sterling effective exchange rate figures were calculated by averaging the daily values sourced from the Bank of England's Interactive Database.
Source: Adapted from Bank of England (2010) *Statistics Interactive Database: Interest and exchange rates*, April 3rd. Reprinted with permission.

have cost less in dollar terms in 2010 than in 2007. We can illustrate the above using data from Table 25.1:

£1 = $2.00   2007
£1 = $1.51   2010

A £100 export from the UK to the US cost $200 in the US in 2007, but costs only $151 in 2010. An import from the US costing $200 would sell for £100 in the UK in 2007 but a higher £132.5 in 2010.

We can therefore conclude that the exchange rate is a key 'price' affecting the competitiveness of UK exporters and UK producers of import substitutes.

- A fall (depreciation) in the sterling exchange rate makes UK exports cheaper abroad (in the foreign currency) and imports into the UK dearer at home (in £ sterling)
- A rise (appreciation) in the sterling exchange rate makes UK exports dearer abroad (in the foreign currency) and imports into the UK cheaper at home (in £ sterling)

Effective exchange rate (EER)

Of course, UK trade with the US is only a part of UK external transactions. The sterling *effective exchange rate* (EER) is a weighted average of the various national currencies involved in trade with the UK, the weights given to each national currency depending on the relative importance of UK trade with each of these nations. Currently, the euro has a weight of over 50%, compared to less than 20% for the dollar when calculating the sterling EER, reflecting the relative importance of these areas in UK trade.

As we can see from Table 25.1, the sterling EER has varied in both directions, but overall has fallen by almost 33% since 1998. This suggests a considerable boost to the competitiveness of UK exporters and UK producers of import substitutes over the past 12 years. As we noted in Chapter 1 (p. 19), a fall in the relative exchange rate will, other things equal, reduce a country's relative unit labour cost (RULC), the single most widely used measure of international competitiveness.

But does the recorded fall in both nominal and effective exchange rates for sterling really mean that UK goods had become more competitive on world markets? Of course the answer depends not only on changes in the exchange rate but on relative inflation rates between the UK and the countries with which

we are comparing it. In other words, we must examine the *real exchange rate*.

Real exchange rates (RER)

Returning again to the *bilateral* exchange rate between sterling and the US dollar, we can now investigate the *real exchange rate* (RER) between the two currencies from 1997 to 2010. As we can see from Table 25.1, although the nominal (bilateral) exchange rate between sterling and US dollar fell substantially over the period, consumer price inflation was somewhat higher in the UK than in the US.

Using the information in Table 25.1 on nominal exchange rates and UK/US consumer prices, we can work out the RERs between pound sterling and US dollar for 2007 and 2010:

$$RER = \frac{nominal\ £/\$}{exchange\ rate} \times \frac{price\ index\ of\ UK\ goods\ in\ £}{price\ index\ of\ US\ goods\ in\ \$}$$

$$RER\ (2007) = 2.00 \times \frac{155.8}{149.2} = 2.09$$

$$RER\ (2010) = 1.51 \times \frac{166.2}{155.6} = 1.61$$

The fall in the RER ($/£) from 2.09 in 2007 to 1.61 in 2010 clearly indicates that by 2010 fewer dollars are needed to be exchanged for each £1 worth of UK products bought in the US. Although inflation was higher in the UK than in the US over the period, the fall in the nominal sterling exchange rate against the US dollar has *more than offset* the higher UK inflation. Whilst sterling depreciated against the dollar by some 25% [(0.49/2.00) × 100] over the period using *nominal* exchange rates, it only depreciated by some 23% [(0.48/2.09) × 100] over the period using *real* exchange rates. In other words, the loss of competitiveness because of higher UK inflation eroded *some* of the exchange rate gains between UK and US producers, though these still remained substantial.

Exchange rate determination

We can distinguish four theoretical approaches to exchange rate determination. It must be emphasized that these are in no sense 'competing' theories. They are simply different ways of looking at what determines the exchange rate, depending on whether we are interested in the short run or the long run, in immediate or more fundamental determinants, and on what we consider to be the most empirically relevant factors at any given time.

Exchange rates and the balance of trade

The *traditional* approach sees the exchange rate simply as the price which brings into equilibrium the supply and demand for currency arising from trade in goods and services and from capital transactions, as explained above. This approach was formulated in the 1950s when capital flows were small in relation to trade flows, and hence its major use is to illustrate the interrelationship between current account flows and exchange rate changes. Nevertheless, it can also accommodate capital account transactions. It is essentially a perspective which concentrates on short-run influences.

Figure 25.1 shows that the demand for pounds will increase as the price falls. This is because customers abroad will perceive that the price of UK exports has fallen in their own currency as sterling depreciates, increasing their demand for UK exports and therefore for pounds with which to buy them. The supply of pounds will rise as the price of sterling rises because the price of imports in sterling falls as the

pound strengthens. With cheaper imports, UK consumers now buy more imported items and firms exchange more pounds in order to buy these imports.[1]

Demand and supply curves can shift for a number of reasons. A shift (increase) in supply from S to S_1 might be due to a change in tastes in favour of foreign goods. A shift (decrease) in demand from D to D_1 might occur because UK interest rates had fallen, leading to a decrease in the demand for pounds as investors switch their funds out of the UK money markets. In either of these cases, there will be a fall in the exchange rate below its original level, P. In a floating exchange rate system the rate will be allowed to fall. Should the monetary authorities wish to keep the exchange rate at its original level, they will be obliged to buy sterling. If the supply of sterling increases to S_1, they will buy up the excess quantity AB; if the demand for sterling has fallen to D_1, they will make up the shortfall by buying up quantity CA. In either case, the price reverts to its original level.

This view of exchange rate determination predicts that the exchange rate will alter in response to macro-economic policy, because the demand for imports (and hence the supply of pounds) will depend in part on the level of income. Fiscal policy, with its impacts on the equilibrium level of national income, will thus affect the exchange rate. So too will monetary policy as short-term capital flows (and hence both demand and supply of pounds) are seen as being sensitive to interest rate changes. Both fiscal and monetary policy will therefore have exchange rate repercussions. Expansionary policies, whether fiscal or monetary, which raise levels of income and employment will cause the S curve to shift to S_1, as imports rise with income. Such policies may cause a balance of payments deficit and a fall in the exchange rate. The converse will be the case when fiscal or monetary policies are contractionary. Where fiscal and monetary policies alter interest rates in a downward direction (as, for instance, if public borrowing is reduced so that fewer bonds need to be issued, bond prices rise and yields fall, or interest rates are reduced directly by the monetary authorities), capital outflows will be triggered – S will move to S_1 as people move their money out of UK financial markets; at the same time D will fall to D_1 as investment in UK money markets is no longer forthcoming.

What this model does not enable us to do is to predict the overall effect of any given policy stance. In the case of an *expansionary monetary policy*, spending

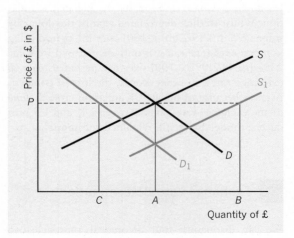

Fig. 25.1 The foreign exchange market.

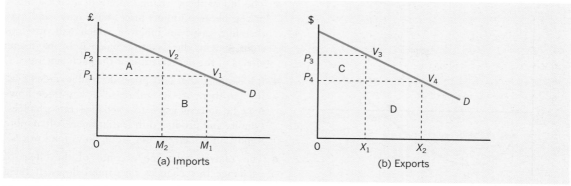

Fig. 25.2 Marshall–Lerner elasticity conditions.

will increase and interest rates will fall, the supply of pounds will increase in both cases and the exchange rate will fall. But in the case of an *expansionary fiscal policy*, expansion may be associated with an increase in government borrowing, which will lead to a fall in bond prices (as the supply of bonds increases) and a rise in the interest rate. The effect on the exchange rate will then be ambiguous, depending on the marginal propensity to import from a rise in income in relation to the interest elasticity of capital flows.

Marshall–Lerner elasticity condition

We have seen how the traditional explanation of exchange rate determination is based on balance of payments flows. However, there is also a 'feedback' effect in that these flows, in particular flows of imports and exports, are themselves partly determined by the level of the exchange rate. Suppose that an exogenous disturbance, such as a change in government policy, leads to a balance of payments deficit and a consequent fall in the exchange rate. Since the demand for exports and imports is dependent on their price, will the new exchange rate level result in a further deterioration in the balance of payments and a further fall in the exchange rate, or will the balance of payments improve and the exchange rate return to its former level?

The answer to this question depends on the elasticities of demand for imports and exports. The 'elasticities' approach to balance of payments adjustment predicts that if the sum of the elasticities of demand for imports and exports is greater than one (the

Marshall–Lerner condition) then the balance between the change in export earnings and import expenditure will be such as to improve the balance of payments, and the exchange rate will rise in consequence.

The Marshall–Lerner condition can be outlined further by reference to Fig. 25.2 where, following a depreciation of the pound, the price of imports increases and the price of exports decreases. In Fig. 25.2(a) a depreciation of the pound has resulted in a rise in the sterling price of imports from P_1 to P_2 and reduced their demand from M_1 to M_2. This leads to an increase in sterling expenditure on imports of area A but a reduction in sterling expenditure on imports of area B. There will be an *overall reduction* in expenditure on imports of (B − A) if the demand for imports is elastic. In Fig. 25.2(b) the depreciation of the pound has resulted in a reduction in the foreign (\$) price of exports from P_3 to P_4 and an expansion in the demand for exports from X_1 to X_2. This will lead to a reduction in expenditure by foreigners on UK exports by area C, but at the same time there will be a rise in expenditure by foreigners on UK exports of area D. There will be an *overall increase* in expenditure by foreigners on UK exports of (D − C) if the demand for exports is elastic.

In terms of the balance of payments, the effect will have been an improvement of (B − A) + (D − C), which will be greater the higher the respective elasticities of demand for imports and exports. However, it can be shown that the cut-off value for these respective elasticities is where the *sum of their values equals 1*. In this situation a fall (depreciation) in the exchange rate will leave the balance of payments unchanged. However, if the sum of these respective

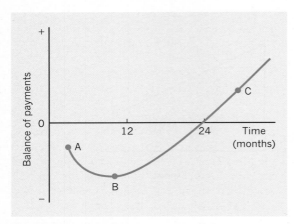

Fig. 25.3 'J' curve effect.

elasticities is *less than 1*, then a fall (depreciation) in the exchange rate will cause the balance of payments to deteriorate. Only if the sum of these elasticities is greater than 1 and the Marshall–Lerner condition is fulfilled, will a depreciation (eventually) improve the balance of payments.

In practice the following factors may influence the balance of payments outcome from any given fall in the exchange rate:

- Trade adjustments take time. The exchange rate may adjust instantaneously, but traders take time to adjust their orders. The initial effect of a depreciation may therefore be to make the deficit larger as export demand is slow to increase at new lower prices, and importers fail to cut back their purchases. There will thus be a 'J-curve' effect (see Fig. 25.3) as the balance of payments deteriorates (A to B) before it improves. It has been estimated from previous falls in the exchange rate that it is only during the second year after the devaluation/depreciation that the gain in export volume offsets the loss in revenue due to lower export prices.

- In a floating exchange rate regime exchange rates will alter again in the time it takes for these adjustments to be made. Stability is therefore unlikely to occur.

- The analysis takes no account of supply conditions. In a full employment situation it may not be possible to cope with the increased demand both for exports and for import-competing goods, so that the beneficial effect of a depreciation may not be realized because of supply constraints.

- The fall in the exchange rate will increase home prices, because import prices have risen, and may therefore cause an inflation which will offset to some extent the positive balance of payments effects of the depreciation of the exchange rate.

- It is assumed that only prices determine trade flows. In fact, there are several reasons why trade flows may be unresponsive to exchange rate changes. Quality and product differentiation are often more important in determining trade flows than prices.

- The analysis takes no account of the effect of exchange rate changes on capital flows. If these latter are quantitatively unimportant this does not matter, but since they currently play a very large part in exchange rate determination the usefulness of the elasticities approach is weakened.

The 'traditional' analysis of exchange rate determination, which sees exchange rates as a function of the current balance of payments position, became less useful as historical circumstances have changed. Two major developments after the 1950s made it necessary to consider alternative theoretical approaches.

One of these was the growing importance of capital flows in the balance of payments accounts. These flows of international investment were partly caused by capital formation by multinational companies (see Chapter 7) but were also due to increasing preferences by asset holders for holding foreign assets as capital restrictions were eased. The last of these restrictions vanished in 1979 when the UK abolished exchange control. The other, later, development was the advent of worldwide inflation in the 1970s. The traditional view outlined earlier took no account of internal price changes when analysing exchange rate variations. In fact, in an inflationary situation internal and external price changes are interactive.

These two developments led to the *monetary* and *portfolio* approaches to exchange rate determination on the one hand, and to the revival of the *purchasing power parity* (PPP) theory on the other. Because the monetary and portfolio approach hinges on the validity of the PPP theory, we deal first with purchasing power parity.

Purchasing power parity

This theory originated in the nineteenth century, and was used in the 1920s to discuss the correct value of currencies in relation to gold. In general terms, the proposition states that equilibrium exchange rates will be such as to enable people to buy the same amount of goods in any country for a given amount of money. For this to be the case, exchange rates must be at the correct level in relation to prices in the different countries. In order to state the proposition more rigorously, we must assume that goods are homogeneous (or that there is only one good), also that there are no barriers to trade or transactions costs, and that there is internal price flexibility. The 'law of one price' will then ensure that the price of a good will be equalized in domestic and foreign currency terms. For instance, the price of a car in the UK in sterling must be equal to the price of a car in US dollars times the exchange rate (the sterling price of dollars). If the exchange rate is too high or too low, it will adjust if exchange rates are flexible. If they are fixed, internal prices will adjust as there is an excess of demand in one country and a shortfall in the other. There are two versions of the proposition.

1 The 'absolute' version of PPP predicts that the exchange rate (E) will equalize the purchasing power of a given income in any two countries, so that

$$E = P(\text{UK})/P(\text{US})$$

2 The 'relative' version of the principle states that changes in exchange rates reflect differences in relative inflation rates. If internal prices rise in one country relative to another, exchange rates will adjust (downwards) to compensate.

It is easy to see how the existence of high inflation rates in the 1970s increased the attractiveness of this theory as an explanation of exchange rate determination, because the theory concentrates on showing the relationship between exchange rates and relative price movements, unlike the more traditional view which, as we have seen, had nothing to say about prices. However, what can we say about the empirical usefulness of the principle? Let us consider the problems of applying the principle first, and then look at the extent to which it was in fact successful in explaining exchange rate changes.

A number of damaging criticisms of the theory can be made.

■ The major problem relates to the choice of price index used to give empirical content to the theory. Any overall price index includes non-traded as well as traded goods, and inflation rates may be differently reflected in these sectors, hence rendering the index unusable. Even the use of export price indices is problematic because the profitability element in export prices may vary over time. The appropriate measure would appear to be a measure of unit labour costs normalized as between countries (relative normalized unit labour costs – RNULC) which reflects differences in wage costs per unit of output and thus includes productivity measures.[2] The RNULC measures are the most accurate way of assessing the relative competitive strength of different countries in the traded goods sector (see also Chapter 1).

■ It is difficult to discuss an 'equilibrium' exchange rate without reference to some base year. The choice of representative year can pose problems in a world where inflation rates vary constantly.

■ Factors other than the prices of traded goods can affect the exchange rate. Barriers to trade such as tariffs can exist. Tastes can change, incomes can change, technology can change. The classic example of the latter is the effect on the exchange rate of North Sea oil.

■ Although in the long run the PPP theory may have some validity, exchange rates in the short run are more likely to be dominated by the effects of capital flows, particularly short-run flows. In other words, exchange rates may 'overshoot'.

Quite apart from these particular criticisms, it is doubtful whether the PPP theory provides us with an adequate explanation of changes in the sterling exchange rate. The theory would predict that if prices rise faster in the UK than in other countries the resultant trade deficit should cause a fall in the exchange rate. We can test this by examining the relationship between the EER and RNULC. When costs rise the UK is becoming less competitive, so we might expect to see a consequent fall in the EER if the 'relative' version of the PPP theory holds. In other words, there should be an inverse relationship between the two measures. However, empirical evidence is rather weak in this respect, with relative prices (proxied by unit labour costs) and the EER often tending to move together rather than inversely. There are various possible explanations for this.

■ Price elasticities for imports and exports may not be such as to cause the exchange rate to improve

Table 25.2 Balance on oil trading account (£m).

1976	1978	1980	1982	1985	1987	1989	1993	1997	2001	2003	2005	2007	2009
−3,947	−1,984	315	4,605	8,163	4,184	1,257	2,442	4,608	5,392	3,376	−1,234	−4,031	−3,237

Source: Adapted from ONS (2010) *UK Balance of Payments*, and previous editions.

with a rise in competitiveness. In fact, with a floating exchange rate a rise in competitiveness may cause the exchange rate to fall (the J-curve effect).

- The EER is influenced by trade in invisibles and by capital flows as well as by the relative prices of manufactured goods entering into trade.

- Price competitiveness is not the only factor affecting trade flows. Non-price competitiveness is also an important determinant. In other words, the crucial assumption of the 'law of one price' – that of homogeneous goods and services – does not hold in the real world.

We must also realize that RNULCs are themselves influenced by the EER. This is because costs of production in the UK will rise faster than those in other countries if the EER depreciates. Raw materials will become more expensive, production costs will rise, and any resulting (cost-push) inflation may trigger wage demands to respond to the price rises, and RNULC will rise in consequence.

We may sum up by saying that the usefulness of the PPP theory as a theory of exchange rate determination is probably best thought of in a long-run context when changes in relative prices between countries represent the workings of inflationary forces rather than transient 'real' effects such as changes in tastes or technology. However, even in the long run it is still not possible to say whether relative price shifts determine exchange rate movements, or whether exchange rate changes influence price movements.

North Sea oil and the exchange rate

We have argued that little of the variation in the EER can be explained by UK price competitiveness. Other factors have been more important: one of these has been the fundamental change in technological possibilities resulting in the ability to undertake deep water oil exploration and extraction, providing the context for the advent of North Sea oil. North Sea

oil came on stream in 1976, and the UK became self-sufficient in oil by 1980. This has been perhaps the main reason why over various periods of time since then, the EER has risen in spite of a loss of competitiveness.

There are three ways in which oil production has improved the balance of payments.

First, since 1976 the UK has been an exporter of oil and has reduced its own dependence on imported oil. As we can see from Table 25.2, the oil trading balance improved steadily from 1976 onwards, and moved into surplus in 1980. However, after 1985 oil production began to decline in volume, and this was reflected in the reduced oil surplus from 1985 to 1993. Nevertheless, a recovery in world oil prices, new oil fields yielding extra output and the lower price of oil exports (after sterling depreciated on leaving the European ERM in 1992) all contributed to an improvement in the oil trade balance in the mid-1990s and early years of the new millennium. There has been a tendency for oil prices to rise in recent years, due partly to uncertainties as to future supplies of oil (e.g. Gulf War 2, hurricanes and oil spills in the Gulf of Mexico) and partly to more effective restrictions on the supply of oil from the OPEC oil cartel.

Second, the inflows of capital needed to fund investment in the oil industry helped the UK balance of payments in the 1970s. However, this positive effect has to some extent been offset since then by outflows of interest, profits and dividends as companies remit their gains back to the country of origin.

Third, the popularity of sterling rose as international asset holders speculated on the strength of sterling deriving from the (then) favourable oil trading balance. Such problems have raised the profile of sterling as a 'petro-currency', attractive to investors at a time of higher oil prices.

The net effect of the balance of payments impact of North Sea oil is likely to have been sufficiently favourable to keep the exchange rate higher than it would otherwise have been over the past few decades.

The monetary approach to exchange rate determination

As we saw earlier, the growth in importance of capital account transactions led to attempts to explain the determination of the exchange rate by analysing financial flows between countries. The monetary approach to exchange rate determination, developed in the early 1970s, sees the exchange rate as the price of foreign money in terms of domestic money, determined in turn by the demand for and supply of money. If people are not willing to hold the existing stock of money there will be a shortfall in demand for it and its price will fall in relation to the currencies of other countries. What it in fact argues is that balance of payments, and hence exchange rate movements, are simply reflections of disequilibria in money markets.

Money is thought of as being an asset, the demand for which depends on income and interest rates. If the central bank in a country increases the money supply, income and interest rates remaining unchanged, people will be unwilling to hold more money and so the excess money holdings will be used to buy more goods from abroad. The result will be a balance of payments deficit and downward pressure on the exchange rate. If the authorities intervene to support the currency they will lose reserves, and so the increase in the money supply will be exactly offset by a reduction in the external component of the money stock (see Chapter 20). On the other hand, if exchange rates are flexible, the fall in the exchange rate will simply result in internal inflation (as the price of imports rises) which will exactly cancel out the original increase in the money supply.

Suppose now that there is no increase in the money supply, but that exogenous factors cause a change in the demand for money. Suppose incomes rise: the increase in demand for money balances will then lead to an appreciation of the exchange rate as less money is available for imports. Or suppose interest rates rise: the demand for money balances will be reduced, people will spend the money on imports, the exchange rate will fall and home inflation will result. (Note that the prediction here is at variance with the usual assumption that a rise in interest rates will cause an appreciation of the exchange rate because capital flows will be attracted into the country.)

The monetary approach to exchange rate determination, incorporating as it does a whole new perspective on the role of money in the balance of payments, provides a monetarist explanation of exchange rate determination. Its strength lies in the fact that it recognizes the importance of asset market changes in determining the exchange rate, as opposed to concentrating merely on the importance of current account flows in the short or long term, as the previous approaches did. That perspective allows for the possibility of introducing the question of the effect of expectations, which is essential if we are to explain exchange rate volatility. However, in evaluating the usefulness of this approach we must first of all remember that the validity of the argument rests on very limited assumptions:

- The demand for money is a stable function of real income and interest rates.
- Prices are determined by the world price level and the exchange rate, i.e. the PPP theory holds.
- There is full employment domestically.

The validity of these assumptions may be criticized on several grounds:

- The impact of a monetary disturbance on prices and hence the exchange rate may not be predictable in the short run because of the instability of the velocity of circulation (see Chapter 20).
- Exchange rates do not conform to the naive PPP model.
- Changes in the money stock may produce short-run changes in output (see Chapter 20) which may make it difficult to identify ultimate effects on prices and the exchange rate.

It may help to remember the restrictiveness of these assumptions when we examine some of the implications of this monetarist view. For instance, it is clear that the theory implies that there is no need to have a balance of payments policy, since deficits are self-correcting, because increases in the money stock are reversed either by exchange market intervention or by the effects of resultant price rises. But perhaps the major problem with the monetary approach to exchange rate determination, and certainly the central problem when it comes to any empirical testing of its usefulness as an explanatory device, is that it considers there to be only one asset – money – which affects exchange rate determination. This is clearly not the case in practice. We must therefore look to a wider interpretation of asset-holding behaviour if we are to account for the actual behaviour of the exchange rate.

The portfolio balance approach to exchange rate determination

The portfolio balance approach to exchange rate determination sees exchange rates as determined mainly by movements on the capital account of the balance of payments. However, it recognizes that there are a wide variety of assets represented by these transactions. Wealth holders will hold their assets in domestic and foreign securities as well as money, and their asset preferences will be determined by their assessment of the relationship between risk and return on these assets. Given the difference between domestic and foreign rates of return, the exchange rate will be determined by investors' assessment of the degree of substitutability between domestic and foreign assets. If domestic interest rates rise, the extent to which this will cause an inflow of capital and a consequent appreciation of the exchange rate will depend on investor expectations. If expectations change, so that the perceived relationship between risk and return alters, the exchange rate will vary accordingly.

This approach, which was developed in the mid-1970s, represents the 'state of the art' in exchange rate theory. It does not discount the influence of the current account in trend movements of the exchange rate, but it does suggest a plausible explanation for the observed short-run variability in the exchange rate. Exchange rates may vary sharply in response to asset-switching behaviour in the face of changing rates of return and expectations. Adherents of this view would argue that the major exchange rate changes of September 1992 were largely caused by asset-switching behaviour by portfolio holders. For example, once expectations moved sharply against the lira and pound sterling holding their central parities in the ERM, it became a 'low-risk' one-way bet to move out of those currencies into 'harder' currencies such as Deutsche mark and yen.

Short-term capital flows and the exchange rate

Here we consider the way in which the exchange rate is influenced by short-term capital flows. These consist mainly of borrowings from, and lending to, overseas residents by banks. Such short-term capital flows respond primarily to interest rate differentials. Asset switching between countries will take place so long as the interest rate differential is greater than any expected changes in the exchange rate. What happens is that if interest rates rise in, for instance, the US, people will buy dollars in order to invest in US money markets. This will drive the dollar rate up, but as people realize their gains by selling dollars the dollar rate will come down again. It is possible to try and hedge against potential loss by selling dollars bought today on today's forward market for delivery at some future date, but that will in turn drive today's forward rate down. In a perfect market the rise in dollar spot rate and the fall in forward rates (as investors try to make sure of their future gains today) will be just sufficient to cancel out the advantages of rising interest rates. But markets are never perfect, and some *arbitrage* is always possible.

We have no firm empirical evidence for such behaviour on the part of asset-holders. There should be a positive correlation between interest rate differentials and exchange rates, as people switch funds into the UK when interest rates rise relative to US interest rates, thereby driving up the sterling exchange rate. However, empirical evidence as regards the UK/US interest rate differential shows as much evidence of negative as of positive correlation. There are various reasons for this. One is that the positive effect of interest rate differentials on the exchange rate may be outweighed by exchange rate *expectations*. For instance, in the period 1980–82, when interest rate differentials were very low because both the UK and the US had high interest rates, the UK exchange rate was high because people believed that a petro-currency such as sterling would remain strong.

Expectations about future exchange rates are formed by assessments about the potential demand for and supply of sterling. If asset-holders see that the UK has a combined current and capital account deficit, they will *expect* the exchange rate to fall, and will move their money out of sterling, thereby exerting a further downward pressure on sterling. If the authorities do not wish this to happen, they must raise interest rates so that they are higher than those of other countries by a margin sufficient to attract funds into sterling.

Of course, it is never possible to predict the effect on capital flows, and hence on the exchange rate, of any given interest rate differential. Capital flows will be more or less responsive, depending on the strength and the nature of expectations. Lacking adequate information in an imperfect market, speculators tend to be influenced by any item of information, however irrelevant. Money supply figures, political developments at home and abroad, unsuccessful summit meetings – all these tend to trigger behavioural responses in terms of flows of 'hot' money in and out of sterling. Exogenous shocks, such as the consequences of oil price rises, or the threat of international conflict, may also lead to major flows of short-term capital. It may happen that, in spite of high interest rates, the exchange rate does depreciate. In this case, there will be consequent structural changes both in competitiveness and in real rates of return on long-term investment.

Expectations would certainly seem to have outweighed interest rate differentials in September 1992, when a number of ERM currencies came under intense speculative attack. Despite sharp rises in Italian and UK interest rates, for example, the speculative pressure against the lira and pound was sustained. In the case of the UK, interest rates rose an unprecedented five percentage points (from 10% to 15%) within 24 hours. Even this, together with an estimated expenditure of £7bn by the Bank of England (roughly one-third of total UK reserves) in purchasing sterling, and further support of over £2bn by the Bundesbank, could not withstand the continued speculative pressure. Eventually the UK was forced to withdraw from the system altogether (see Chapter 27) and the Italians had to reduce the central parity of the lira within the system.

Currency 'warfare'

There has been much discussion amongst nations, analysts and global institutions as to the 'dangers' of currency manipulation for international trade and economic growth. In September 2010 the US House of Representatives passed a law allowing firms to seek tariff protection against countries with undervalued currencies, a key focus of such a law obviously being China.

Figure 25.4 provides useful data for the G20 group of countries which underpins many of these concerns. The key point is, of course, that the balance of payments is an accounting identity, so that there is a corresponding minus sign (deficit) for every plus sign (surplus), with the net total always zero, except for errors and omissions. In other words, the balance of payments corresponds to a zero sum game, and every 'win' for one party involves, by definition, a 'loss' for another party.

The current account balance in Fig. 25.4(a) represents the absolute value (in $bn) of the deficit (−) or surplus (+) for trade in goods and services forecast for 2010 by the IMF in October of that year. Figure 25.4(b) presents the same data, but as a percentage of the GDP of the respective countries. Whilst capital inflows (+) and outflows (−) are not shown in the current account balance, the picture is clearly one of major deficit for some countries and major surplus for other countries. Moreover, the 2010 'snapshot' of trade performance reflects a longer term reality for many countries as regards their trade in goods and services, as is suggested by the substantial growth in foreign exchange reserves for a number of countries over the 2000–2010 period shown in Fig. 25.4(c).

While the US has much the largest *absolute* current account deficit at almost $450bn in 2010, as a proportion of GDP that current account deficit is, at around −3%, smaller in percentage terms than for the current account deficits in Spain (−5.1%), Turkey (−5%) and South Africa (−4.2%). Nevertheless, these current account imbalances, where they are persistent as in the case of the US, are believed by many analysts to be unsustainable, even when mitigated to some extent and for some countries by surpluses on the capital account (capital inflows exceeding capital outflows).

Self-correcting mechanisms

As we note below (p. 544) the so-called floating exchange rate regime can, potentially, help avoid the *persistent* balance of payments deficits and surpluses that are all too prevalent in the global economy. It may be useful at this point to outline the mechanisms that might be expected to provide a degree of 'self-correction' to balance of payments disequilibria, before exploring why such mechanisms seem not to have worked in practice, at least as regards certain major 'players' such as the US and China!

The exchange rate should, under a floating exchange rate regime, be responsive to changing balance of payments outcomes, depreciating for deficit countries

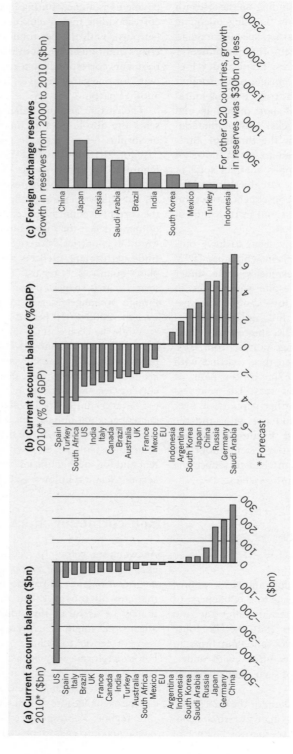

Fig. 25.4 Balance of payments, foreign exchange reserves and currency implications.

Source: Balance of payments, foreign exchange reserves and currency implications, *Financial Times*, 03/11/2010 (Wolf, M.).

and appreciating for surplus countries. Yet despite its huge ($200bn) bilateral balance of payments surplus with the US in 2009/10, the Chinese yuan barely appreciated against the US dollar over that period, rising by less than 1% throughout the whole period! The People's Bank of China (PBOC), the country's central bank, administers China's exchange rate policy, and has clearly acted to stabilize the yuan at close to its current rate, rather than permitting the sharp appreciation of the yuan which might otherwise occur in a free-market system.

Currency-related conflicts

At least three areas of concern were identified in the G20 meeting in October 2010 in South Korea.

First, the allegedly undervalued yuan, with many countries (especially the US) arguing for a significant appreciation, making Chinese exports dearer abroad and imports cheaper within China.

Second, quantitative easing (see Chapter 20, p. 419) and other aspects of monetary policy in the advanced industrialised economies has increased the supply of sterling, dollar, yen and other currencies on foreign exchange markets, tending to lower these countries' exchange rates. With the increase in liquidity, rise in prices and lower interest rates often associated with quantitative easing, China and others argue that these policies artificially depreciate other country exchange rates (a relative appreciation for the yuan). Also the low interest rates and fear of investors that the exchange rates of countries engaged in quantitative easing will fall, both combine to lead to major capital outflows from these advanced economies to the emerging economies such as China and India, putting upward pressures on their exchange rates.

Third, in order to prevent exchange rate appreciation, emerging and other capital receiving economies are intervening more actively, selling their own currencies and buying foreign currencies and/or imposing taxes on foreign capital inflows. Brazil doubled its tax on foreign purchases of domestic debt in 2010 and Thailand announced a new 15% withholding tax for foreign investors in its bonds in October 2010.

What is seen by most analysts of the IMF, G20, OECD, World Bank and others is an urgent need to rebalance global demand for products by switching spending away from the indebted advanced economies and towards the emerging economies.

'Appropriate' exchange rates

Interestingly, the communiqué from the October 23 meeting of G20 finance minutes in South Korea, included the following statement:

> Persistently large (balance of payments) imbalances, assessed against indicative guidelines to be agreed, would warrant an assessment of their nature and the root causes of impediments to adjustment as part of the Mutual Assessment Process, recognizing the need to take into account national or regional circumstances, including [those of] large commodity producers (G20 communiqué, 2010, October).

Despite its complexity, it is interesting to note that both China and the US could agree the above statement. Of course much depends on the discussions regarding implementing this approach, especially agreeing the 'indicative guidelines'! The US has suggested that 4% of GDP might be the target for determining which are the countries with 'persistently large imbalances' and that both surplus and deficit countries breaching this threshold would have an obligation to adjust.

'Big Mac' index

The homogeneous and globally consumed 'Big Mac' has been used for some time as a useful indicator of the extent to which a currency is under- or overvalued. The index is based on the idea of PPP, i.e. that a currency's price should reflect the amount of goods and services which can be bought with that currency. Since it only costs a Chinese consumer 14.5 yuan to buy a Big Mac and a US consumer $3.71, then 1 yuan should exchange against $0.26 on the foreign exchange market. In fact 1 yuan exchanged against $0.15 on the 13th October date of the Big Mac index, suggesting that the yuan is undervalued by around 42% [(0.11/0.26) × 100].

Figure 25.5 uses this approach to identify which currencies are under and overvalued. As we can see, using the US as comparator, Switzerland, Brazil, the Euro area, Canada and Japan are overvalued against the US dollar, and China, Malaysia, Russia, Thailand, Mexico, South Africa, South Korea, Singapore and the UK are undervalued.

IMF approach

The IMF has proposed a rather complex method for its own assessment of under- and overvaluation of an

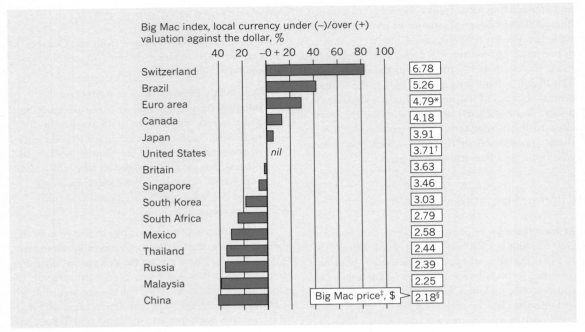

Fig. 25.5 'Big Mac' Index.
*Weighted average of member countries; †Average of four cities; ‡At market exchange rate (Oct 13th); §Average of two cities.
Source: *The Economist* (2010), October 14.

exchange rate. This method incorporates different, but related, approaches with a key element being a calculation of the RER that would be necessary to bring the current account balance into line with a 'norm' identified by the IMF for that country. This 'norm' is based on the country's growth rate, its income per capita, demographic characteristics and budget balance. Another element in the calculation involves establishing the RER which would stabilize the country's foreign assets and liabilities at a 'reasonable' level. This attempt to find a universally accepted definition of under- or overvaluation of a currency is very much in its infancy.

Economic policy and the exchange rate

It has become increasingly clear that there is a direct relationship between changes in the exchange rate and the rate of inflation, because the price of imports enters into the Consumer and Retail Price Indices (CPI and RPI) in different ways. We can illustrate this as follows. In Fig. 25.6 we consider in some detail the impact of a sterling depreciation on UK import prices. Sterling depreciation will raise the cost, expressed in sterling, of imported items. However, both the magnitude and the speed of price rise will vary with the type of import. This can be illustrated for the 1980s by reference to a Bank of England short-term forecasting model. As we can see from Fig. 25.6, the full effect of the sterling depreciation on import prices will only be felt after more than two years. Imported fuel and industrial material prices will, with less elastic demands, respond most substantially and most rapidly to the depreciation. This is in part because the less elastic is demand, the easier it is to pass on cost increases to consumers. Imported finished goods prices rise by a smaller amount, and less quickly, because some of these goods face extensive competition on home markets, i.e. face more elastic demand curves. Imported food prices will tend

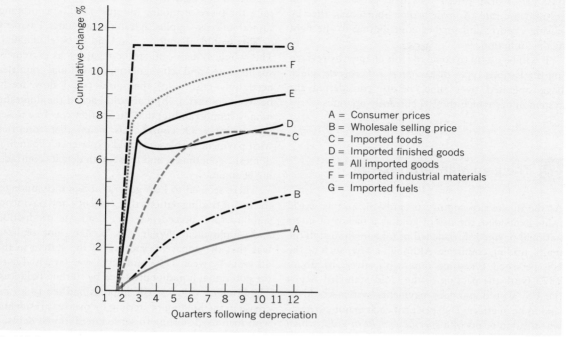

Fig. 25.6 Impact on prices of a 10% depreciation.
Notes:
1 A 10% depreciation of sterling against the dollar is equivalent to an increase of 11.1% in units of sterling per dollar. As it is the latter rate which is relevant in this context, the 10% depreciation leads eventually to a rise slightly greater than 11% in some import prices.
2 The bank's short-term model assumes no wages response. The exchange rate is assumed to remain 10% below the level it would otherwise have been.

to be less affected, at least initially, because of the operation of the Common Agricultural Policy.

The final effect on consumer prices can be seen to be about one-quarter of the sterling depreciation, and then only after more than two years. For any depreciation, the final effect on consumer prices will depend on a number of factors:

- the import content of production;

- the extent to which cost increases can be passed on to consumers, i.e. price elasticity of demand;

- the import content of consumption; and

- the sensitivity of wage demands to cost-of-living increases.

Figure 25.6 is drawn on the assumption of no wage response, i.e. that the sensitivity of wage demands to cost-of-living increases is zero. Any such response would increase wholesale and consumer prices still further.

Whereas a fall in the sterling exchange rate will increase inflation, a rise in the exchange rate will reduce it. There is, of course, another side to the picture. A high sterling exchange rate, although helping the fight against inflation, may adversely affect output and employment. United Kingdom producers may now find it more difficult to sell their goods and services, first, because competition from cheaper imports drives them out of home markets and, second, because UK exports become expensive on foreign markets. Much of the deindustrialization of the early 1980s was attributed to the high pound, and again in the period 1996–2007 (see Chapter 1).

The adherence of governments to a policy of high exchange rates has often been based on a belief that high exchange rates help fight inflation by making imports cheaper, and that on the export side reliance could be placed on the 'law of one price'. In other words, British manufacturers, seeing that they could not sell on world markets unless they observed world prices for their products, would restrain the rate of growth of labour costs, thereby raising exports and further contributing to the fight against inflation.

It will be useful to conclude this chapter by reviewing the various types of *exchange rate regime* which have operated over time, before considering the system under which the UK currently operates.

The gold standard system

As the nineteenth century progressed, and as world trade expanded, the use of gold as a means of international payment broadened to take in almost all the major trading countries. Although a few, such as the US, persisted for some time with silver, by about 1873 (with the passing of the Gold Standard Act in the US) a gold standard payments system could be said to be in effect. The 'price' of each major currency was fixed in terms of a *specific weight of gold*, which meant that the price of each currency was fixed in terms of every other currency, at a rate that could not be altered. The gold standard was therefore a system of *fixed exchange rates*. Any difficulties for the balance of payments had to be resolved by expanding or contracting the domestic economy. A rather stylized account of the adjustment mechanism will highlight the main features of the gold standard system.

Suppose a country moved into balance of payments surplus. Payment would be received in gold which, because domestic money supply was directly related to the gold stock, would raise money supply. This would expand the economy, raising domestic incomes, spending and prices. Higher incomes and prices would encourage imports and discourage exports, thereby helping to eliminate the initial payments surplus. In addition, the extra money supply would lead to a fall in its price (the rate of interest), encouraging capital outflows to other countries which had higher rates of interest – a minus sign in the accounts. A payments surplus would, in these ways, tend to be eliminated. For countries with payments deficits, gold outflow would reduce the gold stock and with it the domestic money supply. This would cause the domestic economy to contract, reducing incomes, spending and prices. Lower incomes and prices would discourage imports and encourage

exports. The reduction in money supply would also raise the price of money (interest rate), encouraging capital inflows – a plus sign in the accounts. Payment deficits would, therefore, also tend to be eliminated. This whole system came to be regarded as extremely sophisticated and self-regulating. Individual countries need only ensure (a) that gold could flow freely between countries, (b) that gold backed the domestic money supply, and (c) that the market was free to set interest rates. Of course, this meant that countries with payment surpluses would experience expanding domestic economies, and those with deficits contracting economies.

There seemed to be a general acceptance amongst the major trading nations that currency and payments stability took precedence over domestic production and employment. What was perhaps not realized was that the apparent 'success' of the system in the 40 years between 1873 and 1913 was largely due to the additional liquidity provided by sterling balances. The growing value of UK imports had led to an increase in the holding of sterling by overseas residents, who then used sterling to settle international debts.

If the supply of gold and other precious commodities could not keep pace with the expansion of world trade, the obvious alternative was to make use of 'paper'. In practice, of course, exporters would accept only paper and a 'paper' system could be used on a worldwide basis only when it fulfilled a number of useful criteria:

1 It had to be freely exchangeable on a global basis.
2 It had to be available in sufficient quantities.
3 It needed to be of a fixed value which did not depreciate rapidly.
4 Its value, ideally, needed to be guaranteed in terms of some other precious commodity such as gold.

The paper currency, in other words, had to be 'as good as gold'.

For a brief period in the late Victorian and early Edwardian eras sterling fulfilled the bulk of this role. Sterling continued to play a part in the funding of international debt in what was called the 'Sterling Area' well into the 1960s.

Although several attempts were made to revive the gold standard after the First World War, these largely failed. The dominance of the UK in world trade began to fade during this period, restricting the supply of sterling as a world currency. The Great

Depression of the late 1920s and early 1930s also encouraged many countries to adopt protectionist measures. In such an atmosphere countries became less willing to abide by the 'rules' of the gold standard. Gold flows were restricted, and money supply and interest rates were adjusted independently of gold flow to help domestic employment rather than international payments. Wages and prices became much more rigid as labour and product markets became less 'perfect', which further impeded the adjustment mechanism. For instance, any deflation that did still occur in deficit countries led *less often* to the reductions in factor and product price needed to restore price competitiveness. Countries began therefore to resort more and more to changes in the exchange rate to regain lost competitiveness.

This breakdown of the gold standard system during the inter-war period found no ready replacement. The result was a rather chaotic period of unstable exchange rates, inadequate world liquidity and protectionism. It was to seek a more ordered system of world trade and payments that the Allies met in Bretton Woods, in the US, even before the Second World War had ended. What emerged from that meeting was an entirely new system, under the auspices of the IMF.

The IMF system

The adjustable-peg exchange rate system

Imbalances in world trading patterns, and imperfections in world money markets have at least three implications:

1 That deficits and surpluses rarely self-correct, so that foreign exchange reserves are required to fund persistent payments deficits.

2 That although surpluses and deficits are supposed to balance as an accounting identity for the world as a whole, in practice surpluses are rarely recycled to debtor countries.

3 That even though in theory the world must be in overall balance, in practice there is a substantial imbalance. As far as these missing balances are concerned, the IMF reported in 1991 a global surplus of over $100bn. A number of factors may be involved: time-lags in reporting transactions, the non-recording of arrangements conducted through tax havens, and the problem of using an appropriate 'price' to evaluate trade deals when exchange rates fluctuate several times between initiation and completion.

In order to settle deficits, theory tells us that deficit countries should be able to run down their foreign exchange reserves, or to borrow from surplus countries. Both methods have, in reality, proved next to impossible. The countries most likely to suffer deficits are those with low per capita incomes and few foreign exchange reserves. They are also in consequence those with low credit ratings on the international banking circuit, making borrowing from surplus countries difficult. It was in order to solve just these sorts of liquidity problems for deficit countries that the IMF was established. As well as providing foreign currencies in times of need, its other major objective was to promote stability in exchange rates, following the uncertainties of the inter-war period.

Exchange rate stability

Under the IMF system, each country could, on joining, assign to itself an exchange rate. It did this by indicating the number of units of its currency it would trade for an ounce of gold, valued at $35. The dollar was therefore the common unit of all exchange rates. A country had a 'right' to change its initial exchange rate (par value) by up to 10%. For changes in par value which, when cumulated, came to more than 10%, the permission of the IMF was required. The IMF would give such permission only if the member could demonstrate that its payments were in 'fundamental disequilibrium'. Since this term was never clearly defined in the Articles of the IMF, any substantial payments imbalance would usually qualify. A rise in par became known as a revaluation; a fall in par, devaluation. As well as changing par value, a member could permit its exchange rate to move in any one year ±1% of par, but no more. Because the IMF system sought stable, but not totally fixed, exchange rates, it became known as the 'adjustable peg' exchange rate system.

The IMF also introduced – in 1961 – the idea of 'currency swaps' by which a country in need of specific foreign exchange could avoid the obvious disadvantages of having to purchase it with its own currency by simply agreeing to 'swap' a certain amount through the Bank of International Settlements. The swap contract would state a rate of exchange which would also apply to the 'repayment' at the end of the contract.

Changes in exchange rate were a means by which deficits or surpluses could be adjusted. For instance, a devaluation would lower the foreign price of exports and raise the domestic price of imports. The IMF system has, however, been criticized in its actual operation for permitting too little flexibility in exchange rates. Between 1947 and 1971 only six adjustments took place: devaluations of the French franc (1958 and 1969) and sterling (1949 and 1967), and revaluations of the DM (1961 and 1969). It is true, of course, that adjustments of exchange rates are subject to an extremely fine balance: too many adjustments and the system loses stability and confidence; too few and the system generates internal tensions of unemployment and/or lower real incomes which may eventually destroy it.

By 1971, continuing US deficits (the expense of the Vietnam War was a major contributory factor), paid in part with US dollars, had led to an overabundance of dollars in the world system. Under the IMF rules all dollars could be converted into gold at $35 per ounce, and as confidence in the dollar declined, US gold stocks came under increasing strain. Although the US, even in 1971, still accounted for 30% of world gold reserves and 15% of total world reserves (gold, foreign currencies and the specially created IMF 'currency', namely Special Drawing Rights), the enormous payments deficits of 1970 and 1971 ($11bn and $30bn respectively) imposed tremendous pressure on its gold and foreign currency reserves. President Nixon announced in August 1971 that the US dollar would no longer be convertible into gold.

The scrapping of dollar convertibility into gold at a *fixed price* caused a crisis in the IMF exchange rate system, which had been founded on that very principle.[3] This was followed by two increases in the 'official price' of gold – in 1971 to $38 per ounce, and in 1973 to $42.22 per ounce – together with revaluations of other currencies against the dollar, and increases in the width of the permitted band within which currencies were allowed to drift from ±1% to ±2.25%. None of these had any lasting effect, however, as first sterling (in 1972) and then the dollar (in 1973) began to float freely against other currencies. By 1976 almost all IMF members had adopted some type of floating exchange rate system. The IMF meeting of that year in Jamaica officially recognized this new situation.

The floating exchange rate system

According to basic economic theory, a system of freely floating exchange rates should be self-regulating. If the cause of a UK deficit were, say, extra imports from the US, then the pound should fall (depreciate) against the dollar. This would result from UK importers *selling* extra pounds sterling on the foreign exchange markets to buy US dollars to pay for those imports. In simple demand/supply analysis, the extra supply of pounds sterling will lower their 'price', i.e. the sterling exchange rate. As we have already seen, provided the Marshall–Lerner elasticity conditions are fulfilled (price-elasticity of demand for UK exports and imports together greater than one), then the lower-priced exports and higher-priced imports will contribute to an improvement in the balance of payments, perhaps after a short time-lag.

As it has developed since 1973, however, the system has not been one of 'freely floating' rates. Instead, governments have tended to intervene from time to time to support the values of their currencies (see Fig. 25.1). For instance, the UK has intervened in recent times to prevent the pound falling when cheap imports were part of its anti-inflationary strategy. The setting, for internal reasons, of particular 'targets' for the exchange rate has therefore resulted in a system of 'managed' exchange rates, picturesquely described as a 'dirty floating system'. The major advantages and disadvantages of fixed versus floating exchange rates are shown in Table 25.3.

Sterling and the ERM

In the last 60 years we have moved, as we have noted, from a fixed to a floating exchange rate regime. With the advent of world inflation in the 1970s it became impossible to maintain fixed exchange rate

Table 25.3 Fixed versus floating exchange rates: pros and cons.

Fixed	Floating
Advantages	*Advantages*
1 Exchange rate stability provides a realistic basis for expectations	1 Automatic eradication of imbalances
2 Stability encourages increased trade	2 Reduced need for reserves – in theory, no need at all
3 Reduced danger from international currency speculation	3 Relative freedom for internal economic policy
4 Imposes increased discipline on internal economic policy	4 Exchange rates change in relatively smooth steps
5 Domestic price stability not endangered through import prices	5 May reduce speculation (rates move freely up or down)
Disadvantages	*Disadvantages*
1 Requires large reserves	1 Increased uncertainty for traders
2 Internal economic policy largely dictated by external factors	2 Domestic price stability may be endangered by rising import prices
3 No automatic adjustment – danger of large changes in rates	3 May increase speculation through coordinated buying or selling

parities between countries because internal prices were accelerating at different rates. As world inflation subsided in the 1980s floating exchange rates became less necessary: in addition, the increased volatility of currencies led the major countries to seek some form of greater stability. The countries of the European Community had a particular problem in that it was clearly not possible to create a unified market without fixed parities.

While it has not proved possible to implement any form of fixed exchange rate regime for countries as a whole, the European economies operated an ERM in the period 1979–1999 (see Chapter 27). This pegged currencies to the central unit, known as the 'ecu', within a permitted band of divergence. The value of the 'ecu' was based on a weighted average of the participating currencies. The ERM of the European Monetary System can now be seen to have been an intermediate step towards the European Monetary Union (EMU) which began its transition phase on 1 January 1999 with the launch of the euro (see Chapter 27).

The UK did not join the ERM when it was established in 1979, as it was feared that sterling would

not be able to maintain its position within the system. After that, when sterling rose as a result of the advent of North Sea oil, it seemed inappropriate to join an exchange rate system where the dominant currency, the mark, was a non-oil currency. After 1987, when the UK signed the Single European Act designed to create the single market by 1993, the question of joining the ERM again became a live issue. In fact, before the then Chancellor, Nigel Lawson, resigned in 1989 it was clear that he was attempting to target the value of sterling at DM3 = £1. However, the UK government expressed a reluctance to join until various conditions were fulfilled. Behind what were clearly political arguments and bargaining positions lay a very real apprehension about the problems which the UK might face on entry. In particular, there was the fear of losing the use of a policy instrument, namely the exchange rate, which might then make it more difficult to use depreciation/devaluation to remedy any trade imbalances with individual countries or the rest of the world. A full discussion of the UK's entry into, and exit from, the ERM can be found in Chapter 27, and more detail on the operation of EMU can also be found in the chapter.

Key points

- The exchange rate is usually quoted as the number of units of the domestic currency that are needed to purchase one unit of a foreign currency.

- Some 66% of transactions in London, the largest centre for foreign exchange trading, are 'spot' on any one day, 24% are forward for periods less than one month and a further 10% forward for periods greater than one month.

- The exchange rate is a key 'price', affecting the competitiveness of a country's exporters and producers of import substitutes.

- A fall (depreciation) in an exchange rate will, other things being equal, make that country's exports cheaper abroad and imports into that country dearer at home.

- The Marshall–Lerner elasticity conditions must be fulfilled if a fall in the exchange rate is to improve the balance of payments. Namely the *sum* of the price

- elasticities of demand for exports and imports must be greater than one.

- Because short-term elasticities are lower than long-term elasticities, the initial one to two years after a depreciation may *not* lead to an improvement in the balance of payments (the so-called 'J-curve' effect).

- The *effective exchange rate* (EER) for sterling is a weighted average of the six national currencies which are most important in terms of trade with the UK.

- The *real exchange rate* (RER) takes account of the nominal exchange rates between the various countries *and* of the relative inflation rates in those countries.

- There is increasing concern that exchange rate manipulation is becoming a policy mechanism to achieve balance of payments targets.

- There is considerable evidence to suggest that some exchange rates are undervalued and others overvalued.

Now try the self-check questions for this chapter on the Companion Website. You will also find useful links to relevant websites.

Notes

1 This analysis assumes that the elasticity of demand for imports is greater than one. In the case of exports, foreign buyers will demand more pounds whatever the elasticity of demand, simply because they are buying more goods as the price in their own currency falls, and the sterling price of exports has not changed.

2 The RNULC are calculated by taking indices of labour costs in the UK and dividing by the weighted geometric average of competitors'

unit labour costs. 'Normalization' involves adjusting the basic indices to allow for short-run variations in productivity – so eliminating cyclical variations.

3 During the exchange rate crisis of September 1992, three countries reintroduced exchange controls aimed at reducing the capacity of international banks to borrow in their money markets and then sell the currency for speculative gain. Portugal permitted only between half and

one-third of escudos in Lisbon's money markets physically to be used for currency speculation. Spain demanded that the banks deposit funds interest free for a year to match the amount they plan to sell for foreign exchange. Ireland insisted that the government now take over the management of currency swaps, with the exception of those that are trade related.

References and further reading

Bank of England (2010) *Statistics Interactive Database*, London.

Bénassy-Quéré, A. and Coeuré, B. (2010) *Economic Policy*, New York, Oxford University Press.

Buxton, T. and Lintner, V. (1998) Cost competitiveness, the ERM and UK economic policy, in Buxton, T., Chapman, P. and Temple, P. (eds), *Britain's Economic Performance* (2nd edn), London, Routledge.

Copeland, L. (2008) *Exchange Rates and International Finance* (5th edn), Harlow, Pearson Education.

Giavazzi, F. and Blanchard, O. (2010) *Macroeconomics: A European Perspective*, Harlow, Financial Times/Prentice Hall.

Goodman, S. (2002) The euro and progress on enlargement, *British Economy Survey*, 31(2): 31–4.

Jones, R. (2002) The Argentinian crisis – a case study in exchange rate inflexibility and national bankruptcy, *British Economy Survey*, 31(2): 35–8.

Kitson, M. and Michie, J. (1994) Fixed exchange rates and deflation: the ERM and the Gold Standard, *Economics and Business Education*, 2(Spring): 11–16.

Krugman, P. and Obstfeld, M. (2010), *International Economics: Theory and Policy*, Harlow, Financial Times/Prentice Hall.

Mercier, P. and Papadia, F. (2011) *The Concrete Euro: Implementing Monetary Policy in the Euro Area*, Oxford, Oxford University Press.

ONS (2010) *UK Balance of Payments – The Pink Book, Various*, London, Office for National Statistics.

Sutherland, A. (1998) Why are exchange rates so important?, *Economic Review*, 16(2).

The Economist (2010) The Big Mac Index. An indigestible problem. Why China needs more expensive burgers, 14 October.

Turner, P. (1997) Britain and the European Monetary System, *Economic Review*, 14(3).

UNDP (2010) *Human Development Report 2010: The Real Wealth of Nations: Pathways to Human Development*, New York, United Nations Development Programme.

UNCTAD (2010) *World Investment Report 2010: Investing in a Low Carbon Economy*, New York and Geneva, United Nations Conference on Trade and Development.

Wolf, M. (2010) Balance of payments, foreign exchange reserves and currency implications, *Financial Times*, 3 November.

World Bank (2010) *World Development Report 2010: Development and Climate Change*, Washington DC.

The following websites are relevant to this chapter:

ONS Economic Trends: http://www.statistics.gov.uk/statbase/product.asp?vlnk=308

ONS Financial Statistics: http://www.statistics.gov.uk/statbase/product.asp?vlnk=376

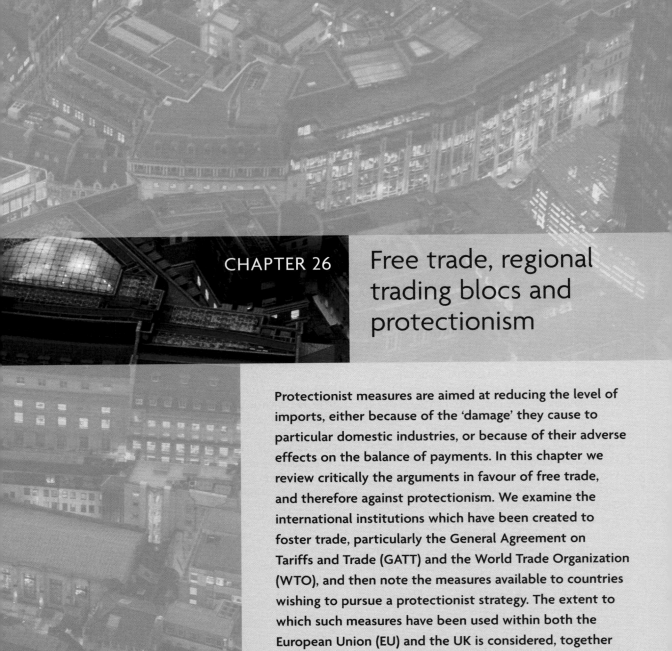

CHAPTER 26

Free trade, regional trading blocs and protectionism

Protectionist measures are aimed at reducing the level of imports, either because of the 'damage' they cause to particular domestic industries, or because of their adverse effects on the balance of payments. In this chapter we review critically the arguments in favour of free trade, and therefore against protectionism. We examine the international institutions which have been created to foster trade, particularly the General Agreement on Tariffs and Trade (GATT) and the World Trade Organization (WTO), and then note the measures available to countries wishing to pursue a protectionist strategy. The extent to which such measures have been used within both the European Union (EU) and the UK is considered, together with their alleged benefits and costs. We also consider the shift in trading patterns towards regional blocs and assess the implications of this development.

Free trade

Free trade was given impetus by 'The Theory of Comparative Advantage', outlined by Ricardo in the nineteenth century. Essentially, Ricardo sought to extend Adam Smith's principle of the division of labour to a global scale, with each country specializing in those goods which it could produce most efficiently. Even if one country was more efficient than another country in the production of all goods, Ricardo showed that it could still gain by specializing in those goods in which its *relative efficiency* was greatest. It was said to have a *comparative* advantage in such goods. This would raise total world output above the level it would otherwise be, with the benefits shared via trade between the two countries. The degree of benefit to any one country after specialization and trade would depend upon the terms of trade, i.e. the ratio of export to import prices.

The use of protectionist measures, such as tariffs, may distort the comparative cost ratios, by raising import prices and encouraging the domestic production of goods that could otherwise have been imported rather more cheaply. In addition to disrupting the efficient allocation of *domestic* resources, such protectionist measures are likely to reduce international specialization and to lead to a less efficient allocation of *world* resources.

Figure 26.1 shows that free trade could, in theory, bring welfare benefits to an economy previously protected. Suppose the industry is initially *completely protected*. The price P_D will then be determined by the interaction of domestic supply (S–S_H) and domestic demand (D–D_H). The government now decides to remove these barriers and to allow foreign competition. For simplicity, we assume a perfectly elastic 'world' supply curve P_W–C, giving a total supply curve (domestic and world) of SAC. Domestic price will then be forced down to the world level, P_W, with domestic demand being $0Q_3$ at this price. To meet this domestic demand, $0Q_2$ will be supplied from domestic sources, with Q_2Q_3 supplied from the rest of the world (i.e. imported). The consumer surplus, which is the difference between what consumers are *prepared* to pay and what they *have* to pay, has risen from DBP_D to DCP_W. The producer surplus, which is the difference between the price the producer receives and the minimum necessary to induce production, has fallen from P_DBS to P_WAS. The gain in consumer

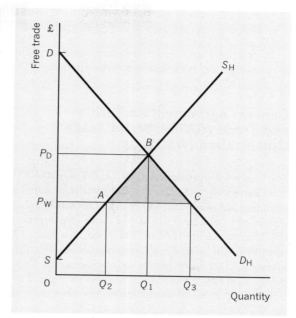

Fig. 26.1 Free trade versus no trade.

surplus outweighs the loss in producer surplus by the area *ABC*, which could then be regarded as the net gain in economic welfare as a result of free trade replacing protectionism.

Critics of free trade suggest that a number of drawbacks may outweigh the net gain shown above:

- The theory is based on a 'full employment' model and fails to appreciate the problems raised by chronic unemployment. For instance, in Fig. 26.1 if domestic supply falls from $0Q_1$ to $0Q_2$ as a result of the removal of tariffs, then the reduced output may lead to unemployment. The welfare loss associated with this may more than offset the net welfare gain (area *ABC*) noted above.

- It fails to analyse how the gains that arise from trade will be distributed. In practice, the stronger economies, through their economic power, have often been able to extract the greater benefits.

- It assumes a purely competitive model of industry. If, in fact, industry includes both large and small firms, then area *ABC* may not represent net gain. For instance, a higher proportion of the remaining domestic output $0Q_2$ in Fig. 26.1 may now be in the hands of a monopoly. This growth in importance of monopoly could be construed as a welfare loss to be set against the area of net gain, *ABC*.

In practice a number of organizations have tried to encourage free trade in the post-war period.

General Agreement on Tariffs and Trade (GATT)/World Trade Organization (WTO)

The General Agreement on Tariffs and Trade (GATT) was signed in 1947 by 23 industrialized nations including the US, Canada, France and the Benelux countries. Its successor, the World Trade Organization (WTO), was established in 1995 and now has 153 members. China was the latest high-profile recruit, joining in 2001, although the newest member is Cape Verde. WTO members in total account for more than 97% of the value of world trade. The objectives of the WTO are essentially the same as GATT's: that is, to reduce tariffs and other barriers to trade and to eliminate discrimination in trade. But the WTO is much more than GATT. Although the latter still provides the principal rulebook for trade in goods, the WTO has broadened out the agreement to also include services (the General Agreement on Trade in Services) and intellectual property such as copyright, trademarks and patents (the Agreement on Trade Related Aspects of Intellectual Property, also known as TRIPS).

Since the GATT was signed there have been eight rounds of negotiations paving the way for considerable cuts in the level of tariffs being applied. In 1947 the average tariff in the industrialized world stood at some 40%, but the figure has now dropped in 2010 to around 5%. The 'Kennedy round' of negotiations in the 1960s was particularly effective, cutting tariffs by around one-third. The 'Tokyo round' in the latter part of the 1970s resulted in further reductions of a similar magnitude.

An important series of multilateral negotiations, known as the Uruguay round, was completed in December 1993. This proved to be a particularly complex and ambitious round of negotiations. It consisted of 28 accords designed to extend fair trade rules to agriculture, services, textiles, intellectual property rights and foreign investment. It was agreed to make further cuts in tariffs on industrial products, to eliminate tariffs entirely in 11 sectors and to substantially reduce the level of farm subsidies. Non-tariff barriers were to be converted into the more viable tariff barriers (Greenaway 1994). Significantly, the most recent series of negotiations, known as the Doha round, begun in 2001 has proved to be even more protracted than the Uruguay round and yet to reach any sort of agreement. A key issue is the vexed subject of agricultural liberalization, with neither the US nor the EU willing to make sufficient concessions in terms of the removal of subsidies to their farmers. We will return to this subject later. In addition, middle-income countries such as Brazil and India are proving reluctant to open their markets for industrial goods until in return there is more on offer from the richer countries.

GATT itself, the accord on services and intellectual property and the codes on government procurement and anti-dumping have now been placed under the umbrella of the WTO. Trade disputes between member states are settled in this arena by a streamlined disputes procedure with the provision for appeals and binding arbitration. Since its creation in January 1995, more than half the cases brought before the WTO have involved the US and the EU, whilst around one-quarter have involved developing countries. Trade disputes which go to arbitration still tend to be fairly lengthy affairs, as can be seen from the case of the importation of polyethylene retail bags from Thailand into the US. Although the complaint was lodged by Thailand in November 2008, it was not until March 2010 that the US informed the WTO that it would implement the recommendations of the body. Moreover, it took a further six-month period before it actually began to do so, meaning all in all, close to two years from start to finish.

Although the aim of the WTO is to reduce tariff barriers, there are a number of circumstances in which a country will be allowed to maintain such barriers. Article 6 of the original GATT permits retaliatory sanctions if 'dumping' can be proven. Article 18 also provides a number of 'escape clauses' for the newly industrializing economies, allowing some protection of both infant industries and of their balance of payments. Article 19 permits any country to abstain from a general tariff cut in situations where rising imports may seriously damage domestic production. Articles 21–25 are concerned with the protection of the national interest, permitting restrictions to be placed on imported products which might affect the nation's security.

Aside from tariff cuts, the WTO/GATT has made efforts to eliminate discrimination in trade by use of the 'most-favoured nation' (MFN) principle. This means that each member country has to treat each of its fellow members equally; any trading advantage granted by one country to another must be accorded to all other member states. The MFN clause is so important that it was actually the first article of the original GATT. It has also been incorporated in the GATS (Article 2) and the TRIPS (Article 4). Some exceptions are allowed from MFN, for example when a free trade area has been established by a specific group of countries. In general, however, the MFN means that no discrimination is permitted in trade relations.

One indication that there is growing understanding of the benefits of free trade is the sharp drop in the number disputes coming before the WTO. In total, WTO members initiated an average of 41 new disputes per year during 1995 to 2000, but this falls to an average of just half this total between 2001 and 2009. The drop is almost entirely due to the US and EU launching fewer cases. Developing countries' use of the disputes process has been steadier and provides some evidence of their commitment to the multilateral rules-based WTO system.

Trade and the world economy

The rapid growth of world trade over the past 100 years or so reflects the fact that nations have become more interrelated as they have attempted to gain the benefits of freer trade. One way of measuring this increasing integration is to compare the *relative growth* of world trade and world output, as seen in Table 26.1.

Table 26.1 shows that the growth rate of world merchandise exports (Trade) has exceeded the growth of world output (GDP) in five of the six periods, clearly suggesting an acceleration of global integration through trade. The only exception to this pattern occurred during 1913–50 when two world wars and a major world depression led to economic depression and the emergence of protectionist trade policies. The post-Second World War period (1950–73) saw an unprecedented growth of world trade which far outstripped the growth of world production. This period of freer trade reflected the desire to reduce the high protective tariffs introduced during the inter-war period as a means of increasing post-war prosperity for all countries. The founding of the GATT in 1947 was a positive step in this direction. Since 1991 it is significant that a more profound move towards globalization of the world economy has seen a further acceleration in the average growth rate of exports. In this regard, it is noteworthy that developing and newly industrializing countries have achieved the fastest expansion of trade. With an average annual rise of close to 10%, their share of world trade has increased from 24 to 40%.

It may be useful to enquire at this stage whether the expanding role of world trade seen in Table 26.1 was accompanied by an increase in the share of that trade conducted on a *regional* basis. It would seem natural that nations would tend to trade more with their immediate neighbours in the first instance, thereby raising the share of world trade occurring between nations within a specific geographical region. This tendency towards *intra-regional* trade can be seen in Table 26.2.

From Table 26.2 it can be seen that the share of intra-regional trade grew most rapidly in Western Europe between 1948 and 1996. However, between 1996 and 2004, North America saw the most rapid growth in intra-regional trade. In the most recent period, it is the Middle East and Latin America that have enjoyed the biggest gains in intra-regional trade. It is also clear from Table 26.2 that intra-regional

Table 26.1 Growth in world GDP and merchandise trade, 1870–2009 (average annual % change).

	1870–1900	1900–13	1913–50	1950–73	1973–1990	1991–2009
GDP	2.9	2.5	2.0	5.1	3.0	2.0
Trade	3.8	4.3	0.6	8.2	4.0	5.0

Sources: WTO, *International Trade: Trends and Statistics*, various; WTO (2010a) *Annual Report*, and previous editions.

Table 26.2 Shares of intra-regional trade in total trade, 1928–2009 (% of each region's total trade in goods occurring between nations located in that region).

	1928	1938	1948	1968	1979	1996	2004	2009
Western Europe	50.7	48.8	41.8	63.0	66.2	68.3	73.8	72.2
CIS							20.7	19.2
North America	25.0	22.4	27.1	36.8	29.9	36.0	56.0	48.0
Latin America	11.1	17.7	17.7	18.7	20.2	21.2	23.2	26.1
Asia	45.5	66.4	38.9	36.6	41.0	51.9	50.3	51.6
Africa	10.3	8.8	8.4	9.1	5.6	9.2	9.9	11.7
Middle East	5.0	3.6	20.3	8.7	6.4	7.4	5.6	15.5

Source: WTO (2010a) *Annual Report*, and previous editions.

trading is not a new phenomenon and that geographically adjacent nations in many areas of the world have been trading with each other for many decades.

Regional trading arrangements (RTAs)

As we have noted above, the resumption of rapid growth in world trade after the Second World War was tied up with the desire for the resumption of *multilateral trade* under the auspices of the GATT. However, this movement towards free trade was accompanied by a parallel movement towards the formation of *regional trading blocs* centred on the EU, North and South America, and East Asia. We noted in Table 26.2 that intra-regional trading is not a new phenomenon and has been active for at least a century or more. However, what is new involves the fact that the nations of a given region have begun to create more *formal* and comprehensive trading and economic links with each other. By 2010 there were more than 280 RTAs in force, many of which had been established over the previous decade.

There are four types of regional trading arrangements:

1 *free trade areas*, where member countries reduce or abolish restrictions on trade between each other while maintaining their individual protectionist measures against non-members;

2 *customs unions*, where, as well as liberalizing trade amongst members, a common external tariff is established to protect the group from imports from any non-members;

3 *common markets*, where the customs union is extended to movements of factors of production as well as products;

4 *economic union*, where national economic policies are also harmonized within the common market.

Three features have characterized post-war regional integration.

1 Regional integration has been primarily centred in Western Europe. More than half of all the RTAs established have involved West European countries, with many of the more recent agreements with the EU involving the Central and Eastern European countries.

2 Only a relatively small number of regional agreements have been concluded by developing countries although this is now changing. This is mainly due to continuing competition between these countries involving trade in similar products (e.g. primary products) together with the difficulty of achieving the political stability in some developing countries which is so vital to trade.

3 The *type* of economic integration between the parties to agreements has varied quite significantly. Most of the notifications made to GATT have involved free trade areas, with the number of customs unions agreement being much smaller.

Table 26.3 provides examples of different types of regional trading arrangements across the globe. For example, the most advanced form of trading bloc is the EU which originated as a customs union but moved towards the common market type of

Table 26.3 Regional Trading Arrangements (RTAs): intra-regional export shares (%).

	1990	1995	2004	2009
NAFTA	42.6	46.1	56.0	47.9
EU	64.9	64.0	68.5	66.7
MERCOSUR	8.9	20.5	12.5	15.2
ASEAN	20.1	25.5	25.0	24.8
ANDEAN	4.2	12.2	7.7	7.7

Source: WTO (2010b) *International Trade Statistics*.

largest RTA in geographic terms, with some 19 members. It is a free trade area which was established in the mid-1990s, has eliminated customs tariffs and is working on the elimination of quantitative restrictions and other non-tariff barriers. In central and eastern Europe, a free trade area was established in the early 1990s (CEFTA), although the three founding members, Poland, Hungary and Czechoslovakia (now the Czech Republic and Slovakia), have since left to join the EU. The remaining members are Albania, Bosnia and Herzegovina, Croatia, Macedonia, Moldova, Montenegro and UKMIK/Kosovo.

From the above examples it is possible to see that trading blocs have adopted various types of arrangements depending on their specific circumstances. Table 26.3 shows the share of *intra-regional exports* of each specific bloc as a percentage of the total exports of that bloc. For example, in 2009 the exports of EU members *to each other* comprised around two-thirds of total EU exports. A significant shift towards intra-regional exports took place in Europe, North and Central America, and Asia between 1960 and 1970, but since that time the tend has moderated.

The completion of the Uruguay round in December 1993 served as a step forward in the cause of *multilateral trade*. However, frustration with the slow progress of the Doha round, and increasing frictions over the level of currencies (fuelled by a depreciating dollar and the renminbi peg), have reinforced concerns that regional trading blocs may begin to look inwards and behave more like 'regional fortresses'. Thus, the trading blocs we have been discussing above have begun to be seen as initiators of a 'new regionalism', leading to potential problems for *inter-bloc* trade. Those who favour the regional approach argue that the setting up of trading blocs can enable individual countries to purchase products at lower prices because tariff walls between the member countries have been removed; this is the *trade creation effect*. They also argue that regional trading arrangements help to harmonize tax policies and product standards, while also helping to reduce political conflicts. Others argue that where the world is already organized into trading blocs, negotiations in favour of free trade are more likely to be successful between, say, three large and influential trading blocs than between a large number of individual countries with little power to bargain successfully for tariff reductions.

arrangement in the 1990s, the majority of members effectively progressing into a type of economic union with the advent of the euro and its related financial arrangements on 1 January 1999. At the start of 2010 the EU consisted of 27 nations with a combined population of over 490 million and accounted for about 38% of world trade. In August 1993 the North American Free Trade Agreement (NAFTA) was signed between the US, Canada and Mexico, having grown out of an earlier Canadian–US Free Trade Agreement (CUFTA). NAFTA, as the name implies, is a free trade arrangement covering a population of 372 million and accounting for around 20% of world trade.

MERCOSUR was established in South America in 1991, evolving out of the Latin American Free Trade Area, the four initial members being Argentina, Brazil, Paraguay and Uruguay. It developed into a partial customs union in 1995 when it imposed a common external tariff covering 85% of total products imported.

In Asia and the Pacific, the rather 'loose' Association of South East Asian Nations (ASEAN) with a population of 300 million was formed in August 1967. In 1991 they agreed to form an ASEAN Free Trade Area (AFTA) by the year 2003. A Common External Preference Tariff (CEPT) came into force in 1994 as a formal tariff-cutting mechanism for achieving free trade in all goods except agricultural products, natural resources and services. One of the latest arrangements initiated covers ASEAN, Australia and New Zealand. This came into force at the start of 2010 and has the explicit goal of liberalizing and facilitating trade within the area.

RTAs have also featured in trade liberalization in Africa over the past decade. The Common Market for Eastern and Southern Africa (COMESA) is the

On the other hand, the critics of regionalism warn that regional trading blocs have, historically, tended to be inward looking, as in the 1930s when discriminatory trade blocs were formed to impose tariffs on non-members. Some also argue that member countries may suffer from being inside a regional bloc because they then have to buy products from *within* the bloc, when cheaper sources are often available from outside, i.e. the *trade diversion effect*. Further, it is argued that regionalism threatens to erode support for multilateralism in that business groups *within* a regional bloc will find it easier to obtain protectionist (trade diversionary) deals via preferential pacts than they would in the world of non-discriminatory trade practices favoured by GATT. Finally, it is argued that regionalism will move the world away from free trade due to the increasing tendency for members of a regional group to resort to the use of *non-tariff barriers* (VERs, anti-dumping duties, etc.) when experiencing a surge of imports from other countries *inside* the group. Such devices, all part of the new protectionism, can then easily be used by individual countries against non-members from other regional groups.

Many studies have been made as to the trade and welfare effects of such regional blocs both on 'internal' participants and on countries outside the bloc.

- Analyses of the customs union formed between the original six members of the European Community (EC) have shown that trade creation exceeded trade diversion in the case of manufactures (Lloyd 1992; Srinivasan *et al.* 1993), but that the reverse was true in the case of trade in agricultural products – leaving the overall effect unclear.

- Studies of EFTA suggest that trade creation just outweighed trade diversion (Lloyd 1992).

- Studies for CUFTA suggest positive benefits for Canada but negligible benefits for the US, while trade with third countries declined (Primo Braga *et al.* 1994).

- For NAFTA, estimates indicate some net trade creation with small trade effects for third countries (Reinert *et al.* 1994).

- Research by Prusa and Teh in 2010 shows anti-dumping cases within RTAs have dropped by between 33 and 55%. However, they found that there has been a 10–30% increase in the number of anti-dumping actions over the same period against countries that are not part of the trading bloc.

The various studies noted above can only give a general idea of the net effects as they do not measure accurately the potential stimulus to third countries resulting from any higher rate of economic growth in the bloc being studied.

What then can be done to make sure that regionalism and multilateralism (general free trade) can coexist? First, it has been suggested that article 24 of GATT which sets the rules for regional arrangements could be modified to allow only customs unions (i.e. regions which require a common external tariff) and to prohibit free trade areas which allow countries to retain a variety of national tariffs against other countries. If this were done, the more liberal members of the region would then be able to force down the overall regional tariff level, which could then be 'locked in' under GATT rules and prevented from being subsequently raised. Second, in order to fight the 'new protectionism', GATT articles 6 (anti-dumping) and 19 (VER) could be strengthened to minimize the use of non-tariff barriers against countries outside the regional arrangement (IMF 1993).

Protectionism

Methods of protection

There are a number of methods which individual countries or regional trading blocs can use to restrict the level of imports into the home market.

Tariff

A tariff is, in effect, a tax levied on imported goods, usually with the intention of raising the price of imports and thereby discouraging their purchase. Additionally, it is a source of revenue for the government. Tariffs can be of two types: lump sum, or specific, with the tariff a fixed amount per unit; and *ad valorem*, or percentage, with the tariff a variable amount per unit.

To examine the effect of a tariff, it helps to simplify Fig. 26.2 if we again assume a perfectly elastic world supply of the good S_W at the going world price P_W, which implies that any amount of the good can be imported into the UK without there being a change in the world price. In the absence of a tariff the domestic price would be set by the world price, P_W in

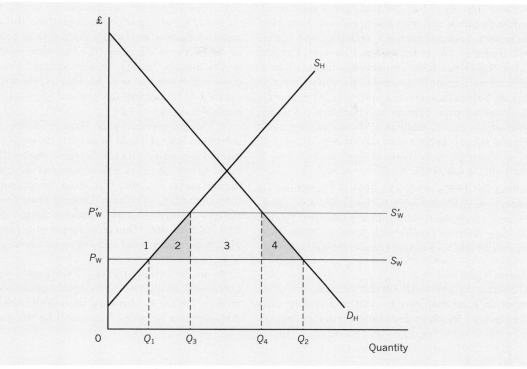

Fig. 26.2 The effect of a tariff.

Fig. 26.2. At this price, domestic demand D_H will be $0Q_2$ though domestic supply S_H will be only $0Q_1$. The excess demand, $Q_2 - Q_1$, will be satisfied by importing the good.

If the government now decides to restrict the level of import penetration, it could impose a tariff of, say, $P_W - P'_W$. A tariff always shifts a supply curve vertically upwards by the amount of the tariff, so that in this case the world supply curve shifts vertically upwards from S_W to S'_W. This would raise the domestic price to S'_W which is above the world price P_W. This higher price will reduce the domestic demand for the good to $0Q_4$, whilst simultaneously encouraging domestic supply to expand to $0Q_3$. Imports will be reduced to $Q_4 - Q_3$. Domestic consumer surplus will decline as a result of the tariff by the area $1 + 2 + 3 + 4$, though domestic producer surplus will rise by area 1, and the government will gain tax revenue of $(P'_W - P_W) + (Q_4 - Q_3)$ (i.e. area 3). These gains would be inadequate to compensate consumers for their loss in welfare, yielding a net welfare loss of area $2 + 4$ as a result of imposing a tariff.

The UK was extensively protected by tariffs until the 1850s. These were progressively dismantled in an era of free trade that lasted until the First World War. The first significant reintroduction of tariffs occurred in 1915 with the 'McKenna duties', a 33.3% *ad valorem* tax on luxuries such as motor cars, watches, clocks, etc. They were designed to discourage unnecessary imports in order to save foreign exchange, and thereby free shipping space for the war effort. In 1921, the Safeguarding of Industry Act extended protection to key industries. This was followed in 1932 by the Import Duties Act, which provided a comprehensive range of protection; a 20% *ad valorem* duty on manufactured goods in general, but 33.3% on articles such as bicycles and chemicals, and 15% on certain industrial raw materials and semi-manufactures.

Since the Second World War, the UK, along with others, has moved away from the protectionist doctrine of the inter-war period. We have already seen that considerable reductions in tariffs took place under the auspices of GATT. However, for the UK, entrance into the EU in 1973 has had a dual effect. Although tariffs on industrial products have been eliminated between member countries, permitting free trade, at the same time a Common External Tariff (CET) has been imposed on industrial trade with all non-member countries, with import tariffs varying by product. For example, whilst the *average* tariff on industrial imports into the EU is 3.5%, the tariff on shoes is as high as 17%. In contrast, most mineral imports carry a zero rate of duty.

Non-tariff barriers

During the 1990s many quantitative restrictions on trade were gradually replaced by tariffs. Exceptions do, however, remain with significant non-tariff barriers affecting trade in textiles and clothing. There are a number of different types of non-tariff barriers.

Quotas

A quota is a physical limit on the amount of an imported good that may be sold in a country in a given period. Its effects are examined in Fig. 26.3. As in the case of a tariff, we assume for simplicity that the world supply curve is perfectly elastic at P_W. Once again, if there is free trade, the domestic price will be set by the world price, P_W. Domestic production would initially be $0Q_1$ though demand would be considerably higher at $0Q_2$. This excess would be satisfied by importing the amount $Q_2 - Q_1$ of the particular good.

If the government were now to decide that it wanted to limit the level of imports to, say, $Q_3 - Q_1$, it could impose a quota to this effect. The total supply curve to the UK market now becomes the domestic supply curve, S_H, plus the fixed quota permitted from abroad, Q. The new domestic price rises from P_W to P'_W which in turn reduces domestic demand from $0Q_2$ to $0Q_5$. Domestic supply will expand to $0Q_4$, with imports reduced to the quota level $Q_3 - Q_1$ $(= Q_5 - Q_4)$.

As in the case of the tariff, the imposition of a quota will involve a loss in consumer surplus (i.e. area $1 + 2 + 3 + 4$). However, in contrast to the tariff, the only area of welfare gain will be the producer

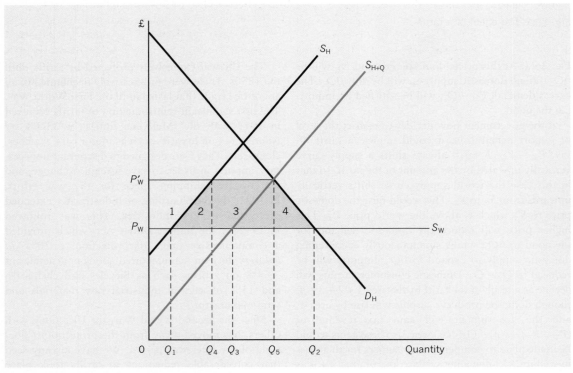

Fig. 26.3 The effect of a quota.

surplus of area 1, since the government receives no increase in tax revenue from the quota. This leaves area 2 + 3 + 4 as the net loss of economic welfare. For *any given price rise*, the welfare loss is then greater for a quota than for a tariff.[1] Import quotas are still used on a whole range of products. They may be applied either unilaterally or as a result of negotiated agreements between the two parties. For instance, the EU has the authority to negotiate quota agreements on behalf of member states, including the UK, and does so on a whole range of products.

One of the most significant quota arrangements, which has now been phased out, was the Multi-Fibre Agreement (MFA). This came into effect in 1974 and controlled the import of textiles from the newly industrialized countries. A major aim of the MFA was to provide greater scope for newly industrialized countries to increase their share of world trade in textile products whilst at the same time maintaining some stability for textile production in the developed economies. The MFA was phased out at the beginning of 2005, but one of the interesting consequences of this was that some of the exporters of textiles suffered in the wake of this development. Lesotho, Swaziland and Madagascar all found themselves unprepared for a more competitive environment. Textile exports fell by almost one-fifth over the following two years as companies based elsewhere were no longer restricted by quotas.

An UNCTAD study (World Bank 1986) concluded that the complete liberalization of trade barriers would bring substantial benefits for developing countries. It was suggested that their total export of clothing would rise by around 135% while textile exports could grow by some 80%. A number of more recent analyses carried out by the World Bank have put the potential gains at an even greater level. These figures seem to indicate quite clearly that the export quotas work against the interest of the *producers* rather than the *consumers*. But there is an argument that the developing countries actually benefited through the MFA arrangement. This is because, it is asserted, they received what may be termed *quota rents*, i.e. higher prices than would be guaranteed through a free market.

Looking back to Fig. 26.3, this benefit would amount to area 3. However research into this by Balassa and Michalopoulos (1985) estimated that the value of lost output to the US exceeds the quota rent by nine times and to the EU by a factor of seven.

Subsidies

The first two forms of protection we have described have both been designed to restrict the volume of imports directly. An alternative policy is to provide a subsidy to domestic producers so as to improve their competitiveness in both the home and world markets. The effect of this is demonstrated in Fig. 26.4.

Once again, we assume that the world supply curve is perfectly elastic at P_W. Under conditions of free trade, the domestic price is set by the world price at P_W. Domestic production is initially $0Q_1$ with imports satisfying the excess level of demand which amounts to $Q_2 - Q_1$. The effect of a general subsidy to an industry would be to shift the supply curve of domestic producers to the right. The domestic price

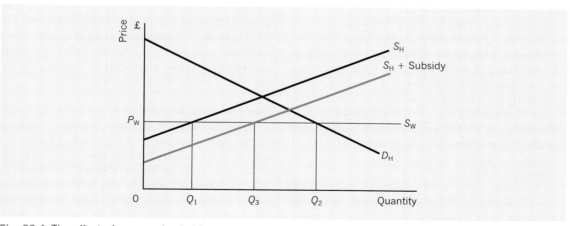

Fig. 26.4 The effect of a general subsidy.

will remain unchanged, but domestic production will rise to $0Q_3$ with imports reduced to Q_2Q_3. If, however, the subsidy is provided solely for *exporters*, the impact on the domestic market could be quite different. The incentive to export may encourage more domestic production to be switched from the home market to the overseas markets which, in turn, could result in an increased volume of imports to satisfy the unchanged level of domestic demand.

Subsidies continue to be widely employed in agriculture alongside other forms of protection. The US and the Cairns group of farm exporters, which includes Australia, Canada and Brazil, is pushing for a liberalization of trade in agricultural products. For example, producer support grant in the OECD area for agriculture still accounted for around $350bn in 2009 with the EU accounting for the largest share of this expenditure (36%) followed by Japan (24%). However, it is noteworthy that the US ranked third in the league table (20%) in terms of providing support for its farmers. Anti-subsidy cases brought before the WTO hit a peak in 1999 with 41 complaints, before falling to as few as six complaints in 2005.

Currency manipulation

The US Treasury stopped short of labelling China a currency manipulator in its latest assessment conducted during 2010. Nevertheless, it continues to argue that the extremely low level of the renminbi is an impediment to free trade and is a key factor explaining the huge bilateral trade imbalance between the two nations, and an impediment to a global economic recovery in the wake of the fall-out from the credit crunch. Indeed, this has become an even bigger issue as the Chinese currency has become more competitive against other emerging market currencies. Morgan Stanley suggested in the middle of 2010 that the Chinese currency would need to rise by at least 15% to bring it closer to 'fair value'. A cheap currency can have significant implications for trade patterns, particularly if it is managed centrally and is thus unable to appreciate sufficiently to reflect market forces. In some ways, this 'currency manipulation' strategy may be viewed as another form of protectionism.

Exchange controls

A system of exchange controls was in force in the UK from the outbreak of the Second World War until 1979 when, in order to allow the free flow of capital, they were abolished. They enabled the government to limit the availability of foreign currencies and so curtail excessive imports; for instance, holding a foreign-currency bank account had required Bank of England permission. Exchange controls could also be employed to discourage speculation and investment abroad.

Safety, technological and environmental standards

These are often imposed in the knowledge that certain imported goods will be unable to meet the requirements. The UK government used such standards to prevent imports of French turkeys and ultra-heat-treated (UHT) milk. Ostensibly the ban on French turkeys was to prevent 'Newcastle disease', a form of fowl pest found in Europe, reaching the UK. The European Court ruled, however, that the ban was merely an excuse to prevent the free flow of imports. In the mid-1990s Germany effectively blocked imports of traffic cones from a UK manufacturer while it 'upgraded' its testing requirements no fewer than 12 times. The cones passed the test each time, but the German authorities refused to issue approval certificates or to publish their standards. Eventually, pressure from the UK led to the standard for cones being published which allowed sales of cones to Germany to proceed. The US, meanwhile, banned shrimp imports from countries that fish using 'Turtle Excluder Devices', a ban that included fish from India. While the policy may appear to have an environmental motive, it was also a form of discrimination. Significantly, it was applied to all Indian exports, whether farmed (as the bulk of shrimps are) or caught in the ocean. A more pertinent issue relates to genetically modified foods. The EU has effectively banned the import of GM products, much to the irritation of the US amongst others. GM crops now account for 75% of the US annual output of soya beans, 71% of its cotton and 34% of its corn. The WTO rules do allow countries to regulate imports on health and environmental grounds, but any restraints must be based on 'sufficient scientific evidence'. In the case of GM foods, this is a point of dispute.

Time-consuming formalities

In 1990, the EU alleged that 'excessive invoicing requirements' required by US importing authorities had hampered exports from member countries to the US. In Asia these problems abound. For example, Indonesian customs officials take at least a week to process imports, and this often involves considerable administrative and capital costs for many companies. A similar problem in China can lead to two or three weeks' delay.

Table 26.4 Anti-dumping cases initiated.

1987	1990	1991	1992	1993	1994	1995	1996	1997	1998	1999	2000	2001	2002	2003	2004	2005	2006	2007	2008
120	165	228	326	299	228	157	225	243	257	356	292	366	312	232	214	200	202	163	208

Source: WTO (2010a) *Annual Report,* and previous editions.

Public sector contracts

Governments often give preference to domestic firms in the issuing of public contracts, despite EU directives requiring member governments to advertise such contracts. A number of Australian states have continued to give price preferences of up to 20% to domestic bidders for public contracts in the latter half of the 1990s. Public contracts are actually placed outside the country of origin in only 1% of cases.

Labour standards

This is not an area currently subject to WTO rules and disciplines, but some countries do believe the issue should be examined as a first step towards bringing the matter of core labour standards within the WTO framework. However, many developing and some developed nations contend that the issue has no place within the WTO framework and see it as little more than a smokescreen for protectionism by the more developed economies from low-wage competition. Areas of particular concern include the issues of child labour and slave labour, but the broader issue of setting minimum labour standards is where opinion tends to diverge. The issue is a bone of contention in the current Doha round of negotiations.

The case for protection

A number of arguments have been used to justify the application of both tariff and non-tariff barriers:

■ to prevent dumping;

■ to protect infant industries;

■ to protect strategically important industries.

Dumping occurs where a good is sold in an overseas market at a price below the real cost of production. Under Article 6 of the GATT, the WTO allows retaliatory sanctions to be applied if it can be shown that the dumping materially affected the domestic industry. As well as using the WTO, countries within the EU can refer cases of alleged dumping for investig-

ation by the European Commission. The Commission is then able to recommend the appropriate course of action, which may range from 'no action' where dumping is found not to have taken place, to either obtaining an 'undertaking' of no further dumping, or imposing a tariff.

Table 26.4 indicates a decline in anti-dumping cases initiated by the WTO in recent years. This is particularly encouraging in view of the severity of the recession that followed the onset of the credit crunch in many large economies.

The US has consistently been one of the main initiators of anti-dumping investigations. Canada, India and the EU have also initiated numerous actions. The main targets of anti-dumping probes have been the EU, China, Taiwan and India, although it is interesting that China has itself taken advantage of this mechanism in recent years. The sectors where anti-dumping measures are most widely applied include chemical products and base metals, in particular steel. In 2010, the US imposed anti-dumping measures on warm water shrimps from Vietnam while China put in place restrictions on flat rolled electrical steel from the US.

The use of protection in order to *establish new industries* is widely accepted, particularly in the case of developing countries. Article 18 of GATT explicitly allows such protection. An infant industry is likely to have a relatively high cost structure in the short run, and in the absence of protective measures may find it difficult to compete with the established overseas industries already benefiting from scale economies. The EU has used this argument to justify protection of its developing high-technology industries.

The protection of industries for *strategic reasons* is widely practised in both the UK and the EU, and is not necessarily contrary to GATT rules (Article 2). The protection of the UK steel industry has in the past been justified on this basis, and the EU has used a similar argument to protect agricultural production throughout the Community under the guise of the CAP. In the Uruguay round of GATT, the developing countries used this argument in seeking to resist calls for the liberalization of trade in the service sector. This has been one of the few sectors recording strong growth in recent years and is still a highly 'regulated' sector in most countries.

Criticisms of protectionism

Retaliation

A major drawback to the imposition of protectionist measures is the possibility of retaliation. For example, in 2007 the EU initiated an anti-dumping investigation over Chinese fastener exports and imposed new duties of up to 85% in January 2009. China responded by initiating its own anti-dumping investigation over EU exports of a different variety of fastener and it imposed new 25% tariffs. Other examples include the WTO approving $4bn worth of trade sanctions to be applied by the EU in response to tax breaks being given by the US government to multinationals such as Boeing and Microsoft and to the imposition of steel tariffs in the US. In most cases, the *threat* of retaliation has been sufficient to produce a compromise, but there is always a danger that a full-blown trade war could result from retaliatory actions.

Misallocation of resources

We saw in Figs 26.1–26.3 that protectionism can erode some of the welfare benefits of free trade. For instance, Fig. 26.2 showed that a tariff (and Fig. 26.3 a quota) raises domestic supply at the expense of imports. If the domestic producers cannot make such products as cheaply as overseas producers, then one could argue that encouraging high-cost domestic production is a misallocation of international resources.

A related criticism also suggests that protectionism leads to resource misallocation on an international scale, but this time concerns the multinational. We saw in Chapter 7 that multinationals are the fastest-growing type of business unit in Western economies, and that they are increasingly adopting strategies which locate particular stages of the production process in (to them) appropriate parts of the world. Protectionism may disrupt the flow of goods from one stage of the production process to another, and in this sense inhibit global specialization.

A number of studies have been carried out in recent years on the impact of protectionism on the global economy. The most recent report produced by the OECD (2006) suggests that a 50% cut in agricultural support and a similar percentage reduction in applied tariffs would boost global GDP by $44bn. Almost two-thirds of the gain would accrue to the farming industry. Other studies generate even more positive outcomes. For example, a World Bank analysis (2005) concluded that if all trade protection were to be eliminated then the global welfare gain would amount to $278bn, with $173bn resulting from removing agricultural subsidies. Meanwhile a group of economists led by Robert Stern estimates that lowering services barriers by one-third under the Doha Development Agenda would raise developing countries' incomes by around $60bn.

Fair trade as well as free trade

We noted earlier that the failure to advance the Doha trade round is in part a function of the reluctance of the rich economies to make sufficient concessions in terms of reducing their own array of protectionist measures. This is rather ironic since the OECD study (2006) referred to above shows that over 90% of the estimated benefit from the reform of agricultural policies goes to the OECD countries themselves.

The uneven outcome of trade negotiations prior to the current Doha round is reflected in the fact that tariff levels in the advanced industrial countries against the *developing* world are four times higher than against the *developed* countries. Indeed, as Joseph Stiglitz (2006) points out, the last round of successful trade negotiations, namely the Uruguay round, actually left the poorer countries worse off. While the developing countries were forced to open up their markets, the advanced economies continued to protect agriculture and to maintain barriers against key products from the developing world.

Conclusion

The current Doha round of trade negotiations is struggling to make very much headway, with attempts to extend the range of goods and services covered under the auspices of the WTO proving difficult. There is clearly a need for the developed economies to make greater concessions and for all countries to recognize that free trade creates many more 'winners' than 'losers', with developed countries themselves benefiting most from reducing their own protectionist barriers.

For the time being, the volume of world trade is continuing to grow. But with the global economy struggling to cope with the legacy of the credit crunch, the risk remains of a retreat towards protectionism. This may conceivably at least initially take the form of competitive currency devaluations, but it could spread beyond that when such a move fails to solve the underlying issues. Unless there is a renewed recognition of the *worldwide costs* of protection, lobbies in various countries may still succeed in curbing the growth of international specialization and trade in a misleading attempt to revive economic fortunes.

Key points

- In a competitive, full employment framework, free trade can be shown to yield a net welfare gain *vis-à-vis* various protectionist alternatives.

- In the more realistic situation of 'market failures', the existence of monopoly power, unemployment, etc. may offset (in part or in whole) these welfare gains.

- The General Agreement on Tariffs and Trade (GATT) established in 1947, and its successor the World Trade Organization (WTO), seek to reduce tariffs and other barriers to trade, and to eliminate discrimination in trade.

- The GATT/WTO have had some success, cutting the average tariff in the industrialized world from 40% in 1947 to less than 5% in 2010.

- Since 1870, the growth of trade has *exceeded* the growth of world GDP in all but the period between the First and Second World Wars.

- *Intra-regional* trade (i.e. trade within a region) has grown substantially in recent decades. For example, around three-quarters of all Western European trade occurs between countries in Western Europe.

- Various types of regional trading arrangement have promoted this trend. Free Trade Areas, Customs Unions (which have an external tariff barrier), Common Markets (in which factors of production can also freely move) and Economic Unions (with harmonization of member policies) have all been used to this end.

- Various types of protection have been used by countries, including tariffs, quotas, currency manipulation, subsidies, exchange controls and a range of restrictions involving technological standards, safety, etc.

- Arguments often advanced in *favour* of protectionist policies include the prevention of dumping, the protection of infant industries and the protection of strategically important industries.

- Arguments *against* protectionist policies include retaliation and a misallocation of resources on both a national and international scale, leading to welfare loss.

Now try the self-check questions for this chapter on the Companion Website. You will also find useful links to relevant websites.

Note

1 It could, however, be argued that the welfare loss is overestimated by this analysis. Area 3, though no longer received by the government as tax revenue, may still be received by importers. Although paying only P_W to the foreign suppliers, the importers now receive P'_W when selling $Q_5 - Q_4$ on the domestic market.

References and further reading

Balassa, B. and Michaelopoulos, M. (1985) *Liberalizing World Trade*, Development Policy Issues Series Report VPERS4, Washington DC, World Bank.

Barrell, R. E. and Pain, N. (1999) Trade restraints and Japanese direct investment flows, *European Economic Review*, 43(1): 29–45.

Bayard, T. O. and Elliot, K. A. (1994) *Reciprocity and Retaliation in US Trade Policy*, Washington DC, Institute for International Economics.

Bénassy-Quéré, A. and Coeuré, B. (2010) *Economic Policy*, New York, Oxford University Press.

Bhagwati, J. (1992) *Regionalism and multilateralism: an overview*, Discussion Paper No. 603, New York, Columbia University.

Booth, P. and Wellings, R. (2009) *Globalization and Free Trade*, Cheltenham, Edward Elgar.

Boughton, J. and Lombardi, D. (2009) *Finance, Development and the IMF*, Oxford, Oxford University Press.

Bown Chad, P. (2010) The WTO dispute settlement system would survive without Doha, *VOX*, 19 June.

De Melo, J. and Panagariya, A. (1992) The new regionalism, *Finance and Development*, December, 37–40.

Dicken, P. (2011) *Global Shift: Reshaping the Global Economic Map in the 21st Century* (6th edn), London, Sage Publications.

Fontaine Thomson (2007) End of quotas hits African textiles, *IMF Survey Magazine*, July 5.

Giavazzi, F. and Blanchard, O. (2010) *Macroeconomics: A European Perspective*, Harlow, Financial Times/Prentice Hall.

Greenaway, D. (1994) The Uruguay Round of trade negotiations, *Economic Review*, 12, November.

Grimwade, N. (1996) Anti-dumping policy after the Uruguay Round, *National Institute Economics Review*, February, 98–105.

Hanson, D. (2010) *Limits to Free Trade: Non-Tariff Barriers in the European Union, Japan and United States*, Cheltenham, Edward Elgar.

IMF (1993) *World Economic Outlook 1993*, Washington DC, International Monetary Fund.

Krugman, P. and Obstfeld, M. (2010) *International Economics: Theory and Policy*, Harlow, Financial Times/Prentice Hall.

Lloyd, P. J. (1992) *Regionalisation and world trade*, OECD Economic Studies, No. 18, Paris, Organisation for Economic Cooperation and Development.

OECD (2006) *Agricultural Policy and Trade Reform: Potential Effects at Global, National and Household Levels*, Paris, Organisation for Economic Cooperation and Development.

Panagariya, A. (1999) The regionalism debate: an overview, *The World Economy*, 22(4): 477–511.

Primo Braga, C. A., Safadi, R. and Yeats, A. (1994) *NAFTA's Implications for East Asian Exports*, Policy Working Paper No. 1351, Washington DC, World Bank.

Prusa, T. J. and Teh, R. (2010) *Protection Reduction and Diversion: PTAs and the Incidence of Anti-dumping Disputes*, NBER Working Paper No. 16276, Cambridge MA, National Bureau of Economic Research.

Reinert, K. A., Roland-Holst, D. W. and Shiells, C. R. (1994) A general equilibrium analysis of North American regional integration, in Francois,

J. F. and Shiells, C. R. (eds), *Modelling Trade Policy: Applied General Equilibrium Analysis of a North American Free Trade Area*, Cambridge, Cambridge University Press.

Schefer, K. N. (2010) *Social Regulation in the WTO: Trade Policy and International Legal Development*, Cheltenham, Edward Elgar.

Smith, F. (2009) *Agriculture and the WTO*, Cheltenham, Edward Elgar.

Srinivasan, T. N., Whalley, J. and Wooton, I. (1993) Measuring the effects of regionalism on trade and welfare, in Anderson, K. and Blackhurst, R. (eds), *Regional Integration*, Hemel Hempstead, Harvester Wheatsheaf.

Stiglitz, J. (2006) Social justice and global trade, *Far Eastern Economic Review*, March, 18–22.

UNCTAD (2010a) *Trade and Development Report 2010: Employment, Globalization and Development*, New York and Geneva, United Nations Conference on Trade and Development.

UNCTAD (2010b) *World Investment Report 2010: Investing in a Low Carbon Economy*, New York and Geneva, United Nations Conference on Trade and Development.

UNDP (2010) *Human Development Report 2010: The Real Wealth of Nations: Pathways to Human Development*, New York, United Nations Development Programme.

Vanston, N. (1993) What price regional integration? *OECD Observer*, No. 181, 4–7.

World Bank (1986) *World Development Report 1986*, Washington DC.

World Bank (2005) *Global Monitoring Report*, Washington DC.

World Bank (2010) *World Development Report 2010: Development and Climate Change.* Washington DC.

WTO (2008) *10 Benefits of the WTO Trading System*, Geneva, World Trade Organization.

WTO (2010a) *Annual Report*, Geneva, World Trade Organization.

WTO (2010b) *International Trade Statistics*, Geneva, World Trade Organization.

Yannopoulos, G. N. (1990) Foreign direct investment and European direct investment: the evidence from the formative years of the European Community, *Journal of Common Market Studies*, **23**(3): 235–59.

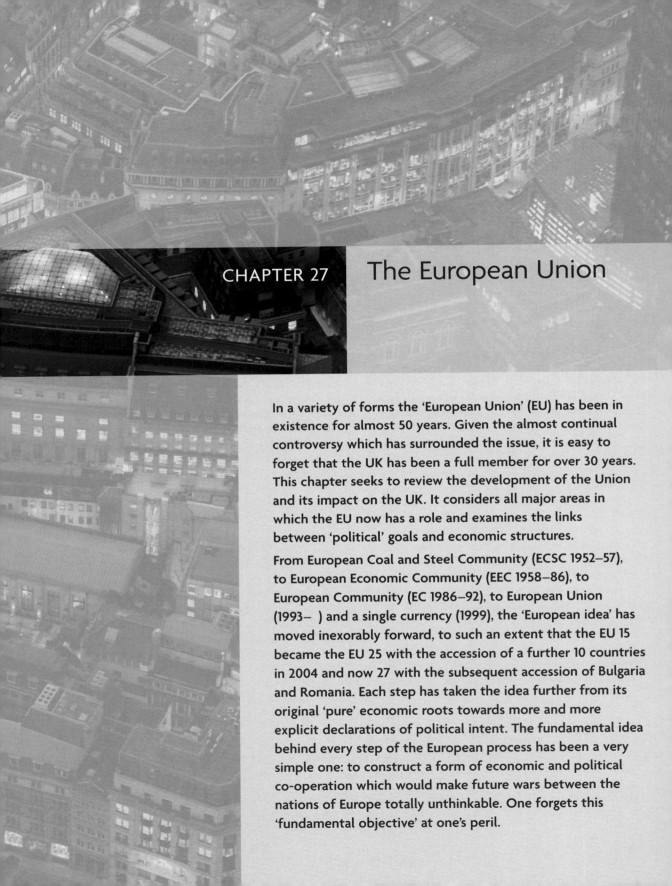

CHAPTER 27

The European Union

In a variety of forms the 'European Union' (EU) has been in existence for almost 50 years. Given the almost continual controversy which has surrounded the issue, it is easy to forget that the UK has been a full member for over 30 years. This chapter seeks to review the development of the Union and its impact on the UK. It considers all major areas in which the EU now has a role and examines the links between 'political' goals and economic structures.

From European Coal and Steel Community (ECSC 1952–57), to European Economic Community (EEC 1958–86), to European Community (EC 1986–92), to European Union (1993–) and a single currency (1999), the 'European idea' has moved inexorably forward, to such an extent that the EU 15 became the EU 25 with the accession of a further 10 countries in 2004 and now 27 with the subsequent accession of Bulgaria and Romania. Each step has taken the idea further from its original 'pure' economic roots towards more and more explicit declarations of political intent. The fundamental idea behind every step of the European process has been a very simple one: to construct a form of economic and political co-operation which would make future wars between the nations of Europe totally unthinkable. One forgets this 'fundamental objective' at one's peril.

Historical background

The historical background to the EU has been covered in some depth elsewhere (see, e.g., Lewis 1993). Since its foundation, the EU has absorbed the two 'communities' which preceded it, i.e. the European Coal and Steel Community (ECSC) and the European Atomic Energy Community (Euratom). The ECSC had been established in 1952 to control the pooled coal and iron and steel resources of the six member countries – France, West Germany, Italy, Belgium, the Netherlands and Luxembourg. By promoting free trade in coal and steel between members and by protecting against non-members, the ECSC revitalized the two war-stricken industries. It was this success which prompted the establishment of the much more ambitious European Economic Community (EEC), subsequently known simply as the European Community (EC). The European Atomic Energy Community (Euratom) had been set up by treaty in 1957 with the same six countries, to promote growth in nuclear industries and the peaceful use of atomic energy.

The EEC was formed on 1 January 1958 after the signing of the Treaty of Rome. This sought to establish a 'common market', by eliminating all restrictions on the free movement of goods, capital and persons between member countries. By dismantling tariff barriers on industrial trade between members and by imposing a common tariff against non-members, the EEC was to become a protected free trade area or 'customs union'. The formation of a customs union was to be the first step in the creation of an 'economic union' with national economic policies harmonized across the member countries. The original 'Six' became 'Nine' in 1973 with the accession of the UK, the Republic of Ireland and Denmark, and 'Ten' in 1981 with the entry of Greece. The accession of Spain and Portugal on 1 January 1986 increased the number of member countries to 12.

With the entry into law of the Single European Act in January 1993 the EC became the European Union (EU). In January 1995 the 12 became 15 as Austria, Finland and Sweden joined, followed by the new EU10 in May 2004 and by Romania and Bulgaria in January 2007, bringing the population of the EU to over 50 million with a GDP of over €12 trillion.

The Single European Act (SEA), as it is widely known, came into force in July 1987. It constituted a major development of the Community and was based on a White Paper, 'Completing the Common Market', which had been presented by the Commission to the Milan meeting of the European Council in June 1985. It represented the first time, since 1957, that the original Treaty of Rome had been amended. The Act looked towards creating a single European economy by 1993. The objective was not simply to create an internal market by removing frontier controls but to remove all barriers to the movement of goods, people and capital. Achieving a single European market has meant, amongst other things, work on standards, procurement, qualifications, banking, capital movements and exchange regulations, tax 'approximation', communications standards and transport.

Since 1987 over 600 separate new directives have been created, ranging from common hygiene rules for meat and regulations on the wholesaling, labelling and advertising of medicines, to capital adequacy rules for investment and credit institutions and a common licensing system for road haulage. The Single Act also had political ramifications in that it formalized the use of qualified majorities for taking decisions in the Council of Ministers and gave the elected European Parliament greater legislating powers.

The European Economic Area

In the 1990s the political and economic problems of the EU itself prevented formal enlargement but did not stand in the way of intermediate arrangements for closer co-operation with certain states. In 1992 the EU signed an agreement with the seven members of the European Free Trade Association (EFTA) which led, on 1 January 1993, to the formation of the 'European Economic Area' (EEA). The EEA then consisted of 19 states which together formed a powerful and wealthy trading bloc.[1] Under the agreement, the EU extended to EFTA all of the EU's own freedoms in the movement of goods, services, people and capital while the EFTA states agreed to abide by the EU's competition rules. Under agreements existing prior to the EEA agreement, industrial tariffs between the 19 countries were already at zero. The 1992 agreement further reduced agricultural tariffs and established a new EEA fund designed to help the poorer EU regions (including Northern Ireland).

The Maastricht Treaty

The Treaty on European Union which was signed at Maastricht on 7 February 1992 represents one of the most fundamental changes to have occurred in the EU since its foundation. Although, legally speaking, merely an extension and amendment to the Treaty of Rome, Maastricht represents a major step for the member states. For the first time, many of the political and social imperatives of the Community have been explicitly agreed and delineated. Maastricht takes the EU beyond a 'merely' economic institution (if it ever was such) and towards the full political, economic and social union foreseen by many of its founders. Some of its major objectives are as follows:

■ to create economic and social progress through an 'area without internal frontiers' and through economic and monetary union (EMU);

■ to develop a common foreign, security and defence policy which 'might lead to common defence';

■ to introduce a 'citizenship of the Union'.

Table 27.1 presents some of the important characteristics of the 27 member countries in 2010. It shows how diverse they are in terms of population, industrial structure, standard of living, unemployment level and inflation rate. In terms of population, the UK is still the third-largest member, with a smaller proportion engaged in agriculture than in other EU countries but the fifth largest in services. In overall wealth, however, the UK drops down the rankings. It has the third-largest GDP in absolute terms, but comes only eleventh in terms of GDP per capita.

Quite apart from the political rationale behind the EU, a number of economic arguments have been advanced in its support:

■ By abolishing industrial tariff and non-tariff barriers at national frontiers, the EU has created a single 'domestic' market of around 490 million people, with opportunities for substantial economies of scale in production. By surrounding this market with a tariff wall, the Common External Tariff (CET), member countries are the beneficiaries of these scale economies.

■ By regulating agricultural production through the Common Agricultural Policy (CAP), the EU has become self-sufficient in many agricultural products.

■ By amending and co-ordinating labour and capital regulations in the member countries, the EU seeks to create a free market in both, leading to a more 'efficient' use of these factors. A further factor, 'enterprise', is to be 'freed' through increased standardization of national laws on patents and licences.

■ By controlling monopoly and merger activities, competition has been encouraged both within and across frontiers.

■ By creating a substantial 'domestic' market and by co-ordinating trade policies, the EU hopes to exert a greater collective influence on world economic affairs than could possibly be achieved by any single nation.

These policies have been supported by a number of other arrangements, including a common form of taxation, a common currency and policies directed towards transport, energy, education, social improvement and regional aid. Although our main concern in this chapter will be economic, we should not overlook the political objectives which lay behind the formation of the EU. As early as 1946, Winston Churchill had called for a 'United States of Europe' as a diplomatic and military counter to the Soviet Union. However, it was two Frenchmen – Robert Schuman and Jean Monnet – who were the founding fathers of the EC, with their vision of using economic involvement to tie Europe's warring countries together. Having attempted, on three occasions, to join the EU during the 1960s, the UK was finally accepted for membership in 1970, signed the Treaty of Accession in 1972, and became a full member with effect from 1 January 1973.

The UK's objectives in signing the Treaty of Accession in 1972 were a combination of the short- to medium-term economic, with the medium- to long-term political. There was an undeniable desire to share in the prosperity which the EU appeared to have stimulated for its six original members since 1958. The fact that the average growth rate of the Six had been 4.8% per annum between 1961 and 1971, compared to the UK's 2.7% per annum, seemed to show that entry into the EU might offer a solution to some of the UK's growth problems. In this chapter we examine the EU and the effect of UK membership of the EU under five broad headings:

Table 27.1 The 27 in 2010: some comparative statistics.

| Member country | Population (m) | Shares of GDP | | | GDP €(bn) | GDP per capita €(000)s | Shares of EU | | Index of GDP per capita | Unemployment[1] (%) | Inflation[2] (%) |
		Agriculture (%)	Industry (%)	Services (%)			GDP (%)	Population (%)			
Austria	8.4	3	29	68	281.1	33.5	2.3	1.7	139.6	6.0	1.3
Belgium	10.8	1	26	73	345.5	32.1	2.9	2.2	133.8	9.9	1.3
France	64.8	2	21	77	1,992.0	30.8	16.5	12.9	128.3	10.2	1.1
Finland	5.4	3	33	64	180.1	30.7	1.5	1.0	127.9	10.2	1.6
Germany	81.9	1	30	69	2,436.0	29.8	20.2	16.3	124.2	9.2	0.6
Greece	11.3	4	20	76	243.0	21.4	2.0	2.2	89.2	10.2	1.4
Ireland	4.5	2	34	64	160.5	35.9	1.3	0.9	149.6	14.0	-0.8
Italy	60.4	2	27	71	1,573.0	26.0	13.1	12.0	108.3	8.7	1.8
Luxembourg	0.5	1	16	83	39.1	79.8	0.3	0.1	332.5	7.3	1.7
The Netherlands	16.6	2	25	73	581.8	35.1	4.8	3.3	146.3	5.4	1.2
Portugal	10.7	3	25	72	164.1	15.4	1.4	2.1	64.2	10.7	1.1
Spain	46.6	3	30	66	1,046.0	22.5	8.7	9.3	93.8	20.0	0.8
EU12	**321.9**	**2**	**26**	**72**	**9,042.1**	**28.1**	**75.1**	**64.1**	**117.1**	**10.7**	**1.1**
Bulgaria	7.6	7	31	62	33.6	4.4	2.8	0.2	1.8	8.0	1.3
Cyprus	0.8	2	19	79	17.8	22.1	0.1	0.2	92.1	6.6	3.3
Czech Rep.	10.5	2	39	59	140.9	13.4	1.2	2.1	55.8	7.9	1.4
Denmark	5.5	1	20	79	230.4	41.7	1.9	1.1	173.8	15.2	1.6
Estonia	1.3	3	26	71	13.4	10.1	0.1	0.3	42.1	20.0	0.8
Hungary	10.1	4	30	66	98.1	10.0	0.8	2.1	41.7	11.3	4.2
Latvia	2.2	3	26	71	16.7	7.5	0.1	0.5	31.3	19.9	-3.7
Lithuania	3.5	4	33	63	24.7	7.4	0.2	0.7	30.8	17.6	-1.2
Malta	0.4	2	19	79	5.8	13.9	0.05	0.1	57.9	7.4	1.6
Poland	38.1	4	31	65	327.0	8.5	2.7	7.6	35.4	9.9	2.0
Romania	21.4	7	37	56	122.9	5.7	1.0	4.3	23.8	8.7	3.6
Slovakia	5.4	4	39	57	69.5	12.8	0.6	1.1	53.3	12.8	2.4
Slovenia	2.0	2	31	65	36.3	17.9	0.3	0.4	74.6	8.3	3.9
Sweden	9.3	1	28	71	312.6	33.7	2.6	1.9	140.4	10.2	-1.0
UK	62.2	1	23	76	1,858.0	29.0	12.9	12.4	104.2	8.7	1.4
EU27	**501.9**	**2**	**27**	**71**	**12,048**	**24.0**	**100.0**	**100.0**	**100.0**	**10.3**	**1.2**
EU15	**398.7**	**2**	**26**	**72**	**11,420**	**27.9**	**94.8**	**79.4**	**116.3**	**6.0**	**1.1**

[1]Eurostat definition of unemployment.
[2]Private consumption deflation.
Sources: Adapted from European Commission (2010c) Statistical Annex of European Economy, Spring; World Bank (2010) World Development Indicators, and previous editions; OECD (2010b) OECD Factbook, 2010.

For each of these headings we discuss both EU policy in general and how it has affected the UK in particular.

Finance and the EU budget

Between 1958 and 1970 the EU was financed by contributions from member states which, although politically determined, were still broadly based on the various countries' ability to pay. However, since 1970 the EU has financed its spending using a system of 'own resources', i.e. income it regards as its own *as of right*. The composition of 'own resources' is shown in Table 27.2 and consists of three main sources of revenue. First, Traditional Own Resources (TOR) includes revenue raised from customs duties such as the CET and agricultural duties. Second, 'VAT' is revenue from each country up to a *maximum* of 1% of its domestic VAT tax base. Third, 'GNP' is a levy of up to a *maximum* of 1.24% of the value of GNP in each member country. This levy, which was originally introduced in 1988, is used as a 'buffer' to equate EU revenue with its expenditure. In other words, the actual percentage of GNP required can vary according to how much revenue is required to balance the EU budget (e.g. 0.40% of GNP in 1997 but 0.56% in 2010). Finally, the table also includes 'other revenue' which consists of revenue from a variety of sources such as interest on late payments, fines, taxes on salaries of employees of EU institutions, etc.

A notable feature of Table 27.2 is the decline in the relative importance of TOR and VAT as sources of revenue and the growth in importance of the GNP element. The impact of trade liberalization on tariff levels (e.g. reductions via GATT rounds) has meant that the total yield from TOR has failed to increase in line with the expansion of world trade, so that the share of TOR in total revenue has decreased. Similarly, the share of VAT in total revenue has also decreased. This is partly because of decisions made by the Commission to decrease the percentage of GNP which acts as the *tax base* for calculating the VAT paid by member states. For example, the VAT base for member states fell from 55% of their GNP in 1995 to 50% of GNP by 2003 and has now been capped at that level, so the tax base cannot be greater than 50% of GNP. Once the absolute amount of the tax base has been calculated for each country, then a VAT tax rate is applied to this amount in order to arrive at the sum which each member has to pay. The maximum rate of VAT applied to this tax base has also fallen from 1.4% in the mid-1990s to 0.75% in 2003 and to 0.3% by 2010, which has further decreased the revenue derived by the EU from the VAT source. These curbs on the VAT source of

Table 27.2 Sources of revenue for the EU budget (€m and %).

	2000	(%)	2006	(%)	2010	(%)
TOR	14,564.9	(16.4)	14,225.1	(12.9)	14,203.1	(11.7)
VAT	32,554.6	(36.7)	15,884.3	(14.3)	13,950.9	(11.5)
GNP	41,593.4	(46.9)	80,562.5	(72.8)	93,352.7	(76.8)
Total 'own resources'	**88,712.9**	**(100.0)**	**110,671.9**	**(100.0)**		**(100.0)**
Other revenue	674.0		1,297.6		1,430.3	
Total revenue	**89,386.9**		**111,969.5**		**122,937.0**	

Source: Adapted from European Commission (2010b) *General Budget of the European Union for the Financial Year 2010*, January, and previous issues.

Table 27.3 Budgetary expenditure of the European communities (€m).

Budget heading	1998	2000	2002	2006	2010
Agriculture	**40,937.0**	**40,993.9**	**45,377**	**50,991.0**	**58,135.6**
EAGGF guarantee	40,937.0	36,889.0	40,761	43,279.7	43,701.2
Rural Development (RDP)	–	4,104.9	4,616	7,711.3	14,431.4
Structural operations	**28,594.7**	**32,678.0**	**32,998**	**35,639.6**	**36,384.9**
Structural Funds	23,084.4	28,105.0	30,316	32,134.1	29,521.9
Community Initiatives	2,558.8	1,743.0	–	–	–
Cohesion Fund	2,648.8	2,659.0	2,682	3,505.5	6,854.9
Others	302.7	325.0	–	–	–
Internal policies	4,678.5	6,027.0	6,793	8,889.2	11,342.3
External policies	4,528.5	4,805.1	4,895	5,369.0	7,787.7
Administration	4,353.4	4,703.7	5,225	6,656.4	7,888.5
Other	437.0	4,072.7	3,754	4,424.3	1,398
Total	**83,529.2**	**93,280.4**	**99,042**	**111,969.6**	**122,937.0**

Source: As for Table 27.2.

revenue reflect the view that it is a regressive tax which tends to disadvantage poorer members of the EU because a greater proportion of their national income is devoted to consumption, resulting in a greater tax burden being placed on them than on richer members. As a result of the trends noted above, the importance of the GNP element in EU revenue has increased in order to fill the revenue gap. This is regarded as a more acceptable source because the contributions of the various member countries to the EU budget are more closely related to their affluence, i.e. to their ability to pay as indicated by GNP.

A breakdown of the expenditure side of the EU budget is shown in Table 27.3. During the early years of the new millennium, around 45% of the EU's total expenditure was spent on the *Guarantee* section of the European Agricultural Guarantee and Guidance Fund (EAGGF). This Fund is used to subsidize the farming community under the EU's CAP in various ways. The Guarantee section is responsible for a wide range of price support programmes but has decreased in importance to only 36% of total EU expenditure by 2010.

The second most important expenditure group is 'Structural Operations' which accounts for some 30% of EU expenditures in 2010. Most of the Structural Funds are designed to meet the convergence objective by developing effective employment and regional policies in the EU. Other objectives of 'Structural Operations' are to improve regional com-

petitiveness and cooperation whilst also providing technical assistance to EU members. Although not shown in Table 27.3, the Structural Fund is made up of four sub-funds:

1 the European Regional Development Fund (ERDF), which aims to reduce the inequality gap between the Community's regions;

2 the European Social Fund (ESF), which is designed to improve the labour market in member countries by increasing employment opportunities, employment flexibility and equal opportunities for the workforce;

3 the EAGGF *Guidance* Fund, which helps to adapt the structure of agriculture by encouraging small (less efficient) farmers to leave the land;

4 the Financial Instrument for Fisheries Guidance (FIFG), which helps the restructuring of the fisheries sector.

These Structural Funds are spent on the EU's three priority-based objectives:

■ *Objective 1* covers regions of the EU in which development is seriously lagging behind the EU average. Member countries can apply to the four funds for assistance under this objective.

■ *Objective 2* covers regions undergoing economic and social conversion, involving industrial restructuring or urban problems. The ERDF and ESF provide the main funding assistance under this objective.

- *Objective 3* covers whole countries and provides support for the adoption of education, training and employment initiatives. This objective is mostly funded by the ESF.

The remaining part of the Structural Fund, i.e. 'Community Initiatives', is designed to stimulate co-operation between EU member states in promoting measures of common interest, e.g. rural development (the expenditures under this heading are no longer recorded separately but are included in the overall Structural Fund).

Finally, the Cohesion Fund is a separate part of the Structural Operations and is designed to help the least prosperous member states of the EU to take part in Economic and Monetary Union. For example, it provides assistance to projects in Greece, Ireland, Portugal, Spain and Poland, such as those which contribute to improvements in the transport infrastructure and transport networks of those countries.

- 'Internal policies' refers to the funds used to help improve EU competitiveness and includes spending on research and development (R&D) projects.
- 'External policies' includes EU foreign aid to states such as the former Eastern bloc countries wishing to progress towards the market economy model.

In 1998 the European Commission reported on the revenue and expenditure aspects of the EU budget (European Commission 1998). On the *revenue* side it was suggested that the performance of the budget should be assessed on five criteria, namely resources adequacy, equity in gross contributions, financial autonomy, transparency and simplicity, and cost-effectiveness. To fulfil these criteria the report proposed changes which would be simpler, fairer and more cost-effective. In particular, there was support for more *revenue* being derived from members' GNP contributions. On the *expenditure* side, the main proposal was to decrease spending on market support policies for agricultural products. Finally, the report suggested that those members with large budget imbalances (i.e. whose contributions are generally greater than their receipts) should be compensated by some form of correction mechanism. For example, Germany, the Netherlands, Austria and Sweden have

found themselves with budgetary deficits which are arguably excessive in relation to their relative standards of living within the EU.

The nature of the imbalances problem can be seen from Table 27.4. This table shows the relative shares of member countries in total EU GNP and in relative contributions to the total revenue for the EU budget, together with figures for the imbalances, both in absolute amounts and as a percentage of the country's GNP (UK figures are net of its rebate). Some important points can be noted from this table. First, the UK had a 13% share of EU GNP but contributed only 8.3% (after rebate) to the total revenue for the EU budget. Second, the UK often had a negative budgetary imbalance with the EU, except in 2001 when it became a net beneficiary because of an unusually high amount of rebate in that year. Third, other countries such as Germany, France, Italy, the Netherlands, Austria and Sweden were also experiencing negative imbalances with the EU. Arguably their situations are less fair in that their negative budgetary imbalance is a much higher percentage of their respective GNPs than for other member states. Germany's problems have been particularly difficult because, as a wealthy country with a relatively small agricultural sector, it attracts low shares of EU spending on both the Structural Funds and the CAP. Fourth, it is clear that the EU budget continues to generate major financial transfers to Greece, Portugal, Spain, Ireland and Poland – the five countries that receive a substantial amount from the Cohesion Fund. In addition, the Baltic States were also net receivers of income from the EU.

In March 1999, the Berlin European Council reached an agreement on an important communication entitled *Agenda 2000: a stronger and wider Europe*. This was directed towards stimulating economic growth, increasing living standards and preparing for the enlargement of Europe over the period 2000–06. On the expenditure side of the new financial framework, the Council agreed to ensure that the EU's budget expenditure would not rise too rapidly (see Table 27.3). On the revenue side, adjustments were to be introduced to ensure that the burden on the least prosperous members would be alleviated by altering the rules on VAT contributions to the EU budget. At the same time, the UK's rebate would be gradually decreased, and adjustments made to the GNP method of revenue calculation (the base) in order to reduce the contributions of Austria,

Table 27.4 Shares of GDP and EU budgetary balances, 2009.

	Share of EU GDP (%)	Share of EU budget (%)	Net budgetary balance (€ million)	Net budgetary balance (% GNI)
Austria	3.1	2.3	−431.5	−0.16
Belgium	3.8	3.4	−1,452.7	−0.43
Bulgaria	0.3	0.4	642.2	1.94
Cyprus	0.2	0.2	6.9	0.04
Czech Republic	1.2	1.3	1,776.8	1.38
Denmark	1.9	2.3	−821.0	−0.36
Estonia	0.1	0.1	582.0	4.34
Finland	1.9	1.8	−430.3	−0.25
France	21.3	19.9	−4,739.4	−0.25
Germany	26.8	18.6	−8,107.3	−0.33
Greece	2.6	2.4	3,251.5	1.41
Hungary	0.8	0.9	2,772.1	3.16
Ireland	1.8	1.4	47.0	0.04
Italy	17.0	14.7	−4,079.3	−0.27
Latvia	0.2	0.2	513.6	2.55
Lithuania	0.2	0.3	1,510.6	5.67
Luxembourg	0.4	0.3	−82.8	−0.32
Malta	0.1	0.1	11.7	0.22
Netherlands	6.4	1.7	−2,026.2	−0.36
Poland	2.6	3.0	6,488.5	2.16
Portugal	1.9	1.6	2,248.8	1.43
Romania	1.0	1.3	+1,755.8	+1.54
Slovakia	0.7	0.7	580.2	0.93
Slovenia	0.4	0.4	261.6	0.76
Spain	11.8	10.8	1,794.3	0.17
Sweden	2.5	1.6	−704.2	−0.24
UK	13.3	8.3	−1,362.9	−0.09
EU27	**100.0**	**100.0**	**0.0**	**0.0**

Note: Imbalances exclude administrative expenditure and include UK correction payments. A positive net balance means that the country is a 'net beneficiary' from the EU budget while a negative figure means that the member is a 'net contributor' to the EU budget.
Sources: European Commission (2010a) *Allocation of 2010 EU budgets*; ECB (2010) *Statistics Pocket Book*, May.

Germany, the Netherlands and Sweden to the EU budget.

The UK and the EU budget

It must be stressed that the terms 'net contributor' and 'net beneficiary' relate only to the EU budget and its relatively tiny amounts of expenditure, and *not* to the members' total experience within the Community. Merely to say that Germany and the UK have usually been large net contributors to the budget has no bearing upon whether they have or have not benefited overall from membership of the EU. It is also important to understand that being a 'net contributor' does not imply a transfer of German or UK funds to the EU. The budget is 'self-financing' to the extent that contributions to it are, by treaty, never the property of the member state. It is intended (although the results in practice are very different) to be a reallocation of resources from rich to poor in much the same way as national income tax. However, it is not so much being in the position of a net contributor to the budget that has worried successive UK governments, as the relative size of that contribution.

The calculation of the UK's net contribution involves the following procedure:

1 customs tariffs paid directly to EU; plus

2 agricultural levies paid directly to EU; minus

3 administrative costs of collecting the above returned to UK government; plus

4 VAT contribution (according to the rate set by Council); plus

5 direct UK government contribution (the GNP element)

   equals gross contribution, *minus*

6 amount due to UK for agricultural support (from Intervention Board); minus

7 Structural Fund payments

   equals net contribution (or benefit for some members).

As a major importer of both manufactured goods and food, the UK collects large amounts under items (1) and (2). The VAT rate as a tax on the value added is, of course, fairly closely related to economic activity and therefore the VAT contribution is reasonably proportional across member countries. Summing items (1)–(5) gives the UK's *gross* contribution to the EU budget. However, the UK must set against this the revenue it receives for agricultural support programmes, item (6), and for regional and social projects, item (7). Subtracting items (6) and (7) from gross contribution gives the UK's *net* contribution (or benefit).

Whereas the UK's gross contribution is relatively high compared with those of other members, its receipts from the EU budget, items (6) and (7), are relatively low. The UK receives little in terms of agricultural support because the operation of the CAP largely benefits less efficient producers, and not efficient ones like the UK. The modest increase in EU support for regional and social projects in the UK has been insufficient to correct this imbalance. As a result the UK has consistently found itself a net contributor.

The UK's net contributions to the EU budget are shown in Table 27.5. The fact that the UK was a large net contributor to the EU was addressed as early as 1984 when, under the Fontainebleau agreement of that year, the UK received a 'rebate' according to a set formula which the Commission calls 'a correction mechanism in favour of the UK'. The rebate was reviewed in 1988 and 1992 and on both occasions the European Commission decided that it should be continued. However, as noted above, under *Agenda 2000* the UK can expect its net payments to the EU to rise over the coming years, especially in view of the substantial rebates shown in Table 27.5.

Table 27.5 UK net contributions to the EU budget (£m), 1996–2010.

	1996	1998	2002	2006	2010[3]
Total contribution[1]	6,721	8,712	6,340	8,857	9,515
VAT and FRA[2]	−4	874			
UK abatement	−2,412	−1,378	−3,099	−3,569	−4,218
Total receipts	4,373	4,115	3,201	4,948	−4,820
Net contribution	**2,348**	**4,597**	**3,138**	**3,909**	**4,695**

[1]Net of VAT, FRA and Abatement.
[2]Fourth Resource Adjustment.
[3]Estimates based on 2009/10.
Sources: Adapted from HM Treasury (2009) *European Community Finances*, May, CM 7640 and previous issues; HM Treasury (2010) *Public Expenditure Statistical Analysis*.

Policy areas

1 Competition policy

The theory behind European competition policy is exactly that which created the original EEC almost 50 years ago. Competition brings consumer choice, lower prices and higher quality goods and services. The Commission has a set of directives in this area which are designed to underpin 'fair and free' competition. They cover cartels (price fixing, market sharing, etc.), government subsidies (direct or indirect subsidies for inefficient enterprises – state and private), the abuse of dominant market position (differential pricing in different markets, exclusive contracts, predatory pricing, etc.), selective distribution (preventing consumers in one market from buying in another in order to maintain high margins in the first market), and mergers and takeovers. The latter powers were given to the Commission in 1990.

Two of the most active areas of competition policy have involved mergers and acquisitions (see Chapter 5) and state aid. In the former, the power of the Commission was widened in 1998 to increase the range of mergers which can be referred to it.

The amendments of 1998 were further strengthened in May 2004 when new rules under Regulation 139/2004 were passed, including changes in the rules on jurisdiction and strengthening of the Commission's powers of investigation and enforcement. Although surveys have found that the EU Commission's decisions have *not* been politically biased and that economic welfare has been its main criterion (Bergman *et al.* 2004), EU mergers policy continues to be controversial. For example, in July 2006 the European Court of First Instance (CFI), the competition watchdog, made the unprecedented decision of annulling the EU Commission's approval of the 2004 merger between Sony Music and BMG. Its judgment was a serious blow to the authority of the EU Commission.

As well as the issue of mergers and acquisitions, the Commission has attempted to restrict the aid paid by member states to their own nationals through Articles 87 and 88 (previously Articles 92 and 93) of the EC Treaty and Articles 4 and 95 of the ECSC Treaty. These Articles cover various aspects of the distorting effect that subsidies can have on competition between member states. However, it is likely that the progressive implementation of Single Market arrangements will result in domestic firms increasing their attempts to obtain state aid from their own governments as a means of helping them meet greater Europe-wide competition. Overall, aid given by member states to their domestic industry has been running at around 2% of their respective GNPs during the 1990s.

In 2009 some €67.4bn was spent by EU members on state aid, equivalent to an average of 0.6% of EU GDP. Most of the subsidies went to manufacturing (59%) and agriculture (23%). Of the new members, Poland tops the list of state subsidies (3.0% of GDP) followed by Malta (2.3%) and Cyprus (2.1%). However, difficulties still arise in that of the €61.6bn spent by EU states on subsidies, 40% is spent by Germany, Italy, France and the UK – arguably giving such economies considerable advantages over 'cohesion' countries such as Greece, Portugal, Spain and Ireland, as well as some of the new economies of the EU10.

2 The Common Agricultural Policy (CAP)

When the Treaty of Rome was signed in 1957, over 20% of the working population of the 'Six' were engaged in agriculture. In the enlarged EU of 27 countries in 2009 that figure is only 6.1%, ranging from the UK with 1.6% to Poland with 20%. Since one in five of the EU's workers were involved in agricultural production in 1957, it came as no surprise that the depressed agricultural sector became the focus of the first 'common' policy, the CAP, established in 1962. The objectives of this policy were to create a single market for agricultural produce and to protect the agricultural sector from imports, the justification being to ensure dependable supplies of food for the EU and stability of income for those engaged in agriculture.

Both the demand for, and the supply of, agricultural products are, for the most part, inelastic, so that a small shift in either schedule will induce a more than proportionate change in price. Fluctuations in agricultural prices will in turn create fluctuations in agricultural incomes and therefore investment and ultimately output. The CAP seeks to stabilize agricultural prices, and therefore incomes and output in the industry, to the alleged 'benefit' of both producers and consumers.

There are, of course, a number of ways of achieving such objectives. Prior to joining the EU, the UK placed great emphasis on supplies of cheap food from the Commonwealth. The UK therefore adopted a system of 'deficiency payments' which operated by letting actual prices be set at world levels, but at the same time guaranteeing to farmers minimum 'prices' for each product. If the world price fell below the guaranteed minimum, then the 'deficiency' would be made up by government subsidy. Under this system the consumer could benefit from the low world prices whilst at the same time farm incomes were maintained. Although the UK system involved some additional features, such as marketing agencies, direct production grants, research agencies, etc., it was by no means as complex as that which has operated in the UK since 1972 under the CAP.

Method of operation

The formal title for the executive body of the CAP is the European Agricultural Guarantee and Guidance Fund (EAGGF), often known by its French translation 'Fonds Européen d'Orientation et de Garantie Agricole' (FEOGA). As its name implies, it has two essential roles: guaranteeing farm incomes and guiding farm production. We shall consider each aspect in turn.

Guarantee system

Different agricultural products are dealt with in slightly different ways, but the basis of the system is the establishment of a 'target price' for each product (Fig. 27.1). The target price is *not* set with reference to world prices, but is based upon the price which producers would need to cover costs, including a profit mark-up, in the highest-cost area of production in the EU. The EU then sets an 'Intervention' or 'guaranteed' price for the product in that area, about 7–10% below the target price. Should the price be in danger of falling below this level, the Commission intervenes to buy up production to keep the price at or above the 'guaranteed' level. The Commission then sets separate target and Intervention prices for that product in *each area* of the Community, related broadly to production costs in that area. As long as the market price in a given area (there are 11 such areas in the UK) is above the Intervention price, the producer will sell his produce at prevailing market prices. In effect, the Intervention price sets a 'floor' below which market price will not be permitted to fall and is therefore the guaranteed minimum price to producers.

In Fig. 27.2, an increase in supply of agricultural products to S_1 would, if no action were taken, lower the market price from P_1 to P_2, below the 'Intervention' or 'guaranteed' price, P^*. At P^* demand is Q' but supply is Q^*. To keep the price at P^* the EAGGF will buy up the excess $Q^* - Q'$. In terms of Fig. 27.2, the demand curve is artificially increased to D_1 by the EAGGF purchase.

If this system of guaranteed minimum prices is to work, then EU farmers must be protected from low-priced imports from overseas. To this end, levies or tariffs are imposed on imports of agricultural products. If in Fig. 27.2 the price of imported food were higher than the EU target price then, of course, there would be no need for an import tariff. If, however,

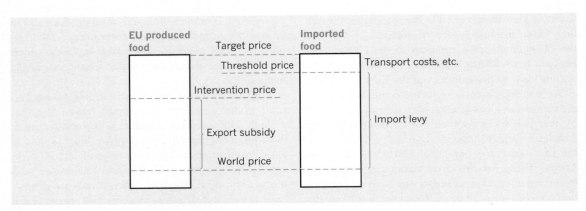

Fig. 27.1 EU agricultural pricing.

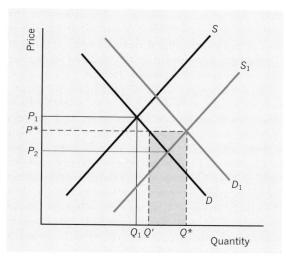

Fig. 27.2 The EU guarantee system.

subsidy systems, e.g. olive oil and tobacco, and some products, such as potatoes, agricultural alcohol and honey, are not covered by EU regulation at all.

Guidance system

The CAP was, as originally established, a simple price-support system. It soon became obvious that agriculture in the 'Six' required considerable structural change because too much output was being produced by small, high-cost, farming units. In 1968 the Commission published a report called *Agriculture 1980*, more usually known as the 'Mansholt Plan' after its originator, the Commissioner for Agriculture, Sicco Mansholt. The plan envisaged taking large amounts of marginal land out of production, reducing the agricultural labour force and creating larger economic farming units. The plan eventually led to the establishment of a Common Structural Policy in 1972, which for political reasons was to be voluntary and administered by the individual member states. The import levies of the EAGGF were to provide funds to encourage small farmers to leave the land and to promote large-scale farming units.

Reform of the CAP

The relative failure of the guidance policy has meant the continued existence of many small, high-cost producers in many agricultural areas of the EU, with correspondingly high 'target' prices. High target prices have in turn encouraged excess supply in a number of products, requiring substantial purchases by the Guarantee section of the EAGGF, resulting in butter and beef mountains, wine lakes, etc. The net effect of the CAP has therefore been, via high prices, to transfer resources from the EU consumer to the EU producer. At the same time, the CAP has led to a less efficient allocation of resources within the EU in that high prices made the use of marginal land and labour-intensive processes economically viable. Arguably, resource allocation has been impaired both within the EU *and* on a world scale, in that the system of agricultural levies distorts comparative advantages by encouraging high-cost production within the EU to the detriment of low-cost production outside the EU. Finally, through its import levies and export subsidies the CAP introduces an element of discrimination against Third World producers of agricultural products, for whom such exports are a major source of foreign earnings.

the import price is below this, say at the 'world price' in Fig. 27.2, then an appropriate tariff must be calculated. This need not quite cover the difference between 'target' and 'world' price, since the importer still has to pay transport costs within the EU to get the food to market. The tariff must therefore be large enough to raise the import price at the EU frontier to the target price minus transport costs, i.e. 'threshold price'. This calculation takes place in the highest-cost area of production in the EU, so that the import tariff set will more than protect EU producers in areas with lower target prices (i.e. lower-cost areas).

Should an EU producer wish to export an agricultural product then an export subsidy will be paid to bring his receipts up to the Intervention price (see Fig. 27.2), i.e. the minimum price he would receive in the home market. Problems involving this form of subsidy of oil-seed exports were a major threat to dealings between the EU and the US, with the latter alleging a breach of GATT rules.

Reforms in the latter part of the 1980s had a significant effect on key sectors such as dairy products. In the cereals and oil-seeds market, intervention buying now occurs only outside the harvest periods. *Maximum Guaranteed Quantities* (MGQs) are also set for most products. If the MGQ is exceeded, then the intervention price is cut by 3% in the following year.

The system outlined above does not apply to all agricultural products in the EU. About a quarter of these products are covered by different direct

The growth of agricultural spending in the early 1980s placed increasing pressure on the EU's 'own resources'. By 1983 the 1% VAT ceiling had been breached and even the steady growth in imports (providing CET revenue) was not sufficient to meet the demands on the budget. The member governments were forced to agree to special additional payments to meet deficits which arose in 1983, 1984, 1985 and 1987. With no agreement on reform during the late 1980s, the CAP began to expand rapidly and the Council was forced to agree a series of 'supplementary' budgets.

The breakthrough occurred at the Brussels Heads of Government meeting in February 1988 during which a further, new source of finance was sanctioned (up to 1.2% of GNP) in return for legislative limits on the CAP. In 1988 the CAP was limited to a fixed sum of 27.5bn ECU (€27.5bn) and from then onwards could only expand, in future years, by three-quarters of the average rate of growth in EU GNP (see Table 27.6). Other significant limits were placed on the CAP in the form of a ceiling on cereal production (160 million tonnes), a cut in producer prices of about 3% and a new 'co-responsibility' levy of 3% on larger farmers.[2]

The reform of CAP took a further step forward in June 1992 when the so-called 'McSharry proposals' for reform were adopted. The purposes of the reforms were, first, to control agricultural production which had been artificially stimulated by CAP; second, to make European agriculture more competitive by reduction of support prices; and third, to discourage very intensive agricultural methods while still maintaining high employment on the land and supporting more marginal and vulnerable farmers.

To achieve these aims, support prices for cereals were to be reduced by some 30%. Also, arable land was taken out of production or 'set aside', with farmers receiving payment based on average yields for what is *not* produced. Livestock farmers were limited to a maximum head of cattle per hectare of available fodder. Other elements of the reform involved direct income-support for farmers in Less Favoured Areas (LFAs) and for those who use environmentally sound methods of farming. Finally, an early 'pre-pension' scheme was introduced to accelerate the retirement of farmers who operated unviable holdings.

In July 1997 the European Commission published *Agenda 2000* which analysed the EU's past policies and considered certain long-term future trends. As far as agriculture was concerned, it recognized the need to extend the agricultural reforms of 1992. The recommendations of 1997 were designed to continue the post-1992 trend of reducing price support to farmers (through the intervention buying system) and providing more money payments direct to producers. For example, in the cereals sector the intervention price was reduced by 15% between 2000 and 2002 to set it closer to world levels (see Fig. 27.1). In the milk sector, the intervention price was cut by 15% in three steps from 2005/06 onwards, although output quotas were raised by 1.5% in three steps from 2000 onwards (from 2003 in the UK) to try to alleviate the problems resulting from a lower intervention price.

Finally, a new Rural Development Policy (RDP) was introduced in January 2000 to boost a variety of restructuring schemes directed towards easing these changes in agricultural policy (see Table 27.3). This is the 'second pillar' of EU agricultural policy and is designed to help stimulate investment in farm business, develop forestry and forestry products, improve training for young farmers and provide help for those older farmers wishing to retire. In the UK, expenditure on the RDP amounted to £1bn between 2000 and 2006 in support of hard-pressed farmers, given the drop in their incomes resulting from lower intervention prices. In fact, since 2002 the European Commission has been involved in discussions relating to reforming the CAP by freezing agricultural spending from 2007 onwards. It has also introduced the

Table 27.6 CAP spending as a proportion of the EU budget, 1984–2010.

	% of EU budget
1984	65.4
1988	65.0
1990	59.4
1992	53.3
1996	50.4
1998	49.0
2002	41.1
2004	39.0
2006	38.0
2008	35.6
2010	35.5

Note: Figures exclude EAGGF guidance.
Sources: As for Table 27.3 and *Eurostat* (various).

idea of 'compulsory modulation' which involves forcing member states to reduce direct payments to agriculture and place more funds into environmental protection and early retirement schemes for workers within the agricultural sector.

Final agreement on the reforms was completed in June 2003 and the implementation by the individual countries took place between 2005 and 2007. The old subsidy system was based on the amount of agricultural output produced, and comprised 11 types of financial support given for growing crops and rearing animals. This system was replaced by a single farm payment (SFP), linked to meeting standards set for the environment, food safety and animal welfare. Recipients will be expected to keep all farmland in good agricultural and environmental condition – this linkage is called 'cross compliance'. Direct payments to larger farms were designed to be reduced and the money used to help finance the new RDP. Decoupling payments from the output produced means that EU support for agriculture will no longer be classified as 'trade distorting', which has been a long-standing criticism of the CAP. However, some member states will retain an element of subsidy in which payments are still linked to output in order to deter farmers from abandoning production and simply taking the single payment for 'environmentally friendly' activities.

Payments made to farmers will depend on each farmer's 'entitlements', which are based on how much the farmer received under the old CAP system. However, this type of payment based on 'historic' entitlement will be phased out gradually and replaced by the flat rate 'single payment' system by 2012. In 2010 UK farmers received around £230 per hectare in SFP payments, as long as they meet standards on the environment, food quality and animal welfare. In the UK, the government expects the new flat rate payment to redistribute subsidies from the more intensive to the less intensive producers, and to land-uses not previously receiving subsidies. Sheep farmers will tend to gain, while beef producers will tend to lose – and in the dairy industry, small producers are expected to gain and large producers to lose. The reformed CAP shows a marked shift of spending towards rural development, where only €7.8m was spent on this area in 2006 as compared to €44.8m on farm subsidies under the CAP. By 2010 the amounts were €14m and €39.2m respectively. In the meantime, the Commission conducted a major review of the CAP in May 2008 to try to make it more efficient. Its proposals included reducing the SFPs to large farms and increasing the funds transferred to the Rural Development budget, and further proposals involved abolishing the set-aside scheme. The CAP is due for renewal in 2013, and it is expected that CAP spending might move towards greater support for innovation, climate and energy. In addition, some proposals have been made to include income insurance schemes for farmers, as 66% of farm earnings are now provided by direct payments from the CAP.

The pressure for agricultural reform has come from many sides – such as consumers who worry that CAP encourages higher prices, ministers afraid of the spiralling budget costs of agricultural subsidies, policymakers aware of the need to shift resources from an EU farming community of 11 million in order to help the 18.5 million Europeans who are unemployed, and supporters of the single currency who accept the need to cut member states' budget deficits in order to meet the Maastricht criteria. Agricultural reform was also accepted as necessary by supporters of EU enlargement who recognized that if price supports were not decreased, then the enlargement of the EU in 2004 would cause severe budgetary difficulties. This was because farm prices in the new entrants were already 20–40% below the EU level and would require extensive (and costly) support to be raised to the EU levels. Such increases in agricultural prices to EU levels could, of course, also cause financial hardship for the consumers in those lower-income countries, as well as giving a cost-push stimulus to inflation.

3 Structural policy

This is the term given to a combination of what used to be called the Regional and Social Policies (together with several other minor policy areas). For clarity, we have separated these two central policy areas in the discussion which follows.

Regional policy

Like the UK's own regional policy, the objective of that for the EU as a whole is to attempt to ease regional economic differences (Chapter 23). Almost a quarter of the current EU budget is devoted to 'regional policy' as part of what are called the 'Structural Funds' (Social plus Regional plus other policies).

Table 27.7 Population covered by EU regional aid, 2007–13.

Country	Population covered (%)	Country	Population covered (%)
Belgium	25.6	Denmark	8.6
Germany	29.9	Estonia	100.0
Greece	100.0	Cyprus	50.0
Spain	59.6	Latvia	100.0
France	18.4	Lithuania	100.0
Ireland	50.0	Hungary	100.0
Italy	34.1	Malta	100.0
Luxembourg	16.0	Poland	100.0
Netherlands	7.5	Romania	100.0
Austria	22.9	Slovenia	100.0
Portugal	76.7	Slovakia	88.9
Finland	33.0	Sweden	15.4
Czech Republic	88.6	UK	21.6
Bulgaria	100.0	EU27	46.4

Sources: European Commission (2010) *Official Journal of the European Union*, and various sources.

Regional policy attempts to improve the structural base of the EU's poorer regions against a background of inequality in income per head, ranging from around 30% of the EU average in some poor regions to over 200% in some rich regions. The disparities in regional income per head have grown still wider with the inclusion of some of the countries in eastern Europe within the EU. Of even greater concern were the findings of an early study by Dunford (1994). This showed that, although the regions of the EU were converging up to 1976, they actually diverged in terms of incomes per head after that date, casting doubt as to the effectiveness of EU regional policy. As a part answer to this problem, a *Cohesion Fund* was introduced in 1993 to help certain countries achieve the convergence criteria necessary for economic and monetary union. Four countries benefited from the Fund because they had GDP per head of less than 90% of the Community average in the early 1990s. They are Spain (75%), Ireland (68%), Portugal (56%) and Greece (47%). To these are now added Poland. Some €41bn was spent on this Cohesion Fund over the 1993–2006 time period.

The accepted wisdom during the 1970s and 1980s was that a European *core* existed which was highly developed and very wealthy. The core consisted of the northern and western parts of Germany, Benelux, most of northern France and south-east England. Outside the core the picture was of a less-developed *periphery*. It is now understood that the EU's pattern of economic wellbeing is more patchy and far more complex than the 'core and periphery' model.

This core–periphery model has become even more complex with the accession of the EU10 countries in 2004 and the reduced entitlements on offer. For example, the EU had already decided to reduce the proportion of the population eligible to receive regional aid as early as 1997 in order to reduce the value of such subsidies to industry. Over the period 2007–13 the aim is to limit the overall coverage of regional aid to 42% of the population. Table 27.7 provides some idea of the projected coverage of regional aid in the EU27 for the period 2007–13, indicating that the percentage of the population covered by regional aid varies from very low coverage in the Netherlands to very high coverage in the EU10, partly reflecting the lower relative incomes per head shown in Table 27.1. New maps showing the areas covered by regional aid in the various countries have been published since January 2007.

Initially the EU will more carefully scrutinize the eligibility of regions for the *Objective 1* status which provides maximum grants, i.e. where GDP per head in the region is less than 75% of the EU average. By 2006, some 50 regions, covering 22% of the EU's population, had received money under Objective 1, accounting for 74% of the total Structural Fund budget. Meanwhile, 18% of the EU population lived in areas that received *Objective 2* money, accounting for 9% of the Structural Fund's resources. Finally, *Objective 3*, whose eligibility is not confined to any particular areas of the EU, received 10.3% of total Structural Fund resources.

In the UK, the EU classified Cornwall and the Isles of Scilly, South Yorkshire, West Wales and the Valleys, and Merseyside as areas eligible for Objective 1 funding over the period 2000–06. These areas cover some 5 million people and each has GDP per head levels of around 70% of the EU average. Northern Ireland and the Highlands and Islands received transitional support until 2006 to help them consolidate the improvements they achieved as a result of previous funding in the 1990s.

Social policy

The development of European social policy has involved both the operation of the *European Social Fund* (ESF) and developments in the 'Social Chapter' of the Maastricht Treaty.

The ESF is designed to develop human resources and improve the workings of the labour market throughout the EU. Expenditure is concentrated in those regions of the EU which are suffering from high unemployment and is designed to help with retraining initiatives, improving skills and providing educational opportunities in order to make the labour force more flexible. In March 1998 the European Commission formally adopted a series of draft regulations which formed the backbone of the ESF's plans for the 2000–06 period. At the centre of these plans was the new European Employment Strategy (EES) which stipulates that each member state must submit an annual employment plan directed towards raising 'employability, entrepreneurship, labour force adaptability and equal opportunities'. A sum of €210bn was allocated to achieving these goals by 2006.

As far as the 'Social Chapter' of the Maastricht Treaty is concerned, the UK had been opposed to many of the regulations and directives associated with the Social Chapter, with successive Conservative governments arguing that attempting to impose regulations in such areas as works councils, maternity/paternity rights, equal pay, part-time workers issues, etc. merely increased labour costs and decreased UK competitiveness. Nevertheless, the government in the UK has adopted many parts of the Social Chapter in order to provide basic minimum standards across Europe even if this does result in some increase in labour costs. In any case, even if the UK had remained outside the Social Chapter it would still have been subject to a great deal of EU social legislation introduced as part of other programmes from which there is no UK 'opt-out'. The UK has adopted the Directives such as the Working Time Directive and the Parent Leave Directive in an attempt to catch up with other EU members which had already adopted these directives (see Chapter 14).

4 Trade policy and balance of payments

The EU is the largest trading bloc in the world. It accounts for 19% of world GDP and around 41% of world trade. The EU runs a deficit on its visible trade with the rest of the world, largely due to its need for substantial imports of fuel and raw materials. As regards invisible trade, the EU is roughly in balance with the rest of the world. By the early 1990s, almost 60% of both EU exports and imports involved other EU countries. The growth of this intra-European trade has been a significant factor in attracting inward investment into the EU (see Chapter 7).

The UK's trade with the EU

The UK's trade with the EU has shown important changes since the late 1960s. First, the area composition of UK visible exports and imports indicates a strong movement towards the Community. In 1969, for example, 29% of total UK visible exports were destined for the EU, whilst 26% of UK visible imports came from the EU. By 2010 the shares had increased significantly, to 57% and 56% respectively. Second, as can be seen from Table 27.8, the UK's trade with the rest of the EU has shown that the UK had a deficit on trade in goods and services with the EU. Thus there is little real evidence that the UK could earn sufficient income from the EU to cover its large trade deficit, especially in manufactures. Any disadvantage for the UK in its trade in manufactures is particularly worrying, since exports and imports of manufactures together constitute some 66% of total trade with the EU whilst food, drink, tobacco and oil together account for only 25%.

The nature of the EU, as a bloc which allows free trade in manufactured goods, has worked to the

Table 27.8 UK current account transactions with the EU, 1996–2009.

£m	1996	1998	2000	2002	2005	2009
Balances						
Trade in goods	−4,870	−6,571	−5,262	−22,194	−36,048	−37,162
Trade in services	−397	244	−1,894	−1,409	−1,852	9,205
Trade in goods and services	−5,267	−6,327	−7,156	−23,603	−37,900	−27,957
Investment income	1,899	7,861	6,378	18,708	11,275	19,508
Current transfers	−6,606	−6,562	−5,521	−4,217	−5,615	−5,926
Current account	**−9,974**	**−5,028**	**−6,299**	**−9,112**	**−32,240**	**−14,375**

Source: Adapted from ONS (2010c) *United Kingdom Balance of Payments*, and previous issues.

disadvantage of many relatively less efficient British manufacturers. Similarly, the fact that the EU remains a relatively closed market with respect to both agricultural goods and invisibles (particularly the two areas of relative British strength – insurance and banking) has tended to restrict the UK from taking advantage of the areas in which it has had a small comparative advantage. Table 27.8 shows the UK's current account transactions with the EU for selected years between 1996 and 2009. The deficit on the goods account continues to be a weakness; whilst trade in services in 2009 has shown significant improvement, it is not clear whether this trend in services will continue. The improvement in the UK's investment income account has continued with the EU, supporting the idea that it is in her trade balance with the EU that most of the UK's problems lie as regards current account transactions.

5 Monetary policy

A single currency permitting trade at 'known prices' has been a long-standing goal of the EU. Such a currency would overcome the uncertainties created by currency fluctuations which discourage medium- and long-term contracts and therefore international trade. A common currency and common exchange reserves, together with a European Central Bank, are the major features of European EMU. The 'Snake', and later the European Monetary System (EMS), were seen by many as steps towards European monetary union.

While now thoroughly integrated into the move towards economic and monetary union, we deal in this section with the background to EMU in the form of the EMS and its precursors and the European Currency Unit (ECU). The discussion of EMU and the euro is presented in a separate section below.

The 'Snake', 1973–79

Consultations between the 'Six' and the three applicant countries between 1970 and 1972 led in 1973 to the establishment of a currency co-operation system called variously the 'Snake', or the 'Snake in the Tunnel'. It required each central bank to maintain its currency within a band of ±2.25% against the US dollar, limiting the fluctuations that could occur between member country currencies. This had the advantage of reducing uncertainty but it did restrict the use of the exchange rate as a policy instrument for adjusting trade deficits and surpluses between members.

The oil crisis of 1973 and ensuing world recession created balance of payments problems for many member countries. Fluctuations in the balance of payments in turn led to more volatile exchange rates, making it more difficult to maintain par values within the narrow bands of the 'Snake'. As a result, the UK remained a member for only a few months, with France also leaving the system in January 1974. Although the 'Snake' itself continued, it did so in a truncated form, with three members outside (UK, the Republic of Ireland and France) and four non-members inside (Norway, Sweden, Austria and Switzerland). In effect, the 'Snake' now contained only currencies with a historically close link to the Deutsch mark (DM) and it was replaced in the late 1970s by the EMS.

European Monetary System (EMS) since 1979

The EMS was created in order to increase co-operation on monetary affairs within the Community, and like the 'Snake' was founded on the ultimate goal of European Monetary Union (EMU). The EMS was established in March 1979 with three main components, a European currency unit (ECU), an Exchange Rate Mechanism (ERM), and the European Monetary Co-operation Fund (EMCF). In 1989 a fourth element was added – the Very Short Term Financing facility (VSTF). This is a means of funding deficits between member states to an unlimited amount, but for very short periods of time.

The ECU was, possibly, the most radical of the EMS innovations. Whilst superficially similar to the old unit of account in which EU dealings used to be denominated, the ECU was far more than a *numéraire*. It was valued according to a weighted basket of all the EU currencies. Being a weighted average it was more stable than the exchange rate of any single currency. In addition to its role as a unit of account, it functioned as an international reserve currency. Each member of the EMS 'bought' ECUs with 20% of their gold and dollar reserves, which were then held by a new EU institution called the European Monetary Co-operation Fund (FECOM according to its French initials). The central banks used their holdings of ECUs to buy each other's currencies and to settle debts. Of course, as of 1 January 1999, the ECU was replaced on a one-to-one basis by the euro.

The second element of the EMS involved the ERM which was, essentially, a development of the 'Snake'. Like its predecessor, the scheme originally set a 2.25% divergence limit, but this time not against the more volatile individual currencies but against the ECU. The new scheme also differed from the old in that it encompassed a formally recognized method of 'warning' governments that they have to take action. Each currency had a 'divergence limit'[3] computed against each of the other currencies in the scheme which, because it did not include the 'home' currency whose divergence against itself was zero, was always slightly less than the official 2.25% limit. If a currency diverged by more than 75% of this limit it had reached its 'divergence threshold' and the government was expected to intervene, either to buy its own currency for ECUs (if the exchange rate has declined) or to sell it for ECUs (if the exchange rate has risen).

The EMCF, the third element in the EMS, consisted of all the heads of the central banks of the member states and was intended to supervise the use of the 'official ECU'. This was the currency unit originally established, and acted as a means of settling deficits between the members; it was supported by an IMF-type system of deposits of gold and foreign currency. It held the members' 20% deposits of gold and dollars, was empowered to lend up to 25bn ECUs to countries in difficulties, and was intended ultimately to become a central bank for Europe acting to support the ECU against the dollar, yen, etc.

Until mid-1987 the development of the ECU as a private currency was hampered by the refusal of the West Germans to recognize it. The ECU had been developing as a major international bond currency and, indeed, as a private European currency, but the objections of the West Germans meant that it could not be truly 'European'. In June 1987, however, the West German government removed their veto on the private holding of ECUs by their citizens and thereby opened the way for further liberalization of capital movements within the Community. Up to 1999 the ECU was used throughout the EU as a basis for travellers' cheques, and the Belgian government even issued 50 ECU gold and 5 ECU silver coins in 1987 to celebrate the thirtieth anniversary of the founding of the EC. After 1999, the ECU was superseded by the euro.

The UK and the EMS

The UK has always been a member of the EMS but, until late 1990, did not join its exchange rate system (known as the 'parity grid'). The UK government felt in 1978 that sterling would be too volatile to cope with the confines of the parity grid system. The UK anticipated a continual need to defend a weak pound within the grid, thereby putting pressure on its gold and foreign exchange reserves. The UK also held that the restricted variation in exchange rate against other member currencies would impede the use of the exchange rate as a policy instrument. Finally, by setting limits for sterling, the exchange rate could less readily be used for economic management in the UK, e.g. a high pound helping to curb inflation.

Up to 1987 there had been 11 realignments in the EMS parity grid. The West Germans felt that these readjustments were too frequent, allowing several countries to avoid the macroeconomic discipline originally intended by adopting the system. Ironically, having remained out of the parity grid due to fears of sterling's weakness, the UK government experienced for a period the exact opposite. At least until the end of 1982 the problem would have been that of having to keep sterling down within the grid rather than of establishing a 'floor' for sterling.

There is considerable evidence to suggest that UK trade has become less sensitive to price factors and therefore less easily influenced by exchange rate adjustment. Further, a third of UK trade is still invoiced in the dollar or in other EMS currencies, reducing the importance of EMS currency fluctuations to the UK. For these reasons, it has been suggested that the restrictions imposed on the *sterling exchange rate* by the EMS parity grid were, from the point of view of trade, less important to the UK than to other EU member countries. It would therefore seem that the restrictions imposed upon *UK demand management*, via the parity grid, proved the greater deterrent to full UK participation within the EMS. However, the arguments in favour of the UK joining the EMS parity grid became stronger as the EU became more important in UK trade, and as dollar-invoiced oil took a smaller share in UK exports. The problem, once the UK joined in 1990, became the ability of the system to cope with three major currencies, in view of the difficulties it had experienced in coping with two, namely, the DM and French franc.

Black Wednesday

The initial phase of UK membership of the EMS lasted less than two years before the Conservative government of John Major withdrew sterling on Wednesday, 16 September 1992 – 'Black Wednesday'.

Underlying the events which led to the withdrawal of sterling and the lira from the EMS in September 1992 were two phenomena: the weakness of the US economy and the resulting low interest rates in that country, and the large amounts of capital required by Germany for economic reconstruction in the eastern part of that country and the resulting high interest rates needed in Germany to reduce inflationary pressure. Finance flowed towards the DM and out of US dollars and sterling. The UK government made it worse by refusing to realign sterling in the ERM in early September and there followed two weeks of momentous pressure on European currencies and the ERM itself.

Downward pressure on the Italian lira forced the Italian government first to increase domestic interest rates twice – first to 15% (4 September) and then to 20% (8 September). Continued speculative selling of the lira then forced the Italians to negotiate the first realignment in the EMS since 1987 – a 7% devaluation of the lira against the other EMS currencies (13 September). Finally, a small reduction in German interest rates (by 0.25% on 14 September) was not enough to prevent the lira being withdrawn from the EMS on Black Wednesday.

Sterling followed a similar path to the lira but without the intermediate rises in interest rates. On 3 September the Chancellor announced that the UK was borrowing £7.25bn in foreign currency to assist in the defence of the pound. At the same time, the government made it clear that they had no intention of allowing sterling to be deflected from its rate and band in the EMS. Both German and French central banks, the Bundesbank and the Bank of France, assisted the Bank of England in trying to defend sterling's central rate in the EMS.

By Wednesday 16 September, however, the financial markets had driven sterling below its 'floor' in the EMS and the British government took drastic measures to attempt to maintain sterling's position. Unprecedented rises in British interest rates – by 2% and then by another 3% (from 10% to 15%) – were announced during Wednesday 16 September, but neither was sufficient to prevent sales of sterling from reducing its rate against the DM well below the EMS 'floor' of DM2.78. Sterling was withdrawn from the EMS system – along with the lira – and allowed to 'float'. Viewed against an EMS central rate of DM2.95 and a 'floor' of DM2.78, sterling quickly fell and continued falling. By October 1992 it had reached DM2.36 – a devaluation of some 20% on its previous central rate in the EMS.

These events seemed to indicate that a fixed system of exchange rates could not stand against the sheer scale of currency movements in the new global financial markets. A number of factors might, however, have exacerbated the situation for the EMS in September 1992 which need not have been allowed to hold sway. In the absence of these factors it might have been that the system could have weathered the period in a more effective manner.

It might have been the case that the attempt – unofficially – to 'fix' the EMS currencies together as early as the late 1980s and early 1990s was just too early. No realignment had taken place since 1987 in spite of significant underlying economic changes in the economies of the member states (reunification in Germany, lower inflation and better industrial performance in France, high inflation and poor economic performance in Italy, and persistent recession and falling industrial production in the UK). Rather than relieving pressures and differentials gradually by occasional realignments, the EMS had resisted changes in parity for five years. At the same time, unusually large divergencies had built up between the US and German economies. Interest rates of 3% in the US and 9% in Germany carried sufficient differential to create massive currency flows between the two and between Germany and other less successful economies. Large amounts of money were required by the German economy to finance reconstruction, and high interest rates were deemed to be required both to encourage this investment and to keep inflation in check. Political and financial uncertainties over the future of the Maastricht Treaty and, therefore, over the future of EMU following the Danish rejection of the Treaty simply added to the problem.

The crisis in the EMS in September 1992 did not imply that such currency arrangements were impractical or irrelevant, only that the member states of the EU needed to gain more experience of their management. The key seems to lie in achieving the correct balance in the degree of 'fixity' of the rates in the system and in ensuring that 'divergence indicators' require both strong and weak currencies to take action. Concerns about the degree of 'fixity' were met in late 1992 by extending the ERM fluctuation bands to ±15%. This band continued in operation for the non-eurozone currencies after the major EMU reforms of 1999.

6 Commercial and industrial policy

The Common Customs Tariff (CCT) is common to all members of the EU and is imposed on all industrial imports from non-EU countries, though with a few exceptions. Tariff rates differ from one kind of import to another. For example, raw materials and some types of semi-manufactured goods that are not produced within the EU tend to benefit from low duty rates. Tariff rates may also be set at a low rate to stimulate competition within some sectors of the EU, e.g. for pharmaceutical and IT-related goods. Since tariffs on industrial products traded between member countries have been dismantled, the application of the CCT has created a protected free trade area or 'customs union' of some 460 million consumers.

The effect of creating a customs union is, however, double-edged. 'Trade creation' is the term used to refer to the extra trade between members of the customs union as a result of removing tariff barriers. Production of certain goods is then transferred from high-cost to low-cost producers within the customs union. It can therefore be argued that trade creation causes resources *within* the customs union to be used more efficiently. However, 'trade diversion' also occurs as a result of the CCT imposed against non-members of the customs union. This may cause some production to be transferred from low-cost producers *outside* the union to high-cost producers inside. We shall see below that the two effects are extremely difficult to quantify. However, in general terms, the higher the original tariff between member countries, and the higher the original tariff against non-members, the more likely it will be that the efficiency gains from trade creation will outweigh the efficiency losses from trade diversion.

A major study of trade in manufactured goods in France, Germany, Italy and the UK over the period 1985–95 showed a strong 'trade-creation' effect from the creation of the Single Market but found little evidence of a 'trade diversion' effect (European Commission 1996). For example, while the share of the domestic demand in these countries met from other member states (i.e. *intra-EU trade*) rose from 16.9% to 21.5% between 1985 and 1995, the share of domestic demand met from outside the EU also increased from 12.7% to 15.6%. In other words, there was a strong trade creation effect (rise in intra-EU trade) and no evidence of a trade diversion effect (fall in *extra-EU trade*).

UK industry and the EU

It is extremely difficult to evaluate the industrial effects of UK entry into the EU. Certainly the hope on entry was that the UK would secure 'dynamic gains' in this sector to offset the expected 'static costs' of the net budget contribution and higher food prices. The 'dynamic gains' were expected to include a boost to output and productivity from a large, protected market, with its potential for scale economies and greater export opportunities. However, for whatever reason,

Table 27.9 Comparisons of manufacturing output (1970 = 100).

	1970	1975	1980	1985	1992	2010*
EU (excluding UK)	100	108	133	133	154	179
Germany	100	104	122	122	138	174
France	100	108	133	133	157	174
Italy	100	107	139	132	160	148
UK	100	102	110	113	128	137

*Second quarter.
Source: Adapted from OECD (2010a) *Main Economic Indicators,* and previous issues.

there seems little evidence in Table 27.9 of those gains in UK manufacturing output anticipated after entry into the EU in 1973. In fact, the real output of UK manufacturing has grown more slowly than that of the other EU countries.

Lord Kaldor suggested, prior to entry, that the alleged 'dynamic gains' might turn out to be 'dynamic costs', as the UK market in industrial products became more exposed to its European competitors with the dismantling of tariffs. It may be that the UK joined the wrong type of 'customs union'! If trade in agriculture and in service activities were freed between member countries, rather than trade in industrial products, then some of the alleged 'dynamic gains' might indeed have materialized. In Chapter 1 we noted that the trend towards service activities, though a feature of all advanced economies, has been most marked in the UK. It is arguable that it is in this sector that the UK's comparative advantages lie. The present industrial policy of the EU, which frees trade in industrial products whilst permitting (along with WTO/GATT) the protection of services, would seem to be to the particular disadvantage of the UK.

Monetary union

European Economic and Monetary Union (EMU)

As long ago as 1969 the Commission funded the 'Werner Report' which acknowledged what it called the 'political wish to establish economic and monetary union' and set a target of completion by 1980. Unfortunately the severe economic traumas of the 1970s intervened and it was 1979 before even the first stage – the setting up of the EMS – was accomplished.

In 1988 the Council decided to look into the matter again and set up a Committee under the then EC President, Jacques Delors. That Committee reported in June 1989 and the Council agreed to enter into Stage 1 on 1 July 1990.

The first stage of the Delors Plan – the establishment of a true Single European Market (SEM) – had, of course, already been put in train by the Single European Act of 1987. As the fundamental base of the EMU structure, the Commission felt that it was necessary to set out clearly what the economic benefits would be. They therefore commissioned a group of senior economists, financiers and business people to investigate the issues. The Committee under the chairmanship of Paulo Ceccini reported in 1988.

The Ceccini Report

Although published as a single report, the 'Ceccini Report' is simply the summary and conclusions of no fewer than 13 separate economic reports on aspects of the single market. It identifies two types of cost associated with what it calls, in shorthand, 'non-Europe', i.e. a Europe of markets separated by physical, technical and fiscal barriers:

■ first, those barriers which have an immediate benefit when they are removed;

■ second, those which will have benefits spread over a period of time.

It should be noted that both types include elements of both static and dynamic benefits.

The parts which made up the 'Ceccini Report' examined the single market from the point of view of microeconomic benefits (the removal of non-tariff barriers, economies of scale, X-efficiencies, etc.) and of macroeconomic benefits (the supply-side shock and its effects on GDP, inflation rates, employment, production, etc.).

Using a variety of methods, the Report came up with significant benefits which might accrue to EU members as a result of the Single Market. These included the following:

- total gains of around 216bn ECU at 1988 prices (between 4.3% and 6.4% of EU GDP);
- price deflation of an average 6.1%;
- an improvement to the EU's external trade of about 1%;
- an improvement to budget balances of about 2.2%; and
- around 1.8 million new jobs (a reduction in unemployment of about 1.5%).

The Maastricht agreement set out a planned system for moving towards EMU, including the creation of a system of European central banks to precede the European Central Bank (ECB). The full schedule was delineated in three 'Stages'.

Stage 1

Theoretically this commenced on 1 January 1993 and involved the creation of an EU 'Monetary Committee' whose role included general monitoring and review of monetary matters in EU states and throughout the EU as a whole, providing advice to the Council of Ministers and contributing to the preparation for the European System of Central Banks (ESCB) and the ECB (see below).

Stage 2

In theory, this Stage was to commence on 1 January 1994 with the establishment of a new 'European Monetary Institute' to strengthen co-operation between EU central banks, co-ordinate monetary policy, monitor the functioning of the EMS and take over the role of the EMCF. The EMI would seek to obtain a 'high degree of sustainable convergence' against four criteria:

1 *Price stability*. This should be close to the performance of the three best performing members. In a protocol to the treaty 'close to' was defined as not more than 1.5% above the average inflation of the three best performers.

2 *Government finance*. This should adhere to a pre-ordained 'reference value' – defined as a government deficit of no more than 3% of GDP at market prices and a government debt of no more than 60% of GDP at market prices.

3 *ERM fluctuations*. Normal margins of fluctuation should not have been breached for *two years*.

4 *Durability of convergence*. This was to be measured by long-term interest rate levels. The rate for long-term government bonds should not have exceeded by more than 2% those of the three best performing countries.

The Maastricht Treaty required that the EMI should specify – by 31 December 1996 at the latest – the regulatory, organizational and logistical framework for the ESCB (to be created in the third stage). It should also set a date for the beginning of the Third Stage. If this date was not set before the end of 1997 it would, according to the Treaty, automatically begin on 1 January 1999.

Stage 3

This stage included the establishment of the ESCB which would hold and manage the official reserves of all the member states. At this stage, exchange rates would be fixed and the ECU would acquire full status as a currency throughout the Community. The ESCB would prepare for the establishment of the ECB which, when founded, would have the exclusive right to issue banknotes throughout the EU. It would accomplish this through the central bank of each of the member states. It would receive some 5bn ECU together with all members' reserves – excepting only member states' foreign currency, ECU holdings, IMF reserve positions and special drawing rights (SDRs). Any reserves over 50bn ECU in value would also be left with the member country (in theory, of course, these would not be required and could be used in any way by the member state). The theoretical total reserves to be held by the ESCB would, therefore, be around 600bn ECU.

Maastricht established the shape and format of all of the institutions it envisaged. The Treaty provided for it to come into force on 1 January 1993 or on the date on which the last member country deposited an instrument of ratification with the Commission.

There were a number of protocols to the Maastricht Treaty involving most of the members. The UK had a lengthy protocol agreed which allowed it not to proceed to Stage 3 if it did not wish to and excluded it from most of the Stage 2 arrangements (in return the UK would not be allowed to have a vote in Council on arrangements to do with the ESCB or the ECB).

The path to EMU settled down into the following timetable:

1996–98	All member countries brought their economies into line to meet the Maastricht criteria (see Table 27.10).
1998	The countries which formed the first members of EMU were selected.
1999	January 1 – the EMU process began with the launch of the euro and the beginning of the transition phase (through to the end of 2001). During this phase national currencies still existed but were irrevocably fixed to each other and to the euro.
2002	January 1 – the euro was introduced in coin and note form. A period of six months was allowed for national currencies to be withdrawn from circulation. Since 1 July 2002 only the euro has been legal tender in EMU member countries.

Single currency: the euro

The launch of the single currency, the 'euro', occurred on 1 January 1999, although it did not become a physical currency until 1 January 2002 (see also Chapter 20). However, from 1999 onwards the euro became a legal currency in its own right and the vehicle for electronic and business-to-business transactions throughout the eurozone. As early as January 1999 some 25% of Barclays Bank customers had already been asked to invoice or pay in euros.

The long-term effects of the euro, and with it EMU, are to change the nature of the way business is carried out in Europe. For consumers, prices are more 'transparent', making it easier to see whether different prices are being charged for the same product in various EU countries. For manufacturers and other traders, the introduction of EMU means the elimination of exchange rate risks, which should benefit smaller businesses which often lack the resources for foreign exchange management.

The EMU might also produce further corporate rationalization as firms merge in an attempt to grow larger in order to derive scale economies from operating within the Single Market. The foreign exchange market is restricted in its dealings as fewer currencies are traded, with most dealings being in currencies outside the euro, together with euro–dollar or euro–yen. It is likely that a new market for government debt denominated in euros and a new pool of euro-denominated equity will be created.

For the potential benefits of the euro and EMU to be realized in the long run, three factors will be decisive:

1   *Sustainable economic convergence.* For the smooth working of the euro, the economies of the participating countries must be in the same stage of the economic cycle and be relatively homogeneous.

2   *Strong political commitments to EMU discipline.* The European Council of Economic and Financial Ministers (ECOFIN), consisting of the finance ministers of the EU, is able to impose severe fines on member states whose budget deficits exceed the ratio of 3% of GDP. The fines could, as noted above, reach as much as 0.5% of GDP.

3   *Credible European Central Bank* (ECB). The ECB's independence is enshrined in the Maastricht treaty, as is its commitment to price stability. Short-term interest rates are set with a view to achieving such price stability. However, political pressure for reflationary policies might arise if the EU experiences slow growth and high unemployment.

The question also remains as to how the national central banks will operate under EMU. Together with the ECB, the national central banks formed the ESCB in June 1998. This body, through its Governing Council and Executive Board, defines and implements monetary policy and foreign exchange and reserves policies. However, the operational responsibility to carry out agreed ESCB policy is retained by the national central banks. As with the federal central banking systems of the US and Germany, the operations of the ESCB are therefore highly decentralized. There is a risk that the national central banks may try to pressurize the independent ECB to adopt policies directed towards growth and employment in situations where the ECB might be more inclined to tighten control of inflation.

Convergence and the Growth and Stability Pact (GSP)

In March 1998 the European Commission announced that 11 members had reached a sufficient degree of sustainable convergence as measured against the Maastricht Treaty criteria. The relevant criteria were (1) consumer price inflation must not exceed that of the three best-performing countries by more than $1\frac{1}{2}$ percentage points; (2) interest rates on long-term government securities must not be more than 2 percentage points higher than those in the same three member states; (3) the financial position must be sustainable. In particular, the general government deficit should be at or below the reference value of 3% of GDP, or, if not, it should have declined substantially and continuously and reached a level close to the reference value, or the excess over the reference value should be temporary and exceptional. The gross debt of general government should be at or below 60% of GDP or, if not, the debt ratio should be sufficiently diminishing and approaching the 60% reference value at a satisfactory pace. The exchange rate criterion is that the currency must have been held within the normal fluctuation margins of the ERM for two years without a realignment at the initiative of the member state in question. Based on these figures it was agreed that 11 members of the EU had reached a sufficient degree of sustainable convergence against the criteria laid down in the Maastricht Treaty. The countries which qualified and wished to join the single currency in January 1999 were Austria, Belgium, Finland, France, Germany, Ireland, Italy, Luxembourg, the Netherlands, Portugal and Spain. Sweden and Greece did not meet the convergence criteria at that time and the UK and Denmark had already decided not to take part in Stage 3 of EMU in 1999.

The European Commission's convergence report of March 2000 concluded that Greece had met the criteria for entering the EMU and Greece was subsequently accepted as a full member from January 2001. Sweden was deemed not to have met the criteria on convergence since its legislation was not compatible with the Treaty and the ESCB Statute, and also its exchange rate had been outside the ERM II and hence fluctuated against the ERM currencies. The UK and Denmark had decided not to take part in Stage 3 of EMU in 1999 and thus remained outside 'Euroland'.

To maintain stability in Euroland, a 'Growth and Stability Pact' has been operating since January 1999 which is designed to ensure that the euro maintains its value over time by committing the participating countries to form 'convergence contracts'. These contracts are necessary to make sure that members of Euroland continue to maintain their economies under the same economic criteria as when they entered. In particular, the Pact was designed to ensure that the medium-term budgetary discipline criteria were met. At least every two years, the Commission and the ECB report to the Council on the fulfilment of the convergence criteria. If member states exceed the criteria for government budget deficit (set at 3% of GDP) or government debt (set at 60% of GDP) they would be penalized. Penalties for *excessive government deficits* can involve members having to lodge with the Commission a fixed, non-interest bearing deposit of 0.2% of the country's GDP and a variable non-interest bearing deposit of 0.1% of GDP for every 0.1% excess over the deficit criteria, up to a ceiling of 0.5% of GDP. The penalty for *excessive government debt* is a fixed amount involving a non-interest bearing deposit of 2% of a country's GDP.

The rationale for introducing budgetary discipline in the form of 'fiscal rules' as the major part of the GSP included the following.

1 There was a need to correct the so-called 'deficit bias' of fiscal policy, i.e. bureaucrats are inclined to spend more than they can afford in the present, and pass the burden of this spending onto future taxpayers. For example, in the mid-1990s, fiscal deficits of 4–5% of GDP were common and these continuously large deficits led to debt as a percentage of GDP rising from 35% in 1980 to 75% by the mid-1990s. To finance such large deficits means that interest rates need to be increased, which in turn cuts back investment and growth.

2 High deficits and debts also have an effect on monetary policy, because fiscal expansion boosts domestic demand and may give rise to inflationary pressures which may require higher interest rates and reduced money supply to curb them.

3 Fiscal rules may also be needed to help stabilize an individual economy because monetary policy is undertaken by the ECB for *all* countries in the eurozone. In other words, individual countries only have their own fiscal policy to deal with their particular problems and fiscal rules may be

necessary to make sure that countries do not expand their budget deficits too much in their attempt to correct an economic downturn.

The actual performance of EU countries, *vis-à-vis* the GSP 'rules', has changed over time. For example, in 1993, when the Maastricht treaty entered into force, the deficit ratio of the euro area stood at a peak of 5.5% of GDP and this was reduced to 3% in 1997,

the year identified for meeting the Maastricht convergence criteria. Fiscal balances improved considerably between 1997 and 2000, but when growth slowed down after 2000 the fiscal balances of some countries quickly deteriorated. Portugal was first to breach the 3% reference value in 2001, and Germany and France followed in 2002, the Netherlands and Greece in 2003, and Italy in 2004. Table 27.10 shows the position for all the 27 countries in 2009 following the

Table 27.10 Performance of the member states in relation to the convergence criteria, 2009.

	Inflation HICP (%) 2009	Deficit (% of GDP)* 2009	Debt (% of GDP) 2009	ERM member 2005	Long-term interest rate 2009
Reference value	1%	3%	60%		
Belgium	0.0	−6.0	96.7	yes	3.0
Germany	0.2	−3.3	73.2	yes	2.4
Greece	1.3	−13.6	115.1	yes	10.7
Spain	−0.2	−11.2	53.2	yes	4.0
France	0.1	−7.5	77.6	yes	2.7
Ireland	−1.7	−14.3	64.0	yes	5.3
Italy	0.8	−5.3	115.8	yes	3.8
Luxembourg	0.0	−0.7	14.5	yes	2.7
Netherlands	1.0	−5.3	60.9	yes	2.6
Austria	0.4	−3.4	66.5	yes	2.8
Portugal	−0.9	−9.4	76.8	yes	5.3
Finland	1.6	−2.2	44.0	yes	2.6
Czech Republic	0.6	−5.9	35.4	no	3.6
Denmark	1.1	−2.7	41.6	no	2.5
Estonia	0.2	−1.7	7.2	no	3.9
Cyprus	3.3	−6.1	56.2	no	4.6
Latvia	4.2	−9.0	36.1	no	10.0
Lithuania	4.0	−8.9	29.3	no	5.2
Hungary	1.8	−4.0	78.3	no	7.1
Malta	4.0	−3.8	69.1	no	4.0
Poland	0.9	−7.1	51.0	no	5.6
Romania	5.6	−8.3	23.7	no	7.2
Bulgaria	2.5	−3.9	14.8	no	6.0
Slovenia	0.9	−5.5	35.9	no	3.7
Slovakia	0.9	−6.8	35.7	no	3.7
Sweden	1.9	−0.5	42.3	no	2.7
UK	2.2	−11.5	68.1	no	2.7
EU27	**1.0**	**−6.8**	**73.6**	**−**	**4.3**

*A negative sign for the government deficit indicates a surplus.
Sources: Eurostat (2010) *Euro indicators*; ECB (2010) *Statistics Pocket Book*, May.

financial shock in 2007/8. Almost all the countries were in breach of the 3% reference, with the average for the 27 countries being 6.8% and the UK's deficit nearing twice the average. With regards to the debt-to-GDP ratio, some 12 countries were breaching the 60% reference value in 2009, with Italy, Greece, Belgium, France and Germany, amongst others, showing figures of over 70%.

Problems with the Growth and Stability Pact (GSP)

Three main problems have been identified for the GSP.

1 *Excessive rigidity*. For example, the 3% deficit limit on each country does not take into consideration important variables such as the stock of public debt, the need for infrastructure investment, or the population age structure – all of which affect the demand for fiscal spending. Hence, the operation of a single figure of 3% as the maximum budget deficit for *all* economies is too rigid. Another rigidity arises because the GSP focuses on annual budgets and therefore overlooks longer-term relationships. For example, governments may be forced to postpone structural reforms, e.g. a pension system that would yield benefits only in the medium-to-long term, in order to meet the annual 'fiscal rule'.

2 *Limiting discretionary fiscal policy* which governments may wish to introduce to help their economy. Germany had to struggle to reduce expenditure and to raise taxes whilst on the brink of a recession in 2003.

3 *Lacking credibility*. The sanctions are decided by ECOFIN, i.e. the economic and finance ministers of the eurozone, in which political motivation has high priority as seen when France and Germany broke the rules in 2003 where no fine was imposed.

The new Growth and Stability Pact

Various problems with the GSP led to its reform in March 2005 in an attempt to meet some of the criticisms outlined above (ECB 2005). The new SGP introduced differentiated 'medium term objectives' (MTOs), which take into account the economic characteristics of each country, especially in relation to the debt-to-GDP ratio. These MTOs will be measured in *cyclically adjusted* terms, i.e. net of one-off and temporary measures to make sure that the focus is on the underlying structural budget position and not on the simple annual budgetary situation as in the original SGP. Second, under the SGP a deficit above 3% of GDP will not necessarily be considered excessive if it can be shown that the breach is 'exceptionally temporary', e.g. a deficit can be considered exceptional if it results from a 'severe economic downturn'. The new GSP provides a list of factors which will be taken into account if the deficit is above 3%, unlike the original GSP. However, the new provisions might make it more difficult to harmonize monetary and fiscal policy and therefore force the ECB to strengthen its stance on interest rates (Al Eyd and Gottschalk 2005).

As a result of the global crisis in 2008, the European Commission adopted an ambitious reform of the pact in July 2010, designed to prevent fiscal ill-discipline. All eurozone members must specify medium-term budget objectives and the growth of public spending must be kept below the medium-term growth of GDP until the target is met. Countries are also required to implement 'best practice' budgetary procedures, such as medium-term planning, fiscal rules, etc. In addition, there is an *explicit* budget deficit limit of 3% of GDP and a target public debt ratio of 60% of GDP. All countries that exceed the debt limit are required to reduce their debt every year at a rate of one-twentieth of the excess debt. For example, a country with a debt of 100%, and thus some 40% from the target, will need to cut the debt by two points (40/20) of GDP every year.

Violation of either budget deficit or debt requirements leads to an 'infringement process' and a fine of 2% of GDP if countries do not comply. In addition, the Commission also envisaged monitoring countries using 'vulnerability indicators' such as private and public debt, competitiveness, productivity growth, the current account and credit expansion. The Commission will open another infringement procedure for 'excessive imbalances' if the country fails to introduce corrective measures – possibly resulting in a fine of 0.1% of GDP.

Advantages/disadvantages of a single currency

A number of advantages have been claimed for the single currency.

■ *Lower costs of exchange.* Importers no longer have to obtain foreign currency to pay exporters from the eurozone.

■ *Reduced exchange rate uncertainty.* All members face fixed exchange rates within the eurozone.

■ *Eliminates competitive depreciations/devaluations.* Historically, countries have tried to match any fall in the exchange rates of rival countries, with such 'competitive depreciations' creating uncertainty and discouraging trade.

■ *Prevents speculative attacks.* Speculators can sometimes force individual currencies to depreciate/devalue their currency by selling large amounts of that currency. The euro, being supported by all member countries, is much better equipped to resist such speculative attacks.

However, critics of the euro point to a number of disadvantages:

■ *Loss of independent exchange rate policy.* Governments can no longer seek to remedy a balance of payment deficit with a member of the eurozone by lowering their exchange rate, thereby making exports cheaper in that country and imports dearer from that country.

■ *Loss of independent monetary policy.* The eurozone has a ECB which determines the money supply and interest rate policy for all member countries.

Conclusion

The purely economic effects of British membership of the EU are extremely difficult to isolate and describe. It is increasingly irrelevant to speak of economic models of what the UK's experience might have been if we had not joined the EEC in 1973.

The economic debate has centred around two different 'models':

1 the UK as a permanent and irrevocable member of the EU; and

2 the UK outside the EU – the 'non-Europe' model.

The viability of any economic argument which describes the UK outside the EU has become more and more suspect as the financial, economic and business environments have become intermeshed since the 1980s. There is little doubt that the UK has experienced a continuing budget deficit with respect to the EU, that its consumers may have suffered a slight welfare loss with respect to food and the policies of the CAP, and that there has been an observable displacement of UK-manufactured goods in our own domestic market.

Alongside these factors one must recognize the interdependence of the member states in almost every commercial and economic area. The EU represents the UK's most important trading partner by far in both visible and invisible trade. Membership of the Community has also been responsible for significant amounts of inward investment from Japan and the US into the UK. Ironically this inward investment has been so large that the UK is becoming a major exporter of motor vehicles and electronic equipment, developing trade surpluses with the EU in these categories. In a similar fashion, London's place as one of the pre-eminent financial centres in the world rests strongly on its position as the financial centre in which US, EU and Japanese banks and investment houses come together. Where portfolio investment is concerned, the EU has become much more important to the UK (see Chapter 7).

The UK's experience in the EMS has been fraught with problems, but it is clear that a number of those problems were of the UK's own devising. International freedom in financial markets meant that – even outside the EMS – the UK had to ensure that sterling 'shadowed' the DM.

However, a further question has to ask why the benefits to the UK have been less than those which have accrued to other members. The UK has not gained massive benefits from Social and Regional Funds and has a relatively efficient agricultural sector. There have been few or no net real benefits from the CAP and we have suffered from having a relatively inefficient manufacturing sector which has been only modestly successful in exporting to Europe. The UK has not, therefore, gained proportional benefits from the free trade area. Outside the EU, however, the UK would still have had to survive, had to manage its own agriculture and had to find markets for its exports in a world in which the ties of the Commonwealth and EFTA would almost certainly have counted for less and less as the years went by.

Key points

- In 2010 there were 27 member states within the EU. The 27-member EU is essentially a regional trading bloc with 501 million people within a protected free trade area, with a high per capita income of €27,900 per annum.

- The EU is the largest trading bloc in the world. It accounts for 19% of world GDP and around 41% of world trade.

- Since 1992, the EU has established the European Economic Area (EEA) which initially included 19 countries altogether.

- Agriculture is the most regulated sector within the EU. Around 42% of the entire EU budget is spent on various price support and intervention policies involving agricultural products.

- The Regional and Social Funds are targeted at poorer regions *within* each member state in order to relieve unemployment and poverty.

- The Social Chapter includes a number of 'directives' establishing minimum working conditions, though the UK has an 'opt-out'.

- The Maastricht Treaty in 1992 sought to widen the scope of the EU beyond a common market (see Chapter 26) to that of an economic and monetary union (EMU).

- Various 'convergence criteria' needed to be fulfilled before countries could join EMU, which began on 1 January 1999. These convergence criteria included consumer price inflation within $1\frac{1}{2}$%, and long-term interest rates within 2% of the average achieved by the 'best three' EU countries. In addition, the public sector borrowing requirement (PSBR) should be no higher than 3% of GDP and total public debt no more than 60% of GDP.

- The Growth and Stability Pact (GSP) aims to maintain fiscal prudence in the EU. A new framework was introduced in 2005 to control excessive budgetary deficits. However, this has been revised in 2010 following the 'strains' experienced in operating the GSP during the major financial problems from 2008 onwards.

Now try the self-check questions for this chapter on the Companion Website. You will also find useful links to relevant websites.

Notes

1 The European Economic Area comprised the (then) 12 members of the EU plus Iceland, Norway, Sweden, Finland, Switzerland, Austria and Liechtenstein, though in 1995 Sweden, Austria and Finland joined the EU.

2 The 'co-responsibility' levy is a method by which farmers are penalized for over-production of agricultural products. Up to a certain level of production the farmer is entitled to sell his goods either on the open market, or to the EU's Intervention stocks. Above that, agreed, level of production the price allowed to the farmer reduced by a specific percentage called the 'co-responsibility' levy.

3 The divergence limit for any currency was calculated by the formula ±2.25 $(1 - w)$ where w was the percentage weight of the currency in the ECU. For Germany this resulted in a limit of 2.25 $(1 - 0.301) = 1.57$%.

References and further reading

Ackrill, R. (1997) *Economic and Monetary Union, Developments in Economics*, Vol. 13, Ormskirk, Causeway Press.

Al Eyd, A. and Gottschalk, S. (2005) The Stability and Growth Pact and slow growth in Europe, *National Institute Economic Review*, April **192**(2): 23–32.

Barnes, I. and Barnes, P. (1995) *The Enlarged European Union* (2nd edn), London, Longman.

Barras, R. and Madhavan, S. (1996) *European Economic Integration and Sustainable Development*, London, McGraw-Hill.

Bénassy-Quéré, A. and Coeuré, B. (2010) *Economic Policy*, New York, Oxford University Press.

Bergman, M. A., Jakobsson, M. and Razo, C. (2004) *An Econometric Analysis of the European Commission's Merger Discussions*, Department of Economics, Working Paper Series No. 6/2003, Uppsala University.

Brittan, L. (1994) *Europe – The Europe We Need*, London, Hamish Hamilton.

De Grauwe, P. (2000) *The Economics of Monetary Integration* (4th edn), Oxford, Oxford University Press.

Dunford, M. (1994) Winners and losers: the new map of economic inequality in the European Union, *European Urban and Regional Studies*, 1(2): 95–114.

ECB (2005) The reform of the Stability and Growth Pact, *ECB Monthly Bulletin*, August, 57–74.

ECB (2010) *Statistics Pocket Book*, May, Frankfurt, European Central Bank.

European Commission (1996) Economic evaluation of the internal market, *European Economy*, 63(4): 1–173.

European Commission (1997) Trade patterns inside the single market, *The Single Market Review*, Subseries IV, Vol. 2, Kogan Page/Earthscan.

European Commission (1998) *Financing the European Union*, 7 October, Brussels, Commission of the European Communities.

European Commission (2010a) *Allocation of the 2010 EU Budgets*, January, Brussels, Commission of the European Communities.

European Commission (2010b) *General Budget of the European Union for the Financial Year 2010*, January, Brussels, Commission of the European Communities.

European Commission (2010c) *Statistical Annex of European Economy*, Spring, Brussels, Commission of the European Communities.

Eurostat (2010) *Economic Indicators*, Brussels, European Commission.

Geradin, D., Layne-Farrar, A. and Petit, N. (2011) *EU Competition Law and Economics*, Oxford, Oxford University Press.

Giavazzi, F. and Blanchard, O. (2010) *Macroeconomics: A European Perspective*, Financial Times/Prentice Hall.

Goodman, S. F. (1996) *The European Union* (3rd edn), London, Macmillan.

Griffiths, A. (1992) *European Community Survey*, London, Longman.

HM Treasury (2009) *European Community Finances*, May, CM 7640, London.

HM Treasury (2010) *Public Expenditure Statistical Analysis*, London.

Johnson, C. (1996) *In with the Euro, out with the Pound*, London, Penguin.

Kenen, P. (1995) *Economic and Monetary Union in Europe*, Cambridge, Cambridge University Press.

Krugman, P. and Obstfeld, M. (2010), *International Economics: Theory and Policy*, Financial Times/Prentice Hall.

Leveque, F. and Shelanski, H. (2009) *Antitrust and Regulation in the EU and US: Legal and Economic Perspectives*, Cheltenham, Edward Elgar.

Lewis, D. W. P. (1993) *The Road to Europe: History, Institutions and Prospects of European Integration 1945–1993*, New York, Peter Lang.

McDonald, F. and Dearden, S. (eds) (1998) *European Economic Integration* (3rd edn), Harlow, Addison Wesley Longman.

Mercier, P. and Papadia, F. (2011) *The Concrete Euro: Implementing Monetary Policy in the Euro Area*, Oxford, Oxford University Press.

OECD (2010a) *Main Economic Indicators*, Paris, Organisation for Economic Cooperation and Development.

OECD (2010b) *OECD Factbook 2010*, Paris, Organisation for Economic Cooperation and Development.

ONS (2010c) *United Kingdom Balance of Payments – The Pink Book*, London, Office for National Statistics.

Rosamond, B. (2000) *Theories of European Integration*, London, Palgrave Macmillan.

Wistrich, E. (1994) *The United States of Europe*, London, Routledge.

Wolf, M. (1996) Thinking the unthinkable, *Financial Times*, 18 June.

World Bank (2010) *World Development Indicators*, Washington DC.

The following websites are relevant to this chapter:

DTI's website for Europe and world trade
http://webarchive.nationalarchives.gov.uk/+/
http://www.dti.gov.uk/ewt/intro.htm

CHAPTER 28

The BRIC economies: Brazil, Russia, India and China

The term BRICs was first used in 2001 by Jim O'Neill, chief economist at the investment bank Goldman Sachs, who used this label to refer to the four largest and fastest growing emerging countries: Brazil, Russia, India and China. Goldman Sachs predicted in 2003 that the four economies would comprise more than 10% of the global output by 2010, and in fact they surpassed this target, reaching 15% by that date. The BRIC four countries, combined, currently account for more than a quarter of the world's land area and more than 40% of the world's population and hold a combined GDP of more than 8 trillion dollars, or close to 16 trillion dollars in purchasing power parity exchange rates (see Chapter 25, p. 532).

This chapter reviews the economic and political context behind the emergence of each of these economies. The demographic and sociocultural contexts of each country are also examined, together with issues of international competitiveness and the impacts on the respective countries of the recent global recession. The chapter concludes by assessing some of the global implications in the coming years stemming from the rise of the BRIC economies.

Rise of BRIC economies

A thousand years ago, China and the region that is now India were the richest and most populous areas of the world. In terms of per capita income, they were then overtaken by various countries in Western Europe, then by some of their European offshoots, such as the US, and finally by some East Asian economies such as Japan and South Korea. This process has now gone into reverse and both China and India are catching up rapidly with the countries which had overtaken them. The acronym BRIC is increasingly used as a symbol of the shift in global economic power away from the developed economies and towards the developing world, and in particular towards Brazil, Russia, India and China. The onset since 1993 of a consistent decline in the global market shares of exports in goods from the advanced industrialized countries has coincided with the emergence of these new players on the world markets. In fact, Goldman Sachs argued in 2003 that the economic potential of Brazil, Russia, India, and China is such that they could become among the four most dominant economies by the year 2050. Goldman Sachs' expectations around BRIC growth were met sooner than predicted. The absolute size of China's economy overtook Germany's economy in 2007, a year earlier than expected, and overtook Japan's in July 2010. Goldman Sachs now believes that the Chinese economy will overtake the US by 2027, with India accounting even now for 10 of the 30 fastest-growing urban areas in the world. With 700 million people projected to move to Indian cities by 2050, India's influence on the world economy will also be larger and faster than was predicted in 2003. Taken together, the BRICs could be larger than the combined contribution of the US and the developed economies of Europe within 40 years. Table 28.1 provides a useful data profile indicating the rapid growth of various indicators across the BRIC economies.

Nevertheless, two of the BRICs are still relatively poor countries when measured by *per capita* income (note that the table uses the terminology GNI, i.e. Gross National Income, but we will use the more usual GDP terminology throughout this chapter). In terms of per capita income: India ($3,020) and China ($6,240) fall below the mean level of GDP per head in the global economy whilst Brazil ($10,180) has a mid-level per capita income and Russia ($19,780) is now relatively affluent (all values in purchasing power

parities – PPP – compared against the UK $38,370). An important expectation is that by 2025, BRICs will bring another 200 million people with incomes above $15,000 into the world economy – a number equal to the combined populations of Germany, France and the UK. This phenomenon will affect world markets as multinational corporations will attempt to take advantage of the enormous potential markets in the BRICs by producing, for example, far cheaper manufactured goods affordable to the consumers within the BRICs rather than concentrating only on the higher priced and 'luxury' models that currently bring the most income when sold to these countries.

The BRICs have some common features including large territories and populations, generally low income levels, fast economic growth and the emergence of a prosperous local middle class. They also, however, show significant differences, not least because they follow different models of economic development. At its simplest level, Russia and Brazil have relied on commodity price rises, particularly energy in the case of the Russia, whereas India and China have relied on low labour costs to take market share in services and manufacturing respectively from the advanced industrialized economies. As a group, their relationship is somewhat symbiotic: higher demand for raw materials in India and China boosts the GDP of Russia and Brazil. Analysts predict that China, Brazil and India respectively will become the dominant global suppliers of manufactured goods and services, while Brazil and Russia will become the dominant global suppliers of raw materials.

It should be noted that of the four countries, Brazil remains the only nation that has the capacity to be *both* a dominant global supplier of manufactured goods and services and a dominant global supplier of raw materials simultaneously. Co-operation is thus seen by many to be a logical next step among the BRICs, with Brazil and Russia together forming the logical raw material and energy suppliers to India and China. They have also taken steps to increase their political co-operation, mainly as a way of influencing the outcome of major global trade accords, and to enhance their role in major global organizations such as the IMF and World Bank. In these ways, the BRICs have the potential to form a powerful economic and political bloc to challenge the modern-day states currently with 'Group of Eight' status.

In the followings sections we look at the countries individually in terms of their recent economic growth,

Table 28.1 Data profiles of the BRIC economies.

	Brazil			Russia			India			China		
	2000	2008	% increase in decade	2000	2008	% increase in decade	2000	2008	% increase in decade	2000	2008	% increase in decade
World view												
Population, total (millions)	174.17	191.97	110%	146.30	141.95	97%	1,015.92	1,139.96	112%	1,262.65	1,324.66	105%
Population growth (annual %)	1.4	1.0		0.0	-0.1		1.7	1.3		0.8	0.5	
Surface area (sq. km) (thousands)	8,514.9	8,514.9		17,098.2	17,098.2		3,287.3	3,287.3		9,598.1	9,598.1	
GNI, Atlas method (current US$) (billions)	673.69	1,438.51	214%	250.31	1,369.14	547%	458.08	1,235.29	270%	1,168.88	4,051.77	347%
GNI per capita, Atlas method (current US$)	3,870	7,490	194%	1,710	9,650	564%	450	1,080	240%	930	3,060	329%
GNI, PPP (current international $) (billions)	1,167.25	1,955.00	167%	972.45	2,807.75	289%	1,553.48	3,442.87	222%	2,895.44	8,262.69	285%
GNI per capita, PPP (current international $)	6,700	10,180	152%	6,650	19,780	297%	1,530	3,020	197%	2,290	6,240	272%
People												
Life expectancy at birth, total (years)	70	72		65	68		61	64		71	73	
Fertility rate, total (births per woman)	2.4	1.9		1.2	1.5		3.3	2.7		1.8	1.8	
Economy												
GDP (current US$) (billions)	644.70	1,638.61	254%	259.71	1,667.60	642%	460.18	1,214.21	264%	1,198.48	4,532.79	378%
GDP growth (annual %)	4.3	5.1		10.0	5.6		4.0	5.1		8.4	9.6	
Mobile cellular subscriptions (per 100 people)	13	78	600%	2	141	7050%	0	30	N/A	7	48	686%
Internet users (per 100 people)	2.9	37.5	1293%	2.0	31.9	1595%	0.5	4.5	900%	1.8	22.5	1250%

Sources: World Bank (2010a) World Development Indicators Database; UNCTAD (2010b) World Investment Report, and previous issues; World Bank (2010b) World Development Report, and previous editions.

their political, economic and sociocultural structures, starting with China, then moving on to India, Brazil and Russia respectively.

China

Background

China's major attraction is its large and fast growing market. It is the most populous country of the world, with its population now standing at 1,324 million people. Economic growth over the past 30 years has been unprecedentedly high, reaching an average annual rate of 9.8% in the first decade of the millennium, though starting from a very low level. The Chinese economy is highly fragmented as is typical of large, fast-growing developing countries with huge regional disparities and a large gap between average incomes in urban and rural areas and wide disparities of per-

sonal incomes in general. In 2008, the Chinese GDP amounted to $4,051 billion, approximately the size of the German economy, although China's GDP *per capita* is still relatively small and amounted to only $3,060 (about 6% of that in the UK), which places China in the 'lower middle income country' category according to the World Bank's definition. However, using PPP, GDP per capita is significantly higher, reaching $6,240 (15% of the UK). China has achieved a more than five-fold increase in real per capita income since 1990 and lifted more than 390 million people out of poverty.

The relatively low level of per capita income is an important reason for Chinese policy-makers to have placed greater emphasis on foreign demand rather than domestic demand! For this reason, China has so far been a larger and more dynamic market for purchasing investment goods from the rest of the world than for purchasing consumer goods. Investment in fixed assets is unusually high, reaching around 50% of GDP, and investment has been the most important driver of growth over recent years, with around half of the investment being private and the other half public. Table 28.2

Table 28.2 China: data profile.

	2000	2005	2007	2008
World view				
Population, total (millions)	1,262.65	1,303.72	1,317.89	1,324.66
Population growth (annual %)	0.8	0.6	0.5	0.5
Surface area (sq. km) (thousands)	9,598.1	9,598.1	9,598.1	9,598.1
Poverty headcount ratio at national poverty line (% of population)	–	–	–	–
GNI, Atlas method (current US$) (billions)	1,168.88	2,292.42	3,284.35	4,051.77
GNI per capita, Atlas method (current US$)	930	1,760	2,490	3,060
GNI, PPP (current international $) (billions)	2,895.44	5,389.52	7,385.91	8,262.69
GNI per capita, PPP (current international $)	2,290	4,130	5,600	6,240
People				
Income share held by lowest 20%	–	5.7	–	–
Life expectancy at birth, total (years)	71	73	73	73
Fertility rate, total (births per woman)	1.8	1.8	1.8	1.8
Adolescent fertility rate (births per 1,000 women ages 15–19)	10	10	10	10
Contraceptive prevalence (% of women ages 15–49)	–	–	–	–
Births attended by skilled health staff (% of total)	–	98	98	–
Mortality rate, under 5 (per 1,000)	36	25	22	21
Malnutrition prevalence, weight for age (% of children under 5)	–	–	–	–
Immunization, measles (% of children ages 12–23 months)	85	86	94	94
Primary completion rate, total (% of relevant age group)	–	–	99	96
Ratio of girls to boys in primary and secondary education (%)	–	–	103	104
Prevalence of HIV, total (% of population ages 15–49)	0.1	0.1	0.1	–

Table 28.2 (*continued*)

	2000	2005	2007	2008
Environment				
Forest area (sq. km) (thousands)	1,770.0	1,972.9	2,054.1	–
Agricultural land (% of land area)	58.4	58.7	59.3	–
Annual freshwater withdrawals, total (% of internal resources)	–	–	22.4	–
Improved water source (% of population with access)	80	86	–	89
Improved sanitation facilities (% of population with access)	49	53	–	55
Energy use (kg of oil equivalent per capita)	865	1,296	1,484	–
CO_2 emissions (metric tons per capita)	2.7	4.3	5.0	–
Electric power consumption (kWh per capita)	993	1,783	2,332	–
Economy				
GDP (current US$) (billions)	1,198.48	2,257.07	3,505.53	4,532.79
GDP growth (annual %)	8.4	11.3	14.2	9.6
Inflation, GDP deflator (annual %)	2.1	3.9	7.6	7.8
Agriculture, value added (% of GDP)	15	12	11	11
Industry, value added (% of GDP)	46	47	47	47
Services, etc., value added (% of GDP)	39	41	42	42
Exports of goods and services (% of GDP)	23	37	38	35
Imports of goods and services (% of GDP)	21	32	30	27
Gross capital formation (% of GDP)	35	44	42	43
Revenue, excluding grants (% of GDP)	–	9.7	17.0	–
Cash surplus/deficit (% of GDP)	–	–1.4	–	–
States and markets				
Time required to start a business (days)	–	48	35	40
Market capitalization of listed companies (% of GDP)	48.5	34.6	177.6	61.6
Military expenditure (% of GDP)	1.8	2.0	1.9	1.9
Mobile cellular subscriptions (per 100 people)	7	30	42	48
Internet users (per 100 people)	1.8	8.6	16.1	22.5
Roads, paved (% of total roads)	–	41	50	–
High-technology exports (% of manufactured exports)	19	31	30	29
Global links				
Merchandise trade (% of GDP)	39.6	63.0	62.1	56.5
Net barter terms of trade index (2000 = 100)	100	86	80	74
External debt stocks, total (DOD, current US$) (millions)	145,711	283,986	373,773	378,245
Total debt service (% of exports of goods, services and income)	9.3	3.1	2.2	2.0
Net migration (thousands)	–786	–2,058	–	–
Workers' remittances and compensation of employees, received (current US$) (millions)	5,237	24,102	38,791	48,524
Foreign direct investment, net inflows (BoP, current US$) (millions)	38,399	79,127	138,413	147,791
Net official development assistance and official aid received (current US$) (millions)	1,712	1,814	1,487	1,489

Source: World Bank (2010a) *World Development Indicators Database*, April.

provides a useful data profile on China using many indicators over the period 2000 to 2008 (World Bank 2010a).

The role of the state

The Chinese economy can be characterized as a hybrid, combining elements of a developing country, a transition country and a 'newly industrializing country'. The institutional and political framework is that of a 'Socialist Market Economy', where the state has a significant influence on the essentially market-driven system and the Communist Party of China has remained the all-embracing power. Due to the dominance of State Owned Enterprises (SOEs) and the relatively high degree of government influence, China is still classified as a 'non-market economy' (NME) by the EU and the US. An important international economic policy goal for many, both inside and outside China, is that China reach 'market economy status' as soon as possible!

Under constitutional law China is a centralist state, but during the economic reforms it has become more decentralized, although on a largely informal basis, in that provinces have received wider discretion in how they implement policy goals set by the central government. Government expenditure is relatively low by international standards (20% of GDP), about half of which is spent by the central government and the other half by local governments. The budget deficit and the total public debt are relatively low, reaching −0.6% and 20% of GDP respectively in the most recent year for which data are available.

The state has a dual function as the owner of large public enterprises and as a powerful regulator of the economy. To regulate the economy, the government applies measures such as interest rate adjustments and tax policies, but also uses more direct measures such as credit controls, export restrictions and licensing. Apart from the long-term development plans and the 'five-year plans', which provide a broad framework for government policy, there are also sectoral policies such as energy plans and plans for industrial development and for important individual industries, e.g. the automotive sector.

The public enterprise sector in China is very heterogeneous: public enterprises may be controlled either by the central government or by local governments, some are fully state-owned while in others the state only has a controlling interest, and some are collectively owned. Because of the difficulty in determining which enterprises are actually state-controlled, there is considerable uncertainty in providing an accurate estimate of the size of the Chinese public sector, but most estimates indicate that 30–40% of the GDP is currently produced by public enterprises of one kind or another.

There has never been an official process of 'privatization'. It was only after 1997 that a comprehensive 'state-owned enterprise reform' (SOE reform) was launched and large numbers of small enterprises were either sold off by various methods (including auctions), made bankrupt or merged with larger ones. The state retained and restructured the largest and most strategic SOEs. Many were turned into joint stock companies and accepted private partners and/or listed on the stock market. SOEs enjoy certain advantages such as better access to loan and equity capital. On the other hand, they may be prompted to actively support government policies, e.g. by keeping employment high, by supplying products at a loss or by investing abroad to secure strategic raw materials, and in return they may receive subsidies.

No enterprises have been sold to foreigners, as has been the case in the Central and Eastern European countries. In most Sino–foreign joint ventures, the Chinese partner is a state-owned enterprise. The 'Guidelines for state-owned enterprise reform' in 2006 give a list of sectors in which the state should be the sole owner or have a majority share. These include power generation and distribution, oil, petrochemicals and natural gas, telecommunications and armaments.

Economic context

Officially, the Chinese economic model is termed 'Building socialism with Chinese characteristics' or a 'socialist market economy', where markets take the pivotal role for the functioning of the economy, but public ownership, direct government intervention and state-led industrial policies remain an integral part of the system. The market-oriented reform of the Chinese command economy began after Mao Tse Tung's death, under the leadership of Deng Xiaoping in 1978. It was a gradual process, as opposed to the 'shock therapy' taken by the Central and East European countries ten years later, which left the Chinese state with substantial power. The reform started in the agricultural sector and proceeded to the industrial sector in 1985 and the services sector only after China's entry into the World Trade Organization (WTO) in 2001. A number of reform steps are still not completed, such as the rules for the acquisitions and transfer of 'land use rights' (all land in China is owned by the state), price reform (prices of important agricultural products such as grain are still regulated and prices of energy and other utilities are also set by the state authorities), establishing a new social security and health system and developing an adequate legal system.

In parallel to the market-oriented reforms starting in 1978, China gradually opened its closed, self-supporting economy following the model of the Asian 'Newly Industrializing Economies' in the 1970s, which attracted labour-intensive, export-oriented foreign direct investment (FDI) from more advanced economies such as the USA and Japan to produce mainly textiles and clothing. In the first step 'Special Economic Zones' (SEZs) were established in the south of China to attract export-oriented FDI from nearby Hong Kong and Taiwan to take advantage of low wage costs and modern infrastructure, and tax privileges and tariff exemptions. More 'special zones' were then established in other coastal provinces such as Shanghai.

Through a 'joint venture law', the state then followed a 'market for technology' strategy such that in exchange for access to the highly protected Chinese market, foreign producers were expected to transfer advanced technology to their Chinese partners. In a second step, after 1992, the system of SEZs was extended to the inland provinces and a greater number of Chinese enterprises were allowed to engage in foreign trade. Tariff rates for intermediate inputs and investment goods were reduced, but remained high for final products. As a consequence FDI grew extremely rapidly and China became the second most important recipient of inward FDI after the US. Since WTO entry, Chinese exports and imports have expanded even more strongly, with exports rising much faster than imports, which has led to a large trade surplus and corresponding bilateral trade deficits with the US and the EU and to the accumulation of large foreign exchange reserves by China. In order to rebalance this trade relationship between China and the developed economies, the latter argue that the renminbi should be allowed to strongly appreciate to make Chinese exports more expensive abroad and

imports less expensive in China, thereby helping to reduce the country's external surplus and, as a side-effect, reduce the US current-account deficit with China (Krugman and Obstfeld 2010). Other experts suggest that measures such as an increase in government spending on social security (including pensions, health and education) and increased public investment in housing could help reduce household precautionary savings and thereby help increase consumer spending in China.

In 2001, the long-term development goal for China was still formulated in quantitative terms, namely 'to quadruple the per capita value of the 2000 GDP by 2020', implying an average growth rate of 8%. The next generation of Chinese leaders, under Hu Jintao, came into power in 2003 and opted for more sustainable growth, clearly emphasizing qualitative instead of quantitative growth. To secure this sustainability, the state should put more emphasis on tackling social problems, reducing regional disparities, improving environmental protection and increasing energy efficiency. The export-led development model should therefore be phased out and transformed into a more domestic-market oriented growth model. In line with these goals, the Chinese economy would then become more balanced between agricultural and industrial development, with industry restructured away from the low value added export-intensive industries and towards the higher value added, technology-intensive industries.

The new development model is putting strong emphasis on the quality of inward FDI that China should absorb, which may reduce the overall size and change the type of FDI inflows into China in the future. China will seek to encourage technology-intensive investment, more control of Sino–foreign mergers and acquisitions and better protection of intellectual property rights. China has a sharply growing number of college graduates and earlier experiences in East Asia suggest that changes in the sectoral structure of an economy, for example linked to the technological upgrading of its export sector, can absorb part of the increased supply of educated workers. This is likely to happen also in China: the slower growth of the labour surplus could make unskilled labour relatively more expensive, and the growing supply of skilled labour could make skilled workers relatively less expensive. As a result, the country's comparative advantage could shift towards more skill-intensive manufactures and services.

In 2002, China introduced the 'go-abroad' policy aimed at making more efficient use of its foreign exchange reserves to secure resources, to acquire technology, to gain access to established distribution networks, and to reduce the risk for Chinese enterprises of getting caught by non-tariff barriers to trade. The longer-term perspective is to generate a group of 30–50 large transnational companies.

China and the global economic crisis

GDP growth fell from 9.9% during the first three-quarters of 2008 to 6.8% in the last quarter of 2008 and reached only 6.1% in the first quarter of 2009. The transmission of the crisis took place in the form of declining exports due to sluggish external demand, which then triggered a slowing-down of industrial production and investments. Because of falling incomes and rising unemployment, private consumption dropped; nor was China spared from the global contraction of FDI, with FDI inflows falling below the previous levels. Real estate investment contracted particularly strongly in the first quarter of 2009 and stock prices in general fell dramatically.

To contain the crisis, the Chinese government announced a 'stimulus package' in November 2008, providing additional funds of more than $600 billion for 2009 and 2010 (equivalent to some 7% of GDP per annum). The funds are being spent mainly on infrastructure, such as highways, railways, airports and rural infrastructure (37.5%); reconstruction of earthquake hit areas (25%); affordable housing (10%); improvement of villages (9.25%); public health and education (3.75%); and restructuring of industry (14.5%).

Thanks to its huge domestic market and its massive and timely stimulus policies, China appears to be the BRIC which has been least affected by the crisis and its economy seemed to bottom-out earlier than those of the advanced economies. GDP growth in the second quarter of 2009 reached 7.9%, almost 2% higher than in the previous quarter. The strongest recovery came from fixed asset investment, pushed up by the extra public expenditures. Private consumption rose too, although moderately. On the supply side, industrial output, which had suffered the heaviest slump of all sectors, rose sharply. Stock prices gained more than 60% during the first half of that year.

In the medium term, the major question is whether the Chinese government will seek to continue its policy of qualitative rather than quantitative growth in the face of the current global financial crisis, with exports and FDI shrinking worldwide.

In recent years, most external estimates for China's long-term economic development until 2020 have been in the range between 6% and 9% average annual growth of GDP, which is also in line with the Chinese government's target of 7–8% average annual growth. The question is whether the current global crisis will affect these estimates. If the crisis is over in one or two years, little will change, but if the world slides into a prolonged recession, China's transition from an export-led to a domestically-oriented economy may proceed slower than envisaged, with FDI inflows and technology transfer slower than expected. Estimates suggest this may result in one to two percentage points less annual growth in China than otherwise. Whatever the prospects for a 'double dip' global recession, there is no doubt that China is moving rapidly from a developing to a developed country and from a regional to a global economic power.

Demographic and sociocultural factors

Because of the one-child policy proclaimed by the Chinese government at the beginning of the 1980s, population growth in China at around 0.6% per annum is much lower than in other countries at a similar stage of economic development, and is only slightly higher than the EU average. China also faces the problem of a rapidly ageing population and rising dependency ratios of the retired on the working population, which will have an important influence on consumption as well as production in the future. It is estimated that the Chinese population of working age will have reached its maximum as early as 2015. Table 28.3 gives a useful breakdown of demographic patterns and trends in China in recent years.

The 'one-child rule' in China is beginning to be lifted as the country faces the future with an increasingly ageing population. For example, for the first time in over 30 years, officials in Shanghai, the country's economic capital, are urging eligible parents to plan for a second child. The move was prompted by the growing demographic imbalance in the city and fears that the younger generation will not be able to support the ageing population. The one-child system,

Table 28.3 China's population (millions), 1994 and 2009.

Age (years)	Male 1994	Female 1994	Male 2009	Female 2009
0–5	59	53	45	40
5–10	62	58	42	39
10–15	53	50	53	44
15–20	51	49	56	50
20–25	64	59	60	54
25–30	64	59	52	49
30–35	48	43	50	46
35–40	46	41	60	58
40–45	44	40	59	57
45–50	30	28	43	42
50–55	25	20	41	39
55–60	23	18	39	36
60–65	20	17	26	21
65–70	18	15	20	20
70–75	11	12	18	17
75–80	6	7	10	12
80–85	2	4	5	7
85–90	1	2	2	4
90–95	1	2	2	3

where all pregnancies are monitored and sometimes terminated by order, was enforced to control a population that is the largest in the world at more than 1.3 billion. 'We advocate eligible couples to have two children because it can help to reduce the proportion of the ageing people and alleviate a workforce shortage in the future,' said Xie Linli, the director of the Shanghai Population and Family Planning Commission.

In practice the one couple, one child family-planning policy has actually been less rigorous than its name suggests. Urban parents have often been permitted to have two children if the husband and wife were themselves from one-child families. In rural areas, couples have often been allowed to have a second child if their first child was a girl. Shanghai's over-60 population already exceeds three million, or 21.6% of registered residents. Zhang Meixin, a spokesman for the Shanghai Commission, said, 'That is already near the average figure of developed countries and is still rising quickly.' By 2020 the proportion of over-60s is expected to rise to 34% of the city's population.

The elderly population is rising at a similar rate across the rest of China, mainly in cities, with the working-age population expected to start shrinking in about 2015. The overall population will peak in 2030, with China becoming the first country to grow old before it grows rich and therefore likely to find it even more difficult to support a nation of pensioners. The US Centre for Strategic and International Studies warned in 2009 that by 2050, China would have more than 100 million people aged 80 or over. The country will by that date only have 1.6 working age adults to support every person aged 60 or above, as compared with 7.7 working age adults in 1975.

Figure 28.1(c) provides a useful summary of Chinese cultural characteristics from the perspective of Gert Hofstede's classification of national cultural characteristics. We will refer back to Fig. 28.1 as we discuss each of the individual BRIC countries, but here our focus in on China.

- *Power distance.* In terms of *power distance* (PDI) China has a much higher score (80) as compared to the world average score of 60, suggesting much greater respect for position within hierarchies and for receiving direct instructions in China as compared to, say, the UK (35), US (40) and most other countries which also have lower PDI scores than China.

- *Individualism.* In terms of *individualism* (IDV) China has a much lower individualism score (20) as compared to the world average score of 44, and the UK (89) and US (91). This indicates the much more collectivist outlook in China as compared to the greater emphasis on self-reliance and relatively loose bonds with others in the UK, US and most other countries.

- *Masculinity.* In terms of *masculinity* (MAS) China has a higher score (66) as compared to the world average score of 50, suggesting a greater emphasis on assertiveness, decisiveness and career focus amongst other predominantly 'male' characteristics.

- *Uncertainty avoidance.* In terms of *uncertainty avoidance* (UAI) China has a much lower score (30) than the world average score of 68. This implies that China is much less concerned with uncertainty avoidance than many other countries, suggesting that China has a much higher degree of

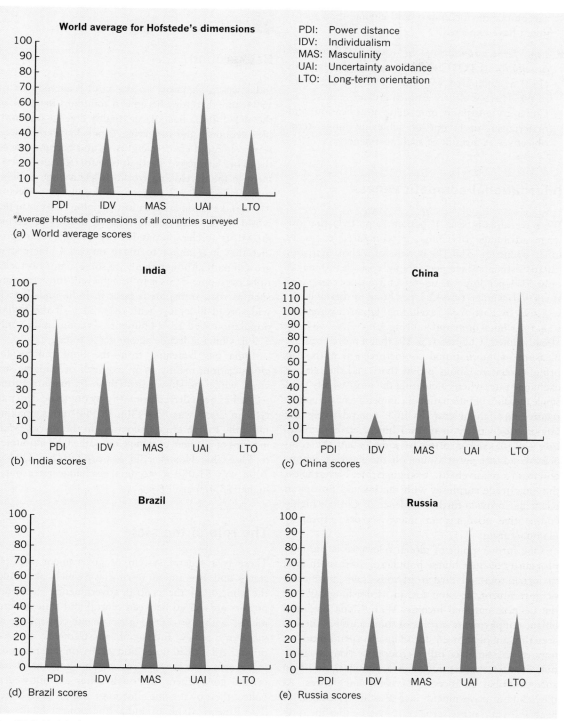

Fig. 28.1 Hofstede scores on five cultural dimensions.
Source: Adapted from Hofstede and Hofstede (2005).

acceptance of uncertainty and change than many might have expected.

- *Long-term orientation.* In terms of *long-term orientation* (LTO) China has a much higher score (118) as compared with the world average score of 44. There is clearly a much greater readiness in China to postpone immediate gratification and materialism in favour of achieving longer-term objectives as a result of such abstinence.

International competitiveness

We have already seen (Chapter 7, p. 131) the low wage advantage of China, as compared to many other countries. The US Bureau of Labor Statistics (2010) estimates average labour costs in China at only $1.4 per hour in manufacturing, as compared to an EU average of $43.3 per hour in manufacturing and an East Asia (excluding Japan) average of $13.3 per hour in manufacturing. Of course we have already noted (Chapter 1, p. 19) that a more accurate measure of international competitiveness must also bring in relative labour productivity and the relative exchange rate, when calculating the most widely used single measure of international competitiveness, namely relative unit labour cost (RULC). The relatively low labour productivity in many Chinese economic sectors will, of course, offset to some extent the competitive advantage of China on the basis of labour costs and a relatively low exchange rate. Nevertheless the huge trade surpluses with the US and Europe in particular provide further evidence of China's highly competitive economy in many sectors, especially manufacturing.

One further point of global relevance is the high propensity of the Chinese population to save. In fact, savings in total, whether from households, businesses or government, account for an astonishing 50% of the Chinese national income. With China having a balance of payments surplus of some $300bn, there is arguably a global 'need' for China to spend more on imports to stimulate other economies (via an injection of extra exports into their economies), and help correct global balance of payment imbalances. As the Chinese government increases its provision of healthcare and other services, it may be that the 'precautionary' need for high savings to guard against adversity may become less pressing!

 India

Background

India was a signatory to the GATT agreements of 1994 and therefore became a founding member of the WTO. India has a large, highly diverse and complex economy and in recent years it has experienced relatively rapid economic growth and become one of the more attractive destinations for foreign investment in the developing world. It has a huge population of around 1.2 billion people and is projected to overtake China as the most populous nation in the world in the near future. India's rate of economic growth is accelerating and many commentators predict that it is about to move onto a Chinese-style growth path although there are some major obstacles to be overcome if this is to be achieved! Infrastructure such as road transport is poor in India and there is widespread illiteracy, with over 20% of the Indian population aged 15–24 illiterate, as compared to only 5% in China a decade ago and 1% today.

India has benefited from the opportunities for globalization, mainly as an exporter of tradable services, while the slower growth in its manufacturing sector has been driven primarily by domestic demand. GNI in 2008 was $3,443bn in PPP terms, making India the fourth largest economy in the world, while in terms of nominal exchange rates, the GNI amounted to $1,235bn. However, in *per capita* terms GNI in 2008 was $1,080 in nominal exchange rates but a higher $3,020 at PPP.

The role of the state

There is a federal system of government with 30 states and five union territories (which are under the control of the central government). Economic powers are shared between central and state governments, with the central government controlling all monetary policy and significant elements of fiscal policy. All direct taxes and taxes on international trade, as well as taxes on services, are collected by the central government, although states are allowed to collect their own value added tax and property taxes. The Reserve Bank of India (the central bank) can determine and constrain the borrowing limits of the state governments, thereby constraining their fiscal policies. State governments that borrow from international organizations such as the World Bank and the Asian Development Bank require the prior permission of the central government. The central government, as well as many states, has passed fiscal responsibilities legislation that puts a limit of 2% of GDP on the fiscal deficit. However, these have been explicitly relaxed during the recent crisis, and even in the past they have often been breached via the internationally familiar method of moving several items of expenditure off-budget!

The recent rapid growth of the economy has placed increased stress on the physical infrastructure such as electricity, railways, roads, ports, airports, irrigation, urban and rural water supply and sanitation. Since all of these already suffered from substantial shortages and lack of capacity, this has made the 'physical infrastructure deficit' even more evident! Total infrastructure investment has amounted to around 5% of GDP in recent years according to the Planning Commission, which also estimated that this ratio would need to rise to 9% to get at least close to meeting the required infrastructure needs of the Indian economy and society. Table 28.4 provides a useful data profile of India and its development path across many indicators.

Economic context

The diversity of India encompasses many different features. The economy includes various different production and distribution systems: from traditional village farming by peasant households, shifting cultivation and pastoralism in some areas, to modern mechanized agriculture; from labour-intensive handicraft production to a wide range of modern industries at different levels of technological development; from low-productivity informal service activities to highly skilled and capital-intensive 'new' services. Geographically India covers a huge area from mountainous and cold or temperate regions to sub-tropical

Table 28.4 India: data profile.

	2000	2005	2007	2008
World view				
Population, total (millions)	1,015.92	1,094.58	1,124.79	1,139.96
Population growth (annual %)	1.7	1.4	1.3	1.3
Surface area (sq. km) (thousands)	3,287.3	3,287.3	3,287.3	3,287.3
Poverty headcount ratio at national poverty line (% of population)	28.6	–	–	–
GNI, Atlas method (current US$) (billions)	458.08	823.09	1,116.93	1,235.29
GNI per capita, Atlas method (current US$)	450	750	990	1,080
GNI, PPP (current international $) (billions)	1,553.48	2,509.01	3,206.74	3,442.87
GNI per capita, PPP (current international $)	1,530	2,290	2,850	3,020
People				
Income share held by lowest 20%	–	8.1	–	–
Life expectancy at birth, total (years)	61	63	63	64
Fertility rate, total (births per woman)	3.3	2.9	2.8	2.7
Adolescent fertility rate (births per 1,000 women ages 15–19)	88	74	69	67
Contraceptive prevalence (% of women ages 15–49)	47	–	–	–
Births attended by skilled health staff (% of total)	43	–	–	–
Mortality rate, under 5 (per 1,000)	93	77	71	68
Malnutrition prevalence, weight for age (% of children under 5)	–	–	–	–
Immunization, measles (% of children ages 12–23 months)	54	64	70	70
Primary completion rate, total (% of relevant age group)	72	85	94	
Ratio of girls to boys in primary and secondary education (%)	79	90	92	–
Prevalence of HIV, total (% of population ages 15–49)	0.5	0.4	0.3	–

Table 28.4 (continued)

	2000	2005	2007	2008
Environment				
Forest area (sq. km) (thousands)	675.5	677.0	677.6	–
Agricultural land (% of land area)	61.4	60.5	60.5	–
Annual freshwater withdrawals, total (% of internal resources)	–	–	51.2	–
Improved water source (% of population with access)	81	85	–	88
Improved sanitation facilities (% of population with access)	25	28	–	31
Energy use (kg of oil equivalent per capita)	450	488	529	–
CO_2 emissions (metric tons per capita)	1.2	1.3	1.4	–
Electric power consumption (kWh per capita)	402	476	542	–
Economy				
GDP (current US$) (billions)	460.18	837.20	1,232.82	1,214.21
GDP growth (annual %)	4.0	9.3	9.6	5.1
Inflation, GDP deflator (annual %)	3.5	4.7	5.3	7.2
Agriculture, value added (% of GDP)	23	19	18	17
Industry, value added (% of GDP)	26	28	29	28
Services, etc., value added (% of GDP)	50	53	53	54
Exports of goods and services (% of GDP)	13	19	21	24
Imports of goods and services (% of GDP)	14	22	25	29
Gross capital formation (% of GDP)	24	34	38	36
Revenue, excluding grants (% of GDP)	11.9	12.1	14.0	14.3
Cash surplus/deficit (% of GDP)	–3.9	–3.2	–1.0	–1.5
States and markets				
Time required to start a business (days)	–	71	33	30
Market capitalization of listed companies (% of GDP)	32.2	66.1	147.6	53.2
Military expenditure (% of GDP)	3.1	2.8	2.4	2.7
Mobile cellular subscriptions (per 100 people)	0	8	21	30
Internet users (per 100 people)	0.5	2.5	4.1	4.5
Roads, paved (% of total roads)	47	–	–	–
High-technology exports (% of manufactured exports)	5	5	5	6
Global links				
Merchandise trade (% of GDP)	20.4	29.0	30.8	42.5
Net barter terms of trade index (2000 = 100)	100	105	127	92
External debt stocks, total (DOD, current US$) (millions)	100,243	120,224	204,992	230,611
Total debt service (% of exports of goods, services and income)	14.5	13.1	13.7	8.7
Net migration (thousands)	–1,400	–1,540	–	–
Workers' remittances and compensation of employees, received (current US$) (millions)	12,883	22,125	37,217	49,941
Foreign direct investment, net inflows (BoP, current US$ (millions)	3,584	7,606	25,127	41,169
Net official development assistance and official aid received (current US$) (millions)	1,373	1,851	1,384	2,108

Source: World Bank (2010a) *World Development Indicators Database*, April.

monsoon regions to arid desert conditions. Linguistically India has the most diverse population in the world, with 14 official languages other than English (which is widely used in government, the organized sector and for inter-state communication) as well as 250 minor languages and several thousand dialects.

India's integration with the world economy increased rapidly in the 1990s, associated with the various economic reform measures. Trade to GDP ratios in India increased from 11% in 1995 to around 24% in the latest data period. The share of agriculture in GDP has fallen in the course of development, but there has been little increase in the share of the secondary sector which has hardly changed since the early 1990s. In India fewer industries have been as export dependent as those in China, and those that are tended to be traditional industries, such as apparel, leather goods and textiles. In most manufacturing categories (at the three-digit SITC – Standard International Trade Classification – level) exports have accounted for less than 20% of production over this period. The most dramatic increase in manufacturing exports has been to China, as India has become a 'player' in the export expansion of the Asian region as a whole, supplying metals and other intermediate products to China for further processing for the US and European markets.

In service exports, India has been much more successful, becoming the foremost exporter of computer and information services in the international economy, with its share in world exports of computer and information services placed at 17% in the most recent data. Indeed, Indian economic growth in recent years has essentially been service-led, as the rate of growth of services within GDP has been much higher than the rate of growth of overall GDP, with more than 60% of the increase in GDP during the past 20 years being due to an increase in GDP from services.

However, despite this rapid growth, the absolute size of the computer and information services sector in India remains relatively small (less than 6% of GDP). It is the vast mass of differentiated but largely low-productivity unorganized services which still accounts for half the GDP and most of the employment in the services sector. Further, the computer and information sector's contribution to employment does not compare with its role in the generation of income and foreign exchange. The total IT industry, including both hardware and software elements as well as IT-enabled services, still employs only around 2 million workers.

India's telecom sector has been possibly the biggest success story of its market-oriented reforms. Deregulation and liberalization of telecommunications laws and policies have prompted rapid growth in this sector. With more than 270 million connections, India's telecommunication network is currently the third largest in the world, and the second largest among the emerging economies of Asia. At present more than 8 million telephone connections are being added every month, and the frenetic pace of expansion continues despite the economic slowdown.

There has been a significant amount of liberalization concerning FDI, with the government moving from fairly strict controls to a much more liberal regime as regards the extent and proportion of shares held in private hands, reductions in the need for permissions and in the constraints placed on profit repatriation, and fewer foreign exchange controls. Similarly FDI policy in India is now thought to be among the most liberal in the emerging economies, with FDI up to 100% now allowed under the 'automatic route', i.e. without prior approval, in most sectors and activities. There is, however, a small list of industrial sectors is which FDI is *not* permitted, including arms and ammunition, atomic energy, railway transport, coal and lignite, and the mining of iron, manganese, chrome, gypsum, sulphur, gold, diamonds, copper and zinc. Whilst there are still limits on FDI permitted in a few key sectors, such as telecommunications, where these still exist the limits have been relaxed significantly.

India and the global economic crisis

India has been adversely affected by the global economic crisis. Rapidly declining exports, reversal of private capital flows and worsening fiscal balances of both the central and state governments have constrained the immediate prospects for growth in the period since 2007, although the impact thus far has been one of slowing down the growth process rather than reversing it with negative output growth. As in some of the Western economies, the earlier emphasis on public spending as the principal stimulus for growth has been replaced in the past 15 or more years with debt-financed sources for housing investment and private consumption for the burgeoning middle classes. This required a relaxation of the terms on which debt was available to households and the private sector, and therefore made the country's financial system more vulnerable to default at various levels, especially in circumstances such as 'contagion' from the sub-prime crisis (see Chapter 30). The Indian government's attempts at recovery have focused on encouraging banks into lending even more, in the hope that there would be enough borrowers who would use that credit to revive flagging domestic demand and make up for sluggish exports. In addition, the recovery strategy has pushed forward infrastructure investment, financed not only with domestic debt but also with external commercial borrowing. While this seems to have had some immediate effects in terms of creating some growth revival, especially in an international context, it does involve further potential problems for the future! It arguably adds to the debt spiral and may involve a currency mismatch inasmuch as infrastructural projects are unlikely to yield foreign exchange revenues that can be used to meet future interest and amortization commitments payable in foreign exchange.

Nevertheless, there remain several reasons to be optimistic about the medium-term outlook for the Indian economy. First, there are basic strengths defined by the potentially huge domestic mass market, which is now beginning to expand in terms of effective purchasing power. Second, new government welfare programmes will act as cushions for the income of the poor and as a demand stimulus (perhaps reducing precautionary savings), especially for the rural economy. Third, the significant increase in funding for education at all levels will also have a positive effect. Thus, while the global crisis is definitely taking its toll on India, there are other forces within the economy that suggest that faster recovery and more positive future growth patterns are still possible.

Demographic and sociocultural factors

India has a population of 1,140 million, growing at an annual rate of 1.3%, with some 30% urban based in 2010, a significant increase on the 25% urban based in 1990. Although the ageing population in India is by no means as severe a problem as in China, India also has a rising 'old age dependency ratio' defined as the population aged 65 years and above

expressed as a percentage of the population of working age (15–64 years of age). This ratio has risen in India from 6.6 in 1990 to 7.7 in 2010, whereas in China it has risen from 8.3 to 11.4 over the same period!

Figure 28.1 earlier (p. 603) provides an outline of India's cultural characteristics using Hofstede's definitions, and comparing these with the other BRIC economies and the world 'average' scores for the individual elements.

As we can see, India is similar to China in terms of *Power Distance* (PDI), with its 'score' of 77 higher than the world average of 60, indicating significant respect for position within hierarchies and for accepting direct instructions. The India score for *Individualism* (IDV) is 48, which is interestingly above the world average (44) and well above that for China (20). This suggests a less collectivist outlook in India than in China and a greater emphasis on self-reliance and less close bonds with others. As regards *Masculinity* (MAS) the Indian score of 56 is again above the world average (50), suggesting a somewhat greater emphasis on decisiveness, career focus, assertiveness and other 'male' characteristics. As regards *Uncertainty Avoidance* (UAI), the Indian score of 40 is well below the world average (68), suggesting a higher degree of acceptance of uncertainty and change in India than perhaps might have been expected! Finally, in terms of *Long-term Orientation* (LTI) the Indian score of 61 is well above the world average (41), suggesting a lesser emphasis on materialism and instant gratification and a greater focus on long-term outcomes than in many other countries.

In terms of religion, all the major religions of the world are represented in the population. The Census of India has indicated that 80.2% of the population is officially described as Hindu, 13.4% as Muslim, 2.3% Christian, 1.9% Sikh, and the remaining 1.9% consists of Buddhists, Jains, Zoroastrians and various other religions. Social divisions extend beyond religious and ethnic groups to caste divisions which are extremely complex.

International competitiveness

We have already seen (Chapter 7, p. 131) the low wage advantage of India, as compared to many other countries. The estimate by the US Bureau of Labor Statistics (2010) is of an average labour cost in India of only $0.9 per hour in manufacturing, lower even than the $1.4 per hour in China and well below the EU average of $43.3 per hour in manufacturing and East Asian (excluding Japan) average of $13.3 per hour in manufacturing. Of course, we have already noted (Chapter 1, p. 19) that a more accurate measure of international competitiveness must also bring in relative labour productivity and relative exchange rate, needed for calculating the most widely used single measure of international competitiveness, namely RULC. The relatively low labour productivity in many lower technology Indian economic sectors and the relatively high exchange rate for the rupee will, of course, offset to some extent the competitiveness advantages on the basis of labour costs alone. Indeed, India has had an overall balance of payments deficit on goods and services since year 2000.

Brazil

Background

Brazil is an emerging world economic power, being the fifth largest country in the world, both in terms of territory (8.5 million km^2) and of population (with an estimated 192 million inhabitants in 2008). Its population is predominantly young and mostly concentrated on or near the Atlantic coast of the south-eastern and north-eastern states.

In recent years, Brazil has been implementing an increasingly assertive foreign policy, playing an active role in positioning itself as a representative of emerging countries and as a staunch defender of poorer countries, particularly in Africa. The country is a member of the G20 group of richest nations, leading the reforms and global responses to the 2008 financial crisis. Brazil plays a key political role within Mercosur pushing for the negotiation of free trade agreements with third counties and for the extension of Mercosur. Brazil has also diversified its bilateral relations, establishing closer links with the other BRIC powers with Arab and African countries, while maintaining balanced relations with the US and EU.

Brazil is classified as an upper-middle-income country with a GNI of $1,439bn and a per capita income of approximately $7,490 ($10,180 measured at PPP) in 2008, being the world's 8th largest consumption market and the world's 10th largest economy. Since 2000 the average GDP growth rate has been over 4%, which is low as compared to those of the other BRICs, but the continuous growth has been stable and has now occurred over an extended period of more than 20 years.

In recent years, the country has also recorded significant trade surpluses and exports have contributed positively to Brazil's GDP growth. This export expansion has been accompanied by a rising importance of non-traditional export markets such as China, whose market share trebled from 2% in 2000 to reach more than 6% today. Exports have been led mainly by agricultural commodities, meat, transport equipment and iron and steel. Significant productivity gains have been made in the agricultural sector turning Brazil into a major agricultural power.

Brazil is the second largest recipient of net FDI among the emerging markets just after China, with the US being the highest inward investor. Most of the inward FDI is via mergers and acquisitions, mainly in public services and telecommunications.

Brazil is also Latin America's largest energy consumer, accounting for over 40% of Latin America's energy. Its energy mix is one of the cleanest in the world, and the country is expected to continue to rely on hydropower to meet most of its power-generation needs. In 2010, Brazil is the world's 15th largest oil producer, with proven reserves of 11.2 billion barrels; oil reserves have increased over eight-fold since 1980, with some 85% of these oil reserves located in offshore fields, increasingly from deep- and ultra-deep waters, which have yielded significant recent discoveries. Table 28.5 gives a useful overview of many of the key indicators for Brazil.

The role of the state

Constitutionally, Brazil is a federal republic made up of 26 states, one federal district (Brasilia) and 5,560 municipalities which has a stable and representative democracy with developed political bodies and institutions. The country's President acts simultaneously as head of state and of the federal government. Each state has a state legislature and a directly elected governor, who heads the state executive and appoints its members. The constitution provides for an independent judiciary.

Table 28.5 Brazil: data profile.

	2000	2005	2007	2008
World view				
Population, total (millions)	174.17	186.07	190.12	191.97
Population growth (annual %)	1.4	1.2	1.0	1.0
Surface area (sq. km) (thousands)	8,514.9	8,514.9	8,514.9	8,514.9
Poverty headcount ratio at national poverty line (% of population)	–	–	–	–
GNI, Atlas method (current US$) (billions)	673.69	747.44	1,166.89	1,438.51
GNI per capita, Atlas method (current US$)	3,870	4,020	6,140	7,490
GNI, PPP (current international $) (billions)	1,167.25	1,560.00	1,826.95	1,955.00
GNI per capita, PPP (current international $)	6,700	8,380	9,610	10,180
People				
Income share held by lowest 20%	–	2.9	3.0	–
Life expectancy at birth, total (years)	70	72	72	72
Fertility rate, total (births per woman)	2.4	2.1	1.9	1.9
Adolescent fertility rate (births per 1,000 women ages 15–19)	88	81	77	75
Contraceptive prevalence (% of women ages 15–49)	–	–	–	–
Births attended by skilled health staff (% of total)	–	–	–	–
Mortality rate, under 5 (per 1,000)	34	26	23	22
Malnutrition prevalence, weight for age (% of children under 5)	–	–	2	–
Immunization, measles (% of children ages 12–23 months)	99	99	99	99
Primary completion rate, total (% of relevant age group)	108	106	–	–
Ratio of girls to boys in primary and secondary education (%)	103	103	102	103
Prevalence of HIV, total (% of population ages 15–49)	0.6	0.6	0.6	–
Environment				
Forest area (sq. km) (thousands)	4,932.1	4,777.0	4,714.9	–
Agricultural land (% of land area)	30.9	31.2	31.1	–
Annual freshwater withdrawals, total (% of internal resources)	–	–	1.1	–
Improved water source (% of population with access)	93	95	–	97
Improved sanitation facilities (% of population with access)	75	78	–	80
Energy use (kg of oil equivalent per capita)	1,086	1,159	1,239	–
CO_2 emissions (metric tons per capita)	1.9	1.9	1.9	–
Electric power consumption (kWh per capita)	1,894	2,017	2,171	–
Economy				
GDP (current US$) (billions)	644.70	882.19	1,365.98	1,638.61
GDP growth (annual %)	4.3	3.2	6.1	5.1
Inflation, GDP deflator (annual %)	6.2	7.2	5.9	7.4
Agriculture, value added (% of GDP)	6	6	6	6
Industry, value added (% of GDP)	28	29	27	27
Services, etc., value added (% of GDP)	67	65	67	67
Exports of goods and services (% of GDP)	10	15	13	14
Imports of goods and services (% of GDP)	12	12	12	14
Gross capital formation (% of GDP)	18	16	17	18
Revenue, excluding grants (% of GDP)	–	–	23.2	23.8
Cash surplus/deficit (% of GDP)	–	–	–1.9	–1.2

Table 28.5 (continued)

	2000	2005	2007	2008
States and markets				
Time required to start a business (days)	–	152	152	152
Market capitalization of listed companies (% of GDP)	35.1	53.8	100.3	36.0
Military expenditure (% of GDP)	1.8	1.5	1.5	1.4
Mobile cellular subscriptions (per 100 people)	13	46	64	78
Internet users (per 100 people)	2.9	21.0	30.9	37.5
Roads, paved (% of total roads)	6	–	–	–
High-technology exports (% of manufactured exports)	19	13	12	12
Global links				
Merchandise trade (% of GDP)	17.7	22.2	21.0	23.2
Net barter terms of trade index (2000 = 100)	100	99	107	110
External debt stocks, total (DOD, current US$) (millions)	241,552	187,431	237,472	255,614
Total debt service (% of exports of goods, services and income)	93.5	44.7	27.8	22.7
Net migration (thousands)	−210	−229	–	–
Workers' remittances and compensation of employees, received (current US$) (millions)	1,649	3,540	4,382	5,089
Foreign direct investment, net inflows (BoP, current US$) (millions)	32,779	15,066	34,585	45,058
Net official development assistance and official aid received (current US$) (millions)	231	243	321	460

Source: World Bank (2010a) *World Development Indicators Database*, April.

The origins of today's Brazilian state and many current issues can be traced to the history of its people. From 1875 until 1960, about 5 million Europeans immigrated to Brazil, settling mainly in the southern states, with such immigrants coming mainly from Italy, Germany, Spain, Japan, Poland, and the Middle East. Pedro Alvares Cabral had claimed Brazil for Portugal as long ago as 1500, and the colony was ruled from Lisbon until 1808, when Dom Joao VI and the rest of the Portuguese royal family fled from Portugal when confronted by Napoleon's army, and established the Brazilian seat of government in Rio de Janeiro. Dom Joao VI returned to Portugal in 1821, but his son declared Brazil's independence from Portugal in 1822, and became emperor. His son, Dom Pedro II, ruled from 1831 to 1889, when a federal republic was established in a coup led by the army.

From 1889 to 1930, the government was a constitutional republic, with the presidency alternating between the dominant states of Sao Paulo and Minas Gerais. This period ended with a military coup that placed Getulio Vargas, a civilian, in the presidency; Vargas remained as dictator until 1945. Between 1945 and 1961, Brazil had six civilian presidents followed by another military coup in 1964. The coup leaders chose senior army officers as consecutive presidents. Geisel began and then Figueiredo (1979–85) permitted the return of politicians exiled or banned from political activity during the 1960s and 1970s. In 1985, the electoral college voted Neves from the opposition Brazilian Democratic Movement Party (PMDB) into office as President. Neves died before his presidential inauguration, and his vice president, Sarney, became president upon Neves' death.

Brazil completed its transition to a popularly elected government in 1989, when Fernando Collor de Mello won 53% of the vote in the first direct presidential election in 29 years. Luiz Inacio Lula da Silva, commonly known as Lula, was elected president in 2002, and was re-elected in 2006 for a second four-year term. Lula, a former union leader, was Brazil's first working-class president. Since taking office he has taken a prudent fiscal path, warning that social reforms would take years and that Brazil had no alternative but to maintain tight fiscal austerity policies. At the same time, he has made the fight against poverty, through conditional transfer payments, an important element of his policies.

Economic context

After a period of economic stability and growth in the 1970s the country suffered from hyperinflation and macroeconomic volatility in the 'lost decade' of the 1980s due to the external debt crisis of 1982. At the beginning of the 1990s, growth was again erratic and the period was marked again by instability and inflation. In 1994 Brazil adopted the 'Plano Real' and succeeded in controlling inflation and aligning its currency, the real, with the US dollar. The combination of the fixed exchange rate with a loose fiscal policy in the second half of the 1990s caused a persistent deterioration of the trade balance, culminating in a major balance of payments crisis in January 1999. The country was then forced to negotiate an adjustment programme with the IMF and launched a package of structural reforms to restore macroeconomic balances. These included the adoption of a floating exchange system for the 'real', a low inflation-target regime and a tight fiscal policy.

The government that came to power in 2003 has maintained the prudent macroeconomic policy that Brazil has been implementing since 1999. Lower inflation rates have permitted a partial reduction in interest rates which, in turn, has set in motion a significant credit expansion in the country. This credit boom, along with well-funded social programmes, has increased the purchasing power of the poorest strata of Brazilian society.

The cautious economic policy also prompted a steep fall in the public debt/GDP ratio (to 35.8%), allowing Brazil to repay all its liabilities to the IMF. The structure of its debt has also improved, with a smaller share of total debt now being denominated in foreign currency.

The success of Brazil's economic policy has paved the way for longer term economic thinking, though problems still exist. The rate of growth in Brazil at present is below 5%. Some experts think this is surprisingly low, given the near 2% increase in the working-age population, the rise in female labour force participation, the advancing urbanization and the trend towards greater average education and schooling of the labour force! Despite the relative successes of its macroeconomic policies, inflation remains a problem in Brazil, with an annual rate of over 7% in recent years.

In the course of its recent history, Brazil's industrial policies were integrated in the strategic plans of development. All of these plans focused on the industrial sector and were influential in the development and integration of modern Brazilian industry. During the 1970s targets were related to the balance of payments, concentrating on import substitution, and on the expansion of manufactured exports. In the 1980s and 1990s, the development plans were left aside and replaced by macroeconomic stabilization plans under the belief that macroeconomic stability would create the necessary and sufficient conditions for the development of the productive sectors. In 1992 Brazil reduced import tariffs, opening the economy and forced a restructuring in large parts of Brazilian industry. At the same time a programme of privatization was started which has been continued under the current government. Public utility sales have involved large mining companies and public telecommunications and electricity suppliers.

Even though Brazil has diversified its industrial activities, the industrial structure is still very concentrated, with small/medium-sized enterprises (SMEs) accounting for around 35% of GDP. By comparison, the US has a similar ratio of SMEs to the number of firms (98%), but their valued added corresponds to 65% of GDP. Productivity and innovation in Brazil is also low, though Brazilian industry is competitive in some high-technology sectors such as aerospace, in which the country holds third position in the world market for commercial aircraft. It is also the second biggest exporter of ethanol, being the technological leader in this product. The automotive sector is one of the biggest industries in the country, accounting for about 10% of total revenues and 6% of employment.

Recent Brazilian industrial policy

In March 2004, the current federal administration announced its first industrial policy after decades advocating that the state should create a favourable environment for industrial development and facilitate entrepreneurship, while holding firm to its commitment to macroeconomic stability. The government set about reducing the external restrictions on inward FDI to increase efficiency. In the medium to long term, it would now foster the development of key activities and technologies to allow Brazil to increase its competitiveness in the international markets, by simplifying trade procedures, helping companies find new markets, stimulating the creation of distribution centres for Brazilian companies abroad and supporting and consolidating the image of Brazil and Brazilian trademarks overseas. The focus on the international market has been one of the differences between this new industrial policy and the ones in previous decades. In May 2008, the Brazilian government announced new tax measures and goals for its industrial policy, including tax incentives for investment, R&D and exports. The National Bank for Economic and Social Development is to provide more than $100bn in finance for innovation projects in industrial and services sectors. The programme contains four macro targets: (i) to increase the ratio of investment to GDP; (ii) to stimulate innovation via an increase in private R&D; (iii) to increase the share of Brazilian exports in world exports; and (iv) to increase the number of SME exporters.

Brazil and the global financial crisis

Brazil has, in general, been more resilient to the crisis than many developed nations. Nevertheless, the Brazilian stock market suffered one of the world's largest losses from May to November 2008, losing practically half of its value. At the beginning of May 2009, however, the index largely recovered, gaining 37% compared to the beginning of the year. Nevertheless, Brazil, as with most of the emerging markets, was facing large capital outflows in 2008, which was accompanied by a sudden freeze in credit lines (including trade credit). Brazil's currency dropped more than 35% against the US dollar between August 2008 and March 2009, with the depreciation of the Brazilian 'real' being the second largest (after the Russian rouble) among major currencies. The depreciation has, however, been seen as mainly positive for the country by increasing the competitiveness of its exports and its import substitutes, even though exports dwindled as the biggest consumers of Brazilian goods saw their own economies move into recession.

In January 2009, export volume fell by 29% in comparison to December 2008 and by 26% in comparison to January 2008.

The response on the part of the monetary authorities has been two-fold. On the exchange rate side, the Brazilian Central Bank (BCB) engaged in several auctions on the foreign exchange markets, raising liquidity. On the domestic credit side, besides extending its re-discount policies, the BCB has eased its long-held strict reserve requirements, in a series of moves that, according to estimates, ended up liberating an amount of liquidity potentially higher than 5.7% of GDP. On the part of the government, the main response to the crisis was an easing of constraints on public banks to acquire the capital of private financial institutions. At the end of March 2009, the government also reduced the tax on certain industrial products, helping reduce prices for the final consumer.

Analysts such as Ernst & Young argue that the country is already on a sustainable growth path and would grow by an average 4% per year in the period 2007–2030. Goldman Sachs concurs, predicting that Brazil will overtake Germany in terms of GDP in 2029. While most countries are in search of products through which they can integrate with the global economy, Brazil is innovative in a number of high-technology activities in agriculture, energy, aircraft, mining products, design, machinery and automobiles, among many others. The country has a diversified economy through which it can sustain growth for many years to come.

Demographic and sociocultural factors

Brazil has a population of some 192 million, with a low population growth rate of around 1% per annum. It also has an ageing population issue, with the 'old age dependency ratio' (see p. 601) rising from 7.4 in 1990 to 10.6 in 2010.

Key social indicators have improved over the past decades. The current government has assigned high priority to social development programmes for the most disadvantaged families, offering financial subsidies as well as a combined access to basic social rights like healthcare, food and education. However, much remains to be done to address rural, urban, gender and racial inequalities and to ensure that access to goods and services benefits all social groups. In 2008 Brazil ranked 70th out of 177 in the UN

Human Development Index, a rather modest position compared with the country's levels of economic development and technological sophistication and there are still regional imbalances between the Northeast and the South and Southeast regions.

The *Human Development Report* (UNDP 2010) estimates that some 18% of the Brazilian population live on less than $2 a day (approximately 36 million people), while a further 22% of the population have a standard of living below the 'poverty line' as defined in Brazil itself. Brazil is also one of the world's most unequal societies: in 2008 the poorest 20% accounted for just 3% of Brazil's national income or consumption.

Figure 28.1 earlier (p. 603) presents the Brazilian cultural characteristics identified by Gert Hofstede's analysis. We can see that Brazil has a higher *Power Distance* score of 69 than the world average (60), suggesting considerable respect for position within hierarchies and a willingness to receive direct instructions. However, its *Individualism* score of 38 is below the world average of 44, suggesting a more collectivist and group-oriented outlook than in many other countries. In terms of *Masculinity* characteristics Brazil's score of 49 is broadly similar to the world average (50), i.e. similar to most countries in terms of assertiveness/materialism. However, its *Uncertainty Avoidance* score of 76 is above the world average (68), suggesting a preference for a more structured and predictable environment, as compared to a less certain one. Finally, in terms of *Long-term Orientation* Brazil has a score of 65, well above the world average (44) and suggesting a greater readiness to look further into the future and to postpone immediate gratification in favour of longer-term goals.

International competitiveness

Brazil is seen in Chapter 7 (Table 7.8, p. 131) to have a total labour cost per hour in manufacturing of only $8.3 (US Bureau of Labor Statistics 2010). This compares favourably with the average of $43.3 per hour in EU manufacturing and $13.3 per hour in East Asia manufacturing (excluding Japan), though well above the $0.9 per hour and $1.5 per hour recorded in India and China respectively. Whilst labour productivity is lower than in many advanced industrialized economies in certain, less high technology sectors this still gives Brazil a competitive edge over many

countries. However, the rapid rise in the Brazilian exchange rate for the 'real' in recent times (see Chapter 25, p. 529) has certainly helped erode this labour cost advantage.

Russia

Background

Nearly 20 years after the collapse of the Soviet Union and despite the considerable structural changes that have occurred during the transition to a market economy, Russia is still very much affected by the heritage of the former one-party political and centrally planned economic system. The effects range from the disintegration of the Soviet Union and the related disruptions of traditional economic linkages, to the loss of perceived superpower status including the loss of former allies in Central and Eastern Europe and the former Soviet Republics, some of which are now members of the EU. Former President Putin viewed the collapse of the Soviet Union as the 'greatest tragedy of the 20th century'. The prevailing Russian view also sees the outcome of the transition-related industrial restructuring of the early and mid-1990s as very much connected with the 'primitivization' of the Russian economy, whereas in contrast in the new EU member states such economic restructuring – despite some setbacks – is broadly viewed as a success. Table 28.6 provides a range of indicators for developments in Russia during the past decade.

The role of the state

Russia's 'economic development model' has undergone marked changes since the 1990s. The heavy reliance on energy and raw materials resources, particularly for exports, and the advanced defence- and space industry-related high-technology sectors represent structural features of the Russian economy associated with its Soviet heritage. It has moved from liberal approaches, where the initial focus was on the liberalization of prices and external trade, mass privatization and devolution of powers from the centre to regions, which had been applied between early 1992 and the late 1990s, to a subsequent path involving backtracking

Table 28.6 Russia: data profile.

	2000	2005	2007	2008
World view				
Population, total (millions)	146.30	143.15	142.10	141.95
Population growth (annual %)	0.0	−0.5	−0.3	−0.1
Surface area (sq. km) (thousands)	17,098.2	17,098.2	17,098.2	17,098.2
Poverty headcount ratio at national poverty line (% of population)	–	–	–	–
GNI, Atlas method (current US$) (billions)	250.31	639.04	1,068.47	1,369.14
GNI per capita, Atlas method (current US$)	1,710	4,460	7,520	9,650
GNI, PPP (current international $) (billions)	972.45	1,655.71	2,320.77	2,807.75
GNI per capita, PPP (current international $)	6,650	11,570	16,330	19,780
People				
Income share held by lowest 20%	–	6.4	5.6	–
Life expectancy at birth, total (years)	65	65	67	68
Fertility rate, total (births per woman)	1.2	1.3	1.4	1.5
Adolescent fertility rate (births per 1,000 women ages 15–19)	32	26	25	25
Contraceptive prevalence (% of women ages 15–49)	–	–	–	–
Births attended by skilled health staff (% of total)	–	99	–	–
Mortality rate, under 5 (per 1,000)	24	17	15	13
Malnutrition prevalence, weight for age (% of children under 5)	–	–	–	–
Immunization, measles (% of children ages 12–23 months)	97	99	99	99
Primary completion rate, total (% of relevant age group)	94	–	94	95
Ratio of girls to boys in primary and secondary education (%)	–	99	98	98
Prevalence of HIV, total (% of population ages 15–49)	0.3	1.1	1.1	–
Environment				
Forest area (sq. km) (thousands)	8,092.7	8,087.9	8,086.0	–
Agricultural land (% of land area)	13.3	13.2	13.2	–
Annual freshwater withdrawals, total (% of internal resources)	–	–	1.8	–
Improved water source (% of population with access)	95	96	–	96
Improved sanitation facilities (% of population with access)	87	87	–	87
Energy use (kg of oil equivalent per capita)	4,170	4,550	4,730	–
CO_2 emissions (metric tons per capita)	9.9	10.6	10.8	–
Electric power consumption (kWh per capita)	5,209	5,785	6,317	–
Economy				
GDP (current US$) (billions)	259.71	764.55	1,300.12	1,667.60
GDP growth (annual %)	10.0	6.4	8.1	5.6
Inflation, GDP deflator (annual %)	37.7	19.2	14.4	18.0
Agriculture, value added (% of GDP)	6	6	5	5
Industry, value added (% of GDP)	38	39	38	37
Services, etc., value added (% of GDP)	56	55	57	58
Exports of goods and services (% of GDP)	44	35	30	31
Imports of goods and services (% of GDP)	24	21	22	22
Gross capital formation (% of GDP)	19	20	24	26
Revenue, excluding grants (% of GDP)	–	–	31.3	33.5
Cash surplus/deficit (% of GDP)	–	–	6.2	5.6

Table 28.6 (continued)

	2000	2005	2007	2008
States and markets				
Time required to start a business (days)	–	35	30	30
Market capitalization of listed companies (% of GDP)	15.0	71.8	115.6	23.8
Military expenditure (% of GDP)	3.7	3.7	3.4	3.5
Mobile cellular subscriptions (per 100 people)	2	84	120	141
Internet users (per 100 people)	2.0	15.2	24.6	31.9
Roads, paved (% of total roads)	–	84	–	–
High-technology exports (% of manufactured exports)	17	8	7	7
Global links				
Merchandise trade (% of GDP)	57.8	48.3	44.4	45.8
Net barter terms of trade index (2000 = 100)	–	–	–	–
External debt stocks, total (DOD, current US$) (millions)	159,993	229,911	368,075	402,453
Total debt service (% of exports of goods, services and income)	9.9	14.6	9.2	11.5
Net migration (thousands)	2,208	964	–	–
Workers' remittances and compensation of employees, received (current US$) (millions)	1,275	3,012	4,713	6,033
Foreign direct investment, net inflows (BoP, current US$) (millions)	2,714	12,886	55,073	75,002
Net official development assistance and official aid received (current US$) (millions)	1,553	–	–	–

Source: World Bank (2010a) *World Development Indicators database*, April.

towards recentralization and a strengthening role of the state, associated mainly with Putin's presidency after 2000.

The Russian economy has been booming during the first decade of the new millennium and most analysts have been busy repeatedly revising GDP growth forecasts upwards, largely owing to surging energy prices. Russian GDP growth has exceeded 8% in recent years, driven by a double-digit expansion of household consumption and even faster growth of investments. Even in 2008, when the global financial turmoil started to bite, GDP growth still reached 5.6%. During the past five years, real GDP has increased by more than 40%. Using PPP figures, Russia's GNI amounted to $2,800bn in 2008. In *per capita* terms, the Russian PPP-based GNI reached $19,780 in 2008 – about 54% of the EU average. During the Putin era consumers have experienced rising income and average wages and decreasing poverty levels, along with rising employment, almost full repayment of the government's external debt and growing foreign exchange reserves.

The application of industrial policy principles over free market approaches, the use of public–private ownership investment schemes, etc. were the economic development model guidelines designed at the end of Putin's presidency to be implemented by his successor Dimitry Medvedev. The global financial crisis and its outbreak in Russia in late 2008 has led to further adjustments in the direction of more centralization and state interventionism while some of the ambitious investment and modernization programmes have had to be scaled down due to the lack of finance.

Economic context

Russian foreign exchange reserves and capital inflows were at record levels at the beginning of 2008 and the government budget had a large surplus (4.9% of GDP) with public foreign largely repaid. These factors translated into double-digit annual inflation (14.1% in 2008) and to a sizeable appreciation of the rouble against the dollar in real terms. The appreciation pressure was reversed only after November 2008: with sharply declining oil prices and export revenues, the rouble started to depreciate – despite massive interventions by the Central Bank of Russia (CBR) which spent around $200bn of its reserves to support the rouble within the three subsequent months.

The recent economic boom has been explained to a large degree by surging world market commodity prices, in particular those of energy. The development of Russian exports has been closely linked to rising oil prices. Indeed, the surging revenues from energy exports have accounted for a major (and growing) share of total export revenues.

The main challenge for the Russian economy in the medium and long run is whether it will succeed in replacing energy exports as the key growth driver by the development of other sectors (diversification towards manufacturing, high-technology branches, services, etc.) and how it will cope with the acute demographic crisis (the population is projected to decline by nearly 10 million in the coming decade). The officially endorsed long-term development programme, prepared by the Ministry of Economic Development and Trade in 2007, envisaged in its 'innovation scenario' an ambitious economic diversification away from the current heavy reliance on energy through a plan to a gradual switch to innovation-based development, supported by various industrial policy instruments, as well as the completion of reforms which aim at an improved climate for investment and entrepreneurship. Growing investment in transport infrastructure, education, health and R&D should help to generate an average annual GDP growth rate above 6% over the next decade. In this scenario, the Russian economy should become more efficient, modern and competitive.

In 2008, Russian economic growth still reached nearly 6%; fixed investments grew by 13% and real money incomes by 8%. However, GDP growth virtually collapsed in the fourth quarter of 2008 and the first quarter of 2009 while inflation remains high and may even accelerate as a consequence of the recent government rescue measures and the depreciation of the rouble.

Russia and the global economic crisis

Despite strong economic fundamentals, Russia was seriously hit by the global crisis, especially after September 2008. The stock market dropped by more than 70% between May 2008 and January 2009 – one of the largest declines among the emerging markets. Market capitalization declined by about $1,000bn over the same period. For the whole of 2008, net capital outflows reached nearly $140bn (net capital inflows exceeded $80bn during 2007). The stocks of a number of Russian blue chip companies (such as Gazprom, Rosneft, Lukoil Sberbank, Norilsk Nickel) were hit particularly hard, reflecting partly investors' over-reaction, although fundamental factors played a role given the recent decline in the world prices for oil and metals and high exposure to short-term foreign debts. Potentially more serious than the poor performance of the stock market is the tightening of credit conditions. Large Russian companies and smaller Russian banks have been facing difficulties servicing and refinancing their outstanding foreign debts. The lack and/or dearth of domestic, especially long-term credit financing have motivated Russian companies, even the state-owned or state-controlled ones such as Gazprom or Roseneft, to seek external financing.

Similar to the US and the EU, the Russian government has adopted various rescue and stimulation packages in order to improve the liquidity of the banking sector and restore confidence. The central bank released more than $100bn out of its reserves in order to provide additional liquidity and to support the rouble exchange rate. New loans to the banking sector with a maturity of up to six months have been provided via the state-owned Vnesheconombank (VEB) with no collateral required. In addition, the VEB will provide credit for refinancing short-term foreign loans, while acquiring shares in those companies as collateral, and the bank guarantee on private deposits was raised to RUB 700,000. More than $200 billion of state assistance in various forms were earmarked in an endeavour to ease liquidity in the financial sector.

Russia's greatest untapped potential lies in efficiency-seeking FDI. With its technological capabilities and human skills, Russia could become a major international engineering hub. But such success may prove challenging to achieve under a scenario of intense global competition for FDI projects, in which case the country would also need to upgrade its investment promotion efforts, including the liberalization of FDI and the provision of targeted incentives. If that happens, Russia could multiply its inward FDI stock within a relatively short period of time. One important caveat is that, before this happens, Russia could become too expensive a location for export-oriented FDI projects.

Demographic and sociocultural factors

The Russian population has been declining due to a combination of high mortality rates and declining birth rates, falling from 146.3 million in 2000 to around 140 million in 2010. The adverse demographic developments and labour shortages are among the major challenges that Russia will be facing in the near future. Russia also has an ageing population issue, with the 'old age dependency ratio' rising from the already high figure of 15.1 in 1990 to 17.9 in 2010.

Key social indicators, however, have improved since year 2000 with the average life expectancy rising from 65 years to 68 years, and a fall in the child mortality rate from 24 per 1,000 in the year 2000 to less than 13 per 1,000 in 2010. However, much remains to be done to address various inequalities. The *Human Development Report* (UNDP 2010) estimates that the poorest 10% of the Russian population receive only 2.6% of National Income, whilst the richest 10% receive 28.4%.

Figure 28.1 earlier (p. 603) presents the Russian cultural characteristics identified by Gert Hofstede's analysis. We can see that Russial has a higher *Power Distance* score of 93 than the world average (60), suggesting considerable respect for position within hierarchies and a willingness to accept direct instructions. However, its *Individualism* score of 39 is below the world average of 44, suggesting a more collectivist and group-oriented outlook than in many other countries. In terms of *Masculinity* characteristics Russia's score of 36 is below the world average (50), i.e. perhaps rather surprisingly suggesting less assertiveness/materialism and other 'male' characteristics! However, its *Uncertainty Avoidance* score of 95 is well above the world average (68), suggesting a strong preference for a more structured and predictable environment, as compared to a less certain one. Finally, in terms of *Long-term Orientation* Russia has a score of 36, below the world average (44) and suggesting a reluctance to look further into the future and to postpone immediate gratification in favour of longer-term goals.

International competitiveness

Russia has a total labour cost per hour in manufacturing of around $28.4, which compares favourably with the average of $43.3 per hour in EU manufacturing and $13.3 per hour in East Asia manufacturing (excluding Japan), though well above the $0.9 per hour and $1.5 per hour recorded in India and China respectively. Whilst labour productivity is lower than in many other advanced industrialized economies, in certain, less high technology sectors this still gives Russia a competitive edge over many countries. However, the rapid rise in the Russian exchange rate for the rouble in recent times has eroded some of this labour cost advantage.

Conclusion

If the last decade from 2000 saw the arrival of the BRICs, what of the second decade of the new millennium through to 2020? Goldman Sachs (2010) predict that BRICs will continue to strengthen, contributing twice as much to global growth over the next decade as the combined G3 of the US, Japan and Germany (Fig. 28.2a). China alone is projected to contribute some 30% of the projected global growth in the next decade, with some 15% contributed by the other BRIC economies. Figure 28.2(b) suggests that rising incomes in the BRICs will create a large new middle class (defined here as people with incomes between $6,000 and $30,000 per annum) with subsequent changes in spending patterns, increased competition for resources and greater pressure on the environment.

It seems likely, therefore, that within a few decades China and India will once again become on their own the largest economies in the world and their per capita incomes will rise dramatically. There may still be poor areas and many poor individuals, but they will both have large and sophisticated manufacturing and service sectors. Brazil and Russia will join them in the list of the world's top 10 economies.

All this will have many diverse implications. Both India and China will become great powers along with Russia (regaining its status), with large well-equipped armed forces and the economic muscle to challenge the present global dominance of the US. This will have

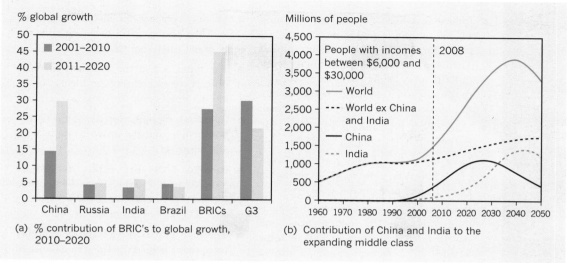

(a) % contribution of BRIC's to global growth, 2010–2020

(b) Contribution of China and India to the expanding middle class

Fig. 28.2 BRICs and global economic prospects.
Source: Goldman Sachs (2010).

profound implications for international politics as the world moves from a unipolar world to a multipolar one. There are also environmental issues to consider as the economic growth of Brazil, China and India is accompanied by a trend growth in CO_2 emissions continuing into the future. The consumption of oil by China has been increasing rapidly, and it appears that China will soon overtake the US as a user of this fuel. The Indian demand for oil is much lower, but if pre-dictions of Indian growth are correct, the country's consumption of oil will also increase rapidly. A large increase in world oil demand could lead to global shortages and higher prices, thereby damaging countries which are heavily dependent on imported oil.

Whatever the specific predictions the rapid emergence of the BRIC economies, with their economic and political developments, will have major impacts on a global scale.

Key points

- The BRIC economies already account for 15% of global output, comprise over 40% of the world's population and contribute around 16 trillion dollars to global output (using PPP exchange rates).

- China has the highest world population, at 1,324 million people, with a GDP per capita of around $6,240 (around 15% of that in the UK, using PPP). China has grown its economy by an average annual rate close to 10% in the first decade of the millennium, but has the problem of a rapidly ageing population.

- The Chinese economic model is sometimes termed a 'socialist market economy', with markets playing a key role in resource allocation, but with public ownership, direct governmental international and state-led industrial polices also an integral part of the system.

- China has a huge balance of payments surplus of some $300 million with the rest of the world. It also has an astonishingly high propensity to save, with almost 50% of its national income being 'saved' by households, businesses or government.

- India has a huge population of around 1.2 billion people, and is expected to surpass China's population in the near future! There is a much higher rate of illiteracy in India than in China, with some 20% of the population aged 15–24 years illiterate in India, compared to only 5% in China.

- India's GNP per capita is $3,020 in PPP, i.e. around half of that in China.

- India has been a highly regulated economy, but deregulation is occurring in many sectors of economic activity.

- Brazil has the 5th largest world population, with some 192 million people and with a GNP per capita in PPP of some $10,180. The average economic growth rate has been over 4% per year over the past decade.

- Brazil is engaged in industrial policies which encourage private markets and entrepreneurship, and has 35% of GDP accounted for by SME activity.

- There is considerable income inequality, with the poorest 20% receiving only 3% of Brazil's national incomes.

- The rapid rise in the Brazilian currency (the 'real') is creating problems for its international competitiveness.

- Russia has a population of some 142 million people, but the growth rate is actually negative!

- Russian GDP per capita is around $19,708 in PPP terms, some 54% of the EU average. Economic growth has been over 8% per annum in recent years.

- The high global energy and commodity prices have helped the Russian balance of payments to be in considerable surplus, although inflation has been over 10% in recent years.

- The rise of the BRIC economics is creating strong growth in the global 'middle class'.

Now try the self-check questions for this chapter on the Companion Website. You will also find useful links to relevant websites.

References and further reading

Abdelal, R. (2010) The promise and peril of Russia's resurgent state, *Harvard Business Review*, Jan/Feb, 125–9.

Black, J. S. and Morrison, A. J. (2010) A cautionary tale for emerging market giants, *Harvard Business Review*, September, 99–103.

Giavazzi, F. and Blanchard, O. (2010) *Macroeconomics: A European Perspective*, Harlow, Financial Times/Prentice Hall.

Goldman Sachs (2010) Global economics, commodities and strategy research, *Global Economics Weekly*, 2 December.

Hofstede, G. and Hofstede, G. J. (2005) *Cultures and Organisations: Software of the Mind*, Maidenhead, McGraw Hill.

Hout, T. and Ghemawat, P. (2010) China versus the world: whose technology is it? *Harvard Business Review*, December, 94–103.

Krugman, P. and Obstfeld, M. (2010), *International Economics: Theory and Policy*, Harlow, Financial Times/Prentice Hall.

Paine, L. (2010) The China Rules! *Harvard Business Review*, June, 103–8.

Rakshit, M. (2011) *Macroeconomics of Post Reform India*, Oxford, Oxford University Press.

Rakshit, M. (2011) *Money and Finance in the Indian Economy*, Oxford, Oxford University Press.

Tse, E. (2010) Is it too late to enter China? *Harvard Business Review*, April, 96–101.

World Bank (2010a) *World Development Indicators Database 2010*, April, Washington DC.

World Bank (2010b) *World Development Report 2010: Development and Climate Change*, Washington DC.

UNCTAD (2009) *The Least Developed Countries Report 2009: The State and Development Governance*, New York and Geneva, United Nations Conference on Trade and Development.

UNCTAD (2010a) *Trade and Development Report 2010: Employment, Globalization and Development*, New York and Geneva, United Nations Conference on Trade and Development.

UNCTAD (2010b) *World Investment Report 2010: Investing in a Low Carbon Economy*, New York and Geneva, United Nations Conference on Trade and Development.

UNDP (2010) *Human Development Report 2010: The Real Wealth of Nations: Pathways to Human Development*, New York, United Nations Development Programme.

US Bureau of Labor Statistics (2010) *International Labor Statistics*.

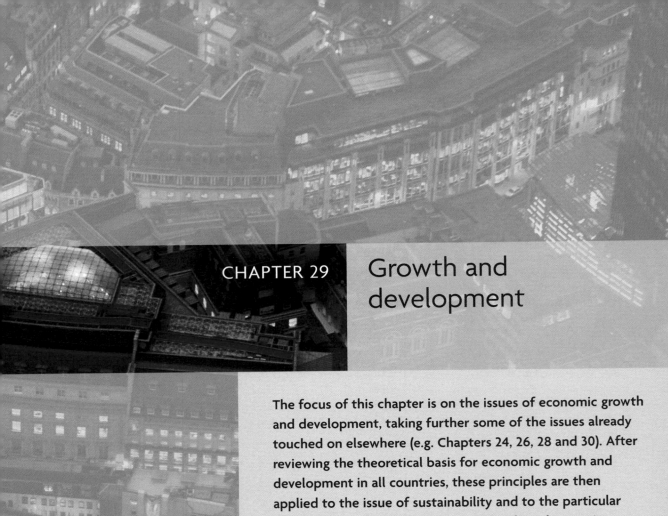

CHAPTER 29

Growth and development

The focus of this chapter is on the issues of economic growth and development, taking further some of the issues already touched on elsewhere (e.g. Chapters 24, 26, 28 and 30). After reviewing the theoretical basis for economic growth and development in all countries, these principles are then applied to the issue of sustainability and to the particular circumstances of the so-called less developed countries (LDCs). It is now acknowledged that political, social, historical and cultural factors work alongside the economic factors when LDCs go through a process of growth and structural change. Although this chapter will focus on the economic issues, reference will be made on occasions to these broader issues. The nature and causes of poverty amongst the nations are very complex, and the remedies are neither easy nor quick. An analysis of the major features of LDCs will shed some light on the peculiar economic and social conditions of production, consumption and distribution of income and wealth which exist in LDCs. This will help us to understand some development approaches and their policy implications. The causes and consequences of the breakdown in the global trade talks at Doha in 2006 are reviewed, as is the 'debt crisis' facing many LDCs as well as the policy responses of the IMF and other international institutions.

Theories of economic growth

It will be useful at the outset to review the classical, neo-classical and modern theories of growth.

Classical growth theory

The 'subsistence real wage' rate plays a key role in *classical growth theory*, i.e. the minimum real wage rate required to maintain life. Whenever the actual real wage exceeds the subsistence real wage, then population grows and this, combined with diminishing returns to labour, ensures that the actual real wage rate falls back to the subsistence level. On the other hand, when the actual real wage falls below the subsistence real wage, then lives are lost and the population declines until the actual real wage rises to the subsistence level. The discouraging prediction of the classical growth theory (Fig. 29.1) is that whatever the increase in levels of investment or the improvements in technology, the long-run growth rate is effectively zero, since equilibrium will only occur with living standards at the subsistence real wage.

In Fig. 29.1 an increase in capital equipment and/or technical change increases the labour marginal revenue product of labour (see Chapter 14, p. 286) and therefore the demand for labour increases from LD_1 to LD_2. The real wage rises from W_s to W_2 in the short run, but the increase in population and labour

supply to LS_2 in the long run reduces the real wage rate, which then falls back to the original subsistence level W_s. This rather dismal prospect was emphasized by analysts of the time such as Thomas Malthus.

Population and natural resources

Thomas Malthus (1766–1834) claimed that the human population would, left unchecked, grow exponentially (in a geometric progression). However, food production would grow only linearly (in an arithmetic progression), restricted by the need to bring new, less productive land into cultivation (an earlier forerunner of the theory of diminishing returns). Population would therefore double every 25 years and food production would be unable to keep pace. Periodic famines and high infant mortality, together with occasional wars, were seen by Malthus as the most likely 'checks' to population explosion. Malthus noted that even in nineteenth-century Britain, food production was already falling short of population growth, as evidenced by the high price of bread and increasing public expenditure on relief of the poor.

Malthus failed, however, to perceive that population growth has turned out to have an internal check: as people grow richer and healthier, they have smaller families. Indeed, the growth rate of the human population reached its peak of more than 2% a year in the early 1960s. The rate of increase has been declining ever since. It is now 1.26% and is expected to fall to 0.46% in 2050. The United Nations has estimated

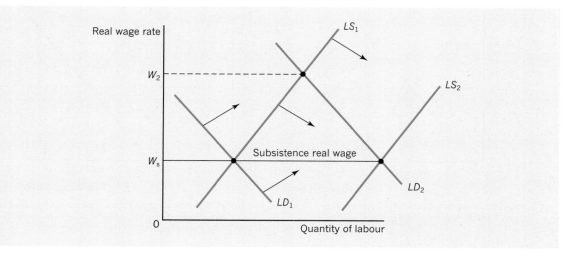

Fig. 29.1 Classical growth theory.

that most of the world's population growth will be over by 2100, with the population stabilizing at just below 11 billion. Malthus also failed to take account of developments in agricultural technology. These have squeezed more and more food out of each hectare of land. It is this application of technology and human ingenuity that has boosted food production, not merely in line with, but ahead of, population growth.

Neoclassical growth theory

Later analysts such as Solow (1957) and Denison (1967) used the production function (relating output to capital and labour inputs respectively) to argue that technical change and additional investment capital could indeed raise national growth rates. However, there is no reason why technical change should be anything other than a chance event under *neoclassical growth theory*, so that there is no prediction that growth can be sustained over time. The neoclassical growth theory is represented in Fig. 29.2. It assumes that savers have in mind a target real interest rate (R_T) that remains constant over time. This target real interest rate, say 5% per annum, is also called the *rate of time preference*.

In Fig. 29.2(a) the starting point is an equilibrium where the supply of capital (KS_1) intersects the demand for capital (KD_1) at the target real interest rate R_T. The supply of capital and the demand for capital are determined by saving and investment decisions. For example, as real interest rates rise, savings rise and the supply of capital expands. However, as real interest rates rise, fewer investment projects are now profitable and the demand for capital contracts (see Chapter 17, pp. 341–42). We now suppose that technical change occurs which raises the output per unit of capital, so that at any given interest rate there is an increased demand for capital investment, raising the amount of capital per person in production. In the short run, this increase in the demand for capital from KD_1 to KD_2 raises the real interest rate to R_2, which is now above the target rate R_T. In Fig. 29.2(b) this above-target return to savers shifts sentiments in favour of still more saving at any given real interest rate, increasing (shifting to the right) the supply of capital from KS_1 to KS_2. As progressively more capital is used per person, the marginal productivity of capital diminishes along the new KD_2 curve. The extra savings and supply of capital will continue until KS_1 has shifted as far as KS_2 in Fig. 29.2(b) and the marginal return on capital has fallen to the target real interest rate R_T and no further savings and capital is supplied. We now have the new equilibrium situation with a higher capital/labour ratio (K_2/L_2) but with the original real target interest rate of R_T.

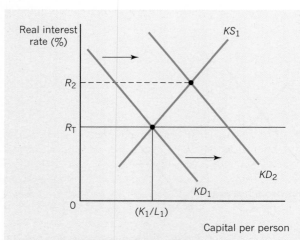

(a) Increase in marginal productivity of capital from unexpected technical change

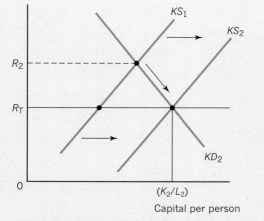

(b) Higher real interest rate increases savings and the supply of capital, until original real interest rate R_T is restored

Fig. 29.2 Neoclassical growth theory.

Whilst real GDP per person will have grown during the transition period from one equilibrium to another, it will now cease to grow once the real rate of interest has returned to its target level R_T. The marginal productivity of (a now higher volume of) capital will have fallen back to its original level and real GDP per person, whilst higher, will cease to grow. In the absence of continuous technical change, there can only be short-term and transient growth periods under the neoclassical theory.

Modern growth theories

The modern approach to growth is sometimes called *endogenous growth theory* (EGT) and is often associated with the pioneering work of Joseph Schumpeter. The emphasis here is on education and training, research and development and other knowledge-accumulating activities building the potential for continuous technical change, progressively increasing the marginal productivities of both capital and labour, and resulting in prolonged and sustainable periods of economic growth. Unlike neoclassical growth theory, technical change is no longer haphazard and down to chance, but can be fostered and promoted by appropriate policies. Moreover, as the foundations for innovation and entrepreneurship are secured, the probabilities of further technical change and associated economic growth occurring rise significantly. Technical change is no longer regarded as 'unexplainable' and due to chance as in neoclassical theory, but in the endogenous growth theories becomes itself a variable which can be influenced by policy decisions and should now be included within production functions, alongside the conventional inputs of labour and capital.

Productivity and growth

The critical role of productivity in economic growth is emphasized in a wide range of cross-country studies. Bosworth and Collins (2003), in their study of 62 developing countries over the period 1960–2000, found that differences in *total factor productivity* (TFP) accounted for over half the recorded differences in GDP growth per worker across those countries. This is an extremely important finding since it

has important implications for the 'sustainability' of growth. If growth is due mainly to factor accumulation (e.g. increases in labour or capital input), then the diminishing marginal returns to factor input can be expected to apply, and higher growth rates, such as those achieved in recent years in East Asia, will be unsustainable in the future. However, if these recorded high growth rates are due to higher TFP of these factor inputs, then such limits to growth need not necessarily apply.

Productivity and 'investment climate'

As noted in Chapter 17, there is substantial empirical evidence to suggest that higher TFP is strongly and positively associated with a favourable 'investment climate'. In other words, where the business environment in which the firm operates is characterized by transparency, policy stability, secure property rights and open and competitive markets, then private investment and innovation (both product and process) are stimulated and higher rates of productivity growth are recorded. Similar conclusions were reached in a major study by the World Bank (2004b). This study correlated 'investment profile', based on measures of contract enforceability, expropriation, profit repatriation and payment delays, with annual percentage growth in private investment. These countries with a more favourable 'investment profile' experienced much faster rates of growth of private investment than those countries with a less favourable 'investment profile'. We consider these issues further later in this chapter.

Productivity and competition

Whilst individual firms might prefer an absence of competition, Joseph Schumpeter and other analysts have noted the benefits to the aggregate of firms of competitive pressures. Schumpeter called the dynamic processes that follow such competition 'creative destruction', rewarding success, penalizing failure and encouraging firms to experiment and learn. In the advanced industrialized economies of the OECD, between 5% and 20% of firms enter and exit the market each year (Bartelsman *et al.* 2004). Firms that leave the market were found to be generally less productive than the new firms which entered the market, with the net productivity gain substantial, contributing on average around 25% of the recorded productivity gains in the countries investigated.

Productivity and policy uncertainty

Uncertainty plays a key role in investment decisions, given that these are, by definition, forward looking and involve expected future returns over the lifespan of a project. In the annual *World Bank Investment Climate Survey*, some 30% of firms in developing countries regularly rate 'policy uncertainty' as the major single deterrent to investment. Various studies have suggested that improving policy predictability can increase the probability of making new investments by over 30% (Kraay 2003; *World Bank* 2005).

Sustainable development

As we noted in Chapter 10 on the Environment, the term 'sustainable development' is now widely used, and its origins can be traced back to the early 1970s, when fears were already growing about globally unsustainable social and economic development with an influential academic report entitled *The Limits to Growth* published in 1972 (Meadows *et al.* 1972). The report explored alternative futures as to what might happen as a result of a rapidly growing global human population, including impacts on food production, natural resources and environmental degradation in a finite world. 'Limits to Growth' was widely received as a message of impending doom and concluded that sooner or later one or more of these interrelated systems would collapse. The report had a significant impact, partly because it reinforced the growing economic and political uncertainty and fuelled the general pessimism of the time. 'Limits to Growth' was followed soon after by the onset of the first oil crisis in late 1973, which compounded fears about finite oil and other energy resources.

Characteristics of sustainable development

The modern understanding of the concept of 'sustainable development' was perhaps most clearly articulated in 1987 through the publication of a United Nations report entitled *Our Common Future*. This was the final report of a process involving the United National World Commission on Environment and Development (WCED). The report is also sometimes known as the Brundtland Report after the Norwegian Prime Minister Gro Harlem Brundtland, the then chair of the WCED. 'Our Common Future' is famous for providing the following most widely cited definition of sustainable development. Sustainable development is 'development which meets the needs of the present without compromising the ability of future generations to meet their own needs' (WCED 1987).

Two years on from the WCED report, preparations began in 1989 for a major international meeting on environment and development. The 'Earth Summit' or, to give it its legal title, the UN Conference on Environment and Development (UNCED), was held in June 1992 in Rio de Janeiro in Brazil. Attended by over 30,000 governmental and nongovernmental organizations from over 170 countries, the Earth Summit laid down key principles for governments to follow to promote sustainability. The Johannesburg 'sustainability conference' a decade later in 2002 revisited and reinforced many of these principles.

The Rio Declaration on Environment and Development

The *Rio Declaration on Environment and Development* aims to establish 'a new and equitable global partnership through the creation of new levels of co-operation among states, key sectors of societies and people' by '. . . working towards international agreements which respect the interests of all and protect the integrity of the global environment and development system' (preamble to the Rio Declaration). The main themes of the Rio Declaration are outlined below. Although the actual text is much longer, this list gives a good idea of the vast range of issues covered (adapted from UNEP 1992).

- *Principle 1*: Humans are at the centre of concerns for sustainable development.
- *Principle 2*: Countries must not cause damage to the environment of other states.
- *Principle 3*: Development must equitably meet developmental and environmental needs of present and future generations.

- *Principle 4*: Environmental protection is an integral part of the development process.
- *Principle 5*: Eradicating poverty is an indispensable requirement for sustainable development.
- *Principle 6*: The special situation and needs of (least) developing countries must be given special priority.
- *Principle 7*: States have common but differentiated responsibilities to conserve, protect and restore the health and integrity of the Earth's ecosystem.
- *Principle 8*: States should reduce and eliminate unsustainable patterns of production and consumption and promote appropriate demographic policies.
- *Principle 9*: States should co-operate to strengthen endogenous capacity-building for sustainable development.
- *Principle 10*: There is a need to improve access to environmental information, public awareness and participation.

The World Summit on Sustainable Development

The Rio Declaration contains many sensible principles and proclamations. However, a major weakness as an international treaty is its lack of any enforcement or compliance system. In legal terms, the Rio Declaration is what is called 'soft law'. Nevertheless, some of these principles are starting to play important roles in the development of a future detailed legal framework around trade and the environment.

The *World Summit on Sustainable Development* (WSSD) or, as it was commonly known, the 'Rio + 10' conference, was held in Johannesburg in 2002. The communiqué from this conference acknowledged shortcomings in attempts by developed economies to implement the Rio principles over the past 10 years. It placed still greater emphasis than Rio on interdependencies, acknowledging that economic, developmental, environmental and social dimensions must be addressed simultaneously if sustainability is to be achieved.

Key conditions for sustainable development

It has already been noted that the Brundtland Commission defined 'sustainable development' (SD) as development that meets the needs of the present generation without compromising the ability of future generations to meet their own needs. This would seem to imply that at least two key aspects need to be present if social and economic development is to be regarded as 'sustainable':

1 *Intergenerational equity*: namely that the development process seeks to minimize any adverse impacts on future generations. These clearly include avoiding adverse environmental impacts such as excessive resource depletion today reducing the stock available for future use, or levels of pollution emission and waste disposal today being beyond the ability of the environment to absorb them, thereby imposing long-term damage.

2 *Intra-generational equity*: namely that the development process seeks to minimize tendencies towards excessive income and wealth inequalities within and between nations and groups of nations at any point of time.

Attempts have been made to operationalize these aspects of sustainable development still further. For example, various 'rules' have been devised to reflect views as to what might constitute 'weak' and 'strong' sustainability practices.

Weak sustainability (WS)

Under *WS rules* practical efforts will be made to fully compensate those adversely affected by development:

- *Future generations*: e.g. depletion of scarce resources 'compensated' by income transfers to future generations or by technological developments increasing the efficiency of future resource use (less resource requirements per unit of output). Significant attempts will be made under WS to 'decouple' adverse environmental effects from economic growth. Support will also be given to the '*constant capital rule*', namely that this generation must pass on to future generations an aggregate capital stock no smaller in value than the one it inherited. Less environmental capital (e.g. fewer natural resources) can be passed on so long as it is replaced by an equivalent value of physical capital (e.g. buildings and infrastructure) since physical capital is seen under this 'rule' as a credible substitute for environmental capital. Attempts will be made to capture environmental impacts within the macroeconomic accounts so that the 'constant capital' rule can be monitored.

■ *Current generations*: e.g. the poor and those disadvantaged by development must be compensated by various support programmes and other policy measures. Higher priority must be given under WS to attempts to tackle poverty both at home and abroad (e.g. debt relief for developing countries).

Strong sustainability (SS)

Under *SS rules* attempts will also be made to compensate those adversely affected by development. However, under SS that compensation must be explicitly 'environmental'.

■ *Future generations*: e.g. the 'constant capital rule' no longer applies. Any loss of environmental capital in this generation must be offset by the addition of an equivalent 'value' of environmental capital to future generations (e.g. deforestation must be fully offset by an equivalent 'value' of tree planting). Physical capital is seen under SS as a highly imperfect substitute for environmental capital. The focus is on the conservation and preservation of ecosystems, landscapes and other 'natural' features.

■ *Current generations*: e.g. although there is still concern under SS for support for individuals disadvantaged by development, the focus shifts from individual valuations and concerns to the collective value ascribed to ecosystems and other environmental assets.

We now review some of the more technical issues underlying the issue of sustainable development.

Sustainable development: a technical approach

Following Pearce (1998), Fig. 29.3 uses wellbeing per capita on the vertical axis and time on the horizontal axis, where time is split into three generations of people. Pearce suggests that an economy that develops along a path like *A* is pursuing *sustainable development*, securing increases in wellbeing that last over future generations. Even an economy developing along path *B* is 'sustainable' because later generations are no worse off than the first one: wellbeing is 'non-declining'. However, the economy on path *C* is not sustainable, because per capita wellbeing grows, then declines for succeeding generations. Note that sustainable development is not necessarily 'optimal' in

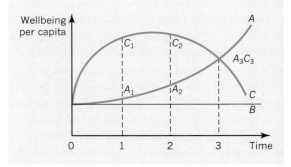

Fig. 29.3 Sustainable and non-sustainable growth paths.

that path *C* ($C_1 + C_2 + C_3$) yields a total wellbeing in excess of path *A* ($A_1 + A_2 + A_3$).

Sustainability 'rules'

Whatever concept of 'wellbeing' is applied (GDP or 'quality of life' indices), the condition for sustainable development is that each generation should leave the next generation a stock of capital assets no less than the stock it 'inherits'. The next generation will then have the capacity to generate the same (or more) 'wellbeing' as the previous generation. At least four types of capital asset are often identified.

1 *Man-made capital* (K_M): factories, machines, roads, computers, etc.

2 *Human capital* (K_H): knowledge, skills embodied in people.

3 *Natural capital* (K_N): the stock of environmental assets that provide natural resources to sustain life, to use in production, to help in the assimilation of wastes and provide amenity attractions.

4 *Social capital* (K_S): values and relationships which give a particular society its sense of identity.

The **weak sustainability rule** is that:

> The total stock of capital ($K_M + K_H + K_N + K_S$) should not fall, though individual elements within it can vary.

The **strong sustainability rule** is that

> Each element within the total stock of capital should not fall.

Sustainable development is a key issue for both developed and developing countries. However, it is clearly the developing countries which will have the greatest problems in conforming to either of these sustainability rules. This is especially true if these capital rules are expressed per capita, given the current and projected rapid population growth for the developing countries. Of course, the 'weak sustainability rule' gives more scope for the developing economies. For example, a fall in K_N (per capita) via, say, deforestation in Amazonia, can, at least in principle, be offset by investing the monies received in education and training, giving an offsetting rise in K_H (per capita).

The extent to which such offsets are feasible depends on how easily one form of capital can be substituted for another form in terms of its contribution to 'wellbeing'. If K_M, K_H or K_S (per capita) can more than offset a decline in K_N (per capita) then achieving 'weak sustainability' for both developed and developing countries will at least be more plausible. It is in this context that many are placing their hopes for sustainable development on further advances in technological capabilities, thereby raising output per unit input of these various types of capital asset.

Measuring sustainable development

It has often been pointed out that an implication for fulfilling the 'weak sustainability rule' is that the total savings of a nation must be greater than the total depreciation of its capital assets ($K_M + K_H + K_N + K_S$). Only then can the nation replenish its capital assets so that they are at least as extensive at the end of the time period as they were at the beginning. The **general savings rule** is that:

> For development to be sustainable (weak form), total savings must at least cover depreciation of the four types of capital.

Estimates (if imperfect) of savings by nations are available from the national accounts as are also estimates of man-made capital depreciation (K_M). Environmental economists have also made progress in developing indicators of natural resources (e.g. oil, timber) and of waste-receiving capabilities (e.g. via pollution) and the environmental 'pluses' of new discoveries of natural resources and growth of renewable resources (see Chapter 10).

Progress has been made in developing indicators of human capital depreciation (K_H), which tends of

course to be substantial and positive in sign in the poorer developing economies, but via increased education, training and improvements in the quality of life to be negative in sign in the developed economies, implying appreciation of K_H. Indicators for social capital depreciation (K_S) remain somewhat elusive.

A dilemma facing the developing economies and particularly the poorer LDC grouping is that, expressed as a percentage of GNP, savings are often insufficient to more than offset any (net) depreciation estimated for the other four capital assets combined. The richer countries would certainly seem to be sustainable in terms of the 'general savings rule' and in a context of 'weak sustainability'. Problems clearly exist elsewhere, as in much of Africa and in the Middle East where assets appear to be depreciating faster than they are being replaced.

Technical change and sustainability

Technical change is not usually included in national savings ratios, although many would argue that it is a factor to be added to general savings. Pearce (1998) suggests that a rich economy such as the US would gain an extra three percentage points on its 'genuine savings' measure by adding on technological change. The number is likely to be far less, perhaps zero in many developing economies. However, a major debate is currently under way on the extent to which technological change might become a major factor in supporting sustainable development in the low-income, developing economies.

Figure 29.4 indicates how technological change can play a key role in development, in terms of our earlier analysis enhancing human capital (K_H), man-made capital (K_M), social capital (K_S) and arguably even natural capital (K_N). The *Human Development Report* of the United Nations (UNDP 2001) emphasizes the benefits of technology for developing economies, producing drought-tolerant plant varieties for farming in uncertain climates, more efficient industrial processing vaccines for infectious diseases, and clean energy sources for domestic and industrial uses. In these ways, new technologies support economic growth through productivity gains in agriculture, industry and service activities and by supporting a healthier, more highly educated and skilled workforce.

Technical change is one of the factors associated with increases in TFP, as noted earlier (p. 625).

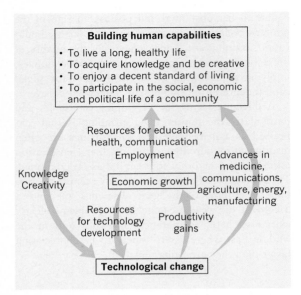

Fig. 29.4 How technological change can influence economic growth.

However, technical change need not be limited to new scientific breakthroughs (*innovations*) of the type which might involve patents. It can include *adaptations* of existing scientific and/or technological processes and products, with estimates of the adaptation:innovation ratio as high as 30:1 (World Bank 2005). This ratio emphasizes the great potential for developing countries to catch up with the more developed countries, by creating a business environment that supports the diffusion and adaptation of existing processes and products as well as the creation of new ones. Parente and Prescott (2000) note that while it took the early industrialized countries 40–60 years to double their incomes in real terms, others have achieved the same outcome much more rapidly in recent times, examples being Costa Rica in 19 years (1961–80), Jordan in 15 years (1965–80) and China and Taiwan in 10 years (1965–75).

GNP data, developed and developing countries

The use of GNP per head as a basis for classifying countries as developed or developing has been much

criticized in recent years. Nevertheless, it does give some indication of the huge disparities in standard of living between countries, as can be seen from Fig. 29.5.

GNP per head

Before moving to alternative indicators of 'economic wellbeing', let us briefly review the usefulness of the GNP per head figures represented in Fig. 29.5, paying particular attention to the situation of the developing economies. Students of macroeconomics will know that GNP can be measured in the local currency using output, income and expenditure methods. By dividing the figure for GNP (converted into US dollars at the official $/country exchange rate) by the country population, we obtain an average figure for output or income per head. Interesting as this figure undoubtedly is, it has a number of flaws as a measure of comparative living standards in the respective countries.

■ *Inappropriate exchange rates*. Converting the value of GNP expressed in the local currency into a US dollar equivalent using the official exchange rate may misrepresent the actual purchasing power in the local economy. This is because the official exchange rate is influenced by a range of complex forces in the foreign exchange markets and may not accurately reflect the purchasing power of one country's currency in another country. A more accurate picture is given if we use purchasing power parities (PPPs) rather than official exchange rates when making this conversion (see Table 29.1 below). Purchasing power parities measure how many units of one country's currency are needed to buy exactly the same basket of goods as can be bought with a given amount of another country's currency. On this basis, Ethiopia's figure rises from $70 to $870 per capita and the Switzerland figure falls from $65,330 to around $46,460 per capita, using purchasing power parities (World Bank 2010).

■ *Differing degrees of non-market economic activity*. GNP per capita includes only the money value of recorded (market) transactions involving goods and services. Non-market transactions are excluded. For example, the output of subsistence agriculture, whereby farmers grow food for their own consumption, is excluded from GNP figures. In many less developed economies where there is often a

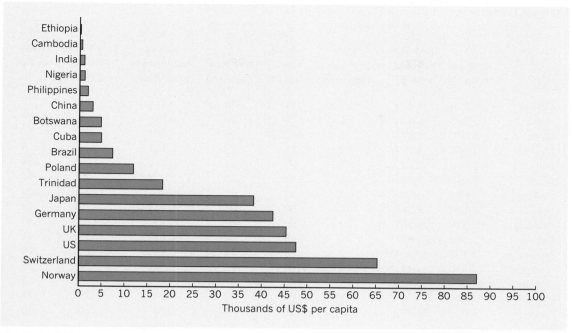

Fig. 29.5 GNP per head in $US, 2008.
Source: Adapted from World Bank (2010) *World Development Report*.

greater degree of non-market economic activity, this fact may lead to GNP figures that underestimate the true living standards.

- *Varying degrees of inequality*. GNP per capita gives an indication of the 'average' standard of living in a country. However, this may reflect the experience of only a small number of people in that country because its income distribution may be highly unequal, being skewed in the direction of the wealthier sections of society. For example, instead of using the arithmetic mean for GNP per capita, the median might be a more useful measure of the 'average', i.e. that figure for which 50% of the population has a higher GNP per capita, and 50% has a lower GNP per capita.

- *Incidence of externalities*. Externalities occur where actions by an individual or group impose costs (or benefits) on others which are not fully 'priced'. Increased pollution is a by-product of many industrial processes, reducing the quality of life for those affected. However, this negative externality may not be reflected in the GNP calculations. Similarly, the GNP figure makes no

allowance for the depletion and degradation of natural resources and for the social costs these may impose, e.g. deforestation as a factor in global warming, etc.

For these and other reasons (differing accounting conventions, economic and social practices), there has been a move towards the use of indicators other than the GNP per capita figure to reflect the 'true' standard of living in various countries, using various 'quality of life' indicators such as life expectancy, medical provision, educational opportunities, etc.

The United Nations has moved on to publish a *Human Development Report* since 1990 in which new methods of classification are presented, including a Human Development Index which we consider below.

Human Development Index (HDI) classification

An interesting issue is whether the conventional GNP per capita figure can be merged with 'quality of life'

Table 29.1 Selected country indicators and rankings (out of 182 countries).

	1 GNP per head ($)	2 Real GNP per head (PPP$)	3 Life expectancy at birth (years)	4 Adult literacy rate (%)	5 Enrolment ratio* (%)	6 Human Development Index (HDI)	7 Rank by real GNP per head (PPP$)	8 Rank by HDI
Ethiopia	280	779	55	36	49	0.414	171	171
Cambodia	600	1,802	61	76	59	0.593	143	137
Cuba	4,870	6,876	79	100	100	0.863	95	51
Nigeria	1,160	1,969	48	72	53	0.511	175	158
India	1,070	2,753	63	66	61	0.612	128	134
China	2,940	5,383	73	93	69	0.772	102	92
Philippines	1,890	3,406	72	93	80	0.751	124	105
Brazil	7,350	9,567	72	90	87	0.813	79	75
Trinidad	18,340	23,507	69	99	61	0.837	64	90
Poland	11,880	15,887	76	99	88	0.888	53	41
Botswana	4,781	13,604	53	83	71	0.699	60	125
Germany	42,440	34,401	80	100	88	0.947	24	22
Norway	87,070	53,433	81	100	98.6	0.971	5	1
UK	45,390	35,130	79	100	89	0.947	20	21
Japan	38,210	33,632	83	100	87	0.96	26	10
US	47,580	45,592	79	100	93	0.956	9	13
Switzerland	65,330	40,658	82	100	87	0.96	13	9

*Percentage of population at Levels 1, 2 and 3 (combined) of *OECD Literacy Survey*.
Sources: Adapted from UNDP (2010) *Human Development Report 2010*; World Bank (2010) *World Development Report 2010*.

indicators to give an overall index of economic well-being. A first step in this direction has in fact been made with the publication of the United Nations' Human Development Index (HDI). In Table 29.1 we present more comprehensive data for 17 countries. We also show the rank of these countries (out of 182 countries) in terms of real GNP per head using PPPs and in terms of the HDI. Before commenting further on these rankings it will help if we explore the background to the HDI a little further.

The Human Development Index (HDI) is based on three indicators.

1 *Standard of living*, as measured by real GNP per capita (PPP$) – column 2 in Table 29.1.

2 *Life expectancy at birth*, in years – column 3 in Table 29.1.

3 *Educational attainment*, as measured by a weighted average of adult literacy (two-thirds weight) and enrolment ratio (one-third weight) – columns 4 and 5 respectively in Table 29.1.

Each of these three indicators is then expressed in index form, with a scale set between a minimum value (index = 0) and a maximum value (index = 1) for each indicator.

■ *Standard of living*: $100 real GNP per capita (PPP$) is the minimum value (index = 0) and $40,000 is the maximum value (index = 1).

■ *Life expectancy at birth*: 25 years is the minimum value (index = 0) and 85 years is the maximum value (index = 1).

■ *Educational attainment*: 0% for both adult literacy and enrolment ratios are the minimum values used for calculating the weighted average (index = 0) and 100% for both adult literacy and enrolment ratios are the maximum values used for calculating the weighted average (index = 1).

An index is then calculated for each of these three indicators, and the average of these three index numbers is then calculated, as shown for each country in column 6 of Table 29.1. This average of the three separate index numbers is the HDI. The closer to 1 is the value of the HDI, the closer the country is to achieving the maximum values defined for each of the three indicators.

From columns 7 and 8 of Table 29.1, we can see that the rankings of the countries (in order from 1 to 182) do vary with the type of indicator used. In other words, using a GNP per head indicator, even adjusted for PPPs, gives a different ranking for countries than using the HDI index which brings quality of life aspects into the equation.

The HDI, by bringing together both economic and quality of life indicators, suggests a smaller degree of under-development for some countries than is indicated by economic data alone. For example, Cuba is 95th out of 182 countries when the GNP per head data is used for ranking (column 7) but rises 44 places to 51st when the HDI is used for ranking (column 8). For Cuba it would seem that the high life expectancy at birth and high adult literacy and enrolment ratios into education have helped raise these indicators and thereby the overall HDI. On the other hand, the HDI suggests a greater degree of under-development for some countries than is indicated by economic data alone. For example, Botswana is 60th out of 182 countries when the GNP per head data is used for ranking (column 7) but falls by 65 places to 125th when the HDI is used for ranking (column 8). For Botswana it would seem that the relatively low life expectancy of a country ravaged by Aids and relatively low adult literacy and enrolment ratios have lowered the overall HDI.

Although only in its infancy, it may be that classification of countries based on indices such as the HDI which bring together both economic and quality of life data may give a more accurate picture of the level of development.

Less developed countries (LDCs)

Clearly the exact definition of which countries are regarded as the LDCs may depend on the types of classification system adopted. In the World Development Report (World Bank 2010) the 'low income economies' are defined as those with a Gross National Income (GNI) per capita of $975 or less. Some 43 out of 196 countries are currently in this category. The 'poverty line' is now defined as $1.25 a day (or $2 a day using PPPs).

Major features of LDCs

Whatever the precise definition of an LDC, a number of features or characteristics are regarded as fairly typical of any country placed within this category:

Low real income per capita

This is a major indicator of under-development. A comparison with the economically developed countries is striking. For instance, in 2008, an average employed adult in the 43 'low income economies' earned less than 3% of the average employed adult in the US. Most LDCs exhibit very low ratios of total income (however defined) to total population, resulting in a low value for real income per capita. This is usually the result of low productivity, low savings, low investment, few resources and backward technology, often allied to high levels of population, the latter being determined by complex socioeconomic factors.

High population growth rate

Many LDCs have experienced a high population growth rate, although some LDCs in Africa and elsewhere are now experiencing population decline due mainly to a rapidly rising death rate from HIV/AIDS. Despite HIV/AIDS, the 43 'low income economies' have grown at a compound rate of 5.8% per annum over the period 2000–2008, compared to only 2.3% per annum for the 'high income developed countries'. A major implication of population growth in LDCs has been the growth in the proportion of people who live on the subsistence or 'poverty' line, defined as the minimum calorie intake necessary to stay alive. Even where the population growth rate is not very high (e.g. China) or falling (e.g. India), the absolute size of the population may be very high.

Large-scale unemployment and under-employment

This has been a common feature of many LDCs. Contributory factors often include a low level of economic activity, particularly in the industrial sector.

Since labour in LDCs tends to be both more abundant than capital and poorly educated, labour productivity is often quite low. Currently some 1.3 billion people, around one-quarter of the world's population, live on $1.25 a day or less, with the majority of these people to be found in East and South Asia, sub-Saharan Africa, Latin America and the Caribbean. Even with low wages, an even lower labour productivity can mean high 'relative unit labour costs' in LDCs, which in turn can mean unemployment.

Inequalities in the distribution of income

The pattern of income distribution tends to be less equal in most LDCs in comparison with the developed countries. For example, the ratio of shares of income between the richest 10% and poorest 10% is over 106 to 1 in Namibia, compared to a ratio of only 6 to 1 in Norway. This reflects the fact that in Namibia the richest 10% have 65% of all income, whereas the poorest 10% have only 0.6% (i.e. just over half of 1%) of all income. In Norway, by way of contrast, the richest 10% have 23.4% of all income, whereas the poorest 10% have 3.9% of all income. A significant disparity in this ratio is evident between developed and developing countries.

Large but neglected agricultural sector

In most LDCs, agriculture accounts for 40–85% of the real national income and about 60–90% of total employment. Nevertheless, policy-makers in many LDCs have opted for industrialization, often at the expense of agricultural development, in order to promote rapid economic growth. Such neglect of agriculture has often led to food shortages, poverty and famines.

Volatile export earnings

Foreign trade has tended to contribute relatively little to the national income of many LDCs. The pattern of foreign trade for most LDCs has often been determined by former colonial trade relationships, with today's LDCs remaining net exporters of primary goods and net importers of finished industrial goods. The export income of LDCs from primary goods (such as food and raw materials) sometimes fluctuates quite sharply, in part because of low price elasticities of demand for primary goods. For example, fluctuations in export earnings of LDCs have, on occasions,

been the result of a substantial increase in supply of primary products allied to a relatively price-inelastic demand curve, resulting in a fall in price and a fall in revenue for the exporter of primary goods. The tendency for such products to have relatively low income elasticity of demand has also meant that rising prosperity in the developed countries has resulted in only modest increases in demand for primary products from developing countries. In addition, the LDCs have historically often depended on a few key markets, with such a narrow market base increasing the risk factor as regards the prospects for a sustained growth of export earnings.

Market imperfections

In many LDCs markets are imperfect; sometimes they do not even exist. The money markets are just such an example of market failure. These money markets are often divided into two broad categories: (a) organized; and (b) unorganized. The organized sector generally consists of a central bank, commercial banks, co-operative credit banks and development banks. Division of labour and specialization does not always exist in such money markets, as with the absence of insurance companies. The unorganized sector mainly consists of moneylenders, indigenous banks, pawnbrokers, traders, merchants, landlords and friends. While the organized sector is amenable to financial control, the unorganized sector is not. In many LDCs the unorganized sector still controls a significant section of the money market, chiefly because of its hold over the rural areas. Clearly the existence of such financial dualism has restricted the use of bank cheques and other means of payment. By reducing the volume of monetary transactions this has led to the (less efficient) growth of transactions supported by barter or goods exchange. Further, this lack of an organized money market has deprived the society of an array of financial assets through which savings could have been more effectively mobilized and converted into investment for promoting economic growth. Evidently, a major policy objective in LDCs should be for the organized sector of the money markets to bring the unorganized sector more closely under its control.

Environmental degradation

There is considerable evidence to point to greater environmental degradation in the developing economies. As Robert Dorfman, a well-known environmental economist, noted, '. . . the poorer countries of the world confront tragic choices. They cannot afford drinking water standards as high as those the industrial countries are accustomed to. They cannot afford to close their pristine areas to polluting industries that would introduce technical knowhow and productive capital and that would earn urgently needed foreign exchange. They cannot afford to bar mining companies from their exploited regions. Nor can they afford to impose anti-pollution requirements on these companies that are as strict and expensive as those in richer industrial countries. They should always realize that environmental protection measures are financed out of the stomachs of their own people; the multinationals cannot be made to pay for them' (Dorfman and Dorfman 1972) The so-called 'pollution haven hypothesis' reflects this type of thinking. The suggestion here is that an increasingly important factor in the decisions by multinational firms to locate production facilities in the developing economies is the absence of the strict environmental controls applied in the developed economies. In this sense the developing economies are acting as 'pollution havens', proving particularly attractive to firms in the more toxic-intensive industries which release relatively large amounts of toxic chemicals per unit output. With many variables involved in locational decisions by multinationals, testing this hypothesis by establishing the significance of the single explanatory variable (environmental standard avoidance) is clearly difficult. Some studies do, however, claim to have found evidence that the more toxic intensive industries have grown most rapidly in the developing economies.

HIV/AIDS

The low levels of education, income and healthcare services in many developing countries have contributed to the spread of HIV/AIDS, with devastating effects on the countries affected, as indicated by the example of Botswana. Botswana has almost 40% of its adult population infected by HIV/AIDS and an average life expectancy of less than 30 years for new-born children, having been as high as 75 years only a decade ago. Those who are dying early from AIDS include the breadwinners as well as the young, and the missing middle generation will not be there to look after either the young or the old in future years.

Poor governance

Developing countries feature prominently in international studies citing poor governance and widespread corruption. For example, Transparency International (TI) is a non-governmental organization founded in 1993 and based in Berlin. It has developed one of the more comprehensive databases on corruption which it defines as an abuse of public office for private gain. The 'TI Corruption Perception Index' correlates a number of surveys, polls and country studies involving the number of bribe requests which those conducting business in some 102 separate countries perceive to have been made to them. A score of 10 indicates a perception that bribe requests are never made in that country, while a score of 0 indicates a perception that bribe requests are always made. A score of 5.0 indicates a perception that there is an equal chance of a bribe being made as not being made. Of the 102 countries included in the 2009 index, 69 scored 5.0 or below; in other words, businessmen perceive that in two-thirds of these countries it is more likely than not that a bribe request will be made in any given transaction. In 2009 Finland scored 10, the UK 8.6, the US 7.8, China 3.9, India 2.7, Pakistan 2.2 and Indonesia 1.9.

Benefits of good governance

The World Bank has pointed out that good governance – including independent agencies, mechanisms for citizens to monitor public behaviour, and rules that constrain corruption – is a key ingredient for growth and prosperity. In an early study Barro (1991) had found a positive correlation between economic growth and measures of political stability for 98 countries surveyed between 1960 and 1985. More recent empirical research points in a similar direction, for example confirming that foreign direct investment (FDI) inflows are inversely related to measures of corruption, as with Lipsey (1999) observing a strong negative correlation between corruption and the locational choice of US subsidiaries across Asian countries. Similarly, Claugue et al. (1999) and Zak (2001) found that productivity and economic growth will improve when governments impartially protect and define property rights. Underpinning these findings is the perception by firms that a non-transparent business environment increases the prevalence of information asymmetries, raises the cost of securing additional information, increases transaction costs (e.g. risk premiums) and creates an uncertain business environment which deters trade and investment. For example, Wallsten (2001) found a strong inverse relationship between investment intentions and the threat of asset expropriation, as well as a propensity for firms to charge higher prices to help pay back their initial capital outlays more rapidly when they felt less secure about the intentions of host governments, the higher prices often inhibiting the penetration and growth phase of product life cycles.

International Development Targets (IDTs)

Today's political orientations towards development are firmly centred on the use of International Development Targets (IDTs). This approach is usefully illustrated by *The UN Millennium Declaration* which included a commitment to a set of *Millennium Development Goals* (MDGs) broken down into targets (see Table 29.2).

Despite growing recognition for these targets, international development targets are not new. Many previous summits have included targets. What does seem to be new, however, is the seriousness of tackling the issue of development on a broad front, bringing into play economic, social, political, environmental and technological elements in a comprehensive and integrative approach. Effectively monitoring and implementing these targets on a global scale will ultimately determine whether a more coherent approach in principle can result in more effective development in practice. Optimists should note, however, that despite the 'make poverty history' campaign for Africa, some ten years into the new millennium many of the targets in Table 29.2 are already well behind schedule if they are to be met by 2015.

Climate change and economic development

We have already reviewed (Chapter 10) the Kyoto Protocol, Copenhagen Accord and other interna-

tional mechanisms for dealing with climate change. Developing countries are especially vulnerable to climate change, with estimates suggesting that some 75–80% of the costs of climate change will be borne by LDCs. A 2 °C warming of the world climate above pre-industrial temperatures could result in a permanent reduction in GDP of 4–5% for Africa and South Asia (World Bank 2010). At the Copenhagen climate change convention in December 2009 (see Chapter 10, p. 204) it was noted that financing for LDCs was crucial, with current financing of LDCs for adaptation and mitigation policies to deal with climate change less than 5% of what is deemed necessary.

Urbanization and developing economies

'Urban areas' are usually defined in terms of concentrations of non-agricultural workers and non-agricultural production sectors. Although individual country definitions differ, most countries regard settlements involving 2,500–25,000 people as urban areas. Larger urban areas are often termed 'metropolitan areas' as they involve networks of geographically adjacent urban areas, including towns and cities (the latter defined in terms of legal status within countries rather than pure size). *Urbanization* is sometimes defined as the tendency of populations in LDCs to concentrate in urban areas during the development process which often involves industrialization.

Reasons for urbanization

Why is it that economic activity is so often concentrated in large, urban areas where land prices are often more than 50 times higher and the cost of living four or five times higher than they are in smaller urban or rural areas, less than 50 miles away? From the firm's point of view, the answer must involve a belief that the perceived benefits more than outweigh the additional costs. Many of these perceived benefits are often grouped under the heading *agglomeration economies*, which refers to the alleged synergies which benefit firms from increases in urban size.

Table 29.2 The UN Millennium Development Goals (MDGs).

Goals	Targets
Goal 1 Eradicate extreme poverty and hunger	*Target 1* Halve, between 1990 and 2015, the proportion of people whose income is less than one dollar a day
	Target 2 Halve, between 1990 and 2015, the proportion of people who suffer from hunger
Goal 2 Achieve universal primary education	*Target 3* Ensure that, by 2015, children everywhere, boys and girls alike, will be able to complete a full course of primary schooling
Goal 3 Promote gender equality and empower women	*Target 4* Eliminate gender disparity in primary and secondary education, preferably by 2005, and to all levels of education no later than 2015
Goal 4 Reduce child mortality	*Target 5* Reduce by two-thirds, between 1990 and 2015, the under-five mortality rate
Goal 5 Improve maternal health	*Target 6* Reduce by three-quarters, between 1990 and 2015, the maternal mortality ratio
Goal 6 Combat HIV/AIDS, malaria and other diseases	*Target 7* Have halted by 2015 and begun to reverse the spread of HIV/AIDS
	Target 8 Have halted by 2015 and begun to reverse the incidence of malaria and other major diseases
Goal 7 Ensure environmental sustainability	*Target 9* Integrate the principles of sustainable development into country policies and programmes and reverse the loss of environmental resources
	Target 10 Halve by 2015 the proportion of people without sustainable access to safe drinking water
	Target 11 By 2020 to have achieved a significant improvement in the lives of at least 100 million slum dwellers
Goal 8 Develop a global partnership for development	*Target 12* Develop further an open, rule-based, predictable, non-discriminatory trading and financial system (includes a commitment to good governance, development and poverty reduction – both nationally and internationally)
	Target 13 Address the special needs of the Least Developed Countries
	Target 14 Address the special needs of landlocked countries and small island developing states
	Target 15 Deal comprehensively with the debt problems of developing countries through national and international measures in order to make debt sustainable in the long term
	Target 16 In cooperation with developing countries, develop and implement strategies for decent and productive work for youth
	Target 17 In cooperation with pharmaceutical companies, provide access to affordable essential drugs in developing countries
	Target 18 In cooperation with the private sector, make available the benefits of new technologies, especially information and communications

Source: Adapted from UN sources.

- *Localization economies*. Firms benefit from locating close to other firms in the same industry since this expands the pool of specialized workers and inputs. It has been shown that in Brazil and the Republic of Korea, if a plant moves from a location shared by 1,000 workers employed by firms in the same industry to one with 10,000 such workers, output will increase by some 15% on average.

- *Urbanization economies*. Firms also benefit from locating close to firms in different industries. The presence of a common pool of labour, materials and services provides benefits for all firms, whatever their sector of economic activity. Geographical proximity to other firms can, for example, help in the more rapid diffusion of knowledge, as in the case of 'information spillovers' via firms observing what others are doing, whatever the activities involved. Evidence using patent citations shows that information flows increase with geographical proximity and deteriorate with geographical distance. 'Transaction costs' also fall when there is a higher degree of industrial concentration, e.g. the lower search costs now involved in matching workers with employment opportunities.

- *Diversification economies*. Large urban areas are less vulnerable to business cycles because of their more diversified economic base.

Impacts of urbanization

Increased urbanization is clearly associated with the transfer of workers from agricultural and rural activities to new industrial and service sector employment in towns and cities. Around 50% of the world's population currently lives in areas classified as urban, a rapid increase on the 34% recorded in 1975. By 2020 over 4 billion people (around 60% of the world's population) will live in towns and cities, with the developing countries being the major contributor to this continued growth in urbanization. The rate of urbanization has passed its peak in the middle to high income industrial countries, but is far from its peak in much of Asia and Africa. The more rapid pace and less regulated nature of the urban growth in the developing economies has created a number of environmental problems.

Urban living conditions such as crowding, sewage connections, waste collections and water access tend to be far inferior in cities with lower levels of average household incomes. The case study below pays particular attention to the issue of sanitation in the context of urbanization within developing economies.

Sanitation, health and urbanization

As the low-income developing countries industrialize over the next 25 years, progressively larger discharges of wastewater and solid wastes can be expected in total and per capita. Inadequate investments in waste collection and disposal mean that large quantities of waste enter both groundwater and surface water. Groundwater contamination is less visible but often more serious because it can take decades for polluted aquifers to cleanse themselves and because large numbers of people drink untreated groundwater.

More environmental damage occurs when people try to compensate for inadequate provision. The lack or unreliability of piped water causes households to sink their own wells, which often leads to overpumping and depletion. In cities such as Jakarta, where almost two-thirds of the population relies on groundwater, the water table has declined dramatically since the 1970s. In coastal areas this can cause saline intrusion, sometimes rendering the water permanently unfit for consumption. In, for example, Bangkok excessive pumping has also led to subsidence, cracked pavements, broken water and sewerage pipes, intrusion of seawater and flooding. Inadequate water supply also prompts people to boil water, thus using energy. The practice is especially common in Asia. In Jakarta more than $50m is spent each year by households for this purpose – an amount equal to 1% of the city's GDP. Investments in water supply can therefore reduce fuelwood consumption and air pollution.

The health benefits from better water and sanitation are substantial: diarrhoeal death rates are typically about 60% lower among children in households with adequate facilities than among those in households without such facilities. Improved environmental sanitation has economic benefits. Consider the case of sewage collection in Santiago, Chile. The principal justification for investments was the need to reduce the extraordinarily high incidence of typhoid fever in the city. A secondary motive was to maintain access to the markets of industrial countries for Chile's increasingly important exports of fruit and vegetables. To ensure the sanitary quality of these exports, it was essential to stop using raw wastewater in their production. In just the first 10 weeks of the cholera epidemic in Peru in the early 1990s, losses from reduced agricultural exports and tourism were estimated at $1 billion – more than three times the amount that the country had invested in water supply and sanitation services during the 1980s.

Despite such problems there are a number of factors which make urbanization so attractive to firms in both developing and developed economies.

Aid, trade and development

Here we briefly examine the role of both aid and trade in development.

Foreign aid and development

In theory, foreign aid should raise both consumption and investment in a developing country, since in the absence of foreign aid an LDC will produce less of both consumption and investment goods given its limited resources. However, if the economy has a very high preference for consumption, then most of the foreign aid might be used for consumption purposes with little addition to its future productive capacity. To counter this, the aid programmes often seek to designate aid for particular purposes; for example, food aid is intended to increase consumption rather than investment, but project aid is usually intended to raise investment rather than consumption.

In the traditional economic models, an increase in access to savings from abroad should raise the growth rate of the borrowing country by increasing its rate of investment. If we aggregate aid from abroad with access to the savings from foreign capital markets, this gives us the variable 'financial resources' (FR). For some LDCs such as Bangladesh and Nepal in Asia and Mali and Senegal in Africa, foreign aid is a significant proportion of the GDP of these economies and hence the impact of additional aid on FR should help increase their growth rates. However, a rise in the flow of FR may raise consumption at the expense of savings/investment so that the overall growth rate suffers. Further, a rise in domestic

consumption due to a rise in FR may increase imports and add to the balance of payment problems of many LDCs. They may then have to deflate aggregate demand to reduce imports, adversely affecting economic growth. In addition, many governments of LDCs have used FR for increasing public expenditure on prestige projects which are relatively unproductive.

On the other hand, foreign aid has the potential to increase domestic economic growth rates by supplementing domestic savings to further increase investment and to allow imports of capital items previously restricted by scarce foreign exchange reserves. In this view, foreign aid could have a positive and significant influence on growth rates for LDCs.

This is not to deny that a corrupt government in a developing country seeking to maximize its own 'utility function' may use aid money to expand non-productive expenditures, e.g. on military capability, corrupt bureaucracy and very inefficient investments. In such cases, the impact of aid on economic growth will indeed tend adversely to affect growth. For aid to be effective may then depend on carefully choosing the countries to support through aid and targeting specific projects to support within those countries. For instance it has been widely acknowledged that, despite the absence of a positive aid–growth correlation in India, aid inflows in the agricultural sector significantly helped to usher in the 'Green Revolution' in the late 1960s and early 1970s, thereby helping to overcome India's acute problems of food insecurity and famines. Such aid was generally well targeted, as in its allocation to specific areas in north-west India where irrigation facilities were available to reap the benefits of new seeds–fertilizer techniques. The inflow of foreign aid to such specific rural areas has helped India to import considerable amounts of new seeds and chemical fertilizers from abroad and to substantially increase the yields of major food crops.

The impact of foreign aid on the economic growth rates of LDCs is clearly likely to vary across different countries. More specially, such impacts will depend on a number of factors:

- the effective targeting of aid by both donor and recipient;
- the effective use of aid by the recipient;
- the current level of economic development and rate of output growth;
- the rates of return on investment in both organized and unorganized financial markets;

- the public infrastructure and the availability of physical human capital; and

- the level and types of economic regulation.

Without a careful analysis of such a complex set of dynamic socioeconomic factors, it is difficult to draw a definite conclusion about the real impact of foreign aid on LDCs.

Trade and development

In recent years the focus has moved to a broader recognition of the key role of trade to economic development. The World Bank (Dollar and Kraay 2000) has argued that increased openness to trade raises average incomes and the incomes of the poor, i.e. that there is no relationship between increased openness to trade and rising inequality, if anything quite the opposite. Sebastian Edwards of the University of California also concludes in a study of 93 countries that there is a close link between openness to trade and rates of productivity growth (Edwards 2000). It has been estimated (World Bank 2004b) that removing trade protection and related distortions in developed countries could provide gains to developing countries of $85bn by 2015.

Some of the ways in which protectionism still pervades much of the trade between developed and developing countries have been considered in Chapter 28. What is clear is that the developing countries have been badly damaged by export subsidies on agricultural and other products by the EU, US and other advanced industrialized countries.

Here we review some of the issues at the heart of the recent Doha round of trade negotiations, between developed and developing nations which failed to reach agreement in July 2006.

Collapse of Doha in 2006

The issue of farm subsidies has been identified by most analysts as the key reason for the breakdown in the global trade talks in Doha in July 2006. Whilst the US had been willing to remove explicit *export subsidies* on farm products, it had insisted on retaining support for domestic farm production, including *domestic subsidies*. Critics of the US argue that these domestic subsidies have exactly the same effect as export subsidies, namely encouraging excessive domestic production of farm products, at artificially

low prices which can then be 'dumped' on export markets.

The World Trade Organization (WTO) classifies farm subsidies into three 'boxes'.

1 *Green box subsidies*. These are defined as not distorting trade and can be unlimited under current WTO rules, e.g. payments to farmers to protect the environment.

2 *Blue box subsidies*. These are defined as only 'mildly distorting' and are not affected by current WTO rules: e.g. payments related to fixed output or to the size of the farms aimed at limiting output beyond agreed target levels.

3 *Amber box subsidies*. These are defined as 'significantly distorting' and the current WTO rules place a ceiling on such subsidies: e.g. payments based on current output or prices.

A fourth category of farm subsidy is also permitted for countries whose total farm subsidy payments for a specific product or group of products is less than 5% of the total value of output. These *de minimis subsidies* can be either 'product specific' (PS) or 'non-product specific' (NPS).

At Doha the US had proposed cutting its 'amber box' subsidies by 60% of the 2006 value, capping its 'blue box' subsidies at the 2006 value, and halving the 2006 value of the 'de minimis' subsidies. However, it had also proposed removing the current ceiling on its 'counter cyclical payments' (CCP), by shifting these from the current amber box to the blue box. The CCP allows US farmers to be compensated for low prices, and such compensation would now be unlimited. The EU and others strongly criticized this aspect of the US proposals, with the EU claiming that it encourages farmers to ignore market forces and keep producing. The EU estimated that the net effect of the US proposals would have been to increase total US farm subsidies by a further 10% on current levels, rather than reducing them. Four US commodities – rice, corn, wheat and cotton – have received around three-quarters of US farm aid over the past decade, products vital to many developing countries (e.g. India, China, Brazil) which, with the EU, were equally critical of the US position.

However, the US and many developing nations were also critical of the EU position. The EU had agreed to eliminate its export subsidies by 2013 and to more than halve the existing tariffs on agricultural imports into the EU. However, these offers were criticized as insufficient by the G20 group of middle-income countries as well as the US.

There are concerns that the failure of these global trade talks will herald an era of increased protectionism and the growth of bilateral agreements between individual nations on trade issues, rather than the multilateral approach of the WTO whereby a trade concession offered to one country is available to all countries ('most favoured nation' clause).

Debt and development

An important economic issue in recent times has been the analysis of the impact of external debt on the economies of the LDCs. The main focus of attention has been the cost of servicing foreign debt and the potential benefits from default. It has been argued that if the cost of debt service is higher than the cost of default, then debt repayment by an LDC is not 'incentive-compatible'. However, a *highly indebted developing country* (LDCs with the highest ratio of debt to GDP) may still have an incentive to repay because of the fear of losing access to the international capital market.

Reasons for LDC borrowing

The practice of borrowing from foreign countries as a method of promoting economic growth is not new. Historically, most of today's developed countries, including the US, depended significantly on the imports of foreign capital for achieving a high standard of living. Besides the lessons of history, there are a number of sound reasons to explain the borrowing of LDCs from abroad.

- Most LDCs have low per capita income and savings. The required rate of economic growth to attain a better standard of living may need a higher level of investment (I) than can be financed by domestic savings (S). Thus, LDCs may wish to borrow foreign capital to eliminate the 'savings gap', i.e. $I - S > 0$.
- Most LDCs suffer from serious shortages in their foreign exchange earnings as their imports (M) are generally much greater than their exports (X). Such an imbalance, i.e. $M - X > 0$, is defined as a 'trade gap' which could be a serious constraint on achieving a higher rate of economic growth and per capita income. Many LDCs depend substantially on the import of capital and intermediate inputs to increase their production. Sometimes food imports may also play a crucial role in averting the threat of hunger and famine. Imports of foreign technology and skills may help ease the trade gap and accelerate economic growth.

Many LDCs suffer from capital scarcity relative to labour supply which, according to orthodox theory, means that they should enjoy higher returns at the margin on capital flows from the developed countries. In capital-abundant countries, the marginal efficiency of capital (MEC) tends to be lower than in the LDCs. It follows that, as long as capital is fully mobile across nations, capital should flow, on efficiency grounds, from the rich to the poor countries to equalize the global MEC. Of course, such capital movements depend on the funds being invested in sectors where the rate of return is higher than the interest rate charged on the use of foreign capital.

Resolving the debt problem

It has become increasingly clear that past debts are unsustainable for many developing countries. The ratio of total debt to GDP is well over 50% for many developing countries and nearly 100% for the 15 most heavily indebted countries, mainly located in Africa and South America. As a result, payment of interest on such debts is often three or four times the annual export earnings of such countries, making it impossible for such countries to invest in the improvements in education, health and infrastructure so important for development. Many attempts have been made over the years to resolve this debt problem, often involving global institutions such as the World Bank and IMF (see below).

The Jubilee 2000 Campaign mobilized world opinion and led to an easing of the debt burden for many countries. Most recently, the meeting of the eight most advanced industrialized economies (G8) at Gleneagles in Scotland in July 2005 announced a package of measures whereby 18 of the world's poorest countries will have their debts to the World Bank and IMF wiped out as part of a £30bn package. A further nine countries qualified for similar debt relief by 2007, rising to 37 countries shortly thereafter. Unlike previous deals, the debts of the initial eight countries would be eliminated immediately, and with them the heavy burden of interest payments in servicing the debt.

Role of the IMF and World Bank

As has been mentioned, both institutions have provided support for LDCs in various ways, but only under specified conditions.

IMF 'stabilization programmes'

IMF stabilization programmes seek to address adverse balance of payments situations whilst retaining price stability and encouraging the resumption of economic growth. As Evers and Nixxon (1997) have indicated, the main components of typical IMF stabilization policies include some or all of the following:

- *fiscal contraction* – a reduction in the public sector deficit through cuts in public expenditure and/or rises in taxation;
- *monetary contraction* – restrictions on credit to the public sector and increases in interest rates;
- *devaluation of the exchange rate* (this is often a precondition for the serious negotiation of a stabilization programme, rather than part of the programme as such);
- *liberalization of the economy* via reduction or elimination of controls, and privatization of public sector assets;
- *incomes policy* – wage restraint and removal of subsidies and reduction of transfer payments.

Various studies of the impact of IMF stabilization policies from Latin America and elsewhere have suggested that stabilization causes a fall in labour's share in the distribution of income. A wage freeze has often been involved, reducing the real value of all incomes from labour, especially those employed in the public sector where a wage freeze can be applied most effectively. Stabilization was often found to be associated with declines in public sector employment. Cuts in public expenditure have been an important part of many stabilization programmes, such as health and education, with disproportionate effects on the poor

and particularly women. Stabilization has had differing effects on the urban and the rural poor, with the urban poor being hardest hit.

Criticisms of IMF action

Criticisms of the IMF's activities can be grouped as follows:

- *That IMF programmes are inappropriate.* The criticism here is that the IMF's approach to policy has been preoccupied with the control of demand, and too little concerned with other weaknesses stemming from the productive system of LDCs, e.g. balance of payments problems. By deflating demand the IMF has imposed large adjustment costs on borrowing countries through losses of output and employment, further impoverishing the poor and even destabilizing incumbent governments.
- *That IMF programmes are inflexible.* The criticism here is that the IMF has imposed its solutions on LDCs rather than negotiated a more flexible package. This has arguably infringed the sovereignty of states and alienated governments from the measures they are supposed to implement.
- *That IMF support has been too small, expensive and short term.* The programmes have been criticized for having been too small in magnitude and too short term in duration for economies whose underlying problems are rooted in structural weaknesses and who often face secular declines in their terms of trade (fall in export prices relative to import prices).
- *That the IMF is dominated by a few major industrial countries.* The criticism here is that the industrial countries have sometimes used their control of the IMF to promote their own interests, as for example in using the IMF to shift a disproportionate amount of the debt burden onto the debtor countries rather than forcing lenders (e.g. banks) to accept some of the debt burden. It has been alleged that successive American governments have used their influence to favour (or oppose) friendly (or hostile) LDCs.

World Bank 'Structural Adjustment Lending' (SAL)

Since 1980 the World Bank has been involved in various types of Structural Adjustment Lending (SAL) which accounts for over 20% of World Bank lending.

These SAL programmes are non-project related; rather they involve lending to support specific programmes of policy which may involve elements of institutional change. These SAL programmes are generally directed towards improving the 'supply side' of the borrowing countries, intending to initiate and fund change which will ultimately raise productive efficiency in various sectors of the economies.

Figure 29.6 provides a rather stereotyped but useful overview of the IMF 'stabilization programmes' and the World Bank 'structural adjustment lending' programmes. It compares the stabilization policies of the IMF (downward and leftward shift in AD) with the structural adjustment policies of the World Bank (downward and rightward shift in AS).

Most of the policies involved in the IMF stabilization programmes have been of a deflationary nature, as can be illustrated using Fig. 29.6. This results in the downward movement, to the left, of the aggregate demand curve (AD) from AD_1 to AD_2, thus reducing the price level (from P_1 to P_2) but also reducing output (from Q_1 to Q_2). The debtor country may be made more competitive in its exports and import-substitute sectors, benefiting its balance of payments and reducing its debt, but at the cost of lost output and employment.

As was noted earlier, most of the World Bank SAL programmes have sought to improve the supply side of the economy. This results in the downward, to the right, movement of the aggregate supply curve (AS) from AS_1 to AS_2 in Fig. 29.6, thus reducing the price

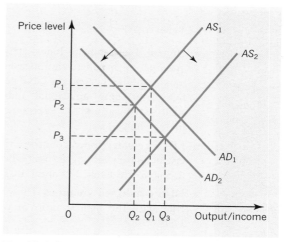

Fig. 29.6 Stabilization versus structural adjustment.

level (from P_2 to P_1 with AD_2) and increasing output (from Q_2 to Q_3). Clearly the 'medicine' via structural adjustment is rather more palatable in that output and employment rise, but only after possibly difficult changes to labour and capital market practices and institutions to improve supply-side conditions. (Note that for diagrammatic purposes we have assumed that the structural adjustment programme of the World Bank occurs at the same time as the IMF stabilization programme. Of course, they may occur independently.)

Key points

- There are different ways of classifying countries, including those regarded as the less developed countries (LDCs).

- The conventional measure of real GNP per head has a number of weaknesses as a measure of the standard of living.

- New measures have been devised which also bring quality of life indicators into the equation, an important example being the Human Development Index (HDI) of the UN.

- The LDCs have a number of features which create additional problems for policies aimed at increasing growth.

- In recent times the focus has shifted away from aid and towards trade as a mechanism for supporting economic development.

- The world debt problem bears down heavily on the LDCs and various initiatives involving the IMF and World Bank have sought to resolve some of these problems.

- There has been considerable criticism of the nature of the support mechanisms provided to LDCs, especially those from the IMF.

Key terms

- **Human Development Index (HDI)** An attempt to broaden the measures of 'quality of life' beyond the GNP per head figure, bringing additional indicators such as education, life expectancy and literacy into focus.

- **LDCs** Less developed countries, the precise definition varying across bodies such as the World Bank, UN and OECD.

- **Highly indebted countries** Those countries with the highest ratio of debt to GDP.

- **Millennium Development Goals (MDGs)** Specific targets set by the UN in 2000 for developing economies, to be achieved by 2015.

- **Urbanization** The tendency of populations in LDCs to concentrate in urban areas during the development process which often involves industrialization.

- **Offshoring** The movement of jobs from developed to developing countries, usually on the basis of lower labour costs.

- **Agglomeration economies** Benefits to firms from the growth in size of urban areas.

Now try the self-check questions for this chapter on the Companion Website. You will also find useful links to relevant websites.

References and further reading

Aghion, P. and Howitt, P. (2009). *The Economics of Growth*, Cambridge MA, MIT Press.

Barro, R. (1991) Economic growth in a cross-section of countries, *Quarterly Journal of Economics*, **106**(20), 407–43.

Bartelsman, E., Haltimanger, J. and Scarpetta, S. (2004) *Microeconomic Evidence of Creative Destruction in Industrial and Developing Countries*, Policy Research Working Paper No. 3436, Washington DC, World Bank.

Bénassy-Quéré, A. and Coeuré, B. (2010) *Economic Policy*, New York, Oxford University Press.

Bosworth, B. and Collins, S. (2003) *The Empirics of Growth: An Update*, Washington DC, The Brookings Institution.

Boughton, J. and Lombardi, D. (2009) *Finance, Development and the IMF*, Oxford, Oxford University Press.

Claugue, C., Keefer, P., Knack, S. and Olson, M. (1999) Contract-intensive money: contract enforcement, property rights and economic performance, *Journal of Economic Growth*, 4, 185–211.

Denison, E. F. (1967) *Why Growth Rates Differ*, Washington DC, Brookings Institution.

Dollar, D. and Kraay, A. (2000) *Growth is Good for the Poor*, Washington DC, World Bank.

Dorfman, R. and Dorfman, N. (1972) *Economics of the Environment*, New York, Norton.

Durlauf, S. and Blume, L. (2010) *Economic Growth*. Basingstoke, Palgrave Macmillan.

Edwards, S. (2000) *Trade Development and Poverty Reduction*, Washington DC, World Bank.

Evers, B. and Nixxon, R. (1997) International institutions and global poverty, *Developments in Economics*, Vol. 13, Ormskirk, Causeway Press.

Kraay, A. (2003) *What Can Cross-country Regressions Tell Us About the Determinants of Poor Growth?* Washington DC, World Bank.

Krugman, P. and Obstfeld, M. (2010) *International Economics: Theory and Policy*, Harlow, Financial Times/Prentice Hall.

Lipsey, R. E. (1999) *The Location and Characteristics of US Affiliates in Asia*, NBER Working Paper 6876, Cambridge MA, National Bureau of Economic Research.

Meadows, D. H., Meadows, D. L., Randers, J. and Behrens, W. W. (1972) *The Limits to Growth*, Washington DC, Potomac Associates.

Parente, S. and Prescott, E. (2000) *Barriers to Riches*, Cambridge MA, MIT Press.

Pearce, D. W. (1998) *Economics and Environment*, Cheltenham, Edward Elgar.

Setterfield, M. (2010) *Handbook of Alternative Theories of Economic Growth*, Cheltenham, Edward Elgar.

Solow, R. M. (1957) Technical change and the aggregate production function, *Review of Economics and Statistics*, 39, 312–20.

Todaro, M. and Smith, S. (2009) *Economic Development* (10th edn), Harlow, Financial Times/Prentice Hall.

UNCTAD (2009) *The Least Developed Countries Report 2009: The State and Development Governance*, New York and Geneva, United Nations Conference on Trade and Development.

UNCTAD (2010a) *Trade and Development Report 2010: Employment, Globalization and Development*, New York and Geneva, United Nations Conference on Trade and Development.

UNCTAD (2010b) *World Investment Report 2010: Investing in a Low Carbon Economy*, New York and Geneva, United Nations Conference on Trade and Development.

UNDP (2001) *Human Development Report 2001: Making New Technologies Work for Human Development*, New York, United National Development Programme.

UNDP (2004) *Human Development Report 2004: Cultural Liberty in Today's Diverse World*, New York, United National Development Programme.

UNDP (2010) *Human Development Report 2010: The Real Wealth of Nations: Pathways to Human Development*, New York, United Nations Development Programme.

UNEP (1992) *Rio Declaration on Environment and Development*, Nairobi, United Nations Environment Programme.

Wallsten, S. (2001) *Ringing in the 20th century*, Policy Research Working Paper No. 2690, Washington DC, World Bank.

World Commission on Environment and Development (WCED) (1987) *Our Common Future*, New York, Oxford University Press.

Weil, D. (2009) *Economic Growth* (2nd edn), Harlow, Pearson Education.

World Bank (2002) *World Development Report 2002: Building Institutions for Markets*, Washington DC.

World Bank (2004a) *Global Economic Prospects 2004: Realising the Development Promise of the Doha Agenda*, Washington DC.

World Bank (2004b) *World Development Indicators*, Washington DC.

World Bank (2005) *World Development Report 2005: A Better Investment Climate for Everyone*, Washington DC.

World Bank (2010) *World Development Report 2010: Development and Climate Change*, Washington DC.

Zak, P. (2001) Institutions, property rights and growth, *Gruter Institute Working Papers*, **2**(1), Article 2.

CHAPTER 30

Managing the global economy: post 'credit crunch'

In this chapter the objectives of macroeconomic policy are discussed, along with the instruments for achieving them! Adjusting the instruments of policy to 'best' meet a set of target values for various objectives seems to fit the actual conduct of policy in various countries, including the UK, at various periods of time. Whilst, on occasions, the UK is used by way of illustration, the principles of macroeconomic management are generally applicable. The emphasis has, however, subsequently tended to shift away from such 'fine-tuning' and towards the adoption of medium- and long-term rules. Various approaches to managing the economy are reviewed, including the Cambridge Economic Policy Group (CEPG), the Keynesian and the monetarist/supply-side approaches. The problems in the global economy associated with the collapse of the sub-prime market and the subsequent 'credit crunch' are reviewed, together with some of the techniques proposed for resolving these problems and for managing the global economy in a more sustainable way.

The chapter builds on the earlier chapters involving both fiscal policy (Chapters 18 and 19) and monetary policy (Chapters 20 and 21).

The objectives of policy

The desire of most individuals is to live and work within an economic framework which gives them the prospect of steady employment, relatively stable prices and a rising standard of living. It is usually recognized that to achieve such a situation the economy must trade and 'pay its way' with other economies. Politicians realize that to attract votes and gain political power they must promise that these aspirations will be met, if only in the long run. Economic objectives at the macroeconomic level are therefore set in terms of full employment, price stability and rapid economic growth, together with long-term equilibrium in the balance of payments. All these objectives have attracted attention in the post-war period. Since they are unlikely to be achieved in their totality, they have usually been expressed in terms of target values. Whilst these target values have not always been explicitly stated, they seem to be influenced by achieved values within the recent past.

Full employment

For instance, it is recognized that full employment can never mean zero registered unemployment if only because of dynamic change within society. Following the Beveridge Report of 1944, a 3% rate of unemployment (about half a million) was used in the 1950s and 1960s in the UK as the 'acceptable' upper limit. In more recent times, UK governments have been reluctant to commit themselves to any specific unemployment target.

Stable prices

Stable prices have always been regarded as unrealistic, but the attainment of an annual inflation rate of around 2.5% seems to have been the approximate target for the UK government in the first two post-war decades. More recently, the reduction of the annual inflation rate to below 4%, or to a rate equivalent to that of our industrial rivals, would appear to have been the target set during much of the 1980s and 1990s. With the advent of the new Labour government in 1997 and the establishment of an independent Monetary Policy Committee (MPC), a specific target of 2.5% for annual inflation was given to the MPC between 1997 and 2003 to guide it in setting interest rate policy. This target was decreased to 2% in December 2003 and remains in place in 2011.

Economic growth

Economic growth (see also Chapter 29) has received relatively little specific emphasis in the UK, although most governments have expressed some enthusiasm for it! We have, generally speaking, enjoyed rising living standards and have compared ourselves (favourably) with our parents and grandparents rather than with our contemporaries in Europe, the US or Japan. A well-known statement concerning economic growth as an objective was made by the late R. A. Butler in 1954, when he suggested a doubling of living standards every 25 years as an explicit target. This was greeted as being over-ambitious, yet it entailed an annual growth rate of GDP of less than 3%. The Economic Plan of 1965 sought a UK growth rate of 3.8% per annum, but this was quickly seen to be unattainable and this attempt at long-term planning was soon abandoned. Between 1997 and 2003 there was a criticism that the Monetary Policy Committee had not been given a growth target to set alongside the 2.5% inflation target when deciding the level of interest rates.

The balance of payments

The balance of payments is often described as an objective of economic policy, the target being either equilibrium or a surplus over a period of time in order that accumulated international debts might be repaid. This can hardly be related to the aspirations of individuals and is thought by many to be more properly described as a constraint upon the achievement of other objectives. Nevertheless, target figures have been set in the past, e.g. the 1953 Economic Survey in the UK called for a surplus of £450m per annum as the target surplus on current account in the 1950s to finance the long-term capital outflow. It was not achieved, and since then the use of target figures has become less important. However, a relatively 'healthy' external account is still an important consideration of policy.

This list of objectives could be extended to include others, such as the redistribution of income and wealth, but target values for employment, inflation and underlying economic growth have received most attention.

The instruments of policy

Governments would have no macroeconomic problems if market forces in the economy automatically led to 'full employment' equilibrium, with stable prices and a rapid economic growth. The bulk of the evidence seems to indicate that market forces alone have failed to achieve these objectives, either in full or even at 'satisfactory' values. Such 'market failure' essentially constitutes the case for intervention by governments. If governments *are* to intervene in the economy, there still remains the problem of selecting the appropriate instruments for achieving the targets they set themselves.

In general terms the policy instruments available to the UK government are fiscal policy, monetary policy, prices and incomes policy and policy instruments aimed at the balance of payments, such as the exchange rate or import controls. These policy instruments are sometimes called 'instrumental variables', i.e. variables over which the government has some control, and the values of which affect the behaviour of the economy itself in some reasonably systematic way.

Fiscal policy

Fiscal policy involves using both government spending and taxation to influence the composition and level of aggregate demand in the economy. Elementary circular flow analysis suggests that by raising the level of government expenditure and/or by reducing taxation, the level of aggregate demand can be raised (by a multiplied amount) with favourable consequences for economic activity and employment. Such an expansionary course of action might result in a larger budget deficit, or a reduced budget surplus, in this way affecting the Public Sector Borrowing Requirement (PSBR), now known as the Public Sector Net Cash Requirement (PSNCR). This somewhat simplistic approach is the basis for fiscal interven-

tionism as advocated by 'Keynesians', and carried out with some success in the UK for over 25 years after the Second World War. The Budget was viewed not as an accounting procedure, with expenditure and revenue to be balanced as a matter of good housekeeping, but as an instrument of policy to be manipulated as a means to an end. Deficits were financed by borrowing, short or long term, from home and abroad, with the increased National Debt seen as a means of spreading the costs of current policy over future generations.

Practical problems abound. Although tax rates can be set, the revenues they will yield are difficult to predict as income levels can vary. Also government expenditure and tax receipts are subject to time-lags, which can have destabilizing effects. For instance, the government may aim to raise spending to stimulate the economy during recession, but the effects may not be felt for several time periods, when the economy may be in a different situation. In other words, fiscal policy may move the economy away from desired values rather than towards them. There is even a problem in identifying the government's fiscal stance. A contractionary fiscal policy will, if successful, reduce incomes and tax yield, and might also have the effect of raising some government expenditures such as unemployment benefit. If we look, therefore, at the Budget *out-turn* for evidence of the government's fiscal stance, we may come to the wrong conclusion – the reduced tax yield and increased government expenditure may be the result of a contractionary fiscal policy, not evidence of an expansionary one! Problems such as these account in part for the relegation of fiscal policy in favour of monetary policy by Conservative governments during the 1980s. Even after the post-1997 Labour government brought some measure of stability into fiscal affairs by introducing its 'fiscal rules' (see Chapter 18), problems still arose in identifying accurate trends for government expenditure and revenue which has remained the case for the Coalition government in the UK which came into power in 2010 and moved away from such fiscal rules.

Monetary policy

Monetary policy aims to influence monetary variables such as the rate of interest and the money supply, in order to achieve the targets set for the four major objectives. Although the rate of interest and the money supply are interrelated (see Chapter 20), for convenience we examine these separately.

The rate of interest – in practice there are many – is thought to be important because it is a cost of borrowing, influencing not only long-term investment decisions by firms but also their short-term borrowing to overcome cash-flow problems. Interest rates may influence consumer spending on durable goods by affecting the cost of hire-purchase finance. Interest rates also influence household decisions as to the composition of the assets they hold. For example, low interest rates offer little reward for those acquiring financial assets, thus encouraging consumer expenditure on goods and services. The balance of payments is also affected by interest rate policy, as capital inflow and outflow depend on UK interest rates relative to those in other countries.

The money supply, as we saw in Chapter 20, 'matters' to both monetarists and Keynesians. To monetarists, money supply mainly affects prices, at least in the long run, whereas to Keynesians, the major impact is on output and employment. The measurement and control of money supply have therefore been widely regarded as an important policy instrument, and we return to this below.

Prices and incomes policy

Prices and incomes policy is used in an attempt to control inflation by directly influencing the rate at which prices, wages and salaries rise. Depending on political and economic belief, such a policy can be viewed as an irrelevance by the monetarists, or as a necessary means of influencing the institutional determinants of inflation by the Keynesians, particularly when expansionary fiscal measures are being used to overcome unemployment.

Since 1960 there have been few occasions on which this instrument of policy was not in use in the UK, either on a voluntary basis or in the form of statutory control. Prices have been directly controlled as well as wages, and wages themselves have been subject to various forms of restraint, such as 'freezes', or 'norms' for wage increases. The impact of the policy has, predictably, fallen most heavily on the public sector. Although during the operation of incomes policy the rate of wage inflation has usually been reduced below the previously prevailing figure, it has often been higher than the 'norm' set, and has always been followed, when controls have been relaxed, by a rapid and sharp increase in the rate of wage inflation. It is difficult to test the overall effects of the use of this instrument of policy, but it is generally regarded as having been less useful in the long term. Prices and incomes policy was last used formally in 1979, but an incomes policy has been used informally since then, with the introduction of cash limits for the public sector acting as a constraint on wage increases. For example, public sector pay has been frozen over the period 2009–11.

The exchange rate

The exchange rate is one of the instruments which can be used to influence the balance of payments. With the exception of the devaluations of 1949 (30%), and 1967 (14%), the sterling exchange rate was essentially fixed under the International Monetary Fund (IMF) system. In 1971 the convertibility of the dollar into gold at a fixed price was abandoned and the IMF fixed exchange rate system broke down. Since mid-1972 the UK exchange rate has fluctuated, in theory according to market forces (a 'clean' float), but in practice often 'managed' by the authorities (a 'dirty' float). Although the pound fell to record low levels against the dollar in early 1983, it would have fallen even lower had the Bank of England not intervened on the foreign exchange market to buy the pound with its foreign currency reserves.

A change in the exchange rate will affect the relative prices of domestic- and foreign-produced goods and services. For example, a lower exchange rate makes UK goods cheaper in the foreign markets, and foreign goods more expensive in the UK market (see Chapter 25). Given appropriate elasticities for exports and imports,[1] a lower exchange rate will improve the balance of payments.

One major difficulty in a lower exchange rate policy is that this will have an adverse effect on domestic costs, both directly and indirectly. The rise in price of imported foodstuffs and finished manufactures will have an immediate and direct effect on the price level, because these items are included in the Retail Price Index (RPI). The rise in price of imported raw materials and semi-finished manufactures will also have an indirect effect on the price level, by raising domestic costs of production. Higher prices could also stimulate higher wage demands to protect real incomes, further fuelling inflation. In these ways, the competitive advantage of devaluation may well be eroded, and the objective of price stability (or reduced inflation) adversely affected. Between 1987 and 1992, the government sought to target the exchange rate at particular levels against various currencies. This was in order to prevent sterling depreciating too rapidly, thereby endangering the control of inflation. The entry of sterling into the Exchange Rate Mechanism (ERM) at a relatively high rate of 2.95 Deutsche marks (DM) to the pound in October 1990 was also to help contain inflationary pressure in the UK. One of the concerns facing the government when the UK left the ERM in September 1992 was the fear that the 14% fall in sterling's value against the DM (and 20% against the US dollar) by late 1992 would rekindle inflationary pressures. As it turned out, such fears proved largely unfounded. Since 1992 there has been no explicit targeting of the exchange rate, despite frequent complaints by UK manufacturers and industrialists of a 'high pound'.

Import controls

Import controls are another policy instrument for affecting the balance of payments, but have been little used in the UK since the Second World War, other than to reduce import tariffs in line with other members of the General Agreement on Tariffs and Trade (GATT). Two examples may serve to illustrate their use. Between 1964 and 1966 there was an import surcharge scheme whereby most imported manufactured goods carried a levy of 15% in an attempt to reduce imports by over £550m per annum. It was a partial success, reducing them by perhaps half the intended sum. In 1968–70 there was an import deposit scheme whereby half the value of imported manufactured goods had to be deposited with the government for six months, with no interest paid. Little effect upon the balance of payments was discerned.

Renewed interest in import tariffs emerged in the early 1980s, stimulated by the Cambridge Economic Policy Group (CEPG) who, initially at least, saw a direct and close relationship between the size of the Budget deficit and the size of the balance of payments deficit. If expansionary domestic fiscal policy is to overcome unemployment and stimulate investment, they advocate imposing tariffs to prevent the extra

domestic spending from being satisfied by overseas suppliers. Their aim was not to reduce imports below the initial pre-expansion figure, but to prevent them from rising above that level.

 ## Problems in managing the economy

Before we consider the theory of economic policy, some general points can be made concerning the objectives of policy and the instruments available to the government.

Trade-off between objectives

The most obvious difficulty is that the objectives 'trade off' against each other. For example, policy instruments that governments use to achieve the objective of lower inflation often impose a cost of higher unemployment. Curbing the money supply may reduce the value of spending,[2] and raise interest rates, resulting in the closure of many firms, with the loss of jobs. Curbing government spending as part of monetary policy can also reduce employment in the public sector. A higher exchange rate during 1981/82, from 1985 to 1988 and again from 1996 to 2002 made UK exports expensive, and imports cheaper, reducing domestic output and employment, especially in the more tradeable manufacturing sector. Lower inflation can therefore be achieved, but at the cost of higher unemployment. High interest rates and low economic activity can also discourage investment, adversely affecting another important policy objective, that of economic growth. This raises the question of 'weighting' the objectives against each other, e.g. how much extra unemployment and lower growth will be tolerated in order to reduce the inflation rate by a further x percentage points?

Interdependence of instruments

Policy instruments are not independent of each other. For example, fiscal policy has implications for the money supply and for the rate of interest. In turn, the domestic rate of interest will, by its effect upon short-term capital flows, influence the sterling exchange rate, and will also affect the money supply.

Instruments as objectives

It has to be recognized that policy instruments sometimes become objectives in their own right. This was the case with the exchange rate instrument which was used only twice in the post-war period up to the early 1970s. This was because preserving the value of the pound had itself become an objective of policy, so that it could no longer be used as a flexible instrument of policy. Again in February 1987 the UK agreed to the Louvre Accord in Paris which stated that a period of exchange rate stability was desirable. This made it more difficult to use the exchange rate as a policy *instrument* and in some respects it then becomes an *objective* of policy instead! This became even more obvious between 1990 and 1992 when maintaining sterling's parity in the ERM was seen as a major objective of policy.

Political constraints

The set of policy objectives chosen, and the instruments used, may be constrained by the fact that it is politicians who are the ultimate decision-takers. Each course of action must therefore be evaluated in its political context. The use of some policy instruments may then be inhibited, as with the Conservative government's reluctance formally to use a prices and incomes policy given its views on the efficacy of a free market system. Similarly, the decision of the government to enter the ERM in October 1990 severely limited its ability to use the exchange rate as an instrument of policy, although its subsequent withdrawal in September 1992 eased this limitation. In 1997 the decision to establish an independent body, the MPC, to set interest rates effectively removed this policy instrument from government control.

The theory of economic policy

Here we look at the basic theory of economic policy, first reviewing the 'fixed targets', the 'variable targets'

and the 'satisficing' approaches to policy formation before briefly considering a number of other approaches.

The fixed targets approach

Perhaps the best-known approach is that of Tinbergen (1952), the so-called fixed targets approach, which establishes the condition for the simultaneous achievement of fixed target values for a number of objectives. *Tinbergen's rule* states that if these target values are to be achieved simultaneously, then there must be at least the same number of instruments as there are objectives. The values of these instruments are determined by the desired-target values of the objectives, and they can then be assessed to see whether they are both feasible and acceptable to the decision-makers.

This rule can be illustrated in Fig. 30.1 where, for simplicity, the two-instrument/two-objective case is illustrated. Instruments I_1 (monetary policy) and I_2 (fiscal policy) are plotted on the axes of the graph. Movements along each axis and away from the origin will be used to indicate 'expansionary' policy. On the horizontal axis, for example, close to the origin we have 'tight' fiscal policy, with high taxation and low government expenditure. Movement along the

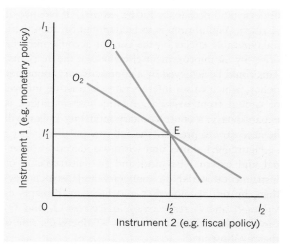

Fig. 30.1 Two-instrument/two-objective case.
Notes:
O_1 = Objective 1 (internal balance) at a particular target value.
O_2 = Objective 2 (external balance) at a particular target value.
I_1 = Instrumental variable 1, e.g. monetary policy.
I_2 = Instrumental variable 2, e.g. fiscal policy.

horizontal axis and away from the origin indicates that fiscal policy becomes 'easier', with taxation falling and government expenditure rising. The Budget moves from surplus into deficit, with the deficit becoming greater as the movement to the right continues. On the vertical axis, points close to the origin indicate restrictive monetary policy, with high interest rates and static, or slowly growing, money supply. Movement along the vertical axis and away from the origin indicates an expansionary monetary policy, the money supply rising rapidly and interest rates falling.

The line O_1 shows the combinations of monetary and fiscal policy required to achieve the objective of *internal balance*, i.e. full employment (or something very close to it) with price stability (or a low and acceptable rate of inflation). O_1 will be negatively sloped, on the assumption that expansionary fiscal policy must be accompanied by contractionary monetary policy, if full employment is to be achieved without price inflation. If contractionary monetary policy did not accompany the expansionary fiscal policy then too high a level of aggregate demand would be generated, and with it price inflation.[3]

The line O_2 shows the combinations of monetary and fiscal policy required to achieve *external balance*, i.e. balance of payments equilibrium. It, too, is negatively sloped, reflecting the fact that expansionary fiscal policy raises domestic incomes, so increasing imports (and perhaps reducing exports). If balance of payments equilibrium is to be maintained, then these unfavourable effects on the current account must be offset by an improvement elsewhere in the accounts. This could be achieved by a contractionary monetary policy, which raises interest rates, attracting inflows of capital from overseas. Again, if fiscal policy is expansionary, a contractionary monetary policy will be necessary to preserve the external balance.[4]

Figure 30.1 shows that with two objectives (internal and external balance) and two instruments or instrumental variables (monetary and fiscal policy) then, by setting monetary and fiscal instruments at values I_1' and I_2' respectively, objectives O_1 and O_2 can be achieved simultaneously.[5] Tinbergen's rule is thereby illustrated.

Suppose now a third objective is added, perhaps a target rate of economic growth (Fig. 30.2). The line O_3 shows the combinations of monetary and fiscal policy required to achieve this target rate of economic growth. O_3 is positively sloped, on the assumption

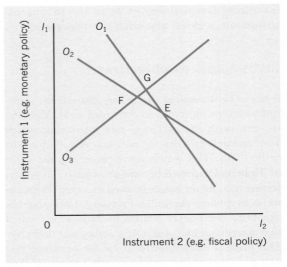

Fig. 30.2 Two-instrument/three-objective case.

that an expansionary fiscal policy, involving extra government spending, will 'crowd out' private sector investment. Total investment can then be kept at the level required to achieve growth rate O_3 only by encouraging private sector investment through low interest rates, i.e. by expansionary monetary policy. Expansionary fiscal *and* monetary policy are in this case required to achieve the target rate of economic growth O_3.

We can now see that it would be a fortunate and unlikely coincidence if O_3 happened to pass through point E, i.e. if all three objectives could be achieved with just two policy instruments. If, as in the figure, it does not, then we can only achieve two of the three objectives with our two policy instruments. For instance, we could be at G (O_1 and O_3 achieved, but not O_2) or at F (O_2 and O_3 achieved, but not O_1) or at E (O_1 and O_2 achieved, but not O_3). To achieve the third objective now requires a third policy instrument, perhaps exchange rate policy![6] If we cannot find extra policy instruments, Tinbergen's rule will be violated, i.e. there will be fewer instruments (here two) than objectives (here three). Except in the fortuitous case that all three objectives intersect, at G, F or E, then an *explicit choice* will have to be made between the conflicting objectives. In our example we must choose between G, F or E.

Tinbergen's approach has the great merit of being fairly simple to understand. It has encouraged governments to be explicit about their macro-economic objectives and has stimulated the search for new policy instruments, such as flexible exchange rates or prices and incomes policy. Its emphasis on 'fine-tuning' the economy by introducing additional policy instruments, and changing their values, reflects the spirit of 'Keynesian' interventionism.

The variable targets approach

In Tinbergen's approach, when we were unable to achieve all three objectives simultaneously because we lacked sufficient policy instruments, the target then became the achievement of any two, i.e. at G, F or E in Fig. 30.2. A choice had to be made between these alternatives. In contrast, Theil (1956) suggested that the target could be more flexible, and that any position could be chosen within the triangle GFE. In this case, no single objective is achieved; instead a compromise between the three is reached, all three being 'missed', but by a narrow margin in each case. This might be preferred to achieving two objectives by missing the third by a considerable margin.

Theil's flexible targets approach therefore presupposes that since all the objectives cannot be met there must be some 'welfare loss' whatever choice of objectives is made. This approach also assumes that a social welfare function can be defined for society as a whole, the aim then being to minimize the welfare loss for any choice made. The welfare function will take into account the *deviation* between the actual value achieved for any objective and its target value, with any such deviation indicating a loss of welfare. The problem then becomes one of minimizing a welfare loss function bearing in mind that the objectives are presumably 'weighted' with respect to each other. For example, in the early 1980s a deviation between the actual and target inflation rate would appear to be weighted more heavily than a deviation between the actual and target unemployment rate. Weights W_1, W_2 and W_3 are introduced into the welfare loss function to be minimized below. The deviations between actual and target levels are conventionally squared in order to eliminate the problem of sign.

It follows that if the three objectives have *actual* values O_1, O_2 and O_3, and target values O_1^*, O_2^* and O_3^*, then the policy-makers would seek to minimize the social welfare loss function defined in terms of those three objectives, i.e.

Minimize $U(O_1, O_2, O_3)$
$= W_1(O_1 - O_1^*)^2 + W_2(O_2 - O_2^*)^2 + W_3(O_3 - O_3^*)^2$

If there had been sufficient instruments to permit the simultaneous achievement of all three objectives, then $O_1 = O_1^*$, $O_2 = O_2^*$ and $O_3 = O_3^*$; in other words, the welfare loss function would equal zero. In terms of Fig. 30.2 all three objective functions (O_1, O_2 and O_3) have coincided at a single point. More sophisticated forms of such functions recognize that it is not only the extent to which the target objectives are fulfilled that matters, but also the values of the instrumental variables themselves. For example, high tax rates or higher interest rates may themselves reduce social welfare and might therefore be included in the loss function.

No-one would suggest that political decision-makers study loss minimization functions of the form indicated above, but the approach is helpful in suggesting that attempts should be made to think seriously about the relative weights given to objectives, and that if fixed target values are unattainable then flexibility might have to be accepted.

The 'satisficing' approach

Both the Tinbergen and the Theil approaches suggest that the economy is 'fine-tuned' by the policy-makers, i.e. instruments are continuously manipulated in order to achieve target welfare-maximizing (or loss-minimizing) values. Mosley (1976) pointed out that in practice policy instruments are periodically manipulated, usually all at once, in response to a crisis. He has proposed a 'satisficing' theory of economic policy, which views the policy-maker as a 'satisficing' agent, i.e. one whose motive is not to achieve the best possible states at all times, but to achieve 'satisfactory' levels of performance. These 'satisfactory' levels are influenced, in the case of macroeconomic objectives, by recently achieved performance and are determined by compromise bargaining between such institutions as the Bank of England, the Treasury and the Cabinet. He suggests that a package of instruments will be used in order to respond to a 'crisis', which might be an unsatisfactory level of performance with respect even to one objective, with the strength of the response depending upon the amount by which the actual value differs from the 'satisfactory' level.

Testing the satisficing approach for the period 1946–71, Mosley found that *any* balance of payments deficit triggered a response – in other words, only a zero or positive balance was regarded as 'satisfactory'. However, the unemployment figure considered 'satisfactory' varied over the years, following a rising trend. In 1953 it was below 1.6%, in 1965 below 2.5%, and by 1971 below 3.6%. Should a figure of below 5% be considered 'satisfactory' in the early years of the new millennium?

The fixed and flexible targets approaches to macroeconomic policy predict that policy-makers will seek to find new and effective instruments of policy in order simultaneously to achieve a growing number of economic objectives. If that search is not successful, then compromises between the target values of the objectives will be sought; more pragmatically, the policy-makers will accept quite broad ranges of values for the objectives and will intervene only when one (or more) of the target values becomes 'unsatisfactory'. In this last, 'satisficing', case the economy is 'managed by exception'.

Until the mid-1970s this reflected the interventionist 'Keynesian' approach which prevailed in the UK after the Second World War. Target values and achieved values for the objectives rarely diverged significantly, and it was generally accepted that policy-makers, armed with the predictions of increasingly sophisticated forecasting models of the economy, and using an increasing range of instrumental variables, could and should manage the economy by 'fine-tuning' it on to a desired path. However, as the 1970s progressed, the fine tuning and satisficing approaches to policy-making were being replaced by theories which began stressing the inherently stable nature of the economy. These advocated the need to set 'rules' which policy-makers should follow in the medium term, instead of concentrating on short-term interventionism.

The Cambridge Economic Policy Group (CEPG) approach

The CEPG differed from traditional Keynesians in seeing fiscal policy as possibly *contributing to* the balance of payments problem rather than correcting it. They identified a strong link between the balance of payments on current account and the size of the public sector surplus/deficit.

In the conventional manner let:

I = investment expenditure,
G = government expenditure,
X = exports,
S = savings,
T = taxation receipts,
M = imports.

Then, for equilibrium:

$$I + G + X = S + T + M$$

Rearranging,

$$X - M = S - I + T - G$$

i.e. the surplus on the balance of payments current account is, by definition, equal to the private sector surplus $(S - I)$ plus the public sector surplus $(T - G)$.

The private sector surplus is the sum of household and company *net* savings and this, it is claimed, is so small that it can be ignored. Household saving in the UK is normally balanced by investment in housing (channelled by building society deposits), and company saving is the major source of company investment. That being so, then:

$$S - I \approx 0$$

and

$$X - M \approx T - G$$

i.e. the balance of payments current account surplus/deficit is approximately equal to the public sector surplus/deficit, and changes in the latter will lead to approximately equal changes in the former. The explanation is that the effect of expansionary fiscal policy will be to raise incomes and imports faster than exports.

The policy implication of the approach typified by the CEPG was that an expansion of domestic demand to alleviate unemployment must be accompanied by the use of import controls. If the expansion is not accompanied by import controls, then the balance of payments will rapidly move into a considerable deficit, with devaluation or depreciation of the exchange rate unable to correct the deficit. The favourable effects for employment of the expansionary fiscal policy will then be dissipated overseas as increased demand in the UK is met by increased purchases of foreign goods rather than domestically produced goods. Their reply to the argument that the imposition of import controls on the part of the

UK would be met with retaliation from other countries is that the aim would not be to *reduce* the level of imports into the UK but to keep the level from rising. If no other country is harmed there will be no need for retaliation! In fact, any rise in UK exports might subsequently create scope for imports to rise.

We have already seen that economists supporting the CEPG analysis believe that 'fine-tuning' the economy by pursuing an interventionist policy is actually counter-productive and destabilizing. They believe that the economy is relatively stable in the medium term and that the most appropriate policy is to apply a 'fiscal rule' within the context of a medium-term strategy. This rule takes the form of a composite tax rate – the par tax rate – set at such a level that desired targets for National Income (employment) and the balance of payments can be achieved in the medium term. This rule should be adhered to, and the par tax rate altered, *only* if the target values are themselves altered, or if there are major disturbances in the world economy, or in the trade-off between the employment and balance of payments objectives.

The monetarists approach

Monetarists similarly eschew the use of an armoury of policy instruments (instrumental variables) to achieve macroeconomic objectives. The monetarist economists believe that if the money stock is increased, real output is not affected in the long run, though prices are, i.e. control of the money supply is the key to the control of inflation.[7] They accept that in the short run changes in money supply will affect output as well as prices. However, there will be time-lags between the change in money supply and changes in output, making it inadvisable to use the manipulation of aggregate demand as a policy instrument for achieving target levels of output and employment. Output and employment will instead be determined at their 'natural' levels by microeconomic factors affecting aggregate supply. These are more easily influenced by measures designed to improve market efficiency or to increase the supply of factors of production.

Policy-makers are therefore encouraged to follow simple 'rules' which will influence the economy in the long run, and will not generally be subject to changes which might cause instability in the short run. The most obvious rule is to control the rate of monetary expansion, and to effect changes in it relatively gradually in order that disruption is not too great. To the monetarist, the target rate for monetary expansion (given flexible exchange rates) becomes the proxy for the target rate of inflation, so that the 'target' is now set in terms of the value of the instrumental variable (money supply) rather than in terms of the objective (inflation). Short-run manipulation of the instrument to achieve the target objective was regarded as neither necessary nor even possible. Instead, the authorities are to control inflation through the long-run rate of monetary expansion. A rule for policy is therefore established.

Supply-side strategy

Monetarists and 'neoclassical' economists generally have sympathy with the view that output and employment are supply-determined, rather than with the Keynesian view that they are demand-determined.

Figure 30.3(a) represents the familiar Keynesian view, with prices and output (real national income) being determined largely by changes in aggregate demand. Our main interest here is to contrast this familiar diagram with Fig. 30.3(b), which uses the same axes to reflect the monetarist or supply-side view of economics.

Keynesian versus supply-side/ monetarist approaches

In the Keynesian case, an increase in real output from Y_1 to Y_2 is most readily achieved by an increase in aggregate demand from AD_1 to AD_2. However, the supply-side view is that an increase in real output from Y_1 to Y_2 is more effectively achieved by a downward (rightward) shift of the short-run aggregate supply (SRAS) curve from $SRAS_1$ to $SRAS_2$. In the former case, the average price level is likely to rise as real output rises, while the supply-side approach predicts a fall in the average price level alongside a rise in real output.

In favouring the supply-side approach, Conservative governments of the 1980s argued that there were certain features of the UK economy which tended to *prevent* the supply curve shifting downwards from

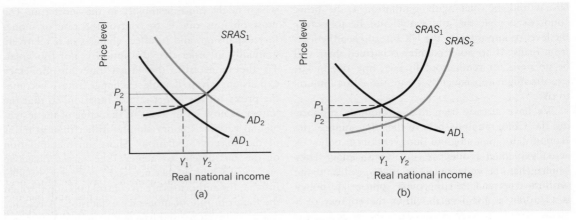

Fig. 30.3 (a) The Keynesian approach; (b) the supply-side approach.

$SRAS_1$ to $SRAS_2$. They felt that the main task of the government was to achieve such a downward shift in SRAS through 'supply-side' policies aimed at increasing productive efficiency in the economy. However, before we look at the various policies advocated since the early 1980s in support of this approach, it is useful to consider the factors which allegedly prevent the SRAS curve from shifting downwards.

First, there is the suggestion that unemployment and social security benefits encourage people to spend more time searching for the type of employment they consider appropriate. As a result, they remain on the unemployment register longer, the unemployment figures are swollen and aggregate output is restricted from the supply side. An ancillary argument is that the difference between some low-paid jobs and the rate of unemployment benefit is so marginal that such jobs are not taken up. This problem is aggravated by the UK tax system, which may result in some workers, previously unemployed, paying marginal tax rates in excess of 100% when moving into low-paid jobs – the 'unemployment trap' (see Chapter 23). Unemployment and social security benefits may in these ways cause the SRAS curve to remain at $SRAS_1$ in Fig. 30.3(b), thereby preventing output from rising to Y_2 and keeping the price level higher than it would otherwise be.

The second suggestion is that, quite apart from the 'unemployment trap', high taxation can affect the supply of labour (and so the level of output) through its disincentive effects. The reverse side of this is that a cut in taxes might so stimulate work effort that real output (and even total tax revenue) rises. In terms of Fig. 30.3(b) tax cuts would shift the supply curve to the right, i.e. from $SRAS_1$ to $SRAS_2$, so that output and employment would rise, and prices fall.

The third suggestion is that labour has priced itself out of the market, thereby reducing employment and output, because the trade unions have forced up the real wages of their members. It was estimated by Minford and Peel (1981) that unions had 'marked up' members' wages by between 12% and 25%, so raising permanent unemployment figures by between 400,000 and 800,000, although more recent research has put the average mark-up at 10% or less. Another important study (Layard and Nickell 1985) showed that the unemployment rate in the UK had risen by 11.83 percentage points between 1956 and 1983 and that union 'push' on wages accounted for 2.27 of those percentage points. The policy implication is that trade union bargaining power should be curbed. In terms of *labour market* analysis, the market wage is kept above the equilibrium wage so that unemployment is higher than market conditions warrant. In terms of the *goods market* in Fig. 30.3(b), the relatively high labour costs tend to keep the SRAS curve artificially high at $SRAS_1$. Output and employment are lower and prices are higher than they would otherwise be.

Finally, there is the suggestion that the very high unemployment and low output figures prevailing in the UK exaggerate the true situation because there is a considerable 'hidden' or 'black' economy, encouraged by a desire to evade taxation. Some of the 'black' economy would be conducted in monetary terms (e.g. payment in cash to a local handyman), some in non-monetary terms by means of barter. The 'black' economy has always been with us, and estimates as to its size vary from 2.5% of GDP (the gap between expenditure and declared income) to 7.5% (Inland Revenue estimates of tax evasion) and even to 15%. New estimates have indicated that the 'black economy' activity of self-employed people in the UK amounts to 10.6% of GDP.

As explained above, successive governments have implemented a wide range of measures consistent with the approach of supply-side economics (shown in Fig. 30.3 as a shift in the SRAS curve downwards to the right). We will briefly summarize some of the practical changes which have to be implemented in an attempt to increase the efficiency of markets.

Other supply-side approaches

Taxation

Successive governments have believed that the taxation structure has become distorted over the years and should be changed in order to create more incentives and to induce more output (supply) responsiveness. For example, the decrease in tax allowances on mortgages in the late 1980s from £30,000 per *person* to £30,000 per *dwelling* was partly designed to curb the amount of investment in housing and to stimulate investment in company shares, i.e. to channel investment into more productive forms which would help stimulate output. Similarly, tax relief on life insurance premiums had been abolished in 1984, in an attempt to encourage people to invest in company equities. Again the rate of Capital Gains Tax (CGT) had long been *less than* the basic rate of income tax, giving, for example, a better return to a person who bought and sold oil paintings than to a person buying company shares. In 1988 the CGT and the basic rate of income tax were equalized to prevent this bias. As well as bringing down personal taxation in order to stimulate incentives, successive governments have also decreased the standard rate of Corporation Tax for large companies, from 52% in 1983/84 to 30% by 2010; for small firms the rate was reduced from 35% to 19% in the same period. Those cuts in Corporation Tax were an attempt to stimulate reinvestment in capital stock.

Labour supply, efficiency and training

Successive governments have also believed in the need to improve the workings of the UK labour market, in order to make it more 'efficient' (i.e. labour should be mobile, well trained and free from institutional – e.g. union – bias). As far as *mobility* is concerned, the government felt that the UK labour market needed to be 'flexible', with workers induced to take up jobs rapidly. It was thought that this process was being inhibited by narrow differentials between the income of those out of work, thereby preventing active job search. Continuous adjustments have therefore been made in National Insurance benefits and income-related benefits over the past years, with the aim of widening the gap in income levels between those in work and those out of work.

To improve the *institutional problems* surrounding the labour market, successive Conservative governments introduced a series of laws to regulate employment and the trade unions. The Employment Acts of 1980, 1982, 1988, 1989 and 1990, together with the Trade Union Act of 1984, all of which were consolidated into the Trade Union and Labour Relations (Consolidation) Act of 1992, have weakened the control of unions (see Chapter 14).

In the area of training, one of the greatest problems for the UK has been the dearth of vocational skills at the intermediate level. As a result of these deficiencies, the UK government introduced a number of initiatives in the early 1990s. For example, by 1991 some 104 Training and Enterprise Councils (TECs) were in operation in Britain. These were independent business-led companies, funded by government, and charged with meeting the training, enterprise and vocational education requirements of local communities and employers. Similarly, the Technical and Vocational Educational Initiative (TVEI) was introduced in the early 1990s to influence the whole curriculum of schools and colleges to prepare pupils of 14–18 for the demands of working life. This process continued under the post-1997 Labour government. A new revised National Curriculum was introduced in September 2000 designed to make more explicit the links between education, employment and enterprise. Meanwhile, in the first few years of the new millennium, various strategies have been introduced to provide a better quality of work experience for pupils (Education–Business links), to encourage more entrepreneurial attitudes (National

Enterprise Campaign), to improve management expertise (Council for Excellence in Management and Leadership), and to increase training initiatives (New Deal). All these policies were designed to focus on increasing the UK's stock of 'human capital'.

These types of initiatives continued with the creation of the Learning and Skills Council (LSC) in April 2001 and then to the Skills Funding Agency and the Young People's Learning Agency in 2009. The Council was designed to raise participation in education and training and to enhance what came to be called Work Force Development (WFD), i.e. a desire to increase the capacity of individuals in the workplace. For example, the 'Train to Gain' service was introduced in the autumn of 2006 to help identify what skills businesses need. The LSC trains 'skill brokers' who help firms assess what skills are needed.

Arguably all these policies are designed to improve efficiency and help shift the supply curve downwards from S_1 to S_2 as in Fig. 30.3(b).

Global economic management: post 'credit crunch'

Here we review some of the key events and policy responses across the global economy in the period since 2006/07.

Sub-prime market and the 'credit crunch'

The term 'sub-prime' is widely used to refer to excessive lending for mortgage purposes in the US to low-income borrowers at high risk. When economic slowdown occurred in the US in 2006/07, many of these high-risk borrowers lost their jobs and/or found themselves unable to pay the higher monthly repayments as US interest rates rose substantially in 2006/07 (by around 4% in a little over one year). Nor did these low-income/high-risk borrowers have assets to help cushion falls in their current income. As a result, many have defaulted on their loans and the bad debt provisions of the lenders have soared, putting huge pressure on themselves and on other financial firms worldwide which have invested in them.

By late-2010, US house prices had fallen by 29%, and share prices by a similar amount, from their 2007 peak. A simulation by economists at the UBS bank suggests that a 10% drop in US house and share prices would reduce US economic growth by as much as 2.6 percentage points. This cut-back in projected economic growth was linked to the expectation of a significant fall in consumer spending in the US, given the *reversal* of the previous 'wealth effect' whereby higher house prices had played a key role in stimulating consumer borrowing and indebtedness. Indeed by late-2010 household wealth in the US had shrunk by $12 trillion, or by 18%, since 2007.

'Contagion' is a word much feared by analysts of the sub-prime market. Many innovative financial instruments developed and used ('securitization') to stimulate extra lending and borrowing are now viewed with much greater suspicion by the financial markets (see Chapter 21). Lending between financial intermediaries themselves has also diminished, as they have become more unsure of the true credit-worthiness of the borrowers, given that there is now serious concern over the value of many of these new financial instruments in their portfolio. This reluctance of financial intermediaries to lend to each other was a key factor in the problems experienced by Northern Rock in the UK, whose business model depended on regular inter-bank loans which were no longer forthcoming. The share price of Northern Rock collapsed in late 2007, forcing the Bank of England to step in as 'lender of last resort' and to avoid a systemic banking failure in the UK.

Financial instruments and the 'credit crunch'

The impacts of the housing market collapse on key financial instruments and markets are reviewed below. Many of these new financial derivatives and instruments had been widely traded across the world, and it has been the collapse in value of these widely held financial instruments which has been a root cause of many of the contemporary issues that have arisen within global finance and international trade. It may be helpful to illustrate these problems by using the market in a wide range of *Structured Investment Vehicles* (SIVs).

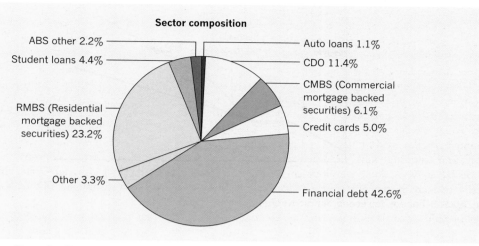

Fig. 30.4 Composition of a Structured Investment Vehicle (SIV).
Source: Wall, Minocha and Rees (2009) *International Business* (3rd edn), Financial Times/Prentice Hall.

Structured Investment Vehicles (SIV) market

These are the financial instruments that have emerged in recent years and which consist of not one but a *variety* of securities, some of which involve mortgage debt (see Fig. 30.4). Before reviewing the contribution of SIVs to current international financial developments, it will help to consider the so-called *sub-prime* market, and the impacts this has had on the value of SIVs, many of which involve a mortgage-backed 'slice' of their overall portfolio.

Problems in this market for SIVs and associated financial instruments such as Collateralized Debt Obligations (CDOs) have played a key role in the events unfolding globally over recent years. It has been the inclusion of (collapsing) mortgage backed assets in the composition of these financially engineered instruments, and the uncertainties as to future return to 'health' of the housing market, that has led

Structured Investment Vehicle (SIV)

1 A structured investment vehicle (SIV) exists to help those acquiring it make a profit from the difference between the low cost of short-term debt funding and the higher returns, or yields, of longer term debt investments.

2 A SIV consists of a pool of debts of financial companies, such as banks and insurers, including asset-backed securities, or bonds, backed by mortgages, loans or other debt (see Fig. 30.4).

3 The SIV funds these more profitable longer term investments by issuing debt itself. A small portion of this debt (between 5 and 12 per cent) is longer term and carries the first risk of losses if assets in the pool of investments start to go bad. This debt is also the last to be repaid, but it shares some of the profits made by the vehicle. This is the *junior debt*, otherwise known as the capital notes.

4 The lion's share of debt issued by the SIV is very low-cost short-term commercial paper, which has a lifespan of days or weeks, and medium-term notes, which have a lifespan of three to six months. This is the *senior debt*.

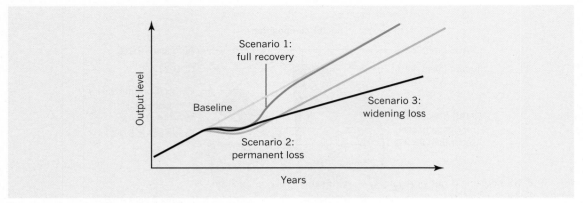

Fig. 30.5 Scenarios for economic recovery.

to the 'junk bond' status of many of these instruments, with seriously damaging effects on the balance sheets of major organizations.

Recovery scenarios

Pimco, the largest global bond manager – based in California – held its five-year planning meeting in May 2009 and predicted that financial markets will 'return to mean'. However, what exactly is meant by 'mean' or 'normal'? Is the 'new normal' a global economy with low growth and high unemployment and a different financial system, or are we to return to previous growth paths and 'business as usual'? Figure 30.5 presents three alternative scenarios.

Milton Friedman used US time-series data to suggest that *Scenario 1: full recovery* is the most likely. His analogy involved using a string stretched taut/ tightly on a board; the more forcefully the string is plucked, the more rapidly it snaps back! Friedman noted that deep recessions are often followed by strong recoveries and a return to the original growth path. However, others see different recovery scenarios. For example, *Scenario 2: permanent loss* sees no recovery back to the original growth path, though the *growth rate* might return to the previous level (parallel to Scenario 1) but on a lower trajectory. *Scenario 3: widening loss* sees even a return to the previous growth rate as unlikely so there is an ever widening loss of output.

Empirical evidence would seem to suggest that Scenarios 2 and 3 are the most likely outcomes. An IMF survey (World Economic Outlook 2009) identified 88 banking crises over the past 40 years and found that, on average, seven years after the deepest point of the recession, an economy's level of output was still around 10% below what it would have been without the banking crisis. This is also borne out by the Japanese experience where output in the period 1992–2005 was estimated at being some 25% below trajectory in 2005, i.e. below what the 2005 output would have been had the 1992 recession not occurred!

A suggestion is often made that the current financial crisis is more damaging than many of its predecessors because the overvalued assets of individuals and organizations in 2007 were accompanied by huge debts/liabilities. The result of this is that the value of liabilities is likely to exceed the value of assets for many years, even after recovery has begun! The legacy of such huge past losses can depress future gains on the balance sheet – additional income going forward being used to restore the balance sheets rather than to be used for new lending.

The future recovery scenarios may depend on the response of *consumers* to the financial crisis. The US saving rate averaged over 8% in the period 1962–67, but had fallen to only 2.7% in the period 2001–07, rising to around 5% in the period 2008–11 (see Fig. 30.6).

We can see from Fig. 30.6 that net worth had risen dramatically from 500% of annual disposable personal income in 2002 to 650% in 2006, i.e. in only four years, before falling again to around 460% in 2009/10. Such increase in wealth is seen by many as a reason for the continued fall in the US savings ratio

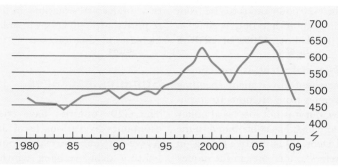

Fig. 30.6 US household net worth as % of disposable personal income.
Source: US Federal Reserve (various).

(see also Chapter 16). Between 2007 and 2010 as many as 30% of US mortgage holders owed more than their homes were worth on the market – i.e. negative equity. In fact the US savings ratio is already rising, from 2.7% in 2006 to over 5% in 2010 and is continuing to rise. A key question is whether US consumers will eventually resume the growth in spending of a few years ago or continue to spend progressively less.

China is an obvious possible source of consumption growth for the global economy (see also Chapter 28), given that it has a substantial balance of payments surplus with the rest of the world. However, the savings ratio in China has been estimated at close to 50% of GDP, when household, company and government savings are aggregated.

Global budgetary problems and the 'credit crunch'

There has been an increasing awareness by governments of the need to reduce government expenditure as a proportion of national income. This concern is common to many countries which have attempted to avoid the recessionary impacts of falling consumer expenditure associated with the 'credit crunch' by increasing government expenditures or reducing government revenues via taxation.

The G20 group of major developed economies all face problems of rapidly increasing public sector deficits as they seek to stimulate their economies in response to the 'credit crunch'. As can be seen in Table 30.1, the National Debt (what the government

Table 30.1 Percentage of GDP.

Country	National Debt 2009	National Debt 2014	Budget deficit[1] 2009	Budget surplus required[2] in 2014
United States	88.8	112.0	−12.3	4.3
Japan	217.4	239.2	−9.0	9.8
Germany	79.8	91.4	−2.3	2.8
France	77.4	95.5	−5.3	3.1
Britain	68.6	99.7	−10.0	3.4
G20	100.6	119.7	−8.6	4.5

[1]Before interest payments.
[2]To keep debt under control.
Source: IMF, *World Economic Outlook* (various).

owes its creditors) of the G20 countries is to rise from 100.6% of G20 GDP in 2009 (it had only been 79% of G20 GDP in 2007) to almost 120% of GDP in 2014.

This increase in National Debt is, of course, the consequence of increased government spending and/or reduced tax revenues from attempts to stimulate national economies. But it is not just fiscal policy but monetary policy too which has contributed to the sharp rise in National Debt. 'Quantitative easing' in the UK, for example, refers to increases in the money supply, often involving the purchases of government debt such as Treasury bills, with cheques drawn on the government itself. This has increased cash and liquidity for the financial institutions and for individuals selling their bills and bonds, but also increased the National Debt!

Other increases in the National Debt have involved sharply increased expenditures by government departments on a wide range of projects to stimulate their respective economies.

The table also shows the average *budget deficit* (G > T) for the G20 countries, recorded at −8.6% of GDP in 2009, a figure significantly higher than the average −1.1% of GDP recorded as recently as 2007 for the G20. This captures both the sharp rise in government spending on 'bail outs' and other activities to stimulate domestic economies and also the fall in revenues from tax cuts also aimed at stimulating domestic economies. For example, VAT was temporarily cut from 17.5% to 15% in the UK for a 12-month period in 2009/10.

The table also shows the projected *budget surplus* required of the G20 countries by 2014 in order 'to keep public debt under control', defined here as bringing the respective national debts back to a maximum of 60% of GDP by 2014. The size of this task can be gauged by the fact that an average annual *budget surplus* of +4.5% will be required by 2014 to achieve this across the G20 countries, as compared to the average annual *budget deficit* of −8.6% in those countries in 2009. It will be a major challenge for many countries to achieve such a turnaround; for the US it will require the budget deficit of −12.3% in 2009 to be transformed to a budget surplus of +4.3% by 2014, and for the UK it will require the budget deficit of −10.0% in 2009 to be transformed to a budget surplus of +3.4% by 2014.

Whatever governments are in power in the various G20 countries, such a dramatic transformation in their budgetary situations in less than five years will require sharp reductions in public expenditure and/or increases in taxation.

Stimulus packages

The G20 countries have tried to stimulate their economies by various fiscal and monetary policies. As we noted above, expansionary fiscal policies have led to a 'debt overhang' which may create problems for global recovery in the coming years. As well as expansionary fiscal policies used to stimulate the economies during recession, many governments have also adopted expansionary monetary policies. 'Quantitative easing' has been reviewed elsewhere (e.g. Chapter 20 and Chapter 21) but is essentially an increase in the money supply, which is usually associated with lower interest rates and a lower exchange rate (see Chapter 25).

 Sovereign wealth funds (SWFs) and sovereign debt

A new emphasis in financial risk management is being placed on *sovereign debt ratings*, linked closely to the growth of *sovereign wealth funds* (SWFs). These are government owned investment vehicles managed separately from the official reserves of the country. They have usually been accumulated by those governments as the result of high global commodity prices for their exports. High energy (e.g. oil), food and other primary product prices over recent years have meant that an estimated $5,000bn is now available for potential investment by countries such as the United Arab Emirates, Saudi Arabia, Dubai, Kuwait, China, Norway, the Russian Federation and Singapore, amongst others. The SWFs will often be invested in projects with higher risks but higher expected future returns. Professional portfolio management techniques are often adopted with a view to generating a sustainable future income stream via investments in bonds, equities and other assets. In 2009 Barclays Bank raised $7bn of funds from this source rather than accept UK government funding to help it cope with the liquidity crisis of the 'credit crunch'. In 2010 there were 70 SWFs in 44 countries with assets ranging in value from $20m (Sao Tome and Principe) to more than $500bn in the United Arab Emirates.

Sovereign debt ratings

There has been much criticism of the credit rating agencies as regards their giving high (triple A) ratings to financial institutions found to be anything but credit-worthy as events in the sub-prime market unfolded! Investors who subsequently lost huge amounts of money complained that they had been misled by the AAA ratings that the agencies had handed out on complex packages of mortgage-related debt. The critics further argue that there is a clear conflict of interest when the credit rating agencies are themselves paid by the issuers to assess their bonds and other debt instruments.

Investor attention has now shifted to sovereign debt risk, and the three big agencies (Fitch, Moody's and Standard & Poor's) again find themselves at the centre of attention. Sovereign debt upgrades actually exceeded downgrades in every year between 1999 and 2007, but that has changed as a result of the financial crisis and over the period 2008–10 sovereign debt downgrades exceeded upgrades by a ratio of 7:1, the exact reverse of previous experiences.

The workings of the financial system make these ratings even more important; for example, should any EU country be downgraded below A–, then that country's bonds become ineligible for use as collateral by the European Central Bank (ECB) under the tighter ECB rules from the end of 2010. This concern was a key factor in persuading the Greek government to accept austerity measures as a condition for the huge €110bn support for its currency from the EU and IMF in 2010. Without such support, a downgrade would have been inevitable. Politicians also place great emphasis on such ratings. Tim Geithner, the US Treasury Secretary, claims that America will 'never' lose its AAA mark. Political parties in the UK have also promised to defend its AAA rating.

Over the long term, the ratings of most developed nations have been remarkably stable. No country rated AAA, AA or A by S&P has gone on to default within a subsequent 15-year period. Indeed, nearly 98% of countries ranked AAA were either at that rating, or the AA level, 15 years later. That stable record may not persist. Investors have been buying government debt for years in the belief it is 'risk-free', almost regardless of the economic fundamentals. But if they lose faith in a government's policies, the situation can change very quickly. Such concerns are especially true since sovereign debt has increased from 62% of world GDP in 2006 to over 85% in 2010.

Some, however, argue that governments and investors place too much importance on credit rating. Canada lost its AAA rating in the 1990s, but then regained it during the past decade, while Japan managed to keep borrowing at a cheap rate, despite losing its triple AAA rating.

The agencies are well aware that ratings changes are highly sensitive. Decisions are therefore made by committee, rather than by an individual, to reduce the scope for outside pressure. Consensus is generally sought before a downgrade is made. The agencies also seek to protect themselves from criticism by being as transparent as possible.

A number of factors help determine whether a country's AAA status can be maintained, including economic and institutional strength, the government's finances and susceptibility to specific shocks. Others argue that the key ratio is not debt-to-GDP but interest payments as a proportion of government revenues. Once that gets beyond 10%, a government may face difficulties.

That does not mean a downgrade is inevitable, however. If the government is implementing a credible plan to cut its deficit, then it may maintain its AAA status. Agencies may also have to make qualitative judgements about a range of other factors, e.g. the willingness of eurozone countries to bail out countries such as Greece when they enter financial difficulties!

Key points

- Macroeconomic policy seeks to achieve various *target* values as regards objectives such as employment, prices, economic growth and the balance of payments.

- To achieve such 'target values', governments use various *policy instruments*, such as fiscal and monetary policy, prices and incomes policy, exchange rate policy and import controls.

- Governments often find that there are complex linkages between policy objectives and policy instruments.

- Tinbergen's *fixed target approach* emphasizes that there must be at least as many policy instruments as policy objectives if target values for a number of objectives are to be achieved simultaneously.

- Theil's *flexible target approach* suggests that no exact target value can be achieved for any single objective or group of objectives. Instead policy instruments are geared to minimizing the (squared) deviations between the actual and target value for one or more objectives in order to minimize overall welfare loss.

- The 'satisficing' approach of Mosley moves away from the fine-tuning of Tinbergen and Theil, and suggests that 'satisfactory' rather than optimum levels of performance should be the aim of macroeconomic policy.

- Macroeconomic policy in the pre-1974 period largely followed Keynesian principles, i.e. managing demand mainly through fiscal policy, allied occasionally to prices and incomes policies.

- Macroeconomic policy after 1974 often moved away from such Keynesian 'fine tuning' and towards the use of 'rules', following a more monetarist standpoint.

- Macroeconomic policy has also involved improving the responsiveness of the economy by concentrating on the *supply side* of the economy, for example by adjusting tax rates and improving labour efficiency and training.

- The global economic crises triggered by the collapse of the sub-prime market, have led to major fiscal and monetary expansion in many countries as governments sought to avoid the worst impacts of the credit crunch on their levels of output and employment.

- The major budgetary deficits have resulted in sharp increases in National Debt for many countries and to current attempts to restore the 'health' of their public finances.

- The growth of sovereign wealth funds (SWFs) brings a new factor into the equation for managing economies which might be the recipient of major capital inflows or outflows of such funds.

- Sovereign debt ratings by credit agencies are of increasing importance, when national (as opposed to corporate) downgrades can have major impacts on economies such as Greece and Spain.

Now try the self-check questions for this chapter on the Companion Website. You will also find useful links to relevant websites.

Notes

1 That is, provided the Marshall–Lerner condition is satisfied, with the sum of price elasticity of demand for UK exports and price elasticity of demand for imports into the UK greater than unity.

2 For instance, in Chapter 20 we noted that the money supply, M, times the velocity of circulation of money, V, would give the monetary value of spending.

3 If points on O_1 indicate internal balance, then points off it indicate imbalance. Check that above and to the right of the line there will be inflation, whereas below and to the left there will be unemployment.

4 Similarly, if points on O_2 indicate external balance, then points off it indicate imbalance. Check that a balance of payments surplus will occur below and to the left of the O_2 line, and a deficit above and to the right.

5 Provided that O_2 and O_1 cross! Economic objective O_2 is shown as having a shallower slope than O_1. Can you see why? Start at E, and move up the O_1, line; expansionary monetary policy reduces interest rates, so that the short-term capital inflow will diminish, and the balance of payments will deteriorate. To keep it in balance, a lower National Income would be necessary in order to reduce the import flow. This could be achieved by contractionary fiscal policy, i.e. above E, O_2 must lie to the left of O_1.

6 If the exchange rate is lowered then O_2 might shift to the right and so pass through point G (which had previously been a balance of payments deficit position). All three objectives are now achieved.

7 If $M.V = P.T$, the equation of exchange where M = money supply, V = average velocity of circulation of money, P = average price level and T = volume of transactions, then, if both V and T are fixed (or change at a known rate), money supply M directly affects price level P. So $\Delta M = \Delta P$, and the inflation rate is determined by the growth of the money supply.

References and further reading

Allsopp, C. (2002) Macroeconomic policy rules in theory and in practice, *Bank of England Quarterly Bulletin*, **42**(4): 485–504.

Balls, E., Grice, J. and O'Donnell, A. (2004) *Microeconomic Reforms in Britain*, Basingstoke, Palgrave.

Bank of England (2010) *Quantitative Easing Explained*, pamphlet, London, 1–14.

Barrell, R. and Gottschalk, S. (2004) The volatility of the output gap in the G7, *National Institute Economic Review*, **188**(1): 100–7.

Beath, J. (2002) UK industrial policy: old tunes on new instruments?, *Oxford Review of Economic Policy*, **18**(2): 221–39.

Bénassy-Quéré, A. and Coeuré, B. (2010) *Economic Policy*, New York, Oxford University Press.

Bray, J., Kuleshov, A., Uysal, A. and Walker, P. (1993) Balance-achieving policies: a comparative policy-optimization study on four UK models, *Oxford Review of Economic Policy*, **9**(3): 69–82.

Britton, A. (2002) Macroeconomics and history, *National Institute Economic Review*, **179**(January): 104–18.

Cowling, K. and Sugden, R. (1993) Industrial strategy: a missing link in British economic policy, *Oxford Review of Economic Policy*, **9**(3): 83–100.

Dungey M., Fry, R., Gonzales-Hermosillo, B. and Martin, V. (2011) *Transmission of Financial Crises and Contagion*, Oxford, Oxford University Press.

Giavazzi, F. and Blanchard, O. (2010) *Macroeconomics: A European Perspective*, Harlow, Financial Times/Prentice Hall.

Gnos, C. (2009) *Monetary Policy and Financial Stability*, Cheltenham, Edward Elgar.

Griffiths, A. (2001) The government's fiscal rules: origins, development and problems, *British Economy Survey*, **31**(1): 17–20.

Healey, N. (1990) Mrs Thatcher's fight against inflation: ten years without cheer, *Economics*, **26**(1): 28–56.

Heibling, T. and Wescott, R. (1995) The global interest rate, *Staff Studies for the World Economic Outlook*, September, Washington DC, International Monetary Fund.

HM Treasury (2002) *Reforming Britain's Economic and Financial Policy*, Basingstoke, Palgrave Macmillan.

Hudson, S. and Fisher, P. (1994) Monetary policy in the United Kingdom, *Economics and Business Education*, **II**, part 2, no. 6, Summer, 79–83.

IMF (1996) World economic situation and short term prospects, *World Economic Outlook*, May, Table 2, Washington DC, International Monetary Fund.

IMF (2009) *World Economic Outlook 2009: Crisis and Recovery*, Washington DC, International Monetary Fund.

Krugman, P. and Obstfeld, M. (2010) *International Economics: Theory and Policy*, Harlow, Financial Times/Prentice Hall.

Layard, R. L. and Nickell, S. (1985) The causes of British unemployment, *National Institute Economic Review*, **111**, February, 62–85.

Lyssiotou, P., Parshardes, P. and Stengos, T. (2004) Estimates of the Black Economy based on consumer demand approaches, *Economic Journal*, July, 622–40.

Mercier, P. and Papadia, F. (2011) *The Concrete Euro: Implementing Monetary Policy in the Euro Area*, Oxford, Oxford University Press.

Minford, P. and Peel, D. (1981) Is the government's economic strategy on course?, *Lloyds Bank Review*, **40**, April, 1–19.

Mosley, P. (1976) Towards a satisficing theory of economic policy, *Economic Journal*, **86**, March, 59–72.

Newman, S., Rickert, C. and Schaap, R. (2011) Investing in the post-recession world, *Harvard Business Review*, January–February, 150–5.

O'Mahony, M. (1998) *Britain's Relative Productivity Performance 1950–1996: Estimates by Sector*, September, London, National Institute of Economic and Social Research.

Oulton, N. (1995) Supply side reform and UK economic growth: what happened to the miracle?, *National Institute Economic Review*, **154**, November, 53–70.

Performance and Innovation Unit (2001) In demand: adult skills in the 21st century, *Performance and Innovation Unit Report*, November, Fig. 12, London, Cabinet Office.

Savage, D. (1982) Fiscal policy, 1974/75–1980/81: description and measurement, *National Institute Economic Review*, **99**, February, 85–95.

Sentance, A. (1998) UK macroeconomic policy and economic performance, in Buxton, T., Chapman, P. and Temple, P. (eds), *Britain's Economic Performance* (2nd edn), London, Routledge.

Steedman, H., McIntosh, S. and Green, A. (2004) *International Comparisons of Qualifications: Skills Audit Update*, Research Report, RR 548, London, Department for Education and Skills.

Theil, H. (1956) On the theory of economic policy, *American Economic Review*, **46**, May, 360–6.

Tinbergen, J. (1952) *On the Theory of Economic Policy*, Amsterdam, North-Holland Publishing Co.

Trade and Industry Committee (1994) *Competitiveness of UK Manufacturing Industry*, Second Report, House of Commons, April, London, HMSO.

UNCTAD (2010) *Trade and Development Report 2010: Employment, Globalization and Development*, New York and Geneva, United Nations Conference on Trade and Development.

UNCTAD (2010) *World Investment Report 2010: Investing in a Low Carbon Economy*, New York and Geneva, United Nations Conference on Trade and Development.

UNDP (2010) *Human Development Report 2010: The Real Wealth of Nations: Pathways to Human Development*, New York, United Nations Development Programme.

Wall, S., Minocha, S. and Rees, B. (2009) *International Business* (3rd edn), Harlow, Financial Times/Prentice Hall.

World Bank (2010) *World Development Report 2010: Development and Climate Change*, Washington DC.

World Economic Outlook (2009) Financial crises tend to have long impact on the economy, *IMFSurvey Magazine: IMF Research*, 22 September.

Wyplosz, C. (2005) Fiscal policy: institutions versus rules, *National Institute Economic Review*, **191**(1): 70–84.

A guide to sources

The following materials will guide you to a wide range of statistical data and other applied materials on the UK, EU and global economy. These materials are presented using the following structure:

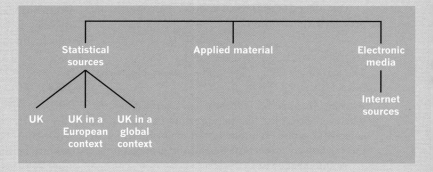

Statistical sources

The following contain important statistical series and, in some cases, articles commenting on those series or on related issues. The addresses given are those for enquiries about *orders* and *subscriptions*.

The UK economy

Guide to Official Statistics   The Stationery Office (TSO), PO Box 29, Norwich NR3 1GN

This is, perhaps, the most useful starting point in any search for statistical sources relating to the UK. It has been published at irregular intervals since 1976 and the latest enlarged edition, compiled by the Office for National Statistics (ONS), was published in 1996. The first chapter of the Guide looks at the organization of the Government Statistical Office and gives the main contact points and publishers of statistics. The remaining 15 chapters contain one subject area per chapter, e.g. population, education, labour market, environment, the economy, etc. For each subject, the main datasets are described and the sources of statistics available are provided. Information on any specific topic can be obtained by using the extensive key word index at the back of the Guide.

The other UK statistical sources we consider are presented alphabetically.

Annual Abstract of Statistics   (AAS)
The Stationery Office (TSO), PO Box 29, Norwich, NR3 1GN

Annual Abstract of Statistics gives annual figures, wherever possible, for the previous 10 years, in some 400 tables. It presents the major statistics of the various government departments, grouped under 18 section headings.

Annual Survey of Hours and Earnings   (ASHE)   The Stationery Office, PO Box 29, Norwich, NR3 1GN

This yearly publication provides detailed and important information relating to the make-up of earnings and hours paid to employees, and its distribution by industry, occupation, region, sex and full/part time status.

Bank of England Quarterly Bulletin
(BEQB)   Publications Group, Bank of England, London, EC2R 8AH

The *Bulletin* is published quarterly, providing detailed statistics on assets and liabilities of the UK monetary sector institutions, though with less detail than in *Financial Statistics* (see below). Data are also provided for money stock components, government debt, official reserves, foreign exchange rates, comparative interest rates and flow of funds analyses. Each issue contains a number of articles on recent economic and financial developments and on other topics in banking and finance. The Bank of England also publishes *Inflation Report* every quarter. This contains six sections covering topics such as the outlook for inflation over the next two years, monetary aggregates, financial market data, firm's pricing behaviour, etc.

Economic and Labour Market Trends
(ELMT)   The Stationery Office (TSO), PO Box 29, Norwich, NR3 1GN

This monthly publication is a fusion of two previous publications in 2007, namely, *Economic Trends* and *Labour Market Trends*. It contains an up-to-date statistical picture of the UK economy and its labour market together with an insight into how the statistics behind the analysis are produced and interpreted. Detailed articles cover such topics as output, employment, finance, wealth distribution, etc. It also has a 'News Release' section which provides issues of topical importance.

Households Below Average Income
(HBAI)   The Stationery Office (TSO), PO Box 29 Norwich NR3 1GN

This yearly publication from the Department of Work and Pensions provides statistics and commentary on the standard of living of various types of households in Great Britain. It provides important information on households at the lower end of the income distribution spectrum.

International Comparisons of Productivity
The Stationery Office (TSO), PO Box 29 Norwich NR3 1GN

This is a twice yearly publication which provides details about UK productivity (output per worker and output per hour) as compared to her main developed country rivals such as Canada, France, Germany, Italy, Japan, the US and the G7 average.

Financial Statistics (FS) The Stationery Office (TSO), PO Box 29, Norwich NR3 1GN

Financial Statistics is a monthly publication of the ONS. Data are provided on a wide range of financial topics, for the latest month or quarter, and for at least the previous five years. Financial accounts are presented for various sectors of the economy, central and local government, the public corporations, the monetary sector, other financial institutions, industrial and commercial companies, the personal sector and the overseas sector.

Monthly Digest of Statistics (MDS) The Stationery Office (TSO), PO Box 29, Norwich NR3 1GN

This is another monthly publication of the ONS. It gives up-to-date statistics on the output of various industries, covering a wide range of industries. Statistics are also presented on the components of National Income and Expenditure, on demographic topics, on the labour market and on a variety of social issues.

Regional Trends (RT) The Stationery Office (TSO), PO Box 29, Norwich NR3 1GN

Regional Trends is an annual publication of the ONS, and presents detailed data on the Standard Planning Regions of the UK. *Regional Trends* includes a wide range of economic, social and demographic indices, highlighting regional disparities in the UK.

Social Trends (ST) The Stationery Office (TSO), PO Box 29, Norwich NR3 1GN

Much of the material in *Social Trends* is of interest to the social scientist in general rather than the economist in particular. Nevertheless, it gives a detailed breakdown of patterns of household wealth, income and expenditure, together with demographic, housing and social trends.

Transport Statistics: Great Britain The Stationery Office (TSO), PO Box 29, Norwich NR3 1GN

Published annually by the Department of Transport, this is the main source of statistics on UK Transport. It is divided into nine parts covering Energy and the Environment, Vehicles and Roads, Road Traffic and Freight, Water and Air Transport and Public Transport. It also contains international transport statistics to place the UK in a global context.

UK Balance of Payments The Stationery Office (TSO), PO Box 29, Norwich NR3 1GN

The so-called *Pink Book* is the most comprehensive single source available for balance of payments statistics. Published annually, it breaks down trade in goods and services, investment income, investment and other capital transactions, official financing and external assets and liabilities, into their various components. Data for the previous 10 years are presented for purposes of comparison.

UK Economic Accounts The Stationery Office (TSO), PO Box 29, Norwich NR3 1GN

Published quarterly by the ONS, this provides a useful update of some of the main components of National Income. It includes the financial accounts of industrial and commercial corporations together with those of central and local government. This publication also provides details of the Balance of Payments on goods, services and investment accounts.

United Kingdom: National Accounts The Stationery Office (TSO), PO Box 29, Norwich NR3 1GN

Published annually by the ONS, the so-called *Blue Book* is the single most comprehensive source of data on National Income, output and expenditure, and their components. As well as data for the current calendar year, those of the previous 10 years are also provided. For some tables, data are even presented for 20 calendar years on a consistent basis and, in an annual supplement, as far back as 1946.

United Kingdom 5,000 largest companies ELC International, 5 Mile Drive, Oxford, OX2 8HT

This publication provides basic details on a large number of individual companies with information including headquarter location, sales, change in sales, profits, profits as a percentage of equity capital, number of employees and sales per employee. It also includes lists of the 250 largest companies as measured by profit, losses and employment.

The UK economy in a European context

European Economy   The Stationery Office (TSO), PO Box 29, Norwich NR3 1GN

European Economy appears three times a year, in March, July and November, and is published by the Commission of the European Union. The November issue contains an annual report on the economic situation within the Union. A statistical annex presents the main economic indicators on an annual basis, and is attached to each issue.

Europe's 15,000 Largest Companies

(ELC)   ELC International, 5 Mile Drive, Oxford OX2 8HT

This publication is regularly updated and contains information on the top companies of Europe. The volume contains data on the sales, profits, total assets, shareholder funds and employment of the largest companies in the industrial, trading and services sectors.

Eurostat   ONS, Room 1.015, Government Buildings, Cardiff Road, Newport, S. Wales NP10 8XG

Annual publications on the major indices of economic activity are provided by the Statistical Offices of the members of the European Union under the *Eurostat* heading.

ECB Statistical Pocket Book   Postfach 16 03 19, 60066 Frankfurt am Main, Germany

The *Statistics Pocket Book* is published each month and provides selected macroeconomic indicators for the individual member states of the European Union, as well as comparisons between the euro area, the United States, and Japan.

ECB Monthly Bulletin   Postfach 16 03 19, 60066 Frankfurt am Main, Germany

Monetary policy decisions taken monthly by the Governing Council of the ECB are explained in the *Monthly Bulletin*. To make the decision more transparent, the *Monthly Bulletin* provides a detailed analysis of the current economic situation and risks to price stability. The editorial summarises the Governing Council's assessment of present data. The data used by the Governing Council are presented chapters such as: the external environment of the euro area, monetary and financial developments, prices and costs, fiscal developments etc

European Central Bank (ECB) statistics

http://www.ecb.int/stats/html/index.en.html

The statistics section of the ECB provides support to the EU's monetary policy by providing detailed monetary statistics on each country together with other vital data relating to economic accounts, balance of payments, labour markets and government finances – as well as information on medium-term plans of the EU. All statistics can be downloaded via the Bank's *Statistical Data Warehouse.*

 ## The UK economy in a global context

International Monetary Fund publications   The Stationery Office (TSO), PO Box 29, Norwich NR3 1GN

World Economic Outlook Published annually since 1980. This presents and analyses short- and medium-term projections for individual countries, together with a discussion of key policy issues. The industrial countries, the oil-exporting countries and the non-oil developing countries are considered as separate groups.

IMF Economic Review is the official research journal which succeeded the previous IMF Staff Papers in mid-2010. It published high quality academic research related to global economic policies, open economy macroeconomics and international finance and trade.

International Financial Statistics is the standard source of statistics on international and domestic finance. Data include balance of payments, international liquidity, money and banking government accounts, etc.

OECD publications   The Stationery Office (TSO), PO Box 29, Norwich NR3 1GN

OECD Economic Surveys Individual country reports for the advanced industrialised economies, published annually in most cases.

OECD Economic Outlook Presents economic trends and prospects in OECD countries. Published twice a year in July and December.

Regional Economic Outlook Reports Published annually, these reports discuss the recent economic developments and prospects for countries in various regions. They also address the factors that have affected economic performance, and discuss the challenges for policy-makers.

The World Bank publications
See 'World Bank' below.

United Nations publications   The Stationery Office (TSO), PO Box 29, Norwich NR3 1GN

Human Development Report Published annually. These reports provide valuable data and analysis on a wide range of topics involving developing and developed nations. There is an annual up-date of the Human Development Index which seeks to use a wide range of indicators, as well as real national income per head, to measure 'wellbeing' across the global economy.

Monthly Bulletin of Statistics Published monthly, this volume contains a section on special statistics compiled for that specific issue and regular information on other statistical series, including population, wages, prices, production, manpower, etc.

UN Statistical Yearbook Published annually, covering a wide variety of indices of economic activity for developed and developing nations.

World Economic Survey Published every second year, examines fluctuations in the world economy, by individual countries and by groups of countries, for a variety of economic indicators. Problems and prospects are examined for the developed market

economies, for centrally planned economies and for the developing countries, together with the outlook for international trade.

World Investment Report This is published yearly by the UN's trade and development arm (UNCTAD). It focuses on flows of foreign direct investment world-wide and provides rankings of the largest transnational corporations in the world and their importance in world trade. It also has in-depth analysis of selected topics and provides insights into policy-making in this area.

World Statistics Pocketbook A useful pocketbook which provides an easy-to-use international compilation of 50 basic economic, social and environmental indicators for 216 countries and areas worldwide. The notes on sources and definitions provide a valuable guide for further research.

World Bank   The World Bank, 1818 H Street, NW, Washington DC, 20433

The World Bank provides a range of data and materials which are extremely useful for analysis of developments throughout the global economy.

World Development Report Published annually, this report provides data on a wide range of development indicators, as well as an analysis of particular issues of relevance to developing economies.

World Trade Organization   The Stationery Office (TSO), PO Box 29, Norwich, NR3 1GN

The World Trade Organization (WTO) is the only global international organisation dealing with the rules of trade between nations. At its heart are the WTO agreements, negotiated and signed by the bulk of the world's trading nations and ratified in their parliaments. The goal is to help producers of goods and services, exporters, and importers conduct their business.

World Trade Report The World Trade Report is an annual publication that aims to deepen understanding about trends in trade, trade policy issues and the multilateral trading system. Each publication provides a summary of the general trade situation in the world and then has a section on different topics each year. Such topics include globalisation and trade, distributional aspects of trade, trade policy and trade agreements, trade in natural resources, etc.

International Trade Statistics Annual publication including detailed analysis and tables for the latest year (leading traders, trade by sector product and region, LDCs, etc.).

Applied materials

The following are a number of useful sources, readily available to the reader interested in applied economic issues.

Business Strategy Review   John Wiley & Sons Limited, 1 Oldlands Way, Bognor Regis, West Sussex, PO22 9SA

Business Strategy Review published four times a year under the aegis of the London Business School analyses and interprets contemporary research on strategic management and the wider business environment, publishing articles which combine disciplines and cross-cultural boundaries. Leading business thinkers from around the world, both academic and managerial, come together in *Business Strategy Review* to debate current issues and present cutting-edge research and ideas

Business Review   Philip Allen Updates, Market Place, Deddington, OX15 0SE

Published four times a year, this journal contains a range of articles that place theory in a real-life business context and address subjects such as marketing, finance, production operations and human resource development. It also provides guidelines on how to tackle examination questions.

Economics Today   Anforme Ltd, Stocksfield Hall, Stocksfield, Northumberland NE43 7TN

This journal is published four times a year and contains a main article section relating to economic problems in both micro- and macro-economics. It also has regular features covering various topic areas,

e.g. essay and multiple choice questions, making sense of economic data, views from the city, etc.

Economic Review   Philip Allan Publishers Ltd, Market Place, Deddington, OX15 0SE

Four issues are published each academic year in September, November, February and April. *Economic Review* is aimed at introductory students in economics, and relates economic theory to contemporary economic problems. Each issue contains main feature articles, and a teaching section which reviews the various ways of tackling typical examination questions.

Far Eastern Economic Review   GPO Box 160, Hong Kong

A weekly publication available from main UK booksellers. It is a major source of up-to-date information about countries of the 'Pacific Rim' (such as SE Asia and Australasia) which have become an important part of the world economy. It contains sections which deal with regional issues in the Far East, and presents important articles on business and society in the different Far East countries.

Fiscal Facts   Institute for Fiscal Studies (IFS), 7 Ridgmount Street, London, WC1 7AE

This is the UK's leading independent microeconomic research institute and is an authority on fiscal facts, public finances, tax and welfare policy, education, inequality and poverty, productivity and innovation, etc. It produces reports, working papers and press releases on these topic areas.

FT Global 500   Financial Times, 1 Southwark Bridge, London SE1 9HL

The annual snapshot of the world's largest companies, ranked by market capitalisation, gives an important picture of how corporate fortunes have changed in the past year. Market values are given by country and sector with the largest rises and falls within the year.

Key British Enterprises   Dun & Bradstreet, Marlow International, Parkway, Marlow SL7 1AJ

This yearly publication covers some 50 000 large and medium-sized UK companies. It provides *financial* details (profit, turnover, etc.), *operational* details (line of business, markets, brand names, etc.) and *corporate* details (registration no., parent company, etc.).

National Institute Economic Review

2 Dean Trench Street, Smith Square, London SW1P 3HE

Published four times a year. Each issue of the *Review* contains comments on the economic situation in the UK and on the world economy as a whole. It also contains interesting articles on various aspects of the UK economy. This source is particularly strong in providing comparisons between the UK and her competitors in particular areas, e.g. labour costs, productivity and education. There is a statistical appendix which offers updates on a wide range of economic variables relating to production, prices/wages, external trade, etc.

Oxford Review of Economic Policy

Oxford University Press, Great Clarendon Street, Oxford OX2 6DP

A quarterly publication which includes articles on various topics of current relevance. Some issues concentrate wholly on *one* contemporary topic, such as Exchange Rates, Education and Training, Finance, Health Economics, etc.

Regional Studies
Routledge, Taylor and Francis Group, Customer Services Dept, 130 Milton Park, Abingdon, Oxon, OX14 4SB

Published ten times a year. This is the standard source of articles for those students who are interested in various aspects of UK and world regional and urban issues.

Teaching Business and Economics

Economics and Business Education Association, 1a Keymer Road, Hassocks, West Sussex BN6 8AD

This is the official journal of the Economics and Business Education Association and is published in October, February and May. As well as containing articles on various aspects of economics, business and related subjects, it also covers up-to-date teaching methods and reviews new literature.

The Economist
25 St James Street, London SW1A 1HG

This is the internationally known weekly, published by The Economist Newspapers Ltd. It includes articles on subjects such as World Politics and Current Affairs, together with Business, Finance and Science. It is an invaluable source of national and international business news and also has a useful update on basic economic statistics.

Who Owns Whom?
Dun and Bradstreet, 5th Floor, Westminster House, Portland Street, Manchester M1 3HU

This is a yearly publication which includes a mass of essential information about companies and their subsidiaries. It enables readers to find the main subsidiaries of UK companies, whether in the UK or abroad. It can also be used to trace the parent firm if the name of the subsidiary is known. This publication is therefore invaluable for unravelling the pattern of ownership and control in UK industry.

Electronic media

Many series of data and sources of information can now be accessed directly on-line or are available on disk or tape.

ONS Databank
ONS Sales Desk, Room 131/4, Office for National Statistics, Government Offices, Great George Street, London SW1P 3AQ

The ONS Databank contains major series such as GDP, PSBR, RPI, Balance of Payments, National Accounts, index of production, etc. Time series data for these items are available on disk or paper.

NOMIS
Suite IL-N, Block 1, Mountjoy Research Centre, Stockton Road, Durham DH1 3SW

The National Online Manpower Information Service (NOMIS) is a database of labour statistics run on behalf of the ONS by the University of Durham. It contains a range of official statistics relating to the labour market. Nomis website (http://www.dur.ac.uk/mountjoy.researchcentre/Nomis.htm) gives the address as Suite IL-N, Block 1, Mountjoy Research Centre, Stockton Road, Durham DH1 3SW.

ESRC Data Archive   University of Essex, Colchester, Essex CO4 3SQ

This archive provides data across the full range of the social sciences and humanities and contains information about most areas of social and economic life including Family Expenditure Surveys, Labour Force Surveys, census data, etc. The Data Archive will locate and obtain research data for those interested.

CD-ROM   Many schools, colleges and public libraries now provide CD-ROM access to a range of UK and EU *databases* and *Information Sources*. The following items are indicative of what may well be available to you via this resource:

1 ABI/INFORM
   Gives 150-word abstracts and indexing to over 800 international academic business, economics and management journals.

2 ANBAR ABSTRACTS
   Abstracts and indexes articles covering business, management and IT topics from mainly UK and European journals.

3 FINANCIAL TIMES
   Full text of back issues of this newspaper.

4 THE GUARDIAN
   Full text of back issues of this newspaper.

5 JUSTIS
   This is the official legal database of the European Union. It contains the full text of most of the treaties, regulations, directives, preparatory work, case law and parliamentary questions dealt with by the EU.

6 THE TIMES
   Full text of back issues of this newspaper.

Internet sources

Use of the Internet as a source of information for economics and business has grown rapidly over the last few years. The usefulness of the material on the Internet largely depends on whether organizations keep their site up-to-date. The sources of information are growing daily so the list given below provides only a very brief idea of the type and range of web-sites available.

UK sites

British Library Integrated Catalogue (http://catalogue.bl.uk)

This will provide details of books published in the UK, enabling a search to be made to identify up-to-date books on many topic areas.

Competition Commission (http://www.Competition-Commission.org.uk)

The Commission is an independent public body which conducts in-depth inquiries into mergers, markets and the regulation of the major regulated industries. This site contains valuable reports on companies referred by the OFT to the Commission.

Department for Business, Innovation and Skills   (BIS)   (http://www.bis.gov.uk)

This site contains significant amounts of information on business innovation, productivity, regional economic development, etc.

Directgov   (http://www.direct.gov.uk/)

This site is an important all round source of information. It will lead to most of the materials published by UK government authorities and public service organisations. It has a valuable A to Z section which allows various government departments and offices to be located, and also has a link to 'Business Links' for those interested in resources available to Business.

Economist   (http://www.economist.com/)

This includes the current week's issue of *The Economist*, book reviews and surveys. It also provides links to other related sites.

HM Treasury   (http://www.hm-treasury.gov.uk)

This site contains press releases, ministers' speeches, lists of research papers, together with sections on the budget, spending reviews, taxation, economic data, economic forecasts, international issues, and enterprise /productivity information.

Institute for Fiscal Studies
(http://www.ifs.org.uk)

This is an independent research organization that does extensive microeconomic analysis on areas such as the budget, public finance, income inequality, etc.

Office for Budget Responsibility
(http://budgetresponsibility.independent.gov.uk/)

This Office was created in May 2010 to carry out independent assessments of the public sector balance sheets and the economy as a whole including areas such as the costs of aging, public service pensions, and Private Finance Initiatives (PFI) contracts.

Office of Fair Trading   (OFT)
(http://oft.gov.uk/)

The OFT's mission is to make markets work well for consumers. It undertakes investigations into abuse of power by companies in the form a monopoly/cartel type activity. It produces reports which provide a wealth of information for those interested in the mechanism and operations of companies and markets.

ONS National Statistics online
(http://www.statistics.gov.uk)

This is the premier statistical source on the UK economy. The latest updated releases of statistics are posted every day. It is possible to browse by theme, or click on the 'virtual bookshelf' to discover the range of statistics available.

Opening up government   (http://data.gov.uk)

This is a site which was formed in January 2010 under the government's transparency agenda and is a source of over 5,600 datasets designed to provide information in a more easily accessible and transparent form. The data information section is organized by publisher and nation while it also has other sections such as 'applications', 'ideas' and 'blog' sections. It also has a 'resources' section where it is possible to access tools to help analyse and share data.

The National Archives
(http://nationalarchives.gov.uk/)

The National Archives is the UK government's official archive, containing over 1,000 years of history. It was formed between 2003–6 by a fusion of four organizations including the HMSO. It gives detailed guidance to various government departments and the public sector as a whole.

TSO (Stationery Office)
(http://www.tso.co.uk)

This is a privately owned company which publishes for the UK government and Parliament. It maintains a catalogue of all official publications – some 450,000 titles in all. It also distributes publications for international bodies. It has a large range of publications in many fields and can be used as a reference point for searching for economic publications and information.

Newspapers

The following list provides a guide to the main newspapers that provide search facilities, and access can be gained to up-to-date articles. Occasionally, the user is asked to register (free) before using the facility, but some of their services are not free.

- Financial Times (http://www.ft.com)
- Guardian Unlimited (http://www.guardian.co.uk)
- Independent (http://www.independent.co.uk)
- Timesonline (http://www.timesonline.co.uk)

European/international

British Library: Help for Researchers
(http://www.bl.uk/reshelp/findhelpsubject/socsci/eurunian/eurounion.html)

This website available at the British Library provides a very comprehensive guide for those wanting to access information relating to the EU. It provides useful contact points and on-line directories and gateways. Other sections include bibliographic databases and guides; news and current awareness sources; contracts, grants and funding; legislative databases; on-line journals and blogs/social media sections.

EU Information (Europa)

(http://europa.eu)

This is the EU's central home page. It is the starting point for a search of the main sources of official information on the EU. It leads to an enormous range of sources, including the publications of the various Directors General (DGs) and Eurostat.

European Central Bank (ECB)

(http://www.ecb.int/)

A significant amount of information on all aspects of European finance.

European Competition Policy

(http://ec.europa.eu/comm/competition/index_en.html)

Significant detail on aspects of anti-trust, mergers, state aid and liberalization issues in the EU.

International Monetary Fund (IMF)

(http://www.imf.org)

This site provides a guide to the material available with the IMF on a wide range of economic issues.

The World Bank   (http://www.worldbank.org/)

See 'World Bank' below.

United Nations   (http://www.un.org)

This site provides details of the publications and activities of the United Nations, e.g. information about its yearly Trade and Development Report.

United States   (US)

There are a large number of sites that give information about the US economy and business. Five useful ones are:

■ *Economic Statistics*   (http://www.whitehouse.gov/ administration/eop/cea/economic-indicators)
This is a central source on current economic data and reports from various US state agencies, e.g. The Economic Report of the President. There is also a resources section on the White House website which is useful.

■ *Statistical Abstract of the United States*   (http:// www.census.gov/compendia/statab/)
This publication is an authoritative and comprehensive summary of statistics on the social, political and economic organization of the United States.

■ *FirstGov*   (http://www.usa.gov)
This site has 51 million pages with information about all aspects of US life and business. It has a 'reference centre' which contains data and law sections.

■ *Fedstats*   (http://www.fedstats.gov/)
This gateway contains statistics from over 100 US Federal Agencies.

■ *CIA World Factbook*   (https://www.cia.gov/ library/publications/the-world-factbook/)
The factbook provides information on the history, geography, economy, government and transnational issues for 267 world entities.

World Bank   (http://www.worldbank.org/)

An invaluable source for information, research and data on economic development of all kinds.

World Trade Organization   (WTO)

(http://www.wto.org)

This site is dedicated to the publications of the WTO in the area of trade and trade policy.

INDEX